Temple Bailey,
Collection novels

In this book:
The Tin Soldier, 1918
Contrary Mary, 1914
Mistress Anne, 1917
The Gay Cockade, 1921
Judy, 1923
The Trumpeter Swan, 1920

Irene Temple Bailey (1885 – 1953) was an American novelist and short story writer. Beginning around 1902, Temple Bailey was contributing stories to national magazines such as The Saturday Evening Post, Cavalier Magazine, Cosmopolitan, The American Magazine, McClure's, Woman's Home Companion, Good Housekeeping, McCall's and others.

In 1914, Bailey wrote the screenplay for the Vitagraph Studios film Auntie, and two of her books were filmed. She also had three of her books on the list of bestselling novels in the United States in 1918, 1922, and 1926 as determined by Publishers Weekly.

In this book:

The Tin Soldier

CHAPTER I
THE TOY SHOP

The lights shining through the rain on the smooth street made of it a golden river.

The shabby old gentleman navigated unsteadily until he came to a corner. A lamp-post offered safe harbor. He steered for it and took his bearings. On each side of the glimmering stream loomed dark houses. A shadowy blot on the triangle he knew to be a church. Beyond the church was the intersecting avenue. Down the avenue were the small exclusive shops which were gradually encroaching on the residence section.

The shabby old gentleman took out his watch. It was a fine old watch, not at all in accord with the rest of him. It was almost six. The darkness of the November afternoon had come at five. The shabby old gentleman swung away from the lamppost and around the corner, then bolted triumphantly into the Toy Shop.

"Here I am," he said, with an attempt at buoyancy, and sat down.

"Oh," said the girl behind the counter, "you are wet."

"Well, I said I'd come, didn't I? Rain or shine? In five minutes I should have been too late—shop closed—" He lurched a little towards her.

She backed away from him. "You—you are—wet—won't you take cold—?"

"Never take cold—glad to get here—" He smiled and shut his eyes, opened them and smiled again, nodded and recovered, nodded and came to rest with his head on the counter.

The girl made a sudden rush for the rear door of the shop. "Look here, Emily. Poor old duck!"

Emily, standing in the doorway, surveyed the sleeping derelict scornfully. "You'd better put him out. It is six o'clock, Jean—"

"He was here yesterday—and he was furious because I wouldn't sell him any soldiers. He said he wanted to make a bonfire of the Prussian ones—and to buy the French and English ones for his son," she laughed.

"Of course you told him they were not for sale."

"Yes. But he insisted. And when he went away he told me he'd come again and bring a lot of money—"

The shabby old gentleman, rousing at the psychological moment, threw on the counter a roll of bills and murmured brokenly:

"'Ten little soldiers fighting on the line,
One was blown to glory, and, then there were nine—!'"

His head fell forward and again he slept.

"Disgusting," said Emily Bridges; "of course we've got to get him out."

Getting him out, however, offered difficulties. He was a very big old gentleman, and they were little women.

"We might call the police—"

"Oh, Emily—"

"Well, if you can suggest anything better. We must close the shop."

"We might put him in a taxi—and send him home."

"He probably hasn't any home."

"Don't be so pessimistic—he certainly has money."

"You don't know where he got it. You can't be too careful, Jean—"

The girl, touching the old man's shoulder, asked, "Where do you live?"

He murmured indistinctly.

"Where?" she bent her ear down to him.

Waking, he sang:

"Two little soldiers, blowing up a Hun—
The darned thing—exploded—
And then there was—One—"

"Oh, Emily, did you ever hear anything so funny?"

3

Emily couldn't see the funny side of it. It was tragic and it was disconcerting. "I don't know what to do. Perhaps you'd better call a taxi."

"He's shivering, Emily. I believe I'll make him a cup of chocolate."

"Dear child, it will be a lot of trouble—"

"I'd like to do it—really."

"Very well." Emily was not unsympathetic, but she had had a rather wearing life. Her love of toys and of little children had kept her human, otherwise she had a feeling that she might have hardened into chill spinsterhood.

As Jean disappeared through the door, the elder woman moved about the shop, setting it in order for the night. It was a labor of love to put the dolls to bed, to lock the glass doors safely on the puffy rabbits and woolly dogs and round-eyed cats, to close the drawers on the tea-sets and Lilliputian kitchens, to shut into boxes the tin soldiers that their queer old customer had craved.

For more than a decade Emily Bridges had kept the shop. Originally it had been a Thread and Needle Shop, supplying people who did not care to go downtown for such wares.

Then one Christmas she had put in a few things to attract the children. The children had come, and gradually there had been more toys—until at last she had found herself the owner of a Toy Shop, with the thread and needle and other staid articles stuck negligently in the background.

Yet in the last three years it had been hard to keep up the standard which she had set for herself. Toys were made in Germany, and the men who had made them were in the trenches, the women who had helped were in the fields—the days when the bisque babies had smiled on happy working-households were over. There was death and darkness where once the rollicking clowns and dancing dolls had been set to mechanical music.

Jean, coming back with the chocolate, found Emily with a great white plush elephant in her arms. His trappings were of red velvet and there was much gold; he was the last of a line of assorted sizes.

There had always been a white elephant in Miss Emily's window. Painfully she had seen her supply dwindle. For this last of the herd, she had a feeling far in excess of his value, such as a collector might have for a rare coin of a certain minting, or a bit of pottery of a pre-historic period.

She had not had the heart to sell him. "I may never get another. And there are none made like him in America."

"After the war—" Jean had hinted.

Miss Emily had flared, "Do you think I shall buy toys of Germany after this war?"

"Good for you, Emily. I was afraid you might."

But tonight a little pensively Miss Emily wrapped the old mastodon up in a white cloth. "I believe I'll take him home with me. People are always asking to buy him, and it's hard to explain."

"I should say it is. I had an awful time with him," she indicated the old gentleman, "yesterday."

She set the tray down on the counter. There was a slim silver pot on it, and a thin green cup. She poked the sleeping man with a tentative finger. "Won't you please wake up and have some chocolate."

Rousing, he came slowly to the fact of her hospitality. "My dear young lady," he said, with a trace of courtliness, "you shouldn't have troubled—" and reached out a trembling hand for the cup. There was a ring on the hand, a seal ring with a coat of arms. As he drank the chocolate eagerly, he spilled some of it on his shabby old coat.

He was facing the door. Suddenly it opened, and his cup fell with a crash.

A young man came in. He too, was shabby, but not as shabby as the old gentleman. He had on a dilapidated rain-coat, and a soft hat. He took off his hat, showing hair that was of an almost silvery fairness. His eyebrows made a dark pencilled line—his eyes were gray. It was a striking face, given a slightly foreign air by a small mustache.

He walked straight up to the old man, laid his hand on his shoulder, "Hello, Dad." Then, anxiously, to the two women, "I hope he hasn't troubled you. He isn't quite—himself."

Jean nodded. "I am so glad you came. We didn't know what to do."

"I've been looking for him—" He bent to pick up the broken cup. "I'm dreadfully sorry. You must let me pay for it."

"Oh, no."

"Please." He was looking at it. "It was valuable?"

"Yes," Jean admitted, "it was one of Emily's precious pets."

"Please don't think any more about it," Emily begged. "You had better get your father home at once, and put him to bed with a hot water bottle."

Now that the shabby youth was looking at her with troubled eyes, Emily found herself softening towards the old gentleman. Simply as a derelict she had not cared what became of him. But as the father of this son, she cared.

"Thank you, I will. We must be going, Dad."

The old gentleman stood up. "Wait a minute—I came for tin soldiers—Derry—"

"They are not for sale," Miss Emily stated. "They are made in Germany. I can't get any more. I have withdrawn everything of the kind from my selling stock."

The shabby old gentleman murmured, disconsolately.

"Oh, Emily," said the girl behind the counter, "don't you think we might—?"

Derry Drake glanced at her with sudden interest. She had an unusual voice, quick and thrilling. It matched her beauty, which was of a rare quality—white skin, blue eyes, crinkled hair like beaten copper.

"I don't see," he said, smiling for the first time, "what Dad wants of tin soldiers."

"To make 'em fight," said the shabby old man, "we've got to have some fighting blood in the family."

The smile was struck from the young man's face. Out of a dead silence, he said at last, "You were very good to look after him. Come, Dad." His voice was steady, but the flush that had flamed in his cheeks was still there, as he put his arm about the shaky old man and led him to the door.

"Thank you both again," he said from the threshold. Then, with his head high, he steered his unsteady parent out into the rain.

It was late when the two women left the shop. Miss Emily, struggling down the block with her white elephant, found, in a few minutes, harbor in her boarding house. But Jean lived in the more fashionable section beyond Dupont Circle. Her father was a doctor with a practice among the older district people, who, in spite of changing administrations and fluctuating populations, had managed, to preserve their family traditions and social identity.

Dr. McKenzie did not always dine at home. But tonight when Jean came down he was at the head of the table. He was a big, handsome man with crinkled hair like his daughter's, copper-colored and cut close to his rather classic head.

Hilda Merritt was also at the table. She was a trained nurse, who, having begun life as the Doctor's office-girl, had, gradually, after his wife's death, assumed the management of his household. Jean was not fond of her. She had repeatedly begged that her dear Emily might take Miss Merritt's place.

"But Hilda is much younger," her father had contended, "and much more of a companion for you."

"She isn't a companion at all, Daddy. We haven't the same thoughts."

But Hilda had stayed on, and Jean had sought her dear Emily's company in the little shop. Sometimes she waited on customers. Sometimes she worked in the rear room. It was always a great joke to feel that she was really helping. In all her life her father had never let her do a useful thing.

The table was lighted with candles, and there was a silver dish of fruit in the center. The dinner was well-served by a trim maid.

Jean ate very little. Her father noticed her lack of appetite, "Why don't you eat your dinner, dear?"

"I had chocolate at Emily's."

"I don't think she ought to go there so often," Miss Merritt complained.

"Why not?" Jean's voice was like the crack of a whip.

"It is so late when you get home. It isn't safe."

"I can always send the car for you, Jean," her father said. "I don't care to have you out alone."

"Having the car isn't like walking. You know it isn't, Daddy, with the rain against your cheeks and the wind—"

Dr. McKenzie's quick imagination was fired. His eyes were like Jean's, lighted from within.

"I suppose it is all right if she comes straight up Connecticut Avenue, Hilda?"

Miss Merritt had long white hands which lay rather limply on the table. Her arms were bare. She was handsome in a red-cheeked, blond fashion.

"Of course if you think it is all right, Doctor—"

"It is up to Jean. If she isn't afraid, we needn't worry."

"I'm not afraid of anything."

He smiled at her. She was so pretty and slim and feminine in her white gown, with a string of pearls on her white neck. He liked pretty things and he liked her fearlessness. He had never been afraid. It pleased him that his daughter should share his courage.

"Perhaps, if I am not too busy, I will come for you the next time you go to the shop. Would walking with me break the spell of the wind and wet?"

"You know it wouldn't. It would be quite—heavenly—Daddy."

After dinner, Doctor McKenzie read the evening paper. Jean sat on the rug in front of the fire and knitted for the soldiers. She had made sweaters until it seemed sometimes as if she saw life through a haze of olive-drab.

"I am going to knit socks next," she told her father.

He looked up from his paper. "Did you ever stop to think what it means to a man over there when a woman says 'I'm going to knit socks'?"

Jean nodded. That was one of the charms which her father had for her. He saw things. It was tired soldiers at this moment, marching in the cold and needing—socks.

Hilda, having no vision, remarked from the corner where she sat with her book, "There's no sense in all this killing—I wish we'd kept out of it."

"Wasn't there any sense," said little Jean from the hearth rug, "in Bunker Hill and Valley Forge?"

5

Hilda evaded that. "Anyhow, I'm glad they've stopped playing the 'Star-Spangled Banner' at the movies. I'm tired of standing up."

Jean voiced her scorn. "I'd stand until I dropped, rather than miss a note of it."

Doctor McKenzie interposed:

"'The time has come,' the Walrus said,
'To talk of many things,
Of shoes—and ships—and sealing wax—
Of cabbages—and kings—'"

"Oh, Daddy," Jean reproached him, "I should think you might be serious."

"I am not just twenty—and I have learned to bank my fires. And you mustn't take Hilda too literally. She doesn't mean all that she says, do you, Hilda?"

He patted Miss Merritt on the shoulder as he went out. Jean hated that. And Hilda's blush.

With the Doctor gone, Hilda shut herself up in the office to balance her books.

Jean went on with her knitting, Hilda did not knit. When she was not helping in the office or in the house, her hands lay idle in her lap.

Jean's mind, as she worked, was on those long white hands of Hilda's. Her own hands had short fingers like her father's. Her mother's hands had been slender and transparent. Hilda's hands were not slender, they had breadth as well as length, and the skin was thick. Even the whiteness was like the flesh of a fish, pale and flabby. No, there was no beauty at all in Hilda's hands.

Once Jean had criticised them to her father. "I think they are ugly."

"They are useful hands, and they have often helped me."

"I like Emily's hands much better."

"Oh, you and your Emily," he had teased.

Yet Jean's words came back to the Doctor the next night, as he sat in the Toy Shop waiting to escort his daughter home.

Miss Emily was serving a customer, a small boy in a red coat and baggy trousers. A nurse stood behind the small boy, and played, as it were, Chorus. She wore a blue cape and a long blue bow on the back of her hat.

The small boy was having the mechanical toys wound up for him. He expressed a preference for the clowns, but didn't like the colors.

"I want him boo'," he informed Miss Emily, "he's for a girl, and she yikes boo'."

"Blue," said the nurse austerely, "you know your mother doesn't like baby talk, Teddy."

"Ble-yew—" said the small boy, carefully.

"Blue clowns," Miss Emily stated, sympathetically, "are hard to get. Most of them are red. I have the nicest thing that I haven't shown you. But it costs a lot—"

"It's a birfday present," said the small boy.

"Birthday," from the Chorus.

"Be-yirthday," was the amended version, "and I want it nice."

Miss Emily brought forth from behind the glass doors of a case a small green silk head of lettuce. She set it on the counter, and her fingers found the key, then clickety-click, clickety-click, she wound it up. It played a faint tune, the leaves opened—a rabbit with a wide-frilled collar rose in the center. He turned from side to side, he waggled his ears, and nodded his head, he winked an eye; then he disappeared, the leaves closed, the music stopped.

The small boy was entranced. "It's boo-ful—"

"Beautiful—" from the background.

"Be-yewtiful—. I'll take it, please."

It was while Miss Emily was winding the toy that Dr. McKenzie noticed her hands. They were young hands, quick and delightful hands. They hovered over the toy, caressingly, beat time to the music, rested for a moment on the shoulders of the little boy as he stood finally with upturned face and tied-up parcel.

"I'm coming adain," he told her.

"Again—."

"Ag-yain—," patiently.

"I hope you will." Miss Emily held out her hand. She did not kiss him. He was a boy, and she knew better.

When he had gone, importantly, Emily saw the Doctor's eyes upon her. "I hated to sell it," she said, with a sigh; "goodness knows when I shall get another. But I can't resist the children—"

He laughed. "You are a miser, Emily."

6

He had known her for many years. She was his wife's distant cousin, and had been her dearest friend. She had taught in a private school before she opened her shop, and Jean had been one of her pupils. Since Mrs. McKenzie's death it had been Emily who had mothered Jean.

The Doctor had always liked her, but without enthusiasm. His admiration of women depended largely on their looks. His wife had meant more to him than that, but it had been her beauty which had first held him.

Emily Bridges had been a slender and diffident girl. She had kept her slenderness, but she had lost her diffidence, and she had gained an air of distinction. She dressed well, her really pretty feet were always carefully shod and her hair carefully waved. Yet she was one of the women who occupy the background rather than the foreground of men's lives—the kind of woman for whom a man must be a Columbus, discovering new worlds for himself.

"Yon are a miser," the Doctor repeated.

"Wouldn't you be, under the same circumstances? If it were, for example, surgical instruments—anaesthetics—? And you knew that when they were gone you wouldn't get any more?"

He did not like logic in a woman. He wanted to laugh and tease. "Jean told me about the white elephant."

"Well, what of it? I have him at home—safe. In a big box—with moth-balls—" Her lips twitched. "Oh, it must seem funny to anyone who doesn't feel as I do."

The door of the rear room opened, and Jean came in, carrying in her arms an assortment of strange creatures which she set in a row on the floor in front of her father.

"There?" she asked, "what do you think of them?"

They were silhouettes of birds and beasts, made of wood, painted and varnished. But such ducks had never quacked, such geese had never waddled, such dogs had never barked—fantastic as a nightmare—too long—too broad—exaggerated out of all reality, they might have marched with Alice from Wonderland or from behind the Looking Glass.

"I made them, Daddy."

"You—."

"Yes, do you like them?"

"Aren't they a bit—uncanny?"

"We've sold dozens; the children adore them."

"And you haven't told me you were doing it. Why?"

"I wanted you to see them first—a surprise. We call them the Lovely Dreams, and we made the ducks green and the pussy cats pink because that's the way the children see them in their own little minds—"

She was radiant. "And I am making money, Daddy. Emily had such a hard time getting toys after the war began, so we thought we'd try. And we worked out these. I get a percentage on all sales."

He frowned. "I am not sure that I like that."

"Why not?"

"Don't I give you money enough?"

"Of course. But this is different."

"How different?"

"It is my own. Don't you see?"

Being a man he did not see, but Miss Emily did. "Any work that is worth doing at all is worth being paid for. You know that, Doctor."

He did know it, but he didn't like to have a woman tell him. "She doesn't need the money."

"I do. I am giving it to the Red Cross. Please don't be stuffy about it, Daddy."

"Am I stuffy?"

"Yes."

He tried to redeem himself by a rather tardy enthusiasm and succeeded. Jean brought out more Lovely Dreams, until a grotesque procession stretched across the room.

"Tomorrow," she announced, triumphantly, "we'll put them in the window, and you'll see the children coming."

As she carried them away, Doctor McKenzie said to Emily, "It seems strange that she should want to do it."

"Not at all. She needs an outlet for her energies."

"Oh, does she?"

"If she weren't your daughter, you'd know it."

On the way home he said, "I am very proud of you, my dear."

Jean had tucked her arm through his. It was not raining, but the sky was full of ragged clouds, and the wind blew strongly. They felt the push of it as they walked against it.

"Oh," she said, with her cheek against his rough coat, "are you proud of me because of my green ducks and my pink pussy cats?"

But she knew it was more than that, although he laughed, and she laughed with him, as if his pride in her was a thing which they took lightly. But they both walked a little faster to keep pace with their quickened blood.

7

Thus their walk became a sort of triumphant progress. They passed the British Embassy with the Lion and the Unicorn watching over it in the night; they rounded the Circle and came suddenly upon a line of motor cars.

"The Secretary is dining a rather important commission," the Doctor said; "it was in the paper. They are to have a war feast—three courses, no wine, and limited meats and sweets."

They stopped for a moment as the guests descended from their cars and swept across the sidewalk. The lantern which swung low from the arched entrance showed a spot of rosy color—the velvet wrap of a girl whose knot of dark curls shone above the ermine collar. A Spanish comb, encrusted with diamonds, was stuck at right angles to the knot.

Beside the young woman in the rosy wrap walked a young man in a fur coat who topped her by a head. He had gray eyes and a small upturned mustache—Jean uttered an exclamation.

"What's the matter?" her father asked.

"Oh, nothing—" she watched the two ascend the stairs. "I thought for a moment that I knew him."

The great door opened and closed, the rosy wrap and the fur coat were swallowed up.

"Of course it couldn't be," Jean decided as she and her father continued on their wonderful way.

"Couldn't be what, my dear?"

"The same man, Daddy," Jean said, and changed the subject.

CHAPTER II
CINDERELLA

The next time that Jean saw Him was at the theater. She and her father went to worship at the shrine of Maude Adams, and He was there.

It was Jean's yearly treat. There were, of course, other plays. But since her very-small-girlhood, there had been always that red-letter night when "The Little Minister" or "Hop-o'-my-Thumb" or "Peter Pan" had transported her straight from the real world to that whimsical, tender, delightful realm where Barrie reigns.

Peter Pan had been the climax!

Do you believe in fairies?

Of course she did. And so did Miss Emily. And so did her father, except in certain backsliding moments. But Hilda didn't. Tonight it was "A Kiss for Cinderella"—! The very name had been enough to set Jean's cheeks burning and her eyes shining.

"Do you remember, Daddy, that I was six when I first saw her, and she's as young as ever?"

"Younger." It was at such moments that the Doctor was at his best. The youth in him matched the youth in his daughter. They were boy and girl together.

And now the girl on the stage, whose undying youth made her the interpreter of dreams for those who would never grow up, wove her magic spells of tears and laughter.

It was not until the first satisfying act was over that Jean drew a long breath and looked about her.

The house was packed. The old theater with its painted curtain had nothing modern to recommend it. But to Jean's mind it could not have been improved. She wanted not one thing changed. For years and years she had sat in her favorite seat in the seventh row of the parquet and had loved the golden proscenium arch, the painted goddesses, the red velvet hangings—she had thrilled to the voice and gesture of the artists who had played to please her. There had been "Wang" and "The Wizard of Oz"; "Robin Hood"; the tall comedian of "Casey at the Bat"; the short comedian who had danced to fame on his crooked legs; Mrs. Fiske, most incomparable Becky; Mansfield, Sothern—some of them, alas, already gods of yesterday!

At first there had been matinées with her mother—"The Little Princess," over whose sorrows she had wept in the harrowing first act, having to be consoled with chocolates and the promise of brighter things as the play progressed.

Now and then she had come with Hilda. But never when she could help it. "I'd rather stay at home," she had told her father.

"But—why—?"

"Because she laughs in the wrong places."

Her father never laughed in the wrong places, and he squeezed her hand in those breathless moments where words would have been desecration, and wiped his eyes frankly when his feelings were stirred.

"There is no one like you, Daddy," she had told him, "to enjoy things." And so it had come about that he had pushed away his work on certain nights and, sitting beside her, had forgotten the sordid and suffering world which he knew so well, and which she knew not at all.

8

As her eyes swept the house, they rested at last with a rather puzzled look on a stout old gentleman with a wide shirt-front, who sat in the right-hand box. He had white hair and a red face.

Where had she seen him?

There were women in the box, a sparkling company in white and silver, and black and diamonds, and green and gold. There was a big bald-headed man, and quite in the shadow back of them all, a slender youth.

It was when the slender youth leaned forward to speak to the vision in white and silver that Jean stared and stared again.

She knew now where she had seen the old gentleman with the wide shirt front. He was the shabby old gentleman of the Toy Shop! And the youth was the shabby son!

Yet here they were in state and elegance! As if a fairy godmother had waved a wand—!

The curtain went up on a feverish little slavey with her mind set on going to the ball, on Our Policeman wanting a shave, on the orphans in boxes, on baked potato offered as hospitality by a half-starved hostess, on a waiting Cinderella asleep on a frozen doorstep.

And then the ball—and Mona Lisa, and the Duchess of Devonshire, and The Girl with the Pitcher and the Girl with the Muff—and Cinderella in azure tulle and cloth-of-gold, dancing with the Prince at the end like mad—.

Then the bell boomed—the lights went out—and after a little moment, one saw Cinderella, stripped of her finery, staggering up the stairs.

Jean cried and laughed, and cried again. Yet even in the midst of her emotion, she found her eyes pulled away from that appealing figure on the stage to those faintly illumined figures in the box.

When the curtain went down, her father, most surprisingly, bowed to the old gentleman and received in return a genial nod.

"Oh, do you know him?" she demanded.

"Yes. It is General Drake."

"Who are the others?"

"I am not sure about the women. The boy in the back of the box is his son, DeRhymer Drake."

Derry!

"Oh,"—she had a feeling that she was not being quite candid with her father—"he's rather swank, isn't he, Daddy?"

"Heavens, what slang! I don't see where you get it. He is rich, if that's what you mean, and it's a wonder he isn't spoiled to death. His mother is dead, and the General is his own worst enemy; eats and drinks too much, and thinks he can get away with it."

"Are they very rich—?"

"Millions, with only Derry to leave it to. He's the child of a second wife."

Oh, lovely, lovely, lovely Cinderella, could your godmother do more than this? To endow two rained-on and shabby gentlemen with pomp and circumstance!

Jean tucked her hand into her father's, as if to anchor herself against this amazing tide of revelation. Then, as the auditorium darkened, and the curtain went up, she was swept along on a wave of emotions in which the play world and the real world were inextricably mixed.

And now Our Policeman discovers that he is "romantical." Cinderella finds her Prince, who isn't in the least the Prince of the fairy tale, but much nicer under the circumstance—and the curtain goes down on a glass slipper stuck on the toes of two tiny feet and a cockney Cinderella, quite content.

"Well," Jean drew a long breath. "It was the loveliest ever, Daddy," she said, as he helped her with her cloak.

And it was while she stood there in that cloak of heavenly blue that the young man in the box looked down and saw her.

He batted his eyes.

Of course she wasn't real.

But when he opened them, there she was, smiling up into the face of the man who had helped her into that heavenly garment.

It came to him, quite suddenly, that his father had bowed to the man—the big man with the classic head and the air of being at ease with himself and the world.

He did things to the velvet and ermine wrap that he was holding, which seemed to satisfy its owner, then he gripped his father's arm. "Dad, who is that big man down there—with the red head—the one who bowed to you?"

"Dr. McKenzie, Bruce McKenzie, the nerve specialist—"

Of course it was something to know that, but one didn't get very far.

"Let's go somewhere and eat," said the General, and that was the end of it. Out of the tail of his eye, Derry Drake saw the two figures with the copper-colored heads move down the aisle, to be finally merged into the indistinguishable stream of humanity which surged towards the door.

Jean and her father did not go to supper at the big hotel around the corner as was their custom.

"I've got to get to the hospital before twelve," the Doctor said. "I am sorry, dear—"

"It doesn't make a bit of difference. I don't want to eat," she settled herself comfortably beside him in the car. "Oh, it is snowing, Daddy, how splendid—"

He laughed. "You little bundle of—ecstasy—what am I going to do with you?"

"Love me. And isn't the snow—wonderful?"

"Yes. But everybody doesn't see it that way."

"I am glad that I do. I should hate to see nothing in all this miracle, but—slush tomorrow—"

"Yet a lot of life is just—slush tomorrow—. I wish you need never find that out—."

When Jean went into the house, and her father drove on, she found Hilda waiting up for her.

"Father had to go to the hospital."

"Did you have anything to eat?"

"No."

"I thought I might cook some oysters."

"I am really not hungry." Then feeling that her tone was ungracious, she tried to make amends. "It was nice of you to think of it—"

"Your father may like them. I'll have them hot for him."

Jean lingered uncertainly. She didn't want the food, but she hated to leave the field to Hilda. She unfastened her cloak, and sat down. "How are you going to cook them?"

"Panned—with celery."

"It sounds good—I think I'll stay down, Hilda."

"As you wish."

The Doctor, coming in with his coat powdered with snow, found his daughter in a big chair in front of the library fire.

"I thought you'd be in bed."

"Hilda has some oysters for us."

"Fine—I'm starved."

She looked at him, meditatively, "I don't see how you can be."

"Why not?"

"Oh, on such a night as this, Daddy? Food seems superfluous."

He sat down, smiling. "Don't ever expect to feed any man over forty on star-dust. Hilda knows better, don't you, Hilda?"

Hilda was bringing in the tray. There was a copper chafing-dish and a percolator. She wore her nurse's outfit of white linen. She looked well in it, and she was apt to put it on after dinner, when she was in charge of the office.

"You know better than to feed a man on stardust, don't you?" the Doctor persisted.

Hilda lifted the cover of the chafing-dish and stirred the contents. "Well, yes," she smiled at him, "you see, I have lived longer than Jean. She'll learn."

"I don't want to learn," Jean told her hotly. "I want to believe that—that—" Words failed her.

"That men can live on star-dust?" her father asked gently. "Well, so be it. We won't quarrel with her, will we, Hilda?"

The oysters were very good. Jean ate several with healthy appetite. Her father, twinkling, teased her, "You see—?"

She shrugged, "All the same, I didn't need them."

Hilda, putting things back on the tray, remarked: "There was a message from Mrs. Witherspoon. Her son is on leave for the week end. She wants you for dinner on Saturday night—both of you."

Doctor McKenzie tapped a finger on the table thoughtfully, "Oh, does she? Do you want to go, Jeanie?"

"Yes. Don't you?"

"I am not sure. I should like to build a fence about you, my dear, and never let a man look over. Ralph Witherspoon wants to marry her, Hilda, what do you think of that?"

"Well, why not?" Hilda laid her long hands flat on the table, leaning on them.

Jean felt little prickles of irritability. "Because I don't want to get married, Hilda."

Hilda gave her a sidelong glance, "Of course you do. But you don't know it."

She went out with her tray. Jean turned, white-faced, to her father, "I wish she wouldn't say such things—"

"My dear, I am afraid you don't quite do her justice."

"Oh, well, we won't talk about her. I've got to go to bed, Daddy."

She kissed him wistfully. "Sometimes I think there are two of you, the one that likes me, and the one that likes Hilda."

With his hands on her shoulders, he gave an easy laugh. "Who knows? But you mustn't have it on your mind. It isn't good for you."

"I shall always have you on my mind—."

"But not to worry about, baby. I'm not worth it—."

Hilda came in with the evening paper. "Have you read it, Doctor?"

"No." He glanced at the headlines and his face grew hard. "More frightfulness," he said, stormily. "If I had my way, it should be an eye for an eye, a tooth for a tooth. For every man they have tortured, there should be one of their men—tortured. For every child mutilated, one of theirs—mutilated. For every woman—."

He stopped. Jean had caught hold of his arm. "Don't, Daddy," she said thickly, "it makes me afraid of you." She covered her face with her hands.

He drew her to him and smoothed her hair in silence. Over her head he glanced at Hilda. She was smiling inscrutably into the fire.

CHAPTER III
DRUSILLA

The thing that Derry Drake had on his mind the next morning was a tea-cup. There were other things on his mind—things so heavy that he turned with relief to the contemplation of cups.

Stuck all over the great house were cabinets of china—his father had collected and his mother had prized. Derry, himself, had not cared for any of it until this morning, but when Bronson, the old man who served him and had served his father for years, came in with his breakfast, Derry showed him a broken bit which he had brought home with him two nights before.

"Have we a cup like this anywhere in the house, Bronson?"

"There's a lot of them, sir, in the blue room, in the wall cupboard."

"I thought so, let me have one of them. If Dad ever asks for it, send him to me. He broke the other, so it's a fair exchange."

He had it carefully wrapped and carried it downtown with him. The morning was clear, and the sun sparkled on the snow. As he passed through Dupont Circle he found that a few children and their nurses had braved the cold. One small boy in a red coat ran to Derry.

"Where are you going, Cousin Derry?"

"Down town."

"To-day is Margaret-Mary's birf-day. I am going to give her a wabbit—."

"Rabbit, Buster. You'd better say it quick. Nurse is on the way."

"Rab-yit. What are you going to give her?"

"Oh, must I give her something?"

"Of course. Mother said you'd forget it. I wanted to telephone, and she wouldn't let me."

"Would a doll do?"

"I shouldn't like a doll. But she is littler. And you mustn't spend much money. Mother said I spent too much for my rab-yit. That I ought to save it for Our Men. And you mustn't eat what you yike—we've got a card in the window, and there wasn't any bacon for bref-fus."

"Breakfast."

"Yes. An' we had puffed rice and prunes—"

Nurse, coming up, was immediately on the job. "You are getting mud on Mr. Derry's spats, Teddy. Stand up like a little gentleman."

"He is always that, Nurse, isn't he? And I should not have on spats at this hour in the morning."

Derry smiled to himself as he left them. He knew that Nurse did not approve of him. He had a way as it were of aiding and abetting Teddy.

But as he went on the smile faded. There were many soldiers on the street, many uniforms, flags of many nations draping doorways where were housed the men from across the sea who were working shoulder to shoulder with America for the winning of the war—. Washington had taken on a new aspect. It had a waked-up look, as if its lazy days were over, and there were real things to do.

The big church at the triangle showed a Red Cross banner. Within women were making bandages, knitting sweaters and socks, sewing up the long seams of shirts and pajamas. A few years ago they had worshipped a Christ among the lilies. They saw him now on the battlefield, crucified again in the cause of humanity.

It seemed to Derry that even the civilians walked with something of a martial stride. Men, who for years had felt their strength sapped by the monotony of Government service, were revived by the winds of patriotism which swept from the four corners of the earth. Women who had lost youth and looks in the treadmill of Departmental life held up their heads as if their eyes beheld a new vision.

Street cars were crowded, things were at sixes and sevens; red tape was loose where it should have been tight and tight where it should have been loose. Little men with the rank of officer sat in swivel chairs and tried to direct big things; big men, without rank, were tied to the trivial. Many, many things were wrong, and many, many things were right, as it is always when war comes upon a people unprepared.

And in the midst of all this clash and crash and movement and achievement, Derry was walking to a toy shop to carry a tea-cup!

He found Miss Emily alone in the big front room.

She did not at once recognize him.

"You remember I was in here the other night—and you wouldn't sell—tin soldiers—."

She flushed a little. "Oh, with your father?"

"Yes. He's a dear old chap—."

It was the best apology he could make, and she loved him for it.

He brought out the cup and set it on the counter. "It is like yours?"

"Yes." But she did not want to take it.

"Please. I brought it on purpose. We have a dozen."

"Of these?"

"Yes."

"But it will break your set."

"We have oodles of sets. Dad collects—you know— There are dishes enough in the house to start a crockery shop."

She glanced at him curiously. It was hard to reconcile this slim young man of fashion with the shabby boy of the other night. But there were the lad's eyes, smiling into hers!

"I should like, too, if you don't mind, to find a toy for a very little girl. It is her birthday, and I had forgotten."

"It is dreadful to forget," Miss Emily told him, "children care so much."

"I have never forgotten before, but I had so much on my mind."

She brought forth the Lovely Dreams—"They have been a great success."

He chose at once a rose-colored cat and a yellow owl. The cat was carved impressionistically in a series of circles. She was altogether celestial and comfortable. The owl might have been lighted by the moon.

"But why?" Derry asked, "a rose-colored cat?"

"Isn't a white cat pink and puffy in the firelight? And a child sees her pink and puffy. If we don't it is because we are blind."

"But why the green ducks and the amethyst cows?"

"The cows are coming tinkling home in the twilight—the green ducks swim under the willows. And they are longer and broader because of the lights and shadows. That's the way you saw them when you were six."

"By Jove," he said, staring, "I believe I did."

"So there's nothing queer about them to the children—you ought to see them listen when Jean tells them."

Jean—!

"She—she tells the children?"

"Yes. Charming stories. I am having them put in a little pamphlet to go with the toys."

"She's Dr. McKenzie's daughter, isn't she? I saw her last night at the play."

"Yes. Such a dear child. She is usually here in the afternoon."

He had hoped until then that Jean might be hidden in that rear room, locked up with the dolls in a drawer, tucked away in a box—he had a blank feeling of the futility of his tea-cup—

Then, suddenly, the gods being in a gay mood, Jean arrived!

At once his errand justified itself. She wore a gray squirrel jacket and a hat to match—and her crinkled copper-colored hair came out from under the hat and over her ears. She carried a little muff. Her eyes—the color of her cheeks! A man might walk to the world's end for less than this—!

He was buying, he told her, pink pussy cats and yellow owls. Had she liked the play last night? He was glad that she adored Maude Adams. He adored—Maude Adams. Did she remember "Peter Pan"? Yes, he had gone to everything—glorified matinées—glorified everything! Wasn't it remarkable that his father knew her father? And she was Jean McKenzie, and he was Derry Drake!

At last there was no excuse for him to linger. "I shall come back for more—Lovely Dreams," he told Miss Emily, and got away.

Alone in the shop the two women looked at each other. Then Emily said, "Jean, darling, how dreadful it must be for him."

"Dreadful—."

"With such a father—."

"Oh, you mean—the other night."

"Yes. He isn't happy, Jean."

"How do you know?"

"He has lonesome eyes."

"Oh, Emily."

"Well, he has, and it must be dreadful."

How dreadful it was neither of them could really know. Derry, having lunched with a rather important committee, went to Drusilla Gray's in the afternoon for a cup of tea. He was called almost at once to the telephone. Bronson was at the other end. "I am sorry, Mr. Derry, but I thought you ought to know—"

Derry, with the sick feeling which always came over him with the knowledge of what was ahead, said steadily, "That's all right, Bronson—which way did he go?"

"He took the Cabin John car, sir. I tried to get on, but he saw me, and sent me back, and I didn't like to make a scene. Shall I follow in a taxi?"

"Yes; I'll get away as soon as I can and call you up out there."

He went back to Drusilla. "Sing for me," he said. Drusilla Gray lived with her Aunt Marion in an apartment winch overlooked Rock Creek. Marion Gray occupied herself with the writing of books. Drusilla had varying occupations. Just now she was interested in interior decoration and in the war.

She was also interested in trying to flirt with Derry Drake. "He won't play the game," she told her aunt, "and that's why I like it—the game, I mean."

"You like him because he hasn't surrendered."

"No. He is a rather perfect thing of his kind, like a bit of jewelled Sèvres or *Sang de boeuf*. And he doesn't know it. And that's another thing in his favor—his modesty. He makes me think of a little Austrian prince I once met at Palm Beach; who wore a white satin shirt with a high collar of gold embroidery, and white kid boots, and wonderful rings—and his nails long like a Chinaman's. At first we laughed at him—called him effeminate—. But after we knew him we didn't laugh. There was the blood in him of kings and rulers—and presently he had us on our knees. And Derry's like that. When you first meet him you look over his head; then you find yourself looking up—"

Marion smiled. "You've got it bad, Drusilla."

"If you think I am in love with him, I'm not. I'd like to be, but it wouldn't be of any use. He's a Galahad—a pocket-edition Galahad. If he ever falls in love, there'll be more of romance in it than I can give him."

It was to this Drusilla that Derry had come. He liked her immensely. And they had in common a great love of music.

She had tea for him, and some rather strange little spiced cakes on a red lacquer tray. There was much dark blue and vivid red in the room, with white woodwork. Drusilla herself was in unrelieved red. The effect was startling but stimulating.

"I am not sure that I like it," she said, "the red and white and blue, but I wanted to see whether I could do it. And Aunt Marion doesn't care. The red things can all be taken out, and the rest toned down. But I have a feeling that a man couldn't sit in this room and be a slacker."

"No, he couldn't," Derry agreed. "You'd better hang out a recruiting sign, Drusilla."

"I should if they would let me. The best I can do is ask them to tea and sing for them."

It was right here that Bronson's message had broken in, and Derry, coming back from the telephone, had said, "Sing for me."

Drusilla lighted two red candles on the piano in the alcove. She began with a medley of patriotic songs. With her voice never soaring above a repressed note, she managed to give the effect of culminating emotion, so that when she reached a climax in the Marseillaise, Derry rose, thrilled, to his feet.

She whirled around and faced him. "They all do that," she said, with a glowing air Of triumph. "It's when I get them."

"Why did you give the Marseillaise last?"

"It has the tramp in it of marching men—I love it."

"But why not the 'Star Spangled Banner'?"

"That's for sacred moments. I hate to make it common—but I'll sing it—now—"

Still standing, he listened. Drusilla held her voice to that low note, but there was the crash of battle in the music that she made, the hush of dawn, the cry of victory—

"Dear girl, you are a genius."

"No, I am not. But I can feel things—and I can make others feel—"

She rose and went to the window. "There's a new moon," she said, "come and see—"

The curtains were not drawn, and the apartment was high up, so that they looked out beyond the hills to a sky in which the daylight blue had faded to a faint green, and saw the little moon and one star.

"Derry," Drusilla said, softly. "Derry, why aren't you fighting?"

It was the question he had dreaded. He had seen it often in her eyes, but never before had she voiced it.

"I can't tell you, Drusilla, but there's a reason—a good one. God knows I would go if I could."

The passion in his voice convinced her.

"Don't you know I'd be in it if I had my way. But I've got to stay on the shelf like the tin soldier in the fairy tale. Do you remember, Drusilla? And people keep asking me—why?"

"I shouldn't have asked it, Derry?"

"You couldn't know. And you had a right to ask—everybody has a right—and I can't answer."

She laid her hand on his shoulder. "When I was a little girl," she said, softly, "I used to cry—because I was so sorry for the—tin soldier—"

"Are you sorry for me, Drusilla?"

"Dreffly sorry."

They stood in silence among the shadows, with only the red candles burning. Then Derry said, heartily, "You are the best friend that a fellow ever had, Drusilla."

And that was as far as he would play the game!

CHAPTER IV
THE QUESTION

Whatever else might be said of General Drake, his Bacchanalian adventures were those of a gentleman. Not for him were the sinister streets and the sordid taverns of the town. When his wild moods came upon him, he struck out straight for open country. Up hill and down dale he trudged, a knight of the road, finding shelter and refreshment at wayside inns, or perchance at some friendly farm.

The danger lay in the lawless folk whom he might meet on the way. Unshaven and unshorn he met them, travelling endlessly along the railroad tracks, by highways, through woodland paths. They slept by day and journeyed by night. By reversing this program, the General as a rule avoided them. But not always, and when the little lad Derry had followed his strange quests, he had come now and then upon his father, telling stories to an unsavory circle, lord for the moment of them all.

"Come, Dad," Derry would say, and when the men had growled a threat, he had flung defiance at them. "My mother's motor is up the road with two men in it. If I don't get back in five minutes they will follow me."

The General had always been tractable in the hands of his son. He adored him. It was only of late that he had found anything to criticise.

Derry, driving along the old Conduit road in the crisp darkness, wondered how long that restless spirit would endure in that ageing body. He shuddered as he thought of the two men who were his father—one a polished gentleman ruling his world, by the power of his keen mind and of his money, the other a self-made vagabond—pursuing an aimless course.

The stars were sharp in a sable sky, the river was a thin line of silver, the bills were blotted out.

Bronson was waiting by the big bridge. "He is singing down there," he said, "on the bank. Can you hear him?"

Leaning over the parapet, Derry listened. The quavering voice came up to him.

"'_He has sounded forth the—trumpet—that shall never call—retreat— He is sifting out the—hearts of men—before his judgment— Oh, be swift, my soul, to answer him! Be jubilant, my feet—'_"

Poor old soldier, beating time to the triumphant tune, stumbling over the words—held pathetically to the memory of those days when he had marched in the glory of his youth, strength and spirit given to a mighty cause!

The pity of it wrung Derry's heart. "Couldn't you do anything with him, Bronson?"

"No, sir, I tried, but he sent me home. Told me I was discharged."

They might have laughed over that, but it was not the moment for laughter. In the last twenty years, the General had discharged Bronson more than once, always without the least idea of being taken at his word. To have lost this faithful servant would have broken his heart.

"I see. It won't do for you to show yourself just now. You'd better go home, and have his hot bath ready."

"Are you sure you can bring him, Mr. Derry?"

"Sure, Bronson, thank you."

Bronson walked a few steps and came back. "It is freezing cold, sir, you'd better take the rug from the car."

Laden thus, Derry made his way down. His flashlight revealed the General, a humped-up figure on the bank of a little frozen stream.

"Go home, Derry," he said, as he recognized his son. "I want to sit by myself."

His tone was truculent.

Derry attempted lightness. "You'll be a lump of ice in the morning, Dad. We'd have to chip you off in chunks."

"You go home with Bronson, son, He is up there. Go home—"

He had once commanded a brigade. There were moments when he was hard pushed that he remembered it.

"Go home, Derry."

"Not till you come with me."

"I'm not coming."

Derry spread his rug on the icy ground. "Sit on this and wrap up your legs—you'll freeze out here."

His father did not move. "I am puf-feckly comfa'ble."

The General rarely got his syllables tangled. Things at times happened to his legs, but he usually controlled his tongue.

"I am puf-feckly comfa'ble—go home, Derry."

"I can't leave you, Dad."

"I want to be left."

He had never been quite like this. There had been moods of rebellion, but usually he had yielded himself to his son's guidance.

"Dad, be reasonable."

"I'd rather sit here and freeze—than go home with a—coward."

It was out at last. It struck Derry like a whiplash. He sprang to his feet. "You don't mean that, Dad. You can't mean it."

"I do mean it."

"I am not a coward, and you know it."

"Then why don't you go and fight?"

Silence! The only sound the chuckle of living waters beneath the ice of the little stream.

"Why don't you go and fight like other men?"

The emphasis was insulting. Derry had only one idea—to escape from that taunting voice. "You'll be sorry for this, Dad," he flung out at white heat, and scrambled up the bank.

When he reached the bridge, he paused. He couldn't leave that old man down there to die of the cold—the wind was rising and rattled in the bare trees.

But Derry's blood was boiling. He sat down on the parapet, thick blackness all about him. Whatever had been his father's shortcomings, they had always clung together—and now they were separated by words which had cut like a knife. It was useless to tell himself that his father was not responsible. Out of the heart the mouth had spoken.

And there were other people who felt as his father did—there had been Drusilla's questions, the questions of others—there had been, too, averted faces. He saw the little figure in the cloak of heavenly blue as she had been the other night,—in her gray furs as she had been this morning—; would her face, too, be turned from him?

Words formed themselves in his mind. He yearned to toss back at his father the taunt that was on his lips. To fling it over the parapet, to shout it to the world—!

He had never before felt the care of his father a sacrifice. There had been humiliating moments, hard moments, but always he had been sustained by a sense of the rightness of the thing that he was doing and of its necessity.

Then, out of the darkness, came a shivering old voice, "Derry, are you there?"

"Yes, Dad."

"Come down—and help me—"

The General, alone in the darkness, had suffered a reaction. He felt chilled and depressed. He wanted warmth and light.

Mounting steadily with his son's arm to sustain him, he argued garrulously for a sojourn at the nearest hostelry, or for a stop at Chevy Chase. He would, he promised, go to bed at the Club, and thus be rid of Bronson. Bronson didn't know his place, he would have to be taught—

Arriving at the top, he was led to Derry's car. He insisted on an understanding. If he got in, they were to stop at the Club.

"No," Derry said, "we won't stop. We are going home."

Derry had never commanded a brigade. But he had in him the blood of one who had. He possessed also strength and determination backed at the moment by righteous indignation. He lifted his father bodily, put him in the car, took his seat beside him, shut the door, and drove off. He felt remarkably cheered as they whirled along at top speed.

The General, yielding gracefully to the inevitable, rolled himself up in the rugs, dropped his head against the padded cushions and, soothed by the warmth, fell asleep.

He waked to find himself being guided up his own stairway by Bronson and the butler.

"Put him into a hot bath, Bronson," Derry directed from the threshold of his father's room, and, the General, quite surprisingly, made no protest. He had his bath, hot drinks to follow, and hot water bags in his bed. When he drifted off finally, into uneasy dreams, he was watched over by Bronson as if he had been a baby.

Derry, looking at his watch, was amazed to find that the evening was yet early. He had lived emotionally through a much longer period than that marked by the clocks.

He had no engagements. He had found himself of late shrinking a little from his kind. The clubs and the hotels were crowded with officers. Private houses, hung with service flags, paid homage to men in uniform. He was aware that he was, perhaps, unduly sensitive, but it was not pleasant to meet the inquiring glance, the guarded question. He was welcomed outwardly as of old. But, then, he had a great deal of money. People did not like to offend his father's son. But if he had not been his father's son? What then?

He dined alone and in state in the great dining room. The portraits of his ancestors looked down on him. There was his mother's grandfather, who had the same fair hair and strongly marked brows. He had been an officer in the English army, and wore the picturesque uniform of the period. There were other men in uniform—ancestors—.

But of what earthly use was an ancestor in uniform to the present situation? It would have been better to have inherited Quaker blood. Derry smiled whimsically as he thought how different he might have felt if there had been benignant men in gray with broad-brimmed hats, staring down.

But to grant a man an inheritance of fighting blood, and then deny him the opportunity to exercise his birthright, was a sort of grim joke which he could not appreciate.

For dessert a great dish of fruit was set before him. He chose a peach!

Peaches in November! The men in the trenches had no peaches, no squabs, no mushrooms, no avacados—for them bully beef and soup cubes, a handful of dates, or by good luck a bit of chocolate.

He left the peach untasted—he had a feeling that he might thus, vicariously, atone for the hardships of those others who fought.

After dinner he walked downtown. Passing Dr. McKenzie's house he was constrained to loiter. There were lights upstairs and down. Was Jean McKenzie's room behind the two golden windows above the balcony? Was she there, or in the room below, where shaded lamps shone softly among the shadows?

He yearned to go in—to speak with her—to learn her thoughts—to read her heart and mind. As yet he knew only the message of her beauty. He fancied her as having exquisite sensibility, sweetness, gentleness, perceptions as vivid as her youth and bloom.

The front door opened, and Jean and her father came out. Derry's heart leaped as he heard her laugh. Then her clear voice, "Isn't it a wonderful night to walk, Daddy?" and her father's response, "Oh, you with your ecstasies!"

They went briskly down the other side of the street. Derry found himself following, found himself straining his ear for that light laugh, found himself wishing that it were he who walked beside her, that her hand was tucked into his arm as it was tucked into her father's.

Their destination was a brilliantly illumined palace on F Street, once a choice little playhouse, now given over to screen productions. The house was packed, and Jean and her father, following the flashlight of the usher, found harbor finally in a box to the left of the stage. Derry settled himself behind them. He was an eavesdropper and he knew it, but he was loath to get out of the range of that lovely laughter.

Yet observing the closeness of their companionship he felt himself lonely—they seemed so satisfied to be together—so sufficient without any other. Once Dr. McKenzie got up and went out. When he came back he brought a box of candy. Derry heard Jean's "Oh, you darling—" and thrilled with a touch of jealousy.

He wondered a little that he should care—his experiences with women had heretofore formed gay incidents in his life rather than serious epochs. He had carried in his heart a vision, and the girl in the Toy Shop had seemed to make that vision suddenly real.

The play which was thrown on the screen had to do with France; with Joan of Arc and the lover who failed her, with the reincarnation of the lover and his opportunity, after long years, to redeem himself from the blot of cowardice.

In the stillness, Derry heard the quick-drawn breath of the girl in front of him. "Daddy, I should hate a man like that."

"But, my dear—"

"I should hate him, Daddy."

The play was over.

The lights went up, and Jean stood revealed. She was pinning on her hat. She saw Derry and smiled at him. "Daddy," she said, "it is Mr. Drake—you know him."

Dr. McKenzie held out his hand. "How do you do? So you young people have met, eh?"

"In Emily's shop, Daddy. He—he came to buy my Lovely Dreams."

The two men laughed. "As if any man could buy your dreams, Jeanie," her father said, "it would take the wealth of the world."

"Or no wealth at all," said Derry quickly.

They walked out together. As they passed the portal of the gilded door, Derry felt that the moment of parting had come.

"Oh, look here, Doctor," he said, desperately, "won't you and your daughter take pity on me—and join me at supper? There's dancing at the Willard and all that—Miss McKenzie might enjoy it, and it would be a life-saver for me."

Light leaped into Jean's eyes. "Oh, Daddy—"

"Would you like it, dear?"

"You know I should. So would you. And you haven't any stupid patients, have you?"

"My patients are always stupid, Drake, when they take me away from her. Otherwise she is sorry for them." He looked at his watch. "When I get to the hotel I'll telephone to Hilda, and she'll know where to find us."

It was the Doctor who talked as they went along—the two young people were quite ecstatically silent. Jean was between her father and Derry. As he kept step with her, it seemed to him that no woman had ever walked so lightly; she laughed a little now and then. There was no need for words.

While her father telephoned, they sat together for a moment in the corridor. She unfastened her coat, and he saw her white dress and pearls. "Am I fine enough for an evening like this?" she asked him; "you see it is just the dress I wear at home."

"It seems to me quite a superlative frock—and I am glad that your hat is lined with blue."

"Why?"

"Your cloak last night was heavenly, and now this—it matches your eyes—"

"Oh." She sat very still.

"Shouldn't I have said that? I didn't think—"

"I am glad you didn't think—"

"Oh, are you?"

"Yes. I hate people who weigh their words—" The color came up finely into her cheeks.

When Dr. McKenzie returned, Derry found a table, and gave his order.

Jean refused to consider anything but an ice. "She doesn't eat at such moments," Doctor McKenzie told his young host. "She lives on star-dust, and she wants me to live on star-dust. It is our only quarrel. She'll think me sordid because I am going to have broiled lobster."

Derry laughed, yet felt that it was after all a serious matter. His appetite, too, was gone. He too wanted only an ice! The Doctor's order was, however, sufficiently substantial to establish a balance.

"May I dance with her?" Derry asked, as the music brought the couples to their feet.

"I don't usually let her. Not in a place like this. But her eyes are begging—and I spoil her, Drake."

Curious glances followed the progress of the young millionaire and his pretty partner. But Derry saw nothing but Jean. She was like thistledown in his arms, she was saying tremendously interesting things to him, in her lovely voice.

"I cried all through the scene where Cinderella sits on the door-step. Yet it really wasn't so very sad—was it?"

"I think it was sad. She was such a little starved thing—starved for love."

"Yes. It must be dreadful to be starved for love."

He glanced down at her. "You have never felt it?"

"No, except after my mother died—I wanted her—"

"My mother is dead, too."

The Doctor sat alone at the head of the table and ate his lobster; he ate war bread and a green salad, and drank a pot of black coffee, and was at peace with the world. Star-dust was all very well for those young things out there. He laughed as they came back to him. "Each to his own joys—the lobster was very good, Drake."

They hardly heard him. Jean had a rosy parfait with a strawberry on top. Derry had another.

They talked of the screen play, and the man who had failed. If he had really loved her he would not have failed, Jean said.

"I think he loved her," was Derry's opinion; "the spirit was willing, but the flesh was weak."

Jean shrugged. "Well, Fate was kind to him—to give him another chance. Oh, Daddy, tell him the story the little French woman told at the meeting of the Medical Association."

"You should have heard her tell it—but I'll do my best. Her eloquence brought us to our feet. It was when she was in Paris—just after the American forces arrived. She stopped at the curb one morning to buy violets of an ancient dame. She found the old flower vendor inattentive and, looking for the cause, she saw across the street a young American trooper loitering at a corner. Suddenly the old woman snatched up a bunch of lilies, ran across the street, thrust them into the hands of the astonished soldier. 'Take them, American,' she said. 'Take the lilies of France and plant them in Berlin.'"

"Isn't that wonderful?" Jean breathed.

"Everything is wonderful to her," the Doctor told Derry, "she lives on the heights."

"But the lilies of France, Daddy—! Can't you see our men and the lilies of France?"

Derry saw them, indeed,—a glorious company—!

"Oh, if I were a man," Jean said, and stopped. She stole a timid glance at him. The question that he had dreaded was in her eyes.

They fell into silence. Jean finished her parfait. Derry's was untouched.

Then the music brought them again to their feet, and they danced. The Doctor smoked alone. Back of him somebody murmured, "It is Derry Drake."

"Confounded slacker," said a masculine voice. Then came a warning "Hush," as Derry and Jean returned.

"It is snowing," Derry told the Doctor. "I have ordered my car."

Late that night when the Doctor rode forth again alone in his own car on an errand of mercy, he thought of the thing which he had heard. Then came the inevitable question: why wasn't Derry Drake fighting?

It was at the Witherspoon dinner that Jean McKenzie first heard the things that were being said about Derry.

"I can't understand," someone had remarked, "why Derry Drake is staying out of it."

"I fancy he'll be getting in," Ralph Witherspoon had said. "Derry's no slacker."

Ralph could afford to be generous. He was in the Naval Flying Corps. He looked extremely well in his Ensign's uniform, and he knew it; he was hoping, in the spring, for active service on the other side.

"I don't see why Derry should fight. I don't see why any man should. I never did believe in getting into other people's fusses."

It was Alma Drew who said that. Nobody took Alma very seriously. She was too pretty with her shining hair and her sea-green eyes, and her way of claiming admiration.

Jean had recognised her when she first came in as the girl she had seen descending from her motor car with Derry Drake on the night of the Secretary's dinner. Alma again wore the diamond-encrusted comb. She was in sea-green, which matched her eyes.

"If I were a man," Alma pursued, "I should run away."

There was a rustle of uneasiness about the table. In the morning papers had been news of Italy—disturbing news; news from Russia—Kerensky had fled to Moscow—there had been pictures of our men in gas masks! It wasn't a thing to joke about. Even Alma might go too far.

Ralph relieved the situation. "Oh, no, you wouldn't run away," he said; "you don't do yourself justice, Alma. Before you know it you will be driving a car over there, and picking me up when I fall from the skies."

"Well, that would be—compensation—." Alma's lashes flashed up and fluttered down.

But she turned her batteries on Ralph in vain. Jean McKenzie was on the other side of him. It would never be quite clear to him why he loved Jean. She was neither very beautiful nor very brilliant. But there was a dearness about her. He hardly dared think of it. It had gone very deep with him.

He turned to her. Her eyes were blazing. "Oh," she said, under her breath, "how can she say things like that? If I knew a man who would run away, I'd never speak to him."

"Of course. That's why I fell in love with you—because you had red blood in your veins."

It was the literal truth. The first time that Ralph had seen Jean McKenzie, he had been riding in Rock Creek Park. She, too, was on horseback. It was in April. War had just been declared, and there was great excitement. Jean, taking the bridle path over the hills, had come upon a band of workers. A long-haired and seditious orator was talking to them. Jean had stopped her horse to listen, and before she knew it she was answering the arguments of the speaker. Rising a little in her stirrups, her riding-crop uplifted to emphasize her burning words, her cheeks on fire, her eyes shining, her hair blowing under her three-cornered hat, she had clearly and crisply challenged the patriotism of the speaker, and she had presented to Ralph's appreciative eyes a picture which he was never to forget.

She had not been in the least embarrassed by his arrival, and his uniform had made him seem at once her ally. "I am sure this gentleman will be glad to talk to you," she had said to her little audience. "I'll leave the field to him," and with a nod and a smile she had ridden off, the applause of the men following her.

Ralph, having put the long-haired one to rout, had asked the men if they knew the young lady who had talked to them. They had, it seemed, seen her riding with Dr. McKenzie. They thought she was his daughter. It had been easy enough after that to find Jean on his mother's visiting list. Mrs. Witherspoon and Mrs. McKenzie had exchanged calls during the life-time of the latter, but they had lived in different circles. Mrs. Witherspoon had aspired to smartness and to the friendship of the new people who brought an air of sophistication to the staid and sedate old capital. Mrs. McKenzie had held to old associations and to old ideals.

Mrs. Witherspoon was a widow and charming. Dr. McKenzie was a widower and an addition to any dinner table. In a few weeks the old acquaintance had been renewed. Ralph had wooed Jean ardently during the short furloughs which had been granted him, and from long distance had written a bit cocksurely. He had sent flowers, candy, books and then, quite daringly; a silver trench ring.

Jean had sent the ring back. "It was dear of you to give it to me, but I can't keep it."

"Why not?" he had asked when he next saw her.

"Because—"

"Because is no reason."

She had blushed, but stood firm. She was very shy—totally unawakened—a little dreaming girl—with all of real life ahead of her—with her innocence a white flower, her patriotism a red one. If only he might wear that white and red above his heart.

As a matter of fact, Jean resented, sub-consciously, his air of possession, the certainty with which he seemed to see the end of his wooing.

"You can't escape me," he had told her.

"As if I were a rabbit," she had complained afterwards to her father. "When I marry a man I don't want to be caught—I want to run to him, with my arms wide open."

"Don't," her father advised; "not many men would be able to stand it. Let them worship you, Jeanie, don't worship."

Jean stuck her nose in the air. "Falling in love doesn't come the way you want it. You have to take it as the good Lord sends it."

"Who told you that?"

"Emily—"

"What does Emily know of love?"

He had laughed and patted her hand. He was cynical generally about romance. He felt that his own perfect love affair with his wife had been the exception. He looked upon Emily as a sentimental spinster who knew practically nothing of men and women.

He did not realize that Emily knew a great deal about dolls that laughed and cried when you pulled a string. And that the world in Emily's Toy Shop was not so very different from his own.

Alma, having turned a cold shoulder to Ralph, was still proclaiming her opinion of Derry Drake to the rest of the table. "He is rich and young and he doesn't want to die—"

"There are plenty of rich young men dying, Alma," said Mrs. Witherspoon, "and it is probably as easy for them as for the poor ones—"

"The poor ones won't mind being muddy and dirty in the trenches," said Alma, "but I can't fancy Derry Drake without two baths a day—"

"I can't quite fancy him a slacker." There was a hint of satisfaction in Mrs. Witherspoon's voice. Her son and Derry Drake had gone to school together and to college. Derry had outdistanced Ralph in every way; but now it was Ralph who was leaving Derry far behind.

Jean wished that they would stop talking. She felt as she might had she seen a soldier stripped of sword and stripes and shamed in the eyes of his fellows.

"Wasn't he in the draft?" she asked Ralph.

"Too old. He doesn't look it, does he? It's a bit hard for the rest of us fellows to understand why he keeps out—"

"Doesn't he ever try to—explain?"

Ralph shook his head. "Not a word. And he's beginning to stay away from things. You see, he knows that people are asking questions, and you hear what they are calling him?"

"Yes," said Jean, "a coward."

"Well, not exactly that—"

"There isn't much difference, is there?"

And now Alma's cool voice summed up the situation. "A man with as much money as that doesn't have to be brave. What does he care about public opinion? After the war everybody will forgive and forget."

Coolly she challenged them to contradict her. "You all know it. How many of you would dare cut the fellow who will inherit his father's millions?"

Mrs. Witherspoon tried to laugh it off; but it was true, and Alma was right. They might talk about Derry Drake behind his back, but they'd never omit sending a card to him.

Jean ate her duckling in flaming silence, ate her salad, ate her ice, drank her coffee, and was glad when the meal ended.

The war from the beginning had been for her a sacred cause. She had yearned to be a man that she might stand in the forefront of battle. She had envied the women of Russia who had formed a Battalion of Death. Her father had laughed at her. "You'd be like a white kitten in a dog fight."

It seemed intolerable that tongues should be busy with this talk of young Drake's cowardice. He had seemed something so much more than that. And he was a man—with a man's right to leadership. What was the matter with him?

The night before she had slept little—Derry's voice—Derry's eyes! She had gone over every word that he had said. She had risen early in the morning to write in her memory book, and she had drawn a most entrancing border about the page, with melting strawberry ice, lilies of France, Cinderella slippers, and red-ink lobsters, rather nightmarishly intermingled!

He had seemed so fine—so—she fell back on her much overworked word *wonderful*—her heart had run to meet him, and now—it would have to run back again. How silly she had been not to see.

After dinner they danced in the Long Room, which was rather famous from a decorative point of view. It was medieval in effect, with a balcony and tapestries, and some precious bits of armor. There was a lion-skin flung over the great chair where Mrs. Witherspoon was enthroned.

Between dances, Jean and Ralph sat on the balcony steps, and talked of many things which brought the red to Jean's cheeks, and a troubled light into her eyes.

And it was from the balcony-steps that, as the evening waned, she saw Derry Drake standing in the great arched doorway.

There was a black velvet curtain behind him which accentuated his fairness. He did not look nineteen. Jean had a fleeting vision of a certain steel engraving of the "Princes in the Tower" which had hung in her grandmother's house. Derry was not in the least like those lovely imprisoned boys, yet she had an overwhelming sense of his kinship to them.

As young Drake's eyes swept the room, he was aware of Jean on the balcony steps. She was in white and silver, with a touch of that heavenly blue which seemed to belong to her. Her crinkled hair was combed quaintly over her ears and back from her forehead. He smiled at her, but she apparently did not see him.

He made his way to Mrs. Witherspoon. "I was so sorry to get here late. But my other engagements kept me. If I could have dined at two places, you should have had at least a half of me."

"We wanted the whole. You know Dr. McKenzie, Derry?"

The two men shook hands. "May I dance with your daughter?" Derry said, smiling.

"Of course. She is up there on the stairs."

Jean saw him coming. Ever since Derry had stood in the door she had been trying to make up her mind how she would treat him when he came. Somebody ought to show him that his millions didn't count. She hadn't thought of his millions last night. If he had been just the shabby boy of the Toy Shop, she would have liked his eyes just as much, and his voice!

But a slacker was a slacker! A coward was a coward! All the money in the world couldn't take away the stain. A man who wouldn't fight at this moment for the freedom of the world was a renegade! She would have none of him.

He came on smiling. "Hello, Ralph. Miss McKenzie, your father says you may dance with me—I hope you have something left?"

The blood sang in her ears, her cheeks burned.

"I haven't anything left—for you—" The emphasis was unmistakable.

"I HAVEN'T ANYTHING LEFT FOR YOU"

[Illustration: "I haven't anything left for you."]

Even then he did not grasp what had happened to him. "Ralph will let me have one of his—be a good sport, Ralph."

"Well, I like that," Ralph began. Then Jean's crisp voice stopped him. "I am not going to dance any more—my head aches. I—I shall ask Daddy to take me—home—"

It was all very young and obvious. Derry gave her a puzzled stare. Ralph protested. "Oh, look here, Jean. If you think you aren't going to dance any more with me."

"Well, I'm not. I am going home. Please take me down to Daddy."

It seemed a long time before the blurred good-byes were said, and Jean was alone with her father in the cozy comfort of the closed car.

"Do you love me, Daddy?"

"My darling, yes."

"May I live with you always—to the end of my days?"

He chuckled. "So that was it? Poor Ralph!"

"You know you are not sorry for him, Daddy. Don't be a hypocrite."

He drew her close to him. "I should be sorry for myself if he took you from me."

She clung to him. "He is not going to take me away."

"Was that what you were telling him on the balcony stairs?"

"Yes. And he said I was too young to know my own mind. That I was a sleeping Princess—and some day he would wake me—up—"

"Oh."

21

"And he is not the Prince, Daddy. There isn't any Prince."

She had shut resolutely away from her the vision of Derry Drake as she had seen him on the night of Cinderella. She would have no white-feathered knight! Princes were brave and rode to battle!

CHAPTER VI
THE PROMISE

It was Alma who gave Derry Drake the key to Jean's conduct.

"Did your ears burn?" she asked, as they danced together after Jean and her father had gone.

"When?"

"We were talking about you at dinner."

"I hope you said nice things."

"I did, of course." Her lashes flashed up and fluttered down as they had flashed and fluttered for Ralph. Every man was for Alma a possible conquest. Derry was big game, and as yet her little darts had not pierced him. She still hoped, however. "I did, but the rest didn't."

He shrank from the things which she might tell him. "What did they say?" His voice caught.

"I shan't tell you. But it was about the war, and your not fighting. As if it made any difference. You are as brave as any of them."

He glanced down at her with somber eyes. Quite unreasonably he hated her for her defense of him. If all women defended men who wouldn't fight, what kind of a world would it be? Women who were worth anything girded their men for battle.

He knew now the reason for Jean's high head and burning cheeks, and in spite of his sense of agonizing humiliation, he was glad to think of that high-held head.

For such women, for such women men died!

But not for women like Alma Drew!

He got away from her as soon as possible. He got away from them all. He had a morbid sense of whispering voices and of averted glances. He fancied that Mrs. Witherspoon touched his hand coldly as he bade her "good-night."

Well, he would not come again until he could meet their eyes.

It was a perfectly clear night, and he walked home. With his face turned up to the stars, he told himself that the situation was intolerable—tomorrow morning, he would go to his father.

When he reached home, his father was asleep. Derry looked in on him and found Bronson sitting erect and wide-eyed beside a night lamp which threw the rest of the room into a sort of golden darkness. The General was in a great lacquered bed which he had brought with him years ago from China. Gilded dragons guarded it and princes had slept in it. Heavy breathing came from the bed.

"I think he has caught cold, sir," Bronson whispered. "I'm a bit afraid of bronchitis."

Derry's voice lacked sympathy. "I shouldn't worry, Bronson. He usually comes around all right."

"Yes, sir. I hope so, sir," and Bronson's spare figure rose to a portentous shadow, as he preceded Derry to the door.

On the threshold he said, "Dr. Richards has gone to the front. Shall I call Dr. McKenzie if we need someone—?"

"Has he been left in charge?"

"Yes, sir."

Derry stood for a moment undecided. "I suppose there's no reason why you shouldn't call McKenzie. Do as you think best, Bronson."

On his way to his own room, Derry paused for a moment at the head of the great stairway. His mother's picture hung on the landing. The dress in which she was painted had been worn to a dinner at the White House during the first Cleveland Administration. It was of white brocade, with its ostrich feather trimming making it a rather regal robe. It had tight sleeves, and the neck was square. Around her throat was a wide collar of pearls with diamond slides. Her fair hair was combed back in the low pompadour of the period, and there were round flat curls on her temples. The picture was old-fashioned, but the painted woman was exquisite, as she had always been, as she would always be in Derry's dreams.

The great house had given to the General's wife her proper setting. She had trailed her satins and silks up and down the marble stairway. Her slender hands, heavy with their rings, had rested on its balustrade, its mirrors had reflected the diamond tiara with which the General had crowned her. In the vast drawing room, the gold and jade and ivory treasures in the cabinets had seemed none too fine for this greatest treasure of them all. In the dining room the priceless porcelains had been cheapened by her greater worth. The General had travelled far and wide, and he had brought the wealth of the world to lay at the feet of his young wife. He adored her and he adored her son.

22

"It is just you and me, Derry," the old man had said in the first moment of bereavement; "we've got to stick it out together—"

And they had stuck it out until the war had come, and patriotism had flared, and the staunch old soldier had spurned this—changeling.

It seemed to Derry that if his mother could only step down from the picture she might make things right for him. But she would not step down. She would go on smiling her gentle painted smile as if nothing really mattered in the whole wide world.

Thus, with his father asleep in the lacquered bed, and his mother smiling in her gilded frame, the son stood alone in the great shell of a house which had in it no beating heart, no throbbing soul to answer his need.

Derry's rooms were furnished in a lower key than those in which his father's taste had been followed. There were gray rugs and gray walls, some old mahogany, the snuff-box picture of Napoleon over his desk, a dog-basket of brown wicker in a corner.

Muffin, Derry's Airedale, stood at attention as his master came in. He knew that the length of his sojourn depended on his manners.

A bright fire was burning, a long chair slanted across the hearthrug. Derry got into a gray dressing gown and threw himself into the chair. Muffin, with a solicitous sigh, sat tentatively on his haunches. His master had had no word for him. Things were very bad indeed, when Derry had no word for his dog.

At last it came. "Muffin—it's a rotten old world."

Muffin's tail beat the rug. His eager eyes asked for more.

It came—"Rotten."

Derry made room among the pillows, and Muffin curled up beside him in rapturous silence. The fire snapped and flared, flickered and died. Bronson tiptoed in to ask if Derry wanted him. Young Martin, who valeted Derry when Bronson would let him, followed with more proffers of assistance.

Derry sent them both away. "I am going to bed."

But he did not go to bed. He read a letter which his mother had written before she died. He had never broken the seal until now. For on the outside of the envelope were these words in fine feminine script: "Not to be opened until the time comes when my boy Derry is tempted to break his promise."

It began, "Boy dear—"

"I wonder if I shall make you understand what it is so necessary that you should understand? It has been so hard all of these years when your clear little lad's eyes have looked into mine to feel that some day you might blame—me. Youth is so uncompromising, Derry, dear—and so logical—so demanding of—justice. And life isn't logical—or just—not with the sharp-edged justice which gives cakes to the good little boys and switches to the bad ones. And you have always insisted on the cakes and switches, Derry, and that's why I am afraid of you.

"Even when you were only ten and I hugged you close in the night—those nights when we were alone, Derry, and your father was out on some wild road under the moonlight, or perhaps with the snow shutting out the moon, you used to whisper, 'But he oughtn't to do it, Mother—' And I knew that he ought not, but, oh, Derry, I loved him, and do you remember, I used to say, 'But he's so good to us, Laddie,—and perhaps we can love him enough to make him stop.'

"But you are a man now, Derry. I am sure you will be a man before you read this, for my little boy will obey me until he comes to man's estate, and then he may say 'She was only a foolish loving woman, and why should I be bound?'

"I know when that moment comes that all your father's money will not hold you. You will not sell your soul's honor for your inheritance. Haven't I known it all along? Haven't I seen you a little shining knight ready to do battle for your ideals? And haven't I seen the clash of those ideals with the reality of your father's fault?

"Well, there's this to think of now, Derry, now that you are a man—that life isn't white and black, it isn't sheep and goats—it isn't just good people and bad people with a great wall between. Life is gray and amethyst, it is a touch of dinginess on the fleece of the whole flock, and the men and women whom you meet will be those whose great faults are balanced by great virtues and whose little meannesses are contradicted by unexpected generosities.

"I am putting it this way because I want you to realize that except for the one fault which has shadowed your father's life, there is no flaw in him. Other men have gone through the world apparently untouched by any temptation, but their families could tell you the story of a thousand tyrannies, their clerks could tell you of selfishness and hardness, their churches and benevolent societies could tell you of their lack of charity. Oh, there are plenty of good men in the world, Derry, strong and fine and big, I want you to believe that always, but I want you to believe, too, that there are men who struggle continually with temptation and seem to fail, but they fight with an enemy so formidable that I, who have seen the struggle, have shut my eyes—afraid to look—.

"And now I shall go back to the very beginning, and tell you how it all happened. Your father was only a boy when the Civil War broke out. He came down from Massachusetts with a regiment which had in it the blood of the farmers who fired the shot heard round the world—. He felt that he was fighting for Freedom—he had all of your ideals, Derry; plus, perhaps, a few of his own.

"You know how the war dragged, four years of it—and much of the time that Massachusetts regiment was in swamp and field, on the edge of fever-breeding streams, never very well fed, cold in winter, hot in summer.

"They were given for medicine quinine and—whiskey. It kept them alive. Sometimes it kept them warm, sometimes it lifted them above reality and granted them a moment's reckless happiness.

"It was all wrong, of course. I am making no plea for its rightness; and it unchained wild beasts in some of the men. Your father for many years kept his chained, but the beasts were there.

"He was almost fifty when I married him, and he was not a General. That title was given to him during the Spanish War. I was twenty when I came here a bride. There was no deception on your father's part. He told me of the dragon he fought—he told me that he hoped with God's help and mine to conquer. And I hoped, too, Derry. I did more than that. I was so sure of him—my King could do no wrong.

"But the day came when he went on one of those desolate pilgrimages where you and I so often followed in later years. I am not going to try to tell you how we fought together, Derry; how I learned with such agony of soul that a man's will is like wax in the fire of temptation—oh, Derry, Derry—.

"I am telling you this for more reasons than one. What your father has been you might be. With all your ideals there may be in you some heritage of weakness, of appetite. Wild beasts can conquer you, too, if you let them in. And that's why I have preached and prayed. That's why I've kept you from that which overcame your father. You are no better, no stronger, than he was in the glory of his youth. But I have barred the doors against the flaming dragon.

"I have no words eloquent enough to tell you of his care of me, his consideration, his devotion. Yet nothing of all this helped in those strange moods that came upon him. Then you were forgotten, I was forgotten, the world was forgotten, and he let everything go—.

"I have kept what I have suffered to some extent from the world. If people have pitied they have had the grace at least not to let me see. The tragedy has been that you should have been sacrificed to it, your youth shadowed. But what could I do? I felt that you must know, must see, and I felt, too, that the salvation of the father might be accomplished through the son.

"And so I let you go out into the night after him, I let you know that which should, perhaps, have been hidden from you. But I loved him, Derry—I loved you—I did the best I could for both of you.

"And now because of the past, I plead for the future. I want you to stay with him, Derry. No matter what happens I beg that you will stay—for the sake of the boy who was once like you, for the sake of the man who held your mother always close to his heart, for the sake of the mother who in Heaven holds you to your promise."

The great old house was very still. Somewhere in a shadowed room an old man slept heavily with his servant sitting stiff and straight beside him, at the head of the stairway a painted bride smiled in the darkness, the dog Muffin stirred and whined.

Derry's head was buried deep in the cushion. His hands clutched the letter which had cut the knot of his desperate decision.

No—one could not break a promise to a mother in Heaven....

He waked heavily in the morning. Bronson was beside his bed. "I am sorry to disturb you, sir, but Dr. McKenzie would like to speak to you."

"McKenzie?"

"Yes, sir. I had to call him last night. Your father was worse."

"Bring him right in here, Bronson, and have some coffee for us."

When Dr. McKenzie was ushered into Derry's sitting room, he found a rather pale and languid young man in the long chair.

"I hated to wake you, Drake. But it was rather necessary that I should talk your father's case over with you."

"Is he very ill?"

"It isn't that—there are complications that I don't care to discuss with servants."

"You mean he has been drinking?"

"Yes. Heavily. You realize that's a rather serious thing for a man of his age."

"I know it. But there's nothing to be done."

"What makes you say that?"

"We've tried specialists—cures. I've been half around the world with him."

The Doctor nodded. "It's hard to pull up at that age."

"My mother's life was spent in trying to help him. He's a dear old chap, really."

"There is, of course, the possibility that he may get a grip on himself."

Derry's languor left him. "Do you think there's the least hope of it? Frankly? No platitudes?"

"We are making some rather interesting experiments—psycho-analysis—things like that—"

He stood up. He was big and breezy. "What's the matter with you this morning? You ought to be up and out."

Derry flushed. "Nothing—much."

The Doctor sat down again. "I'd tell most men to take a cold shower and a two hours' tramp, but it's more than that with you—."

"It's a ease of suspended activity. I want to get into the war—"

"Why don't you?"

"I can't leave Dad. Surely you can see that."

"I don't see it. He must reap, every man must."

"But there's more than that. My mother tied me by a promise. And people are calling me a coward—even Dad thinks I am a slacker, and I can't say to him, 'If you were more than the half of a man I might be a whole one.'"

"Your mother couldn't have foreseen this war."

"It would have made no difference. Her world was centered in him. You know, of course, Doctor, that I wouldn't have spoken of this to anyone else—"

"My dear fellow, I am father confessor to half of my patients." The Doctor's eyes were kind. "My lips will be sealed. But if you want my advice I should throw the old man overboard. Let him sink or swim. Your life is your own."

"It has never been my own." He went to a desk and took out an envelope. "It's a rather sacred letter, but I want you to read it—I read it for the first time last night."

When at last the Doctor laid the letter down, Derry said very low, "Do you blame me?"

"My dear fellow; she had no right to ask it."

"But having asked—?"

"It is a moving letter, and you loved her—but I still contend she had no right to ask."

"I gave my sacred word."

"I question whether any promise should stand between a man and his country's need of him."

They faced each other. "I wonder—" Derry said, "I—I must think it over, Doctor."

"Give yourself a chance if you do. We can go too far in our sacrifice for others—." He resumed his brisk professional manner. "In the meantime you've a rather sick old gentleman on your hands. You'd better get a nurse."

CHAPTER VII

HILDA

The argument came up at breakfast two days before Thanksgiving. It was a hot argument. Jean beat her little hands upon the table. Hilda's hands were still, but it was an irritating stillness.

"What do you think, Daddy?"

"Hilda is right. There is no reason why we should go to extremes."

"But a turkey—."

"Nobody has said that we shouldn't have a turkey on Thanksgiving—not even Hoover." Hilda's voice was as irritating as her hands.

"Well, we have consciences, Hilda. And a turkey would choke me."

"You make so much of little things."

"Is it a little thing to sacrifice our appetites?"

"I don't think it is a very big thing." The office bell rang, and Hilda rose. "If I felt as you do I should sacrifice something more than things to eat. I'd go over there and nurse the wounded. I could be of real service. But you couldn't. With all your big ideas of patriotism you couldn't do one single practical thing."

It was true, and Jean knew that it was true, but she fired one more shot. "Then why don't you go?" she demanded fiercely.

"I may," Hilda said slowly. "I have been thinking about it. I haven't made up my mind."

Dr. McKenzie glanced at her in surprise. "I didn't dream you felt that way."

"I don't think I do mean it in the way you mean. I should go because there was something worth doing—not as a grandstand play."

She went out of the room. Jean stared after her.

The Doctor laughed. "She got you there, girlie."

"Yes, she did. Do you really think she intends to go, Daddy?"

"It is news to me."

"Good news?"

He shook his head. "She is a very valuable nurse. I should hate to lose her." He sat for a moment in silence, then stood up. "I shouldn't hold out for a turkeyless Thanksgiving if I were you. It isn't necessary."

"Are you taking Hilda's part, Daddy?"

"No, my dear, of course not." He came over and kissed her. "Will you ride with me this morning?"

"Oh, yes—how soon?"

"In ten minutes. After I see this patient."

In less time than that she was ready and waiting for him in her squirrel coat and hat and her little muff.

Her father surveyed her. "Such a lovely lady."

"Do you like me, Daddy?"

"What a question—I love you."

Safe in the car, with the glass screen shutting away the chauffeur, Jean returned to the point of attack.

"Hilda makes me furious, Daddy. I came to talk about her."

"I thought you came because you wanted to ride with me."

"Well, I did. But for this, too."

Over her muff, her stormy eyes surveyed him. "You think I am unreasonable about meatless and wheatless days. But you don't know. Hilda ignores them, Daddy—you should see the breadbox. And the other day she ordered a steak for dinner, one of those big thick ones—and it was Tuesday, and I happened to go down to the kitchen and saw it—and I told the cook that we wouldn't have it, and when I came up I told Hilda, and she laughed and said that I was silly.

"And I said that if she had that steak cooked I would not eat it, and I should ask you not to eat it, and she just stood with her hands flat on your desk, you know the way she does—I hate her hands—and she said that of course if I was going to make a fuss about it she wouldn't have the steak, but that it was simply a thing she couldn't understand. The steak was there, why not eat it? And I said it was because of the psychological effect on other people. And she said we were having too much psychology and not enough common sense in this war!

"Well, after that, I went to my Red Cross meeting at the church. I expected to have lunch there, but I changed my mind and came home. Hilda was at the table alone, and, Daddy, she was eating the steak, the whole of it—." She paused to note the effect of her revelation.

"Well?"

"She was eating it when all the world needs food! She made me think of those dreadful creatures in the fairy books. She's—she's a ghoul—"

"My dear."

"A ghoul. You should have seen her, with great chunks of bread and butter."

"Hilda has a healthy appetite."

"Of course you defend her."

"My dear child—"

"Oh you do, Daddy, always, against me—and I'm your daughter—"

She wept a tear or two into her muff, then raised her eyes to find him regarding her quizzically. "Are you going to spoil my ride?"

"You are spoiling mine."

"We won't quarrel about it. And we'll stop at Small's. Shall it be roses or violets, to-day, my dear?"

She chose violets, as more in accord with her pensive mood, lighting the bunch, however, with one red rose. The question of Hilda was not settled, but she yielded as many an older woman has yielded—to the sweetness of tribute—to man's impulse to make things right not by justice but by the bestowal of his bounty.

From the florist's, they went to Huyler's old shop on F Street, where the same girl had served Jean with ice-cream sodas and hot chocolate for fifteen years. Administrations might come and administrations go, but these pleasant clerks had been cup-bearers to them all—Presidents' daughters and diplomats' sons—the sturdy children of plain Congressmen, the scions of noble families across the seas.

It was while Jean sat on a high stool beside her father, the sunshine shining on her through the wide window, that Derry Drake, coming down Twelfth, saw her!

Well, he wanted a lemonade. And the fact that she was there in a gray squirrel coat and bunch of violets with her copper-colored hair shining over her ears wasn't going to leave him thirsty!

He went in. He bowed to the Doctor and received a smile in return. Jean's eyes were cold above her chocolate. Derry bought his check, went to a little table on the raised platform at the back of the room, drank his lemonade and hurried out.

"A nice fellow," said the Doctor, watching him through the window. "I wonder why he didn't stop and speak to us?"

"I'm glad he didn't."

"My dear, why?"

"I've found out things—"

"What things?"

"That he's a—coward," with tense earnestness. "He won't fight."

"Who told you that?"

"Everybody's saying it."

"Everybody is dead wrong."

"What do you mean, Daddy?"

"What I have just said. Everybody is dead wrong."

"How do you know?"

"A doctor knows a great many things which he is not permitted to tell. I am rather bound not to tell in this case."

"Oh, but you could tell me."

"Hardly—it was given in confidence."

"Did he? Oh, Daddy, did he tell you?"

"Yes."

"And he isn't a slacker?"

"No."

"I knew it—."

"You didn't. You thought he was a coward."

"Well, I ought to have known better. He looks brave, doesn't he?"

"I shouldn't call him exactly a heroic figure."

"Shouldn't you?"

She finished her chocolate in silence, and followed him in silence to his car. They sped up F Street, gay with its morning crowd.

Then at last it came. "Isn't it a wonderful day, Daddy?"

He smiled down at her. "There you go."

"Well, it is wonderful." She fell again into silence, then again bestowed upon him her raptures. "Wouldn't it be dreadful if we had loveless days, Daddy, as well as meatless ones and wheatless?"

That night, after Jean had gone to bed, the Doctor, having dismissed his last patient, came out of his inner office. Hilda, in her white nurse's costume, was busy with the books. He stood beside her desk. His eyes were dancing. "Jean told me about the steak."

"I knew she would—I suppose it was an awful thing to do. But I was hungry, and I hate fish—" She smiled at him lazily, then laughed.

He laughed back. He felt that it would be unbearable for Hilda to go hungry, to spoil her red and white with abstinence.

"My dear girl," he said, "what did you mean when you spoke of going away?"

"Haven't you been thinking of going?"

The color came up in his cheeks. "Yes, but how did you know it?"

"Well, a woman knows. Why don't you make up your mind?"

"There's Jean to think of."

"Emily Bridges could take care of her. And you ought to go. Men are seeing things over there that they'll never see again. And women are."

"If my country needs me—"

Hilda was cold. "I shouldn't go for that. As I told Jean, I am not making any grand stand plays. I should go for all that I get out of it, the experience, the adventure—."

He looked at her with some curiosity. Jean's words of the afternoon recurred to him. "She's a ghoul—"

Yet there was something almost fascinating in her frankness. She tore aside ruthlessly the curtain of self-deception, revealing her motives, as if she challenged him to call them less worthy than his own.

"If I go, it will be because I want to become a better nurse. I like it here, but your practice is necessarily limited. I should get a wider view of things. So would you. There would be new worlds of disease, men in all conditions of nervous shock."

"I know. But I'd hate to think I was going merely for selfish ends."

She shrugged. "Why not that as well as any other?"

He had a smouldering sense of irritation.

"When I am with Jean she makes me feel rather big and fine; when I am with you—" He paused.

"I make you see yourself as you are, a man. She thinks you are more than that."

27

All his laughter left ham. "It is something to be a hero to one's daughter. Perhaps some day I shall be a little better for her thinking so."

She saw that she had gone too far. "You mustn't take the things I say too seriously."

The bell of the telephone at her elbow whirred. She put the receiver to her ear. "It is General Drake's man; he thinks you'd better come over before you go to bed."

"I was afraid I might have to go. He is in rather bad shape, Hilda."

She packed his bag for him competently, and telephoned for his car. "I'll have a cup of coffee ready for you when you get back," she said, as she stood in the door. "It is going to be a dreadful night."

The streets were icy and the sleet falling. "You'd better have your overshoes," Hilda decided, and went for them.

As he put them on, she stood under the hall light, smiling. "Have you forgiven me?" she asked as he straightened up.

"For telling me the truth? Of course. You take such good care of me, Hilda."

Upstairs in her own room Jean was writing a letter. It was a very pretty room, very fresh and frilly with white dimity and with much pink and pale lavender. The night-light which shone through the rose taffeta petticoats of a porcelain lady was supplemented at the moment by a bed-side lamp which flung a ring of gold beyond Jean's blotter to the edge of the lace spread. For Jean was writing in bed. All day her mind had been revolving around this letter, but she had had no time to write. She had spent the afternoon in the Toy Shop with Emily, and in the evening there had been a Red Cross sale. She had gone to the sale with Ralph Witherspoon and his mother. She had not been able to get out of going. All the time she had talked to Ralph she had thought of Derry. She had rather hoped that he might be there, but he wasn't.

The letter required much thought. She tore up, extravagantly, several sheets of note-paper with tiny embossed thistles at the top. Doctor McKenzie was intensely Scotch, and he was entitled to a crest, but he was also intensely American, and would have none of it. He had designed Jean's note-paper, and it was lovely. But it was also expensive, and it was a shame to waste so much of it on Derry Drake.

The note when it was finished seemed very simple. Just one page in Jean's firm, clear script:

"Dear Mr. Drake:—

"Could you spare me one little minute tomorrow? I shall be at home at four. It is very important—to me at least. Perhaps when you hear what I have to say, it will seem important to you. I hope it may.

"Very   sincerely   yours,
"JEAN MCKENZIE."

She read it over several times. It seemed very stiff and inadequate. She sealed it and stamped it, then in a panic tore it open for a re-reading. She was oppressed by doubts. Did nice girls ask men to come and see them? Didn't they wait and weary like Mariana of the Moated Grange—? "He cometh not, she said?"

New times! New manners! She had branded a man as a coward. She had condemned him unheard. She had slighted him, she had listened while others slandered—why should she care what other women had done? Would do? Her way was clear. She owed an apology to Derry Drake, and she would make it.

So with a new envelope, a new stamp, the note was again sealed.

It had to be posted that night. She felt that under no circumstance could she stand the suspense of another day.

She had heard her father go out. Hilda was coming up, the maids were asleep. She waited until Hilda's door was shut, then she slipped out of bed, tucked her toes into a pair of sandals, threw a furry motor coat around her, and sped silently down the stairs. She shrank back as she opened the front door. The sleet rattled on the steps, the pavements were covered with white.

The mail-box was in front of the house. She made a rush for it, dropped in the precious letter, and gained once more the haven of the warm hall.

She was glad to get back to her room. As she settled down among her pillows, she had a great sense of adventure, as if she had travelled far in a few moments.

As a matter of fact, she had made her first real excursion into the land of romance. She found her thoughts galloping.

At the foot of the bed her silver Persian, Polly Ann, lay curled on her own gray blanket.

"Polly Ann," Jean said, "if he doesn't come, I shall hate myself for writing that note."

Polly Ann surveyed her sleepily.

"But it would serve me right if he didn't, Polly Ann."

She turned off the light and tried to sleep. Downstairs the telephone rang. It rang, too, in Hilda's room. Hilda's door opened and shut. She came across the hall and tapped on Jean's door. "May I come in?"

"Yes."

"Your father has just telephoned," Hilda said from the threshold, "that General Drake's nurse is not well, and will have to be taken off the case. I shall have to go in her place. There is a great shortage at the hospital. Will you be afraid to stay alone, or shall I wake up Ellen and have her sleep on the couch in your dressing room?"

"Of course I am not afraid, Hilda. Nothing can happen until father comes back."

As Hilda went away, Jean had a delicious feeling of detachment. She would be alone in the house with her thoughts of Derry.

She got out of bed to say her prayers. With something of a thrill she prayed for Derry's father. She was not conscious as she made her petitions of any ulterior motive. Yet a placated Providence would, she felt sure, see that the General's sickness should not frustrate the plans which she had quite daringly made for his son.

CHAPTER VIII
THE SHADOWED ROOM

Derry had dined that night with his cousin, Margaret Morgan. Margaret's husband was somewhere in France with Pershing's divisions. Margaret was to have news of him this evening, brought by a young English officer, Dawson Hewes, who had been wounded at Ypres, and who had come on a recruiting mission, among his countrymen in America.

The only other guest was to be Drusilla Gray.

Derry had gone over early to have the twilight hour with Margaret's children. There was Theodore, the boy, and Margaret-Mary, on the edge of three. They had their supper at five in the nursery, and after that there was always the story hour, with nurse safely downstairs for her dinner, their mother, lovely in a low-necked gown, and father coming in at the end. For several months their father had not come, and the best they could do was to kiss his picture in the frame with the eagle on it, to put flowers in front of it, and to say their little prayers for the safety of men in battle.

It was Cousin Derry who dropped in now at the evening hour. He was a famous story-teller, and they always welcomed him uproariously.

Margaret Morgan, perhaps better than any other, knew in those days what was in Derry's heart. She knew the things against which he had struggled, and she had rebelled hotly, "Why should he be sacrificed?" she had asked her husband more than once during the three years which had preceded America's entrance into the war. "He wants to be over there driving an ambulance—doing his bit. Aunt Edith always idealized the General, and Derry is paying the price."

"Most women idealize the men they love, honey-girl." Winston Morgan was from the South, and he drew upon its store of picturesque endearments to express his joy and pride in his own Peggy. "And if they didn't where should we be?"

She had leaned her head against him. "I don't need to idealize you," she had said, comfortably, "but the General is different. Aunt Edith made Derry live his father's life, not his own, and it has moulded him into something less than he might have been if he had been allowed more initiative."

Winston had shaken his head. "Discipline is a mighty good thing in the Army, Peggy, and it's a mighty good thing in life. Derry Drake is as hard as steel, and as finely tempered. If he ever does break loose, he'll be all the more dynamic for having held himself back."

Margaret, conceding all that, was yet constrained to pour out upon Derry the wealth of her womanly sympathy. It was perhaps the knowledge of this as well as his devotion to her children which brought him often to her door.

Tonight she was sitting on a low-backed seat in front of the fire with a child on each side of her. She was in white, her dark hair in a simple shining knot, a little pearl heart which had been Captain Morgan's parting gift, her only ornament.

"Go on with your story," he said, as he came in. "I just want to listen and do nothing."

She glanced up at him. He looked tired, unlike himself, depressed.

"Anything the matter?"

"Father isn't well. Dr. McKenzie has taken the case. Richards has gone to the front. Bronson will call me if there are any unfavorable developments."

Margaret-Mary, curled up like a kitten in the curve of Cousin Derry's arm, was exploring his vest pocket. She found two very small squares of Washington taffy wrapped in wax paper, one for herself and one for Teddy. It was Derry's war-time offering. No other candies were permitted by Margaret's patriotism. Her children ate molasses on their bread, maple sugar on their cereal. Her soldier was in France, and there were other soldiers, not one of whom should suffer because of the wanton waste of food by the people who stayed softly at home.

"You tell us a story, Uncle Derry," Teddy pleaded as he ate his taffy.

"I'd rather listen to your mother."

"They are tired of me," Margaret told him.

"We are not ti-yard," her small son enunciated carefully, "but you said you had to fix the f'owers."

"Well, I have. May I turn them over to you, Derry?"

"For a minute. But you must come back."

She came back presently, to find the lights out and only the glow of the fire to illumine faintly the three figures on the sofa. She stood unseen in the door and listened.

"And so the Tin Soldier stood on the shelf where the little boy had put him, and nothing happened in the old, old house. There was just an old, old man, and walls covered with old, old portraits, and knights in armor, and wooden trumpeters carved on the door who blew with all their might, 'Trutter-a-trutt, Trutter-a-trutt'—. But the old man and the portraits and the wooden trumpeters had no thought for the Tin Soldier who stood there on the shelf, alone and longing to go to the war. And at last the Tin Soldier cried out, 'I can't stand it. I want to go to the wars—I want to go to the wars!' But nobody listened or cared."

"Poor 'itte sing," Margaret-Mary crooned.

"If I had been there," Teddy proclaimed, "I'd have put him on the floor and told him to run and run and run!"

"But there was nobody to put him on the floor," said Derry, "so at last the Tin Soldier could stand it no longer. 'I will go to the wars, I will go to the wars,' he cried, and he threw himself down from the shelf."

The story stopped suddenly. "Go on, go on," urged the little voices in the dark.

"Perhaps you think that was the end of it, and that the Tin Soldier ran away to the wars, to help his country and save the world from ruin. But Fate wasn't as kind to him as that. For when the little boy came again to the old house, he looked for the Tin Soldier. But he wasn't on the shelf. And he looked and looked and, the old man looked, and the wooden trumpeters blew out their cheeks, 'Trutter-a-trutt, trutter-a-trutt—where is the Tin Soldier?—trutter-a-trutt—.'

"But they did not find him, for the Tin Soldier had fallen through a crack in the floor, and there he lay as in an open grave."

Drusilla's voice was heard in the lower hall, and the deeper voice of Captain Hewes. Margaret sped down to meet them, leaving the story, reluctantly, in that moment of heart-breaking climax.

When later Derry followed her, she had a chance to say, "I hope you gave it a happy ending."

"Oh, did you hear? Yes. They found him in time to send him away to war. But Hans Andersen didn't end it that way. He knew life."

She stared at him in amazement. Was this the Derry whose supply of cheerfulness had seemed inexhaustible? Whose persistent optimism had been at times exasperating to his friends?

Throughout the evening she was aware of his depression. She was aware, too, of the mistake which she had made in bringing Derry and Captain Hewes together.

The Captain had red hair and a big nose. But he was a gentleman in the fine old English sense; he was a soldier with but one idea, that every physically able man should fight. Every sentence that he spoke was charged with this belief, and every sentence carried a sting for Derry.

More than once Peggy found it necessary to change the subject frantically. Drusilla supplemented her efforts.

But gradually the Captain's manner froze. With a sort of military sixth sense, he felt that he had been asked to break bread and eat salt with a slacker, and he resented it.

After dinner Drusilla sang for them. Sensitive always to atmosphere, she soothed the Captain with old and familiar songs, "Flow gently, sweet Afton," and "Believe me if all those endearing young charms."

Then straight from these to "I'm going to marry 'Arry on the Fifth of January."

"Oh, I say—Harry Lauder," was Captain Hewes' eager comment. "I heard him singing to the chaps in the trenches just before I sailed—a little stocky man in a red kilt. He'd laugh, and you'd want to cry."

Drusilla gave them "Wee Hoose among the Heather," with the touch of pathos which the little man in the red kilt had imparted to it as he had sung it in October in New York before an audience which had wept as it had welcomed him.

"Queer thing," Captain Hewes mused, "what the war has done to him, set him preaching and all that."

"Oh, it isn't queer," Margaret was eager. "That is one of the things the war is doing, bringing men back to—God—" A sob caught in her throat.

Drusilla's hands strayed upon the keys, and into the Battle Hymn of the Republic.

> "I have seen Him in the watch fires of a hundred circling camps,
> They have builded Him an altar in the evening dews and damps,

I can read His righteous sentence by the dim and flaring lamps,
His day is marching on—"

It was an old tune, but the words were new to Captain Hewes—as the girl chanted them, in that repressed voice that yet tore the heart out of him.

"He has sounded forth the trumpet that shall never call retreat,
He is sifting out the hearts of men before His judgment seat,
Oh, be swift, my soul, to answer Him, be jubilant my feet,
Our God is marching on—"

The Captain sat on the edge of his chair. His face was illumined.

"By Jove," he ejaculated, "that's topping!"

Drusilla stood up with her back to the piano, and sang without music.

"In the beauty of the lilies, Christ was born across the sea—
With the glory in His bosom that transfigures you and me,
As He died to make men holy, let us die to make men free,
While God is marching on—"

She wore a gown of sheer dull blue, there was a red rose in her hair—her white arms, her white neck, the blue and red, youth and fire, strength and purity.

When she finished the room was very still. The big Englishman had no words for such a moment. The music had swept him up to unexpected heights of emotion. While Drusilla sang he had glimpsed for the first time the meaning of democracy, he had seen, indeed, in a great and lofty sense, for the first time—America.

Among the shadows a young man shrank in his seat. His vision was not of Democracy, but of a freezing night—of a ragged old voice rising from the blackness of a steep ravine—

"Oh, be swift, my soul—to answer—Him—
Be jubilant my feet—"

Why had Drusilla chosen that of all songs? Oh, why had she sung at all?

A maid came in to say that Mr. Drake was wanted at the telephone. The message was from Dr. McKenzie. The General was much worse. It might be well for Derry to come home.

So Derry, with a great sense of relief, got away from the frigid Captain, and from the flaming Drusilla, and from Peggy with her flushed air of apology, and went out into the stormy night. He had preferred to walk, although his shoes were thin. "It isn't far," he had said when Margaret expostulated, "and I'll send my car for Drusilla and Captain Hewes."

The sleet drove against his face. His feet were wet before he reached the first corner, the wind buffeted him. But he felt none of it. He was conscious only of his depression and of his great dread of again entering the big house where a sick man lay in a lacquered bed and where a painted lady smiled on the stairs. Where there was nothing alive, nothing young, nothing with lips to welcome him, or with hands to hold out to him.

He found when at last he arrived that the Doctor had sent for Hilda Merritt.

She came presently, in her long blue cloak and small blue bonnet. Hilda made no mistakes in the matter of clothes. She realized the glamour which her nurse's uniform cast over her. In evening dress she was slightly commonplace. In ordinary street garb not an eye would have been turned upon her, but the nun's blue and white of her uniform added the required spiritual effect to her rather full-blown beauty.

As she passed the painted lady at the head of the stairway she gave her a slight glance. Then on and up she went to her appointed task.

"It is pneumonia," Dr. McKenzie told Derry; "that's why I wanted Miss Merritt. She is very experienced, and in these days of war it is hard to get good nurses."

Derry found his voice shaking. "Is there any danger?"

"Naturally, at his age. But I think we are going to pull him through."

Derry went into the shadowed room. His father was breathing heavily. Something clutched at the boy's heart—the fear of the Thing which lurked in the darkness—a chill and sinister figure with a skeleton hand.

He could not have his father die. He would feel as if his thoughts had killed him—a murderer in intention if not in deed. Not thus must the Obstacle be removed. He raised haggard eyes to the Doctor's face. "You—you mustn't think that I store things up against him. He's all I have."

The Doctor's keen glance appraised him. "Don't get morbid over it; he has everything in his favor—and Miss Merritt is famous in such cases."

Hilda took his praise with downcast eyes. Her manner with the Doctor when others were present was professionally deferential. It was only when they were alone that the nurse was submerged in the woman.

With her bonnet off and a white cap in its place, she moved about the room. "I shall be very comfortable," she said, when Derry inquired if anything could be done for her.

"We haven't any women about the place but Cook," he explained. "She has been in our family forever—"

"I'll put a day nurse on tomorrow," the Doctor said, "but I want Hilda with him at night; she can call me up if there's any change, and I'll come right over."

When the Doctor had gone, Derry, seeking his room, found Muffin waiting. Bronson bustled in to see that his young master got out of his wet clothes and into a hot bath. "All the time the Doctor was talking to you, I was worrying about your shoes. Your feet are soaked, sir. Whatever made you walk in the rain?"

"I couldn't ride—I couldn't."

The old man on his knees removing the wet shoes looked up. "Restless, sir?"

"Yes. There are times, Bronson, when I want my mother."

He could say it in this room to Bronson and Muffin—to the gray old dog and the gray old man who adored him.

Bronson put him to bed, settled Muffin among his blankets in a basket by the hot water pipes, opened the windows wide, said "God bless you," and went away.

"Sweet dreams, Muffin," said Derry from the big bed.

The old dog whuffed discreetly.

It was their nightly ceremony.

The sleet came down in golden streaks against the glow of the street lights. Derry lay watching it, and it was a long time before he slept. Not since his mother's death had he been so weighed down with heaviness.

He kept seeing Jean with her head up, declining to dance with him; on the high stool at the confectioner's, her eyes cold above her chocolate; the English Captain and his contemptuous stare; Alma, basely excusing him; Drusilla, in her red and blue and white—singing—!

He waked in the morning with a sore throat. Young Martin came in to light the fire and draw the water for his bath. Later Bronson brought his breakfast and the mail.

"You'd better stay in bed, Mr. Derry."

"I think I shall. How is Dad?"

"The nurse says he is holding his own."

"I am glad of that."

Bronson, feeding warm milk and toast to Muffin, ventured an opinion, "I am not sure that I like the nurse, sir."

"Why not?"

"She's not exactly a lady, and she's not exactly a nurse."

"I see." Derry, having glanced over a letter or two, had picked up an envelope with embossed thistles on the flap. "But she is rather pretty, Bronson."

"Pretty is as pretty does," sententiously.

Silence. Bronson looked across at the young man propped up among the pillows. He was rereading the letter with the thistles on the flap. The strained look had gone out of his eyes, and his lips were smiling.

"I think I'll get up."

"Changed your mind, sir?"

"Yes." He threw back the covers. "I've a thousand things to do."

But there was just one thing which he was going to do which stood out beyond all others. Neither life nor death nor flood nor fire should keep him from presenting himself at four o'clock at Jean McKenzie's door, in response to the precious note which in a moment had changed the world for him.

CHAPTER IX
ROSE-COLOR!

Jean found the day stretching out ahead of her in a series of exciting events. At the breakfast table her father told her that Hilda would stay on General Drake's case, and that she had better have Emily Bridges up for a visit.

"I don't like to have you alone at night, if I am called away."

"It will be heavenly, Daddy, to have Emily—"

And how was he to know that there were other heavenly things to happen? She had resolved that if Derry came, she would tell her father afterwards. But he might not come, so what was the use of being premature?

She sallied down to the Toy Shop in high feather. "You are to stay with us, Emily."

"Oh, am I? How do you know that I can make it convenient?"

"But you will, darling."

Jean's state of mind was beatific. She painted Lovely Dreams with a touch of inspiration which resulted in a row of purple camels: "Midnight on the Desert," Jean called them.

"Oh, Emily," she said, "we must have them in the window on Christmas morning, with the Wise Men and the Star—"

Emily, glancing at the face above the blue apron, was struck by the radiance of it.

"Is it because Hilda is away?" she asked.

"Is what—?"

"Your—rapture."

Jean laughed. "It is because Hilda is away, and other things. But I can't tell you now."

Then for fear Emily might be hurt by her secrecy, she flew to kiss her and again call her "Darling."

At noon she put on her hat and ran home, or at least her heart ran, and when she reached the house she sought the kitchen.

"I am having company for tea, Ellen—at four. And I want Lady-bread-and-butter, and oh, Ellen, will you have time for little pound cakes?"

She knew of course that pound cakes were—*verboten*. She felt, however, that even Mr. Hoover might sanction a fatted calf in the face of this supreme event.

She planned that she would receive Derry in the small drawing room. It was an informal room which had been kept by her mother for intimate friends. There was a wide window which faced west, a davenport in deep rose velvet, some chairs to match, and there were always roses in an old blue bowl.

Jean knew the dress she was going to wear in this room—of blue to match the bowl, with silver lace, and a girdle of pink brocade.

Alone in her room with Polly-Ann to watch proceedings, she got out the lovely gown.

"Oh, I do want to be pretty, Polly-Ann," she said with much wistfulness.

Yet when she was all hooked and snapped into it, she surveyed herself with some dissatisfaction in the mirror.

"Why not?" she asked the mirror. "Why shouldn't I wear it?"

The mirror gave back a vision of beauty—but behind that vision in the depths of limitless space Jean's eyes discerned something which made her change her gown. Quite soberly she got herself into a little nun's frock of gray with collars and cuffs of transparent white, and above it all was the glory of her crinkled hair.

Neither then nor afterwards could she analyze her reasons for the change. Perhaps sub-consciously she was perceiving that this meeting with Derry Drake was to be a serious and stupendous occasion. Throughout the world the emotions of men and women were being quickened to a pace set by a mighty conflict. Never again would Jean McKenzie laugh or cry over little things. She would laugh and cry, of course, but back of it all would be that sense of the world's travail and tragedy, made personal by her own part in it.

Julia, the second maid, was instructed to show Mr. Drake into the little drawing room. Jean came down early with her knitting, and sat on the deep-rose Davenport. The curtains were not drawn. There was always the chance of a sunset view. Julia was to turn on the light when she brought in the tea.

There was the whir of a bell, the murmur of voices. Jean sat tense. Then as her caller entered, she got somewhat shakily on her feet.

But the man in the door was not Derry Drake!

33

In his intrusive and impertinent green, pinched-in as to waist, and puffed-out as to trousers, his cheeks red with the cold, his brown eyes bright with eagerness, Ralph Witherspoon stood on the threshold.

"Of all the good luck," he said, "to find you in."

She shook hands with him and sat down.

"I thought you had gone back to Bay Shore. You said yesterday you were going."

"I got my orders in the nick of time. We are to go to Key West. I am to join the others on the way down."

"How soon?"

He sat at the other end of the davenport. "In three days, and anything can happen in three days."

He moved closer. She had a sense of panic. Was he going to propose to her again, in this room which she had set aside so sacredly for Derry Drake?

"Won't you have some tea?" she asked, desperately. "I'll have Julia bring it in."

"I'd rather talk."

But she had it brought, and Julia, wheeling in the tea-cart, offered a moment's reprieve. And Ralph ate the Lady-bread-and-butter, and the little pound cakes with the nuts and white frosting which had been meant for Derry, and then he walked around the tea-cart and took her hand, and for the seventh time since he had met her he asked her to marry him.

"But I don't love you." She was almost in tears.

"You don't know what love is—I'll teach you."

"I don't want to be taught."

"You don't know what it means to be taught—"

Jean had a stifling sense as of some great green tree bending down to crush her. She put out her hand to push it away.

In the silence a bell whirred—.

Derry Drake, ushered in by Julia, saw the room in the rosy glow of the lamp. He saw Ralph Witherspoon towering insolently in his aviator's green. He saw Jean, blushing and perturbed. The scene struck cold against the heat of his anticipation.

He sat down in one of the rose-colored chairs, and Julia brought more tea for him, more Lady-bread-and-butter, more pound cakes with nuts and frosting.

Ralph was frankly curious. He was also frankly jealous. He was aware that Derry had met Jean for the first time at his mother's dinner dance. And Derry's millions were formidable. It did not occur to Ralph that Derry, without his millions, was formidable. Ralph's idea of a man's attractiveness for women was founded on his belief in their admiration of good looks, and their liking for the possession of, as he would himself have expressed it, "plenty of pep" and "go." From Ralph's point of view Derry Drake was not handsome, and he was utterly unaware that back of Derry's silver-blond slenderness and apparent languidness were banked fires which could more than match his own.

And there was this, too, of which he was unconscious, that Derry's millions meant nothing to Jean. Had he remained the shabby son of the shabby old man in the Toy Shop, her heart would still have followed him.

So, fatuously hopeful, Ralph stayed. He stayed until five, until half-past five. Until a quarter of six.

And he talked of the glories of war!

Derry grew restless. As he sat in the rose-colored chair, he fingered a tassel which caught back one of the curtains of the wide window. It was a silk tassel, and he pulled at one strand of it until it was flossy and frayed. He was unconscious of his work of destruction, unconscious that Jean's eyes, lifted now and then from her knitting, noted his fingers weaving in and out of the rosy strands.

Ralph talked on. With seeming modesty he spoke of the feats of other men, yet none the less it was Ralph they saw, poised like a bird at incredible heights, looping the loop, fearless, splendid—beating the air with strong wings.

Six o'clock, and at last Ralph rose. Even then he hesitated and hung back, as if he expected that Derry might go with him. But Derry, stiff and straight beside the rose-colored chair, bade him farewell!

And now Derry was alone with Jean!

They found themselves standing close together in front of the fire. The garment of coldness and of languor which had seemed to enshroud Derry had dropped from him. The smile which he gave Jean was like warm wine in her veins.

"Well—?"

"I asked you to come—to say—that I am,—sorry—," her voice breaking. "Daddy told me that he knew why—you couldn't fight—"

"I didn't intend that he should tell."

"He didn't," eagerly, "not your reasons. He said it was a—confidence, and he couldn't break his word. But he knew that you were brave. That the things the world is saying are all wrong. Oh, I ought to go down on my knees."

Her face was white, her eyes deep wells of tears.

"It is I," he said, very low, "who should be on my knees—do you know what it means to me to have you tell me this?"

"I wasn't sure that I ought to write. To some men I couldn't have written—"

His face lighted. "When your note came—I can't tell you what it meant to me. I shouldn't like to think of what this day would have been for me if you had not written. Everybody is calling me—a coward. You know that. You heard Witherspoon just now pitying me, not in words, but his manner."

"Oh, Ralph," how easily she disposed of him. "Ralph crows, like a—rooster."

They looked at each other and tried to laugh. But they were not laughing in their hearts.

He lifted her hand and kissed it—then he stood well away from her, anchoring himself again to the silken tassel. "Now that you know a part," he said, from that safe distance, "I'd like to tell you all of it, if I may."

As he talked her fingers were busy with her knitting, but there came moments when she laid it down and looked up at him with eyes that mirrored his own earnestness.

"It—it hasn't been easy," he said in conclusion, "but—but if you will be my friend, nothing will be hard."

She tried to speak—was shaken as if by a strong wind, and her knitting went up as a shield.

"My dear, you are crying," he said, and was on his knees beside her.

And now they were caught in the tide of that mighty wave which was sweeping the world!

When at last she steadied herself, he was again anchored to the rose-colored tassel.

"You—you must forgive me—but—it has been so good to talk it out—to some one—who cared. I had never dreamed until that night in the Toy Shop of anybody—like you. Of anybody so—adorable. When your note came this morning, I couldn't believe it. But now I know it is true. And that night of Cinderella you were so—heavenly."

It was a good thing that Miss Emily came in at that moment—for his eloquence was a burning flood, and Jean was swept up and on with it.

The entrance of Emily, strictly tailored and practical, gave them pause.

"You remember Mr. Drake, don't you, Emily?"

Emily did, of course. But she had not expected to see him here. She held out her hand. "I remember that he was coming back for more of your Lovely Dreams."

"I want all of her dreams," said Derry, and something in the way that he said it took Miss Emily's breath away. "Please don't sell them to anyone else. You have a wholesale order from me."

Miss Emily looked from one to the other. She was conscious of something which touched the stars—something which all her life she had missed, something which belongs to youth and ecstasy.

"Wholesale orders are not in my line," she said. "You can settle that with Jean."

She surveyed the tea-wagon. "I'm starved. And if I eat I shall spoil my dinner."

"I can ring for hot water, Emily, and there are more of the pound cakes."

"My dear, no. I must go upstairs and dress. Your father sent for my bag, and Julia says it is in my room."

She bade Derry a cheerful good-bye, and left them alone.

"I must go, too," said Derry, and took Jean's hand. He stood looking down at her. "May I come tomorrow?"

"Oh,—yes—"

"There's one thing that I should like more than anything, if we could go to church together—to be thankful that—that we've found each other—"

Tears in the shining eyes!

"Why are you crying?"

"Because it is so—sweet."

"Then you'll go?"

"I'd love it."

He dropped her hand and got away. She was little and young, so divinely innocent. He felt that he must not take unfair advantage of that mood of exaltation.

He drove straight downtown and ordered flowers for her. Remembering the nun's dress, he sent violets in a gray basket, with a knot on the handle of heavenly blue.

The flowers came while Jean was at dinner. Emily was in Hilda's place, a quiet contrast in her slenderness and modest black to Hilda's opulence. Dr. McKenzie had not had time to dress.

"I am so busy, Emily."

"But you love the busy-ness, don't you? I can't imagine you without the hours crammed full."

"Just now I wish that I could push it away as Richards pushed it—"

Jean looked up. "But Dr. Richards went to France, Daddy."

"I envy him."

"Oh, do you—?" Then her flowers came, and she forgot everything else.

The Doctor whistled as Julia set the basket in front of Jean. "Ralph is generous."

Jean had opened the attached envelope and was reading a card. A wave of self-conscious color swept over her cheeks. "Ralph didn't send them. It—it was Derry Drake."

"Drake? How did that happen?"

35

"He was here this afternoon for tea, and Ralph, and Emily—only Emily was late, and the tea was cold—"

"So you've made up?"

"We didn't have to make up much, Daddy, did we?" mendaciously.

Miss Emily came to the rescue. "He seems very nice."

"Splendid fellow. But I am not sure that I want him sending flowers to my daughter. I don't want anyone sending flowers to her."

Miss Emily took him up sharply. "That's your selfishness. Life has always been a garden where you have wandered at will. And now you want to shut the gate of that garden against your daughter."

"Well, there are flowers that I shouldn't care to have her pluck."

"Don't you know her well enough to understand that she'll pluck only the little lovely blooms?"

His eyes rested on Jean's absorbed face. "Yes, thank God. And thank you, too, for saying it, Emily."

After dinner they sat in the library. Doctor McKenzie on one side of the fire with his cigar, Emily on the other side with her knitting. Jean between them in a low chair, a knot of Derry's violets fragrant against the gray of her gown, her fingers idle.

"Why aren't you knitting?" the Doctor asked.

"I don't have to set a good example to Emily."

"And you do to Hilda?" He threw back his head and laughed.

"You needn't laugh. Isn't it comfy with Emily?"

"It is." He glanced at the slender black figure. He was still feeling the fineness of the thing she had said about Jean. "But when she is here I am jealous."

"Oh, Daddy."

"And I am never jealous of Hilda. If you had Emily all the time you'd love her better than you do me."

He chuckled at their hot eyes. "If you are teasing," Jean told him, "I'll forgive you. But Emily won't, will you, Emily?"

"No." Emily's voice was gay, and he liked the color in her cheeks. "He doesn't deserve to be forgiven. Some day he is going to be devoured by a green-eyed monster, like a bad little boy in a Sunday School story."

Her needles clicked, and her eyes sparkled. There was no doubt that there was a sprightliness about Emily that was stimulating.

"But one's only daughter, Emily. Isn't jealousy pardonable?"

"Not in you."

"Why not?"

"Well," with obvious reluctance, "you're too big for it."

"Oh," he was more pleased than he was willing to admit, "did you hear that, Jean?"

But Jean, having drifted away from them, came back with, "I am going to church with him tomorrow."

"Him? Whom?"

"Derry Drake, Daddy, and may I bring him home to dinner?"

"Do you think a man like that goes begging for invitations? He has probably been asked to a dozen places to eat his turkey."

"He can't eat it at a dozen places, Daddy. And anyhow I should like to ask him. I—I think he is lonely—"

"A man with millions is never lonely."

She did not attempt to argue. She felt that her father could not possibly grasp the truth about Derry Drake. Her own understanding of his need had been a blinding, whirling revelation. He had said, "I wanted some one—who cared—." Not for a moment since then had the world been real to her. She had seemed in the center of a golden-lighted sphere, where Derry's voice spoke to her, where Derry's smile warmed her, where Derry, a silver-crested knight, knelt at her feet.

Julia came in to say that Miss Jean was wanted at the telephone.

Miraculously Derry's voice came over the wire. Was she going to the dance at the Willard? The one for the benefit of the Eye and Ear Hospital? The President and his wife would be there—the only ball they had attended this season—everybody would be there. Could he come for Jean and her father? And he'd bring Drusilla and Marion Gray. She knew Drusilla?

Jean on tiptoe. Oh, yes. But she was not sure about her father.

"But you—you—?"

"I'll ask."

She flew on winged feet and explained excitedly.

"Tonight? *Tonight*, Jean?"

"Yes, Daddy."

"But what time is it?"

"Only ten. He'll come at eleven—"

"But you can't leave Emily alone, dear."

"Emily won't mind—darling—will you, Emily?"

"Of course not. I am often alone."

It was said quietly, without bitterness, but Dr. McKenzie was quite suddenly and unreasonably moved by the thought of all that Emily had missed. He felt it utterly unfair that she should sit alone by an empty hearth while he and Jean frivolled. He had never thought of Hilda by an empty hearth—and she had been often alone—but there was this which made the difference, he would not have asked Hilda to meet his daughter's friends. She had her place in his household, but it was not the place which Emily filled.

Yet he missed her. He missed her blond picturesqueness at the dinner table, her trim whiteness as she served him in his office.

He came back to the question of Emily. "You can tell Drake we will go, if Emily can accompany us."

"But, Doctor, I'd rather not."

"Why not?"

"I'm not included in the invitation."

"Don't be self-conscious."

"And I haven't anything to wear."

"You never looked better than you do at this moment. And Jean can get you that scarf of her mother's with the jet and spangles."

"The peacocky one—oh, yes, Daddy." Jean danced back to the telephone.

Derry was delighted to include Miss Bridges. "Bring a dozen if you wish."

"I don't want a dozen. I want just Daddy and Emily."

"And me?"

"Of course—silly—"

Laughter singing along the wire. "May I come now?"

"I have to change my dress."

"In an hour, then?"

"Yes."

"I can't really believe that we are going together!"

"Together—"

CHAPTER X

A MAN WITH MONEY

White and silver for Jean, the peacocky scarf making Emily shine with the best of them, Dr. McKenzie called away at the last moment, and promising to join them later; Derry catching his breath when he saw his violets among Jean's laces; Drusilla wondering a little at this transfigured Derry; Marion Gray settling down to the comfort of a chat with Emily—what had these to do with a Tin Soldier on a shelf?

"How is your father, Derry?"

"Better, Drusilla. He has a fine nurse. Dr. McKenzie sent her."

"And I have Emily," Jean sang from the corner of the big car where Derry had her penned in, with the fragrance of her violets sweeping over him as he sat next to her. "I want Emily always, but Daddy has to have a nurse in the office, and Emily won't give up her toys. And in the meantime Hilda and I are ready to scratch each other's eyes out. Please keep her as long as you can on your father's case, Mr. Drake."

"Say 'Derry,'" he commanded under cover of the light laughter of the women.

"Not before—everybody—"

"Whisper it, then."

"Derry, Derry."

His pulses pounded. During the rest of the drive, he spoke to his other guests and seemed to listen, but he heard nothing—nothing but the whisper of that beloved voice.

As Derry had said, all the world of Washington was at the ball. The President and his wife in a flag-draped box, she in black with a turquoise fan, he towering a little above her, more than President in these autocratic days of war. They looked down on men in the uniforms of the battling world—Scot and Briton and Gaul—in plaid and khaki and horizon blue—.

They looked down on women knitting.

Mrs. Witherspoon and a party of young people sat in a box adjoining Derry's. Ralph was there and Alma Drew, and Alma was more than ever lovely in gold-embroidered tulle.

Ralph knew what had happened when he saw Jean dancing with Derry. There was no mistaking the soft raptures of the youthful pair. In the days to come Ralph was to suffer wounds, but none to tear his heart like this. And so when he danced with Jean a little later he did not spare her.

"A man with money always gets what he wants."

"I don't know what you mean."

"I think you do. You are going to marry Derry Drake."

She shrank at this. She had in her meetings with Derry never looked beyond the bliss of the moment. To have Ralph's rough fingers tearing at the veil of her future was revolting.

She breathed quickly. "I shan't dance with you, if you speak of it again."

"You shall dance with me," grimly, "this moment is my own—"

She was like wax in his strong arms. "Oh, how dare you." She was cold with auger. "I want to stop."

"And I could dance forever. That's the irony of it—that I cannot make you. But if I had Drake's money, I'd make you."

"Do you think it is his money?"

"Perhaps not. But the world will think it."

"If—if he wanted me, I'd marry him if he were a beggar in the streets."

"Has it gone as far as that? But you wouldn't marry a beggar. A troubadour beneath your balcony, yes. But not a beggar. You'd want him silken and blond and singing, and staying at home while other men fought—"

She stopped at once. "If you knew what you were talking about; I'd never speak to you again. But because I was fool enough once to believe that Derry Drake was a coward, I am going to forgive you. But I shall not dance with you again; ever—"

Making her way back alone to the box, she saw with a throb of relief that her father had joined Emily and Marion Gray.

He uttered a quick exclamation as she came up. "What's the matter, daughter?"

Her throat was dry. "I can't tell you now—there are too many people. It was Ralph. I hate him, Daddy."

"My dear—"

"I do."

"But why?"

"Please, I don't want to talk about it—wait until we get home."

Looking out over the heads of the swaying crowd, she saw that Derry was dancing with Alma Drew. And it was Alma who had said at the Witherspoon dinner, "Everybody will forgive a man with money."

And that was what Ralph had thought of her, that she was like Alma—that money could buy her—that she would sell the honor of her country for gold—.

But worse than any hurt of her own was the hurt of the thing for Derry. Ralph Witherspoon had dared to point a finger of scorn at him—other people had dared—

She suffered intensely, not as a child, but as a woman.

Alma, out on the floor, was saying to Derry, "I saw you dancing with Jean McKenzie. She's a quaint little duck."

"Not a duck, Alma," he was smiling, "a white dove—or a silver swan." The look that he sent across the room to Jean was a revelation.

Like Ralph, she grew hateful. "So that's it? Well, a man with money can get anything."

He had no anger for her. Jean might blaze in his defense, but his own fires were not to be fanned by any words of Alma Drew. If he lost his fortune, Jean would still care for him. It was fore-ordained, as fixed as the stars.

So he went back to her, and when she saw him coming, the burden of her distress fell from her. The world became once more hers and Derry's, with everybody else shut out. When they had supper with the Witherspoon party joining them, and Ralph palely repentant beside her, she even, to the utter bewilderment of her father, smiled at him, and talked as if their quarrel had never been.

Drusilla watched her with more than a tinge of envy. She was aware that her own vivid charm was shadowed and eclipsed by the white flame of Jean's youth and innocence. "And he loves her," she thought with a tug of her heartstrings; "he loves her, and there'll never be anything like it for him again."

She sat rather silently between Captain Hewes and Dr. McKenzie. Dr. McKenzie had always admired Drusilla, but tonight his attention was rather more than usual fixed upon her by a remark which Captain Hewes had made when the two men had stood alone together watching the dancers. "I have seen very little of American women—but to me Drusilla Gray seems the supreme type."

"She is very attractive."

"She is more than that. She is inspiring, the embodiment of your best ideals. When she sings one wonders that all men have not fought for democracy."

That was something to say of a woman. Doctor McKenzie wondered if it could be said of his own daughter. Set side by side with Drusilla, Jean seemed a childish creature, unstable, swayed by the emotion of the moment. Yet her fire matched Drusilla's, her dreams outran Drusilla's dreams.

Two officers passed the table.

"How any man can keep out of it," Drusilla said. "Some day I shall put on a uniform and pass for a boy—"

"Why not go over as you are?"

"They won't let me now. But some day they will. I can drive a car—there ought to be a place for me."

"There is one for me," he said, "and my decision must be made tonight. They are asking me to head a hospital staff in France. A letter came this morning, and I've got to answer it."

Her eyes went to the flame-white maiden on the other side of the table. "What does Jean say?"

"I haven't asked her. She wouldn't keep me back. But I am all she has, and it would hurt."

"It would hurt. But you are not all that she has—you might as well try to sweep back the sea as to stop what is going on over there. I have been sitting here green with envy. Oh, if love might only come to me like that."

"Like what?"

"Heaven-sent—never a doubt, never a speculation; just knowing and believing—souls stripped bare of all pretence."

How splendid she was—how beautiful! He bent down to her. "Why shouldn't it come to you?"

"Men don't love me that way. They admire and respect and then love. But Jean? She's a moon maiden, luring them to—madness." She smiled up at him.

"Captain Hewes says you are the supreme type—the perfect American."

"Yes, but he thinks of me as a type. Some day perhaps he will think of me as a woman."

She brought the conversation back to Jean. "You need not let the thought of her loneliness trouble you."

"You think then that I am going to lose her?"

"You have lost her already."

Sparks burned in the Doctor's eyes. "I don't believe it. She has known him a few days—and I've given her my whole life."

"'Forsaking all others,'" murmured Drusilla.

"Yet she loves me."

"It isn't that she loves you less—she loves him more."

"Don't," he lifted his hand. "I am not sure that I can stand it."

"It makes your way clear. That's why I have said it. There will be nothing now to keep you back from France."

Once upon a time she had said to Derry, "I can feel things, and I can make others feel." She had, perhaps, tonight, been a little cruel, but she had been cruel with a purpose.

All the way home Doctor McKenzie was very silent. When he kissed his daughter before she went upstairs, he held her close and smoothed her hair, but not a word did he say of the thing which had come to him.

He asked Emily, however, to wait a moment. "I have a letter to answer. I should like your advice."

Wondering a little, she sat down by the fire. The peacocky scarf gave out glittering lights of blue and green. She was tired and there were shadows under her eyes.

He came at once to his proposition. "I am thinking of going to France, Emily. If I do, can you stay with Jean?"

She turned her startled gaze upon him. "To France? Why?"

He told her. "They have been writing to me for weeks, and now the moment for my decision has come. I haven't said anything to Jean. But she won't keep me back. You know how she feels. But unless you can come, I can't leave her."

"I should have to be all day in my shop."

"I know, but you could be here in the evening and at night, and she could, of course, be with you in the shop, she likes that—and it would keep her from brooding. Or, if you will give up the shop, I should like to make it financially possible for you, Emily."

She shook her head. "No. You will be coming back, and then my occupation would be gone." She hesitated. "But if I come—what of Hilda?"

"She may decide to go over, too, as a nurse. We work well together."

She was silent, searching for the words which she felt that she ought to say. So that was it? They would go together, and the tongues of the world would wag. And Hilda would know that they were wagging, and would not care. But he, with his mind on bigger things, would never know, and would blunder unseeing into the net which was set for him. She felt that she ought to warn him, that the good friendship which existed between them demanded it. Yet it was a hard thing to say, and she hated it. So the moment passed.

It was he who spoke first—of Jean and Derry. "What do you think of it, Emily?"

"He is very much in love with her."

"And Jean?"

"Oh, I think you know. You saw her tonight."

He felt a sudden sense of age and loneliness. "She won't miss me, then?"

"Do you think that anyone could make up to your little Jean for the loss of her father?"

He covered his face with his hand. "You are feeling it like that?" she asked, gently.

"Yes. She is all I have, Emily. And I am jealous—desperately—desperately."

She searched for words to comfort him, and at last they came. "She will be very proud of her Daddy in France."

"Do you think she will?"

"I know it."

"And yet—I am not really worthy of all that she gives—"

She leaned forward, her white hands in her lap. Jean's comment echoed once more in his ears. "I like Emily's hands much better than Hilda's." They seemed, indeed, to represent all that was lovely in Emily, her refinement, her firmness, her gentle spirit.

"Bruce," she said—she rarely called him that—"your dear wife would never have loved you if you hadn't been worthy of love."

"I need her—to hold me to my best."

"Hold yourself to it, Bruce—" She stood up. "I must go to bed, and so must you. We have busy days before us."

He spoke impulsively. "You are a good woman, Emily—there's no one in the world that I would trust to stay with Jean but you."

She smiled a little wistfully as she went upstairs. She had perhaps comforted him, but she had left unsaid the words she should have spoken. "You must not take Hilda with you. If you take her with you, will your Jean be proud of her Daddy in France?"

CHAPTER XI
HILDA WEARS A CROWN

At two o'clock on Thanksgiving morning the light burned low in the General's room. Hilda, wide awake, was reading. Derry stopped at the door.

She rose at once and went to him.

"Is he all right, Miss Merritt?"

"Yes. He's sound asleep."

"Then you think he's better?"

"Much better."

"Good. I hope you can stay on the case. Dr. McKenzie says it is all because of your splendid care of him. I just left McKenzie, by the way. I took him and his daughter to the ball at the Willard. We had a corking time."

Her eyes saw a change in him. This was not the listless Derry with whom she had talked the day before—here were flushed cheeks and shining eyes—gay youth and gladness—.

"A corking time," Derry reiterated. "The President was there, and his wife—and we danced a lot—and—" he caught himself up. "Well, good-night, Miss Merritt."

"Good-night." She went back to the shadowed room.

Bronson, following Derry, came back in a half hour with a dry, "Is there anything I can do for you, Miss Merritt?" and then the house was still.

And now Hilda was alone with the old man in the lacquered bed. There would be no interruptions until morning. It was the moment for which she had waited ever since the hour when the General had sent her into his wife's room for a miniature of Derry, which was locked in the safe.

The suite which had belonged to Mrs. Drake consisted of three rooms—a sitting room, a bedroom and a sun-parlor which had been Derry's nursery. Nothing had been changed since her death. Every day a maid cleaned and dusted, and at certain seasons the clothes in the presses were brushed and aired and put back again. In a little safe in the wall were jewels, and the key was on the General's ring. He had given the key to Hilda when he had sent her for the miniature. His fever had been high, and he had not been quite himself. Even a nurse with a finer sense of honor might have argued, however, that her patient must be obeyed. So she knew now where his treasure was kept—behind a Chinese scroll, which when rolled up revealed the panel which hid the safe.

Hilda had never worn a jewel of value in her life. She possessed, it is true, a few trinkets, a gold ring with her monogram engraved in it, a string of Roman pearls, and a plain wrist watch. But such brilliance as that which met her startled eyes when she had first looked into the safe was beyond anything conceived by her rather limited imagination.

She opened the door between the rooms quietly, and went in, leaving a crack that she might hear any movement on the part of her patient. She crossed the sitting room in the dark. Reaching the bedroom she pulled the chain of the lamp, then set a screen to hide any ray of light which might escape.

The room was furnished with a feeling for delicate color—gold and ivory—Japanese prints—pale silks and crêpes—a bit of jade—a cabinet inlaid with mother-of-pearl. But Hilda's eyes were not for these. Indeed, she knew nothing of their value, nothing, indeed, of the value of the Chinese scroll which so effectually hid the panel in the wall.

Within the safe was a large velvet box, and several smaller ones. It was from the big box that Hilda had taken the miniature, and it contained also the crown which she yearned to wear.

She called it a crown! It was a tiara of diamonds, peaked up to a point in front. There was, also, the wide collar of pearls with the diamond slides which had been worn by the painted lady on the stairs. In the smaller boxes were more pearls, long strings of them; sapphires like a midnight sky, opals, fire in a mist; rubies, emeralds—. They should have been locked in a vault at the General's bank, but he had wanted nothing taken away, nothing disturbed. Yet with that touch of fever upon him he had given the key to Hilda.

She took off her cap and turned in the neck of her white linen gown. The pearl collar was a bit small for her, but she managed to snap the three slides. She set the sparkling circlet on her head.

Then she stood back and surveyed herself in the oval mirror!

Gone was the Hilda Merritt whom she had known, and in her place was a queen with a crown! She smiled at her reflection and nodded. For once she was swayed from her stillness and stolidity. She loaded her long hands with rings, and held them to her cheeks; then, struck by the contrast of her white linen sleeve, she rummaged in one of the big closets, and threw on the bed a drift of exquisite apparel.

The gowns were all too small for her, but there was a cloak of velvet and ermine. The General's wife had worn it to the White House dinner over the gown in which she had been painted. Hilda drew the cloak about her shoulders, and laughed noiselessly. She could look like this, and she had never known it! But now that she knew—!

There was the soft click of the telephone in the General's room. Fearful lest the sound should waken her patient, she tore off the tiara, turned up the neck of her dress to hide the shining collar, dropped the cloak, pulled the chain of the lamp, then sped breathless to the shadowed room.

Dr. McKenzie was at the other end of the wire.

"I am coming over, Hilda."

"You need not,"—her voice was a whisper—"he is sound asleep."

"I want to see you for a moment. It is very important."

She hesitated. "It is very late."

"Has young Drake arrived?"

"Yes. He has gone to bed."

"I'll be there in ten minutes. You can meet me downstairs."

The General stirred. "Miss Merritt."

She hung up the receiver and went to him at once.

"Has the Doctor come?"

"No. But he has just telephoned. He will be here shortly."

His sick old eyes surveyed her. "I never saw you before without your cap—"

"No."

"You are very pretty."

She smiled down at him. "It is nice of you to say it."

"Don't wear your cap again, I don't like uniforms for women."

"But when I am on duty I must wear it. You know enough of discipline to understand that I must."

"Yes. But women don't need discipline, God bless 'em." His old eyes twinkled. "Has Derry come in?"

"Yes, and gone to bed. He asked after you."

"And it's Thanksgiving morning?"

"Yes."

"And no turkey for me. But you'll get me a glass of wine?"

"I'm not sure. I'll ask the Doctor."

She sat beside him until he again dozed. Then made her way once more to the room where the lovely gowns were piled high on the bed, and the jewels sparkled on the dressing-table. Quickly and noiselessly she put them in place. Then she tried to take off the collar, but the snaps held. She tugged and pressed, but with no result. She was afraid to pull too hard lest she break the snaps.

At last she was forced to button the collar of her linen gown above it. She smoothed her hair and put on her cap. The room as she surveyed it showed no sign of her occupation. She put out the light and returned to her patient.

She was at the front door to let the Doctor in when he arrived.

"The General is awake, and wants to see you. I'll come down when you go, and we can talk."

As they entered the shadowed room together, the old man opened his eyes. "Hello, McKenzie. Nurse, what made you put on your cap? I don't like it."

"I shouldn't dare leave it off when the Doctor's here."

"Does she have to take your orders or mine, McKenzie?"

"Mine," smiling; "that's one of the perquisites of my profession, to have all the nurses under my thumb."

"Don't you try to please your patients?"

"Yes."

"Then tell her to leave off her cap."

He began to cough. The Doctor bent over him. Hilda helped to make the old man comfortable.

When at last the General drifted into slumber, the two went down together. The hall clock pointed to four.

They stood at the foot of the great stairway. From the landing the painted lady smiled at them.

"Hilda, I am going to France."

She expressed no surprise. "When did you make up your mind?"

"In a sense it is not made up. I think I am waiting for you to confirm my decision. They want me at the head of a hospital staff, to deal with cases of shock. I should like to have you in charge of my nurses."

She meditated. "I am not sure that I care to go."

He showed his surprise. "I understood that if I went, you would go—"

"I don't think I said that."

"Perhaps not. But it didn't occur to me that you would back out." His voice showed the irritation of a man balked in the thing he wants.

"I haven't backed out. I don't know what I want to do. I have to think it over."

He ran his fingers through his hair. "What made you change your mind?"

"I like to be comfortable. And it isn't comfortable over there."

"For Heaven's sake, Hilda—don't make yourself out as selfish as that."

"I am not any more selfish than other people, but I am honest. I don't go around deceiving myself with the idea that if I go I shall be doing something wonderful. But you—that's why you are going—to be wonderful in your own eyes, and Jean's eyes and in the eyes of the world."

"I don't think it is that," he said soberly. "I hope not. I have tried to see straight. I sometimes think it is you who are seeing crooked, Hilda."

They faced each other squarely. Her chin was slightly lifted. He caught the gleam of jewels at her throat.

"Hilda," he said, sharply, "where did you get those diamonds?"

Her hand flew up to them. She was not in the least disconcerted. "I might as well tell you. They belonged to the General's wife. I didn't have anything to do tonight, so I've been trying them on. There isn't any harm in that, is there?"

"It's rather dangerous," slowly; "why didn't you take the collar off?"

"The snap caught just as you came, and I couldn't unfasten it."

"Did the General know that you tried them on?"

"Of course not. He was asleep."

"Bend your head down, and let me look at the snap."

She leaned towards him, bringing her neck against his hand. The little curls of bright hair sprang up towards his fingers as he worked at the obstinate catch. But he did his work steadily, and as she straightened up again, he dropped the collar into her hand.

"If you will take my advice," he said, "you won't do a thing like that again. People might not understand."

"You mean that they might think I had stolen it? I am not a thief, Doctor—"

"Of course not. Do you think you have to tell me that? And are we quarrelling, Hilda?"

She swung back to her normal calm. "I am tired and cross—"

"I know you are tired. I hope the day nurse will relieve you. I can get two nurses, and let you off entirely."

She shook her head. "I'll stay here. I am interested in the case. And I want to see it through. By the way, he has asked again for wine."

"He can't have it, I told you. You must say that my orders are strict."

He held out his hand. "Then you won't go to France with me?"

"Let me sleep on it,"—her fingers were firm on his own—"and don't scold me any more."

"Did I scold?"

"Yes."

"I am sorry."

She smiled at him. The slow smile which transformed her. "I'll forgive you. Call me up in the morning, please."

She let him out, and went silently up the stairs. The General was again awake. "I want to talk," he told her; "take off your cap, and sit where I can look at you."

He was still feverish, still not quite responsible for what he might say.

She sat with the light falling full upon her. She never made an unnecessary movement, and her stillness soothed him. She was a good listener, and he grew garrulous.

At last he spoke of his wife. "Sometimes I think she is here and I find myself speaking. A little while ago, I thought I heard her moving in her room, but when I opened my eyes you were bending over me. Sometimes I seem to hear her singing—there is never a moment that I do not miss her. If I were good enough I might hope to meet her—perhaps the Lord will let the strength of my love compensate for the weakness of my will."

So on and on in the broken old voice.

Bronson came at six, and Hilda went away to have some sleep. While the General drowsed she had put the collar safely away behind the Chinese scroll.

As she passed through the hall, she stopped for a moment at the head of the stairs. The painted lady smiled at her, the painted lady who was loved by the old man in the shadowed room.

No, Hilda was not a thief. Yet as she stood there, in the cold dawn of that Thanksgiving morning, she had it in her mind to steal from the painted lady things more precious than a pearl collar or an ermine cloak or the diamonds in a crown!

CHAPTER XII
WHEN THE MORNING STARS SANG

Jean was having her breakfast in bed. Emily had slipped downstairs to drink an early cup of coffee with the Doctor and to warn him, "Don't tell her to-day."

"Why not?"

"It will spoil her feast. Derry Drake is coming to dinner."

"The robber—"

"Do you really feel that way about it?"

"I don't know how I feel."

He rose and went to the window. "It's a rotten morning."

"It is Thanksgiving."

"I haven't much to be thankful for," moodily. "I am, you tell me, about to lose my daughter. I am, also, it would seem, to part company with my best nurse."

"Hilda?"

"Yes. I wanted her to take charge of things for me in France. She elects to stay here."

"But why?"

"She's a—woman."

"You don't mean that. And I must say that I am rather glad that she is not going."

It was out at last! She had a feeling as if she had taken a cold plunge and had survived it!

"Glad? What do you mean, Emily?"

"Every time I waked in the night, I thought of Jean and of how she would feel if Hilda went with you. Do you realize that if she goes, there are things that the world will say?"

His face was stern. "You are very brave to tell me that, Emily."

"It had to be said, and last night I shirked it."

"But Hilda is a very good nurse."

"Do you think of her only as a—good nurse?"

He turned that over in his mind. "No. In a sense she's rather attractive. She satisfies a certain side of me—."

"The best side?"

He avoided an answer to that. "When she is away I miss her."

And now Miss Emily, shaking a little, but not showing it, made him face the situation squarely.

"Have you ever thought that, missing her, you might want to marry her?"

"I have thought of it. Why not, Emily?"

"Have you thought that it would make her your Jean's—mother—?"

His startled look met her steadfast one. His mind flew back to Hilda as she had bent down to him the night before, that he might unfasten the necklace. He thought of the evil that her eyes saw in him, and in the rest of the world. He thought of Jean, and of her white young dreams.

"No," he said, as if to himself, "not that—"

She laid her hand on his arm, "Go by yourself—there's a big work over there, and you can do it best—alone."

He looked down at her, smiling a little, but smiling sadly. "If Jean's mother had lived I should not have been such a weathercock. Will you write to me—promise me that you will write."

"Of course," cheerfully. "Oh, by the way, Julia tells me that dinner will be at three, and that two soldier boys are coming. I rather think I shall like that."

He ran his fingers through his crinkled hair. "What a lot you get out of life, Emily."

"What makes you say that?"

"Little things count so much with you. You are like Jean. She is in seventh Heaven over a snowstorm—or a chocolate soda. It's the youth in her—and it's the youth, too, in you—"

She liked that, and flushed a little. "Perhaps it is because there have been so few big things, Bruce, that the little ones look big."

He had a fleeting sense of what Emily would be like with some big thing in her life—how far would it swing her from her sedate course?

"You have done me a lot of good," he said heartily when she left him to go upstairs to Jean.

Jean was still in bed. "I must run down to the shop," Emily informed her. "But I'll be back in plenty of time to dress for dinner."

"Darling—" Jean reminded her, "you must go to church."

"Of course. I shall stop on my way down."

"Pray for me, Emily." She reached out her arms. Emily came to them and they clung together. "I am so happy, darling—" Jean whispered, "but there isn't anything to tell, not really—yet—Emily—"

When Emily had gone, Jean got out her memory books. She had made of breakfast a slight affair. How could one eat in the face of such astounding events. Already this morning flowers had arrived for her, heather and American Beauties. And Derry had written on his card, "The heather because of you—the roses because of the day—"

There were two hours on her hands before church. She could dress in one—the intervening time must be filled.

Her memory books were great fat volumes kept on a shelf by themselves, and forming a record of everything that had happened to her since her first day at boarding school. They were in no sense diaries, nor could they be called scrap-books. They had, rather, been compiled with an eye to certain red-letter events—and their bulkiness had been enhanced by the insertion between the leaves of various objects not intended for such limited space. There was a mask which she had worn at Hallowe'en; the tulle which had tied her roses at graduation; a little silver ring marking a childish romance; a flattened and much-dried chocolate drop with tender associations; dance-favors, clippings, photographs, theater programs, each illumined and emphasized by a line or two of sentiment or of nonsense in Jean's girlish scrawl.

Even now, as she turned the leaves, she found herself laughing over a rhyme which her father had cut from his daily paper, and had sent in response to her wild plea for a box of something good to eat:

"Mary had a little lamb,
A little pork, a little jam,
A little egg on toast,
A little potted roast,
A little stew with dumplings white,
A little shad,
For Mary had,
A little appetite."

The big box had followed—how *dear* Daddy had always been—but had she ever wanted to eat like that?

There were letters which her father had written, pasted in, envelopes and all, to be read in certain longing moments when she had missed him and her mother. There were love letters from certain callow college boys—*love*—! She laughed now as she thought of the pale passion they had offered her.

Derry had had no word for her the night before when he had left her at her door. Her father had been with her, so Derry could only press her hand and watch her as she went in. But there had been no need for words. All the evening what they had felt had flamed between them—.

So with the desire to preserve a record of these marvellous moments which were crowding into her life, she chose a perfectly new book to be devoted to Derry. And on the first page she pasted, not the faded violet from the basket which had come to her yesterday—oh, day of days!—not the dance program on which Derry's name was most magically scrawled, nor the spring of heather, nor a handful of rose leaves from the offering of the morning—no, the very first thing that went into Jean's memory book was a frayed silken tassel that had been cut from a rose-colored curtain! She had carried down her little scissors the night before, and had snipped it, and here it was—an omen for her own rose-colored future!

Starry-eyed she lay back among her pillows.

"Oh, Polly-Ann, Polly-Ann," she said tensely, to the small cat on the cushions, "if I should ever wake up and find that it wasn't true—"

Polly-Ann stared at her with mystical green orbs. She could offer no help, but she served as a peg upon which Jean could hang her eloquence. She stretched herself luxuriously and purred.

"But it is true, Polly-Ann," Jean said, "and I am going to church with him—wasn't it beautiful that he should think of going to church with me on Thanksgiving morning, Polly-Ann?"

She dressed herself presently, making a sort of sacred rite of it—because of Derry. She was glad that she was pretty—because of Derry. Glad that her gray fur coat was becoming—glad of the red rose against it.

He came in his car, but they decided to walk.

"I always walk to church," said Jean.

"There's sleet falling," said Derry.

"I don't care," said Jean.

"Nor I," said Derry.

And so they started out together!

It was a dismal day, but they did not know it. They knelt together in the old church. They prayed together. And when at last the benediction had been said and they stood together for a moment alone in the pew, Derry looked down at her and said, "Beloved," and the morning stars sang—!

When they went out, the sleet was coming thick and fast, and Derry's car was waiting. And when they were safe inside, he turned to her and his voice exulted, "I haven't even told you that I love you—I haven't asked you to marry me—I haven't done any of the conventional things—it hasn't needed words, and that's the wonder of it."

"Yes."

"But you knew."

"Yes."

"From the first?"

"I think it was from the first—"

"In the Toy Shop?"

"Yes."

"And you thought I was poor—and I thought you were just the girl in the shop?"

"Isn't it wonderful?"

It was more wonderful than they knew.

"Do you know that my money has always been more important to some people than I have been? I have thought they cared for me because of it."

"Ralph said last night that I cared—for the money."

She would not tell him of the other things that Ralph had said. And even as she thought of him, across the path of her rapture fell the shadow of Ralph's scorn of Derry.

He bent down to her. "Jean, if I had been that shabby boy that you first saw in the shop would you have been happy with me, in a plain little house? Would you?"

Up the streets came the people from the churches—the crowds of people who had thanked the Lord soberly, feeling meantime a bit bewildered as to the workings of His Providence. Most of them were going home to somewhat modified feasts. Many of them were having a soldier or two to dine with them. And presently these soldiers whom they feasted would be crossing the sea to that dread land of death and desolation.

Should they thank the Lord for that?

Some of the clergymen, craving light, had sought it in the Old Testament. But one, more inspired than the rest, had found it in the New.

"And there was war in Heaven; Michael and his angels fought against the dragon; and the dragon fought and his angels. And prevailed not—neither was their place found any more in Heaven."

Those who came from that church spoke of a Holy War, and were thankful that there were men in America going forth to fight the Dragon.

The two soldiers who were to dine at Dr. McKenzie's were plain young fellows from an upper county in Maryland. They were waiting somewhat awkwardly in the drawing-room when Jean arrived. She took them at once to the less formal library, left Derry with them and went upstairs to dress.

As she came into the fresh and frilly room so identified with her child life and her girl life, she stopped on the threshold.

45

Oh, little room, little room, the child that once lived here will never come again!

She knelt beside the bed, her face buried in her hands. No words came, but in her heart she was saying, "My beloved is mine—and I am his—"

When she went down, Dr. McKenzie was there, and Emily, and the two young soldiers had lost their awkwardness. When they found out afterwards that the young Drake who talked to them so simply and unaffectedly was DeRhymer Drake, the multi-millionaire, they refused to believe it. "He was a mighty nice chap. He didn't put on a bit of side, and the dinner was some feast."

And how could they know that Derry was envying them their cavalry yellow and their olive drab?

As for Jean, throughout the afternoon they gazed upon her as upon an enchanting vision. When they told her "Good-bye" it was the boldest who asked, with a flush on his hard cheek, if he might have a bit of the heather which she wore. "I am Scotch myself, and my mother was, and it would seem a sort of mascot."

If she hesitated for a moment it was only Derry who noticed it. And he helped her out. "It will be a proud day for the heather."

So she gave away a part of his gift, and thanked him with her eyes.

It was after the boys had gone that Derry had a talk alone with Dr. McKenzie.

"But you haven't known her a month—"

"I have wanted her all my life."

"I see—how old are you?"

"Thirty-one."

"You don't look it."

"No. And I don't feel it. Not to-day."

"And you think that she cares?"

"What do you think, sir?"

The Doctor threw up his hands. "Oh, lad, lad, there's all the wonder of it in her eyes when she looks at you."

When Derry went at last to find Jean, she was not in the library. He crossed the hall to the little drawing-room. His love sat by the fire alone.

"My darling—"

Thus she came to his arms. But even then he held her gently, worshipping her innocence and respecting it.

The next morning he brought her a ring. It was such a wonderful ring that she held her breath. She sat on the rose-colored davenport while he put it on her finger.

"If I had been the girl in the Toy Shop," she told him, "and you had been the shabby boy, you would have given me a gold band with three little stones—and I should have liked that, too."

"You shall have the gold ring some day, and it won't have stones in it—and it will be a wedding ring."

"Oh—"

"And when yon wear it I shall call you—Friend Wife—"

CHAPTER XIII
ARE MEN MADE ONLY FOR THIS?

In the afternoon the lovers made a triumphant pilgrimage to the place where they had first met. All the toys in the little shop stared at them—the clowns and the dancers in pink and yellow and the bisque babies and the glassy-eyed dogs and cats.

The white elephant was again in the window. "He seemed so lonely," Emily explained, "and with Christmas coming I couldn't feel comfortable to think of him away from it all."

Jean showed Derry her midnight camels. "I am going to do peacocks next," she told him. "I am so proud."

He bought all of the camels and a lot of other things. "We'll take them to Margaret Morgan's kiddies tomorrow; I want you to meet her."

Miss Emily found her lavish customer interesting, but demoralizing. "Run away with him, Jean," she said. "I am not used to Croesuses. He won't leave anything to sell, and then what shall I say to the people who want to buy?"

"Shut up your shop and go to tea with us at Chevy Chase," Derry suggested.

Emily smiled at him. "It is good of you to ask me, but I can't. I am not in love, and I have my day's work to do. But I think if you would like to take Jean—"

"Alone?" eagerly. "Do you think I might?"

"Why not?"

"I was almost afraid to suggest it."

"I am not a dragon. And there will never be a day like this for you again."

Jean broke in at that. "Oh, Emily, they will be wonderfuller!"

"But not this day—"

Derry knew what she meant. "How sweet you are."

Miss Emily, flushing, was a transformed Miss Emily. "Well, old people are apt to forget, and I have not forgotten."

"Darling, darling," Jean chanted. "I am going to paint dragons, and they shall all have lovely faces, and I shall call them the Not-Forgetting Dragons."

It was all very superlative. Miss Emily tried to send them away, but they still lingered. Jean set the music boxes going to celebrate the occasion, then stopped them because the only tunes they played were German tunes.

Derry laughed at her, then came to silence before a box of tin soldiers. They were little French soldiers, flat on their backs, bright with paint—

"I wonder how they feel about it?" he asked Jean.

"About what?"

"Shut up in a box, doing nothing—"

As the lovers drove away, Emily stood at the window looking after them. There was one customer in the shop, but Miss Emily had a feeling that he would keep himself amused until she was ready to wait on him. She had intuitions about the people who came to buy, and this tall spare man with the slight droop of his shoulders, his upstanding bush of gray hair, his shell glasses on a black ribbon was, she was aware, having the time of his life. No little boy could have spent more time over the toys. He fingered them lovingly as he peered through his big horn glasses.

He saw Miss Emily looking at him and smiling. "It was the white elephant that brought me in. He was made in Germany?"

"Yes."

"It is not easy to get them any more?"

"No. You see I have a little card on him 'Not for sale.'"

He nodded. "I should like to buy him—"

She shook her head. "I have refused many offers."

"I can understand that. Yet, perhaps if I should tell you?"

There was a slight trace of foreign accent in his speech. She stiffened. She felt that he was capable of calling her "Fräulein." There was not the least doubt in her mind as to the Teutonic extraction of this gentleman who was shamelessly trying to induce her to sell her elephant.

"I can't imagine any reason that would make me change my mind."

"My father is German; he makes toys."

She showed her surprise. "Makes toys?"

"Yes. He is an old man—eighty-five. He was born in Nuremberg. Until he was twenty-five he made elephants like the one in your window. Now do you see?"

She was not sure that she did see. "Well?"

"I want him for my father's Christmas present."

"Impossible," coldly; "he is not for sale."

He was still patient. "He will make you another—many others."

He had her attention now. "Make—elephants?"

"Yes. He needs only a pattern. There are certain things he has forgotten. I should like to make him happy."

Miss Emily, hostilely convinced that it was not her business to contribute to the happiness of any octogenarian Hun, shook her head, "I'm sorry."

"Then you won't sell him?"

"Certainly not."

He still lingered. "You love your toys—I have been here before, and I have watched you. They are not just sawdust and wood and cloth and paint to you—they are real—"

"Yes."

"My father is like that. They are real to him. There's an old wax doll that was my mother's. He loves her and talks to her—. Because she was made in that Germany which is dead—"

The fierceness in his voice, the flash of his eye; the thrust of his hand as if it held a rapier!

"Dead?"

"The Germany he knew died when Prussia throttled her. Her poetry died, her music—there is no echo now from the Rhine but that of—guns."

"You feel—that way—?"

"Yes."

"Then sit down and tell me—tell me—" She was eager.

"Tell you what?"

"About your father, about the toys, about the Germany that is—dead."

He was glad to tell her. It poured forth, with now and then an offending phrase, "Gott in Himmel, do they think we have forgotten? My father came to America because he loved freedom—he fought in the Civil War for freedom—he loves freedom still; and over there they are fighting for slavery. The slavery of the little nations, the slavery of those who love democracy. They want Prussia, and more Prussia, and more Prussia—" He struck his hand on the counter so that all the dolls danced.

"They are fighting to get the whole world under an iron heel—to crush—to grind—to destroy. My father reads it and weeps. He is an old man, Fräulein, and his mind goes back to the Germany which sang and told fairy tales, and made toys; do you see?

"Yet there are people here who do not understand, who point their fingers at him, at me. Who think because I am Ulrich Stölle that I am not—American. Yet what am I but that?"

He got up and walked around the room restlessly. "I am an American. If I was not born here, can I help that? But my heart has been moulded here. For me there is no other country. Germany I love—yes, but as one loves a woman who has been led away—because one thinks of the things she might have been, not of the thing she is."

He came back to her. "Will you sell me your elephant, Fräulein?"

She held out her hand to him. Her eyes were wet. "I will lend him to your father. Indeed, I cannot sell him."

He took her hand in a strong grasp. "I knew you were kind. If you could only see my father."

"Bring him here some day."

"He is too old to be brought. He sticks close to his chair. But if you would come and see him? You and perhaps the young lady who waited on me when I came before, and who was here to-day with the young man whose heart is singing."

"Oh, you saw that?"

"It was there for the whole world to see, was it not? A man in love hides nothing. You will bring them then? We have flowers even in December in our hothouses; you will like that, and you shall see my father. I think you will love my father, Fräulein."

After he had gone she wondered at herself. She had trusted her precious elephant to a perfect stranger. He might be anything, a spy, a thief, with his "Gotts in Himmel" and his "Fräuleins"—how Jean would laugh at her for her softheartedness!

Oh, but he wasn't a thief, he wasn't a spy. He was a poet and a gentleman. She made very few mistakes in her estimates of the people who came to her shop. She had made, she was sure, no mistake in trusting Ulrich Stölle.

Jean and Derry motoring to Chevy Chase were far away from the world of the Toy Shop. As they whirled along the country roads the bare trees seemed to bud and bloom for them, the sky was gold.

The lovely clubhouse as they came into it was gay with big-flowered curtains and warm with its roaring fires.

As they crossed the room together, they attracted much attention. There was about them a fine air of exaltation—.

"Young blood, young blood," said an old gentleman in a corner. "Gad, I envy him. Look at her eyes—!"

But there was more than her eyes to look at. There were her cheeks, and her crinkled copper hair under the little hat, and the flower that she wore, and her white hands as she poured the tea.

They drank unlimited quantities of Orange Pekoe, and ate small mountains of toast. They were healthily happy and quite unexpectedly hungry, and the fact that they were sitting alone at the table gave the whole thing an enchanting atmosphere of domesticity.

"Ralph spoiled it the other day," Jean confided, "I had everything ready for you."

"How I hated him when I came in."

"Oh, did you?"

"Of course," and then they both laughed, and the old gentleman in the corner said to the woman who sat with him, "Let's get away. I can't stand it."

"I don't see why."

"You wouldn't see. But there was a time once when I loved a girl like that."

Drusilla and Captain Hewes coming in, after a canter through the Park, broke in upon the Paradise of the young pair.

Drusilla in riding togs still managed to preserve the picturesque quality of her beauty—a cockade in her hat, a red flower in her lapel, a blue tie against her white shirt.

"And she does it so well," Derry said, as the two came towards them. "In most women it would have an air of bad taste, but Drusilla never goes too far—"

Captain Hewes in tow showed himself a captured man. "I didn't know that American women could ride until Miss Gray showed me—today. It was rippin'."

Drusilla laughed. "It is worth more than the ride to have you say 'rippin' like that."

"She makes fun of me," the Captain complained; "some day I shall take her over to England and show her how our gentle maidens look up to me."

"Your gentle maidens," Drusilla stated, "are driving ambulances or making munitions. When the Tommies come marching home again they will find comrades, not clinging vines."

"And they'll jolly well like it," said the big Englishman; "a man wants a woman who understands—"

This was law and gospel to Derry. "Of course. Jean, dear, may I tell Drusilla?"

"As if you had to tell me," Drusilla scoffed; "it is written all over you."

"Is it?" Derry marvelled.

"It is. The whole room is lighted up with it. You are a lucky man, Derry,"—for a moment her bright eyes were shadowed—"and Jean is a lucky girl." She leaned down and kissed the woman that Derry loved. "Oh, you Babes in the Wood—"

"By Jove," the Captain ejaculated, much taken by the little scene, "do you mean that they are going to be married?"

"Rather," Drusilla mocked him. "But don't shout it from the housetops. Derry is a public personage, and it might get in the papers."

"It is not to get in the papers yet," Derry said. "Dr. McKenzie won't let me tell Dad—he's too ill—but we told you because you are my good friend, Drusilla."

She might have been more than that, but he did not know it. When he went away with Jean, she looked after him wistfully.

"Good-bye, little Galahad," she said.

The Captain stared. "Oh, I say, do you call him that?"

She nodded.

"He's a knight in shining armor—"

"I can't understand why he's not fightin'."

"Nobody understands. There's something back of it, and meantime people are calling him a coward—"

"Doesn't look like a slacker."

"He isn't. I have sometimes thought," said wise Drusilla, "that it might be his father. He's a gay old bird, and Derry has to jack him up."

"Drink?"

"Yes. They say that Derry has followed him night after night—getting him home if he could; if not, staying with him."

"Hard lines—"

"And yet he is asking little Jean to marry him. I wonder if she will keep step with him."

"Why shouldn't she?"

"Because Derry is going to travel far and fast in the next few months," Drusilla prophesied.

Her face settled into tired lines. For the first time the Captain saw her divorced from her radiance. He set himself to cheer her.

"What is troubling you, dear woman?"

She was very frank, and she told him the truth. "I should have been glad to keep step with him myself."

He laid his hand over hers. "If you had, where would I be? From the moment I saw you, you filled my heart."

So, after all, she had been to him from the first, not a type but a woman. It had come to him like that, but not to her.

"You're the bravest and best man I have ever met," she told him, "but I don't love you."

"I should be glad to wait," said the poor Captain, "until you could find something in me to like."

"I find a great deal to like," she said, "but it wouldn't be fair to give you anything less than love."

"At least you'll let me have your friendship—to take back with me."

She looked at him, startled. "Oh, you are going back?"

"I may get my orders any day. There are things I can be doing over there."

Some day she was to see him "over there," to see him against a background of fire and flame and smoke, to see him transfigured by heroism, and she was to remember then with an aching heart this moment when he had told her that he loved her.

It was dark when Derry brought Jean home. There had been a sunset and an afterglow, and a twilight, and an evening star to ravish them as they rode, to say nothing of the moon—they came to the Doctor's door quite dizzy with the joy of it.

Derry was loath to leave. "Can't we all go to a play tonight?" he asked Jean's father. "You and Miss Bridges and the two of us?"

"Certainly not. Jean has done enough to-day. She isn't made of iron."

"She is made of fire and dew," Derry flung at him, lightly.

"Heavens, has it come to that? Well, she is still my daughter. I won't have her ill on my hands."

"But, Daddy!"

"You are to have a quiet dinner with me, my dear, and go to bed—and young Lochinvar may call for you in the morning—"

Young Lochinvar was repentant. "I didn't think it would tire her."

"Henceforth you will have to think."

"I know, sir."

He was so meek that the Doctor melted. "Run along and say 'Good-bye' to her. I'll give you ten minutes."

They wanted ten eternities. But there was, of course, tomorrow. They comforted themselves with that.

At dinner, the Doctor spoke of Derry's father. "All real danger is past, but he will have to be careful."

"When is Hilda coming back?"

"She told me last night that she'd rather stay until there was no further need for a nurse. The General hates a change, and he has asked her to stay."

"Does she like it?"

"She is very comfortable."

"Derry says that his father is an old dear."

"He would think so, naturally."

There were things about the General's case which were troubling Dr. McKenzie, and of which he could not speak. The old man had, undoubtedly been given something to drink on Thanksgiving Day.

Hilda had had strict orders, and the day nurse, and the only other person who had had access to the General's room was Bronson. He had made up his mind to speak to Derry about Bronson.

The meal progressed rather silently. The Doctor was preoccupied, taciturn. Miss Emily made futile efforts at conversation. Jean dallied with her dinner.

"My dear," the Doctor commented as she pushed away her salad, "you can't live on love."

"I'm not hungry. We had tea at the Club. Drusilla was there—and—we told her."

"Told her what?"

Blushing furiously, "That Derry and I are going to be—married."

"But you are not. Not for months. If that cub thinks he can carry you off from under my eyes he is mistaken. You've got to get acquainted with each other—I have seen too many unhappy marriages."

"But we are not going to be unhappy, Daddy."

"How do you know?"

Her cheeks were blazing. Miss Emily interposed. "Don't tease her, she's too tired."

"If he is teasing, I don't care," Jean said, "but it always sounds as if he meant it."

After dinner, the Doctor laid his hand on his daughter's shoulder. "I want to talk to you, daughter."

"Is it about Derry, Daddy?"

"About myself."

Emily, understanding, left them alone. Jean sat in her low chair in front of the fire, her earnest eyes on her father. "Well, Daddy."

He patted her hand. It was hard for him to speak.

She saw his emotion. "Is—is it because I am going to marry Derry?"

"That, and more than that. Jean, dear, I must go to France—"

"To France?"

"Yes. They want me to head a hospital. I don't see how I can refuse, and keep my self-respect. But it means—leaving you."

"Leaving me—"

"My little girl—don't look like that." He reached out his arms to her.

She came, and clung to him. "How soon?"

"As soon as I can wind things up here."

"It—it seems as if I couldn't let you."

"Then you'll miss me, dearest?"

"You know I will, Daddy."

"But you will have your Derry." His jealousy forced that.

"As if it makes any difference about—you."

She hid her face against his coat. She felt suddenly that the war was assuming a new and very personal aspect. Of course men had to go. But she and her father had never been separated—not for more than a day or week, or a month when she was at the shore.

"How long, Daddy?"

"God knows, dearest. Until I am not needed."

"But—" her lip trembled.

"You are going to be my brave little girl."

"I'll try—" the tears were running down her cheeks.

"You wouldn't have me not go, would you?"

She shook her head and sobbed on his shoulder. He soothed her and presently she sat up. Quite gallantly she agreed that she would stay with Emily. If he thought she was too young to marry Derry now, she would wait. If Derry went into it, it might be easier to let him go as a lover than as a husband—she thought it might be easier. Yes, she would try to sleep when she went upstairs—and she would remember that her old Daddy loved her, loved her, and she was to ask God to bless him—and keep him—when they were absent one from the other—.

She kissed him and clung to him and then went upstairs. She undressed and said her prayers, put Polly-Ann on her cushion, turned off the light, and got into bed.

Then she lay in the dark, facing it squarely.

The things she had said to her father were not true. She didn't want him to go to France. She didn't want Derry to go. She was glad that Derry's mother had made him promise. She didn't care who called him a coward. She cared only to keep her own.

There wasn't any sense in it, anyhow. Why should Daddy and Derry be blown to pieces—or made blind—or not come back at all? Just because a barbarian had brought his hordes into Belgium? Well, let Belgium take care of herself—and France.

She shuddered deeper down into the bed. She wasn't heroic. Hilda had been right about that. She was willing to knit miles and miles of wool, to go without meat, to go without wheat, to wear old clothes, to let the furnace go out and sit shivering in one room by a wood fire, she was willing to freeze and to starve, but she was not willing to send her men to France.

She found herself shaking, sobbing—.

Hitherto war had seemed a glorious thing, an inspiring thing. She had thrilled to think that she was living in a time which matched the days of Caesar and Alexander and of Napoleon, of that first Richard of England, of Charlemagne, of Nelson and of Francis Drake, of Grant and Lee and Lincoln.

Even in fiction there had been Ivanhoe and—and Alan Breck—and even poor Rawdon Crawley at Waterloo—fighters all, even the poorest of them, exalted in her eyes by their courage and the clash of arms.

But there wasn't any glory, any romance in this war. It was machine guns and bombs and dirt, and cold and mud; and base hospitals, and men screaming with awful wounds—and gas, and horrors, and nerve-shock and—frightfulness. She had read it all in the papers and in the magazines. And it had not meant anything to her, it had been just words and phrases, and now it was more than words and phrases—.

When the hordes of people had swept into Washington, changing it from its gracious calm into a seething and unsettling center of activities, she had been borne along on the wings of enthusiasm and of high endeavor. She had scolded women who would not work, she had scorned mothers and wives who had sighed and sobbed because their men must go. She had talked of patriotism!

Well, she wasn't patriotic. Derry would probably hate her when she told him. But she was going to tell him. She wouldn't have him blown to pieces or made blind or not come back at all. And in the morning, she would beg Daddy—she would beg and beg!

As she sat up in bed and looked wildly about her, it seemed as if all the corners of the little room were haunted by specters. A long time ago she had seen Maude Adams in "L'Aiglon." She remembered now those wailing voices of the dead at Wagram. And in this war millions of men had died. It seemed to her that their souls must be pressing against the wall which divided them from the living—that their voices must penetrate the stillness which had always shut them out. "How dare you go on with it? Are men made only for this?"

She remembered now the thing that her father had said on the night after "Cinderella."

"If I had my way, it should be an eye for an eye, a tooth for a tooth. For every man that they have tortured, we must torture one of theirs. For every child mutilated, we must mutilate a child—for every woman—"

Her Daddy had said that. Her kind and tender Daddy. Was that what the war made of men? Would Daddy and Derry, when they went over, do that? Torture and mutilate? Would they, would they? And would they come back after that and expect her to love them and live with them?

Well, she wouldn't. She would *not*. She would be afraid of them—of both of them.

If they loved her, they would stay with her. They wouldn't go away and leave her to be afraid—alone and crying in the dark, with all of those dead voices.

Emily tapped at the door. Came in. "My dear, my dear—. Oh, my poor little Jean."

51

After a long time her father was there, and he was giving her a white tablet and a drink of water.
"It will quiet her nerves, Emily. I didn't dream that she would take it like this."

CHAPTER XIV
SHINING SOULS

The next morning Jean was ill. Derry, having the news conveyed to him over the telephone, rushed in to demand tragically of Dr. McKenzie, "Was it my fault?"

"It was the fault of too much excitement. Seventh heaven with you for hours, and then my news on top of it."

"What news?"

The Doctor explained. "It is going to tear me to pieces if she takes it like this. She was half-delirious all night, and begged and begged—"

"She doesn't want you to go?"

The Doctor ran his fingers through his hair. "Well, we've been a lot to each other. But she's such a little sport—and patriotic—nobody more so. She won't feel this way when she's herself again."

Derry stood drearily at the window looking out. "You think then she won't be able to see me for several days? I had planned such a lot of things."

The Doctor dropped a hand on the boy's shoulder. "Life has a way of spoiling our plans, hasn't it? I had hoped for old age with Jean's mother."

That was something for youth to think of—of life spoiling things—of lonely old age!

"I wish," Derry said, after a pause, "that you'd let me marry her before you go."

"No, no," sharply, "she's too young, Drake. And you haven't known each other long enough."

"Things move rapidly in these days, sir."

The Doctor agreed. "It is one of the significant developments. We had become material. And now fire and flame. But all the more reason why I should keep my head. Jean will be safe here with Emily. And you may go any day."

"I wish I might think so. I'd be there now if I weren't bound."

"It won't hurt either of you to wait until I come back," was the Doctor's ultimatum, and Derry, longing for sympathy, left him presently and made his way to the Toy Shop.

"If we were to wait ten years do you think I'd love her any more than I do now?" he demanded of Emily. "I should think he'd understand."

"Men never do understand," said Emily—"fathers. They think their own romance was unique, or they forget that there was ever any romance."

"If you could put in a word for us," ventured Derry.

"I am not sure that it would do any good; Bruce is a Turk."

A customer came, and Derry lingered disconsolately while Emily served her. More customers, among them a tall spare man with an upstanding bush of gray hair. He had a potted plant in his arms, wrapped in tissue paper. He set it on the counter and went away.

When Miss Emily discovered the plant, she asked Derry, "Who put it there?"

Derry described the man. "You were busy. He didn't stop."

The plant was a cyclamen, blood-red and beautiful.

Miss Emily managed to remark casually that she had loaned his father an elephant, perhaps he had felt that he ought to make some return—but he needn't—.

"*An elephant?*"

"Not a real one. But the last of my plush beauties."

She set the cyclamen on a shelf, and wrapped up the parcel of toys which Derry had bought the day before, "I may as well take them to Margaret Morgan's kiddies," he told her. "I want to tell her about Jean."

After Derry had gone, Miss Emily stood looking at the cyclamen on the shelf. It was a lovely thing, with a dozen blooms. She wished that her benefactor had stayed to let her thank him. She was not sure that she even knew where to send a note. She hunted him up in the telephone book, and found him—Ulrich Stölle. His hot-houses were on the old Military Road. She remembered now to have seen them, and to have remarked the house, which was peaked up in several gables, and had quaint brightly-colored iron figures set about the garden—with pointed caps like the graybeards in Rip van Winkle, or the dwarf in Rumpelstiltzkin.

When Derry's car slid up to Margaret's door, he saw the two children at an upper window. They waved to him as he rang the bell. He waited several moments and no one came to open the door. He turned the knob and, finding it unlatched, let himself in.

As he went through the hall he was aware of a strange stillness. Not a maid was in sight. Passing Margaret's room on the second floor he heard voices.

The children were alone in the nursery. He was flooded with sunlight. Margaret-Mary's pink wash frock, Teddy's white linen—yellow jonquils in a blue bow—snowy lambs gambolling on a green frieze—Bo-peeps, flying ribbons—it was a cheering and charming picture.

"How gay you are," said Derry.

"We are not gay in our hearts," Teddy told him.

"Why not?"

"Mother's crying—we heard her, and then Nurse went down and left us, and we looked out of the window and you came." Derry's heart seemed to stop beating. "Crying?"

Even as he spoke, Margaret stood on the threshold. There were no tears, but it was worse than tears.

He started towards her, but with a gesture she stopped him.

"I am so glad you are—here," she said.

"My dear—what is it?"

She put her hand up to her head. "Teddy, dearest," she asked, "can you take care of Margaret-Mary until Cousin Derry comes back? I want to talk to him."

Teddy's grave eyes surveyed her. "You've been cryin'," he said, "I told Cousin Derry—"

"Yes. I have had—bad news. But—I am not going to cry—any more. And you'll take care of sister?"

"I tell you, old chap," said Derry resourcefully, "you and Margaret-Mary can open my parcel, and when I come back we'll all play together."

Outside with Margaret, with the door shut on the children, he put his arm about her. "Is it Win—is he—hurt?"

"He is—oh, Derry, Derry, he is dead!"

Even then she did not cry. "The children mustn't know. Not till I get a grip on myself. They mustn't think of it as—sad. They must think of it as—glorious—that he went—that way—."

Held close in his arms, she shook with sobs, silent, hard. He carried her down to her room. The maids were gathered there—Nurse utterly useless in her grief. It came to Derry, as he bent over Margaret, that he had always thought of Nurse as a heartless automaton, playing Chorus to Teddy, yet here she was, a weeping woman with the rest of them.

He sent all of the servants away, except Nurse, and then Margaret told him, "He was in one of the French towns which the Germans had vacated, and he happened to pick up a toy—that some little child might have dropped—-and there was an explosive hidden in it—and that child's toy killed him, Derry, killed him—"

"My God, Margaret—"

"They had put it there that it might kill a—child!"

"Derry, the children mustn't know how it happened. They mustn't think of him as—hurt. They know that something is the matter. Can you tell them, Derry? So that they will think of him as fine and splendid, and going up to Heaven because God loves brave men—?"

It was a hard task that she had set him, and when at last he left her, he went slowly up the stairs.

The children had strung the Midnight Camels across the room, the purple, patient creatures that Jean had made.

"The round rug is an oasis," Teddy explained, "and the jonquil is a palm—and we are going to save the dates and figs from our lunch."

"I want my lunch," Margaret-Mary complained.

Derry looked at his watch. It was after twelve. The servants were all demoralized. "See here," he said, "you sit still for a moment, and I'll go down for your tray."

He brought it up himself, presently, bread and milk and fruit.

They sat on the oasis and ate, with the patient purple camels grouped in the shade of the jonquil palm.

Then Derry asked, "Shall I tell you the story of How the Purple Camels Came to Paradise?"

"Yes," they said, and he gathered little Margaret-Mary into his arms, and Teddy lay flat on the floor and looked up at him, while Derry made his difficult way towards the thing he had to tell.

53

"You see, the purple camels belonged to the Three Wise Men, the ones who journeyed, after the Star—do you remember? And found the little baby who was the Christ? And because the purple camels had followed the Star, the good Lord said to them, 'Some day you shall journey towards Paradise, and there you shall see the shining souls that dwell in happiness.'"

"Do their souls really shine?" Teddy asked.

"Yes."

"Why?"

"Because of the light in Paradise—the warm, sweet light, clearer than the sunshine, Teddy, brighter than the moon and the stars—."

The children sighed rapturously. "Go on," Teddy urged.

"So the patient camels began their wonderful pilgrimage—they crossed the desert and rounded a curve of the sea, and at last they came to Paradise, and the gate was shut and they knelt in front of it, and they heard singing, and the sound of silver trumpets, and at last the gate swung back, and they saw—what do you think they saw?"

"The shining souls," said Teddy, solemnly.

"Yes, the shining souls in all that lovely light—there were the souls of happy little children, and of good women, but best of all," his voice wavered a little, "best of all, there were the souls of—brave men."

"My father is a brave man."

Was, oh, little Teddy!

"And the purple camels said to the angels who guarded the gate, 'We have come because we saw the little Christ in the manger.'

"And the angel said, 'It is those who see Him who enter Paradise,' So the patient purple camels went in and the gates were shut behind them, and there they will live in the warm, sweet light throughout the deathless ages."

"What are de-yethless ages, Cousin Derry?"

"Forever and ever."

"Is that all?"

"It is all about the camels—but not all about the shining souls."

"Tell us the rest."

He knew that he was bungling it, but at last he brought them to the thought of their father in Paradise, because the dear Lord loved to have him there.

"But if he's there, he can't be here," said the practical Teddy.

"No."

"I want him here. Doesn't Mother want him here?"

"Well—yes."

"Is she glad to have him go to Paradise?"

"Not exactly—glad."

"Was that why she was crying?"

"Yes. Of course she will miss him, but it is a wonderful thing just the same, Teddy, when you think of it—when you think of how your own father went over to France because he was sorry for all the poor little children who had been hurt, and for all the people who had suffered and suffered until it seemed as if they must not suffer any more—and he wanted to help them, and—and—"

But here he stumbled and stopped. "I tell you, Teddy," he said, as man to man, "it is going to hurt awfully, not to see him. But you've got to be careful not to be too sorry—because there's your Mother to think of."

"Is she crying now?"

"Yes. Down there on her bed. Could you be very brave if you went down, and told her not to be sorry?"

"Brave, like my Daddy?"

"Yes."

Margaret-Mary was too young to understand—she was easily comforted. Derry sang a little song and her eyes drooped.

But downstairs the little son who was brave like his father, sat on the edge of the bed, and held his mother's hand. "He's in Paradise with the purple camels, Mother, and he's a shining soul—."

It was a week before Jean went with Derry to see Margaret. It had been a week of strange happenings, of being made love to by Derry and of getting Daddy ready to go away. She had reached heights and depths, alternately. She had been feverishly radiant when with her lover. She had resolved that she would not spoil the wonder of these days by letting him know her state of mind.

The nights were the worst. None of them were as bad as the first night, but her dreams were of battles and bloodshed, and she waked in the mornings with great heaviness of spirit.

What Derry had told her of Margaret's loss seemed but a confirmation of her fears. It was thus that men went away and never returned—. Oh, how Hilda would have triumphed if she could have looked into Jean's heart with its tremors and terrors!

She came, thus, into the room, where Margaret sat with her children.

"I want you two women to meet," Derry said, as he presented Jean, "because you are my dearest—"

"He has told me so much about you,"—Margaret put her arm about Jean and kissed her—"and he has used all the adjectives—yet none of them was adequate."

Jean spoke tensely. "It doesn't seem right for us to bring our happiness here."

"Why not? This has always been the place of happiness?" She caught her breath, then went on quickly, "You mustn't think that I am heartless. But if the women who have lost should let themselves despair, it would react on the living. The wailing of women means the weakness of men. I believe that so firmly that I am afraid to—cry."

"You are braver than I—" slowly.

"No. You'd feel the same way, dear child, about Derry."

"No. I should not. I shouldn't feel that way at all. I should die—if I lost Derry—"

Light leaped in her lover's eyes. But he shook his head. "She'd bear it like other brave women. She doesn't know herself, Margaret."

"None of us do. Do you suppose that the wives and mothers of France ever dreamed that it would be their fortitude which would hold the enemy back?"

"Do you think it did, really?" Jean asked her.

"I know it. It has been a barrier as tangible as a wall of rock."

"You put an awful responsibility upon the women."

"Why not? They are the mothers of men."

They sat down after that; and Jean listened frozenly while Margaret and Derry talked. The children in front of the fire were looking at the pictures in a book which Derry had brought.

Teddy, stretched at length on the rug in his favorite attitude, was reading to Margaret-Mary. His mop of bright hair, his flushed cheeks, his active gestures spoke of life quick in his young body—.

And his father was—dead—!

Oh, oh, Mothers of men—!

CHAPTER XV

HILDA BREAKS THE RULES

It was Dr. McKenzie who told Hilda of Jean's engagement to Derry Drake.

"I thought it best for them not to say anything to the General until he is better. So you may consider it confidential, Hilda."

"Of course."

She had come to his office to help him with his books. The nurse who somewhat inadequately supplied her place was having an afternoon off. The Doctor had been glad to see her, and had told her so. "I am afraid things are in an awful muddle."

"Not so bad that they can't be straightened out in an hour or two."

"I don't see why you insist upon staying on the General's case. I shouldn't have sent you if I had thought you'd keep at it like this."

"I always keep at things when I begin them, don't I?"

He knew that she did. It was one of the qualities which made her valuable. "I believe that you are staying away to let me see how hard it is to get along without you."

"It wouldn't be a bad idea, but that's not the reason. I am staying because I like the case." She shifted the topic away from herself.

"People will say that Jean has played her cards well."

He blazed, "What do you mean, Hilda?"

"He has a great deal of money."

"What has that to do with it?"

Her smile was irritating. "Oh, I know you are not mercenary. But a million or two won't come amiss in any girl's future—and two country houses, and a house in town."

"You seem to know all about it."

"The General talks a lot—and anyhow, all the world knows it. It's no secret."

"I rather think that Jean doesn't know it. I haven't told her. She realizes that he is rich, but it doesn't seem to have made much impression on her."

"Most people will think she is lucky to have caught him."

"He is not a fish," with rising anger, "and as for Jean, she'd marry him if he hadn't a penny, and you know it, Hilda."

Hilda considered that for a moment. Then she said, "Is it his money or his father's?"

"Belongs to the old man. Derry's mother had nothing but an irreproachable family tree."

Hilda's long hands were clasped on the desk, her eyes were upon them. "If he shouldn't like his son's marriage, he might make things uncomfortable."

"Why shouldn't he like my Jean?"

"He probably will. But there's always the chance that he may not. He may be more ambitious."

Dr. McKenzie ran his fingers through his crinkled hair. "She's good enough for—a king."

"You think that, naturally, but he isn't the doting father of an only daughter."

"If he thinks that my daughter isn't good enough for his son—"

"You needn't shout at me like that," calmly; "but he knows as well as you do that Derry Drake's millions could get him any girl."

He had a flashing sense of the coarse fiber of Hilda's mental make-up. "My Jean is a well-born and well-bred woman," he said, slowly. "It is a thing that money can't buy."

"Money buys a very good counterfeit. Lots of the women who come here aren't ladies, not in the sense that you mean it, but on the surface you can't tell them apart."

He knew that it was true. No one knows better than a doctor what is beneath the veneer of social convention and personal hypocrisy.

"And as for Jean," her quiet voice analyzed, "what do you know of her, really? You've kept her shut away from the things that could hurt her, but how do you know what will happen when you open the gate?"

Yet Emily had said—? His hand came down on top of the desk. "I think we won't discuss Jean."

"Very well, but you brought it on yourself. And now please go away, I've got to finish this and get back—"

He went reluctantly, and returned to say, "You'll come over again before I sail, and straighten things out for me?"

"Of course."

"You don't act as if you cared whether I went or not."

"I care, of course. But don't expect me to cry. I am not the crying kind." The little room was full of sunlight. She was very pink and white and self-possessed. She smiled straight up into his face. "What good would it do me to cry?"

After she had left him he was restless. She had been for so long a part of his life, a very necessary and pleasant part of it. She never touched his depths or rose to his heights. She seemed to beckon, yet not to care when he came.

He spoke of her that night to Emily. "Hilda was here to-day and she reminded me that people might think that my daughter is marrying Derry Drake for his money."

"She would look at it like that."

"When Hilda talks to me"—he was rumpling his hair—"I have a feeling that all the people in the world are unlovely—"

"There are plenty of unlovely people," said Emily, "but why should we worry with what they think?"

She was knitting, and he found himself watching her hands. "You have pretty hands," he told her, unexpectedly.

She held them out in front of her. "When I was a little girl my mother told me that I had three points of beauty—my hands, my feet, and the family nose," she smiled whimsically, "and she assured me that I would therefore never be commonplace. 'Any woman may be beautiful,' was her theory, 'but only a woman with good blood in her veins can have hands and feet and a nose like yours—.' I was dreadfully handicapped in the beginning of my life by my mother's point of view. I am afraid that even now if the dear lady looks down from Heaven and sees me working in my Toy Shop she will feel the family disgraced by this one member who is in trade. It was only in the later years that I found myself, that I realized how I might reach out towards things which were broader and bigger than the old ideals of aristocratic birth and inherited possessions."

He thought of Hilda. "Yet it gave you something, Emily," he said, slowly, "that not every woman has: good-breeding, and the ability to look above the sordid. You are like Jean—all your world is rose-colored."

She was thoughtful. "Not quite like Jean. I heard a dear old bishop ask the other day why we should see only the ash cans and garbage cans in our back yards when there was blue sky above? I know there are ash cans and garbage cans, but I make myself look at the sky. Jean doesn't know that the cans are there."

"The realists will tell you that you should keep your eyes on the cans."

"I don't believe it," said Miss Emily, stoutly; "more people are made good by the contemplation of the fine and beautiful than by the knowledge of evil. Eve knew that punishment would follow the eating of the apple. But she ate it. If I had a son I should tell him of the strength of men, not of their weaknesses."

He nodded. "I see. And yet there is this about Hilda. She does not deceive herself;—perhaps you do—and Jean."

"Perhaps it is Hilda who is deceived. All the people in the world are not unlovely—all of them are not mercenary and deceitful and selfish." Her cheeks were flushed.

"Nobody knows that better than a doctor, Emily. I am conscious that Hilda draws out the worst in me—yet there is something about her that makes me want to find things out, to explore life with her—"

He was smiling into the fire. Miss Emily girded herself and gave him a shock. "The trouble with you is that you want the admiration of every woman who comes your way. Most of your patients worship you—Jean puts you on a pedestal—even I tell you that you have a soul. But Hilda withholds the admiration you demand, and you want to conquer her—to see her succumb with the rest of us."

"The rest of you! Emily, you have never succumbed."

"Oh, yes, I have. I seem to be saying, 'He may have a few weaknesses, but back of it all he is big and fine.' But Hilda's attitude indicates, 'He is not fine at all.' And you hate that and want to show her."

He chuckled. "By Jove, I do, Emily. Perhaps it is just as well that I am getting away from her."

"I wouldn't admit it if I were you. I'd rather see you face a thing than run away."

"If Eve had run away from the snake in the apple tree, she would not have lost her Eden—poor Eve."

"Poor Adam—to follow her lead. He should have said, 'No, my dear, apples are not permitted by the Food Administrator; we must practice self-denial.'"

"I think I'd rather have him sinning than such a prig."

"It depends on the point of view."

He enjoyed immensely crossing swords with Emily. There was never any aftermath of unpleasantness. She soothed him even while she criticised.

They spoke presently of Jean and Derry.

"They want to get married."

"Well, why not?"

"She's too young, Emily. Too ignorant of what life means—and he may go to France any day. He is getting restless—and he may see things differently—that his duty to his country transcends any personal claim—and then what of Jean?—a little wife—alone."

"She could stay with me."

"But marriage, *marriage*, Emily—why in Heaven's name should they be in such a hurry?"

"Why should they wait, and miss the wonder of it all, as I have missed it—all the color and glow, the wine of life? Even if he should go to France, and die, she will bear his beloved name—she will have the right to weep."

He had never seen her like this—the red was deep in her cheeks, her voice was shaken, her bosom rose and fell with her agitation.

"Emily, my dear girl—"

"Let them marry, Bruce, can't you see? Can't you see. It is their day—there may be no tomorrow."

"But there are practical things, Emily. If she should have a child?"

"Why not? It will be his—to love. Only a woman with empty arms knows what that means, Bruce."

And this was Emily, this rose-red, wet-eyed creature was Emily, whom he had deemed unemotional, cold, self-contained!

"Men forget, Bruce. You wouldn't listen to reason when you wooed Jean's mother. You were a demanding, imperative lover—you wanted your own way, and you had it."

"But I had known Jean's mother all my life."

"Time has nothing to do with it."

"My dear girl—"

"It hasn't."

She was illogical, and he liked it. "If I let them marry, what then?"

"They will love you for it."

"They ought to love you instead."

"I shall be out of it. They will be married, and you will be in France, and I shall sell—toys—"

She tried to laugh, but it was a poor excuse. He glanced at her quickly. "Shall you miss me, Emily?"

Her hands went out in a little gesture of despair. "There you go, taking my tears to yourself."

He was a bit disconcerted. "Oh, I say—"

"But they are not for you. They are for my lost youth and romance, Bruce. My lost youth and romance."

Leaning back in his chair he studied her. Her eyes were dreamy—the rose-red was still in her cheeks. For the first time he realized the prettiness of Emily; it was as if in her plea for others she had brought to life something in herself which glowed and sparkled.

"Look here," he said. "I want you to write to me."

"I am a busy woman."

"But a letter now and then—"

"Well, now and then—"

He was forced to be content with that. She was really very charming, he decided as he got into his car. She was such a gentlewoman—she created an atmosphere which belonged to his home and hearth.

When he came in late she was not waiting up for him as Hilda had so often waited. There was a plate of sandwiches on his desk, coffee ready in the percolator to be made by the turning on of the electricity. But he ate his lunch alone.

Yet in spite of the loneliness, he was glad that Emily had not waited up for him. It was a thing which Hilda might do—Hilda, who made a world of her own. But Emily's world was the world of womanly graciousness and dignity—the world in which his daughter moved, the world which had been his wife's. For her to have eaten alone with him in his office in the middle of the night would have made her seem less than he wanted her to be.

Before he went to bed, he called up Hilda. "I forgot to tell you when you were here this afternoon that I asked young Drake about Bronson. He says that it isn't possible that the old man is giving the General anything against orders. You'd better watch the other servants and be sure of the day nurse—"

"I am sure of her and of the other servants—but I still have my doubts about Bronson."

"But Drake says—"

"I don't care what he says. Bronson served the General before he served young Drake—and he's not to be trusted."

"I should be sorry to think so; he impresses me as a faithful old soul."

"Well, my eyes are rather clear, you know."

"Yes, I know. Good-night, Hilda."

She hung up the receiver. She had talked to him at the telephone in the lower hall, which was enclosed, and where one might be confidential without feeing overheard.

She sat very still for a few moments in the little booth, thinking; then she rose and went upstairs.

The General was awake and eager.

"Shall I read to you?" Hilda asked.

"No, I'd rather talk."

She shaded the light and sat beside the little table. "Did you like your dinner?"

"Yes. Bronson said you made the broth. It was delicious."

"I like to cook—-when I like the people I cook for."

He basked in that.

"There are some patients—oh, I have wanted to salt their coffee and pepper their cereal. You have no idea of the temptations which come to a nurse."

"Are you fond of it—nursing?"

"Yes. It is nice in a place like this—and at Dr. McKenzie's. But there are some houses that are awful, with everybody quarrelling, the children squalling—. I hate that. I want to be comfortable. I like your thick carpets here, and the quiet, and the good service. And the good things to eat, and the little taste of wine that we take together." Her low laugh delighted him.

"The wine? You are going to drink another glass with me before I go to sleep."

"Yes. But it is our secret. Dr. McKenzie would kill me if he knew, and a nurse must obey orders."

"He need never know. And it won't hurt me."

"Of course not. But he has ideas on the subject."

"May I have it now?"

"Wait until Bronson goes to bed."

"Bronson has nothing to do with it. A servant has neither ears nor eyes."

"It might embarrass him if the Doctor asked him. And why should you make him lie?"

Bronson, pottering in, presently, was told that he would not be needed. "Mr. Derry telephoned that he would be having supper after the play at Miss Gray's. You can call him there if he is wanted."

"Thank you, Bronson. Good-night."

When the old man had left them, she said to the General, "Do you know that your son is falling in love?"

"In love?"

"Yes, desperately—at first sight?"

He laughed. "With whom?"

"Dr. McKenzie's daughter."

"What?" He raised himself on his elbow.

"Yes. Jean McKenzie. I am not sure that I ought to tell you, but somehow it doesn't seem right that you are not being told—"

He considered it gravely. "I don't want him to get married," he said at last. "I want him to go to war. I can't tell you, Miss Merritt, how bitter my disappointment has been that Derry won't fight."

"He may have to fight."

"Do you think I want him dragged to defend the honor of his country? I'd rather see him dead." He was struggling for composure.

"Oh, I shouldn't have told you," she said, solicitously.

"Why not? It is my right to know."

"Jean is a pretty little thing, and you may like her."

"I like McKenzie," thoughtfully.

She glanced at him. His old face had fallen into gentler lines. She gave a hard laugh. "Of course, a rich man like your son rather dazzles the eyes of a young girl like Jean."

"You think then it is his—money?"

"I shouldn't like to say that. But, of course, money adds to his charms."

"He won't have any money," grimly, "unless I choose that he shall. I can stop his allowance tomorrow. And what would the little lady do then?"

She shrugged. "I am sure I don't know. She'd probably take Ralph Witherspoon. He's in the race. She dropped him after she met your son."

The General's idea of women was somewhat exalted. He had an old-fashioned chivalry which made him blind to their faults, the champion of their virtues. He had always been, therefore, to a certain extent, at the mercy of the unscrupulous. He had loaned money and used his influence in behalf of certain wily and weeping females who had deserved at his hands much less than they got.

In his thoughts of a wife for Derry, he had pictured her as sweet and unsophisticated—a bit reserved, like Derry's mother—

The portrait which Hilda had subtly presented was of a mercenary little creature, lured by the glitter of gold—off with the old and on with the new, lacking fineness.

"I can stop his allowance," he wavered. "It would be a good test. But I love the boy. The war has brought the first misunderstandings between Derry and me. It would have hurt his mother."

Hilda was always restless when the name was introduced of the painted lady on the stairs. When the General spoke of his wife, his eyes grew kind—and inevitably his thoughts drifted away from Hilda to the days that he had spent with Derry's mother.

"She loved us both," he said.

Hilda rose and crossed the room. A low bookcase held the General's favorite volumes. There was a Globe edition of Dickens on the top shelf, little fat brown books, shabby with much handling. Hilda extracted one, and inserted her hand in the hollow space back of the row. She brought out a small flat bottle and put the book back.

"I always keep it behind 'Great Expectations,'" she said, as she approached the bed. "It seems rather appropriate, doesn't it?"

The old eyes, which had been soft with memories, glistened.

She filled two little glasses. "Let us drink to our—secret."

Then while the wine was firing his veins, she spoke again of Jean and Derry. "It really seems as if he should have told you."

"I won't have him getting married. He can't marry unless he has money."

"Please don't speak of it to him. I don't want to get into trouble. You wouldn't want to get me into trouble, would you?"

"No."

She filled his glass again. He drank. Bit by bit she fed the fire of his doubts of his son. When at last he fell asleep in his lacquered bed he had made up his mind to rather drastic action.

She sat beside him, her thoughts flying ahead into the years. She saw things as she wanted them to be—Derry at odds with his father; married to Jean; herself mistress of this great house, wearing the diamond crown and the pearl collar; her portrait in the place of the one of the painted lady on the stairs; looking down on little Jean who had judged her by youth's narrow standards—whose husband would have no fortune unless he chose to accept it at her hands.

Thus she weighed her influence over the sleeping sick man, thus she dreamed, calm as fate in her white uniform.

CHAPTER XVI
JEAN-JOAN

Drusilla Gray's little late suppers were rather famous. It was not that she spent so much money, but that she spent much thought.

Tonight she was giving Captain Hewes a sweet potato pie. "He has never eaten real American things," she said to Jean. "Nice homey-cooked things—"

"No one but Drusilla would ever think of pie at night," said Marion Gray, "but she has set her heart on it."

There were some very special hot oyster sandwiches which preceded the pie—peppery and savory with curls of bacon.

"I hope you are hungry," said Drusilla as her big black cook brought them in. "Aunt Chloe hates to have things go back to the kitchen."

Nothing went back. There was snow without, a white whirl in the air, piling up at street corners, a night for young appetites to be on edge.

"Jove," said the Captain, as he leaned back in his chair, "how I shall miss all this!"

Jean turned her face towards him, startled. "Miss it?"

"Yes. I am going back—got my orders today."

Drusilla was cutting the pie. "Isn't it glorious?"

Jean gazed at her with something like horror. Glorious! How could Drusilla go on, like Werther's Charlotte, *calmly cutting bread and butter*? Captain Hewes loved her, anybody with half an eye could see that—and whether she loved him or not, he was her friend—and she called his going "glorious!"

"I was afraid my wound might put me on the shelf," the Captain said.

"He is ordered straight to the front," Drusilla elucidated. "This is his farewell feast."

After that everything was to Jean funeral baked meats. The pie deep in its crust, rich with eggs and milk, defiant of conservation, was as sawdust to her palate.

Glorious!

Well, she couldn't understand Margaret. She couldn't understand Drusilla. She didn't want to understand them.

"Some day I shall go over," Drusilla was saying. "I shall drive something—it may be a truck and it may be an ambulance. But I can't sit here any longer doing nothing."

"I think you are doing a great deal," said Jean. "Look at the committees you are managing."

"Oh, things like that," said Drusilla contemptuously. "Women's work. I'm not made to knit and keep card indexes. I want a man's job."

There was something almost boyish about her as she said it. She had parted her hair on the side, which heightened the effect. "In the old days," she told Captain Hewes, "I should have worn doublet and hose and have gone as your page."

"Happy old days—."

"And I should have written a ballad about you," said Marion, "and have sung it to the accompaniment of my harp—and my pot-boilers would never have been. And we should all have worn trains and picturesque headdresses instead of shirtwaists and sports hats, and I should have called some man 'my Lord,' and have listened for his footsteps instead of ending my days in single blessedness with a type-writer as my closest companion."

Everybody laughed except Jean. She broke her cheese into small bits with her fork, and stared down at it as if cheese were the most interesting thing in the whole wide world.

It was only two weeks since they had had the news of Margaret's husband—only a month since he had died. And Winston had been Captain Hewes' dear friend; he had been Derry's. Would anybody laugh if Derry had been dead only fourteen days?

She tried, however, to swing herself in line with the others. "Shall you go before Christmas?" she asked the Captain.

"Yes. And Miss Gray had asked me to dine with her. You can see what I am missing—my first American Christmas."

"We are going to have a little tree," said Drusilla, "and ask all of you to come and hang presents on it."

Jean had always had a tree at Christmas time. From the earliest days of her remembrance, there had been set in the window of the little drawing room, a young pine brought from the Doctor's country-place far up in Maryland. On Christmas Eve it had been lighted and the doors thrown open. Jean could see her mother now, shining on one side of it, and herself coming in, in her nurse's arms.

There had been a star at the top, and snow powdered on the branches—and gold and silver balls—and her presents piled beneath—always a doll holding out its arms to her. There had been the first Rosie-Dolly, more beloved than any other; made of painted cloth, with painted yellow curls, and dressed in pink with a white apron. Rosie was a wreck of a doll now, her features blurred and her head bald with the years—but Jean still loved her, with something left over of the adoration of her little girl days. Then there was Maude, named in honor of the lovely lady who had played "Peter Pan," and the last doll that Jean's mother had given her. Maude had an outfit for every character in which Jean had seen her prototype—there were the rowan berries and shawl of "Babbie," the cap and jerkin of "Peter Pan," the feathers and spurs of "Chantecler"— such a trunkful, and her dearest mother had made them all—.

And Daddy! How Daddy had played Santa Claus, in red cloth and fur with a wide belt and big boots, every year, even last year when she was nineteen and ready to make her bow to society. And now he might never play Santa Claus again—for before Christmas had come he would be on the high seas, perhaps on the other side of the seas—at the edge of No Man's

Land. And there would be no Star, no dolls, no gold and silver balls—for the nation which had given Santa Claus to the world, had robbed the world of peace and of goodwill. It had robbed the world of Christmas!

She came back to hear the Captain saying, "I want you to sing for me—Drusilla."

They rose and went into the other room.

"Tired, dearest?" Derry asked, as he found a chair for her and drew his own close to it.

"No, I am not tired," she told him, "but I hate to think that Captain Hewes must go."

"I'd give the world to be going with him."

Her hands were clasped tightly. "Would you give me up?"

"You? I should never have to give you up, thank God. You would never hold me back."

"Shouldn't I, Derry?"

"My precious, don't I know? Better than you know yourself."

Drusilla and the Captain were standing by the wide window which looked out over the city. The snow came down like a curtain, shutting out the sky.

"Do you think she loves him?" Jean asked.

"I hope so," heartily.

"But to send him away so—easily. Oh, Derry, she can't care."

"She is sending him not easily, but bravely. Margaret let her husband go like that."

"Would you want me to let you go like that, Derry?"

"Yes, dear."

"Wouldn't you want me to—cry?"

"Perhaps. Just a little tear. But I should want you to think beyond the tears. I should want you to know that for us there can be no real separation. You are mine to the end of all eternity, Jean."

He believed it. And she believed it. And perhaps, after all, it was true. There must be a very separate and special Heaven for those who love once, and never love again.

Drusilla came away from the window to sing for them—a popular song. But there was much in it to intrigue the imagination—a vision of the heroic Maid—a hint of the Marseillaise—and so the nations were singing it—.

> "Jeanne d'Arc, Jeanne d'Arc,
> Oh, soldats! entendez vous?
> 'Allons, enfants de la patrie,'
> Jeanne d'Arc, la victoire est pour vous—"

There was a new note in Drusilla's voice. A note of tears as well as of triumph—and at the last word she broke down and covered her face with her hands.

In the sudden stillness, the Captain strode across the room and took her hands away from her face.

"Drusilla," he said before them all, "do you care as much as that?"

She told him the truth in her fine, frank fashion.

"Yes," she said, "I do care, Captain, but I want you to go."

"And oh, Derry, I am so glad she cried," Jean said, when they were driving home through the snow-storm. "It made her seem so—human."

Derry drew her close. "Such a thing couldn't have happened," he said, "at any other time. Do you suppose that a few years ago any of us would have been keyed up to a point where a self-contained Englishman could have asked a girl, in the face of three other people, if she loved him, and have had her answer like that? It was beautiful, beautiful, Jean-Joan—"

She held her breath. "Why do you call me that?"

"She lived for France. You shall live for France—and me."

The snow shut them in. There was the warmth of the car, of the fur rugs and Derry's fur coat, Jean's own velvet wrap of heavenly blue, the fragrance of her violets. Somewhere far away men were fighting—there was the mud and cold of the trenches—somewhere men were suffering.

She tried not to think of them. Her cheek was against Derry's. She was safe—safe.

Captain Hewes went away that night Drusilla's accepted lover. He put a ring on her finger and kissed her "good-bye," and with his head high faced the months that he must be separated from her.

"I will come back, dear woman."

"I shall see you before that," she told him. "I am coming over."

"I shall hate to have you in it all. But it will be Heaven to see you."

When he had gone, Drusilla went into Marion Gray's study.

Marion looked up from her work. She was correcting manuscript, pages and pages of it. "Well, do you want me to congratulate you, Drusilla?"

Drusilla sat down. "I don't know, Marion. He is the biggest and finest man I have ever met, but—"

"But what?"

"I wanted love to come to me differently, as it has come to Jean and Derry—without any doubts. I wanted to be sure. And I am not sure. I only know that I couldn't let him go without making him happy."

"Then is it—pity?"

"No. He means more to me than that. But I gave way to an impulse—the music, and his sad eyes. And then I cried, and he came up to me—fancy a man coming up before you all like that—"

"It was quite the most dramatic moment," said the lady who wrote. "Quite unbelievable in real life. One finds those things occasionally in fiction."

"It was as if there were just two of us alone in the world," Drusilla confessed, "and I said what I did because I simply couldn't help it. And it was true at the moment; I think it is always going to be true. If I marry him I shall care a great deal. But it has not come to me just as I had—dreamed."

"Nothing is like our dreams," said Marion, and dropped her pen. "That's why I write. I can give my heroine all the bliss for which she yearns."

Drusilla stood up. "You mustn't misunderstand me, Marion. I am very happy in the thought of my good friend, of my great lover. It is only that it hasn't quite measured up to what I expected."

"Nothing measures up to what we expect."

"And now Jean belongs to Derry, and I belong to my gallant and good Captain. I shall thank God before I sleep tonight, Marion."

"And he'll thank God—."

They kissed each other, and Drusilla went to bed, and the next morning she wrote a letter to her Captain, which he carried next to his heart and kissed when he got a chance.

CHAPTER XVII

THE WHITE CAT

Derry, going quietly to his room that night, did not stop at the General's door. He did not want to speak to Hilda, he did not want to speak to anyone, he wanted to be alone with his thoughts of Jean and that perfect ride with her through the snow.

He was, therefore, a little impatient to find Bronson waiting up for him.

"I thought I told you to go to bed, Bronson."

"You did, sir, but—but I have something to tell you."

"Can't it wait until morning?"

"I should like to say it now, Mr. Derry." The old man's eyes were anxious. "It's about your father—"

"Father?"

"Yes. I told you I didn't like the nurse."

"Miss Merritt? Well?"

"Perhaps I'd better get you to bed, sir. It's a rather long story, and you'd be more comfortable."

"You'd be more comfortable, you mean, Bronson." The impatient note had gone out of Derry's voice. Temporarily he pigeon-holed his thoughts of Jean, and gave his attention to this servant who was more than a servant, more even than a friend. To Derry, Bronson wore a sort of halo, like a good old saint in an ancient woodcut.

Propped up at last among his pillows, pink from his bath and in pale blue pajamas, Derry listened to what the old man had to say to him.

Bronson sat on the edge of a straight-backed chair with Muffin at his knees. "From the first day I had a feeling that she wasn't just—straight. I don't know why, but I felt it. She had one way with the General and another with us servants. But I didn't mind that, not much, until she went into your mother's room."

"My mother's room?" sharply. "What was she doing there, Bronson?"

"That's what I am going to tell you, sir. You know that place on the third floor landing, where I sits and looks through at your father when he ain't quite himself, and won't let me come in his room? Well, there was one night that I was there and watched her—"

Derry's quick frown rebuked him. "You shouldn't have done that, Bronson."

"I had a feeling, sir, that things were going wrong, and that the General wasn't always himself. I shouldn't ever have said a thing to you, Mr. Derry," earnestly, "if I hadn't seen what I did."

He cleared his throat. "That first night I saw her open the door between your father's room and the sitting room, and she did it careful and quiet like a person does when they don't want anybody to know. The sitting room was dark, but I went down and stood behind the curtain in the General's door, and I could see through, and there was a light in your mother's room and a screen set before it."

"I took a big chance, but I slid into the sitting room, and I could see her on the other side of the screen, and she had opened the safe behind the Chinese scroll, and she was trying on your mother's diamonds."

"What!"

Bronson nodded solemnly. "Yes, sir, she had 'em on her head and her neck and her fingers—."

"You don't mean—that she took anything."

"Oh, no, sir, she's no common thief. But she looked at herself in the glass and strutted up and down, up and down, up and down, bowing and smiling like a—fool."

"Then the telephone rang, and I had to get out pretty quick, before she came to answer it. I went to bed, but I didn't sleep much, and the next night I watched her again. I watch every night."

Derry considered the situation. "I don't like it at all, Bronson. But perhaps it was just a woman's vanity. She wanted to see how she looked."

"Well, she's seen—and she ain't going to be satisfied with that. She'll want to wear them all the time—"

"Of course, she can't, Bronson. She isn't as silly as to think she can."

"Perhaps not, sir." Bronson opened his lips and shut them again.

"There's something else, sir," he said, after a pause. "I've found out that she's giving the General things to drink."

"Hilda?" Derry said, incredulously. "Oh, surely not, Bronson, The Doctor has given her strict orders—."

"She's got a bottle behind the books, and she pours him a glass right after dinner, and another before he goes to sleep, and—and—you know he'd sell his soul for the stuff, Mr. Derry."

Derry did know. It had been the shame of all his youthful years that his father should stoop to subterfuge, to falsehood, to everything that was foreign to his native sense of honor and honesty, for a taste of that which his abnormal appetite demanded.

"If anyone had told me but you, Bronson, I wouldn't have believed it."

"I didn't want to tell you, but I had to. You can see that, can't you, sir?"

"Yes. But how in the world did she know where the diamonds were?"

"He gave her his key one day when I was there—made me get it off his ring. He sent her for your picture—the one that your mother used to wear. I thought then that he wasn't quite right in his head, with the fever and all, or he would have sent me. But a woman like that—"

"Dr. McKenzie has the greatest confidence in her."

"I know, sir, and she's probably played square with him—but she ain't playing square here."

"It can't go on, of course. I shall have to tell McKenzie."

Bronson protested nervously. "If she puts her word against mine, who but you will believe me? I'd rather you saw it yourself, Mr. Derry, and left my name out of it."

"But I can't sit on the steps and watch."

"No, sir, but you can come in unexpected from the outside—when I flash on the third floor light for you."

Derry slept little that night. Ahead of him stretched twenty-four hours of suspense—twenty-four hours in which he would have to think of this thing which was hidden in the big house in which his mother had reigned.

In the weeks since he had met Jean, he had managed to thrust it into the back of his mind—he had, indeed, in the midst of his happiness, forgotten his bitterness, his sense of injustice—he wondered if he had not in a sense forgotten his patriotism. Life had seemed so good, his moments with Jean so transcendent—there had been no room for anything else.

But now he was to take up again the burden which he had dropped. He was to consider his problem from a new angle. How could he bring Jean here? How could he let her clear young eyes rest on that which he and his mother had seen? How could he set, as it were, all of this sordidness against her sweetness? Money could, of course, do much. But his promise held him to watchfulness, to brooding care, to residence beneath this roof. His bride would be the General's daughter, she would live in the General's house, she would live, too, beneath the shadow of the General's tragic fault.

Yet—she was a brave little thing. He comforted himself with that. And she loved him. He slept at last with a desperate prayer on his lips that some new vision might be granted him on the morrow.

63

But the first news that came over the telephone was of Jean's flitting. "Daddy wants me to go with him to our old place in Maryland. He has some business which takes him there, and we shall be gone two days."

"Two days?"

"Yes. We are to motor up."

"Can't I go with you?"

"I think—Daddy wants me to himself. You won't mind, Derry—some day you'll have me all the time."

"But I need you now, dearest."

"Do you really," delightedly. "It doesn't seem as if you could—"

"If you knew how much."

She could not know. He hung up the receiver. The day stretched out before him, blank.

But it passed, of course. And Hilda, having slept her allotted number of hours, was up in time to superintend the serving of the General's dinner. Later, Derry stopped at the door to say that he was going to the theater and might be called there. The General, propped against his pillows and clothed in a gorgeous mandarin coat, looked wrinkled and old. The ruddiness had faded from his cheeks, and he was much thinner.

Hilda, sitting by the little table, showed all the contrast of youth and bloom. Her long hands lay flat on the table. Derry had a fantastic feeling, as if a white cat watched him under the lamp.

"Are you going alone, son?" the General asked.

"Yes."

"Why don't you take a girl?" craftily.

Derry smiled.

"The only girl I should care to take is out of town."

The white cat purred. "Lucky girl to be the only one."

Derry's manner stiffened. "You are good to think so."

After Derry had gone, Hilda said, "You see, it is Jean McKenzie. The Doctor said that he and Jean would be up in Maryland for a day or two. She has a good time. She doesn't know what it means to be poor, not as I know it. She doesn't know what it means to go without the pretty things that women long for. You wouldn't believe it, General, but when I was a little girl, I used to stand in front of shop windows and wonder if other girls really wore the slippers and fans and parasols. And when I went to Dr. McKenzie's, and saw Jean in her silk dressing gowns, and her pink slippers and her lace caps, she seemed to me like a lady in a play. I've worn my uniforms since I took my nurse's training, and before that I wore the uniform of an Orphans' Home. I—I don't know why I am telling you all this—only it doesn't seem quite fair, does it?"

He had all of an old man's sympathy for a lovely woman in distress. He had all of any man's desire to play Cophetua.

"Look here," he said. "You get yourself a pink parasol and a fan and a silk dress. I'd like to see you wear them."

She shook her head. "What should I do with things like that?" Her voice had a note of wistfulness. "A woman in my position must be careful."

"But I want you to have the things," he persisted.

"I shouldn't have a place to wear them," sadly. "No, you are very good to offer them. But I mustn't."

The General slept after that. Hilda read under the lamp—a white cat watched by a little old terrier on the stairs!

And now the big house was very still. There were lights in the halls of the first and second floors. Bronson crouching in the darkness of the third landing was glad of the company of the painted lady on the stairs. He knew she would approve of what he was doing. For years he had served her in such matters as this, saving her husband from himself. When Derry was too small, too ignorant of evil, too innocent, to be told things, it was to the old servant that she had come.

He remembered a certain night. She was young then and new to her task. She and the General had been dining at one of the Legations. She was in pale blue and very appealing. When Bronson had opened the door, she had come in alone.

"Oh, the General, the General, Bronson," she had said. "We've got to go after him."

She was shaking with the dread of it, and Bronson had said, "Hadn't you better wait, ma'am?"

"I mustn't. We stopped at the hotel as we came by, and he said he would run in and get a New York paper. And we waited, and we waited, and he didn't come out again, and at last I sent McChesney in, and he couldn't find him. And then I went and sat in the corridor, thinking he might pass through. It isn't pleasant to sit alone in the corridor with the men—staring at you—at night. And then I asked the man at the door if he had seen him, and he said, 'yes,' that he had called a cab, and then I came home."

They had gone out again together, with Bronson, who was young and strong, taking the place of the coachman, McChesney, because Mrs. Drake did not care to have the other servants see her husband at times like these. "You know how good he is," had been her timid claim on him from the first, "and you know how hard he tries." And because Bronson knew, and because he had helped her like the faithful squire that he was, she had trusted him more and more with this important but secret business.

She had changed her dress for something dark, and she had worn a plain dark hat and coat. She had not cried a tear and she would not cry. She had been very brave as they travelled a beaten path, visiting the places which the General frequented, going on and on until they came to the country, and to a farm-house where they found him turning night into day, having roused the amazed inmates to ask for breakfast.

He had paid them well for it, and was ready to set forth again with the dawn when his wife drove in.

"My dear," he had said, courteously, as his little wife's face peered out at him from the carriage, "you shouldn't have come."

Sobered for the moment, he had made a handsome figure, as he stood with uncovered head, his dark hair in a thick curl between his eyes. The morning was warm and he carried his overcoat on his arm. His patent leather shoes and the broadcloth of his evening clothes showed the dust and soil of his walk through the fields. He had evidently dismissed his cab at the edge of the city and had come crosscountry.

His wife had reached out her little hand to him. "I came because I was lonely. The house seems so big when you are—away—"

It had wrung Bronson's heart to see her smiling. Yet she had always met the General with a smile and with the reminder of her need of him. There had been never a complaint, never a rebuke—at these moments. When he was himself, she strove with him against his devils. But to strive when he was not himself, would be to send him away from her.

Her hands were clasped tightly, and her voice shook as she talked on the way back to the husband who seemed so unworthy of the love she gave.

Yet she had not thought him unworthy. "If I can only save him," she had said so many times. "Oh, Bronson, I mustn't let him go down and down, with no one who loves him to hold him back."

In the years that had followed, Bronson had seen her grow worn and weary, but never hopeless. He had seen her hair grow gray, he had seen the light go out of her face so that she no longer smiled as she had smiled in the picture.

But she had never given up the fight. Not even at the last moment. "You will stay with him, Bronson, and help Derry."

And now this other woman had come to undo all the work that his beloved mistress had done. And there in the shadowed room she was weaving her spells.

Outside, snug against the deadly cold in his warm closed car, Derry waited alone for Bronson's signal.

There was movement at last in the shadowed room. The General spoke from the bed. Hilda answered him, and rose. She arranged a little tray with two glasses and a plate of biscuits. Then she crossed the room towards the bookcase.

Bronson reached up his hand and touched the button which controlled the lights on the third floor. He saw Hilda raise a startled head as the faint click reached her. She listened for a moment, and he withdrew himself stealthily up and out of sight. If she came into the hall she might see him on the stairs. He had done what he could. He would leave the rest to Derry.

"What's the matter?" the General asked.

"I thought I heard a sound—but there's no one up. This is our hour, isn't it?"

She brought the bottle out from behind the books. Then she came and stood by the side of the bed.

"Will you drink to my happiness, General?"

She was very handsome. "To our happiness," he said, eagerly, and unexpectedly, as he took the glass.

Hilda, pouring out more wine for herself, stood suddenly transfixed. Derry spoke from the threshold. "Dr. McKenzie has asked you repeatedly not to give my father wine, Miss Merritt."

He was breathing quickly. His hat was in his hand and he wore his fur coat. "Why are you giving it to him against the Doctor's orders?"

The General interposed. "Don't take that tone with Miss Merritt, Derry. I asked her to get it for me, and she obeyed my orders. What's the matter with that?"

"Dr. McKenzie said, explicitly, that you were not to have it."

"Dr. McKenzie has nothing to do with it. You may tell him that for me, I am not his patient any longer."

"Father—"

"Certainly not. Do you think I am going to take orders from McKenzie—or from you?"

"But, Miss Merritt is his nurse, under his orders."

"She is not going to be his nurse hereafter. I have other plans for her."

Derry stood staring, uncomprehending. "Other plans—"

"I have asked her to be my wife."

Oh, lovely painted lady on the stairs, has it come to this? Have your prayers availed no more than this? Have the years in which you sacrificed yourself, in which you sacrificed your son, counted no more than this?

Derry felt faint and sick. "You can't mean it, Dad."

"I do mean it. I—am a lonely man, Derry. A disappointed man. My wife is dead. My son is a slacker—"

It was only the maudlin drivel of a man not responsible for what he was saying. But Derry had had enough. He took a step forward and stood at the foot of the bed. "I wouldn't go any farther if I were you, Dad. I've not been a slacker. I have never been a slacker. I am not a coward. I have never been a coward. I am going to tell you right now why I am not in France. Do you think I should have stayed out of it for a moment if it hadn't been for you? Has it ever crossed your mind that if you had been half a man I might have acted like a whole one? Have you ever looked back at the years and seen me going out into the night to follow you and bring you back? I am not whining. I loved you, and I wanted to do it; but it wasn't easy. And I should still be doing it; but of late you've said things that I can't forgive. I've stood by you because I gave a promise to my mother—that I wouldn't leave you. And I've stayed. But now I shan't try any more. I am going to France. I am going to fight. I am not your son, sir. I am the son of my mother."

Then the General said what he would never have said if he had been himself.

"If you are not my son, then, by God, you shan't have any of my money."

"I don't want it. Do you think that I do? I shall get out of here tonight, and I shan't come back. There is only one thing that I want besides my own personal traps—and that is my mother's picture on the stairs."

The General was drawing labored breaths. "Your mother's picture—?"

"Yes, it has no place here. Do you think for as instant that you can meet her eyes?"

There was a look of fright on the drawn old face. "I am not well, give me the wine."

Derry reached for the bottle. "He shall not have it."

Hilda came up to him swiftly. "Can't you see? He must. Look at him."

Derry looked and surrendered. Then covered his face with his hands.

All that night, Derry, trying to pack, with Bronson in agitated attendance, was conscious of the sinister presence of Hilda in the house. There was the opening and shutting of doors, her low orders in the halls, her careful voice at the telephone, and once the sound of her padded steps as she passed Derry's room on her way to her own. The new doctor came and went. Hilda sent, at Derry's request, a bulletin of the patient's condition. The General must be kept from excitement; otherwise there was not reason for alarm.

But Derry was conscious, as the night wore on, and Bronson left him, and he sat alone, of more than the physical evidences of Hilda's presence; he was aware of the spiritual effect of her sojourn among them. She had stolen from them all something that was fine and beautiful. From Derry his faith in his father. From the General his constancy to his lovely wife. The structure of ideals which Derry's mother had so carefully reared for the old house had been wrecked by one who had first climbed the stairs in the garb of a sister of mercy.

He saw his father's future. Hilda, cold as ice, setting his authority aside. He saw the big house, the painted lady smiling no more on the stairs. Hilda's strange friends filling the rooms, the General's men friends looking at them askance, his mother's friends staying away.

Poor old Dad, poor old Dad. All personal feeling was swept away in the thought of what might come to his father. Yet none the less his own path lay straight and clear before him. The time had come for him to go.

BOOK TWO
Through the Crack

"I will go to the wars! I will go to the wars!" the Tin Soldier cried as loud as he could, and he threw himself from the shelf....

What could have become of him? The old man looked, and the little boy looked. "I shall find him," the old man said, but he did not find him. For the Tin Soldier had fallen through a crack in the floor, and there he lay as in an open grave.

The Doctor's house in Maryland was near Woodstock, and from the rise of the hill where it stood one could see the buildings of the old Jesuit College, and the river which came so soon to the Bay.

In his boyhood the priests had been great friends of Bruce McKenzie. While of a different faith, he had listened eagerly to the things they had to tell him, these wise men, the pioneers of missionary work in many lands, teachers and scholars. His imagination had been fired by their tales of devotion, and he had many arguments with his Covenanter grandfather, to whom the gold cross on the top of the college had been the sign and symbol of papacy.

"But, grandfather, the things we believe aren't so very different, and I like to pray in their chapel."

"Why not pray in your own kirk?"

"It's so bare."

"There's nothing to distract your thoughts."

"And I like the singing, and the lights and the candles—"

"We need no candles; we have light enough in our souls."

But Bruce had loved the smell of the incense, and the purple and red of the robes, and, seeing it all through the golden haze of the lights, his sense of beauty had been satisfied, as it was not satisfied in his own plain house of worship.

Yet it had been characteristic of the boy as it was of the man that neither kirk nor chapel held him, and he had gone through life liking each a little, but neither overmuch.

Something of this he tried to express to Jean as, arriving at Woodstock in the early afternoon, they passed the College. "I might have been a priest," he said, "if I hadn't been too much of a Puritan or a Pagan. I am not sure which held me back—"

Jean shuddered. "How can people shut themselves away from the world?"

"They have a world of their own, my dear," said the Doctor, thoughtfully, "and I'm not sure that it isn't as interesting as our own."

"But there isn't love in it," said Jean.

"There's love that carries them above self—and that's something."

"It is something, but it isn't much," said his small daughter, obstinately. "I don't want to love the world, Daddy. I want to love Derry—"

The Doctor groaned. "I thought I had escaped him, for a day."

"You will never escape him," was the merciless rejoinder, but she kissed him to make up for it.

In spite of the fact of her separation for the moment from her lover, she had enjoyed the ride. There had been much wind, and a little snow on the way. But now the air was clear, with a sort of silver clearness—the frozen river was gray-green between its banks, there were blue shadows flung by the bare trees. As they passed the College, a few black-frocked fathers and scholastics paced the gardens.

Jean wished that Derry were there to see it all. It was to her a place of many memories. Most of the summers of her little girlhood had been spent there, with now and then a Christmas holiday.

The house did not boast a heating plant, but there were roaring open fires in all the rooms, except in the Connollys' sitting room, which was warmed by a great black stove.

The Connollys were the caretakers. They occupied the left wing of the house, and worked the farm. They were both good Catholics, and Mrs. Connolly looked after the little church at the crossroads corner, where the good priests came from the College every week to say Mass. She was a faithful, hard-working, pious soul, with her mind just now very much on her two sons who had enlisted at the first call for men, and were now in France.

She talked much about them to Jean, who came into the kitchen to watch her get supper. The deep, dark, low-ceiled room was lighted by an oil lamp. The rocking chair in which Jean sat had a turkey-red cushion, and there was another turkey-red cushion in the rocking chair on the other side of the cookstove. They ate their meals on the table under the lamp. It was only when guests were in the house that the dining room was opened.

The Doctor and Jim Connolly were at the barn, where were kept two fat mules, a fat little horse, a fat little cow, and a pair of fat pigs. There were also a fat house dog, and a brace of plump pussies, for the Connollys were a plump and comfortable couple who wanted everything about them comfortable, and who had had little to worry them until the coming of the war.

Yet even the war could not shake Mrs. Connolly's faith in the rightness of things.

"I was glad to have our country get into it, and to have my sons go. If they had stayed at home, I shouldn't have felt satisfied."

"Didn't it nearly break your heart?"

Mrs. Connolly, beating eggs for an omelette, shook her head. "Women's hearts don't break over brave men, Miss Jean. It is the sons who are weak and wayward who break their mothers' hearts—not the ones that go to war."

She poured the omelette into a pan. "When I have a bad time missing them, I remember how the Mother of God gave her blessed Son to the world. And He set the example, to give ourselves to save others. No, I don't want my boys back until the war is over."

Jean said nothing. She rocked back and forth and thought about what Mary Connolly had said. One of the fat pussies jumped on her lap and purred. It was all very peaceful, all as it had been since some other cook made omelettes for the little aristocrat of an Irish grandmother who would not under any circumstances have sat in the kitchen on terms of familiarity with a dependent. The world had progressed much in democracy since those days. Those who had fought in this part of the country for liberty and equality had not really known it. They had seen the Vision, but it was to be given to their descendants to realize it.

Jean rocked and rocked. "I hate war," she said, suddenly. "I didn't until Daddy said he was going, and then it seemed to come—so near—all the time I am trying to push the thought of it away. I wouldn't tell him, of course. But I don't want him to go."

"No, I wouldn't tell him. We women may be scared to death, but it ain't the time to tell our men that we are scared."

"Are you scared to death, Mrs. Connolly?"

The steady eyes met hers. "Sometimes, in the night, when I think of the wet and cold, and the wounded groaning under the stars. But when the morning comes, I cook the breakfast and get Jim off, and he don't know but that I am as cheerful as one of our old hens, and then I go over to the church, and tell it all to the blessed Virgin, and I am ready to write to my boys of how proud I am, and how fine they are—and of every little tiny thing that has happened on the farm."

Thus the heroic Mary Connolly—type of a million of her kind in America—of more than a million of her kind throughout the world—hiding her fears deep in her heart that her men might go cheered to battle.

The omelette was finished, and the Doctor and Jim Connolly had come in. "The stars are out," the Doctor said. "After supper we'll walk a bit."

Jean was never to forget that walk with her father. It was her last long walk with him before he went to France, her last intimate talk. It was very cold, and he took her arm, the snow crunched under their feet.

Faintly the chimes of the old College came up to them. "Nine o'clock," said the Doctor. "Think of all the years I've heard the chimes, I have lived over half a century—and my father before me heard them—and they rang in my grandfather's time. Perhaps they will ring in the ears of my grandchildren, Jean."

They had stopped to listen, but now they went on. "Do you know what they used to say to me when I was a little boy?

'The Lord watch
Between thee and—me—'"

"My mother and I used to repeat it together at nine o'clock, and when I brought your mother here for our honeymoon—that first night we, too, stood and listened to the chimes—and I told her what they said.

"Men drift away from these things," he continued, with something of an effort. "I have drifted too far. But, Jean, will you always remember this, that when I am at my best, I come back to the things my mother taught her boy? If anything should happen, you will remember?"

"IF ANYTHING SHOULD HAPPEN, YOU WILL REMEMBER?"

[Illustration: "If anything should happen, you will remember?"]

She clung to his arm. She had no words. Never again was she to hear the chimes without that poignant memory of her father begging her to remember the best—.

"I have been thinking," he said, out of a long silence, "of you and Derry. I—I want you to marry him, dear, before I go."

"Before you go—Daddy—"

"Yes. Emily says I have no right to stand in the way of your happiness. And I have no right. And some day, perhaps, oh, my little Jean, my grandchildren may hear the chimes—"

White and still, she stood with her face upturned to the stars. "Life is so wonderful, Daddy."

And this time she said it out of a woman's knowledge of what life was to mean.

They went in, to find that the Connollys had retired. Jean slept in a great feather-bed. And all the night the chimes in the College tower struck the hours—

In the morning, Jean went over to the church with Mrs. Connolly. It was Saturday, and things must be made ready for the services the next day. Jean had been taught as a child to kneel reverently while Mrs. Connolly prayed. To sit quietly in a pew while her good friend did the little offices of the altar.

Jean had always loved to sit there, to wonder about the rows of candles and the crucifix, to wonder about the Sacred Heart, and St. Agnes with the lamb, and St. Anthony who found things when you lost them, and St. Francis in the brown frock with the rope about his waist, and why Mrs. Connolly never touched any of the sacred vessels with bare hands.

But most of all she had wondered about that benignant figure in the pale blue garments who stood in a niche, with a light burning at her feet, and with a baby in her arms.

Mary—

Faintly as she gazed upon it on this winter morning, Jean began to perceive the meaning of that figure. Of late many women had said to her, "Was my son born for this, to be torn from my arms—to be butchered?"

Well, Mary's son had been torn from her arms—butchered—her little son who had lain in a manger and whom she had loved as much as any less-worshipped mother,—and he had told the world what he thought of sin and injustice and cruelty, and the world had hated him because he had set himself against these things—and they had killed him, and from his death had come the regeneration of mankind.

And now, other men, following him, were setting themselves against injustice and cruelty, and they were being killed for it. But perhaps their sacrifices, too, would be for the salvation of the world. Oh, if only it might be for the world's salvation!

She walked quite soberly beside Mrs. Connolly back to the house. She took her knitting to the kitchen. Mrs. Connolly was knitting socks. "I don't mind the fighting as much as I do the chance of their taking cold. And I'm afraid they won't have the sense to change their socks when they are wet. I have sent them pairs and pairs—but they'll never know enough to change—

"It is funny how a mother worries about a thing like that," she continued. "I suppose it is because you've always worried about their taking cold, and you've never had to worry much about their being killed. I always used to put them to bed with hot drinks and hot baths, and a lot of blankets, and I keep thinking that there won't be anybody to put them to bed."

Jean knitted a long row, and then she spoke. "Mrs. Connolly, I'm going to be married, before Daddy leaves for France."

"I am happy to hear that, my dear."

"I didn't know it until last night—Daddy wasn't willing. I—I feel as if it couldn't be really true—that I am going to be married, Mrs. Connolly."

There was a tremble of her lip and clasping of her little hands.

Mary Connolly laid down her work. "I guess you miss your mother, blessed lamb. I remember when she was married. I was young, too, but I felt a lot older with my two babies, and Jim and I were so glad the Doctor had found a wife. He needed one, if ever a man did—for he liked his gay good time."

"Daddy?" said Jean, incredulously. It is hard for youth to visualize the adolescence of its elders. Dr. McKenzie's daughter beheld in him none of the elements of a Lothario. He was beyond the pale of romance! He was fifty, which settled at once all matters of sentiment!

"Indeed, he was gay, my dear, and he had broken half the hearts in the county, and then your mother came for a visit. She didn't look in the least like you, except that she was small and slender. Her hair was dark and her eyes. You have your father's eyes and hair.

"But she was so pretty and so loving—and you never saw such a honeymoon. They were married in the spring, and the orchards were in bloom, and your father filled her room with apple blossoms, and the first day when Jim drove them up from the station, your father carried her in his arms over the threshold and up into that room, and when she came down, she said, 'Mary Connolly, isn't life—wonderful?'"

"Did she say that, Mrs. Connolly, really? Daddy always teases me when I go into raptures. He says that I think everything is wonderful from a sunset to a chocolate soda."

"Well, she did, too. Her husband was the most wonderful man, and her baby was the most wonderful baby—and her house was the most wonderful house. You make me think of her in every way. But you won't have apple blossoms for your honeymoon, my dear."

"No. But, oh, Mrs. Connolly—it won't make any real difference."

"Not a bit. And if you'll come up here, Jim and I will promise not to be in the way. Your mother said we were never in the way. And I'll serve your meals in front of the sitting-room fire. They used to have theirs out of doors. But you'll be just as much alone, with me and Jim eating in the kitchen."

It was very easy after that to tell Mrs. Connolly all about it. About Derry, and how he had fallen in love with her when he had thought she was just the girl in the Toy Shop. But there were things which she did not tell, of the shabby old gentleman and of the shadow which had darkened Derry's life.

Then when she had finished, Mary Connolly asked the thing which everybody asked—"Why isn't he fighting?"

Jean flushed. "He—he made a promise to his mother."

"I'd never make my boys promise a thing like that. And if I did, I'd hope they'd break it."

"Break it?" tensely.

"Of course. Their honor's bigger than anything I could ever ask them. And they know it."

"Then you think that Derry ought to break his promise?"

"I do, indeed, my dear."

"But—. Oh, Mrs. Connolly, I don't know whether I want him to break it."

"Why not?"

With her face hidden. "I don't know whether I could let him—go."

"You'd let him go. Never fear. When the moment came, the good Lord would give you strength—"

There were steps outside. Jean leaned over and kissed Mary Connolly on the cheek. "You are such a darling—I don't wonder that my mother loved you."

"Well, you'll always be more than just yourself to me," said Mary. "You'll always be your mother's baby. And after I get lunch for you and the men I am going back to the church and ask the blessed Virgin to intercede for your happiness."

So it was while Mary was at church, and the two men had gone to town upon some legal matter, that Jean, left alone, wandered through the house, and always before her flitted the happy ghost of the girl who had come there to spend her honeymoon. In the great south chamber was a picture of her mother, and one of her father as they looked at the time of their marriage. Her mother was in organdie with great balloon sleeves, and her hair in a Psyche knot. She was a slender little thing, and the young doctor's picture was a great contrast in its blondness and bigness. Daddy had worn a beard then, pointed, as was the way with doctors of his day, and he looked very different, except for the eyes which had the same teasing twinkle.

The window of this room looked out over the orchard, the orchard which had been bursting with bloom when the bride came. The trees now were slim little skeletons, with the faint gold of the western sky back of them, and there was much snow. Yet so vivid was Jean's impression of what had been, that she would have sworn her nostrils were assailed by a delicate fragrance, that her eyes beheld wind-blown petals of white and pink.

The long mirror reflecting her showed her in her straight frock of dark blue serge, with the white collars and cuffs. The same mirror had reflected her mother's organdie. It, too, had been blue, Mary had told her, but blue with such a difference! A faint forget-me-not shade, with a satin girdle, and a stiff satin collar!

Two girls, with a quarter of a century between them. Yet the mother had laughed and loved, and had looked forward to a long life with her gay big husband. They had had ten years of it, and then there had been just her ghost to haunt the old rooms.

Jean shivered a little as she went downstairs. She found herself a little afraid of the lonely darkening house. She wished that Mary would come.

Curled up in one of the big chairs, she waited. Half-asleep and half-awake; she was aware of shadow-shapes which came and went. Her Scotch great-grandfather, the little Irish great-grandmother; her copper-headed grandfather, his English wife, her own mother, pale and dark-haired and of Huguenot strain, her own dear father.

From each of these something had been given her, some fault, some virtue. If any of them had been brave, there must have been handed down to her some bit of bravery—if any of them had been cowards—

But none of them had been cowards.

"*We came to a new country,*" *said the great-grandparents.* "*There were hardships, but we loved and lived through them—*"

"*The Civil war tore our hearts,*" *said the grand-parents.* "*Brother hated brother, and friend hated friend, but we loved and lived through it—*"

"*We were not tested,*" *said her own parents.* "*You are our child and test has come to you. If you are brave, it will be because we have given to you that which came first to us—*"

Jean sat up, wide-awake—"*I am not brave,*" she said.

She stood, after that, at a lower window, watching. Far down the road a big black motor flew straight as a crow towards the hill on which the Doctor's house stood. It stopped at the gate. A man stepped out. Jean gave a gasp, then flew to meet him.

"Oh, Derry, Derry—"

He came in and shut the door behind him, took her in his arms, kissed her, and kissed her again. "I love you," he said, "I love you. I couldn't stay away—"

It seemed to Jean quite the most wonderful thing of all the wonderful things that had happened, that he should be here in this old house where her parents had come for their honeymoon—where her own honeymoon was so soon to be—.

She saved that news for him, however. He had to tell her first of how he had taken the wrong road after he had left Baltimore. He had gone without his lunch to get to her quickly. No, he wasn't hungry, and he was glad Mary Connolly was out, "I've so much to say to you."

Then, too, she delayed the telling so that he might see the farm before darkness fell. She wrapped herself in a hooded red cloak in which he thought her more than ever adorable.

The sun rested on the rim of the world, a golden disk under a wind-blown sky. It was very cold, but she was warm in her red cloak, he in his fur-lined coat and cap.

She told him about her father's honeymoon, hugging her own secret close. "They came here, Derry, and it was in May. I wish you could see the place in May, with all the appleblooms.

"It seems queer, doesn't it, Derry, to think of father honeymooning. He always seems to be making fun of things, and one should be serious on a honeymoon."

She flashed a smile at him and he smiled back. "I shall be very serious on mine."

"Of course. Derry, wouldn't you like a honeymoon here?"

"I should like it anywhere—with you—"

"Well," she drew a deep breath, "Daddy says we may—"

"We may what, Jean-Joan?"

"Get married—"

"Before he goes?"

"Yes."

She leaned forward to get the full effect of his surprise, to watch the dawn of his delight.

But something else dawned. Embarrassment? Out of a bewildering silence she heard him say, "I am not sure, dear, that it will be best for us to marry before he goes."

She had a stunned feeling that, quite unaccountably, Derry was failing her. A shamed feeling that she had offered herself and had been rejected.

Something of this showed in her face. "My dear, my dear," he said, "let us go in. I can tell you better there."

Once more in the warm sitting room with the door shut behind them, he lifted her bodily in his arms. "Don't you know I want it," he whispered, tensely. "Tell me that you know—"

When he set her down, his own face showed the stress of his emotion. "You are always to remember this," he said, "that no matter what happens, I am yours, yours—always, till the end of time."

Instinctively she felt that this Derry was in some way different from the Derry she had left the day before. There was a hint of masterfulness, a touch of decision.

"Will you remember?" he repeated, hands tight on her shoulders.

"Yes," she said, simply.

He bent and kissed her. "Then nothing else will matter." He placed a big chair for her in front of the fire, and drew another up in front of it. Bending forward, he took her hands. "I am glad I found you alone. What luck it was to find you alone!"

He tried then to tell her what he had come to tell. Yet, after all there was much that he left unsaid. How could he speak to her of the things he had seen in his father's shadowed house? How fill that delicate mind with a knowledge of that which seemed even to his greater sophistication unspeakable?

So she wondered over several matters. "How can he want to marry Hilda? I can't imagine any man wanting Hilda."

"She is handsome in a big fine way."

"But she is not big and fine. She is little and mean, but I could never make Daddy see it."

He wondered if McKenzie would see it now.

Mary Connolly, coming in through the back door to her warm kitchen, heard voices. Standing in the dark hall which connected the left wing with the house, she could see through into the living room where Jean sat with her lover.

There was much dark wood and the worn red velvet—low bookshelves lining the walls, a grand piano on a cover by the window. In the dimness Jean's copper head shone like the halo of a saint. Mary decided that Derry was "queer-looking," until gathering courage, she went in and was warmed by his smile.

"He hasn't had any lunch, Mary," Jean told her, "and he wouldn't let me get any for him."

"I'll have something in three whisks of a lamb's tail," said Mary with Elizabethan picturesqueness, and away she went on her hospitable mission.

"Marrying just now," said Derry, picking up the subject, where he had dropped it, when Mary came in, "is out of the question."

"Did you think that I was marrying you for your money?"

"No. But two months' pay wouldn't buy a gown like this,"—he lifted a fold with his forefinger—"to say nothing of your little shoes." He dropped his light tone. "Oh, my dear, can't you see?"

"No. I can't see. Daddy would let us have this house, and I have a little money of my own from my mother, and—and the Connollys would take care of everything, and we should see the spring come, and the summer."

He rose and went and stood with his back to the fire. "But I shan't be here in the spring and summer."

She clasped her hands nervously. "Derry, I don't want you to go."

"You don't mean that."

"I do. I do. At least not yet. We can be married—and have just a little, little month or two—and then I'll let you go—truly."

He shook his head. "I've stayed out of it long enough. You wouldn't want me to stay out of it any longer, Jean-Joan."

"Yes, I should. Other men can go, but I want to keep you—it's bad enough to give—Daddy—. I haven't anybody. Mary Connolly has her husband, but I haven't anybody—" her voice broke—and broke again—.

He came over and knelt beside her. "Let me tell you something," he said. "Do you remember the night of the Witherspoon dinner? Well, that night you cut me dead because you thought I was a coward—and I thanked God for the women who hated cowards."

"But you weren't a coward."

"I know, and so I could stand it—could stand your scorn and the scorn of the world. But what if I stayed out of it now, Jean?

"What if I stayed out of it now? You and I could have our little moment of happiness, while other men fought that we might have it. We should be living in Paradise, while other men were in Hell. I can't see it, dearest. All these months I have been bound. But now, my dear, my dear, do you love me enough not to keep me, but to let me go?"

There was a beating pause. She lifted wet eyes. "Oh, Derry, darling, I love you enough—I love you—"

Thus, in a moment, little Jean McKenzie unlatched the gate which had shut her into the safe and sunshiny garden of pampered girlhood and came out upon the broad highway of life, where men and women suffer for the sake of those who travel with them, sharing burdens and gaining strength as they go.

Dimly, perhaps, she perceived what she had done, but it was not given to her to know the things she would encounter or the people she would meet. All the world was to adventure with her, throughout the years, the poor distracted world, dealing death and destruction, yet dreaming ever of still waters and green pastures.

CHAPTER XIX

HILDA SHAKES A TREE

When Dr. McKenzie and Jim Connolly arrived, Derry said apologetically as he shook hands with the Doctor, "You see, you can't get rid of me—but I have such a lot of things to talk over with you."

It was after Jean had gone to bed, however, that they had their talk, and before that Derry and Jean had walked in the moonlight and had listened to the chimes.

There had, perhaps, never been such a moon. It hung in a sky that shimmered from horizon to horizon. Against this shimmering background the college buildings were etched in black—there was a glint of gold as the light caught the icicles and made candles of them.

In the months to come that same moon was to sail over the cantonment where Derry slept heavily after hard days. It was to sail over the trenches of France, where, perhaps, he slept not at all, or slept uneasily in the midst of mud and vermin. But always when he looked up at it, he was to see the Cross on the top of the College, and to hear the chimes.

They talked that night of the things that were deep in their hearts. She wanted him to go—yes, she wanted him to go, but she was afraid.

"If something should happen to you, Derry."

"Sometimes I wonder," he said, in his grave, young voice, "why we are so—afraid. I think we have the wrong focus. We want life, even if it brings unhappiness, even if it brings suffering, even if it brings disgrace. Anything seems better than to—die—"

"But to have things stop, Derry." She shuddered. "When there's so much ahead."

"Perhaps they don't stop, dear."

"If I could only believe that—"

"Why not? Do you remember 'Sherwood,' where Blondin rides through the forest singing:

"'Death, what is death?" he cried, "I must ride on—'"

His face was lifted to the golden sky. She was never to forget the look upon it. And with a great ache and throb of passionate renunciation, she told herself that it was for this that the men of her generation had been born, that they might fight against the powers of darkness for the things of the spirit.

She lay awake a long time that night, thinking it out. Of how she had laughed at other women, scolded, said awful things to them of how their cowardice was holding the world back. She had thought she understood, but she had not understood. It was giving your own—your own, which was the test. *Oh, let those who had none of their own to give keep silent.*

With her breath almost stopping she thought of those glorious young souls riding on and on through infinite space, the banner of victory floating above them. No matter what might come to the world of defeat or of disaster, these souls would never know it, they had given themselves in the cause of humanity—for them there would always be the sound of silver trumpets, the clash of cymbals, the song of triumph!

Downstairs, Dr. McKenzie was listening with a frowning face to what Derry had to tell him.

"Do you mean to say that Hilda was giving him—wine?"

"Yes. Bronson told me. But he didn't want you to depend upon his unsupported testimony. So we fixed up a scheme, and I stayed outside until he flashed a light for me; and then I went in and caught her."

"It is incredible. Why should she do such a thing? She has always been a perfect nurse—a perfect nurse, Drake." He rose and walked the floor. "But deliberately to disobey my orders—what could have been her object?"

Derry hesitated.

"I haven't told you the worst."

Doctor McKenzie stopped in front of him. "The worst?"

"Dad is going to marry her."

"What?"

Derry repeated what he had said.

The Doctor dropped into a chair. "Who told you?"

"Dad."

"And she admitted that it was—true?"

"Yes."

Derry gave the facts. "He wasn't himself, of course, but that doesn't change things for me."

The Doctor in the practice of his profession had learned to conceal his emotions. He concealed now what he was feeling, but a close observer might have seen in the fading of the color in his cheeks, the beating of his clenched fist on the arm of his chair, something of that which was stirring within him.

"And this has been going on ever since she went there. She has had it in mind to wear your mother's jewels—" Derry had graphically described Bronson's watch on the stairs—"to get your father's money. I knew she was cold-blooded, but I had always thought it a rather admirable quality in a woman of her attractive type."

Before his eye came the vision of Hilda's attractiveness by his fireside, at his table. And now she would sit by the General's fire, at his table.

"She didn't say a word," Derry's young voice went on, "when he told me that I was no longer—his son. I can't tell you how I felt about her. I've never felt that way about anyone before. I've always liked people—but it was as if some evil thing had swooped down on the old house."

The lad saw straight! That was the thought which suddenly illumined Dr. McKenzie's troubled mind. Hilda was not beautiful. So beauty of body could offset the ugliness of her distorted soul.

"And so I am poor," Derry was saying, heavily, "and I must wait to marry Jean."

The red surged up in the Doctor's face. He jerked himself forward in his chair. "You shall not wait. After this you are my son, if you are not your father's."

He laid his hand on Derry's shoulder. "I've money enough, God knows. And I shan't need it. It isn't a fortune, but it is enough to make all of us comfortable for the rest of our days—and I want Jean to be happy. Do you think I am going to let Hilda Merritt stand between my child and happiness?"

"It's awfully good of you, sir," Derry's voice was husky with feeling, "but—"

"There are no 'buts.' You must let me have my own way; I shall consider it a patriotic privilege to support one soldier and his little wife."

He was riding above the situation splendidly. He even had visions of straightening things out. "When I go back I shall tell Hilda what I think of her, I shall tell her that it is preposterous—that her professional reputation is at stake."

"What will she care for her professional reputation when she is my father's wife?"

The thought of Hilda with the world, in a sense, at her feet was maddening. The Doctor paced the floor roaring like an angry lion. "It may not do any good, but I've got to tell her what I think of her."

Derry had a whimsical sense of the meeting of the white cat and this leonine gentleman—would she purr or scratch?

"The sooner you and Jean are married the better. If Hilda thinks she is going to keep you and Jean apart she is mistaken."

"Oh—did she know of the engagement?"

"Yes," the Doctor confessed. "I told her the other day when she came to fix the books."

"Then that accounts for it."

"For what?"

"Dad's attitude. I thought it was queer he should fly up all in a moment. She wanted to make trouble, Doctor, and she has made it."

Long after Derry had gone to bed, the Doctor sat there pondering on Hilda's treachery. He was in some ways a simple man—swayed by the impulse of the moment. The thought of deliberate plotting was abhorrent. In his light way he had taken her lightly. He had laughed at her. He had teased Jean, he had teased Emily, calling their intuition jealousy. Yet they had known better than he. And why should not women know women better than men know them? Just as men know men in a way that women could never know. Sex erected barriers—there was always the instinct to charm, to don one's gayest plumage; even Hilda's frankness had been used as a lure; she knew he liked it. Would she have been so frank if she had not felt its stimulus to a man of his type? And, after all, had she really been frank?

Such a woman was like a poisonous weed; and he had thought she might bloom in the same garden with Jean—until Emily had told him.

He turned to the thought of Emily with relief. Thank God he could leave Jean in her care. If Derry went, there would still be Emily with her sweet sanity, and her wise counsels.

He felt very old as he went upstairs. He stood for a long time in front of his wife's picture. How sweet she had been in her forget-me-not gown—how little and tender! Their love had burned in a white flame—there would never be anything like that for him again.

He waked in the morning, however, ready for all that was before him. He was a man who dwelt little on the past. There was always the day's work, and the work of the day after.

His appetite for the work of the coming day was, it must be confessed, whetted somewhat by the thought of what he would say to Hilda.

They had an early breakfast, with Jean between her father and Derry and eating nothing for very happiness.

There was the start in the opal light of the early morning, with a faint rose sky making a background for the cross on the College, and the chimes saying "Seven o'clock."

Jim and Mary Connolly came out in the biting air to see them off. Then Mary went over to the church to pray for Jean and Derry. But first of all she prayed for her sons.

The Doctor, arriving at his office, at once called up Hilda.

"I must see you as soon as possible."

"What has Derry Drake been telling you?"

"How do you know that he has told me anything?"

"By your voice. And you needn't think that you are going to scold me."

"I shall scold you for disobeying orders. I thought you were to be trusted, Hilda."

"I am not a saint. You know that. And I am not sure that I want you to come. I shall send you away if you scold."

She hung up the receiver and left him fuming. Her high-handed indifference to his authority sent him storming to Derry, "I've half a mind to stay away."

"I think I would. It won't do any good to go—"

But the Doctor went. He still hoped, optimistically, that Hilda might be induced to see the error of her ways.

She received him in the blue room, where the General's precious porcelain was set forth in cabinets. It was a choice little room which had been used by Mrs. Drake for the reception of special guests. Hilda was in her uniform, but without her cap. It was as if in doffing her cap, she struck her first note of independence against the Doctor's rule.

He began professionally. "Doctor Bryer telephoned this morning that his attendance of the case had been only during my absence. That he did not care to keep it unless I definitely intended to withdraw. I told him to go ahead. I told him also that you were a good nurse. I had to whitewash my conscience a bit to say it, Hilda—"

Her head went up. "I am a good nurse. But I am more than a nurse, I am a woman. Oh, I know you are blaming me for what you think I have done. But if you stood under a tree and a great ripe peach hung just out of your reach, could you be blamed for shaking the tree? Well, I shook the tree."

She was very handsome as she gave her defense with flashing eyes.

"The General asked me to marry him, and that's more than you would ever have done. You liked to think that I was half in love with you. You liked to pretend that you were half in love with me. But would you ever have offered me ease and rest from hard work? Would you ever have thought that I might some day be your daughter's equal in your home? Oh, I have wanted good times. I used to sit night after night alone in the office while you and Jean went out and did the things I was dying to do. I wanted to go to dances and to the theater and to supper with a gay crowd. But you never seemed to think of it. I am young and I want pretty clothes—yet you thought I was satisfied to have you come home and say a few careless pleasant words, and to tease me a little. That was all you ever did for me—all you ever wanted.

"But the General wants more than that. He wants me here in the big house, to be his wife, and to meet his friends. He had a man come up the other day with a lot of rings, and he bought me this." She showed the great diamonds flashing on her third finger. "I have always wanted a ring like this, and now I can have as many as I want. Do you blame me for shaking the tree?"

He sat, listening, spellbound to her sophistry. But was it sophistry? Wasn't some of it true? He saw her for the first time as a woman wanting things like other women.

She swept out her hand to include the contents of the little room. "I have always longed for a place like this. I don't know a thing about china. But I know that all that stuff in the cabinet cost a fortune. And it's a pretty room, and some day when I am the General's wife, I'll ask you here to take tea with me, and I'll wear a silver gown like your daughter wears, and I think you'll be surprised to see that I can do it well."

He flung up his hand. "I can't argue it, Hilda. I can't analyze it. But it is all wrong. In all the years that you worked for me, while I laughed at you, I respected you. But I don't respect you now."

She shrugged. "Do you think I care? And a man's respect after all is rather a cold thing, isn't it? But I am sorry you feel as you do about it. I should have been glad to have you wish me happiness."

"Happiness—" His anger seemed to die suddenly. "You won't find happiness, Hilda, if you separate a son from his father."

"Did he tell you that? I had nothing to do with it. His father was angry at his—interference."

He stood up. "We won't discuss it. But you may tell him this. That I am glad his son is poor, for my daughter will marry now the man and not his money."

"Then he will marry her?"

"Yes. On Christmas Day."

She wished that she might tell him the date of her own wedding, but she did not know it. The General seemed in no hurry. He had carefully observed the conventions; had hired a housekeeper and a maid, and there was, of course, the day nurse. Having thus surrounded his betrothed with a sort of feminine bodyguard, he spoke of the wedding as happening in the spring. And he was hard to move. As has been said, the General had once commanded a brigade. He was immensely entertained and fascinated by the lady who was to be his wife. But he was not to be managed by her. She found herself, as he grew stronger, quite strangely deferring to his wishes. She found herself, indeed, rather unexpectedly dominated.

She came back to the Doctor. "Aren't you going to wish me happiness?"

"No. How can I, Hilda?"

After he had left her, she stood very still in the middle of the room. She could still see him as he had towered above her—his crinkled hair waving back from his handsome head. She had always liked the youth of him and his laughter and his boyish fun.

The rich man upstairs was—old—.

CHAPTER XX
THE VISION OF BRAVE WOMEN

And now the Tin Soldier was to go to the wars!

Derry, swinging downtown, found himself gazing squarely into the eyes of the khaki-clad men whom he met. He was one of them at last!

He was on his way to meet Jean. The day before they had gone to church together. They had heard burning words from a fearless pulpit. The old man who had preached had set no limits on his patriotism. The cause of the Allies was the cause of humanity, the cause of humanity was the cause of Christ. He would have had the marching hymn of the Americans "Onward, Christian Soldiers." His Master was not a shrinking idealist, but a prophet unafraid. "Woe unto thee, Chorazin! Woe unto thee, Bethsaida!… It shall be more tolerable for Tyre and Sidon in the day of Judgment than for you. And thou, Capernaum, which art exalted unto Heaven, shall be brought down to hell …"

"I am too old to go myself," the old man had said, "but I have sent my sons. In the face of the world's need, no man has a right to hold another back. Personal considerations which might once have seemed sufficient must now be set aside. Things are at stake which involve not only the honor of a nation but the honor of the individual. To call a man a coward in the old days was to challenge his physical courage. To know him as a slacker in these modern times is to doubt the quality of his mind and spirit. 'I pray thee have me excused' is the word of one lost to the high meanings of justice—of love and loyalty and liberty—"

Stirring words. The lovers had thrilled to them. Derry's hand had gone out to Jean and her own hand clasped it. Together they saw the vision of his going forth, a shining knight, girded for the battle by a beloved woman—saw it through the glamour of high hopes and youthful ardor!

A troop of cavalry on the Avenue! Jackies in saucer caps, infantry, artillery, aviation! Blue and red and green cords about wide-brimmed hats. Husky young Westerners, slim young Southerners, square-chinned young Northerners—a great brotherhood, their faces set one way—and he was to share their hardships, to be cold and hungry with the best of them, wet and dirty with the worst. It would be a sort of glorified penance for his delay in doing the thing which too long he had left undone.

He was to have lunch with Jean in the House restaurant—he was a little early, and as he loitered through the Capitol grounds, in his ears there was the echo of fairy trumpets—"*trutter-a-trutt, trutter-a-trutt—*"

The old Capitol had always been for Derry a place of dreams. He loved every inch of it. The sunset view of the city from the west front; the bronze doors on the east, the labyrinthine maze of the corridors; the tesselated floors, the mottled marble of the balustrades; the hushed approach to the Supreme Court; the precipitous descent into the galleries of House and Senate, the rap of the Speaker's gavel—the rattle of argument as political foes contended in the legislative arena; the more subdued squabbles on the Senate floor; the savory smell of food rising from the restaurants in the lower regions; the climb to the dome, the look of the sky when one came out at the top; Statuary Hall and its awesome echoes; the Rotunda with its fringe of tired tourists, its frescoed frieze—Columbus, Cortez, Penn, Pizarro—; the mammoth paintings—Pocahontas, and the Pilgrims, De Soto, and the Surrender of Cornwallis, the Signing of the Declaration, and Washington's Resignation as Commander-in-Chief—Indian and Quaker, Puritan and Cavalier—these were some of the things which had ravished the eyes of the boy Derry in the days when his father had come to the Capitol to hobnob with old cronies, and his son had been allowed to roam at will.

But above and beyond everything else, there were the great mural paintings on the west wall of the House side, above the grand marble staircase.

"*Westward the Course of Empire takes its way—!*"

Oh, those pioneers with their faces turned towards the Golden West! The tired women and the bronzed men! Not one of them without that eager look of hope, of a dream realized as the land of Promise looms ahead!

Derry had often talked that picture over with his mother. "It was such men, Derry, who made our country—men unafraid—North, South, East and West, it was these who helped to shape the Nation's destiny, as we must help to shape it for those who come after us."

It was in front of this picture that he was to meet Jean. He had wanted to share with her the inspiration of it.

She was late, and he waited, leaning on the marble rail which overlooked the stairway. People were going up and down passing the picture, but not seeing it, their pulses calm, their blood cold. The doors of the elevators opened and shut, women came and went in velvet and fur, laughing. Men followed them, laughing, and the picture was not for them.

Derry wondered if it were symbolic, this indifference of the crowd. Was the world's pageant of horrors and of heroism thus unseen by the eyes of the unthinking?

And now Jean ascended, the top of her hat first—a blur of gray, then the red of the rose that he had sent her, a wave of her gray muff as she saw him. He went down to meet her, and stood with her on the landing. Beneath the painting, on one side, ran the inscription, "No pent up Utica confines our powers, but the boundless Continent is ours," on the other side, "The Spirit moves in its allotted space; the mind is narrow in a narrow sphere."

Thousands of men and women came and went and never read those words. But boys read them, sitting on the stairs or leaning over the rail—and their minds were carried on and on. Old men, coming back after years to read them again, could testify what the words had meant to them in the field of high endeavor.

Jean had seen the painting many times, but now, standing on the upper gallery floor with Derry, it took on new meanings. She saw a girl with hope in her eyes, a young mother with a babe at her breast; homely middle-aged women redeemed from the commonplace by that long gaze ahead of them; old women straining towards that sunset glow. She saw, indeed, the Vision of Brave Women. "If it could only be like that for me, Derry. Do you see—they go with their husbands, those women, and I must stay behind."

"You will go with me, beloved, in spirit—"

They fell into silence before the limitless vista.

And now more people were coming up the stairs, a drawling, familiar voice—Alma Drew on the landing below. With her a tall young man. She was turning on him all her batteries of charm.

Alma passed the picture and did not look at it, she passed the lovers and did not see them. And she was saying as she passed, "I don't know why any man should be expected to fight. I shouldn't if I were a man."

Jean drew a long breath. "There, but for the grace of God, goes Jean McKenzie."

Derry laughed. "You were never like that. Not for the least minute. You were afraid for the man you loved. It isn't fear with Alma."

But the thought of Alma did not trouble them long. There was too much else in their world today. As they walked through the historic halls, they had with them all the romance of the past—and so Robert Fulton with his boats, Père Marquette with his cross and beads, Frances Willard in her strange old-fashioned dress spoke to them of the dreams which certain inspired men and women have translated into action.

They talked of these things while they ate their lunch. The black waiter, who knew Derry, hovered about them. His freedom, too, had been the culmination of a dream.

"Men laugh at the dreamers," Derry said, "then honor them after they are dead."

"That's the cruelty, the sadness of it, isn't it?"

"Not to the dreamer. Do you think that Père Marquette cared for what smaller minds might think, or Frances Willard? They had their vision backed by a great faith in the rightness of things, and so Marquette followed the river and planted the cross, and Frances Willard blazed the way for the thing which has come to pass."

After lunch they motored to Drusilla's. They used one of Dr. McKenzie's cars. Derry had ceased to draw upon his father's establishment for anything. He lived at the club, and met his expenses with the small balance which remained to his credit in the bank.

"You can give Jean whatever you think best," he told the Doctor, "but I shall try to live on what I have until I go, and then on my pay."

"Your pay, my dear boy, will just about equal what you now spend in tips."

"I think I shall like it. It's an adventure for rich men when they have to be poor. That's why a lot of fellows have gone into it. They are tired of being the last word in civilization. They want to get down to primitive things."

"Mrs. Witherspoon can't imagine Derry Drake without two baths a day."

"Can't she? Well, Mrs. Witherspoon may find that Derry Drake is about like the rest of the fellows. No better and no worse. There is no disgrace in liking to be clean. The disgrace comes when one kicks against a thing that can't be helped."

In the Doctor's car, therefore, they arrived at Drusilla's.

"We have come to tell you that we are going to be married."

"You Babes in the Wood!"

"Will you come to the wedding?

"Of course I'll come. Marion, do you hear? They are going to be married."

"And after that, Drusilla,"—he smiled as he phrased it—"your Tin Soldier will go to the wars."

Jean glanced from one to the other. "Is that what she called you—a Tin Soldier?"

"It is what I called myself."

Marion having come forward to say the proper thing, added, "Drusilla's going, too."

"Drusilla?"

"Yes, with my college unit—to run errands in a flivver."

The next day, encountering Derry on the street, Drusilla opened her knitting bag and brought out a tiny parcel. "It's my wedding gift to you. I found it in Emily's toy shop."

It was a gay little French tin soldier. "For a mascot;" she told him, seriously. "Derry, dear, I shall not try to tell you how I feel about your marriage to Jean. About your going. If I could sing it, you'd know. But I haven't any words. It—it seems so—perfect that the Tin Soldier should go—to the wars—and that the girl he leaves behind him should be a little white maid like—Jean."

Thus Drusilla, with a shake in her voice, renouncing a—dream.

Derry, who was on his way to Margaret's showed the tin soldier to Teddy and his little sister. "He is going to the wars."

"With you?"

"Yes."

"When are you going?"

"As soon as I can—"

"I should think you wouldn't like to leave us."

"Well, I don't. But I am coming back."

"Daddy didn't come back."

"But some men do."

"Perhaps God doesn't love you as much as He did Daddy, and He won't want to keep you."

"Perhaps not—"

The things which the child had spoken stayed with Derry all that day. His feeling about death had always been that of a man who has long years before him. He had rather jauntily conceded that some men die young, but that the chances in his case were for a green old age. He might indeed have fifty years before him, and in fifty years one could—get ready—age had to do with serious things, people were peaceful and prepared.

But to get ready now. To face the thing squarely, saying, "I may not come back—there are, indeed, a thousand chances that I shall not come." Lacking those fifty years in which to grow towards the thought of dissolution, what ought one to do? Should a man make himself fit in some special fashion?

There was, too, the thought of those whom he might leave behind. Of Jean—his wife—whom he would leave. She would break her heart—at first. And then—? Would she remember? Would she forget? Would he and those millions of others who had gone down in battle become dim memories—pale shadows against the vivid background of the hurrying world? He felt that he could not, must not speak of these things to Jean. So he talked of them to Emily.

"If anything should happen to me," he said, "I couldn't, of course, expect that Jean would go on—caring—. And if there should ever be anyone else—I—I should want her to be happy."

"Don't try to be magnanimous," Miss Emily advised. "You are human, and it isn't in the heart of man to want the woman he loves ever to turn to another. Let the years take care of that. But you can be very sure of one thing—that no one will ever take your place with Jean."

"But she may marry."

"Why should you torture yourself with that? You have given her something that no one else can ever give—the wonder and rapture of first love. And the heroes of a war like this will be in a very special manner set apart! 'A glorious company, the flower of men, to serve as models for the mighty world!'"

She laid her hand on his shoulder. "You must think now only of love and life and of coming back to Jean."

He reached up his hand and caught hers in a warm clasp. "Do you know you are the nearest, thing to a mother that I've known since I lost mine?"

He spoke, too, rather awkwardly, of the feeling about—getting ready.

"I have always thought that if I tried to live straight—I've thought, too, that it wouldn't come until I was old—that I should have plenty of time—and that by then, I should be more—spiritual."

"You will never be more spiritual than you are at this moment. Youth is nearer Heaven than age. I have always thought that. As we grow old—we are stricken by—fear—of poverty, of disease—of death. It is youth which has faith and hope."

Before he left her, he gave her a sacred charge. "If anything happens, I know what you'll be to—Jean—and I can't tell you what a help you've been this morning."

She was thrilled by that. And after he left her she thought much about him. Of what it would have meant to her to have a son like that.

Women had said to her, "You should be glad that you have no boy to send—." But she was not glad. Were they mad, these mothers, to want to hold their boys back? Had the days of peace held no dangers that they should be so afraid for them now?

For peace had dangers—men and women had been worshipping false gods. They had set up a Golden Calf and had bowed before it—and their children, lured by luxury, emasculated by ease of living, had wanted more ease, more luxury, more time in which to—play!

And now life had become suddenly a vivid Crusade, with everybody marching in one direction, and the young men were manly in the old ways of strength and heroism, and the young women were womanly in the old way of sending their lovers forth, and in a new way, when, like Drusilla, they went forth themselves to the front line of battle.

To have children in these days, meant to have something to give. One need not stand before suffering humanity empty-handed!

War was a monstrous thing, a murderous thing—but surely this war was a righteous one—a fire which would cleanse the world. Men and women, because of it, were finding in themselves something which could suffer for others, something in themselves which could sacrifice, something which went beyond body and mind, something which reached up and touched their souls.

So, in the midst of darkness, Miss Emily had a vision of Light. After the war was over, things could never be as they had been before. The spirit which had sent men forth in this Crusade, which had sent women, would survive, please God, and show itself in a greater sense of fellowship—of brotherhood. Might not men, even in peace, go on praying as they were praying it now in war, the prayer of Cromwell's men, "Oh, Lord, it's a hard battle, but it's for the rights of the common people—" Might not the rich young men who were learning to be the brothers of the poor, and the poor young men who were learning in a large sense of the brotherhood of the rich—might these not still clasp hands in a sacred cause?

Yes, she was sorry that she had no son. Slim and gray-haired, a little worn by life's struggle, her blood quickened at the thought of a son like Derry. The warmth of his handclasp, the glimpse of that inner self which he had given her, these were things to hold close to her heart. She had known on that first night that he was—different. She had not dreamed that she should hold him—close.

Rather pensively she arranged her window. It was snowing hard, and in spite of the fact that Christmas was only three days away, customers were scarce.

The window display was made effective by the use of Jean's purple camels—a sandy desert, a star overhead, blazing with all the realism of a tiny electric bulb behind it, the Wise Men, the Inn where the Babe lay, and in a far corner a group of shepherds watching a woolly flock—

Her cyclamen was dead. A window had been left open, and when she arrived one morning she had found it frozen.

She had thanked Ulrich Stölle for it, in a pleasantly worded note. She had not dared express her full appreciation, lest she seem fulsome. Few men in her experience had sent her flowers. Never in all the years of her good friendship with Bruce McKenzie had he bestowed upon her a single bloom.

Several days had passed, and there had been no answer to the note. She had not really expected an answer, but she had thought he might come in.

He came in now, with a great parcel in his arms. He was a picturesque figure in an enveloping cape and a soft hat pulled down over his gray hair, and with white flakes powdered over his shoulders.

"Good morning, Miss Bridges," he said; "did you think I was never coming?"

His manner of assuming that she had expected him quite took Emily's breath away. "I am glad you came," she said, simply. "It is rather dreary, with the snow, and this morning I found my cyclamen frozen on the shelf."

He glanced up at it. "We have other flowers," he said, and, with a sure sense of the dramatic effect, untied the string of his parcel.

Then there was revealed to Miss Emily's astonished eyes not the flowers that she had expected, but four small plush elephants, duplicates in everything but size of the one she had loaned to Ulrich, and each elephant carried on his back a fragrant load of violets cunningly kept fresh by a glass tube hidden in his trappings.

"There," said Ulrich Stölle, "my father sent them. It is his taste, not mine—but I knew that you would understand."

"But," Miss Emily gasped, "did he make them?"

"Most certainly. With his clever old fingers—and he will make as many more as you wish."

Thus came white elephants back to Miss Emily's shelves. "It seems almost too good to be true," she said, sniffing the violets and smiling at him.

"Nothing is too good to be true," he told her, "and now I have something to ask. That you will come and see my father."

"With pleasure."

He glanced around the empty shop. "Why not now? There are no customers—and the gray light makes things dreary—. And it is spring in my hothouses—there are a thousand cyclamens for the one you have lost, a thousand violets for every one on the backs of these little elephants—narcissus and daffodils—. Why not?"

Why not, indeed? Why not, when Adventure beckoned, go to meet it? She had tied herself for so many years to the commonplace and the practical.

And so Miss Emily closed her shop, and went in Ulrich's car, leaving a card tucked in the shop door, "Will reopen at three."

It was at one o'clock that Dr. McKenzie came and found that door shut against him. He shook the knob with some impatience, and stamped his foot impotently when no one answered. His orders had come and he must leave for France tomorrow. He had not told Jean, he had come to Emily to ask her to break the news—.

He stood there in the snow feeling quite unexpectedly forlorn. Heretofore he had always been able to put his finger on Emily when he had wanted her. He had needed only to beckon and she had followed.

And how could he know that she was at that very moment following other beckonings? That she had responded to a call that was not the call of selfish need, but of a subtle understanding of her rare charm. Bruce McKenzie had, perhaps, subconsciously felt that Emily would be fortunate to have a place by his fireside, to bask in his presence—Ulrich Stölle leading Emily through the moist fragrance of his hot-houses counted himself blessed by the gods to have her there. "You see," he said, "that here it is spring."

It was indeed spring, with birds singing, not in cages, but free to fly as they pleased; with the sound of water, as a little artificial stream wound its way over moss-covered rocks set where it might splash and fall over them—with ferns bending down to it and tiny flashing fish following it.

"My father did that," Ulrich explained, "when he was younger and stronger. But now he sits in his chair and works at his toys."

The workshop of Franz Stölle was entered through the door of the last hothouse; he had thus always a vista of splashing color—red and purples and yellows—great stretches, and always with the green to rest his eyes; with the door opened between there came to him the fragrance, and the singing of birds, and the sound of the little stream.

He sat in a big chair, bent a little, plump and ruddy-faced, with a fringe of white hair. He wore horn spectacles—and a velvet coat. He rose when Emily entered, elegant of manner, in spite of his rotundity.

"So it is the lady of the elephants, Ulrich? When you telephoned I thought it was too good to be true."

"Your son says that nothing is too good to be true," Emily told him, sitting down in the chair that Ulrich placed for her, "but I have a feeling that this will all vanish in a moment like Aladdin's palace—" She waved her hands towards the shelves that went around the room. "I never expected to see such toys again."

For there they were—the toys of Germany. The quaint Noah's arks, the woolly dogs and the mewing cats—the moon-faced dolls.

"I don't see how you have made them all."

"Many of them were made years ago, Fräulein, and I have kept them for remembrance, but many of them are new. When my son told me that it was hard for you to get toys, I gathered around me a few old friends who learned their trade in Nuremberg. We have done much in a few days. We will do more. We are all patriotic. We will show the Prussians that the children of America do not lack for toys. What does the Prussian know of play? He knows only killing and killing and killing."

The old man beat his fist upon the table, "Killing!"

"You see," Ulrich said to Emily, "there are many of us who feel that way. Yet unthinking people cannot see that we are loyal, that our hearts beat with the hearts of those who have English blood and French blood and Italian blood and Dutch blood in their veins, and who have but one country—America."

The old man had recovered himself. "We are not here to talk of killing, but of what I and my friends shall make for you. And you are to have lunch with us? I have planned it, and I won't take 'no,' Fräulein. You and I have so much to say to each other."

Emily wondered if it were really her middle-aged and prosaic self who sat later at the table, being waited on by a very competent butler, and deferred to by the two men as if she were a queen.

It was she and the old man who did most of the talking, but always she was conscious of Ulrich's attentive eyes, of the weight of the quiet words which he interjected now and then in the midst of his father's volubility.

"Germany, my mother, is dead," wailed the old man. "I have wept over her grave; those who wage this war against humanity are bastards, the real sons and daughters of that sweet old Germany are here in America—they have come to their foster-mother, and they love her.

"If I had been younger," he went on, "I should have fought. My son would have fought. But as it is we can make toys—and we shall say to the Prussians across the sea, 'You have killed our mother—your people are no longer our people, nor your God our God.'"

Ulrich took Emily home. She carried with her a Noah's Ark, and a precious pot of cyclamen. She had chosen the cyclamen out of all the rest. "It is such a cheerful thing blooming in my shop."

"There are other cheerful things in your shop," he told her.

As she met his smiling eyes, she smiled back, "Do you mean that I am a cheerful thing?"

"A rose, mein Fräulein, when your cheeks are red, like this."

Emily, alone at last in the Toy Shop, took off her hat in front of the mirror and saw her red cheeks. She set the cyclamen safely in a warm corner. The four elephants with their fragrant freight of violets made an exotic and incongruous addition to the Christmas scene in the window.

Bruce McKenzie, coming in, asked, "Where did you get them?"

"The elephants? Ulrich Stölle brought them. Do you know him?"

"Yes. But I didn't know that you did."

"His father makes toys. I lent him my white elephant, and he made these—"

She spoke without self-consciousness, and McKenzie's mind was on his own matters, so they swept away from the subject of Ulrich Stölle. "Emily," Bruce said, "I have my orders. Tomorrow at twelve I must leave for France."

She gazed at him stupidly. "Tomorrow—?"

"Yes."

"But—Jean—?"

"I haven't told her. I don't know how to tell her."

"You won't be here for the wedding—?"

"No."

"It will break her heart."

"You needn't tell me that. Don't I know it?" His voice was sharp with the tension of suppressed emotion.

He dropped into a chair, then jumped up and placed one for her. "Sit down, sit down," he said, "and don't make me forget my manners. Somehow this thing gets me as nothing has ever gotten me before. It isn't that I mind going—I mind hurting—Jean—"

"You have always hated to hurt people," Emily said. "In some ways it's a sign of weakness."

"Don't scold," he begged. "I know I'm not much of a fellow, but you'll be sorry for me a little, won't you, Emily?"

She did not melt as he had expected to the appeal in his voice. "The thing we have to think of now," she said, "is not being sorry for you, but how we can get Jean married before twelve o'clock tomorrow—"

"Oh, of course we can't."

"Of course we can—if we make up our minds to it, and it's the only thing to do."

"But nothing is ready."

"Things can be made ready. They can stand up in the rose drawing-room at ten, and you can give her away."

He looked at her admiringly. "I didn't know that you had so much initiative."

She might have told him that it was a quality on which she rather prided herself, but that hitherto it had not seemed to attract him. "There are several things as yet undiscovered by you," she remarked casually, as she locked up her toys.

Watching her, he wondered idly if there were really worlds to discover in Emily. It might be interesting to—find out—.

"Shall you miss me?" he asked.

"Of course. And now if you'll see that the back shutters are barred, we'll be ready to go."

Thus she checked his small attempt at sentiment, and on the way home they talked about Jean. "If Derry goes, you and she must live together in my house. Let that be understood. I'd rather have her with you than with anyone else in the whole wide world."

Thus again the sacred charge, but this time not as a favor, but in lordly fashion, as one who claims a right.

Jean and Derry were having tea at the club, but could not be reached by phone. "They had probably motored out into the country," Emily decided. "We'll have to do things before they come."

The things that she did were stupendous.

She had a florist up in two hours—and the rose-colored drawing room was rosier than ever, and as fragrant as a garden.

She telephoned the clergyman—"At ten o'clock tomorrow."

She telephoned the caterer—"A wedding breakfast—"

She telephoned the dressmaker—"Miss McKenzie's gown—"

She telephoned Margaret and Marion Gray—.

"Is there anyone else?" she asked the Doctor. "I suppose we really ought to tell the General."

"Certainly not."

"But Bronson—? Derry will want him."

"If he can keep a secret—yes."

Jean and Derry, arriving after dark, were swept into a scene of excitement.

Florists on the stairs!

A frenzied dressmaker waiting with Jean's wedding gown!

Maids with mops and men with vacuums!

Julia and the cook helping at loose ends and dinner late!

What did it all mean?

"It means," said the Doctor, "that you are going to be married, my dear, at ten o'clock in the morning."

"But why, Daddy—" fear showed in her eyes—

"Ask Emily."

"Is he—going away,—Emily?"

"Yes, dear."

"But he mustn't. Derry, do you hear? He is going to France—and he mustn't—"

Derry took her trembling hands in his firm clasp. "He must go, you know that, dearest." His touch steadied her.

He leaned down to her and sang:—

"Jeanne D'Arc, Jeanne D'Arc—
Jeanne D'Arc, la victoire est pour vous."

Her head went up. The color came back to her cheeks.

"Of course," she said, and put away childish things that she might measure up to the stature of her lover's faith in her.

And it was Jean, the Woman, who talked long that night with her father before he went to France.

CHAPTER XXI
DERRY'S WIFE

It snowed hard the next morning. The General, waking, found the day nurse in charge. Bronson came in to get him ready for his breakfast. There was about the old man an air of suppressed excitement. He hurried a little in his preparations for the General's bath. But everything was done with exactness, and it was not until the General was shaved and sitting up in his gorgeous mandarin robe that Bronson said, "I'd like to go out for an hour or two this morning, if you can spare me, sir—"

"In this snow? I thought you hated snow. You've always been a perfect pussy cat about the cold, Bronson."

"Yes, sir, but this is very important, sir."

The General ran his eye over the spruce figure.

"And you are all dressed up. I hope you are not going to be married, Bronson."

It was an old joke between them. Bronson was a pre-destined bachelor, and the General knew it.

But he liked to tease him.

"No, sir. I'll be back in time to look after your lunch, sir."

The General had been growing stronger, so that he spent several hours each day in his chair. When Bronson had gone, he rose and moved restlessly about the room. The day nurse cautioned him. "The Doctor doesn't want you to exert yourself, General Drake."

He was always courteous, but none the less he meant to have his own way. "Don't worry, Miss Martin. I'll take the responsibility."

He shuffled out into the hall. When she would have followed, he waved her back. "I am perfectly able to go alone," he told her.

She stood on the threshold watching him. She was very young and she was a little afraid of him. Her eyes, as she looked upon him, saw an obstinate old man in a gay dressing gown. And the man in the gay dressing gown felt old until he faced suddenly his wife's picture on the stairs.

It had been weeks since he had seen it, and in those weeks much had happened. Her smiling presence came to him freshly, as the spring might come to one housed through a long winter, or the dawn after a dark night.

"Edith!"

He leaned upon the balustrade. The nurse, coming out, warned him. "Indeed, you'd better stay in your room."

"I'm all right. Please don't worry. You 'tend to your knitting, and I'll take care of myself."

She insisted, however, on bringing out a chair and a rug. "Perhaps it will be a change for you to sit in the hall," she conceded, and tucked him in, and he found himself trembling a little from weakness, and glad of the support which the chair gave him.

It seemed very pleasant to sit there with Edith smiling at him. For the first time in many weeks his mind was at rest. Ever since Hilda had come he had felt the pressure of an exciting presence. He felt this morning free from it, and glad to be free. What a wife Edith had been! Holding him always to his highest and best, yet loving him even when he stumbled and fell. Bending above him in her beautiful charity and understanding, raising him up, fostering his self-respect in those moments of depression when he had despised himself.

What other woman would have done it? What other woman would have kept her love for him through it all? For she had loved him. It had never been his money with her. She would have clung to him in sickness and in poverty.

But Hilda loved his money. He knew it now as absolutely as if she had said it. For the first time in weeks he saw clearly. Last night his eyes had been opened.

He had been roused towards morning by those soft sounds in the second room, which he had heard more than once in the passing weeks. In his feverish moments, it had not seemed unlikely that his wife might be there, coming back to haunt, with her gentle presence, the familiar rooms. There was, indeed, her light step, the rustle of her silken garments—.

Half-asleep he had listened, then had opened his eyes to find the night-lamp burning, Hilda's book under it and Hilda gone!

The minutes passed as still his ears were strained. There was not a sound in the house but that silken rustle. He wondered if he sought Edith if she would speak to him. He rose and reached for his dressing gown.

Hilda had grown careless; there was no screen in front of the second door, and the crack was wide. The General standing in the dark saw her before his wife's mirror, wearing his wife's jewels, wrapped in the cloak which his wife had worn—triumphant—beautiful!

It was that air of triumph which repelled him. It was a discordant note in the Cophetua theme. He had liked her in her nurse's white. In the trappings which did not belong to her she showed herself a trifle vulgar—less than a lady.

He had crept back to bed, and wide-awake, he had worked it all out in his mind. It was his money which Hilda wanted, the things that he could give her; he meant to her pink parasols and satin slippers, and diamonds and pearls and ermines and sables, and a check-book, with unlimited credit everywhere.

And to get the things that she wanted, she had given him that which had stolen away his brains, which might indeed have done more than that—which might have killed his soul.

He had heard her come in, but he had simulated sleep. She had seated herself by the little table, and had gone on with her book. Between his half-closed eyes he had studied her—seeing her with new eyes—the hard line of her lips, the long white hands, the heaviness of her chin.

Then he had slept, and had waked to find the day nurse on duty. He felt that he should be glad never to see Hilda again. He dreaded the night when he must once more speak to her.

He was very tired sitting there in his chair. The rug had slipped from his knees. He tried to reach for it and failed. But he did not want to call the day nurse. He wanted some one with him who—cared. He raised his poor old eyes to the lady in the picture. He was cold and tired.

He wished that Bronson would come back—good old Bronson, to pull up the rug. He wished that Derry might come.

A door below opened and shut. Some one was ascending the stairs. Some one who walked with a light step—some one slim and youthful, in a white gown—!

"Edith—?"

But Edith's hair had not been crinkled and copper-colored, and Edith would have come straight up to him; she would not have hesitated on the top step as if afraid to advance.

"Who are you?"

"Jean—"

"Jean?"

"Derry's wife."

"Come here." He tried to reach out his hand to her, but could not. His tongue felt thick—.

She knelt beside his chair. Her head was bare. She wore no wrap. "We were married this morning. And my own father has gone—to France—and I wanted a father—"

"Did Derry tell you to come?"

"Bronson begged me. He was at the wedding—"

"Old Bronson?" He tried to smile, but the smile was twisted.

She was looking up at him fearfully, but her voice did not falter. "I came to tell you that Derry loves you. He doesn't want your money, oh, you know that he doesn't want it. But he is going away to the—war, and he may be killed, so many men are—killed. And he—loves you—"

"Where is he?"

"I wouldn't let him come. You see, you said things which were hard for him to forgive. I was afraid you might say such things again."

He knew that he would never say them. "Tell him that—I love him." He tried to sit up. "Tell him that he is—my son."

He fell back. He heard her quick cry, "Bronson—"

Bronson came running up the stairs, and the nurse who had watched the scene dazedly from the threshold of the General's room ran, too.

Weighted down by a sense of increasing numbness he lifted his agonized eyes to Jean. "Stay with me—stay—"

Hilda, waked by the day nurse, raged. "You should have called me at once when he left his room. Why didn't you call me?"

"Because I felt myself competent to manage the case."

"You see how you have managed it—I will be down in a minute. Get everybody out—"

Her composed manner when she came down showed nothing of that which was seething within her.

She found Jean in bridal-white sitting by the bed and holding the General's hand. The doctor had been sent for, Derry had been sent for—things were being swept out of her hands. She blamed it, still hiding her anger under a quiet manner, on Jean.

"He has had a stroke. It was probably the excitement of your coming."

The day nurse intervened. "It was before she came, Miss Merritt, that I saw him reach for the rug. I was puzzled and started to investigate, and then I saw her on the stairs—" She smiled at Jean. Never in her limited young life had the day nurse seen such a lovely bride, and she did not in the least like Miss Merritt.

Derry coming a little later held Jean's hand in his while he faced Hilda. "What does the doctor say?"

The truth came reluctantly. "He may be unconscious for days. He may never wake up—"

"I do not think we shall need your services—. I will send you a check for any amount you may name."

"But—"

"Whatever claim you may have upon him will be settled when he is in a condition to settle anything; until then, my wife and I shall stay—"

Hilda went upstairs and packed her bag. So her house of dreams tumbled about her. So she left behind her the tiara and the pearl collar with the diamond slides, and the velvet cloak with the ermine collar. Poor Hilda, with her head held high, going out of the shadowed house.

And taking Hilda's place, oh, more than taking her place, was Jean—and this was her wedding day. The little rose-colored drawing room had needed all of its rose to counteract the gray of the world outside, with the snow and Daddy's car standing ready to take him to the station.

But always there had been the thought of Derry to uphold her, and the wonder of their love. Nothing could rob her of that.

He had held her in his arms the night before, and had said, "Tomorrow we shall be in Woodstock, and shall listen to the chimes—"

And now it was tomorrow, and they were here in this great grim house with Death at the door.

Quite miraculously Emily arrived, and she and Bronson made a boudoir of Derry's sitting-room. They filled it with flowers, as was fitting for a bridal-bower. Jean's little trunk had been sent on to Woodstock, but there was her bag, and a supply of things which Emily brought from home.

A new night nurse came, and Miss Martin was retained for the day. The snow still fell, and the old man in the lacquered bed was still unconscious, his stertorous breathing sounding through the house.

And it was her wedding day!

They dined in the great room where Derry's ancestors gazed down on them. Emily was there, and it was a bridal feast, with things ordered hurriedly. Bronson, too, had seen to that. But they ate little. Emily talked and Derry ably supplemented her efforts.

84

But Jean was silent. It was all so different from what one might expect—! She still wore her white dress. It was a rather superlative frock with much cobwebby lace that had been her mother's, and in the place of her own small string of pearls was the longer string which had been her father's last gift to her. She had worn no veil, her crinkled copper hair in all its beauty had been uncovered.

"I can't believe that the lovely, lovely lady at the other end of the table is my wife," Derry told Miss Emily.

Jean smiled at him. She felt as if she were smiling from a great distance—and she had to look at him over a perfect thicket of orchids. "Shall I always have to sit so far away from you, Derry?" she asked in a very small voice.

"My dearest, no—" and he came and stood behind her, and reached for her little coffee cup and drank where her lips had touched, shamelessly, before the eyes of the sympathetic and romantic Miss Emily.

And now Emily had gone! And at last Jean and Derry were alone in the bridal bower, and Jean was telling Derry again what his father had said. "He begged me to stay—"

Their eyes met. "Dearest, dearest," Derry said, "what is life doing to me?"

"It has given you me, Derry"—such a little, little whisper.

"My beloved—yes."

The next morning they talked it over.

"What am I to do? He needs me more than ever—"

"There must be some way out, Derry."

But what way? The Tin Soldier had jumped from the shelf, but he had fallen through a crack! And the war was going on without him—!

CHAPTER XXII
JEAN PLAYS PROXY

Christmas morning found the General conscious. He was restless until Jean was brought to him. He had a feeling that she had saved him from Hilda. He wanted her where he could see her. "Don't leave me," he begged.

She slipped away to eat her Christmas dinner with Derry and Emily and Margaret. It was an early dinner on account of the children. They ate in the big dining room, and after dinner there was a tree, with Ulrich Stölle playing Father Christmas. It had come about quite naturally that he should be asked. It had been unthinkable that Derry could enter into the spirit of it, so Emily had ventured to suggest Ulrich. "He will make an ideal Santa Claus."

But it developed that he was not to be Santa Claus at all. He was to be Father Christmas, with a wreath of mistletoe instead of a red cap.

Teddy was intensely curious about the change. "But why isn't he Santa Claus?" he asked.

"Well, Santa Claus was—made in Germany."

"Oh!"

"But now he has joined the Allies and changed his name."

"Oh!"

"And he wears mistletoe, because mistletoe is the Christmas bush, and red caps don't really mean anything, do they?"

"No, but Mother—"

"Yes?"

"If Santa Claus has joined the Allies what will the little German children do?"

What indeed?

Jean had trimmed a little tree for the General, and the children carried it up to him carefully and sang a carol—having first arranged on his table, under the lamp, the purple camels, to create an atmosphere.

"'We three kings of Orient are,
Bearing gifts we traverse far
Field and fountain, moor and mountain,
Following yonder star—'"

"Yonner 'tar," piped Margaret-Mary.
"Yon-der-er ste-yar," trailed Teddy's falsetto.

"'Oh,   star   of   wonder,   star   of   might,
Star   with   royal   beauty   bright,
Westward   leading,   still   proceeding,
Guide us to the perfect light—'"

Twenty-four hours ago Hilda's book had lain where the purple camels now played their little part in the great Christmas drama. In the soul of the stricken old man on the bed entered something of the peace of the holy season.

"Oh, 'tar of wonner—"

"Ste-yar of wonder-er—" chimed the little voices.

When the song was finished, Margaret-Mary made a little curtsey and Teddy made a manly bow, and then they took their purple camels and left the tree on the table with its one small candle burning.

The General laid his left hand over Jean's—his right was useless—and said to Derry: "Your mother's jewels are my Christmas gift to her. No matter what happens, I want her to have them."

The evening waned, and the General still held Jean's hand. Every bone in her body ached. Never before had she grown weary in the service of others. She told herself as she sat there that she had always been a sort of sugar-and-spice-and-everything-nice sort of person. It was only fair that she should have her share of hardness.

The nurse begged her in a whisper to leave the General. "He won't know." But when Jean moved, that poor left hand tightened on hers and she shook her head.

Then Derry came and sat with his arm about her.

"My darling, you must rest."

She laid her head against her husband's shoulder, as he sat beside her. After a while she slept, and the nurse unlocked the clinging old fingers, and Derry carried his little wife to bed.

And so Christmas passed, and the other days, wonderful days in spite of the shadow which hung over the big house. For youth and love laugh at forebodings and they pushed as far back into their minds as possible, the thought of the thing which had to be faced.

But at last Derry faced it. "It is my self-respect, Jean."

They were sitting in her room with Muffin, wistful and devoted, on the rug at Jean's feet. The old dog, having been banished at first by Bronson, had viewed his master's wife with distrust. Gradually she had won him over, so that now, when she was not in the room, he hunted up a shoe or a glove, and sat with it until she came back.

"It is my self-respect, Jean-Joan."

She admitted that. "But—?"

"I can't stay out of the fighting and call myself a man. It has come to that with me."

She knew that it had come to that. She had thought a great deal about it. She lay awake at night thinking about it. She thought of it as she sat by the General's bed, day after day, holding his hand.

The doctor's report had been cautious, but it had amounted to this—the General might live to a green old age, some men rallied remarkably after such a shock. He rather thought the General might rally, but then again he might not, and anyhow he would be tied for months, perhaps for years, to his chair.

The old man was giving to his daughter-in-law an affection compounded of that which he had given to his wife and to his son. It was as if in coming up the stairs in her white gown on her wedding day, Jean had brought a bit of Edith back to him. For deep in his heart he knew that without her, Derry would not have come.

So he clung pathetically to that little hand, which seemed the only anchor in his sea of loneliness. Pathetically his old eyes begged her to stay. "You won't leave me, Jean?" And she would promise, and sit day after day and late into the night, holding his hand.

And as she sat with him, there grew up gradually within her a conviction which strengthened as the days went by. She could tell the very moment when she had first thought of it. She had left the General with Bronson while she went to dress for dinner. Derry was waiting for her, and usually she would have flown to him, glad of the moment when they might be together. But something halted her at the head of the stairs. It was as if a hand had been put in front of her, barring the way. The painted lady was looking at her with smiling eyes, but back of the eyes she seemed to discern a wistful appeal—"I want you to stay. No matter what happens I beg that you will stay."

But Jean didn't want to stay. All the youth in her rebelled against the thing that she saw ahead of her. She yearned to be free—to live and love as she pleased, not a prisoner in that shadowed room.

So she pushed it away from her, and so there came one morning a letter from her father.

"Drusilla went over on the same boat. It was a surprising thing to find her there. Since I landed, I haven't seen her. But I met Captain Hewes in Paris, and he was looking for her.

"I had never known how fine she was until those days on the boat. It was wonderful on the nights when everything was darkened and we were feeling our way through the danger zone, to have her sing for us. I believe we should all have gone to the bottom singing with her if a submarine had sunk us.

"I am finding myself busier than I have ever been before, finding myself, indeed, facing the most stupendous thing in the world. It isn't the wounded men or the dead men or the heart-breaking aspect of the refugees that gets me, it is the sight of the devastated country—made barren and blackened into hell not by devils, but by those who have called themselves men. When I think of our own country, ready soon to bud and bloom with the spring, and of this country where spring will come and go, oh, many springs, before there will be bud and bloom, I am overwhelmed by the tragic contrast. How can we laugh over there when they are crying here? Perhaps more than anything else, the difference in conditions was brought home to me as I motored the other day through a country where there was absolutely no sign of life, not a tree or a bird—except those war birds, the aeroplanes, hovering above the horizon.

"Well, as we stopped our car for some slight repairs, there rose up from a deserted trench, a lean cat with a kitten in her mouth. Oh, such a starved old cat, Jean, gray and war-worn. And her kitten was little and blind, and when she had laid it at our feet, she went back and got another. Then she stood over them, mewing, her eyes big and hungry. But she was not afraid of us, or if she was afraid, she stood her ground, asking help for those helpless babies.

"Jean, I thought of Polly Ann. Of all the petted Polly Anns in America, and then of this starved old thing, and they seemed so typical. You are playing the glad game over there, and it is easy to play it with enough to eat and plenty to wear, and away from the horror of it all. But how could that old pussy-cat be glad, how could she be anything but frightened and hungry and begging my help?

"Well, we took her in. We had some food with us, and we gave her all she could eat, and then she curled up on a pile of bags in the bottom of the car, and lay there with her kittens, as happy as if we were not going lickety-split over the shell-torn spaces.

"And that your tender heart may be at rest, I may as well tell you that she and the kittens are living in great content in a country house where one of the officers who was in the car with us is installed. We have named her Dolores, but it is ceasing to be appropriate. She is no longer sad, and while she is on somewhat slim fare like the rest of us, she is a great hunter and catches mice in the barn, so that she is growing strong and smooth, and she is not, perhaps, to be pitied as much as Polly Ann on her pink cushion.

"And here I am writing about cats, while the only thing that is really in my heart is—You.

"Ever since the moment I left you, I have carried with me the vision of you in your wedding gown—my dear, my dear. Perhaps it is just as well that I left when I did, for I am most inordinately jealous of Derry, not only because he has you, but because he has love and life before him, while I, already, am looking back.

"My work here is, as you would say, 'wonderful.' How I should like to hear you say it! There are things which in all my years of practice, I have never met before. How could I meet them? It has taken this generation of doctors to wrestle with the problem of treating men tortured by gas, and with nerves shaken by sights and sounds without parallel in the history of the world.

"But I am not going to tell you of it. I would rather tell you how much I love you and miss you, and how glad I am that you are not here to see it all. Yet I would have all Americans think of those who are here, and I would have you help until it—hurts. You must know, my Jean, how moved I am by it, when I ask you, whom I have always shielded, to give help until it hurts—

"I have had a letter from Hilda. She wants to come over. I haven't answered the letter. But when I do, I shall tell her that there may be something that she can do, but it will not be with me. I need women who can see the pathos of such things as that starved cat and kittens out there among the shell-holes, and Hilda would never have seen it. She would have left the cat to starve."

Jean found herself crying over the letter. "I am not helping at all, Derry."

"My dear, you are."

"I am not. I am just sitting on a pink cushion, like Polly Ann—"

It was the first flash he had seen for days of her girlish petulance. He smiled. "That sounds like the Jean of yesterday."

"Did you like the Jean of yesterday better than the Jean of to-day?"

"There is only one Jean for me—yesterday, today and forever."

She stood a little away from him. "Derry, I've been thinking and thinking—"

He put a finger under her chin and turned her face up to him. "What have you been thinking, Jean-Joan?"

"That you must go—and I will take care of your father."

"You?"

"Yes. Why not, Derry?"

"I won't have you sacrificed."

"But you want me to be brave."

"Yes. But not burdened. I won't have it, my dear."

"But—you promised your mother. I am sure she would be glad to let me keep your promise."

She was brave now. Braver than he knew.

"I can't see it," he said, fiercely. "I can see myself leaving you with Emily, in your own house—to live your own life. But not to sit in Dad's room, day after day, sacrificing your youth as I sacrificed my childhood and boyhood—my manhood—. I am over thirty, Jean, and I have always been treated like a boy. It isn't right, Jean; our lives are our own, not his."

"It is right. Nobody's life seems to be his own in these days. And you must go—and I can't leave him. He is so old, and helpless, Derry, like the poor pussy-cat over there in France. His eyes are like that—hungry, and they beg—. And oh, Derry, I mustn't be like Polly Ann, on a pink cushion—."

She tried to laugh and broke down. He caught her up in his arms. Light as thistledown, young and lovely!

She sobbed on his heart, but she held to her high resolve. He must go—and she would stay. And at last he gave in.

He had loved her dearly, but he had not looked for this, that she would give herself to hardness for the sake of another. For the first time he saw in his little wife something of the heroic quality which had seemed to set his mother apart and above, as it were, all other women.

BOOK THREE
The Bugle Calls

The wooden trumpeters that were carved on the door blew with all their might, so that their cheeks were much larger than before. Yes, they blew "Trutter-a-trutt—trutter-a-trutt—" …

CHAPTER XXIII
THE EMPTY HOUSE

Jean's world was no longer wonderful—not in the sense that it had once been, with all the glamour of girlish dreams and of youthful visions.

She had never thought of life as a thing like this in the days when she had danced down to the confectioner's, intent on good times.

But now, with her father away, with Derry away, with the city frozen and white, and with not enough coal to go around, with many of the rooms in the house shut that fuel might be conserved, with Margaret and the children and Nurse installed as guests at the General's until the weather grew warmer, with Emily transforming her Toy Shop into a surgical dressings station, and with her father-in-law turning over to her incredible amounts of money for the Red Cross and Liberty Bonds and War Stamps, life began to take on new aspects of responsibility and seriousness.

She could never have kept her balance in the midst of it all, if Derry had not written every day. Her father wrote every day, also, but there were long intervals between his letters, and then they were apt to arrive all at once, a great packet of them, to be read and re-read and passed around.

But Derry's letters, brought to her room every morning by Bronson, contained the elixir which sent her to her day's work with shining eyes and flushed cheeks. Sometimes she read bits of them to Bronson. Sometimes, indeed, there were only a few lines for herself, for Derry was being intensively trained in a Southern camp, working like an ant, with innumerable other ants, all in olive-drab, with different colored cords around their hats.

Sometimes she read bits of the letters to Margaret at breakfast, and after breakfast she would go up to the General and read everything to him except the precious words which Derry had meant for her very own self.

And then she and the General would tell each other how really extraordinary Derry was!

It was a never-failing subject, of intense interest to both of them. For there was always this to remember, that if the world was no longer a radiant and shining world, if the day's task was hard, and if now and then in the middle of the night she wept tears of loneliness, if there were heavy things to bear, and hard things and sad things, one fact shone brilliantly above all others, Derry was as wonderful as ever!

"There was never such a boy," the General would chant in his deep bass.

"Never," Jean would pipe in her clear treble.

And when they had chorused thus for a while, the General would dictate a letter to Derry, for his hand was shaky, and Jean would write it out for him, and then she would write a letter of her own, and after that the day was blank, and the night until the next morning when another letter came. So she lived from letter to letter.

"You have never seen Washington like this," she wrote one day in February, "we keep only a little fire in the furnace, and I am wearing flannels for the first time in my life. We dine in sweaters, and the children are round and rosy in the cold. And the food steams in the icy air of the dining room, and you can't imagine how different it all is—with the servants bundled up like the rest of us. We keep your father warm by burning wood in the fireplace of his room, and we have given half the coal in the cellar to people who haven't any."

"I am helping Cook with the conservation menus, and it is funny to see how topsy-turvy everything is. It is perfectly patriotic to eat mushrooms and lobsters and squabs and ducklings, and it is unpatriotic to serve sausages and wheat cakes. And Cook can't get adjusted to it. She will insist upon bacon for breakfast, because well-regulated families since the Flood have eaten bacon—and she feels that in some way we are sacrificing self-respect or our social status when we refrain.

"Your father is such an old dear, Derry. He has war bread and milk for lunch, and I carry it to him myself in the pretty old porcelain bowl that he likes so much.

"It was one day when I brought the milk that he spoke of Hilda. 'Where is she?'

"I told him that she was still in town, and that you had given her a check which would carry her over a year or two, and he said that he was glad—that he should not like to see her suffer. The porcelain bowl had reminded him of her. She had asked him once what it cost, and after she had found out, she had never used it. She evidently stood quite in awe of anything so expensive.

"Your mother and I are getting to be very good friends, dearest. When I am dreadfully homesick for you, I go and sit on the stairs, and she smiles at me. It is terribly cold in the hall, and I wrap myself up in your fur coat, and it is almost like having your arms around me."

She was surely making the best of things, this little Jean, when she found comfort in being mothered by a painted lady on the stairs, and in being embraced by a fur coat which had once been worn by her husband!

She kept Derry's tin soldier, which Drusilla had given him, on her desk. "You shall have him when you go to France, but until then he is a good little comrade, and I say; 'Good-morning' to him and 'Good-night.' Yet I sometimes wonder whether he likes it there on the shelf, and whether he is crying, 'I want to go to the wars—'"

She was very busy every morning in Emily's room, working on the surgical dressings. She hated it all. She hated the oakum and the gauze, the cotton and the compresses, the pneumonia jackets and the split-irrigation pads, the wipes, the triangulars, the many-tailed and the scultetus. Other women might speak lightly of five-yard rolls as dressing for stumps, of paper-backs "used in the treatment of large suppurating wounds." Jean shivered and turned white at these things. Her vivid imagination went beyond the little work-room with its white-veiled women to those hospitals back of the battle line where mutilated men lay waiting for the compresses and the wipes and the bandages, men in awful agony—.

But the lesson she was learning was that of harnessing her emotions to the day's work; and if her world was no longer wonderful in a care-free sense, it was a rather splendid world of unselfishness and self-sacrifice, although she was not conscious of this, but felt it vaguely.

She wore now, most of the time, her nun's frock of gray, which had seemed to foreshadow something of her future on that glorified day when Derry had first come to her. She had laid away many of her lovely things, and one morning Teddy remarked on the change.

"You don't dwess up any more."

Nurse stood back of his chair. "Dress—"

"Dur-wess."

"Don't you like this dress, Teddy?"

"I liked the boo one."

"Blue—"

"Ble-yew, an' the pink one, and all the shiny ones you used to wear at night."

"Blue dresses and pink dresses and shiny dresses cost a lot of money, Teddy, and I shouldn't have any money left for Thrift Stamps."

Thrift stamps were a language understood by Teddy, as he would not have understood the larger transactions of Liberty Bonds. He and the General held long conversations as to the best means of obtaining a large supply of stamps, and the General having listened to Margaret who wanted the boy to work for his offering, suggested an entrancing plan. Teddy was to feed the fishes in the dining-room aquarium, he was to feed Muffin, and he was to feed Polly Ann.

It sounded simple, but there were difficulties. In the first place he had to face Cook, and Cook hated to have children in the kitchen.

"But you'd have to face more than that if you were grown up and in the trenches. And Hodgson is really very kind."

"Well, she doesn't look kind, Mother."

"Why not?"

"Well, she doesn't smile, and her face is wed."

"Red, dear."

"Ur-ed—. And when I ask her for milk for Polly, she says 'Milk for cats,' and when she gets it out, she slams the 'frigerator door."

"Refrigerator, dear."

"Rif-iggerator."

But in the main Teddy went to his task valiantly. He conserved bones for Muffin and left-over corn-meal cakes. Polly Ann dined rather monotonously on fish boiled with war-bread crusts, on the back of Cook's big range. Hodgson was conscientious and salted it and cooled it, and kept it in a little covered granite pail, and it was from this pail that Teddy ladled stew into Polly Ann's blue saucer. "Mother says it is very good of you, Hodgson, to take so much trouble."

Hodgson, whose face was redder than ever, as she broiled mushrooms for lunch, grunted, "I'd rather do it than have other people messin' around."

Teddy surveyed her anxiously. "You don't mind having me here, do you, Hodgson?"

His cheeks were rosy, his bronze hair bright, his sturdy legs planted a trifle apart, Polly's dish in one hand, the big spoon in the other. "No, I don't mind," she admitted, but it was some time before she acknowledged even to herself how glad she was when that bright figure appeared.

Feeding the fishes presented few problems, and gradually thrift stamps filled the little book, and there was a war stamp, and more thrift stamps and more war stamps, and Muffin and Polly Ann waxed fat and friendly, and were a very lion and lamb for lying down together.

Then there came a day when Teddy, feeding the fishes in the aquarium, heard somebody say that Hodgson's son was in the war.

He went at once to the kitchen. "Why didn't you tell me?" he asked the cook, standing in front of her where she sat cutting chives and peppers and celery on a little board for salad.

"Tell you what?"

"That your boy was in Fwance."

Hodgson's red face grew redder, and to Teddy's consternation, a tear ran down her cheek.

He stood staring at her, then flew upstairs to his mother. "Cook's cryin'."

"Teddy—"

"She is. Because her son is in Fwance."

After that when he went down to get things for Muffin and Polly Ann, he said how s'prised he was and how nice it was now that he knew, and wasn't she pr-roud? And he fancied that Hodgson was kinder and softer. She told him the name of her son. It was Charley, and she and Teddy talked a great deal about Charley, and Teddy sent him some chocolate, and Hodgson told Margaret. "He's a lovely boy, Mrs. Morgan. May you never raise him to fight."

"I should want him to be as brave as his father, Hodgson."

"Yes. My boy's brave, but it was hard to let him go." Then, struck by the look on Margaret's face, she said, "Forgive me, ma'am; if mine is taken from me, I'd like to feel as you do. You ain't makin' other people unhappy over it."

"I think it is because my husband still lives for me, Hodgson."

Hodgson cried into her apron. "It ain't all of us that has your faith. But if I loses him, I'll do my best."

And so the painted lady on the stairs saw all the sinister things that Hilda had brought into the big house swept out of it. She saw Hodgson the cook trying to be brave, and bringing up Margaret's tea in the afternoons for the sake of the moment when she might speak of her boy to one who would understand; she saw Emily, coming home dead tired after a hard day's work, but with her face illumined. She saw Margaret smiling, with tears in her heart, she saw Jean putting aside childish things to become one of the women that the world needed.

Brave women all of them, women with a vision, women raised to heroic heights by the need of the hour!

The men, too, were heroic. Indeed, the General, trying to control his appetite, was almost pathetically heroic. He had given up sugar, although he hated his coffee without it, and he had a little boy's appetite for pies and cakes.

"When the war is over," he told Teddy, "we will order a cake that's as high as a house, and we will eat it together."

Teddy giggled. "With frostin'?"

"Yes. I remember when Derry was a lad that we used to tell him the story of the people who baked a cake so big that they had to climb ladders to reach the top. Well, that's the kind of cake we'll have."

Yet while he made a joke of it, he confessed to Jean. "It is harder than fighting battles. I'd rather face a gun than deny myself the things that I like to eat and drink."

Bronson was contributing to the Red Cross and buying Liberty Bonds, and that was brave of Bronson. For Bronson was close, and the hardest thing that he had to do was to part with his money, or to take less interest than his rather canny investments had made possible.

And Teddy, the man of his family, came one morning to his mother. "I've just got to do it," he said in a rather shaky voice.

"Do what, dear?"

"Send my books to the soldiers."

She let him do it, although she knew how it tore his heart. You see, there were the Jungle Books, which he knew the soldiers would like, and "Treasure Island," and "The Swiss Family Robinson," and "Huckleberry Finn." He brought his fairy books, too, and laid them on the altar of patriotism, and "Toby Tyler," which had been his father's, and "Under the Lilacs," which he adored because of little brown-faced Ben and his dog, Sancho.

He was rapturously content when his mother decided that the fairy books and Toby and brown-faced Ben might still be his companions. "You see the soldiers are men, dear, and they probably read these when they were little boys."

"But won't I wead them when I grow up, Mother?"

"You may want to read older books."

But Teddy was secretly resolved that age should not wither nor custom stale the charms of the beloved volumes. And that he should love them to the end. His mother thought that he might grow tired of them some day and told him so.

"I can wead them to my little boys," he said, hopefully, "and to their little boys after that," and having thus established a long line of prospective worshippers of his own special gods, he turned to other things.

General Drake, growing gradually better, went now and then in his warm closed car for a ride through the Park. Usually Jean was with him, or Bronson, and now and then Nurse with the children.

It was one morning when the children were with him that he said to Nurse: "Take them into the Lion House for a half hour, I'll drive around and come back for you."

Nurse demurred. "You are sure that you won't mind being left, sir?"

"Why not?" sharply. "I am perfectly able to take care of myself."

He watched them go in, then he gave orders to drive at once to the Connecticut Avenue entrance.

A woman stood by the gate, a tall woman in a long blue cloak and a close blue bonnet. In the clear cold, her coloring showed vivid pink and white. The General spoke through the tube; the chauffeur descended and opened the door.

"If you will get in," the General said to the woman, "you can tell me what you have to say—"

"Perhaps I should not have asked it," Hilda said, hesitating, "but I had seen you riding in the Park, and I thought of this way—I couldn't of course, come to the house."

"No." He had sunk down among his robes. "No."

"I felt that perhaps you had been led to—misunderstand." She came directly to the point. "I wanted to know—what I had done—what had made the difference. I couldn't believe that you had not meant what you said."

He stirred uneasily. "I have been very ill—"

Her long white hands were ungloved, the diamonds that he had given her sparkled as she drew the ring off slowly. "I felt that I ought to give you this—if it was all really over."

"It is all over. But keep it—please."

"I should like to keep it," she admitted frankly, "because, you see, I've never had a ring like this."

It was the Cophetua and Beggar Maid motif but it left him cold. "Hilda," he said, "I saw you that night trying on my wife's jewels. That was my reason."

She was plainly disconcerted. "But that was child's play. I had never had anything—it was like a child—dressing up."

"It was not like that to me. I think I had been a rather fatuous fool—thinking that there might be in me something that you might care for. But I knew then that without my money—you wouldn't care—"

"People's motives are always mixed," she told him. "You know that."

"Yes, I know."

"You liked me because I was young and made you feel young. I liked you because you could give me things."

"Yes. But now the glamour is gone. You make me feel a thousand years old, Hilda."

"Why?" in great surprise.

"Because I know that if I had no wealth to offer you, you would see me for what I am, an aged broken creature for whom you have no tenderness—"

It was time for him to be getting back to the Lion House. They stopped again at the gate. "If you will keep the ring," he said, "I shall be glad to think that you have it. Jean gays Derry gave you a check. If it is not enough to buy pink parasols, will you let me give you another?" He was speaking with the ease of his accustomed manner.

"No; I am not an—adventuress, though you seem to think that I am, and to condemn me for it."

"I condemn you only for one thing—for that flat bottle behind the books."

"But you wanted it."

"For that reason you should have kept it away. You should have obeyed orders."

"You asked me to doff my cap, so I—doffed my discipline." She was standing on the ground, holding the door open as she talked; again he was aware of the charm of her pink and white.

"Good-bye, Hilda." He reached out his hand to her.

She took it. "I am going to France."

"When?"

"As soon as I can." She stepped back and the door was shut between them. As the car turned, Hilda waved her hand, and the General had a sense of sudden keen regret as the tall cloaked figure with its look of youth and resoluteness faded into the distance.

When he reached the Lion House the children were waiting. "Did you hear him roar?" Teddy asked as he climbed in.

"No."

"Well, he did, and we came out 'cause it fwightened Peggy."

"Frightened—" from Nurse.

"Fr-ightened. But I liked the leopards best."

"Why?"

"Because they're pre-itty."

"You can't always trust—pretty things."

"Can't you tre-ust—leopards—General Drake?"

The General was not sure, and presently he fell into silence. His mind was on a pretty woman whom he could not trust.

That night he said to Jean, "Hilda is going to France."

"Oh—how do you know?"

"I met her in the Park."

He was sitting, very tired, in his big chair. Jean's little hand was in his.

"Poor Hilda," he said at last, looking into the fire, as if he saw there the vision of his lost dreams.

"Oh, no—" Jean protested.

"Yes, my dear, there is so much that is good in the worst of us, and so much that is bad in the best—and perhaps she struggles with temptations which never assail you."

Jean's lips were set in an obstinate line. "Daddy was always saying things like that about Hilda."

"Well, we men are apt to be charitable—to beauty in distress." The General was keenly and humorously aware that if Hilda had been ugly, he might not have been so anxious about the pink parasol. He might not, indeed, have pitied her at all!

And now in Jean's heart grew up a sharply defined fear of Hilda. In the old days there had been cordial dislike, jealousy, perhaps, but never anything like this. The question persisted in the back of her mind. If Hilda went to France, would she see Daddy and weave her wicked spells. To find the General melting into pity, in spite of the chaos which Hilda's treachery had created, was to wonder if Daddy, too, might melt.

She wrote to Derry about it.

"I would try and see her if I knew what to say, but when I even think of it I am scared. I never liked her, and I feel now as if I should be glad to pin together the pages of my memory of her, as I pinned together the pages of one of my story books when I was a little girl. There was a shark under water in the picture and two men were trying to get away from him. I hated that picture and shivered every time I looked at it, so I stuck in a pin and shut out the sight of it.

"Your father has had two letters from her since the day when he saw her in the Park. Bronson always brings the mail to me, and you know what a distinctive hand Hilda writes, there is no mistaking it. Your father dropped the letters into the fire, but she ought not to write to him, Derry, and I should like to tell her so.

"But if I told her, she would laugh at me, and that would be the end of it. For you can't rage and tear and rant at a thing that is as cold as stone. Oh, my dearest, I need you so much to tell me what to do, and yet I would not have you here—

"I met Alma Drew the other day, and she said, as lightly as you please, 'Do you know, I can't quite fancy Derry Drake in the trenches.'

"I looked at her for a minute before I could answer, and then I said, 'I can fancy him with his back to the wall, fighting a thousand Huns—!'

"She shrugged her shoulders, 'You're terribly in love.'

"'I am,' I said, and I hope I said it calmly, 'but there's more than love in a woman's belief in her husband's bravery—there's respect. And it's something rather—sacred, Alma.' And then I choked up and couldn't say another word, and she looked at me in a rather stunned fashion for a moment, and then she said, 'Gracious Peter, do you love him like that?' and I said, 'I do,' and she laughed in a funny little way, and said, 'I thought it was his millions.'

"I was perfectly furious. But you can't argue with such people. I know I was as white as a sheet. 'If anything should happen to Derry,' I said, 'do you think that all the money in the world would comfort me?'

"She stopped smiling. 'It would comfort me,' then suddenly she held out her hand. 'But I fancy you're different, and Derry is a lucky fellow.' which was rather nice and human of her, wasn't it?

"Life is growing more complicated than ever here in Washington. The crowds pour in as if the Administration were a sort of Pied Piper and had played a time, and the people who have lived here all their lives are waking to something like activity. Great buildings are going up as if some Aladdin had rubbed a lamp—. None of us are doing the things we used to do. We don't even talk about the things we used to talk about, and we go around in blue gingham and caps, and white linen and veils, and we hand out sandwiches to the soldiers and sailors, and drive perfectly strange men in our cars on Government errands, and make Liberty Bond Speeches from many platforms, and all the old theories of what women should do are forgotten in the rush of the things which must be done by women. It is as if we had all been bewitched and turned into somebody else.

"Well, I wish that Hilda could be turned into somebody else. Into somebody as nice as—Emily—. But she won't be. She hasn't been changed the least bit by the war, and everybody else has, even Alma, or she wouldn't have said that about your being lucky to have me. Are you lucky, Derry?

"And when Hilda sets her mind on a thing—. Oh, I can't seem to talk of anything but Hilda—when she sets her mind on anything, she gets it in one way or another—and that's why I am afraid of her."

Derry wrote back.

"Don't be afraid of anything, Jean-Joan. And it won't do any good to talk to Hilda. I don't want you to talk to her. You are too much of a white angel to contend against the powers of darkness.

"As for my luck in having you, it is something which transcends luck—it just hits the stars, dearest.

"I wonder what the fellows do who haven't any wives to anchor themselves to in a time like this? Through, all the day I have this hour in mind when I can write to you—and I think there are lots of other fellows like that—for I can see them all about me here in the Hut, bending over their letters with a look on their faces which isn't there at any other time.

"By Jove, Jean-Joan, I never knew before what women meant in the lives of men. Here we are marooned, as it were, on an island of masculinity, yet it isn't what the other fellows think of us that counts, it is what you think who are miles away. Always in the back of our minds is the thought of what you expect of us and demand of us, and added to what we demand and expect of ourselves, it sways us level. We don't talk a great deal about you, but now and then some fellow says, 'My wife,' and we all prick up our ears and want to hear the rest of it.

"It is a great life, dearest, in spite of the hard work, in spite of the stress and strain. And to me who have known so little of the great human game it is a great revelation.

"In the first place, there has been brought to me the knowledge of the joy of real labor. I shall never again be sorry for the man who toils. You see, I had never toiled, not in the sense that a man does whose labor counts. I was always a rather anxious and lonely little boy, looking after my father and trying to help my mother, and feeling a bit of a mollycoddle because I had a tutor and did not go to school with the other chaps. In the eyes of the world I was looked upon as a lucky fellow, but I know now what I have missed. In these days I am rubbing elbows with fellows who have had to hustle, and I am discovering that life is a great game, and that I have missed the game. If Dad had been different, he might have pushed me into things, as some men with money push their sons, making them stand on their own feet. But Dad liked an easy life, and he was perhaps entitled to ease, for he had struggled in his younger years. But I have never struggled. I have always had somebody to brush my clothes and to bring my breakfast, and I think I have had a sort of hazy idea that life was like that for everybody—or if it wasn't, then the people who couldn't be brushed and breakfasted by others were much to be pitied.

"Oh, I've been a Tin Soldier, Jean-Joan, left out not only of the war but of life. I've been on the shelf all these years in our big house, with the wooden trumpets blowing, 'Trutter-a-trutt' while other men have striven.

"When I first came here I had a sort of detached feeling. I had no experiences to match with the experiences of other men. I had never had to rush in the morning to catch a subway, I had never eaten, to put it poetically, by candlelight, so that I might get to the store by eight. I had never sold papers, or plowed fields, or stood behind a counter. I had never sat at a desk, I had never in fact done anything really useful, I had just been rich, and that isn't much of a background as I am beginning to see it here—.

"I find myself having a rather strange feeling of exaltation as the days go by, because for the first time I am a cog in a great machine, for the first time I am toiling and sweating as I rather think it was intended that men should toil and sweat. And the friends that I am making are the sign and seal of the levelling effects of this great war. Not one of the men of what you might call my own class interests me half as much as Tommy Tracy, who before he entered the service drove the car of one of Dad's business associates. I have often ridden behind Tommy, but he doesn't know it. And I don't intend that he shall. He rather fancies that I am a scholarly chap torn from my books, and he patronizes me on the strength of his knowledge of practical things.

"Tommy likes to eat, and he talks a great deal about his mother's cooking. He says there was always tripe for Sunday mornings, and corned beef and cabbage on Mondays, and Monday was wash-day!

"I wish you could hear him tell what wash-day meant to him. It is a sort of poem, the way he puts it. He doesn't know that it is poetry, though Vachell Lindsay would, or Masters, or some of those fellows.

"It seems that he used to help his mother, because he was a strong little fellow, and could turn the wringer, and they would get up very early because he had to go to school, and in the spring and summer they washed out of doors, under a tree in the yard, and his mother's eyes were bright and her cheeks were red and her arms were white, and she was always laughing. There's a memory for a man on the battlefield, dearest, a healthy, hearty memory of the day's work of a boy, and of a bright-eyed mother, and of a good dinner at the end of hours of toil.

"Perhaps with such a mother it isn't surprising that Tommy has made so much of himself. He has aspirations far beyond driving some other man's car, and if he keeps on he'll have a little flivver of his own before he knows it—when the war ends, and he can strike out, with his energy at the boiling point.

"There are a lot of men who have belonged not to the idle rich, but to the idle poor, and the discipline of this life is just the thing for them as it is for me. It rather contradicts the kindergarten idea of play as a preparation for life. These busy men, forced to be busy, are a thousand times more self-respecting than if left to lead the listless lives that were theirs before their country called them. I wonder if, after all, Kipling isn't right, and that the hump and hoof and haunch of it all isn't obedience? Not slavish obedience, but obedience founded on a knowledge of one's place and value in the pack?"

Jean, striving to follow Derry's point of view, found herself floundering.

"I am glad you like it, but I don't see how you can. And you mustn't say that you've always been a Tin Soldier on a shelf. I won't have it. And you have played the game of life just as bravely as Tommy Tracy, only your problems were different—. And if you can't remember wash days you can remember other days—. But I like to have you tell me about it, because I can see you, listening to Tommy and laughing at him. I adore your laugh, Derry, though I shouldn't be telling you, should I—? I have pasted the picture you sent me of you and Tommy in my memory book and have written under it, 'When you and I were young, Tommy' and I've drawn a cloud of steam above Tommy, with washboilers—and tubs—and cabbages and soap suds, and his mother's face smiling in the midst of it all—. And in your cloud is your mother smiling, too, with her little crown on her head, and gold spoons for a border—and a frosted cake with candles—and a mountain of ice-cream. Perhaps you have other memories, but I had to do the best I could with my poor little rich boy—"

It was about this time that Jean's memory book! became chaotic. Most of the things in it had to do with Derry, a bit of pine from a young plume which Derry had sent her from the south—triangles cut from the letter paper on which he sometimes wrote—post-cards to say "Good-morning," telegrams to say "Good-night"—a service pin with its one sacred star.

There were reminders, too, of the things which were happening across the sea, a cartoon or two, a small reproduction of a terrible Raemaeker print; verse, much of it—

They have taken your bells, O God,
The bells that hung in your towers,
That cried your grace in a lovely song,
And counted the praying hours!
The little birds flew away!
They will tell the clouds and the wind,
Till the uttermost places know
The sin that the Hun has sinned!

Jean thought a great deal about the Huns. She always called them that. She hated to think about them, but she had to. She couldn't pin the pages together, as it were, of her thoughts. And the Huns were worse than the sharks that had frightened her in her little girl days. Oh, they were much worse than sharks, for the shark was only following an instinct when it killed, and the Huns had worked out diabolically their murderous, monstrous plan.

In the days when she had argued with Hilda, she had been told of the power and perfection of Prussian rule. "Everything is at loose ends in America," had been Hilda's accusation.

"Well, what if it is?" Jean had flung back at her hotly. "Having things in place isn't the end and aim of happiness. Just because a house is swept and garnished isn't any sign that it is a blissful habitation. When I was a child I used to visit my two great-aunts in Maryland. I loved to go to Aunt Mary's, but I dreaded Aunt Anne's. And the reason was this. Everything in Aunt Anne's house went by clock-work, and everything was polished and scrubbed and dusted within an inch of its life. When we arrived, we scraped our shoes before we kissed Aunt Anne, and when we departed, we felt that she literally swept us out—. We had hours for everything, and nobody thought of doing as she pleased. It was always as Aunt Anne pleased, and the meals were always on time, and nobody was ever expected to be late, and if she was late she was scolded or punished; and nobody ever dared throw a newspaper on the floor, or go out to the kitchen and make fudge, or pop corn by the sitting-room fire. Yet Aunt Anne was so efficient that her house-keeping was the admiration of the whole State.

"But we loved Aunt Mary's. She would come smiling down the stone walk to meet us, and she would leave the morning's work undone to wander with us in the fields or woods. And we had some of our meals under the trees, and some of them in the house, and when we made taffy, and it stuck to things, Aunt Mary smiled some more and said it didn't matter. And we loved the freedom of our life, and we went to Aunt Mary's as often as we could, and stayed away when we could from Aunt Anne's.

"And that's the way with America. It isn't perfect, it isn't efficient, but it is a lovely place to live in, because in a sense we can live as we please.

"Did you ever know a man who wanted to go back to slavery? As a slave he was fed and clothed and kept by his master, with no thought of responsibility—. Yet it was freedom he wanted, even though he had to go hungry now and then for the sake of it—"

"I like law and order," Hilda said. "We don't always have it here."

"I'd rather be a gipsy on the road," had been Jean's passionate declaration, "and free, than a princess with a 'verboten' sign at all the palace gates."

There were wisps of gauze, too, in her memory book, a red cross, drawings in which were caricatured some of the women who worked in the surgical dressing rooms.

"Emily," Jean asked, as she showed one of the pictures to her friend, "do such women come because it's fashion or because they really feel—?"

"I fancy their motives are mixed," said Emily, "and you mustn't think because they wear high heels and fluff their hair out over their ears that they haven't any hearts."

"No, I suppose not," Jean admitted, "but I wonder what they think the veils are for when they fluff out their hair.

"And their rings," she went on. "You see, when they all have on white aprons and veils you can't tell whether they are Judy O'Grady or the Colonel's lady—so they load their hands with diamonds. As if the hands wouldn't tell the tale themselves. Why, Emily, if you and Hilda were hidden, all but your hands, the people would know the Colonel's lady from Judy O'Grady."

Emily smiled abstractedly, she was counting compresses. She stopped long enough to ask, "Is Hilda still in town?"

"Yes. I saw her yesterday on the other side of the street. I didn't speak, but some day when I get a good opportunity I am going to tell her what I think of her."

But when the opportunity came she did not say all that she had meant to say!

She went over one morning to her father's house to get some papers which he had left in his desk. The house had been closed for weeks and the hall, as she entered it, was cold with a chill that reached the marrow of her bones—it was dim with the half-gloom of drawn curtains and closed doors. Even the rose-colored drawing-room as she stood on the threshold held no radiance—it had the stiff and frozen look of a soulless body. Yet she remembered how it had throbbed and thrilled on the night that Derry had come to her. The golden air had washed in waves over her.

She shivered and went over to the window. She pulled up a curtain and looked out upon the grayness of the street. The clouds were low, and a strong wind was blowing. Those who passed, bent to the wind. She was slightly above the level of the street, and nobody looked up at her. She might have been a ghost in the ghostly house.

Well, she had to get the papers. She turned to face the gloom, and as she turned she heard a sound in the room above her.

It was the rather startling sound of muffled steps. She dared not go into the hall. She felt comparatively safe by the window—. If—anything came, she could open the window and call.

But she did not call, for it was Hilda who came presently on rubber-heels and stood in the door.

"I thought I heard some one," she said, calmly.

"How did you get in?" was Jean's abrupt demand.

"I had my key. I have never given it up."

"But this is no longer your home."

"It was never home," said Hilda, darkly. "It was never home. I lived here with you and your father, but it was never home."

Jean, more than ever afraid of this woman, had a sudden sense of something tragic in the fact of Hilda's homelessness.

"I don't quite see what you mean," she said, slowly.

"You couldn't see," Hilda told her, "and you will never see. Women like you don't."

"We didn't get on very well together," Jean said, almost timidly, "but that was because we were different."

"It wasn't because we were different that we didn't get on," Hilda said. "It was because you were afraid of me. You knew your father liked me."

With her usual frankness she spoke the truth as she saw it.

"I was not afraid," Jean faltered.

"You were. But we needn't talk about that. I am going to France."

"When?"

"As soon as I can get there. That's why I came here. To take away some things I wanted."

"Oh—"

96

"And one of the things I wanted was the picture of your father which hung in your room. I have taken that. You can get more of them. I can't. So I have taken it."

They faced each other, this shining child and this dark woman.

"But—but it is mine—Hilda."

"It is mine now, and if I were you, I shouldn't make a fuss about it."

"Hilda, how dare you!" Jean began in the old indignant way, and stopped. There was something so sinister about it all. She hated the thought that she and Hilda were alone in the empty house—

"Hilda, if you go to France, shall you see Daddy?"

"I shall try. I had a letter from him the other day. He told me not to come. But I am going. There is work to do, and I am going."

Jean had a stunned feeling, as if there was nothing left to say, as if Hilda were indeed a rock, and words would rebound from her hard surface.

"But after all, you didn't really care for Daddy—"

"What makes you say that?"

"You were going to marry the General."

"Well, I wanted a home. I wanted some of the things you had always had. I'm not old, and I am tired of being a machine."

For just one moment her anger blazed, then she laughed with something of toleration.

"Oh, you'd never understand if I talked a year. So what's the use of wasting breath?"

She said "Good-bye" after that, and Jean watched her go, hearing the padded steps—until the front door shut and there was silence.

After that, with almost a sense of panic, she sped through the empty rooms, finding the papers after a frantic search, and gaining the street with a sense of escape.

Yet even then, it was sometime before her heart beat normally, and always after that when she thought of Hilda, it was against the chill and gloom of the empty house, with that look upon her face of dark resentment.

CHAPTER XXIV
THE SINGING WOMAN

Somewhere in France, Drusilla had found the Captain. Or, rather, he had found her. He had come upon her one rainy afternoon, and had not recognized her in her muddy uniform, with a strap under her chin. Then all at once he had heard her voice, crooning a song to a badly wounded boy whose head lay in her lap.

The Captain had stopped in his tracks. "Drusilla—"

The light in her eyes gave him his welcome, but she waved him away.

The boy died in her arms. When she joined her lover, she was much moved. "It is not my work to look after the wounded; I carry blankets and things to refugees. But now and then—it happens. A shell burst in the street, and that poor lad—! He asked me to sing for him—you see, I have been singing for them as they go through, and he remembered—"

He was holding both of her hands in his. "Dear woman, dear woman—" There were people all about them, but there were no conventions in war times, and nobody cared if he held her hands.

Her face was dirty, her hair wind-blown. She was muddy and without a trace of the smartness for which she had been famous. She was simply a hard-worked woman in clothes of masculine cut, yet never had she seemed so beautiful to her lover. He bent and kissed her in the market-place. He was an undemonstrative Englishman, but there was that in her eyes which carried him away from self-consciousness.

"I saw McKenzie in Paris," he said. "He told me that you were here."

"We came over together. Did you get my letter?"

"I have had no letters. But now that I have you, nothing matters."

"Really? Somehow I don't feel that I deserve it."

"Deserve what?"

"All that you are giving me. But I have liked to think of it. It has been a prop to lean on—"

"Only that—?"

"A shield and a buckler, dearest, a cross held high—" Her breath came quickly.

  * * * * * *

They sat side by side on the worn doorstep of a shattered building and talked.

"I am in a shack—a *baraque*,—they call it," Drusilla told him, "with three other women. We have fixed up one room a little better than the others, and whenever the men come through the town some of them drift in and are warmed by our fire, and I sing to them; they call me 'The Singing Woman.'"

She did not tell him how she had mothered the lads. She was not much older than some of them, but they had instinctively recognized the maternal quality of her interest in them. With all her beauty they had turned to her for that which was in a sense spiritual.

Hating the war, Drusilla yet loved the work she had to do. There was, of course, the horror of it, but there was, too, the stimulus of living in a world of realities. She wondered if she were the same girl who had burned her red candles and had served her little suppers, safe and sound and far away from the stress of fighting.

She wondered, too, if women over there were still thinking of their gowns, and men of their gold. Were they planning to go North in the summer and South in the winter? Were they still care-free and comfortable?

People over here were not comfortable, but how little they cared, and how splendid they were. She had seen since she came such incredibly heroic things—men as tender as women, women as brave as men—she had seen human nature at its biggest and best.

"I have never been religious," she told the Captain, earnestly; "our family is the kind which finds sufficient outlet in a cool intellectual conclusion that all's right with the world, and it doesn't make much difference what comes hereafter. You know the attitude? 'If there is future life, we shall be glad to explore, and if there isn't, we shall be content to sleep!'

"But since I have been over here, I have carried a little prayer-book, and I've read things to the men, and when I have come to that part 'Gladly to die—that we may rise again,' I have known that it is true, Captain—"

He laid his hand over hers. "May I have your prayer-book in exchange for mine?" He was very serious. With all his heart he loved her, and never more than at this moment when she had thrown aside all reserves and had let him see her soul.

She drew the little book from her pocket. It was bound in red leather, with a thin black cross on the cover. His own was in khaki.

"I want something else," he said, as he held the book in his hand.

"What?"

"This." He touched a lock of hair which lay against her cheek. "A bit of it—of you—"

A band of *poilus*—marching through the street, saw him cut it off. But they did not laugh. They had great respect for a thing like that—and it happened every day—when men went away from their women.

They separated with a promise of perhaps a reunion in Paris, if he could get leave and if she could be spared. Then she drove away through the mud in her little car, and he went back to his men.

Thus they were swept apart by that tide of war which threatened to submerge the world.

Drusilla, arriving late at her *baraque*, made tea, and sat by an infinitesimal stove.

She found herself alone, for the other women were away on various errands. She uncovered all the glory of her lovely hair, and in her little mirror surveyed pensively the ragged lock over her left ear.

A man like that, oh, a man like that. What more could a woman ask—than love like that?

Yet even in the midst of her thought of him, came the feeling that she was not predestined for happiness. She must go on riding over rough roads on her errands of mercy. Nothing must interfere with that, not love or matters of personal preference—nothing.

She was very tired. But there was no time for rest. A half dozen kilted Highlanders hailed her through the open door and asked for a song. She gave them "Wee Hoose Amang the Heather—" standing on the step. It was still raining, and they took with them a picture of a girl with glorious uncovered hair, and that cut tell-tale lock against her cheek.

Drusilla watching them go, wondered if she would ever see them again, with their pert caps, the bare knees of them—the strong swing of their bodies.

She stretched her arms above her head. "Oh, oh, I'm tired—"

She went in and poured another cup of tea. She left the door open. Indeed it always stood open that the room might shine its welcome.

Snatching forty winks, she waked to find a woman standing over her—a tall woman in a blue cloak and bonnet, who held in her hand a dripping umbrella.

She felt that she still dreamed. "It can't be Hilda Merritt?"

"Yes, it is." Hilda set the umbrella in the wood box. "I knew you were here."

"Who told you?"

"Dr. McKenzie."

"Oh, you are with him, then?"

"He won't have me. That's why I came to you."

"To me?"

"Yes. I want you to tell him not to—turn me away."

98

Drusilla showed her bewilderment. "But, surely nothing that I could say would have more weight with him than your own arguments."

"You are his kind. He'd listen. Things that you say count with him."

"I don't know what you mean."

"Well, I've offended him. And he won't forgive me. Not even for the sake of the work. And I'm a good nurse, Miss Gray. But he's as hard as nails. And—and he sent me away."

"Oh, I'm sorry," Drusilla said gently. Hilda was a dark figure of tragedy, as she sat there statuesquely in her blue cloak.

"You could make him see how foolish it is to refuse to have a good worker; men may die whom I could save. He thinks that—those things don't mean anything to me, that I am arguing from a personal standpoint. He wouldn't think that of you."

"I'll do what I can, of course," Drusilla said slowly. She was not sure that she wanted to get into it, but she was sorry for Hilda.

"Won't you have a cup of tea," she said impulsively, "and take off your cloak? I am afraid I haven't seemed a bit hospitable. I was so surprised."

Hilda gave a little laugh. "I'm not used to such courtesies—so I didn't miss it. But I should like the tea, and something to eat with it. I left Dr. McKenzie's hospital early this morning, and I haven't eaten since—I didn't want anything to eat—"

She watched Drusilla curiously as she set forth the food. "It must seem strange to you to live in a room like this."

"I like it."

"But you have always had such an easy life, Miss Gray."

Drusilla smiled. "It may have looked easy to you. But I give you my word that keeping up with the social game is harder than this."

"You say that," Hilda told her crisply, "not because it's true, but because it sounds true. Do you mean to tell me that you like to be muddy and dirty and live in a place like this?"

"Yes, I like it." Something flamed in the back Of Drusilla's eyes. "I like it because it means something, and the other didn't."

"Well, I don't like it," Hilda stated. "But nursing is all I am fit for. I came over with a lot of other nurses, and they tell me at the hospital I am the best of the lot—and in war times you can't afford to miss the experience. But then I am used to a hard life, and you are not."

"Neither are the men in the trenches used to it. That's the standard I apply to myself—for every hard thing I am doing, it is ten times harder for them. I wish all the people at home could see how wonderful they are."

"That's Jean McKenzie's word—wonderful. Everything was wonderful, and now she has married Derry Drake."

"Yes, she has married Derry," Drusilla stood staring into the little round stove.

She roused herself presently. "I call them Babes in the Wood. They seem so young, and yet Derry isn't really young—it is only that there's such a radiant air about him."

Hilda's bitterness broke forth. "Why shouldn't he be radiant? Life has given him everything. It has given her everything; in a way it has given you everything. I am the one who goes without—it looks as if I should always go without the things I want."

"Don't think that," Drusilla said in her pleasant fashion. "Nobody is set apart—and some day you will see it. Did you know that Derry may be over now at any time, and that Jean is to stay with the General?"

"Yes," Hilda moved restlessly. There came to her a vision of the big house, of the shadowed room, of the room beyond, and of herself in a tiara, with ermine on her cloak.

What a dream it had been, and she had waked to this!

She rose. "If Dr. McKenzie doesn't take me back he may be sorry. Will you write to him?"

"I shall see him Saturday—in Paris. I have promised to dine with him. Captain Hewes is coming, too, if he can."

Hilda, going away in the rain, dwelt moodily on Drusilla's opportunities. If only she, too, might dine in Paris with men like Dr. McKenzie and Captain Hewes. There were indeed, men who might ask her to dine with them, but not as Drusilla had been asked, as an equal and as a friend.

The way was long, the road was muddy. There was not much to look towards at the end. It was not that she minded the dreadfulness of sights and sounds—she had been too much in hospitals for that. But she hated the ugliness, the roughness, the grinding toil.

Yet had she been with Dr. McKenzie, she would have toiled gladly for him. There would have been the sight of his crinkled copper head, the sound of his voice, his teasing laugh to sustain her. And now it was Drusilla who would see him, who would sit with him at the table, who would tempt his teasing laugh.

Well—if he didn't take her back, he would be sorry. There had been a patient in the hospital who in his delirium had whispered things. When he had come to himself, she had told him calmly, "You are a spy." He had not whitened, but had measured her with a glance. "Help me, and you shall see the Emperor. There will be nothing too good for you."

Drusilla, after Hilda's departure, sat by her little stove and thought it over. She divined something which did not appear on the surface. She was glad that she had promised to plead Hilda's cause. The woman's face haunted her.

And now the other workers who shared Drusilla's shack returned, bringing news of many wounded and on the way. Then came the darkness of the night, the long line of ambulances, the ghastly procession that trailed behind.

And all through the night Drusilla sang to men who rested for a moment on their weary way, out of the shadows came eager voices asking for this song and that—then they would pass on, and she would throw herself down for a little sleep, to rouse again and lift her voice, while the other women poured the coffee.

She was hoarse in the morning, and white with fatigue, but when one of the women said, "You can't keep this up, Drusilla, you can't stand it," she smiled. "They stand it is the trenches, and some of them are so tired."

She was as fresh as paint, however, on Saturday, when she met Dr. McKenzie in Paris. "I have had two hot baths, and all my clothes are starched and ironed and fluted by an adorable Frenchwoman who opened her house for me," she announced as she sat down with him at a corner table. "I never wore fluted things before, but you can't imagine how civilizing it is after you've been letting yourself down."

The Doctor was tired, and he looked it. "No one has starched and fluted me."

"Poor man. I'm glad you ran away from it all for a minute with me. Captain Hewes thought he might be able to come. But I haven't heard from him, have you?"

"No. But he may blow in at any moment. It seems queer, doesn't it, Drusilla, that you and I should be over here with all the rest of them left behind."

She hesitated, then brought it out without prelude. "Hilda came to see me."

"To see you? Why?"

"She is broken-hearted because you won't let her work with you."

"I told her I could not. And she hasn't any heart to break."

"I wonder if you'd mind," Drusilla ventured, "telling me what's the matter."

"A rather squalid story," but he told it. "She wanted to marry the General."

"Poor thing."

He glanced at her in surprise. "Then you defend her?"

"Oh, no—no. But think of having to marry to get the—the fleshpots, and to miss all of the real meanings. I talked to Hilda for a long time, and somehow before she left she made me feel sorry. She wants so much that she will never have. And she will grow hard and bitter because life isn't giving her all that she demands."

"Did she ask you to plead her cause?"

"Yes," frankly. "She feels that you ought to give her another chance."

He ran his fingers through his crinkled hair. "I don't want her. I'm afraid of her."

"Afraid?"

"She sees the worst that is in me, and brings it to the surface. And when I protest, she laughs and insists that I don't know myself. That I am a sort of Dr. Jekyll, with the Mr. Hyde part of me asleep—"

"And you let her scare you like that?"

He nodded. "Every man has a weak spot, and mine is wanting the world to think well of me."

"Think well of yourself. What would Jean say if she heard you talking like this?"

"Jean?" she was startled by the breaking up of his face into deep lines of trouble. "Do you know what she is doing, Drusilla? She is staying in that great old house playing daughter to the General."

"Marion says the General's affection for her is touching—he doesn't want her out of his sight."

"And because he doesn't want her out of his sight, she must stay a prisoner. I say that he hasn't done anything to deserve such devotion, Drusilla. He hasn't done anything to deserve it."

"You are jealous."

"No. It isn't that. Though I'll confess that something pulls at my heart when I think of it—. But I want her to be happy."

"I think she is happy. Life is giving her the hard things—but you and I would not be without the—hard things; we have reached out our hands for them, because the world needs us. Are you going to deny your daughter that?"

"Oh, I suppose not. But I hate it. Women ought to be happy—care-free, not shut up in sick rooms or running around in the rain."

"Oh, you men, how little you know what makes a woman happy." She stopped, and half rose from her chair. "Captain Hewes is coming."

"I don't know that I am glad, Drusilla," the Doctor turned to survey the beaming officer, "for now you won't have eyes or ears for me."

But she was glad.

While the Captain held her hand in his as if he would never let her go, she told him about being fluted and starched. "I don't look as dishevelled as I did the other day."

"You looked beautiful the other day," he assured her with fervor, "but this is better, because you are rested and some of the sadness has gone out of your eyes."

Dr. McKenzie watched them enviously, "I realize," he reminded them, "that I am the fifth wheel, or any other superfluous thing, but you can't get rid of me. I am homesick—somebody's got to cheer me up."

"We don't want to get rid of you," Drusilla told him, smiling.

But he knew that her loveliness was all for the Captain. She was lighted up by the presence of her betrothed, made exquisite, softer, more womanly. Love had come slowly to Drusilla, but it had come at last.

When the Doctor left them, he was in a daze of loneliness. He wanted Jean, he wanted sympathy, understanding, good-comradeship.

For just one little moment temptation assailed him. There was of course, Hilda. She would bring with her the atmosphere of familiar things which he craved. There would be the easy give and take of speech which was such a relief after his professional manner, there would be his own teasing sense of how much she wanted, and of how little he had to give. There would be, too, the stimulus to his vanity.

A broken-hearted Hilda, Drusilla had said. There was something provocative in the situation—elements of drama. Why not?

He thought about it that night when once more back at his work he and his head nurse discussed a case of shell shock—a pitiful case of fear, loss of memory, complete prostration.

The nurse was a plain little thing, very competent, very quiet. She was, perhaps, no more competent than Hilda in the mechanics of her profession, but she had qualities which Hilda lacked. She was not very young, and there were younger nurses under her. Yet in spite of her plainness and quietness, she wielded an influence which was remarkable. The whole hospital force was feeling the effect of that influence. It was as if every nurse had in some rather high and special way dedicated herself—as nuns might to the conventual life, or sisters of charity to the service of the poor. There was indeed a heroic aspect to it, a spiritual aspect, and this plain little woman was setting the pace.

And Hilda, coming in, would spoil it all. Oh, he knew how she would spoil it. With her mocking laugh, her warped judgments, her skeptical point of view.

No, he did not want Hilda. The best in him did not want her, and please God, he was giving his best to this cause. However he might fail in other things, he would not fail in his high duty towards the men who came out of battle shattered and broken, holding up their hands to him for help.

"I am going to let Miss Shelby have the case," the plain little nurse was saying, "when he begins to come back. She will give him what he needs. She is so strong and young, so sure of the eternal rightness of things—and she's got to make him sure."

The Doctor nodded. "Some of us are not sure—"

She agreed gravely. "But we are learning to be sure, aren't we, over here? Don't you feel that all the things you have ever done are little compared to this? That men and women are better and bigger than you have believed?"

"If anyone could make me feel it," he said, "it would be you."

When she had gone, he wrote letters.

He wrote to Jean—he wrote every day to Jean.

He wrote to Hilda.

"You are splendidly fitted for just the thing that you are doing. Men come and go and you care for their wounds. But we have to care here for more than men's bodies, we care for their minds and souls—we piece them together, as it were. And we need women who believe that God's in his Heaven. And you don't believe it, Hilda. I fancy that you see in every man his particular devil, and like to lure it out for him to look at—"

He stopped there. He could see her reading what he had written. She would laugh a little, and write back:

"Are you any better than I? If I am too black to herd with the white sheep, what of you; aren't you tarred with the same brush—?"

He tore up the letter and sent a brief note. Why explain what he was feeling to Hilda? She was of those who would never know nor understand.

And he felt the need tonight of understanding—of sympathy.

And so he wrote to Emily.

CHAPTER XXV
WHITE VIOLETS

Bruce McKenzie's letter arriving in due time at the Toy Shop, found Emily very busy. There were many women to be instructed how to do things with gauze and muslin and cotton, so she tucked the letter in her apron pocket. But all day her mind went to it, as a feast to be deferred until the time came to enjoy it.

In the afternoon Ulrich Stölle arrived, bearing the inevitable tissue paper parcel.

"Do you know what day it is?" he asked.

"Thursday."

"There are always Thursdays. But this is a special Thursday."

"Is it?"

"And you ask me like that? It is a Thursday for valentines."

"Of course. But how could you expect me to remember? Nobody ever sends me valentines."

"My father has sent you one." It was a heart-shaped basket of pink roses; "but mine I couldn't bring. You must come and see it. Will you dine with us tonight?"

"Oh, I am so busy."

"You are not too busy for that. Let your little Jean take charge."

Jean, all in white with her white veil and red crosses was more than ever like a little nun. She was remote, too, like a nun, wrapped not in the contemplation of her religion, but of her love.

She still made toys, and the proceeds of the sale of Lovely Dreams had been contributed by herself and Emily for Red Cross purposes. There were rows and rows of the fantastic creatures behind glass doors on the shelves, and for Valentine's Day Jean had carved and painted pale doves which carried in their beaks rosy hearts and golden arrows and whose wings were outspread—.

There were also on the shelves the white plush elephants which Franz Stölle and his friends had made, and which were, too, being sold to swell the Red Cross fund.

Thus had the Toy Shop come into its own. "I have enough to live on," Emily had said, "at least for a while, and I am taking no more chances for future living, than the men who give up everything to fight."

So enlisted in this cause of mercy as men had enlisted in the cause of war, Miss Emily led where others followed, and the old patriarch of all the white elephants, who had been born in a country of blood and iron, looked down on women working to heal the wounds which his country had made.

"Let your little Jean look after things," Ulrich repeated.

"Do you mind, my dear?"

"Mind what, Emily—?"

"If I go with Mr. Stölle—to see his father about the—toys."

"Darling—no;" Jean kissed her. "I don't mind in the least, and the ride will do you good."

"But you are not going to see my father about toys," Ulrich told her, twinkling, as he followed her to the back of the shop. "Do you think I was going to tell her that?"

She put on her coat and hat and off she went with Ulrich, leaving still unread in the pocket of the big apron the letter which Bruce McKenzie had written her.

All the way out Ulrich was rather silent. It was not, however, the silence of moodiness or dullness, it was rather as if he wanted to hear her speak. It was, indeed, a responsive, stimulating silence, and she glowed under his glance.

It seemed to her, as she talked, that these adventures with Ulrich Stölle were in every way the most splendid thing that had happened to her. They were always unexpected, and they were packed to the brim with pleasure of a rare quality.

When they reached their destination, Ulrich took her at once to the hothouses. As they passed down the fragrant aisles, she found that all the men and gone, their day's work over; only she and Ulrich were under the great glass roof.

"Anton comes back later," Ulrich explained, "but at this hour the houses are empty, and dinner will not be ready for as hour. We have it all to ourselves, Emily."

Her name, spoken with so much ease, without a sign of self-consciousness, startled her. Her inquiring glance showed her that he was utterly unaware that he had spoken it. Her breath came quickly.

The birds sang and the stream sang, and suddenly her heart began to sing.

You see it had been so many years since Emily had known romance;—indeed, she had never known it—there had always been, in her mother's time, her sense of the proper thing, and her sense of duty, and her sense of making the best of things—and now for the first time in her life there was no make-believe. This was a world of realities, with Ulrich leading the way, his hands gathering flowers for her.

He stopped at last at the entrance of a sort of grotto where great ferns towered—at their feet was a bed of white violets.

"You see," he said, "I could not bring it. I came here this morning to pick the violets—for you—to let them say, 'I love you'—"

Even the birds seemed silent, and the little stream!

"And suddenly they spoke to me, 'Let her see us here, where you have so often thought of her. Tell her here that you love her—'

"How much I love you," and now she found her hands in his, "I cannot tell you. It seems to me that the thought of you as my wife is so exquisite that I cannot believe it will ever come to pass. And I have so little to offer you. Even my name is hated because it is a German name, and my old house is German, and my father—

"But my heart's blood is for America. You know that, and so I have dared to ask it, not that you will love me now, but that you may come to think of loving me, so that some day you will care a little."

The birds were singing madly, the streams were shouting—Emily was trembling. Nobody had ever wanted her like this—nobody had ever made her feel so young and lovely and—wanted—. She had had a proposal or two, but there had been always the sense that she had been chosen for certain staid and sensible qualities; there had been nothing in it of red blood and rapture.

"If you should come to us, to me and my father, you would be a queen on a throne. If you could love me just a little in return—"

She could not answer, she just stood looking up at him, and suddenly his arms went around her. "Tell me, beloved."

An hour later they went in to his father, and after that Emily was lifted up on the wings of an enthusiasm which left her breathless, but beatified. "I knew when I first saw you what we desired," said the old man, "and my son knew. All that I have is yours both now and afterwards—"

Dinner was a candle-lighted feast, with heart-shaped ices at the end.

"How sure you were," Emily told her lover, smiling.

"I was not sure. But I set the stage for success. It was only thus that I kept up my courage. There were so many chances that the curtain might drop on darkness—," his hand went over hers. "If it had been that way, I should have let the ices melt and the violets die—."

After dinner they went over the house. "Why should we wait," Ulrich had said, "you and I? There is nothing to wait for. Tell me what you want changed in this old house, and then come to it, and to my heart."

It was, she found, such a funny old place. It had been furnished by men, and by German men at that. There was heaviness and stuffiness, and all the bric-a-brac was fat and puffy, and all the pictures were highly-colored, with the women in them blonde and buxom, and the men blond and bold—.

But Ulrich's room was not stuffy or heavy. The windows were wide open, and the walls were white, and the cover on the canopy bed was white, and there were two pictures, one of Lincoln and one of Washington, and that was all.

"And when I have your picture, it will be perfect," he told her. "Where I can see you when I wake, and pray to you before I go to sleep."

"But why," she probed daringly, "do you want my picture?"

"Because you are so—beautiful—"

It was not to be wondered that such worship went to Miss Emily's head. She slipped out of the dried sheath of the years which had saddened and aged her, and emerged lovely as a flower over which the winter has passed and which blooms again.

"I don't want to change anything," Emily told her lover as they went downstairs, "at least not very much. I shall keep all of the lovely old carved things—with the fat cupids."

As she lay awake that night, reviewing it all, she thought suddenly of Bruce McKenzie's letter in her apron pocket. The apron was in the Toy Shop, and it was not therefore until the next morning that she read the letter.

In it Dr. McKenzie asked her to marry him.

"I should like to think that when I come back, you will be waiting for me, Emily. I am a very lonely man. I want someone who will sympathize and understand. I want someone who will love Jean, and who will hold me to the best that is in me, and you can do that, Emily; you have always done it."

It was a rather touching letter, and she felt its appeal strongly. Indeed, so stern was her sense of self-sacrifice, that she had an almost guilty feeling when she thought of Ulrich. If he had not come into her life at the psychological moment, she might have given herself to Bruce McKenzie.

But the letter had come too late. Oh, how glad she was that she had left it in her apron pocket!

She answered it that night.

"I am going to be very frank with you, Bruce, because in being frank with you I shall be frank with myself. If Ulrich Stölle had not come into my life, I should probably have thought I cared for you. Even now when I am saying 'no,' I realize that your charm has always held me, and that the prospect of a future by your pleasant fireside holds many attractions. But since you left Washington, something has happened which I never expected, and all of my preconceived ideas of myself have been overturned. Bruce, I am no longer the Emily you have known—a little staid, gray-haired, with pretty hands, but with nothing else very pretty about her; a lady who would, perhaps, fill gracefully, a position for which her aristocratic nose fits her. I am no longer the Emily of the Toy Shop, wearing spectacles on a black ribbon, eating her lunches wherever she can get them. No, I am an Emily who is young and beautiful, a sort of fairy-tale Princess, an Emily who, if she wishes, shall sit on a cushion and sew a fine seam, but who doesn't wish it because she hates to sew, and would much rather work in her silver-bell-and-cockle shell garden—oh, such a wonderful garden as it is!

"And I am all this, Bruce, I am young and beautiful and all the rest, because I am seeing myself through the eyes of my lover.

"He is Ulrich Stölle, as I have said, and you mustn't think because his name is German that he is to be cast into outer darkness. He is as American as you with your Scotch blood, or as I with my English blood. And he is as loyal as any of us. He is too old to be accepted for service, but he is giving time and money to the cause.

"And he loves me rapturously, radiantly, romantically. He doesn't want me as a cushion for his tired head, he doesn't want me because he thinks it would be an act of altruism to provide a haven for me in my old age, he wants me because he thinks I am the most remarkable woman in the whole wide world, and that he is the most fortunate man to have won me.

"And you don't feel that way about it, Bruce. You know that I am not beautiful, there is no glamour in your love for me. You know that I am not wonderful, or a fairy Princess—. And you are right and he is wrong. But it is his wrongness which makes me love him. Because every woman wants to be beautiful to her lover, and to feel that she is much desired.

"You will ask why I am telling you all this. Well, there was one sentence in your letter which called it forth. You say that you want me because I will hold you to the best that is in you.

"Oh, Bruce, what would you gain if I held you? Wouldn't there be moments when in spite of me you would swing back to women like Hilda? You are big and fine, but you are spoiled by feminine worship—it is a temptation which assails clergymen and doctors—who have, as it were, many women at their feet.

"Does that sound harsh? I don't mean it that way. I only want you to come into your own. And if you ever marry I want you to find some woman you can love as you loved your wife, someone who will touch your imagination, set you on fire with dreams, and I could never do it.

"Yet even as I finish this letter, I am tempted to tear it up and tell you only of my real appreciation of the honor you have conferred upon me in asking me to be your wife. I know that you are offering me more in many ways than Ulrich Stölle. I don't like his name, because something rises up in me against Teuton blood and Teuton nomenclature. But he loves me, and you do not, and because of his love for me and mine for him, everything else seems too small to consider.

"Oh, you'd laugh at his house, Bruce, but I love even the fat angels that are carved on everything from the mahogany chests to the soup tureens. It is all like some old fairy-tale. I shall make few changes; it seems such a perfect setting for Ulrich and his busy old gnome of a father.

"When you get this, pray for my happiness. Oh, I do want to be happy. I have made the best of things, but there has been much more of gray than rose-color, and now as I turn my face to the setting sun, I am seeing—loveliness and light—"

She read it over and sealed it and sent it away. It was several weeks before it reached Doctor McKenzie. He was very busy, for the spring drive of the Germans had begun, and shattered men were coming to him faster than he could handle them. But he found time at last to read it, and when he laid it down he sat quite still from the shock of it.

And the next time he saw Drusilla he said to her, "Emily Bridges is going to be married, and she is not going to marry me."

"I am glad of it," Drusilla told him.

"My dear girl, why?"

"Because you don't love her, and you never did."

CHAPTER XXVI
THE HOPE OF THE WORLD

The great spring drive of the Germans brought headlines to the papers which men and women in America read with dread, and scoffed at when they talked it over.

"They'll never get to Paris," were the words on their lips, but in their hearts they were asking, "Will they—?"

Easter came at the end of March, and Good Friday found Jean working very early in the morning on fawn-colored rabbits with yellow ears. She worked in her bedroom because it was warmed by a feeble wood fire, and Teddy came up to watch her.

"The yellow in their ears is the sun shining through," Jean told him. "We used to see them in the country on the path in front of the house, and the light from the west made their ears look like tiny electric bulbs."

Margaret-Mary entranced by one small bunny with a splash of white for a cotton tail, sang, "Pitty sing, pitty sing."

"They don't weally lay eggs, do they?" Teddy ventured.

"I wouldn't ask such questions if I were you, Teddy."

"Why not?"

"Because you might find out that they didn't lay eggs, and then you'd feel terribly disappointed."

"Well, isn't it better to know?"

Jean shook her head. "I'm not sure—it's nice to think that they do lay eggs—blue ones and red ones and those lovely purple ones, isn't it?"

"Yes."

"And if they don't lay them, who does?"

"Hens," said Teddy, rather unexpectedly, "and the rab-yits steal them."

"Who told you that?"

"Hodgson. And she says that she ties them up in rags and the colors come off on the eggs."

"Well, I wouldn't listen to Hodgson."

"Why not? I like to listen."

"Because she hasn't any imagination."

"What's 'magination?"

They were getting in very deep. Jean gave it up. "Ask your mother, Teddy."

So Teddy sought his unfailing source of information. "What's 'magination, Mother."

"It is seeing things, Teddy, with your mind instead of your eyes. When I tell you about the poor little children in France who haven't any food or any clothes except what the Red Cross gives them, you don't really see them with your eyes, but your mind sees them, and their cold little hands, and their sad little faces—"

"Yes." He considered that for a while, then swept on to the things over which his childish brain puzzled.

"Mother, if the Germans get to Paris what will happen?"

He saw the horror in her face.

"Do you hate the Germans, Mother?"

"My darling, don't ask me."

After he had gone downstairs, Margaret got out her prayer-book, and read the prayers for the day.

"Oh, merciful God, who hast made all men and hatest nothing that thou hast made, nor desirest the death of a sinner, but rather that he should be converted and live, have mercy on all Jews, Turks, infidels and heretics, and take from them all ignorance, hardness of heart, and contempt of Thy word, and so fetch them home, blessed Lord, to Thy flock, that they may be saved—"

She shut the book. No, she could not go on. She did not love her enemies. She was not in the least sure that she wanted the Germans to be saved!

On Easter morning, however, Teddy was instructed to pray for his enemies. "We mustn't have hate in our hearts."

"Why mustn't we, Mother?"

"Well, Father wouldn't want it. We hate the evil they do, but we must pray that they will be shown their wickedness and repent."

"If they re-pyent will they stop fighting?"

"My dearest, yes."

"How would they stop?"

Jean, who was ready for church and waiting, warned, "You'd better not try to give an answer to that, Margaret, there isn't any."

Teddy ignored her. "How would they stop, Mother?"

"Well, they'd just stop, dear—"

"Would they say they were sorry?"

Would William of Prussia ever be sorry?

"Can God stop it, Mother?"

Margaret wrenched her mind away from the picture which his words had painted for her, the Kaiser on his knees! *Miserere mei, Deus—*

With quick breath, "Yes, dear."

"Then why doesn't He stop it, Mother?"

Why? Why? Why? Older voices were asking that question in agony.

"He will do it in His own good time, dearest. Perhaps the world has a lesson to learn."

With Teddy walking ahead with nurse, Jean proclaimed to Margaret, "I shan't pray for them."

"I know how you feel."

"Shall you?"

"Yes," desperately, "I must."

"Why must you?"

"Because of—Win," Margaret said simply. In her widow's black, with her veil giving her height and dignity, she had never been more beautiful. "Because of Win, I must. There are wives in Germany who suffer as I suffer—who are not to blame. There are children, like my children, asking the same questions—. This drive has seemed to me like the slaughter of sheep, with a great Wolf behind them, a Wolf without mercy, sending them down to destruction, to—death—"

"And the Wolf—?"

Margaret raised her hand and let it drop, "God knows."

And now soldiers were being rushed overseas. Trains swept across the land loaded with men who gazed wistfully at the peaceful towns as they passed through, or chafed impotently when, imprisoned in day coaches, they were side-tracked outside of great cities.

And on the battle line those droves and droves of gray sheep were driven down and down—to death—by the Wolf.

The war was coming closer to America. A look of care settled on the faces of men and women who had, hitherto, taken things lightly. Fathers, who had been very sure that the war would end before their sons should go to France, faced the fact that the end was not in sight, and that the war would take its toll of the youth of America. Mothers, who had not been sure of anything, but had hidden their fears in their hearts, stopped reading the daily papers. Wives, who had looked upon the camp experiences of their husbands as a rather great adventure, knew now that there might be a greater adventure with a Dark Angel. The tram-sheds in great cities were crowded with anxious relatives who watched the troops go through, clutching at the hope of a last glimpse of a beloved face, a few precious moments in which to say farewell.

Yes, the war was coming near!

Derry wrote that he might go at any moment, but hoped for a short furlough. It was on this hope that Jean lived. She worked tirelessly, making the much-needed surgical dressings. When Emily tried to get her to rest, Jean would shake her head.

"Darling, I must. They are bringing the wounded over."

"But you mustn't get too tired."

"I want to be tired. So that I can sleep."

She was finding it hard to sleep. Often she rose and wrote in her memory book, which was becoming in a sense a diary because she confided to its pages the things she dared not say to Derry. Some day, perhaps, she might show him what she had written. But that would be when the war was over, and Derry had come back safe and sound. Until then she would have to smile in her letters, and she did not always feel like smiling!

But that was what Derry called them, "Smiling letters!"

"They smile up at me every morning, Jean."

So she wrote to him bravely, cheerfully, of her busy days, of how she missed him, of her love and longing, but not a word did she say of her world as it really was.

But there was no laughter in the things she said to the old memory book.

"I don't like big houses—not houses like this, with grinning porcelain Chinese gods at every turn of the hall, and gold dragons on the bed-posts. There are six of us here besides the servants, yet we are like dwarfs in a giant palace. Perhaps if we had the usual fires it wouldn't seem quite so forlorn. But the china in the cabinets is so cold—and the ceilings are so high—and the marble floors—.

"Perhaps if everyone were happy it would be different. But only Emily is happy. And I don't see how she can be. She is going to marry a Hun! Of course, he isn't really, and he'd be a darling dear if it weren't for his German name, and his German blood, and the German things he has in his house. But Emily says she loves his house, that it speaks to her of a different Germany—of the sweet old gay Germany that waltzed and sang and loved simple things. It seems so funny to think of Emily in love—she's so much older than people are usually when they are engaged and married.

"But Emily is the only happy one, except the children, and I sometimes think that even they have the shadow on them of the dreadful things that are happening. Margaret-Mary tries to knit, and tires her stubby little fingers with the big needles, and Teddy, poor chap, seems to feel that he must be the man of the family and take his father's place, and he is pathetically careful of his mother.

"I wonder if Margaret feels as I do about it all? She is so sweet and smiling—and yet I know how her heart weeps, and I know how she longs for her own house and her own hearth and her own husband—

"Oh, when my Derry comes back safe and sound—and he will come back safe, I shall say it over and over to myself until I make it true—when Derry comes back, we'll build a cottage, with windows that look out on trees and a garden—and there'll be cozy little rooms, and we'll take Polly Ann and Muffin—and live happy ever after—.

"I wonder how father stands it to be always with people who are sick? I never knew what it meant until now. The General is an old dear—but sometimes when I sit in that queer room of his with its lacquer and gold and see him in his gorgeous dressing gown, I feel afraid. It is rather dreadful to think that he was once young and strong like Derry, and that he will never be young and strong again.

"Oh, I want the war to end—I want Derry, and sunshine and well people. It seems a hundred years since I did anything just for the fun of doing it. It seems a million years since Daddy and I drove downtown together and drank chocolate sodas—

"But then nobody is drinking chocolate sodas—at least no one is doing it light-heartedly. You can't be light-hearted when the person you love best in the world is going to war. You can be brave, and you can make your lips laugh, but you can't make your heart laugh—you can't—you can't—.

"I talk a great deal to the women who come to Emily's Toy Shop. And I am finding out that some of those that seem fluffy-minded are really very much in earnest. There is one little blonde, who always wears white silk and chiffon, she looks as if she had just stepped from the stage. And at first I simply scorned her. I felt that she would be the kind to leave ravellings in her wipes, and things like that. But she doesn't leave a ravelling. She works slowly, but she does her work well—. But now and then her hands tremble and the tears fall; and the other day I went and sat down beside her and I found out that her husband is flying in France, and that her two brothers are at the front—. And one of them is among the missing; he may be a prisoner and he may be dead—. And she is trying to do her bit and be brave. And now I don't care if she does wear her earlocks outside of her veil and load her hands with diamonds—she's a dear—and a darling. But she's scared just as I am—and as Mary Connolly is, and as all the women are, though they don't show it—. I wonder if Joan of Arc was afraid—in her heart as the rest of us are? Perhaps she wasn't, because she was in the thick of it herself, and we aren't. Perhaps if we were where we could see it and have the excitement of it all, we should lose our fear.

"But when women tell me that the women have the worst of it—that they must sit at home and weep and wait, I don't believe it. We suffer—of course, and there's the thought of it all like a bad dream, and when we love our loved ones—it is heartbreak. But the men suffer, daily, in all the little things. The thirst and the vermin, and the cold and wet—and the noise—and the frightfulness. And they grow tired and hungry and homesick,—and death is on every side of them, and horror—. Some of the women who come to the shop sentimentalize a lot. One woman recited, 'Break, break, break—, the other day, and the rest of them cried into the gauze, *cried for themselves*, if you please; 'For men must work and women must weep.' And then my little blonde told them what she thought of them. Her name is 'Maisie,' wouldn't you know a girl like that would be called 'Maisie'?

"'If you think,' she said, 'that you suffer—what in God's name will you think before the war is over? It hasn't touched you. You won't know what suffering means until your men begin to come home. You talk about hardships; not one of you has gone hungry yet—and the men over there may be cut off at any moment from food supplies, and they are always at the mercy of the camp cooks, who may or may not give them things that they can eat. And they lie out under the stars with their wounds, and if any of you has a finger ache, you go to bed with hot water bottles and are coddled and cared for. But our boys,—there isn't anyone to coddle them—they have to stick it out. And we've got to stick it out—and not be sorry for ourselves. Oh, why should we be sorry for ourselves!' The tears were streaming down her cheeks when she finished, and a gray-haired woman who had wept with the others got up and came over to her. 'My dear,' she said, 'I shall never pity myself again. My two sons are over there, and I've been thinking how much I have given. But they have given their young lives, their futures—their bodies, to be broken—' And then standing right in the middle of the Toy Shop that mother prayed for her sons, and for the sons of other women, and for the husbands and lovers, and that the women might be brave.

"Oh, it was wonderful—as she stood there like a white-veiled prophetess, praying.

"Yet a year ago she would have died rather than pray in public. She is a conservative, aristocratic woman, the kind that doesn't wear rings or try to be picturesque—and she has always kept her feelings to herself, and said her prayers to herself—or in church, but never in all her life has she been so fine as she was the other day praying in the Toy Shop.

"Yet in a way I am sorry for myself. Not for me as I am to-day, but for the Jean of Yesterday, who thought that patriotism was remembering Bunker Hill!

"Of course in a way it is that—for Bunker Hill and Lexington and Valley Forge are a part of us because our grandfathers were there, and what they felt and did is a part of our feeling and doing.

"I have always thought of those old days as a sort of picture—the embattled farmers in their shirt-sleeves and with their hair blowing, and the Midnight Ride, and the lantern in the old North Church—and the Spirit of '76. And it was the same with the Civil War; there was always the vision of cavalry sweeping up and down slopes as they do in the movies, and of the bugles calling, and bands playing 'Marching through Georgia' or 'Dixie' as the case might be—and flags flying—isn't it glorious to think that the men in gray are singing to-day, 'The Star Spangled Banner' with the rest of us?

"But my thoughts never had anything to do with money, though I suppose people gave it then, as they are giving now. But you can't paint pictures of men and women making out checks, and children putting thrift stamps in little books, so I suppose that in future the heroes and heroines of the emptied pocket-books will go down unsung—.

"It isn't a bit picturesque to give until it hurts, but it helps a lot. I saw Sarah Bernhardt the other day in a wonderful little play where she's a French boy, who dies in the end—and she dies, exquisitely, with the flag of France in her arms—the faded, lovely flag—I shall never forget. The tears ran down my cheeks so that I couldn't see, but her voice, so faint and clear, still rings in my ears—

"If she had died clutching a Liberty Bond or wearing a Red Cross button, it would have seemed like burlesque. Yet there are men and women who are going without bread and butter to buy Liberty Bonds, and who are buying them not as a safe investment, as rich men buy, but because the boys need the money. And there ought to be poems written and statues erected to commemorate some of the sacrifices for the sake of the Red Cross.

"Yet I think that, in a way, we have not emphasized enough the picturesque quality of this war, not on this side. They do it in France—they worship their great flyers, their great generals, their crack regiments, everything has a personality, they are tender with their shattered cathedrals as if something human had been hurt, and the result is a quickening on the part of every individual, a flaming patriotism which as yet we have not felt. We don't worship anything, we don't all of us know the words of 'The Star Spangled Banner'; fancy a Frenchman not knowing the words of the 'Marseillaise' or an Englishman forgetting 'God Save the King.' We don't shout and sing enough, we don't cry enough, we don't feel enough—and that's all there is to it. If we were hot for the triumph of democracy, there would be no chance of victory for the Hun. Perhaps as the war comes nearer, we shall feel more, and every day it is coming nearer—"

It was very near, indeed. Thousands of those gray sheep were lying dead on the plains of Picardy—the Allies fought with their backs to the wall—Americans who had swaggered, secure in the prowess of Uncle Sam, swaggered no longer, and pondered on the parable of the Wise and Foolish Virgins.

Slowly the nation waked to what was before it. In America now lay the hope of the world. The Wolf must be trapped, the sheep saved in spite of themselves, those poor sheep, driven blindly to slaughter.

The General was not quite sure that they were sheep, or that they were being driven. He held, rather, that they knew what they were about—and were not to be pitied.

Teddy, considering this gravely, went back to previous meditations, and asked if he prayed for his enemies.

"Bless my soul," said the old gentleman, "why should I?"

"Well, Mother says we must, and then some day they'll stop and say they are sorry—"

The General chuckled, "Your mother is optimistic."

"What's 'nopt'mistic?"

"It means always believing that nice things will happen."

"Don't you believe that nice things will happen?"

"Sometimes—"

"Don't you believe that the war will stop?"

"Not until we've thrown the full force of our fighting men into it—at what a sacrifice."

"Can't God make it stop?"

"He can, but He won't, not if He's a God of justice," said this staunch old patriot, "until America has brought them to their knees—"

"Will they say they are sorry then?"

"It won't make very much difference what they say—"

But Teddy, having been brought up to understand the things which belong to an officer and a gentleman, had his own ideas on the subject. "Well, I should think they'd ought to say they were sorry—."

CHAPTER XXVII
MARCHING FEET

The end of April brought much rain; torrents swept down the smooth streets, and the beauty of the carefully kept flower beds in the parks was blurred by the wet.

The General, limping from window to window, chafed. He wanted to get out, to go over the hills and far away; with the coming of the spring the wander-hunger gripped him, and with this restless mood upon him he stormed at Bronson.

"It's a dog's life."

"Yes, sir," said Bronson, dutifully.

"It is dead lonesome, Bronson, and I can't keep Jean tied here all of the time. She is looking pale, don't you think she is looking pale?"

"Yes, sir. I think she misses Mr. Derry."

"Well, she'll miss him a lot more before she gets him back," grimly. "He'll be going over soon—"

"Yes, sir."

"I wish I were going," the old man was wistful. "Think of it, Bronson, to be over there—in the thick of it, playing the game, instead of rotting here—"

It was, of course, the soldier's point of view. Bronson, being hopelessly civilian, did his best to rise to what was expected of him. "You like it then, sir?"

"Like it? It is the only life. We've lost something since men took up the game of business in place of the game of fighting."

"But you see, sir, there's no blood—in business." Bronson tried to put it delicately.

"Isn't there? Why, more men are killed in accidents in factories than are killed in war—murdered by money-greedy employers."

"Oh, sir, not quite that."

"Yes, quite," was the irascible response. "You don't know what you are talking about, Bronson. Read statistics and find out."

"Yes, sir. Will you have your lunch up now, sir?"

"I'll get it over and then you can order the car for me."

"But the rain—?"

"I like rain. I'm not sugar or salt."

Bronson, much perturbed, called up Jean. "The General's going out."

"Oh, but he mustn't, Bronson."

"I can't say 'mustn't' to him, Miss," Bronson reported dismally. "You'd better see what you can do—"

But when Jean arrived, the General was gone!

"We'll drive out through the country," the old man had told his chauffeur, and had settled back among his cushions, his cane by his side, his foot up on the opposite seat to relieve him of the weight.

And it was as he rode that he began to have a strange feeling about that foot which no longer walked or bore him lightly.

How he had marched in those bygone days! He remembered the first time he had tried to keep step with his fellows. The tune had been Yankee Doodle—with a fife and drum—and he was a raw young recruit in his queer blue uniform and visored cap—.

And how eager his feet had been, how strongly they had borne him, spurning the dust of the road—as they would bear him no more—.

There were men who envied him as he swept past them in the rain, men who felt that he had more than his share of wealth and ease, yet he would have made a glad exchange for the feet which took them where they willed.

He came at last to one of his old haunts, a small stone house on the edge of the Canal. From its wide porch he had often watched the slow boats go by, with men and women and children living in worlds bounded by weather-beaten decks. To-day in the rain there was a blur of lilac bushes along the tow path, but no boats were in sight; the Canal was a ruffled gray sheet in the April wind.

Lounging in the low-ceiled front room of the stone house were men of the type with whom he had once foregathered—men not of his class or kind, but interesting because of their very differences—human derelicts who had welcomed him.

But now, for the first time he was not one of them. They eyed his elegances with suspicion—his fur coat, his gloves, his hat—the man whose limousine stood in front of the door was not one of them; they might beg of him, but they would never call him "Brother."

So, because his feet no longer carried him, and he must ride, he found himself cast out, as it were, by outcasts.

He ordered meat and drink for them, gave them money, made a joke or two as he limped among them, yet felt an alien. He watched them wistfully, seeing for the first time their sordidness, seeing what he himself had been, more sordid than any, because of his greater opportunities.

Sitting apart, he judged them, judged himself. If all the world were like these men, what kind of world would it be?

"Why aren't you fellows fighting?" he asked suddenly.

They stared at him. Grumbled. Why should they fight? One of them wept over it, called himself too old—.

But there were young men among them. "For God's sake get out of this—let me help you get out." The General stood up, leaned on his cane. "Look here, I've done a lot of things in my time—things like this—" his arm swept out towards the table, "and now I've only one good foot—the other will never be alive again. But you young chaps, you've got two good feet—to march. Do you know what that means, to march? Left, right, left, right and step out bravely—. Yankee Doodle and your heads up, flags flying? And you sit here like this?"

Two of the men had risen, young and strong. The General's cane pounded—he had their eyes! "Left, right, left, right—all over the world men are marching, and you sit here—"

The years seemed to have dropped from him. His voice rang with a fire that had once drawn men after him. He had led a charge at Gettysburg, and his men had followed!

And these two men would follow him. He saw the dawn of their resolve in their faces. "There's fine stuff in both of you," he said, "and the country needs you. Isn't it better to fight than to sit here? Get into my car and I'll take you down."

"Aw, what's eatin' you," one of the older men growled. "What game's this? Recruitin'?"

But the young men asked no questions. They came—glad to come. Roused out of a lethargy which had bound them. Waked by a ringing old voice.

The General was rather quiet when he reached home. Jean and Bronson, who had suffered torments, watched him with concerned eyes. And, as if he divined it, he laid his hand over Jean's. "I did a good day's work, my dear. I got two men for the Army, and I'm going to get more—"

And he did get more. He went not only in the rain, but in the warmth of the sun, when the old fruit trees bloomed along the tow path, and the backs of the mules were shining black, and the women came out on deck with their washing.

And always he spoke to the men of marching feet—. Now and then he sang for them in that thin old voice whose thinness was so overlaid by the passion of his patriotism that those who listened found no flaw in it.

"He has sounded forth the trumpet that has never called retreat,
He is sifting forth the hearts of men before his Judgment seat,
O be swift my soul to answer him, be jubilant my feet,
Our God is marching on—"

There was no faltering now, no fumbled words. With head up, singing—"Be jubilant, my feet—"

Sometimes he took Jean with him, but not always. "There are places that I don't like to have you go, my dear, but those are where I get my men."

At other times when he came out to where she sat in the car there would flash before his eyes the vision of his wife's face, as she, too, had once sat there, waiting—

Sometimes he took the children, and rode with them on a slow-moving barge from one lock to another, with the limousine meeting them at the end.

So he travelled the old paths, innocently, as he might have travelled them throughout the years.

Yet if he thought of those difficult years, he said never a word. He felt, perhaps, that there was nothing to say. He took to himself no credit for the things he was doing. If age and infirmity had brought to him a realization of all that he had missed, he was surely not to be praised for doing that which was, obviously, his duty.

Yet it gave him a new zest for life, and left Jean freer than she had been before. It left her, too, without the fear of him, which had robbed their relationship of all sense of security.

"You see, I never knew," she wrote in her memory book, "what might happen. I had visions of myself going after him in the night as Derry had gone and his mother. I used to dream about it, and dread it."

Yet she had said nothing of her dread to Derry in her smiling letters, and as men think of women, he had thought of her in the sick room as a guardian angel, shining and serene.

And now, faint and far came to the men in the cantonments the sound of battles across the sea. The bugles calling them each morning seemed to say, "Soon, soon, you will go, you will go, you will go—"

To Derry, listening, it seemed the echo of the fairy trumpets, "*Trutter-a-trutt, trutter-a-trutt, you will go, you will go, you will go—*"

It was strange how the thought of it drew him, drew him as even the thoughts of Jean his bride did not draw—. He remembered that years ago he had smiled with a tinge of tolerant sophistication over the old lines:

"I   could   not   love   thee,   dear,   so   much,
Loved I not honor more—"

Yet here it was, a truth in his own life. A woman meaning more to him than she could ever have meant in times of peace, because he could go forth to fight for her, his life at stake, for her. It was for her, and for other women that his sword was unsheathed.

"If only they could understand it," he wrote to Jean. "You haven't any idea what rotten letters some of the women write. Blaming the men for going over seas. Blaming them for going into it at all. Taking it as a personal offense that their lovers have left them. 'If you had loved me, you couldn't have left me,' was the way one woman put it, and I found a poor fellow mooning over it and asked him what was the matter. 'It isn't a question of what we want to do, it is a question of what we've got to do, if we call ourselves men,' he said. But she couldn't see that, she was measuring her emotions by an inch rule.

"But, thank God, most of the women are the real thing—true as steel and brave. And it is those women that the men worship. It is a masculine trait to want to be a sort of hero in the eyes of the woman you love. When she doesn't look at it that way, your plumes droop!"

And now the bugles rang with a clearer note—not, "You will go, you will go—" but, "Do not wait, do not wait, do not wait."

The cry from abroad was Macedonian. "Come over and help us!" It was to America that the ghosts of those fighting hordes appealed.

"Take up our quarrel with the foe,
To you from falling hands we throw
The torch—be yours to hold it high.
If ye break faith with us who die,
We shall not sleep, though poppies grow
In Flanders' field—"

111

Gradually there had grown up in the hearts of simple men a flaming response to that sacred charge. Men whose dreams had never reached beyond a day's frivolity, found springing up in their souls a desire to do some deed to match that of the other fellow who slept "in Flanders field."

"To you from falling hands we throw the torch—be yours to hold it high—," the little man who had measured cloth behind a counter, the boy who had sold papers on the streets, the bank clerk who had bent over his books, the stenographer who had been bound to the wheel of everlasting dictation, were lighted by the radiance of that vision, "to hold it high—."

"Gee, I never used to think," said Tommy Tracy, "that I might have a chance to do a stunt like that."

"Like what?" Derry asked.

Tommy found it a thing rather hard to express. "Well, when you've been just a common sort of chap, to die—for the other fellow—"

So men's bodies grew and their muscles hardened. But their souls grew, too, expanding to the breadth and height of the things which were waiting for them to do across the sea.

And one morning Derry was granted a furlough, and started home. He sent no word ahead of him. He wanted to come upon them unawares. To catch the light that would be on Jean's face when she looked up and saw him.

There was rain and more rain when at last he arrived in Washington. The trees as his taxi traversed the wide avenues showed clear green, melting into vistas of amethyst and gray. The parks as he passed were starred with the bright yellow and pinks of flowering shrubs. Washington, in spite of the rain, was as lovely as a woman whose color blooms behind a veil.

He came into the great house unannounced, having his key with him. The General was out for a ride, the children with him, Margaret and Emily and Jean away, the servants in the back of the house.

Derry, going up the stairs, two steps at a time, stopped on the landing with head uncovered to greet his mother.

Oh, lovely painted lady, is this the little white-faced lad you loved, the big bronzed man, fresh from hardships, strong in the sense of the thing he has to do?

No promise made to you could hold him now. He has weighed your small demands is the balance with the world's great need.

He did not tarry long. Straight as an eagle to its mate, he swept through the hall and knocked at the door of Jean's room. There was no response. He knocked again, turned the handle, entered, and found the room empty. The tin soldier on the shelf shouted, "Welcome, welcome—comrade," but Derry had no ears to hear. Everywhere were signs of Jean; her fat memory book open on her desk, the ivory and gold appointments of her dressing table, her pink slippers, her prayer book—his own picture with flowers in front of it as before a shrine.

"My dear, my darling," his heart said when he saw that. What, after all, was he that she should worship him?

Impatient, he rang for Bronson, and the old man came—bewildered, hurried, joyful. "It's a great surprise, sir, but it's good to see you."

"It's good to see you, Bronson. Where's Miss Jean?"

"At Miss Emily's shop, sir."

"As late as this?"

"Sometimes later. She tries to get home in time for dinner."

"Where's Dad?"

"Driving with the children, and the ladies are out on war work."

A year ago women had played bridge at this hour in the afternoon, but there was no playing now.

"Don't tell Dad that I am here. I'll come back presently with Mrs. Drake."

And now down the hall came an old gray dog, wild with delight, outracing Polly Ann, who thought it was a play and leaped after him—Muffin had found his master!

But Derry left Muffin, left Bronson, left Polly Ana, a wistful trio at the front door. He must find Jean!

The day was darkening, and a light burned far back on the Toy Shop. Derry, standing outside, saw a room which was the very wraith of the gay little shop as he had left it—with its white tables, its long counters piled high with finished dressings; the white elephants in a spectral row behind glass doors on the top shelf the only reminder of what it once had been.

He saw, too, a small nun-like figure behind the counter, a figure all in white, with a white veil banded about her forehead and flowing down behind.

All of her bright hair was hidden, her eyes were on the compresses that she was counting. It seemed to him that there was a sharpened look on the little face.

112

He had not expected this. He had felt that he would find her glowing as she had been on that first night when he had followed his father through the rain—his dream had been of crinkled copper hair, of silver and rose, of youth and laughter and lightness—.

Her letters had been like that—gay, sparkling—there had been times when they had seemed almost too exuberant, times when he had wondered if she had really waked to the seriousness of the great struggle, and the part he was to play in it.

Yet now he saw signs of suffering. He opened the door. "Jean," he cried.

With the blood all drained from her face, she stared at him as if she saw a specter—"Derry," she whispered.

With his strong arms, he lifted her over the counter. "Jean-Joan, Jean-Joan—"

When at last she released herself, it was to laugh through her tears. "Derry, pull down the shades; what will people think?"

He cared little what people would think. And, anyway, very few people were passing at that late hour in the rain. But he pulled them down, and when he came back, he held her off at arm's length. "What have you been doing to yourself, dearest? You are a feather-weight."

"Well, I've been working."

"How does it happen that you are here alone?"

"Emily had to go down to order supplies, and Margaret went to a Liberty Loan meeting. I often stay like this to count and tie."

"Don't you get dreadfully tired?"

"Yes. But I think I like to get tired. It keeps me from thinking too much."

He drew her to him. "Take off your veil," he said, almost roughly. "I want to see your hair."

Divested of her headcovering, she was more like herself, but even then he was not content. He loosed a hairpin here and there and ran his fingers through the crinkled gold. "If you knew how I've dreamed of it, Jean-Joan."

But he had not dreamed of the dearness of the little face. "My darling, you have been pining, and I didn't know it."

"Well, didn't you like my smiling letters?"

"So that was it? You've been trying to cheer me up, and letting yourself get like this."

"I didn't want to worry you."

"Didn't you know that I'd want to be worried with anything that pertained to you? What's a husband for, dearest, if you can't tell him your troubles?"

"Yes, but a soldier-husband, Derry, is different. You've got to keep smiling—"

Her lips trembled and she clung to him. "It is so good to have you here, Derry."

She admitted, later, that she had confided her troubles to her memory book. "There weren't any big things, really—just missing you and all that—"

He was jealous of the memory book. "I shall read every word of it."

"Not until you come back from the war—and then we can laugh at it together."

They fell into silence after that. With his arms about her he thought that he might not come back, and she clinging to him had the same thought. But neither told the other.

"Do you know," she said at last, sitting up and sticking the hairpins into her crinkled knot. "Do you know that it's almost time for dinner, and that the General will wonder where I am?"

"I told Bronson not to tell him."

"Oh, really, Derry? Let's make it a great surprise."

Providentially the General was late. He and the children came home to find the house quite remarkably illumined, and Margaret flushed and excited, and in white.

"Is it a party, Mother?" Teddy asked, lending his shoulder manfully to the General's hand, as, with the chauffeur on the other side, they helped the old man up the stairs.

"No, but on such a rainy night Bronson and I thought we'd have a little feast. Don't you think that would be fun?"

The General was tired. "I had planned not to come down again—"

"Please do," she begged,

Bronson, knowing his master's moods, was on tip-toe with anxiety. "I've your things all laid out, sir."

"Well, well, I'll see."

Teddy, somewhat out of breath as they reached the top landing was inspired to remark, "We'll be 'spointed if you don't come down—"

"You want me, eh?"

"Yes, I do. There isn't any other man—"

The General chuckled. "Well, that's reason enough—. You can count on me, Ted, for masculine support."

The table was laid for six. Teddy appearing presently in the dining room pointed out the fact to Bronson, who was taking a last look.

"Is Margaret-Mary coming down?"

"She may later, for the sweets."

"Those aren't her spoons and forks."

"Well, well," said Bronson, "so they aren't"; but he did not have them changed.

The General in his dinner coat, perfectly groomed, immaculate, found Jean in rose and silver waiting for him.

"How gay we are," he said, and pinched her cheek.

Teddy in white linen and patent leathers also approved. "You've got on your spangly dwess, and it makes you pwetty—"

"Oh, Ted, is it just my clothes that make me pretty?"

"I didn't mean that. Only tonight you're so nice and—shining."

She shone, indeed, with such effulgence, that it was a wonder that the General did not suspect. But he did not, even when she said, "We have a surprise for you."

"For me, my dear?"

"Yes. A parcel—it came this afternoon. We want you to untie the string."

"Where is it?" Teddy demanded.

"On the table in the blue room."

Teddy rushed in ahead of the rest, came back and reported, "It's a big one."

It was a big one, cone-shaped and tied up in brown paper. It was set on a heavy carved table, a length of tapestry was under it and hid the legs of the table.

"It looks like a small tree," the General remarked. "But why all this air of mystery?"

He was plainly bored by the fuss they were making. He was tired, and he wanted his dinner.

But Jean, in an excited voice, was telling him to cut the string, and Bronson was handing him a knife.

And then—the paper dropped and everybody was laughing, and Teddy was screaming wildly and he was staring at the khaki-clad upper half of a tall young soldier whose silver-blond hair was clipped close, and whose hand went up in salute.

"It's Cousin Derry. It's Cousin Derry," Teddy was shouting, and Margaret-Mary piped up, "It's Tousin Dee."

Derry stepped out from behind the table, where leaning forward and wrapped up he had lent himself to the illusion, and put both hands on the General's shoulders. "Glad to see me, Dad?"

"Glad; my dear boy—" It was almost too much for him.

Yet as supported by his son's arm, they went a moment later into the dining room, he had a sense of renewed strength in the youth and vigor of this youth who was bone of his bone, flesh of his flesh. If his own feet could not march here were feet which would march for him.

There were flowers on the table, most extravagantly, for these war times, orchids; and there were tall white candles in silver holders.

Jean shining between the candles was a wonder for the world to gaze upon. Derry couldn't keep his eyes off her. This was no longer a little nun of the Toy Shop, yet he held the vision of the little nun in his heart, lest he should forget that she had suffered.

He talked to them all. But beating like a wave against his consciousness was always the thought of Jean. Of the things he had to tell her which he could tell to no one else. He knew now that he could reveal to her the depths of his nature. He had withheld so much, fearing to crush her butterfly wings, but she was not a butterfly. They had been playing at cross purposes, and writing letters that merely skimmed the surface of their emotions. It had taken those moments in the Toy Shop to teach them their mistake.

Teddy, feeling that the occasion called for a relaxing of the children-should-be-seen-and-not-heard rule, asked questions.

"How long can you stay?"

"Ten days."

"Are you going to Fwance?"

"I hope so."

"Mother says I've got to pray for the Germans."

"Teddy," Margaret admonished.

"Well, I rather think I would," Derry told him. "They need it."

This was a new angle. "Shall you hate to kill them?"

There was a stir about the table. The old man and the women seemed to hang on Derry's answer.

"Yes, I shall hate it. I hate all killing, but it's got to be done."

He spoke presently, at length, of what many men thought of war.

"We are red-blooded enough, we Americans, but I think we hate killing the other man rather more than we fear being killed. It's sickening—bayonet practice. Killing at long range is different. The children of my generation were trained to tender-heartedness. We looked after the birds and rescued kittens, and were told that wars were impossible—long wars. But war is not impossible, and it has come upon us, and we are finding that men must be brave not merely in the face of losing their own lives, but in the face of taking the lives of—others. I sometimes wonder what it must have seemed to those Germans who went first into Belgium. Some of them must have been kind—some of them must have asked to be shot rather than be set at the work of butchery.

"I sometimes think," he pursued, "that if we could give moving pictures of the war just as it is—in all its horror and hideousness—show the pictures in every little town in every country in the world, that war would stop at once. If the Germans could see themselves in those towns in Belgium—if the world could see them. If we could see men mowed down—wounded, close up, as our soldiers see them. If our people should be forced to look at those pictures, as the people of war-ridden countries have been forced to gaze upon realities, money would be provided and men provided in such amounts and numbers that those who began the war would be forced to end it on the terms the world would set for them.

"The fact that men are going into this war in spite of their aversion to killing shows the stuff of which they are made. It is like drowning kittens," he smiled a little. "It has to be done or the world would be overrun by cats."

Teddy, wide-eyed, was listening. "Do people drown kittens?" he asked. "Oh, I didn't think they would." It was a sad commentary on the conditions of war that he was more heavily oppressed by the thought of drowned little cats than by the murder of men.

"My dear fellow," Derry said, "we won't talk about such things. I must beg your pardon for mentioning it."

The talk flowed on then in lighter vein. "Ralph Witherspoon is in town," Jean vouchsafed. "He had a bad fall and was sent home to get over it. Mrs. Witherspoon has asked me there to dine. I shall take you with me."

"I didn't know that people were dining out in these times."

"Mrs. Witherspoon prides herself on her conservation menus. She says that she serves war things, that she gives us nothing to eat that the men need, and she likes her friends about her."

"We shall miss Drusilla," Derry said. "I've been worried about her since the Huns recaptured those towns in France."

"Daddy wrote that she is not far from his hospital, doing splendid work, and that the men adore her."

"They would," said Derry. "She is a great-hearted creature. I can fancy her singing to them over there. You know what a wonder she was at that sort of thing—"

After dinner the General was eager to have his son to himself. "The women will excuse us while we smoke and talk."

Derry's eyes wandered to Jean. "All right," he said with an effort.

The General's heart tightened. His son was his son. The little girl in silver and rose was in a sense an outsider. She had not known Derry throughout the years, as his father had known him. How could she care as much?

Yet she did care. He realized how Derry's coming had changed her. He heard her laugh as she had not laughed in all the weeks of loneliness. She came up and stood beside Derry, and linked her arm in his and looked up at him with shining eyes.

"Isn't he—wonderful?" she asked, with a catch of her breath.

"Oh, take her away," the old gentleman said. "Go and talk to her somewhere."

Derry's face brightened. "You don't mind?"

"Of course not," stoutly. "Bronson says that the rain has stopped. There's probably a moon somewhere, if you'll look for it."

Margaret went up to put the children to bed. Emily, promising to come back, withdrew to write a letter. The old man sat alone.

He limped into the blue room, and gazed indifferently around on its treasures. Once he had cared for these plates and cups—his quest for rare porcelains had been eager.

And now he did not care. The lovely glazed things were for the eye, not for the heart. He would have given them all for the touch of a loving hand, for a voice that grew tender—.

There was the patter of little feet on the polished floor. Margaret-Mary in a diminutive blue dressing gown and infinitesimal slippers, with her curls brushed tidily up from the back of her neck and skewered with a hairpin, came over and laid her hand on his knee. "Dus a 'itte 'tory?" she asked ingratiatingly. She adored stories.

He picked her up, and she curled herself into the corner of his arm.

Her mother found her there. "Mother's naughty little girl," she said, "to run away—"

"Let her stay," the General begged. "Somehow my heart needs her tonight."

CHAPTER XXVIII
SIX DAYS

Four days of Derry's furlough had passed, four palpitating days, and now the hours that the lovers spent together began to take on the poignant quality of coming separation. Every moment counted, nothing must be lost, nothing must be left unsaid, nothing must be left undone which should emphasize their oneness of thought and purpose.

They read together, they walked together, they rode together, they went to church together. If they included the General in their plans it was because they felt his need of them, not theirs of him. They lived in a world created to survive for ten days and then to collapse like a pricked bubble—

And it was because of the dread of collapse that Jean began to plan a structure of remembrance which should endure after Derry's departure.

"Darling," she said, "there are only six days—What shall we do with them?"

THE FIFTH DAY

It was Sunday, and in the morning they went dutifully to church. They ate their luncheon dutifully with the whole family, and motored dutifully afterwards with the General. Then at twilight they sought the Toy Shop.

They had it all to themselves, and they had told Bronson that they would not be home for dinner. So Jean made chocolate for Derry as she had made it on that first night for his father. They toasted war bread on the electric grill, and there were strawberries.

They were charmed with their housekeeping. "It would have been like this," Derry said—all eyes for her loveliness, "if you had been the girl in the Toy Shop and I had been the shabby boy—"

Jean pondered. "I wonder if a big house is ever really a home?"

"Not ours. Mother tried to make it—but it has always been a sort of museum with Dad's collections."

"Do you think that some day we could have a little house?"

"We can have whatever you want." His smile warmed her.

"Wouldn't you want it, Derry?"

"If you were in it."

"Let's talk about it, and plan it, and put dream furniture in it, and dream friends—"

"More Lovely Dreams?"

"Well, something like that—a House o' Dreams, Derry, without any gold dragons or marble balls or queer porcelain things; just our own bits of furniture and china, and a garden, and Muffin and Polly Ann—" Her eyes were wistful.

"You shall have it now if you wish."

"Not until you can share it with me—"

And that was the beginning of their fantastic pilgrimage. In the time that was left to them they were to find a house of dreams, and as Jean said, expansively, "all the rest."

"We will start tonight," Derry declared. "There's such a moon."

It was the kind of moon that whitened the world; one swam in a sea of light. Derry's runabout was a fairy car. Jean's hair was molten gold, her lover's pale silver—as with bare heads, having passed the city limits, they took the open road.

It was as warm as summer, and there were fragrances which seemed to wash over them in waves as they passed old gardens and old orchards. There was bridal-wreath billowing above stone fences, snow-balls, pale globes among the green, beds of iris, purple-black beneath the moon.

They forded a stream—more silver, and a silver road after that.

"Where are we going?" Jean breathed.

"I know a house—"

It was a little house set on top of a hill, where indeed no little house should be set, for little houses should nestle, protected by the slopes back of them. But this little house was set up there for the view—the Monument a spectral shaft, miles away, the Potomac broadening out beyond it, the old trees of the Park sleeping between. This was what the little house saw by night; it saw more than that by day.

It was not an empty house. One window was lighted, a square of gold in a lower room.

They did not know who lived in the house. They did not care. For the moment it was theirs. Leaving the car, they sat on the grass and surveyed their property.

"Of course it is ours," Jean said, "and when you are over there, you can think of it with the moon shining on it."

"I like the sloping roof," her lover took up the refrain, "and the big chimney and the wide windows."

"I can sit on the window seat and watch for you, Derry, and there will be smoke coming out of the chimney on cold days, and a fire roaring on the hearth when you open the door—"

They decided that there ought to be eight rooms—, and they named them. The Log-Fire Room; The Room of Little Feasts; the Place of Pots and Pans—

"That's the first floor," said Jean.

"Yes."

The upper floor was harder—The Royal Suite; The Friendly Boom, for the dream maid of all work; The Spare Chamber—

"My grandmother had a spare chamber," Jean explained, "and I always liked the sound of it, as if she kept her hospitality pressed down and running over—"

Derry, who had written it all by the light of the moon, held his pencil poised. "There is one more," he said, "the little room towards the West—"

Jean hesitated for the breadth of a second. "Well, we may need another," she said, and left it nameless.

The door opened and a man came out. If he saw them, they meant nothing to him—a pair of lovers by the wayside; there were many such.

He paced back and forth on the gravel walk. They could hear the crunch of it under his feet. They saw the shining tip of his cigar—smelt its fragrance—.

Again the door opened, to frame a woman. She called and her voice was young.

"Dearest, it is late. Are you coming in?"

His young voice answered. His far-flung cigar-end trailed across the darkness, his eager steps gave quick response—the door was shut—.

"Oh, Derry, I'd call you like that—"

"And I should come."

The light went out on the lower floor, and presently in a room above a window was illumined.

THE SIXTH DAY

A dream house must have dream furniture. There are old shops in Alexandria, where, less often than in earlier years, one may find treasures, bow-legged chairs and gate-legged tables, yellowed letters written by famous pens, steel engravings which have hung in historic halls, pewter and plate, Luster and Sèvres, Wedgwood and Willow, Chippendale and Hepplewhite, Adams and Empire, everything linked with some distinguished name, everything with a story, real or invented. One may buy an ancestor for a song, or at least the portrait of one, and silver with armorial bearings, and no one will know if you do not tell them that your heirlooms have come from a shop.

And Alexandria, as all the world knows, is reached from Washington by motor and trolley, train or ferry.

It was by ferry that the lovers preferred to go in the glory of this May morning, feeling the breeze fresh in their faces as with a motley crowd they stood on the lower deck and looked towards the old town.

Thus they came to the wharves, flanked by ancient warehouses in a straggly row along the water line. The windows of these ancient edifices had looked down on Revolutionary heroes, the old brick walls had echoed to the sound of fife and drum—the old streets had once been thronged by men in blue and buff. Since those days the quaint little city had basked in the pride of her traditions. She had tolerated nothing modern until within this very year she had waked to find that her red-coat enemy was now her friend, that the roads which George Washington had travelled were being trod once more by marching men; that in the church where he had worshipped prayers were being said once more for men in battle.

And into the shops, with their storied antiques, drifted now men in olive-drab and men in blue, and men in forester's green, who laughed at the flint locks and powder horns, saluted the Father of his Country whenever they passed his picture, gazed with reverence on ancient swords and uniforms, dickered for such small articles as might be bought out of their limited allowances, and paid in the end, cheerfully, prices which would have been scorned by any discriminating buyer.

"There must be a table for the Log-Fire Room," Jean told her husband, "and a fire-bench, not too high, and a big chair for you, and another chair for me—"

"And a stool for your little feet—."

"And a desk for you, Derry."

"And an oval mirror with a gold frame, for me to see your face in, Jean-Joan—"

Then there was a four-poster bed with pineapples, and an Adams screen, an old brass-bound chest, the most adorable things in Sheffield and crystal, and to crown it all, a picture of George Washington—a print, faintly colored, with the country's coat of arms carved on the frame.

Yet not one thing did they buy except a quite sumptuous and splendid marriage coffer which suggested itself at once as the only wedding present for Emily.

The price took Jean's breath away. "But, dearest—"

"Nothing is too good for Emily, Jean-Joan."

That night Derry drew a picture of the house in Jean's memory book.

"I'll put a garden in front—"

"How can you put in a garden, Derry, when there isn't one?"

She wore a lace robe and a lace cap, and there were pink ribbons threaded in, and her cheeks were pink. "You can't put in a garden until there is one, Derry. When we find it, it must be a lovesome garden, with the old-fashioned flowers, and a fountain with a cupid—and a fish-pond."

With this settled, he proceeded, with facile pen, to furnish the house. There was the Log-Fire Room, with the print of George Washington over the mantel, with Jean's knitting on the table; Muffin on one side of the fire, and Polly Ann on the other. He even started to put Jean in one of the big chairs, but she made him rub it out. "Not yet, Derry. You see, I am not living in it yet. I am living here, with you alive and loving—"

He caught her to him. "When you are away from me," she whispered, "I'll live in it—and you'll be there—and I shall never feel alone—"

Yet later, Derry coming in unexpectedly after a talk with his father, found her sobbing with her head on the fat old book. "My darling—"

"It isn't that I am unhappy, Derry—. It is just for that one little minute, I wanted it to be real—"

THE SEVENTH DAY

It was on the morning of the seventh day that a letter came from Drusilla.

"*Dear Babes in the Wood*:

"I am writing this to tell you that the next time I see Captain Hewes, I am going to marry him. That sounds a little like a hold-up, doesn't it? But it is the way we are doing things over here. He has wanted it for so long, and I am beginning to know that I want it, too. It has been hard to tell just what was really best in the face of all that is happening. It has seemed sometimes as if it were a sacrilege to think of love and life in the midst of death and destruction.

"I shan't have any trousseau; I shan't have a wedding journey. He will just blow in some day, and the chaplain will marry us, and the little old curé of this village will give us his blessing.

"I never expected to be married like this. You know the kind of mind I have. I must always see the picture of myself doing things, and there had always been a sort of dream of some great church with a blur of gold light at the far end, and myself floating up the aisle in a cloud of white veil, and a hushed crowd and the organ playing.

"And it won't be a bit like that. I shall wear a uniform and a flannel shirt, and I'll be lucky if my boots are not splashed with mud. It will seem queer to be married with my boots on, as men died in old romances.

"Perhaps by the time this reaches you, Drusilla Gray will be Drusilla Hewes, and so I ask your blessing, and your prayers.

"I should never have asked for your prayers a year ago. I should have been thanking you for your wedding present of glass and silver, and asking you to dine with me on Tuesday or Thursday as the case might be. But now, the only thought that holds me is whether God will give my Captain back to me, and the hope that if not, I may have the strength to bear it—.

"I am sure that Derry will feel the sublimity of it all when he comes—death is so near, yet so little feared; the men know that tonight or tomorrow they may be beyond the shadows, and it holds them to something bigger than themselves.

"But be sure of this, my dears, that when Derry goes the seas will not part you—. Spirit touches spirit, space has nothing to do with it. Often when I am alone, the Captain comes to me, speaks to me, cheers me; I think if he should die in battle, he would still come.

"If ever I have a home of my own, I shall build an altar not to the Unknown God but to the God whom I had lost and have found again. I go into old churches here to pray, and it is no longer a matter of feeling, no longer a matter of form, it is something more than that.

"And now I can't ask you to dance at my wedding, but I can ask you to wish me happiness and a long life with my lover, or failing that, the strength to give him up—"

She signed herself, "Always loving you both, DRUSILLA."

"Such a dear letter," said Jean.

"And such a different Drusilla. Do you think that the Drusilla of the old days would have built an altar?"

And it was because of Drusilla's letter that Derry took Jean that afternoon to the great Library with the gold dome and guided her to a corridor made beautiful by the brush of an artist who had painted "The Occupations of the Day"; in one lunette a primitive man and woman knelt before a pile of stones on which burned a sacred flame. Above them was blue sky—flowers grew within reach of their hands—the fields stretched beyond.

"We must build an altar, dearest."

"In our hearts—"

"And in our House of Dreams—"

THE EIGHTH DAY

There was no getting out of the Witherspoon dinner, and it was when Ralph greeted Jean that he said to her, "You are lovelier than ever."

She smiled at him. "It is because my heart is singing—"

"Do you feel like that?"

She nodded. "In three days the song will cease—the lights will go out, and the curtain will fall—the end of the world will come."

"Drake goes in three days?"

"He goes back to camp. I don't expect to see him again before he sails."

"Lucky fellow."

"To go?"

"To have you."

"Please don't."

"Let me say this—that I acted like a cad; I'd like to feel that you've forgiven me."

"I have forgotten, which is better, isn't it?"

"How sweet you are—and all the sweetness is Derry's. Well, when I go over, will you pray for me, my dear?"

He was in dead earnest. "There are so few women—who pray—but I rather fancy that you must—"

All around them was surging talk. "How strange it seems," Jean said, "that we should be speaking of such things, here—"

"No," Ralph said, "it is not strange. I have a feeling that I shan't come back."

Alma Drew on the other side of him claimed his attention. "War is the great sensational opportunity. And there are people who like patriotism of the sound-the-trumpet-beat-the-drum variety—"

"You said that rather cleverly, Alma," Ralph told her, "but you mustn't forget that was the kind of patriotism our forefathers had, and it seemed rather effective."

"Men aren't machines," Jean said hotly. "They are flesh and blood, and so are women—a fife and drum or a bag-pipe means more to them than just crude music; the blood of their ancestors thrilled to the sound."

"As savages thrill to a tom-tom."

They stared at her.

"It is all savage," Alma said, crisply and coolly, "We are all murderers. We are teaching our men to run Germans through with bayonets, and trying to make ourselves think that they aren't breaking the sixth commandment. Yet in times of peace, when a man kills he goes to the electric chair—"

It was Derry who answered that. "If in times of peace I heard you scream and saw you set upon by thieves and murderers, and stood with my hands in my pockets while you were tortured and killed, would you call my non-interference laudable?"

"That's different."

"It is the same thing. The only difference lies in the fact that thousands of defenceless women and little children are calling. Would you have the nation stand with its hands in its pockets?"

Alma, cold as ice, challenged him: "Why should they call to us? We'll be sorry some day that we went into it."

Out of a dead silence, a man said: "Not long ago, I went into a sweet shop in England. A woman came in with two children. They were rosy children and round. They carried muffs.

"She bought candy for them—and when she gave it to them, I saw that they had—no hands—"

A gasp went round the table.

"They were Belgian children."

That night Jean said to Derry with a sternness which set strangely upon her, "We must have friends in our House of Dreams. The latchstrings will always be out for people like Emily and Marion, and Drusilla, and Ulrich and Ralph—"

"Yes—"

"But not for Hilda and Alma."

THE NINTH DAY

It was on the ninth day that Derry waked his wife at dawn. "I've ordered the car. It rained in the night, and now—oh, there was never such a morning; there may never be such a morning for us again."

"What time is it, Derry?"

"Sunrise time—come and see."

Her window faced the east, and she saw all the pearl of it, and the faint rose and the amethyst and gold.

"We shall eat our breakfast ten miles from town," Derry said, as their car carried him out into the country, "and there's a lovesome garden—"

"With old-fashioned flowers and a fountain and a Cupid?"

"With all that—and more—"

The garden belonged to an old woman. For years and years she had planted flowers——tulips and hyacinths and poppies and lilies and gladiolus and larkspur and phlox and ladyslipper—there had always been a riot of color.

She had an old gardener, and she would stand over him, leaning on her silver-topped ebony cane, with a lace scarf covering her hair, and would point out the places to plant things.

But now in her garden she had strawberries and Swiss chard and sweet herbs, and rows and rows of peas and young onions and potatoes, with a place left for corn at the back, and tomatoes in every spare space.

And there was lettuce, and an asparagus bed, and everything on this May morning was shouting to the sun.

"I had always thought," said the old lady to Derry, when he presented Jean, "that a vegetable garden was uninteresting. But it is a little world—with class distinctions of its own, if you please. All the really useful vegetables we call common; it is the ones we can do without which are the aristocrats. The potatoes and cabbages and onions are really important, but I am proudest of my young peas and my peppers and cucumbers and tomatoes, and that's the way of the world, isn't it? If there was only an aristocracy things would stop, but the common folk could go on alone until the end of time."

She gave Jean a blue bowl to pick strawberries in; and Derry dug asparagus—the creamy shoots were tipped with pale purple and pink, deepening into green where they had stood too long in the sun.

"Aren't there any flowers?" Jean was anxious.

"Come and see." The old woman went ahead of them, her cane tap-tapping on the stone flags.

She opened a gate which was flanked by brick walls. "These," she said, whimsically, "are my jewels."

"THESE ARE MY JEWELS"

[Illustration: "These are my jewels."]

All the sweetness which had once spread over her domain was concentrated here, fragrance and flame—roses, iris, peonies—honeysuckle—ruby and emerald, amethyst and gold; a Cupid riding a swan, with water pouring from his quiver into a shallow marble basin.

"I should not have dared keep this, if it had not been for the other—" the old woman told them. "I am very sure that in these days God walks in vegetable gardens—"

For breakfast they had strawberries and radishes, thin little corn cakes—and two fresh eggs from the chickens which most triumphantly occupied the conservatory.

"This is the only way I can do my bit," the old lady explained, "by helping with the world's food supply. My eyes are bad and I cannot sew, my fingers are twisted and I cannot knit, and Dennis is old—but we plan the garden and plant—"

And that night Jean said to Derry, "I am glad there were flowers to make it lovesome—and I am glad there were vegetables to make it right."

So he drew a waving field of corn back of the dream cottage, and tomatoes and peas to the right and left—with onions in a stiff row along the border, and potatoes storming the hillside. But the gate which led to the Lovesome Garden was open wide, so that one might see the Cupid as he rode his swan.

THE LAST DAY

121

It was on the tenth day that Derry said, "We have our house and the furniture for it, and we have built an altar, and found our friends, and we have planted a garden—what shall we do on the last day?"

And Jean said, rather unexpectedly, "We will go to the circus."

"To the circus?"

"Yes. And take the children—they are dying to go, and Margaret can't. It is up to you and me, Derry."

Even Nurse was to stay behind. "We'll have them all to ourselves."

Derry was dubious, a little hurt. "It seems rather queer, doesn't it, on our last day?"

"I—I think I should like it better than anything else, Derry."

And so they went.

It was warm with a hint of showers in the air, and both of the children were in white. Jean was also in white. They rode in the General's limousine to where the big tent with all its flags flying covered a vast space.

"Cousin Derry, Mother said I might have some peanuts."

"All right, old man."

"And Margaret-Mary mustn't. But there are some crackers in a bag."

It was all most entrancing, the gilded wagons, the restless beasts behind their bars, the spotted ponies, the swaying elephants, the bands playing, the crowds streaming—.

Teddy held tight to Jean's hand. Margaret-Mary was carried high on Derry's shoulder. All of her curls were bobbing, and her eyes were shining. Now and then she dropped a light kiss on the silver blond hair of her cavalier.

"Tousin Dee," she murmured, affectionately.

"She's an adorable kiddie," Derry told Jean as they found their seats.

"Cousin Derry," Teddy reminded him, "don't forget the peanuts."

And now the trumpets blared and the drums boomed, and the great parade writhed like a glittering serpent around the huge circle, then broke up into various groups as the performance began in the rings.

After that one needed all of one's eyes. Teddy sat spellbound for a while, but found time at last to draw a long breath.

"Cousin Derry, that is the funniest clown—"

"The little one?"

"The big one; oh, well, the little one, too."

Silence again while the elephants did amazing things in one ring, with Japanese tumblers in another, with piebald ponies beyond, and things being done on trapezes everywhere.

Teddy slipped his hand into Derry's. "It's—it's almost like having Daddy," he confided. "I know he's glad I'm here."

Derry's big hand closed over the small one. "I'm glad, too, old chap."

Margaret-Mary having gazed her fill, slept comfortably in Jean's arms.

"Let me hold her," Derry said.

Jean shook her head. "I love to have her here."

She had taken off her hat, and as she bent above the child her hair made a halo of gold. In the midst of all the tawdriness she was a still and sacred figure—a Madonna with a child.

Teddy, when he reached home, told the General all about it.

"It was be-yeutiful—but Cousin Jean cwied—"

"Cried?"

"I saw a tear rwunning down her cheek, and it splashed on Margaret-Mary's nose—"

And that night Derry said, "My darling, what shall I draw in our book?"

"The thing that you want most to remember, Derry."

So he drew her all in white, bending over a child of dreams.

The next morning, she told him "Good-bye." They had come along to the Toy Shop for their farewell, so that there was only the old white elephant to see her tears, and the Lovely Dreams to be sorry for her.

Yet her head was held high at the very last, and she was not sorry for herself. "I am glad and proud to have you go, dearest. I am glad and proud—"

And after he had gone, she worked until lunch time on the bandages and wipes, and rode with the General in the afternoon, with her hand in his, knowing that it comforted him.

But very late that night, when every one else is the big house was fast asleep, she crept out into the hall in her lace robe and lace cap and pink slippers and stood beneath the picture of the painted lady. "He will come back," she said. "He must come back—and—oh, oh, Derry's mother in Heaven—you must tell me how to live—without him—."

CHAPTER XXIX
"AND, AFTER ALL, HE CAME TO THE WARS!"

A perfect day, with men lying dead by thousands on the battlefield; twilight, with a young moon; night and the stars— Drusilla's throat was dry with singing—there had been so many hurt, and she had found that it helped them to hear her, so when a moaning, groaning, cursing ambulance load stopped a moment, she sang; when walking wounded came through sagging with pain and dreadful weariness, she sang; and when night fell, and an engine was stalled, and she took in her own car a man who must be rushed to the first collecting station, she found herself still singing—. And this time it was "The Battle Hymn of the Republic."

The man propped up beside her murmured, "My Captain liked that—he used to sing it—"

"Yes?" She was listening with only half an ear. There were so many Captains.

"He was engaged to an American."

She listened now. "Your Captain—?"

"Captain Hewes."

She guided the car steadily. "Dawson Hewes?"

"Yes. Do you know him?"

"I—I am the girl he is going to marry—"

He froze into silence. She bent towards him. "What made you say—*was*—?"

"He's—gone West—"

"Dead?"

"Yes."

"When?" She still drove steadily through the dark.

"To-day."

She looked up at the stars. So—he would never come blowing in with the sweet spring winds.

"I'd rather have been—shot—than to have told you that—" the man beside her was saying, "but, you see, I didn't know you were the girl—"

"Of course you couldn't. You mustn't blame yourself."

She delivered her precious charge at the hospital and put up her car for the night. Standing alone under the stars she wondered what she should do next. There was no one to tell—the women who had worked with her in the town which had since been recaptured by the Germans had gone to other towns. But she had stayed as near the front as possible, and she had never felt lonely because at any moment her lover might come—there had always been the thought that he might come—.

And now he would never come!

She had a room in the house of an old woman, all of whose sons were in the war. So far two of them had escaped death. But the old woman said often, fatalistically, "They will not always escape—but it will be for France."

The old woman had soup on the fire for Drusilla's supper. The room was faintly lighted. "What is it?" she asked, as the girl dropped down on the doorstep.

"My Captain is dead—"

The old woman rose and stood over her. "It comes to all."

"I know."

"Will you eat your soup? When the heart fails, the body must have strength."

Drusilla covered her face with her bands. The room was very still. The old woman went back to her chair by the fire and waited. At last she rose and filled a small bowl with the soup—she broke into it a small allowance of bread. Then she came and sat on the step beside the girl.

"Eat, Mademoiselle," she said, with something like authority, and Drusilla obeyed. And when she gave back the bowl, the old woman set it on the floor, and drew the girl's head to her breast.

And Drusilla lay there, crying softly, a lonely American mothered by this indomitable old woman of France.

Days passed, days in which men came and men went and Drusilla sang to them. And now new faces were seen among the tired and war-worn ones. Eager young Americans, pressing forward towards the front, found a countrywoman in the little town; and they wrote home about her. "She's a beauty, by jinks, and when she sings it pulls the heart out of you. She's the kind you want to say your prayers to."

So her fame went forth and took on gradually something of the supernatural—her tall, straight slenderness, her steady eyes, her halo of red hair grew to have a sort of sacred significance, like that of some militant young saint.

Then came a day when Derry's regiment marched through the town to the trenches, spent an interval, and came back, awed by what it had seen, but undaunted.

Drusilla, sitting on the doorstep of the stone house, saw a tall figure striding down the street. He stopped to speak to an old woman and doffed his hat, showing a clipped silver-blond head.

Drusilla went flying through the dusk. "Derry, Derry!"

He stared and stared again. "Is it you?" he asked. Nothing was vivid now about Drusilla except her hair.

"Yes."

He took her hands in his. "My dear girl." It was hard for either of them to speak.

"Did Bruce McKenzie tell you that my Captain has—gone West?"

"I had a letter. I haven't seen him. His hospital isn't far from here, I understand."

"Just outside. He—he has been a great help—to me, Derry."

She took him back to her doorstep and they sat down.

"Tell me about Jean."

He tried to tell her, wavered a little and spoke the truth. "The hardest thing was leaving her. I don't mind the fighting. I don't mind anything but the fact that she's over there and I'm over here. But it had to be—of course."

"Yes, everything had to be, Derry. I am believing that more and more. When my Captain went—I found how much I cared. I hadn't always been sure. But I am sure now, and I am sure, too, that he knows—"

"Love—in these times, Derry—isn't building a nest—and singing songs in the tree tops on a May morning; it goes beyond just the man and the woman; it even goes beyond the child. It goes as far as the future of mankind. What the future of the world will be depends not so much on how much you love Jean or she loves you, or on how much I loved and was loved, but on how much that love will mean to the world. If we can't give up our own for the sake of the world's ideal then love hasn't meant what it should to you and to me, Derry—"

She rose as a group of men approached. "They want me to sing for them. You won't mind?"

"My dear girl, I have heard of you everywhere. I believe that some of the fellows say their prayers to you at night—"

She stood up and sang. Her hair caught the light from the room back of her. She gave them a popular air or two, a hymn, "The Marseillaise—"

He missed nothing in her then. In spite of her paleness, the old fire was there, the passion of patriotism—there was, too, a new note of triumphant faith.

She needed no candles now, no red and white and blue for a background—she did not even need her beauty, her voice was enough—

When she sat down and the men had gone she said to Derry, "Do you remember when I last sang the 'Marseillaise' for you?"

"Yes."

He brought out from his pocket a tiny object and set it on the step, so that the light from the open door shone on it.

"You gave it to me, Drusilla."

"Oh, my little tin soldier."

"And after all, he came to the wars—"

Very proudly the little soldier shouldered his musket.

He had indeed come to the wars, and the winds of France blew upon him, the stars of France were over his head, the soil of France was beneath his feet.

Trutter-a-trutt, trutter-a-trutt—blew all the bugles of France, and the little tin soldier was at last content!

Derry had, too, in his pocket a letter from Jean; he read to Drusilla the part that belonged to her.

"Tell Drusilla that there's a chair in our dream house for her. I often shut my eyes and see her in it, and I see Daddy and you, Derry, all home safe from the war and the world at peace—"

"Safe and at home and the world at peace—. Will the time ever come, Derry?"

"You know it will come. It must—"

It was three days later that Dr. McKenzie motored over for a late supper with Drusilla and Derry. They were served by the old woman who had mothered the lonely girl.

"To think," the Doctor said, as they sat at their frugal board, "to think that we three should be here in the midst of all this; and yet a year ago I was wondering what to do with the rest of my life, Drusilla was running around telling people what kind of pictures to put on their walls, and what kind of draperies to put at their windows, and Derry was trying to pretend that he was not an elegant idler; and now—we are seeing a world made over—"

"You are seeing the world of men made over," said Drusilla, "but the most wonderful thing is seeing the women made over."

"I don't want to see the women made over," the Doctor groaned. "They are nice enough as it is. I want my little Jean gay and smiling—and Derry tells me that she is a nun in a white veil."

"She is more than that," Derry said, and a great light came into his eyes. "I sometimes feel that she and Drusilla are holding hands across the sea—two brave women in different spheres."

Drusilla, wise Drusilla pondered. "Perhaps the war will teach men like Bruce that women aren't playthings—"

"Don't be too hard on me, Drusilla."

"I am not hard. I am telling the truth."

"I'll forgive you, because in these weeks you've taught me a lot—" Bruce McKenzie's world would not have recognized in this tired and serious gentleman its twinkling, teasing man of medicine. Weary feet on the stones—

"I must go to them," Drusilla said.

She went out on the step. They saw the men cluster about her—French and English, Scotch—a few Americans.

Her voice soared:

"In the beauty of the lilies, Christ was born across the sea,
With the glory in his bosom which transfigures you and me.
As he died to make men holy, let us die to make men free—
While God is marching on—"

"Look," said the Doctor. "Do you see their faces, Derry?"

Gazing up at her as if they drank her in, the men listened. She was the daughter of a nation of dreamers, the daughter of a nation *which made its dreams come true*.

Tired and spent, they saw in her hope personified. They saw America coming fresh and unworn to fight a winning battle to the end. So they turned their faces towards Drusilla. She was more to them than a singing woman. Behind her stood a steadfast people—and God was marching on.

125

Contrary Mary

In Which Silken Ladies Ascend One Stairway, and a Lonely Wayfarer Ascends Another and Comes Face to Face With Old Friends.

The big house, standing on a high hill which overlooked the city, showed in the moonlight the grotesque outlines of a composite architecture. Originally it had been a square substantial edifice of Colonial simplicity. A later and less restrained taste had aimed at a castellated effect, and certain peaks and turrets had been added. Three of these turrets were excrescences stuck on, evidently, with an idea of adornment. The fourth tower, however, rounded out and enlarged a room on the third floor. This room was one of a suite, and the rooms were known as the Tower Rooms, and were held by those who had occupied them to be the most desirable in the barn-like building.

To-night the house had taken on an unwonted aspect of festivity. Its spaciousness was checkered by golden-lighted windows. Delivery wagons and automobiles came and went, some discharging loads of deliciousness at the back door, others discharging loads of loveliness at the front.

Following in the wake of one of the front door loads of fluttering femininity came a somewhat somber pedestrian. His steps lagged a little, so that when the big door opened, he was still at the foot of the terrace which led up to it. He waited until the door was shut before he again advanced. In the glimpse that he thus had of the interior, he was aware of a sort of pink effulgence, and in that shining light, lapped by it, and borne up, as it were, by it toward the wide stairway, he saw slender girls in faint-hued frocks—a shimmering celestial company.

As he reached the top of the terrace the door again flew open, and he gave a somewhat hesitating reason for his intrusion.

"I was told to ask for Miss Ballard—Miss Mary Ballard."

It seemed that he was expected, and that the guardian of the doorway understood the difference between his business and that of the celestial beings who had preceded him.

He was shown into a small room at the left of the entrance. It was somewhat bare, with a few law books and a big old-fashioned desk. He judged that the room might have been put to office uses, but to-night the desk was heaped with open boxes, and odd pieces of furniture were crowded together, so that there was left only a small oasis of cleared space. On the one chair in this oasis, the somber gentleman seated himself.

He had a fancy, as he sat there waiting, that neither he nor this room were in accord with the things that were going on in the big house. Outside of the closed door the radiant guests were still ascending the stairway on shining wings of light. He could hear the music of their laughter, and the deeper note of men's voices, rising and growing fainter in a sort of transcendent harmony.

When the door was finally opened, it was done quickly and was shut quickly, and the girl who had entered laughed breathlessly as she turned to him.

"Oh, you must forgive me—I've kept you waiting?"

If their meeting had been in Sherwood forest, he would have known her at once for a good comrade; if he had met her in the Garden of Biaucaire, he would have known her at once for more than that. But, being neither a hero of ballad nor of old romance, he knew only that here was a girl different from the silken ladies who had ascended the stairs. Here was an air almost of frank boyishness, a smile of pleasant friendliness, with just enough of flushing cheek to show womanliness and warm blood.

Even her dress was different. It was simple almost to the point of plainness. Its charm lay in its glimmering glistening sheen, like the inside of a shell. Its draperies were caught up to show slender feet in low-heeled slippers. A quaint cap of silver tissue held closely the waves of thick fair hair. Her eyes were like the sea in a storm—deep gray with a glint of green.

These things did not come to him at once. He was to observe them as she made her explanation, and as he followed her to the Tower Rooms. But first he had to set himself straight with her, so he said: "I was sorry to interrupt you. But you said—seven?"

"Yes. It was the only time that the rooms could be seen. My sister and I occupy them—and Constance is to be married—to-night."

This, then, was the reason for the effulgence and the silken ladies. It was the reason, too, for the loveliness of her dress.

"I am going to take you this way." She preceded him through a narrow passage to a flight of steps leading up into the darkness. "These stairs are not often used, but we shall escape the crowds in the other hall."

Her voice was lost as she made an abrupt turn, but, feeling his way, he followed her.

Up and up until they came to a third-floor landing, where she stopped him to say, "I must be sure no one is here. Will you wait until I see?"

She came back, presently, to announce that the coast was clear, and thus they entered the room which had been enlarged and rounded out by the fourth tower.

It was a big room, ceiled and finished in dark oak, The furniture was roomy and comfortable and of worn red leather. A strong square table held a copper lamp with a low spreading shade. There was a fireplace, and on the mantel above it a bust or two.

But it was not these things which at once caught the attention of Roger Poole.

Lining the walls were old books in stout binding, new books in cloth and fine leather—the poets, the philosophers, the seers of all ages. As his eyes swept the shelves, he knew that here was the living, breathing collection of a true book-lover—not a musty, fusty aggregation brought together through mere pride of intellect. The owner of this library had counted the heart-beats of the world.

"This is the sitting-room," his guide was telling him, "and the bedroom and bath open out from it." She had opened a connecting door. "This room is awfully torn up. But we have just finished dressing Constance. She is down-stairs now in the Sanctum. We'll pack her trunks to-morrow and send them, and then if you should care to take the rooms, we can put back the bedroom furniture that father had. He used this suite, and brought his books up after mother died."

He halted on the threshold of that inner room. If the old house below had seemed filled with rosy effulgence, this was the heart of the rose. Two small white beds were side by side in an alcove. Their covers were of pink overlaid with lace, and the chintz of the big couch and chairs reflected the same enchanting hue. With all the color, however, there was the freshness of simplicity. Two tall glass candlesticks on the dressing table, a few photographs in silver and ivory frames—these were the only ornaments.

Yet everywhere was lovely confusion—delicate things were thrown half-way into open trunks, filmy fabrics floated from unexpected places, small slippers were held by receptacles never designed for shoes, radiant hats bloomed in boxes.

On a chair lay a bridesmaid's bunch of roses. This bunch Mary Ballard picked up as she passed, and it was over the top of it that she asked, with some diffidence, "Do you think you'd care to take the rooms?"

Did he? Did the Peri outside the gates yearn to enter? Here within his reach was that from which he had been cut off for five years. Five years in boarding-houses and cheap hotels, and now the chance to live again—as he had once lived!

"I do want them—awfully—but the price named in your letter seems ridiculously small——"

"But you see it is all I shall need," she was as blissfully unbusinesslike as he. "I want to add a certain amount to my income, so I ask you to pay that," she smiled, and with increasing diffidence demanded, "Could you make up your mind—now? It is important that I should know—to-night."

She saw the question in his eyes and answered it, "You see—my family have no idea that I am doing this. If they knew, they wouldn't want me to rent the rooms—but the house is mine——I shall do as I please."

She seemed to fling it at him, defiantly.

"And you want me to be accessory to your—crime."

She gave him a startled glance. "Oh, do you look at it—that way? Please don't. Not if you like them."

For a moment, only, he wavered. There was something distinctly unusual in acquiring a vine and fig tree in this fashion. But then her advertisement had been unusual—it was that which had attracted him, and had piqued his interest so that he had answered it.

And the books! As he looked back into the big room, the rows of volumes seemed to smile at him with the faces of old friends.

Lonely, longing for a haven after the storms which had beaten him, what better could he find than this?

As for the family of Mary Ballard, what had he to do with it? His business was with Mary Ballard herself, with her frank laugh and her friendliness—and her arms full of roses!

"I like them so much that I shall consider myself most fortunate to get them."

"Oh, really?" She hesitated and held out her hand to him. "You don't know how you have helped me out—you don't know how you have helped me——"

Again she saw a question in his eyes, but this time she did not answer it. She turned and went into the other room, drawing back the curtains of the deep windows of the round tower.

"I haven't shown you the best of all," she said. Beneath them lay the lovely city, starred with its golden lights. From east to west the shadowy dimness of the Mall, beyond the shadows, a line of river, silver under the moonlight. A clock tower or two showed yellow faces; the great public buildings were clear-cut like cardboard.

Roger drew a deep breath. "If there were nothing else," he said, "I should take the rooms for this."

And now from the lower hall came the clamor of voices.

127

"*Mary! Mary!*"

"I must not keep you," he said at once.

"*Mary!*"

Poised for flight, she asked, "Can you find your way down alone? I'll go by the front stairs and head them off."

"*Mary——!*"

With a last flashing glance she was gone, and as he groped his way down through the darkness, it came to him as an amazing revelation that she had taken his coming as a thing to be thankful for, and it had been so many years since a door had been flung wide to welcome him.

CHAPTER II

In Which Rose-Leaves and Old Slippers Speed a Happy Pair; and in Which Sweet and Twenty Speaks a New and Modern Language, and Gives a Reason for Renting a Gentleman's Library.

In spite of the fact that Mary Ballard had seemed to Roger Poole like a white-winged angel, she was not looked upon by the family as a beauty. It was Constance who was the "pretty one," and tonight as she stood in her bridal robes, gazing up at her sister who was descending the stairs, she was more than pretty. Her tender face was illumined by an inner radiance. She was two years older than Mary, but more slender, and her coloring was more strongly emphasized. Her eyes were blue and her hair was gold, as against the gray-green and dull fairness of Mary's hair. She seemed surrounded, too, by a sort of feminine *aura*, so that one knew at a glance that here was a woman who would love her home, her husband, her children; who would lean upon masculine protection, and suffer from masculine neglect.

Of Mary Ballard these things could not be said at once. In spite of her simplicity and frankness, there was about her a baffling atmosphere. She was like a still pool with the depths as yet unsounded, an uncharted sea—with its mystery of undiscovered countries.

The contrast between the sisters had never been more marked than when Mary, leaning over the stair-rail, answered the breathless, "Dearest, where have you been?" with her calm:

"There's plenty of time, Constance."

And Constance, soothed as always by her sister's tranquillity, repeated Mary's words for the benefit of a ponderously anxious Personage in amber satin.

"There's plenty of time, Aunt Frances."

That Aunt Frances *was* a Personage was made apparent by certain exterior evidences. One knew it by the set of her fine shoulders, the carriage of her head, by the diamond-studded lorgnette, by the string of pearls about her neck, by the osprey in her white hair, by the golden buckles on her shoes.

"It is five minutes to eight," said Aunt Frances, "and Gordon is waiting down-stairs with his best man, the chorus is freezing on the side porch, and *everybody* has arrived. I don't see *why* you are waiting——"

"We are waiting for it to be eight o'clock, Aunt Frances," said Mary. "At just eight, I start down in front of Constance, and if you don't hurry you and Aunt Isabelle won't be there ahead of me."

The amber train slipped and glimmered down the polished steps, and the golden buckles gleamed as Mrs. Clendenning, panting a little and with a sense of outrage that her nervous anxiety of the preceding moment had been for naught, made her way to the drawing-room, where the guests were assembled.

Aunt Isabelle followed, gently smiling. Aunt Isabelle was to Aunt Frances as moonlight unto sunlight. Aunt Frances was married, Aunt Isabelle was single; Aunt Frances wore amber, Aunt Isabelle silver gray; Aunt Frances held up her head like a queen, Aunt Isabelle dropped hers deprecatingly; Aunt Frances' quick ears caught the whispers of admiration that followed her, Aunt Isabelle's ears were closed forever to all the music of the universe.

No sooner had the two aunts taken their places to the left of a floral bower than there was heard without the chanted wedding chorus, from a side door stepped the clergyman and the bridegroom and his best man; then from the hall came the little procession with Mary in the lead and Constance leaning on the arm of her brother Barry.

They were much alike, this brother and sister. More alike than Mary and Constance. Barry had the same gold in his hair, and blue in his eyes, and, while one dared not hint it, in the face of his broad-shouldered strength, there was an almost feminine charm in the grace of his manner and the languor of his movements.

There were no bridesmaids, except Mary, but four pretty girls held the broad white ribbons which marked an aisle down the length of the rooms. These girls wore pink with close caps of old lace. Only one of them had dark hair, and it was the dark-haired one, who, standing very still throughout the ceremony, with the ribbon caught up to her in lustrous festoons, never took her eyes from Barry Ballard's face.

And when, after the ceremony, the bride turned to greet her friends, the dark-haired girl moved forward to where Barry stood, a little apart from the wedding group.

"Doesn't it seem strange?" she said to him with quick-drawn breath.

He smiled down at her. "What?"

"That a few words should make such a difference?"

"Yes. A minute ago she belonged to us. Now she's Gordon's."

"And he's taking her to England?"

"Yes. But not for long. When he gets the branch office started over there, they'll come back, and he'll take his father's place in the business here, and let the old man retire."

She was not listening. "Barry," she interrupted, "what will Mary do? She can't live here alone—and she'll miss Constance."

"Oh, Aunt Frances has fixed that," easily; "she wants Mary to shut up the house and spend the winter in Nice with herself and Grace—it's a great chance for Mary."

"But what about you, Barry?"

"Me?" He shrugged his shoulders and again smiled down at her. "I'll find quarters somewhere, and when I get too lonesome, I'll come over and talk to you, Leila."

The rich color flooded her cheeks. "Do come," she said, again with quick-drawn breath, then like a child who has secured its coveted sugar-plum, she slipped through the crowd, and down into the dining-room, where she found Mary taking a last survey.

"Hasn't Aunt Frances done things beautifully?" Mary asked; "she insisted on it, Leila. We could never have afforded the orchids and the roses; and the ices are charming—pink hearts with cupids shooting at them with silver arrows——"

"Oh, Mary," the dark-haired girl laid her flushed cheek against the arm of her taller friend. "I think weddings are wonderful."

Mary shook her head. "I don't," she said after a moment's silence. "I think they're horrid. I like Gordon Richardson well enough, except when I think that he is stealing Constance, and then I hate him."

But the bride was coming down, with all the murmuring voices behind her, and now the silken ladies were descending the stairs to the dining-room, which took up the whole lower west wing of the house and opened out upon an old-fashioned garden, which to-night, under a chill October moon, showed its rows of box and of formal cedars like sharp shadows against the whiteness.

Into this garden came, later, Mary. And behind her Susan Jenks.

Susan Jenks was a little woman with gray hair and a coffee-colored skin. Being neither black nor white, she partook somewhat of the nature of both races. Back of her African gentleness was an almost Yankee shrewdness, and the firm will which now and then degenerated into obstinacy.

"There ain't no luck in a wedding without rice, Miss Mary. These paper rose-leaf things that you've got in the bags are mighty pretty, but how are you going to know that they bring good luck?"

"Aunt Frances thought they would be charming and foreign, Susan, and they look very real, floating off in the air. You must stand there on the upper porch, and give the little bags to the guests."

Susan ascended the terrace steps complainingly. "You go right in out of the night, Miss Mary," she called back, "an' you with nothin' on your bare neck!"

Mary, turning, came face to face with Gordon's best man, Porter Bigelow.

"Mary," he said, impetuously, "I've been looking for you everywhere. I couldn't keep my eyes off you during the service—you were—heavenly."

"I'm not a bit angelic, Porter," she told him, "and I'm simply freezing out here. I had to show Susan about the confetti."

He drew her in and shut the door. "They sent me to hunt for you," he said. "Constance wants you. She's going up-stairs to change. But I heard just now that you are going to Nice. Leila told me. Mary—you can't go—not so far away—from me." His hand was on her arm.

She shook it off with a little laugh.

"You haven't a thing to do with it, Porter. And I'm not going—to Nice."

"But Leila said——"

Her head went up. It was a characteristic gesture. "It doesn't make any difference what *any one* says. I'm not going to Nice."

Once more in the Tower Rooms, the two sisters were together for the last time. Leila was sent down on a hastily contrived errand. Aunt Frances, arriving, was urged to go back and look after the guests. Only Aunt Isabelle was allowed to remain. She could be of use, and the things which were to be said she could not hear.

"Dearest," Constance's voice had a break in it, "dearest, I feel so selfish—leaving you——"

Mary was kneeling on the floor, unfastening hooks. "Don't worry, Con. I'll get along."

"But you'll have to bear—things—all alone. It isn't as if any one knew, and you could talk it out."

"I'd rather die than speak of it," fiercely, "and I sha'n't write anything to you about it, for Gordon will read your letters."

"Oh, Mary, he won't."

"Oh, yes, he will, and you'll want him to—you'll want to turn your heart inside out for him to read, to say nothing of your letters."

She stood up and put both of her hands on her sister's shoulders. "But you mustn't tell him, Con. No matter how much you want to, it's my secret and Barry's—promise me, Con——"

"But, Mary, a wife can't."

"Yes, she *can* have secrets from her husband. And this belongs to us, not to him. You've married him, Con, but we haven't."

Aunt Isabelle, gentle Aunt Isabelle, shut off from the world of sound, could not hear Con's little cry of protest, but she looked up just in time to see the shimmering dress drop to the floor, and to see the bride, sheathed like a lily in whiteness, bury her head on Mary's shoulder.

Aunt Isabelle stumbled forward. "My dear," she asked, in her thin troubled voice, "what makes you cry?"

"It's nothing, Aunt Isabelle." Mary's tone was not loud, but Aunt Isabelle heard and nodded.

"She's dead tired, poor dear, and wrought up. I'll run and get the aromatic spirits."

With Aunt Isabella out of the way, Mary set herself to repair the damage she had done. "I've made you cry on your wedding day, Con, and I wanted you to be so happy. Oh, tell Gordon, if you must. But you'll find that he won't look at it as you and I have looked at it. He won't make the excuses."

"Oh, yes he will." Constance's happiness seemed to come back to her suddenly in a flood of assurance. "He's the best man in the world, Mary, and so kind. It's because you don't know him that you think as you do."

Mary could not quench the trust in the blue eyes. "Of course he's good," she said, "and you are going to be the happiest ever, Constance."

Then Aunt Isabelle came back and found that the need for the aromatic spirits was over, and together the loving hands hurried Constance into her going away gown of dull blue and silver, with its sable trimmed wrap and hat.

"If it hadn't been for Aunt Frances, how could I have faced Gordon's friends in London?" said Constance. "Am I all right now, Mary?"

"Lovely, Con, dear."

But it was Aunt Isabelle's hushed voice which gave the appropriate phrase. "She looks like a bluebird—for happiness."

At the foot of the stairway Gordon was waiting for his bride—handsome and prosperous as a bridegroom should be, with a dark sleek head and eager eyes, and beside him Porter Bigelow, topping him by a head, and a red head at that.

As Mary followed Constance, Porter tucked her hand under his arm.

"Oh, Mary, Mary, quite contrary,
Your eyes they are so bright,
That the stars grow pale, as they tell the tale
To the other stars at night,"

he improvised under his breath. "Oh, Mary Ballard, do you know that I am holding on to myself with all my might to keep from shouting to the crowd, 'Mary isn't going away. Mary isn't going away.'"

"Silly——"

"You say that, but you don't mean it. Mary, you can't be hard-hearted on such a night as this. Say that I may stay for five minutes—ten—after the others have gone——"

They were out on the porch now, and he had folded about her the wrap which she had brought down with her. "Of course you may stay," she said, "but much good may it do you. Aunt Frances is staying and General Dick—there's to be a family conclave in the Sanctum—but if you want to listen you may."

And how the rose-leaves began to flutter! Susan Jenks had handed out the bags, and secretly, and with much elation had leaned over the rail as Constance passed down the steps, and had emptied her own little offering of rice in the middle of the bride's blue hat!

It was Barry, aided and abetted by Leila, who brought out the old slippers. There were Constance's dancing slippers, high-heeled and of delicate hues, Mary's more individual low-heeled ones, Barry's outworn pumps, decorated hurriedly by Leila for the occasion with lovers' knots of tissue paper.

And it was just as the bride waved "Good-bye" from Gordon's limousine that a new slipper followed the old ones, for Leila, carried away by the excitement, and having at the moment no other missile at hand, reached down, and plucking off one of her own pink sandals, hurled it with all her might at the moving car. It landed on top, and Leila, with a gasp, realized that it was gone forever.

"It serves you right." Looking up, she met Barry's laughing eyes.

She sank down on the step. "And they were a new pair!"

"Lucky that it's your birthday next week," he said. "Do you want pink ones?'"

"*Barry!*"

Her delight was overwhelming. "Heavens, child," he condoned her, "don't look as if I were the grand Mogul. Do you know I sometimes think you are eight instead of eighteen? And now, if you'll take my arm, you can hippity-hop into the house. And I hope that you'll remember this, that if I give you pink slippers you are not to throw them away."

In the hall they met Leila's father—General Wilfred Dick. The General had married, in late bachelorhood, a young wife. Leila was like her mother in her dark sparkling beauty and demure sweetness. But she showed at times the spirit of her father—the spirit which had carried the General gallantly through the Civil War, and had led him after the war to make a success of the practice of law. He had been for years the intimate friend and adviser of the Ballards, and it was at Mary's request that he was to stay to share in the coming conclave.

He told Leila this. "You'll have to wait, too," he said. "And now, why are you hopping on one foot in that absurd fashion?"

"Dad, dear, I lost my shoe——"

"Her very best pink one," Barry explained; "she threw it after the bride, and now I've got to give her another pair for her birthday."

The General's old eyes brightened as he surveyed the young pair. This was as it should be, the son of his old friend and the daughter of his heart.

He tried to look stern, however. "Haven't I always kept you supplied with pink shoes and blue shoes and all the colors of the rainbow shoes!" he demanded. "And why should you tax Barry?"

"But, Dad, he wants to." She looked eagerly at Barry for confirmation. "He wants to give them to me—for my birthday———"

"Of course I do," said Barry, lightly. "If I didn't give her slippers, I should have to give her something else—and far be it from me to know what—little—lovely—Leila—wants——"

And to the tune of his chant, they hippity-hopped together up the stairs in a hunt for some stray shoe that should fit little-lovely-Leila's foot!

A little later, the silken ladies having descended the stairway for the last time, Aunt Frances took her amber satin stateliness to the Sanctum.

Behind her, a silver shadow, came Aunt Isabelle, and bringing up the rear, General Dick, and the four young people; Leila in a pair of mismated slippers, hippity-hopping behind with Barry, and Porter assuring Mary that he knew he "hadn't any business to butt in to a family party," but that he was coming anyhow.

The Sanctum was the front room on the second floor. It had been the Little Mother's room in the days when she was still with them, and now it had been turned into a retreat where the young people drifted when they wanted quiet, or where they met for consultation and advice. Except that the walnut bed and bureau had been taken out nothing had been changed, and their mother's books were still in the low bookcases; religious books, many of them, reflecting the gentle faith of the owner. On mantel and table and walls were photographs of her children in long clothes and short, and then once more in long ones; there was Barry in wide collars and knickerbockers, and Constance and Mary in ermine caps and capes; there was Barry again in the military uniform of his preparatory school; Constance in her graduation frock, and Mary with her hair up for the first time. There was a picture of their father on porcelain in a blue velvet case, and another picture of him above the mantel in an oval frame, with one of the Little Mother's, also in an oval frame, to flank it. In the fairness of the Little Mother one traced the fairness of Barry and Constance. But the fairness and features of the father were Mary's.

Mary had never looked more like her father than now when, sitting under his picture, she stated her case. What she had to say she said simply. But when she had finished there was the silence of astonishment.

In a day, almost in an hour, little Mary had grown up! With Constance as the nominal head of the household, none of them had realized that it was Mary's mind which had worked out the problems of making ends meet, and that it was Mary's strength and industry which had supplemented Susan's waning efforts in the care of the big house.

131

"I want to keep the house," Mary repeated. "I had to talk it over to-night, Aunt Frances, because you go back to New York in the morning, and I couldn't speak of it before to-night because I was afraid that some hint of my plan would get to Constance and she would be troubled. She'll learn it later, but I didn't want her to have it on her mind now. I want to stay here. I've always lived here, and so has Barry—and while I appreciate your plans for me to go to Nice, I don't think it would be fair or right for me to leave Barry."

Barry, a little embarrassed to be brought into it, said, "Oh, you needn't mind about me——"

"But I do mind." Mary had risen and was speaking earnestly. "I am sure you must see it, Aunt Frances. If I went with you, Barry would be left to—drift—and I shouldn't like to think of that. Mother wouldn't have liked it, or father." Her voice touched an almost shrill note of protest.

Porter Bigelow, sitting unobtrusively in the background, was moved by her earnestness. "There's something back of it," his quick mind told him; "she knows about—Barry——"

But Barry, too, was on his feet. "Oh, look here, Mary," he was expostulating, "I'm not going to have you stay at home and miss a winter of good times, just because I'll have to eat a few meals in a boarding-house. And I sha'n't have to eat many. When I get starved for home cooking, I'll hunt up my friends. You'll take me in now and then, for Sunday dinner, won't you, General?—Leila says you will; and it isn't as if you were never coming back—Mary."

"If we close the house now," Mary said, "it will mean that it won't be opened again. You all know that." Her accusing glance rested on Aunt Frances and the General. "You all think it ought to be sold, but if we sell what will become of Susan Jenks, who nursed us and who nursed mother, and what shall we do with all the dear old things that were mother's and father's, and who will live in the dear old rooms?" She was struggling for composure. "Oh, don't you see that I—I can't go?"

It was Aunt Frances' crisp voice which brought her back to calmness. "But, my dear, you can't afford to keep it open. Your income with what Barry earns isn't any more than enough to pay your running expenses; there's nothing left for taxes or improvements. I'm perfectly willing to finance you to the best of my ability, but I think it very foolish to sink any more money—here——"

"I don't want you to sink it, Aunt Frances. Constance begged me to use her little part of our income, but I wouldn't. We sha'n't need it. I've fixed things so that we shall have money for the taxes. I—I have rented the Tower Rooms, Aunt Frances!"

They stared at her stunned. Even Leila tore her adoring eyes from Barry's face, and fixed them on the girl who made this astounding statement.

"Mary," Aunt Frances gasped, "do you meant that you are going to take—lodgers——?"

"Only one, Aunt Frances. And he's perfectly respectable. I advertised and he answered, and he gave me a bank reference."

"*He*. Mary, is it a man?"

Mary nodded. "Of course. I should hate to have a woman fussing around. And I set the rent for the suite at exactly the amount I shall need to take me through this year, and he was satisfied."

She turned and picked up a printed slip from the table.

"This is the way I wrote my ad," she said, "and I had twenty-seven answers. And this seemed the best——"

"Twenty-seven!" Aunt Frances held out her hand. "Will you let me see what you wrote to get such remarkable results?"

Mary handed it to her, and through the diamond-studded lorgnette Aunt Frances read:

"To let: Suite of two rooms and bath; with Gentleman's Library. House on top of a high hill which overlooks the city. Exceptional advantages for a student or scholar."

"I consider," said Mary, as Aunt Frances paused, "that the Gentleman's Library part was an inspiration. It was the bait at which they all nibbled."

The General chuckled, "She'll do. Let her have her own way, Frances. She's got a head on her like a man's."

Aunt Frances turned on him. "Mary speaks what is to me a rather new language of independence. And she can't stay here alone. She *can't*. It isn't proper—without an older woman in the house."

"But I want an older woman. Oh, Aunt Frances, please, may I have Aunt Isabelle?"

She had raised her voice so that Aunt Isabelle caught the name. "What does she want, Frances?" asked the deaf woman; "what does she want?"

"She wants you to live with her—here." Aunt Frances was thinking rapidly; it wasn't such a bad plan. It was always a problem to take Isabelle when she and her daughter traveled. And if they left her in New York there was always the haunting fear that she might be ill, or that they might be criticized for leaving her.

"Mary wants you to live with her," she said, "While we are abroad, would you like it—a winter in Washington?"

Aunt Isabelle's gentle face was illumined. "Do you really *want* me, my dear?" she asked in her hushed voice. It had been a long time since Aunt Isabelle had felt that she was wanted anywhere. It seemed to her that since the illness which had sent her into a world of silence, that her presence had been endured, not coveted.

Mary came over and put her arms about her. "Will you, Aunt Isabelle?" she asked. "I shall miss Constance so, and it would almost be like having mother to have—you——"

No one knew how madly the hungry heart was beating under the silver-gray gown. Aunt Isabella was only forty-eight, twelve years younger than her sister Frances, but she had faded and drooped, while Frances had stood up like a strong flower on its stem. And the little faded drooping lady yearned for tenderness, was starved for it, and here was Mary in her youth and beauty, promising it.

"I want you so much, and Barry wants you—and Susan Jenks——"

She was laughing tremulously, and Aunt Isabelle laughed too, holding on to herself, so that she might not show in face or gesture the wildness of her joy.

"You won't mind, will you, Frances?" she asked.

Aunt Frances rose and shook out her amber skirts "I shall of course be much disappointed," she pitched her voice high and spoke with chill stateliness, "I shall be very much disappointed that neither you nor Mary will be with us for the winter. And I shall have to cross alone. But Grace can meet me in London. She's going there to see Constance, and I shall stay for a while and start the young people socially. I should think you'd want to see Constance, Mary."

Mary drew a quick breath. "I do want to see her—but I have to think about Barry—and for this winter, at least, my place—is here."

Then from the back of the room spoke Porter Bigelow.

"What's the name of your lodger?"

"Roger Poole."

"There are Pooles in Gramercy Park," said Aunt Frances. "I wonder if he's one of them."

Mary shook her head. "He's from the South."

"I should think," said Porter, slowly, "that you'd want to know something of him besides his bank reference before you took him into your house."

"Why?" Mary demanded.

"Because he might be—a thief, or a rascal," Porter spoke hotly.

Over the heads of the others their eyes met. "He is neither," said Mary. "I know a gentleman when I see one, Porter."

Then the temper of the redhead flamed. "Oh, do you? Well, for my part I wish that you were going to Nice, Mary."

CHAPTER III

In Which a Lonely Wayfarer Becomes Monarch of All He Surveys; and in Which One Who Might Have Been Presented as the Hero of This Tale is Forced, Through No Fault of His Own, to Take His Chances With the Rest.

When Roger Poole came a week later to the big house on the hill, it was on a rainy day. He carried his own bag, and was let in at the lower door by Susan Jenks.

Her smiling brown face gave him at once a sense of homeyness. She led the way through the wide hall and up the front stairs, crisp and competent in her big white apron and black gown.

As he followed her, Roger was aware that the house had lost its effulgence. The flowers were gone, and the radiance, and the stairs that the silken ladies had once ascended showed, at closer range, certain signs of shabbiness. The carpet was old and mended. There was a chilliness about the atmosphere, as if the fire, too, needed mending.

But when Susan Jenks opened the door of the Tower Room, he was met by warmth and brightness. Here was the light of leaping flames and of a low-shaded lamp. On the table beside the lamp was a pot of pink hyacinths, and their fragrance made the air sweet. The inner room was no longer a rosy bower, but a man's retreat, with its substantial furniture, its simplicity, its absence of non-essentials. In this room Roger set down his bag, and Susan Jenks, hanging big towels and little ones in the bathroom, drawing the curtains, and coaxing the fire, flitted cozily back and forth for a few minutes and then withdrew.

It was then that Roger surveyed his domain. He was monarch of all of it. The big chair was his to rest in, the fire was his, the low lamp, all the old friends in the bookcases!

He went again into the inner room. The glass candlesticks were gone and the photographs in their silver and ivory frames, but over the mantel there was a Corot print with forest vistas, and another above his little bedside table. On the table was a small electric lamp with a green shade, a new magazine, and a little old bulging Bible with a limp leather binding.

As he stood looking down at the little table, he was thrilled by the sense of safety after a storm. Outside was the world with its harsh judgments. Outside was the rain and the beating wind. Within were these signs of a heart-warming hospitality. Here was no bleak cleanliness, no perfunctory arrangement, but a place prepared as for an honored guest.

Down-stairs Mary was explaining to Aunt Isabelle. "I'll have Susan Jenks take some coffee to him. He's to get his dinners in town, and Susan will serve his breakfast in his room. But I thought the coffee to-night after the rain—might be comfortable."

The two women were in the dining-room. The table had been set for three, but Barry had not come.

The dinner had been a simple affair—an unfashionably nourishing soup, a broiled fish, a salad and now the coffee. Thus did Mary and Susan Jenks make income and expenses meet. Susan's good cooking, supplementing Mary's gastronomic discrimination, made a feast of the simple fare.

"What's his business, my dear?"

"Mr. Poole's? He's in the Treasury. But I think he's studying something. He seemed to be so eager for the books——"

"Your father's books?"

"Yes. I left them all up there. I even left father's old Bible. Somehow I felt that if any one was tired or lonely that the old Bible would open at the right page."

"Your father was often lonely?"

"Yes. After mother's death. And he worked too hard, and things went wrong with his business. I used to slip up to his bedroom sometimes in the last days, and there he'd be with the old Bible on his knee, and mother's picture in his hand." Mary's eyes were wet.

"He loved your mother and missed her."

"It was more than that. He was afraid of the future for Constance and me. He was afraid of the future for—Barry——"

Susan Jenks, carrying a mahogany tray on which was a slender silver coffee-pot flanked by a dish of cheese and toasted biscuit, asked as she went through the room: "Shall I save any dinner for Mr. Barry?"

"He'll be here," Mary said. "Porter Bigelow is taking us to the theater, and Barry's to make the fourth."

Barry was often late, but to-night it was half-past seven when he came rushing in.

"I don't want anything to eat," he said, stopping at the door of the dining-room where Mary and Aunt Isabelle still waited. "I had tea down-town with General Dick and Leila's crowd. And we danced. There was a girl from New York, and she was a little queen."

Mary smiled at him. To Aunt Isabella's quick eyes it seemed to be a smile of relief. "Oh, then you were with the General and Leila," she said.

"Yes. Where did you think I was?"

"Nowhere," flushing.

He started up-stairs and then came back. "I wish you'd give me credit for being able to keep a promise, Mary. You know what I told Con——"

"It wasn't that I didn't believe——" Mary crossed the dining-room and stood in the door.

"Yes, it was. You thought I was with the old crowd. I might as well go with them as to have you always thinking it."

"I'm not always thinking it."

"Yes, you are, too," hotly.

"Barry—please——"

He stood uneasily at the foot of the stairs. "You can't understand how I feel. If you were a boy——"

She caught him up. "If I were a boy? Barry, if I were a boy I'd make the world move. Oh, you | men, you have things all your own way, and you let it stand still——"

She had raised her voice, and her words floating up and up reached the ears of Roger Poole, who appeared at the top of the stairway.

There was a moment's startled silence, then Mary spoke.

"Barry, it is Mr. Poole. You don't know each other, do you?"

The two men, one going up the stairway, the other coming down, met and shook hands. Then Barry muttered something about having to run away and dress, and Roger and Mary were left alone.

It was the first time that they had seen each other, since the night of the wedding. They had arranged everything by telephone, and on the second short visit that Roger had made to his rooms, Susan Jenks had looked after him.

It seemed to Roger now that, like the house, Mary had taken on a new and less radiant aspect. She looked pale and tired. Her dress of white with its narrow edge of dark fur made her taller and older. Her fair waved hair was parted at the side and dressed compactly without ornament or ribbon. He was again, however, impressed by the almost frank boyishness of her manner as she said:

"I want you to meet Aunt Isabella. She can't hear very well, so you'll have to raise your voice."

As they went in together, Mary was forced to readjust certain opinions which she had formed of her lodger. The other night he had been divorced from the dapper youths of her own set by his lack of up-to-dateness, his melancholy, his air of mystery.

But to-night he wore a loose coat which she recognized at once as good style. His dark hair which had hung in an untidy lock was brushed back as smoothly and as sleekly as Gordon Richardson's. His dark eyes had a waked-up look. And there was a hint of color in his clean-shaven olive cheeks.

"I came down," he told her as he walked beside her, "to thank you for the coffee, for the hyacinths; for the fire, for the—welcome that my room gave me."

"Oh, did you like it? We were very busy up there all the morning, Aunt Isabelle and I and Susan Jenks."

"I felt like thanking Susan Jenks for the big bath towels; they seemed to add the final perfect touch."

She laughed and repeated his remark to Aunt Isabelle.

"Think of his being grateful for bath towels, Aunt Isabelle."

After his presentation to Aunt Isabelle, he said, smiling:

"And there was another touch—the big gray pussy cat. She was in the window-seat, and when I sat down to look at the lights, she tucked her head under my hand and sang to me."

"*Pittiwitz*? Oh, Aunt Isabelle, we left Pittiwitz up there. She claims your room as hers," she explained to Roger. "We've had her for years. And she was always there with father, and then with Constance and me. If she's a bother, just put her on the back stairs and she will come down."

"But she isn't a bother. It is very pleasant to have something alive to bear me company."

The moment that his remark was made he was afraid that she might interpret it as a plea for companionship. And he had no right—— What earthly right had he to expect to enter this charmed circle?

Susan Jenks came in with her arms full of wraps. "Mr. Porter's coming," she said, "and it's eight o'clock now."

"We are going out——" Mary was interested to note that her lodger had taken Aunt Isabelle's wrap, and was putting her into it without self-consciousness.

Her own wrap was of a shimmering gray-green velvet which matched her eyes, and there was a collar of dark fur.

"It's a pretty thing," Roger said, as he held it for her. "It's like the sea in a mist."

She flashed a quick glance at him. "I like that," she said in her straightforward way. "It is lovely. Aunt Frances brought it to me last year from Paris. Whenever you see me wear anything that is particularly nice, you'll know that it came from Aunt Frances—Aunt Isabelle's sister. She's the rich member of the family. And all the rest of us are as poor as poverty."

Outside a motor horn brayed. Then Porter Bigelow came in—a perfectly put together young man, groomed, tailored, outfitted according to the mode.

"Are you ready, Contrary Mary?" he said, then saw Roger and stopped.

Porter was a gentleman, so his manner to Roger Poole showed no hint of what he thought of lodgers in general, and this one in particular. He shook hands and said a few pleasant and perfunctory things. Personally he thought the man looked down and out. But no one could tell what Mary might think. Mary's standards were those of the dreamer and the star gazer. What she was seeking she would never find in a Mere Man. The danger lay however, in the fact that she might mistakenly hang her affections about the neck of some earth-bound Object and call it an Ideal.

As for himself, in spite of his Buff-Orpington crest, and his cock-o'-the-walk manner, Porter was, as far Mary was concerned, saturated with humility. He knew that his money, his family's social eminence were as nothing in her eyes. If underneath the weight of these things Mary could find enough of a man in him to love that could be his only hope. And that hope had held him for years to certain rather sedate ambitions, and had given him moral standards which had delighted his mother and had puzzled his father.

"Whatever I am as a man, you've made me," he said to Mary two hours later, in the intermission between the second and third acts of the musical comedy, which, for a time, had claimed their attention. Aunt Isabelle, in front of the box, was smiling gently, happy in the golden light and the nearness of the music. Barry was visiting Leila and the General who were just below, in orchestra chairs.

"Whatever I am as a man, you've made me," Porter repeated, "and now, if you'll only let me take care of you——"

Hitherto, Mary had treated his love-making lightly, but to-night she turned upon him her troubled eyes. "Porter, you know I can't. But there are times when I wish—I could——"

"Then why not?"

She stopped him with a gesture. "It wouldn't be right. I'm simply feeling lonely and lost because Constance is so far away. But that isn't any reason for marrying you. You deserve a woman who cares, who really cares, heart and soul. And I can't, dear boy."

"I was a fool to think you might," savagely, "a man with a red head is always a joke."

"As if that had anything to do with it."

"But it has, Mary. You know as well as I do that when I was a youngster I was always Reddy Bigelow to our crowd—Reddy Bigelow with a carrot-head and freckles. If I had been poor and common, life wouldn't have been worth living. But mother's family and Dad's money fixed that for me. And I had an allowance big enough to supply the neighborhood with sweets. You were a little thing, but you were sorry for me, and I didn't have to buy you. But I'd buy you now—with a house in town and a country house, and motor cars and lovely clothes—if I thought it would do any good, Mary."

"You wouldn't want me that way, Porter."

"I want you—any way."

He stopped as the curtain went up, and darkness descended. But presently out of the darkness came his whisper, "I want you—any way."

They had supper after the play, Leila and the General joining them at Porter's compelling invitation.

Pending the serving of the supper, Barry detained Leila for a moment in a palm-screened corner of the sumptuous corridor.

"That girl from New York, Leila—Miss Jeliffe? What is her first name?"

"Delilah."

"It isn't."

Leila's light laughter mocked him. "Yes, it is, Barry. She calls herself Lilah and pronounces it as I do mine. But she signs her cheques De-lilah."

Barry recovered. "Where did you meet her?"

"At school. Her father's in Congress. They are coming to us to-morrow. Dad has asked me to invite them as house guests until they find an apartment."

"Well, she's dazzling."

Leila flamed. "I don't see how you can like—her kind——"

"Little lady," he admonished, "you're jealous. I danced four dances with her, and only one with your new pink slippers."

She stuck out a small foot. "They're lovely, Barry," she said, repentantly, "and I haven't thanked you."

"Why should you? Just look pleasant, please. I've had enough scolding for one day."

"Who scolded?"

"Mary."

Leila glanced into the dining-room, where, in her slim fairness, Mary was like a pale lily, among all the tulip women, and poppy women, and orchid women, and night-shade women of the social garden.

"If Mary scolded you, you deserved it," she said, loyally.

"You too? Leila, if you don't stick to me, I might as well give up."

His face was moody, brooding. She forgot the Delilah-dancer of the afternoon, forgot everything except that this wonderful man-creature was in trouble.

"Barry," she said, simply, like a child, "I'll stick to you until I—die."

He looked down into the adoring eyes. "I believe you would, Leila," he said, with a boyish catch in his voice; "you're the dearest thing on God's great earth!"

The chilled fruit was already on the table when they went in, and it was followed by a chafing dish over which the General presided. Red-faced and rapturous, he seasoned and stirred, and as the result of his wizardry there was placed before them presently such plates of Creole crab as could not be equaled north of New Orleans.

"To cook," said the General, settling himself back in his chair and beaming at Mary who was beside him, "one must be a poet—to me there is more in that dish than merely something to eat. There's color—the red of tomatoes, the green of the peppers, the pale ivory of mushrooms, the snow white of the crab—there's atmosphere—aroma."

"The difference," Mary told him, smiling, "between your cooking and Susan Jenks' is the difference between an epic—and a nursery rhyme. They're both good, but Susan's is unpremeditated art."

"I take off my hat to Susan Jenks," said the General—"when her poetry expresses itself in waffles and fried chicken."

Mary was devoting herself to the General. Porter Bigelow who was on the other side of her, was devoting himself to Aunt Isabelle.

Aunt Isabelle was serenely content in her new office of chaperone.

"I can hear so much better in a crowd." she said, "and then there's so much to see."

"And this is the time for the celebrities," said Porter, and wrote on the corner of the supper card the name of a famous Russian countess at the table next to them. Beyond was the Speaker of the House; the British Ambassador with his fair company of ladies; the Spanish Ambassador at a table of darker beauties.

Mary, listening to Porter's pleasant voice, was constrained to admit that he could be charming. As for the freckles and "carrot-head," they had been succeeded by a fine if somewhat florid complexion, and the curled thickness of his brilliant crown gave to his head an almost classic beauty.

As she studied him, his eyes met hers, and he surprised her by a quick smile of understanding.

"Oh, Contrary Mary," he murmured, so that the rest could not hear, "what do you think of me?"

She found herself blushing, "*Porter.*"

"You were weighing me in the balance? Red head against my lovely disposition?"

Before she could answer, he had turned back to Aunt Isabelle, leaving Mary with her cheeks hot.

After supper, the young host insisted that Leila and the General should go home in his limousine with Barry and Aunt Isabelle.

"Mary and I will follow in a taxi," he said in the face of their protests.

"Young man," demanded the twinkling General, "if I accept, will you look upon me in the light of an incumbrance or a benefactor?"

"A benefactor, sir," said Porter, promptly, and that settled it.

"And now," said Porter, as, having seen the rest of the party off, he took his seat beside the slim figure in the green velvet wrap, "now I am going to have it out with you."

"But—Porter!"

"I've a lot to say. And we are going to ride around the Speedway while I say it."

"But—it's raining."

"All the better. It will be we two and the world away, Mary."

"And there isn't anything to say."

"Oh, yes, there is—*oodles*."

"And Aunt Isabelle will be worried."

He drew the rug up around her and settled back as placidly as if the hands on the moon face of the clock on the post-office tower were not pointing to midnight. "Aunt Isabelle has been told," he informed her, "that you may be a bit late. I wrote it on the supper card, and she read it—and smiled."

He waited in silence until they had left the avenue, and were on the driveway back of the Treasury which leads toward the river.

"Porter, this is a wild thing to do."

"I'm in a wild mood—a mood that fits in with the rain and wind, Mary. I'm in such a mood that if the times were different and the age more romantic, I would pick you up and put you on my champing steed and carry you off to my castle."

He laughed, and for the moment she was thrilled by his masterfulness. "But, alas, my steed is a taxi—the age is prosaic—and you—I'm afraid of you, Contrary Mary."

They were on the Speedway now, faintly illumined, showing a row of waving willow trees, spectrally outlined against a background of gray water.

"I'm afraid of you. I have always been. Even when you were only ten and I was fifteen. I would shake in my shoes when you looked at me, Mary; you were the only one then—you are the only one—now."

Her hand lay on the outside of the rug. He put his own over it.

"Ever since you said to-night that you didn't care—there's been something singing—in my brain, and it has said, 'make her care, make her care.' And I'm going to do it. I'm not going to trouble you or worry you with it—and I'm going to take my chances with the rest. But in the end I'm going to—win."

"There aren't any others."

"If there aren't there will be. You've kept yourself protected so far by that little independent manner of yours, which scares men off. But some day a man will come who won't be scared—and then it will be a fight to the finish between him—and me."

"Oh, Porter, I don't want to think of marrying—not for ten million years."

"And yet," he said prophetically, "if to-morrow you should meet some man who could make you think he was the Only One, you'd marry him in the face of all the world."

"No man of that kind will ever come."

"What kind?"

"That will make me willing to lose the world."

The rain was beating against the windows of the cab.

"Porter, please. We must go home."

"Not unless you'll promise to let me prove it—to let me show that I'm a man—not a—boy."

"You're the best friend I've ever had. I wish you wouldn't insist on being something else."

"But I do insist——"

"And I insist upon going home. Be good and take me."

It was said with decision, and he gave the order to the driver. And so they whirled at last up the avenue of the Presidents and along the edges of the Park, and arrived at the foot of the terrace of the big house.

There was a light in the tower window.

"That fellow is up yet," Porter said. He had an umbrella over her, and was shielding her as best he could from the rain. "I don't like to think of him in the house."

"Why not?"

"Oh, he sees you every day. Talks to you every day. And what do you know of him? And I who've known you all my life must be content with scrappy minutes with other people around. And anyhow—I believe I'd be jealous of Satan himself, Mary."

They were under the porch now, and she drew away from him a bit, surveying him with disapproving eyes.

"You aren't like yourself to-night, Porter."

He put one hand on her shoulder and stood looking down at her. "How can I be? What am I going to do when I leave you, Mary, and face the fact that you don't care—that I'm no more to you—than that fellow up there in the—tower?"

He straightened himself, then with the madness of his earlier mood upon him, he said one thing more before he left her: "Contrary Mary, if I weren't such a coward, and you weren't so—wonderful—I'd kiss you now—and *make* you—care———"

CHAPTER IV

In Which a Little Bronze Boy Grins in the Dark; and in Which Mary Forgets That There is Any One Else in the House.

Up-stairs among his books Roger Poole heard Mary come in. With the curtains drawn behind him to shut out the light, he looked down into the streaming night, and saw Porter drive away alone.

Then Mary's footstep on the stairs; her raised voice as she greeted Aunt Isabelle, who had waited up for her. A door was shut, and again the house sank into silence.

Roger turned to his books, but not to read. The old depression was upon him. In the glow of his arrival, he had been warmed by the hope that things could be different; here in this hospitable house he had, perchance, found a home. So he had gone down to find that he was an outsider—an alien—old where they were young, separated from Barry and Porter and Mary by years of dark experience.

To him, at this moment, Mary Ballard stood for a symbol of the things which he had lost. Her youth and light-heartedness, her high courage, and now, perhaps, her romance. He knew the look that was in Porter Bigelow's eyes when they had rested upon her. The look of a man who claims—his own. And behind Bigelow's pleasant and perfunctory greeting Roger had felt a subtle antagonism. He smiled bitterly. No man need fear him. He was out of the running. He was done with love, with romance, with women, forever. A woman had spoiled his life.

Yet, if before the other, he had met Mary Ballard? The possibilities swept over him. His life to-day would have been different. He would be facing the world, not turning his back to it.

Brooding over the dying fire, his eyes were stern. If it had been his fault, he would have taken his punishment without flinching. But to be overthrown by an act of chivalry—to be denied the expression of that which surged within him. Daily he bent over a desk, doing the work that any man might do, he who had been carried on the shoulders of his fellow students, he whose voice had rung with a clarion call!

In the lower hall, a door was again opened, and now there were footsteps ascending. Then he heard a little laugh. "I've found her—Aunt Isabelle, she insists upon going up."

He clicked off his light and very carefully opened his door. Mary was in the lower hall, the heavy gray cat hugged up in her arms. She wore a lace boudoir cap, and a pale blue dressing-gown trailed after her. Seen thus, she was exquisitely feminine. Faintly through his consciousness flitted Porter Bigelow's name for her—Contrary Mary. Why Contrary? Was there another side which he had not seen? He had heard her flaming words to Barry, "If I were a man—I'd make the world move———" and he had been for the moment repelled. He had no sympathy with modern feminine rebellions. Women were women. Men were men. The things which they had in common were love, and that which followed, the home, the family. Beyond these things their lives were divided, necessarily, properly.

He groped his way back through the darkness to the tower window, opened it and leaned out. The rain beat upon his face, the wind blew his hair back, and fluttered the ends of his loose tie. Below him lay the storm-swept city, its lights faint and flickering. He remembered a test which he had chosen on a night like this.

"O Lord, Thou art my God. I will exalt Thee, I will praise Thy name, for Thou hast done wonderful things; Thou hast been a strength to the poor, a strength to the needy in distress … a refuge from the storm———"

How the words came back to him, out of that vivid past. But to-night—why, there was no—God! Was he the fool who had once seen God—in a storm?

He shut the window, and finding a heavy coat and an old cap put them on. Then he made his way, softly, down the tower steps to the side door. Mary had pointed out to him that this entrance would make it possible for him to go and come as he pleased. To-night it pleased him to walk in the beating rain.

At the far end of the garden there was an old fountain, in which a bronze boy rode on a bronze dolphin. The basin of the fountain was filled with sodden leaves. A street lamp at the foot of the terrace illumined the bronze boy's face so that it seemed to wear a twisted grin. It was as if he laughed at the storm and at life, defying the elements with his sardonic mirth. Back and forth, restlessly, went the lonely man, hating to enter again the rooms which only a few hours before had seemed a refuge. It would have been better to have stayed in his last cheap boarding-house, better to have kept away from this place which brought memories—better never to have seen this group of young folk who were gay as he had once been gay—better never to have seen—Mary Ballard!

He glanced up at the room beneath his own where her light still burned. He wondered if she had stayed awake to think of the young Apollo of the auburn head. Perhaps he was already her accepted lover. And why not?

Why should he care who loved Mary Ballard?

He had never believed in love at first sight. He didn't believe in it now. He only knew that he had been thrilled by a look, warmed by a friendliness, touched by a frankness and sincerity such as he had found in no other woman. And because he had been thrilled and warmed and touched by these things, he was feeling to-night the deadly mockery of a fate which had brought her too late into his life.

Coming in, shivering and excited after her ride with Porter, Mary had found evidence of Aunt Isabelle's solicitous care for her. Her fire was burning brightly, the covers of her bed were turned down, her blue dressing-gown and the little blue slippers were warming in front of the blaze.

"No one ever did such things for me before," Mary said with appreciation, as the gentle lady came in to kiss her niece good-night. "Mother wasn't that kind. We all waited on her. And Susan Jenks is too busy; it isn't right to keep her up. And anyway I've always been more like a boy, taking care of myself. Constance was the one we petted, Con and mother."

"I love to do it," Aunt Isabelle said, eagerly. "When I am at Frances' there are so many servants, and I feel pushed out. There's nothing that I can do for any one. Grace and Frances each have a maid. So I live my own life, and sometimes it has been—lonely."

"You darling." Mary laid her cool young lips against the soft cheek. "I'm dead lonely, too. That's why I wanted you."

Aunt Isabelle stood for a moment looking into the fire. "It has been years since anybody wanted me," she said, finally.

There was no bitterness in her tone; she simply stated a fact. Yet in her youth she had been the beauty of the family, and the toast of a county.

"Aunt Isabelle," Mary said, suddenly, "is marriage the only way out for a woman?"

"The only way?"

"To freedom. It seems to me that a single woman always seems to belong to her family. Why shouldn't you do as you please? Why shouldn't I? And yet you've never lived your own life. And I sha'n't be able to live mine except by fighting every inch of the way."

A flush stained Aunt Isabelle's cheeks. "I have always been poor, Mary——"

"But that isn't it," fiercely. "There are poor girls who aren't tied—I mean by conventions and family traditions. Why, Aunt Isabelle, I rented the Tower Rooms not only in defiance of the living—but of the dead. I can see mother's face if we had thought of such a thing while she lived. Yet we needed the money then. We needed it to help Dad—to save him——" The last words were spoken under her breath, and Aunt Isabelle did not catch them.

"And now everybody wants me to get married. Oh, Aunt Isabelle, sit down and let's talk it out. I'm not sleepy, are you?" She drew the little lady beside her on the high-backed couch which faced the fire. "Everybody wants me to get married, Aunt Isabelle. And to-night I had it out with—Porter."

"You don't love him?"

"Not—that way. But sometimes—he makes me feel as if I couldn't escape him—as if he would persist and persist, until he won. But I don't want love to come to me that way. It seems to me that if one loves, one knows. One doesn't have to be shown."

"My dear, sometimes it is a tragedy when a woman knows."

"But why?"

"Because men like to conquer. When they see love in a woman's eyes, their own love—dies."

"I should hate a man like that," said Mary, frankly. "If a man only loves you because of the conquest, what's going to happen when you are married and the chase is over? No, Aunt Isabelle, when I fall in love, it will be with a man who will know that I am the One Woman. He must love me because I am Me—Myself. Not because some one else admires me, or because I can keep him guessing. He will know me as I know him—as his Predestined Mate!"

Thus spoke Sweet and Twenty, glowing. And Sweet and Forty, meeting that flame with her banked fires, faltered. "But, my dear, how can you know?"

"How did you know?"

The abrupt question drove every drop of blood from Aunt Isabelle's face. "Who told you?"

"Mother. One night when I asked her why you had never married. You don't mind, do you?"

Aunt Isabelle shook her head. "No. And, Mary, dear, I've faced all the loneliness, all the dependence, rather than be untrue to that which he gave me and I gave him. There was one night, in this old garden. I was visiting your mother, and he was in Congress at the time, and the garden was full of roses—and it was—moonlight. And we sat by the fountain, and there was the soft splash of the water, and he said: 'Isabelle, the little bronze boy is throwing kisses at you—do you see him—smiling?' And I said, 'I want no kisses but yours'—and that was the last time. The next day he was killed—thrown from his horse while he was riding out here to see—me.

"It was after that I was so ill. And something teemed to snap in my head, and one day when I sat beside the fountain I found that I couldn't hear the splash of the water, and things began to go; the voices I loved seemed far away, and I could tell that the wind was blowing only by the movement of the leaves, and the birds rounded out their little throats—but I heard—no music———"

Her voice trailed away into silence.

"But before the stillness, there were others who—wanted me—for I hadn't lost my prettiness, and Frances did her best for me. And she didn't like it when I said I couldn't marry, Mary. But now I am glad. For in the silence, my love and I live, in a world of our own."

"Aunt Isabelle—darling. How lovely and sweet, and sad———" Mary was kneeling beside her aunt, her arm thrown around her, and Aunt Isabelle, reading her lips, did not need to hear the words.

"If I had been strong, like you, Mary, I could have held my own against Frances and have made something of myself. But I'm not strong, and twenty-five years ago women did not ask for freedom. They asked for—love."

"But I want to find freedom in my love. Not be bound as Porter wants to bind me. He'd put me on a pedestal and worship me, and I'd rather stand shoulder to shoulder with my husband and be his comrade. I don't want him to look up too far, or to look down as Gordon looks down on Constance."

"Looks down? Why, he adores her, Mary."

"Oh, he loves her. And he'll do everything for her, but he will do it as if she were a child. He won't ask her opinion in any vital matter. He won't share his big interests with her, and so he'll never discover the big fine womanliness. And she'll shrivel to his measure of her."

Aunt Isabelle shook her head, smiling. "Don't analyze too much, Mary. Men and women are human—and you may lose yourself in a search for the Ideal."

"Do you know what Porter calls me, Aunt Isabelle? Contrary Mary. He says I never do things the way the people expect. Yet I do them the way that I must. It is as if some force were inside of me—driving me—on."

She stood up as she said it, stretching out her arms in an eager gesture. "Aunt Isabelle, if I were a man, there'd be something in the world for me to do. Yet here I am, making ends meet, holding up my part of the housekeeping with Susan Jenks, and taking from the hands of my rich friends such pleasures as I dare accept without return."

Aunt Isabelle pulled her down beside her. "Rebellious Mary," she said, "who is going to tame you?"

They laughed a little, clinging to each other, and than Mary said, "You must go to bed, Aunt Isabelle. I'm keeping you up shamefully."

They kissed again and separated, and Mary made ready for bed. She took off her cap, and all her lovely hair fell about her. That was another of her contrary ways. She and Constance had been taught to braid it neatly, but from little girlhood Mary had protested, and on going to bed with two prim pigtails had been known to wake up in the middle of the night and take them down, only to be discovered in the morning with all her fair curls in a tangle. Scolding had not availed. Once, as dire punishment, the curls had been cut off. But Mary had rejoiced. "It makes me look like a boy," she had told her mother, calmly, "and I like it."

Another of her little girl fancies had been to say her prayers aloud. She said them that way to-night, kneeling by her bed with her fair head on her folded hands.

Then she turned out the light, and drew her curtains back. As she looked out at the driving rain, the flare of the street lamp showed a motionless figure on the terrace. For a moment she peered, palpitating, then flew into Aunt Isabelle's room.

"There's some one in the garden."

"Perhaps it's Barry."

"Didn't he come with you?"

"No. He went on with Leila and the General."

"But it is two o'clock, Aunt Isabelle."

"I didn't know; I thought perhaps he had come."

Going back into her room, Mary threw on her blue dressing-gown and slippers and opened her door. The light was still burning in the hall. Barry always turned it out when he came. She stood undecided, then started down the back stairs, but halted as the door opened and a dark figure appeared.

"Barry——"

Roger Poole looked up at her. "It isn't your brother," he said. "I—I must beg your pardon for disturbing you. I could not sleep, and I went out——" He stopped and stammered. Poised there above him with all the wonder of her unbound hair about her, she was like some celestial vision.

She smiled at him. "It doesn't matter," she said; "please don't apologize. It was foolish of me to be—frightened. But I had forgotten that there was any one else in the house."

She was unconscious of the effect of her words. But his soul shrank within him. To her he was the lodger who paid the rent. To him she was, well, just now she was, to him, the Blessed Damosel!

Faintly in the distance they heard the closing of a door. "It's Barry," Mary said, and suddenly a wave of self-consciousness swept over her. What would Barry think to find her at this hour talking to Roger Poole? And what would he think of Roger Poole, who walked in the garden on a rainy night?

Roger saw her confusion. "I'll turn out this light," he said, "and wait——"

And she waited, too, in the darkness until Barry was safe in his own room, then she spoke softly. "Thank you so much," she said, and was gone.

CHAPTER V

In Which Roger Remembers a Face and Delilah Remembers a Voice—and in Which a Poem and a Pussy Cat Play an Important Part.

Since the night of his arrival, Roger had not intruded upon the family circle. He had read hostility in Barry's eyes as the boy had looked up at him; and Mary, in spite of her friendliness, had forgotten that he was in the house! Well, they had set the pace, and he would keep to it. Here in the tower he could live alone—yet not be lonely, for the books were there—and they brought forgetfulness.

He took long walks through the city, now awakening to social and political activities. Back to town came the folk who had fled from the summer heat; back came the members of House and of Senate, streaming in from North, South, East and West for the coming Congress. Back came the office-seekers and the pathetic patient group whose claims were waiting for the passage of some impossible bill.

There came, too, the sightseers and trippers, sweeping from one end of the town to the other, climbing the dome of the Capitol, walking down the steps of the Monument, venturing into the White House, piloted through the Bureau where the money is made, riding on "rubber-neck wagons," sailing about in taxis, stampeding Mt. Vernon, bombarding Fort Myer, and doing it all gloriously under golden November skies.

And because of the sightseers and statesmen, and the folk who had been away for the summer, the shops began to take on beauty. Up F Street and around Fourteenth into H swept the eager procession, and all the windows were abloom for them.

Roger walked, too, in the country. In other lands, or at least so their poets have it, November is the month of chill and dreariness. But to the city on the Potomac it comes with soft pink morning mists and toward sunset, with amethystine vistas. And if, beyond the city, the fields are frosted, it is frost of a feathery whiteness which melts in the glory of a warmer noon. And if the trees are bare, there is yet pale yellow under foot and pale rose, where the leaves wait for the winter winds which shall whirl them later in a mad dance like brown butterflies. And there's the green of the pines, and the flaming red of five-fingered creepers.

It was on a sunny November day, therefore, as he followed Rock Creek through the Park that Roger came to the old Mill where a little tea room supplied afternoon refreshment.

As it was far away from car lines, its patronage came largely from those who arrived in motors or on horseback, and a few courageous pedestrians.

Here Roger sat down to rest, ordering a rather substantial repast, for the long walk had made him hungry.

It was while he waited that a big car arrived with five passengers. He recognized Porter Bigelow at once, and there were besides two older men and two young women.

The taller of the two young women had eyes that roved. She had blue black hair, and she wore black—a small black hat with a thin curved plume, and a tailored suit cut on lines which accentuated her height and slenderness. Her furs were of leopard skins. Her cheeks were touched with high color under her veil.

The other girl had also dark hair. But she was small and bird-like. From head to foot she was in a deep dark pink that, in the wool of her coat and the chiffon of her veil, gave back the hue of the rose which was pinned to her muff.

But it was on the girl in black that Roger fixed his eyes. Where had he seen her?

They chose a table near him, and passed within the touch of his hand. Porter did not recognize him. The tall man in the old overcoat and soft hat was not linked in his memory with that moment of meeting in Mary's dining-room.

"Everybody mixes up our names, Porter," the girl with the rose was saying as they sat down; "the girls did at school, didn't they, Lilah?"

"Yes," the girl in black did not need many words with her eyes to talk for her.

"Was it big Lilah and little Leila?" Porter asked.

"No," the dark eyes above the leopard muff widened and held his gaze. "It was dear Leila, and dreadful Lilah. I used to shock them, you know."

The three men laughed. "What did you do?" demanded Porter, leaning forward a little.

Men always leaned toward Delilah Jeliffe. She drew them even while she repelled.

"I smoked cigarettes, for one thing," she said; "everybody does it now. But then—I came near being expelled for it."

The little rose girl broke in hotly. "I think it is horrid still, Lilah," she said.

Lilah smiled and shrugged. "But that wasn't the worst. One day—I eloped."

She was making them all listen. The old men and the young one, and the man at the other table.

"I eloped with a boy from Prep. He was nineteen, and I was two years younger. We started by moonlight in Romeo's motor car—it was great fun. But the clergyman wouldn't marry us. I think he guessed that we were a pair of kiddies from school—and he scolded us and sent me back in a taxi——"

The tall, thin old gentleman was protesting. "My dear——"

"Oh, you didn't know, Daddy darling," she said. "I got back before I was discovered, and let myself in by the door I had unlocked. But I couldn't keep it from the girls—it was such fun to make them—shiver."

"And what became of Romeo?" Porter asked.

"He found another Juliet—a lovely little blonde and they are living happy ever after."

Leila's eyes were round. "But I don't see," she began.

"Of course you don't, duckie. To me, the whole thing was an adventure along the road—to you, it would have been a heart-break."

Her words came clearly to Roger. That, then, was what love meant to some women—an adventure along the road. One man served for pleasuring, until at some curve in the highway she met another.

Lilah was challenging her audience. "And now you see why I was dreadful Lilah. I fit the name they had for me, don't I?"

Her question was put at Porter, and he answered it. "It is women who set the pace for us," he said; "if they adventure, we venture. If they lead, we follow."

General Dick broke in. With his halo of white hair and his pink face, he looked like an indignant cherub. "The way you young people treat serious subjects is appalling;" then he felt his little daughter's hand upon his arm.

"Lilah is always saying things that she doesn't mean, Dad. Please don't take her seriously."

"Nobody takes me seriously," said Lilah, "and that's why nobody knows me as I really am."

"I know you," said her father, "and you're like a little mare that I used to drive out on the ranch. As long as I'd let her have her head, she was lovely. But let me try to curb her, and she'd kick over the traces."

They all laughed at that; then their tea came, and a great plate of toast, and the conversation grew intermittent and less interesting.

Yet the man at the other table had his attention again arrested when Lilah said to Porter, as she drew on her gloves:

"We are invited to Mary Ballard's for Thanksgiving, and you're to be there."

"Yes—mother and father are going South, so I can escape the family feast."

"Mary Ballard is—charming——" It was said tentatively, with an upward sweep of her lashes.

But Porter did not answer; and as he stood behind her chair, there was a deeper flush on his florid cheeks. Mary's name he held in his heart. It was rarely on his lips.

Mary had not wanted Delilah and her father for Thanksgiving. "But we can't have Leila and the General without them," she said to Barry, after a conversation with Leila over the telephone, "and it wouldn't seem like Thanksgiving without the Dicks."

"Delilah," said Barry, comfortably, "is good fun. I'm glad she is coming."

"She may be good fun," said Mary, slowly, "but she isn't—our kind."

"Leila said that to me," Barry told her. "I don't quite see what you girls mean."

"Well, you wouldn't," Mary agreed; "men don't see. But I should think when you look at Leila you'd know the difference. Leila is like a little wild rose, and Delilah Jeliffe is a—tulip."

"I like tulips," murmured Barry, audaciously.

Mary laughed. What was the use? Barry was Barry. And Delilah Jeliffe would flit in and out of his life as other girls had flitted; but always there would be for him—Leila.

"If you were a woman," she said, "you'd know by her clothes, and the pink of her cheeks, and by the way she does her hair—she's just a little too much of—everything—Barry."

"There's just enough of Delilah Jeliffe," said Barry, "to keep a man guessing."

"Guessing what?" Mary demanded with a spark in her eyes.

"Oh, just guessing," easily.

"Whether she likes you?"

Barry nodded.

"But why should you want to know, Barry? You're not in love with her."

His blue eyes danced. "Love hasn't anything to do with it, little solemn sister; it's just in the—game."

Later they had a tilt over inviting Mary's lodger.

"It seems so inhospitable to let him spend the day up there alone."

"I don't see how he could possibly expect to dine with us," Barry said, hotly. "You don't know anything about him, Mary. And I agree with Porter—a man's bank reference isn't sufficient for social recognition. And anyhow he may not have the right kind of clothes."

"We are to have dinner at three o'clock," she said, "just as mother always had it on Thanksgiving Day. If you don't want me to ask Roger Poole, I won't. But I think you are an awful snob, Barry."

Her eyes were blazing.

"Now what have I done to deserve that?" her brother demanded.

"You haven't treated him civilly," Mary said. "In a sense he's a guest in our house, and you haven't been up to his rooms since he came—and he's a gentleman."

"How do you know?"

"Because I do."

"Yet the other day you hinted that Delilah Jeliffe wasn't a lady, not in your sense of the word—and that I couldn't see the difference because was a man. I'll let you have your opinion of Delilah Jeliffe if you'll let me have mine of Roger Poole."

So Mary compromised by having Roger down for the evening. "We shall be just a family party for dinner," she said. "But later, we are asking some others for candle-lighting time. We want everybody to come prepared to tell a story or recite, or to sing, or play—in the dark at first, and then with the candles."

His pride urged him to refuse—to spurn this offer of hospitality from the girl who had once forgotten that he was in the house!

But as he stood there on the threshold of the Tower Rooms, her smile seemed to draw him, her voice called him, and he was young—and desperately lonely.

So as he dressed carefully on Thanksgiving afternoon, he had a sense of exhilaration. For one night he would let himself go. He would be himself. No one should snub him. Snubs came from self-consciousness—he who was above them need not see them.

When at last he entered the drawing-room, it was unillumined except for the flickering flame of a fire of oak logs. The guests, assembling wraith-like among the shadows, were given, each, an unlighted candle.

Roger found a place in a big chair beside the piano, and sat there alone, interested and curious. And presently Pittiwitz, stealing toward the hearth, arched her back under his hand, and he reached down and lifted her to his knee, where she stretched herself, sphinx-like, her amber eyes shining in the dusk.

With the last guest seated, Barry stood before them, and gave the key to the situation.

"Everybody is to light a candle with some stunt," he explained. "You know the idea. All of you have some parlor tricks, and you're to show them off."

There were no immediate volunteers, so Barry pounced on Leila.

"You begin," he said, and drew her into the circle of the firelight.

She looked very childish and sweet as she stood there with her unlighted candle, and sang a lullaby. Mary Ballard played her accompaniment softly, sitting so near to Roger in his dim corner that the folds of her velvet gown swept his foot.

And when the song was finished, Leila touched a match to her candle and stood on tiptoe to set it on the corner of the mantel, where it glimmered bravely.

General Dick and Mr. Jeliffe came next. Solemnly they placed two cushions on the hearth-rug, solemnly they knelt thereon, facing each other. Then intently and conscientiously they played the old game of "Pease porridge hot, pease porridge cold." The General's fat hands met Mr. Jeliffe's thin ones alternately and in unison. Not a mistake did they make, and, ending out of breath, the General found it hard to rise, and had to be picked by Porter, like a plump feather pillow.

And now the candles were three!

Then Barry and Delilah danced, a dance which they had practiced together. It had in it just a hint of wildness, and just a hint of sophistication, and Delilah in her dress of sapphire chiffon, with its flaring tunic of silver net, seemed in the nebulous light like some strange bird of the night.

And now the candles were five!

Following, Leila went to the piano, and Porter and Mary gave a minuet. They had learned it at dancing-school, and it had been years since they had danced it. But they did it very well; Porter's somewhat stiff bearing accorded with its stateliness, and Mary, having added to her green velvet gown a little Juliet cap of lace and a lace fan, showed the radiant, almost boyish beauty which had charmed Roger on the night of the wedding.

His pulses throbbed as he watched her. They were a well-matched pair, this young millionaire and the pretty maid. And as their orderly steps went through the dance, so would their orderly lives, if they married, continue to the end. But what could Porter Bigelow teach Mary Ballard of the things which touch the stars?

And now the candles were seven! And the spirit of the carnival was upon the company. Song was followed by story, and story by song—until at last the room seemed to swim in a golden mist.

And through that mist Mary saw Roger Poole! He was leaning forward a little, and there was about him the air of a man who waited.

She spoke impetuously.

"Mr. Poole," she said, "please——"

There was not a trace of awkwardness, not a hint of self-consciousness in his manner as he answered her.

"May I sit here?" he asked. "You see, my pussy cat holds me, and as I shall tell you about a cat, she gives the touch of local color."

And then he began, his right hand resting on the gray cat's head, his left upon his knee.

He used no gestures, yet as he went on, the room became still with the stillness of a captured audience. Here was no stumbling elocution, but a controlled and perfect method, backed by a voice which soared and sang and throbbed and thrilled—the voice either of a great orator, or of a great actor.

The story that he told was of Whittington and his cat. But it was not the old nursery rhyme. He gave it as it is written by one of England's younger poets. Since he lacked the time for it all, he sketched the theme, rounding it out here and there with a verse—and it seemed to Mary that, as he spoke, all the bells of London boomed!

> "'_Flos Mercatorum_,' moaned the bell of All Hallowes,
> 'There was he an orphan, O, a little lad, alone!'
> 'Then we all sang,' echoed happy St. Saviour's,
> 'Called him and lured him, and made him our own.'"

And now they saw the little lad stealing toward the big city, saw all the color and glow as he entered upon its enchantment, saw his meeting with the green-gowned Alice, saw him cold and hungry, faint and footsore, saw him aswoon on a door-step.

> "'Alice,' roared a voice, and then, O like a lilied angel,
> Leaning from the lighted door, a fair face unafraid,
> Leaning over Red Rose Lane, O, leaning out of Paradise
> Drooped the sudden glory of his green-gowned maid!"

Touching now a lighter note, his voice laughed through the lovely lines; of the ship which was to sail beyond the world; of how each man staked such small wealth as he possessed; "for in those days Marchaunt adventurers shared with their prentices the happy chance of each new venture."

But Whittington had nothing to give. "Not a groat," he tells sweet Alice. "I staked my last groat in a cat!"

144

> "'Ay, but we need a cat,'
> The Captain said. So when the painted ship
> Sailed through a golden sunrise down the Thames,
> A gray tail waved upon the misty poop,
> And Whittington had his venture on the seas!"

The ringing words brought tumultuous applause. Pittiwitz, startled, sat up and blinked. People bent to each other, asking: "Who is this Roger Poole?" Under his breath Barry was saying, boyishly, "Gee!" He might still wonder about Mary's lodger, he would never again look down on him. And Delilah Jeliffe sitting next to Barry murmured, "I've heard that voice before—but where?"

Again the bells boomed as the story swept on to the fortune which came to the prentice lad—the price paid for his cat in Barbary by a king whose house was rich in gems but sorely plagued with rats and mice.

Then Whittington's offer of his wealth to Alice, her refusal, and so—to the end.

> "'I know a way,' said the Bell of St. Martin's.
> 'Tell it and be quick,' laughed the prentices below!
> 'Whittington shall marry her, marry her, marry her!
> Peal for a wedding,' said the Big Bell of Bow."

Roger stopped there, and with Pittiwitz in his arms, rose to light his candle. All about him people were saying things, but their words seemed to come to him through a beating darkness. There was only one face—Mary's, and she was leaning toward him, or was it above him? "It was wonderful," she said.

"It is a great poem."

"I don't mean that—it was the way you—gave it."

Outwardly calm, he carried his candle and set it in its place.

Then he came back to Mary—Mary with the shining eyes. This was his night! "You liked it, then?"

For a moment she did not speak, then she said again, "It was wonderful."

There were other people about them now, and Roger met them with the ease of a man of the world. Even Barry had to admit that his manners were irreproachable, and his clothes. As for his looks, he was not to be matched with Mary's auburn Apollo—one cannot compare a royal stag and a tawny-maned lion!

During the rest of the program, Roger sat enthroned at Mary's side, and listened. He watched the candles, an increasing row of little pointed lights. He went down to supper, and again sat beside Mary—and knew not what he ate. He saw Porter's hot eyes upon him. He knew that to-morrow he must doff his honors and be as he had been before. However, "who knows but the world may end to-night," he told himself, desperately.

Thus he played with Fate, and Fate, turning the tables, brought him at last to Delilah Jeliffe as the guests were saying "good-bye."

"Somewhere I've heard your voice," she said with the upsweep of her lashes. "It isn't the kind that one is likely to forget."

"Yet you have forgotten," he parried.

"I shall remember," she said. "I want to remember—and I shall want to hear it again."

He shook his head. "It was my—swan song——"

"Why?"

He shrugged. "One isn't always in the mood——"

And now it was she who shook her head. "It isn't a mood with you, it's your life."

She had him there, so he carried the conversation lightly to another topic. "I had not thought to give Whittington until I saw Pittiwitz."

"And Mary's green gown?"

Again he parried. "It was dark. I could not see the color of her gown."

"But 'love has eyes.'" The words were light and she meant them lightly. And she went away laughing.

But Roger did not laugh.

And when Mary came to look for him he was gone.

And up-stairs, his evening stripped of its glamour, he told himself that he had been a fool! The world would *not* end tonight. He had to live the appointed length of his days, through all the dreary years.

CHAPTER VI

In Which Mary Brings Christmas to the Tower Rooms; and in Which Roger Declines a Privilege for Which Porter Pleads.

On Christmas Eve, Mary and Susan Jenks brought up to Roger a little tree. It was just a fir plume, but it was gay with tinsel and spicy with the fragrance of the woods, and it was topped by a wee wax angel.

In vain Mary and Barry and even Aunt Isabelle had urged Roger to join their merrymaking downstairs. Aunt Frances, having delayed her trip abroad until January, was coming; and except for Leila and General Dick and Porter Bigelow, it was to be strictly a family affair.

But Roger had refused. "I'm not one of you," he had told Mary. "I'm a bee, not a butterfly, and I shouldn't have joined you on Thanksgiving night. When you're alone, if I may, I'll come down—but please—not with your guests."

He had not joined them often, however, and he had never again shown the mood which had possessed him when his voice had charmed them. Hence they grew, as the days went on, to know him as quiet, self-contained man, whose eyes burned now and then, when some subject was broached which moved him, but who, for the most part, showed at least an outward serenity.

They grew to like him, too, and to depend upon him. Even Aunt Isabelle went to him for advice. He had such an attentive manner, and when he spoke, he gave his opinion with an air of comforting authority.

But always he avoided Porter Bigelow, he avoided Leila, and most of all, he avoided Delilah Jeliffe, although that persistent young person would have invaded the Tower Rooms, if Mary had not warned her away.

"He is very busy, Lilah," she said, "and when he isn't, he comes down here."

"Don't you ever go up?" Delilah's tone was curious.

"No," said Mary, "Why should I?"

Delilah shrugged. "If a man," she said, "had looked at me as he looked at you on Thanksgiving night, I should be, to say the least—interested——"

Mary's head was held high. "I like Roger Poole," she said, "and he's a gentleman. But I'm not thinking about the look in his eyes."

Yet she did think of it, after all, for such seed does the Delilah-type of woman sow. She thought of him, but only with a little wonder—for Mary was as yet unawakened—Porter's passionate pleading, the magic of Roger Poole's voice—these had not touched the heart which still waited.

"Since Mahomet wouldn't come to the mountain," Mary remarked to her lodger as Susan deposited her burden, "the mountain had to come to Mahomet. And here's a bit of mistletoe for your door, and of holly for your window."

He took the wreaths from her. "You are like the spirit of Christmas in your green gown."

"This?" She was wearing the green velvet—with a low collar of lace. "Oh, I've had this for ages, but I like it——" She broke off to say, wistfully, "It seems as if you ought to come down—as if up here you'd be lonely."

Susan Jenks, hanging the mistletoe over the door, was out of range of their voices.

"I am lonely," Roger said, "but now with my little tree, I shall forget everything but your kindness."

"Don't you love Christmas?" Mary asked him. "It's such a friendly time, with everybody thinking of everybody else. I had to hunt a lot before I found the wax angel. It needed such a little one—but I always want one on my tree. When I was a child, mother used to tell me that the angel was bringing a message of peace and good will to our house."

"If the little angel brings me your good will, I shall feel that he has performed his mission."

"Oh, but you have it," brightly. "We are all so glad you are here. Even Barry, and Barry hated the idea at first of our having a lodger. But he likes you."

"And I like Barry," he said. "He is youth—incarnate."

"He's a dear," she agreed. Then a shadow came into her eyes. "But he's such a boy, and—and he's spoiled. Everybody's too good to him. Mother was—and father, though father tried not to be. And Leila is, and Constance—and Aunt Isabelle excuses him, and even Susan Jenks."

Susan Jenks, having hung all the wreaths, had departed, and was not there to hear this mention of her shortcomings.

"I see—and you?" smiling.

She drew a long breath. "I'm trying to play Big Sister—and sometimes I'm afraid I'm more like a big brother—I haven't the—patience."

His attentive face invited further confidence. It was the face of a man who had listened to many confidences, and instinctively she felt that others had been helped by him.

"You see I want Barry to pass the Bar examination. All of the men of our family have been lawyers, But Barry won't study, and he has taken a position in the Patent Office. He's wasting these best years as a clerk."

Then she remembered, and begged, "Forgive me——"

"There's nothing to forgive," he said. "I suppose I am wasting my years as a clerk in the Treasury Department—but there's this difference, your brother's life is before him—mine is behind me. His ambitions are yet to be fulfilled. I have no—ambitions."

"You don't mean that—you can't mean it?"

"Why not?"

"Because you're a man! Oh, I should have been the man of our family—and Barry and Constance should have been the girls." Her eyes blazed.

"You think then, as I heard you say the other night on the stairs, that the world is ours; yet we men let it stand still."

Her head went up. "Yes. Perhaps you do have to fight for what you get. But I'd rather die fighting than smothered."

He laughed a good boyish laugh. "Does Barry know that you feel that way?"

"I'm afraid," penitently, "that I make him feel it, sometimes. And he doesn't know that it is because I care so much. That it is because I want him to be like—father."

He smiled into her misty eyes. "Perhaps if you weren't so militant—in your methods——"

"Oh, that's the trouble with Barry. Everybody's too good to him. And when I try to counteract it, Barry says that I nag. But he doesn't understand."

Her voice broke, and by some subtle intuition he was aware that her burden was heavier than she was willing to admit.

She stood up and held out her hand. "Thank you so much—for letting me talk to you."

He took her hand and stood looking down at her.

"Will you remember that always—when you need to talk things out—that the Tower Room—is waiting?"

And now there were steps dancing up the stairs, and Barry whirled in with Little-Lovely Leila.

"Mary," he said, "we are ready to light the tree, and Aunt Frances is having fits because you aren't down. You know she always has fits when things are delayed. Poole, you are a selfish hermit to stay off up here with a tree of your own."

Roger, who had stepped forward to speak to Leila, shook his head. "I don't deserve to be invited. And you're all too good to me."

"Oh, but we're not," Leila spoke in her pretty childish way; "we'd love to have you down. Everybody's just crazy about you, Mr. Poole."

They shouted at that.

"Leila," Barry demanded, "are you crazy about him? Tell me now and get the agony over."

Leila, tilting herself on her pink slipper toes almost crowed with delight at his teasing: "I said, *everybody*——"

Barry advanced to where she stood in the doorway.

"Leila Dick," he announced, "you're under the mistletoe, and you can't escape, and I'm going to kiss you. It's my ancient and hereditary privilege—isn't it, Poole? It's my ancient and hereditary privilege," he repeated, and now he was bending over her.

"Barry," Mary expostulated, "behave yourself."

But it was Leila who stopped him. Her little hands held him off, her face was white. "Barry," she whispered, "Barry—*please*——"

He dropped her hands.

"You blessed baby," he said, with all his laughter gone. "You're like a little sweet saint in an altar shrine!"

Then, with another sudden change of mood, he whirled her away as quickly as he had come, and Mary, following, stopped on the threshold to say to Roger:

"We shall all be away to-morrow. We are to dine at General Dick's. But I am going to church in the morning—the six o'clock service. It's lovely with the snow and the stars. There'll be just Barry and me. Won't you come?"

He hesitated. Then, "No," he said, "no," and lest she should think him unappreciative, he added, "I never go to church."

She came back to him and stood by the fire. "Don't you believe in it?" She was plainly troubled for him. "Don't you believe in the angels and the shepherds, and the wise men, and the Babe in the Manger?"

"No," he said dully, "I don't believe."

"Oh," it was almost a cry, "then what does Christmas mean to you? What can it mean to anybody who doesn't believe in the Babe and the Star in the East?"

147

"It means this, Mary Ballard," he said, impetuously, "that out of all my unbelief—I believe in you—in your friendliness. And that is my star shining just now in the darkness."

She would have been less than a woman if she had not been thrilled by such a tribute. So she blushed shyly. "I'm glad," she said and smiled up at him.

But as she went down-stairs, the smile faded. It was as if the shadow of the Tower Rooms were upon her. As if the loneliness and sadness of Roger Poole had become hers. As if his burden was added to her other burdens.

Aunt Frances, more regal than ever in gold and amethyst brocade, was presiding over a mountainous pile of white boxes, behind which the unlighted tree spread its branches.

"My child," she said reprovingly, as Mary entered, "I wonder if you were ever in time for anything."

And Porter whispered in Mary's ear as he led her to the piano: "Is this a merry Christmas or a Contrary-Mary Christmas? You look as if you had the weight of the world on your shoulders."

She shook her head. Tears were very near the surface. He saw it and was jealously unhappy. What had brought her in this mood from the Tower Rooms?

And now Barry turned off the lights, and in the darkness Mary struck the first chords and began to sing, "Holy Night——" As her voice throbbed through the stillness, little stars shone out upon the tree until it was all in shining glory.

Up-stairs, Roger heard Mary singing. He went to his window and drew back the curtains. Outside the world was wrapped in snow. The lights from the lower windows shone on the fountain, and showed the little bronze boy in a winding sheet of white.

But it was not the little bronze boy that Roger Poole saw. It was another boy—himself—singing in a dim church in a big city, and his soul was in the words. And when he knelt to pray, it seemed to him that the whole world prayed. He was bathed in reverence. In his boyish soul there was no hint of unbelief—no doubt of the divine mystery.

He saw himself again in a church. And now it was he who spoke to the people of the Shepherds and the Star. And he knew that he was making them believe. That he was bringing to them the assurance which possessed his own soul—and again there were candles on the altar, and again he sang, and the choir boys sang, and the song was the one that Mary Ballard was singing——

He saw himself once more in a church. But this time there was no singing. There were no candles, no light except such as came faintly through the leaded panes. He was alone in the dimness, and he stood in the pulpit and looked around at the empty pews. Then the light went out behind the windows, and he knelt in the darkness; but not to pray. His head was hidden in his arms. Since then he had never shed a tear, and he had never gone to church.

———————————

Mary's song was followed by carols in which the other voices joined—Porter's and Barry's and Leila's; General Dick's breathy tenor, Aunt Isabelle's quaver, Aunt Frances' dominant note—with Susan Jenks and the colored maid who helped her on such occasions, piping up like two melodious blackbirds in the hall.

Then General Dick played Santa Claus, handing out the parcels with felicitous little speeches.

Constance had sent a big box from London. There were fads and fripperies from Grace Clendenning in Paris, while Aunt Frances had evidently raided Fifth Avenue and had brought away its treasures.

"It looks like a French shop," said Leila, happy in her own gifts of gloves and silk stockings and slipper buckles and beads, and the crowning bliss of a little pearl heart from Barry.

Porter's offering to Mary was a quaint ring set with rose-cut diamonds and emeralds.

Aunt Frances, hovering over it, exclaimed at its beauty. "It's a genuine antique?"

He admitted that it was, but gave no further explanation.

Later, however, he told Mary, "It was my grandmother's. She belonged to an old French family. My grandfather met her when he was in the diplomatic service. He was an Irishman, and it is from him I get my hair."

"It's a lovely thing. But—Porter—it mustn't bind me to anything. I want to be free."

"You are free. Do you remember when you were a kiddie that I gave you a penny ring out of my popcorn bag? You didn't think that ring tied you to anything, did you? Well, this is just another penny prize package."

So she wore it on her right hand and when he said "Good-night," he lifted the hand and kissed it.

"Girl, dear, may this be the merriest Christmas ever!"

And now the tears overflowed. They were alone in the lower hall and there was no one to see. "Oh, Porter," she wailed, "I'm missing Constance dreadfully—it isn't Christmas—without her. It came over me all at once—when I was trying to think that I was happy."

"Poor little Contrary Mary—if you'd only let me take care of you."

She shook her head. "I didn't mean to be—silly, Porter."

"You're not silly." Then after a silence, "Shall you go to early service in the morning?"

"Yes."

"May I go?"

"Of course. Barry's going, too."

"You mean that you won't let me go with you alone."

"I mean nothing of the kind. Barry always goes. He used to do it to please mother, and now he does it—for remembrance."

"I'm so jealous of my moments alone with you. Why can't Leila stay with you to-night, then there will be four of us, and I can have you to myself. I can bring the car, if you'd rather."

"No, I like to walk. It's so lovely and solemn."

"Be sure to ask Leila."

She promised, and he went away, having to look in at a dance given by one of his mother's friends; and Mary, returning to join the others, pondered, a little wistfully, on the fact that Porter Bigelow should be so eager for a privilege which Roger Poole had just declined.

CHAPTER VII

In Which Aunt Frances Speaks of Matrimony as a Fixed Institution and is Met by Flaming Arguments; and in Which a Strange Voice Sings Upon the Stairs.

Aunt Frances stayed until after the New Year. But before she went she sounded Aunt Isabelle.

"Has Mary said anything to you about Porter Bigelow?"

"About Porter?"

"Yes," impatiently, "about marrying him. Anybody can see that he's dead in love with her, Isabelle."

"I don't think Mary wants to marry anybody. She's an independent little creature. She should have been the boy, Frances."

"I wish to heaven she had," Aunt Frances' tone was fervent. "I can't see any future for Barry, unless he marries Leila. If he were not so irresponsible, I might do something for him. But Barry is such a will-o'-the-wisp."

Aunt Isabelle went on with her mending, and Aunt Frances again pounced upon her.

"And it isn't just that he is irresponsible. He's—— Did you notice on Christmas Day, Isabelle—that after dinner he wasn't himself?"

Aunt Isabelle had noticed. And it was not the first time. Her quick eyes had seen things which Mary had thought were hidden. She had not needed ears to tell the secret which was being kept from her in that house.

Yet her sense of loyalty sealed her lips. She would not tell Frances anything. They were dear children.

"He's just a boy, Frances," she said, deprecatingly, "and I am sorry that General Dick put temptation in his way."

"Don't blame the General. If Barry's weak, no one can make him strong but himself. I wish he had some of Porter Bigelow's steadiness. Mary won't look at Porter, and he's dead in love with her."

"Perhaps in time she may."

"Mary's like her father," Aunt Frances said shortly. "John Ballard might have been rich when he died, if he hadn't been such a dreamer. Mary calls herself practical—but her head is full of moonshine."

Aunt Frances made this arraignment with an uncomfortable memory of a conversation with Mary the day before. They had been shopping, and had lunched together at a popular tea room. It was while they sat in their secluded corner that Aunt Frances had introduced in a roundabout way the topic which obsessed her.

"I am glad that Constance is so happy, Mary."

"She ought to be," Mary responded; "it's her honeymoon."

"If you would follow her example and marry Porter Bigelow, my mind would be at rest."

"But I don't want to marry Porter, Aunt Frances. I don't want to marry anybody."

Aunt Frances raised her gold lorgnette, "If you don't marry," she demanded, "how do you expect to live?"

"I don't understand."

"I mean who is going to pay your bills for the rest of your life? Barry isn't making enough to support you, and I can't imagine that you'd care to be dependent on Gordon Richardson. And the house is rapidly losing its value. The neighborhood isn't what it was when your father bought it, and you can't rent rooms when nobody wants to come out here to live. And then what? It's a woman's place to marry when she meets a man who can take care of her—and you'll find that you can't pick Porter Bigelows off every bush—not in Washington."

Thus spoke Worldly-Wisdom, not mincing words, and back came Youth and Romance, passionately. "Aunt Frances, a woman hasn't any right to marry just because she thinks it is her best chance. She hasn't any right to make a man feel that he's won her when she's just little and mean and mercenary."

"That sounds all right," said the indignant dame opposite her, "but as I said before, if you don't marry,—what are you going to do?"

Faced by that cold question, Mary met it defiantly. "If the worst comes, I can work. Other women work."

"You haven't the training or the experience." Aunt Frances told her coldly; "don't be silly, Mary. You couldn't earn your shoe-strings."

And thus having said all there was to be said, the two ate their salad with diminished appetite, and rode home in a taxi in stiff silence.

Aunt Frances' mind roamed back to Aunt Isabelle, and fixed on her as a scapegoat. "She's like you, Isabelle," she said, "with just the difference between the ideals of twenty years ago and to-day. You haven't either of you an idea of the world as a real place—you make romance the rule of your lives—and I'd like to know what you've gotten out of it, or what she will."

"I'm not afraid for Mary." There was a defiant ring in Aunt Isabelle's voice which amazed Aunt Frances. "She'll make things come right. She has what I never had, Frances. She has strength and courage."

It was this conversation with Aunt Frances which caused Mary, in the weeks that followed, to bend for hours over a yellow pad on which she made queer hieroglyphics. And it was through these hieroglyphics that she entered upon a new phase of her friendship with Roger Poole.

He had gone to work one morning, haggard after a sleepless night.

As he approached the Treasury, the big building seemed to loom up before him like a prison. What, after all, were those thousands who wended their way every morning to the great beehives of Uncle Sam but slaves chained to an occupation which was deadening?

He flung the question later at the little stenographer who sat next to him. "Miss Terry," he asked, "how long have you been here?"

She looked up at him, brightly. She was short and thin, with a sprinkle of gray in her hair. But she was well-groomed and nicely dressed in her mannish silk shirt and gray tailored skirt.

"Twenty years," she said, snapping a rubber band about her note-book.

"And always at this desk?"

"Oh, dear, no. I came in at nine hundred, and now I am getting twelve hundred."

"But always in this room?"

She nodded. "Yes. And it is very nice. Most of the people have been here as long as I, and some of them much longer. There's Major Orr, for example, he has been here since just after the War."

"Do you ever feel as if you were serving sentence?"

She laughed. She was not troubled by a vivid imagination. "It really isn't bad for a woman. There aren't many places with as short hours and as good pay."

For a woman? But for a man? He turned back to his desk. What would he be after twenty years of this? He waked every morning with the day's routine facing him—knowing that not once in the eight hours would there be a demand upon his mentality, not once would there be the thrill of real accomplishment.

At noon when he saw Miss Terry strew bird seed on the broad window sill for the sparrows, he likened it to the diversions of a prisoner in his cell. And, when he ate lunch with a group of fellow clerks in a cheap restaurant across the way, he wondered, as they went back, why they were spared the lockstep.

In this mood he left the office at half-past four, and passing the place where he usually ate, inexpensively, he entered a luxurious up-town hotel. There he read the papers until half-past six; then dined in a grill room which permitted informal dress.

Coming out later, he met Barry coming in, linked arm in arm with two radiant youths of his own kind and class. Musketeers of modernity, they found their adventures on the city streets, in cafes and cabarets, instead of in field and forest and on the battle-field.

Barry, with a flower in his buttonhole, welcomed Roger uproariously. "Here's Whittington," he said. "You ought to hear his poem, fellows, about a little cat. He had us all hypnotized the other night."

Roger glanced at him sharply. His exaggerated manner, the looseness of his phrasing, the flush on his cheeks were in strange contrast to his usual frank, clean boyishness.

"Come on, Poole," Barry urged, "we'll motor out in Jerry's car to the Country Club, and you can give it to us out there—about Whittington and the little cat."

Roger declined, and Barry took quick offense. "Oh, well, if you don't want to, you needn't," he said; "four's a crowd, anyhow—come on, fellows."

Roger, vaguely troubled, watched him until he was lost in the crowd, then sighed and turned his steps homeward.

As Roger ascended to his Tower, the house seemed strangely silent. Pittiwitz was asleep beside the pot of pink hyacinths. She sat up, yawned, and welcomed him with a little coaxing note. When he had settled himself in his big chair, she came and curled in the corner of his arm, and again went to sleep.

Deep in his reading, he was roused an hour later by a knock at his door.

He opened it, to find Mary on the threshold.

"May I come in?" she asked, and she seemed breathless. "It is Susan's night out, and Aunt Isabelle is at the opera with some old friends. Barry expected to be here with me, but he hasn't come. And I sat in the dining-room—and waited," she shivered, "until I couldn't stand it any more."

She tried to laugh, but he saw that she was very pale.

"Please don't think I'm a coward," she begged. "I've never been that. But I seemed suddenly to have a sort of nervous panic, and I thought perhaps you wouldn't mind if I sat with you—until Barry—came——"

"I'm glad he didn't come, if it is going to give me an evening with you." He drew a chair to the fire.

They had talked of many things when she asked, suddenly, "Mr. Poole, I wonder if you can tell me—about the examinations for stenographers in the Departments—are they very rigid?"

"Not very. Of course they require speed and accuracy."

She sighed. "I'm accurate enough, but I wonder if I can ever acquire speed."

He stared. "You——?"

She nodded. "I haven't mentioned it to any one. One's family is so hampering sometimes—they'd all object—except Aunt Isabelle, but I want to be prepared to work, if I ever need to earn my living."

"May you never need it," he said, fervently, visions rising of little Miss Terry and her machine-made personality. What had this girl with the fair hair and the shining eyes to do with the blank life between office walls?

"May you never need it," he repeated. "A woman's place is in the home—it's a man's place to fight the world."

"But if there isn't a man to fight a woman's battles?"

"There will always be some one to fight yours."

"You mean that I can—marry? But what if I don't care to marry merely to be—supported?"

"There would have to be other things, of course," gravely.

"What, for example?"

"Love."

"You mean the 'honor and obey' kind? But don't want that when I marry. I want a man to say to me, 'Come, let us fight the battle together. If it's defeat, we'll go down together. If its victory, we'll win.'"

This was to him a strange language, yet there was that about it which thrilled him.

Yet he insisted, dogmatically, "There are men enough in the world to take care of the women, and the women should let them."

"No, they should not. Suppose I should not marry. Must I let Barry take care of me, or Constance—and go on as Aunt Isabelle has, eating the bread of dependence?"

"But you? Why, one only needs to look at you to know that there'll be a live-happy-ever-after ending to your romance."

"That's what they thought about Aunt Isabelle. But she lost her lover, and she couldn't love again. And if she had had an absorbing occupation, she would have been saved so much humiliation, so much heart-break."

She told him the story with its touching pathos. "And think of it," she ended, "right here in our garden by the fountain, she saw him for the last time."

Chilled by the ghostly breath of dead romance, they sat for a while in silence, then Mary said: "So that's why I'm trying to learn something—that will have an earning value. I can sing and play a little, but not enough to make—money."

She sighed, and he set himself to help her.

"The quickest way," he said, "to acquire speed, is to have some one read to you."

"Aunt Isabelle does sometimes, but it tires her."

"Let me do it. I should never tire."

"Oh, wouldn't you mind? Could we practice a little—now?"

And so it began—the friendship in which he served her, and loved the serving.

He read, slowly, liking to see, when he raised his eyes, the slim white figure in the big chair, the firelight on the absorbed face.

Thus the time slipped by, until with a start, Mary looked up.

"I don't see what is keeping Barry."

Then Roger told her what he had been reluctant to tell. "I saw him down-town. I think he was on his way to the Country Club. He had been dining with some friends."

"Men friends?"

"Yes. He called one of them Jerry."

He saw the color rise in her face. "I hate Jerry Tuckerman, and Barry promised Constance he'd let those boys alone."

Her voice had a sharp note in it, but he saw that she was struggling with a gripping fear.

This, then, was the burden she was bearing? And what a brave little thing she was to face the world with her head up.

"Would you like to have me call the Country Club—I might be able to get your brother on the wire."

"Oh; if you would."

But he was saved the trouble. For, even while they spoke of him, Barry came, and Mary went down to him.

A little later, there were stumbling steps upon the stairs, and a voice was singing—a strange song, in which each verse ended with a shout.

Roger, stepping out into the dark upper hall, looked down over the railing. Mary, a slender shrinking figure; was coming with her brother up the lower flight. Barry had his arm around her, but her face was turned from him, and her head drooped.

Then, still looking down, Roger saw her guide those stumbling steps to the threshold of the boy's room. The door opened and shut, and she was alone, but from within there still came the shouted words of that strange song.

Mary stood for a moment with her hands clenched at her sides, then turned and laid her face against the closed door, her eyes hidden by her upraised arm.

CHAPTER VIII

In Which Little-Lovely Leila Sees a Picture in an Unexpected Place; and in Which Perfect Faith Speaks Triumphantly Over the Telephone.

Whatever Delilah Jeliffe might lack, it was not originality. The apartment which she chose for her winter in Washington was like any other apartment when she went into it, but the changes which she made—the things which she added and the things which she took away, stamped it at once with her own individuality.

The peacock screen before the fireplace, the cushions of sapphire and emerald and old gold on the couch, the mantel swept of all ornament except a seven-branched candlestick; these created the first impression. Then one's eyes went to an antique table on which a crystal ball, upborne by three bronze monkeys, seemed to gather to itself mysteriously all the glow of firelight and candlelight and rich color. At the other end of the table was a low bowl, filled always with small saffron-hued roses.

In this room, one morning, late in Lent, Leila Dick sat, looking as out of place as an English daisy in a tropical jungle.

Leila did not like the drawn curtains and the dimness. Outside the sun was shining, gloriously, and the sky was a deep and lovely blue.

She was glad when Lilah sent for her.

"You are to come right to her room," the maid announced.

"Heavens, child," said the Delilah-beauty, who was combing her hair, "I didn't promise to be up with the birds."

"The birds were up long ago," Leila perched herself on an old English love-seat. "We're to have lunch before we go to Fort Myer, and it is almost one now."

Lilah yawned, "Is it?" and went on combing her hair with the air of one who has hours before her. She wore a silken négligée of flamingo red which matched her surroundings, for this room was as flaming as the other was subdued. Yet the effect was not that of crude color; it was, rather, that of color intensified deliberately to produce a contrast. Delilah's bedroom was high noon under a blazing sun, the sitting-room was midnight under the stars.

With her black hair at last twisted into wonderful coils, Delilah surveyed her face reflectively in the mirror, and having decided that she needed no further aid from the small jars on her dressing table, she turned to her friend.

"What shall I wear, Leila?"

"If I told you," was the calm response, "you wouldn't wear it."

Delilah laughed. "No, I wouldn't. I simply have to think such things out for myself. But I meant what kind of clothes—dress up or motor things?"

"Porter will take us out in his car. You'll need your heavy coat, and something good-looking underneath, for lunch, you know."

"Is Mary Ballard going?"

"Of course. We shouldn't get Porter's car if she weren't."

"Mary wasn't with us the day we had tea with him in the Park."

"No, but she was asked. Porter never leaves her out."

"Are they engaged?"

"No, Mary won't be."

"She'll never get a better chance," Delilah reflected. "She isn't pretty, and she's rather old style."

Leila blazed. "She's beautiful——"

"To you, duckie, because you love her. But the average man wouldn't call Mary Ballard beautiful."

"I don't care—the un-average one would. And Mary Ballard wouldn't look at an ordinary man."

"No man is ordinary when he is in love."

"Oh, with you," Leila's tone was scornful, "love's just a game."

Lilah rose, crossed the room with swift steps, and kissed her. "Don't let me ruffle your plumage, Jenny Wren," she said; "I'm a screaming peacock this morning."

"What's the matter?"

"I'm not the perfect success I planned to be. Oh, I can see it. I've been here for three months, and people stare at me, but they don't call on me—not the ones I want to know. And it's because I am too—emphasized. In New York you have to be emphatic to be anything at all. Otherwise you are lost in the crowd. That's why Fifth Avenue is full of people in startling clothes. In the mob you won't be singled out simply for your pretty face—there are too many pretty faces; so it is the woman who strikes some high note of conspicuousness who attracts attention. But you're like a flock of cooing doves, you Washington girls. You're as natural and frank and unaffected as a—a covey of partridges. I believe I am almost jealous of your Mary Ballard this morning."

"Not because of Porter?"

"Not because of any man. But there are things about her which I can't acquire. I've the money and the clothes and the individuality. But there's a simplicity about her, a directness, that comes from years of association with things I haven't had. Before I came here, I thought money could buy anything. But it can't. Mary Ballard couldn't be anything else. And I—I can be anything from a siren to a soubrette, but I can't be a lady—not the kind that you are—and Mary Ballard."

Saying which, the tropic creature in flamingo red sat down beside the cooing dove, and continued:

"You were right just now, when you said that the un-average man would love Mary Ballard. Porter Bigelow loves her, and he tops all the other men I've met. And he'd never love me. He will laugh with me and joke with me, and if he wasn't in love with Mary, he might flirt with me—but I'm not his kind—and he knows it."

She sighed and shrugged her shoulders. "There are other fish in the sea, of course, and Porter Bigelow is Mary's. But I give you my word, Leila Dick, that when I catch sight of his blessed red head towering above the others—like a lion-hearted Richard, I can't see anybody else."

For the first time since she had known her, Leila was drawn to the other by a feeling of sympathetic understanding.

"Are you in love with him, Lilah?" she asked; timidly.

Lilah stood up, stretching her hands above her head. "Who knows? Being in love and loving—perhaps they are different things, duckie."

With which oracular remark she adjourned to her dressing-room, where, in long rows, her lovely gowns were hung.

Leila, left alone, picked up a magazine on the table beside her glanced through it and laid it down; picked a bonbon daintily out of a big box and ate it; picked up a photograph——

"Mousie," said Lilah, coming back, several minutes later, "what makes you so still? Did you find a book?"

No, Leila had not found a book, and the photograph was back where she had first discovered it, face downward under the box of chocolates. And she was now standing by the window, her veil drawn tightly over her close little hat, so that one might not read the trouble in her telltale eyes. The daisy drooped now, as if withered by the blazing sun.

But Delilah saw nothing of the change. She wore a saffron-hued coat, which matched the roses in the other room, and her leopard skins, with a small hat of the same fur.

As she surveyed herself finally in the long glass, she flung out the somewhat caustic remark:

"When I get down-stairs and look at Mary Ballard, I shall feel like a Beardsley poster propped up beside a Helleu etching."

153

After lunch, Porter took Aunt Isabelle and Barry and the three girls to Fort Myer. The General and Mr. Jeliffe met them at the drill hall, and as they entered there came to them the fresh fragrance of the tan bark.

As the others filed into their seats, Barry held Leila back. "We will sit at the end," he said. "I want to talk to you."

Through her veil, her eyes reproached him.

"No," she said; "no."

He looked down at her in surprise. Never before had Little-Lovely Leila refused the offer of his valuable society.

"You sit beside—Delilah," she said, nervously, "She's really your guest."

"She is Porter's guest," he declared. "I don't see why you want to turn her over to me." Then as she endeavored to pass him, he caught her arm.

"What's the matter?" he demanded.

"Nothing," faintly,

"Nothing——" scornfully. "I can read you like a book. What's happened?"

But she merely shook her head and sat down, and then the bugle sounded, and the band began to play, and in came the cavalry—a gallant company, through the sun-lighted door, charging in a thundering line toward the reviewing stand—to stop short in a perfect and sudden salute.

The drill followed, with men riding bareback, men riding four abreast, men riding in pyramids, men turning somersaults on their trained and intelligent steeds.

One man slipped, fell from his horse, and lay close in the tan bark, while the other horses went over him, without a hoof touching, so that he rose unhurt, and took his place again in the line.

Leila hid her eyes in her muff. "I don't like it," she said. "I've never liked it. And what if that man had been killed?"

"They don't get killed," said Barry easily. "The hospital is full of those who get hurt, but it is good for them; it teaches them to be cool and competent when real danger comes."

And now came the artillery, streaming through that sun-lighted entrance, the heavy wagons a featherweight to the strong, galloping horses. Breathless Leila watched their manoeuvres, as they wheeled and circled and crisscrossed in spaces which seemed impossibly small—horses plunging, gun-wagons rattling, dust flying—faster, faster—— Again she shut her eyes.

But Mary Ballard, cheeks flushed, eyes dancing, turned to Porter. "Don't you love it?" she asked.

"I love you——" audaciously. "Mary, you and I were born in the wrong age. We belong to the days of King Arthur. Then I could have worn a coat of mail and have stormed your castle, and I shouldn't have cared if you hurled defiance from the top turret. I'd have known that, at last, you'd be forced to let down the drawbridge; and I would have crossed the moat and taken you prisoner, and you'd have been so impressed with my strength and prowess that you would——"

"No, I wouldn't," said Mary quickly.

"Wait till I finish," said Porter, coolly. "I'd have shut you up in a tower, and every night I'd have come and sung beneath your window, and at last you'd have dropped a red rose down to me."

They were laughing together now, and Delilah on the other side of Porter demanded, "What's the joke?"

"There isn't any," said Porter; "it is all deadly earnest—for me, if not for Mary."

And now a horse was down; there was a quick bugle-note, silence. Like clockwork, everything had stopped.

People were asking, "Is anybody hurt?"

Barry looked down at Leila. Then he leaned toward her father. "I'm going to take this child outside," he said; "she's as white as a sheet. She doesn't like it. We will meet you all later."

Leila's color came back in the sunshine and air and she insisted that Barry should return to the hall.

"I don't want you to miss it," she said, "just because I am so silly. I can stay in Porter's car and wait."

"I don't want to see it—it's an old story to me."

So they walked on toward Arlington, entering at last the gate which leads into that wonderful city of the nation's Northern dead, which was once the home of Southern hospitality. In a sheltered corner they sat down and Barry smiled at Little-Lovely Leila.

"Are you all right now, kiddie?"

"Yes," but she did not smile.

He bent down and peered through her veil. "Take it off and let me look at your eyes."

With trembling hands, she took out a pin or two and let it fall.

"You've been crying."

"Oh, Barry," the words were a cry—the cry of a little wounded bird.

He stopped smiling. "Blessed one, what is it?"

"I can't tell you."

"You must."

"No."

A low-growing magnolia hid them from the rest of the world; he put masterful hands on her shoulders and turned her face toward him—her little unhappy face.

"Now tell me."

She shook herself free. "Don't, Barry."

He flushed suddenly and sensitively. "I know I'm not much of a fellow."

She answered with a dignity which seemed to surmount her usual childishness, "Barry, if a man wants a woman to believe in him, he's got to make himself worthy of it."

"Well," defiantly, "what have I done?"

"WHAT HAVE I DONE?"

[Illustration: "What have I done?"]

"Don't you know?"

"No-o."

"Then I'll tell you. Yes, I *will* tell you," with sudden courage. "I was at Delilah's this morning, and I saw your picture, and what you had written on it——"

He stared at her, with a sense of surging relief. If it was only that he had to explain about—Lilah. A smile danced in his eyes.

"Well?"

"I know you like to—play the game—but I didn't think you'd go as far as that——"

"How far?"

"Oh, you know."

"I don't."

"*Barry!*"

"I don't. I wish you'd tell me what you mean, Leila."

"I will." Her eyes were not reproachful now, they were blazing. She had risen, and with her hands tucked into her muff, and her veil blowing about her flushed cheeks, she made her accusation. "You wrote on that picture, 'To the One Girl— Forever.' Is that the way you think of Delilah, Barry?"

"No. It is the way I think of you. And how did that picture happen to be in Delilah's possession? I sent it to you."

"To me?"

"Yes, I took it over to you yesterday, and left it with one of the maids—a new one. I intended, to go in and give it to you, but when she said you had callers, I handed her the package——"

"And I thought—oh, Barry, what else could I think?"

She was so little and lovely in her tender contrition, that he flung discretion to the winds. "You are to think only one thing," he said, passionately, "that I love you—not anybody else, not ever anybody else. I haven't dared put it into words before. I haven't dared ask you to marry me, because I haven't anything to offer you yet. But I thought you—knew——"

Her little hand went out to him. "Oh, Barry," she whispered, "do you really feel that way about me?"

"Yes. More than I have said. More than I can ever say."

He drew her down beside him on the bench. "Our world won't want us to get married, Leila; they will say that I am such a boy. But you will believe in me, dear one?"

"Always, Barry."

"And you love me?"

"Oh, you know it."

"Yes, I know it," he said, in a moved voice, as he raised her hands and kissed them, "I know it—thank God."

After the drill, Porter took the whole party back to Delilah's for tea. And when her guests had gone, and the black-haired beauty went to her flamingo room to dress for dinner, she found a note on her pincushion.

"I have taken Barry's picture, because he meant it for me; it was a mistake, your getting it. He left it with the new maid one day when you were at our house, and she handed it to you instead of to me—she mixed up our names, just as the maids used to mix them up at school. And I know you won't mind my taking it, because with you it is just a game to play at love—with Barry. But it is my life, as you said that day in the Park. And to-day Barry told me that it is his life, too. And I am very happy. But this is our secret, and please let it be your secret until we let the rest of the world know——"

Delilah, reading the childish scrawl, smiled and shook her head. Then she went to the telephone and called up Leila.

"Duckie," she said, "I'll dance at your wedding. Only don't love him too much—no man is worth it."

Then, triumphant from the other end of the line, came the voice of Perfect Faith—"Oh, Barry's worth it. I've known him all my life, Lilah, and I've never had a single doubt."

CHAPTER IX

In Which Roger Sallies Forth in the Service of a Damsel in Distress, and in Which He Meets Dragons Along the Way.

In the weeks which followed the trip to Fort Myer, Mary found an astonishing change in her brother. For the first time in his life he seemed to be taking things seriously. He stayed at home at night and studied. He gave up Jerry Tuckerman and the other radiant musketeers. She did not know the reason for the change but it brought her hope and happiness.

Barry saw Leila often, but, as yet, no one but Delilah Jeliffe knew of the tie between them.

"I ought to tell Dad," Leila had said, timidly; "he'd be very happy. It is what he has always wanted, Barry."

"I must prove myself a man first," Barry told her, "I've squandered some of my opportunities, but now that I have you to work for, I feel as strong as a lion."

They were alone in the General's library. "It is because you trust me, dear one," Barry went on, "that I am strong."

She slipped her little hand into his. "Barry—it seems so queer to think that I shall ever be—your wife."

"You had to be. It was meant from the—beginning."

"Was it, Barry?"

"Yes."

"And it will be to the end. Oh, I shall always love you, dearly, dearly——"

It was idyllic, their little love affair—their big love affair, if one judged by their measure. It was tender, sweet, and because it was their secret, because there was no word of doubt or of distrust from those who were older and wiser, they brought to it all the beauty of youth and high hope.

Thus the spring came, and the early summer, and Barry passed his examinations triumphantly, and came home one night and told Mary that he was going to marry Leila Dick. As he told her his blue eyes beseeched her, and loving him, and hating to hurt him, Mary withheld the expression of her fears, and kissed him and cried a little on his shoulder, and Barry patted her cheek, and said awkwardly: "I know you think I'm not worthy of her, Mary. But she will make a man of me."

Alone, afterward, Mary wondered if she had been wise to acquiesce—yet surely, surely, love was strong enough to lift a man up to a woman's ideal—and Leila was such a—darling.

She put the question to Roger Poole that night. In these warmer days she and Roger had slipped almost unconsciously into close intimacy. He read to her for an hour after dinner, when she had no other engagements, and often they sat in the old garden, she with her note-book on the arm of the stone bench—he at the other end of the bench, under a bush of roses of a hundred leaves. Sometimes Aunt Isabelle was with them, with her fancy work, sometimes they were alone; but always when the hour was over, he would close his book and ascend to his tower, lest he might meet those who came later. There were many nights that he thus escaped Porter Bigelow—nights when in the moonlight he heard the murmur of voices, mingled with the splash of the fountain; and there were other nights when gay groups danced upon the lawn to the music played by Mary just within the open window.

Yet he thanked the gods for the part which he was allowed to play in her life. He lived for that one hour out of the twenty-four. He dared not think what a day would be if he were deprived of that precious sixty minutes.

Now and then, when she had been very sure that no one would come, he had stayed with her in the moonlight, and the little bronze boy had smiled at him from the fountain, and there had been the fragrance of the roses, and Mary Ballard in white on the stone bench beside him, giving him her friendly, girlish confidences; she discussed problems of genteel poverty, the delightful obstinacies of Susan Jenks, the dominance of Aunt Frances. She gave him, too, her opinions—those startling untried opinions which warred constantly with his prejudices.

And now to-night—his advice.

"Do you think love can change a man's nature? Make a weak man strong, I mean?"

He laid down his book. "You ask that as if I could really answer it."

"I think you can. You always seem to be able to put yourself in the other person's place, and it—helps."

"Thank you. And now in whose place shall put myself?"

"The girl's," promptly.

He considered it. "I should say that the man should be put to the test before marriage."

"You mean that she ought to wait until she is sure that he is made over?"

"Yes."

"Oh, I feel that way. But what if the girl believes in him? Doesn't dream that he is weak—trusts him absolutely, blindly? Should any one try to open her eyes?"

"Sometimes it is folly to be wise. Perhaps for her he will always be strong."

"Then what's the answer?"

"Only this. That the man himself should make the test. He should wait until he knows that he is worthy of her."

She made a little gesture of hopelessness, just the lifting of her hands and letting them drop; then she spoke with a rush of feeling.

"Mr. Poole—it is Barry and Leila. Ought I to let them marry?"

He smiled at her confidence in her ability to rule the destinies of those about her.

"I fancy that you won't have anything to do with it. He is of age, and you are only his sister. You couldn't forbid the banns, you know."

"But if I could convince him——"

"Of what?" gravely. "That you think him a boy? Perhaps that would tend to weaken his powers."

"Then I must fold my hands?"

"Yes. As things are now—I should wait."

He did not explain, and she did not ask, for what she should wait. It was as if they both realized that the test would come, and that it would come in time.

And it did come.

It was while Leila was on a trip to the Maine coast with her father.

July was waning, and already an August sultriness was in the air. Those who were left in town were the workers—every one who could get away was gone. Mary, with the care of her house on her hands, refused Aunt Frances' invitation for a month by the sea, and Aunt Isabelle declined to leave her.

"I like it better here, even with the heat," she told her niece, "than running around Bar Harbor with Frances and Grace."

Barry wrote voluminous letters to Leila, and received in return her dear childish scrawls. But the strain of her absence began to tell on him. He began to feel the pull toward old pleasures and distractions. Then one day Jerry Tuckerman arrived on the scene. The next night, he and Barry and the other radiant musketeers motored over to Baltimore by moonlight. Barry did not come home the next day, nor the next, nor the next. Mary grew white and tense, and manufactured excuses which did not deceive Aunt Isabelle. Neither of the tired pale women spoke to each other of their vigils. Neither of them spoke of the anxiety which consumed them.

Then one night, after a message had come from the office, asking for an explanation of Barry's absence; after she had called up the Country Club; after she had called up Jerry Tuckerman and had received an evasive answer; after she had exhausted all other resources, Mary climbed the steps to the Tower Rooms.

And there, sitting stiff and straight in a high-backed chair, with her throat dry, her pulses throbbing, she laid the case before Roger Poole.

"There is no one else—I can speak to—about it. But Barry's been away for nearly a week from the office and from home—and nobody knows where he is. And it isn't the first time. It began before father died, and it nearly broke his heart. You see, he had a brother—whose life was ruined because of this. And Constance and I have done everything. There will be months when he is all right. And then there'll be a week—away. And after it, he is dreadfully depressed, and I'm afraid." She was shivering, though the night was hot.

Roger dared not speak his sympathy. This was not the moment.

So he said, simply, "I'll find him, and when I find him," he went on, "it may be best not to bring him back at once. I've had to deal with such cases before. We will go into the country for a few days, and come back when he is completely—himself."

"Oh, can you spare the time?"

"I haven't taken any vacation, and—so there are still thirty days to my credit. And I need an outing."

He prepared at once to go, and when he had packed a little bag, he came down into the garden. There was moonlight and the fragrance and the splashing fountain. Roger was thrilled by the thought of his quest. It was as if he had laid upon himself some vow which was sending him forth for the sake of this sweet lady. As Mary came toward him, he wished that he might ask for the rose she wore, as his reward. But he must not ask. She gave him her friendship, her confidence, and these were very precious things. He must never ask for more—and so he must not ask for a rose.

And now he was standing just below her on the terrace steps, looking up at her with his heart in his eyes.

"I'll find him," he said, "don't worry."

She reached out and touched his shoulder with her hand. "How good you are," she said, wistfully, "to take all of this trouble for us. I feel that I ought not to let you do it—and yet—we are so helpless, Aunt Isabelle and I."

There was nothing of the boy about her now. She was all clinging dependent woman. And the touch of her hand on his shoulder was the sword of the queen conferring knighthood. What cared he now for a rose?

So he left her, standing there in the moonlight, and when he reached the bottom of the hill, he turned and looked back, and she still stood above him, and as she saw him turn, she waved her hand.

In days of old, knights fought with dragons and cut off their heads, only to find that other heads had grown to replace those which had been destroyed.

And it was such dragons of doubt and despair which Roger Poole fought in the days after he had found Barry.

The boy had hidden himself in a small hotel in the down-town district of Baltimore. Following one clue and then another, Roger had come upon him. There had been no explanations. Barry had seemed to take his rescue as a matter of course, and to be glad of some one into whose ears he could pour the litany of his despair.

"It's no use, Poole. I've fought and fought. Father helped me. And I promised Con. And I thought that my love for Leila would make me strong. But there's no use trying. I'll be beaten. It is in the blood. I had an uncle who drank himself to death. And back of him there was a grandfather."

They had been together for two days. Barry had agreed to Roger's plans for a trip to the country, and now they were under the trees on the banks of one of the little brackish rivers which flow into the Chesapeake. They had fished a little in the early morning, then had brought their boat in, for Barry had grown tired of the sport. He wanted to talk about himself.

"It's no use," he said again; "it's in the blood."

Roger was propped against a tree, his hat off, his dark hair blown back from his fine thin face.

"Our lives," he said, "are our own. Not what our ancestors make them."

"I don't believe it," Barry said, flatly. "I've fought a good fight, no one can say that I haven't. And I've lost. After this do you suppose that Mary will let me marry Leila? Do you suppose the General will let me marry her?"

"Will you let yourself marry her?"

Barry's face flamed. "Then you think I'm not worthy?"

"It is what you think, Ballard, not what I think."

Barry pulled up a handful of grass and threw it away, pulled up another handful and threw it away. Then he said, doggedly, "I'm going to marry her, Poole; no one shall take her away from me."

"And you call that love?"

"Yes. I can't live without her."

Roger with his eyes on the dark water which slipped by the banks, taking its shadows from the darkness of the thick branches which bent above it said quietly, "Love to me has always seemed something bigger than that—it has seemed as if love—great love took into consideration first the welfare of the beloved."

There was a long silence, out of which Barry said tempestuously, "It will break her heart if anything comes between us. I'm not saying that because am a conceited donkey. But she is such a constant little thing."

Roger nodded. "That's all the more reason why you've got to pull up now, Ballard."

"But I've tried."

"I knew a man who tried—and won."

"How?" eagerly.

"I met him in the pine woods of the South. I was down there to recover from a cataclysm which had changed—my life. This man had a little shack next to mine. Neither of us had much money. We lived literally in the open. We cooked over fires in front of our doors. We hunted and fished. Now and then we went to town for our supplies, but most of our things we got from the schooner-men who drove down from the hills. My neighbor was married. He had a wife and three children. But he had come alone. And he told me grimly that he should never go back until he went back a man."

"Did he go back?"

"Yes. He conquered. He looked upon his weakness not merely as a moral disease, but as a physical one. And it was to be cured like any other disease by removing the cause. The first step was to get away from old associations. He couldn't resist temptation, so he had come where he was not tempted. His occupation in the city had been mental, here it was largely physical. He chopped wood, he tramped the forest, he whipped the streams. And gradually he built up a self which was capable of resistance. When he went back he was a different man, made over by his different life. And he has cast out his—devil."

The boy was visibly impressed.

"His way might not be your way," Roger concluded, "but the fact that he fought a winning battle should give you hope."

The next day they went back. Mary met them as if nothing had happened. The basket of fish which they had brought to be cooked by Susan Jenks furnished an unembarrassing topic of conversation. Then Barry went to his room, and Mary was alone with Roger.

She had had a letter from him, and a message by telephone; thus her anxiety had been stilled. And she was very grateful—so grateful that her voice trembled as she held out her hands to him.

"How shall I ever thank you?" she said.

He took her hands in his, and stood looking down at her.

He did not speak at once, yet in those fleeting moments Mary had a strange sense of a question asked and answered. It was as if he were calling upon her for something she was not ready to give—as if he were drawing from her some subconscious admission, swaying her by a force that was compelling, to reveal herself to him.

And, as she thought these things, he saw a new look in her eyes, and her breath quickened.

He dropped her hands.

"Don't thank me," he said. "Ask me again to do something for you. That shall be my reward."

CHAPTER X

In Which a Scarlet Flower Blooms in the Garden; and in Which a Light Flares Later in the Tower.

In September everybody came back to town, Porter Bigelow among the rest.

He telephoned at once to Mary, "I'm coming up."

She was radiant. "Constance and Gordon arrived Monday, and I want you for dinner. Leila will be here and the General and Aunt Frances and Grace from New York."

His growl came back to her. "And that means that I won't have a minute alone with you."

"Oh, Porter—please. There are so many other girls in the world—and you've had the whole summer to find one."

"The summer has been a howling wilderness. But mother has put me through my paces at the resorts. Mary, I've learned such a lot of new dances to teach you."

"Teach them to Grace."

He groaned. "You know what I think of Grace Clendenning."

"Porter, she's beautiful. She wears little black frocks with wide white collars and cuffs and looks perfectly adorable. To-night she's going to wear a black tulle gown and a queer flaring black tulle head-dress, and with her red hair—you won't be able to drag your eyes from her."

"I've enough red hair of my own," Porter informed her, "without having to look at Grace's."

"I'll put you opposite her at dinner. Come and see, and be conquered."

Roger Poole was also invited to the home-coming dinner. Mary had asked nobody's advice this time. Of late Roger and Barry had been much together, and it was their friendship which Mary had exploited, when Constance, somewhat anxiously, had asked, on the day preceding the dinner, if she thought it was wise to include the lonely dweller in the Tower Rooms.

"He's really very nice, Constance. And he has been a great help to Barry."

It was the first time that they had spoken of their brother. And now Constance's words came with something of an effort. "What of Barry, Mary?"

"He is more of a man, Con. He is trying hard for Leila's sake."

"Gordon thinks they really ought not to be engaged."

The sisters were in Mary's room, and Mary at her little desk was writing out the dinner list for Susan Jenks. She looked up and laid down her pen. "Then you've told Gordon?"

"Yes. And he says that Barry ought to go away."

"Where?"

"Far enough to give Leila a chance to get over it."

"Do you think she would ever get over it, Con?"

"Gordon thinks she would."

Mary's head went up. "I am not asking what Gordon thinks. What do you think?"

"I think as Gordon does." Then as Mary made a little impatient gesture, she added, "Gordon is very wise. At first it seemed to me that he was—harsh, in his judgment of Barry. But he knows so much of men—and he says that here, in town, among his old associations—Barry will never be different. And it isn't fair to Leila."

Mary knew that it was not fair to Leila. She had always known it. Yet she was stubbornly resentful of the fact that Gordon Richardson should be, as it were, the arbiter of Barry's destiny.

"Oh, it is all such a muddle, Con," she said, and put the question aside. "We won't talk about it just now. There is so much else to say—and it is lovely to have you back, dearest—and you are so lovely."

Constance was curled up on Mary's couch, resting after her journey. "I am so happy, Mary. No woman knows anything about it, until she has had it for herself. A man's strength is so wonderful—and Gordon's care of me—oh, Mary, if there were only another man in the world for you like Gordon I should be perfectly content."

It was a fervent gentle echo of Aunt Frances' demand upon her, and Mary suppressing her raging jealousy of the man who had stolen her sister, asked somewhat wistfully, "Can you talk about me, for a minute, and forget that you have a husband?"

"I don't need to forget Gordon," was the serene response. "I can keep him in the back of my mind."

Mary picked up her pen, and underscored "*Soup*"; then: "Constance, darling," she said, "would you feel dreadfully if I went to work?"

"What kind of work, Mary?"

"In one of the departments,—as stenographer."

"But you don't know anything about it."

"Yes, I do, I've been studying ever since you went away."

"But why, Mary?"

"Because—oh, can't you see, Constance? I can't be sure of—Barry—for future support. And I won't go with Aunt Frances. And this house is simply eating up the little that father left us. When you married, I thought the rental of the Tower Rooms would keep things going, but it won't. And I won't sell the house. I love every old stick and stone of it. And anyhow, must I sit and fold my hands all the rest of my life just because I am a woman?"

"But Mary, dear, you will marry—there's Porter."

"Constance, I couldn't think of marriage that way—as a chance to be taken care of. Oh, Con, I want to wait—for love."

"Dearest, of course. But you can live with us. Gordon would never consent to your working—he thinks it is dreadful for a woman to have to fight the world."

Mary shook her head. "No, it wouldn't be fair to you. It is never fair for an outsider to intrude upon the happiness of a home. If your duet is ever to be a trio, it must not be with my big blundering voice, which could make only a discord, but a little piping one."

She looked up to meet Constance's shy, self-conscious eyes.

Mary flew to her, and knelt beside the couch. "Darling, darling?"

And now the list was forgotten and Susan Jenks coming up for it was made a party to that tremulous secret, and the fate of the dinner was threatened until Mary, coming back to realities, kissed her sister and went to her desk, and held herself sternly to the five following courses of the family dinner which was to please the palates of those fresh from Paris and London and from castles by the sea; and which was to test to the utmost the measure of Susan's culinary skill.

At dinner the next night, Gordon Richardson looked often and intently at Roger Poole, and when, under the warmth of the September moon, the men drifted out into the garden to smoke, he said, "I've just placed you."

Roger nodded. "I thought you'd remember. You were one of the younger boys at St. Martin's—you haven't changed much, but I couldn't be sure."

Gordon hesitated. "I thought I heard from someone that you entered the Church."

"I had a church in the South—for three years."

Gordon tried to keep the curiosity out of his voice.

"And you gave it up?"

"Yes. I gave it up."

That was all. Not a word of the explanation for which he knew Gordon was waiting. Nothing but the bare statement, "I gave it up."

They talked a little of St. Martin's after that, of their boyish experiences. But Roger was conscious that Gordon was weighing him, and asking of himself, "Why did he give it up?"

The two men were sitting on the stone bench where Roger had so often sat with Mary. The garden was showing the first signs of the season's blight. Fading leaf and rustling vine had replaced the unspringing greenness and the fragrant growth of the summer. There were, to be sure, dahlias and chrysanthemums and cosmos. But the glory of the garden was gone.

Then into the garden came Mary!

She was wrapped in a thin silken, scarlet cloak that belonged to Constance. As she passed through the broad band of light made by the street lamp. Roger had a sudden memory of the flame-like blossoming of a certain slender shrub in the spring. It had been the first of the flowers to bloom, and Mary had picked a branch for the vase on his table in the Tower sitting-room.

"Constance wants you, Gordon," Mary said, as she came nearer; "some one has called up to arrange about a dinner date, and she can't decide without you."

She sat down on the stone bench, and Roger, who had risen at her approach, stood under the hundred-leaved bush from which all the roses were gone.

"Do you know," he said, without warning or preface, "that it seemed to me that, as you came into the garden, it bloomed again."

Never before had he spoken thus. And he said it again. "When you came, it was as if the garden bloomed."

He sat down beside her. "Is any one going to claim you right away? Because if not, I have something I want to say."

"Nobody will claim me. At least I hope nobody will. Grace Clendenning is telling Porter about the art of woman's dress. She takes clothes so seriously, you know. And Porter is interested in spite of himself. And Barry and Leila are on the terrace steps, looking at the moon over the river, and Aunt Frances and Aunt Isabelle and General Dick are in the house because of the night air, so there's really no one in the garden but you and me."

"Just you—and—me——" he said, and stopped.

She was plainly puzzled by his manner. But she waited, her arms wrapped in her red cloak.

At last he said, "Your brother-in-law and I went to school together."

"Gordon?"

"Yes. St. Martin's. He was younger than I, and we were not much together. But I knew him. And after he had puzzled over it, he knew me."

"How interesting."

"And he asked me something about myself, which I have never told you; which I want to tell you now."

He was finding it hard to tell, with her eyes upon him, bright as stars.

"Your brother said he had heard that I had gone into the Church—that I had a parish. And what he had heard was true. Until five years ago, I was rector of a church in the South."

"*You?*" That was all. Just a little breathed note of incredulity.

"Yes. I wanted to tell you before he should have a chance to tell, and to think that I had kept from you something which you should have been told. But I am not sure, even now, that it should be told."

"But on Christmas Eve, you said that you did not believe——"

"I do not."

"And was that the reason you gave it up?"

"No. It is a long story. And it is not a pleasant one. Yet it seems that I must tell it."

The wind had risen and blew a mist from the fountain. The dead leaves rustled.

Mary shivered.

"Oh, you are cold," Roger said, "and I am keeping you."

"No," she said, mechanically, "I am not cold. I have my cloak. Please go on."

But he was not to tell his story then, for a shaft of strong light illumined the roadway, and a big limousine stopped at the foot of the terrace steps. They heard Delilah Jeliffe's high laugh; then Porter's voice in the garden. "Mary, are you there?"

"Yes."

"Grace Clendenning and her mother are going, and Delilah and Mr. Jeliffe have motored out to show you their new car."

There was deep disapproval in his voice. Mary rose reluctantly as he joined them. "Oh, Porter, must I listen to Delilah's chatter for the rest of the evening?"

"You made me listen to Grace's. This is your punishment."

"I don't want to be punished. And I am very tired, Porter."

This was a new word in Mary Ballard's vocabulary, and Porter responded at once to its appeal.

"We will get rid of Delilah presently, and then Gordon and Constance will go with us for a spin around the Speedway. That will set you up, little lady."

Roger stood silent by the fountain. Through the veil of mist the little bronze boy seemed to smile maliciously. During all the years in which he had ridden the dolphin, he had seen men and women come and go beneath the hundred-leaved bush. And he had smiled on all of them, and by their mood they had interpreted his smiles.

Roger's mood at this moment was one of impotent rebellion at Porter's air of proprietorship, and it was with this air intensified that, as Mary shivered again Porter drew her wrap about her shoulders, fastening the loop over the big button with expert fingers and said, carelessly, "Are you coming in with us, Poole?"

"No. Not now."

Above the head of the little bronze boy, level glance met level glance, as in the moonlight the men surveyed each other. Then Mary spoke.

"Mr. Poole, I am so sorry not to hear the rest of the—story."

"You shall hear it another time."

She hesitated, looking up at him. It was as if she wanted to speak but could not, with Porter there to listen.

So she smiled, with eyes and lips. Just a flash, but it warmed his heart.

Yet as she went away with Porter, and passed once more through the broad band of the street lamp's light which made of her scarlet cloak a flaming flower, he looked after her wistfully, and wondered if when she had heard what he had to tell she would ever smile at him like that again.

Delilah, fresh from a triumphal summer, was in the midst of a laughing group on the porch.

As Mary came up, she was saying: "And we have taken a dear old home in Georgetown. No more glare or glitter. Everything is to be subdued to the dullness of a Japanese print—pale gray and dull blue and a splash of black. This gown gives the keynote."

She was in gray taffeta, with a girdle of soft old blue, and a string of black rose-beads. No color was on her cheeks—there was just the blackness of her hair and the whiteness of her fine skin.

"It's great," Barry said,

Delilah nodded. "Yes. It has taken me several years to find out some things." She looked at Grace and smiled. "It didn't take you years, did it?"

Grace smiled back. The two women were as far apart as the poles. Grace represented the old Knickerbocker stock, Lilah, a later grafting. Grace studied clothes because it pleased her to make fashions a fine art. Delilah studied to impress. But each one saw in the other some similarity of taste and of mood, and the smile that they exchanged was that of comprehension.

Aunt Frances did not approve of Delilah. She said so to Grace going home.

"My dear, they live on the West Side—in a big house on the Drive. My calling list stops east of the Park."

Grace shrugged. "Mother," she said, "I learned one thing in Paris—that the only people worth knowing are the interesting people, and whether they live on the Drive or in Dakota, I don't care. And we've an awful lot of fossils in our set."

Mrs. Clendenning shifted the argument. "I don't see why General Dick allows Leila to be so much with Miss Jeliffe."

"They were at school together, and the General and Mr. Jeliffe are old friends."

162

Her mother shrugged. "Well, I hope that if we stay here for the winter that they won't be forced upon us. Washington is such a city of climbers, Grace."

Grace let the matter drop there. She had learned discretion. She and her mother viewed life from different angles. To attempt to reconcile these differences would mean, had always meant, strife and controversy, and in these later years, Grace had steered her course toward serenity. She had refused to be blown about by the storms of her mother's prejudices. In the midst of the conventionality of her own social training, she had managed to be untrammeled. In this she was more like Mary than the others of her generation. And she loved Mary, and wanted to see her happy.

"Mother," she asked abruptly, "who is this Roger Poole?"

Mrs. Clendenning told her that he was a lodger in the Tower Rooms—a treasury clerk—a mere nobody.

Grace challenged the last statement. "He's a brilliant man," she said. "I sat next to him at dinner. There's a mystery somewhere. He has an air of authority, the ease of a man of the world."

"He is in love with Mary," said Mrs. Clendenning, "and he oughtn't to be in the house."

"But Mary isn't in love with him—not yet."

"How do you know?"

In the darkness Grace smiled. How did she know? Why, Mary in love would be lighted up by a lamp within! It would burn in her cheeks, flash in her eyes.

"No, Mary's not in love," she said.

"She ought to marry Porter Bigelow."

"She ought not to marry Porter. Mary should marry a man who would utilize all that she has to give. Porter would not utilize it."

"Now what do you mean by that?" said Mrs. Clendenning, impatiently. "Don't talk nonsense, Grace."

"Mary Ballard," Grace analyzed slowly, "is one of the women who if she had been born in another generation would have gone singing to the lions for the sake of an ideal; she would have led an army, or have loaded guns behind barricades. She has courage and force, and the need of some big thing in her life to bring out her best. And Porter doesn't need that kind of wife. He doesn't want it. He wants to worship. To kneel at her feet and look up to her. He would require nothing of her. He would smother her with tenderness. And she doesn't want to be smothered. She wants to lift up her head and face the beating winds."

Mrs. Clendenning, helpless before this burst of eloquence on the part of her usually restrained daughter, asked, tartly, "How in the world do you know what Porter wants or Mary needs?"

"Perhaps," said Grace, slowly, "it is because I am a little like Mary. But I am older, and I've learned to take what the world gives. Not what I want. But Mary will never be content with compromise, and she will always go through life with her head up."

Mary's head was up at that very moment, as with cheeks flaming and eyes bright, she played hostess to her guests, while in the back of her brain were beating questions about Roger Poole.

Freed from the somewhat hampering presence of Mrs. Clendenning, Delilah was letting herself go, and she drew even from grave Gordon Richardson the tribute of laughter.

"It was an artist that I met at Marblehead," she said, "who showed me the way. He told me that I was a blot against the sea and the sky, with my purples and greens and reds and yellows. I will show you his sketches of me as I ought to be. They opened my eyes; and I'll show you my artist too. He's coming down to see whether I have caught the idea."

And now she moved down the steps. "Father will be furious if I keep him waiting any longer. He's crazy over the car, and when he drives, it is a regular Tam O'Shanter performance. I won't ask any of you to risk your necks with him yet, but if you and the General are willing to try it, Leila, we will take you home."

"I haven't fought in fifty battles to show the white feather now," said the General, and Leila chirruped, "I'd love it," and presently, with Barry in devoted attendance, they drove off.

Mary, waiting on the porch for Porter to telephone for his own car, which was to take them around the Speedway, looked eagerly toward the fountain. The moon had gone under a cloud, and while she caught the gleam of the water, the hundred-leaved bush hid the bench. Was Roger Poole there? Alone?

She heard Porter's voice behind her. "Mary," he said, "I've brought a heavy wrap. And the car will be here in a minute."

Aunt Isabelle had given him the green wrap with the fur. She slipped into it silently, and he turned the collar up about her neck.

"I'm not going to have you shivering as you did in that thin red thing," he said.

She drew away. It was good of him to take care of her, but she didn't want his care. She didn't want that tone, that air of possession. She was not Porter's. She belonged to herself. And to no one else. She was free.

With the quick proud movement that was characteristic of her, she lifted her head. Her eyes went beyond Porter, beyond the porch, to the Tower Rooms where a light flared, suddenly. Roger Poole was not in the garden; he had gone up without saying "Good-night."

CHAPTER XI

In Which Roger Writes a Letter; and in Which a Rose Blooms Upon the Pages of a Book.

In the Tower Rooms, Midnight——

It is best to write it. What I might have said to you in the garden would have been halting at best. How could I speak it all with your clear eyes upon me—all the sordid history of those years which are best buried, but whose ghosts to-night have risen again?

If in these months—this year that I have lived in these rooms, I have seemed to hide that which you will now know, it was not because I wanted to set myself before you as something more than I am. Not that I wished to deceive. It was simply that the thought of the old life brought a surging sense of helplessness, of hopelessness, of rebellion against fate, Having put it behind me, I have not wished to talk about it—to think about it—to have it, in all its tarnished tragedy, held up before your earnest, shining eyes.

For you have never known such things as I have to tell you, Mary Ballard. There has been sorrow in your life, and, I have seen of late, suffering for those you love. But, as yet, you have not doffed an ideal. You have not bowed that brave young head of yours. You have never yet turned your back upon the things which might have been.

As I have turned mine. I wish sometimes that you might have known me before the happening of these things which I am to tell you. But I wish more than all, that I might have known you. Until I came here, I did not dream that there was such a woman in the world as you. I had thought of women first, as a chivalrous boy thinks, later, as a disillusioned man. But of a woman like a young and ardent soldier, on fire to fight the winning battles of the world—of such a woman I had never dreamed.

But this year has taught me. I have seen you pushing away from you the things which would have charmed most women I have seen you pushing away wealth, and love for the mere sake of loving. I have seen you willing to work that you might hold undimmed the ideal which you had set for your womanhood. Loving and love-worthy, you have not been willing to receive unless you could give, give from the fulness of that generous nature of yours. And out of that generosity, you have given me your friendship.

And now; as I write the things which your clear eyes are to read, I am wondering whether that friendship will be withdrawn. Will you when you have heard of my losing battle, find anything in me that is worthy—will there be anything saved out of the wreck of your thought of me?

Well, here it is, and you shall judge:

I will skip the first years, except to say that my father was one of the New York Pooles who moved South after the Civil War. My mother was from Richmond. We were prosperous folk, with an unassailable social position. My mother, gracious and charming, is little more than a memory; she died when I was a child. My father married again, and died when I was in college. There were three children by this second marriage, and when the estate was settled, only a modest sum fell to my share.

I had been a lonely little boy—at college I was a dreamy, idealistic chap, with the saving grace of a love of athletics. Your brother-in-law will tell you something of my successes on our school team. That was my life—the day in the open, the nights among my books.

As time went on, I took prizes in oratory—there was a certain commencement, when the school went wild about me, and I was carried on the shoulders of my comrades.

There seemed open to me the Church and the law. Had I lived in a different environment, there would have been also the stage. But I saw only two outlets for my talents, the Church, toward which my tastes inclined, and the law, which had been my father's profession.

At last I chose the Church. I liked the thought of my scholarly future—of the power which my voice might have to sway audiences and to move them.

I am putting it all down, all of my boyish optimism, conceit—whatever you may choose to call it.

Yet I am convinced of this, and my success of a few years proved it, that had nothing interfered with my future, I should have made an impression on ever-widening circles.

164

But something came to interfere.

In my last years at the Seminary, I boarded at a house where I met daily the daughter of the landlady. She was a little thing, with yellow hair and a childish manner. As I look back, I can't say that I was ever greatly attracted to her. But she was a part of my life for so long that gradually there grew up between us a sort of good fellowship. Not friendship in the sense that I have understood it with you; there was about it nothing of spiritual or of mental congeniality. But I played the big brother. I took her to little dances; and to other college affairs. I gave both to herself and to her widowed mother such little pleasures as it is possible for a man to give to two rather lonely women. There were other students in the house, and I was not conscious that I was doing anything more than the rest of them.

Then there came a day when the yellow-haired child—shall I call her Kathy?—wanted to go to a pageant in a neighboring town. It was to last two days, and there was to be a night parade, and floats and a carnival. Many of the students were going, and it was planned that Kathy and I should take a morning train on the first day, so that we might miss nothing. Kathy's mother would come on an afternoon train, and they would spend the night at a certain quiet hotel, while I was to go with a lot of fellows to another.

Well, when that afternoon train arrived, the mother was not on it. Nor did she come. Without one thought of unconventionality, I procured a room for Kathy at the place where she and her mother would have stopped. Then I left her and went to the other hotel to join my classmates. But carnival-mad; they did not come in at all, and went back on an express which passed through the town in the early morning.

When Kathy and I reached home at noon, we found her mother white and hysterical. She would listen to no explanations. She told me that I should have brought Kathy back the night before—that she had missed her train and thus her appointment with us. And she told me that I was in honor bound to marry Kathy.

As I write it, it seems such melodrama. But it was very serious then. I have never dared analyze the mother's motives. But to my boyish eyes her anxiety for her daughter's reputation was sincere, and I accepted the responsibility she laid upon me. Well, I married her. And she put her slender arms about my neck and cried and thanked me.

She was very sweet and she was my—wife—and when I was given a parish and had introduced her to my people, they loved her for the white gentleness which seemed purity, and for acquiescent amiability which seemed—goodness.

I have myself much to blame in this—that I did not love her. All these years I have known it. But that I was utterly unawakened I did not know. Only in the last few months have I learned it.

Perhaps she missed what I should have given her. God knows. And He only knows whether, if I had adored her, worshiped her, things would have been different.

I was very busy. She was not strong. She was left much to herself. The people did not expect any great efforts on her part—it was enough that she should look like a saint—that she should lend herself so perfectly to the ecclesiastical atmosphere.

And now comes the strange, the almost unbelievable part. One morning when we had been married two years, I left the house to go to the office of one of my most intimate friends in the parish—a doctor who lived near us, who was unmarried, and who had prescribed now and then for my wife. As I went out, Kathy asked me to return to him a magazine which she handed me. It was wrapped and tied with a string. I had to wait in the doctor's office, and I unwrapped the magazine and untied the string, and between the leaves I found a note to—my friend.

Why do people do things like that? She might have telephoned what she had to say; she might have written it, and have sent it through the mails. But she chose this way, and let me carry to another man the message of her love for him.

For that was what the note told. There was no doubt, and I walked out of the office and went home. In other times with other manners, I might have killed him. If I had loved her, I might; I cannot tell. But I went home.

She seemed glad that I knew. And she begged that I would divorce her and let her marry him.

Dear Clear Eyes, who read this, what do you think of me? Of this story?

And what did I think? I who had dreamed, and studied and preached, and had never—lived? I who had hated the sordid? I who had thought myself so high?

As I married her, so I gave her a divorce. And as I would not have her name and mine smirched, I separated myself from her, and she won her plea on the ground of desertion.

Do you know what that meant in my life? It meant that I must give up my church. It meant that I must be willing to bear the things which might be said of me. Even if the truth had been known, there would have been little difference, except in the sympathy which would have been vouchsafed me as the injured party. And I wanted no man's pity.

And so I went forth, deprived of the right to lift up my voice and preach—deprived of the right to speak to the thousands who had packed my church. And now—what meaning for me had the candles on the altar, what meaning the voices in the choir? I had sung too, in the light of the holy candles, but it was ordained that my voice must be forever still.

I fought my battle out one night in the darkness of my church. I prayed for light and I saw none. Oh, Clear Eyes, why is light given to a man whose way is hid? I went forth from that church convinced that it was all a sham. That the lights meant nothing; that the music meant less, and that what I had preached had been a poetic fallacy.

Some of the people of my church still believe in me. Others, if you should meet them, would say that she was a saint, and that I was the sinner. Well, if my sin was weakness, I confess it. I should, perhaps, never have married her; but having married her, could I have held her mine against her will?

She married him. And a year after, she died. She was a frail little thing, and I have nothing harsh to say of her. In a sense she was a victim, first of her mother's ambition, next of my lack of love, and last of all, of his pursuit.

Perhaps I should not have told you this. Except my Bishop, who asked for the truth, and to whom I gave it, and whose gentleness and kindness are never-to-be-forgotten things—except for him, you are the only one I have ever told; the only one I shall ever tell.

But I shall tell you this, and glory in the telling. That if I had a life to offer of honor and of achievement, I should offer it now to you. That if I had met you as a dreaming boy, I would have tried to match my dreams to yours.

You may say that with the death of my wife things have changed. That I might yet find a place to preach, to teach—to speak to audiences and to sway them.

But any reëntrance into the world means the bringing up of the old story—the question—the whispered comment. I do not think that I am a coward. For the sake of a cause, I could face death with courage. But I cannot face questioning eyes and whispering lips.

So I am dedicated for all my future to mediocrity. And what has mediocrity to do with you, who have "never turned your back, but marched face forward"?

And so I am going away. Not so quickly that there will be comment. But quickly enough to relieve you of future embarrassment in my behalf.

I do not know that you will answer this. But I know that whatever your verdict, whether I am still to have the grace of your friendship or to lose it forever, I am glad to have lived this one year in the Tower Rooms. I am glad to have known the one woman who has given me back—my boyish dreams of all women.

And now a last line. If ever in all the years to come you should have need of me, I am at your service. I shall count nothing too hard that you may ask. I am whimsically aware that in the midst of all this darkness and tragedy my offer is that of the Mouse to the Lion. But there came a day when the Mouse paid its debt. Ask me to pay mine, and I will come—from the ends of the earth.

This was the letter which Mary found the next morning on her desk in the little office room into which Roger had been shown on the night of the wedding. She recognized his firm script and found herself trembling as she touched the square white envelope.

But she laid the letter aside until she had given Susan her orders, until she had given other orders over the telephone, until she had interviewed the furnace man and the butcher's boy, and had written and mailed certain checks.

Then she took the letter with her to her own room, locked the door and read it.

Constance, knocking a little later, was let in, and found her sister dressed and ready for the street.

"I've a dozen engagements," Mary said. She was drawing on her gloves and smiling. She was, perhaps, a little pale, but that the Mary of to-day was different from the Mary if yesterday was not visible from outward signs.

"I am going first to the dressmaker, to see about having that lovely frock you bought me fitted for Delilah's tea dance; then I'll meet you at Mrs. Carey's luncheon. And after that will be our drive with Porter, and the private view at the Corcoran, then two teas, and later the dinner at Mrs. Bigelow's. I'm afraid it will be pretty strenuous for you, Constance."

"I sha'n't try to take in the teas. I'll come home and lie down before I have to dress for dinner."

As she followed out her programme for the day, Mary was conscious that she was doing it well. She made conscientious plans with her dressmaker, she gave herself gayly to the light chatter of the luncheon; during the drive she matched Porter's exuberant mood with her own, she viewed the pictures and made intelligent comments.

After the view, Constance went home in Porter's car, and Mary was left at a house on Dupont Circle. Porter's eyes had begged that she would let him come with her, but she had refused to meet his eyes, and had sent him off.

As she passed through the glimmer of the golden rooms, she bowed and smiled to the people that she knew, she joked with Jerry Tuckerman, who insisted on looking after her and getting her an ice. And then, as soon as she decently could, she got away, and came out into the open air, drawing a long breath, as one who has been caged and who makes a break for freedom.

She did not go to the other tea. All day she had lived in a dream, doing that which was required of her and doing it well. But from now until the time that she must go home and dress for dinner, she would give herself up to thoughts of Roger Poole.

She turned down Connecticut Avenue, and walking lightly and quickly came at last to the old church, where all her life she had worshiped. At this hour there was no service, and she knelt for a moment, then sat back in her pew, glad of the sense of absolute immunity from interruption.

And as she sat there in the stillness, one sentence from his letter stood out.

"And now what meaning for me had the candles on the altar, what meaning the voices in the choir? I had sung, too, in the light of the candles, but it was ordained that my voice must be forever still."

This to Mary was the great tragedy—his loss of courage, his loss of faith—his acceptance of a passive future. Resolutely she had conquered all the shivering agony which had swept over her as she had read of that sordid marriage and its sequence. Resolutely she had risen above the faintness which threatened to submerge her as the whole of that unexpected history was presented to her; resolutely she had fought against a pity which threatened to overwhelm her.

Resolutely she had made herself face with clear eyes the conclusion; life had been too much for him and he had surrendered to fate.

To say that his letter in its personal relation to herself had not thrilled her would be to underestimate the warmth of her friendship for him; if there was more than friendship, she would not admit it. There had been a moment when, shaken and stirred by his throbbing words, she had laid down his letter and had asked herself, palpitating, "has love come to me—at last?" But she had not answered it. She knew that she would never answer it until Roger Poole found a meaning in life which was, as yet, hidden from him.

But how could she best help him to find that meaning? Dimly she felt that it was to be through her that he would find it. And he was going away. And before he went, she must light for him some little beacon of hope.

It was dark in the church now except for the candle on the altar.

She knelt once more and hid her face in her hands. She had the simple faith of a child, and as a child she had knelt in this same pew and had asked confidently for the things she desired, and she had believed that her prayers would be answered.

It was late when she left the church. And she was late in getting home. All the lower part of the house was lighted, but there was no light in the Tower Rooms. Roger, who dined down-town, would not come until they were on their way to Mrs. Bigelow's.

As she passed through the garden, she saw that on a bush near the fountain bloomed a late rose. She stooped and picked it, and flitting in the dusk down the path, she entered the door which led to the Tower stairway.

And when, an hour later, Roger Poole came into the quiet house, weary and worn from the strain of a day in which he had tried to read his letter with Mary's eyes, he found his room dark, except for the flicker of the fire.

Feeling his way through the dimness, he pulled at last the little chain of the electric lamp on his table. The light at once drew a circle of gold on the dark dull oak. And within that circle he saw the answer to his letter.

Wide open and illumined, lay John Ballard's old Bible. And across the pages, fresh and fragrant as the friendship which she had given him, was the late rose which Mary had picked in the garden.

CHAPTER XII

In Which Mary and Roger Have Their Hour; and in Which a Tea-Drinking Ends in What Might Have Been a Tragedy.

To Mary, possessed and swayed by the letter which she had received from Roger, it seemed a strange thing that the rest of the world moved calmly and unconsciously forward.

The letter had come to her on Saturday. On Sunday morning everybody went to church. Everybody dined afterward, unfashionably, at two o'clock, and later everybody motored out to the Park.

That is, everybody but Mary!

She declined on the ground of other things to do.

"There'll be five of you anyhow with Aunt Frances and Grace," she said, "and I'll have tea for you when you come back."

So Constance and Gordon and Aunt Isabelle had gone off, and with Barry at Leila's, Mary was at last alone.

Alone in the house with Roger Poole!

Her little plans were all made, and she went to work at once to execute them.

It was a dull afternoon, and the old-fashioned drawing-room, with its dying fire, and pale carpet, its worn stuffed furniture and pallid mirrors looked dreary.

Mary had Susan Jenks replenish the fire. Then she drew up to it one of the deep stuffed chairs and a lighter one of mahogany, which matched the low tea-table which was at the left of the fireplace. She set a tapestry screen so that it cut off this corner from the rest of the room and from the door.

Gordon had brought, the night before, a great box of flowers, and there were valley lilies among them. Mary put the lilies on the table in a jar of gray-green pottery. Then she went up-stairs and changed the street costume which she had worn to church for her old green velvet gown. When she came down, the fire was snapping, and the fragrance of the lilies made sweet the screened space—Susan had placed on the little table a red lacquered tray, and an old silver kettle.

Susan had also delivered the note which Mary had given her to the Tower Rooms.

Until Roger came down Mary readjusted and rearranged everything. She felt like a little girl who plays at keeping house. Some new sense seemed waked within her, a sense which made her alive to the coziness and comfort and seclusion of this cut-off corner. She found herself trying to see it all through Roger Poole's eyes.

When he came at last around the corner of the screen, she smiled and gave him her hand.

"This is to be our hour together. I had to plan for it. Did you ever feel that the world was so full of people that there was no corner in which to be—alone?"

As he sat down in the big chair, and the light shone on his face, she saw how tired he looked, as if the days and the nights since she had seen him, had been days and nights of vigil.

She felt a surging sense of sympathy, which set her trembling as she had trembled when she had touched his letter as it had laid on her desk, but when she spoke her voice was steady.

"I am going to make you a cup of tea—then we can talk."

He watched her as she made it, her deft hands unadorned, except by the one quaint ring, the whiteness of her skin set on by her green gown, the whiteness of her soul symbolized by the lilies.

He leaned forward and spoke suddenly. "Mary Ballard," he said, "if I ever reach paradise, I shall pray that it may be like this, with the golden light and the fragrance, and you in the midst of it."

Earnestly over the lilies, she looked at him. "Then you believe in Paradise?"

"I should like to think that in some blessed future state I should come upon you in a garden of lilies."

"Perhaps you will." She was smiling, but her hand shook.

She felt shy, almost tongue-tied. She made him his tea, and gave him a cup; then she spoke of commonplaces, and the little kettle boiled and bubbled and sang as if there were no sorrow or sadness in the whole wide world.

She came at last timidly to the thing she had to say.

"I don't quite know how to begin about your letter. You see when I read it, it wasn't easy for me at first to think straight. I hadn't thought of you as having any such background to your life. Somehow the outlines I had filled in were—different. I am not quite sure what I had thought—only it had been nothing like—this."

"I know. You could not have been expected to imagine such a past."

"Oh, it is not your past which weighs so heavily—on my heart; it is your future."

Her eyes were full of tears. She had not meant to say it just that way. But it had come—her voice breaking on the last words.

He did not speak at once, and then he said: "I have no right to trouble you with my future."

"But I want to be troubled."

"I shall not let you. I shall not ask that of your friendship. Last night when I came back to my rooms I found a rose blooming upon the pages of a book. It seemed to tell me that I had not lost your friendship; and you have given me this hour. This is all I have a right to ask of your generosity."

She moved the jar of lilies aside, so that there might be nothing between them. "If I am your friend, I must help you," she said, "or what would my friendship be worth?"

"There is no help," he said, hurriedly, "not in the sense that I think you mean it. My past has made my future. I cannot throw myself into the fight again. I know that I have been called all sorts of a coward for not facing life. But I could face armies, if it were anything tangible. I could do battle with a sword or a gun or my fists, if there were a visible adversary. But whispers—you can't kill them; and at last they—kill you."

"I don't want you to fight," she said, and now behind the whiteness of her skin there was a radiance. "I don't want you to fight. I want you to deliver your message."

"What message?"

"The message that every man who stands in the pulpit must have for the world, else he has no right to stand there."

"You think then that I had no message?"

"I think," and now her hand went out to him across the table, as if she would soften the words, "I think that if you had felt yourself called to do that one thing, that nothing would have swayed you from it—there are people not in the churches, who never go to church, who want what you have to give—there are the highways and hedges. Oh, surely, not all of the people worth preaching to are the ones in the pews."

She flung the challenge at him directly.

And he flung it back to her, "If I had had such a woman as you in my life——"

"Oh, don't, *don't*." The radiance died. "What has any woman to do with it? It is you—yourself, who must stand the test."

After the ringing words there was dead silence. Roger sat leaning forward, his eyes not upon her, but upon the fire. In his white face there was no hint of weakness; there was, rather, pride, obstinacy, the ruggedness of inflexible purpose.

"I am afraid," he said at last, "that I have not stood the test."

Her clear eyes met his squarely. "Then meet it now."

For a moment he blazed. "I know now what you think of me, that I am a man who has shirked."

"You know I do not think that."

He surrendered. "I do know it. And I need your help."

Shaken by their emotion, they became conscious that this was indeed their hour. She told him all that she had dreamed he might do. Her color came and went as she drew the picture of his future. Some of the advice she gave was girlish, impracticable, but through it all ran the thread of her faith to him. She felt that she had the solution. That through service he was to find—God.

It was a wonderful hour for Roger Poole. An hour which was to shine like a star in his memory. Mary's mind had a largeness of vision, the ability to rise above the lesser things in order to reach the greater, which seemed super-feminine. It was not until afterward when he reviewed what they had said, that he was conscious that she had placed the emphasis on what he was to do. Not once had she spoken of what had been done—not once had she spoken of his wife.

"You mustn't bury yourself. You must find a way to reach first one group and then another. And after a time you'll begin to feel that you can face the world."

He winced. As she put it into words, he began to see himself as others must have seen him. And the review was not a pleasant one.

In a sense that hour with Mary Ballard in the screened space by the fire was the hour of Roger Poole's spiritual awakening. He realized for the first time that he had missed the meaning of the candles on the altar, the voices in the choir; he had missed the knowledge that one must spend and be spent in the service of humanity.

"I must think it over," he said. "You mustn't expect too much of me all at once."

"I shall expect—everything."

As she spoke and smiled, and it seemed to him that his old garment of fear slipped from him—as if he were clothed in the shining armor of her confidence in him.

They had little time to talk after that, for it was not long before they heard without the bray of a motor horn.

Roger rose at once.

"I must go before they come," he said.

But she laid her hand upon his arm. "No," she said, "you are not to go. You are never going to run away from the world again. Set aside the screen, please—and stay."

Porter, picked up on the way, came in with the others, to behold that glowing corner, and those two together.

With his red crest flaming, he advanced upon them.

"Somebody said 'tea.' May I have some, Mary?"

"When the kettle boils." She had risen, and was holding out her hand to him.

As the two men shook hands, Porter was conscious of some subtle change in Roger. What had come over the man—had he dared to make love to Mary?

And Mary? He looked at her.

She was serenely filling her tea ball. She had lighted the lamp beneath her kettle, and the blue flame seemed to cast her still further back among the shadows of her corner.

Grace Clendenning and Aunt Frances had come back with the rest for tea. Grace's head, with Porter's, gave the high lights of the scene. Barry had nicknamed them the "red-headed woodpeckers," and the name seemed justified.

While Porter devoted himself to Grace, however, he was acutely conscious of every movement of Mary's. Why had she given up her afternoon to Roger Poole? He had asked if he might come, and she had said, "after four," and now it was after four, and the hour which she would not give him had been granted to this lodger in the Tower Rooms.

It has been said before that Porter was not a snob, but to him Mary's attitude of friendliness toward this man, who was not one of them, was a matter of increasing irritation. What was there about this tall thin chap with the tired eyes to attract a woman? Porter was not conceited, but he knew that he possessed a certain value. Of what value in the eyes of the world was Roger Poole—a government clerk, without ambition, handsome in his dark way, but pale and surrounded by an air of gloom?

But to-night it was as if the gloom had lifted. To-night Roger shone as he had shone on the night of the Thanksgiving party—he seemed suddenly young and splendid—the peer of them all.

It came about naturally that, as they drank their tea, some one asked him to recite.

"Please "—it was Mary who begged.

Porter jealously intercepted the look which flashed between them, but could make nothing of it.

"The Whittington one is too long," Roger stated, "and I haven't Pittiwitz for inspiration—but here's another."

Leaning forward with his eyes on the fire, he gave it.

It was a man's poem. It was in the English of the hearty times of Ben Jonson and of Kit Marlowe—and every swinging line rang true.

> "What will you say when the world is dying?
> What when the last wild midnight falls,
> Dark, too dark for the bat to be flying
> Round the ruins of old St. Paul's?
> What will be last of the lights to perish?
> What but the little red ring we knew,
> Lighting the hands and the hearts that cherish
> A fire, a fire, and a friend or two!"
>
> CHORUS:
> "Up now, answer me, tell me true.
> What will be last of the stars to perish?
> --The fire that lighteth a friend or two."

As the last brave verse was ended, Gordon Richardson said, "By Jove, how it comes back to me—you used to recite Poe's 'Bells' at school."

Roger laughed. "Yes. I fancy I made them boom toward the end."

"You used to make me shiver and shake in my shoes."

Aunt Frances' voice broke in crisply, "What do you mean, Gordon; were you at school with Mr. Poole?"

"Yes. St. Martin's, Aunt Frances."

The name had a magic effect upon Mrs. Clendenning; the boys of St. Martin's were of the elect.

"Poole?" she said. "Are you one of the New York Pooles?"

Roger nodded. "Yes. With a Southern grafting—my mother was a Carew."

He was glad now to tell it. Let them follow what clues they would. He was ready for them. Henceforth nothing was to be hidden.

"I am going down next week," he continued, "to stay for a time with a cousin of my mother's—Miss Patty Carew. She lives still in the old manor house which was my grandfather's—she hadn't much but poverty and the old house for an inheritance, but it is still a charming place."

Aunt Frances was intent, however, on the New York branch of his family tree.

"Was your grandfather Angus Poole?"

"Yes."

Grace was wickedly conscious of her mother's state of mind. No one could afford to ignore any descendant of Angus Poole. To be sure, a second generation had squandered the fortune he had left, but his name was still one to conjure with.

"I never dreamed——" said Aunt Frances.

"Naturally," said Roger, and there was a twinkle in his eyes. "I am afraid I'm not a credit to my hard-headed financier of a grandfather."

It seemed to Mary that for the first time she was seeing him as he might have been before his trouble came upon him. And she was swept forward to the thought of what he might yet be. She grew warm and rosy in her delight that he should thus show himself to her people. She looked up to find Porter's accusing eyes fixed on her; and in the grip of a sudden shyness, she gave herself again to her tea-making.

"Surely some of you will have another cup?"

It developed that Aunt Frances would, and that the water was cold, and that the little lamp was empty of alcohol.

Mary filled it, and, her hand shaking from her inward excitement, let the alcohol overflow on the tray and on the kettle frame. She asked for a match and Gordon gave her one.

Then, nobody knew how it happened! The flames seemed to sweep up in a blue sheet toward the lace frills in the front of Mary's gown. It leaped toward her face. Constance screamed. Then Roger reached her, and she was in his arms, her face crushed against the thickness of his coat, his hands snatching at her frills.

It was over in a moment. The flames were out. Very gently, he loosed his arms. She lay against his shoulder white and still. Her face was untouched, but across her throat, which the low collar had left exposed, was a hot red mark. And a little lock of hair was singed at one side, her frills were in ruins.

He put her into a chair, and they gathered around her—a solicitous group. Porter knelt beside her. "Mary, Mary," he kept saying, and she smiled weakly, as his voice broke on "Contrary Mary."

Gordon had saved the table from destruction. But the flame had caught the lilies, crisping them, and leaving them black. Constance was shaken by the shock, and Aunt Frances kept asking wildly, "How did it happen?"

"I spilled the alcohol when I filled it," Mary said. "It was a silly thing to do—if I had had on one of my thinner gowns——" She shuddered and stopped.

"I shall send you an electric outfit to-morrow," Porter announced. "Don't fool with that thing again, Mary."

Roger stood behind her chair, with his arms folded on the top and said nothing. There was really nothing for him to say, but there were many things to think. He had saved that dear face from flame or flaw, the dear eyes had been hidden against his shoulder—his fingers smarted where he had clutched at her burning frills.

Porter Bigelow might take possession of her now, he might give her electric outfits, he might call her by her first name, but it had not been Porter who had saved her from the flames; it had not been Porter who had held her in his arms.

CHAPTER XIII

In Which the Whole World is at Sixes and Sevens, and in Which Life is Looked Upon as a Great Adventure.

It had been decided that, for a time at least, Gordon and Constance should stay with Mary. In the spring they would again go back to London. Grace Clendenning and Aunt Frances were already installed for the winter at their hotel.

The young couple would occupy the Sanctum and the adjoining room, and Mary was to take on an extra maid to help Susan Jenks.

In all her planning, Mary had a sense of the pervasiveness of Gordon Richardson. With masculine confidence in his ability, he took upon himself not only his wife's problems, but Mary's. Mary was forced to admit, even while she rebelled, that his judgments were usually wise. Yet, she asked herself, what right had an outsider to dictate in matters which pertained to herself and Barry? And what right had he to offer her board for Constance? Constance, who was her very own?

But when she had indignantly voiced her objection to Gordon, he had laughed. "You are like all women, Mary," he had said, "and of course I appreciate your point of view and your hospitality. But if you think that I am going to let my wife stay here and add to your troubles and expense without giving adequate compensation, you are vastly mistaken. If you won't let us pay, we won't stay, and that's all there is to it."

Here was masculine firmness against which Mary might rage impotently. After all, Constance was Gordon's wife, and he could carry her off.

"Of course," she said, yielding stiffly, "you must do as you think best."

"I shall," he said, easily, "and I will write you a check now, and you can have it to settle any immediate demands upon your exchequer. I shall be away a good deal, and I want Constance to be with you and Aunt Isabelle. It is a favor to me, Mary, to have her here. You mustn't add to my obligations by making me feel too heavily in your debt."

He smiled as he said it, and Gordon had a nice smile. And presently Mary found herself smiling back.

"Gordon," she said, in a half apology, "Porter calls me Contrary Mary. Maybe I am—but you see, Constance was my sister before she was your wife."

He leaned back in his chair and looked at her. "And you've had twenty years more of her than I—but please God, Mary, I am going to have twenty beautiful years ahead of me to share with her—I hope it may be three times twenty."

His voice shook, and in that moment Mary felt nearer to him than ever before.

"Oh, Gordon," she said, "I'm a horrid little thing. I've been jealous because you took Constance away from me. But now I'm glad you—took her, and I hope I'll live to dance at your—golden wedding." And then, most unexpectedly, she found herself sobbing, and Gordon was patting her on the back in a big-brotherly way, and saying that he didn't blame her a bit, and that if anybody wanted to take Constance away from him, they'd have to do it over his dead body.

Then he wrote the check, and Mary took it, and in the knowledge of his munificence, felt the relief from certain financial burdens.

Before he left her, Gordon, hesitating, referred gravely to another subject.

"And it will be better for you to have Constance here if Barry goes away."

"Barry?" breathlessly.

"Yes. Don't you think he ought to go, Mary?"

"No," she said, stubbornly; "where could he go?"

"Anywhere away from Leila. He mustn't marry that child. Not yet—not until he has proved himself a man."

The blow hit her heavily. Yet her sense of justice told her that he was right.

"I can't talk about it," she said, unsteadily; "Barry is all I have left."

He rose. "Poor little girl. We must see how we can work it out. But we've got to work it out. It mustn't drift."

Left alone, Mary sat down at her desk and faced the future. With Roger gone, and Barry going——

And the Tower Rooms empty!

She shivered. Before her stretched the darkness and storms of a long winter. Even Constance's coming would not make up for it. And yet a year ago Constance had seemed everything.

She crossed the hall to the dining-room and looked out of the window. The garden was dead. The fountain had ceased to play. But the little bronze boy still flung his gay defiance to wind and weather.

Pittiwitz, following her, murmured a mewing complaint. Mary picked her up; since Roger's going the gray cat had kept away from the emptiness of the upper rooms.

With the little purring creature hugged close, Mary reviewed her worries—the world was at sixes and sevens. Even Porter was proving difficult. Since the Sunday when Roger had saved her from the fire, Porter had adopted an air of possession. He claimed her at all times and seasons; she had a sense of being caught in a web woven of kindness and thoughtfulness and tender care, but none the less a web which held her fast and against her will.

Whimsically it came to her that the four men in her life were opposed in groups of two: Gordon and Porter stood arrayed on the side of logical preferences; Barry and Roger on the side of illogical sympathies.

Gordon had conveyed to her, in rather subtle fashion, his disapproval of Roger. It was only in an occasional phrase, such as "Poor Poole," or "if all of his story were known." But Mary had grasped that, from the standpoint of her brother-in-law, a man who had failed to fulfil the promise of his youth might be dismissed as a social derelict.

As for Barry—the situation with regard to him had become acute. His first disappearance after the coming of Constance had resulted in Gordon's assuming the responsibility of the search for him. He had found Barry in a little town on the upper Potomac, ostensibly on a fishing trip, and again there was a need for fighting dragons.

But Gordon did not fight with the same weapons as Roger Poole. His arguments had been shrewd, keen, but unsympathetic. And the result had been a strained relation between him and Barry. The boy had felt himself misunderstood. Gordon had sat in judgment. Constance had tearfully agreed with Gordon, and Mary, torn between her sense of Gordon's rightness, and her own championship of Barry, had been strung to the point of breaking.

She turned from the window, and went up-stairs slowly. In the Sanctum, Constance and Aunt Isabelle were sewing. At last Aunt Isabelle had come into her own. She spent her days in putting fine stitches into infinitesimal garments. There was about her constantly the perfume of the sachet powder with which she was scenting the fine lawn and lace which glorified certain baskets and bassinets. When she was not sewing she was knitting—little silken socks for a Cupid's foot, little warm caps, doll's size; puffy wool blankets on big wooden needles.

The Sanctum had taken on the aspect of a bower. Here Constance sat enthroned—and in her gentleness reminded Mary more and more of her mother. Here was always the sweetness of the flowers with which Gordon kept his wife supplied; here, too, was an atmosphere of serene waiting for a supreme event.

Mary, entering with Pittiwitz in her arms, tried to cast away her worries on the threshold. She must not be out of tune with this symphony. She smiled and sat down beside Constance. "Such lovely little things," she said; "what can I do?"

It seemed that there was a debate on, relative to the suitability of embroidery as against fine tucks.

Mary settled it. "Let me have it," she said; "I'll put in a few tucks and a little embroidery—I shall be glad to have my fingers busy."

"You're always so occupied with other things," Constance complained, gently. "I don't see half enough of you."

"You have Gordon," Mary remarked.

"You say that as if it really made a difference."

"It does," Mary murmured. Then, lest she trouble Constance's gentle soul, she added bravely, "But Gordon's a dear. And you're a lucky girl."

172

"I know I am." Constance was complacent. "And I knew you'd recognize it, when you'd seen more of Gordon."

Mary felt a rising sense of rebellion. She was not in a mood to hear a catalogue of Gordon's virtues. But she smiled, bravely. "I'll admit that he is perfect," she said; "we won't quarrel over it, Con, dear."

But to herself she was saying, "Oh, I should hate to marry a perfect man."

All the morning she sat there, her needle busy, and gradually she was soothed by the peace of the pleasant room. The world seemed brighter, her problems receded.

Just before luncheon was announced came Aunt Frances and Grace.

They brought gifts, wonderful little things, made by the nuns of France—sheer, exquisite, tied with pale ribbons.

"We are going from here to Leila's," Aunt Frances informed them; "we ordered some lovely trousseau clothes and they came with these."

Trousseau clothes? Leila's? Mary's needle pricked the air for a moment.

"They haven't set the day, you know, Aunt Frances; it will be a long engagement."

"I don't believe in long engagements," Aunt Frances' tone was final; "they are not wise. Barry ought to settle down."

Nobody answered. There was nothing to say, but Mary was oppressed by the grim humor of it all. Here was Aunt Frances bearing garments for the bride, while Gordon was planning to steal the bridegroom.

She stood up. "You better stay to lunch," she said; "it is Susan Jenks' hot roll day, and you know her rolls."

Aunt Frances peeled off her long gloves. "I hoped you'd ask us, we are so tired of hotel fare."

Grace laughed. "Mother is of old New York," she said, "and better for her are hot rolls and chops from her own kitchen range, than caviar and truffles from the hands of a hotel chef—in spite of all of our globe trotting, she hasn't caught the habit of meals with the mob."

Grace went down with Mary, and the two girls found Susan Jenks with the rolls all puffy and perfect in their pans.

"There's plenty of them," she said to Mary, "an' if the croquettes give out, you can fill up on rolls."

"Susan," Grace said, "when Mary gets married will you come and keep house for me?"

Susan smiled. "Miss Mary ain't goin' to git married."

"Why not?"

"She ain't that kind. She's the kind that looks at a man and studies about him, and then she waves him away and holds up her head, and says, 'I'm sorry, but you won't do.'"

The two girls laughed. "How did you get that idea of me, Susan?" Mary asked.

"By studyin' you," said Susan. "I ain't known you all your life for nothin'.

"Now Miss Constance," she went on, as she opened the oven and peeped in, "Miss Constance is just the other way. 'Most any nice man was bound to git her. An' it was lucky that Mr. Gordon was the first."

"And what about me?" was Grace's demand.

"Go 'way," said Susan, "you knows yo'se'f, Miss Grace. You bats your eyes at everybody, and gives your heart to nobody."

"And so Mary and I are to be old maids—oh, Susan."

"They don't call them old maids any more," Susan said, "and they ain't old maids, not in the way they once was. An old maid is a woman who ain't got any intrus' in life but the man she can't have, and you all is the kin' that ain't got no intrus' in the men that want you."

They left her, laughing, and when they reached the dining-room they sat down on the window-seat; where Mary had gazed out upon the dead garden and the bronze boy.

"And now," said Grace, "tell me about Roger Poole."

"There isn't much to tell. He's given up his position in the Treasury, and he's gone down to his cousin's home for a while. He's going to try to write for the magazines; he thinks that stories of that section will take."

"He's in love with you, Mary. But you're not in love with him—and you mustn't be."

"Of course not. I'm not going to marry, Grace."

Grace gave her a little squeeze. "You don't know what you are going to do, darling; no woman does. But I don't want you to fall in love with anybody yet. Flit through life with me for a time. I'll take you to Paris next summer, and show you my world."

"I couldn't, unless I could pay my own way."

"Oh, Mary, what makes you fight against anybody doing anything for you?"

"Porter says it is my contrariness—but I just can't hold out my hands and let things drop into them."

"I know—and that's why you won't marry Porter Bigelow."

Mary flashed at her a surprised and grateful glance. "Grace," she said, solemnly, "you're the first person who has seemed to understand."

"And I understand," said Grace, "because to me life is a Great Adventure. Everything that happens is a hazard on the highway—as yet I haven't found a man who will travel the road with me; they all want to open a gate and shut me in and say, 'Stay here.'"

Mary's eyes were shining. "I feel that, too."

Grace kissed her. "You'd laugh, Mary, if I told the dream which is at the end of my journey."

"I sha'n't laugh—tell me."

There was a rich color in Grace's cheeks. In her modish frock of the black which she affected, and which was this morning of fine serge set on by a line of fur at hem and wrist, and topped by a little hat of black velvet which framed the vividness of her glorious hair, she looked the woman of the world, so that her words gained strength by force of contrast.

"Nobody would believe it," she prefaced, "but, Mary Ballard, some day when I'm tired of dancing through life, when I am weary of the adventures on the road, I'm going to build a home for little children, and spend my days with them."

So the two girls dreamed dreams and saw visions of the future. They sang and soared, they kissed and confided.

"Whatever comes, life shall never be commonplace," Mary declared, and as the bell rang and she went to the table, she felt that now nothing could daunt her—the hard things would be merely a part of a glorious pilgrimage.

Susan's hot rolls were pronounced perfect, and Susan, serenely conscious of it, banished the second maid to the kitchen and waited on the table herself.

Here were five women of one clan. She understood them all, she loved them all. She gave even to Aunt Frances her due. "They all holds their heads high," she had confided on one occasion to Roger Poole, "and Miss Frances holds hers so high that she almost bends back, but she knows how to treat the people who work for her, and she's always been mighty good to me."

Mary's mood of exaltation lasted long after her guests had departed. She found herself singing as she climbed the stairs that night to her room. And it was with this mood still upon her that she wrote to Roger Poole.

Her letter, penned on the full tide of her new emotion, was like wine to his thirsty soul. It began and ended formally, but every line throbbed with hope and courage, and responding to the note which she had struck, he wrote back to her.

CHAPTER XIV

In Which Mary Writes From the Tower Rooms; and in Which Roger Answers From Among the Pines.

The Tower Rooms.
Dear Mr. Poole:

I have taken your rooms for mine, and this is my first evening in them. Pittiwitz is curled up under the lamp. She misses you and so do I. Even now, it seems as if your books ought to be on the table; and that I ought to be talking to you instead of writing.

I liked your letter. It seemed to tell me that you were hopeful and at home. You must tell me about the house and your Cousin Patty—about everything in your life—and you must send me your first story.

Here everything is the same. Constance will be with me until spring, and we are to have a quiet Thanksgiving and a quiet Christmas with just the family, and Leila and the General. Porter Bigelow goes to Palm Beach to be with his mother. I don't know why we always count him in as one of the family except that he never waits for an invitation, and of course we're glad to have him. Mother and father used to feel sorry for him; he was always a sort of "Poor-little-rich-boy" whose money cut him out from lots of good times that families have who don't live in such formal fashion as Mr. and Mrs. Bigelow seem to enjoy.

As soon as Constance leaves, I am going to work. I haven't told any one, for when I hinted at it, Constance was terribly upset, and asked me to live with her and Gordon. Grace wants me to go to Paris with her; Barry and Leila have stated that I can have a home with them.

But I don't want a home with anybody. I want to live my own life, as I have told you. I want to try my wings. I don't believe you quite like the idea of my working. Nobody does, not even Grace Clendenning, although Grace seems to understand me better than any one else.

Grace and I have been talking to-day about life as a great adventure. And it seems to me that we have the right idea. So many people go through life as just something to be endured, but I want to make things happen, or rather, if big things don't happen, I want to see in the little things something that is interesting. I don't believe that any life need be commonplace. It is just the way we look at it. I'm copying these words which I read in one of your books; perhaps you've seen them, but anyhow it will tell you better than I what I mean.

"But life is a great adventure, and the worst of all fears is the fear of living. There are many forms of success, many forms of triumph. But there is no other success that in any way approaches that which is open to most of the many men and women who have the right idea. These are the men and the women who see that it is the intimate and homely things that count most. They are the men and women who have the courage to strive for the happiness which comes only with labor and effort and self-sacrifice, and only to those whose joy in life springs in part from power of work and sense of duty."

Aren't those words like a strong wind blowing from the sea? I just love them. And I know you will. I am so glad that I can talk to you of such things. Everybody has to have a friend who can understand—and that's the fine thing about our friendship—that we both have things to overcome, and that our letters can be reports of progress.

Of course the things which I have to overcome are just little fussy woman things—but they are big to me because I am breaking away from family traditions. All the women our household have followed the straight and narrow path of conventional living. Even Grace does it, although she rebels inwardly—but Aunt Frances keeps her to it. Once Grace tried to be an artist, and she worked hard in Paris, until Aunt Frances swooped down and carried her off—Grace still speaks of that time in Paris as her year out of prison. You see she worked hard and met people who worked, too, and it interested her. She had a studio apartment, and was properly chaperoned by a little widow who went with her and shared her rooms.

But Aunt Frances popped in on them suddenly one day and found a Bohemian party. There wasn't anything wrong about it, Grace says, but you know Aunt Frances! She has never ceased to talk about the frumpy crowd she met there. She hated the students in their velvet coats and the women with their poor queer clothes. And Grace loved them. But she's given up the idea of ever living there again. She says you can't do a thing twice and have it the same. I don't know. I only know that Grace may seem frivolous on the outside, but that underneath she is different. She has taken up advanced ideas about women, and she says that I have them naturally, and that she didn't expect such a thing in Washington where everybody stops to think what somebody else is going to say. But I haven't arrived at the point where I am really interested in Suffrage and things like that. Grace says that I must begin to look beyond my own life, and perhaps when I get some of my own problems settled, I will. And then I shall be taking up the problems of the girls in factories and the girls in laundries and the girls in the big shops, as Grace is. She says that she may live like a bond-slave herself, but she'd like to help other women to be free.

And now I must tell you about Delilah Jeliffe. She had a house-warming last week. The old house in Georgetown is a dream. Delilah hasn't a superfluous or gorgeous thing in it. Everything is keyed to the old-family note. Some of the things are even shabby. She has done away with flamingo colors, and her monkeys with the crystal ball and the peacock screen. She has little stools in her drawing-room with faded covers of canvas work, and she has samplers and cracked portraits, and the china doesn't all match. There isn't a sign of "new richness" in the place. She keeps colored servants, and doesn't wear rings, and her gowns are frilly flowing white things which make her look like one of those demure grandmotherly young persons of the early sixties.

Her little artist is a charming blond who doesn't come up to her shoulders, and Delilah hangs on every word he says. For the moment he obscures all the other men on her horizon. He made sketches of the way every room in her house ought to look. And what seems to be the result of years of formal pleasant living really is the result of the months of hunting and hard work which he and Delilah have put in. He even indicates the flowers she shall wear, and those which are to bloom next summer in her garden. She affects heliotrope, and on the night of her house-warming she carried a tight bunch of it with a few pink rosebuds.

Really, in her new rôle Delilah is superb. And, people are beginning to notice her and to call on her. Even in this short time she has been invited to some very good houses. She has a new way with her eyes, and drops her lashes over them, and is very still and lovely.

Do you remember her leopard skins of last year? Well, now she wears moleskins—a queer dolman-shaped wrap of them, and a little hat with a dull blue feather, and she drapes a black lace veil over the hat and looks like a duchess.

Grace Clendenning says that Delilah and her artist will achieve a triumph if they keep on. They aren't trying to storm society, they are trying to woo it, and out of it the artist gets the patronage of the people whom he meets through Delilah. Perhaps it will end by Delilah's marrying him. But Grace says not. She says that Delilah simply squeezes people dry, like so many oranges, and when she has what she wants, she throws them aside.

Yet Grace and Delilah get along very well together. Grace has always made a study of clothes, because it is the only way in which she can find an outlet for her artistic tastes. And she is interested in Delilah's methods. She says that they are masterly.

But I am forgetting to tell you what Delilah said of you. It was on the night of her house-warming. She asked about you, and when I said that you had gone south to get atmosphere for some stories you were writing, she said:

"Do you know it came to me yesterday, while I was in church, where I had seen him. It was the same text, and that was what brought it back. He was *preaching*, my dear. I remember that I sat in the front pew and looked up at him, and thought that I had never heard such a voice; and now, tell me why he has given it up, and why he is burying himself in the South?"

175

At first I didn't know just what to say, and then I thought it best to tell the truth. So I looked straight at her, and said: "He made a most unhappy marriage, and gave up his life-work. But now his wife is dead, and some day he may preach again." Was it wrong for me to say that? I do hope you are going to preach; somehow I feel that you will. And anyhow while people need never know the details of your story, they will have to know the outlines. It seemed to me that the easiest way was to tell it and have it over.

Of course Gordon has asked some questions, and I have told what I thought should be told. I hope that you won't feel that I have been unwise. I thought it best to start straight, and then there would be nothing to hide.

And now may I tell you a little bit about Barry? They want him to go away—back to England with Gordon and Constance. You see Gordon looks at it without sentiment. Gordon's sentiment stops at Constance. He thinks that Barry should simply give Leila up, go away, and not come back until he can show a clear record.

Of course I know that Gordon is right. But I can't bear it—that's why I haven't been able to face things with quite the courage that I thought I could. But since my talk with Grace, I am going to look at it differently. I shall try to feel that Barry's going is best, and that he must ride away gallantly, and come back with trumpets blowing and flags flying.

And that's the way you must some day come into your own.—I like to think about it. I like to think about victory and conquest, instead of defeat and failure. Somehow thinking about a thing seems to bring it, don't you think?

Oh, but this is such a long letter, and it is gossipy, and scrappy. But that's the way we used to talk, and you seemed to like it.

And now I'll say "Good-night." Pittiwitz waked up a moment ago, and walked across this sheet, and the blot is where she stepped on a word. So that's her message. But my message is Psalms 27:14. You can look it up in father's Bible—I am so glad you took it with you. But perhaps you don't have to look up verses; you probably know everything by heart. Do you?

Sincerely ever,

MARY BALLARD.

Among the Pines.

My good little friend:

I am not going to try to tell you what your letter meant to me. It was the bluebird's song in the spring, the cool breeze in the desert, sunlight after storm—it was everything that stands for satisfaction after a season of discomfort or of discontent.

Yet, except that I miss the Tower Rooms, and miss, too, the great happiness I found in pursuing our friendship at close range, I should have no reason here either for discomfort or lack of content—if I feel the world somewhat barren, it is not because of what I have found, but because of what I have brought with me.

I like to think of you in the Tower Rooms. You always belonged there, and I felt like a usurper when I came and discovered that all of your rosy belongings had been moved down-stairs and my staid and stiff things were in their place. It is queer, isn't it, the difference in the atmosphere made by a man and by a woman. A man dares not surround himself with pale and pretty colors and delicate and dainty things, lest he be called effeminate—perhaps that's why men take women into their lives, so that they may have the things which they crave without having their masculinity questioned.

Yet the atmosphere which seems to fit you best is not merely one of rosiness and prettiness; it is rather that of sunshine and out-of-doors. When you talk or write to me I have the sensation of being swept on and on by your enthusiasms—I seem to fly on strong wings—the quotation which you gave is the utterance of some one else, but you unerringly selected, and passed it on to me, and so in a sense made it your own. I am going to copy it and illumine it, and keep it where I can see it at all times.

I find that I do not travel as fast as you toward my future. I have shut myself up for many years. I have been so sure that all the wine of life was spilled, that the path ahead of me was dreary, that I cannot see myself at all with trumpets blowing, with flags flying and the rest of it. Perhaps I shall some day—and at least I shall try, and in the trying there will be something gained. Some day, perhaps, I shall reach the upper air where you soar—perhaps I shall "mount as an eagle."

Your message——! Dear child—do you know how sweet you are? I don't know all the verses—but that one I do know. Yet I had let myself forget, and you brought it back to me with all its strong assurance.

Your decision that it was best to tell what there is to tell, to let nothing be hidden, is one which I should have made long ago. Only of late have I realized that concealment brings in its train a thousand horrors. One lives in fear, dreading that which must inevitably come. Yet I do not think I must be blamed too much. I was beaten and bruised by the knowledge of my overthrow. I only wanted to crawl into a hole and be forgotten.

Even now, I find myself unfolding slowly. I have lived so long in the dark, and the light seems to blind my eyes!

It is strange that I should have remembered Delilah Jeliffe, but not strange that she should have remembered me; for I stood alone in the pulpit, but she was one of a crowd. Since your letter, I have been thinking back, and I can see her as she sat reading in the front pew, big and rather fine with her black hair and her bold eyes. I think that perhaps the thing which made me remember her was the fleeting thought that her type stood usually for the material in woman, and I wondered if in her case outward appearances were as deceptive as they were in my wife—with her saint's eyes, and her distorted moral vision. Perhaps I was intuitively right, and that beneath Delilah Jeliffe's exterior there is a certain fineness, and that these funny fads of dress and decorations are merely in some way her striving toward the expression of her real self.

What you tell me of your talk with your cousin Grace interests me very much. I fancy she is more womanly than she is willing to admit. Yet she should marry. Every woman should marry, except you—who are going to be my friend! There peeps out my selfishness—but I shall let it stand.

No, I don't like the idea that you must work. I don't want you to try your wings. I want you to sit safe in your nest in the top of the Tower, and write letters to me!

Labor, office drudgery, are things which sap the color from a woman's cheeks, and strength from her body. She grows into a machine, and you are a bird, to fly and light on the nearest branch and sing!

But now you will want to know something of my life, and of the house and of Cousin Patty.

The house has suffered from the years of poverty since the War. Yet it has still about it something of the dignity of an ancient ruin. It is a big frame structure with the Colonial pillars which belong to the period of its building. Many of the rooms are closed. My own suite is on the second floor—Cousin Patty's opposite, and adjoining her rooms those of an old aunt who is a pensioner.

There is little of the old mahogany which once made the rooms stately, and little of the old silver to grace the table. Cousin Patty's poverty is combined, happily, with common sense. She has known the full value of her antiques, and has preferred good food to family traditions. Yet there are the old portraits and in her living-room a few choice pieces. Here we have an open fire, and here we sit o' nights.

Cousin Patty is small, rather white and thin, and she is fifty-five. I tell you her age, because in a way it explains many things which would otherwise puzzle you. She was born just before the war. She knew nothing of the luxury of the days of slavery. She has twisted and turned and economized all of her life. She has struggled with all the problems which beset the South in Reconstruction times, and she has come out if it all, sweet and shrewd, and with a point of view about women which astonishes me, and which gives us a chance for many sprightly arguments. Her black hair is untouched with gray, she wears it parted and in a thick knot high on her head. Her gowns are invariably of black silk, well cut and well made. She makes them herself, and gets her patterns from New York! Can you see her now?

Our arguments are usually about women, and their position in the world to-day. You know I am conservative, clinging much to old ideals, old fashions, to the beliefs of gentler times—but Cousin Patty in this backwater of civilization has gone far ahead of me. She believes that the hope of the South is in its women. "They read more than the men," she says, "and they have responded more quickly to the new social ideals."

But of our arguments more in another letter—this will serve, however, to introduce you to some of the astonishing mental processes of this little marooned cousin of mine.

For in a sense she is marooned. Once upon a time when Cotton was king, and slave labor made all things possible, there was prosperity here, but now the land is impoverished. So Cousin Patty does not depend upon the land. She read in some of her magazines of a woman who had made a fortune in wedding cake. She resolved that what one woman could do could be done by another. Hence she makes and sells wedding cake, and while she has not made a fortune she has made a living. She began by asking friends for orders; she now gets orders from near and far.

So all day there is the good smell of baking in the house, and the sound of the whisking of eggs. And every day little boxes have to be filled. Will you smile when I tell you that I like the filling of the little boxes? And that while we talk o' nights, I busy myself with this task, while Cousin Patty does things with narrow white ribbon and bits of artificial orange blossoms, so that the packages which go out may be as beautiful and bride-y as possible.

It is strange, when one thinks of it, that I came to your house on a wedding night, and here I live in a perpetual atmosphere of wedding blisses.

In the morning I write. In the afternoon I do other things. The weather is not cold—it is dry and sunshiny—windless. I take long walks over the hills and far away. Some of it is desolate country where the boxed pines have fallen, or where an area has been burned but one comes now and then upon groves of shimmering and shining young trees,—is there any tree as beautiful as a young pine with the sunshine on it?

It is rare to find a grove of old pines, yet there are one or two estates where for years no trees have been cut or burned, and beneath these tall old singing monarchs I sit on the brown needles, and write and write—to what end I know not.

I have not one finished story to show you, though the beginnings of many. The pen is not my medium. My thoughts seem to dry up when I try to put them on paper. It is when I talk that I grow most eloquent. Oh, little friend, shall I ever make the world listen again?

I am going to tell you presently of those who have listened, down here—such an audience—and in such an amphitheater!

My walks take me far afield. The roads are sandy, and I do not always follow them, preferring, rather, the dunes which remind me so much of those by the sea. Once upon a time this ground was the ocean's bed—I have the feeling always that just beyond the low hills I shall glimpse the blue.

Now and then I meet some darkey of the old school with his cheery greeting; now and then on the highroad a schooner wagon sails by. These wagons give one the queer feeling of being set back to pioneer days,—do you remember the Pike's Peak picture at the Capitol with all the eager faces turned toward the setting sun?

Now and then I run across a hunting party from one of the big hotels which are getting to be plentiful in this healthy region, but these people with their sporting clothes and their sophistication always seem out of place among the pines.

And now, since you have written to me of life as a journey on the highroad, I will tell you of my first adventure.

There's a schooner-man who comes from the sandhills on his way to the nearest resort with his chickens and eggs. It is a three days' journey, and he camps out at night, sleeping in his wagon, building his fire in the open.

One day he passed me as I sat tired by the wayside, and offered to give me a lift toward home. I accepted, and rode beside him. And thus began an acquaintance which interests me, and evidently pleases him.

He is tall and loosely put together, this knight of the Sandy Road, but with the ease of manner which seems to belong to his kind. There's good blood in these sand-hill people, and it shows in a lack of self-consciousness which makes one feel that they would meet a prince or an emperor without embarrassment. Yet there's nothing of forwardness, nothing of impertinence. It is a drawing-room manner, preserved in spite of generations of illiteracy and degeneration.

He is not an unpicturesque object. Given a plumed hat, a doublet and hose, and he would look the part, and his manner would fit in with it. Given good English, his voice would never betray him for what he is. For another thing that these people have preserved is a softness of voice and an inflection which is Elizabethan rather than twentieth century American.

Having grown to know him fairly well, I fished for an invitation to visit his home. I wanted to see where this gentlemanly backwoodsman spent the days which were not lived on the road.

I carried a rug with me, and slept for the first night under the open sky. Have you ever seen a southern sky when it was studded with stars? If not, there's something yet before you. There's no whiteness or coldness about these stars, they are pure gold, and warm with light.

My schooner-man slept in his wagon, covered with an old quilt. His mules were picketed close by, the dog curled himself beside his master, each getting warmth from the other.

We cooked supper and breakfast over the coals—chickens broiled for our evening meal, ham and eggs for the morning. We gave the dog the bones and the crusts. I took bread with me, for Cousin Patty warned me that I must not depend upon my squire for food. Cooking among these people is a lost art. Cousin Patty believes that the regeneration of the poor whites of the South will be accomplished through the women. "When they learn to cook," she says, "the men won't need whiskey. When the whiskey goes, they'll respect the law."

A mile before we reached the end of our journey, we were met by the children of my schooner-squire. Five of them—two boys, two girls, and a baby in the arms of the oldest girl. They all had the gentle quiet and ease of the father—but they were unkempt little creatures, uncombed, unwashed, in sad-colored clothes. That's the difference between the negro and the white man of this region. The negro is cheerful, debonair, he sings, he dances, and he wears all the colors of the rainbow. An old black woman who carries home my wash wore the other day a purple petticoat with a scarlet skirt looped above it, an old green sweater, and, tied over her head, a pink wool shawl. Against the neutral background of sandy hill she was a delight to the eye. The whites on the other hand seem like little animals, who have taken on the color of the landscape that they may be hidden.

But to go back to my sad children. It seemed to me that in them I was seeing the South with new eyes, perhaps because I have been away just long enough to get the proper perspective. And my life has been, you see, lived in the Southern cities, where one touches rarely the primitive.

The older boys are, perhaps, ten and twelve, blue-eyed and tow-headed. I saw few signs of affection or intelligence. They did not kiss their father when he came, except the small girl, who ran to him and was hugged; the others seemed to practice a sort of incipient stoicism, as if they were too old, too settled, for demonstration.

The mother, as we entered, was like her children. None of them has the initiative or the energy of the man. They are subdued by the changeless conditions of their environment; his one adventure of the week keeps him alert and alive.

It is a desolate country, charred pines sticking up straight from white sand. It might be made beautiful if for every tree that they tapped for turpentine they would plant a new one.

But they don't know enough to make things beautiful. The Moses of this community will be some man who shall find new methods of farming, new crops for this soil, who will show the people how to live.

And now I come to a strange fairy-tale sort of experience—an experience with the children who have lived always among these charred pines.

178

All that evening as I talked, their eyes were upon me, like the eyes of little wild creatures of the wood—a blank gaze which seemed to question. The next day when I walked, they went with me, and for some distance I carried the baby, to rest the arms of the big girl, who is always burdened.

It was in the afternoon that we drifted to a little grove of young pines, the one bit of pure green against the white and gray and black of that landscape. The sky was of sapphire, with a buzzard or two blotted against the blue.

Here with a circle of the trees surrounding us, the children sat down with me. They were not a talkative group, and I was overcome by a sense of the impossibility of meeting them on any common ground of conversation. But they seemed to expect something—they were like a flock of little hungry birds waiting to be fed—and what do you think I gave them? Guess. But I know you have it wrong.

I recited "Flos Mercatorum," my Whittington poem!

It was done on an impulse, to find if there was anything in them which would respond to such rhyme and rapture of words. I gave it in my best manner, standing in the center of the circle. I did not expect applause. But I got more than applause. I am not going to try to describe the look that came into the eyes of the oldest boy—the nearest that I can come to it is to say that it was the look of a child waked from a deep sleep, and gazing wide-eyed upon a new world.

He came straight toward me. "Where—did you—git—them words?" he asked in a breathless sort of way.

"A man wrote them—a man named Noyes."

"Are they true?"

"Yes."

"Say them again."

It was not a request. It was a command. And I did say them, and saw a soul's awakening.

Oh, there are people who won't believe that it can be done like that—in a moment. But that boy was ready. He had dreamed and until now no one had ever put the dreams into words for him. He cannot read, has probably never heard a fairy tale—the lore of this region is gruesome and ghostly, rather than lovely and poetic.

Perhaps, 'way back, five, six generations, some ancestor of this lad may have drifted into London town, perhaps the bells sang to him, and subconsciously this sand-hill child was illumined by that inherited memory. Somewhere in the back of his mind bells have been chiming, and he has not known enough to call them bells. However that may be, my verses revealed to him a new heaven and a new earth.

Without knowing anything, he is ready for everything. Perhaps there are others like him. Cousin Patty says there are girls. She insists that the girls need cook-books, not poetry, but I am not sure.

I shall go again to the pines, and teach that boy first by telling him things, then I shall take books. I haven't been as interested in anything for years as I am in that boy.

So, will you think of me as seeing, faintly, the Vision? Your eyes are clearer than mine. You can see farther; and what you see, will you tell me?

And now about Barry. I know how hard it is to have him leave you, and that under all your talk of trumpets blowing and flags flying, there's the ache and the heart-break. I cannot see why such things should come to you. The rest of us probably deserve what we get. But you—I should like to think of you always as in a garden—you have the power to make things bloom. You have even quickened the dry dust of my own dead life, so that now in it there's a little plot of the pansies of my thoughts of you, and there's rosemary, for remembrance, and there's the little bed of my interest in that boy—what seeds did you plant for it?

It is raining here to-night. I wonder it the rain is beating on the windows of the Tower Rooms, and if you are snug within, with Pittiwitz purring and the fire snapping, and I wonder if throughout all that rain you are sending any thought to me.

Perhaps I shouldn't ask it. But I do ask for another letter. What the last was to me I have told you. I shall live on the hope of the next.

Faithfully   and   gratefully   always,

ROGER POOLE.

CHAPTER XV

In Which Barry and Leila Go Over the Hills and Far Away; and in Which a March Moon Becomes a Honeymoon.

179

The news that Barry must go away had been a blow to Leila's childish dreams of immediate happiness. She knew that Barry was bitter, that he rebelled against the plans which were being made for him, but she did not know that Gordon had told the General frankly and flatly the reason for this delay in the matrimonial arrangements.

The General, true to his ancient code, had protested that "a man could drink like a gentleman," that Barry's good blood would tell. "His wild oats aren't very wild—and every boy must have his fling."

Gordon had listened impatiently, as to an ancient and outworn philosophy. "The business world doesn't take into account the wild oats of a man, General," he had said. "The new game isn't like the old one,—the convivial spirit is not the popular one among men of affairs. And that isn't the worst of it, with Barry's temperament there's danger of a breakdown, moral and physical. If it were not for that, he could come into your office and practice law, as you suggest. But he's got to get away from Washington. He's got to get away from old associations, and you'll pardon me for saying it, he's got to get away from Leila. She loves him, and is sorry for him, even though we've kept from her the knowledge of his fault. She thinks we are all against him and her sympathy weakens him. It was the same with her mother, Constance tells me. She wouldn't believe that her boy could be anything but perfect, and John Ballard wasn't strong enough to counteract her influence. Mary was the only one, and now that it has come to an actual crisis, even Mary blames me for trying to do what I know is best for Barry. I want to take him over to the other side, cut him away from all that hampers him here, and bring him back to you stronger in fiber and more of a man."

The General shook his head. "Perhaps," he said, "but I can't bear to think of the hurt heart of my little Leila."

"They should never have been engaged," Gordon said, "but it won't make matters any better to let things go on. If Leila doesn't marry Barry, she won't have to bear the burdens he will surely bring to her. She'd better be unhappy with you to take care of her, than tied to him and unhappy."

"But I'm an old man, and she is such a child. Life for me is so short, and for her so long."

"We must do what seems best for the moment, and let the future take care of itself. Barry's only a boy. They are neither of them ready for marriage—a few years of waiting won't hurt them."

It was in this strain that Gordon talked to Barry.

"It won't hurt you to wait."

"Wait for what?" Barry flamed; "until Leila wears her heart out? Until you teach her that I'm not—fit? Until somebody else comes along and steals her, while I'm gone?"

"Is that the opinion you have of her constancy?"

"No," Barry said, huskily, "she's as true as steel. But I can't see the use of this, Gordon. If I marry Leila, she'll make a man of me."

"She hasn't changed you during these last months," Gordon stated, inexorably, "and you mustn't run the risk of making her unhappy. It is a mere business proposition that I am putting before you, Barry. You must be able to support a wife before you marry one, and Washington isn't the place for you to start. In a business like ours, a man must be at his best. You are wasting your time here, and you've acquired the habit of sociability, which is just a habit, but it grows and will end by paralyzing your forces. A man who's always ready to be with the crowd isn't the man that's ready for work, and he isn't the man who's usually onto his job. I am putting this not from any moral or spiritual ideal, but from the commercial. The man who wins out isn't the one with his brain fuddled; he's the one with his brain clear. Business to-day is too keen a game for any one to play who isn't willing to be at it all the time."

Thus practical common sense met the boy at every turn. And he was forced at last for pride's sake to consent to Gordon's plans for him. But he had gone to Mary, raging. "Is he going to run our lives?"

"He is doing it for your good, Barry."

"Why can't I go South with Roger Poole?—if I must go away? He told me of a man who stayed in the woods with him."

"That would simply be temporary, and it would delay matters. Gordon's idea is that in this way you'll be established in business. If you went South you'd be without any remunerative occupation."

"Doesn't Poole make a living down there?"

"He hasn't yet. He's to try story-writing."

"Are you corresponding with him, Mary?"

Resenting his catechism, she forced herself to say, quietly, "We write now and then."

"What does Porter think of that?"

"Porter hasn't anything to do with it."

"He has, too. You know you'll marry him, Mary."

"I shall not. I haven't the least idea of marrying Porter."

"Then why do you let him hang around you?"

"Barry," she was blazing, "I don't let him hang around. He comes as he has always come—to see us all."

"Do you think for a moment that he'd come if it weren't for you? He isn't craving my society, or Aunt Isabelle's, or Susan Jenks'."

Barry was glad to blame somebody else for something—he was aware of himself as the blackest sheep in the fold, but let those who had other sins hear them.

He flung himself away from her—out of the house. And for days he did not come home. They kept the reason of his absence from Leila, and as far as they could from Constance. But Mary went nearly wild with anxiety, and she found in Gordon a strength and a resourcefulness on which she leaned.

When Barry came back, he offered no further objections to their plans. Yet they could see that he was consenting to his exile only because he had no argument with which to meet theirs. He refused to resign from the Patent Office until the last moment, as if hoping for some reprieve from the sentence which his family had pronounced. He was moody, irritable, a changed boy from the one who had hippity-hopped with Leila on Constance's wedding night.

Even Leila saw the change. "Barry, dear," she said one evening as she sat beside him in her father's library, "Barry—is it because you hate to leave—me?"

He turned to her almost fiercely. "If I had a penny of my own, Leila, I'd pick you up, and we'd go to the ends of the earth together."

And she responded breathlessly, "It would be heavenly, Barry."

He dallied with temptation. "If we were married, no one could take you away from me."

"No one will ever take me away."

"I know. But they might try to make you give me up."

"Why should they?"

"They'll say that I'm not worthy—that I'm a poor idiot who can't earn a living for his wife."

"Oh, Barry," she whispered, "how can any one say such things?" She knelt on a little stool beside him, and her brown hair curled madly about her pink cheeks. "Oh, Barry," she said again, "why not—why not get married now, and show them that we can live on what you make, and then you needn't go—away."

He caught at that hope. "But, sweetheart, you'd be—poor."

"I'd have you."

"I couldn't take you to our old house. It—belongs to Mary. Father knew that Constance was to be married, so he tried to provide for Mary until she married; after that the property will be divided between the two girls. He felt that I was a man, and he spent what money he had for me on my education."

"I don't want to live in Mary's house. We could live with Dad."

"No," sharply. Barry had been hurt when the General had seemed to agree so entirely with Gordon. He had expected the offer of a place in the General's office, and it had not come.

"If we marry, darling," he said, "we must go it alone. I won't be dependent on any one."

"We could have a little apartment," her eyes were shining, "and Dad would furnish it for us, and Susan Jenks could teach me to cook and she could tell me your favorite things, and we'd have them, and it would be like a story book. Barry, please."

He, too, thought it would be like a story book. Other people had done such things and had been happy. And once at the head of his own household he would show them that he was a man.

Yet he tried to put her away from him. "I must not. It wouldn't be right."

But as the days went on, and the time before his departure grew short, he began to ask himself, "Why not?"

And it was thus, with Romance in the lead, with Love urging them on, and with Ignorance and Innocence and Impetuosity hand in hand, that, at last, in the madness of a certain March moon, Leila and Barry ran away.

Leila had a friend in Rockville—an old school friend whom she often visited. Barry knew Montgomery County from end to end. He had fished and hunted in its streams, he had motored over its roads, he had danced and dined at its country houses, he had golfed at its country clubs, he had slept at its inns and worshiped in its churches.

So it was to Montgomery County and its county seat that they looked for their Gretna Green, and one night Leila kissed her father wistfully, and told him that she was going to see Elizabeth Dean.

"Just for Saturday, Dad. I'll go Friday night, and come back in time for dinner Saturday."

"Why not motor out?"

"The train will be easier. And I'll telephone you when I get there."

She took chances on the telephoning—for had he called her up, he would have found that she did not reach Rockville on Friday night, nor was she expected by Elizabeth Dean until Saturday in time for lunch.

There was thus an evening and a night and the morning of the next day in which Little-Lovely Leila was to be lost to the world.

She took the train for Rockville, but stopped at a station half-way between that town and Washington, and there Barry met her. They had dinner at the little station restaurant—a wonderful dinner of ham and eggs and boiled potatoes, but the wonderfulness had nothing to do with the food; it had to do rather with Little-Lovely Leila's shining eyes and blushes, and

Barry's abounding spirits. He was like a boy out of school. He teased Leila and wrote poetry on the fly-specked dinner card, reading it out loud to her, reveling in her lovely confusion.

When they finished, Leila telephoned to her father that she had arrived at Rockville and was safe. If her voice wavered a little as she said it, if her eyes filled at the trustfulness of his affectionate response, these things were soon forgotten, as Barry caught up her little bag, and they left the station, and started over the hills in search of happiness.

The way was rather long, but they had thought it best to avoid trolley or train or much-traveled roads, lest they be recognized. And so it came about that they crossed fields, and slipped through the edges of groves, and when the twilight fell Little-Lovely Leila danced along the way, and Barry danced, too, until the moon came up round and gold above the blackness of the distant hills.

Once they came to a stream that was like silver, and once they passed through a ghostly orchard with budding branches, and once they came to a farmhouse where a dog barked at them, and the dog and the orchard and the budding trees and the stream all seemed to be saying:

"*You are running away—-you are running away.*"

And now they had walked a mile, and there was yet another.

"But what's a mile?" said Barry, and Little-Lovely Leila laughed.

She wore a frock of pale yellow, with a thick warm coat of the same fashionable color. Her hat was demurely tied under her little chin with black velvet ribbons. She was like a primrose of the spring—and Barry kissed her.

"May I tell Dad, when I get home to-morrow night?" she asked.

"We'll wait until Sunday. April Fool's Day, Leila. We'll tell him, and he will think it's a joke. And when he sees how happy we are, he will know we were right."

So like children they refused to let the thought of the future mar the joy of the present.

Once they rested on a fallen log in a little grove of trees. The wind had died down, and the air was warm, with the still warmth of a Southern spring. Between the trees they could see a ribbon of white road which wound up to a shadowy church.

"The minister's house is next to the church," Barry told her; "in a half hour from now you'll be mine, Leila. And no one can take you away from me."

In the wonder of that thought they were silent for a time, then:

"How strange it will seem to be married, Barry."

"It seems the most natural thing in the world to me. But there will be those who will say I shouldn't have let you."

"I let myself. It wasn't you. Did you want my heart to break at your going, Barry?"

For a moment he held her in his arms, then he kissed her, gently, and let her go. When they came back this way, she would be his wife.

The old minister asked few questions. He believed in youth and love; the laws of the state were lenient. So with the members of his family for witnesses, he declared in due time that this man and woman were one, and again they went forth into the moonlight.

And now there was another little journey, up one hill and down another to a quaint hostelry—almost empty of guests in this early season.

A competent little landlady and an old colored man led them to the suite for which Barry had telephoned. The little landlady smiled at Leila and showed the white roses which Barry had sent for her room, and the old colored man lighted all the candles.

There was a supper set out on the table in their sitting-room, with cold roast chicken and hot biscuits, a bottle of light wine, and a round cake with white frosting.

Leila cut the cake. "To think that I should have a wedding cake," she said to Barry.

So they made a feast of it, but Barry did not open the bottle of wine until their supper was ended. Then he poured two glasses.

"To you," he whispered, and smiled at his bride.

Then before his lips could touch it, he set the glass down hastily, so that it struck against the bottle and broke, and the wine stained the white cloth.

Leila looking up, startled, met a strange look. "Barry," she whispered, "Barry, dear boy."

He rose and blew out the candles.

"Let me tell you—in the dark," he said. "You've got to know, Leila."

And in the moonlight he told her why they had wanted him to go away.

"It is because I've got to fight—devils."

At first she did not understand. But he made her understand.

She was such a little thing in her yellow gown. So little and young to deal with a thing like this.

But in that moment the child became a woman. She bent over him.

"My husband," she said, "nothing can ever part us now, Barry."

So love taught her what to say, and so she comforted him.

The next morning Elizabeth Dean met Leila Dick at the station. That she was really meeting Leila Ballard was a thing, of course, of which she had no knowledge. But Leila was acutely conscious of her new estate. It seemed to her that the motor horn brayed it, that the birds sang it, that the cows mooed it, that the dogs barked it, "*Leila Ballard, Leila Ballard, Leila Ballard, wife of Barry—you're not Leila Dick, you're not, you're not, you're not.*"

"I never knew you to be so quiet," Elizabeth said at last, curiously. "What's the matter?"

Leila brought herself back with an effort. "I like to listen," she said, "but I am usually such a chatterbox that people won't believe it."

Somehow she managed to get through that day. Somehow she managed to greet and meet the people who had been invited to the luncheon which was given in her honor. But while in body she was with them, in spirit she was with Barry. Barry was her husband—her husband who loved her and needed her in his life.

His confession of the night before had brought with it no deadening sense of hopelessness. To her, any future with Barry was rose-colored.

But it had changed her attitude toward him in this, that she no longer adored him as a strong young god who could stand alone, and whom she must worship because of his condescension in casting his eyes upon her.

He needed her! He needed little Leila Dick! And the thought gave to her marriage a deeper meaning than that of mere youthful raptures.

He had put her on the train that morning reluctantly, and had promised to call her up the moment she reached town.

So her journey toward Washington on the evening train was an hour of anticipation. To those who rode with her, she seemed a very pretty and self-contained young person making a perfectly proper and commonplace trip on the five o'clock express—in her own mind, she was set apart from all the rest by the fact of her transcendant romance.

Her father met her at the station and put her into a taxi. All the way home she sat with her hand in his.

"Did you have a good time?" he asked.

"Heavenly, Dad."

They ate dinner together, and she talked of her day, wishing that there was nothing to keep from him, wishing that she might whisper it to him now. She had no fear of his disapproval. Dad loved her.

No call had come from Barry. She finished dinner and wandered restlessly from room to room.

When nine o'clock struck, she crept into the General's library, and found him in his big chair reading and smoking.

She sat on a little stool beside him, and laid her head against his knee. Presently his hand slipped from his book and touched her curls. And then both sat looking into the fire.

"If your mother had lived, my darling," the old man said, "she would have made things easier for you."

"About Barry's going away?"

"Yes."

"It seems silly for him to go, Dad. Surely there's something here for him to do."

"Gordon thinks that the trip will bring out his manhood, make him less of a boy."

"I don't think Gordon understands Barry."

"And you do, baby? I'm afraid you spoil him."

"Nobody could spoil Barry."

"Don't love him too much."

"As if I could."

"I'm not sure," the old man said, shrewdly, "that you don't. And no man's worth it. Most of us are selfish pigs—we take all we can get—and what we give is usually less than we ask in return."

But now she was smiling into the fire. "You gave mother all that you had to give, Dad, and you made her happy."

"Yes, thank God," and now there were tears on the old cheeks; "for the short time that I had her—I made her happy."

When Barry came, he found her curled up in her father's arms. Over her head the General smiled at this boy who was some day to take her from him.

But Barry did not smile. He greeted the General, and when Leila came to him, tremulously self-conscious, he did not meet her eyes, but he took her hand in his tightly, while he spoke to her father.

"You won't mind, General, if I carry Leila off to the other room. I've a lot of things to say to her."

"Of course not. I was in love once myself, Barry."

They went into the other room. It was a long and formal parlor with crystal chandeliers and rose-colored stuffed furniture and gilt-framed mirrors. It had been furnished by the General's mother, and his little wife had loved it and had kept it unchanged.

It was dimly lighted now, and Leila in her white dinner gown and Barry tall and slender in his evening black were reflected by the long mirrors mistily.

Barry took her in his arms, and kissed her. "My wife, my wife," he said, again and again, "my wife."

At first she yielded gladly, meeting his rapture with her own. But presently she became aware of a wildness in his manner, a broken note in his whispers.

So she released herself, and stood back a little from him, and asked, breathing quickly, "Barry, what has happened?"

"Everything. Since I left you this morning I've lost my place. I found the envelope on my desk this morning—telling of my discharge. They said that I'd been too often away without sufficient excuse, and so they have dropped me from the rolls. And you see that what Gordon said was true. I can't earn a living for a wife. Now that I have you, I can't take care of you—it is not much of a fellow that you've married, Leila."

Oh, the little white face with the shining eyes!

Then out of the stillness came her cry, like a bird's note, triumphant. "But I'm your wife now, and nothing can part us, Barry."

He caught up her hands in his. "Dearest, dearest—don't you see that I can't ever tell them of our marriage until I can show them——"

"Show them what, Barry?"

"That I can take care of you."

"Do you mean that I mustn't even tell Dad, Barry?"

"You mustn't tell any one, not until I come back."

Every drop of blood was drained from her face.

"Until you come back. Are you going—away?"

"I promised Gordon to-day that I would."

She swayed a little, and he caught her. "I had to promise, Leila. Don't you see? I haven't a penny, and I can't confess to them that I've married you. I wanted to tell him that you were mine—that all your sweetness and dearness belonged to me. I wanted to shout it to the world. But I haven't a penny, and I'm proud, and I won't let Gordon think I've been a—fool."

"But Dad would help us."

"Do you think I'd beg him to give me what he hasn't offered, Leila? I've got to show them that I'm not a boy."

She struggled to bring herself out of the strange numbness which gripped her. "If I could only tell Dad."

"Surely it can be our own sweet secret, dearest."

She laid her cheek against his arm, in a dumb gesture of surrender, and her little bare left hand crept up and rested like a white rose petal against the blackness of his coat.

He laid his own upon it. "Poor little hand without a wedding ring," he said.

And now the numbness seemed to engulf her, to break——

"Hush, Leila, dear one."

But she could not hush. That very morning they had slipped the wedding ring over a length of narrow blue ribbon, and Barry had tied it about her neck. To-morrow, he had promised, she should wear it for all the world to see.

But she was not to wear it. It must be hidden, as she had hidden it all day above her heart.

"Leila, you are making it hard for me."

It was the man's cry of selfishness, but hearing it, she put her own trouble aside. He needed her, and her king could do no wrong.

So she set herself to comfort him. In the month that was left to them they would make the most of their happiness. Then perhaps she could get Dad to bring her over in the summer, and he should show her London, and all the lovely places, and there would be the letters; she would write everything—and he must write.

"You little saint," he said when he left her, "you're too good for me, but all that's best in me belongs to you—my precious."

She went to the door with him and said "good-night" bravely.

Then she shut the door and shivered. When at last she made her way through the hall to the library, she seemed to be pushing against some barrier, so that her way was slow.

On the threshold of that room she stopped.

"Dad," she said, sharply.

"My darling."

He sprang to his feet just in time and caught her.

She lay against his heart white and still. The strain of the last two days had been too great for her, and Little-Lovely Leila had fainted dead away.

184

In Which a Long Name is Bestowed Upon a Beautiful Baby; and in Which a Letter in a Long Envelope Brings Freedom to Mary.

The christening of Constance's baby brought together a group of feminine personalities, which, to one possessed with imagination, might have stood for the evil and beneficent fairies of the old story books.

The little Mary-Constance Ballard Richardson, in spite of the dignity of her hyphenated name, was a wee morsel. Swathed in fine linen, she showed to the unprejudiced eye no signs of great beauty. With a wrinkly-red skin, a funny round nose, a toothless mouth—she was like every other normal baby of her age, but to her family and friends she was a rare and unmatched object.

Even Aunt Frances succumbed to her charms. "I must say," she remarked to Delilah Jeliffe, as they bent over the bassinet, "that she is remarkable for her age."

Delilah shrugged. "I'm not fond of them. They're so red and squirmy."

Leila protested hotly. "Delilah, she's lovely—such little perfect hands."

"Bird's claws!"

Mary took up the chant. "Her skin's like a rose leaf."

And Grace: "Her hair is going to be gold, like her mother's."

"Hair?" Delilah's tone was incredulous. "She hasn't any."

Aunt Frances expertly turned the small morsel on its back. "What do you call that?" she demanded, indignantly.

Above the fat crease of the baby's neck stuck out a little feathery duck's-tail curl—bright as a sunbeam.

"What do you call that?" came the chorus of worshipers.

Delilah gave way to quiet, mocking laughter. "That isn't hair," she said; "it is just a sample of yellow silk."

Porter, coming up, was treated to a repetition of this remark.

"Let us thank the Gods that it isn't red," was his fervent response.

Grace's hands went up to her own lovely hair.

"Oh," she reproached him.

Porter apologized. "I was thinking of my carroty head. Yours is glorious."

"Artists paint it," Grace agreed pensively, "and it goes well with the right kind of clothes."

Delilah looked from one to the other.

"You two would make a beautiful pair of saints on a stained glass window," she said reflectively, "with a spike of lilies and halos back of your heads."

"Most women are ready for halos," Porter said, "and wings, but I can't see myself balancing a spike of lilies."

"Nor I," Grace rippled; "you'd better make it hollyhocks, Delilah—do you know the old rhyme

"'A beau never goes
Where the hollyhock blows'?"

"You've never lacked men in your life," Delilah told her, shrewdly, "but with that hair you won't be one of the comfortable married kind—it will be either a *grande passion* or a career for you. If you don't find your Romeo, you'll be Mother Superior in a convent, the head of a deaconess home, or a nurse on a battle-field."

Grace's eyes sparkled. "Oh, wise Delilah, you haven't drifted so very far away from my dreams. Where did you get your wisdom?"

"I'm learning things from Colin Quale. We study types together. It's great fun for me, but he's perfectly serious."

Colin Quale was Delilah's artist. "Why didn't you bring him?" Constance asked.

"Because he doesn't belong in this family group; and anyhow I had something for him to do. He's making a sketch of the gown I am to wear at the White House garden party. It will keep him busy for the afternoon."

185

"Delilah," Leila looked up from her worship of Mary-Constance, "I don't believe you ever see in people anything but the way they look."

"I don't, duckie. To me—you are a sort of family art gallery. I hang you up in my mind, and you make a rather nice little collection."

Barry, coming in, caught up her words, with something of his old vivacity.

"The baby belongs to the Dutch school—with that nose."

There was a chorus of protest.

"She looks like you," Delilah told him. "Except for her nose, she's a Ballard. There's nothing of her father in her, except her beautiful disposition."

She flashed a challenging glance at Gordon. He stiffened. Such women as Delilah Jeliffe might have their place in the eternal scheme of femininity, but he doubted it.

"She is a Ballard even in that," he said, formally; "it is Constance whose disposition is beyond criticism, not mine."

"And now that you've carried off Constance, you're going to take Barry," Delilah reproached him.

Leila dropped the baby's hand.

"Yes," Gordon discussed the subject with evident reluctance, "he's going over with me, to learn the business—he may never have a better opportunity."

The light went out of Barry's eyes. He left the little group, wandered to the window, and stood looking out.

"Mary will go next," Delilah prophesied. "With Constance and Barry on the other side, she won't be able to keep away."

Mary shook her head. "What would Aunt Isabelle and Susan Jenks and Pittiwitz do without me?"

"What would I do without you?" Porter demanded, boldly. "Don't put such ideas in her head, Delilah; she's remote enough as it is."

But Mary was not listening. Barry had slipped from the room, and presently she followed him. Leila had seen him go, and had looked after him longingly, but of late she had seemed timid in her public demonstrations; it was as if she felt when she was under the eye of others that by some sign or look she might betray her secret.

Mary found Barry down-stairs in the little office, his head in his hands.

"Dear boy," she said, and touched his bright hair with hesitating fingers.

He reached up and caught her hand.

"Mary," he said, brokenly, "what's the use? I began wrong—and I guess I'll go on wrong to the end."

And now she spoke with earnestness, both hands on his shoulders.

"Oh, Barry, boy—if you fight, fight with all your weapons. And don't let the wrong thoughts go on molding you into the wrong thing. If you think you are going to fail, you'll fail. But if you think of yourself as conquering, triumphant—if you think of yourself as coming back to Leila, victorious, why you'll come that way; you'll come strong and radiant, a man among men, Barry."

It was this convincing optimism of Mary Ballard's which brought to weaker natures a sense of actual achievement. To hear Mary say, "You can do it," was to believe in one's own powers. For the first time in his life Barry felt it. Hitherto, Mary had seemed rather worrying when it came to rules of conduct—rather unreasonable in her demands upon him. But now he was caught up on the wings of her belief in him.

"Do you think I can?" a light had leaped into his tired eyes.

"I know you can, dear boy," she bent and kissed him.

"You'll take care of Leila," he begged, and then, very low, "I'm afraid I've made an awful mess of things, Mary."

"You mustn't think of that—just think, Barry—of the day when you come back! How all the wedding bells will ring!"

But he thought of a wedding where there had been no bells. He thought of Little-Lovely Leila, in her yellow gown on the night of the mad March moon.

"You'll take care of her," he said again, and Mary promised.

And now the Bishop arrived, and certain old friends of the family. As Barry and Mary made their way up-stairs, they met Susan with the mail. There was one long letter for Mary, which she tore open with eagerness, glanced at it, and tucked it into her girdle, then went on with winged feet.

Porter, glancing at her as she came in, was struck by the radiance of her aspect. How lovely she was with that flush on her cheek, and with her sweet shining eyes!

With due formality and with the proper number of godfathers and godmothers, little Mary-Constance Ballard Richardson was officially named.

During the ceremony, Leila sat by her father's side, her hand in his. In these days the child clung to the strong old soldier. When she had come back to consciousness on the night that she had fainted on the threshold of the library, he had asked, "My darling, what is it?"

And she had cried, "Oh, Dad, Dad," and had wept in his arms. But she had not told him that she was Barry's wife. It was because of Barry's going, she had admitted; it seemed as if her heart would break.

The General talked the situation over with Mary. "How will she stand it, when he is really gone?"

"It will be better when the parting is over, and she settles down to other things."

Yet that day, after the christening, Mary wondered if what she had said was true. What would life hold for Leila when Barry was gone?

Her own life without Roger Poole was blank. Reluctantly, she was forced to admit it. Constance, the baby, Porter, these were the shadows, Roger was the substance.

The letters which had passed between them had shown her depths in him which had hitherto been unrevealed. Comparing him with Porter Bigelow, she realized that Porter could never say the things which Roger said; he could not think them.

And while in the eyes of the world Roger was a defeated man, and Porter a successful one, yet there was this to think of, that Porter's qualities were negative rather than positive. With all of his opportunities, he was narrowing his life to the pursuit of pleasure and his love for her. Roger had shirked responsibility toward his fellow man by withdrawal; Porter was shirking by indifference.

So she found herself, as many another woman has found herself, fighting the battle of the less fortunate. Roger wanted her, yet pressed no claim. Porter wanted her and meant to have her.

He had shown of late his impatience at the restraint which she had put upon him. He had encroached more and more upon her time—demanded more and more. He had been kept from saying the things which she did not want him to say only by the fact that she would not listen.

She knew that he was expecting things which could never be—and that by her silence she was giving sanction to his expectations. Yet she found herself dreading to say the final word which would send him from her.

The friendship between a man and a woman has this poignant quality—it has no assurance of permanence. For, if either marries, the other must suffer loss; if either loves, the other must put away that which may have become a prized association. As her friend, Mary valued Porter highly. She had known him all her life. Yet she was aware that she was taking all and returning nothing; and surely Porter had the right to ask of life something more than that.

She sighed, and going to her desk, took out of it the letter which she had received in the morning mail.

She knew that the moment that she announced the contents of that letter would be a dramatic one. Even if she did it quietly, it would have the effect of a bomb thrown into the midst of a peaceful circle. She had a fancy that it would be best to tell Porter first. He was to come back to dinner, so she dressed and went down early.

He found her in the garden. There were double rows of hyacinths in the paths now, with tulips coming up between, and beyond the fountain was an amethyst sky where the young moon showed.

She rose to greet him, her hands full of fragrant blossoms.

He held her hand tightly. "How happy you look, Mary."

"I am happy."

"Because I'm here? If you could only say that once truthfully."

"It is always good to have you,"

"But you won't tell a lie, and say you're happier, because of my coming? Oh, Contrary Mary!"

She shook her head. "If I said nice things to you, you'd misunderstand."

"Perhaps. But why this radiance?"

"Good news."

"From whom?"

"A man."

"What man?" with rising jealousy.

"One who has given me the thing I want."

He was plainly puzzled.

"I don't know what you mean."

"A letter came this morning—a lovely letter in a long envelope."

She took a paper out of a magazine which lay on the stone bench by her side. "Read that," she said.

He read and his face went perfectly white, so that it showed chalkily beneath his red hair.

"Mary," he said, "what have you done this for? You know I'm not going to let you."

"You haven't anything to do with it."

"But I have. It is ridiculous. You don't know what you are doing. You've never been tied to an office desk—you've never fought and struggled with the world."

187

"YOU DON'T KNOW WHAT YOU ARE DOING"

[Illustration: "You don't know what you are doing."]

"Neither have you, Porter."

"Well, if I haven't, is it my fault?" he demanded, "I was born into the world with this millstone of money around my neck, and a red head. Dad sent me to school and to college, and he set me up in business. There wasn't anything left for me to do but to keep straight, and I've done that for you."

"I know," she was very sweet as she leaned toward him, "but, Porter, sometimes, lately, I've wondered if that's all that is expected of us."

"All? What do you mean?"

"Aren't we expected to do something for others?"

"What others?"

She wanted to tell him about Roger Poole and the boy in the pines. Her eyes glowed. But her lips were silent.

"What others, Mary?"

"The people who aren't as fortunate as we are."

"What people?"

Mary was somewhat vague. "The people who need us—to help."

"Marry me, and you can be Lady Bountiful—dispensing charity."

"It isn't exactly charity." She had again the vision of Roger Poole and the boy. "People don't just want our money—they want us to—understand."

He was not following her. "To think that you should want to go out in the world—to work. Tell me why you are doing it."

"Because I need an outlet for my energies—the girl of limited income in these days is as ineffective as a jellyfish, if she hasn't some occupation."

"You could never be a jellyfish. Mary, listen, listen. I need you, dear. I've kept still for a year—Mary!"

"Porter, I can't."

And now he asked a question which had smouldered long in his breast.

"Is there any one else?"

Was there? Her thoughts leaped at once to Roger. What did he mean to her? What could he ever mean? He had said himself that he could expect nothing. Perhaps he had meant that she must expect nothing.

"Mary, is it—Roger Poole?"

Her eyes came up to meet his; they were like stars. "Porter, I don't—know."

He took the blow in silence. The shadows were on them now. In all the beauty of the May twilight, the little bronze boy grinned at love and at life.

"Has he asked you, Mary?"

"No. I'm not sure that he wants to marry me—I'm not sure that I want to marry him—I only know that he is different." It was like Mary to put it thus, frankly.

"No man could know you without wanting to marry you. But what has he to offer you—oh, it is preposterous."

She faced him, flaming. "It isn't preposterous, Porter. What has any man to offer any woman except his love? Oh, I know you men—you think because you have money—but if—if—both of you loved me—you'd stand before me on your merits as men—there would be nothing else in it for me but that."

"I know. And I'm willing to stand on my merits." The temper which belonged to Porter's red head was asserting itself. "I'm willing to stand on my merits. I offer you a past which is clean—a future of devotion. It's worth something, Mary—in the years to come when you know more of men, you'll understand that it is worth something."

"I know," she said, her hand on his, "it is worth a great deal. But I don't want to marry anybody." It was the old cry reiterated. "I want to live the life I have planned for a little while—then if Love claims me, it must be *love*—not just a comfortable getting a home for myself along the lines of least resistance. I want to work and earn, and know that I can do it. If I were to marry you, it would be just because I couldn't see any other way out of my difficulties, and you wouldn't want me that way, Porter."

He did want her. But he recognized the futility of wanting her. For a little while, at least, he must let her have her way. Indeed, she would have it, whether he let her or not. But Roger Poole should not have her. He should not. All that was primitive in Porter rose to combat the claims which she made for his rival.

"I knew there'd be trouble when you let the Tower Rooms," he said heavily at last; "a man like that always appeals to a girl's sense of romance."

The Tower Rooms! Mary saw Roger as he had stood in them for the first time amid all the confusion of Constance's flight from the home nest. That night he had seemed to her merely a person who would pay the rent—yet the money which she had received from him had been the smallest part.

She drifted away on the tide of her dreams, and Porter felt sharply the sense of her utter detachment from him.

"Mary," he said, tensely, "Mary, oh, my little Contrary Mary—you aren't going to slip out of my life. Say that you won't."

"I'm not slipping away from you," she said, "any more than I am slipping away from my old self. I don't understand it, Porter. I only know that what you call contrariness is a force within me which I can't control. I wish that I could do the things which you want me to do, I wish I could be what Gordon and Constance and Barry and even Aunt Frances want—but there's something which carries me on and on, and seems to say, 'There's more than this in the world for you'—and with that call in my ears, I have to follow."

He rose, and his head was up. "All my life, I have wanted just one thing which has been denied me—and that one thing is you. And no other man shall take you from me. I suppose I've got to set myself another season of patience. But I can wait, because in the end I shall get what I want—remember that, Mary."

"Don't be too sure, Porter."

"I am so sure," lifting the hand which was weighted with the heavy ring, "I am so sure, that I will make a wager with fortune, that the day will come when this ring shall be our betrothal ring, I'll give you others, Mary, but this shall be the one which shall bind you to me."

She snatched her hand away. "You speak as if you were—sure," she said.

"I am. I'm going to let you work and do as you please for a little while, if you must. But in the end I'm going to marry you, Mary."

At dinner Mary announced the contents of her letter in the long envelope. "I have received my appointment as stenographer in the Treasury, and I'm to report for duty on the twentieth."

It was Aunt Frances who recovered first from the shock. "Well, if you were my child——"

Grace, with little points of light in her eyes, spoke smoothly, "If Mary were your child, she would be as dutiful as I am, mother. But you see she isn't your child."

Aunt Frances snorted—"Dutiful."

Gordon was glowering. "It is rank foolishness."

Mary flared. "That's your point of view, Gordon. You judge me by Constance. But Constance has always been feminine and sweet—and I've never been particularly feminine, nor particularly sweet."

Barry followed up her defense. "I guess Mary knows how to take care of herself, Gordon."

"No woman knows how to take care of herself," Gordon was obstinate, "when it comes to the fight with economic conditions. I should hate to think of Constance trying to earn a living."

"Gordon, dear," Constance's voice appealed, "I couldn't—but Mary can—only I hate to see her do it."

"I don't," said Grace, stoutly. "I envy her."

Aunt Frances fixed her daughter with a stern eye. "Don't encourage her in her foolishness, Grace," she said; "each of you should marry and settle down with some nice man."

"But what man, mother?" Grace, leaning forward, put the question, with an irritating air of doubt.

"There are a half dozen of them waiting."

"Nice boys! But a man. Find me one, mother, and I'll marry him."

"The trouble with you and Mary," Porter informed her, "is that you don't want a man. You want a hero."

Grace nodded. "With a helmet and plume, and riding on a steed—that's my dream—but mother refuses to let me wander in Arcady where such knights are found."

"I think," Constance remarked happily, "that now and then they are found in every-day life, only you and Mary won't recognize them."

From the other side her husband smiled at her. "She thinks I'm one," he said, and his fine young face was suffused by faint color. "She thinks I'm one. I hope none of you will ever undeceive her."

Under the table Leila's little hand was slipped into Barry's big one. She could not proclaim to the world that she had found her knight, and loved him.

Aunt Frances, very stiff and straight in her jetted dinner gown, resumed, "I wish it were possible to give girls a dose of common sense, as you give them cough syrup."

"*Mother!*"

But Aunt Frances, mounted on her grievance, rode it through the salad course. She had wanted Grace to marry—her beauty and her family had entitled her to an excellent match. But Grace was single still, holding her own against all her mother's arguments, maintaining in this one thing her right to independent action.

Isabelle, straining her ears to hear what it was all about, asked Mary, late that night, "What upset Frances at dinner?"

Mary told her.

"Do you think I'm wrong, Aunt Isabelle?" she asked.

The gentle lady sighed, "If you feel that it is right, it must be right for you. But you're trying to be all head, dear child. And there's your heart to reckon with."

Mary flushed "I know. But I don't want my heart to speak—yet."

Aunt Isabelle patted her hand. "I think it has—spoken," she said softly.

Mary clung to her. "How did you know?"

"We who have dull ears have often clear eyes—it is one of our compensations, Mary."

CHAPTER XVII

In Which an Artist Finds What All His Life He Has Been Looking For; and in Which He Speaks of a Little Saint in Red.

It might have been by chance that Delilah Jeliffe driving in her electric through a broad avenue on the afternoon following the christening of Constance's baby, met Porter Bigelow, and invited him to go home with her for a cup of tea.

There were certain things which Delilah wanted of Porter. Perhaps she wanted more than she would ever get. But to-day she had it in her mind to find out if he would go with her to the White House garden party.

Colin Quale was little and blond. Because of his genius, his presence had added distinction to her entrances and exits. But at the coming function, she knew that she needed more than the prestige of genius—among the group of distinguished guests who would attend, the initial impression would mean much. Porter's almost stiff stateliness would match the gown she was to wear. His position, socially, was impregnable; he had wealth, and youth, and charm. He would, in other words, make a perfectly correct background for the picture which she designed to make of herself.

The old house at Georgetown, to which they came finally, was set back among certain blossoming shrubs and bushes. A row of tulips flamed on each side of the walk. Small and formal cedars pointed their spired heads toward the spring sky.

In the door, as they ascended the steps, appeared Colin Quale.

"Come in," he said, "come in at once. I want you to see what I have done for you."

He spoke directly to Delilah. It was doubtful if he saw Porter. He was blind to everything except the fact that his genius had designed for Delilah Jeliffe a costume which would make her fame and his.

They followed him through the wide hall to the back porch in which he had set up his easel. There, where a flowering almond bush flung its branches against a background of green, he had worked out his idea.

A water-color sketch on the easel showed a girl in white—a girl who might have been a queen or an empress. Her gown partook of the prevailing mode, but not slavishly. There was distinction in it, and color here and there, which Colin explained.

"It must be of sheer white, with many flowing flounces, and with faint pink underneath like the almond bloom. And there must be a bit of heavenly blue in the hat, and a knot of green at the girdle—and a veil flung back—you see?—there'll be sky and field and flowers and a white cloud—all the delicate color and bloom———"

Still explaining, he was at last induced to leave the picture, and have tea. While Delilah poured, Porter watched the two, interested and diverted by enthusiasms which seemed to him somewhat puerile for a man who could do real things in the world of art.

Yet he saw that Delilah took the little man very seriously, that she hung on his words of advice, and that she was obedient to his demands upon her.

"She'll marry him some day," he said to himself, and Delilah seemed to divine his thought, for when at last Colin had rushed back to his sketch, she settled herself in her low chair, and told Porter of their first meeting.

"I'll begin at the beginning," she said; "it is almost too funny to be true, and it could not possibly have happened to any one but me and Colin.

"It was last summer when I was on the North Shore. Father and I stayed at a big hotel, but I was crazy to get acquainted with the cottage colony.

"But somehow I didn't seem to make good—you see that was in my crude days when I wanted to be a cubist picture instead of a daguerreotype. I liked to be startling, and thought that to attract attention was to attract friends—but I found that I did not attract them.

"One night in August there was a big dance on at one of the hotels, and I wanted a gown which should outshine all the others—the ball was to be given for the benefit of a local chanty, and all the cottage colony would attend. I sent an order for a gown to my dressmaker, and she shipped out a strange and wonderful creation. It was an imported affair—you know the kind—with a bodice of a string of jet and a wisp of lace—with a tulle tunic, and a skirt of gold brocade that was so tight about my feet that it had the effect of Turkish trousers. For my head she sent a strip of gold gauze which was to be swathed around and around my hair in a sort of nun's coif, so that only a little knot could show at the back and practically none in front. It was the last cry in fashions. It made me look like a dream from the Arabian Nights, and I liked it."

She laughed, and, in spite of himself, Porter laughed with her.

"I wore it to the dance, and it was there that I met Colin Quale. I wish I could make you see the scene—the great ballroom, and all the other women staring at me as I came in—and the men, smiling.

"I was in my element. I thought, in those days, that the test of charm was to hold the eyes of the multitude. To-day I know that it is to hold the eyes of the elect, and it is Colin who has taught me.

"I had danced with a dozen other men when he came up to claim me. I scarcely remembered that I had promised him a dance. When he was presented to me I had only been aware of a pale little man with eye-glasses and nervous hands who had stared at me rather too steadily.

"We danced in silence for several minutes and he danced divinely.

"He stopped suddenly. 'Let's get out of here,' he said. 'I want to talk to you.'

"I looked at him in amazement. 'But I want to dance.'

"'You can always dance,' he said, quietly, 'but you cannot always talk to me.'

"There was nothing in his manner to indicate the preliminaries of a flirtation. He was perfectly serious and he evidently thought that he was offering me a privilege. Curiosity made me follow him, and he led the way down the hall to a secluded reception room where there was a long mirror, a little table, and a big bunch of old-fashioned roses in a bowl.

"On our way we passed a row of chairs, where some one had left a wrap and a scarf. Colin snatched up the scarf—it was a long wide one of white chiffon. The next morning I returned it to him, and he found the owner. I am not sure what explanation he made for his theft, but it was undoubtedly attributed to the eccentricities of genius!

"Well, when, as I said, we reached the little room, he pulled a chair forward for me, so that I sat directly in front of the mirror.

"I remember that I surveyed myself complacently. To my deluded eyes, my appearance could not be improved. My head, swathed in its golden coif, seemed to give the final perfect touch."

She laughed again at the memory, and Porter found himself immensely amused. She had such a cool way of turning her mental processes inside out and holding them up for others to see.

"As I sat there, stealing glances at myself, I became conscious that my little blond man was studying me. Other men had looked at me, but never with such a cold, calculating gaze—and when he spoke to me, I nearly jumped out of my shoes—his voice was crisp, incisive.

"'Take it off,' he said, and touched the gauze that tied up my head.

"I gasped. Then I drew myself up in an attempt at haughtiness. But he wasn't impressed a bit.

"'I suppose you know that I am an artist, Miss Jeliffe,' he said, 'and from the moment you came into the room, I haven't had a bit of peace. You're spoiling your type—and it affects me as a chromo would, or a crude crayon portrait, or any other dreadful thing.'

"Do you know how it feels to be called a 'dreadful thing' by a man like that? Well, it simply made me shrivel up and have shivers down my spine.

"'But why?' I stammered.

"'Women like you,' he said, 'belong to the stately, the aristocratic type. You can be a *grande dame* or a duchess—and you are making of yourself—what? A soubrette, with your tango skirt and your strapped slippers, and your hideous head-dress—take it off.'

"'But I can't take it off,' I said, almost tearfully; 'my hair underneath is—awful.'

"'It doesn't make any difference about your hair underneath—it can't be worse than it is,' he roared. 'I want to see your coloring—take it off.'

"And I took it off. My hair was perfectly flat, and as I caught a glimpse of myself in the mirror, I wanted to laugh, to shriek. But Colin Quale was as solemn as an owl. 'Ah,' he said, 'I knew you had a lot of it!'

"He caught up the scarf which he had borrowed and flung it over my shoulders. He gave a flick of his fingers against my forehead and pulled down a few hairs and parted them. He whisked a little table in front of me, and thrust the bunch of roses into my arms.

"'Now look at yourself,' he commanded.

"I looked and looked again. I had never dreamed that I could be like that. The scarf and the table hid every bit of that Paris gown, and showed just a bit of white throat. My plain parted hair and the roses—I looked," and now Delilah was blushing faintly, "I looked as I had always wanted to look—like the lovely ladies in the old English portraits.

"'Do you like it?' Colin asked.

"He knew that I liked it from my eyes, and for the first time since I had met him, he laughed.

"'All my life,' he said, 'I have been looking for just such a woman as you. A woman to make over—to develop. We must be friends, Miss Jeliffe. You must let me know where I can see you again.'

"Well, I didn't dance any more that night. I wrapped the scarf about my head, and went back to my hotel. Colin Quale went with me. All the way he talked about the sacredness of beauty. He opened my eyes. I began to see that loveliness should be suggested rather than emphasized. And I have told you this because I want you to understand about Colin. He isn't in love with me. I rather fancy that back home in Amesbury or Newburyport, or whatever town it is that he hails from, there's somebody whom he'll find to marry. To him I am a statue to be molded. I am clay, marble, a tube of paint, a canvas ready for his brush. It was the same way with this old house. He wanted a setting for me, and he couldn't rest until he had found it. He has not only changed my atmosphere, he has changed my manner—I was going to say my morals—he brings to me portraits of Romney ladies and Gainsborough ladies—until I seem positively to swim in a sea of stateliness. And what I said just now about manners and morals is true. A woman lives up to the clothes she wears. If you think this change is on the surface, it isn't. I couldn't talk slang in a Gainsborough hat, and be in keeping, so I don't talk slang; and a perfect lady in a moleskin mantle must have morals to match; so in my little mantle I cannot tell a lie."

To see her with lowered lashes, telling it, was the funniest thing in the world, and Porter shouted. Then her lashes were, for a moment, raised, and the old Delilah peeped out, shrewd, impish.

"He wants me to change my name. No, don't misunderstand me—not my last one. But the first. He says that Delilah smacks of the adventuress. I don't think he is quite sure of the Bible story, but he gets his impressions from grand opera—and he knows that the Delilah of the Samson story wasn't nice—not in a lady-like sense. My middle name is Anne. He likes that better."

"Lady Anne? You'll look the part in that garden party frock he is designing for you."

And now she had reached the question toward which she had been working. "Shall you go?"

He shook his head. "I doubt it. It isn't a function from which one will be missed. And the Ballards won't be there. Mary is going over to New York with Constance for a few days before the sailing. I'm to join them on the final day."

"And you won't go to the garden party without Mary?"

He found himself moved, suddenly, to speak out to her.

"She wouldn't go if she were here—not with me."

"Contrary Mary?" she drawled the words, giving them piquant suggestion.

"It isn't contrariness. Her independence is characteristic. She won't let me do things because she wants to do them by herself. But some day she'll let me do them."

He said it grimly, and Delilah flashed a glance at him, then said carefully, "It would be a pity if she should fancy—Roger Poole."

"She won't."

"You can't tell—pity leads to the softer feeling, you know."

"Why should she pity him?"

"There's his past."

"His past? Roger Poole's? What do you know of it, Delilah?"

As he leaned forward to ask the eager question, he knew that by all the rules of the game he should not be discussing Mary with any one. But he told himself hotly that it was for Mary's good. If things had been hidden, they should be revealed—the sooner the better.

Delilah gave him the details dramatically.

"Then his wife is dead?"

"Yes. But before that the scandal lost him his church. Nobody seems to know much of it all, I fancy. Mary only gave me the outline."

"And she knows?"

"Yes. Roger told her."

"The chances are that there's—another side."

He knew that it was a small thing to say. He would not have said it to any one but Delilah. She would not think him small. To her all things would be fair for a lover.

Before he went, that afternoon, he had promised to go with Delilah to the White House garden party.

Hence a week later there floated within the vision of the celebrities and society folk, gathered together on the spacious lawn of the executive mansion, a lovely lady in faint rose-white, with a touch of heavenly blue in her wide hat, from which floated a veil which half hid her down-drooped eyes.

People began at once to ask, "Who is she?"

When it was discovered that her name was Jeliffe, and that she was not a distinguished personage, it did not matter greatly. There was about her an air of distinction—a certain quiet atmosphere of withdrawal from the common herd which had nothing in it of haughtiness, but which seemed to set her apart.

Porter, following in her wake as she swept across the green, thought of the girl in leopard skins, whose unconventionality had shocked him. Surely in this woman was developed a sense of herself as the center of a picture which was almost uncanny. He found himself contrasting Mary's simplicity and lack of pose.

Mary's presence here to-day would have meant much to a few people who knew and loved her; it would have meant nothing to the crowd who stared at Delilah Jeliffe.

Colin Quale was there to enjoy the full triumph of the transformation. He hovered at a little distance from Delilah, worshiping her for the genius which met and matched his own.

"I shall paint her in that," he said to Porter. "It will be my masterpiece. And if you could have seen her on the night I met her——"

"She told me." Porter was smiling.

"It was like one of the old masters daubed by a novice, or like a room whitewashed over rare carvings—everything was hidden which should have been shown, and everything was shown which should have been hidden. It was monstrous.

"There are few women," he went on, "whom I could make over as I have made her over. They have not the adaptability—the temperament. There was one whom I could have transformed. But I was not allowed. She was little and blonde and the wife of a clergyman; she looked like a saint——and she should have worn straight things of clear green or red, or blue. But she wore black. I've sometimes wondered if she was such a saint as she looked. There was a divorce afterward, I believe, and another man. And she died."

Porter, listening idly, came back. "What type was she?"

"Fra Angelico—to perfection. I should have liked to dress her."

"Did you ever tell her that you wanted to do it?"

"Yes. And she listened. It was then that I gained my impression—that she was not a saint. One night there was a little entertainment at the parish house and I had my way. I made of her an angel, in a red robe with a golden lyre—and I painted her afterward. She used to come to my studio, but I'm not sure that Poole liked it."

"Poole?" Porter was tense.

"Her husband. He could not make her happy."

"Was she—the one in fault?"

Colin shrugged. "There are always two stories. As I have said, she looked like a saint."

"I should like to see—the picture." Porter tried to speak lightly. "May I come up some day to your rooms?"

Colin's face beamed.

"I'm getting into new quarters. I shall want your opinion—call me up before you come."

It was Colin who went home with Delilah in Porter's car. Porter pleaded important business, and walked for an hour around the Speedway, his brain in a whirl.

Then Mary knew—Mary *knew*—and it had made no difference in her thought of Roger Poole!

CHAPTER XVIII

In Which Mary Writes of the Workaday World, and in Which Roger Writes of the Dreams of a Boy.

In the Tower Rooms—June.

I have been working in the office for a week, and it has been the hardest week of my life. But please don't think that I have any regrets—it is only that the world has been so lovely outside, and that I have been shut in.

I am beginning to understand that the woman in the home has a freedom which she doesn't sufficiently value. She can run down-town in the morning; or slip out in the afternoon, or put off until to-morrow something which should have been done to-day. But men can't run out or slip away or put off—no matter if the sun is shining, or the birds singing, or the wind calling, or the open road leading to adventure.

Yet there are compensations, and I am trying to see them. I am trying to live up to my theories. And I am sustained by the thought that at last I am a wage-earner—independent of any one—capable of buying my own bread and butter, though all masculine help should fail!

Aunt Isabelle is a dear, and so is Susan Jenks. And that's another thing to think about. What will the wage-earning part of the world do, when there are no home-keepers left? If it were not for Aunt Isabelle and Susan, there wouldn't be any one to trail after me with cushions for my tired back, and cold things for me to drink on hot days, and hot things to drink on cool days.

I begin to perceive faintly the masculine point of view. If I were a man I should want a wife for just that—to toast my slippers before the fire as they do in the old-fashioned stories, to have my dinner piping hot, and to smooth the wrinkles out of my forehead.

That's why I'm not sure that I should make a comfortable sort of wife. I can't quite see myself toasting the slippers. But I can see Constance toasting them, or Leila—but Grace and I—you see, after all, there are home women and the other kind, and I fancy that I'm the other kind.

This, you'll understand, is a philosophy founded on the vast experience of a week in the workaday world—I'll let you know later of any further modification of my theories.

Well, the house seems empty with just the three of us, and Pittiwitz. I miss Constance beyond words, and the beautiful baby. Constance wanted to name her for me, but Gordon insisted that she should be called after Constance, so they compromised on Mary-Constance, such a long name for such a mite.

We all went to New York to see them off. By "all," I mean our crowd—Aunt Frances and Grace, Leila and the General—oh, poor little Leila—Delilah and Colin Quale, Aunt Isabelle and I, Susan Jenks with the baby in her arms until the very last minute—and Porter Bigelow.

At the boat Leila went all to pieces. I could never have believed that our gay little Leila would have taken anything so hard—and it was pitiful to see Barry. But I can't talk about that—I can't think about it.

Porter was dear to Leila. He treated her as if she were his own little sister, and it was lovely. He took her right away from the General, when the ship was leaving the dock.

"Brace up, little girl," he said; "he'll be back before you know it."

He literally carried her to a taxi and put her in, and then began such a day. We did all of the delightful things that one can do in New York on a summer day, beginning with breakfast at a charming inn on Long Island, and ending with a roof garden at night. And that night Leila was so tired that she went to sleep all in a minute, like a child, and forgot to grieve.

Since we came back to Washington, Porter has kept it up, not letting Leila miss Barry any more than possible, and playing big brother to perfection.

It is queer how we misjudge people. If any one had told me that Porter could be so sweet and tender to anybody, I wouldn't have believed it. But perhaps Leila brings out that side of him. Now I am independent, and aggressive, and I make Porter furious, and most of the time we fight.

As I said, the house seems empty—but I am not in it much now. If I had not had my work, I think I should have gone crazy. That's why men don't get silly and hysterical and morbid like women—they are saved by the day's work. I simply have to forget my troubles while I transcribe my notes on the typewriter.

Of course you know what life in the Departments is without my telling you. But to me it isn't monotonous or machine-like. I am awfully interested in the people. Of course my immediate work is with the nice old Chief. I'm glad he is old, and gray-haired. It makes me feel comfortable and chaperoned. Do you know that I believe the reason that most girls hate to go out to work is because of the loss of protection. You see we home girls are always in the care of somebody. I've been more than usually independent, but there has always been some one to play propriety in the background. When I was a tiny tot there was my nurse. Later at kindergarten I was sent home in a 'bus with all the other babies, and with a nice teacher to see that we arrived safely. Then there was mother and father and Barry and Constance, some of them wherever I went—and finally, Aunt Isabella.

But in the office, I am not Mary Ballard, Daughter of the Home. I am Mary Ballard, Independent Wage-Earner—stenographer at a thousand a year. There's nobody to stand between me and the people I meet. No one to say, "Here is my daughter, a woman of refinement and breeding; behind her I stand ready to hold you accountable for everything you may do to offend her." In the wage-earning world a woman must stand for what she is—and she must set the pace. So, in the office I find that I must have other manners than those in my home. I can't meet men as frankly and freely. I can't laugh with them and talk with them as I would over a cup of tea at my own little table. If you and I had met, for example, in the office, I should have put up a barrier of formality between us, and I should have said, "Good-morning" when I met you and "Good-night" when I left you, and it would have taken us months to know as much about each other as you and I knew after a week in the same house.

I suppose if I live here for years and years, that I shall grow to look upon my gray-haired chief as a sort of official grandfather, and my fellow-clerks will be brothers and sisters by adoption, but that will take time.

I wonder if I shall work for "years and years"? I am not sure that I should like it. And there you have the woman of it. A man knows that his toiling is for life; unless he grows rich and takes to golf. But a woman never looks ahead and says, "This thing I must do until I die." She always has a sense of possible release.

I am not at all sure that I am a logical person. In one breath I am telling you that I like my work; and in the next I am saying that I shouldn't care to do it all my life. But at least there's this for it, that just now it is a heavenly diversion from the worries which would otherwise have weighed.

What did you do about lunches? Mine are as yet an unsolved problem. I like my luncheon nicely set forth on my own mahogany, with the little scalloped linen doilies that we've always used. And I want my own tea and bread and butter and marmalade, and Susan's hot little made-overs. But here I am expected to rush out with the rest, and feast on impossible soups and stews and sandwiches in a restaurant across the way. The only alternative is to bring my lunch in a box, and eat it on my desk. And then I lose the breath of fresh air which I need more than the food.

Oh, these June days! Are they hot with you? Here they are heavenly. When the windows are open, the sweet warm air blows up from the river and across the White Lot, and we get a whiff of roses from the gardens back of the President's house; and when I reach home at night, the fragrance of the roses in our own garden meets me long before I can see the house. We have wonderful roses this year, and the hundred-leaved bush back of the bench by the fountain is like a rosy cloud. I made a crown of them the other day, and put them on the head of the little bronze boy, and I took a picture which I am sending. Somehow the boy of the fountain has always seemed to me to be alive, and to have in him some human quality, like a faun or a dryad.

Last night I sat very late in the garden, and I thought of what you said to me that night when you tried to tell me about your life. Do you remember what you said—that when I came into it, it seemed to you that the garden bloomed? Well, I came across this the other day, in a volume of Ruskin which father gave me, and which somehow I've never cared to read—but now it seems quite wonderful:

"You have heard it said that flowers flourish rightly only in the garden of some one who loves them. I know you would like that to be true; you would think it a pleasant magic if you could flush your flowers into brighter bloom by a kind look upon them; if you could bid the dew fall upon them in the drought, and say to the south wind, 'Come thou south wind and breathe upon my garden that the spices of it may flow forth.' This you would think a great thing. And do you not think it a greater thing that all this you can do for fairer flowers than these—flowers that have eyes like yours and thoughts like yours, and lives like yours; which, once saved, you save forever.

"Will you not go down among them—far among the moorlands and the rocks—far in the darkness of the terrible streets; these feeble florets are lying with all their fresh leaves torn and their stems broken—will you never go down to them, not set them in order in their little fragrant beds, nor fence them in their shuddering from the fierce wind?"

There's a lot more of it—but perhaps you know it. I think I have always done nice little churchly things, and charitable things, but I haven't thought as much, perhaps, about my fellow man and woman as I might. We come to things slowly here in Washington. We are conservative, and we have no great industrial problems, no strikes and unions and things like that. Grace says that there is plenty here to reform, but the squalor doesn't stick right out before your eyes as it does in some of the dreadful tenements in the bigger cities. So we forget—and I have forgotten. Until your letter came about that boy in the pines.

Everything that you tell me about him is like a fairy tale. I can shut my eyes and see you two in that circle of young pines. I can hear your voice ringing in the stillness. You don't tell me of yourself, but I know this, that in that boy you've found an audience—and he is doing things for you while you are doing them for him. You are living once more, aren't you?

And the little sad children. I was so glad to pick out the books with the bright pictures. Weren't the Cinderella illustrations dear? With all the gowns as pink as they could be and the grass as green as green, and the sky as blue as blue. And the yellow frogs in "The frog he would a wooing go," and the Walter Crane illustrations for the little book of songs.

You must make them sing "Oh, What Have You Got for Dinner, Mrs. Bond?" and "Oranges and Lemons" and "Lavender's blue, Diddle-Diddle."

Do you know what Aunt Isabelle is making for the little girls? She is so interested. Such rosy little aprons of pink and white checked gingham—with wide strings to tie behind. And my contribution is pink hair ribbons. Now won't your garden bloom?

You must tell me how their little garden plots come on. Surely that was an inspiration. I told Porter about them the other night, and he said, "For Heaven's sake, who ever heard of beginning with gardens in the education of ignorant children?"

But you and I begin and end with gardens, don't we? Were the seeds all right, and did the bulbs come up? Aunt Isabelle almost cried over your description of the joy on the little faces when the crocuses they had planted appeared.

I am eager to hear more of them, and of you. Oh, yes, and of Cousin Patty. I simply love her.

There's so much more to say, but I mustn't. I must go to bed, and be fresh for my work in the morning.

Ever   sincerely,

MARY BALLARD.

Among the Pines.

I shall have to begin at the last of your letter, and work toward the beginning, for it is of my sad children that I must speak first—although my pen is eager to talk about you, and what your letter has meant to me.

The sad children are no longer sad. Against the sand-hills they are like rose petals blown by the wind. Their pink aprons tied in the back with great bows, and the pink ribbons have transformed them, so that, except for their blank eyes, they might be any other little girls in the world.

I have taught them several of the pretty songs; you should hear their piping voices—and with their picture books and their gardens, they are very busy and happy indeed.

Their mother is positively illumined by the change her young folks. Never in her life has she seen any country but this one of charred pines and sand. I find her bending over the Cinderella book, liking it, and liking the children's little gardens.

"We ain't never had no flower garden," she confided to me. "Jim he ain't had time, and I ain't had time, and I ain't never had no luck nohow."

But the boy still means the most to me. And you have found the reason. It isn't what I am doing for him, it is what he is doing for me. If you could see his eyes! They are a boy's eyes now, not those of a little wild animal. He is beginning to read the simple books you sent. We began with "Mother Goose," and I gave him first "The King of France and Forty Thousand Men." The "Oranges and Lemons" song carried on the Dick Whittington atmosphere which he had liked in my poem, with its bells of Old Bailey and Shoreditch. He'll know his London before I get through with him.

But we've struck even a deeper note. One Sunday I was moved to take out with me your father's old Bible. There's a rose between its leaves, kept for a talisman against the blue devils which sometimes get me in their grip. Well, I took the old Bible out to our little amphitheater in the pines, and read, what do you think? Not the Old Testament stories.

I read the Beatitudes, and my boy listened, and when I had finished, he asked, "What is blessed? And who said that?"

I told him, and brought back to myself in the telling the vision of myself as a boy. Oh, how far I have drifted from the dreams of that boy! And if it had not been for you I should never have turned back. And now this boy in the pines, and the boy who was I are learning together, step by step. I am trying to forget the years between. I am trying to take up life where it was before I was overthrown. I can't quite get hold of things yet as a man, for when I try, I feel a man's bitterness. But the boy believes, and I have shut the man in me away, until the boy grows up.

Does this sound fantastic? To whom else would I dare write such a thing, but to you? But you will understand. I feel that I need make no apology.

Coming now to you and your work. I can bring no optimism to bear, I suppose I should say that it is well. But there is in me too much of the primitive masculine for that. When a man cares for a woman he inevitably wants to shield her. But what would you? Shall a man let the thing which he would cherish be buffeted by the winds?

I don't like to think of you in an office, with all your pretty woman instincts curbed to meet the stern formality of such a life. I don't like to think that any chief, however fatherly, shall dictate to you not only letters but rules of conduct. I don't like to think of you as hustled by a crowd at lunch time. I don't like to think of the great stone walls which shut you in. I don't want your wings clipped for such a cage.

And there is this I must say, that all men do not need wives to toast their slippers or to serve their meals piping hot, or even to smooth the wrinkles, although I confess that there's an appeal in this last. Some of us need wives for inspiration, for spiritual and mental uplift, for the word of cheer when our hearts are weary—for the strength which believes in our strength—one doesn't exactly think of Juliet as toasting slippers, or of Rosalind, or of Portia, yet such women never for one moment failed their lovers.

My Cousin Patty says that work will do you good, and we have great arguments. I have told her of you, not everything, because there are some things which are sacred. But I have told her that life for me, since I have known you, has taken on new meanings.

She glories in your independence and wants to know you. Some day, it is written, I am sure, that you two shall meet. In some things you are much alike—in others utterly different, with the differences made by heredity and environment.

My little Cousin Patty is the composite of three generations. Amid her sweets and spices, she is as domestic as her grandmother, but her mind sweeps on to the future of women in a way which makes me gasp.

Politics are the breath of her life. She comes of a long line of statesmen, and having no father or brother or husband to uphold the family traditions of Democracy, she upholds them herself. She is intensely interested just now in the party nominations. A split among the Republicans gives her hope of the election of the Democratic candidate. She's such a feminine little creature with her soft voice and appealing manner, with her big white aprons covering her up, and curling wisps of black hair falling over her little ears, that the contrasts in her life are almost funny. In our evenings over the little white boxes, we mix questions of State Rights and Free Trade with our bridal decorations, and it seems to me that I shall never again go to a wedding without a vision of my little Cousin Patty among her orange blossoms, laying down the law on current politics.

The negro question in Cousin Patty's mind is that of the Southerner of the better class. It isn't these descendants of old families who hate the negro. Such gentlefolk do not, of course, want equality, but they want fair treatment for the weaker race. Find me a white man who raves with rabid prejudice against the black, and I will show you one whose grandfather belonged not to the planter but to the cracker class, or a Northerner grafting on Southern Stock. Even in slave times there was rancor between the black man and what he called "po' white trash" and it still continues.

The picture of the little bronze boy with his crown of roses lies on my desk. I should like much to sit with you on the bench beneath the hundred-leaved bush. What things I should have to say to you! Things which I dare not write, lest you never let me write again.

You glean the best from everything. That you should take my little talk about gardens, and fit it to what Ruskin has said, is a gracious act. You speak of that night in the garden. Do you remember that you wore a scarlet wrap of thin silk? I could think of nothing as you came toward me, but of some glorious flower of almost supernatural bloom. All about you the garden was dying. But you were Life—Life as it springs up afresh from a world that is dead.

I know how empty the old house seems to you, without Barry, without Constance, without the beautiful baby whom I have never seen. To me it can never seem empty with you in it. Is the saying of such things forbidden? Please believe that I don't mean to force them on you, but I write as I think.

By this post Cousin Patty is sending a box of her famous cake, for you and Aunt Isabelle. There's enough for an army, so I shall think of you as dispensing tea in the garden, with your friends about you—lucky friends—and with the little bronze boy looking on and laughing.

To Mary of the Garden, then, this letter goes with all good wishes.

CHAPTER XIX

In Which Porter Plants an Evil Seed Which Grows and Flourishes; and in Which Ghosts Rise and Confront Mary.

As has been said, Porter Bigelow was not a snob, and he was a gentleman. But even a gentleman can, when swayed by primal emotions, convince himself that high motives rule, even while performing acts of doubtful honor.

It was thus that Porter proved to himself that his interest in Roger Poole's past was purely that of the protector and friend of Mary Ballard. Mary must not throw herself away. Mary must be guarded against the tragedy of marriage with a man who was not worthy. And who could do this better than he?

In pursuance of his policy of protection he took his way one afternoon in July to Colin's studio.

"I'm staying in town," Colin told him, "because of Miss Jeliffe. Her father is held by the long Session. I'm painting another picture of her, and fixing up these rooms in the interim—how do you like them?"

In his furnishing, Colin had broken away from conventional tradition. Here were no rugs hung from balconies, no rich stuffs and suits of armor. It was simply a cool little place, with a big window overlooking one of the parks. Its walls were tinted gray, and there were a few comfortable rattan chairs, with white linen cushions. A portrait of Delilah dominated the room. He had painted her in the costume which she had worn at the garden party—in all the glory of cool greens and faint pink, and heavenly blue.

Porter surveying the portrait said, slowly, "You said that you had painted—other women?"

"Yes—but none so satisfactory as Miss Jeliffe."

"There was the little saint—in red."

"You remember that? It is just a small canvas."

"You said you'd show it to me."

Colin, rummaging in a second room, called back, "I've found it, and here's another, of a woman who seemed to fit in with a Botticelli scheme. She was the long lank type."

Porter was not interested in the Botticelli woman, nor in Colin's experiments. He wanted to see Roger Poole's wife, so he gave scant attention to Colin's enthusiastic comments on the first canvas which he displayed.

"She has the long face. D'you see? And the thin long body. But I couldn't make her a success. That's the joy of Delilah Jeliffe. She has the temperament of an actress and simply lives in her part. But this woman couldn't. And lobster suppers and lovely lank ladies are not synonymous—so I gave her up."

But Porter was reaching for the other sketch.

With it in his hand, he surveyed the small creature with the angel face. In her dress of pure clear red, with the touch of gold in the halo, and a lyre in her hand, she seemed lighted by divine fire, above the earth, appealing.

"I fancy it must have been the man's fault if marriage with such a wife was a failure," he ventured.

Colin shrugged. "Who can tell?" he said. "There were moments when she did not seem a saint."

"What do you mean?" Porter's voice was almost irritable.

"It is hard to tell," the little artist reflected—"now and then a glance, a word—seemed to give her away."

"You may have misunderstood."

"Perhaps. But men who know women rarely misunderstand—that kind."

"Did you ever hear Roger Poole preach?" Porter asked, abruptly.

"Several times. He promised to be a great man. It was a pity."

"And you say she married again."

"Yes, and died shortly after."

The subject ended there, and Porter went away with the vision in his mind of Roger's wife, and of what the picture of the little saint in red would mean to Mary Ballard if she could see it.

The thought, having lodged like an evil seed, grew and flourished.

198

Of late he had seen comparatively little of Mary. He was not sure whether she planned deliberately to avoid him, or whether her work really absorbed her. That she wrote to Roger Poole he knew. She did not try to hide the fact, but spoke frankly of Roger's life in the pines.

The flames of his jealous thought burned high and hot. He refused to go with his father and mother to the northern coast, preferring to stay and swelter in the heat of Washington where he could be near Mary. He grew restless and pale, unlike himself. And he found in Leila a confidante and friend, for the General, like Mr. Jeliffe, was held in town by the late Congress.

Little-Lovely Leila was Little-Lonely Leila now. Yet after her collapse at the boat, she had shown her courage. She had put away childish things and was developing into a steadfast little woman, who busied herself with making her father happy. She watched over him and waited on him. And he who loved her wondered at her unexpected strength, not knowing that she was saying to herself, "I am a wife—not a child. And I mustn't make it hard for father—I mustn't make it hard for anybody. And when Barry comes back I shall be better fitted to share his life if I have learned to be brave."

She wrote to Barry—such cheerful letters, and one of them sent him to Gordon.

"It would have been better if I had brought her with me," he said, as he read extracts; "she's a little thing, Gordon, but she's a wonder. And she's the prop on which I lean."

"Presently you will be the prop," Gordon responded, "and that's what a husband should be, Barry, as you'll find out when you're married."

When!—if Gordon had only known how Barry dreamed of Leila—in her yellow gown, trudging by his side toward the church on the hill—dancing in the moonlight, a primrose swaying on its stem. How unquestioning had been her faith in him! And he must prove himself worthy of that faith.

And he did prove it by a steadiness which astonished Gordon, and by an industry which was almost unnatural, and he wrote to Leila, "I shall show them, dear heart, and then they'll let me have you."

It was on the night after Leila received this letter that Porter came to take her for a ride.

"Ask Mary to go with us," he said; "she won't go with me alone."

Leila's glance was sympathetic. "Did she say she wouldn't?"

"I asked her. And she said she was—tired. As if a ride wouldn't rest her," hotly.

"It would. You let me try her, Porter."

Leila's voice at the telephone was coaxing. "I want to go, Mary, dear, and Dad is busy at the Capitol, and——"

"But I said I wouldn't."

"Porter won't care, just so he gets you. He's at my elbow now, listening. And he says you are to ask Aunt Isabelle, and sit with her on the back seat if you want to be fussy."

"Leila," Porter was protesting, "I didn't say anything of the kind."

She went on regardless, "Well, if he didn't say it he meant it. And we want you, both of us, awfully."

Leila hanging up the receiver shook her head at Porter. "You don't know how to manage Mary. If you'd stay away from her for weeks—and not try to see her—she'd begin to wonder where you were."

"No she wouldn't." Porter's tone was weighted with woe. "She'd simply be glad, and she'd sit in her Tower Rooms and write letters to Roger Poole, and forget that I was on the earth."

It was out now—all his flaming jealousy. Leila stared at him. "Oh, Porter," she asked, breathlessly, "do you really think that she cares for Roger?"

"I know it."

"Has she told you?"

"Not—exactly. But she hasn't denied it. And he sha'n't have her. She belongs to me, Leila."

Leila sighed. "Oh, why should love affairs always go wrong?"

"Mine shall go right," Porter assured her grimly. "I'm not in this fight to give up, Leila."

When they took Mary in and Aunt Isabelle, Mary insisted that Leila should keep her seat beside Porter. "I'm dead tired," she said, "and I don't want to talk."

And now Porter, aiming strategically for Colin Quale's studio, took them everywhere else but in the direction of his objective point. But at last, after a long ride, they crossed the park which was faced by Colin's rooms.

"Have you seen Delilah's portrait?" Porter asked, casually.

They had not, and he knew it.

"If Colin's in, why not stop?"

They agreed and found Delilah there, and her father. The night was very hot, the room was faintly illumined by a hanging silver lamp in an alcove. From among the shadows, Delilah rose. "Colin is telephoning to the club for lemonades and things," she said; "he'll be back in a minute."

"We came to see your picture," Mary informed her.

"He is painting me again," Delilah said, "in the moonlight, like this."

She seated herself in the wide window, so that back of her was the silver haze of the glorious night Her dress of thin fine white was unrelieved.

Colin, coming in, set down his tray hastily and hastened to change the pose of her head. "It will be hard to get just the effect I want," he told them. "It must not be hard black and white, but luminous."

"I want them to see the other picture," Porter said.

Colin switched on the lights. "I'll never do better than this," he said.

"Do you like it, Mary?" Delilah asked. "It is the garden party dress."

"I love it," Mary said. "It isn't just the dress, Delilah. It's you. It's so joyous—as if you were expecting much of life."

"I am," Delilah said. "I'm expecting everything."

"And you'll get it," Colin stated. "You won't wait for any one to hand it to you; you'll simply reach out and take it."

Porter's eyes were searching. "Look here, Quale," he said, at last, "do you mind letting us see the others?—that Botticelli woman and the Fra Angelico—they show your versatility."

Colin hesitated. "They are crude beside this."

But Porter insisted. "They're charming. Trot them out, Quale."

So out they came—-the picture of the lank lady with the long face, and the picture of the little saint in red.

It was to the girl in red that they gave the most attention.

"How lovely she is," Mary said, "and how sweet."

But Delilah, observing closely, did not agree with her. "I'm not sure. Some women look like that who are little fiends. You haven't shown me this before, Colin. Who was she?"

Colin evaded. "Some one I knew a long time ago."

Porter was shaken inwardly by the thought that the little blond artist was proving himself a gentleman. He would not proclaim to the world what he had told Porter in confidence.

Porter's instincts, however, were purely primitive. He wanted to shout to the housetops, "That's the picture of Roger Poole's wife. Look at her and see how sweet she is. And then decide if she made her own unhappiness."

But he did not shout. He kept silent and watched Mary. She was still studying the picture attentively. "I don't see how you can say that she could be anything but sweet, Delilah. I think it is the face of a truthful child."

Porter's heart leaped. The time would come when he would tell her that the picture of the little trustful child was the picture of Roger Poole's wife. And then——

Colin had turned off the lights again. They sat now among the shadows and drank cool things and ate the marvelous little cakes which were a specialty of the pastry cook around the corner.

"In a week we'll all be away from here," Delilah said. "I wonder why we are so foolish. If it weren't for the fact that we've got the habit, we'd be just as comfortable at home."

"I shall be at home," Mary said. "I'm not entitled yet to a vacation."

"Don't you hate it?" Delilah demanded frankly.

Mary hesitated. "No, I don't. I can't say that I really like it—but it gave me quite a wonderful feeling to open my first pay envelope."

"Women have gone mad," Porter said. "They are deliberately turning away from womanly things to make machines of themselves."

Delilah, taking up the cudgels for Mary, demanded, "Is Mary turning her back on womanly things any more than I? I am making a business of capturing society—Mary is simply holding down her job until Romance butts into her life."

Colin stopped her. "I wish you'd put your twentieth century mind on your mid-Victorian clothes," he said, "and live up to them—in your language."

Delilah laughed. "Well, I told the truth if I didn't do it elegantly. We are both working for things which we want. Mary wants Romance and I want social recognition."

Leila sighed. "It isn't always what we want that we get, is it?" she asked, and Porter answered with decision, "It is not. Life throws us usually brickbats instead of bouquets."

Colin did not agree. "Life gives us sometimes more than we deserve. It has given me that picture of Miss Jeliffe. And I consider that a pretty big slice of good fortune."

"You're a nice boy, Colin," Delilah told him, "and I like you—and I like your philosophy. I fancy life is giving me as much as I deserve."

The others were silent. Life was not giving Leila or Porter or Mary at that moment the things that they wanted. Porter's demands on destiny were definite. He wanted Mary. Leila wanted Barry. Mary did not know what she wanted; she only knew that she was unsatisfied.

Porter took Leila home first, then drove Mary and Aunt Isabelle back through the park to the old house on the hill.

"I'm coming in," he said, as he helped Mary out of the car.

"But it is so late, Porter."

"I've been here lots of times as late as this. I won't be sent home, Mary, not to-night."

Aunt Isabelle, tired and sleepy, went at once up-stairs. Mary sat on the porch with Porter. Below them lay the city in the white moonlight. For a while they were silent, then Porter said, suddenly:

"Mary, there's something I want to tell you. You may think that I'm interfering in your affairs, but I can't help it. I can't see you doing things which will make you unhappy."

"I'm not unhappy. What do you mean, Porter?"

"You will be—if you go on as you are going. Mary—I took you to Colin's to-night on purpose, so that you could see the picture of the little saint in red, the Fra Angelico one."

"Yes."

"You know what you said about her—that she had such a trustful, childish face?"

"Yes."

"That was the picture of Roger Poole's wife, Mary."

She sat as still in her white dress as a marble statue.

At last she asked, "How do you know?"

"Quale told me. I fancy he hadn't heard that Poole had lived here, and that we knew him. So he let the name drop carelessly."

"Well?"

He turned on her flaming. "I know what you mean by that tone, Mary. But you're unjust. You think I've been meddling. But I haven't. It is only this. If Poole could break the heart of one woman, he can break the heart of another—and he sha'n't break yours."

"Who told you that he broke her heart?"

"You've seen the picture. Could a woman with a face like that do anything bad enough to wreck a man's life? I can't believe it, Mary. There are always two sides of a question."

She did not answer at once. Then she said, "How did you know about—Roger?"

"Delilah told me—he couldn't expect to keep it secret."

"He did not expect it; and he had much to bear."

"Then he has told you, and has pleaded with eloquence? But that child's face in the picture pleads with me."

It did plead. Remembering it, Mary was assailed by her first doubts. It was such a child's face, with saint's eyes.

Porter's voice was proceeding. "A man can always make out a case for himself. And you have only his word for what he did. Oh, I suppose you'll think I'm all sorts of a cad to talk this way. But I can't see you drifting, drifting toward a danger which may wreck your life."

"Why should it wreck my life?"

"Because Poole, whatever the merits of the case—doesn't seem to me strong enough to shape his destiny and yours. Was it strong for him to let go as he did, just because that woman failed him? Was it strong for him to hide himself here—like—like a criminal? A strong man would have faced the world. He would have tried to rise out of his wreck. His actions all through spell weakness. I could bear your not marrying me, Mary. But I can't bear to see you marry a man who isn't worthy of you. To see you unhappy would be torture for me."

In his earnestness he had struck a genuine note, and she recognized it.

"I know," she said, unsteadily. "I believe that you think you are fighting my battle, instead of your own. But I don't think Roger Poole would—lie."

"Not consciously. But he'd create the wrong impression—we can never see our own faults—and he would blame her, of course. But the man who has made one woman unhappy would make another unhappy, Mary."

Mary was shaken.

"Please don't put it so—inevitably. Roger hasn't any claim on me whatever."

"Hasn't he? Oh, Mary, hasn't he?"

There was hope in his voice, and she shrank from it.

"No," she said, gently, "he is just—my friend. As yet I can't believe evil of him. But I don't love him. I don't love anybody—I don't want any man in my life."

She thought that she meant it. She thought it, even while her heart was crying out in defense of the man he had maligned.

"How can one know the truth of such a thing?" she went on, unsteadily. "One can only believe in one's friends."

"Mary," eagerly, "you've known Poole only for a few months. You've known me always. I can give you a devotion equal to anybody's. Why not drop all this contrariness—and come to me?"

"Why not?" she asked herself. Roger Poole was obscure, and destined to be obscure. More than that, there would always be people like Porter who would question his past. "It is the whispers that kill," Roger had said. And people would always whisper.

She rose and walked to the end of the porch. Porter followed her, and they stood looking down into the garden. It was in a riot of summer bloom—and the fragrance rushed up to them.

201

The garden! And herself a flower! It was such things that Roger Poole could say, and which Porter could never say. And he could not say them because he could not think them. The things that Porter thought were commonplace, the things which Roger thought were wonderful. If she married Porter Bigelow, she would walk always with her feet firmly on the ground. If she married Roger Poole they would fly in the upper air together.

"Mary," Porter was insisting, "dear girl."

She held up her hand. "I won't listen," she said, almost passionately; "don't imagine things about me, Porter. I have my work—and my freedom—I won't give them up for anybody."

If she said the words with something less than her former confidence he was not aware of it. How could he know that she was making a last desperate stand?

When at last she sent him away, he went with an air of depression which touched her.

"I've risked being thought a cad," he said, "but I had to do it."

"I know. I don't blame you, dear boy."

She gave him her hand upon it, and he went away, and she was left alone in the moonlight.

And when the last echo of his purring car had died away into silence she went down and sat in the garden on the bench beside the hundred-leaved bush. Aunt Isabelle's light was still burning, and presently she would go up and say "Good-night," but for the moment she must be alone. Alone to face the doubts which were facing her. Suppose, oh, suppose, that the things which Roger had told her about his marriage had been distorted to make his story sound plausible? Suppose the little wife had suffered, had been driven from him by coldness, by cruelty? One never knew the real inner histories of such domestic tragedies. There was Leila, for example, who knew nothing of Barry's faults, and Barry had not told her. Might not other men have faults which they dared not tell? The world was full of just such tragedies.

When at last Mary reached the Tower Rooms, she undressed in the dark. She said her prayers in the dark, out loud, as had been her childish habit. And this was what she said: "Oh, Lord, I want to believe in Roger. Let me believe—don't let me doubt—let me believe."

When at last she slept, it was to dream and wake and to dream again. And waking or dreaming, out of the shadows came ghostly creatures, who whispered, "His little wife was a saint—how could she make him unhappy?" And again, "He may have been cruel, how do you know that he was not cruel?" And again, "If you were his wife, you would be thinking always of that other wife—thinking—thinking—thinking."

CHAPTER XX

In Which Mary Faces the Winter of Her Discontent; and in Which Delilah Sees Things in a Crystal Ball.

The summer slipped by, monotonously hot, languidly humid. And it was on these hot and humid days that Mary felt the grind of her new occupation. She grew to dread her entrance into the square close office room, with its gaunt desks and its unchanging occupants. She waxed restless through the hours of confinement, escaping thankfully at the end of a long day. She longed for a whiff of the sea, for the deeps of some forest, for the fields of green which must be somewhere beyond the blue-gray haze which had settled over the shimmering city.

She began to show the effects of her unaccustomed drudgery. She grew pale and thin. Aunt Isabelle was worried. The two women sat much by the fountain. Mary had begged Aunt Isabelle to go away to some cooler spot. But the gentle lady had refused.

"This is home to me, my dear," she had said, "and I don't mind the heat. And there's no happiness for me in big hotels."

"There'd be happiness for me anywhere that I could get a breath of coolness," Mary said, restlessly. "I can hardly wait for the fall days."

Yet when the cooler days came, there was the dreariness of rain and of sighing winds. And now it was November, and Roger Poole had been away a year.

The garden was dead, and Mary was glad. Dead gardens seemed to fit into her mood better than those which bloomed. Resolutely she set herself to be cheerful; conscientiously, she told herself that she must live up to the theories which she had professed; sternly, she called herself to account that she did not exult in the freedom which she had craved. Constantly her mind warred with her heart, and her heart won; and she faced the truth that all seasons would be dreary without Roger Poole.

Her letters to him of late had lacked the spontaneity which had at first characterized them. She knew it, and tried to regain her old sense of ease and intimacy. But the doubts which Porter had planted had borne fruit. Always between her and Roger floated the vision of the little saint in red.

It was inevitable that Roger's letters should change. He ceased to show her the side which for a time he had so surprisingly revealed. Their correspondence became perfunctory—intermittent.

"It is my own fault," Mary told herself, yet the knowledge did not make things easier.

And now began the winter of her discontent. If any one had told her in her days of buoyant self-confidence that she would ever go to bed weary and wake up hopeless, she would have scorned the idea; yet the fact remained that the fruit of her independence was Dead Sea apples.

It was a letter from Barry which again brought her head up, and made her life march once more to a martial tune.

"I have found the work for which I am fitted," he wrote; "you don't know how good it seems. For so many years I went to my desk like a boy driven to school. But now—why, I work after hours for the sheer love of it—and because it seems to bring me nearer to Leila."

This from Barry, the dawdler! And she who had preached was whimpering about heat and cold, about long hours and hard work—as if these things matter!

Why, life was a Great Adventure, and she had forgotten!

And now she began to look about her—to find, if she could, some ray to illumine her workaday world.

She found it in the friendliness and companionship of her office comrades—good comrades they were—fighting the battle of drudgery shoulder to shoulder, sharing the fortunes of the road, needing, some of them, the uplift of her courage, giving some of them more than they asked.

As Mary grew into their lives, she grew away somewhat from her old crowd. And if, at times, her gallant fight seemed futile—if at times she could not still the cry of her heart, it was because she was a woman, made to be loved, fitted for finer things and truer things than writing cabalistic signs on a tablet and transcribing them, later, on the typewriter.

Leila had refused to be dropped from Mary's life. She came, whenever she could, to walk a part of the way home with her friend, and the two girls would board a car and ride to the edge of the town, preferring to tramp along the edges of the Soldiers' Home or through the Park to the more formal promenade through the city streets.

It was during these little adventures that Mary became conscious of certain reserves in the younger girl. She was closely confidential, yet the open frankness of the old days was gone.

Once Mary spoke of it. "You've grown up, all in a minute, Leila," she said. "You're such a quiet little mouse."

Leila sighed. "There's so much to think about."

Watching her, Mary decided. "It is harder for her than for Barry. He has his work. But she just waits and longs for him."

In waiting and longing, Little-Lovely Leila grew more mouse-like than ever. And at last Mary spoke to the General. "She needs a change."

He nodded. "I know it. I am thinking of taking her over in the spring."

"How lovely. Have you told her?"

"No—I thought it would be a grand surprise."

"Tell her now, dear General. She needs to look forward."

So the General, who had been kept in the house nearly all winter by his rheumatism, spoke of certain baths in Germany.

"I thought I'd go over and try them," he informed his small daughter, on the day after his talk with Mary, "and you could stop and call on Barry."

"Barry!" She made a little rush toward him. "Dad, *Dad*, do you mean it?"

"Yes."

She tucked her head into his shoulder and cried for happiness. "Dad, I've missed him so."

With this hope held out to her, Little-Lovely Leila grew radiant. Once more her feet danced along the halls, and the music of her voice trilled bird-like in the big rooms.

Delilah, discussing it with her artist, said: "Leila makes me believe in Romance with a big R. But I couldn't love like that."

Colin smiled. "You'd love like a lioness. I've subdued you outwardly, but within you are still primitive."

"I wonder——" Delilah mused.

"The man for you," Colin turned to her suddenly, "is Porter Bigelow. Of course I'm taking it from the artist's point of view. You're made for each other—a pair of young gods—his red head just topping your black one—It was that way at the garden party; any one could see it."

Delilah laughed. "His eyes aren't for me. With him it is Mary Ballard. If I were in love with him, I should hate Mary. But I don't; I love her. And she's in love with Roger Poole."

Colin looked up from the samples from which he and Delilah were choosing her spring wardrobe.

"Poole? I knew his wife," he said abruptly; "it was her picture that I showed you the other night—the little saint in the Fra Angelico pose—it didn't come to me until afterward that he might be the same Poole of whom I had heard you speak."

Delilah swept across the room, and turned the canvas outward. "Roger Poole's wife," she said, "of all things!" Then she stood staring silently.

"You didn't tell us who she was."

"No," he was weighing mentally Porter's attitude in the matter, "no one knew but Bigelow."

"And he showed this to Mary?" They looked at each other, and laughed. "Perhaps all's fair in love," Delilah murmured, at last, "but I wouldn't have believed it of him."

As she turned the picture toward the wall, Delilah decided, "Mary Ballard is worth a hundred of such women as this."

"A woman like you is worth a hundred of them," Colin stated deliberately.

Delilah flushed faintly. Colin Quale was giving to her something which no other man had given. And she liked it.

"Do you know what you are doing to me?" she said, as she sat down by the window. "You are making me think that I am like the pictures you paint of me."

"You are," was the quiet response; "it's just a matter of getting beneath the surface."

There was a pause during which his fingers and eyes were busy with the shining samples—then Delilah said: "If Leila and her father go to Germany in May, I'm going to get Dad to go too. I don't suppose you'd care to join us? You'll want to get back to that girl in Amesbury or Newburyport, or whatever it is."

"What girl?"

"The one you are going to marry."

"There is no girl," said Colin quietly, "in Amesbury or Newburyport; there never has been and there never will be." Coming close, he held against her cheek a sample of soft pale yellow. "Leila Dick wears that a lot, but it's not for you." He stood back and gazed at her meditatively.

"Colin," she protested, "when you look at me that way, I feel like a wooden model."

He smiled, "That's what you have come to mean to me," he said; "I don't want to think of you as a woman."

"Why not?" asked daring Delilah.

"Because it is, to say the least, disturbing."

He occupied himself with his samples, shaking his head over them.

"None of these will do for the Secretary's dinner. You must have lace with many flounces caught up in the new fashion. And I shall want your hair different. Take it down."

She was used to him now, and presently it fell about her in all its shining sable beauty; and as he separated the strands, it was like a thing alive under his hands.

He crowned her head with the braids in a sort of old-fashioned coronet. And so arranged, the old fashion became a new fashion, and Delilah was like a queen.

"You see—with the lace and your pearl ornaments. There is nothing startling; but no one will be like you."

And there was no one like her. And because of the dress, which Colin had planned, and because of the way which he had taught her to do her hair, Delilah annexed to her train of admirers on the night of the Secretary's dinner a distinguished titled gentleman, who was looking for a wife to grace his ancestral halls—and who was impressed mightily by the fact that Delilah looked the part to perfection.

He proposed to her in three weeks, and was so sure of his ability to get what he wanted that he was stunned by her answer: "Perhaps I'll make up my mind to it. I'll give you your answer when I come over in the spring."

"But I want my answer now."

"I'm sorry. But I can't."

When she told Colin of her abrupt dismissal of the discomfited gentleman, she asked, almost plaintively, "Why couldn't I say 'yes' at once? It is the thing I've always wanted."

"Have you really wanted it?"

"Of course."

"Not of course. You want other things more."

"What for example?"

"I think you know."

She did know, and she drew a quick breath. Then laughed.

"You're trying to teach me to understand my—emotions, Colin, as you have taught me to understand my clothes."

"You're an apt pupil."

Tea came in, just then, and she poured for him, telling his fortune afterward in his teacup.

"Are you superstitious?" she asked him, having worked out a future of conventional happiness and success.

"Not enough to believe what you have told me." He was flickering his pale lashes and smiling. "Life shall bring me what I want because I shall make it come."

"Oh, you think that?"

"Yes. All things are possible to those of us who believe they are possible."

"Perhaps to a man. But—to a woman. There's Leila, for example. I'm afraid——"

"You mustn't be. Life will come right for her."

"How do you know?"

"It comes right for all of us, in one way or another. You'll find it works out. You're afraid for your little friend because of Ballard—he's pretty gay, eh?"

"Yes. More, I think, than she understands. But everybody else knows that they sent him away for that. And I can't see any way out. If he marries her he'll break her heart; if he doesn't marry her he'll break it—and there you have it."

"You must not put these 'ifs' in their way. There'll be some way out."

She rose and went to a table to a little cabinet which she unlocked.

"You wouldn't let me have my crystal ball in evidence," she said, "because it doesn't fit in with the rest of my new furnishings—but it tells things."

"What things?"

"I'll show you." She set it on the table between them. "Put your hand on each side of it."

He grasped it with his flexible fingers. "Don't invent——" he warned.

She began to speak slowly, and she was still at it when Porter's big car drove up to the door, and he came in with Mary and Leila.

"I picked up these two on their way home," Porter explained; "it is raining pitchforks, and I'm in my open car. And so, kind lady, dear lady, will you give us tea?"

Colin and Delilah, each a little pale, breathing quickly, rose to greet their guests.

"She's been telling my fortune," Colin informed them, while Delilah gave orders for more hot water and cups. "It's a queer business."

Porter scoffed. "A fake, if there ever was one."

Colin mused. "Perhaps. But she has the air of a seeress when she says it all—and she has me slated for a—masterpiece—and marriage."

Leila, standing by the table, touched the crystal globe with doubtful fingers. "Do you really see things, Delilah?"

"Sit down, and I'll prove it."

Leila shrank. "Oh, no."

But Porter insisted. "Be a sport, Leila."

So she settled herself in the chair which Colin had occupied, her curly locks half hiding her expectant eyes.

And now Delilah looked, bending over the ball.

There was a long silence. Then Delilah seemed to shake herself, as one shakes off a trance. She pushed the ball away from her with a sudden gesture. "There's nothing," she said, in a stifled voice; "there's really nothing to tell, Leila."

"I knew that you'd back out with all of us here to listen," Porter triumphed.

But Colin saw more than that.

"I think we want our tea," he said, "while it is hot," and he handed Delilah the cups, and busied himself to help her with the sugar and lemon, and to pass the little cakes, and all the time he talked in his pleasant half-cynical, half-earnest fashion, until their minds were carried on to other things.

When at last they had gone, he came back to her quickly.

"What was it?" he asked. "What did you see in the ball?"

She shivered. "It was Barry. Oh, Colin, I don't really believe in it—perhaps it was just my imagination because I am worried about Leila, but I saw Barry looking at me with such a white strange face out of the dark."

CHAPTER XXI

In Which a Little Lady in Black Comes to Washington to Witness the Swearing-in of a Gentleman and a Scholar.

It was in February that Roger wrote somewhat formally to ask if his Cousin Patty might have a room in Mary's big house during the coming inauguration.

"She is supremely happy over the Democratic victory, but in spite of her advanced ideas, she is a timid little thing, and she has no knowledge of big cities. I feel that many difficulties would be avoided if you could take her in. I want her, too, to know you. I had thought at first that I might come with her. But I think not. I am needed here."

He did not say why he was needed. He said little of himself and of his work. And Mary wondered. Had his enthusiasm waned? Was he, after all, swayed by impulse, easily discouraged? Was Porter right, and was Roger's failure in life due not to outside forces, but to weakness within himself?

She wrote him that she should be glad to have Cousin Patty, and it was on the first of March that Cousin Patty came.

Once in four years the capital city takes on a supreme holiday aspect. In other years there may be parades, in other years there may be pageants—it is an every-day affair, indeed, to hear up and down the Avenue the beat of music, and the tramp of many feet. There are funerals of great men, with gun carriages draped with the flag, and with the Marine Band playing the "Dead March." There are gay cavalcades rushing in from Fort Myer, to escort some celebrity; there are pathetic files of black folk, gorgeous in the insignia of some society which gives to its dead members the tribute of a conspicuousness which they have never known in life. There are circus parades, and suffrage parades, minstrel parades and parades of the boys from the high schools—all the display of military and motley by which men advertise their importance and their wares.

But the Inauguration is the one great and grand effort. All work stops for it; all traffic stops for it; all of the policemen in the town patrol it; half the detectives in the country are imported to protect it. All of fashion views it from the stands up-town; all of the underworld gazes at it from the south side of the street down-town. Packed trains bring the people. And the people are crowded into hotels and boarding-houses, and into houses where thresholds are never crossed at any other time by paying guests.

To the inauguration of 1913 was added another element of interest—the parade of the women, on the day preceding the changing of presidents. Hence the red and white and blue of former decorations were enlivened by the yellow and white and purple of the Suffrage colors.

Cousin Patty wore a little knot of yellow ribbon when Porter met her at the station.

Porter was not inclined to welcome any cousin of Roger Poole's with open arms. But he knew his duty to Mary's guests. He had offered his car, and had insisted that Mary should make use of it.

"For Heaven's sake, don't make me utterly miserable by refusing to let me do anything for you, Mary," he had said, when she had protested. "It is the only pleasure I have."

Cousin Patty, in spite of Porter's preconceived prejudices, made at once a place for herself. She gave him her little bag, and with a sigh of such infinite relief, her eyes like a confiding child's, that he laughed and bent down to her.

"Mary Ballard is in my car outside. I didn't want her to get into this crowd."

Cousin Patty shuddered. "Crowd! I've never seen anything like—the people. I didn't know there were so many in the world. You see, I've never been far away from home. And they kept pouring in from all the stations, and when I reached here and stood on the steps of the Pullman, and saw the masses streaming in ail directions, I felt faint—but the conductor pointed out the way to go, and then I saw your—lovely head."

She said it so sincerely that Porter laughed.

"Miss Carew," he said, "I believe you mean it."

"Mean what?"

"That it's a lovely head."

"It is." The dark eyes were shining. "You were so tall that I could see you above the people, and Roger had described how you would look. Mary Ballard had said you would surely be here to meet me, and now—oh, I'm really in Washington!"

If she had said, "I'm really in Paradise," it could not have expressed more supreme bliss.

"I never expected to be here," Cousin Patty went on to explain, as they crossed the concourse, and Porter guided her through the crowd. "I never expected it. And now Roger's beautiful Mary Ballard has promised to show me everything."

Roger's beautiful Mary Ballard, indeed!

"Miss Ballard," he said, stiffly, "is taking a week off from her work. And she is going to devote it to sightseeing with you."

"Yes, Roger told me. Is that Mary smiling from that big car? Oh, Mary Ballard, I knew you'd be just—like this."

Well, nobody could resist Cousin Patty. There was that in her charming voice, in her vivid personality which set her apart from other middle-aged and well-bred women of her type.

Porter made a wide sweep to take in the Capitol and the Library; then he flew up the Avenue, disfigured now by the stands from which people were to view the parade.

But Cousin Patty's eyes went beyond the stand to the tall straight shaft of the Monument in the distance, and when they passed the White House, she simply settled back in her seat and sighed.

"To think that, after all these years, there'll be a gentleman and a scholar to live there."

"There have been other scholars—and gentlemen," Mary reminded her.

"Of course, my dear. But this is different. You see, in our section of the country a Republican is just a—Republican. And a Democrat is a—gentleman."

Mary's eyes were dancing. "Cousin Patty," she said, "may I call you Cousin Patty? What will you do when women vote? Will the women who are Republicans be ladies?"

"Oh, now you are laughing at me," Cousin Patty said, helplessly.

Mary gave Cousin Patty the suite next to Aunt Isabelle's, and the two gentle ladies smiled and kissed in the fashion of their time, and became friends at once.

When Cousin Patty had unpacked her bag, and had put all of her nice little belongings away, she tripped across the threshold of the door between the two rooms, to talk to Aunt Isabelle.

"Mary said that we should be going to the theater to-night with Mr. Bigelow. You must tell me what to wear, please. You see I've been out of the world so long."

"But you are more of it than I," Aunt Isabelle reminded her.

Cousin Patty, in her pretty wrapper, sat down in a rocking-chair comfortably to discuss it. "What do you mean?"

"Mary has been telling me how far ahead of me your thoughts have flown. You're taking up all the new questions, and you're a successful woman of business. I have envied you ever since I heard about the wedding cake."

"It's a good business," said Cousin Patty, "and I can do it at home. I couldn't have gone out in the world to make my fight for a living. I can defy men in theory; but I'm really Southern and feminine—if you know what that means," she laughed happily. "Of course I never let them know it, not even Roger."

And now Mary came in, lovely in her white dinner gown.

"Oh," she accused them, "you aren't ready."

Cousin Patty rose. "I wanted to know what to wear, and we've talked an hour, and haven't said a word about it."

"Don't bother," Mary said; "there'll be just four of us."

"But I want to bother. Roger helped me to plan my things. He remembered every single dress you wore while he was here."

"Really?" The look which Roger had loved was creeping into Mary's clear eyes. "Really, Cousin Patty?"

"Yes. He drew a sketch of your velvet wrap with the fur, and I made mine like it, only I put a frill in place of the fur." She trotted into her room and brought it back for Mary's inspection. "Is it all right?" she asked, anxiously, as she slipped it on, and craned her neck in front of Aunt Isabelle's long mirror to see the sweep of the folds.

"It is perfect; and to think he should remember."

Cousin Patty gave her a swift glance. "That isn't all he has remembered," she said, succinctly.

It developed when they went down for dinner that Roger had ordered a box of flowers for them—purple violets for Aunt Isabelle and Cousin Patty, white violets for Mary.

"How lovely," Mary said, bending over the box of sweetness. "I am perfectly sure no one ever sent me white violets before."

There were other flowers—orchids from Porter.

"And now—which will you wear?" demanded sprightly Cousin Patty, an undercurrent of anxiety in her tone.

Mary wore the violets, and Porter gloomed all through the play.

"So my orchids weren't good enough," he said, as she sat beside him on their way to the hotel where they were to have supper.

"They were lovely, Porter."

"But you liked the violets better? Who sent them, Mary?"

"Don't ask in that tone."

"You don't want to tell me."

"It isn't that—it's your manner." She broke off to say pleadingly, "Don't let us quarrel over it. Let me forget for to-night that there's any discord in the world—any work—any worry. Let me be Contrary Mary—happy, care-free, until it all begins over again in the morning."

Very softly she said it, and there were tears in her voice. He glanced down at her in surprise. "Is that the way life looks to you—you poor little thing?"

"Yes, and when you are cross, you make it harder."

Thus, woman-like, she put him in the wrong, and the question of violets vs. orchids was shelved.

Presently, in the great red dining-room, Porter was ordering things for Cousin Patty's delectation of which she had never heard. Her enjoyment of the novelty of it all was refreshing. She tasted and ate and looked about her as frankly as a happy child, yet never, with it all, lost her little air of serene dignity, which set her apart from the flaming, flaring type of femininity which abounds in such places.

The great spectacle of the crowded rooms made a deep impression on Cousin Patty. To her this was no gathering of people who were eating too much and drinking too much, and who were taking from the night the hours which should have been given to sleep. To her it was—fairy-land; all of the women were lovely, all of the men celebrities—and the gold of the lights, the pink of the azaleas which were everywhere in pots, the murmur of voices, the sweet insistence of the

207

music in the balcony, the trail of laughter over it all—these were magical things, which might disappear at any moment, and leave her among her boxes of wedding cake, after the clock struck twelve.

But it did not disappear, and she went home happy and too tired to talk.

At breakfast the next morning, Mary announced their programme for the day.

"Delilah has telephoned that she wants us to have lunch with her at the Capitol. Her father is in Congress, Cousin Patty, and they will show us everything worth seeing. Then we'll go for a ride and have tea somewhere, and the General and Leila have asked us for dinner. Shall you be too tired?"

"Tired?" Cousin Patty's laugh trilled like the song of a bird. "I feel as if I were on wings."

Cousin Patty trod the steps of the historic Capitol with awe. To her these halls of legislation were sacred to the memory of Henry Clay and of Daniel Webster. Every congressman was a Personage—and many a simple man, torn between his desire to serve his constituents, and his need to placate the big interests of his state, would have been touched by the faith of this little Southern lady in his integrity.

"A man couldn't walk through here, with the statues of great men confronting him, and the pictures of other great men looking down on him, and the shades of those who have gone before him haunting the shadows and whispering from the galleries, without feeling that he was uplifted by their influence," she whispered to Mary, as from the Member's Gallery she gazed down at the languid gentlemen who lounged in their seats and listened with blank faces to one of their number who was speaking against time.

Colin Quale, who lunched with them, was delighted with her.

"She is an example of what I've been trying to show you," he said to Delilah. "She is so well bred that she absolutely lacks self-consciousness, and she is so clear-minded that you can't muddy her thoughts with scandals of this naughty world. She is a type worthy of your study."

"Colin," Delilah questioned, with a funny little smile, "is this a 'back to grandma' movement that you are planning for me?"

The pale little man flickered his blond lashes, but his face was grave.

"No," he said, "but I want you to be abreast of the times. There's going to be a reaction from this reign of the bizarre. We've gone long enough to harems and odalisques for our styles and our manners and presently we are going to see the blossoming of old-fashioned beauty."

"And do you think the old manners and morals will come?"

He shrugged. "Who knows? We can only hope."

It was to Colin that Cousin Patty spoke confidingly of her admiration of Delilah. "She's beautiful," she said. "Mary says that you plan her dresses. I never thought that a man could do such things until Roger took such an interest."

"Men of to-day take an interest," Colin said. "Woman's dress is one branch of art. It is worthy of a man's best powers because it adds to the beauty of the world."

"That's the funny part of it," Cousin Patty ventured; "women are taking up men's work, and men are taking up women's—it is all topsy turvy."

The little artist pondered. "Perhaps in the end they'll understand each other better."

"Do you think they will?"

"Yes. The woman who does a man's work learns to know what fighting means. The man who makes a study of feminine things begins to see back of what has seemed mere frivolity and love of admiration a desire for harmony and beauty, and self-expression. Some day women will come back to simplicity and to the home, because they will have learned things from men and will have taught things to men, and by mutual understanding each will choose the best."

Cousin Patty was inspired by the thought. "I never heard any one put it that way before."

"Perhaps not—but I have seen much of the world—and of men—and of women."

"Yet all women are not alike."

"No." His eyes swept the table. "You three—Miss Ballard, Miss Jeliffe—how far apart—yet you're all women—all, I may say, awakened women—refusing to follow the straight and narrow path of the old ideal. Isn't it so?"

"Yes. I'm in business—none of our women has ever been in business. Mary won't marry for a home—yet all of her women have, consciously or unconsciously, married for a home. And Miss Jeliffe I don't know well enough to judge. But I fancy she'll blaze a way for herself."

His eyes rested on Delilah. "She has blazed a way," he said, slowly; "she's a most remarkable woman."

Delilah, looking up, caught his glance and smiled.

"Are they in love with each other?" Cousin Patty asked Mary that night.

Mary laughed. "Delilah's a will-o'-the-wisp; who knows?"

With their days filled, there was little time for intimacy or confidential talks between Mary and Cousin Patty. And since Mary would not ask questions about Roger, and since Cousin Patty seemed to have certain reserves in his direction, it was only meager information which trickled out; and with this Mary was forced to be content.

Grace marched in the Suffrage Parade, and they applauded her from their seats on the Treasury stand. Aunt Frances, who sat with them, was filled with indignation.

"To think that *my* daughter——"

Cousin Patty threw down the gauntlet: "Why not your daughter, Mrs. Clendenning?"

"Because the women of our family have always been—different."

"So have the women of my family," calmly, "but that's no reason why we should expect to stand still. None of the women of my family ever made wedding cake for a living. But that isn't any reason why I should starve, is it?"

Aunt Frances shifted the argument. "But to march—on the street."

"That's their way of expressing themselves. Men march—and have marched since the beginning. Sometimes their marching doesn't mean anything, and sometimes it does. And I'm inclined," said Cousin Patty with an emphatic nod of her head, "to think that this marching means a great deal."

On and on they came, these women who marched for a Cause, heads up, eyes shining. There had been something to bear at the other end of the line where the crowd had pressed in upon them, and there had been no adequate police protection, but they were ready for martyrdom, if need be, perhaps, some of them would even welcome it.

But Grace was no fanatic. She met them afterward, and told of her experience gleefully.

"You should have been with me, Mary," she said.

Porter rose in his wrath. "What has bewitched you women?" he demanded. "Do you all believe in it?"

And now Leila piped, "I don't want to march. I don't want to do the things that men do. I want to have a nice little house, and cook and sew, and take care of somebody."

They all laughed. But Porter surveyed Leila with satisfaction.

"Barry's a lucky fellow," he said.

"Oh, Porter," Mary reproached him, as he helped her down from her high seat on the stand.

"Well, he is. Leila couldn't keep her nice little house any better than you, Mary. But the thing is that she *wants* to keep it for Barry. And you—you want to march on the street—and laugh—at love."

She surveyed him coldly. "That shows just how much you understand me," she said, and turned her back on him and accepted an invitation to ride home in the Jeliffes' car.

On the day of the Inauguration, the same party had seats on the stand opposite the one in front of the White House from which the President reviewed the troops.

And it was upon the President that Cousin Patty riveted her attention. To be sure her little feet beat time to the music, and she flushed and glowed as the soldiers swept by, and the horses danced, and the people cheered. But above and beyond all these things was the sight of the man, who in her eyes represented the resurrection of the South—the man who should sway it back to its old level in the affairs of the nation.

"I couldn't have dreamed," she emphasized, as she talked it over that night with Mary, "of anything so satisfying as his smile. I shall always think of him as smiling out in that quiet way of his at the people."

Mary had a vision of another Inauguration and of another President who had smiled—a President who had captured the hearts of his countrymen as perhaps this scholar never would. It was at the shrine of that strenuous and smiling President that Mary still worshiped. But they were both great men—it was for the future to tell which would live longest in the hearts of the people.

The two women were in Cousin Patty's room. They were too excited to sleep, for the events of the day had been stimulating. Cousin Patty had suggested that Mary should get into something comfortable, and come back and talk. And Mary had come, in a flowing blue gown with her fair hair in shining braids. They were alone together for the first time since Cousin Patty's arrival. It was a moment for which Mary had waited eagerly, yet now that it had come to her, she hardly knew how to begin.

But when she spoke, it was with an impulsive reaching out of her hands to the older woman.

"Cousin Patty, tell me about Roger Poole."

Cousin Patty hesitated, then asked a question, almost sharply, "My dear, why did you fail him?"

The color flooded Mary's face. "Fail him?" she faltered.

"Yes. When he first came to me, there were your letters. He used to read bits of them aloud, and I could see inspiration in them for him. Then he stopped reading them to me, and they seemed to bring heaviness with them—I can't tell you how unhappy he was until he began to make his work fill his life. Do you mind telling me what made the change in you, my dear?"

Mary gazed into the fire, the blood still in her face.

"Cousin Patty, did you know his wife?"

"Yes. Is it because of her, Mary?"

"Yes. After Roger went away, I saw her picture. Colin had painted it. And, Cousin Patty, it seemed the face of such a little—saint."

"Yet Roger told you his story?"

"Yes."

"And you didn't believe him?"

"Oh, I don't know what to believe."

"I see," but Cousin Patty's manner was remote.

Mary slipped down to the stool at Cousin Patty's feet, and brought her clear eyes to the level of the little lady's. "Dear Cousin Patty," she implored, "if you only know how I *want* to believe in Roger Poole."

Cousin Patty melted. "My dear," she said with decision, "I'm going to tell you everything."

And now woman's heart spoke to woman's heart. "I visited them in the first year of their marriage. I wanted to love his wife, and at first she seemed charming. But I hadn't been there a week before I was puzzling over her. She was made of different clay from Roger. In the intimacy of that home I discovered that she wasn't—a lady—not in our nice old-fashioned sense of good manners, and good morals. She said things that you and I couldn't say, and she did things. I felt the catastrophe in the air long before it came. But I couldn't warn Roger. I just had to let him find out. I wasn't there when the blow fell; but I'll tell you this, that Roger may have been a quixotic idiot in the eyes of the world, but if he failed it was because he was a dreamer, and an idealist, not a coward and a shirk." Her eyes were blazing. "Oh, if you could hear what some people said of him, Mary."

Mary could fancy what they had said.

"Oh, Cousin Patty, Cousin Patty," she cried, "Do you think he will ever forgive me? I have let such people talk to me, and I have listened!"

CHAPTER XXII

In Which the Garden Begins to Bloom; and in Which Roger Dreams.

March, which brings to the North sharp winds and gray days, brings to the sand-hill country its season of greatest beauty. Straight up from the unpromising soil springs the green—the pines bud and blossom, everywhere there is the delicate tracery of pale leafage, there is the white of dogwood, the pink of peach trees and of apple bloom, and again the white of cherry trees and of bridal bush. There are amethystine vistas, and emerald vistas, and vistas of rose and saffron—the cardinals burn with a red flame in the magnolias, the mocking-birds sing in the moonlight.

It was through the awakened world that Roger drove one Sunday to preach to his people.

He did not call it preaching. As yet his humility gave it no such important name. He simply went into the sand-hills and talked to those who were eager to hear. Beginning with the boy, he had found that these thirsty souls drank at any spring. The boys listened breathless to his tales of chivalry, the men to his tales of what other men had achieved, the women were reached by stories of what their children might be, and the children rose to his bait of fairy books and of colored pictures.

Gradually he had gone beyond the tales of chivalry and the achievements of men. Gradually he had brought them up and up. Other men had preached to them, but their preaching had not been linked with lessons of living. Others had cried, "Repent," but not one of them had laid emphasis on the fact that repentance was evidenced by the life which followed.

But Roger stood among them, his young face grave, his wonderful voice persuasive, and told them what it meant to be—saved. Planting hope first in their hearts, he led them toward the Christ-ideal. Manhood, he said, at its best was godlike; one must have purity, energy, education, growth.

And they, who listened, began to see that it was a spiritual as well as practical thing to set their houses in order, to plant and to till and to make the soil produce. They saw in the future a community which was orderly and law-abiding, they saw their children brought out of the bondage of ignorance and into the freedom of knowledge. And they saw more than that— they saw the Vision, faintly at first, but with ever-increasing clearness.

It was a wonderful task which Roger had set for himself, and he threw himself into his work with flaming energy. He hired a buggy and a little fat horse, and spent some of his nights *en route* in the houses of his friends along the way; other nights—and these were the ones he liked best—he slept under the pines. With John Ballard's old Bible under his arm, and his prayer-book in his pocket, he went forth each week, and always he found a congregation ready and waiting.

Over the stretches of that barren country they came to hear him, sailing in their schooner-wagons toward the harbor of the hope which he brought to them.

When he had preached from his pulpit, he had talked to men and women of culture and he had spent much of his time in polishing a phrase, or in rounding out a sentence. But now he spent his time in search of the clear words which would carry his—message.

For Mary had said that every man who preached must have a message.

Mary!

How far she had receded from him. When he thought of her now it was with a sense of overwhelming loss. She had chosen to withdraw herself from him. In every letter he had seen signs of it—and he could not protest. No man in his position could say to a woman, "I will not let you go." He had nothing to offer her but his life in the pines, a life that could not mean much to such a woman.

But it meant much to himself. Gradually he had come to see that love alone could never have brought to him what his work was bringing. He had a sense of freedom such as one must have whose shackles have been struck off. He began to know now what Mary had meant when she had said, "I feel as if I were flying through the world on strong wings." He, too, felt as if he were flying, and as it his wings were carrying him up and up beyond any heights to which he had hitherto soared.

He slept that night in one of the rare groves of old pines. He made a couch of the brown needles and threw a rug over them. The air was soft and heavy with resinous perfume. As he lay there in the stillness, the pines stretched above him like the arches of some great cathedral. His text came to him, "Come thou south wind and blow upon my garden." It was a simple people to whom he would talk on the morrow, but these things they could understand—the winds of heaven, and the stars, and the little foxes that could spoil the grapes.

When he woke there was a mocking-bird singing. He had gone to sleep obsessed by his sermon, uplifted. He woke with a sense of loneliness—a great longing for human help and understanding—a longing to look once more into Mary Ballard's clear eyes and to draw strength from the source which had once inspired him.

John Ballard's Bible lay on the rug beside him. He opened it, and the leaves fell apart at a page where a rose had once been pressed. The rose was dead now, and had been laid away carefully, lest it should be lost. But the impress was still there, as the memory of Mary's frank friendliness was still in his mind.

It was a long time before he closed the book. But at last he sighed and rose from his couch. It was inevitable, this drifting apart. Fate would hold for Mary some brilliant future. As for him, he must go on with his work alone.

Yet he realized, even in that moment of renunciation, that it was a wonderful thing that he could at last go on alone. A year ago he had needed all of Mary's strength to spur him to the effort, all of her belief in him. Now with his heart still crying out for her, needing her, he could still go on alone!

He drew a long breath, and looked up through the singing tree-tops to the bit of sky above. He stood there for a long time, silent, looking up into the shining sky.

At ten o'clock when he entered the circle of young pines, his congregation was ready for him, sitting on the rough seats which the men had fashioned, their eager faces welcoming him, their eyes lighted.

The children whom he had taught led in the singing of the simple old hymns, and Roger read a prayer.

Then he talked. He withheld nothing of the poetry of his subject; and they rose to his eloquence. And when light began to fill a man's eyes or tears to fill a woman's—Roger knew that the work of the soul was well begun.

Afterward he went among them, becoming one of them in friendliness and sympathy, but set apart and consecrated by the wisdom which made him their leader.

Among a group of men he spoke of politics. "There's the new President," he said; "it has been a great week in Washington. His administration ought to mean great things for you people down here."

Thus he roused their interest; thus he led them to ask questions; thus he drew them into eager controversy; thus he waked their minds into activity; thus he roused their sluggish souls.

But he found his keenest delight in the children's gardens.

They were such lovely little gardens now—with violets blooming in their borders, with daffodils and jonquils and hyacinths. Every bit of bloom spoke to him of Mary. Not for one moment had she lost her interest in the children's gardens, although she had ceased, it seemed, to have interest in any other of his affairs.

Before he went, the children had to have their fairy tale. But to-night he would not tell them Cinderella or Red Riding Hood. The day seemed to demand something more than that, so he told them the story of the ninety and nine, and of the sheep that was lost.

He made much of the story of the sheep, showing to these children, who knew little of shepherds and little of mountains, a picture which held them breathless. For far back, perhaps, the ancestors of these sand-hill folk had herded sheep on the hills of Scotland.

Then he sang the song, and so well did he tell the story and so well did he sing the song that they rejoiced with him over the sheep that was found—for he had made it a little lamb—helpless and bleating, and wanting very much its mother.

The song, borne on the wings of the wind, reached the ears of a man with a worn face, who slouched in the shadow of the pines.

211

Later he spoke to Roger Poole. "I reckon I'm that lost sheep," he said, soberly, "an' nobody ain't gone out to find me—yit."

"Find yourself," said Roger.

The man stared.

"Find yourself," Roger said; "look at those little gardens over there that the children have made. Can you match them?"

"I reckon I've got somethin' else to do beside make gardens," drawled the man.

"What have you got to do that's better?" Roger demanded.

The man hesitated and Roger pressed his point. "Flowers for the children—crops for men—I'll wager you've a lot of land and don't know what to do with it. Let's try to make things grow."

"Us? You mean you and me, parson?"

"Yes. And while we plant and sow, we'll talk about the state of your soul." Roger reached out his hand to the lean and lank sinner.

And the lean and lank sinner took it, with something beginning to glow in the back of his eyes.

"I reckon I ain't got on to your scheme of salvation," he remarked shrewdly, "but somehow I have a feelin' that I ain't goin' to git through those days of plantin' crops with you without your plantin' somethin' in me that's bound to grow."

In such ways did Roger meet men, women and children, reaching out from his loneliness to their need, giving much and receiving more.

It was on Tuesday morning that he came back finally to the house which seemed empty because of Cousin Patty's absence. The little lady was still in Washington, whence she had written hurried notes, promising more when the rush was over.

At the gate he met the rural carrier, who gave him the letters. There was one on top from Mary Ballard.

Roger tore it open and read it, as he walked toward the house. It contained only a scribbled line—but it set his pulses bounding.

"DEAR ROGER POOLE:

"I want to be friends again. Such friends as we were in the Tower Rooms. I know I don't deserve it—but—please.

"MARY BALLARD."

It seemed to him, as he finished it that all the world was singing, not merely the mocking-birds in the magnolias, but the whole incomparable chorus of the universe. It seemed an astounding thing that she should have written thus to him. He had so adjusted himself to the fact of repeated disappointment, repeated failure, that he found it hard to believe that such happiness could be his. Yet she had written it; that she wanted to be—his friend.

At first his thoughts did not fly beyond friendship. But as he sat down on the porch steps to think it over he began, for the first time since he had known her, to dream of a life in which she should be more to him than friend.

And why not? Why shouldn't he dream? Mary was not like other women. She looked above and beyond the little things. Might not a man offer her that which was finer than gold, greater than material success? Might not a man offer her a life which had to do with life and love—might he not share with her this opportunity to make this garden in the sand-hills bloom?

And now, while the mocking-birds sang madly, Roger Poole saw Mary—here beside him on the porch on a morning like this, with the lilacs waving perfumed plumes of mauve and white, with the birds flashing in blue and scarlet and gold from pine to magnolia, and from magnolia back to pine—with the sky unclouded, the air fresh and sweet.

He saw her as she might travel with him comfortably toward the sand-hills, in a schooner-wagon made for her use, fitted with certain luxuries of cushions and rugs. He saw her with him in deep still groves, coming at last to that circle of young pines where he preached, meeting his people, supplementing his labor with her loveliness. He saw—oh, dream of dreams—he saw a little white church among the sand-hills, a little church with a bell, such a bell as the boy had not heard before Whittington rang them all for him. Later, perhaps, there might be a rectory near the church, a rectory with a garden—and Mary in the garden.

So, tired after his journey, he sat with unseeing eyes, needing rest, needing food, yet feeling no fatigue as his soul leaped over time and space toward the goal of happiness.

He was aroused by the appearance of Aunt Chloe, the cook.

"I'se jus' been lookin' fo' you, Mr. Roger," she said. "A telegraf done come, yestiddy, and I ain't knowed what to do wid it." She handed it to him, and watched him anxiously as he opened it.

It was from Cousin Patty.

"Mary has had sad news of Barry. We need you. Can you come?"

CHAPTER XXIII

In Which Little-Lovely Leila Looks Forward to the Month of May; and in Which Barry Rides Into a Town With Narrow Streets.

It was when Little-Lovely Leila was choosing certain gowns for her trip abroad that she had almost given away her secret to Delilah.

"I want a yellow one," she had remarked, "with a primrose hat, like I wore when Barry and I——" She stopped, blushing furiously.

"When you and Barry what?" demanded Delilah.

Leila having started to say, "When Barry and I ran away to be married," stumbled over a substitute, "Well, I wore a yellow gown—when—when——"

"Not when he proposed, duckie. That was the day at Fort Myer. I knew it the minute I came out and saw your face; and then that telephone message about the picture. Were you really jealous when you found it on my table?"

"Dreadfully." Leila breathed freely once more. The subject of the primrose gown was shelved safely.

"You needn't have been. All the world knew that Barry was yours."

"And he's mine now," Leila laughed; "and I am to see him in—May."

In the days which followed she was a very busy little Leila. On every pretty garment that she made or bought, she embroidered in fine silk a wreath of primroses. It was her own delicious secret, this adopting of her bridal color. Other brides might be married in white, but she had been different—her gown had been the color of the great gold moon that had lighted their way. What a wedding journey it had been—and how she and Barry would laugh over it in the years to come!

For the tragedy which had weighed so heavily began now to seem like a happy comedy. In a few weeks she would see Barry, in a few weeks all the world would know that she was his wife!

So she packed her fragrant boxes—so she embroidered, and sang, and dreamed.

Barry had written that he was "making good"; and that when she came he would tell Gordon. And the General should go on to Germany, and he and Leila would have their honeymoon trip.

"You must decide where we shall go," he had said, and Leila had planned joyously.

"Dad and I motored once into Scotland, and we stopped at a little town for tea. Such a queer little story-book town, Barry, with funny houses and with the streets so narrow that the people leaned out of their windows and gossiped over our heads, and I am sure they could have shaken hands across. There wasn't even room for our car to turn around, and we had to go on and on until we came to the edge of the town, and there was the dearest inn. We stopped and stayed that night—and the linen all smelled of lavender, and there was a sweet dumpling of a landlady, and old-fashioned flowers in a trim little garden—and all the hills beyond and a lake. Let's go there, Barry; it will be beautiful."

They planned, too, to go into lodgings afterward in London.

The thought of lodgings gave Leila a thrill. She hunted out her fat little volume of Martin Chuzzlewit and gloated over Ruth Pinch and her beef-steak pie. She added two or three captivating aprons to the contents of the fragrant boxes. She even bought a cook-book, and it was with a sigh that she laid the cook-book away when Barry wrote that in such lodgings as he would choose the landlady would serve their meals in the sitting-room. And this plan would give Leila more time to see the sights of London!

But what cared Little-Lovely Leila for seeing sights? Anybody could see sights—any dreary and dried-up fossil, any crabbed and cranky old maid—the Tower and Westminster Abbey were for those who had nothing better to do. As for herself, her horizon just now was bounded by primrose wreaths and fragrant boxes, and the promise of seeing Barry in May!

But fate, which has strange things in store for all of us, had this in store for little Leila, that she was not to see Barry in May, and the reason that she was not to see him was Jerry Tuckerman.

Meeting Mary in the street one day early in February, Jerry had said, "I am going to run over to London this week. Shall I take your best to Barry?"

Mary's eyes had met his squarely. "Be sure you take *your* best, Jerry," she had said.

He had laughed his defiance. "Barry's all right—but you've got to give him a little rope, Mary."

When he had left her, Mary had walked on slowly, her heart filled with foreboding. Barry was not like Jerry. Jerry, coarse of fiber, lacking temperament, would probably come to middle age safely—he would never be called upon to pay the piper as Barry would for dancing to the tune of the follies of youth.

She wrote to Gordon, warning him. "Keep Barry busy," she said. "Jerry told me that he intended to have 'the time of his young life'—and he will want Barry to share it."

Gordon smiled over the letter. "Poor Mary," he told Constance; "she has carried Barry for so long on her shoulders, and she can't realize that he is at last learning to stand alone."

But Constance did not smile. "We never could bear Jerry Tuckerman; he always made Barry do things."

"Nobody can make me do things when I don't want to do them," said Gordon comfortably and priggishly, "and Barry must learn that he can't put the blame on anybody's shoulders but his own."

Constance sighed. She did not quite share Gordon's sense of security. Barry was different. He was a dear, and trying so hard; but Jerry had always had some power to sway him from his best, a sinister inexplicable influence.

Jerry, arriving, hung around Barry for several days, tempting him, like the villain in the play.

But Barry refused to be tempted. He was busy—and he had just had a letter from Leila.

"I simply can't run around town with you, Tuckerman," he explained. "Holding down a job in an office like this isn't like holding down a government job."

"So they've put your nose to the grindstone?" Jerry grinned as he said it, and Barry flushed. "I like it, Tuckerman; there's something ahead, and Gordon has me slated for a promotion."

But what did a promotion mean to Jerry's millions? And Barry was good company, and anyhow—oh, he couldn't see Ballard doing a steady stunt like this.

"Motor into Scotland with me next week," he insisted; "get a week off, and I'll pick up a gay party. It's a bit early, but we'll stop in the big towns."

Barry shook his head.

"Leila and the General are coming over in May—she wants to take that trip—and, anyhow, I can't get away."

"Oh, well, wait and take your nice little ride with Leila," Jerry said, good-naturedly enough, "but don't tie yourself too soon to a woman's apron string, Ballard—wait till you've had your fling."

But Barry didn't want a fling. He, too, was dreaming. On half-holidays and Sundays he haunted neighborhoods where there were rooms to let. And when one day he chanced on a sunshiny suite where a pot of primroses bloomed in the window, he lingered and looked.

"If they're empty a month from now I'll take them," he said.

"A guinea down and I'll keep them for you," was the smiling response of the pleasant landlady.

So Barry blushingly paid the guinea, and began to buy little things to make the rooms beautiful—a bamboo basket for flowers—a Sheffield tray—a quaint tea-caddy—an antique footstool for Leila's little feet.

Yet there were moments in the midst of his elation when some chill breath of fear touched him, and it was in one of these moods that he wrote out of his heart to his little bride.

"Sometimes, when I think of you, sweetheart, I realize how little there is in me which is deserving of that which you are giving me. When your letters come, I read them and think and think about them. And the thing I think is this: Am I going to be able all my life to live up to your expectations? Don't expect too much, dear heart. I wonder if I am more cowardly about facing life than other men. Now and then things seem to loom up in front of me—great shadows which block my way—and I grow afraid that I can't push them out of your path and mine. And if I should not push them, what then? Would they engulf you, and should I be to blame?"

Mary found Leila puzzling over this letter. "It doesn't sound like Barry," she said, in a little frightened voice. "May I read it to you, Mary?"

Mary had stopped in for tea on her way home from the office. But the tea waited.

"Barry is usually so—hopeful," Leila said, when she had finished; "somehow I can't help—worrying."

Mary was worried. She knew these moods. Barry had them when he was fighting "blue devils." She was afraid—haunted by the thought of Jerry. She tried to speak cheerfully.

"You'll be going over soon," she said, "and then all the world will be bright to him."

Leila hesitated. "I wish," she faltered, "that I could be with him now to help him—fight."

Mary gave her a startled glance. Their eyes met.

"Leila," Mary said, with a little gasp, "who told you?"

214

"Barry"—the tea was forgotten—"before—before he went away." The vision was upon her of that moment when he had knelt at her feet on their bridal night.

Haltingly, she spoke of her lover's weakness. "I've wanted to ask you, Mary, and when this letter came, I just had to ask. If you think it would be better—if we were married, if I could make a home for him."

"It wouldn't be better for you."

"I don't want to think about myself," Leila said, passionately; "everybody thinks about me. It is Barry I want to think of, Mary."

Mary patted the flushed cheek. "Barry is a fortunate boy," she said. Then, with hesitation, "Leila, when you knew, did it make a difference?"

"Difference?"

"In your feeling for Barry?"

And now the child eyes were woman eyes. "Yes," she said, "it made a difference. But the difference was this—that I loved him more. I don't know whether I can explain it so that you will understand, Mary. But then you aren't like me. You've always been so wonderful, like Barry. But you see I've never been wonderful. I've always been just a little silly thing, pretty enough for people to like, and childish enough for everybody to pet, and because I was pretty and little and childish, nobody seemed to think that I could be anything else. And for a long time I didn't dream that Barry was in love with me. I just knew that I—cared. But it was the kind of caring that didn't expect much in return. And when Barry said that I was the only woman in the world for him—I had the feeling that it was a pleasant dream, and that—that some day I'd wake up and find that he had made a mistake and that he should have chosen a princess instead of just a little goosie-girl. But when I knew that Barry had to fight, everything changed. I knew that I could really help. More than the princess, perhaps, because you see she might not have cared to bother—and she might not have loved him enough to—overlook."

"You blessed child," Mary said with a catch in her voice, "you mustn't be so humble—it's enough to spoil any man."

"Not Barry," Leila said; "he loves me because I am so loving."

Oh, wisdom of the little heart. There might be men who could love for the sake of conquest; there might be men who could meet coldness with ardor, and affection with indifference. Barry was not one of these. The sacred fire which burned in the heart of his sweet mistress had lighted the flame in his own. It was Leila's love as well as Leila that he wanted. And she knew and treasured the knowledge.

It was when Mary left that she said, with forced lightness, "You'll be going soon, and what a summer you will have together."

It was on Leila's lips to cry, "But I want our life together to begin now. What's one summer in a whole life of love?"

But she did not voice her cry. She kissed Mary and smiled wistfully, and went back into the dusky room to dream of Barry—Barry her young husband, with whom she had walked in her little yellow gown over the hills and far away.

And while she dreamed, Barry, in Jerry Tuckerman's big blue car, was flying over other hills, and farther away from Leila than he had ever been in his life.

It was as Mary had feared. Barry's strength in his first resistance of Jerry's importunities had made him over-confident, so that when, at the end of the month, Jerry had returned and had pressed his claim, Barry had consented to lunch with him.

At luncheon they met Jerry's crowd and Barry drank just one glass of golden sparkling stuff.

But the one glass was enough to fire his blood—enough to change the aspect of the world—enough to make him reckless, boisterous—enough to make him consent to join at once Jerry's party in a motor trip to Scotland.

In that moment the world of work receded, the world of which Leila was the center receded—the life which had to do with lodgings and primroses and Sheffield trays was faint and blurred to his mental vision. But this life, which had to do with laughter and care-free joyousness and forgetfulness, this was the life for a man who was a man.

Jerry was saying, "There will be the three of us and the chauffeur—and we will take things in hampers and things in boxes, and things in bottles."

Barry laughed. It was not a loud laugh, just a light boyish chuckle, and as he rose and stood with his hand resting on the table, many eyes were turned upon him. He was a handsome young American, his beautiful blond head held high. "You mustn't expect," he said, still with that light laughter, "that I am going to bring any bottles. Only thing I've got is a tea-caddy. Honest—a tea-caddy, and a Sheffield tray."

Then some memory assailing him, he faltered, "And a little foolish footstool."

"Sit down," Jerry said. There was something strangely appealing in that gay young figure with the shining eyes. In spite of himself, Jerry felt uncomfortable. "Sit down," he said.

So Barry sat down, and laughed at nothing, and talked about nothing, and found it all very enchanting.

He packed his bag and left a note for Gordon and when he piled finally with the others into Jerry's car, he was ready to shout with them that it was a long lane which had no turning, and that work was a bore and would always be.

And so the ride which Leila had planned for herself and her young husband became a wild ride, in which these young knights of the road pursued fantastic adventures, with memories blank, and with consciences soothed.

215

For days they rode, stopping at various inns along the way, startling the staid folk of the villages by their laughter late into the night; making boon companions in an hour, and leaving them with tears, to forget them at the first turn of the corner.

Written as old romance, such things seem of the golden age; looked upon in the light of Barry's future and of Leila's, they were tragedy unspeakable.

And now the car went up and up, to come down again to some stretch of sand, with the mountains looming black against one horizon, the sea a band of sapphire against another.

And so, fate drawing them nearer and nearer, they came at last to the little town which Leila had described in her letter.

Going in, some one spoke the name, and Barry had a stab of memory. Who had talked of narrow streets, across which people gossiped—and shook hands?—who had spoken of having tea in that little shop?

He asked the question of his companions, "Who called this a story-book town?"

They laughed at him. "You dreamed it."

Steadily his mind began to work. He fumbled in his pocket, and found Leila's letter.

Searching through it, he discovered the name of the little place. "I didn't dream it," he announced triumphantly; "my wife told me."

"Wake up," Jerry said, "and thank the gods that you are single."

But Barry stood swaying. "My little wife told me—*Leila*!"

With a sudden cry, he lurched forward. His arm struck the arm of the driver beside him. The car gave a sudden turn. The streets were narrow—so narrow that one might almost shake hands across them!

And there was a crash!

Jerry was not hurt, nor the other adventurers. The chauffeur was stunned. But Barry was crumpled up against the stone steps of one of the funny little houses, and lay there with Leila's letter all red under him.

It was Porter and Mary who told Leila. The General had begged them to do it. "I can't," he had said, pitifully. "I've faced guns, but I can't face the hurt in my darling's eyes."

So Mary's arms were around her when she whispered to the child-wife that Barry was—dead.

Porter had faltered first something about an accident—that the doctors were—afraid.

Leila, shaking, had looked from one to the other. "I must go to him," she had cried. "You see, I am his wife. I have a right to go."

"*His wife*?" Of all things they had not expected this.

"Yes, we have been married a year—we ran away."

"When, dear?"

"Last March—to Rockville—and—and we were going to tell everybody the next day—and then Barry lost his place—and we couldn't."

Oh, poor little widow, poor little child! Mary drew her close. "Leila, Leila," she whispered, "dear little sister, dear little girl, we must love and comfort each other."

And then Leila knew.

But they did not tell her how it had happened. The details of that last ride the woman who loved him need never know. Barry was to be her hero always.

CHAPTER XXIV

In Which Roger Comes Once More to the Tower Rooms; and in Which a Duel is Fought in Modern Fashion.

It was Cousin Patty who had suggested sending for Roger. "He can look after me, Mary. If you won't let me go home, I don't want you to have the thought of me to burden you."

"You couldn't be a burden. And I don't know what Aunt Isabelle and I should have done without you."

216

She began to cry weakly, and Cousin Patty, comforting her, said in her heart, "There is no one but Roger who can say the right things to her."

As yet no one had said the right things. It seemed to Mary that she carried a wound too deep for healing. Gordon had softened the truth as much as possible, but he could not hide it from her. She knew that Barry, her boy Barry, had gone out of the world defeated.

It was Roger who helped her.

He came first upon her as she sat alone in the garden by the fountain. It was a sultry spring day, and heavy clouds hung low on the horizon. Thin and frail in her black frock, she rose to meet him, the ghost of the girl who had once bloomed like a flower in her scarlet wrap.

Roger took her hands in his.

"You poor little child," he said; "you poor little child."

She did not cry. She simply looked up at him, frozen-white. "Oh, it wasn't fair for him to go—that way. He tried so hard. He tried so hard."

"I know. And it was a great fight he put up, you must remember that."

"But to fail—at the last."

"You mustn't think of that. Somehow I can see Barry still fighting, and winning. One of a glorious company."

"A glorious company—Barry?"

"Yes. Why not? We are judged by the fight we make, not by our victory."

She drew a long breath. "Everybody else has been sorry. Nobody else could seem to understand."

"Perhaps I understand," he said, "because I know what it is to fight—and fail."

"But you are winning now." The color swept into her pale cheeks. "Cousin Patty told me."

"Yes. You showed me the way—I have tried to follow it."

"Oh, how ignorant I was," she cried, tempestuously, "when I talked to you of life. I thought I knew everything."

"You knew enough to help me. If I can help you a little now it will be only a fair exchange."

It helped her merely to have him there. "You spoke of Barry's still fighting and winning. Do you think that one goes on fighting?"

"Why not? It would seem only just that he should conquer. There are men who are not tempted, whose goodness is negative. Character is made by resistance against evil, not by lack of knowledge of it. And the judgments of men are not those which count in the final verdict."

He said more than this, breaking the bonds of her despair. Others had pitied Barry. Roger defended him. She began to think of her brother, not as her imagination had pictured him, flung into utter darkness, but with his head up—his beautiful fair head, a shining sword in his hand, fighting against the powers of evil—stumbling, falling, rising again.

He saw her relax as she listened, and his love for her taught him what to say.

And as he talked, her eyes noted the change in him.

This was not the Roger Poole of the Tower Rooms. This was a Roger Poole who had found himself. She could see it in his manner—she could hear it in his voice, it shone from his eyes. Here was a man who feared nothing, not even the whispers that had once had power to hurt.

The clouds were sweeping toward them, hiding the blue; the wind whirled the dead leaves from the paths, and stirred the budding branches of the hundred-leaved bush—touched with its first hint of tender green. The mist from the fountain was like a veil which hid the mocking face of the bronze boy.

But Mary and Roger had no eyes for these warnings; each was famished for the other, and this meeting gave to Mary, at least, a sense of renewed life.

She spoke of her future. "Constance and Gordon want me to come to them. But I hate to give up my work. I don't want to be discontented. Yet I dread the loneliness here. Did you ever think I should be such a coward?"

"You are not a coward—you are a woman—wanting the things that belong to you."

She sat very still. "I wonder—what are the things which belong to a woman?"

"Love—a home—happiness."

"And you think I want these things?"

"I know it."

"How do you know?"

"Because you have tried work—and it has failed. You have tried independence—and it has failed. You have tried freedom, and have found it bondage."

He was once more in the grip of the dream which he had dreamed as he had sat with Mary's letter in his hand on Cousin Patty's porch. If she would come to him there would be no more loneliness. His love should fill her life, and there would be, too, the love of his people. She should win hearts while he won souls. If only she would care enough to come.

It was the fear that she might not care which suddenly gripped him. Surely this was not the moment to press his demands upon her—when sorrow lay so heavily on her heart.

So blind, and cruel in his blindness, he held back the words which rose to his lips.

"Some day life will bring the things which belong to you," he said at last. "I pray God that it may bring them to you some day."

A line of Browning's came into her mind, and rang like a knell—"Some day, meaning no day."

She shivered and rose. "We must go in; there's rain in those clouds, and wind."

He rose also and stood looking down at her. Her eyes came up to his, her clear eyes, shadowed now by pain. What he might have said to her in another moment would have saved both of them much weariness and heartache. But he was not to say it, for the storm was upon them driving them before it, slamming doors, banging shutters in the big house as they came to it—a miniature cyclone, in its swift descent.

And as if he had ridden in on the wings of the storm came Porter Bigelow, his red mane blown like a flame back from his face, his long coat flapping.

He stopped short at the sight of Roger.

"Hello, Poole," he said; "when did you arrive?"

"This morning."

They shook hands, but there was no sign of a welcome in Porter's face.

"Pretty stiff storm," he remarked, as the three of them stood by the drawing-room window, looking out.

The rain came in shining sheets—the lightning blazed—the thunder boomed.

"It is the first thunder-storm of the season," Mary said. "It will wake up the world."

"In the South," Roger said, "the world is awake. You should see our gardens."

"I wish I could; Cousin Patty asked me to come."

"Will you?" eagerly.

"There's my work."

"Take a holiday, and let me show you the pines."

Porter broke in impatiently, almost insolently.

"Mary needs companionship, not pines. I think she should go to Constance. Leila and the General will go over as they planned in May, and the Jeliffes——"

"There's more than a month before May—which she could spend with us."

Porter stared. This was a new Roger, an insistent, demanding Roger. He spoke coldly. "Constance wants Mary at once. I don't think we should say anything to dissuade her. Aunt Isabelle and I can take her over."

And now Mary's head went up.

"I haven't decided, Porter." She was fighting for freedom.

"But Constance needs you, Mary—and you need her."

"Oh, no," Mary said, brokenly, "Constance doesn't need me. She has Gordon and the baby. Nobody needs me—now."

Roger saw the quick blood flame in Porter's face. He felt it flame in his own. And just for one fleeting moment, over the bowed head of the girl, the challenging eyes of the two men met.

Aunt Frances, who came over with Grace in the afternoon, went home in a high state of indignation.

"Why Patty Carew and Roger Poole should take possession of Mary in that fashion," she said to her daughter at dinner, "is beyond me. They don't belong there, and it would have been in better taste to leave at such a time."

"Mary begged Cousin Patty to stay," Grace said, "and as for Roger Poole, he has simply made Mary over. She has been like a stone image until to-day."

"I don't see any difference," Aunt Frances said. "What do you mean, Grace?"

"Oh, her eyes and the color in her cheeks, and the way she does her hair."

"The way she does her hair?" Aunt Frances laid down her fork and stared.

"Yes. Since the awful news came, Mary has seemed to lose interest in everything. She adored Barry, and she's never going to get over it—not entirely. I miss the old Mary." Grace stopped to steady her voice. "But when I went up with her to her room to talk to her while she dressed for dinner, she put up her hair in that pretty boyish way that she used to wear it, and it was all for Roger Poole."

"Why not for Porter?"

"Because she hasn't cared how she looked, and Porter has been there every day. He has been there too often."

"Do you think Roger will try to get her to marry him?"

"Who knows? He's dead in love with her. But he looks upon her as too rare for the life he leads. That's the trouble with men. They are afraid they can't make the right woman happy, so they ask the wrong one. Now if we women could do the proposing——"

"Grace!"

"Don't look at me in that shocked way, mother. I am just voicing what every woman knows—that the men who ask her aren't the ones she would have picked out if she had had the choice. And Mary will wait and weary, and Roger will worship and hang back, and in the meantime Porter will demand and demand and demand—and in the end he'll probably get what he wants."

Aunt Frances beamed. "I hope so."

"But Mary will be miserable."

"Then she'll be very silly."

Grace sighed. "No woman is silly who asks for the best. Mother, I'd love to marry a man with a mission—I'd like to go to the South Sea Islands and teach the natives, or to Darkest Africa—or to China, or India, anywhere away from a life in which there's nothing but bridge, and shopping, and deadly dullness."

She was in earnest now, and her mother saw it.

"I don't see how you can say such things," she quavered. "I don't see how you can talk of going to such impossible places—away from me."

Grace cut short the plaintive wail.

"Of course I have no idea of going," she said, "but such a life would furnish its own adventures; I wouldn't have to manufacture them."

It was with the wish to make life something more than it was that Grace asked Roger the next day, "Is there any work here in town like yours for the boy—you see Mary has told me about him."

He smiled. "Everywhere there are boys and girls, unawakened—if only people would look for them; and with your knowledge of languages you could do great things with the little foreigners—turn a bunch of them into good citizens, for example."

"How?"

"Reach them first through pictures and music—then through their patriotism. Don't let them learn politics and plunder on the streets; let them find their place in this land from you, and let them hear from you of the God of our fathers."

Grace felt his magnetism. "I wish you could go through the streets of New York saying such things."

He shook his head. "I shall not come to the city. My place is found, and I shall stay there; but I have faith to believe that there will yet be a Voice to speak, to which the world shall listen."

"Soon?"

"Everything points to an awakening. People are beginning to say, 'Tell us,' where a few years ago they said, 'There is nothing to tell.'"

"I see—it will be wonderful when it comes—I'm going to try to do my little bit, and be ready, and when Mary comes back, she shall help me."

His eyes went to where Mary sat between Porter and Aunt Frances.

"She may never come back."

"She must be made to come."

"Who could make her?"

"The man she loves."

She flashed a sparkling glance at him, and rose.

"Come, mother," she said, "it is time to go." Then, as she gave Roger her hand, she smiled. "Faint heart," she murmured, "don't you know that a man like you, if he tries, can conquer the—world?"

She left Roger with his pulses beating madly. What did she mean? Did she think that—Mary——? He went up to the Tower Rooms to dress for dinner, with his mind in a whirl. The windows were open and the warm air blew in. Looking out, he could see in the distance the shining river—like a silver ribbon, and the white shaft of the Monument, which seemed to touch the sky. But he saw more than that; he saw his future and Mary's; again he dreamed his dreams.

If he had hoped for a moment alone that night with the lady of his heart, he was doomed to disappointment, for Leila and her father came to dinner. Leila was very still and sweet in her widow's black, the General brooding over her. And again Roger had the sense that in this house of sorrow there was no place for love-making. For the joy that might be his—he must wait; even though he wearied in the waiting.

And it was while he waited that he lunched one day with Porter Bigelow. The invitation had surprised him, and he had felt vaguely troubled and oppressed by the thought that back of it might be some motive as yet unrevealed. But there had been nothing to do but accept, and at one o'clock he was at the University Club.

For a time they spoke of indifferent things, then Porter said, bluntly, "I am not going to beat about the bush, Poole. I've asked you here to talk about Mary Ballard."

"Yes?"

"You're in love with her?"

"Yes—but I question your right to play inquisitor."

"I haven't any right, except my interest in Mary. But I claim that my interest justifies the inquisition."

"Perhaps."

"You want to marry her?"

Roger shifted his position, and leaned forward, meeting Porter's stormy eyes squarely. "Again I question your right, Bigelow."

"AGAIN I QUESTION YOUR RIGHT"

[Illustration: "Again I question your right."]

"It isn't a question of right now, Poole, and you know it. You're in love with her, I'm in love with her. We both want her. In days past men settled such things with swords or pistols. You and I are civilized and modern; but it's got to be settled just the same."

"Miss Ballard will have to settle it—not you or I."

"She can't settle it. Mary is a dreamer. You capture her with your imagination—with your talk of your work—and your people and the little gardens, and all that. And she sees it as you want her to see it, not as it really is. But I know the deadly dullness, the awfulness. Why, man, I spent a winter down there, at one of the resorts and now and then we rode through the country. It was a desert, I tell you, Poole, a desert; it is no place for a woman."

"You saw nothing but the charred pines and the sand. I could show you other things."

"What, for example?"

"I could show you an awakened people. I could show you a community throwing off the shackles of idleness and ignorance. I could show you men once tied to old traditions, meeting with eagerness the new ideals. There is nothing in the world more wonderful than such an awakening, Bigelow. But one must have the Vision to grasp it. And faith to believe it. It is the dreamers, thank God, who see beyond to-day into to-morrow. I haven't wealth or position to offer Mary, but I can offer her a world which needs her. And if I know her, as I think I do, she will care more for my world than for yours."

He did not raise his voice, but Porter felt the force of his restrained eloquence, as he knew Mary would feel it if it were applied to her.

220

And now he shot his poisoned dart.

"At first, perhaps. But when it came to building a home, there'd be always the stigma of your past, and she's a proud little thing, Poole."

Roger winced. "My past is buried. It is my future of which we must speak."

"You can't bury a past. You haven't even a pulpit to preach from."

Roger pushed back his chair. "I am tempted to wish," his voice was grim, "that we were not quite so civilized, not quite so modern. Pistols or swords would seem an easier way than this."

"I'm fighting for Mary. You've got to let go. None of her friends want it—Gordon would never consent."

It seemed to Roger that all the whispers which had assailed him in the days of long ago were rushing back upon him in a roaring wave of sound.

He rose, white and shaken. "Do you call it victory when one man stabs another through the heart? Well, if this is your victory, Bigelow—you are welcome to it."

CHAPTER XXV

In Which Mary Bids Farewell to the Old Life; and in Which She Finds Happiness on the High Seas.

Contrary Mary was Contrary Mary no longer. Since Roger had gone, taking Cousin Patty with him—gone without the word to her for which she had waited, she had submitted to Gordon's plans for her, and to Aunt Frances' and Porter's execution of them.

Only to Grace did she show any signs of her old rebellion.

"Did you ever think that I should be beaten, Grace?" she said, pitifully. "Is that the way with all women? Do we reach out for so much, and then take what we can get?"

Grace pondered. "Things tie us down, but we don't have to stay tied—and I am beginning to see a way out for myself, Mary."

She told of her talk with Roger and of her own strenuous desire to help; but she did not tell what she had said to him at the last. There was something here which she could not understand. Mary persistently refused to talk about him. Even now she shifted the topic.

"I don't want to strive," she said, "not even for the sake of others. I want to rest for a thousand years—and sleep for the next thousand."

And this from Mary, buoyant, vivid Mary, with her almost boyish strength and energy.

The big house was to be closed. Aunt Isabelle would go with Mary. Susan Jenks and Pittiwitz would be domiciled in the kitchen wing, with a friend of Susan's to keep them company.

Mary, wandering on the last day through the Tower Rooms, thought of the night when Roger Poole had first come to them. And now he would never come again.

She had not been able to understand his abrupt departure. Yet there had been nothing to resent—he had been infinitely kind, sympathetic, strong, helpful. If she missed something from his manner which had been there on the day of his arrival, she told herself that perhaps it had not been there, that her own joy in seeing him had made her imagine a like joy in his attitude toward her.

Cousin Patty had cried over her, kissed her, and protested that she could not bear to go.

"But Roger thinks it is best, my dear. He is needed at home."

It seemed plausible that he might be needed, yet in the back of Mary's mind was a doubt. What had sent him away? She was haunted by the feeling that some sinister influence had separated them.

A pitiful little figure in black, she made the tour of the empty rooms with Pittiwitz mewing plaintively at her heels. The little cat, with the instinct of her kind, felt the atmosphere of change. Old rugs on which she had sprawled were rolled up and reeking with moth balls. The little white bed, on which she had napped unlawfully, was stripped to the mattress. The cushions on which she had curled were packed away—the fire was out—the hearth desolate.

Susan Jenks, coming up, found Mary with the little cat in her lap.

"Oh, honey child, don't cry like that."

"Oh, Susan, Susan, it will never be the same again, never the same."

And now once more in the garden, the roses bloomed on the hundred-leaved bush, once more the fountain sang, and the little bronze boy laughed through a veil of mist—but there were no gay voices in the garden, no lovers on the stone seat. Susan Jenks kept the paths trim and watered the flowers, and Pittiwitz chased butterflies or stretched herself in the sun, lazily content, forgetting, gradually, those who had for a time made up her world.

But Mary, on the high seas, could not forget what she had left behind. It was not Susan Jenks, it was not Pittiwitz, it was not the garden which called her back, although these had their part in her regrets—it was the old life, the life which had belonged to her childhood and her girlhood the life which had been lived with her mother and father and Constance—and Barry.

As she lay listless in her deck chair, she could see nothing in her future which would match the happiness of the past. The days lived in the old house had never been days of great prosperity; her father had, indeed, often been weighed down with care—there had been times of heavy anxieties—but, there had been between them all the bond of deep affection, of mutual dependence.

In Gordon's home there would be splendors far beyond any she had known, there would be ease and luxury, and these would be shared with her freely and ungrudgingly, yet to a nature like Mary Ballard's such things meant little. The real things in life to her were love and achievement; all else seemed stale and unprofitable.

Of course there would be Constance and the baby. On the hope of seeing them she lived. Yet in a sense Gordon and the baby stood between herself and Constance—they absorbed her sister, satisfied her, so that Mary's love was only one drop added to a full cup.

It was while she pondered over her future that Mary was moved to write to Roger Poole. The mere putting of her thoughts on paper would ease her loneliness. She would say what she felt, frankly, freely, and when the little letters were finished, if her mood changed she need not send them.

So she began to scribble, setting down each day the thoughts which clamored for expression.

Porter complained that now she was always writing.

"I'd rather write than talk," Mary said, wearily; and at last he let the matter drop.

In Mid-Sea.
DEAR FRIEND O' MINE:

You asked me to write, and you will think that I have more than kept my promise when you get this journal of our days at sea. But it has seemed to me that you might enjoy it all, just as if you were with us, instead of down among your sand-hills, with your sad children (are they really sad now?) and Cousin Patty's wedding cakes.

There's quite a party of us. Leila and her father and the Jeliffes and Colin kept to their original plan of coming in May, and we decided it would be best to cross at the same time, so there's Aunt Frances and Grace and Aunt Isabelle, and Porter—and me—ten of us. If you and Cousin Patty were here, you'd round out a dozen. I wish you were here. How Cousin Patty would enjoy it—with her lovely enthusiasms, and her interest in everything. Do give her much love. I shall write to her when I reach London, for I know she will be traveling with us in spirit; she said she was going to live in England by proxy this summer, and I shall help her all I can by sending pictures, and you must tell her the books to read.

To think that I am on my way to the London of your Dick Whittington! I call him yours because you made me really see him for the first time.

"There was he an orphan, O, a little lad alone."

And I am to hear all the bells, and to see the things I have always longed to see! Yet—and I haven't told this to any one but you, Roger Poole, the thought doesn't bring one little bit of gladness—it isn't London that I want, or England. I want my garden and my old big house, and things as they used to be.

But I am sailing fast away from it—the old life into the new!

So far we have had fair weather. It is always best to speak of the weather first, isn't it?—so that we can have our minds free for other things. It hasn't been at all rough; even Leila, who isn't a good sailor, has been able to stay on deck and people are so much interested in her. She seems such a child for her widow's black. Oh, what children they were, my boy Barry and his little wife, and yet they were man and woman, too. Leila has been letting me see some of his letters; he showed her a side which he never revealed to me, but I am not jealous. I am only glad that, for her, my boy Barry became a man.

But I am going to try to keep the sadness out of my scribbles to you, only now and then it will creep in, and you must forgive it, because you see it isn't easy to think that we are all here who loved him, and he, who loved so much to be with us, is somewhere—oh, where is he, Roger Poole, in that vast infinity which stretches out and out, beyond the sea, beyond the sky, into eternity?

All day I have been lying in my deck chair, and have let the world go by. It is clear and cool, and the sea rises up like a wall of sapphire. Last night we seemed to plough through a field of gold. The world is really a lovely place, the big outside world, but it isn't the outside world which makes our happiness, it is the world within us, and when the heart is tired——

But now I must talk of some one else besides my self.

Shall I tell you of Delilah? She attracts much attention, with her gracious manner and her wonderful clothes. All the people are crazy about her. They think she is English, and a duchess at least. Colin is as pleased as Punch at the success he has made of her, and he just stands aside and watches her, and flickers his pale lashes and smiles. Last night she danced some of the new dances, and her tango is as stately as a minuet. She and Porter danced together—and everybody stopped to look at them. The gossip is going the rounds that they are engaged. Oh, I wish they were—I wish they were! It would be good for him to meet his match. Delilah could hold her own; she wouldn't let him insist and manage until she was positively mesmerized, as I am. Delilah has such a queenly way of ruling her world. All the men on board trail after her. But she makes most of them worship from afar. As for the women, she picks the best, instinctively, and the ice which seems congealed around the heart of the average Britisher melts before her charm, so that already she is playing bridge with the proper people, and having tea with the inner circle. Even with these she seems to assume an air of remoteness, which seems to set her apart—and it is this air, Grace says, which conquers.

When people aren't coupling Porter's name with Delilah's, they are coupling it with Grace's. You should see our "red-headed woodpeckers," as poor Barry used to call them. When they promenade, Grace wears a bit of a black hat that shows all of her glorious hair, and Porter's cap can't hide his crown of glory. At first people thought they were brother and sister, but since it is known that they aren't I can see that everybody is puzzled.

It is all like a play passing in front of me. There are charming English people—charming Americans and some uncharming ones. Oh, why don't we, who began in such simplicity, try to remain a simple people? It just seems to me sometimes as if everybody on board is trying to show off. The rich ones are trying to display their money, and the intellectual ones their brains. Is there any real difference between the new-rich and the new-cultured, Roger Poole? One tells about her three motor cars, and the other tells about her three degrees. It is all tiresome. The world is a place to have things and to know things, but if the having them and knowing them makes them so important that you have to talk about them all the time there's something wrong.

That's the charm of Grace. She has money and position—and I've told you how she simply carried off all the honors at college; she paints wonderfully, and her opinions are all worth listening to. But she doesn't throw her knowledge at you. She is interested in people, and puts books where they belong. She is really the only one whom I welcome without any misgivings, except darling Aunt Isabelle. The others when they come to talk to me, are either too sad or too energetic.

Doesn't all that sound as if I were a selfish little pig? Well, some day I shall enjoy them all—but now—my heart is crying—and Leila, with her little white face, hurts. Mrs. Barry Ballard! Shall I ever get used to hearing her called that? It seems to set her apart from little Leila Dick, so that when I hear people speak to her, I am always startled and surprised.

And now—what are you doing? Are you still planting little gardens, and talking to your boy—talking to your sad people? Cousin Patty has told me of your letter to your bishop, who was so kind during your—trouble—and of his answer—and of your hope that some day you may have a little church in the sand-hills, and preach instead of teach.

Surely that would make all of your dreams come true, all of *our* dreams, for I have dreamed too—that this might come.

Sometimes as I lie here, I shut my eyes, and I seem to see you in that circle of young pines, and I pretend that I am listening; that you are saying things to me, as you say them to those poor people in the pines—and now and then I can make myself believe that you have really spoken, that your voice has reached across the miles. And so I have your little sermons all to myself—out here at sea, with all the blue distance between us—but I listen, listen—just the same.

In the Fog.

Out of the sunshine of yesterday came the heavy mists of to-day. The sea slips under us in silver swells. Everybody is wrapped to the chin, and Porter has just stopped to ask me if I want something hot sent up. I told him "no," and sent him on to Leila. I like this still world, and the gray ghosts about the deck. Delilah has just sailed by in a beautiful smoke-colored costume—with her inevitable knot of heliotrope—a phantom lady, like a lovely dream.

Did I tell you that a very distinguished and much titled gentleman wants to marry Delilah, and that he is waiting now for her answer? Porter thinks she will say "yes." But Leila and I don't. We are sure that she will find her fate in Colin. He dominates her; he dives beneath the surface and brings up the real Delilah, not the cool, calculating Delilah that we once knew, but the lovely, gracious lady that she now is. It is as if he had put a new soul inside of the worldly shell that was once Delilah. Yet there is never a sign between them of anything but good comradeship. Grace says that Colin is following the fashionable policy of watchful waiting—but I'm not sure. I fancy that they will both wake up suddenly to what they feel, and then it will be quite wonderful to see them.

Porter doesn't believe in the waking-up process. He says that love is a growth. That people must know each other for years and years, so that each can understand the faults and virtues of the other. But to me it seems that love is a flame, illumining everything in a moment.

Porter came while I was writing that—and made me walk with him up and down, up and down. He was afraid I might get chilled. Of course he means to be kind, but I don't like to have him tell me that I must "make an effort"—it gives me a sort of Mrs. Dombey feeling. I don't wonder that she just curled up and died to get rid of the trouble of living.

I knew while I walked with Porter that people were wondering who I was—in my long black coat, with my hair all blown about. I fancy that they won't link my name, sentimentally, with the Knight of the Auburn Crest. Beside Grace and Delilah I look like a little country girl. But I don't care—my thick coat is comfortable, and my little soft hat stays on my head, which is all one needs, isn't it? But as I write this I wonder where the girl is who used to like pretty clothes. Do you remember the dress I wore at Constance's wedding? I was thinking to-day of it—and of Leila hippity-hopping up the stairs in her one pink slipper. Oh, how far away those days seem—and how strong I felt—and how ready I was to face the world, and now I just want to crawl into a corner and watch other people live.

Leila is much braver than I. She takes a little walk every morning with her father, and another walk every afternoon with Porter—and she is always talking to lonesome people and sick people; and all the while she wears a little faint shining smile, like an angel's. Yet I used to be quite scornful of Leila, even while I loved her. I thought she was so sweetly and weakly feminine; yet she is steering her little ship through stormy waters, while I have lost my rudder and compass, and all the other things that a mariner needs in a time of storm.

Before the storm.

The fog still hangs over us, and we seem to ride on the surface of a dead sea. Last night there was no moon and to-day Aunt Frances has not appeared. Even Delilah seems to feel depressed by the silence and the stillness—not a sound but the beat of the engines and the hoarse hoot of the horns. This paper is damp as I write upon it, and blots the ink, but—I sha'n't rewrite it, because the blots will make you see me sitting here, with drops of moisture clinging to my coat and to my little hat, and making my hair curl up in a way that it never does in dry weather.

I wonder, if you were here, if you would seem a ghost like all the others. Nothing is real but my thoughts of the things that used to be. I can't believe that I am on my way to London, and that I am going to live with Constance, and go sightseeing with Aunt Frances and Grace, and give up my plans for the—Great Adventure. Aunt Isabelle sat beside me this morning, and we talked about it. She will stay with Aunt Frances and Grace, and we shall see each other every day. I couldn't quite get along at all if it were not for Aunt Isabelle—she is such a mother-person, and she doesn't make me feel, as the rest of them do, that I must be brave and courageous. She just pats my hand and says, "It's going to be all right, Mary dear—it is going to be all right," and presently I begin to feel that it is; she has such a fashion of ignoring the troublesome things of this world, and simply looking ahead to the next. She told me once that heaven would mean to her, first of all, a place of beautiful sounds—and second it would mean freedom. You see she has always been dominated by Aunt Frances, poor thing.

Do you remember how I used to talk of freedom? But now I'm to be a bird in a cage. It will be a gilded cage, of course. Even Grace says that Constance's home is charming—great lovely rooms and massive furniture; and when we begin to go again into society, I am to be introduced to lots of grand folk, and perhaps presented.

And I am to forget that I ever worked in a grubby government office—indeed I am to forget that I ever worked at all.

And I am to forget all of my dreams. I am to change from the Mary Ballard who wanted to do things to the Mary Ballard who wants them done for her. Perhaps when you see me again I shall be nice and clinging and as sweetly feminine as you used to want me to be—Roger Poole.

The mists have cleared, and there's a cloud on the horizon—I can hear people saying that it means a storm. Shall I be afraid? I wonder. Do you remember the storm that came that day in the garden and drove us in? I wonder if we shall ever be together again in the dear old garden?

After the storm.

Last night the storm waked us. It was a dreadful storm, with the wind booming, and the sea all whipped up into a whirlpool.

But I wasn't frightened, although everybody was awake, and there was a feeling that something might happen. I asked Porter to take me on deck, but he said that no one was allowed, and so we just curled up on chairs and sofas and waited

224

either for the storm to end or for the ship to sink. If you've ever been in a storm at sea, you know the feeling—that the next minute may bring calm and safety, or terror and death.

Porter had tucked a rug around me, and I lay there, looking at the others, wondering whether if an accident happened Delilah would face death as gracefully as she faces everything else. Leila was very white and shivery and clung to her father; it is at such times that she seems such a child.

Aunt Frances was fussy and blamed everybody from the captain down to Aunt Isabelle—as if they could control the warring elements. Surely it is a case of the "ruling passion."

But while I am writing these things, I am putting off, and putting off and putting off the story of what happened after the storm—not because I dread to tell it, but because I don't know quite how to tell it. It involves such intimate things—yet it makes all things clear, it makes everything so beautifully clear, Roger Poole.

It was after the wind died down a bit that I made Porter take me up on deck. The moon was flying through the ragged clouds, and the water was a wild sweep of black and white. It was all quite spectral and terrifying and I shivered. And then Porter said; "Mary, we'd better go down."

And I said, "It wasn't fear that made me shiver, Porter. It was just the thought that living is worse than dying."

He dropped my arm and looked down at me.

"Mary," he said, "what's the matter with you?"

"I don't know," I said. "It is just that my courage is all gone—I can't face things."

"Why not?"

"I don't know—I've lost my grip, Porter."

And then he asked a question. "Is it because of Barry, Mary?"

"Some of it."

"And the rest?"

"I can't tell you."

We walked for a long time after that, and I was holding all the time tight to his arm—for it wasn't easy to walk with that sea on—when suddenly he laid his hand over mine.

"Mary," he said, "I've got to tell you. I can't keep it back and feel—honest. I don't know whether you want Roger Poole in your life—I don't know whether you care. But I want you to be happy. And it was I who sent him away from you."

And now, Roger Poole, what can I say? What can *any* woman say? I only know this, that as I write this the sun shines over a blue sea, and that the world is—different. There are still things in my heart which hurt—but there are things, too, which make it sing!

MARY.

When Mary Ballard came on deck on the morning after the storm, everybody stared. Where was the girl of yesterday—the frail white girl who had moped so listlessly in her chair, scribbling on little bits of paper? Here was a fair young beauty, with her head up, a clear light shining in her gray eyes—a faint flush on her cheeks.

Colin Quale, meeting her, flickered his lashes and smiled: "Is this what the storm did to you?"

"What?"

"This and this." He touched his cheeks and his eyes. "To-day, if I painted you, I should have to put pink on my palette—yesterday I should have needed only black and white."

Mary smiled back at him. "Do you interpret things always through the medium of your brush?"

"Why not? Life is just that—a little color more or less, and it all depends on the hand of the artist."

"What a wonderful palette He has!" Her eyes swept the sea and the sky. "This morning the world is all gold and blue."

"And yesterday it was gray."

Mary flashed a glance at him. His voice had changed. Delilah was coming toward them. "There's material I like to work with," he said, "there's something more than paint or canvas—living, breathing beauty."

"He's saying things about you," Mary said, as Delilah joined them.

Delilah, coloring faintly, cast down her eyes. "I'm afraid of him, Mary," she said.

Colin laughed. "You're not afraid of any one."

"Yes, I am. You analyze my mental processes in such a weird fashion. You are always reading me like a book."

"A most interesting book," Colin's lashes quivered, "with lovely illustrations."

They laughed, and swept away into a brisk walk, followed by curious eyes.

If to others Mary's radiance seemed a miracle of returning health, to Porter Bigelow it was no miracle. Nothing could have more completely rung the knell of his hopes than this radiance.

Her attitude toward him was irreproachable. She was kinder, indeed, than she had been in the days when he had tried to force his claims upon her. She seemed to be trying by her friendliness to make up for something which she had withdrawn from him, and he knew that nothing could ever make up.

So it came about that he spent less and less of his time with her, and more and more with Leila—Leila who needed comforting, and who welcomed him with such sweet and clinging dependence—Leila who hung upon his advice, Leila who, divining his hurt, strove by her sweet sympathy to help him.

Thus they came in due time to London. And when Leila and her father left for the German baths, Porter went with them.

It was when he said "Good-bye" to Mary that his voice broke.

"Dear Contrary Mary," he said, "the old name still fits you. You never could, and you never would, and now you never will."

Followed for Mary quiet days with Constance and the beautiful baby, days in which the sisters were knit together by the bonds of mutual grief. The little Mary-Constance was a wonderful comfort to both of them; unconscious of sadness, she gurgled and crowed and beamed, winning them from sorrowful thoughts by her blandishments, making herself the center of things, so that, at last, all their little world seemed to revolve about her.

And always in these quiet days, Mary looked for a letter from across the high seas, and at last it came in a blue envelope.

It arrived one morning when she was at breakfast with Constance and Gordon. Handed to her with other letters, she left it unopened and laid it beside her plate.

Gordon finished his breakfast, kissed his wife, and went away. Constance, looking over her mail, read bits of news to Mary. Mary, in return, read bits of news to Constance. But the blue envelope by her plate lay untouched, until, catching her sister's eye, she flushed.

"Constance," she said, "it is from Roger Poole."

"Oh, Mary, and was that why Porter went away?"

"Yes." It came almost defiantly.

For a moment the young matron hesitated, then she held out her arms. "Dearest girl," she said, "we want you to be happy."

Mary, with eyes shining, came straight to that loving embrace.

"I am going to be happy," she said, almost breathlessly, "and perhaps my way of being happy won't be yours, Con, darling. But what difference does it make, so long as we are both—happy?"

The letter, read at last in the shelter of her own room, was not long.

Among the Pines.

Even now I can't quite believe that your letter is true—I have read it and reread it—again and again, reading into it each time new meanings, new hope. And to-night it lies on my desk, a precious document, tempting me to say things which perhaps I should not say—tempting me to plead for that which perhaps I should not ask.

Dear woman—what have I to offer you? Just a home down here among the sand-hills—a little church that will soon stand in a circle of young pines, a life of work in a little rectory near the little church—for your dreams and mine are to come true, and the little church will be built within a year.

Yet, I have a garden. A garden of souls. Will you come into it? And make it bloom, as you have made my life bloom? All that I am you have made me. When I sat in the Tower Rooms hopeless, you gave me hope. When I lost faith in myself, it shone in your eyes. When I saw your brave young courage, my courage came back to me. It was you who told me that I had a message to deliver.

And I am delivering the message—and somehow I cannot feel that it is a little thing to offer, when I ask you to share in this, my work.

Other men can offer you a castle—other men can give to you a life of ease. I can bring to you a life in which we shall give ourselves to each other and to the world. I can give you love that is equal to any man's. I can give you a future which will make you forget the past.

Not to every woman would I dare offer what I have to give——but you are different from other women. From the night when you first met me frankly with your brave young head up and your eyes shining, I have known that you were different from the rest—a woman braver and stronger, a woman asking more of life than softness.

And now, will you fight with me, shoulder to shoulder? And win?

Somehow I feel that you will say "Yes." Is that the right attitude for a lover? But surely I can see a little way into your heart. Your letter let me see.

If I seem over-confident, forgive me. But I know what I want for myself. I know what I want for you. I am not the Roger Poole of the Tower Rooms, beaten and broken. I am Roger Poole of the Garden, marching triumphantly in tune with the universe.

As I write, I have a vision upon me of a little white house not far from the little white church in the circle of young pines—a house with orchards sweeping up all pink behind it in April, and with violets in the borders of the walk in January, and with roses from May until December.

And I can see you in that little house. I shall see you in it until you say something which will destroy that vision. But you won't destroy it. Surely some day you will hear the mocking-birds sing in the moonlight—as I am hearing them, alone, to-night.

I need you, I want you, and I hope that it is not a selfish cry. For your letter has told me that you, too, are wanting—what? Is it Love, Mary dear, and Life?

ROGER.

CHAPTER XXVI

In Which a Strange Craft Anchors in a Sea of Emerald Light; and in Which Mocking-Birds Sing in the Moonlight.

Sweeping through a country of white sand and of charred trees run hard clay highways. When motor cars from the cities and health resorts began to invade the pines, it was found that the old wagon trails were inadequate; hence there followed experiments which resulted in intersecting orange-colored roads, throughout the desert-like expanse.

It was on a day in April that over the road which led up toward the hills there sailed the snowy-white canopy of one of the strange land-craft of that region—a schooner-wagon drawn by two fat mules who walked at a leisurely but steady pace, seemingly without guidance from any hand.

Yet that, beneath the hooded cover, there was a directing power, was demonstrated, as the mules turned suddenly from the hot road to a wagon path beneath the shelter of the pines.

It was strewn thick with brown needles, and the sharp hoofs of the little animals made no sound. Deeper and deeper they went into the wood, until the swinging craft and its clumsy steeds seemed to swim in a sea of emerald light.

On and on breasting waves of golden gloom, where the sunlight sifted in, to anchor at last in a still space where the great trees sang overhead.

Then from beneath the canopy emerged a man in khaki.

He took off his hat, and stood for a moment looking up at the great trees, then he called softly, "Mary."

She came to the back of the wagon and he lifted her down.

"This is my cathedral," he said; "it is the place of the biggest pines."

She leaned against him and looked up. His arm was about her. She wore a thin silk blouse and a white skirt. Her soft fair hair was blown against his cheek.

"Roger," she said, "was there ever such a honeymoon?"

"Was there ever such a woman—such a wife?"

After that they were silent. There was no need for words. But presently he spread a rug for her, and built their fire, and they had their lunch. The mules ate comfortably in the shade, and rested throughout the long hot hours of the afternoon.

Then once more the strange craft sailed on. On and on over miles of orange roadway, passing now and then an orchard, flaunting the rose-color of its peach trees against the dun background of sand; passing again between drifts of dogwood, which shone like snow beneath the slanting rays of the sun—sailing on and on until the sun went down. Then came the shadowy twilight, with the stars coming out in the warm dusk—then the moonlight—and the mocking-birds singing.

The Gay Cockade

From the moment that Jimmie Harding came into the office, he created an atmosphere. We were a tired lot. Most of us had been in the government service for years, and had been ground fine in the mills of departmental monotony.

But Jimmie was young, and he wore his youth like a gay cockade. He flaunted it in our faces, and because we were so tired of our dull and desiccated selves, we borrowed of him, remorselessly, color and brightness until, gradually, in the light of his reflected glory, we seemed a little younger, a little less tired, a little less petrified.

In his gay and gallant youth there was, however, a quality which partook of earlier times. He should, we felt, have worn a feather in his cap—and a cloak instead of his Norfolk coat. He walked with a little swagger, and stood with his hand on his hip, as if his palm pressed the hilt of his sword. If he ever fell in love, we told one another, he would, without a doubt, sing serenades and apostrophize the moon.

He did fall in love before he had been with us a year. His love-affair was a romance for the whole office. He came among us every morning glorified; he left us in the afternoon as a knight enters upon a quest.

He told us about the girl. We pictured her perfectly before we saw her, as a little thing, with a mop of curled brown hair; an oval face, pearl-tinted; wide, blue eyes. He dwelt on all her small perfections—the brows that swept across her forehead in a thin black line, the transparency of her slender hands, the straight set of her head on her shoulders, the slight halt in her speech like that of an enchanting child.

Yet she was not in the least a child. "She holds me up to my best, Miss Standish," Jimmie told me; "she says I can write."

We knew that Jimmie had written a few things, gay little poems that he showed us now and then in the magazines. But we had not taken them at all seriously. Indeed, Jimmie had not taken them seriously himself.

But now he took them seriously. "Elise says that I can do great things. That I must get out of the Department."

To the rest of us, getting out of the government service would have seemed a mad adventure. None of us would have had the courage to consider it. But it seemed a natural thing that Jimmie should fare forth on the broad highway—a modern D'Artagnan, a youthful Quixote, an Alan Breck—!

We hated to have him leave. But he had consolation. "Of course you'll come and see us. We're going back to my old house in Albemarle. It's a rotten shack, but Elise says it will be a corking place for me to write. And you'll all come down for week-ends."

We felt, I am sure, that it was good of him to ask us, but none of us expected that we should ever go. We had a premonition that Elise wouldn't want the deadwood of Jimmie's former Division. I know that for myself, I was content to think of Jimmie happy in his old house. But I never really expected to see it. I had reached the point of expecting nothing except the day's work, my dinner at the end, a night's sleep, and the same thing over again in the morning.

Yet Jimmie got all of us down, not long after he was married, to what he called a housewarming. He had inherited a few pleasant acres in Virginia, and the house was two hundred years old. He had never lived in it until he came with Elise. It was in rather shocking condition, but Elise had managed to make it habitable by getting it scrubbed very clean, and by taking out everything that was not in keeping with the oldness and quaintness. The resulting effect was bare but beautiful. There were a great many books, a few oil-portraits, mahogany sideboards and tables and four-poster beds, candles in sconces and in branched candlesticks. They were married in April, and when we went down in June poppies were blowing in the wide grass spaces, and honeysuckle rioting over the low stone walls. I think we all felt as if we had passed through purgatory and had entered heaven. I know I did, because this was the kind of thing of which I had dreamed, and there had been a time when I, too, had wanted to write.

The room in which Jimmie wrote was in a little detached house, which had once been the office of his doctor grandfather. He had his typewriter out there, and a big desk, and from the window in front of his desk he could look out on green slopes and the distant blue of mountain ridges.

We envied him and told him so.

"Well, I don't know," Jimmie said. "Of course I'll get a lot of work done. But I'll miss your darling old heads bending over the other desks."

"You couldn't work, Jimmie," Elise reminded him, "with other people in the room."

"Perhaps not. Did I tell you old dears that I am going to write a play?"

That was, it seems, what Elise had had in mind for him from the beginning—a great play!

"She wouldn't even, have a honeymoon"—Jimmie's arm was around her; "she brought me here, and got this room ready the first thing."

"Well, he mustn't be wasting time," said Elise, "must he? Jimmie's rather wonderful, isn't he?"

They seemed a pair of babies as they stood there together. Elise had on a childish one-piece pink frock, with sleeves above the elbow, and an organdie sash. Yet, intuitively, the truth came to me—she was ages older than Jimmie in spite of her twenty years to his twenty-four. Here was no Juliet, flaming to the moon—no mistress whose steed would gallop by wind-swept roads to midnight trysts. Here was, rather, the cool blood that had sacrificed a honeymoon—*and, oh, to honeymoon with Jimmie Harding*!—for the sake of an ambitious future.

She was telling us about it "We can always have a honeymoon, Jimmie and I. Some day, when he is famous, we'll have it. But now we must not."

"I picked out the place"—Jimmie was eager—"a dip in the hills, and big pines—And then Elise wouldn't."

We went in to lunch after that. The table was lovely and the food delicious. There was batter-bread, I remember, and an omelette, and peas from the garden.

Duncan Street and I talked all the way home of Jimmie and his wife. He didn't agree with me in the least about Elise. "She'll be the making of him. Such wives always are."

But I held that he would lose something,—that he would not be the same Jimmie.

Jimmie wrote plays and plays. In between he wrote pot-boiling books. The pot-boilers were needed, because none of his plays were accepted. He used to stop in our office and joke about it.

"If it wasn't for Elise's faith in me, Miss Standish, I should think myself a poor stick. Of course, I can make money enough with my books and short stuff to keep things going, but it isn't just money that either of us is after."

Except when Jimmie came into the office we saw very little of him. Elise gathered about her the men and women who would count in Jimmie's future. The week-ends in the still old house drew not a few famous folk who loathed the commonplaceness of convivial atmospheres. Elise had old-fashioned flowers in her garden, delectable food, a library of old books. It was a heavenly change for those who were tired of cocktail parties, bridge-madness, illicit love-making. I could never be quite sure whether Elise really loved dignified living for its own sake, or whether she was sufficiently discriminating to recognize the kind of bait which would lure the fine souls whose presence gave to her hospitality the stamp of exclusiveness.

They had a small car, and it was when Jimmie motored up to Washington that we saw him. He had a fashion of taking us out to lunch, two at a time. When he asked me, he usually asked Duncan Street. Duncan and I have worked side by side for twenty-five years. There is nothing in the least romantic about our friendship, but I should miss him if he were to die or to resign from office. I have little fear of the latter contingency. Only death, I feel, will part us.

In our moments of reunion Jimmie always talked a great deal about himself. The big play was, he said, in the back of his mind. "Elise says that I can do it," he told us one day over our oysters, "and I am beginning to think that I can. I say, why can't you old dears in the office come down for Christmas, and I'll read you what I've written."

We were glad to go. There were to be no other guests, and I found out afterward that Elise rarely invited any of their fashionable friends down in winter. The place showed off better in summer with the garden, and the vines hiding all deficiencies.

We arrived in a snow-storm on Christmas Eve, and when we entered the house there was a roaring fire on the hearth. I hadn't seen a fire like that for thirty years. You may know how I felt when I knelt down in front of it and warmed my hands.

The candles in sconces furnished the only other illumination. Elise, moving about the shadowy room, seemed to draw light to herself. She wore a flame-colored velvet frock and her curly hair was tucked into a golden net. I think that she had planned the medieval effect deliberately, and it was a great success. As she flitted about like a brilliant bird, our eyes followed her. My eyes, indeed, drank of her, like new wine. I have always loved color, and my life has been drab.

I spoke of her frock when she showed me my room.

"Oh, do you like it?" she asked. "Jimmie hates to see me in dark things. He says that when I wear this he can see his heroine."

"Is she like you?"

"Not a bit. She is rather untamed. Jimmie does her very well. She positively gallops through the play."

"And do you never gallop?"

She shook her head. "It's a good thing that I don't. If I did, Jimmie would never write. He says that I keep his nose to the grindstone. It isn't that, but I love him too much to let him squander his talent. If he had no talent, I should love him without it. But, having it, I must hold him up to it."

She was very sure of herself, very sure of the rightness of her attitude toward Jimmie. "I know how great he is," she said, as we went down, "and other people don't. So I've got to prove it."

It was at dinner that I first noticed a change in Jimmie. It was a change which was hard to define. Yet I missed something in him—the enthusiasm, the buoyancy, the almost breathless radiance with which he had rekindled our dying fires. Yet he looked young enough and happy enough as he sat at the table in his velvet studio coat, with his crisp, burnt-gold hair catching the light of the candles. He and his wife were a handsome pair. His manner to her was perfect. There could be no question of his adoration.

After dinner we had the tree. It was a young pine set up at one end of the long dining-room, and lighted in the old fashion by red wax candles. There were presents on it for all of us. Jimmie gave me an adorably illustrated *Mother Goose*.
"You are the only other child here, Miss Standish," he said, as he handed it to me. "I saw this in a book-shop, and couldn't resist it."
We looked over the pictures together. They were enchanting. All the bells of old London rang out for a wistful Whittington in a ragged jacket; Bo-Peep in panniers and pink ribbons wailed for her historic sheep; Mother Hubbard, quaint in a mammoth cap, pursued her fruitless search for bones. There was, too, an entrancing Boy Blue who wound his horn, a sturdy darling with his legs planted far apart and distended rosy cheeks.
"That picture is worth the price of the whole book," said Jimmie, and hung over it. Then suddenly he straightened up. "There should be children in this old house."
I knew then what I had missed from the tree. Elise had a great many gifts—exquisite trifles sent to her by sophisticated friends—a wine-jug of seventeenth-century Venetian glass, a bag of Chinese brocade with handles of carved ivory, a pair of ancient silver buckles, a box of rare lacquer filled with Oriental sweets, a jade pendant, a crystal ball on a bronze base—all of them lovely, all to be exclaimed over; but the things I wanted were drums and horns and candy canes, and tarletan bags, and pop-corn chains, and things that had to be wound up, and things that whistled, and things that squawked, and things that sparkled. And Jimmie wanted these things, but Elise didn't. She was perfectly content with her elegant trifles.
It was late when we went out finally to the studio. There was snow everywhere, but it was a clear night with a moon above the pines. A great log burned in the fireplace, a shaded lamp threw a circle of gold on shining mahogany. It seemed to me that Jimmie's writing quarters were even more attractive in December than in June.
Yet, looking back, I can see that to Jimmie the little house was a sort of prison. He loved men and women, contact with his own kind. He had even liked our dingy old office and our dreary, dried-up selves. And here, day after day, he sat alone—as an artist must sit if he is to achieve—*es bildet ein Talent sich in der Stille*.
We sat around the fire in deep leather chairs, all except Elise, who had a cushion on the floor at Jimmie's feet.
He read with complete absorption, and when he finished he looked at me. "What do you think of it?"
I had to tell the truth. "It isn't your masterpiece."
He ran his fingers through his hair with a nervous gesture. "I told Elise that it wasn't."
"But the girl"—Elise's gaze held hot resentment—"is wonderful. Surely you can see that."
"She doesn't seem quite real."
"Then Jimmie shall make her real." Elise laid her hand lightly on her husband's shoulder. Her gown and golden net were all flame and sparkle, but her voice was cold. "He shall make her real."
"No"—it seemed to me that as he spoke Jimmie drew away from her hand—"I am not going to rewrite it, Elise. I'm tired of it."
"Jimmie!"
"I'm tired of it—"
"Finish it, and then you'll be free—"
"Shall I ever be free?" He stood up and turned his head from side to side, as if he sought some way of escape. "Shall I ever be free? I sometimes think that you and I will stick to this old house until we grow as dry as dust. I want to live, Elise! I want to live—!"

But Elise was not ready to let Jimmie live. To her, Jimmie the artist was more than Jimmie the lover. I may have been unjust, but she seemed to me a sort of mental vampire, who was sucking Jimmie's youth. Duncan Street snorted when I told him what I thought. Elise was a pretty woman, and a pretty woman in the eyes of men can do no wrong.

"You'll see," I said, "what she'll do to him."
The situation was to me astounding. Here was Life holding out its hands to Elise, glory of youth demanding glorious response, and she, incredibly, holding back. In spite of my gray hair and stiff figure, I am of the galloping kind, and my soul followed Jimmie Harding's in its quest for freedom.
But there was one thing that Elise could not do. She could not make Jimmie rewrite his play. "I'll come to it some day," he said, "but not yet. In the meantime I'll see what I can do with books."

230

He did a great deal with books, so that he wrote several best-sellers. This eased the financial situation and they might have had more time for things. But Elise still kept him at it. She wanted to be the wife of a great man.

Yet as the years went on, Duncan and I began to wonder if her hopes would be realized. Jimmie wrote and wrote. He was successful in a commercial sense, but fame did not come to him. There was gray in his burnt-gold hair; his shoulders acquired a scholarly droop, and he wore glasses on a black ribbon. It was when he put on glasses that I began to feel a thousand years old. Yet always when he was away from me I thought of him as the Jimmie whose youth had shone with blinding radiance.

His constancy to Duncan and to me began to take on a rather pathetic quality. The others in the office drifted gradually out of his life. Some of them died, some of them resigned, some of them worked on, plump or wizened parodies of their former selves. I was stouter than ever, and stiffer, and the top of Duncan's head was a shining cone. And the one interesting thing in our otherwise dreary days was Jimmie.

"You're such darling old dears," was his pleasant way of putting it.

But Duncan dug up the truth for me. "We knew him before he wrote. He gets back to that when he is with us."

I had grown to hate Elise. It was not a pleasant emotion, and I am not sure that she really deserved it. But Duncan hated her, too. "You're right," he said one day when we had lunched with Jimmie; "she's sucked him dry." Jimmie had been unusually silent. He had laughed little. He had tapped the table with his finger, and had kept his eyes on his finger. He had been absent-minded. "She has sucked him dry," said Duncan, with great heat.

But she hadn't. That was the surprising thing. Just as we were all giving up hope of Jimmie's proving himself something more than a hack, he did the great thing and the wonderful thing that years ago Elise had prophesied. His play, "The Gay Cockade," was accepted by a New York manager, and after the first night the world went wild about it.

I had helped Jimmie with the name. I had spoken once of youth as a gay cockade. "That's a corking title," Jimmie had said, and had written it in his note-book.

When his play was put in rehearsal, Duncan and I were there to see. We took our month's leave, traveled to New York, and stayed at an old-fashioned boarding-house in Washington Square. Every day we went to the theatre. Elise was always there, looking younger than ever in the sables bought with Jimmie's advance royalty, and with various gowns and hats which were the by-products of his best-sellers.

The part of the heroine of "The Gay Cockade" was taken by Ursula Simms. She was, as those of you who have seen her know, a Rosalind come to life. With an almost boyish frankness she combined feminine witchery. She had glowing red hair, a voice that was gay and fresh, a temper that was hot. She galloped through the play as Jimmie had meant that she should gallop in that first poor draft which he had read to us in Albemarle, and it was when I saw Ursula in rehearsal that I realized what Jimmie had done—he had embodied in his heroine all the youth that he had lost—she stood for everything that Elise had stolen from him—for the wildness, the impetuosity, the passion which swept away prudence and went neck to nothing to fulfilment.

Indeed, the whole play partook of the madness of youth. It bubbled over. Everybody galloped to a rollicking measure. We laughed until we cried. But there was more than laughter in it. There was the melancholy which belongs to tender years set in exquisite contrast to the prevailing mirth.

Jimmie had a great deal to do with the rehearsals. Several times he challenged Ursula's reading of the part.

"You must not give your kisses with such ease," he told her upon one occasion; "the girl in the play has never been kissed."

She shrugged her shoulders and ignored him. Again he remonstrated. "She's frank and free," he said. "Make her that. Make her that. Men must fight for her favors."

She came to it at last, helped by that Rosalind-like quality in herself. She was young, as he had wanted Elise to be, clean-hearted, joyous—girlhood at its best.

Gradually Jimmie ceased to suggest. He would sit beside us in the dimness of the empty auditorium, and watch her as if he drank her in. Now and then he would laugh a little, and say, under his breath: "How did I ever write it? How did it ever happen?"

Elise, on the other side of him, said, at last, "I knew you could do it, Jimmie."

"You thought I could do great things. You never knew I could do—this—"

It was toward the end of the month that Duncan said to me one night as we rode home on the top of a 'bus, "You don't suppose that he—"

"Elise thinks it," I said. "It's waking her up."

Elise and Jimmie had been married fifteen years, and had never had a honeymoon, not in the sense that Jimmie wanted it—an adventure in romance, to some spot where they could forget the world of work, the world of sordid things, the world that was making Jimmie old. Every summer Jimmie had asked for it, and always Elise had said, "Wait."

But now it was Elise who began to plan. "When your play is produced, we'll run away somewhere. Do you remember the place you always talked about—up in the hills?"

He looked at her through his round glasses. "I can't get away from this"—he waved his hand toward the stage.

"If it's a success you can, Jimmie."

"It will be a success. Ursula Simms is a wonder. Look at her, Elise. Look at her!"

Duncan and I could look at nothing else. As many times as I had seen her in the part, I came to it always eagerly. It was her great scene—where the girl, breaking free from all that has bound her, takes the hand of her vagabond lover and goes forth, leaving behind wealth and a marriage of distinction, that she may wander across the moors and down on the sands, with the wild wind in her face, the stars for a canopy!

It tugged at our hearts. It would tug, we knew, at the heart of any audience. It was the human nature in us all which responded. Not one of us but would have broken bonds. Oh, youth, youth! Is there anything like it in the whole wide world?

I do not think that it tugged at the heart of Elise. Her heart was not like that. It was a stay-at-home heart. A workaday-world heart. Elise would never under any circumstance have gone forth with a vagabond on a wild night.

But here was Ursula doing it every day. On the evening of the first dress-rehearsal she wore clothes that showed her sense of fitness. As if in casting off conventional restraints, she renounced conventional attire; she came down to her lover wrapped in a cloak of the deep-purple bloom of the heather of the moor, and there was a pheasant's feather in her cap.

"*May you never regret it, my dear, my dear*," said the lover on the stage.

"*I shall love you for a million years*," said Ursula, and we felt that she would, and that love was eternal, and that any woman might have it if she would put her hand in her lover's and run away with him on a wild night!

And it was the genius of Jimmie Harding that made us feel that the thing could be done. He sat forward in his chair, his arms on the back of the seat in front of him. "Jove!" he kept saying under his breath. "It's the real thing. It's the real thing—"

When the scene was over, he went on the stage and stood by Ursula. Elise from her seat watched them. Ursula had taken off the cap with the pheasant's feather. Her glorious hair shone like copper, her hand was on her hip, her little swagger matched the swagger that we remembered in the old Jimmie. I wondered if Elise remembered.

I am not sure what made Ursula care for Jimmie Harding. He was no longer a figure for romance. But she did care. It was, perhaps, that she saw in him the fundamental things which belonged to both of them, and which did not belong to Elise.

As the days went on I was sorry for Elise. I should never have believed that I could be sorry, but I was. Jimmie was always punctiliously polite to her. But he was only that.

"She's getting what she deserves," Duncan said, but I felt that she was, perhaps, getting more than she deserved. For, after all, it was she who had kept Jimmie at it, and it was her keeping him at it which had brought success.

Neither Duncan nor I could tell how Jimmie felt about Ursula. But the thought of her troubled my sleep. Stripped of her art, she was not in the least the heroine of Jimmie's play. She was of coarser clay, commoner. And Jimmie was fine. The fear I had was that he might clothe her with the virtues which he had created, and the thought, as I have said, troubled me.

At last Duncan and I had to go home, although we promised to return for the opening night. Ursula gave a farewell supper for us. She lived alone with a housekeeper and maid. Her apartment was furnished in good taste, with, perhaps, a touch of over-emphasis. The table had unshaded purple candles and heather in glass dishes. Ursula wore woodland green, with a chaplet of heather about her glorious hair. Elise was in white with pearls. She was thirty-five, but she did not look it. Ursula was older, but she would always be in a sense ageless, as such women are—one would thrill to Sara Bernhardt were she seventeen or seventy.

Jimmie seemed to have dropped the years from him. He was very confident of the success of his play. "It can't fail," he said, "with Ursula to make it sure—"

I wondered whether it was Ursula or Elise who had made it sure. Could he ever have written it if Elise had not kept him at it? Yet she had stolen his youth!

And now Ursula was giving his youth back to him! As I saw the cock of his head, heard the ring of his gay laughter, I felt that it might be so. And suddenly I knew that I didn't want Jimmie to be young again. Not if he had to take his youth from the hands of Ursula Simms!

There were many toasts before the supper ended—and the last one Jimmie drank "To Ursula"! As he stood up to propose it, his glasses dangled from their ribbon, his shoulders were squared. In the soft and shaded light we were spared the gray in his hair—it was the old Jimmie, gay and gallant!

"To Ursula!" he said, and the words sparkled. "To Ursula!"

I looked at Elise. She might have been the ghost of the woman who had flamed in the old house in Albemarle. In her white and pearls she was shadowy, unsubstantial, almost spectral, but she raised her glass. "To Ursula!" she said.

All the way home on the train Duncan and I talked about it. We were scared to death. "Oh, he mustn't, he must not," I kept saying, and Duncan snorted.

"He's a young fool. She's not the woman for him—"

"Neither of them is the woman," I said, "but Elise has made him—"

"No man was ever held by gratitude."

"He'd hate Ursula in a year."

"He thinks he'd live—"

"And lose his soul—"

Jimmie's play opened to a crowded house. There had been extensive advertising, and Ursula had a great following.

Elise and Duncan and I had seats in an upper box. Elise sat where she was hidden by the curtains. Jimmie came and went unseen by the audience. Between acts he was behind the scenes. Elise had little to say. Once she reached over and laid her hand on mine.

"I—I think I'm frightened," she said, with a catch of her breath.

"It can't fail, my dear—"

"No, of course. But it's very different from what I expected."

"What is different?"

"Success."

As the great scene came closer, I seemed to hold my breath. I was so afraid that the audience might not see it as we had seen it at rehearsal. But they did see it, and it was a stupendous thing to sit there and watch the crowd, and know that Jimmie's genius was making its heart beat fast and faster. When Ursula in her purple cloak and pheasant's feather spoke her lines at the end of the third act, "*I shall love you for a million years*," the house went wild. Men and women who had never loved for a moment roared for this woman who had made them think they could love until eternity. They wanted her back and they got her. They wanted Jimmie and they got him. Ursula made a speech; Jimmie made a speech. They came out for uncounted curtain-calls, hand-in-hand. The play was a success!

The last act was, of course, an anti-climax. Before it was finished, Elise said to me, in a, stifled voice, "I've got to get back to Jimmie."

It seemed significant that Jimmie had not come to her. Surely he had not forgotten the part she had played. For fifteen years she had worked for this.

We found ourselves presently behind the scenes. The curtain was down, the audience was still shouting, everybody was excited, everybody was shaking hands. The stage-people caught at Elise as she passed, and held her to offer congratulations. I was not held and went on until I came to where Jimmie and Ursula stood, a little separate from the rest. Although I went near enough to touch them, they were so absorbed in each other that they did not see me. Ursula was looking up at Jimmie and his head was bent to her.

"Jimmie," she said, and her rich voice above the tumult was clear as a bell, "do you know how great you are?"

"Yes," he said. "I—I feel a little drunk with it, Ursula."

"Oh," she said, and now her words stumbled, "I—I love you for it. Oh, Jimmie, Jimmie, let's run away and love for a million years—"

All that he had wanted was in her words—the urge of youth, the beat of the wind, the song of the sea. My heart stood still. He drew back a little. He had wanted this. But he did not want it now—with Ursula. I saw it and she saw it.

"What a joke it would be," he said, "but we have other things to do, my dear."

"What things?"

The roar of the crowd came louder to their ears. "Harding, Harding! Jimmie Harding!"

"Listen," he said, and the light in his eyes was not for her. "Listen, Ursula, they're calling me."

She stood alone after he had left her. I am sure that even then she did not quite believe it was the end. She did not know how, in all the years, his wife had molded him.

When he had satisfied the crowd, Jimmie fought his way to where Elise and Duncan and I stood together.

Elise was wrapped in a great cloak of silver brocade. There was a touch of silver, too, in her hair. But she had never seemed to me so small, so childish.

"Oh, Jimmie," she said, as he came up, "you've done it!"

"Yes"—he was flushed and laughing, his head held high—"you always said I could do it. And I shall do it again. Did you hear them shout, Elise?"

"Yes."

"Jove! I feel like the old woman in the nursery rhyme, 'Alack-a-daisy, do this be I?'" He was excited, eager, but it was not the old eagerness. There was an avidity, a greediness.

She laid her hand on his arm. "You've earned a rest, dearest. Let's go up in the hills."

"In the hills? Oh, we're too old, Elise."

"We'll grow young."

"To-night I've given youth to the world. That's enough for me"—the light in his eyes was not for her—"that's enough for me. We'll hang around New York for a week or two, and then we'll go back to Albemarle. I want to get to work on another play. It's a great game, Elise. It's a great game!"

She knew then what she had done. Here was a monster of her own making. She had sacrificed her lover on the altar of success. Jimmie needed her no longer.

I would not have you think this an unhappy ending. Elise has all that she had asked, and Jimmie, with fame for a mistress, is no longer an unwilling captive in the old house. The prisoner loves his prison, welcomes his chains.

But Duncan and I talk at times of the young Jimmie who came years ago into our office. The Jimmie Harding who works down in Albemarle, and who struts a little in New York when he makes his speeches, is the ghost of the boy we knew. But he loves us still.

THE HIDDEN LAND

The mystery of Nancy Greer's disappearance has never been explained. The man she was to have married has married another woman. For a long time he mourned Nancy. He has always held the theory that she was drowned while bathing, and the rest of Nancy's world agrees with him. She had left the house one morning for her usual swim. The fog was coming in, and the last person to see her was a fisherman returning from his nets. He had stopped and watched her flitting wraith-like through the mist. He reported later that Nancy wore a gray bathing suit and cap and carried a blue cloak.

"You are sure she carried a cloak?" was the question which was repeatedly asked. For no cloak had been found on the sands, and it was unlikely that she had worn it into the water. The disappearance of the blue cloak was the only point which seemed to contradict the theory of accidental drowning. There were those who held that the cloak might have been carried off by some acquisitive individual. But it was not likely; the islanders are, as a rule, honest, and it was too late in the season for "off-islanders."

I am the only one who knows the truth. And as the truth would have been harder for Anthony Peak to bear than what he believed had happened, I have always withheld it.

There was, too, the fear that if I told they might try to bring Nancy back. I think Anthony would have searched the world for her. Not, perhaps, because of any great and passionate need of her, but because he would have thought her unhappy in what she had done, and would have sought to save her.

I am twenty years older than Nancy, her parents are dead, and it was at my house that she always stayed when she came to Nantucket. She has island blood in her veins, and so has Anthony Peak. Back of them were seafaring folk, although in the foreground was a generation or two of cosmopolitan residence. Nancy had been educated in France, and Anthony in England. The Peaks and the Greers owned respectively houses in Beacon Street and in Washington Square. They came every summer to the island, and it was thus that Anthony and Nancy grew up together, and at last became engaged.

As I have said, I am twenty years older than Nancy, and I am her cousin. I live in the old Greer house on Orange Street, for it is mine by inheritance, and was to have gone to Nancy at my death. But it will not go to her now. Yet I sometimes wonder—will the ship which carried her away ever sail back into the harbor? Some day, when she is old, will she walk up the street and be sorry to find strangers in the house?

I remember distinctly the day when the yacht first anchored within the Point. It was a Sunday morning and Nancy and I had climbed to the top of the house to the Captain's Walk, the white-railed square on the roof which gave a view of the harbor and of the sea.

Nancy was twenty-five, slim and graceful. She wore that morning a short gray-velvet coat over white linen. Her thick brown hair was gathered into a low knot and her fine white skin had a touch of artificial color. Her eyes were a clear blue. She was really very lovely, but I felt that the gray coat deadened her—that if she had not worn it she would not have needed that touch of color in her cheeks.

She lighted a cigarette and stood looking off, with her hand on the rail. "It is a heavenly morning, Ducky. And you are going to church?"

I smiled at her and said, "Yes."

Nancy did not go to church. She practiced an easy tolerance. Her people had been, originally, Quakers. In later years they had turned to Unitarianism. And now in this generation, Nancy, as well as Anthony Peak, had thrown off the shackles of religious observance.

"But it is worth having the churches just for the bells," Nancy conceded on Sunday mornings when their music rang out from belfry and tower.

234

It was worth having the churches for more than the bells. But it was useless to argue with Nancy. Her morals and Anthony's were irreproachable. That is, from the modern point of view. They played cards for small stakes, drank when they pleased, and, as I have indicated, Nancy smoked. She was, also, not unkissed when Anthony asked her to marry him. These were not the ideals of my girlhood, but Anthony and Nancy felt that such small vices as they cultivated saved them from the narrow-mindedness of their forebears.

"Anthony and I are going for a walk," she said. "I will bring you some flowers for your bowls, Elizabeth."

It was just then that the yacht steamed into the harbor—majestically, like a slow-moving swan. I picked out the name with my sea-glasses, *The Viking*.

I handed the glasses to Nancy. "Never heard of it," she said. "Did you?"

"No," I answered. Most of the craft which came in were familiar, and I welcomed them each year.

"Some new-rich person probably," Nancy decided. "Ducky, I have a feeling that the owner of *The Viking* bought it from the proceeds of pills or headache powders."

"Or pork."

I am not sure that Nancy and I were justified in our disdain—whale-oil has perhaps no greater claim to social distinction than bacon and ham or—pills.

The church bells were ringing, and I had to go down. Nancy stayed on the roof.

"Send Anthony up if he's there," she said; "we will sit here aloft like two cherubs and look down on you, and you will wish that you were with us."

But I knew that I should not wish it; that I should be glad to walk along the shaded streets with my friends and neighbors, to pass the gardens that were yellow with sunlight, and gay with larkspur and foxglove and hollyhocks, and to sit in the pew which was mine by inheritance.

Anthony was down-stairs. He was a tall, perfectly turned out youth, and he greeted me in his perfect manner.

"Nancy is on the roof," I told him, "and she wants you to come up."

"So you are going to church? Pray for me, Elizabeth."

Yet I knew he felt that he did not need my prayers. He had Nancy, more money than he could spend, and life was before him. What more, he would ask, could the gods give?

I issued final instructions to my maids about the dinner and put on my hat. It was a rather superlative hat and had come from Fifth Avenue. I spend the spring and fall in New York and buy my clothes at the smartest places. The ladies of Nantucket have never been provincial in their fashions. Our ancestors shopped in the marts of the world. When our captains sailed the seas they brought home to their womenfolk the treasures of loom and needle from Barcelona and Bordeaux, from Bombay and Calcutta, London and Paris and Tokio.

And perhaps because of my content in my new hat, perhaps because of the pleasant young pair of lovers which I had left behind me in the old house, perhaps because of the shade and sunshine, and the gardens, perhaps because of the bells, the world seemed more than ever good to me as I went on my way.

My pew in the church is well toward the middle. My ancestors were modest, or perhaps they assumed that virtue. They would have neither the highest nor the lowest seat in the synagogue.

It happens, therefore, that strangers who come usually sit in front of me. I have a lively curiosity, and I like to look at them. In the winter there are no strangers, and my mind is, I fancy, at such times, more receptive to the sermon.

I was early and sat almost alone in the great golden room whose restraint in decoration suggests the primitive bareness of early days. Gradually people began to come in, and my attention was caught by the somewhat unusual appearance of a man who walked up the aisle preceded by the usher.

He was rather stocky as to build, but with good, square military shoulders and small hips. He wore a blue reefer, white trousers, and carried a yachtsman's cap. His profile as he passed into his pew showed him young, his skin slightly bronzed, his features good, if a trifle heavy.

Yet as he sat down and I studied his head, what seemed most significant about him was his hair. It was reddish-gold, thick, curled, and upstanding, like the hair on the head of a lovely child, or in the painting of a Titian or a Tintoretto.

In a way he seemed out of place. Young men of his type so rarely came to church alone. Indeed, they rarely came to church at all. He seemed to belong to the out-of-doors—to wide spaces. I was puzzled, too, by a faint sense of having seen him before.

It was in the middle of the sermon that it all connected up. Years ago a ship had sailed into the harbor, and I had been taken down to see it. I had been enchanted by the freshly painted figurehead—a strong young god of some old Norse tale, with red-gold hair and a bright blue tunic. And now in the harbor was *The Viking*, and here, in the shadow of a perfectly orthodox pulpit, sat that strong young god, more glorious even than my memory of his wooden prototype.

He seemed to be absolutely at home—sat and stood at the right places, sang the hymns in a delightful barytone which was not loud, but which sounded a clear note above the feebler efforts of the rest of us.

It has always been my custom to welcome the strangers within our gates, and I must confess to a preference for those who seem to promise something more than a perfunctory interchange.

235

So as my young viking came down the aisle, I held out my hand. "We are so glad to have you with us."

He stopped at once, gave me his hand, and bent on me his clear gaze. "Thank you." And then, immediately: "You live here? In Nantucket?"

"Yes."

"All the year round?"

"Practically."

"That is very interesting." Again his clear gaze appraised me. "May I walk a little way with you? I have no friends here, and I want to ask a lot of questions about the island."

The thing which struck me most as we talked was his utter lack of self-consciousness. He gave himself to the subject in hand as if it were a vital matter, and as if he swept all else aside. It is a quality possessed by few New Englanders; it is, indeed, a quality possessed by few Americans. So when he offered to walk with me, it seemed perfectly natural that I should let him. Not one man in a thousand could have made such a proposition without an immediate erection on my part of the barriers of conventionality. To have erected any barrier in this instance would have been an insult, to my perception of the kind of man with whom I had to deal.

He was a gentleman, individual, and very much in earnest; and more than all, he was immensely attractive. There was charm in that clear blue gaze of innocence. Yet it was innocence plus knowledge, plus something which as yet I could not analyze.

He left me at my doorstep. I found that he had come to the island not to play around for the summer at the country clubs and on the bathing beach, but to live in the past—see it as it had once been—when its men went down to the sea in ships. And because there was still so much that we had to say to each other, I asked him to have a cup of tea with me, "this afternoon at four."

He accepted at once, with his air of sweeping aside everything but the matter in hand. I entered the house with a sense upon me of high adventure. I could not know that I was playing fate, changing in that moment the course of Nancy's future.

Dinner was at one o'clock. It seems an impossible hour to people who always dine at night. But on the Sabbath we Nantucketers eat our principal meal when we come home from church.

Nancy and Anthony protested as usual. "Of course you can't expect us to dress."

Nancy sat down at the table with her hat on, and minus the velvet coat. She was a bit disheveled and warm from her walk. She had brought in a great bunch of blue vetch and pale mustard, and we had put it in the center of the table in a bowl of gray pottery. My dining-room is in gray and white and old mahogany, and Nancy had had an eye to its coloring when she picked the flowers. They would not have fitted in with the decorative scheme of my library, which is keyed up, or down, to an antique vase of turquoise glaze, or to the drawing-room, which is in English Chippendale with mulberry brocade.

We had an excellent dinner, served by my little Portuguese maid. Nancy praised the lobster bisque and Anthony asked for a second helping of roast duck. They had their cigarettes with their coffee.

Long before we came to the coffee, however, Anthony had asked in his pleasant way of the morning service.

"Tell us about the sermon, Elizabeth."

"And the text," said Nancy.

I am apt to forget the text, and they knew it. It was always a sort of game between us at Sunday dinner, in which they tried to prove that my attention had strayed, and that I might much better have stayed at home, and thus have escaped the bondage of dogma and of dressing up.

I remembered the text, and then I told them about Olaf Thoresen.

Nancy lifted her eyebrows. "The pills man? Or was it—pork?"

"It was probably neither. Don't be a snob, Nancy."

She shrugged her shoulders. "It was you who said 'pork,' Elizabeth."

"He is coming to tea."

"To-day?"

"Yes."

"Sorry," said Nancy. "I'd like to see him, but I have promised to drive Bob Needham to 'Sconset for a swim."

Anthony had made the initial engagement—to play tennis with Mimi Sears, "Provided, of course, that you have no other plans for me," he had told Nancy, politely.

She had no plans, nor would she, under the circumstances, have urged them. That was their code—absolute freedom. "We'll be a lot happier if we don't tie each other up."

236

It was to me an amazing attitude. In my young days lovers walked out on Sunday afternoons to the old cemetery, or on the moor, or along the beach, and came back at twilight together, and sat together after supper, holding hands.

I haven't the slightest doubt that Anthony held Nancy's hands, but there was nothing fixed about the occasions. They had done away with billing and cooing in the old sense, and what they had substituted seemed to satisfy them.

Anthony left about three, and I went up to get into something thin and cool, and to rest a bit before receiving my guest. I heard Nancy at the telephone making final arrangements with the Drakes. After that I fell asleep, and knew nothing more until Anita came up to announce that Mr. Thoresen was down-stairs.

Tea was served in the garden at the back of the house, where there were some deep wicker chairs, and roses in a riot of bloom.

"This is—enchanting—" said Olaf. He did not sit down at once. He stood looking about him, at the sun-dial, and the whale's jaw lying bleached on a granite pedestal, and at the fine old houses rising up around us. "It is enchanting. Do you know, I have been thinking myself very fortunate since you spoke to me in church this morning."

After that it was all very easy. He asked and I answered. "You see," he explained, finally, "I am hungry for anything that tells me about the sea. Three generations back we were all sailors—my great-grandfather and his fathers before him in Norway—and far back of that—the vikings." He drew a long breath. "Then my grandfather came to America. He settled in the West—in Dakota, and planted grain. He made money, but he was a thousand miles away from the sea. He starved for it, but he wanted money, and, as I have said, he made it. And my father made more money. Then I came. The money took me to school in the East—to college. My mother died and my father. And now the money is my own. I bought a yacht, and I have lived on the water. I can't get enough of it. I think that I am making up for all that my father and my grandfather denied themselves."

I can't in the least describe to you how he said it. There was a tenseness, almost a fierceness, in his brilliant blue eyes. Yet he finished up with a little laugh. "You see," he said, "I am a sort of Flying Dutchman—sailing the seas eternally, driven not by any sinister force but by my own delight in it."

"Do you go alone?"

"Oh, I have guests—at times. But I am often my own—good company—"

He stopped and rose. Nancy had appeared in the doorway. She crossed the porch and came down toward us. She was in her bathing suit and cap, gray again, with a line of green on the edges, and flung over her shoulders was a gray cloak. She was on her way to the stables—it was before the day of motor-cars on the island, those halcyon, heavenly days. The door was open and her horse harnessed and waiting for her. She could not, of course, pass us without speaking, and so I presented Olaf.

Anita had brought the tea, and Nancy stayed to eat a slice of thin bread and butter. "In this air one is always hungry," she said to Olaf, and smiled at him.

He did not smile back. He was surveying her with a sort of frowning intensity. She spoke of it afterward, "Does he always stare like that?" But I think that, in a way, she was pleased.

She drove her own horse, wrapped in her cloak and with an utter disregard to the informality of her attire. She would, I knew, gather up the Drakes and Bob Needham, likewise attired in bathing costumes, and they would all have tea on the other side of the island, naiad-like and utterly unconcerned. I did not approve of it, but Nancy did not cut her life to fit my pattern.

When she had gone, Olaf said to me, abruptly, "Why does she wear gray?"

"Oh, she has worked out a theory that repression in color is an evidence of advanced civilization. The Japanese, for example—"

"Why should civilization advance? It has gone far enough—too far—And she should wear a blue cloak—sea-blue—the color of her eyes—"

"And of yours." I smiled at him.

"Yes. Are they like hers?"

They were almost uncannily alike. I had noticed it when I saw them together. But there the resemblance stopped.

"She belongs to the island?"

"She lives in New York. But every drop of blood in her is seafaring blood."

"Good!" He sat for a moment in silence, then spoke of something else. But when he was ready to go, he included Nancy in an invitation. "If you and Miss Greer could lunch with me to-morrow on my yacht—"

I was not sure about Nancy's engagements, but I thought we might. "You can call us up in the morning."

Nancy brought the Drakes and Bob Needham back with her for supper, and Mimi Sears was with Anthony. Supper on Sunday is an informal meal—everything on the table and the servants out.

Nancy, clothed in something white and exquisite, served the salad. "So your young viking didn't stay, Elizabeth?"

"I didn't ask him."

It was then that she spoke of his frowning gaze. "Does he always stare like that?"

Anthony, breaking in, demanded, "Did he stare at Nancy?"

I nodded. "It was her eyes."

They all looked at me. "Her eyes?"

"Yes. He said that her cloak should have matched them."

Anthony flushed. He has a rather captious code for outsiders. Evidently Olaf had transgressed it.

"Is the man a dressmaker?"

"Of course not, Anthony."

"Then why should he talk of Nancy's clothes?"

"Well," Nancy remarked, "perhaps the less said about my clothes the better. I was in my bathing suit."

Anthony was irritable. "Well, why not? You had a right to wear what you pleased, but he did not have a right to make remarks about it."

I came to Olaf's defense. "You would understand better if you could see him. He is rather different, Anthony."

"I don't like different people," and in that sentence was a summary of Anthony's prejudices. He and Nancy mingled with their own kind. Anthony's friends were the men who had gone to the right schools, who lived in the right streets, belonged to the right clubs, and knew the right people. Within those limits, humanity might do as it pleased; without them, it was negligible, and not to be considered.

After supper the five of them were to go for a sail. There was a moon, and all the wonder of it.

Anthony was not keen about the plan. "Oh, look here, Nancy," he complained, "we have done enough for one day—"

"I haven't."

Of course that settled it. Anthony shrugged his shoulders and submitted. He did not share Nancy's almost idolatrous worship of the sea. It was the one fundamental thing about her. She bathed in it, swam in it, sailed on it, and she was never quite happy away from it.

I heard Anthony later in the hall, protesting. I had gone to the library for a book, and their voices reached me.

"I thought you and I might have one evening without the others."

"Oh, don't be silly, Anthony."

I think my heart lost a beat. Here was a lover asking his mistress for a moment—and she laughed at him. It did not fit in with my ideas of young romance.

Yet late that night I heard the murmur of their voices and looked out into the white night. They stood together by the sun-dial, and his arm was about her, her head on his shoulder. And it was not the first time that a pair of lovers had stood by that dial under the moon.

I went back to bed, but I could not sleep. I lighted my bedside lamp, and read *Vanity Fair*. I find Thackeray an excellent corrective when I am emotionally keyed up.

Nancy, too, was awake; I could see her light shining across the hall. She came in, finally, and sat on the foot of my bed.

"Your viking was singing as we passed his boat—"

"Singing?"

"Yes, hymns, Elizabeth. The others laughed, Anthony and Mimi, but I didn't laugh. His voice is—wonderful—"

She had on a white-crêpe *peignoir*, and there was no color in her cheeks. Her skin had the soft whiteness of a rose petal. Her eyes were like stars. As I lay there and looked at her I wondered if it was Anthony's kisses or the memory of Olaf's singing which had made her eyes shine like that.

I had heard him sing, and I said so, "in church."

Her arms clasped her knees. "Isn't it queer that he goes to church and sings hymns?"

"Why queer? I go to church."

"Yes. But you are different. You belong to another generation, Elizabeth, and he doesn't look it."

I knew what she meant. I had thought the same thing when I first saw him walking up the aisle. "He has asked us to lunch with him to-morrow on his boat."

It was the first time that I had mentioned it. Somehow I had not cared to speak of it before Anthony.

She showed her surprise. "So soon? Doesn't that sound a little—pushing?"

"It sounds as if he goes after a thing when he wants it."

"Yes, it does. I believe I should like to accept. But I can't to-morrow. There's a clambake, and I have promised the crowd."

"He will ask you again."

"Will he? You can say 'yes' for Wednesday then. And I'll keep it."

"I am not sure that we had better accept."

"Why not?"

"Well, there's Anthony."

She slid from the bed and stood looking down at me. "You think he wouldn't like it?"

"I am afraid he wouldn't. And, after all, you are engaged to him, Nancy."

"Of course I am, but he is not my jailer. He does as he pleases and I do as I please."

"In my day lovers pleased to do the same thing."

238

"Did they? I don't believe it. They just pretended, and there is no pretense between Anthony and me"—she stooped and kissed me—"they just pretended, Elizabeth, and the reason that I love Anthony is because we don't pretend."

After that I felt that I need fear nothing. Nancy and Anthony—freedom and self-confidence—why should I try to match their ideals with my own of yesterday? Yet, as I laid my book aside, I resolved that Olaf should know of Anthony.

I had my opportunity the next day. Olaf came over to sit in my garden and again we had tea. He was much pleased when he knew that Nancy and I would be his guests on Wednesday.

"Come early. Do you swim? We can run the launch to the beach—or, better still, dive in the deeper water near my boat."

"Nancy swims," I told him. "I don't. And I am not sure that we can come early. Nancy and Anthony usually play golf in the morning."

"Who is Anthony?"

"Anthony Peak. The man she is going to marry."

He hesitated a moment, then said, "Bring him, too." His direct gaze met mine, and his direct question followed. "Does she love him?"

"Of course."

"It is not always 'of course.'" He stopped and talked of other things, but in some subtle fashion I was aware that my news had been a shock to him, and that he was trying to adjust himself to it, and to the difference that it must make in his attitude toward Nancy.

When I told Nancy that Anthony had been invited, she demanded, "How did Olaf Thoresen know about him?"

"I told him you were engaged."

"But why, Elizabeth? Why shout it from the housetops?"

"Well, I didn't want him to be hurt."

"You are taking a lot for granted."

I shrugged my shoulders. "We won't quarrel, and a party of four is much nicer than three."

As it turned put, however, Anthony could not go. He was called back to Boston on business. That was where Fate again stepped in. It was, I am sure, those three days of Anthony's absence which turned the scale of Nancy's destiny. If he had been with us that first morning on the boat Olaf would not have dared....

Nancy wore her white linen and her gray-velvet coat, and a hat with a gull's wing. She carried her bathing suit. "He intends, evidently, to entertain us in his own way."

Olaf's yacht was modern, but there was a hint of the barbaric in its furnishings. The cabin into which we were shown and in which Nancy was to change was in strangely carved wood, and there was a wolfskin on the floor in front of the low bed. The coverlet was of a fine-woven red-silk cloth, weighed down by a border of gold and silver threads. On the wall hung a square of tapestry which showed a strange old ship with sails of blue and red and green, and with golden dragon-heads at stem and stern.

Nancy, crossing the threshold, said to Olaf, who had opened the door for us, "It is like coming into another world; as if you had set the stage, run up the curtain, and the play had begun."

"You like it? It was a fancy of mine to copy a description I found in an old book. King Olaf, the Thick-set, furnished a room like this for his bride."

Olaf, the Thick-set! The phrase fitted perfectly this strong, stocky, blue-eyed man, who smiled radiantly upon us as he shut the door and left us alone.

Nancy stood in the middle of the room looking about her. "I like it," she said, with a queer shake in her voice. "Don't you, Elizabeth?"

I liked it so much that I felt it wise to hide my pleasure in a pretense of indifference. "Well, it is original to say the least."

But it was more than original, it was poetic. It was—Melisande in the wood—one of Sinding's haunting melodies, an old Saga caught and fixed in color and carving.

In this glowing room Nancy in her white and gray was a cold and incongruous figure, and when at last she donned her dull cap, and the dull cloak that she wore over her swimming costume, she seemed a ghostly shadow of the bright bride whom that other Olaf had brought—a thousand years before—to his strange old ship.

I realize that what comes hereafter in this record must seem to the unimaginative overdrawn. Even now, as I look back upon it, it has a dream quality, as if it might never have happened, or as if, as Nancy had said, it was part of a play, which would be over when the curtain was rung down and the actors had returned to the commonplace.

But the actors in this drama have never returned to the commonplace. Or have they? Shall I ever know? I hope I may never know, if Nancy and Olaf have lost the glamour of their dreams.

Well, we found Olaf on deck waiting for us. In a sea-blue tunic, with strong white arms, and the dazzling fairness of his strong neck, he was more than ever like the figurehead on the old ship that I had seen in my childhood. He carried over his arm a cloak of the same sea-blue. It was this cloak which afterward played an important part in the mystery of Nancy's disappearance.

His quick glance swept Nancy—the ghostly Nancy in gray, with only the blue of her eyes, and that touch of artificial pink in her cheeks to redeem her from somberness. He shook his head with a gesture of impatience.

"I don't like it," he said, abruptly. "Why do you deaden your beauty with dull colors?"

Nancy's eyes challenged him. "If it is deadened, how do you know it is beauty?"

"May I show you?" Again there was that tense excitement which I had noticed in the garden.

"I don't know what you mean," yet in that moment the color ran up from her neck to her chin, the fixed pink spots were lost in a rush of lovely flaming blushes.

For with a sudden movement he had snatched off her cap, and had thrown the cloak around her. The transformation was complete. It was as if he had waved a wand. There she stood, the two long, thick braids, which she had worn pinned close under her cap, falling heavily like molten metal to her knees, the blue cloak covering her—heavenly in color, matching her eyes, matching the sea, matching the sky, matching the eyes of Olaf.

I think I must have uttered some sharp exclamation, for Olaf turned to me. "You see," he said, triumphantly, "I have known it all the time. I knew it the first time that I saw her in the garden."

Nancy had recovered herself. "But I can't stalk around the streets in a blue cloak with my hair down."

He laughed with her. "Oh, no, no. But the color is only a symbol. Modern life has robbed you of vivid things. Even your emotions. You are—afraid—" He caught himself up. "We can talk of that after our swim. I think we shall have a thousand things to talk about."

Nancy held out her hand for her cap, but he would not give it to her. "Why should you care if your hair gets wet? The wind and the sun will dry it—"

I was amazed when I saw that she was letting him have his way. Never for a moment had Anthony mastered her. For the first time in her life Nancy was dominated by a will that was stronger than her own.

I sat on deck and watched them as they swam like two young sea gods, Nancy's bronze hair bright under the sun. Olaf's red-gold crest....

The blue cloak lay across my knee. Nancy had cast it off as she had descended into the launch. I had examined it and had found it of soft, thick wool, with embroidery of a strange and primitive sort in faded colors. Yet the material of the cloak had not faded, or, if it had, there remained that clear azure, like the Virgin's cloak in old pictures.

I knew now why Olaf had wanted Nancy on board, why he had wanted to swim with her in the sea which was as blue as her eyes and his own. It was to reveal her to himself as the match of the women of the Sagas. I found this description later in one of the old books in the ship's library:

Then Hallgerd was sent for, and came with two women. She wore a blue woven mantle ... her hair reached down to her waist on both sides, and she tucked it under her belt.

And there was, too, this account of a housewife in her "kyrtil":

The dress-train was trailing,
The skirt had a blue tint;
Her brow was brighter,
Her neck was whiter
Than pure new fallen snow.

In other words, that one glance at Nancy in the garden, when he had risen at her entrance, had disclosed to Olaf the fundamental in her. He had known her as a sea-maiden. And she had not known it, nor I, nor Anthony.

Luncheon was served on deck. We were waited on by fair-haired, but very modern Norsemen. The crew on *The Viking* were all Scandinavians. Most of them spoke English, and there seemed nothing uncommon about any of them. Yet, in the mood of the moment, I should have felt no surprise had they served us in the skins of wild animals, or had set sail like pirates with the two of us captive on board.

I will confess, also, to a feeling of exaltation which clouded my judgment. I knew that Olaf was falling in love with Nancy, and I half guessed that Nancy might be falling in love with Olaf, yet I sat there and let them do it. If Anthony should ever know! Yet how can he know? As I weigh it now, I am not sure that I have anything with which to reproach myself, for the end, at times, justifies the means, and the Jesuitical theory had its origin, perhaps, in the profound knowledge that Fate does not always use fair methods in gaining her ends.

I can't begin to tell you what we talked about. Nancy had dried her hair, and it was wound loosely, high on her head. The blue cloak was over her shoulders, and she was the loveliest thing that I ever hope to see. By the flame in her cheeks and the light in her eyes, I was made aware of an exaltation which matched my own. She, too, was caught up into the atmosphere of excitement which Olaf created. He could not take his eyes from her. I wondered what Anthony would have said could he have visioned for the moment this blue-and-gold enchantress.

When coffee was served there were no cigarettes or cigars. Nancy had her own silver case hanging at her belt. I knew that she would smoke, and I did not try to stop her. She always smoked after her meals and she was restless without it.

It was Olaf who stopped her. "You will hate my bad manners," he said, with his gaze holding hers, "but I wish you wouldn't."

She was lighting her own little wax taper and she looked her surprise.

"My cigarette?"

He nodded. "You are too lovely."

"But surely you are not so—old-fashioned."

"No. I am perhaps so—new-fashioned that my reason might take your breath away." He laughed but did not explain.

Nancy sat undecided while the taper burned out futilely. Then she said, "Of course you are my host—"

"Don't do it for that reason. Do it because"—he stopped, laughed again, and went on—"because you are a goddess—a woman of a new race—"

With parted lips she looked at him, then tried to wrench herself back to her attitude of light indifference.

"Oh, we've grown beyond all that."

"All what?"

"Goddess-women. We are just nice and human together."

"You are nice and human. But you are more than that."

Nancy put her unlighted cigarette back in its case. "I'll keep it for next time," she said, with a touch of defiance.

"There will be no next time," was his secure response, and his eyes held hers until, with an effort, she withdrew her gaze.

Then he rose, and his men placed deep chairs for us in a sheltered corner, where we could look out across the blue to the low hills of the moor. There was a fur rug over my chair, and I sank gratefully into the warmth of it.

"With a wind like this in the old days," Olaf said, as he stood beside me looking out over the sparkling water, "how the sails would have been spread, and now there is nothing but steam and gasoline and electricity."

"Why don't you have sails then," Nancy challenged him, "instead of steam?"

"I have a ship. Shall I show you the picture of it?"

He left to get it, and Nancy said to me, "Ducky, will you pinch me?"

"You mean that it doesn't seem real?"

She nodded.

"Well, maybe it isn't. He said he was a sort of Flying Dutchman."

"I should hate to think that he wasn't real, Elizabeth. He is as alive as a—burning coal."

Olaf came back with the pictures of his ship, a clean-cut, beautiful craft, very up-to-date, except for the dragon-heads at prow and stem.

"If I could have had my way," he told us, "I should have built it like the ship on the tapestry in there—but it wasn't practical—we haven't manpower for the oars in these days."

He had other pictures—of a strange house, or, rather, of a collection of buildings set in the form of a quadrangle, and inclosed by low walls. There were great gateways of carved wood with ironwork and views of the interior—a wide hall with fireplaces—a raised platform, with carved seats that gave a throne-like effect. The house stood on a sort of high peninsula with a forest back of it, and the sea spreading out beyond.

"The house looks old," Olaf said, "but I planned it."

He had, he explained, during one of his voyages, come upon a hidden harbor. "There is only a fishing village and a few small boats at the landing place, but the people claim to be descendants of the vikings. They are utterly isolated, but a God-fearing, hardy folk.

"It is strangely cut off from the rest of the world. I call it 'The Hidden Land.' It is not on any map. I have looked and have not found it."

"But why," was Nancy's demand, "did you build there?"

It was a question, I think, for which he had waited. "Some day I may tell you, but not now, except this—that I love the sea, and I shall end my days where, when I open my gates, my eyes may rest upon it ... where its storms may beat upon my roof, and where the men about me shall sail it, and get their living from it.

"I have told your cousin," he went on, "something of the life of my grandfather and of my father. With all of their sea-blood, they were shut away for two generations from the sea. Can you grasp the meaning of that to me?—the heritage of suppressed longings? I think my father must have felt it as I did, for he drank heavily before he died. My grandfather sought an outlet in founding the family fortunes. But when I came, there was not the compelling force of poverty to make me work, and I had before me the warning of my father's excesses. But this sea-madness! It has driven me on and on, and at last it has driven me here." He stopped, then took up the theme again in his tense, excited fashion, "It will drive me on again."

"Why should it drive you on?"

When Nancy asked that question, I knew what had happened. The thrill of her voice was the answer of a bird to its mate. When I think of her, I see her always as she was then, the blue cloak falling about her, her hair blowing, her cheeks flaming with lovely color.

I saw his fingers clench the arm of his chair as if in an effort of self-control. Then he said: "Perhaps I shall tell you that, too. But not now." He rose abruptly. "It is warmer inside, and we can have some music. I am sure you must be tired of hearing me talk about myself."

He played for us, in masterly fashion, the Peer Gynt suite, and after that a composition of his own. At last he sang, with all the swing of the sea in voice and accompaniment, and the song drew our hearts out of us.

Nancy was very quiet as we drove from the pier, and it was while I was dressing for dinner that she came into my room.

"Elizabeth," she said, "I am not sure whether we have been to a Methodist revival or to a Wagner music-drama—"

"Neither," I told her. "There's nothing artificial about him. You asked me back there if he was real. I believe that he is utterly real, Nancy. It is not a pose. I am convinced that it is not a pose."

"Yes," she said, "that's the queer thing. He's not—putting it on—and he makes everybody else seem—stale and shallow—like ghosts—or—shadow-shapes—"

I read *Vanity Fair* late into the night, and the morning was coming on before I tried to sleep. I waked to find Nancy standing by my bed.

"His boat is gone."

"Gone?"

"Yes. It went an hour ago. I saw it from the roof."

"From the roof?"

"Yes. I got up—early. I—I could not sleep. And when I looked—it was gone—your glasses showed it almost out of sight."

She was wrapped in the blue cloak. Olaf had made her bring it with her. She had protested. But he had been insistent.

"I found this in the pocket," Nancy said, and held out a card on which Olaf had written, "When she lifted her arms, opening the door, a light shone on them from the sea, and the air and all the world were brightened for her."

"What does it mean, Elizabeth?"

"I think you know, my dear."

"That he cares?"

"What do you think?"

Her eyes were like stars. "But how can he? He has seen me—twice—"

"Some men are like that."

"If you only hadn't told him about Anthony."

"I am glad that I told him."

"Oh, but he might have stayed."

"Well?"

"And I might have loved him." She was still glowing with the fires that Olaf had lighted in her.

"But you are going to marry Anthony."

"Yes," she said, "I am going to marry Anthony. I am going to flirt and smoke cigarettes and let him—flirt—when I might have been a—goddess."

It was after breakfast on the same day that a letter came to me, delivered into my own hands by messenger. It was from Olaf, and he left it to me whether Nancy should see it. It covered many pages and it shook my soul, but I did not show it to Nancy.

There were nights after that when I found it hard to sleep, nights in which I thought of Olaf sailing toward the hidden land, holding in his heart a hope which it was in my power to crown with realization or dash to the ground. Yet I had Nancy's happiness to think of, and, in a sense, Anthony's. It seemed almost incredible that I must carry, too, on my heart, the burden of the happiness of Olaf Thoresen.

When Anthony came back, he and Nancy were caught in a net of engagements, and I saw very little of them. Of course they romped in now and then with their own particular crowd, and treated me, as it were, to a cross-section of modern life. Except for two things, I should have judged that Nancy had put away all thoughts of Olaf, but these two things were significant. She had stopped smoking, and she no longer touched her cheeks with artificial bloom.

Anthony's amazement, when he offered her a cigarette and she refused, had in it a touch of irritation. "But, my dear girl, why not?"

"Well, I have to think of my complexion, Tony."

I think he knew it was not that and was puzzled. "I never saw you looking better in my life."

She was wearing a girdle of blue with her clear, crisp white, and her fairness was charming. She had, indeed, the look which belongs to young Catholic girls dedicated to the Virgin who wear her colors.

It was not, however, until Anthony had been home for a week that he saw the blue cloak. We were all on the beach—Mimi Sears and Bob Needham and the Drakes, myself and Anthony. Nancy was late, having a foursome to finish on the golf grounds. She came at last, threading her way gayly through the crowd of bathers. She was without her cap, and her hair was wound in a thick braid about her head. I saw people turning to look at her as they had never turned to look when she had worn her shadowy gray.

"Great guns!" said a man back of me. "What a beauty!"

A deep flush stained Anthony's face, and I knew at once that he did not like it. It was as if, having attuned his taste to the refinement of a Japanese print, he had been called upon to admire a Fra Angelico. He hated the obvious, and Nancy's loveliness at this moment was as definite as the loveliness of the sky, the sea, the moon, the stars. Later I was to learn that Anthony's taste was for a sophisticated Nancy, a mocking Nancy, a slim, mysterious creature, with charms which were caviar to the mob.

But Bob Needham spoke from the depths of his honest and undiscriminating soul. "Heavens! Nancy. Where did you get it?"

"Get what?"

"That cloak."

"Do you like it?"

"Like it—! I wish Tony would run away while I tell you."

Anthony, forcing a smile, asked, "Where did you get it, Nan?"

"It was given to me." She sat down on the sand and smiled at him.

Mrs. Drake, feeling the thickness and softness, exclaiming over the embroidery, said finally: "It is a splendid thing. Like a queen's robe."

"You haven't told us yet," Anthony persisted, "where you got it."

"No? Well, Elizabeth will tell you. It's rather a long story. I am going into the water. Come on, Bob."

She left the cloak with me. Anthony followed her and the others. I sat alone under a great orange umbrella and wondered if Anthony would ask me about the cloak.

He did not, and when Nancy came back finally with her hair down and blowing in the wind to dry, Anthony was with her. The cloud was gone from his face, in the battle with the wares he had forgotten his vexation.

But he remembered when he saw the cloak. "Tell me about it, Nancy."

"I got it from Elizabeth's viking."

That was the calm way in which she put it.

"He isn't my viking," I told her.

"Well, you were responsible for him."

"Do you mean to say," Anthony demanded, "that you accepted a gift like that from a man you didn't know?"

Nancy, hugging herself in the cloak, said, "I felt that I knew him very well."

"How long was he here?"

"Three days. I saw him twice."

"I don't think I quite like the—idea—" Anthony began, then broke off. "Of course you have a right to do as you please."

"Of course," said Nancy, with a flame in her cheek.

"But it would please me very much if you would send it back to him."

"If I wanted to," she told him, "I couldn't."

"Why not?"

"Can you mail parcel post packages to the—Flying Dutchman? Or express things to—to Odin?"

"I don't in the least know what you are talking about, Nancy."

"Well, he sailed in and he sailed out. He didn't leave any address. He left the cloak—and a rather intriguing memory, Anthony."

That was all the satisfaction she would give him. And I am not sure that he deserved more at her hands. The agreement between them had been—absolute freedom.

I am convinced that if it had not been for the garden party I should never have shown Olaf's letter to Nancy. The garden party is an annual event. We always hold it in August, when the "off-islanders" crowd the hotels, and when money is more plentiful than at any other time during the year.

Nancy had charge of the fish pond. I had helped her to make the fish, which were gay objects of painted paper, numbered to indicate a corresponding prize package, and to be caught with a dangling line from a lily-wreathed artificial pool.

The day of the garden party was a glorious one—with the air so clear that the flying pennants of the decorated booths, and the gowns of the women, gained brilliancy and beauty from the shining atmosphere.

Nancy wore a broad blue hat which matched her eyes, one of her clear white dresses, and a silken scarf of the same blue as her hat. She loved children, and as she stood in a circle of them all the afternoon, untiring, eager—bending down to them, hooking the fish on the dangling line—handing out the prizes, smiling into the flushed eager faces, helping the very littlest ones to achieve a catch, I sat in a chair not far away from her and watched. I saw Anthony come and go, urging her to let some one else take her place, pressing a dozen reasons upon her for desertion of her task, and coming back, when she refused, to complain to me:

"Such things are a deadly bore."

"Not to Nancy."

"But they used to be. She's changed, Elizabeth."

"Beautifully changed."

"I am not sure. She was always such, a good sport."

"And isn't she now?"

"She is different," he caught himself up, "but of course—adorable."

Mimi Sears joined us, and she and Anthony went off together. Bob Needham hung around Nancy until she sent him away. At last the hour arrived for the open-air play which was a special attraction, and the crowds surged toward the inclosure. The booths were deserted, and only one rapturous child remained by the fish pond.

Nancy sat down and lifted the baby to her lap. She had taken off her hat, and her blue scarf fell about her. Something tugged at my heart as I looked at her. With that little head in the hollow of her arm she was the eternal mother.

I saw Anthony approaching. He stopped, and I caught his words. "You must come now, Nancy. I am saving a seat for you."

She shook her head, and looked down at the child. "I told his nurse to go and he is almost asleep."

He flung himself away from her and came over to me. "I have good seats for both of you in the enclosure. But Nancy won't go."

I rose and went with him, although I should have been content to sit there by the fish pond and feast my eyes on Nancy.

"It is perfectly silly of her to stay," Anthony fumed as we walked on together.

"But she loves the children."

"I hate children."

I am sure that he did not mean it. What he hated was the fact that the child had for the moment held Nancy from him. It was as if, looking forward into the future, he could see like moments, and set himself against the thought of any interruption of what might be otherwise an untrammeled and independent partnership. He had, I think, little jealousy where men were concerned. He was willing to give Nancy the reins and let her go, believing that she would inevitably come back to him. He was not, perhaps, so willing to trust her with ties which might prove more absorbing than himself.

If I had not had Olaf's letter, I might not have weighed Anthony's attitude so carefully, but against those burning words and their comprehension of the divinity and beauty of my Nancy's nature, Anthony's querulous complaint struck cold.

I think it was then, as we walked toward the inclosure, that I made up my mind to let Nancy hear what Olaf had to say to her.

She stayed out late that night—there was a dinner and a dance—and Anthony brought her home. I confess that I felt like a traitor as I heard the murmur of his voice in the hall.

But when he had gone, and Nancy passed my door on her way to her room, I called her, and she came in.

I was in bed, and I had the letter in my hand. "I want you to read it," I said. "It is from Olaf Thoresen."

She looked at it, and asked, "When did it come?"

"Two months ago. The day that he left."

"Why haven't you shown it to me?"

"I couldn't make up my mind. I do not know even now that I am right in letting you see it. But I feel that you have a right to see it. It is you who must answer it. Not I."

When she had gone, I turned to the chapter in my book where Becky weeps crocodile tears over poor Rawdon Crawley on the night before Waterloo. There is no scene in modern literature to match it. But I couldn't get my mind on it. Nancy was reading Olaf's letter!

I kept a copy of it, and here it is:

"I knew when I first saw her in the garden that she was the One Woman. I had wanted sea-blood, and when she came, ready for a dip in the sea, it seemed a sign. One knows these things somehow, and I knew. I shan't attempt to explain it.

"When you told me of her lover, I felt that Fate had played a trick on me. I could not now with honor pursue the woman who was promised to another. Yet I permitted myself that one day—the day on my boat.

"I learned in those hours that I spent with her that she had been molded by the man she is to marry and that in the years to come she will shrink to the measure of his demands upon her. She is feminine enough to be swayed by masculine will. That is at once her strength and her weakness. Loving a man who will love her for the wonder of her womanhood, she will fulfill her greatest destiny. Loving, on the other hand, one who aspires only to fit her into some attenuated social scheme, she will wither and fade. I think you know that this is true, that you will not accuse me of being unfair to any one.

"And now may I tell you what my dreams have been for her?

"I am not young. I mean I am past those hot and early years when men play—Romeo. The dream that is mine is one which has come to a man of thirty, who, having seen the world, has weighed it and wants—something more.

"I have told you of my house in that hidden land which is washed by the sea. I want to spend the rest of my days there, and I had hoped that some woman might be found whose love of life, whose love of adventure, whose love of me, might be so strong that she would see nothing strange in my demand that she forsake all others and cleave only to me.

"By forsaking all others, I mean, literally, what I say. I should want to cut her off entirely from all former ties. To let any one into our secret, to reveal that hidden land to a gaping world, would be to destroy it. We should be followed, tracked by the newspapers, written up, judged eccentric—mad. And I do not wish to be judged at all. My separation from my kind would have in it more than a selfish whim, an obsession for solitude. I want to get back to primitive civilization. I want my children to face a simpler world than the one I faced. Do you know what it means for a man to inherit money, with nothing back of it for two generations but hard work, although back of that there were, perhaps, kings? It means that I had, unaided, to fit myself into a social scheme so complex that I have not yet mastered its intricacies. I do not want to master them. I do not want my sons to master them. I want them to find life a thing of the day's work, the day's worship, the day's out-of-door delights. I want them to have time to think and to dream. And then some day they shall come back if they wish to challenge civilization—young prophets, perhaps, out of the wilderness—seeing a new vision of God and man because of their detachment from all that might have blinded them.

"I have a feeling that your Nancy might, if she knew this, dream with me of a new race, rising to the level of the needs of a new world. She might see herself as the mother of such a race—sheltered in my hidden land, sailing the seas with me, held close to my heart. I think I am a masterful man, but I should be masterful only to keep her to her best. If she faltered I should strengthen her. And I should make her happy. I know that I could make her happy. And for me there will never be another.

"I am leaving it to you to decide whether you will show her this. I want her to see it, because it seems to me that she has a right to decide between the life that I can offer her and the life she must live if she marries Anthony Peak. But it all involves a point of honor which I feel that I am not unprejudiced enough to decide. So to-morrow I shall go away. I shall sail far in the two months that I shall give myself before I come back. And when I come, you will let me know whether I am to turn once more to the trackless seas, or stay to find my happiness."

This letter when I had first read it had stirred me profoundly, as I think it must have stirred any man or woman who has yearned amid the complexities of modern existence to find some land of dreams. Even to my island, comparatively untouched by the problems of existence in crowded centers, come the echoes of discord, of social unrest, of political upheavals, of commercial greed. In this hidden land of Olaf's would be life stripped of its sordidness, love free from the blight of cynicism and disillusion—faith, firm in its nearness to God and the wonder of His works. I envied Olaf his hidden land as I envied Nancy her opportunity. My blood is the same as Nancy's, and I love the sea. And as we grow older our souls adventure!

When Nancy came in to me, she had put on her white *peignoir*, and she had Olaf's letter in her hand.

"Ducky," she said, and her voice shook, "I have read it twice—and—I shouldn't dare to think he was in earnest."

"Why not?"

"I should want to go, Elizabeth."

"And leave the world behind you?"

"Oh, I haven't any world. It might be different if mother were alive, or daddy. There'd be only you, Ducky, my dear, dear Ducky." She caught my hand and held it.

"And Anthony—"

"Anthony would get over it"—sharply. "Wouldn't he, Elizabeth? You know he would."

"My dear, I don't know."

"But I know. If I hadn't been in his life, Mimi Sears would have been, just as Bob Needham would have been in my life if it hadn't been for Anthony. There isn't any question between Anthony and me of—one woman for one man. You know that, Elizabeth. But with Olaf—if he doesn't have me, there will be no one else—ever. He—he will go sailing on—alone—"

"My dear, how do you know?"

She flung herself down beside me, a white rose, all fragrance. "I don't know"—she began to cry. "How silly I am," she sobbed against my shoulder. "I—I don't know anything about him, do I, Elizabeth—? But it would be wonderful to be loved—like that."

All through the night she slept on my arm, with her hand curled in the hollow of my neck as she had slept as a child. But I did not sleep. My mind leaped forward into the future, and I saw my world without her.

Nancy stayed with me through September. Anthony's holiday was up the day after the garden party, and he went back to Boston, keeping touch with Nancy in the modern way by wire, special delivery, and long-distance telephone.

It was on a stormy night with wind and beating rain that Nancy told me Anthony was insisting that she marry him in December.

"But I can't, Elizabeth. I am going to write to him to-night."

"When will it be?"

"Who knows? I—I'm not ready. If he can't wait—he can let me go."

She did not stay to listen to my comment on her mutiny—she swept out of the library and sat down at the piano in the other room, making a picture of herself between the tall white candles which illumined the dark mahogany and the mulberry brocades.

I leaned back in my chair and watched her, her white fingers straying over the keys, her thin blue sleeves flowing back from her white arms. Now and then I caught a familiar melody among the chords, and once I was aware of the beat and the swing of the waves in the song which Olaf had once sung.

She did not finish it. She rose and wandered to the window, parting the curtain and looking out into the streaming night.

"It's an awful storm, Ducky."

"Yes, my dear. On nights like this I always think of the old days when the men were on the sea, and the women waited."

"I'd rather think of my man on the sea, even if I had to wait for him, Ducky, than shut up in office, stagnating."

The door-bell rang suddenly. It was a dreadful night for any one to be out, but Anita, undisturbed and crisp in her white apron and cap, came through the hall. A voice asked a question, and the blood began to pound in my body. Things were blurred for a bit, and when my vision cleared—I saw Olaf in the shine of the candles in the room beyond, with Nancy crushed to him, his bright head bent, the sheer blue of her frock infolding him—the archway of the door framing them like the figures of saints in the stained glass of a church window!

I knew then that I had lost her. But she did not yield at once.

"I love him, of course. But a woman couldn't do a thing like that," was the way she put it to me the next morning.

I felt, however, that Olaf would master her. Will was set against will, mind against mind. And at last she showed him the way. "A thousand years ago you would have carried me off."

I can see him now as he caught the idea and laughed at her. "Whether you go of your own accord or I carry you, you will be happy." He lifted her in his strong hands as if she were a feather, held her, kissed her, and flashed a glance at me. "You see how easy it would be, and there's a chaplain on board."

There is not much more to tell. Nancy went down one morning to the beach for her bath—and the fog swallowed her up. I have often wondered whether she planned it, or whether, knowing that she would be there, he had come in his launch and had borne her away struggling, but not, I am sure, unwilling. However it happened, the cloak went with her, and I like to think that she was held in his arms, wrapped in it, when they reached the ship.

I like to think, too, of my Nancy in the glowing room with the wolfskins and the strange old tapestry—and the storms beating helpless against her happiness.

I like to think of her as safe in that hidden land, where most of us fain would follow her—the mistress of that guarded mansion, the wife of a young sea god, the mother of a new race.

But, most of all, I like to think of the children. And I have but one wish for a long life, which might otherwise weigh upon me, that the years may bring back to the world those prophets from a hidden land, those young voices crying from the wilderness—the children of Olaf and of Nancy Greer.

I

A woman, who under sentence of death could plan immediately for a trip to the circus, might seem at first thought incredibly light-minded.

You had, however, to know Anne Dunbar and the ten years of her married life to understand. Her husband was fifteen years her senior, and he had few illusions. He had fallen in love with Anne because of a certain gay youth in her which had endured throughout the days of a dreadful operation and a slow convalescence. He had been her surgeon, and, propped up in bed, Anne's gray eyes had shone upon him, the red-gold curls of her cropped hair had given her a look of almost boyish beauty, and this note of boyishness had been emphasized by the straight slenderness of the figure outlined beneath the white covers.

Anne had married Ridgeley Dunbar because she loved him. And love to Anne had been all fire and flame and spirit. It did not take her long to learn that her husband looked upon love and life as matters of flesh and blood—and bones. By degrees his materialism imposed itself upon Anne. She admired Ridgeley immensely. She worshiped, in fact, the wonder of his day's work. He healed the sick, he cured the halt and blind, and he scoffed at Anne's superstitions—"I can match every one of your Bible miracles. There's nothing to it, my dear. Death is death and life is life—so make the most of it."

Anne tried to make the most of it. But she found it difficult. In the first place her husband was a very busy man. He seemed to be perfectly happy with his cutting people up, and his medical books, and the articles which he wrote about the intricate clockwork inside of us which ticks off the hours from birth to death. Now and then he went out to the theatre with his wife or to dine with friends. But, as a rule, she went alone. She had a limousine, a chauffeur, a low swung touring car—and an electric. Her red hair was still wonderful, and she dressed herself quite understanding in grays and whites and greens. If she did not wear habitually her air of gay youth, it was revived in her now and then when something pleased or excited her. And her eyes would shine as they had shone in the hospital when Ridgeley Dunbar had first bent over her bed.

They shone on Christopher Carr when he came home from the war. He was a friend of her husband. Or rather, as a student in the medical school, he had listened to the lectures of the older man, and had made up his mind to know him personally, and had thus, by sheer persistence, linked their lives together.

Anne had never met him. He had been in India When she had married Ridgeley, and then there had been a few years in Egypt where he had studied some strange germ, of which she could never remember the name. He had plenty of money, hence he was not tied to a practice. But when the war began, he had offered his services, and had made a great record. "He is one of the big men of the future," Ridgeley Dunbar had said.

But when Christopher came back with an infected arm, which might give him trouble, it was not the time to talk of futures. He was invited to spend July at the Dunbars' country home in Connecticut, and Ridgeley brought him out at the week-end.

The Connecticut estate consisted of a rambling stone house, an old-fashioned garden, and beyond the garden a grove of white birches.

"What a heavenly place," Christopher said, toward the end of dinner; "how did you happen to find it?"

"Oh, Anne did it. She motored for weeks, and she bought it because of the birches."

Anne's eyes were shining. "I'll show them to you after dinner."

She had decided at once that she liked Christopher. He still wore his uniform, and had the look of a soldier. But it wasn't that—it was the things he had been saying ever since the soup was served. No one had talked of the war as he talked of it. There had been other doctors whose minds had been on arms and legs—amputated; on wounds and shell shock—And there had been a few who had sentimentalized. But Christopher had seemed neither to resent the frightfulness nor to care about the moral or spiritual consequences. He had found in it all a certain beauty of which he spoke with enthusiasm—"A silver dawn, and a patch of Blue Devils like smoke against it—;" ... "A blood-red sunset, and a lot of airmen streaming across—"

He painted pictures, so that Anne saw battles as if a great brush had splashed them on an invisible canvas. There were just four at the table—the two men, Anne, and her second cousin, Jeanette Ware, who lived the year round in the Connecticut house, and was sixty and slightly deaf, but who wore modern clothes and had a modern mind.

It was not yet dark, and the light of the candles in sconces and on the table met the amethyst light that came through, the wide-flung lattice. Anne's summer gown was something very thin in gray, and she wore an Indian necklace of pierced silver beads. Christopher had sent it to her as a wedding-present and she had always liked it.

When they rose from the table, Christopher said, "Now for the birches."

Somewhere in the distance the telephone rang, and a maid came in to say that Dr. Dunbar was wanted. "Don't wait for me," he said, "I'll follow you."

Jeanette Ware hated the night air, and took her book to the lamp on the screened porch, and so it happened that Anne and Christopher came alone to the grove where the white bodies of the birches shone like slender nymphs through the dusk. A little wind shook their leaves.

"No wonder," said Christopher, looking down at Anne, "that you wanted this—but tell me precisely why."

She tried to tell him, but found it difficult. "I seem to find something here that I thought I had lost."

"What things?"

"Well—guardian angels—do you believe in them?" She spoke lightly, as if it were not in the least serious, but he felt that it was serious.

"I believe in all beautiful things—"

"I used to think when I was a little girl that they were around me when I was asleep—
'Matthew, Mark, Luke, and John—
Bless the bed that I lie on—'"

her laugh was a bit breathless—"but I don't believe in them any more. Ridgeley doesn't, you know. And it does seem silly—"

"Oh, no, it isn't—"

"Ridgeley feels that it is a bit morbid—and perhaps he is right. He says that we must eat and drink and—be merry," she flung out her hands with a little gesture of protest, "but he really isn't merry—"

"I see. He just eats and drinks?" He smiled at her.

"And works. And his work is—wonderful."

They sat down on a stone bench which had been hewn out of solid gray rock. "I wish Ridgeley had time to play," Anne said; "it would be nice for both of us—"

The amethyst light had gone, and the dusk descended. Anne's gray dress was merged into the gray of the rock. She seemed just voice, and phantom outline, and faint rose fragrance. Christopher recognized the scent. He had sent her a precious vial in a sandalwood box. Nothing had seemed too good for the wife of his old friend Dunbar.

"Life for you and Ridgeley," he told her, "should be something more than work or play—it should be infinite adventure."

"Yes. But Ridgeley hasn't time for adventure."

"Oh, he thinks he hasn't—"

As Christopher talked after that, Anne was not sure that he was in earnest. He complained that romance had fallen into disrepute. "With all the modern stories—you know the formula—an ounce of sordidness, a flavor of sensationalism, a dash of sex—" One had to look back for the real thing—Aucassin and Nicolette, and all the rest. "That's why I haven't married."

"Well, I have often wondered."

"If I loved a woman, I should want to make her life all glow and color—and mine—with her—"

Anne's eyes were shining. What a big pleasant boy he was. He seemed so young. He had a way of running his fingers up through his hair. She was aware of the gesture in the dark. Yes, she liked him. And she felt suddenly gay and light-hearted, as she had felt in the days when she first met Ridgeley.

They talked until the stars shone in the tips of the birch trees. Ridgeley did not come, and when they went back to the house, they found that he had been called to New York on an urgent case. He would not return until the following Friday.

Anne and Christopher were thus left together for a week to get acquainted. With only old Jeanette Ware to play propriety.

II

It did not take Christopher long to decide that Ridgeley was no longer in love with his wife. "Of course he would call it love. But he could live just as well without her. He has made a machine of himself."

He spoke to Dunbar one night about Anne. "Do you think she is perfectly well?"

"Why not?"

"There's a touch of breathlessness when we walk. Are you sure about her heart?"

"She has never been strong—" and that had seemed to be the end of it.

But it was not the end of it for Christopher. He watched Anne closely, and once when they climbed a hill together and she gave out, he carried her to the top. He managed to get his ear against her heart, and what he heard drained the blood from his face.

As for Anne, she thought how strong he was—and how fair his hair was with the sun upon it, for he had tucked his cap in his pocket.

That night Christopher again spoke to Ridgeley. "Anne's in a bad way." He told of the walk to the top of the hill.

Ridgeley listened this time, and the next day he took Anne down into his office, and did things to her. "But I don't see why you are doing all this," she complained, as he stuck queer instruments in his ears, and made her draw long breaths while he listened.

"Christopher says you get tired when you walk."

"Well, I do. But there's nothing really the matter, is there?"

There was a great deal the matter, but there was no hint of it in his manner. If she had not been his wife, he would probably have told her the truth—that she had a few months, perhaps a few years ahead of her. He was apt to be frank with his patients. But he was not frank with Anne. He had intended to tell Christopher at once. But Christopher was away for a week.

In the week that he was separated from her, Christopher learned that he loved Anne; that he had been in love with her from the moment that she had stood among the birches—like one of them in her white slenderness—and had talked to him of guardian angels;—"*Matthew, Mark, Luke, and John*!"

He did not believe in saints, nor in the angels whose wings seemed to enfold Anne, but he believed in beauty—and Anne's seemed lighted from within, like an alabaster lamp.

Yet she was very human—and the girl in her and the boy in him had met in the weeks that he had spent with her. They had found a lot of things to do—they had fished in shallow brown streams, they had ridden through miles of lovely country. They had gone forth in search of adventure, and they had found it; in cherries on a tree by the road, and he had climbed the tree and had dropped them down to her, and she had hung them over her ears—He had milked a cow in a pasture as they passed, and they had drunk it with their sandwiches, and had tied up a bill in Anne's fine handkerchief and had knotted it to the halter of the gentle, golden-eared Guernsey.

But they had found more than adventure—they had found romance—shining upon them everywhere. "If I were a gipsy to follow the road, and she could follow it with me," Christopher meditated as he sat in the train on his way back to Anne.

But there was Anne's husband, and Christopher's friend—and more than all there were all the specters of modern life—all the hideous wheels which must turn if Anne were ever to be his—treachery to Ridgeley—the divorce court—and then, himself and Anne, living the aftermath, of it all, facing, perhaps, disillusion—

"Oh, not *that*," Christopher told himself, "she'd never grow less—never anything less than she is—if she could once—care—"

For he did not know whether Anne cared or not. He might guess as he pleased—but there had not been a word between them.

Once more the thought flashed, "If I were a gipsy to follow the road—"

As his train sped through the countryside, he became aware of flaming bill-boards—a circus was showing in the towns—the fences fairly blazed with golden chariots, wild beasts, cheap gods and goddesses, clowns in frilled collars and peaked hats. He remembered a glorious day that he had spent as a boy!

"I'll take Anne," was his sudden decision.

He laughed to himself, and spent the rest of the way in seeing her at it. They would drink pink lemonade, and there would be pop-corn balls—the entrancing smell of sawdust—the beat of the band. He hoped there would be a tom-tom, and some of the dark people from the Far East.

He reached his destination at seven o'clock. Dunbar met him at the station. Anne sat with her husband, and Jeanette was in the back seat. Christopher had, therefore, a side view of Anne as she turned a little that she might talk to him. The glint of her bright hair under her gray sports hat, the light of welcome in her eyes—!

"I am going to take you to the circus to-morrow. Ridgeley, you'll go too?"

Dunbar shook his head. "I've got to get back to town in the morning. And I'm not sure that the excitement will be good for Anne."

"Why not?" quickly. "Aren't you well, Anne?"

She shrugged her shoulders. "Ridgeley seems to think I'm not. But the circus can't hurt me."

Nothing more was said about it. Christopher decided to ask Ridgeley later. But the opportunity did not come until Anne had gone up-stairs, and Dunbar and Christopher were smoking a final cigar on the porch.

"What's the matter with her?" Christopher asked.

Dunbar told him, "She can't get well."

III

Anne, getting ready for bed, on the evening of Christopher's arrival, felt unaccountably tired. His presence had been, perhaps, a bit over-stimulating. It was good to have him back. She scarcely dared admit to herself how good. After dinner she and Ridgeley and Christopher had walked down to the grove of birches. There had been a new moon, and she and Ridgeley had sat on the stone bench with Christopher at their feet. She had leaned her head against her husband's shoulder, and he had put his arm about her in the dark and had drawn her to him. He was rarely demonstrative, and his tenderness had to-night for some reason hurt her. She had learned to do without it.

She had talked very little, but Christopher had talked a great deal. She had been content to listen. He really told such wonderful things—he gave her to-night the full story of her silver beads, and how they had been filched from an ancient temple—and he had bought them from the thief. "Until I saw you wear them, I always had a feeling that they ought to go back to the temple—to the god who had perhaps worn them for a thousand years. If I had known which god, I might have carried them back. But the thief wouldn't tell me."

"It would have done no good to carry them back," Ridgeley had said, "and they are nice for Anne." His big hand had patted his wife's shoulder.

"Oh," Christopher had been eager, "I want you to hear those temple bells some day, Anne. Why won't you take her, Dunbar? Next winter—drop your work, and we'll all go—"

"I've a fat chance of going."

"Haven't you made money enough?"

"It isn't money. You know that. But my patients would set up a howl—"

"Let 'em howl. You've got a life of your own to live, and so has Anne."

Dunbar had hesitated for a moment—then, "Anne's better off here."

Anne, thinking of these things as she got out of her dinner dress and into a sheer negligee of lace and faint blue, wondered why Ridgeley should think she was better off. She wanted to see the things of which Christopher had told her—to hear the temple bells in the dusk—the beat of the tom-tom on white nights.

She stood at the window looking out at the moon. She decided that she could not sleep. She would go down and get a book that she had left on the table. The men were out-of-doors, on the porch; she heard the murmur of their voices.

The voices were distinct as she stood in the library, and Christopher's words came to her, "What's the matter with Anne?"

Then her husband's technical explanation, the scientific name which meant nothing to her, then the crashing climax, "She can't get well."

She gave a quick cry, and when the men got into the room, she was crumpled up on the floor.

Her husband reached her first. "My dear," he said, "you heard?"

"Yes. Do you mean that I am—going to die, Ridgeley?"

There was, of course, no way out of it. "It means, my dear, that I've got to take awfully good care of you. Your heart is bad."

Christopher interposed. "People live for years with a heart like that."

But her eyes sought her husband's. "How long do they live?"

"Many months—perhaps years—without excitement—"

This then had been the reason for his tenderness. He had known that she was going to die, and was sorry. But for ten years she had wanted what he might have given her—what he couldn't give her now—life as she had dreamed of it.

She drew a quivering breath—"It isn't quite fair—is it?"

It didn't seem fair. The two doctors had faced much unfairness of the kind of which she complained. But it was the first time that, for either of them, it had come so close.

They had little comfort to give her, although they attempted certain platitudes, and presently Ridgeley carried her to her room.

IV

She insisted the next morning on going to the circus with Christopher. She had not slept well, and there were shadows under her eyes. The physician in Christopher warred with the man. "You ought to rest," he said at breakfast. Dunbar had gone to New York in accordance with his usual schedule. There were other lives to think of; and Anne, when he had looked in upon her that morning, had seemed almost shockingly callous.

"No, I don't want to stay in bed, Ridgeley. I am going to the circus. I shall follow your prescription—to eat and drink and be merry—"

"I don't think I have put it quite that way, Anne."

"You have. Quite. 'Death is death and life is life—so make the most of it.'"

Perhaps she was cruel. But he knew, too, that she was afraid. "My dear," he said gently, "if you can get any comfort out of your own ideas, it might be better."

"But you believe they are just my own ideas—you don't believe they are true?"

"I should like to think they were true."

"You ought to rest," said Christopher at the breakfast table.

"I ought not. There are to be no more oughts—ever—"

He nodded as if he understood, leaning elbows on the table.

"I am going to pack the days full"—she went on. "Why not? I shall have only a few months—and then—annihilation—"
She flung her question across the table. "You believe that, don't you?"

He evaded. "We sleep—'perchance to dream.'"

"I don't want to dream. They might be horrid dreams—"

250

And then Jeanette came down, and poured their coffee, and asked about the news in the morning paper.

Dressed for her trip to the circus, Anne looked like a girl in her teens—white skirt and short green coat—stout sports shoes and white hat. She wore her silver beads, and Christopher said, "I'm not sure that I would if I were you."

"Why not?"

"In such a crowd."

But she kept them on.

They motored to the circus grounds, and came in out of the white glare to the cool dimness of the tent as if they had dived from the sun-bright surface of the sea. But there the resemblance ceased. Here was no silence, but blatant noise—roar and chatter and shriek, the beat of the tom-tom, the thin piping of a flute—the crash of a band. But it was the thin piping which Christopher followed, guiding Anne with his hand on her arm.

Following the plaintive note, they came at last to the snake-charmer—an old man in a white turban. The snakes were in a covered basket. He sat with his feet under him and piped.

Christopher spoke to him in a strange tongue. The piping broke off abruptly and the man answered with eagerness. There was a quick interchange of phrases.

"I know his village," Christopher said; "he is going to show you his snakes."

A crowd gathered, but the snake-charmer saw only the big man who had spoken to his homesick heart, and the girl with the silver beads. He knew another girl who had had a string of beads like that—and they had brought her luck—a dark-skinned girl, his daughter. Her husband had bestowed the beads on her marriage night, and her first child had been a son.

He put the thin reed to his lips, and blew upon it. The snakes lifted their heads. He drew them up and out of the basket, and put them through their fantastic paces. Then he laid aside his pipe, shut them in their basket, and spoke to Christopher.

"He says that no evil can teach you while you wear the beads," Christopher told Anne.

The old man, with his eyes on her intent face, spoke again. "What you think is evil—cannot be evil," Christopher interpreted. "The gods know best."

They moved toward the inner tent.

"Are you tired?" Christopher asked. "We don't have to stay."

"I want to stay," and so they went in, and presently with a blare of trumpets the great parade began. They looked down on men and women in Roman chariots, men on horseback, women on horseback, on elephants, on camels—painted ladies in howdahs, painted ladies in sedan chairs—Cleopatra, Pompadour—history reduced to pantomime, color imposed upon color, glitter upon glitter, the beat of the tom-tom, the crash of the band, the thin piping, as the white-turbaned snake-charmer showed in the press of the crowd.

Christopher's eyes went to Anne. She was leaning forward, one hand clasping the silver beads. He would have given much to know what was in her mind. How little she was and how young. And how he wanted to get her away from the thing which hung suspended over her like a keen-edged sword.

But to get her away—how? He could never get her away from her thoughts. Unless....

Suddenly he heard her laughing. Two clowns were performing with a lot of little dogs. One of the dogs was a poodle who played the fool. "What a darling," Anne was saying.

There was more than they could look at—each ring seemed a separate circus—one had to have more than a single pair of eyes. Christopher was blind to it all—except when Anne insisted, "Look—look!"

Six acrobats were in the ring—four men and two women. Their tights were of a clear shimmering blue, with silver trunks. One could not tell the women from the men, except by their curled heads, and their smaller stature. They were strong, wholesome, healthy. Christopher knew the quality of that health—hearts that pumped like machines—obedient muscles under satin skins. One of the women whirled in a series of handsprings, like a blue balloon—her body as fluid as quicksilver. If he could only borrow one-tenth of that endurance for Anne—he might keep her for years.

Then came Pantaloon, and Harlequin and Columbine. The old man was funny, but the youth and the girl were exquisite—he, diamond-spangled and lean as a lizard, she in tulle skirts and wreath of flowers. They did all the old tricks of masks and slapping sticks, of pursuit and retreat, but they did them so beautifully that Anne and Christopher sat spellbound—what they were seeing was not two clever actors on a sawdust stage, but love in its springtime—girl and boy—dreams, rapture, radiance.

Then, in a moment, Columbine was dead, and Harlequin wept over her—frost had killed the flower—love and life were at an end.

Christopher was drawing deep breaths. Anne was tense. But now—Columbine was on her feet, and Harlequin was blowing kisses to the audience!

"Let's get out of this," Christopher said, almost roughly, and led Anne down the steps and into the almost deserted outer tent. They looked for the snake-charmer, but he was gone. "Eating rice somewhere or saying his prayers," Christopher surmised.

"How could he know about the gods?" Anne asked, as they drove home.

"They know a great deal—these old men of the East," Christopher told her, and talked for the rest of the way about the strange people among whom he had spent so many years.

V

Ridgeley did not come home to dinner. He telephoned that he would be late. It was close and warm. Christopher, sitting with Anne and Jeanette on the porch, decided that a storm was brewing.

Anne was restless. She went down into the garden, and Christopher followed her. She wore white, and he was aware of the rose scent. He picked a rose for her as he passed through the garden. "Bend your head, and I'll put it in your hair."

"I can't wear pink."

"It is white in the dusk—" He put his hands on her shoulders, stopped her, and stuck the rose behind her ear. Then he let her go.

They came to the grove of birches, and sat down on the stone seat. It had grown dark, and the lightning flashing up from the horizon gave to the birches a spectral whiteness—Anne was a silver statue.

"It was queer," she said, "about the old man at the circus."

"About the beads?"

"Yes. I wonder what he meant, Christopher? *What you think is evil—cannot be evil'?* Do you think he meant—Death?"

He did not answer at once, then he said, abruptly, "Anne, how did it happen that you and Ridgeley drifted apart?"

"Oh, it's hard to tell."

"But tell me."

"Well, when we were first married, I expected so much ... things that girls dream about—that he would always have me in his thoughts, and that our lives would be knit together. I think we both tried hard to have it that way. I used to ride with him on his rounds, and he would tell me about his patients. And at night I'd wait up for him, and have something to eat, and it was—heavenly. Ridgeley was so ... fine. But his practice got so big, and sometimes he wouldn't say a word when I rode with him.... And he would be so late coming in at night, and he'd telephone that I'd better go to bed.... And, well, that was the beginning. I don't think it is really his fault or mine ... it's just ... life."

"It isn't life, and you know it," passionately. "Anne, if you had married me ... do you think...?" He reached out in the dark and took her hand. "Oh, my dear, we might as well talk it out."

She withdrew her hand. "Talk what out?"

"You know. I've learned to care for you an awful lot. I had planned to go away. But I can't go now ... not and leave you to face things alone."

He heard her quick breath. "But I've got to face them."

"But not alone. Anne, do you remember what you said ... this morning? That you were going to pack the days full? And you can't do that without some one to help you. And Ridgeley won't help. Anne, let me do it. Let me take you away from here ... away from Ridgeley. We will go where we can hear the temple bells. We'll ride through the desert ... we'll set our sails for strange harbors. We'll love until we forget everything, but the day, the hour,—the moment! And when the time comes for endless dreams...."

"Christopher...."

"Anne, listen."

"You mustn't say things like that to me ... you must not...!"

"I must. I want you to have happiness. We'll crowd more in to a few short months than some people have in a lifetime. And you have a right to it."

"Would it be happiness?"

"Why not? In a way we are all pushing death ahead of us. Who knows that he will be alive to-morrow? There's this arm of mine ... there's every chance that I'll have trouble with it. And an automobile accident may wreck a honeymoon. You've as much time as thousands who are counting on more."

The lightning flashed and showed the birches writhing.

"But afterward, Christopher, *afterward*...?"

"Well, if it is Heaven, we'll have each other. And if it is Hell ... there were Paolo and Francesca ... and if it is sleep, I'll dream eternally of you! Anne ... Anne, do you love me enough to do it?"

"Christopher, please!"

But the storm was upon them—rain and wind, and the thunder a cannonade. Christopher, brought at last to the knowledge of its menace, picked Anne up in his arms, and ran for shelter. When they reached the house, they found Ridgeley there. He was stern. "It was a bad business to keep her out. She's afraid of storms."

"Were you afraid?" Christopher asked her, as Ridgeley went to look after the awnings.

"I forgot the storm," she said, and did not meet his eyes.

Lying awake in her wide bed, Anne thought it over. She was still shaken by Christopher's vehemence. She had believed him her friend, and had found him her lover—and oh, he had brought back youth to her. If he left her now, how could she stand it—the days with no one but Jeanette Ware, and the soul-shaking knowledge of what was ahead?

And Ridgeley would not care—much. In a week be swallowed up by his work....

She tried to read, but found it difficult. Across each page flamed Christopher's sentences.... "We'll ride through the desert.... We'll set our sails for strange harbors...."

Was that what the old man had meant at the circus.... "What you think is evil—cannot be evil"? Would Christopher give her all that she had hoped of Ridgeley? If she lived to be eighty, she and Ridgeley would—jog. Was Christopher right— "You'll have more happiness in a few months than some people in a lifetime?"

She heard her husband moving about in the next room, the water booming in his bath. A thin line of light showed under his door.

She shut her book and turned out her lamp. The storm had died down and the moon was up. Through the open window she could see beyond the garden to the grove of birches.

Hitherto, the thought of the little grove had been as of a sanctuary. She was aware, suddenly, that it had become a place of contending forces. Were the guardian angels driven out...?

But there weren't any guardian angels! Ridgeley had said that they were silly. And Christopher didn't believe in them. She wished that her mother might have lived to talk it over. Her mother had had no doubts.

The door of her husband's room opened, and he was silhouetted against the light. Coming up to the side of her bed, he found her wide-eyed.

"Can't you sleep, my dear?"

"No."

"I don't want to give you anything."

"I don't want anything."

He sat down by the side of the bed. He had on his blue bathrobe, and the open neck showed his strong white throat. "My dear," he said, "I've been thinking of what you said this morning—about my lack of belief and the effect it has had on yours. And—I'm sorry."

"Being sorry doesn't help any, does it, Ridgeley?"

"I should like to think that you had your old faiths to—comfort you."

She had no answer for that, and presently he said, "Are you warm enough?" and brought an extra blanket, because the air was cool after the storm, and then he bent and kissed her forehead. "Shut your eyes and sleep if you can."

But of course she couldn't sleep. She lay there for hours, weighing what he had said to her against what Christopher had said. Each man was offering her something—Christopher, life at the expense of all her scruples. Ridgeley, the resurrection of burnt-out beliefs.

She shivered a bit under the blanket. It would be heavenly to hear the temple bells—with youth beside her. To drink the wine of life from a brimming cup. But all the time she would be afraid, nothing could take away that fear.—Nothing, nothing, *nothing*.

She was glad that her husband was awake. The thin line of light still showed beneath his door. It would be dreadful to be alone—in the dark. At last she could stand it no longer. She got out of bed, wrapped herself in a robe that lay at the foot of it, and opened the door.

"May I leave it open?"

As her husband turned in his chair, she saw his hand go quickly, as if to cover the paper on which he was writing. "Of course, my dear. Are you afraid?"

"I am always afraid, Ridgeley. Always—"

She put her hands up to her face and began to cry. He came swiftly toward her and took her in his arms. "Hush," he said, "nothing can hurt you, Anne."

VII

When she waked in the morning, it was with, the remembrance of his tenderness. Well, of course he was sorry for her. Anybody would be. But Christopher was sorry, too. And Christopher had something to offer her—more than Ridgeley— yes, it was more—

She was half afraid to go down-stairs. Christopher would be at breakfast on the porch. Jeanette would be there, pouring coffee, and perhaps Ridgeley if he had no calls. And Christopher would talk in his gay young voice—and Ridgeley would read the newspaper, and she and Christopher would make their plans for the day—

She rose and began to dress, but found herself suddenly panic-stricken at the thought of the plans that Christopher might make. If they motored off together, he would talk to her as he had talked in the grove of birches—of the temple bells, and of the desert, and the strange harbors—and how could she be sure that she would be strong enough to resist—and what if she listened, and let him have his way?

She decided to eat her breakfast in bed, and rang for it. A note came up from Christopher. "Don't stay up-stairs. Ridgeley left hours ago, and I shan't enjoy my toast and bacon if you aren't opposite me. I have picked a white rose to put by your plate. And I have a thousand things to say to you—"

His words had a tonic effect. Oh, why not—? What earthly difference would it make? And hadn't Browning said something like that—"*Who knows but the world may end to-night?*"

She was not sure that was quite the way that Browning had put it, and she thought she would like to be sure—she could almost see herself saying it to Christopher.

So she went into her husband's room to get the book.

Ridgeley's books were on the shelf above his desk. They had nothing to do with his medical library—that was down-stairs in his office, and now and then he would bring up a great volume. But he had a literary side, and he had revealed some of it to Anne in the days before he had been too busy. His Browning was marked, and it was not hard to find "The Last Ride." She opened at the right page, and stood reading—an incongruous figure amid Ridgeley's masculine belongings in her sheer negligee of faint blue.

She closed the book, put it back on the shelf, and was moving away, when her eyes were caught by two words—"For Anne," at the top of a sheet of paper which lay on Ridgeley's desk. The entire page was filled with Ridgeley's neat professional script, and in a flash the gesture which he had made the night before returned to her, as if he were trying to hide something from her gaze.

She bent and read....

Oh, was this the way he had spent the hours of the night? Searching for words which might comfort her, might clear away her doubts, might bring hope to her heart?

And he had found things like this: "*My little sister, Death,*" said good St. Francis; ... "*The darkness is no darkness with thee, but the night is as clear as day; the darkness and light to thee are both alike ...*" "*Yea, though I Walk through the Valley of the Shadow ...*" These and many others, truths which had once been a part of her.

She read, avidly. Oh, she had been thirsty—for this! Hungry for this! And *Ridgeley*—! The tears dripped so that she could hardly see the lines. She laid her cheek against the paper, and her tears blistered it.

She carried it into her room. Christopher's note still lay on her pillow. She read it again, but she had no ears now for its call. She rang for her maid. "I shall stay in bed and write some letters."

She wrote to Christopher, after many attempts. "We have been such good, *good* friends. And we mustn't spoil it. Perhaps if you could go away for a time, it would be best for both of us. I am going to believe that some day you will find great happiness. And you would never have found happiness with me, you would have found only—fear. And I know now what the old man meant about the beads—'What you think is evil—cannot be evil.' Christopher, death isn't evil, if it isn't the end of things. And I am going to believe that it is not the end ..."

Christopher went into town before lunch, and later Anne sat alone on the stone bench in her grove of birches. They were serene and still in the gold of the afternoon. Yet last night they had writhed in the storm. She, too, had been swept by a storm.... She missed her playmate—but she had a sense of relief in the absence of her tempestuous lover.

Ridgeley came home that night with news of Christopher's sudden departure. "He found telegrams. He told me to say 'good-bye' to you."

"I am sorry," Anne said, and meant it. Sorry that it had to be—but being sorry could not change it.

After dinner Ridgeley had a call to make, and Anne went up to bed. But she was awake when her husband came in, and the thin line of light showed. She waited until she heard the boom of water in his bath, and then she slipped out of bed and opened the door between. She was propped up in her pillows when he reappeared in his blue bathrobe.

"Hello," he called, "did you want me?"

"Yes, Ridgeley."

He came in. "Anything the matter?"

"No. I'm not sick. But I want to talk."

"About what?"

"This—" She showed him the paper with its caption, "For Anne."

"Ridgeley, did you write it because I was—afraid?" her hand went out to him.

His own went over it. "I think I wrote it because I was afraid."

"You?"

His grip almost hurt her. "My dear, my dear, I haven't believed in things. How could I ... with all the facts that men like me have to deal with? But when I faced ... losing you...! love's *got* to be eternal ..."

"Ridgeley."

"I won't ... lose you. Oh, I know. We've grown apart. I don't know how a man is going to help it ... in this darned whirlpool.... But you've always been right ... here.... I've felt I might ... have you, if I ever had time ..." his voice broke.

"And I thought you didn't care."

"I was afraid of that, and somehow I couldn't get ... back ... to where we began. I was always thinking I would.... And then this came....

"I always hated to kill the things that you believed, Anne. I thought I had to be honest ... that it would be better for you to face the truth.... But which one of us knows the Truth? Not a man among us. And I came across this ... '*Thou fool, that which thou sowest is not quickened except it die* ....' We are all fools—the wisest of us...."

She held out her arms to him, and he gathered her close. She felt that it had been a thousand years since she had prayed, yet she heard herself speaking.... And when he laid her back upon her pillows, she was aware that together they had approached some height from which they would never again descend.

"I'll leave the door open," he said, as he left her. "I shall be reading, and you can see the light."

It seemed as if the light from his room flooded the world. The four posts of her bed once more were tipped with shining saints! She turned on her pillow—beyond the garden, the grove of white birches was steeped in celestial radiance.

"*My little sister, Death*," said good St. Francis.

With her hand under her cheek, she slept at last, as peacefully as a child.

THE EMPEROR'S GHOST

I

I had not known Tom Randolph a week before I was aware that life was not real to him. All his world was a stage, with himself as chief player. He dramatized everything—actions, emotions, income. Thus he made poverty picturesque, love a thing of the stars, the day's work a tragedy, or, if the professors proved kind, a comedy. He ate and drank, as it were, to music, combed his hair and blacked his boots in the glare of footlights; made exits and entrances of a kind unknown to men like myself who lacked his sense of the histrionic.

He was Southern and chivalric. His traditions had to do with the doffed hat and the bent knee. He put woman on a pedestal and kept her there. No man, he contended, was worthy of her—what she gave was by the grace of her own sweet charity!

It will be seen that in all this he missed the modern note. As a boy he had been fed upon Scott, and his later reading had not robbed him of his sense of life as a flamboyant spectacle.

He came to us in college with a beggarly allowance from an impoverished estate owned by his grandfather, a colonel of the Confederacy, who after the war had withdrawn with his widowed daughter to his worthless acres. In due time the daughter had died, and her child had grown up in a world of shadows. On nothing a year the colonel had managed, in some miraculous fashion, to preserve certain hospitable old customs. Distinguished guests still sat at his table and ate ducks cooked to the proper state of rareness, and terrapin in a chafing-dish, with a dash of old sherry. If between these feasts there was famine the world never knew.

It was perhaps from the colonel that Randolph had learned to make poverty picturesque. His clothes were old and his shoes were shabby. But his strength lay in the fact that he did not think of himself as poor. He had so much, you see, that the rest of us lacked. He was a Randolph. He had name, position, ancestry. He was, in short, a gentleman!

I do not think he looked upon any of us as gentlemen, not in the Old Dominion sense. He had come to our small Middle-Western college because it was cheap and his finances would not compass education anywhere else.

In an older man his prejudices would have been insufferable, but his youth and charm made us lenient. We contented ourselves with calling him "Your Highness," and were always flattered when he asked us to his rooms.

His strong suit was hospitality. It was in his blood, of course. When his allowance came he spent it in giving the rest of us a good time. His room was as shabby as himself—a table, an ink-spotted desk, a couch with a disreputable cover, a picture of Washington, a half-dozen books, and a chafing-dish.

The chafing-dish was the hump and the hoof of his festivities. He made rarebits and deviled things with an air that had been handed down from generations of epicures. I can see him now with his black hair in a waving lock on his forehead, in worn slippers and faded corduroy coat, sitting on the edge of the table smoking a long pipe, visualizing himself as the lord of a castle—the rest of us as vassals of a rather agreeable and intelligent sort!

It was perfectly natural that he should stage his first love-affair, and when he was jilted that he should dramatize his despair. For days after Madge Ballou had declared her preference for Dicky Carson, Randolph walked with melancholy. He came to my rooms and sat, a very young and handsome Hamlet, on my fire-bench, with his chin in his hand.

"Why should she like Dicky best?"

"She has no imagination."

"But Dicky's a—beast—"

"With a fat bank-account."

"Money wouldn't count with Madge."

"I'm not so sure—"

"Women are not like that, MacDonald."

I saw, as he went on with his arguments, that she had become to him an Ophelia, weakly led. Women in his lexicon of romance might be weak but never mercenary. I think he finally overthrew her in his mind with "*Get thee to a nunnery!*" I know that he burned her picture; he showed me the ashes in a silver stamp-box.

He had, of course, his heroes—there were moments when unconsciously he aped them. It was after a debate that the boys began to call him "Bonaparte." He had defended the Little Corporal, and in defending him had personified him. With that dark lock over his forehead, his arms folded, he had flung defiance to the deputies, and for that moment he had been not Tom Randolph but the Emperor himself.

He won the debate, amid much acclaim, and when he came down to us I will confess to a feeling, which I think the others shared, of a soul within his body which did not belong there. Tom Randolph was, of course, Tom Randolph, but the voice which had spoken to us had rung with the power of that other voice which had been stilled at St. Helena!

The days that followed dispelled the illusion, but the name clung to him. I think he liked it, and emphasized the resemblance. He let his hair grow long, sunk his head between his shoulders, was quick and imperious in his speech.

Then came the war. Belgium devastated, France invaded. Randolph was fired at once.

"I'm going over."

"But, my dear fellow—"

"There's our debt to Lafayette."

With his mind made up there was no moving him. The rest of us held back. Our imaginations did not grasp at once the world's need of us.

But Randolph saw himself a Henry of Navarre—*white plumes*; a Richard of the Lion Heart—*crusades and red crosses*; a Cyrano without the nose—"*These be cadets of Gascony—*"

"You see, MacDonald," he said, flaming, "we Randolphs have always done it."

"Done what?"

"Fought. There's been a Randolph in every war over here, and before that in a long line of battles—"

He told me a great deal about the ancient Randolphs, and the way they had fought on caparisoned steeds with lances.

"War to-day is different," I warned him. "Not so pictorial."

But I knew even then that he would make it pictorial. He would wear his khaki like chain armor.

He gave us a farewell feast in his room. It was the season for young squirrels, and he made us a Brunswick stew. It was the best thing I had ever tasted, with red peppers in it and onions, and he served it with an old silver ladle which he had brought from home.

While we ate he talked of war, of why men should fight—"for your own honor and your country's."

There were pacifists among us and they challenged him. He flung them off; their protests died before his passion.

"We are men, not varlets!"

Nobody laughed at him. It showed his power over us that none of us laughed. We simply sat there and listened while he told us what he thought of us.

At last one who was braver than the rest cried out: "Go to it, Bonaparte!"

In a sudden flashing change Randolph hunched his shoulders, set his slouched hat sidewise low on his brows, wrapped the couch-cover like a cloak about him. His glance swept the room. There was no anger in it, just a sort of triumphant mockery as he gave the famous speech to Berthier.

"They send us a challenge in which our honor is at stake—a thing a Frenchman has never refused—and since a beautiful queen wishes to be a witness to the combat, let us be courteous, and in order not to keep her waiting, *let us march without sleeping as far as Saxony—*!"

I can't tell you of the effect it had on us. We were gripped by the throats, and the room was so still that we heard ourselves breathe. Four of the fellows left next day with Randolph. I think he might have taken us all if we had not been advised and held back by the protests of our professors, who spoke of war with abhorrence.

II

Three years later I saw him again, in France. Our own country had gotten into the fight by that time, and I was caught in the first draft. I had heard now and then from Randolph. He had worked for nearly three years with the Ambulance Corps, and was now fighting for democracy with his fellows.

We had been shivering in the rain for a week in one of the recaptured French towns when a group of seasoned officers were sent to lick us into shape. Among the other officers was Randolph, and when he came upon me he gave a shout of welcome.

"Good old MacDonald—at last!"

I'll confess that his "at last" carried a sting, and I remember feeling the injustice of our equal rank, as I set his years of privation and hardship against my few weeks in a training camp.

He was very glad to see me, and the very first night he made me a Brunswick stew. This time there were no squirrels, but he begged young rabbits from the old couple who had once been servants in the château where we were billeted. They had trudged back at once on the retirement of the Boches, and were making the best of the changed conditions.

There was, of course, no chafing-dish, and the stew was cooked in an iron pot which hung over an open fire in the ancient kitchen. Before they sold the rabbits the old people had made one condition:

"If we may have a bit for mademoiselle—?"

"For mademoiselle?"

"She is here with us, monsieur. She had not been well. We have been saving the rabbits for her."

Randolph made the grand gesture that I so well remembered.

"My good people—if she would dine with us—?"

The old woman shook her head. She was not sure. She would see.

Perhaps she said pleasant things of us, perhaps mademoiselle was lonely. But whatever the reason, mademoiselle consented to dine, coming out of her seclusion, very thin and dark and small, but self-possessed.

I have often wondered what she thought, in those first moments of meeting, of Randolph, as with a spoon for a sceptre, the manner of a king, he presided over the feast. She spoke very good English, but needed to have many things explained.

"Do gentlemen cook in your country?"

Randolph sketched life as he had known it on his grandfather's plantation—negroes to do it all, except when gentlemen pleased.

She drew the mantle of her distaste about her. "Black men? I shouldn't like it."

Well, I saw before the evening ended that Randolph had met his peer. For every one of his aristocratic prejudices she matched him with a dozen. And he loved her for it! At last here was a lady who would buckle on his armor, watch his shield, tie her token on his sleeve!

He sat on the edge of the table in his favorite attitude—hunched-up shoulders, folded arms. His hair was cut too short now for the dark lock, but even without it I saw her glance at him now and then in a puzzled fashion, as if she weighed some familiar memory.

But it was one of the peasants who voiced it—the old man carrying away the remains of the stew muttered among the shadows to his wife:

"C'est Napoleon."

Mademoiselle caught her breath. "Oui, Gaston." Then to me, in English: "Do you see it?"

"Yes. We called him that at school."

"Bonaparte?"

"Yes."

She was thin and dark no longer—illumined, the color staining her cheeks. "Oh, if he were here—to save France!"

I protested. "An emperor against an emperor?"

"He was a great democrat—he loved the common people. For a little while power spoiled him—but he loved the people. And the Bourbons did not love them—Louis laughed at them—and lost his head. And Napoleon never laughed. He loved France—if he had lived he would have saved us."

Out of the shadows the old woman spoke. "They say he will come again."

"Oui, Margot." Mademoiselle was standing, with her hand on her heart. Randolph's eyes devoured her. He had taken no part in the conversation. It was almost uncanny to see him sitting there, silent, arms folded, shoulders hunched, sparkling eyes missing nothing. "It is true," mademoiselle told us earnestly, "that the tra-dee-tion says he will come back—when France needs him—the soldiers talk of it."

"In almost every country," I said, "there is a story like that, of heroes who will come again."

"But Napoleon, monsieur—surely he would not fail France?"

The thing that followed was inevitable. Randolph and Mademoiselle Julie fell in love with each other. He drew her as he had drawn us at school. She was not a Madge Ballou, mundane and mercenary; she was rather a Heloise, a Nicolette, a Jeanne d'Arc, self-sacrificing, impassioned. She met Randolph on equal ground. They soared together—mixed love of country with love of lovers. They rose at dawn to worship the sun, they walked forth at twilight to adore together the crescent moon.

And all the while war was at the gates; we could hear the boom of big guns. The spring drive was on and the Germans were coming back.

257

I shall never forget the night that Randolph and I were ordered to the front. Mademoiselle had come in with her hands full of violets. Randolph, meeting her for the first time after a busy day, took her hands and the frail blossoms in his eager clasp. He was an almost perfect lover—Aucassin if you will—Abelard at his best.

"Violets," he said. "May I have three?"

"Why three, monsieur?"

"For love, mademoiselle, and truth and constancy."

He took his prayer-book from his pocket, and she gave him the violets. He touched them to her lips, then crushed them to his own. I saw it—sitting back in the shadows. I should never have thought of kissing a girl like that. But it was rather wonderful.

He shut the violets in the little book.

They sat very late that night by the fire. I went in and out, not disturbing them. I saw him kneel at her feet as he left her, and she bent forward and kissed his forehead.

He talked of her a great deal after that. More than I would have talked of love, but his need of an audience drove him to confidences. He felt that he must make himself worthy of her—to go back to her as anything less than a hero might seem to belittle her. I am not sure that he was braver than other men, but his feeling for effect gave him a sort of reckless courage. Applause was a part of the game—he could not do without it.

And so came that night when a small band of us were cut off from the rest. We were intrenched behind a small eminence which hid us from our enemies, with little hope of long escaping their observation. It had been wet and cold, and there had been no hot food for days. We, French and Americans, had fought long and hard; we were in no state to stand suspense, yet there was nothing to do but wait for a move on the other side, a move which could end in only one way—bayonets and bare hands, and I, for one, hated it.

I think the others hated it, too, all but Randolph. The rain had stopped and the moon flooded the world. He turned his face up to it and dreamed.

The knowledge came to us before midnight that the Huns had found us. It became only a matter of moments before they would be upon us, the thing would happen which we hated—bayonets and bare hands, with the chances in favor of the enemy!

Somewhere among our men rose a whimper of fear, and then another. You see, they were cold and hungry and some of them were wounded, and they were cut off from hope. It wasn't cowardice. I call no man a coward. They had faced death a thousand times, some of them. Yet there was danger in their fears.

Randolph was next to me. "My God, MacDonald," he said, "they've lost their nerve—"

There wasn't a second to spare. I saw him doing something to his hat.

As I have said, there was a moon. It lighted that battle-scarred world with a sort of wild beauty, and suddenly in a clear space above us on the little hill a figure showed, motionless against the still white night—a figure small yet commanding, three-cornered hat pulled low—oh, you have seen it in pictures a thousand times—Napoleon of Marengo, of Austerlitz, of Jena, of Friedland—but over and above everything, Napoleon of France!

Of course the Germans shot him. But when they came over the top they were met by Frenchmen who had seen a ghost. "C'est l'Empereur! C'est l'Empereur!" they had gasped. "He returns to lead us."

They fought like devils, and—well, the rest of us fought, too, and all the time, throughout the bloody business, I had before me that vision of Randolph alone in the moonlight. Or was it Randolph? Who knows? Do great souls find time for such small business? And was it small?

His medals were, of course, sent to the colonel. But the violets in the little book went back to mademoiselle. And the old hat, crushed into three-cornered shape, went back. And I told her what he had done.

She wrote to me in her stiff English:

"I have loved a great man. For me, monsieur, it is enough. Their souls unite in victory!"

THE RED CANDLE

It was so cold that the world seemed as stiff and stark as a poet's hell. A little moon was frozen against a pallid sky. The old dark houses with their towers and gables wore the rigid look of iron edifices. The saint over the church door at the corner had an icicle on his nose. Even the street lights shone faint and benumbed through clouded glass.

Ostrander, with his blood like ice within his veins, yearned for a Scriptural purgatory with red fire and flame. To be warm would be heaven. It was a wise old Dante who had made hell cold!

As he crossed the threshold of his filthy tenement he felt for the first time a sense of its shelter. Within its walls there was something that approached warmth, and in his room at the top there was a bed with a blanket.

Making his way toward the bed and its promise of comfort, he was stopped on the second stairway by a voice which came out of the dark.

"Mr. Tony, you didn't see our tree."

Peering down, he answered the voice: "I was going up to get warm."

"Milly said to tell you that we had a fire."

"A real fire, Pussy? I didn't know that there was one in the world."

He came down again to the first floor. Pussy was waiting—a freckled dot of a child tied up in a man's coat.

The fire was in a small round stove. On top of the stove something was boiling. The room was neat but bare, the stove, a table, and three chairs its only furnishing. In a room beyond were two beds covered with patchwork quilts.

On the table was a tree. It was a Christmas tree—just a branch of pine and some cheap spangly things. The mother of the children sewed all day and late into the night. She had worked a little longer each night for a month that the children might have the tree.

There was no light in the room but that of a small and smoky lamp.

Milly spoke of it. "We ought to have candles."

Ostrander, shrugged close to the stove, with his hands out to its heat, knew that they ought to have electric lights, colored ones, a hundred perhaps, and a tree that touched the stars!

But he said: "When I go out I'll bring you a red candle—a long one—and we'll put it on the shelf over the table."

Milly, who was resting her tired young body in a big rocker with the baby in her arms, asked: "Can we put it in a bottle or stand it in a cup? We haven't any candlestick."

"We can do better than that," he told her, "with a saucer turned upside down and covered with salt to look like snow."

Pussy, economically anxious, asked, "Can we eat the salt afterward?"

"Of course."

"Then, may we do it, Milly?"

"Darling, yes. How nice you always fix things, Mr. Tony!"

Long before he had known them he had fixed things—things which would have turned this poor room into an Aladdin's palace. There was that Christmas Eve at the Daltons'. It had been his idea to light the great hall with a thousand candles when they brought in the Yule log, and to throw perfumed fagots on the fire.

He came back to the round stove and the tiny tree. "I like to fix things," he said. "Once upon a time—"

They leaned forward eagerly to this opening.

"Of course you know it isn't true," he prefaced.

"Of course it couldn't be true"—Pussy was reassuringly sceptical—"the things that you tell us couldn't really happen— ever—"

"Well, once upon a time, there was a tree in a great house by a great river, and it was set in a great room with squares of black-and-white marble for a floor, and with a fountain with goldfish swimming in its basin, and there were red-and-blue parrots on perches, and orange-trees in porcelain pots, and the tree itself wasn't a pine-tree or a fir or a cedar; it was a queer round, clipped thing of yew, and it had red and blue and orange balls on it, and in the place of a wax angel on top there was a golden Buddha, and there were no candles—but the light shone out and out of it, like the light shines from the moon."

"Was it a Christmas tree?" Pussy asked, as he paused.

"Yes, but the people who trimmed it and the ones who came to see it didn't believe in the Wise Men, or the Babe in the Manger, or the shepherds who watched their flocks by night—they just worshiped beauty and art—and other gods—but it was a corking tree—"

"You use such funny words," Pussy crowed ecstatically. "Who ever heard of a corking tree?"

He smiled at her indulgently. He was warmer now, and as he leaned back in his chair and unbuttoned his coat he seemed to melt suddenly into something that was quite gentlemanly in pose and outline. "Well, it really was a corking tree, Pussy."

"What's a Buddha?" Milly asked, making a young Madonna of herself as she bent over the baby.

"A gentle god that half of the world worships," Ostrander said, "but the people who put him on the tree didn't worship anything—they put him there because he was of gold and ivory and was a lovely thing to look at—"

"Oh," said Pussy, with her mouth round to say it, "oh, how funny you talk, Mr. Tony!" She laughed, with her small hands beating her knees.

She was presently, however, very serious, as she set the table. There was little formality of service. Just three plates and some bread.

Milly, having carried the baby into the other room, was hesitatingly hospitable. "Won't you have supper with us, Mr. Tony?"

He wanted it. There was a savory smell as Milly lifted the pot from the stove. But he knew there would be only three potatoes—one for Pussy and one for Milly and one for the mother who was almost due, and there would be plenty of gravy. How queer it seemed that his mind should dwell on gravy!

259

"Onions are so high," Milly had said, as she stirred it. "I had to put in just a very little piece."

He declined hastily and got away.

In the hall he met their mother coming in. She was a busy little mother, and she did not approve of Ostrander. She did not approve of any human being who would not work.

"A merry Christmas," he said to her, standing somewhat wistfully above her on the stairs.

She smiled at that. "Oh, Mr. Tony, Mr. Tony, they want a man in the shop. It would be a good way to begin the New Year."

"Dear lady, I have never worked in a shop—and they wouldn't want me after the first minute—"

Her puzzled eyes studied him. "Why wouldn't they want you?"

"I am not—dependable—"

"How old are you?" she asked abruptly.

"Twice your age—"

"Nonsense—"

"Not in years, perhaps—but I have lived—oh, how I have lived—!"

He straightened his shoulders and ran his fingers through his hair. She had a sudden vision of what he might be if shorn of his poverty. There was something debonair—finished—an almost youthful grace—a hint of manner—

She sighed. "Oh, the waste of it!"

"Of what?"

She flamed. "Of you!"

Then she went in and shut the door.

He stood uncertainly in the hall. Then once again he faced the cold.

Around the corner was a shop where he would buy the red candle. The ten cents which he would pay was to have gone for his breakfast. He had sacrificed his supper that he might not go hungry on Christmas morning. He had planned a brace of rolls and a bottle of milk. It had seemed to him that he could face a lean night with the promise of these.

There were no red candles in the shop. There were white ones, but a red candle was a red candle—with a special look of Christmas cheer. He would have no other.

The turn of a second corner brought him to the great square. Usually he avoided it. The blaze of gold on the west side was the club.

A row of motors lined the curb. There was Baxter's limousine and Fenton's French car. He knew them all. He remembered when his own French car had overshadowed Fenton's Ford.

There were wreaths to-night in the club windows, and when Sands opened the doors there was a mass of poinsettia against the hall mirror.

How warm it looked with all that gold and red!

In the basement was the grill. It was a night when one might order something heavy and hot. A planked steak—with deviled oysters at the start and a salad at the end.

And now another motor-car was poking its nose against the curb. And Whiting climbed out, a bear in a big fur coat.

Whiting's car was a closed one. And it would stay there for an hour. Ostrander knew the habits of the man. From the office to the club, and from the club—home. Whiting was methodical to a minute. At seven sharp the doors would open and let him out.

The clock on the post-office tower showed six!

There was a policeman on the east corner, beating his arms against the cold. Ostrander did not beat his arms. He cowered frozenly in the shadow of a big building until the policeman passed on.

Then he darted across the street and into Whiting's car!

Whiting, coming out in forty minutes, found his car gone. Sands, the door man, said that he had noticed nothing. The policeman on the corner had not noticed.

"I usually stay longer," Whiting said, "but to-night I wanted to get home. I have a lot of things for the kids."

"Were the things in your car?" the policeman asked.

"Yes. Toys and all that—"

Ostrander, with his hand on the wheel, his feet on the brakes, slipped through the crowded streets unchallenged. It had been easy to unlock the car. He had learned many things in these later years.

It was several minutes before he was aware of faint fragrances—warm tropical fragrances of flowers and fruits and spices—Christmas fragrances which sent him back to the great kitchen where his grandmother's servants had baked and brewed.

He stopped the car and touched a button. The light showed booty. He had not expected this. He had wanted the car for an hour, to feel the thrill of it under his fingers, to taste again the luxury of its warmth and softness. He had meant to take it back unharmed—with nothing more than the restless ghost of his poor desires to haunt Whiting when again he entered it.

But now here were toys and things which Whiting, in a climax of generosity, had culled from bake-shop and grocer, from flower-shop, fruit-shop, and confectioner.

He snapped out the light and drove on. He had still a half-hour for his adventure.

It took just three of the thirty minutes to slide up to the curb in front of the tall tenement. He made three trips in and up to the top floor. He risked much, but Fate was with him and he met no one.

Fate was with him, too, when he left the car at a corner near the club, and slipped out of it like a shadow, and thence like a shadow back to the shop whence his steps had tended before his adventures.

When he returned to the tall tenement the small family on the first floor had finished supper, and the mother had gone back to work. The baby was asleep. Milly and Pussy, wrapped up to their ears, were hugging the waning warmth of the little stove.

"Mr. Tony, did you get the candle?" Pussy asked as he came in.

"Yes. But I've been thinking"—his manner was mysterious—"I don't want to put it on the shelf. I want it in the window—to shine out—"

"To shine out—why?"

"Well, you know, there's St. Nicholas."

"Oh—"

"He ought to come here, Pussy. Why shouldn't he come here? Why should he go up-town and up-town, and take all the things to children who have more than they want?"

Milly was philosophic. "St. Nicholas is fathers and mothers—"

But Pussy was not so sure. "Do you think he'd come—if we did? Do you really and truly think he would?"

"I think he might—"

The candle set in the window made a fine show from the street. They all went out to look at it. Coming in, they sat around the stove together.

Pussy drew her chair very close to Ostrander. She laid her hand on his knee. It was a little hand with short, fat fingers. In spite of lean living, Pussy had managed to keep fat. She was adorably dimpled.

Ostrander, looking down at the fat little hand, began: "Once upon a time—there was a doll—a Fluffy Ruffles doll, in a rosy gown—"

"Oh!" Pussy beat the small, fat hand upon his knee.

"And pink slippers—and it traveled miles to find some one to—love it. And at last it said to St. Nicholas, 'Oh, dear St. Nick, I want to find a little girl who hasn't any doll—'"

"Like me?" said Pussy.

"Like you—"

"And St. Nicholas said, 'Will you keep your pink slippers clean and your nice pink frock clean if I give you to a poor little girl?' and the Fluffy Ruffles doll said 'Yes,' so St. Nicholas looked and looked for a poor little girl, and at last he came to a window—with a red candle—"

The fat little hand was still and Pussy was breathing hard.

"With a red candle, and there was a little girl who—didn't have any doll—"

Pussy threw herself on him bodily. "Is it true? Is it true?" she shrieked.

Milly, a little flushed and excited by the story, tried to say sedately: "Of course it isn't true. It couldn't be—true—"

"Let's wish it to be true—" Ostrander said, "all three of us, with our eyes shut—"

With this ceremony completed the little girls were advised gravely to go to bed. "If Fluffy Ruffles and old St. Nick come by and find you up they won't stop—"

"Won't they?"

"Of course not. You must shut the door and creep under your quilt and cover up your head, and if you hear a noise you mustn't look."

Milly eyed him dubiously. "I think it is a shame to tell Pussy such—"

"Corking things?" He lifted her chin with a light finger and looked into her innocent eyes. "Oh, Milly, Milly, once upon a time there was a Princess, with eyes like yours, and she lived in a garden where black swans swam on a pool, and she wore pale-green gowns and there were poppies in the garden. And a Fool loved her. But she shut him out of the garden. He wasn't good enough even to kneel at her feet, so she shut him out and married a Prince with a white feather in his cap."

He had a chuckling sense of Whiting as the white-feathered Prince. But Milly's eyes were clouded. "I don't like to think that she shut the poor Fool out of the garden."

For a moment he cupped her troubled face in his two hands. "You dear kiddie." Then as he turned away he found his own eyes wet.

As he started up-stairs Pussy peeped out at him.

"Wouldn't it be—corking—to see a Fluffy Ruffles doll—a-walking up the street?"

In a beautiful box up-stairs the Fluffy Ruffles doll stared at him. She was as lovely as a dream, and as expensive as they make 'em. There was another doll in blue, also as expensive, also as lovely. Ostrander could see Milly with the blue doll matching her eyes.

There were toys, too, for the baby. And there was a bunch of violets. And boxes of candy. And books. And there were things to eat. Besides the fruits a great cake, and a basket of marmalades and jellies and gold-sealed bottles and meat pastes in china jars, and imported things in glass, and biscuits in tins.

Ostrander, after some consideration, opened the tin of biscuits and, munching, he wrote a note. Having no paper, he tore a wrapper from one of the boxes. He had the stub of a pencil, and the result was a scrawl.

"MY DEAR WHITING:

"It was I who borrowed your car—and who ran away with your junk. I am putting my address at the head of this, so that if you want it back you can come and get it. But perhaps you won't want it back.

"I have a feeling that to you and your wife I am as good as dead. If you have any thought of me it is, I am sure, to pity me. Yet I rather fancy that you needn't. I am down and out, and living on ten dollars a month. That's all I got when the crash came—it is all I shall ever get. I pay four dollars a month for my room and twenty cents a day for food. Sometimes I pay less than twenty cents when I find myself in need of other—luxuries. Yet there's an adventure in it, Whiting. A good little woman who lives in this house begs me to work. But I have never worked. And why begin? I've a heritage of bad habits, and one does not wish to seem superior to one's ancestors.

"The winters are the worst. I spend the summers on the open road. Ask Marion if she remembers the days when we read Stevenson together in the garden? Tell her it is like that—under the stars—Tell her that I am getting more out of it than she is—with you—

"But the winters send me back to town—and this winter Fate has brought me to an old house in a shabby street just a bit back from the Club. On the first floor there is a little family. Three kiddies and a young mother who works to keep the wolf from the door. There's a Pussy-Kiddie, and a Milly-Kiddie, and a baby, and they have adopted me as a friend.

"And this Christmas I had nothing to give them—but a red candle to light their room.

"When I got into your car it was just for the adventure. To breathe for a moment the air I once breathed—to fancy that Marion's ghost might sit beside me for one little moment, as she will sit beside you to the end of your days.

"I have played all roles but that of robber—but when I saw the things that you had bought with Marion's money for Marion's children—it went to my head—and I wanted them in the worst way for those poor kiddies—who haven't any dolls or Christmas dinners.

"I am playing Santa Claus for them to-night. I shall take the things down and leave them in their poor rooms. It will be up to you to come and take them away. It will be up to you, too, to give this note to the police and steal my freedom.

"You used to be a good sport, Whiting. I have nothing against you except that you stole Marion—perhaps this will square our accounts. And if your children are, because of me, without their dolls to-morrow, you can remember this, that the kiddies are happy below stairs—since Dick Turpin dwells aloft!

"From among the rest I have chosen for myself a squat bottle, a box of biscuits, and a tin of the little imported sausages that you taught me to like.

"Well, my dear fellow, happy days! To-morrow morning I shall breakfast at your expense, unless you shall decide that I must breakfast behind bars.

"If you should come to-night, you will find in the window a red candle shining. They have put it there to guide St. Nicholas and a certain Fluffy Ruffles doll!

"Ever   yours,
    "Tony."

He found an envelope, sealed, and addressed it. Then he went to work.

Four trips he made down the stairs. Four times he tiptoed into the shadowed room, where the long red candle burned. And when he turned to take a last look there on the table beside the tree stood the blue doll for Milly and the Fluffy Ruffles doll for Pussy and the rattles and rings and blocks for the baby, and on the chairs and the shelf above the tree were the other things—the great cake and the fruit and the big basket and the boxes of candy.

And for the little mother there were the violets and a note:

"The red candle winked at your window and brought me in. It is useless to search for me—for now and then a Prince passes and goes on. And he is none the less a Prince because you do not know him."

And now there was that other note to deliver. Out in the cold once more, he found the moon gone and the snow falling. As he passed the saint on the old church, it seemed to smile down at him. The towers and gables were sheeted with white. His footsteps made no sound on the padded streets.

He left the note at Whiting's door. He fancied that, as the footman held it open, he saw Marion shining on the stairs!

He was glad after that to get home and to bed, and to the warmth of his blanket. There was the warmth, too, of the wine.

In a little while he was asleep. On the table by his untidy bed was the box of biscuits and the bottle and the tin of tiny sausages.

If all went well he would feast like a lord on Christmas morning!

RETURNED GOODS

Perhaps the most humiliating moment of Dulcie Cowan's childhood had been when Mary Dean had called her Indian giver. Dulcie was a child of affluence. She had always had everything she wanted; but she had not been spoiled. She had been brought up beautifully and she had been taught to consider the rights of others. She lived in an old-fashioned part of an old city, and her family was churchly and conscientious. Indeed, so well-trained was Dulcie's conscience that it often caused her great unhappiness. It seemed to her that her life was made up largely of denying herself the things she wanted. She was tied so rigidly to the golden rule that her own rights were being constantly submerged in the consideration of the rights of others.

So it had happened that when she gave to Mary Dean a certain lovely doll, because her mother had suggested that Dulcie had so many and Mary so few, Dulcie had spent a night of agonized loneliness. Then she had gone to Mary.

"I want my Peggy back."

"You gave her to me."

"But I didn't know how much I loved her, Mary. I'll buy you a nice new doll, but I want my Peggy back."

It was then that Mary had called her Indian giver. Mary had been a sturdy little thing with tight-braided brown hair. She had worn on that historic occasion a plain blue gingham with a white collar. To the ordinary eye she seemed just an every-day freckled sort of child, but to Dulcie she had been a little dancing devil, as she had stuck out her forefinger and jeered "Indian giver!"

Dulcie had held to her point and had carried her Peggy off in triumph. Mary, with characteristic independence, had refused to accept the beautiful doll which Dulcie bought with the last cent of her allowance and brought as a peace offering. In later years they grew to be rather good friends. They might, indeed, have been intimate, if it had not been for Dulcie's money and Mary's dislike of anything which savored of patronage.

It was Mary's almost boyish independence that drew Mills Richardson to her. Mills wrote books and was the editor of a small magazine. He came to board with Mary's mother because of the quiet neighborhood. He was rather handsome in a dark slender fashion. He had the instincts of a poet, and he was not in the least practical. He needed a prop to lean on, and Mary gradually became the prop.

She was teaching by that time, but she helped her mother with the boarders. When Mills came in late at night she would have something for him in the dining-room—oysters or a club sandwich or a pot of coffee—and she and her mother and Mills would have a cozy time of it. In due season Mills asked her to marry him, and his dreams had to do with increased snugness and with shelter from the outside world.

They had been engaged three months when Dulcie came home from college. There was nothing independent or practical about Dulcie. She was a real romantic lady, and she appealed to Mills on the æsthetic side. He saw her first in church with the light shining on her from a stained-glass window. In the middle of that same week Mrs. Cowan gave a garden party as a home-coming celebration for her daughter. Dulcie wore embroidered white and a floppy hat, and her eyes when she talked to Mills were worshipful.

He found himself swayed at last by a grand passion. He thought of Dulcie by day and dreamed of her by night. Then he met her by accident one afternoon on Connecticut Avenue, and they walked down together to the Speedway, where the willows were blowing in the wind and the water was ruffled; and there with the shining city back of them and the Virginia hills ahead, Mills, flaming, declared his passion, and Dulcie, trembling, confessed that she too cared.

Mills grew tragic: "Oh, my beloved, have you come too late?"

Dulcie had not heard of his engagement to Mary. Mills told her, and that settled it. She had very decided ideas on such matters. A man had no right to fall in love with two women. If such a thing happened, there was only one way out of it. He had given his promise and he must keep it. He begged, but could not shake her. She cared a great deal, but she would not take him away from Mary.

Mary knew nothing of what had occurred; she thought that Mills was working too hard. She was working hard herself, but she was very happy. She had a hope chest and sat up sewing late o' nights.

Before Mary and Mills were married Dulcie's mother died, and Dulcie went abroad to live with an aunt. Five years later she married an American living in Paris. He was much older than she, and it was rumored that she was not happy. Ten years after her marriage she returned to Washington a widow.

It was at once apparent that she had changed. She wore charming but sophisticated clothes, made on youthful lines so that she seemed nearer twenty-five than thirty-five. Her hair was still soft and shining. She had been a pretty girl, she was a beautiful woman. But the greatest change was in her attitude toward life. In Paris her golden-rule philosophy had been turned topsy-turvy.

Hence when she met Mills and found the old flames lighted in his eyes, she stirred the ashes of her dead romance and discovered a spark. It was pleasant after that to talk with him in dim corners at people's houses. Now and then she invited him and Mary to her own big house with plenty of other guests, so that she was not missed if she walked with Mills in the garden. She meant no harm and she was really fond of Mary.

The years had not been so kind to Mills as to Dulcie. They had stolen some of his slenderness, and his hair was thin at the back. But he wrote better books, and it was Mary who had helped him write them. She had made of his house a home. She was still the same sturdy soul. Her bright color had faded and her hair was gray. Life with Mills had not been an easy road to travel. She had traveled it with loss of youth, perhaps, but with no loss of self-respect. She knew that her husband was in some measure what he was because of her. She had kept the children away from his study door; she had seen that he was nourished and sustained. She had prodded him at times to increased activities. He had resented the prodding, but it had resulted in a continuity of effort which had added to his income.

Dulcie came into Mary's life as something very fresh and stimulating. She spoke of it to Mills.

"It is almost as if I had been abroad to hear her talk. She has had such interesting experiences."

It was not Dulcie's experiences which interested Mills; it was the loveliness of her profile, the glint of her hair, the youth in her, the renewed urge of youth in himself.

Priscilla Dodd saw what had happened. Priscilla was the aunt with whom Dulcie had lived in Paris; and she was a wise, if worldly, old woman. She saw rocks ahead for Dulcie.

"He's in love with you, my dear."

Dulcie, in a rose satin house coat which shone richly in the flame of Aunt Priscilla's open fire, was not disconcerted.

"I know. Mary doesn't satisfy him, Aunt Cilla."

"And you do?"

"Yes."

"The less you see of him the better."

"I'm not sure of that."

"Why not?"

"I can inspire him, be the torch to illumine his path."

"So that's the way you are putting it to yourself! But how will Mary like that?"

"Oh, Mary"—Dulcie moved restlessly—"I don't want to hurt Mary. I don't want to hurt Mary," she said again, out of a long silence, "but after all I have a right to save Mills' soul for him, haven't I, Aunt Cilla?"

"Saving souls had better be left to those who make a business of it."

"I mean his poetic soul." Dulcie studied the toes of her rosy slippers. "A man can't live by bread alone."

Yet Mills had thrived rather well on the bread that Mary had given him, and there was this to say for Mills, he was very fond of his wife. She was not the love of his life, but she had been a helpmate for many years. He felt that he owed many things to her affection and strength. Like Dulcie, he shrank from making her unhappy.

It was because of Mary, therefore, that the lovers dallied. Otherwise, they said to each other, Mills would cast off his shackles, ask for his freedom, and then he and Dulcie would fly to Paris, where nobody probed into pasts and where they could make their dreams come true.

They found many ways in which to see each other. Dulcie had a little town car, and she picked Mills up at all hours and took him on long and lovely rides, from which he returned ecstatic, with wild flowers in his coat and a knowledge of work left undone.

Gossip began to fly about. Aunt Priscilla warned Dulcie.

"It is a dangerous thing to do, my dear. People will talk."

"What do Mills and I care for people? Oh, if it were not for Mary—" She had just come in from a ride with Mills, and her eyes were shining.

"I wish we were not dining there to-night," said Aunt Priscilla. "I wonder how Mary manages a dinner of eight with only one servant."

"She is so splendid and competent, Aunt Cilla. Mills says so. Everybody says it. Things are easy for her that would be hard for other people."

"I wonder what she thinks of you?"

Dulcie, drawing off her gloves, meditated.

"I fancy she likes me. I know I love her, but not so much as I love Mills."

Fifteen years ago Dulcie would have died rather than admit her love for a married man. But since then she had seen life through the eyes of a worldly-minded old husband, and it had made a difference.

At dinner that night Dulcie was exquisite in orchid tulle with a string of pearls that hung to her knees. Her hair was like ripe corn, waved and parted on the side with a girlish knot behind. Her skin was as fresh as a baby's. Mary was in black net. She had been very busy helping the cook, and she had had little time to spend on her hair. She looked ten years older than Dulcie, and her mind was absolutely on the dinner. The dinner was really very good. Mills had been extremely anxious about it. He had called up Mary from down-town to tell her that he was bringing home fresh asparagus. He wanted it served as an extra course with Hollandaise sauce. Mary protested, but gave in. It was the Hollandaise sauce that had kept her from curling her hair.

There were orchids for a centerpiece—in harmony with Dulcie's gown. In fact, the whole dinner seemed keyed up to Dulcie. The guests were for the most part literary folk, to whom Mills wanted to display his Egeria. After dinner Dulcie sang for them. She had set to music the words of one of Mills' poems, and she was much applauded.

After everybody had gone Mary went to bed with a headache. She was glad that it was Saturday, for Sunday promised a rest. She decided to send the children over to her mother and to have a quiet day with Mills. She wouldn't even go to church in the morning. There was an afternoon service; perhaps she and Mills might go together.

But Mills had other plans. He walked as far as the church door with Mary, and left her there. Mary wasn't sorry to be left; her headache had returned, and she was glad to sit alone in the peaceful dimness. But the pain proved finally too much for her, so she slipped out quietly and went home.

Clouds had risen, and she hurried before the shower. It was a real April shower, wind with a rush and a silver downpour. Mary, coming into the dark living-room, threw herself on the couch in a far corner and drew a rug over her. The couch was backed up against a table which held a lamp and a row of books. Mary had a certain feeling of content in the way the furniture seemed to shut her in. There was no sound but the splashing of rain against the windows.

She fell asleep at last, and waked to find that Mills and Dulcie had come in. No lights were on; the room was in twilight dimness.

Mills had met Dulcie at her front door. "How dear of you to come," she had told him.

He had spoken of his desertion of Mary. "But this day was made for you, Dulcie."

They had walked on together, not heeding where they went, and when the storm had caught them they were nearer Mills' house than Dulcie's and so he had taken her there. They had entered the apparently empty room.

"Mary is still at church. Come and dry your little feet by my fire, Dulcie." Mills knelt and fanned the flame.

Mary, coming slowly back from her dreams, heard this and other things, and at last Dulcie's voice in protest:

"Dear, we must think of Mary."

"Poor Mary!"

Now the thing that Mary hated more than anything else in the whole world was pity. Through all the shock of the astounding revelation that Mills and Dulcie cared for each other came the sting of their sympathy. She sat up, a shadow among the shadows.

"I mustn't stay, Mills," Dulcie was declaring.

"Why not?"

"I feel like a—thief—"

"Nonsense, we are only taking our own, Dulcie. We should have taken it years ago. Loving you I should never have married Mary."

"I had a conscience then, Mills, and you had promised."

"But now you see it differently, Dulcie?"

"Perhaps."

Mills was on his knees beside Dulcie's chair, kissing her hands. The fire lighted them. It was like a play, with Mary a forlorn spectator in the blackness of the pit.

"Let me go now, Mills."

"Wait till Mary comes—we'll tell her."

"No, oh, poor Mary!"

Poor Mary indeed!

"Anyhow you've got to stay, Dulcie, and sing for me, and when Mary comes back she'll get us some supper and I'll read you my new verses."

Among the shadows Mary had a moment of tragic mirth. Then she set her feet on the floor and spoke:

"I'm sorry, Mills, but I couldn't cook supper to-night if I died for it—"

From their bright circle of light they peered at her.

"Oh, my poor dear!" Dulcie said.

"I'm not poor," Mary told her, "but I'm tired, dead tired, and my head aches dreadfully, and if you want Mills you can have him."

"Have him?" Dulcie whispered.

"Yes. I don't want him."

Mills exploded.

"What?"

"I don't want you, Mills. I'm tired of being a prop; I'm tired of planning your meals, I'm tired of deciding whether you shall have mushrooms with your steak or—onions. You can have him, Dulcie. I know you think I've lost my mind." She came forward within the radius of the light. "But I haven't. As long as I thought Mills cared I could stick it out. But I have learned to-night that he loved you before he married me. You gave him to me, Dulcie, and now you want him back."

Indian giver! Like a flash Dulcie's mind went to the little Mary of the pigtails and pointing forefinger.

"You want him and you can have him. Perhaps if you had taken him years ago he might have been different. I don't know. Perhaps even now he can live up to all the lovely, lovely things that you and he are always talking about. But I've had to talk to Mills about what he likes to eat and what we have to pay for things; I've had to push him and prod him and praise him, and it has been hard work. If you want him you can have him, Dulcie."

Mills had a stunned look.

"Don't you love me, Mary?"

"I think I've proved it," she said quietly; "but I couldn't possibly go on loving you now. You have Dulcie to love you, and one woman is enough for any man. I don't know what you are planning to do, but you needn't run away or do anything spectacular. I'll make it as easy for you as possible. And now if you don't mind I'll go up and take a headache powder; my head is splitting."

Left alone, they tried to regain their air of high romance.

"Poor Mary!"

But the words rang hollow. One couldn't possibly call a woman poor who had given away so much with a single gesture.

They tried to talk it over but found nothing to say. At last Mills took Dulcie home. She asked him in and he went. Aunt Priscilla was out, and tea was served for the two of them from a lacquered tea cart—Orange Pekoe and Japanese wafers. It was delicious but unsubstantial. Dulcie with her coat off was like a wood sprite in leaf green. Her hair was gold, her eyes wet violets; but Mills missed something. He had a feeling that he wanted to get home and talk things over with Mary.

At last he rose, and it was then that Dulcie laid her hand on his arm.

"Mills, I can't."

"Can't what?"

"Let you leave Mary."

"Why not?"

"It wouldn't be right."

"It would be as right as it has ever been, Dulcie."

"I know how it must look to you, but—but I knew all the time that wrong is wrong. I thought I was a different Dulcie from the girl of long ago, but I'm not. I still have a conscience; I can't take you away from Mary."

"You're not taking me away. You heard what she said—she doesn't want me."

And Dulcie didn't want him! He saw it in that moment! The things that Mary had said had scared her. She didn't want to prod and push and praise. She didn't want to decide what he should have for dinner. She didn't want to weigh the merits of beefsteak and mushrooms or beefsteak and onions—onions!

He felt suddenly old, fat, bald-headed! The glow had faded from everything. He did not protest or attempt to persuade her. He took his hat, kissed her hand and got away.

Aunt Priscilla coming in found Dulcie in tears by the fire.

"I've given him up, Aunt Cilla."

"Why?"

"Well, it wouldn't be right."

She came into Aunt Priscilla's bedroom later to talk it over. She had on the rosy house coat. She spoke of going back to Paris.

"It will be better for both of us. After all, Aunt Cilla, we are what we are fundamentally, and we Puritans can't get away from our consciences, can we?"

"Some of us," said Aunt Priscilla, "can't."

The old woman lay awake a long time that night, thinking it out. She was glad that Dulcie had stopped the thing in time. But she had a feeling that the solution of the situation could not be laid to an awakened conscience. She hoped that some day Dulcie would tell her the truth.

It was still raining when Mills reached home. The house was dark, the fire had died down. He went up-stairs. The boys were in bed. There was a light in Mary's room. He opened the door. Mary was propped up on her pillows reading a book. He stopped, uncertain, on the threshold.

"Come in," she said, "my head's better."

He crossed the room and stood beside her.

"Oh, Mary," he said, and his face worked. He dropped on his knees by the bed and cried like a child.

She laid her hand on his head and smoothed his thin hair.

"Poor Mills!" she said softly; "poor old Mills!" Then after a moment, brightly: "It will do us both good to have some coffee. Run along, Mills, and start the percolator; I'll be down in a minute to get the supper."

BURNED TOAST

I

Perry Cunningham and I had been friends for years. I was older than he, and I had taught him in his senior year at college. After that we had traveled abroad, frugally, as befitted our means. The one quarrel I had with fate was that Perry was poor. Money would have given him the background that belonged to him—he was a princely chap, with a high-held head. He had Southern blood in his veins, which accounted perhaps for an almost old-fashioned charm of manner, as if he carried on a gentlemanly tradition.

We went through the art galleries together. There could have been nothing better than those days with him—the Louvre, the Uffizi, the Pitti Palace. Perry's search for beauty was almost breathless. We swept from Filippo Lippi to Botticelli and Bellini, then on to Ghirlandajo, Guido Reni, Correggio, Del Sarto—the incomparable Leonardo.

"If I had lived then," Perry would say, glowing, "in Florence or in Venice!"

And I, smiling at his enthusiasm, had a vision of him among those golden painters, his own young beauty enhanced by robes of clear color, his thirst for loveliness appeased by the sumptuous settings of that age of romance.

Then when the great moderns confronted us—Sorolla and the rest—Perry complained, "Why did I study law, Roger, when I might be doing things like this?"

"It is not too late," I told him.

I felt that he must not be curbed, that his impassioned interest might blossom and bloom into genius if it were given a proper outlet.

So it came about that he decided to paint. He would stay in Paris a year or two in a studio, and test his talent.

But his people would not hear of it. There had been lawyers in his family for generations. Since the Civil War they had followed more or less successful careers. Perry's own father had made no money, but Perry's mother was obsessed by the idea that the fortunes of the family were bound up in her son's continuance of his father's practice.

So Perry went home and opened an office. His heart was not in it, but he made enough to live on, and at last he made money enough to marry a wife. He would have married her whether he had enough to live on or not. She was an artist, and she was twenty when Perry met her. We had been spending a month in Maine, on an island as charming as it was cheap. Rosalie was there with a great-aunt and uncle. She was painting the sea on the day that Perry first saw her, and she wore a jade-green smock. Her hair was red, drawn back rather tightly from her forehead, but breaking into waves over her ears. With the red of her cheeks and the red of her lips she had something of the look of Lorenzo Lotto's lovely ladies, except for a certain sharp slenderness, a slenderness which came, I was to learn later, from an utter indifference to the claims of appetite. She was one of those who sell bread to buy hyacinths.

I speak of this here because Rosalie's almost ascetic indifference to material matters, in direct contrast to Perry's vivid enjoyment of the good things of life, came to have a tragic significance in later days. Perry loved a warm hearth in winter, a cool porch in summer. He had the Southerner's epicurean appreciation of the fine art of feasting. The groaning board had been his inheritance from a rollicking, rackety set of English ancestors, to whom dining was a rather splendid ceremony. On his mother's table had been fish and game from Chesapeake, fruits and vegetables in season and out—roast lamb when prices soared high in the spring, strawberries as soon as they came up from Florida. There had always been money for these in the Cunningham exchequer, when there had been money for nothing else.

Rosalie, on the other hand, ate an orange in the morning, a square of toast at noon, a chop and perhaps a salad for dinner. One felt that she might have fared equally well on dew and nectar. She had absolutely no interest in what was set before her, and after she married Perry this attitude of mind remained unchanged.

She was a wretched cook, and made no effort to acquire expertness. She and Perry lived in a small but well-built bungalow some miles out from town, and they could not afford a maid. When I dined with them I made up afterward for the deficiencies of their menu by a square meal at the club. There was no chance for Perry to make up, and I wondered as the years went on how he stood it.

He seemed to stand it rather well, except that in time he came to have that same sharpened look of delicacy which added a spiritual note to Rosalie's rich bloom. He always lighted up when he spoke of his wife, and he was always urging me to come and see them. I must admit that except for the meals I liked to go. Rosalie's success at painting had been negligible, but her love of beauty was expressed in the atmosphere she gave to her little home; she had achieved rather triumphant results in backgrounds and in furnishing.

267

I remember one spring twilight. I was out for the week-end, and we dined late. The little house was on a hill, and with the French windows wide open we seemed to hang above an abyss of purple sky, cut by a thin crescent. White candles lighted the table, and there were white lilacs. There was a silver band about Rosalie's red hair.

There was not much to eat, and Perry apologized, "Rose hates to fuss with food in hot weather."

Rosalie, as mysterious in that light as the young moon, smiled dreamily.

"Why should one think about such things—when there is so much else in the world?"

Perry removed the plates and made the coffee. Rosalie did not drink coffee. She wandered out into the garden, and came back with three violets, which she kissed and stuck in Perry's coat.

The next morning when I came down Rosalie was cutting bread for toast. She was always exquisitely neat, and in her white linen and in her white-tiled kitchen she seemed indubitably domestic. I was hungry and had hopes of her efforts.

"Peer is setting the table", she told me.

She always called him "Peer". She had her own way of finding names for people. I was never "Roger", but "Jim Crow". When questioned as to her reason for the appellation she decided vaguely that it might be some connection of ideas—dances—Sir Roger de Coverley—and didn't somebody "dance Jim Crow"?

"You don't mind, do you?" she had asked, and I had replied that I did not.

I did not confess how much I liked it. I had always been treated in a distinctly distant and dignified fashion by my family and friends, so that Rosalie's easy assumption of intimacy was delightful.

Well, I went out on the porch and left Rosalie to her culinary devices. I found the morning paper, and fifteen minutes later there came up across the lawn a radiant figure.

Rosalie, hearing the garden call, had chucked responsibility—and her arms were full of daffodils!

We had burned toast for breakfast! Rosalie had forgotten it and Perry had not rescued it until it was well charred. There was no bread to make more, so we had to eat it.

For the rest we had coffee and fruit. It was an expensive season for eggs, and Rosalie had her eye on a bit of old brocade which was to light a corner of her studio. She breakfasted contentedly on grapefruit, but Perry was rather silent, and I saw for the first time a shadow on his countenance. I wondered if for the moment his mind had wandered to the past, and to his mother's table, with Sunday waffles, omelet, broiled bacon. Yet—there had been no bits of gay brocade to light the mid-Victorian dullness of his mother's dining-room, no daffodils on a radiant morning, no white lilacs on a purple twilight, no slender goddess, mysterious as the moon.

It was in the middle of the following winter that I began to realize that Perry was not well. He had come home on a snowy night, tired and chilled to the bone. He was late and Rosalie had kept dinner waiting for him. It was a rather sorry affair when it was served. Perry pushed his chair back and did not eat. I had as little appetite for it as he, but I did my best. I had arrived on an earlier train, with some old prints that I wanted to show him. Rosalie and I looked at them after dinner, but Perry crouched over the fire and coughed at intervals.

At last I couldn't stand it any longer.

"He needs some hot milk, a foot bath, and to be tucked up in bed."

Rosalie stared at me above the prints. "Perry?"

"Yes. He isn't well."

"Don't croak, Jim Crow."

But I knew what I was talking about. "I am going to get him to bed. You can have the milk ready when I come down."

It developed that there was no milk. I walked half a mile to a road house and brought back oysters and a bottle of cream. I cooked them myself in the white-tiled kitchen, and served them piping hot in a bowl with crackers.

Perry, propped up in bed, ate like a starved bird.

"I've never tasted anything better," he said; and, warmed and fed, he slept after a bit as soundly as a satisfied baby.

It was while he was eating the oysters that Rosalie came to the door and looked at him. He was not an æsthetic object—I must admit that no sick man is—and I saw distaste in her glance, as if some dainty instinct in her shrank from the spectacle.

When I went down I found her sitting in front of the fire, wrapped in a Chinese robe of black and gold. You can imagine the effect of that with the red of her hair and the red of her cheeks and lips. Her feet, in black satin slippers, were on a jade-green cushion, and back of her head was the strip of brocade that she had bought with her housekeeping money. It was a gorgeous bit, repeating the color of the cushion, and with a touch of blue which matched her eyes.

She wanted me to show her the rest of the prints. I tried to talk to her of Perry's health, but she wouldn't.

"Don't croak, Jim Crow," she said again.

As I look back at the two of us by the fire that night I feel as one might who had been accessory to a crime. Rosalie's charm was undoubted. Her quickness of mind, her gayety of spirit, her passion for all that was lovely in art and Nature—made her indescribably interesting. I stayed late. And not once, after my first attempt, did we speak of Perry.

It was in March that I made Perry see a doctor. "Nothing organic," was Perry's report. Beyond that he was silent. So I went to the doctor myself.

"What's the matter with him?"

"He is not getting the proper nourishment," the doctor told me. "He must have plenty of milk and eggs, and good red meat."

It sounded easy enough, but it wasn't. Rosalie couldn't grasp the fact that diet in Perry's case was important. For the first time I saw a queer sort of obstinacy in her.

"Oh, my poor Peer!" And she laughed lightly. "Do they want to make a stuffed pig of you?"

Well, you simply couldn't get it into her head that Perry needed the bread that she sold for hyacinths. She cooked steaks and chops for him, and served them with an air of protest that took away his appetite.

Of course there remained the eggs and milk, but he didn't like them. What Perry really needed was three good meals a day according to the tradition of his mother's home.

But he couldn't have them. His mother was dead, and the home broken up. The little bungalow, with its old brocades, its Venetian glass, its Florentine carvings, its sun-dial and its garden, was the best that life could offer him. And I must confess that he seemed to think it very good. He adored Rosalie. When in moments of rebellion against her seeming indifference I hinted that she lacked housewifely qualities he smiled and shifted the subject abruptly.

Once he said, "She feeds—my soul."

Of course she loved him. But love to her meant what it had meant in those first days on the Maine coast when she had seen him, slender and strong, his brown hair blowing back from his sun-tanned skin; it meant those first days in their new home when, handsome and debonair in the velvet coat which she had made him wear, he had added a high light to the picture she had made of her home.

This new Perry, pale and coughing—shivering in the warmth of the fire—did not fit into the picture. Her dreams of the future had not included a tired man who worked for his living, and who was dying for lack of intelligent care.

To put it into cold words makes it sound ghoulish. But of course Rosalie was not really that. She was merely absorbed in her own exalted theories and she was not maternal. I think when I compared her, unthinking, to the young moon, that I was subconsciously aware of her likeness to the "orbed maiden" whose white fire warms no one.

She tried to do her best, and I am quite sure that Perry never knew the truth—that he might have been saved if she could have left her heights for a moment and had become womanly and wifely. If she had mothered him a bit—poured out her tenderness upon him—oh, my poor Perry. He loved her too much to ask it, but I knew what it would have meant to him.

All through his last illness Rosalie clung to me. I think it grew to be a horror to her to see him, gaunt and exhausted, in the west room. He had a good nurse, toward the last, and good food. I had had a small fortune left to me, too late, by a distant relative. I paid for the cook and the nurse, and I sent flowers to Rosalie that she might take them to Perry and let his hungry eyes feed upon her.

It was in the winter that he died, and after all was over Rosalie and I went out and stood together on the little porch. There was snow on the ground and the bright stars seemed caught in the branches of the pines.

Rosalie shook and sobbed.

"I hate—death," she said. "Oh, Jim Crow, why did God let my poor Peer die?" She was completely unstrung. "Death is so—ugly."

I said, "It is not ugly. Peer will live again—like the daffodils in the spring."

"Do you believe that, Jim Crow?"

I did believe it, and I told her so—that even now her Peer was strong and well; and I think it comforted her. It gave her lover back to her, as it were, in the glory of his youth.

She did not wear mourning, or, rather, she wore mourning which was like that worn by no other woman. Her robes were of purple. She kept Perry's picture on the table, and out of the frame his young eyes laughed at us, so that gradually the vision of that ravaged figure in the west room faded.

I went to see her once a week. It seemed the only thing to do. She was utterly alone, with no family but the great-aunt and uncle who had been with her when she met Perry. She was a child in business matters, and Perry had left it to me to administer the affairs of his little estate. Rosalie had her small bungalow, Perry's insurance, and she turned her knowledge of painting to practical account. She made rather special things in lamp-shades and screens, and was well paid for them.

I went, as I have said, once a week. A woman friend shared part of her house, but was apt to be out, and so I saw Rosalie usually alone. I lived now at the club and kept a car. Rosalie often dined with me, but I rarely ate at the bungalow. Now and then in the afternoon she made me a cup of tea, rather more, I am sure, for the picturesque service with her treasured Sheffield than for any desire to contribute to my own cheer or comfort.

And so, gradually, I grew into her life and she grew into mine. I was forty-five, she twenty-five. In the back of my mind was always a sense of the enormity of her offense against Perry. In my hottest moments I said to myself that she had sacrificed his life to her selfishness; she might have been a Borgia or a Medici.

269

Yet when I was with her my resentment faded; one could as little hold rancor against a child.

Thus the months passed, and it was in the autumn, I remember, that a conversation occurred which opened new vistas. She had been showing me a parchment lamp-shade which she had painted. There was a peacock with a spreading tail, and as she held the shade over the lamp the light shone through and turned every feathered eye into a glittering jewel. Rosalie wore one of her purple robes, and I can see her now as I shut my eyes, as glowing and gorgeous as some of those unrivaled masterpieces in the Pitti Palace.

"Jim Crow," she said, "I shall do a parrot next—all red and blue, with white rings round his eyes."

"You will never do anything better than that peacock."

"Shan't I?" She left the shade over the lamp and sat down. "Do you think I shall paint peacocks and parrots for the rest of my life, Jim Crow?"

"What would you like to do?" I asked her.

"Travel." She was eager. "Do you know, I have never been to Europe? Perry used to tell me about it—Botticelli and Raphael—and Michaelangelo—"

"We had a great time," I said, remembering it all—that breathless search for beauty.

"He promised that some day he and I would go—together."

"Poor Perry!"

She rose restlessly.

"Oh, take me out somewhere, Jim Crow! I feel as if this little house would stifle me."

We motored to the country club. She wore the color which she now affected, a close little hat and a straight frock. People stared at her. I think she was aware of their admiration and liked it.

She smiled at me as she sat down at the table. "I always love to come with you, Jim Crow."

"Why?"

"You do things so well, and you're such a darling."

I do not believe that it was intended as flattery. I am sure that she meant it. She was happy because of the lights and the lovely old room with its cavernous fireplace and its English chintzes; and out of her happiness she spoke.

She could not, of course, know the effect of her words on me. No one had ever called me a darling or had thought that I did things well.

She used, too, to tell me things about my looks. "You'd be like one of those distinguished gentlemen of Vandyke's if you'd wear a ruff and leave off your eye-glasses."

I wonder if you know how it seemed to have a child like that saying such things. For she was more than a child, she was a beautiful woman, and everything surrounding her was beautiful. And there had been a great many gray years before I met Perry and before the money came which made pleasant living possible.

"I like you because you are strong," was another of her tributes.

"How do you know I am strong?"

"Well, you look it. And not many men could have carried me so easily up-stairs."

She had sprained her ankle in getting out of my car on the night that we had dined at the country club. She had worn high-heeled slippers and had stepped on a pebble.

It was on that night that I first faced the fact that I cared for her. In my arms she had clung to me like a child, her hair had swept my cheek, there had been the fragrance of violets.

I did not want to care for her. I remembered Perry—the burned toast which had seemed to mark the beginning of their tragedy—those last dreadful days. I knew that Perry's fate would not be mine; there would be no need to sell bread to buy hyacinths. There was money enough and to spare, money to let her live in the enjoyment of the things she craved; money enough to—travel.

The more I thought of it the more I was held by the thought of what such a trip would mean to me. It would be like that pilgrimage with young Perry. There would be the same impassioned interest—there would be more than that—there would be youth and loveliness—all mine.

I felt that I was mad to think of it. Yet she made me think of it. It was what she wanted. She was not in the least unwomanly, but she was very modern in her frank expression of the pleasure she felt in my companionship.

"Oh, what would I do without you, Jim Crow?" was the way she put it.

I grew young in my months of association with her. I had danced a little in my college days, but I had given it up. She taught me the new steps—and we would set the phonograph going and take up the rugs.

When I grew expert we danced together at the country club and at some of the smart places down-town. It was all very delightful. I made up my mind that I should marry her.

I planned to ask her on Christmas Eve. I had a present for her, an emerald set in antique silver with seed pearls. It was hung on a black ribbon, and I could fancy it shining against the background of her velvet smock. I carried flowers, too, and a book. I was keen with anticipation. The years seemed to drop from me. I was a boy of twenty going to meet the lady of my first romance.

When I arrived at the bungalow I found that Rosalie had with her the old great-aunt and uncle who had been with her when we first met in Maine. They had come on for Christmas unexpectedly, anticipating an eager welcome, happy in their sense of surprise.

Rosalie, when we had a moment alone, expressed her dismay.

"They are going to stay until to-morrow night, Jim Crow. And I haven't planned any Christmas dinner."

"We'll take them to the country club."

"How heavenly of you to think of it!"

I gave her the flowers and the book. But I kept the jewel for the high moment when I should ask her for a greater gift in exchange.

But the high moment did not come that night. The old uncle and aunt sat up with us. They had much to talk about. They were a comfortable pair—silver-haired and happy in each other—going toward the end of the journey hand in hand.

The old man went to the door with me when I left, and we stood for a moment under the stars.

"Mother and I miss hanging up the stockings for the kiddies," he said.

"Were there many kiddies?"

"Three. Two dead and one married and out West. Rosalie seemed the nearest that we had, and that's why we came. I thought mother might be lonely in our big old house."

The next day at the country club the old gentleman was genial but slightly garrulous. The old lady talked about her children and her Christmas memories. I saw that Rosalie was frankly bored.

As for myself, I was impatient for my high moment.

But I think I gave the old folks a good time and that they missed nothing in my manner. And, indeed, I think that they missed nothing in Rosalie's. They had the gentle complacency of the aged who bask in their own content.

It was toward the end of dinner that I caught a look in Rosalie's eyes which almost made my heart stop beating. I had not seen it since Perry's death. I had seen it first when she had stood in the door of his room on the night that I tucked him up in bed and gave him the hot oysters. It was that look of distaste—that delicate shrinking from an unpleasant spectacle.

Following her gaze I saw that the old gentleman had sunk in his chair and was gently nodding. His wife leaned toward me. "Milton always takes a cat nap after meals," she said, smiling. And I smiled back, she was so rosy and round and altogether comfortable.

Rosalie and I went with them to the train, and it was as we drove back that I spoke of them.

"They are rather great dears, aren't they?"

Rosalie was vehement. "I hate old people!"

A chill struck to my bones. "You hate them? Why?"

"They're—ugly, Jim Crow. Did you see how they had shrunk since I last saw them—and the veins in their hands—and the skull showing through his forehead?"

She was twenty-five, and I was almost twice her age. When I was old she would still be young—young enough to see my shrunken body and the skull showing through!

The look that had been in her eyes for Perry would some day be in her eyes for me. And I knew that if I ever saw it it would strike me dead. It might not kill me physically, but it would wither like a flame all joy and hope forever.

When we reached the bungalow I built up a fire, and Rosalie, leaving me for a little, came back in something sheer and lovely in green. It was the first time since Perry's death that she had discarded her purple robes. She sank into a big chair opposite me and put her silver-slippered feet on the green cushion.

"Isn't it heavenly to be alone, Jim Crow?"

It was the high moment which I had planned, but I could not grasp it. Between me and happiness stood the shadow of that other Rosalie, shrinking from me when I was old as she had shrunk from Perry.

"My dear," I said, and I did not look at her, "I've been thinking a lot about you."

Her chin was in her hand. "I know."

But she didn't know.

"I've been thinking, Rosalie; and I want to give you something for Christmas which will make you happy throughout the year."

"You are such a darling, Jim Crow."

"And I have thought of this—a trip to Europe. You'll let me do it, won't you? There'll be the art galleries, and you can stay as long as you like."

I could see that she was puzzled. "Do you mean that I am to go—alone?" she asked slowly.

"There may be some one going. I'll find out."

There was dead silence.

"You will let me do it?" I asked finally.

She came over to my chair and stood looking down at me.

"Why are you sending me alone, Jim Crow?"

I think, then, that she saw the anguish in my eyes. She sank on her knees beside my chair.

"I don't want to go alone, Jim Crow. I want to stay—with—you."

Well, the jewel is on her breast and a ring to match is on her finger. And when the spring comes we are to sail for Italy, for France.

Perhaps we shall never come back. And I am going to give Rosalie all the loveliness that life can hold for her. Now and then she whispers that she never knew love until I taught it to her. That what she felt for Perry was but the echo of his own need of her.

"But I'd tramp the muddy roads with you, Jim Crow."

I wonder if she really means it. I wish with all my heart that I might know it true. I have never told her of my fears and I believe that I can make her happy. I shall try not to look too far beyond the days we shall have in the Louvre and the Uffizi and the Pitti Palace. We shall search for beauty, and perhaps I can teach her to find it, before it is too late, in the things that count.

PETRONELLA

"If you loved a man, and knew that he loved you, and he wouldn't ask you to marry him, what would you do?"

The Admiral surveyed his grand-niece thoughtfully. "What do you expect to do, my dear?"

Petronella stopped on the snowy top step and looked down at him. "Who said I had anything to do with it?" she demanded.

The Admiral's old eyes twinkled. "Let me come in, and tell me about it."

Petronella smiled at him over her big muff. "If you'll promise not to stay after five, I'll give you a cup of tea."

"Who's coming at five?"

The color flamed into Petronella's cheeks. In her white coat and white furs, with her wind-blown brown hair, her beauty satisfied even the Admiral's critical survey, and he hastened to follow his question by the assertion, "Of course I'll come in."

Petronella, with her coat off, showed a slenderness which was enhanced by the straight lines of her white wool gown, with the long sleeves fur-edged, and with fur at the top of the high, transparent collar. She wore her hair curled over her ears and low on her forehead, which made of her face a small and delicate oval. In the big hall, with a roaring fire in the wide fireplace, she dispensed comforting hospitality to the adoring Admiral. And when she had given him his tea she sat on a stool at his feet. "Oh, wise great-uncle," she said, "I am going to tell you about the Man!"

"Have I ever seen him?"

"No. I met him in London last year, and—well, you know what a trip home on shipboard means, with all the women shut up in their cabins, and with moonlight nights, and nobody on deck—"

"So it was an affair of moonlight and propinquity?"

After a pause: "No, it was an affair of the only man in the world for me."

"My dear child—!"

Out of a long silence she went on: "He thought I was poor. You know how quietly I traveled with Miss Danvers. And he didn't associate Nell Hewlett with Petronella Hewlett of New York and Great Rock. And so—well, you know, uncle, he let himself go, and I let myself go, and then—"

She drew a long breath. "When we landed, things stopped. He had found out who I was, and he wrote me a little note, and said he would never forget our friendship—and that's—all."

She finished drearily, and the bluff old Admiral cleared his throat. There was something wrong with the scheme of things when his Petronella couldn't have the moon if she wanted it!

"And what can I do—what can any woman do?" Petronella demanded, turning on him. "I can't go to him and say, 'Please marry me.' I can't even think it"; her cheeks burned. "And he'd die before *he'd* say another word, and I suppose that now we'll go on growing old, and I'll get thinner and thinner, and he'll get fatter and fatter, and I'll be an old maid, and he'll marry some woman who's poor enough to satisfy his pride, and—well, that will be the end of it, uncle."

"The end of it?" said the gentleman who had once commanded a squadron. "Well, I guess not, Petronella, if you want him. Oh, the man's a fool!"

"He's not a fool, uncle." The sparks in Petronella's eyes matched the sparks in the Admiral's.

"Well, if he's worthy of you—"

Petronella laid her cheek against his hand. "The question is not," she said, faintly, "of his worthiness, but of mine, dear uncle."

Dumbly the Admiral gazed down at that drooping head. Could this be Petronella—confident, imperious, the daughter of a confident and imperious race?

He took refuge in the question, "But who is coming at five?"

"He is coming. He is passing through Boston on his way to visit his mother in Maine. I asked him to come. I told him I was down here by the sea, and intended to spend Christmas at Great Rock because you were here, and because this was the house I lived in when I was a little girl, and that I wanted him to see it; and—I told him the truth, uncle."

"The truth?"

"That I missed him. That was all I dared say, and I wish you had read his note of assent. Such a stiff little thing. It threw me back upon myself, and I wished that I hadn't written him—I wished that he wouldn't come. Oh, uncle, if I were a man, I'd give a woman the right to choose. That's the reason there are so many unhappy marriages. Nine wrong men ask a woman, and the tenth right one *won't*. And finally she gets tired of waiting for the tenth right one, and marries one of the nine wrong ones."

"There are women to-day," said the Admiral, "who are preaching a woman's right to propose."

Petronella gazed at him, thoughtfully. "I could preach a doctrine like that—but I couldn't practice it. It's easy enough to say to some other woman, 'Ask him,' but it's different when you are the woman."

"Yet if he asked you," suggested the Admiral, "the world might say that he wanted your money."

"Why should we care what the world would say?" Petronella was on her feet now, defending her cause vigorously. "Why should we care? Why, it's our love against the world, uncle! Why should we care?"

The Admiral stood up, too, and paced the rug as in former days he had paced the decks. "There must be some way out," he said at last, and stopped short. "Suppose I speak to him—"

"And spoil it all! Oh, uncle!" Petronella shook him by the lapels of his blue coat. "A man never knows how a woman feels about such things. Even you don't, you old darling. And now will you please go; and take this because I love you," and she kissed him on one cheek, "and this because it is a quarter to five and you'll have to hurry," and she kissed him on the other cheek.

The Admiral, being helped into his big cape in the hall, called back, "I forgot to give you your Christmas present," and he produced a small package.

"Come here and let me open it," Petronella insisted. And the Admiral, without a glance at the accusing clock, went back. And thus it happened that he was there to meet the Man.

It must be confessed that the Admiral suffered a distinct shock as he was presented to the hero of Petronella's romance. Here was no courtly youth of the type of the military male line of Petronella's family, but a muscular young giant of masterful bearing. The Hewlett men had commanded men; one could see at a glance that Justin Hare had also commanded women. This, the wise old Admiral decided at once, was the thing which had attracted Petronella—Petronella, who had held her own against all masculine encroachments, and who was heart-free at twenty-five!

"Look what this dearest dear of an uncle has given me," said Petronella, and held up for the young surgeon's admiration a string of pearls with a sapphire clasp. "They belonged to my great-aunt. I was named for her, and uncle says I look like her."

"You have her eyes, my dear, and some of her ways. But she was less independent. In her time women leaned more, as it were, on man's strength."

Justin Hare looked at them with interest—at the slender girl in her white gown, at the tall, straight old man with his air of command.

"Women in these days do not lean," he said, with decision; "they lead."

A spark came into Petronella's eyes. "And do you like the modern type best?" she challenged.

He answered with smiling directness, "I like you."

The Admiral was pleased with that, though he was still troubled by this man's difference from the men of his own race. Yet if back of that honest bluntness there was a heart which would enshrine her—well, that was all he would ask for this dearest of girls.

He glanced at the clock, and spoke hurriedly: "I must be going, my dear; it is long after five."

"Must you really go?" asked the mendacious Petronella.

An hour later she was alone. The visit had been a failure. She admitted that, as she gazed with a sort of agonized dismay through the wide window to where the sea was churned by the wildness of the northeast gale. Snow had come with the wind, shutting out the view of the great empty hotels on the Point, shutting out, too, the golden star of hope which gleamed from the top of the lighthouse.

Petronella turned away from the blank scene with a little shudder. Thus had Justin Hare shut her out of his life. He had talked of his mother in Maine, of his hospital plans for the winter, but not a word had he said of those moonlight nights when he had masterfully swayed her by the force of his own passion, had wooed her, won her.

273

And now there was nothing that she could do. There was never anything that a woman could do! And so she must bear it. Oh, if she could bear it!

A little later, when a maid slipped in to light the candles, Petronella said out of the shadows, "When Jenkins goes to the post-office, I have a parcel for the mail."

"He's been, miss, and there won't be any train out to-night; the snow has stopped the trains."

"Not any train!" At first the remark held little significance, but finally the fact beat against her brain. If the one evening train could not leave, then Justin Hare must stay in town, and he would have to stay until Christmas morning!

Petronella went at once to the telephone, and called up the only hotel which was open at that season. Presently she had Hare at the other end of the line.

"You must come to my house to dinner," she said. "Jenkins has told me about your train. Please don't dress—there'll be only Miss Danvers and uncle; and you shall help me trim my little tree."

Although she told him not to dress, she changed her gown for one of dull green velvet, built on the simple lines of the white wool she had worn in the afternoon. The square neck was framed by a collar of Venetian point, and there was a queer old pin of pearls.

The Admiral, arriving early, demanded: "My dear, what is this? I was just sitting down to bread and milk and a handful of raisins, and now I must dine in six courses, and drink coffee, which will keep me awake."

She laid her cheek against his arm. "Mr. Hare's train couldn't get out of town on account of the snow."

"And he's coming?"

"Yes."

"But what of this afternoon, my dear?"

She slipped her hand into his, and they stood gazing into the fire. "It was dreadful, uncle. I had a feeling that I had compelled him to come—against his will."

"Yet you have asked him to come again to-night?"

She shivered a little, and her hand was cold. "Perhaps I shall regret it—but oh, uncle, can't I have for this one evening the joy of his presence? And if to-morrow my heart dies—"

"Nella, my dear child—"

The Admiral's own Petronella had never drawn in this way upon his emotions. She had been gentle, perhaps a little cold. But then he had always worshiped at her shrine. Perhaps a woman denied the lore she yearns for learns the value of it. At any rate, here in his arms was the dearest thing in his lonely life, sobbing as if her heart would break.

When Justin came, a half-hour later, he found them still in front of the fire in the great hall, and as she rose to welcome him he saw that Petronella had been sitting on a stool at her uncle's feet.

"When I was a little girl," she explained, when Hare had taken a chair on the hearth and she had chosen another with, a high, carved back, in which she sat with her silken ankles crossed and the tips of her slipper toes resting on a leopard-skin which the Admiral had brought back from India—"when I was a little girl we always spent Christmas Eve in this house by the sea instead of in town. We were all here then—mother and dad and dear Aunt Pet, and we hung our stockings at this very fireplace—and now there is no one but Miss Danvers and me, and uncle, who lives up aloft in his big house across the way, where he has a lookout tower. I always feel like calling up to him when I go there, 'Oh, Anne, Sister Anne, do you see anybody coming?'"

She was talking nervously, with her cheeks as white as a lily, but with her eyes shining. The Admiral glanced at Hare. The young man was drinking in her beauty. But suddenly he frowned and turned away his eyes.

"It was very good of you to ask me over," he said, formally.

That steadied Petronella. Her nervous self-consciousness fled, and she was at once the gracious, impersonal hostess.

The Admiral glowed with pride of her. "She'll carry it off," he said to himself; "it's in her blood."

"Dinner is served," announced Jenkins from the doorway, and then Miss Danvers came down and greeted Justin, and they all went out together.

There was holly for a centerpiece, and four red candles in silver holders. The table was of richly carved mahogany, and the Admiral, following an old custom, served the soup from a silver tureen, upheld by four fat cupids. From the wide arch which led into the great hall was hung a bunch of mistletoe; beyond the arch, the roaring fire made a background of gleaming, golden light.

To the young surgeon it seemed a fairy scene flaming with the color and glow of a life which he had never known. He had lived so long surrounded by the bare, blank walls of a hospital. Even Petronella's soft green gown seemed made of some mystical stuff which had nothing in common with the cool white or blue starchiness of the uniforms of nurses.

They talked of many things, covering with, their commonplaces the tenseness of the situation. Then suddenly the conversation took a significant turn.

"I love these stormy nights," Petronella had said, "with the snow blowing, and the wind, and the house all warm and bright."

"Think of the poor sailors at sea," Hare had reminded her.

"Please—I don't want to think of them. We have done our best for them, uncle and I. We have opened a reading-room down by the docks, so that all who are ashore can have soup and coffee and sandwiches, and there's a big stove, and newspapers and magazines."

"You dispense charity?"

"Why not?" she asked him, confidently. "We have plenty—why shouldn't we give?"

"Because it takes away from their manhood to receive."

The Admiral spoke bluntly. "The men don't feel it that way. This charity, as you call it, is a memorial to my wife. The grandfathers of these boys used to see her light in the window of the old house on stormy nights, and they knew that it was an invitation to good cheer. More than one crew coming in half frozen were glad of the soup and coffee which were sent down to them in cans with baskets of bread. And this little coffee-room has been the outgrowth of just such hospitality. There are too many of the men to have in my house. I simply entertain them elsewhere, and I like to go and talk to them, and sometimes Petronella goes."

"There's a picture of dear Aunt Pet hanging there," said Petronella, "and you can't imagine how it softens the manners of the men. It is as if her spirit brooded over the place. They have made it into a sort of shrine, and they bring shells and queer carved things to put on the shelf below it."

"In the city we are beginning to think that such methods weaken self-respect."

"That's because," said the wise old Admiral, "in the city there isn't any real democracy. You give your friend a cup of coffee and think nothing of it, yet when I give a cup of coffee to a sailor whose grandfather and mine fished together on the banks, you warn me that my methods tend to pauperize. In the city the poor are never your friends—in this little town no man would admit that he is less than I. They like my coffee and they drink it."

Petronella, seeing her chance, took it. "I think people are horrid to let money make a difference."

"You say that," said Hare, "because you have never had to accept favors—you have, in other words, never been on the other side."

The Admiral, taking up cudgels for his niece, answered, "If she had been on the other side, she would have taken life as she takes it now—like a gentleman and a soldier," and he smiled at Petronella.

Hare had a baffled sense that the Admiral was right—that Petronella's fineness and delicacy would never go down in defeat or despair. She would hold her head high though the heavens fell. But could any man make such demands upon her? For himself, he would not.

So he answered, doggedly, "We shall hope she need never be tested." And Petronella's heart sank like lead.

But presently she began to talk about the little tree. "We have always had it in uncle's lookout tower. That was another of dear Aunt Pet's thoughts for the sailors. On clear nights they looked through their glasses for the little colored lights, and on stormy nights they knew that back of all the snow was the Christmas brightness."

"I never had a tree," said Justin. "When I was a kiddie we had pretty hard times, and the best Christmas I remember was one when mother made us boys put up a shelf for our books, and she started our collection with 'Treasure Island' and 'Huckleberry Finn.'"

In the adjoining room, volumes reached from floor to ceiling, from end to end. Petronella had a vision of this vivid young giant gloating over his two books on a rude shelf. And all her life she had had the things she wanted! Somehow the thought took the bitterness out of her attitude toward him. How strong he must be to deny himself now the one great thing that he craved when his life had held so little.

"How lovely to begin with just those two books," she said, softly, and the radiance of her smile was dazzling.

When she showed him her presents she was still radiant. There was a queer opera-bag of Chinese needlework, with handles of jade, a Damascus bowl of pierced brass, a tea-caddy in quaint Dutch *repoussé*; there was a silver-embroidered altar-cloth for a cushion, a bit of Copenhagen faience, all the sophisticated artistry which is sent to those who have no need for the commonplace. There were jewels, too: a bracelet of topazes surrounded by brilliants, a pair of slipper buckles of turquoises set in silver, a sapphire circlet for her little finger, a pendant of seed pearls.

As she opened the parcels and displayed her riches Justin felt bewildered. His gifts to his mother had included usually gloves and a generous check; if he had ventured to choose anything for Petronella he would not have dared go beyond a box of candy or a book; he had given his nurses pocketbooks and handkerchiefs. And the men of Petronella's world bestowed on her brass bowls and tea-caddies!

Miss Danvers vanished up-stairs. The Admiral, having admired, slipped away to the library, encouraged by Petronella's whispered: "Oh, uncle dear, leave us alone for just a little minute. I've found a way!"

Then Petronella, with that radiance still upon her, sat down on her little stool in front of the fire, and looked at Justin on the other side of the hearth.

"You haven't given me anything," she began, reproachfully.

"What could I give that would compare with these?" His hand swept toward the exquisite display. "What could I give—"

"There's one thing," softly.

"What?"

"That copy of 'Treasure Island' that your mother gave you long ago."

Dead silence. Then, unsteadily: "Why should you want that?"

"Because your mother—loved you."

Again dead silence. Hare did not look at her. His hand clenched the arm of his chair. His face was white. Then, very low, "Why do you—make it hard for me?"

"Because I want—the book"; she was smiling at him with her eyes like stars. "I want to read it with the eyes of the little boy—with the eyes of the little boy who looked into the future and saw life as a great adventure; who looked into the future—and dreamed."

He had a vision, too, of that little boy, reading, in the old house in the Maine woods, by the light of an oil-lamp, on Christmas Eve, with the snow blowing outside as it blew to-night.

"And your mother loved you because she loved your father," the girl's voice went on, "and you were all very happy up there in the forest. Do you remember that you told me about it on the ship?—you were happy, although you were poor, and hadn't any books but 'Treasure Island' and 'Huckleberry Finn.' But your mother was happy—because she—loved your father."

As she repeated it, she leaned forward. "Could you think of your mother as having been happy with any one else but your father?" she asked. "Could you think of her as having never married him, of having gone through the rest of her days a half-woman, because he would not—take her—into his life? Can you think that all the money in the world—all the money in the whole world—would—would have made up—"

The room seemed to darken. Hare was conscious that her face was hidden in her hands, that he stumbled toward her, that he knelt beside her—that she was in his arms.

"Hush," he was saying in that beating darkness of emotion. "Hush, don't cry—I—I will never let you go—"

When the storm had spent itself and when at last she met his long gaze, he whispered, "I'm not sure now that it is right—"

"You will be sure as the years go on," she whispered back; then, tremulously: "but I—I could never have—talked that way if I had thought of you as the man. I had to think of you as the little boy—who dreamed."

THE CANOPY BED

"My great-grandfather slept in it," Van Alen told the caretaker, as she ushered him into the big stuffy bedroom.

The old woman set her candlestick down on the quaint dresser. "He must have been a little man," she said; "none of my sons could sleep in it. Their feet would hang over."

Van Alen eyed the big bed curiously. All his life he had heard of it, and now he had traveled far to see it. It was a lumbering structure of great width and of strangely disproportionate length. And the coverlet and the canopy were of rose-colored chintz.

"I think I shall fit it," he said slowly.

Mrs. Brand's critical glance weighed his smallness, his immaculateness, his difference from her own great sons.

"Yes," she said, with the open rudeness of the country-bred; "yes, you ain't very big."

Van Alen winced. Even from the lips of this uncouth woman the truth struck hard. But he carried the topic forward with the light ease of a man of the world.

"My grandfather had the bed sawed to his own length," he explained; "did you ever hear the story?"

"No," she said; "I ain't been here long. They kept the house shut up till this year."

"Well, I'll tell you when I come down," and Van Alen opened his bag with a finality that sent the old woman to the door.

"Supper's ready," she told him, "whenever you are."

At the supper table the four big sons towered above Van Alen. They ate with appetites like giants, and they had big ways and hearty laughs that seemed to dwarf their guest into insignificance.

But the insignificance was that of body only, for Van Alen, fresh from the outside world and a good talker at all times, dominated the table conversationally.

To what he had to say the men listened eagerly, and the girl who waited on the table listened.

She was a vivid personality, with burnished hair, flaming cheeks, eyes like the sea. Her hands, as she passed the biscuits, were white, and the fingers went down delicately to little points. Van Alen, noting these things keenly, knew that she was out of her place, and wondered how she came there.

At the end of the meal he told the story of the Canopy Bed.

"My great-grandfather was a little man, and very sensitive about his height. In the days of his early manhood he spent much time in devising ways to deceive people into thinking him taller. He surrounded himself with big things, had a big bed made, wore high-heeled boots, and the crown of his hat was so tall that he was almost overbalanced.

"But for all that, he was a little man among the sturdy men of his generation, and if it had not been for the Revolution I think he would have died railing at fate. But the war brought him opportunity. My little great-grandfather fought in it, and won great honors, and straight back home he came and had the bed sawed off! He wanted future generations to see what a little man could do, and his will provided that this house should not be sold, and that, when his sons and grandsons had proved themselves worthy of it by some achievement, they should come here and sleep. I think he swaggered a little when he wrote that will, and he has put his descendants in an embarrassing position. We can never sleep in the canopy bed without taking more upon ourselves than modesty permits!"

He laughed, and instinctively his eyes sought those of the girl who waited on the table. Somehow he felt that she was the only one who could understand.

She came back at him with a question: "What have you done?"

"I have written a book," he told her.

She shook her head, and there were little sparks of light in her eyes. "I don't believe that was what your grandfather meant," she said, slowly.

They stared at her—three of the brothers with their knives and forks uplifted, the fourth, a blond Titanic youngster, with his elbows on the table, his face turned up to her, as to the sun.

"I don't believe he meant something done with your brains, but something fine, heroic—" There was a hint of scorn in her voice.

Van Alen flushed. He was fresh from the adulation of his bookish world.

"I should not have come," he explained, uncomfortably, "if my mother had not desired that I preserve the tradition of the family."

"It is a great thing to write a book"—she was leaning forward, aflame with interest—"but I don't believe he meant just that—"

He laughed. "Then I am not to sleep in the canopy bed?"

The girl laughed too. "Not unless you want to be haunted by his ghost."

With a backward flashing glance, she went into the kitchen, and Van Alen, lighting a cigarette, started to explore the old house.

Except for the wing, occupied by the caretaker, nothing had been disturbed since the family, seeking new fortunes in the city, had left the old homestead to decay among the desolate fields that yielded now a meagre living for Mrs. Brand and her four strapping sons.

In the old parlor, where the ancient furniture showed ghostlike shapes in the dimness, and the dead air was like a tomb, Van Alen found a picture of his great-grandfather.

The little man had been painted without flattery. There he sat—Lilliputian on the great charger! At that moment Van Alen hated him—that Hop-o'-my-Thumb of another age, founder of a pigmy race, who, by his braggart will, had that night brought upon this one of his descendants the scorn of a woman.

And even as he thought of her, she came in, with the yellow flare of a candle lighting her vivid face.

"I thought you might need a light," she said; "it grows dark so soon."

As he took the candle from her, he said abruptly: "I shall not sleep in the canopy bed; there is a couch in the room."

"Oh," her tone was startled, "you shouldn't have taken all that I said in earnest."

"But you meant it?"

"In a way, yes. I have been in here so often and have looked at your grandfather's picture. He was a great little man—you can tell from his eyes—they seem to speak at times."

"To you?"

"Yes. Of how he hated to be little, and how he triumphed when fame came at last."

"I hate to be little—"

It was the first time that he had ever owned it. Even as a tiny boy he had brazened it out, boasting of his mental achievements and slurring the weakness of his stunted body.

"I know," she had shut the kitchen door behind her, and they were standing in the hallway alone, "I know. Every man must want to be big."

She was only the girl who had waited on the table, but as she stood there, looking at him with luminous eyes, he burned with dull resentment, envying the blond boy who had sprawled at the head of the supper table. After all, it was to such a man as Otto Brand that this woman would some day turn.

He spoke almost roughly: "Size isn't everything." She flushed. "How rude you must think me," she said; "but I have been so interested in dissecting your grandfather that I forgot—you—"

Van Alen was moved by an impulse that he could not control, a primitive impulse that was not in line with his usual repression.

"I am tempted to make you remember me," he said slowly, and after that there was a startled silence. And then she went away.

277

As he passed the sitting-room on his way up-stairs, he looked in, and spoke to Otto Brand.

More than any of the other brothers, Otto typified strength and beauty, but in his eyes was never a dream, his brain had mastered nothing. He was playing idly with the yellow cat, but he stopped at Van Alen's question.

"Her great-grandfather and yours were neighbors," the boy said, with his cheeks flushing; "they own the next farm."

"The Wetherells?" Van Alen inquired.

The boy nodded. "They ain't got a cent. They're land poor. That's why she's here. But she don't need to work."

"Why not?"

"There's plenty that wants to marry her round about," was the boy's self-conscious summing up.

With a sense of revolt, Van Alen left him, and, undressing in the room with the canopy bed, he called up vaguely the vision of a little girl who had visited them in the city. She had had green eyes and freckles and red hair. Beyond that she had made no impression on his callowness. And her name was Mazie Wetherell.

He threw himself on the couch, and the night winds, coming in through the open window, stirred the curtains of the canopy bed with the light touch of a ghostly hand.

Then dreams came, and through them ran the thread of his hope of seeing Mazie Wetherell in the morning.

But even with such preparation, her beauty seemed to come upon him unawares when he saw her at breakfast. And again at noon, and again at night. But it was the third day before he saw her alone.

All that day he had explored the length and breadth of the family estate, finding it barren, finding that the population of the little village at its edge had decreased to a mere handful of laggards, finding that there was no lawyer within miles and but one doctor; gaining a final impression that back here in the hills men would come no more where once men had thronged.

It was almost evening when he followed a furrowed brown road that led westward. Above the bleak line of the horizon the sun hung, a red gold disk. There were other reds, too, along the way—the sumac flaming scarlet against the gray fence-rails; the sweetbrier, crimson-spotted with berries; the creeper, clinging with ruddy fingers to dead tree-trunks; the maple leaves rosy with first frosts.

And into this vividness came the girl who had waited on the table, and her flaming cheeks and copper hair seemed to challenge the glow of the autumn landscape.

She would have passed him with a nod, but he stopped her.

"You must not run away, Mazie Wetherell," he said; "you used to treat me better than that when you were a little girl."

She laughed. "Do you remember my freckles and red hair?"

"I remember your lovely manners."

"I had to have nice manners. It is only pretty children who can afford to be bad."

"And pretty women?" he asked, with his eyes on the color that came and went.

She flung out her hands in a gesture of protest "I have seen so few."

His lips were opened to tell her of her own beauty, but something restrained him, some perception of maidenly dignity that enfolded her and made her more than the girl who had waited on the table.

"You were a polite little boy," she recalled, filling the breach made by his silence. "I remember that you carried me across the street, to save my slippers from the wet. I thought you were wonderful. I have never forgotten."

Neither had Van Alen forgotten. It had been a great feat for his little strength. There had been other boys there, bigger boys, but he had offered, and had been saved humiliation by her girlish slimness and feather weight.

"I was a strong little fellow then," was his comment: "I am a strong little fellow now."

She turned on him reproachful eyes. "Why do you always harp on it?" she demanded.

"On what?"

"Your size. You twist everything, turn everything, so that we come back to it."

He tried to answer lightly, but his voice shook. "Perhaps it is because in your presence I desire more than ever the full stature of a man."

He was in deadly earnest. Hitherto he had been willing to match his brain, his worldly knowledge, his ancestry, against the charms of the women he had met; but here with this girl, standing like a young goddess under the wide, sunset sky, he felt that only for strength and beauty should she choose her mate.

He wondered what he must seem in her eyes; with his shoulder on a level with hers, with his stocky build that saved him from effeminacy, his carefulness of attire—which is at once the burden and the salvation of the small man.

As for his face, he knew that its homeliness was redeemed by a certain strength of chin, by keen gray eyes, and by a shock of dark hair that showed a little white at the temples. There were worse-looking men, he knew, but that, at the present moment, gave little comfort.

She chose to receive his remark in silence, and, as they came to a path that branched from the road, she said:

"I am going to help take care of a child who is sick. You see I am mistress of all trades—nurse, waitress, charwoman, when there is nothing else."

He glanced at her hands. "I cannot believe that you scrub," he said.

"I sit up at night to care for my hands"—there was a note of bitterness in her tone—"and I wear gloves when I work. There are some things that one desires to hold on to, and my mother and my grandmother were ladies of leisure."

"Would you like that—to be a lady of leisure?"

She turned and smiled at him. "How can I tell?" she asked; "I have never tried it."

She started to leave him as she said it, but he held her with a question: "Shall you sit up all night?"

She nodded. "His mother has had no sleep for two nights."

"Is he very ill?"

The girl shrugged her shoulders. "Who knows? There is no doctor near, and his mother is poor. We are fighting it out together."

There was something heroic in her cool acceptance of her hard life. He was silent for a moment, and then he said: "Would you have time to read my book to-night?"

"Oh, if I might," she said eagerly, "but you haven't it with you."

"I will bring it," he told her, "after supper."

"But," she protested.

"There are no 'buts,'" he said, smiling; "if you will read it, I will get it to you."

The sky had darkened, and, as he went toward home, he faced clouds in the southeast.

"It is going to rain," Otto Brand prophesied as they sat down to supper.

The other three men hoped that it would not. Already the ground was soaked, making the cutting of corn impossible, and another rain with a frost on top of it would spoil all chance of filling the silo.

Van Alen could not enter into their technical objections. He hoped it would not rain, because he wanted to take a book to Mazie Wetherell, and he had not brought a rain-coat.

But it did rain, and he went without a rain-coat!

The house, as he neared it, showed no light, and under the thick canopy of the trees there was no sound but the drip, drip of the rain. By feeling and instinct he found the front door, and knocked.

There was a movement inside, and then Mazie Wetherell asked softly: "Who's there?"

"I have brought the book."

The bolt was withdrawn, and in the hall, scarcely lighted by the shaded lamp in the room beyond, stood the girl, in a loose gray gown, with braided shining hair—a shadowy being, half-merged into the shadows.

"I thought you would not come," in a hushed tone, "in such a storm."

"I said I should come. The book may help you through the long night."

She caught her breath quickly. "The child is awfully ill."

"Are you afraid? Let me stay."

"Oh, no, no. His mother is sleeping, and I shall have your book."

She did not ask him in, and so he went away at once, beating his way back in the wind and rain, fording a little stream where the low foot-bridge was covered, reaching home soaking wet, but afire with dreams.

Otto Brand was waiting for him, a little curious as to what had taken him out so late, but, getting no satisfaction, he followed Van Alen up-stairs, and built a fire for him in the big bedroom. And presently, in the light of the leaping flames, the roses on the canopy of the bed glowed pink.

"Ain't you goin' to sleep in the bed?" Otto asked, as he watched Van Alen arrange the covers on the couch.

"No," said Van Alen shortly, "the honor is too great. It might keep me awake."

"My feet would hang over," Otto said. "Funny thing, wasn't it, for a man to make a will like that?"

"I suppose every man has a right to do as he pleases," Van Alen responded coldly. He was not inclined to discuss the eccentricities of his little old ancestor with this young giant.

"Of course," Otto agreed, and his next remark was called forth by Van Alen's pale blue pajamas.

"Well, those are new on me."

Van Alen explained that in the city they were worn, and that silk was cool, but while he talked he was possessed by a kind of fury. For the first time the delicate garments, the luxurious toilet articles packed in his bag, seemed foppish, unnecessary, things for a woman. With all of them, he could not compete with this fair young god, who used a rough towel and a tin basin on the kitchen bench.

"Maybe I'd better go," the boy offered. "You'll want to go to bed."

But Van Alen held him. "I always smoke first," he said, and, wrapped in his dressing-gown, he flung himself into a chair on the opposite side of the fireplace.

And after a time he brought the conversation around to Mazie Wetherell.

He found the boy rather sure of his success with her.

"All women are alike," he said; "you've just got to keep after them long enough."

279

To Van Alen the idea of this hulking youngster as a suitor for such a woman seemed preposterous. He was not fit to touch the hem of her garment. He was unmannerly, uneducated; he was not of her class—and even as he analyzed, the boy stood up, perfect in his strong young manhood.

"I've never had much trouble making women like me," he said; "and I ain't goin' to give up, just because she thinks she's better than the rest round about here."

He went away, and Van Alen stared long into the fire, until the flames left a heart of opal among the ashes.

He had not been unsuccessful with women himself. Many of them had liked him, and might have loved him if he had cared to make them. But until he met Mazie Wetherell he had not cared.

Desperately he wished for some trial of courage where he might be matched against Otto Brand. He grew melodramatic in his imaginings, and saw himself at a fire, fighting the flames to reach Mazie, while Otto Brand shrank back. He stood in the path of runaway horses, and Otto showed the white feather. He nursed her through the plague, and Otto fled fearfully from the disease.

And then having reached the end of impossibilities, he stood up and shook himself.

"I'm a fool," he said to the flames, shortly, and went to bed, to lie awake, wondering whether Mazie Wetherell had reached that chapter of his book where he had written of love, deeply, reverently, with a foreknowledge of what it might mean to him some day. It was that chapter which had assured the success of his novel. Would it move her, as it had moved him when he reread it? That was what love ought to be—a thing fine, tender, touching the stars! That was what love might be to him, to Mazie Wetherell, what it could never be to Otto Brand.

At breakfast the next morning he found Mrs. Brand worrying about her waitress.

"I guess she couldn't get back, and I've got a big day's work."

"I'll go and look her up," Van Alen offered; but he found that he was not to go alone, for Otto was waiting for him at the gate.

"I ain't got nothin' else to do," the boy said; "everything is held up by the rain."

It was when they came to the little stream that Van Alen had forded the night before that they saw Mazie Wetherell.

"I can't get across," she called from the other side.

The bridge, which had been covered when Van Alen passed, was now washed away, and the foaming brown waters overflowed the banks.

"I'll carry you over," Otto called, and straightway he waded through the stream, and the water came above his high boots to his hips.

He lifted her in his strong arms and brought her back, with her bright hair fluttering against his lips, and Van Alen, raging impotently, stood and watched him.

It seemed to him that Otto's air was almost insultingly triumphant as he set the girl on her feet and smiled down at her. And as she smiled back, Van Alen turned on his heel and left them.

Presently he heard her running after him lightly over the sodden ground.

And when she reached his side she said: "Your book was wonderful."

"But he carried you over the stream."

Her eyes flashed a question, then blazed. "There, you've come back to it," she said. "What makes you?"

"Because I wanted to carry you myself."

"Silly," she said; "any man could carry me across the stream—but only you could write that chapter in the middle of the book."

"You liked it?" he cried, radiantly.

"Like it?" she asked. "I read it once, and then I read it again—on my knees."

Her voice seemed to drop away breathless. Behind them Otto Brand tramped, whistling; but he might have been a tree, or the sky, or the distant hills, for all the thought they took of him.

"I wanted to beg your pardon," the girl went on, "for what I said the other day—it is a great thing to write a book like that—greater than fighting a battle or saving a life, for it saves people's ideals; perhaps in that way it saves their souls."

"Then I may sleep in the canopy bed?" His voice was calm, but inwardly he was much shaken by her emotion.

Her eyes, as she turned to him, had in them the dawn of that for which he had hoped.

"Why not?" she said, quickly. "You are greater than your grandfather—you are—" She stopped and laughed a little, and, in this moment of her surrender, her beauty shone like a star.

"Oh, little great man," she said, tremulously, "your head touches the skies!"

I

"No man," said O-liver Lee, "should earn more than fifteen dollars a week. After that he gets—soft."

"Soft nothing!"

O-liver sat on a box in front of the post-office. He was lean and young and without a hat. His bare head was one of the things that made him unique. The other men within doors and without wore hats—broad hats that shielded them from the California sun; or, as in the case of Atwood Jones, who came from the city, a Panama of an up-to-the-minute model.

But O-liver's blond mane waved in every passing breeze. It was only when he rode forth on his mysterious journeys that he crowned himself with a Chinese straw helmet.

Because he wore no hat his skin was tanned. He had blue eyes that twinkled and, as I have said, a blond mane.

"Fifteen dollars a week," he reaffirmed, "is enough."

Fifteen dollars was all that O-liver earned. He was secretary to an incipient oil king. As the oil king's monarchy was largely on paper he found it hard at times to compass even the fifteen dollars that went to his secretary.

The other men scorned O-liver's point of view and told him so. They were a rather prosperous bunch, all except Tommy Drew, who dealt in a dilettante fashion in insurance, and who sat at O-liver's feet and worshiped him.

It was Saturday and some of the men had drifted in from the surrounding ranches; others from the cities, from the mountains, from the valleys, from the desert, from the sea. Tinkersfield had assumed a sudden importance as an oil town. All of the men had business connected in some way with Tinkersfield. And all of them earned more than fifteen dollars a week.

Therefore they disputed O-liver's statement. "If you had a wife—" said one.

"Ah," said O-liver, "if I had—"

"Ain't you got any ambition?" Henry Bittinger demanded. Henry was pumping out oil in prodigious quantities. He had bought a motor car and a fur coat. It was too hot most of the time for the coat, but the car stood now at rest across the road—long and lovely—much more of an aristocrat than the man who owned it.

"Ambition for what?" O-liver demanded.

Henry's eyes went to the pride of his heart.

"Well, I should think you'd want a car."

"I'd give," said O-liver, "my kingdom for a horse, but not for a car."

O-liver's little mare stood quite happily in the shade; she was slim as to leg, shining as to coat, and with the eyes of a loving woman.

"I should think you'd want to get ahead," said Atwood Jones, who sold shoes up and down the coast. He was a junior member of the firm, but still liked to go on the road. He liked to lounge like this in front of the post-office and smoke in the golden air with a lot of men sitting round. Atwood had been raised on a ranch. He had listened to the call of the city, but he was still a small-town man.

"Ahead of what?" asked O-liver.

Atwood was vague. He felt himself a rising citizen. Some day he expected to marry and set his wife up in a mansion in San Francisco, with seasons of rest and recreation at Del Monte and Coronado and the East. If the shoe business kept to the present rate of prosperity he would probably have millions to squander in his old age.

He tried to say something of this to O-liver.

"Well, will you be any happier?" asked the young man with the bare head. "I'll wager my horse against your car that when you're drunk with dollars you'll look back to a day like this and envy yourself. It's happiness I'm talking about."

"Well, are you happy?" Atwood challenged.

"Why not?" asked the young man lightly. "I have enough to eat, money for tobacco, a book or two—an audience." He waved his hand to include the listening group and smiled.

It was O-liver's lightness which gave him the whip hand in an argument. They were most of them serious men; not serious in a Puritan sense of taking thought of their souls' salvation and the world's redemption, but serious in their pursuit of wealth. They had to be rich. If they weren't they couldn't marry, or if they were married they had to be rich so that their wives could keep up with the wives of the other fellows who were getting rich. They had to have cars and money to spend at big hotels and for travel, money for diamonds and furs, money for everything.

But here was O-liver Lee, who said lightly that money weighed upon him. He didn't want it. He'd be darned if he wanted it. Money brought burdens. As for himself, he'd read and ride Mary Pick.

"Anyhow," said Henry, with his hands folded across his stomach—Henry had grown fat riding in his car—"anyhow, when you get old you'll be sorry."

"I shall never grow old," said O-liver, and stood up. "I shall be young—till I—die."

They laughed at him outwardly, but in their hearts they did not laugh. They could not think of him as old. They felt that in a hundred years he would still be strong and sure, his blond mane untouched by gray, his clear blue eyes unblurred.

Atwood rounding them all up for a drink found that O-liver wouldn't drink.

"Drank too much, once upon a time," he confessed frankly. "But I'll give you a toast."

He gave it, poised on his box like a young god on the edge of the world.

"Here's to poverty! May we learn to love her for the favors she denies!"

"Queer chap," said Atwood to Henry later.

Henry nodded. "He's queer, but he's great company. Always has a crowd round him. But no ambition."

"Pity," said Atwood. "How'd he get that name—O-liver?"

"One of the fellows got gay and called him 'Ollie.' Lee stopped him. 'My name is Oliver Lee. If you want a nickname you can say "O-liver." But I'm not "Ollie" from this time on, understand?' And I'm darned if the fellow didn't back down. There was something about O-liver that would have made anybody back down. He didn't have a gun; it was just something in his voice."

"Say, he's wasted," said Atwood. "A man with his line of talk might be President of the United States."

"Sure he might," Henry agreed. "I've told him a lot of times he's throwing away his chance."

II

The office of the incipient oil king was on the main street of the straggling town. At the back there was a window which gave a view of a hill or two and a mountain beyond. The mountain stuck its nose into the clouds and was whitecapped.

It was this view at the back which O-liver faced when he sat at his machine. When he rested he liked to fix his eyes on that white mountain. O-liver had acquired of late a fashion of looking up. There had been a time when he had kept his eyes on the ground. He did not care to remember that time. The work that he did was intermittent, and between his industrious spasms he read a book. He had a shelf at hand where he kept certain volumes—Walt Whitman, Vanity Fair, Austin Dobson, Landor's Imaginary Conversations, and a rather choice collection of Old Mission literature. He had had it in mind that he might some day write a play with Santa Barbara as a background, but he had stopped after the first act. He had ridden down one night and had reached the mission at dawn. The gold cross had flamed as the sun rose over the mountain. After that it had seemed somehow a desecration to put it in a painted scene. O-liver had rather queer ideas as to the sacredness of certain things.

Tommy Drew, who had a desk in the same office, read Vanity Fair and wanted to talk about it. "Say, I don't like that girl, O-liver."

"What girl?"

"Becky."

"Why not?"

"Well, she's a grafter. And her husband was a poor nut."

"I'm afraid he was," said O-liver.

"He oughta of dragged her round by the hair of her head."

"They don't do it, Tommy," O-liver was thoughtful. "After all a woman's a woman. It's easier to let her go."

An astute observer might have found O-liver cynical about women. If he said nothing against them he certainly never said anything for them. And he kept strictly away from everything feminine in Tinkersfield, in spite of the fact that his good looks won him more than one glance from sparkling eyes.

"He acts afraid of skirts," Henry had said to Tommy on one occasion.

"He?" Tommy was scornful. "He ain't afraid of anything!"

Henry knew it. "Maybe it's because you can't do much with women on fifteen a week."

"Well, I guess that's so," said Tommy, who made twenty and who had a hopeless passion.

His hopeless passion was Jane. Jane lived with her mother in a small rose-bowered bungalow at the edge of the town. She and her mother owned the bungalow, which was fortunate; they hadn't a penny for rent. Jane's father had died of a weak lung and the failure of his oil well. He had left the two women without an income. Jane's mother was delicate and Jane couldn't leave her to go out to work. So Jane dug in the little garden, and they lived largely on vegetables. She sewed for the neighbors, and bought medicine and now and then a bit of meat. She was young and strong and she had wonderful red hair. Tommy thought it was the most beautiful hair in the world. Jane was for him a sort of goddess woman. She was, he felt, infinitely above him. She knew a great deal that he didn't, about books and things—like O-liver. She sewed for his mother, and that was the way he had met her. He would go over and sit on her front steps and talk. He felt that she treated him like a little dog that she wouldn't harm, but wouldn't miss if it went away. He told her of Vanity Fair and of how he felt about Becky.

"If she had been content to earn an honest living," Jane stated severely, "the story would have had a different ending."

"Well, she wanted things," Tommy said.

"Most women do." Jane jabbed her needle into a length of pink gingham which, when finished, would be rompers for a youngster across the street. "I do; and I intend to have them."

"How?" asked the interested Tommy.

"Work for them."

"O-liver says that fifteen dollars a week is enough for anybody to earn."

Jane had heard of O-liver. Tommy sang his constant praises.

"Why fifteen?"

"After that you get soft."

Jane laid down the length of pink gingham and looked at him. She hated to sew on pink; it clashed dreadfully with her hair.

"I should say," she stated with scorn, "that your O-liver's lazy."

"No, he isn't. He only wants enough to eat and enough to smoke and enough to read."

"That sounds all right, but it isn't. What's he going to do when he's old?"

"He ain't ever going to grow old. He said so, and if you'd see him you'd know."

Jane felt within her the stirring of curiosity. But she put it down sternly. She had no time for it.

"Tommy," she said, "I've been thinking. I've got to earn more money, and I want your help."

Tommy's faithful eyes held a look of doglike affection.

"Oh, if I can——" he quavered.

"I've got to get ahead." Jane was breathless. Her eyes shone.

"I've got to get ahead, Tommy. I can't live all my life like this." She held up the pink strip. "Even if I am a woman, there ought to be something more than making rompers for the rest of my days."

"You might," said the infatuated Tommy, "marry."

"Marry? Marry whom?"

Tommy wished that he might shout "Me!" from the housetops. But he knew the futility of it.

"I shall never marry," she said, "until I find somebody different from anything I've ever seen."

Jane's ideas of men were bounded largely by the weakness of her father and the crudeness of men like Henry Bittinger, Atwood Jones and others of their kind. She didn't consider Tommy at all. He was a nice boy and a faithful friend. His mother, too, was a faithful friend. She classed them together.

Her plan, told with much coming and going of lovely color, was this: She had read that the way to make money was to find the thing that a community lacked and supply it. Considering it seriously she had decided that in Tinkersfield there was need of good food.

"There's just one horrid little eating house," she told Tommy, "when the men come in from out of town."

"Nothing fit to eat either," Tommy agreed; "and they make up on booze."

She nodded. "Tommy," she said, and leaned toward him, "I had thought of sandwiches—home-made bread and slices of ham—wrapped in waxed paper; and of taking them down and selling them in front of the post-office on Saturday nights."

Tommy's eyes bulged. "You take them down?"

"Why not? Any work is honorable, Tommy."

Tommy felt that it wouldn't be a goddess role.

"I can't see it." The red crept up into his honest freckled face. "You know the kind of women that's round on Saturday nights."

"I am not that kind of woman." She was suddenly austere.

He found himself stammering. "I didn't mean—"

"Of course you didn't. But it's a good plan, Tommy. Say you think it's a good plan."

He would have said anything to please her. "Well, you might try."

The next day he found himself talking it over with O-liver. "She wants to sell them on Saturday nights."

"Tell her," said O-liver, "to stay at home."

"But she's got to have some money."

"Money," said O-liver, "is the root of evil. You say she has a garden. Let her live on leeks and lettuce."

"Leeks and lettuce?" said poor Tommy, who had never heard of leeks.

"Her complexion will be better," said O-liver, "and her peace of mind great."

"Her complexion is perfect," Tommy told him, "and she isn't the peaceful kind. Her hair is red."

"Red-haired women"—O-liver had his eye on Vanity Fair—"red-haired women always flaunt themselves."

Tommy, softening O-liver's words a bit, gave them in the form of advice to Jane: "He thinks you'd better live on leeks and lettuce than go down-town like that."

Jane gasped. "Leeks and lettuce? Me? He doesn't know what he's talking about! And anyhow, what can you expect of a man like that?"

A week later Jane in a white shirt-waist and white apron came down with her white-covered basket into the glare of the town's white lights. The night was warm and she wore no hat. Her red hair was swept back from her forehead with a droop over the ears. She had white skin and strong white teeth. Her eyes were as gray as the sea on stormy days. Tommy came after her with a wooden box, which he set on end, and she placed her basket on it. The principal stores of the small town, the one hotel and the post-office were connected by a covered walk which formed a sort of arcade, so that the men lounging against doorways or tip-tilted in chairs seemed in a sort of gallery from which they surveyed the Saturday-night crowd which paraded the street.

Jane folded up the cloth which covered her basket and displayed her wares. "Don't stick round, Tommy," she said. "I shall do better alone."

But as she raised her head and saw the eyes of the men upon her a rich color surged into her cheeks.

She put out her little sign bravely:

HOME-MADE SANDWICHES—TWENTY CENTS

With a sense of adventure upon them the men flocked down at once. They bought at first because the wares were offered by a pretty girl. They came back to buy because never had there been such sandwiches.

Jane had improved upon her first idea. There were not only ham sandwiches; there were baked beans between brown bread, thin slices of broiled bacon in hot baking-powder biscuit. Henry Bittinger said to Atwood Jones afterward: "The food was so good that if she had been as ugly as sin she'd have got away with it."

"She isn't ugly," said Atwood, and had a fleeting moment of speculation as to whether Jane with her red hair would fit into his plutocratic future.

Jane had made fifty sandwiches. She sold them all, and took ten dollars home with her.

"I shall make a hundred next time," she said to Tommy, whom she picked up on the way back. "And—it wasn't so dreadful, Tommy."

But that night as she lay in bed looking out toward the mountain, silver-tipped in the moonlight, she had a shivering sense of the eyes of some of the men—of Tillotson, who kept the hotel, and of others of his kind.

O-liver had stayed at home that Saturday night to write a certain weekly letter. He had stayed at home also because he didn't approve of Jane.

"But you haven't seen her," Tommy protested.

"I know the type."

On Sunday morning Tommy brought him a baked-bean sandwich. "It isn't as fresh as it might be. But you can see what she's giving us."

There were months of O-liver's life which had been spent with a grandmother in Boston. His grandmother had made brown bread and she had baked beans. And now as he ate his sandwich there was the savor of all the gastronomic memories of a healthy and happy childhood.

"It's delicious," he said, "but she'd better not mix with that crowd."

"She doesn't mix," said Tommy.

"She'll have to." O-liver had in mind a red-haired woman, raw-boned, with come-hither eyes. Her kind was not uncommon. Tommy's infatuation would of course elevate her to a pedestal.

"She's going to make a hundred sandwiches next week," Tommy vouchsafed.

O-liver's mind could scarcely compass one hundred sandwiches. "She'd better stick to her leeks and lettuce."

He rode away the next Saturday night. It was his protest against the interest roused in the community by this Jane who sold sandwiches. He heard of her everywhere. Some of the men were respectful and some were not. It depended largely on the nature of the particular male.

O-liver rode Mary Pick and wore his straw helmet. His way led down into the valley and up again and down, until at last he came to the sea. Then he followed the water's edge, letting Mary Pick dance now and then on the hard beach, with the waves curling up like cream, and beyond the waves a stretch of pale azure to the horizon.

He reached finally a fantastic settlement. Against the sky towered walls which might have inclosed an ancient city—walls built of cloth and wood instead of stone. Beyond these walls were thatched cottages which had no occupants; a quaint church which had no congregation; a Greek temple which had no vestals, no sacred fire, no altar; hedges which had no roots. O-liver weighing the hollowness of it all had thought whimsically of an old nursery rime:

The first sent a goose without a bone;
The second sent a cherry without a stone;
The third sent a blanket without a thread;
The fourth sent a book that no man could read.

At the end of the settlement was a vast studio lighted by a glass roof. Entering, O-liver was transported at once to the dance hall on the Barbary Coast—a great room with a bar at one end, the musicians on a platform at the other, a stairway leading upward. Groups of people waited for a signal to dance, to drink, to act whatever part had been assigned them—people with unearthly pink complexions. The heat was intense.

With her face upturned to the director, who was mounted on a chair, stood a childish creature who was pinker, if possible, than the rest. She had fluffy hair of pale gold. She ran up the stairway presently, and the light was turned on her. It made of her fluffy hair a halo. In the strong glare everything about her was overemphasized, but O-liver knew that when she showed up on the screen she would be entrancing.

He had first seen her on the screen. He had met her afterward at her hotel. She had seemed as ingenuous as the parts she played. Perhaps she was. He could never be quite sure. Perhaps the money she had made afterward had spoiled her. She had jumped from fifty dollars a week to a thousand.

After that O-liver could give her nothing. He had an allowance from his mother of three thousand a year. Fluffy Hair made as much as that in three weeks. Where he had been king of his own domain he became a sort of gentleman footman, carrying her sables and her satchels. But that was not the worst of it. He found that they had not a taste in common. She laughed at his books, at his love of sea and sky. She even laughed at his Mary Pick, whose name suggested a hated rival. And so he left her—laughing.

A certain sense of responsibility, however, took him to her once a month, and a letter went to her every week. She was his wife. He continued in a sense to watch over her. Yet she resented his watching.

From her stairway she had seen him, and when a rest was granted she came down to him.

"I'll be through presently," she said. "We can go to my hotel."

Her rooms in the hotel overlooked the sea. There was a balcony, and they sat on it in long lazy chairs and had iced things to drink.

O-liver drank lemonade. His wife had something stronger.

"I have not been well," she said; "it's a part of the doctor's prescription."

She had removed the pink from her face, and he saw that she was pale.

"You are working too hard," he told her. "You'd better take a month in the desert, out of doors."

She shivered. She hated the out-of-doors that he raved about. They had spent their honeymoon in a tent. She had been wild to get back to civilization. It had been their first moment of disillusion.

She showed him before he went some of the things she had acquired since his last visit—an ermine coat, a string of pearls.

"I saw them in your last picture," he told her. "You really visit me by proxy. I find your name on the boards, and walk in with a lot of other men and look at you. And not one of them dreams that I've ever seen the woman on the screen."

"Well, they wouldn't of course." She had never taken his name. Her own was too valuable.

When he told her good-bye he asked a question: "Are you happy?"

For a moment her face clouded. "I'm not quite sure. Is anybody? But I like the way I am living, Ollie."

He had a sense of relief. "So do I," he said. "I earn fifteen dollars a week. The papers say that you earn fifteen hundred—and you're not quite twenty."

"There isn't a man in this hotel that makes so much," she told him complacently. "The women try to snub me, but they can't. Money talks."

It seemed to him that in her case it shouted. As he rode back on Mary Pick he thought seriously of his fifteen dollars a week and her fifteen hundred; and of how little either weighed in the balance of happiness.

IV

It was not until the following Saturday that he saw Jane. She had made two hundred sandwiches. She had got Tommy's mother to help her. She had invented new combinations, always holding to the idea of satisfying the substantial appetites of men.

There would be no use, she argued, in offering five-o'clock-tea combinations.

She was very busy and very happy and very hopeful.

"If this keeps up," she told her mother, "I shall rent a little shop and sell them over the counter."

Her mother had an invalid's pessimism. "They may tire of them."

They were not yet tired. They gave Jane and her basket vociferous greeting, crowding round her and buying eagerly. Atwood and Henry having placed orders hung back, content to wait for a later moment when she might have leisure to talk to them.

Tommy helped Jane to hand out sandwiches and make change. He felt like the faithful squire of a great lady. He had read much romantic literature, and he served as well if not as picturesquely as a page in doublet and hose.

So O-liver saw them. He had been riding all the afternoon on Mary Pick. He had gone up into the Cañon of the Honey Pots. No one knew it by that name but O-liver, but at all the houses one could buy honey. Up and down the road were little stands on which were set forth glasses and jars of amber sweet. The bees flashed like motes in the sunlight, the air was heavy with the fragrance of the flowers which yielded their largess to the marauders.

It was dark when he rode down toward the town. It lay before him, all twinkling lights. Above it hung a thin moon and countless stars. It might have been a fairy town under the kindly cover of the night.

But when he reached the central square the illusion ceased. It was what men had made it—sordid, cheap. He stopped Mary Pick under a pepper tree and surveyed the scene.

Jane and her basket were the center of an excited group. She had almost reached the end of her supplies, and some one had suggested auctioning off the remainder. Jane had protested, but her protests had not availed. She had turned to Tommy for help, to Henry, to Atwood. They had done their best. But the man who led the crowd had an object in his leadership. It was Tillotson of the little hotel—red-faced, whisky-soaked.

"Sandwich Jane, Sandwich Jane!" he shouted. "That's the name for her, boys."

And they took it up and shouted "Sandwich Jane!"

It was at this moment that O-liver stopped under the pepper tree. The bright light fell directly on Jane's distressed face. He saw the swept-back brightness of her hair, her clear-cut profile, her white skin, her white teeth. But he saw more than this. "By Jove," he said, "she's a lady!"

If he had been talking to the men he would have said "Gosh!" It was only when he was alone that he permitted himself the indulgence of more formal language.

That Jane was harried he could see. And suddenly he rode forward on Mary Pick.

The crowd made way for him expectantly. There were always interesting developments when O-liver was on the scene.

"Gentlemen," he said, "let the lady speak for herself. I am not sure what you are trying to do, but it is evidently something she doesn't want done."

Jane flashed a grateful glance up at him. He was the unknown knight throwing down the gauntlet in her defense. He was different from the others—his voice was different.

"They want to auction off my sandwiches," she explained, "and they won't listen."

"I'm sure they will listen." O-liver on Mary Pick, with his hat off and his mane tossed back, might have been Henry of the white plumes. "Of course they'll listen."

And they did!

Jane stood on her box and addressed them.

"I don't want to get any more for my sandwiches than they are worth," she said earnestly. "I make good ones, and I sell them for twenty cents because they are the best of their kind. I am glad you like them. I want to earn my living and my mother's. She is sick, and I have to stay at home with her. And I don't mind being called 'Sandwich Jane.' It's a good name and I shall use it in my business. But I don't like being treated as you have treated me to-night. If it happens again I shall have to stop selling sandwiches; and I'd be sorry to have that happen, and I hope you'd be sorry too."

Her little speech was over. She stepped down composedly from the box, folded her cloth and picked up her basket. She said "Thank you" to O-liver, "Come on" to Tommy, and walked from among them with her light step and free carriage; and they stared after her.

O-liver sitting later in front of the post-office with his satellites round him found himself compelled to listen to praise of Jane.

"She's made a hit," Atwood said earnestly. "When a woman talks like that it's the straight goods."

Henry agreed. "She's got grit. It's her kind that get ahead. But it's a pity that she's got to work to make a living."

Atwood, too, thought it was a pity. And presently he and Henry fell into silence as they fitted Jane into various dreams. Atwood's dream had to do with a mansion high on Frisco's hills. But Henry saw her beside him in his long and lovely car. He saw her, too, in a fur coat.

V

"I feel," said Jane, "like a murderer." Tommy and O-liver had stopped at her front gate to leave her some books.

"Why?" It was O-liver who asked it.

"Come and see." She led them round the house. Death and destruction reigned.

"I poured gasoline into the ants' nests and set them on fire—and now look at them!"

There were a few survivors toiling among the ruins.

"They are taking out the dead bodies," Jane explained. "It's so human that it's tragic. I'll never do it again."

"You can't let them eat you up."

"I know. It's one of the puzzles." She sat looking down at them. "How busy they are!"

"Too busy," O-liver stated. "They are worse than bees. There are at least some drones in the hive."

"Poor drones," said Jane.

"Why?" quickly.

"To miss the best."

"Is work the best?"

She said "Yes," adding after a little: "I don't just mean making sandwiches. That's just a beginning. There's everything ahead."

She said it as if the world were hers. O-liver, in spite of himself, was thrilled. "How do you know that everything is ahead?"

"I shall make it come"—securely.

They sat in silence for a while; then O-liver said: "I have brought you a book."

It was an old copy of Punch.

"I shall like it," she said. "Sometimes the evenings are dull when my work is over."

"Dullness comes for me when work begins."

Her straight gaze met his. "You say that with your lips; you don't mean it."

"How do you know?"

"I'm not sure how I know. But you haven't found the thing yet that you like—the incentive."

"Tommy wants me to go into politics. He and Henry Bittinger. Henry says I ought to be President." O-liver chuckled.

But she took it seriously. "Why not? You've the brains and the magnetism. Can't you see how the crowd draws to you on Saturday nights?"

"Like bees round a honey pot? Yes." His face grew suddenly stern. "But so will mosquitoes buzz round a stagnant pool."

"You're not a stagnant pool and you know it."

"What am I?"

She made a sudden gesture as if she gave him up. "Sometimes I think you are like the sea—on a lazy day—with a storm brewing."

He wondered as he went home—what storm?

He had seen a good deal of Jane since that Saturday night when he had championed her cause. It had been fall then, with the hills brown and the berries red on the pepper trees. It was spring now, with all the world green and growing.

She had spoken of him to Tommy, and Tommy had been a faithful go-between. He had played upon their mutual love of books. At first O-liver had sent her books, then he had taken them. He had met her mother, had seen her in her home doing feminine things, sewing on lengths of pink and blue—filling the vases with the flowers that he brought.

And as they had met and talked his veins had been filled with new wine. He had never known intimately such a woman. His mother transplanted from the East by her marriage to a Western man had turned her eyes always backward. Her son had been born in the East, he had spent his holidays and vacations with his Eastern relatives. He had gone to an Eastern school to prepare for an Eastern college. Except for this one obsession with regard to her son's education his mother was self-centered. She was an idolized wife, a discontented woman—— she had shown O-liver no heights to which to aspire.

And so he had not aspired. He had spent his days in what might be termed, biblically, riotous living. His mother had hoped for an aristocratic and Eastern marriage. When he married Fluffy Hair she had allowed him three thousand a year and had asked him not to bring his wife to see her. His father had refused to give him a penny. O-liver's wild oats and wilfulness cut him off, he ruled, from parental consideration. "You are not my son," he had said sternly. "If the time ever comes when you can say you are sorry, I'll see you."

O-liver having married Fluffy Hair had found her also self-centered—not a lady like his mother, but fundamentally of the same type. Neither of them had made him feel that he might be more than he was. They had always shrunk him to their own somewhat small patterns.

Jane's philosophy came to him therefore like a long-withheld stimulant. "You might be President of the United States."

When Henry or Atwood or Tommy had said it to him he had laughed. When Jane said it he did not laugh.

VI

And so it came about that one day he rose and went to his father. And he said: "Dad, will you kill the fatted calf?"

His father lived in a great Tudor house which gave the effect of age but was not old. It had a minstrels' gallery, a big hall and a little hall, mullioned windows and all the rest of it. It had been built because of a whim of his wife's. But O-liver's father in the ten years he had lived in it had learned to love it. But more than he loved the house he loved the hills that sloped away from it, the mountains that towered above it, the sea that lay at the foot of the cliff.

"It is God's country," he would say with long-drawn breath. He had been born and bred in this golden West. All the passion he might have given to his alien wife and alien son was lavished on this land which was bone of his bone and flesh of his flesh.

And now his son had ridden up to him over those low hills at the foot of the mountain and had said: "Father, I have sinned."

O-liver had not put it scripturally. He had said: "I'm sorry, dad. You said I needn't come back until I admitted the husks and swine."

There was a light on the fine face of the older man. "Oliver, I never hoped to hear you say it." His hand dropped lightly on the boy's shoulders. "My son which was dead is alive again?"

"Yes, dad."

"What brought you to life?"

"A woman."

The hand dropped. "Not—"

"Not my wife. Put your hand back, dad. Another woman."

He sat down beside his father on the terrace. The sea far below them was sapphire, the cliffs pink with moss—gorgeous color. Orange umbrellas dotted the distant beach.

"Your mother is down there," Jason Lee said. "Sun baths and all that. You said there was another woman, Oliver."

"Yes." Quite simply and honestly he told him about Sandwich Jane. "She's made me see things."

"What things?"

"Well, she thinks I've got it in me to get anywhere. She insists that if I'd put my heart into it I might be—President."

One saw their likeness to each other in their twinkling eyes!

"She says that men follow me; and they do. I've found that out since I went to Tinkersfield. She wants me to go into politics—there's a gang down there that rules the town—rotten crowd. It would be some fight if I did."

His father was interested at once. "It was what I wanted—when I was young—politics—clean politics, with a chance at statesmanship. Yes, I wanted it. But your mother wanted—money."

"Money hasn't any meaning to me now, dad. If I slaved until I dropped I couldn't make fifteen hundred a week."

"Does—your wife make that now?"

"Yes. She's making it and spending it, I fancy."

Silence. Then: "What of this—other woman. What are you going to do about her?"

O-liver leaned forward, speaking earnestly. "I love her. But I'm not free. It's all a muddle."

"Does she know you're married?"

"No. I've got to tell her. But I'll lose her if I do. Her comradeship, I mean. And I don't want to give it up."

"There is of course a solution."

"What solution?"

"Divorce."

"It wouldn't be a solution for Jane. She's not that kind. Marriage with her means till death parts. I'll have to lose her. But it hurts."

VII

It was when Jane rented an empty room fronting on the arcade and set up a sandwich shop that Tillotson saw how serious the thing was going to be.

He had had all the restaurant and hotel trade. Men coming up in motors or on horseback, dusty and tired, had eaten and drunk at his squalid tables, swearing at the food but unable to get anything better. And now here was a woman who covered her counters with snowy oilcloth—who had shining urns of coffees, delectable pots of baked beans, who put up in neat boxes lunches that made men rush back for more and more and more—and whose sandwiches were the talk of the coast!

It had to be stopped.

The only way to stop it was to make it uncomfortable for Jane. There were many ways in which the thing could be done— by small and subtle persecutions, by insinuations, by words bandied from one man's evil mouth to another. Tillotson had done the thing before. But he found as the days went on that he had not before had a Jane to deal with. She was linked in the minds of most of the men with a whiteness like that of her own spotless shop.

Gradually Jane became aware of a sinister undercurrent. She found herself dealing with forces that threatened her. There were men who came into her shop to buy, and who stayed to say things that set her cheeks flaming. She mentioned none of these things to Henry or Atwood or Tommy. But she spoke once to O-liver.

"Tillotson must be at the bottom of it. Two drunken loafers stumbled in the other day, straight from the hotel. And when I telephoned to Tillotson to come and get them he laughed at me."

Tillotson was the sheriff. It was an office which he did not honor. In a month or two his term would be up. O-liver riding alone into the mountains stated the solution: "I've got to beat Tillotson."

But first he had things to say to Jane. Since his talk with his father he had known that it must come. He had stayed away from her as much as possible. It had not been a conspicuous withdrawal, for she was very busy and had little time for him. Tommy's mother kept her little home in order and looked after the invalid, so that Jane could give undivided attention to her growing business. O-liver saw her most often at the shop, when he stopped in for a pot of beans—eating them on the spot and discoursing on many things.

288

"My Boston grandmother baked beans like this," he told her on one occasion. "She was a great little woman, Jane, as essentially of the East as you are of the West. She held to the traditions of the past; you are blazing new ways for women, selling sandwiches in the market-place. By Jove, it was superb the way you did it, Jane!"

She was always in a glow when he left her. Here was a man different from her father, different from Henry Bittinger and Atwood Jones. She smiled a little as she thought of Atwood. He had asked her to marry him. He had told her of the things he had ahead of him that he wanted her to share. And he had been much downcast when she had refused him. She had, he felt, smudged the brightness of his splendid future. He couldn't understand a woman throwing away a thing like that.

But he bore her no grudge and was still her friend. Henry, too, was her friend. He had not yet tried his fate with Jane, but he still dreamed of her as lovely in his long car and a fur coat. And he hoped to make his dreams come true.

Tommy had set aside all selfish hopes. He had a feeling that Jane liked O-liver. He loved them both. If he could not have Jane he wanted O-liver to have her. He kept a wary eye therefore on Henry and Atwood.

It was Tommy who found out first about Fluffy Hair. She had never cared to have the world know of her marriage. She had felt that those who loved her on the screen would prefer her fancy free. But it was known at the studio, and some one drifting up to Tinkersfield recognized O-liver and told Tommy.

Tommy for once in his life was stern. "He oughta of told Jane. Somebody's got to tell her."

So the next day he took it on himself—feeling a traitor to his friend.

"Jane," he said, sitting on a high stool in her little sandwich shop—"Jane, O-liver's married."

Jane on the other side of the spotless counter gave him her earnest glance. "Yes," she said; "he told me."

"He did? Well, I'm glad. It wasn't a thing to keep, was it?"

"No," said Jane; "it wasn't. But you mustn't blame him, Tommy, and now that we both know, everything is all right, isn't it?"

"Yes," Tommy agreed; "if Tillotson doesn't get hold of it."

For it had been decided that O-liver was to run against Tillotson in the next election, and beat him if he could.

O-liver had told Jane about his marriage on the night before Tommy came to her. He had asked her to ride with him. "If you'll go this afternoon at four you shall have Mary Pick, and I'll take Tommy's horse."

They had carried their lunch with them and had eaten it at sunset in a lovely spot where the cañon opened out to show a shining yellow stretch of sea, with the hills like black serpents running into it.

Yet it was dark, with the stars above them and the sea a faint gray below, before O-liver said to her what he had brought her there to say.

He told her of his father and mother. Of Fluffy Hair.

"I waked up at last to the fact that I was letting two women support me. So I came here and began to work at fifteen dollars a week. And for the first time in my life I respected myself—and was content. And then I met you and saw things ahead. You made me see them."

He turned toward her in the dark. "Jane, I'm finding that I love you—mightily." He tried to speak lightly. "And I'm not free. And because I love you I've got to keep away. But I want you to understand that my friendship is the same—that it will always be the same. But I've got to keep away."

She was very honest about it. "I didn't dream that you felt like that—about me."

"No, you wouldn't. That's a part of your splendidness. Never taking anything to yourself. Jane, will you believe this—that what I may be hereafter will be because of you? If I ever do a big thing or a fine thing it will be because I came upon you that night with your head high and that rabble round you. You were light shining into the darkness of Tinkersfield. Jove, I wish I were a painter to put you on canvas as you were that night!"

They had ridden down later under the stars, and as they had stood for a moment overlooking the lights of the little town O-liver had said: "I make my big speech to-morrow night to beat Tillotson. I want you to be there. Will you? If I know you are there somewhere in the dark I shall pour out my soul—to you."

Was it any wonder that Jane, talking to Tommy the next morning about O-liver, felt her pulses pounding, her cheeks burning? She had lain awake all night thinking of the things he had said to her. It seemed a very big and wonderful thing that a man could love her like that. As toward morning the moonlight streamed in and she still lay awake she permitted herself to let her mind dwell for a moment on what her future might mean if he were in it. She was too busy and healthy to indulge in useless regrets. But she knew in that moment in the moonlight if he was not to be in her future no other man would ever be.

VIII

O-liver's speech was made in the open. There was a baseball park in Tinkersfield, bounded at the west end by a grove of eucalyptus. With this grove as a background a platform had been erected. From the platform the rival candidates would speak. At this time of the year it would be daylight when the meeting opened. Tillotson was not to speak for himself. He had brought a man down from San Francisco, a big politician with an oily tongue. O-liver would of course present his own case. The thing, as Atwood told Henry, promised to be exciting.

Jane came with Tommy. There was a sort of rude grand stand opposite the platform, and she had a seat well up toward the top. She wore a white skirt, a gray sweater and a white hat. She had a friendly smile for the people about her. And they smiled back. They liked Jane.

O-liver spoke first. Bare-headed, slender, with his air of eternal youth, he was silhouetted against the rose red of the afterglow.

When he began he led them lightly along paths of easy thought. He got their attention as he had so often got it in front of the post-office. He made them smile, he made them laugh, he led them indeed finally into roaring laughter. And when he had brought them thus into sympathy he began with earnestness to speak of Tinkersfield.

Jane, leaning forward, not missing a word, felt his magnetism. He spoke of the future of Tinkersfield. Of what must be done if it was to fulfill its destiny as a decent town. He did not mince his words.

"It will be just what you make up your minds now to have it—good and honest and clean, a place that the right kind of people will want to live in, or the place that will attract loungers and loafers."

He laid upon them the burden of individual responsibility. If a town was honest, he said, it was because the men in it were honest; if it was clean it was because its men were clean. It was for each man to decide at this election whether Tinkersfield should have a future of darkness or of light. There were men in that crowd who squared their shoulders to meet the blows of his eloquence, who kept them squared as they made their decision to do their part in the upbuilding of Tinkersfield.

Yet it was not perhaps so much the things that O-liver said as the way he said them. He had the qualities of leadership—a sincerity of the kind that sways men level with their leaders—the sincerity of a Lincoln, a Roosevelt. For him a democracy meant all the people. Not merely plain people, not indeed selected classes. Rich man, poor man, one, working together for the common good.

Back of his sincerity there was fire—and gradually his audience was lighted by his flame. They listened in a tense silence, which broke now and then into cheers. To Jane sitting high up on the benches he was a prophet—the John the Baptist of Tinkersfield.

"And he's mine, he's mine!" she exulted. This fineness of spirit, the fire and flame were hers. "If I know you are there somewhere in the dark I shall pour out my soul—to you—"

The darkness had not yet fallen, but the dusk had come. The platform was illumined by little lights like stars. Back of the platform the eucalyptus trees were now pale spectres, their leaves hanging nerveless in the still air.

O-liver sitting down amid thunders of applause let his eyes go for the moment to Jane. A lamp hung almost directly over her head. She had taken off her wide hat and her hair was glorious. She was leaning forward a little, her lips parted, her hands clasped, as if he still spoke to her.

As Tillotson's sponsor rose Jane straightened up, smiled at Tommy, and again set herself to listen.

The unctuous voice of the speaker was a contrast to O-liver's crisp tones. There were other contrasts not so apparent. This man was in the game for what he could get out of it. He wanted Tillotson to win because Tillotson's winning would strengthen his own position politically. He meant indeed that Tillotson should win. He was not particular as to methods.

He said the usual things: Tinkersfield was no Sunday school; and they weren't slaves to have their liberty taken from them by a lot of impractical reformers. And Lee was that kind. What had he ever done to prove that he'd make good? They knew Tillotson. They didn't know Lee. Who was Lee anyhow?

He flung the interrogation at them. "What do you know about Lee?"

The pebble that he threw had widening circles. People began to ask themselves what, after all, they knew of O-liver. From somewhere in the darkness went up the words of an evil chant:

What's the matter with O-liver, O-liver,

White-livered O-liver?

Ask Jane, Sandwich Jane,

O-liver, white liver,

Jane, Jane, Jane.

Jane felt her heart stand still. Back of her she heard Tommy swearing: "It's all their damned wickedness!" She saw O-liver start from his chair and sink back, helpless against the insidiousness of this attack.

The speaker went on. It would seem, he said, from what he could learn, that Tillotson's honorable opponent was sailing under false colors. He was a married man. He had deserted his wife. He sat among them as a saint, when he was really a sinner.

"A sinner, gentlemen." The speaker paused for the effect, then proceeded with his argument. Of course they were all sinners, but they weren't hypocrites. Tillotson wasn't a hypocrite. He was a good fellow. He didn't want Tinkersfield to be a Sunday school. He wanted it to be a town. You know—a town that every fellow would want to hit on Saturday night.

290

There were those in the crowd who began to feel that a weak spot had been found in O-liver's armor. Secrecy! They didn't like it. There were signs of wavering among some who had squared their shoulders. After all, they didn't want to make a Sunday school of Tinkersfield. They wondered, too, if there wasn't some truth in the things that were being hinted by that low chant in the darkness:

Ask Jane, Sandwich Jane,

O-liver, white liver,

Jane, Jane, Jane.

O-liver was restless, his hands clenched at his sides. Atwood and Henry were restless. Tommy was restless. They couldn't let such insults go unnoticed. Somebody had to fight for Jane!

Tillotson's supporters kept the thing stirring. If the meeting could end in a brawl the odds would be in favor of Tillotson. The effect of O-liver's uplift would be lost. Even his friends couldn't sway a fighting crowd back to him.

But they had forgotten to reckon with Jane!

She had seen in a sudden crystal flash the thing which might happen. A fight would end it all for O-liver. She had seen his efforts at self-control. She knew his agony of soul. She knew that at any moment he might knock somebody down—Tillotson or Tillotson's sponsor. And it would all be in the morning papers. There would be innuendo—the hint of scandalous things. And O-liver's reputation would pay the price. It was characteristic that she did not at the moment think of her own reputation. It was O-liver who must be saved!

And so when Tillotson's backer sat down Jane stood up.

"Please, listen!" she said; and the crowd turned toward her. "Please, listen, and stop singing that silly song. I never heard anything so silly as that song in my life!"

Before her scorn the chant died away in a gasp!

"The thing you've got to think about," she went on, "isn't Tillotson or O-liver Lee. It's Tinkersfield. You want an honest man. And O-liver Lee's honest. He doesn't want your money. He's got enough of his own. His father's the richest man in his part of the state and his wife's a movie actress and makes as much as the President. It sounds like a fairy tale, but it isn't. If O-liver Lee wanted to live on his father or his wife he could hold out his hand and let things drop into it. But he'd rather earn fifteen dollars a week and own his soul. And he isn't a hypocrite. His friends knew about his marriage. Tommy Drew knew, and I knew. And there wasn't any particular reason why he should tell the rest of you, was there? There wasn't any particular reason why he should tell Tillotson?"

A murmur of laughter followed her questions. There was a feeling in the crowd that the joke was on Tillotson.

"I wonder how many of you have told your pasts to Tinkersfield! How many of you have made Tillotson your father confessor?

"As for me"—her head was high—"I sell sandwiches. I am very busy. I hardly have time to think. But when I do think it is of something besides village gossip."

She grew suddenly earnest; leaned down to them. "You haven't time to think of it either," she told them; "have you, men of Tinkersfield?"

Her appeal was direct, and the answer came back to her in a roar from the men who knew courage when they saw it; who knew, indeed, innocence!

"No!"

And it was that "No" which beat Tillotson.

"The way she put it over," Atwood exulted afterward, "to a packed crowd like this!"

"The thing about Jane"—Henry was very seriously trying to say the thing as he saw it—"the thing about Jane is that she sees things straight. And she makes other people see."

IX

Well, Tillotson was beaten, and the men who supported O-liver came out of the fight feeling as if they had killed something unclean.

And the morning after the election O-liver had a little note from Jane.

"I've got to go away. I didn't want to worry you with it before this. I have saved enough money to start in at some college where I can work for a part of my tuition. I have had experience in my little lunch room that ought to be a help somewhere.

"When I finish college I'm going into some sort of occupation that will provide a pleasant home for mother and me. I want books, and lovely things, and a garden; and I'd like to speak a language or two and have cultured friends. Then some day when you are made President you can say to yourself: 'I am proud of my friend, Jane.' And I'll come to your inauguration and watch you ride to the White House, and I'll say to myself as I see you ride, 'I've loved him all these years.'

"But I shan't let myself say it now. And that's why I'm going away. And I'm going without saying good-bye because I think it will be easier for both of us. You and I can't be friends. What we feel is too big. I found that out about myself that

291

night when you sat there on the platform, and I wanted to save you from Tillotson. If I'm going to work and be happy in my work I've got to get away. And you will work better because I am gone. I mustn't be here—O-liver."

Jane had indeed seen straight. O-liver laid the note down on his desk and looked up at the mountain. He needed to look up. If he had looked down for a moment he would have followed Jane.

X

And now there was no sandwich stand in Tinkersfield. But there was a good hotel. O-liver saw to that. He got Henry Bittinger to put up the money, with Tommy and his mother in charge. O-liver lived in the hotel in a suite of small rooms, and when Atwood Jones passed that way the four men dined together as O-liver's guests.

"Some day we'll eat with you in Washington," was Atwood's continued prophecy.

They always drank "To Jane." Now and then Atwood brought news of her. First from the college, and then as the years passed from the beach resort where she had opened a tea room. She was more beautiful than ever, more wonderful. Her tea room and shop were most exclusive and artistic.

"Sandwich Jane!" said O-liver. "How long ago it seems!"

It was five years now and he had not seen her. And next month he was to go to Washington. Not as President, but representing his district in Congress. Tommy's hotel had outgrown the original modest building and was now modern and fireproof. Henry was married, he had had several new cars, and his wife wore sables and seal.

The old arcade was no more; nor the old post-office. But O-liver still talked to admiring circles in the hotel lobby or to greater crowds in the town hall.

He still would take no money from his father, but he saw much of him, for Mrs. Lee was dead. The Tudor house was without a mistress. It seemed a pity that O-liver had no wife to grace its halls.

The newspapers stated that Fluffy Hair's income had doubled. Whether this was true or not it sounded well, and Fluffy Hair still seemed young on the screen. Jane would go now and then and look at her and wonder what sort of woman this was who had laughed at O-liver.

Then one day a telegram came to O-liver in his suite of rooms. And that day and for two nights he rode Mary Pick over the hills and through the cañon and down to the sea, and came to a place where Jane's tea room was met in the center of a Japanese garden—a low lovely building, with its porches open to the wide Pacific.

He had not seen her for so long that he was not quite prepared for the change. She was thinner and paler and more beautiful, with an air of distinction that was new. It was as if in visualizing his future she had pictured herself in it—as first lady of the land. Such a silly dream for Sandwich Jane!

They were quite alone when he came to her. It was morning, and the porches were empty of guests. Jane was in a long wicker chair, with her pot of coffee on an hour-glass table. Far down on the terrace two Jap gardeners clipped and cut and watered and saw nothing.

"You are younger than ever," Jane said when they had clasped hands. "Will you ever grow old, O-liver?"

"The men say not." He seated himself opposite her. "Jane, Jane, it's heavenly to see you. I've been—starved!"

She had hungered and thirsted for him. Her hand shook a little as she poured him a cup of coffee.

"I told you not to come, O-liver."

He laid the telegram before her. Fluffy Hair was dead!

The yellow sheet lay between, defying them to speak so soon of happiness.

"To-morrow," O-liver said, "I go to Washington. When will you come to me, Jane?"

Her hand went out to him. Her breath was quick. "In time to hear your first speech, O-liver. I'll sit in the gallery, and lean over and listen and say to myself, 'He's mine, he's mine!'"

She heard many speeches in the months that followed, and sometimes Tommy or Atwood or Henry, traveling across the continent, came and sat beside her. And Atwood always clung to his prophecy: "He'll be governor next; and then it'll be the White House. Why not?"

And Jane, dreaming, asked herself "Why?"

The East had had its share. Had the time not come for a nation to seek its leader in the golden West?

LADY CRUSOE

Billy and I came down from the North and opened a grocery store at Jefferson Corners. It is a little store and there aren't many houses near it—just the railroad station and a big shed or two. Beyond the sheds a few cabins straggle along the road, and then begin the great plantations, which really aren't plantations any more, because nobody around here raises much of anything in these days. They just sit and sigh over the things that are different since the war.

292

That's what Billy says about them. Billy is up-to-date and he has a motor-cycle. He made up his mind when he came that he was going to put some ginger into the neighborhood. So he rides miles every morning on his motor-cycle to get orders, and he delivers the things himself unless it is barrels of flour or cans of kerosene or other heavy articles, and then he hires somebody to help him. At first he had William Watters and his mule. William is black and his mule is gray, and they are both old. It took them hours to get anywhere, and I used to feel sorry for them. But when I found out that compared to Billy and me they lived on flowery beds of ease, I stopped sympathizing. They both have enough, to eat, and they work only when they want to. Billy and I work all the time. We have our way to make in the world, and we feel that it all depends on ourselves. We started out with nothing ahead of us but my ambitions and Billy's energy, and a few hundred dollars which my guardian turned over to me when I married Billy on my twenty-first birthday.

As soon as we were married, we came to Virginia. Billy and I had an idea that everything south of the Mason and Dixon line was just waiting for us, and we wanted to earn the eternal gratitude of the community by helping it along. But after we had lived at Jefferson Corners for a little while, we began to feel that there wasn't any community. There didn't seem to be any towns like our nice New England ones, with sociable trolley-cars connecting them and farmhouses in a lovely line between. You can ride for miles through this country and never pass anything but gates. Then way up in the hills you will see a clump of trees, and in the clump you can be pretty sure there is a house. In the winter when the leaves are off the trees you can see the house, but in the summer there is no sign of it. In the old days they seemed to feel that they were lacking somewhat in delicacy if they exposed their mansions to the rude gaze of the public.

There was one mansion that Billy took me to now and then. It was empty, and that was why we went. The big houses which were occupied were not open to us, except in a trades-person sort of fashion, and Billy and I are not to be condescended to—we had a pair of grandfathers in the *Mayflower*. But that doesn't count down here, where everybody goes back to William the Conqueror.

That great big empty house was a fine place for our Sunday afternoon outings. We always went to church in the morning, and people were very kind, but it was kindness with a question-mark. You see Billy and I live over the store, and none of them had ever lived on anything but ancestral acres.

So our Sunday mornings were a bit stiff and disappointing, but our afternoons were heavenly. We discovered the Empty House in the spring, and there was laurel on the mountains and the grass was young and green on the slopes, and the sky was a faint warm blue with the sailing buzzards black against it. Billy and I used to stop at the second gate, which was at the top of the hill, and look off over the other hills where the pink sheep were pastured. I am perfectly sure that there are no other sheep in the whole wide world like those Albemarle sheep. The spring rains turn the red clay into a mud which sticks like paint, and the sheep are colored a lovely terra-cotta which fades gradually to pink.

The effect is impressionistic, like purple cows. Billy doesn't care for it, but I do. And I adore the brilliant red of the roads. Billy says he'll take good brown earth and white flocks. He might be reconciled to black sheep but never to pink ones.

We used to eat our supper on the porch of the Empty House. It had great pillars, and it was rather awe-inspiring to sit on the front steps and look up the whole length, of those Corinthian columns. Billy and I felt dwarfed and insignificant, but we forgot it when we turned our eyes to the hills.

The big door behind us and the blank windows were shut and shuttered close. There were flying squirrels on the roof and little blue-tailed lizards on the stone flagging in front of the house; and there was an old toad who used to keep us company. I called him Prince Charming, and I am sure he was as old as Methuselah, and lived under that stone in some prehistoric age.

We just loved our little suppers. We had coffee in our thermos bottle, and cold fried chicken and bread and butter sandwiches and chocolate cake. We never changed, because we were always afraid that we shouldn't like anything else so well, and we were sure of the chicken and the chocolate cake.

And after we had eaten our suppers we would talk about what kind of house we would build when our ship came in. Billy and I both have nice tastes, and we know what we want; and we feel that the grocery store is just a stepping-stone to better things.

The sunsets were late in those spring days, and there would be pink and green and pale amethyst in the western sky, and after that deep sapphire and a silver moon. And as it grew darker the silver would turn to gold, and there would be a star— and then more stars until the night came on.

I can't tell you how we used to feel. You see we were young and in love, and life was a pretty good thing to us. There was one perfect night when the hills were flooded with moonlight. We seemed all alone in a lovely world and I whispered:

"Oh, Billy, Billy, and some folks think that there isn't any God—"

And Billy put his arm around me and patted my cheek, and we didn't say anything for a long time.

It was just a week later that Lady Crusoe came. I knew that some one was in the house as soon as we passed the second gate. The door was still closed, and the shutters were not opened, but I heard a clock strike—a ship's clock—with bells.

I clutched Billy. "Listen," I said.

He heard it, too; "Who in the dickens?" he demanded.

"There's somebody in the house—"

"Nonsense—"

"Billy, there must be, and we can't sit on the porch."

"You stay here, and I'll go around to the back."

But I wouldn't let him go alone. At the back of the house a window was open, and then we were sure.

"We'd better leave," I said, but Billy insisted that we stay. "If they are new people, I'll find out their names, and come up to-morrow and get their orders."

We went around to the front door and knocked and knocked, but nobody answered. So we sat down on the front step and presently Billy said that we might as well eat our supper, for very evidently nobody was at home.

I didn't feel a bit comfortable about it, but I opened our basket and got out our cups and plates, and Billy poured the coffee and passed the chicken and the bread and butter sandwiches. And just then the door creaked and the knob turned!

My first impulse was to gather up the lunch and tumble it into the basket; but I didn't. I just sat there looking up as calmly as if I were serving tea at my own table, and Billy sat there too looking up.

The door opened and a voice said, "Oh, if you are eating supper, may I have some?"

It was a lovely voice, and Billy jumped to his feet. A lovely head came after the voice. Just the head, peeping around—the body was hidden by the door. On the head was a lace cap with a gold rose, and the hair under the cap was gold.

"You see, I just got up," said the voice, "and I haven't had any breakfast—"

Billy and I gasped. It was seven P.M., and the meal that we were serving was supper!

"Do you mind my coming out?" said the voice. "I am not exactly clothed and in my right mind, but perhaps I'll do."

She opened the door wider and stepped down. I saw that her slippers had gold roses and that they were pale pink like the sunset. She wore a motor coat of tan cloth which covered her up, but I had a glimpse of a pink silk negligee underneath.

She sat quite sociably on the steps with us. "I am famished," she said. "I haven't had a thing to eat for twenty-four hours."

We gasped again. "How did it happen?"

"I was—shipwrecked," she said, "in a motor-car—I am the only survivor—"

Her eyes twinkled. "I'll tell you all about it presently." Then she broke off and laughed.

"But first will you feed a starving castaway?"

Yet she didn't really tell us anything. She ate and ate, and it was the prettiest thing to see her. She was dainty and young and eager like a child at a party.

"How good everything is!" she said, at last with a sigh. "I don't think I was ever so hungry in my life."

Billy and I didn't eat much. You see we were too interested, and besides we had had our dinner.

As I have said, she didn't really tell us anything. "It was an accident, and I came up here. And the old clock that you heard strike belonged to my grandfather. He was an admiral, and it was his clock. I used to listen to it as a child."

"What happened to the rest—?" Billy asked, bluntly. He was more concerned about the automobile accident than about her ancestors.

"Oh, do you mean the others in the car?" she came reluctantly back from the admiral and his ship's clock. "I am sure I don't know. And I am very sure that I don't care."

"But were any of them killed?"

"No—they are all alive—but you see—it was a shipwreck—and I floated away—by myself—and this is my island, and you are the nice friendly savages—" she touched Billy on the arm. He drew away a bit. I knew that he was afraid she had lost her mind, but I had seen her twinkling eyes. "Oh, it's all a joke!" I said.

She shook her head. "It isn't exactly a joke, but it might look like that to other people."

"Are you going to stay?"

"Yes."

"I'll come up in the morning for orders," said Billy promptly. "I keep the grocery store at Jefferson Corners."

"Oh," she said, and seemed to hesitate; "there won't be any orders."

Billy stared at her. "But there isn't any other store."

"Robinson Crusoe didn't have stores, did he? He found things and lived on the land. And I am Lady Crusoe."

"Really?" I asked her.

"I've another name—but—if people around here question you—you won't tell them, will you, that I am here—?"

She said it in such a pretty pleading fashion that of course we promised. It was late when we had to go. I insisted that we should leave what remained of the supper, and she seemed glad to get it. "You are nice friendly savages," she said, with that twinkle in her eyes, "and I am very grateful. Come into the house and let me show you my clock—"

She showed us more than the clock. I hadn't dreamed in those days when Billy and I sat alone on the steps of the treasures that were shut up behind us. The old furniture was dusty, but all the dust in the world couldn't hide its beauty. The dining-room was hung with cobwebs, but when the candles were lighted we saw the Sheffield on the old sideboard, the Chinese porcelains, the Heppelwhite chairs, the painted sheepskin screen—

She picked out a lovely little pitcher and gave it to me. I did not learn until afterward that it was pink lustre and worth a pretty penny. She paid in that way, you see, for her supper, and something in her manner made me feel that I must not refuse it.

She did not ask us to come again, yet I was sure that she liked us. I felt that perhaps it was the grocery store which had made her hesitate. But whatever it was, I must confess that I was a little lonely as I went away. You see we had come to look forward to our welcome at the Empty House. We had known that we were the honored guests of the flying squirrels and the lizards and of old Prince Charming. But now that the house was no longer empty, we would not be welcome. I was sorry that I had accepted the pink pitcher. I should have preferred to feel that I owed no favor to the lady with the twinkling eyes.

It wasn't long after our adventure at the Empty House that Billy asked William Watters to take a big load to a customer two miles out. But William couldn't. He was working, he said, at a regular place. We couldn't imagine William as being regular about anything. He and his mule were so irregular in their habits. They came and went as they pleased, and they would take naps whenever the spirit moved them. But now, as William said, he was "wukin' regular," and he refused to say for whom he worked. But we found out one day when he drove Lady Crusoe down in a queer old carriage with his mule as a prancing steed.

He helped her descend as if she had been a queen, and she came in and talked to Billy. "You see, I've hunted up my friendly savages," she said. "I've reached the end of my resources." She gave a small order, and told Billy that she wasn't at all sure when she could pay her bill, but that there were a lot of things in her old house which he could have for security.

Billy said gallantly that he didn't need any security, and that her account could run as long as she wished and that he was glad to serve her. And he got out his pad and pencil and stood in that nice way of his at attention.

I listened and looked through a window at the back. I had seen her drive up, and she was stunning in the same tan motor-coat that she had worn when we first saw her. But she had on a brown hat and veil and brown shoes instead of the lace cap and rosy slippers.

She asked about me, and Billy told her that I was in the garden. And I was in the garden when she came out; but I had to run. She sat down in a chair on the other side of my little sewing-table and talked to me. It is such a scrap of a garden that there is only room for a tiny table and two chairs, but a screen of old cedars hides it from the road, and there's a twisted apple-tree, and the fields beyond and a glimpse of the mountains.

"How is the island?" Billy asked her.

She twinkled. "I have a man Friday."

"William Watters?"

She nodded. "The Watters negroes have been our servants for generations. And William thinks that he belongs to me. He cooks for me and forages. He shot two squirrels one morning and made me a Brunswick stew. But I couldn't stand that. You see the squirrels are my friends."

I thought of the flying squirrels and the blue-tailed lizards and the old toad, and I knew how she felt. And I said so. She looked at me sharply, and then she laid her hand over mine: "Are you lonely, my dear?"

I said that I was—a little. Billy had gone in to wait on a customer, so I dared say it. I told her that nobody had called.

"But why not?" she demanded.

"I think," I said slowly, "it is because we live—over the store."

"I see." And she did see; it was in her blood as well as in the blood of the rest of them.

Presently she stood up and said that she must go, and it was then that she noticed the work that was in my basket on the table. She lifted out a little garment and the red came into her cheeks. "Oh, oh!" she said, and stood looking at it. When she laid it down, she came around the table and kissed me. "What a dear you are!" she said, and then she went away.

William Watters came in very often after that; but he said very little about Lady Crusoe. He was a faithful old thing, and he had evidently had instructions. But one morning he brought a fine old Sheffield tray to Billy and asked him to take his pay out of it, and let Lady Crusoe have the rest in cash. William Watters didn't call her "Lady Crusoe," he called her "Miss Lily," which didn't give us the key to the situation in the least. Billy didn't know how to value the tray, so he asked me. I knew more than he did, but I wasn't sure. I told him to advance what he thought was best, and to send it to the city and have it appraised, or whatever they call it, so he did; and when the check from the antique shop came it was a big one.

It wasn't long after that that Lady Crusoe called on me. It was a real call, and she left a card. And she said as she laid it on the table: "As I told you, I'd rather the rest of the natives didn't know—they haven't seen me since I was a child, and they think that I am just some stranger who rents the old place and who wants to be alone."

After she had gone I picked up the card, and what I read there nearly took my breath away. There are certain names which mean so much that we get to look upon them as having special significance. The name that was on Lady Crusoe's card had always stood in my mind for money—oceans of it. I simply couldn't believe my eyes, and I took it down to Billy.

"Look at that," I said, and laid it before him, "and she has asked us to supper for next Sunday!"

Well, we couldn't make anything of it. Why was a woman with a name like that down here with nothing to eat but the things that William Watters could forage for, and that Billy could supply from his little store, and that she paid for with Sheffield trays?

We had supper that Sunday night in the great dining-room. There was a five-branched candlestick with tall white candles in the center of the shining mahogany table and William Watters acted as butler. You never would have believed how well he did it. And after supper we had coffee on the front porch and looked out over the hills at the sunset, and the silver moon and the old toad came out from under his stone and sat with us.

Lady Crusoe was in a thin white dress which she had made for herself, and she talked of the old place and of her childhood there. But not a word did she say of why she had come back to live alone on the Davenant ancestral acres.

It was her mother, we learned, who was a Davenant, and it was her mother's father who was the old admiral. She said nothing of the man whose name was on her card. It was as if she stopped short when she came to that part of her life, or as if it had never been.

She took me up-stairs after a while and left Billy to smoke on the porch. She said that she had something that she wanted me to see. Her room was a huge square one at the southwest corner of the house. There was a massive four-poster bed with faded blue satin curtains, and there was a fireplace with fire-dogs and an Adam screen. Lady Crusoe carried a candle, and as she stood in the center of the room she seemed to gather all of the light to her, like the saints in the old pictures. She was so perfectly lovely that I almost wanted to cry. I can't explain it, but there was something pathetic about her beauty.

She set the candle down and opened an old brass-bound chest. She took out a roll of cloth and brought it over and laid it on the table beside the candle.

"I bought it with some of the money that your Billy got for my Sheffield tray," she said. Then she turned to me with a quick motion and laid her hands on my shoulders. "Oh, you very dear—when I saw you making those little things—I knew that—that the good Lord had led me. Will you—will you—show me—how?"

I told Billy about it on the way home.

"She doesn't know anything about sewing, and she hasn't any patterns, and I am to go up every day, and William Watters will come for me with his mule—"

Then I cried about her a little, because it seemed so dreadful that she should be there all alone, without any one to sustain her and cherish her as Billy did me.

"Oh, Billy, Billy," I said to him, "I'd rather live over a grocery store with you than live in a palace with anybody else—"

And Billy said, "Don't cry, lady love, you are not going to live with anybody else."

And he put his arm around me, and as we walked along together in the April night it was like the days when we had been young lovers, only our joy in each other was deeper and finer, for then we had only guessed at happiness, and now we knew—

Well, I went up every day. William Watters came for me, and I carried my patterns and we sat in the big west room, and right under the window a pair of robins were building a nest.

We watched them as they worked, and it seemed to us that no matter how hard we toiled those two birds kept ahead. "I never dreamed," Lady Crusoe remarked one morning, "that they were at it all the time like this."

"You wait until they begin to feed their young," I told her. "People talk about being as free as a bird. But I can tell you that they slave from dawn until dark. I have seen a mother bird at dusk giving a last bite to one squalling baby while the father fed another."

Lady Crusoe laid down her work and looked out over the hills. "The father," she said, and that was all for a long time, and we stitched and stitched, but at last she spoke straight from her thoughts: "How dear your husband is to you!"

"That's what husbands are made for."

"Some of them are not, dear," her voice was hard, "some of them expect so much and give so little—"

I kept still and presently she began again. "They give money—and they think that is—enough. They give jewels—and think we ought to be profoundly grateful."

"Well, my experience," I told her, "is that the men give as much love as the women—"

She looked at me. "What do you mean?"

"Love costs them a lot."

"In what way?"

"They work for us. Now there's Billy's grocery store. If Billy didn't have me, he'd be doing things that he likes better. You wouldn't believe it, but Billy wanted to study law, but it meant years of hard work before he could make a cent, and he and I would have wasted our youth in waiting—and so he went into business—and that's a big thing for a man to do for a woman—to give up a future that he has hoped for—and that's why I feel that I can't do enough for Billy—"

"I don't see why you should look at it in that way," she said, and her eyes were big and bright. "Women are queens, and they honor men when they marry them—"

"If women are queens," I told her, "men are kings—Billy honored me—"

She smiled at me. "Oh, you blessed dear—" she said, and all of a sudden she came over and knelt beside me. "What would you think of a man who married a woman whom the world called beautiful and brilliant, and whom—whom princes wanted to marry—And he was a very plain man, except that he had a lot of money—millions and millions—and after he married the woman whom he had said that he worshiped, he wanted to make just an every-day wife of her. He wanted her to stay at home and look after his house. He told her one night that it would be a great happiness for him if he could come in and find her warming—his slippers. And he said that his ideal of a woman was one who—who—held a child in her arms—"

I looked down at her. "Well, right in the beginning," I said, "I should like to know if the woman loved the man—"

She stared at me and then she stood up. "If she did, what then? She had not married to be—his slave—"

I pointed to the mother robin on the branch below. "I wonder if she calls it slavery! You see—she is so busy—building her nest she hasn't time to think whether Cock Robin is singing fewer love songs than he sang early in the spring."

She laughed and was down on her knees beside me again. "Oh, you funny little practical thing! But it wasn't because I missed the love songs. He sang them. But because I couldn't be an every-day wife—"

"What kind of wife did you want to be?"

"I wanted to travel with him alone—I planned a honeymoon in the desert, and we had it—and I planned after that to sail the seas to the land of Nowhere—and we sailed—and then—I wanted to go to the high plains—and ride and camp—and into the forests to hunt and fish—but he wouldn't. He said that we had wandered enough. He wanted to build a house—and have me warm—his slippers—"

"And so you quarreled?"

"We quarreled—great hot heavy quarrels—and we said things—horrid things—that we can't forgive—"

She was sobbing on my shoulder and I said softly: "Things that *you* can't forgive?"

"Yes. And that *he* can't. That's why I ran away from him."

I waited.

"I couldn't stand it to see him going around with his face stern and set and not like my lover's. And he didn't speak to me except to be polite. And he asked people to go with us—everywhere. And we were never alone—"

"What had you said to make him—like that?"

She raised her head. "I told him that I—hated him—"

"Oh, oh—"

She knelt back on her heels.

"It was a dreadful thing to say, wasn't it? That's why I ran away. I couldn't stand it. I knew it was a thing no man—could—forgive—"

I smoothed her hair and rocked her back and forth while she cried. It was strange how much of a child she seemed to me. And I was only the wife of a country grocer and lived over the store, and she was the wife of a man whose name was known from east to west, and all around the world. But you see she hadn't learned to live. Neither have I, really. But Billy has taught me a lot.

I think it was a comfort for her to feel that she had confided in me. But she made me promise that whatever happened I wouldn't let him know.

"Unless I—die," she said, and she was as white as a lily, "unless I die, and then you can—set him—free—"

Billy was sorry that I had promised. "Somehow I feel responsible, sweetheart, and I'll bet her poor husband is almost crazy."

"Would you be, Billy?"

He caught me to him so quickly that he almost shook the breath out of me. "Don't ask a thing like that," he said, and his voice didn't sound like his own. "If anything should happen to you—if anything should happen—I should—I should—oh, why will women ask things like that—?"

In the days that followed, Billy didn't want me out of his sight. He even hated to have me go up to the Davenant house with William Watters. "Take care of her, William," he would say, and stand looking after us.

William and I got to be very good friends. He was a wise old darky, and he was devoted to Lady Crusoe. He usually served tea for us out under the trees, unless it was a rainy day, and then we had it in the library.

It was on a rainy day that Lady Crusoe said: "I wonder what has become of William. I haven't seen him since you came. I have hunted and called, and I can't find him."

He appeared at tea time, however, with a plate of hot waffles with powdered sugar between. When his mistress asked him about his mysterious disappearance, he said that he had cleaned the attic.

"But, William, on such a day?"

"I kain't wuk out in the rain, Miss Lily, so I wuks in—"

That was all he would say about it, and after we had had our tea, she said to me, "There are a lot of interesting things in the attic. Let's go up and see what Willie has been doing—"

297

The dim old place was as shining as soap and water could make it, and there was the damp smell of suds. There was the beat of the rain on the roof, and the splash of it against the round east window. Through the west window came a pale green light, and there was a view over the hills. As we became accustomed to the dimness our eyes picked out the various objects—an old loom like a huge spider under a peaked gable, a chest of drawers which would have set a collector crazy, Chippendale chairs with the seats out, Windsor chairs with the backs broken, gilt mirror frames with no glass in them—boxes—books—bottles—all the flotsam and jetsam of such old establishments. Most of the things had been set back against the wall, but right in the middle of the floor was an object which I took at first for a small trunk.

Lady Crusoe reached it first, and knelt beside it. She gave a little cry. "My dear, come here!" and I went to her, and in another moment, I, too, was on my knees. For the dark object was a cradle—a lovely hooded thing of mahogany, in which the Davenants had been rocked for generations.

"William got it out," Lady Crusoe said, "ready to be carried down. Oh, my good old man Friday! Do you mind if I cry a little, you very dear?"

It rained a great deal that summer, and it was hot and humid. Billy and I longed for the cold winds that sweep across the sea on the North Shore, but we didn't complain, for we had each other, and I wouldn't exchange Billy for any breeze that blows.

Lady Crusoe suffered less than I, for she was on her native heath, and in the afternoon when we sewed together William Watters made lemonade, and in the evening when Billy came up for me we sat out under the stars until whispers of wind stirred the trees, and then we went away and left our dear lady alone.

As the time went on we hated more and more to leave her, but she was very brave about it. "I have my good man Friday," she told us, "to protect me, and my grandfather's revolver."

So the summer passed, and the fall came, and the busy robin and all of her red-breasted family started for the South, and there was rain and more rain, so that when October rolled around the roads were perfect rivers of red mud, and the swollen streams swept under the bridges in raging torrents of terra-cotta, and the sheep on the hills were pinker than ever. There was no lack of color in those gray days, for the trees burst through the curtain of mist in great splashes of red and green and gold. But now I did not go abroad with William Watters behind his old gray mule, for things had happened which kept me at home.

It was on a rainy November night that I came down to the store to call Billy to supper. I had brought a saucer for old Tid, the store cat, and when he had finished Billy had cut him a bit of cheese and he was begging for it. We had taught Tid to sit up and ask, and he looked so funny, for he is fat and black and he hates to beg, but he loves cheese. We were laughing at him when a great flash of light seemed to sweep through the store, and a motor stopped.

Billy went forward at once. The front door opened, and a man in a rain-coat was blown in by the storm.

"Jove, it's a wet night!" I heard him say, and I knew it wasn't any of Billy's customers from around that part of the country. This was no drawling Virginia voice. It was crisp and clear-cut and commanding.

He took off his hat, and even at that distance I could see his shining blond head. He towered above Billy, and Billy isn't short. "I wonder if you could help me," he began, and then he hesitated, "it is a rather personal matter."

"If you'll come up-stairs," Billy told him, "there'll be only my wife and me, and I can shut up the store for the night."

"Good!" he said, and I went ahead of them with old Tid following, and presently the men arrived and Billy presented the stranger to me.

He told us at once what he wanted. "I thought that as you kept the store, you might hear the neighborhood news. I have lost—my wife—"

"Dead?" Billy inquired solicitously.

"No. Several months ago we motored down into this part of the country. Some miles from here I had trouble with my engine, and I had to walk to town for help. When I came back my wife was gone—"

I pinched Billy under the table. "Gone?" I echoed.

"Yes. She left a note. She said that she could catch a train at the station and that she would take it. Some one evidently gave her a lift, for she had her traveling bag with her. She said that she would sail at once for France, and that I must not try to follow her. Of course I did follow her, and I searched through Europe, but I found no trace, and then it occurred to me that after all she might still be in this part of the country—"

I held on to Billy. "Had you quarreled or anything?"

He ran his fingers through his hair. "Things had gone wrong somehow," he said, uncertainly, "I don't know why. I love her."

If you could have heard him say it! If *she* could have heard him! There was a silence out of which I said: "Did you ask her to warm your slippers?"

He stared at me, then he reached out his hands across the table and caught hold of mine in such a strong grip that it hurt. "You've seen her," he said, "*you've seen her*—?"

Then I remembered. "I can't say any more. You see—I've promised—"

"That you wouldn't tell me?"

"Yes."

He threw back his head and laughed. "If she's in this part of the country, I'll find her." And I knew that he would. He was the kind of man you felt wouldn't know there were obstacles in the way when he went after the thing he wanted.

I made him stay to supper. It was a drizzly cold night and he looked very tired.

"Jove," he said, "you're comfortable here, with your fire and your pussy-cat, and your teakettle on the hearth! This is the sort of thing I like—"

"You wouldn't like living over a grocery store," I told him.

"Why not?"

"Oh, nobody around here ever has, and they are all descended from signers of the Declaration of Independence and back of that from William the Conqueror, and they stick their noses in the air."

"Shades of Jefferson!—why should they?"

"They shouldn't. But they do—"

He came back to the subject of his wife. "I didn't want her to warm my slippers. It was only that I wanted her to feel like warming them," he appealed to Billy, and Billy nodded. Billy positively purrs when I make him comfortable after his day's work. He says that it is the homing instinct in men and that women ought to encourage it.

"Does she warm yours?" he asked Billy.

"Not now, she's too busy—" and then as if the stage were set for it, there came from the next room a little, little cry.

I went in and brought out—Junior! He was only a month old, but you know how heavenly sweet they are with their rose-leaf skins, and their little crumpled hands and their downy heads—Junior's down was brown, for Billy and I are both dark.

"You see he keeps me busy," I said.

I was so proud I am perfectly sure it stuck out all over me, and as for Billy he beamed on us in a funny fatherly fashion that he had adopted from the moment that he first called me "Little Mother."

"Do you wonder that she hasn't time to warm my slippers?" was his question.

The stranger held out his arms—"Let me hold the little chap." And he sat there, without a smile, looking down at my baby. When he raised his head he said in a dry sort of fashion, "I thought the pussy-cat and the teakettle were enough—but this seems almost too good to be true—"

I can't tell you how much I liked him. He seemed so big and fine—and tender. I came across a poem the other day, and he made me think of it:

" ... the strong"
The Master whispered, "are the tenderest!"

Before he went away, he took my hand in his. "I want you to play a game with me. Do you remember when we were children that we used to hide things, and then guide the ones who hunted by saying 'warmer' when we were near them, and 'colder' when they wandered away? Will you say 'warm' and 'cold' to me? That won't be breaking your promise, will it?"

"No."

"Then let's begin now. To-morrow morning I shall go to the north and east—"

"Cold!"

"To the south and west—"

"Warmer."

"Up a hill?"

"Very warm. But you mustn't ask me any more."

"All right. But I am coming again, and we will play the game."

Billy went down with him, and when he came back we stood looking into the fire, and he said, "You didn't tell him?"

"Of course not. That's the lovely, lovely thing that he must find out for himself—"

The next day I went to see Lady Crusoe. William Watters took me. "They's a man been hangin' round this mawnin'," he complained, "an' a dawg—"

"What kind of man, William?"

"He's huntin', and Miss Lily she doan' like things killed—"

Half-way up, we passed the man. His hat came off when he saw me. "It's cold weather we're having," he said pleasantly.

"It's getting warmer," I flung back at him, and William drove on with a grunt.

I had Junior with me, and when I reached the house I went straight up-stairs. In the very center of the room in the hooded mahogany cradle was another crumpled rose-leaf of a child. But this was not a "Junior."

"Robin-son," Lady Crusoe had whispered, when I had first bent over her and had asked the baby's name.

"Because of the robins?" I had asked.

She shook her head. "I couldn't call him Crusoe, could I?"

So there he lay, little Robinson Crusoe, in a desert expanse of polished floor, and there he crowed a welcome to my own beautiful baby!

Lady Crusoe was in a big chair. She was not strong, and William Watters had brought his sister Mandy to wait on her. She was very pale, this lovely lady, and there were shadows under her eyes. As I sat down beside her, she said: "I shall have to have your Billy sell some more things for me. You see the servants must be paid, and my Robin must be comfy. There's a console-table that ought to bring a lot from a city dealer."

"I wish that you needn't be worried," I said. "I wish—I wish—that you'd let me send for Robin's father—"

"Robin's father!" she drew a quick breath, "how funny it sounds!—*Robin's father*—"

I waited for that to sink in, and then I said: "I know how you feel. When I think of Billy as Junior's father it is different from thinking of him as my husband, and it makes a funny sensation in my throat as if I wanted to cry—"

"You've nothing to cry about," she told me fiercely, "nothing, but I sometimes feel as if I could weep rivers of tears!"

I realized that I must be careful, so I changed the subject. "William," I said after a pause, "is worrying about a man who is hunting over the grounds."

"He told me. I can't understand why any one should trespass when the place is posted. I sent William to tell him, but it didn't seem to have any effect. I haven't heard him shoot. When I do, I shall go out and speak to him myself."

I wondered if Fate were going to settle it in that way, and I wondered too if it would be breaking my promise to tell him to shoot! We sewed in silence for a while, but Lady Crusoe was restless. At last she wandered to the window. It was a long French window which opened on a balcony. She parted the velvet curtains and looked out. "There he is again," she said, with irritation, "by the gate with his gun and dog—"

I rose and joined her. The man stood by the gate-post, and the dog sat at his feet. They might have been a pair of statues planted on the round top of the hill, with the valleys rolling away beneath them and the mountain peaks and the golden sky beyond. Lady Crusoe was much stirred up over it.

"I'll send William again, when he comes with our tea. I won't have my wild things shot. There was a covey of partridges on the lawn this morning, and my squirrels come up to the porch to be fed. Men are cruel creatures with their guns and their traps."

"Women are cruel, too," I told her, and now I took my courage in my hands. "Suppose, oh, suppose, that the mother robin had stolen her nest and had never let the father robin share her happiness, wouldn't you call that cruel?"

"What do you mean?" her voice shook.

"You have stolen your—nest—"

"Why shouldn't I steal it? I had always felt that when I wanted a real home it would be here. And the time had come when I wanted a—home. So I planned to come—with him. It was to be my surprise—he doesn't even know that the old place belongs to me. He thought it was just another of my restless demands, but he let me have my way. We had friends with us when we started; they left us at Washington. It was after we were alone that—we quarreled—and I ran away. I left a note and told him that I had gone to France. I suppose he followed and didn't find me. I am not even sure that he wants to find me."

"Do you want to be found?"

"I don't know. I'd rather not talk about it."

William came in with the tea and was told to send the intruder off.

"I done sent him, Miss Lily," he said, with dignity, "but he ain't gwine to go. He say he ain't, and I kain't make him."

She went again to the window, and this time she drew back the faded hangings and stepped out on the balcony.

I heard her utter a cry; then the whole room seemed to whirl about me as she came in, dragging the curtains together behind her. Every drop of blood was drained from her face.

"William," she said, sharply, "that man—is coming toward the house! If he asks for me—I am not—at home."

"Nawm," and William went down to answer the blows of the brass knocker.

We heard him open the door, we heard the crisp, quick voice. We heard William's stately response. Then the quick voice said: "Will you tell your mistress that I shall wait?"

William came up with the message. "He's settin' on the po'ch, an' he looks like he was makin' out to set there all night."

"Let him sit," said Lady Crusoe inelegantly. "Lock all of the doors, William, and serve the tea."

She sat there and drank a cup of it scalding hot, with her head in the air and her foot tapping the floor. But I couldn't drink a drop. I was just sick with the thought of how he loved her, and of how she had hardened her heart.

At last I couldn't stand it any longer. The tears rolled down my cheeks. Lady Crusoe set her cup on the tray and stared at me in amazement. "What's the matter?"

"Oh, how can you—when he loves you?"

I don't know how I dared say it, for her eyes were blazing in her white face, and my heart was thumping, but there was Robinson Crusoe crowing in his hooded cradle, and Robin's father was on the front step, with the old oak door shut and barred against him.

She leaned forward, and I knew what was coming. "How did you know it was—my husband?"

My eyes met hers squarely. "He came to the store. He was looking for you."

"And you told him that I was here?"

300

"No. I wanted to. But I had promised."

For a little while neither of us spoke. The silence was broken by a thud, as if a flying squirrel had dropped from the roof to the balcony. A stick of wood fell apart in the grate, and the crow of the baby in the hooded cradle was answered by the baby on my lap.

Lady Crusoe hugged her knees with her white arms as if she were cold, although the room was hot with the blazing fire. "I think you might have told me. It would have been the friendly thing to have told me—"

"Billy thought it wasn't best."

"What had Billy to do with it?"

"Billy has everything to do with me. I talked it over with him—and—and Billy's such a darling to talk things over—"

I broke down and sobbed and sobbed, and the tears dripped on Junior's precious head. And at last she said, her face softened, "You silly little thing, what do you want me to do?"

"If it were Billy, I should ask him in—and show him—the baby—"

"If it were Billy, you would set your heart under his heel for him to step on. I am not like that—"

Another squirrel dropped to the balcony. The sun was setting, and between the velvet curtains I could see it blood-red behind the hills.

Lady Crusoe rose, pacing the room restlessly. The wind rising rattled the long windows. A shadow blotted out the sun.

"I suppose if you were I," she said at last, "you'd take your baby in your arms, and go down and say to that man on the steps, 'Come in and be lord of the manor and the ruler of your wife and child.'"

I held Junior close and my voice trembled. "I should never say a thing like that to—Billy—"

"What would you say?"

"I should say"—I choked over it, and broke down at the end—"oh, lover, lover, this is your son—and I am his happy mother—"

She stopped in front of me and stood looking down, with the anger all gone from her eyes. Then, before she could turn or cry out, the long windows were struck open by something that was stronger than the wind. There had been no flying squirrels on the balcony, and the shadow which had hidden the sun was the breadth and height of the big man who stood between the velvet curtains! He crossed the room at a stride.

"Did you think that bolts and bars could keep me from you?" he asked, and took Lady Crusoe's hands in a tight grip and drew her toward him. She resisted for a moment. Then her white slenderness was crushed in his hungry arms.

Well, as soon as I could gather up Junior and his belongings, I went down to wait for Billy. But before I went I saw her drop on her knees beside the hooded cradle and lift out little Robin, and, still kneeling, hold him up toward his father, as the nun holds up Galahad in the Holy Grail.

And what do you think I heard her say?

"Oh, lover, lover, this is your son—and I am his happy mother!"

Billy came in glowing from his walk in the sharp air, and I can't tell you how good it seemed to feel his cold cheek against my cheek, and his warm lips on mine. We were a rapturous trio in front of the library fire, and there we were joined presently by the rapturous trio from above stairs. They treated Billy and me as if we were a pair of guardian angels. Then we had dinner together, with Mandy and William in the background beaming.

And that night I told Billy all about it. "Isn't it beautiful, Billy? They are going to live on the old Davenant place, and it is to be their home."

Everybody calls on us now. You see, Lady Crusoe's family is older than any of the others, and then there's her husband's money. And I shine in her reflected light, for our friendship, as she says, is founded on a rock. But Billy says it is founded on a wreck. Yet while he jokes about it, I know that he is proud of his friendship with Robin's father. And when the spring comes, we are to take old Tid and our blessed Junior and our family effects to an adorable cottage with a garden on all four sides of it and set well back from the road. You see, we feel that we can afford it, for we have the exclusive business of supplying the needs of the Davenant estate, and we are thus financially on our feet.

A REBELLIOUS GRANDMOTHER

Mrs. Cissy Beale and her daughter Cecily sat together in the latter's bedroom—a bewitching apartment, in which pale-gray paper and pale-gray draperies formed an effective background for the rosewood furniture and the French mirrors and tapestried screens.

Between the two women was a bassinet and a baby.

"You act," said Cecily, "as if you were sorry about—the baby."

Her mother, who lay stretched at ease on a pillowed couch, shook her head.

"I'm not sorry about the baby—she's a darling—but you needn't think I'm going to be called 'grandmother,' Cecily. A grandmother is a person who settles down. I don't expect to settle down. My life has been hard. I struggled and strove through all those awful years after your father—left me. I educated you and Bob. And now you've both married well, and I've a bit of money ahead from my little book. For the first time in my life I can have leisure and pretty clothes; for the first time in my life I feel young; and then, absolutely without warning, you come back from Europe with your beautiful Surprise, and expect me to live up to it—"

"Oh, no!" Cecily protested.

"Yes, you do," insisted little Mrs. Beale. She sat up and gazed at her daughter accusingly. With the lace of her boudoir cap framing her small, fair face, she looked really young—as young almost as the demure Cecily, who, in less coquettish garb, was taking her new motherhood very seriously.

"Yes, you do," Mrs. Beale repeated. "I know just what you expect of me. You expect me to put on black velvet and old lace and diamonds. I shan't dare to show you my new afternoon frock—it's *red*, Cecily, geranium *red*; I shan't dare to wear even the tiniest slit in my skirts; I shan't dare to wear a Bulgarian sash or a Russian blouse, or a low neck—without expecting to hear some one say, disapprovingly, 'And she's a *grandmother*!'" She paused, and Cecily broke in tumultuously:

"I should think you'd be proud of—the baby."

"No, I'm not proud." Mrs. Beale thrust her toes into a pair of silver-embroidered Turkish slippers and stood up. "I'm not proud just at this moment, Cecily. You see—there's Valentine Landry."

"Mother—!"

"Now please don't say it that way, Cecily. He's half in love with me, and I'm beginning to like him, awfully. I've never had a bit of romance in my life. I married your father when I was too young to know my own mind, and he was much older than I. Then came the years of struggle after he went away.... I was a good wife and a good mother. I worshiped you and Bob, and I gave my youth for you. I never thought of any other man while your father lived, even though he did not belong to me. And now he is dead. You'll never know—I hope you may *never* know—what drudgery means as I have known it. I've written my poor little screeds when I was half-dead with fatigue; I've been out in cold and rain to get news; I've interviewed all sorts of people when I've hated them and hated the work. And if now I want to have my little fling, why not? Everybody effervesces some time. This is my moment—and you can't expect me to spoil it by playing the devoted grandmother."

The baby was wailing, a little hungry call, which made her mother take her up and say, hastily: "It's time to feed her. You won't mind, mother?"

"Yes, I *do* mind," said the little lady. "I don't like that Madonna effect, with the baby in your arms. It makes me feel horribly frivolous and worldly, Cecily. But it doesn't change my mind a bit."

After a pause, the Madonna-creature asked, "Who is Valentine Landry?"

Mrs. Beale had her saucy little cap off, and was brushing out her thin, light locks in which the gray showed slightly. But she stopped long enough to explain. "He isn't half as sentimental as his name. I met him in Chicago at the Warburtons', just before I made a success of my book. I was very tired, and he cheered me a lot. He's from Denver, and he made his money in mines. He hasn't married, because he hasn't had time. We're awfully good friends, but he doesn't know my age. He knows that I have a daughter, but not a grand-daughter. He thinks of me as a young woman—not as a grandmother-creature in black silk and mitts—"

"*Mother*! nobody expects you to wear black silk and mitts—"

"Well, you expect me to have a black-silk-and-mitt mind. You know you are thinking this very minute that there is no idiot like an old one—Cecily—"

The girl flushed. "I don't think you are quite kind, mother."

Mrs. Beale laughed and forgot to be cynical. "I know what you'd like to have me, dearie, but this is my moment of emancipation." She crossed the room and looked down at the tiny bit of humanity curled like a kitten in the curve of her daughter's arm. "I'm not going to be your grandmother, yet, midget," she announced, with decision. Then, "Cecily, I think when she's old enough I shall have her call me—Cupid—"

And laughing in the face of her daughter's horrified protest, the mutinous grandparent retired precipitately to her own room.

Three hours later, Mrs. Cissy Beale went forth to conquer, gowned in a restaurant frock of shadow lace topped by a black tulle hat.

Valentine Landry, greeting her in Cecily's white-and-gold drawing-room, was breezy and radiant. "You're as lovely as ever," he said, as he took her hand; "perhaps a bit lovelier because you are glad to see me."

"I am glad," she assured him; "and it is so nice to have you come before the summer is at an end. We can have a ride out into Westchester, and come back by daylight to dinner."

"And no chaperons?"

302

"No." She was looking up at him a little wistfully. "We know each other too well to have to drag in a lot of people, don't we? It is the men whom women trust with whom they go alone."

He met her glance gravely. "Do you know," he said, "that you have the sweetest way of putting things? A man simply has to come up to your expectations. He'd as soon think of disappointing a baby as of disappointing you."

His selection of a simile was unfortunate. Mrs. Beale's eyes became fixed upon a refractory button of her glove.

"Please help me," she said; "your fingers are stronger," and as he bent above her hand she forgot the baby, forgot her new estate, forgot everything except the joy she felt at having his smooth gray head so close to her own.

When he had her safely beside him in his big car he asked, "What made you run away from me in Chicago?"

"My daughter came home from Europe."

"I can't quite think of you with a grown daughter."

"Cecily's a darling." Mrs. Beale's voice held no enthusiasm.

Landry, noting her tone, looked faintly surprised. "You and she must have great good times together."

"Oh, yes—"

Mrs. Beale wished that he wouldn't talk about Cecily. Cecily had married before good times were possible. They had never played together—she and the little daughter for whom she had toiled and sacrificed.

Landry's voice broke in upon her meditations: "I should like to meet Cecily."

Mrs. Beale switched him away from the topic expeditiously. He should not see her as yet in the bosom of her family. *He should not*. He should not see Cecily with her air of mature motherliness. He should not see Victor, Cecily's husband, who was ten years older than Cecily and only ten years younger than herself. He should not hear her big son Bob call her "Grandma." He should not gaze upon the pretty deference of Bob's little wife toward the queen-dowager!

Dining later opposite Landry in a great golden palace, Cissy seemed like some gay tropical bird. In her new and lovely clothes she was very pretty, very witty, almost girlishly charming. Yet Landry was conscious of a vague feeling of disappointment. She had been more serenely satisfying in Chicago—not so brilliantly hard, not so persistently vivacious. How could he know that the change was one of desperation? Cissy, as grandmother, felt that she must prove, even to herself, that she was not yet a back number.

With this rift in the lute of their budding romance, they ate and drank and went to the play and had what might otherwise have been an enchanted ride home in the moonlight. But when Landry said "Good-night" Cissy felt the loss of something in his manner. His greeting that afternoon had had in it something almost of tenderness; his farewell was commonplace and slightly constrained.

As Mrs. Beale went through the dimly lighted hall to her room, she met Cecily in a flowing garment, pacing back and forth with the baby in her arms.

"She isn't well," Cecily whispered, as the little lady in the lace frock questioned her. "I don't know whether I ought to call a doctor or not."

Mrs. Beale poked the tiny mite with an expert finger. "I'll give her a drink of hot water with a drop of peppermint in it," she said, "as soon as I get my hat off, and you'd better go back to bed, Cecily; you aren't well enough to worry with her."

Cecily looked relieved. "I was worried," she confessed. "It's nurse's night out and Victor had to go to a board meeting unexpectedly—and with you away—I lost my nerve. It seemed dreadful to be alone, mother."

Mrs. Beale knew how dreadful it was. She had carried the wailing Cecily in her arms night after night in the weeks which followed the crushing knowledge of her husband's infidelity. But she had carried a heavier burden than the child—the burden of poverty, of desertion, of an unknown future.

But these things were not to be voiced. "You go to bed, Cecily," she said. "I'll look after her."

Walking the floor later with the baby in her arms, Mrs. Beale's mind was on Landry. "Heavens! if he could see me now!" was her shocked thought, as she stopped in front of a mirror to survey the picture she made.

Her hair was down and the grayest lock of all showed plainly. She had discarded frills and furbelows and wore a warm gray wrapper. She looked nice and middle-aged, yet carried, withal, a subtle air of girlishness—would carry it, in spite of storm or stress, until the end, as the sign and seal of her undaunted spirit.

The baby stirred in her arms, and again Mrs. Beale went back and forth, crooning the lullaby with which she had once put her own babies to bed.

In the morning the baby was much better, but Mrs. Beale was haggard. She stayed in bed until eleven o'clock, however. Cecily, coming in at twelve, found her ready to go out. In response to an inquiry, Mrs. Beale spoke of a luncheon engagement with Valentine Landry.

"Mother—are you going to marry him?"

Cissy, studying the adjustment of her veil, confessed, "He hasn't asked me."

"But he will—"

Mrs. Beale shrugged her shoulders. "Who knows?"

In the weeks which followed, the little lady was conscious that things were not drawing to a comfortable climax. By all the rules of the game, Landry should long ago have declared himself. But he seemed to be slipping more and more into the fatal role of good friend and comrade.

Cissy's pride would not let her admit, even to herself, that she had failed to attract at the final moment. But there was something deeper than her pride involved, and she found her days restless and her nights sleepless. One night in the dense darkness she faced the truth relentlessly. "You're in love, Cissy Beale," she told herself, scornfully. "You're in love for the first time in your life—and you a—grandmother!"

Then she turned over on her pillow, hid her face in its white warmth, and cried as if her heart would break.

In the meantime the baby drooped. Cecily, worried, consulted her mother continually. Thus it came about that Mrs. Beale lived a double life. From noon until midnight she was of to-day—smartly gowned, girlish; from midnight until dawn she was of yesterday—waking from her fitful slumbers at the first wailing note, presiding in gray gown and slippers over strange brews of catnip and of elderflower.

Cecily's doctor, being up-to-date, remonstrated at this return to the primitive, but was forced to admit, after the baby had come triumphantly through a half-dozen critical attacks, that Cissy's back-to-grandma methods were effective.

It was on a morning following one of these struggles that Cissy said to her daughter, wearily, "I can't escape it—"

"Escape what?" demanded Cecily, who, in the pale-gray bedroom was endeavoring to observe the doctor's injunction to let the wailing baby stay in her bassinet, instead of walking the floor with her.

"The black-silk-and-mitt destiny," said the depressed lady.

"What has happened?" Cecily demanded.

"Nothing has happened," responded her weary little mother, and refused to discuss the matter further.

But to herself she was beginning to admit that she had lost Landry. An hour later she had a telephone message from him.

"I want you to go with me for a last ride together," he said. "I leave to-morrow."

"To-morrow!" Her voice showed her dismay.

"But why this sudden decision—"

"I have played long enough," he said; "business calls—"

As Mrs. Beale made ready for the ride she surveyed herself wistfully in her mirror. There were shadows under her eyes, and faint little lines toward the corners of her lips—it even seemed to her that her chin sagged. She had a sudden sense of revolt. "If I were young, *really* young," she thought, "he would not be going away—"

With this idea firmly fixed in her mind, she exerted herself to please him; and her little laugh made artificial music in his ears, her fixed smile wore upon his nerves, her staccato questions irritated him.

Again they had dinner together, and as she sat opposite him, gorgeous and gay in her gown of geranium red, he began to talk with her of her daughter.

"I've never met her. It has seemed to me that you might have let me see her—"

Cissy flushed. "She's such a great grown-up," she said. "Somehow when I'm with her I feel—old—"

"You will never seem old," he said, with the nearest approach to tenderness that had softened his voice for days. "You have in you the spirit of eternal youth—"

Then he floundered on. "But a mother and a daughter—when you used to speak of her in Chicago, it seemed to me that I could see you together, and I liked the sweetness and womanliness of the thought; but I have never seen you together."

With a sense of recklessness upon her, Cissy suddenly determined to tell him the truth. "Cecily hasn't been going out much. You see, there's the baby—"

He stared. "The baby—?"

"Her baby—Cecily's—"

"*Then you're a grandmother?*"

It seemed to Cissy that the whole restaurant rang with the emphasis of the words. Yet he had not spoken loudly; not a head was turned in their direction; even the waiter stood unmoved.

When she came to herself Landry was laughing softly. "When are you going to let me see—the baby—?"

"Never—"

"Why not?"

Cissy went on to her doom. "Because you'll want to put me on the shelf like all the rest of them. You'll want to see me with—my hair—parted—and spectacles. And my eyes are perfectly good—and my hair is my own—"

She stopped. Landry was surveying her with hard eyes.

"Don't you love—the baby—?"

Cissy shrugged. "Perhaps. I don't know yet. Some day I may when I haven't anything to do but sit in a chimney-corner."

Thus spoke Cissy Beale, making of herself a heartless creature, flinging back into the face of Valentine Landry his most cherished ideals.

But what did it matter? She had known from the moment of her confession that he would be repelled. What man could stand up in the face of the world and marry a grandmother!—the idea was preposterous.

She finished dinner with her head in the air; she was hypocritically lively during the drive home; she said "Good-night" and "Good-bye" without feeling, and went up-stairs with her heart like lead to find the nurse weeping wildly on the first landing.

The baby, it appeared, was very ill. And the baby's father and mother, having left the little cherub sleeping peacefully, were motoring somewhere in the wide spaces of the world. The family doctor was out. She had called up another doctor, and he would come as soon as he could. But in the meantime the baby was dying—

"Nonsense, Kate," said Cissy Beale, and pulling off her gloves as she ran, she made for the pale-gray room.

Now, as it happened, Valentine Landry, driving away in a priggish state of mind, was suddenly overwhelmed by miserable remorse. Reviewing the evening, he seemed to see, for the first time, the unhappiness in the eyes of the little woman who had borne herself so bravely. In a sudden moment of illumination he realized all that she must have been feeling. Perhaps it had not been heartlessness; perhaps it had been—heart hunger.

Leaning forward, he spoke to his chauffeur. They stopped at the first drug-store, and Landry called up Cissy. Her voice from the other end answered, sharply, then broke as he gave his name.

"I thought it was the doctor," she said. "Can you come back, please? The baby, oh, the baby is very ill!"

Five minutes later the nurse let him into the house. He followed her up the stairs and into the nursery. Cissy sat with the baby in her arms. The baby was in a blanket and Cissy was in her gray wrapper. She had donned it while the nurse held the baby in the hot bath which saved its life. Cissy's hair was out of curl and the color was out of her cheeks. But to Valentine Landry she was beautiful.

"It was a convulsion," she told him, simply. "I am afraid she will have another. We haven't been able to get a doctor—will you get one for us?"

Out he went on his mission for the lady of his heart, and the lady of his heart, sitting wet and worried in the pale-gray bedroom, was saying to herself, monotonously, "It's all over now—no man could see me like this and love me—"

Cecily and her husband and the doctor and Landry came in out of the darkness together. They went up-stairs together, then stopped on the threshold as Cissy held up a warning hand.

She continued to croon softly the lullaby which had belonged to her own babies: "Hushaby, sweet, my own—"

It was Cecily and the doctor who went in to her, and Landry, standing back in the shadows, waited. He spoke to Cissy as she came out.

"I am going so early in the morning," he said, "will you give me just one little minute now?"

In that minute he told her that he loved her.

And Cissy, standing in the library in all the disorder of uncurled locks and gray kimono, demanded, after a rapturous pause, "But why didn't you tell me before?"

He found it hard to explain. "I didn't quite realize it—until I saw you there so tender and sweet, with the baby in your arms—"

"A Madonna-creature," murmured Cissy Beale.

But he did not understand. "It isn't because I want you to sit in a chimney-corner—it wasn't fair of you to say that—"

Then in just one short speech Cissy Beale showed him her heart. She told of the years of devotion, always unrewarded by the affection she craved. "And here was the baby," she finished, "to grow up—and find somebody else, and forget me—"

As he gathered her into his protecting embrace, his big laugh comforted her.

"I'm yours till the end of the world, little grandmother," he whispered. "I shall never find any one else—and I shall never forget."

WAIT—FOR PRINCE CHARMING

Kingdon Knox was not conscious of any special meanness of spirit. He was a lawyer and a good one. He was fifty, and wore his years with an effect of youth. He exercised persistently and kept his boyish figure. He had keen, dark eyes, and silver in his hair. He was always well groomed and well dressed, and his income provided him with the proper settings. His home in the suburb was spacious and handsome and presided over by a handsome and socially successful wife. His office was presided over by Mary Barker, who was his private secretary. She was thirty-five and had been in his office for fifteen years. She had come to him an unformed girl of twenty; she was now a perfect adjunct to his other office appointments. She wore tailored frocks, her hair was exquisitely dressed in shining waves, her hands were white and her nails polished, her slender feet shod in unexceptional shoes.

Nannie Ashburner, who was also in the office and who now and then took Knox's dictation, had an immense admiration for Mary. "I wish I could wear my clothes as you do," she would say as they walked home together.

"Clothes aren't everything."

"Well, they are a lot."

"I would give them all to be as young as you are."

"You don't look old, Mary."

"Of course I take care of myself," said Mary, "but if I were as young as you I'd begin over again."

"How do you mean 'begin,' Mary?"

But Mary was not communicative. "Oh, well, I'd have some things that I might have had and can't get now," was all the satisfaction that she gave Nannie.

It was through Mary that Nannie had obtained her position in Kingdon Knox's office. Mary had boarded with Nannie's mother for five years. Nannie was fourteen when Mary came. She had finished high school and had had a year in a business college, and then Mrs. Ashburner had asked Mary if there was any chance for her in Kingdon Knox's office.

Mary had considered it, but had seemed to hesitate. "We need another typist, but I am not sure it is the place for her."

"Why not?"

Mary did not say why. "I wish she didn't have to work at all. She ought to get married."

"Dick McDonald wants her. But she's too young, Mary."

"You were married at nineteen."

"Yes, and a lot I got out of it." Mrs. Ashburner was sallow and cynical. "I kept boarders to make a living for my husband, Mary; and since he died I've kept boarders to make a living for Nannie and me."

"But Dick gets good wages."

"Well, he can wait till he saves something."

"Don't make him wait too long."

It was against her better judgment that Mary Barker spoke to her employer about Nannie. "I should want her to help me. She is not expert enough to take your dictation, but she could relieve me of a lot of detail."

"Well, let me have a look at her," Kingdon Knox had said.

So Nannie had come to be looked over, and she had blushed a little and had been rather breathless as she had talked to Mr. Kingdon, and he had been aware of the vividness of her young beauty; for Nannie had red hair that curled over her ears, and her skin was warm ivory, and her eyes were gray.

Her clothes were not quite up to the office standard, but Knox, having hired her, referred the matter to Mary. "You might suggest that she cut out thin waists and high heels," he had said; "you know what I like."

Mary knew, and Nannie's first month's salary had been spent in the purchase of a serge one-piece frock.

Mrs. Ashburner had rebelled at the expense. But Mary had been firm. "Mr. Knox won't have anybody around the office who looks slouchy or sloppy. It will pay in the end."

Nannie thought Mr. Knox wonderful. "He says that he wants me to work hard so that I can handle some of his letters."

"When did he tell you that?"

"Last night, while you were taking testimony in the library."

The office library was lined with law books. There were a handsome long mahogany table, green covered, and six handsome mahogany chairs. Mary, shut in with three of Knox's clients and a consulting partner, had had a sense of uneasiness. It was after hours. Nannie was waiting for her in the outer office. Everybody else had gone home except Knox, who was waiting for his clients.

Mary remembered how, when she was Nannie's age, she had often sat in that outer office after hours, and Knox had talked to her. He had been thirty-five and she, twenty. He had a wife and a handsome home; she had nothing but a hall room. And he had made her feel that she was very necessary to him. "I don't know how we should ever get along without you," he had said.

He had said other things.

It was because he had spoken of her lovely hair that she had kept it brushed and shining. It was because his eyes had followed her pencil that she had rubbed cold cream on her hands at night and had looked well after her nails. It was because she had learned his taste that she wore simple but expensive frocks. It was because of her knowledge that nothing escaped him that she shod her pretty feet in expensive shoes.

He had set standards for her, and she had followed them. And now he would set standards for Nannie!

She spoke abruptly. "Is Dick McDonald coming to-night?"

"Yes. He has had a raise, Mary. He telephoned—"

The two girls were in Mary's room. Dinner was over and Mary had slipped on a Chinese coat of dull blue and had settled down for an evening with her books. Mary's room was charming. In fifteen years she had had gifts of various kinds from Knox. They had always been well chosen and appropriate. Nothing could have been in better taste as an offering from an employer to an employee than the embossed leather book ends and desk set, the mahogany reading lamp with its painted parchment shade, the bronze Buddha, the antique candlesticks, the Chelsea teacups, the Sheffield tea caddy. Mary's comfortable salary had permitted her to buy the book shelves and the tea table and the mahogany day bed. There was a lovely rug which Mrs. Knox had sent her on the tenth anniversary of her association with the office. Mrs. Knox looked upon Mary as a valuable business asset. She invited her once a year to dinner.

Nannie wore her blue serge one-piece frock and a new winter hat. The hat was a black velvet tam.

"You need something to brighten you up," Mary said; "take my beads."

The beads were jade ones which Mr. Knox had brought to Mary when he came back from a six months' sojourn in the Orient. Mary had looked after the office while he was away. He had clasped the beads about her neck. "Bend your head while I put them on, Mary," he had commanded. He had been at his desk in his private office while she sat beside him with her note-book. And when he had clasped the beads and she had lifted her head, he had said with a quick intake of his breath: "I've been a long time away from you, Mary."

Nannie with the jade beads and her red hair and her velvet tam was rather rare and wonderful. "Dick is going to take me to the show to celebrate. He's got tickets to Jack Barrymore."

"Dick is such a nice boy," said Mary. "I'm glad you are going to marry him, Nannie."

"Who said I was going to marry him?"

"That's what he wants, Nannie, and you know it."

"Mr. Knox says it is a pity for a girl like me to get married."

Mary's heart seemed to stop beating. She knew just how Knox had said it.

She spoke quietly. "I think it would be a pity for you not to marry, Nannie."

"I don't see why. You aren't married, Mary."

"No."

"And Mr. Knox says that unless a girl can marry a man who can lift her up she had better stay single."

The same old arguments! "What does he mean by 'lift her up,' Nannie?"

"Well"—Nannie laughed self-consciously—"he says that any one as pretty and refined as I might marry anybody; that I must be careful not to throw myself away."

"Would it be throwing yourself away to marry Dick?"

"It might be. He looked all right to me before I went into the office. But after you've seen men like Mr. Knox—well, our kind seem—common."

Mrs. Ashburner was calling that Dick McDonald was down-stairs. Nannie, powdering her nose with Mary's puff, was held by the earnestness of the other woman's words.

"Let Dick love you, Nannie. He's such a dear."

Dick was, Nannie decided before the evening was over, a dear and a darling. He had brought her a box of candy and something else in a box. Mrs. Ashburner had shown him into the dining-room, which she and Nannie used as a sitting-room when the meals were over. The boarders occupied the parlor and were always in the way.

"Say, girlie, see here," Dick said as he brought out the box; and Nannie had gazed upon a ring which sparkled and shone and which looked, as Dick said proudly, "like a million dollars."

"I wanted you to have the best." His arm went suddenly around her. "I always want you to have the best, sweetheart."

He kissed her in his honest, boyish fashion, and she took the ring and wore it; and they went to the play in a rosy haze of happiness, and when they came home he kissed her again.

"The sooner you get out of that office the better," he said. "We'll get a little flat, and I've saved enough to furnish it."

Nannie was lighting the lamp under the percolator. Mrs. Ashburner had left a plate of sandwiches on one end of the dining-room table. Nannie was young and Mrs. Ashburner was old-fashioned. Her daughter was not permitted to eat after-the-theatre suppers in restaurants. "You can always have something here."

"Don't let's settle down yet," Nannie said, standing beside the percolator like a young priestess beside an altar. "There's plenty of time——"

"Plenty of time for what?" asked her lover. "We've no reason to wait, Nannie."

So Dick kissed her, and she let him kiss her. She loved him, but she would make no promises as to the important day. Dick went away a bit puzzled by her attitude. He wanted her at once in his home. It hurt him that she did not seem to care to come to him.

It was a cold night, with white flakes falling, and the policeman on the beat greeted Dick as he passed him. "It is a nice time in the morning for you to be getting home."

"Oh, hello, Tommy! I'm going to be married. How's that?"

"Who's the girl?"

"Nannie Ashburner."

"That little redhead?"

"You're jealous, Tommy."

"I am; she'll cook sausages for you when you come home on cold nights, and kiss you at your front door, and set the talking machine going, with John McCormack shouting love songs as you come in."

Dick laughed. "Some picture, Tommy. And a lot you know about it. Why don't you get married and try it out?"

Tommy, who was tall and ruddy and forty, plus a year or two, gave a short laugh. "I might find somebody to cook the sausages, but there's only one that I'd care to kiss."

"So that's it. She turned you down, Tommy?"

"She did, and we won't talk about it."

"Oh, very well. Good-night, Tommy."

"Good-night."

So Dick passed on, and Tommy Jackson beat his hands against his breast as he made his way through the whirling snow, his footsteps deadened by the frozen carpet which the storm had spread.

Mary Barker was delighted when Nannie told of her engagement to Dick. She talked it over with Mrs. Ashburner. "It will be the best thing for her."

Mrs. Ashburner was not sure. "I've drudged all my life and I hate to see her drudge."

"She won't have it as hard as you have had it," Mary said. "Dick will always make a good income."

"She will have a harder time than you've had, Mary," said Mrs. Ashburner, and her eyes swept the pretty room wistfully. "Many a time when I've been down in my steaming old kitchen I have thought of you up here in your blue coat and your pretty slippers, with your hair shining, and I've wished to heaven that I had never married."

"Things haven't been easy for you," said Mary gently.

"They have been harder than nails, Mary. You've escaped all that."

"Yes." Mary's eyes did not meet Mrs. Ashburner's. "I have escaped—that."

Nannie and her mother slept in the back parlor of the boarding-house. They had single beds and it was in the middle of the night that Mrs. Ashburner said: "Are you awake, Nannie?"

"Yes, I am."

"Well, I can't seem to get to sleep. Maybe it's the coffee and maybe it's because I have you on my mind. I keep thinking that I hate to have you get married, honey."

"Oh, mother, don't you like Dick?"

"Yes. It ain't that. But it's nice for you in the office and you don't have to slave."

Nannie sat up in bed, and the light from the street lamp shone in and showed her wide-eyed, with her hair in a red glory. "I shan't slave," she said. "I told Dick."

"Men don't know." Mrs. Ashburner spoke with a sort of weary bitterness. "They'll promise anything."

"And I am not going to be married in a hurry, mother. Dick's got to wait for me if he wants me."

It sounded very worldly-minded and decisive and Mrs. Ashburner gained an envious comfort in her daughter's declaration. She had never set herself against a man's will in that way. Perhaps, after all, Nannie would make a success of marriage.

But Nannie was not so resolute as her words might have seemed to imply. Long after her mother slept she lay awake in the dark and thought of Dick, of the break in his voice when he had made his plea, the light in his eyes when he had won a response, his flaming youth, his fine boy's reverence for her own youth and innocence. It would be—rather wonderful, she whispered to her heart, and fell asleep, dreaming.

The next morning was very cold, and Nannie, coming early into Kingdon Knox's office to take his letters, was in a glow after her walk through the snowy streets. Her cheeks were red, her eyes sparkled, and the ring on her finger sparkled.

Knox at once noticed the ring. "So that's it," he said, and leaned back in his chair. "Let's talk about it a little."

They talked about it more than a little, and the burden of Kingdon Knox's argument was that it was a pity. She was too young and pretty to marry a poor man and live in a funny little flat and do her own work and spoil her nails with dishwashing. "Personally, I think it's rather dreadful. A waste of you, if you want the truth."

Poor Nannie, listening, saw her castles falling. It would be rather dreadful—dishwashing and a gas stove and getting meals.

"He is awfully in love with me," she managed to say at last.

"And you?" He leaned forward a little. Nannie was aware of the feeling of excitement which he could always rouse in her. When he spoke like that she saw herself as something rather perfect and princesslike.

"Wait—for Prince Charming," he said.

Nannie was sure that when Prince Charming came he would be like Mr. Knox; younger perhaps, but with that same lovely manner.

"Of course," Mr. Knox said gently, "I suppose I ought not to advise, but if I were you"—he touched the sparkling ring—"I should give it back to him."

So after several absorbing talks with her employer on the subject, Nannie gave the ring back, and when poor Dick passed his friend the policeman on his way home he stopped and told his story.

"They are all like that," Tommy said, "but if I were you I wouldn't take 'no' for an answer."

Dick brightened. "Wouldn't you?"

"Not if I had to carry her off under my arm," said Tommy between his teeth.

"But I can't carry her off, Tommy—and she won't go."

"She'll go if you ain't afraid of her," Tommy told him with solemn emphasis. "I was afraid."

They were under the street lamp, and Dick stared at him in astonishment. "I didn't know you were afraid of anything."

"I didn't know it either," was Tommy's grim response, "until I met her. But I've known it ever since."

"Well, it's hard luck."

"It is hardest at Christmas time," said Tommy, "and my beat ain't the best one to make me cheerful. There are too many stores. And dolls in the windows. And drums. And horns. And Santa Claus handing out things to kids. And I've got to see it, with money just burning in my pocket to buy things and to have a tree of my own and a turkey in my oven and a table with some one who cares at the other end. And all I'll get out of the merry season is a table d'hôte at Nitti's and a box of cigars from the boys."

"Ain't women the limit, Tommy?"

"Well"—Tommy's tone held a note of forced cheerfulness—"that little redhead must have had some reason for not wanting you, Dick. Maybe we men ain't worth it."

"Worth what?"

"Marrying. A woman's got a square deal coming to her, and she doesn't always get it."

"She'd get it with you, and she'd get it with me; you know that, Tommy."

"She might," said Tommy pessimistically, "if the good Lord helped us."

Nannie on the day after her break with Dick was blushingly aware of the bareness of her third finger as she took Kingdon Knox's dictation. When he had finished his letters, Knox smiled at her. "So you gave it back," he said.

"Yes."

"Good little girl. You'll find something much better if you wait. And I don't want you wasted." He opened a drawer and took out a long box. He opened it and lifted a string of beads. They were of carved ivory, and matched the cream of Nannie's complexion. They were strung strongly on a thick thread of scarlet silk, and there was a scarlet tassel at the end.

"They are for you," he said. "It is my first Christmas present to you; but I hope it won't be the last."

Nannie's heart beat so that she could almost hear it. "Oh, thank you," she said breathlessly; "they're so beautiful."

But she did not know how rare they were, nor how expensive until she wore them in Mary's room that night.

"Where did you get them, Nannie?"

"Mr. Knox gave them to me."

There was dead silence, then Mary said: "Nannie, you ought not to take them."

"Why not?"

"They cost such an awful lot, Nannie. They look simple, but they aren't. The carving is exquisite."

"Well, he gave you beads, Mary."

Mary's face was turned away. "It was different. I have been such a long time in the office."

"I don't think it is much different, and I don't see how I can give them back, Mary."

Mary did not argue, but when a little later Nannie told of her broken engagement, Mary said sharply: "But, Nannie—why?"

"Well, mother doesn't care much for the idea. She—she thinks a girl is much better off to keep on at the office."

Mary was lying in her long chair under the lamp. She had a cushion under her head, and her hand shaded her eyes. "Did—Mr. Knox have anything to do with it?"

"What makes you ask that, Mary?"

"Did he?"

"Well, yes. You know what I told you; he thinks I'd be—wasted."

"On Dick?"

"Yes."

Mary lay for a long time with her hand over her eyes; then she said: "If you don't marry Dick, what about your future, Nannie?"

"There's time enough to think about that. And—and I can wait."

"For what?"

Nannie blushed and laughed a little. "Prince Charming."

After that there was a silence, out of which Nannie asked: "Does your head ache, Mary?"

"A little."

"Can't I get you something?"

"No. After I've rested a bit I'll take a walk."

Mary's walk led her by the lighted shop windows. The air was keen and cold and helped her head. But it did not help her heart. She had a sense of suffocation when she thought of Nannie.

She stopped in front of one of the shops. There were dolls in the window, charming, round-eyed, ringleted. One of them was especially captivating, with fat blond curls, fat legs, blue silk socks and slippers, crisp frills and a broad blue hat.

"How I should have loved her when I was a little girl," was Mary's thought as she stood looking in. Then: "How a child of my own would have loved her."

She made up her mind that she would buy the doll—in the morning when the shop opened. It was a whimsical thing to do, to give herself a doll at her time of life. But it would be in a sense symbolic. She had no child to which to give it; she would give it to the child who was once herself.

She came home with a lighter heart and with the knowledge of what she had to do. She put on her blue house coat and sat down to her desk with its embossed leather fittings, and there under the lovely, lamp which Kingdon Knox had given her she wrote to Nannie.

She gave the letter to Nannie the next morning. "I want you to read it when you are all alone. Then tear it up. It must always be just between you and me, Nannie."

Nannie read the letter in the lunch hour. She got her lunch at a cafeteria and there was a rest room. It was very quiet and she had a corner to herself. She wondered what Mary had to say to her, and why she didn't talk it out instead of writing about it.

But Mary had felt that she could not trust herself to speak. There would have been Nannie's eyes to meet, questions to answer; and this meant so much. Paper and pen were impersonal.

"It isn't easy to talk such things out, Nannie. I should never have written this if I had not realized last night that your feet were following the path which my own have followed for fifteen years. And I knew that you were envying me and wanting to be like me; and I am saying what I shall say in this letter so that I may save you, Nannie.

"When I first came into Mr. Knox's office I was young like you, and I had a lover, young and fine like Dick, and he satisfied me. We had our plans—of a home and the happiness we should have together. If I had married him, I should now have sons and daughters growing up about me, and when Christmas came there would be a tree and young faces smiling, and my husband, smiling.

"But Mr. Knox talked to me as he talked to you. He told me, too, to wait—for Prince Charming. He told me I was too fine to be wasted. He hinted that the man I was planning to marry was a plain fellow, not good enough for me. He talked and I listened. He opened vistas. I saw myself raised to a different sphere by some man like Mr. Knox—just as well groomed, just as distinguished, just as rich and wonderful.

"But such men don't come often into the lives of girls like you and me, Nannie. I know that now. I did not know it then. But Mr. Knox should have known it. Yet he held out the hope; and at last he robbed me of my future, of the little home, my fine, strong husband. He robbed me of my woman's heritage of a child in my arms.

"And in return he gave me—nothing. I have found in the years that I have been with him that he likes to be admired and looked up to by pretty women. He likes to mold us into something exquisite and ornamental, he likes to feel that he has molded us. He likes to see our blushes. All these years that I have been with him, he has liked to feel that I looked upon him as the ideal toward which all my girlish dreams tended.

"He is not in love with me, and I am not in love with him. But he has always known that if he had been free and had wooed me, I should have felt that King Cophetua had come to the beggar maid. Yet, too late, I can see that if he had been free he would never have wooed me. His ambition would have carried him up and beyond anything I can ever hope to be, and he would have sought some woman of his own circle who would have contributed to his material success.

"And now he is trying to spoil your life, Nannie—to make you discontented with your future with Dick. You look at him and see in your life some day a Prince Charming. But I tell you this, Nannie, that Prince Charming will never come. And after a time all you will have to show for the years that you have spent in the office will be just a pretty room, a few bits of wood and leather and bronze in exchange for warm, human happiness, clinging hands, a husband like Dick, who adores you, who comes home at night, eager—for you!

"You can have all this—and I have lost it. And there isn't much ahead of me. I shan't always be ornamental, and then Mr. Knox will let me drop out of his life, as he has let others drop out. And there'll be loneliness and old age and—nothing else.

"Oh, Nannie, I want you to marry Dick. I want you to know that all the rest is dust and ashes. I feel tired and old; and when I think of your youth, and beauty, I want Dick to have it, not Mr. Knox, who will flatter and—forget.

"Tear this letter up, Nannie. It hasn't been easy to write. I don't want anybody but you to read it."

But Nannie did not tear it up.

She tucked it in her bag and went to telephone to Dick.

And would he meet her on the corner under the street lamp that night when she came home from the office? She had something to tell him.

Dick met Nannie, and presently they pursued their rapturous way. A little later Tommy Jackson passed by. Something caught his eye.

A bit of white paper.

He stooped and picked it up. It was Mary's letter to Nannie. Nannie had cried into her little handkerchief while she talked to Dick, and in getting the handkerchief out of the bag the letter had come with it and had dropped unnoticed to the ground.

It had been years since Tommy had seen any of Mary's writing. A sentence caught his eye, and he read straight through. After all, there are things permitted an officer of the law which might be unseemly in the average citizen.

And when he had read, Tommy began to say things beneath his breath. And the chances are that had Kingdon Knox appeared at that moment things would have fared badly with him.

But it was Mary Barker who came. She had under her arm in a paper parcel the fat doll with the blond curls and the blue socks. She did not see Tommy until she was almost upon him.

Then she said: "What are you doing here, Tommy?"

"Why shouldn't I be here?"

"This isn't your beat."

"It has been my beat since two weeks ago. I've seen you go by every night, Mary."

She stood looking up at him. And he looked down at her; and so, of course, their gaze met, and something that she saw in Tommy's eyes made Mary's overflow.

"Mary, darling," said Tommy tenderly.

"You said you wouldn't forgive me."

"That was fifteen years ago."

"Tommy, I'm sorry."

Tommy stood very straight as became an officer of the law with, the eyes of the world upon him.

"May," he said, "I just read your letter to Nannie. She dropped it. If I'd known the things in that letter fifteen years ago I'd have stayed on my job until I got you. But I thought you didn't care."

"I thought so too," said Mary.

"But the letter told me that you wanted a husband's loving heart and a strong arm," said Tommy, "and, please God, you are going to have them, Mary. And now you run along, girl, dear. I can't be making love when I'm on duty. But I'll come and kiss you at nine."

So Mary ran along, and her heart sang. And when she got home she unwrapped the fat doll and kissed every curl of her, and she set her under the lovely lamp; and then she got a long box and put something in it and wrapped it and addressed it to Kingdon Knox.

And after that she went to the window and stood there, watching until she saw Tommy coming.

And the next morning when Kingdon Knox found the long box on his desk, addressed in Mary's handwriting, he thought it was a Christmas present, and he opened it, smiling.

But his smile died as he read the note which lay on top of a string of jade beads:

"I am sending them back, Mr. Knox, with my resignation. I should never have taken them. But somehow you made me feel that I was a sort of fairy princess, and that jade beads belonged to me, and everything beautiful, and that some day life would bring them. But life isn't that, and you knew it and I didn't. Life is just warm human happiness, and a home, and work for those we love. And so, after all, I am going to marry Tommy. And Nannie is going to marry Dick. In a way it is a happy ending, and in a way it isn't, because I've grown away from the kind of life I must live with Tommy, and I am afraid that in some ways I am not fitted for it. But Tommy says that I am silly to be afraid. And in the future I am going to trust Tommy."

And so Mary went out of Kingdon Knox's life. And on Christmas Day at the head of a great table, with servants to the right of him and servants to the left, he carved a mammoth turkey; and there was silver shining, and glass sparkling and lovely women smiling, all in honor of the merry season.

But Kingdon Knox was not merry as he thought of the jade beads and of Mary's empty desk.

BEGGARS ON HORSEBACK

I

With the Merryman girls economy was a fine art. Money was spent by them to preserve the family traditions. Nothing else counted. Everything was sacrificed to the gods of yesterday.

Little Anne Merryman had shivered all her short life in the bleakness of this domestic ideal.

"Why can't I have butter on my bread?" she had demanded in her long-legged schoolgirl days, when she had worn her fair hair in a fat braid down her back.

The answers had never been satisfying. Well-bred people might, Amy indicated, go without butter. Their income was not elastic, and there were things more important.

"What things? Amy, I'm so hungry I could eat a house."

It was these expressions of Anne's about food which shocked Amy and Ethel.

"I'd sell my soul for a slice of roast beef."

"Anne!"

"Well, I would!"

"I—I don't see how you can be so ordinary, Anne."

"Ordinary" in the lexicon of Amy and Ethel meant "plebeian." No one in the Merryman family had ever been so ordinary as Anne. Hitherto the Merrymans had been content to warm themselves by the fires of their own complacency, to feed themselves on past splendors; for the Merrymans were as old as Norman rule in England. They had come to America with grants from the king, they had family portraits and family silver and family diamonds, and now in this generation of orphaned girls, two of them at least were fighting the last battles of family pride. The fortunes of the Merrymans had declined, and Amy and Ethel, with their backs, as it were, to the wall, were making a final stand.

"We must have evening clothes, we must entertain our friends, we must pay for the family pew"; this was their nervous litany. The Merrymans had always dressed and entertained and worshiped properly; hence it was for lace or tulle or velvet, as the case might be, that their money went. It went, too, for the very elegant and exclusive little dinners to which, on rare occasions, their friends were bidden; and it went for the high place in the synagogue from which they prayed their pharisaical prayers.

"We thank thee, Lord, that we are not as others," prayed Amy and Ethel fervently.

But Anne prayed no such prayers. She wanted to be like other people. She wanted to eat and drink with the multitude, she wanted a warm, warm heart, a groaning board. She wanted snugness and coziness and comfort. And she grew up loving these things, and hating the pale walls of their old house in Georgetown, the family portraits, the made-over dinner gowns that her sisters wore, her own made-over party frocks.

"Can't I have a new one, Amy?"

"It's Ethel's turn."

So it was when Anne went to a certain diplomatic reception in a made-over satin slip, hidden by a cloud of snowy tulle, that Murray Flint first waked to the fact of her loveliness.

He had waked ten years earlier to the loveliness of Amy, and five years later to the beauty of Ethel.

And now here was Anne!

"She's different though," he told old Molly Winchell; "more spiritual than the others."

It was Anne's thinness which deceived him. It was an attractive thinness. She was pale, with red lips, and the fat fair braids had given way to a shining knot. She wore the family pearls, and the effect was, as Murray had said, spiritual. Anne had the look, indeed, of one who sees heavenly visions.

Amy had never had that look. She was dark and vivid. If at thirty the vividness was emphasized by artificial means the fault lay in Amy's sacrifice to her social ideals, She needed the butter which she denied herself. She needed cream, and eggs, and her doctor had told her so. And Amy had kept the knowledge to herself.

Ethel, eating as little as Amy—or even less—had escaped, miraculously, attenuation. At twenty she had been a plump little beauty. She was still plump. Her neck in her low-cut gown was lovely. Her figure was not fashionable, and she lacked Amy's look of race.

"They are all charming," Molly Winchell said. "Why don't you marry one of them, Murray?"

"Marriage," said Murray, "would spoil it."

"Spoil what?"

Murray turned on her his fine dark eyes. "They are such darlings—the three of them."

"You Turk!" Molly surveyed him over the top of her sapphire feather fan. "So that's it, is it? You want them all."

Murray thought vaguely it was something like that. For ten years he had had Amy and Ethel—Amy at twenty, fire and flame, Ethel at fifteen, with bronze locks and lovely color. In those years Anne had promised little in the way of beauty or charm. She had read voraciously, curled up in chairs or on rugs, and had waked now and then to his presence and a hot argument.

"Why don't you like Dickens, Murray?"

"Oh, his people, Anne—clowns."

"They're not!"

"Boors; beggars." He made a gesture of distaste.

"They're darlings—Mark Tapley and Ruth Pinch. Murray, if I had a beefsteak I'd make a beefsteak pie."

There was more of pathos in this than Murray imagined. There had been no beef on the Merryman table for many moons.

"Murray, did you ever eat tripe?"

"My dear child—"

"It sounds dee-licious when Toby Veck has it on a cold morning. And there's the cricket on the hearth and the teakettle singing. I'd love to hear a kettle sing like that, Murray; wouldn't you?"

But Murray wouldn't. He had the same kind of mind as Amy and Ethel. He did not like robust and hearty things or robust and hearty people. He wore a corset to keep his hips small, and stood up at teas and receptions with an almost military carriage. Of course he had to sit down at dinners, but he sat very straight. He, too, had family portraits and family silver, and he lived scrupulously up to them. His fortunes, unlike the Merrymans', had not declined. He had money enough and to spare. He could have made Amy or Ethel very comfortable if he had married either of them. But he had not wanted to marry. There had been a time when he had liked to think of Amy as presiding over his table. She would have fitted in perfectly with the old portraits and old silver and the family diamonds. Then Ethel had come along. She had not fitted in with the diamonds and portraits and silver, but she had stirred his pulses.

"Anywhere else but in Georgetown," old Molly Winchell was saying, "those girls would have been snapped up long ago. It's a poor matrimonial market."

Murray was complacently aware that he was geographically the only eligible man on the Merryman horizon. Unless Amy and Ethel could marry with distinction they would not marry at all. It was not lack of attraction which kept them single, but lack of suitors in their own set.

And now here was Anne, with Ethel's loveliness and Amy's look of race. There was also that look of angelic detachment from the things of earth.

So Murray's eyes rested on Anne with great content as she came and sat beside Molly Winchell.

Other eyes rested on her—Amy's with quick jealousy. "So now it's Anne," she said to herself as she perceived Murray's preoccupation. Five years ago she had said, "Now it's Ethel," as she had seen him turn to the fresher beauty. Before that she had dreamed of herself as loving and beloved. It had been hard to shut her eyes to that vision.

Yet—better Anne than an outsider. Amy had a fierce sense of proprietorship in Murray. If she gave him to Ethel, to Anne, he would be still in a sense hers. With Anne or Ethel she would share his future, partake of his present.

A third pair of eyes surveyed Anne with interest as she sat by Molly.

"Corking kid," said the owner of the eyes to himself.

His name was Maxwell Sears. He was not in the least like Murray Flint. He was from the Middle West, he was red-blooded, and he cared nothing for the past. He held it as a rather negligible honor that he had a Declaration-signing ancestor. The important things to Maxwell were that he was representing his district in Congress; that he was still young enough to carry his college ideals into politics, and that he had just invested a small portion of the fortune which his father had left him in a model stock farm in Illinois.

For the rest, he was big, broad-shouldered, clean-minded. Now and then he looked up at the stars, and what he saw there swayed him level with the men about him. Because of the stars he called no man a fool, except such as deemed himself wiser than the rest. Because he believed in the people they believed in him. It was that which had elected him. It was that which would elect him again.

"Corking kid," said Maxwell Sears, with his smiling eyes on Anne.

II

In the course of the evening Maxwell managed an introduction. He found Anne quaint and charming. That she was reading Dickens amused him. He had thought that no one read Dickens in these days. How did it happen?

She said that she had discovered him for herself—many years ago.

How many years?

Well, to be explicit, ten. She had been eleven when she had found a new world in the fat little books. They had a lot of old books. She loved them all. But Dickens more than any. Didn't he?

He did. "His heart beat with the heart of the common people. It was that which made him great."

"Murray hates him."

"Who is Murray?"

Anne pondered. "Well, he's a family friend. We girls were brought up on him."

"Brought up on him?"

"Yes. Anything Murray likes we are expected to like. If he doesn't like things we don't."

"Oh."

"He's over there by Mrs. Winchell."

Maxwell looked and knew the type. "But you don't agree about Dickens?"

"No. And Amy says that Murray's wiser than I. But I'm not sure. Amy thinks that all men are wiser than women."

Maxwell chuckled. Anne was refreshing. She was far from modern in her modes of thought. She was—he hunted for the word and found it—mid-Victorian in her attitude of mind.

He wondered what Winifred Reed would think of her. Winifred lived in Chicago. She was athletic and intellectual. She wrote tabloid dramas, drove her own car, dressed smartly, and took a great interest in Maxwell's career. She wrote to him once a week, and he always answered her letters. Now and then she failed to write, and he missed her letters and told her so. It was altogether a pleasant friendship.

313

She hated the idea of Maxwell's farm. She thought it a backward step. "Are you going to spend the precious years ahead of you in the company of cows?"

"There'll be pigs too, Winifred; and chickens. And, of course, my horses."

"You belong in a world of men. It's the secret of your success that men like you."

"My cows like me—and there's great comfort after the stress of a stormy session in the reposefulness of a pig."

"I wish you'd be serious."

"I am serious. Perhaps it's a throwback, Winifred. There is farmer blood in my veins."

It was something deeper than that. It was his virile joy in fundamentals. He loved his golden-eared Guernseys and his black Berkshires and his White Wyandottes—not because of their choiceness but because they were cows and pigs and chickens; and he kept a pair of pussy cats, half a dozen dogs, and as many horses, because man primitively had made friends of the dumb brutes upon whom the ease and safety of his life depended.

There was, rather strangely, something about Anne which fitted in with this atavistic idea. She was, more than Winifred, a hearthstone woman. A man might carry her over his threshold and find her when he came home o' nights. It was hard to visualize Winifred as waiting or watching or welcoming. She was always going somewhere with an air of having important things to do, and coming back with an air of having done them. Maxwell felt that these important things were not connected in any way with domestic matters. One did not, indeed, expect domesticity of Winifred.

Thus Anne, drawing upon him by mysterious forces, drew him also by her beauty and a certain wistfulness in her eyes. He had once had a dog, Amber Witch, whose eyes had held always a wistful question. He had tried to answer it. She had grown old on his hearth, yet always to the end of her eyes had asked. He hoped now that in some celestial hunting ground she had found an answer to that subtle need.

He told Anne about Amber Witch. "I have one of her puppies on my farm."

She was much interested. "I've never had a dog; or a cat."

He had, he said, a big pair of tabbies who slept in the hay and came up to the dairy when the milk was strained. There were two blue porcelain dishes for their sacred use. There was, he said, milk and to spare. He grew eloquent as he told of the number of quarts daily. He bragged of his butter. His cheeses had won prizes at county fairs. As for chickens—they had fresh eggs and broilers without end. He had his own hives, too, white-clover honey. And his housekeeper made hot biscuit. In a month or two there'd be asparagus and strawberries. Say! Yes, he was eloquent.

Anne was hungry. There had been a meagre dinner that evening. The other girls had not seemed to care. But Anne had cared.

"I'm starved," she had said as she had surveyed the table. "Let's pawn the spoons and have one square meal."

"Anne!"

"Oh, we're beggars on horseback"—bitterly—"and I hate it."

It was her moment of rebellion against the tyranny of tradition. Amy had had such a moment years ago when her mother had taken her away from school. Amy had a brilliant mind, and she had loved study, but her mother had brought her to see that there was no money for college. "You'd better have a year or two in society, Amy. And this craze for higher education is rather middle-class."

Ethel's rebellion had come when she had wanted to marry a round-faced chap who lived across the street. They had played together from childhood. His people were pleasant folks but lacked social background. So Ethel's romance had been nipped in the bud. The round-faced chap had married another girl. And now Amy at thirty and Ethel at twenty-five were crystallizing into something rather hard and brilliant, as Anne would perhaps crystallize if something didn't happen.

The something which happened was Maxwell Sears. Anne listened to the things he said about his farm and felt that they couldn't be true.

"It sounds like a fairy tale."

"It isn't. And it's all tremendously interesting."

He looked very much alive as he said it, and Anne felt the thrill of his energy and enthusiasm. Murray was never enthusiastic; neither were Amy and Ethel. They were all indeed a bit petrified.

Before he left her Maxwell asked Anne if he could call. He came promptly two nights later and brought with him a bunch of violets and a box of chocolates. Anne pinned the violets in the front of the gray frock that gave her the look of a cloistered nun, and ate up the chocolates.

Amy was shocked. "Anne, you positively gobbled—"

"I didn't."

"Well, you ate a pound at least."

Anne protested. Maxwell had eaten a lot, and Ethel and Amy had eaten a few, and Murray had come in.

"You remember, Amy, Murray came in."

"He didn't touch one, Anne. He never eats chocolates."

"He's afraid of getting fat."

"Anne!"

"He is. When he takes me out to lunch he thinks of himself, not of me. The last time we had grapefruit and broiled mushrooms and lettuce; and I wanted chops."

Maxwell had been glad to see Anne eat the chocolates. She had seemed as happy as a child, and he had liked that. There was nothing childish about Winifred. She had been always grown-up and competent and helpful. He felt that he owed Winifred a great deal. They were not engaged, but he rather hoped that some day they might marry. Of course that would depend upon Winifred. She would probably make him give up the farm and he would hate that. But a man might give up a farm for a woman like Winifred and still have more than he deserved.

It will be seen that Maxwell was modest, especially where women were concerned. The complacency of Murray Flint, weighing Amy against Ethel and Ethel against Amy and Anne against both, would have seemed infamous to Maxwell. He felt that it was only by the grace of God that any woman gave herself to any man. He had a sense of honor which was founded on decency rather than on convention. He had also a sense of high romance which belonged more fittingly to the fifteenth than to the twentieth century. He was not, however, aware of it. He looked upon himself as a plain and practical chap who had a few things to work out politically before he settled down to the serious business of farming. Of course if he married Winifred he wouldn't settle down to the farm, but he would settle down to something.

In the meantime here was Anne, reading Dickens, eating chocolates, and leaning over the rail of the House Gallery to listen to his speeches.

It was rather wonderful to have her there. She wore a gray cape with a chinchilla collar made out of Amy's old muff. A straight sailor hat of rough straw came well down over her forehead and showed fluffs of shining hair at the sides. Her little gray-gloved hands clasped the violets he had given her. Above the violets her eyes were a deeper blue.

She came always alone. "Amy doesn't know," she had told him frankly; "she wouldn't let me, come if she did."

"Why not?"

"I am supposed to be chaperoned."

"My dear child, I told you to bring either or both of your sisters."

"I don't want them. They would spoil it."

"How?"

She tried to explain. He and she could see things in the old Capitol that Amy and Ethel couldn't.

He laughed, but knew it true. Anne's imagination met his in a rather remarkable fashion. When they walked through Statuary Hall they saw not Fulton and Père Marquette and Carroll of Carrollton; they saw, rather, a thousand ships issuing forth on the steam of a teakettle; they saw civilization following a black-frocked prophet; they saw aristocracy raising its voice in the interest of democracy.

As for the mysterious whispering echo, they repudiated all talk of acoustics. It was for them an eerie thing, like the laughter of elves or the shriek of a banshee.

"Don't say every-day things to me," Anne had instructed Maxwell when he had first placed her behind a mottled marble pillar before leaving for the spot where he could speak to her by this unique wireless.

There came to her, therefore, a part of a famous speech; the murmured words flung back by that strange sounding board rang like a bell:

"Give me liberty or give me death!"

She emerged from her corner, starry-eyed. "It was as if I heard him say it."

"Perhaps it was he, and I was only a mouthpiece."

"I should think they'd like to come back. Will you come?"

He laughed. "Who knows? I'll come if you are here."

To have brought a third into these adventures would have robbed them of charm. Knowing this he argued that the child was safe with him. Why worry?

They always lunched together before he took her up to the Members' Gallery, and went himself to the floor of the House. He let her order what she pleased and liked The definite way in which she did it. They had usually, chops and peas, or steak, and ice-cream at the end.

III

Then suddenly; things stopped. The reason that they stopped was Murray. He saw Anne one day in the House Gallery and asked Amy about it.

"How did she happen to be up there alone?"

Amy asked Anne. Anne told the truth.

"I've had lunch three times with Mr. Sears, and I've listened to his speeches. It's something about the League of Nations. He believes in it, but thinks we've got to be careful about tying ourselves up."

Amy did not care in the least what Maxwell Sears believed. The thing that worried her was Murray. She wanted him to approve of Anne. If Amy had thought in a less limited circle she might have worked the thing out that if Maxwell married

315

Anne it would narrow Murray's choice down to herself and Ethel. But there was always that vague fear of some outside siren who would capture Murray. If he had Anne, he would then be safely in the family.

She realized, in the days following the revelation of the clandestine meetings with Maxwell, that Murray was depending upon her to see that Anne's affections did not stray into forbidden paths. He said as much one afternoon when he found Amy alone in an atmosphere of old portraits, old books, old bronzes. She sat in a Jacobean chair and poured tea for him. The massive lines of the chair made her proportions seem wraithlike. Her white face with its fixed spots of red was a high light among the shadows.

"Where's Anne?"

"She and Ethel have gone to the matinée with Molly Winchell."

"Why didn't you go?"

"Molly never takes but two of us and, of course, this is Anne's first winter out. I have to step back—and let her have her chance."

He chose to be gallant. "You are always lovely, Amy."

His compliment fell cold. Amy felt old and tired. She had a pain in her side. It had been getting very bad of late, and she coughed at night. She had been to her doctor, and again he had emphasized the need of a change of climate and of nourishing food. Amy had come away unconvinced.

She would have a chance in July when she and her sisters would go to the Eastern Shore for their annual visit to their Aunt Elizabeth. As for different food, she ate enough—all the doctors in the world couldn't make her spend any more money on the table.

Murray stood up very straight by the mantelpiece, under the portrait of one of the Merryman great-grandfathers in a bag wig, and talked of Anne:

"I believe I am falling in love with her, Amy."

Amy's heart said, "It has come at last." Her brain said, "He has discovered it because of Maxwell Sears." Her lips said, "I don't wonder. She's a dear child, Murray."

"She's beautiful."

Murray swayed up a little on his toes. It made him seem thinner and taller. He could see himself reflected in the long mirror on the opposite wall. He liked the reflection of the thin tall man.

"She's beautiful, Amy. I am going to ask her to marry me. I can't have some other fellow running off with her. She belongs to Georgetown."

He seemed to think that settled it. The pain in Amy's side was sharper. She felt that she couldn't quite stand seeing Murray happy with Anne. "She's—she's such a child." Her voice shook.

"Well," said Murray, glancing at the tall thin man in the mirror, "of course she is young. But Maxwell Sears is coming here a lot. Is he in love with her?"

"I'm not sure. She amuses him. She isn't in love with him or with anybody."

"Not even with me?" Murray laughed a little. "But we can remedy that, can't we, Amy? But you might hint at what I'm expecting of her. I don't want to startle her." He came and sat down beside her. "You are always a great dear about doing things for me."

The pain stabbed her like a knife. "I'll do my best."

She had a nervous feeling that she must keep Murray from talking to her like that. She rang for hot water, and their one maid, Charlotte, brought it in a Sheffield jug. Then Ethel and Anne and Molly Winchell arrived, and once more Murray stood up, tall and self-conscious as he stole side glances at himself in the mirror.

Maxwell Sears had brought the three women home. He had a fashion of following up Anne's engagements and putting his car at her disposal. When Amy had vetoed any more adventures at the Capitol he had conceded good-naturedly that she was right. After that he had always included Amy or Ethel in his invitations.

"They are very pretty dragons," he had written to Winifred, "and little Anne is like a princess shut in a tower."

Winifred, reading the letter, had brooded upon it. "He's falling in love. A child like that—she'll spoil his future."

Congress was having night sessions. "If I could only have you up there," Maxwell had said to Anne as he had driven her home from the matinée, with old Molly and Ethel on the back seat. "I should steal you if I dared."

"Please dare."

"Do you mean it?"

"Yes. To-night. Ethel and Amy are going to a Colonial Dames meeting with Molly Winchell. I never go. I hate ancestors."

"I shouldn't let you do it," he hesitated, "but ghosts walk after dark in the Capitol corridors."

"I know," she nodded. "Washington, Jefferson, Lincoln."

"Yes. Then you'll come?"

"Of course."

It was the thought of her rendezvous with him that lighted her eyes when she talked to Murray. But Murray did not know. So he swayed up on his toes and glanced in the glass and was glad of his thinness and tallness.

Maxwell came for Anne promptly. "You must get me back by ten," she told him. "I have a key, and Charlotte's out."

It was a night of nights, never to be forgotten. Maxwell did not take Anne into the Gallery. He had not brought her there to hear speeches or to be conspicuous in the glare of lights. He led her through shadowy corridors—up wide dim stairways.

At one turn he touched her arm. "Look!" he whispered.

"What?"

"Lafayette passed us—on the stairs."

It was a great game! On the east front Columbus spoke to them of ships that sailed toward the sunset; in the Rotunda they kept a tryst with William Penn; from the west-front portico they saw a city beautiful—the streets under the moon were rivers of light—the great monument reached like the soul of Washington toward the stars!

Out there in the moonlight Maxwell spoke of another great soul, gone of late to join a glorious company.

"It was he who taught me that life is an adventure."

"Greatheart?"

"Yes."

"You loved him too?"

"Yes."

Anne caught her breath. "To think of him dead—to think of them all—dead."

Maxwell looked down at her. "They live somewhere. You believe that, don't you?"

"Yes."

He was silent for a moment; then he laid his hand lightly on her shoulder. "I feel to-night as if they pressed close."

Oh, it was a rare game to meet great souls in odd corners! They could scarcely tear themselves away. But he got her home before her sisters arrived, and Anne went to bed soberly, and lay long awake, thinking it out. She had never before had such a playmate. In all these years she had starved for other things than food.

IV

In due time Congress adjourned, but Maxwell did not go home. He continued to see Anne. Amy was at last driven to her duty by Murray. She could not forbid Maxwell the house. There was nothing to do but talk to Anne.

Having made up her mind she sought Anne's room at once. Anne, in a cheap cotton kimono, was braiding her hair for the night. The sleeves of the kimono were short and showed her thin white arms. Amy had on a blanket wrapper. Her hair was in metal curlers. She looked old and tired, and now and then she coughed.

Anne got into bed and drew the covers up to her chin. "I'm so cold, I believe there are icicles on my eyebrows. Amy, my idea of heaven is a place where it is as hot as—Hades."

"I don't see where you get such ideas. Ethel and I don't talk that way. We don't even think that way, Anne."

"Maybe when I am as old as you—" Anne began, and was startled at the look on Amy's face.

"I'm not old!" Amy said passionately. "Anne, I haven't lived at all, and I'm only thirty."

Anne stared at her. "Oh, my darling, I didn't mean—"

"Of course you didn't. And it was silly of me to say such a thing. Anne, I'm cold. I'm going to sit on the foot of your bed and wrap up while I talk to you."

Anne's bed had four pineapple posts and a pink canopy. The governor of a state had slept in that bed for years. He was one of the Merryman grandfathers. Amy could have bought mountains of food for the price of that bed. But she would have starved rather than sell it.

Anne under the pink canopy was like a rose—a white rose with a faint flush. The color in Amy's cheeks was fixed and hard. Yet even with her oldness and tiredness and metal curlers she had the look of race which attracted Murray.

"Anne," she said, "Murray and I had a long talk about you the other day."

"Murray always talks—long." Anne was yawning.

"Please be serious, Anne. He wants to marry you."

"Marry me!" incredulously. "I thought it was you; or Ethel."

"Well, it isn't," wearily. "And it's a great opportunity—for you, Anne."

"Opportunity for what?"

Amy had a sense of the futility of trying to explain.

"There aren't many men like him."

"Fortunately."

"Anne, how can you? He's really paying you a great compliment."

"Why didn't he ask me himself?"

"He didn't want to startle you. You're so young. Murray has extreme fineness of feeling."

Anne tilted her chin. "I don't see what he finds in me."

"You're young"—with a tinge of bitterness—"and he says you are beautiful."

317

Anne threw off the covers and set her bare feet on the floor. "Beautiful!" she scoffed, but went to the mirror. "I'm thin," she meditated, "but I've got nice hair."

"We all have nice hair," said Amy; "but you've got Ethel's complexion and my figure."

"I don't think I want to be loved for my complexion." Anne turned suddenly and faced her sister. "Or my figure. I'd rather be loved for my mind."

"Men don't love women for their minds," said Amy wearily. "You'll learn that when you have lived as long as I have. Get back into bed, Anne. You'll freeze."

But Anne, shivering in the cotton kimono, argued the question hotly: "I should think Murray would want to marry someone with congenial tastes. He hates everything that I like."

"He'll make an excellent husband. You ought to be happy to know that he—cares."

She began to cough—a racking cough that left her exhausted.

Anne, bending over her, said, "Why, Amy, are you sick?"

"I'm—I'm rather wretched, Anne."

"Are you taking anything for your cough?"

"Yes."

"You ought to have a doctor."

"I have had one."

"What did he say?"

Amy put her off. "I'll feel better in the morning, Anne. Don't worry." Again the cough tore her. Anne flew to Ethel.

"See what you can do for her. There is blood on her handkerchief! I am going to call a doctor."

The doctor, arriving, checked the cough. Later he told Anne that Amy must have a change and strengthening food.

"At once. She's in a very serious state. I've told her, but she won't listen."

In the days that followed Anne arraigned herself hotly. "I've been a selfish pig—eating up everything—and Amy needed it."

In this state of mind she fasted—and was famished.

Maxwell, noting her paleness, demanded, "What's the matter? Aren't you well?"

She wanted to cry out, "I'm hungry." But she, too, had her pride.

"Amy's ill."

He got it out of her finally. "The doctor is much worried about her. He says she needs a change."

"You need it too."

She needed food, but she couldn't tell him that. The state of their exchequer was alarming. It had been revealed to her since Amy's illness that there was really nothing coming in until the next quarter.

"Why didn't you let Charlotte go, Ethel?"

"We've always had a maid. What would people think?"

"And because of what people think, Amy is to starve?"

"Anne, how can you?"

"Well, it comes to that. She needs things; and we don't need Charlotte."

But when they spoke to Amy of sending Charlotte away she was feverishly excited. "There's nobody to do the work."

"I can do it," said Anne.

"We Merrymans have never worked," Amy began to cry. "I'd rather die," she said, "than have people think we are— poor."

V

Maxwell was a man of action. When he saw Anne pale he sought a remedy. "Look here, why can't you and your sisters come out to my farm?"

Anne, remembering certain things—broilers and fresh eggs—was thrilled by the invitation. "I'd love it! But Amy won't accept."

"Why not?"

"She's terribly stiff."

He laughed. "Perhaps I can talk her over."

Amy, lying on her couch, very weary, facing a shadowy future, felt his magnetism as he talked to her. It was as if life spoke through his lips. Murray had sat there beside her only an hour before. He had brought her roses but he had brought no hope.

Fear had for weeks kept Amy company. Through her nights and days it had stalked, a pale spectre. And now Maxwell was saying: "You'll be well in a month. Of course you'll come! There's room for half a dozen. You three won't half fill the house."

It was decided, however, that Ethel must stay in town. Amy had a nervous feeling that with the house closed Murray might slip away from them.

Old Molly Winchell, summing up the situation, said to Murray: "Of course Anne will marry Maxwell Sears. There's nothing like propinquity."

Murray, startled, admitted the danger. "It would be an awful thing for Anne."

"Why?"

"He's rather a bounder."

Old Molly Winchell hit him on the arm with her fan. Her eyes twinkled maliciously. "He's nothing of the sort, and you know it. You're jealous, Murray."

Murray's jealousy was, quite uniquely, not founded on any great depth of love for Anne. His appropriation of the three sisters had been a pretty and pleasant pastime. When he had finally decided upon Anne as the pivotal center of his universe he had contemplated a future in which the other sisters also figured—especially Amy. He had, indeed, not thought of a world without Amy.

Her illness had troubled him, but not greatly. Things had always come to him as he had wanted them, and he was quite sure that if Anne was to be the flame to light his future, Providence would permit Amy to be, as it were, the keeper of the light.

He felt it necessary to warn Anne: "Don't fall in love with Sears."

"Don't be silly, Murray."

"Is it silly to say that I love you, Anne?"

They were alone in the old library, with its books and bronzes and bag-wigged ancestors. And Murray sat down beside Anne and took her hand in his and said, "I love you, Anne."

It was a proposal which was not to be treated lightly. In spite of herself, Anne was flattered. Murray had always loomed on her horizon as something of a bore but none the less a person of importance.

She caught her breath quickly. "Please, Murray"—her blushes were bewitching—"I'm too young to think about such things. And I'm not in love with anybody."

Murray raised her hand to his lips. "Keep yourself for me, little Anne." He rose and stood looking down at her. "You're a very charming child," he said. "Do you know it?"

Anne, gazing at herself in the glass later, wondered if it were true. It was nice of Murray to say it. But she was not in the least in love with Murray. He was too old. And Maxwell was too old. Anne's dreams of romance had to do with glorified youth. She wanted a young Romeo shouting his passion to the stars!

She packed her bag, however, in high anticipation. Maxwell was a splendid playmate, and she thought of his farm as flowing with milk and honey!

Maxwell wrote to Winifred that he was coming home and bringing guests.

"Run down and meet them. Anne's a corking kid."

Winifred knew what had happened. Some girl had got hold of Maxwell. It was always the way with men like that—big men; they were credulous creatures where women were concerned, and it would make such a difference to Maxwell's future if he married the wrong woman.

She decided to go down as soon as she could. She felt that she ought to hurry, but there were things that held her. And so it happened that before she reached the farm Maxwell had asked Anne to marry him. There had been a cool evening when the scent of lilacs had washed in great waves through the open windows. Amy had gone to bed and he and Anne had dined alone with the flare of candles between them, and the rest of the room in pleasant shadow. And then their coffee had been served, and Aunt Mittie, his housekeeper, had asked if there was anything else, and had withdrawn, and he had risen and had walked round to Anne's place and had laid his hands on her shoulders.

"Little Anne," he had said, "I should like to see you here always."

"Here?"

"As my wife."

"Oh!"

She had had a rapturous week at the farm. She had never known anything like it. Aunt Elizabeth, of the Eastern Shore, lived in a sleepy town, and Anne's other brief vacations had been spent in more or less fashionable resorts. But here was a paradise of plenty; the big wide house, the spreading barns, the opulent garden, the rolling fields, the enchanting creatures who were sheltered by the barns and fed by the fields, and who in return gave payment of yellow cream and warm white eggs, and who lowed at night and cackled in the morning, and whose days were measured by the rising and the setting of the sun.

She loved it all—the purring pussies, the companionable pups, the steady, faithful older dogs, the lambs in the pasture, the good things to eat.

She was glowing with gratitude, and Maxwell was asking insistently, "Won't you, Anne?"

She had never been so happy, and he was the source of her happiness. Against this background of vivid life the thought of Murray was a pale memory.

So her wistful eyes met Maxwell's. "It would be lovely—to live here—always."

Later, when she had started up-stairs with her candle, he had kissed her, leaning over the rail to watch her as she went up, and Anne had gone to sleep tremulous with the thought that her future would lie here in this great house with this fine and kindly man.

Winifred, coming down at last, found that she had come too late. Maxwell told her as they motored up from the station. "Wish me happiness, Win. I am going to marry little Anne."

It did not enter his head for a moment that the woman by his side loved him. He had thought that if she ever married him it would be a sort of concession on her part, a sacrifice to her interest in his future. He had a feeling that she would be glad if such a sacrifice were not demanded.

But Winifred was not glad. "You are sure you are making no mistake, Max?"

"Wait till you see her."

Winifred waited and saw. "She's not in the least in love with him. She likes the warm nest she has fallen into. And she'll spoil his future. He'll settle down here, and he belongs to the world."

He belonged at least to his constituency.

"I've got to make a speech," he told the three women one morning, "in a town twenty miles away. If you girls would like the ride you can motor over with me. You needn't listen to my speech if you don't want to."

Amy and Winifred said that of course they wanted to listen. Anne smiled happily and said nothing. She was, of course, glad to go, but Maxwell's speeches were to her the abstract things of life; the concrete things at this moment were the delicious dinner which was before her and the fact that in the barn, curled up in the hay, was a new family of kittens—little tabbies like their adoring mother.

"Isn't it a lovely world?" she had said to her lover as she had sat in the loft with the cuddly cats in her lap.

"Yes."

He knew that it was not all lovely, that somewhere there were lean and hungry kittens and lean and hungry folks—but why remind her at such a moment?

VI

On the way over Anne sat with Winifred. She had insisted that Amy should have the front seat with Max. Amy was much better. Life had begun to flow into her veins like wine. She had written to Murray: "It is as if a miracle had happened."

Winifred, on the back seat, talked to Anne. She had a great deal to say about Maxwell's future. "I am sorry he bought the farm."

"Oh, not really." Anne's attention strayed. She had one of the puppies in her lap. He kept peeping out from between the folds of her cape with his bright eyes. "Isn't he a darling, Winifred?"

"He ought to sell it." Winifred liked dogs, but at this moment she wanted Anne's attention. "He ought to sell the farm. He has a great future before him. Everybody says it. He simply must not settle down."

"Oh, well, he won't," said Anne easily.

"He will if you let him."

"If I let him?"

"If he thinks you like it."

There was a deep flush on Winifred's cheeks. She was really a very handsome girl, with bright brown hair and brown eyes. She wore a small brown hat and a sable collar. The collar was open and showed her strong white throat.

"If he thinks you like it," she repeated, "he will stay; and he belongs to the world; nobody must hold him back. He's the biggest man in his party to-day. There is no limit to his powers."

Anne stared at her. "Of course there isn't." She wondered why Winifred seemed so terribly in earnest about it. She pulled the puppy's ears. "But I should hate to have him sell the farm."

Winifred settled back with a sharp sigh and gazed at the long gray road ahead of her. She gazed indeed into a rather blank future. Her talents would be, she felt, to some extent wasted. If Max rose to greater heights of fame it would be because of his own unaided efforts. This child would be no help to him.

The speech Max made to his constituents was not cool and clear-cut like the speeches which Anne had heard him make to his colleagues in the House. He spoke now with warmth and persuasiveness. Anne, sitting in the big car on the edge of the crowd, found herself listening intently. She was aware, as he went on, of a new Max. The mass of men who had gathered were largely foreigners who knew little of the real meanings of democracy. Max was telling them what it meant to be a good American. He told it simply, but he was in dead earnest. Anne felt that this earnestness was the secret of his power. He wanted men to be good Americans, he wanted them to know the privileges they might enjoy in a free country, and he was telling them how to keep it free-not by violence and mob rule but by remembering their obligations as citizens. He told them that they must be always on the side of law and order, that they must fight injustice not with the bomb and the red flag but with their votes.

"Vote for the man you trust, and not for the man who inflames your passions. Your vote is a sacred thing; when you sell it you dishonor yourself. Respect yourself, and you'll respect the country that has made a man of you."

The response was immediate, the applause tumultuous. After his speech they crowded about him. They knew him for their friend. But they knew him for more than that. He asked nothing of their manhood but the best. He preached honesty and practiced it.

Yet as he climbed into the car Anne had little to say to him. Winifred, leaning forward, was emphatic in her praise:

"You have no right to bury yourself, Max."

"My dear girl, I'm not dead yet." He was a bit impatient. He had hoped for a word from Anne. But she sat silent, pulling the puppy's ears.

"He's asleep," she said finally as she caught the inquiry in her lover's eyes. "He's tired out, poor darling."

She seemed indifferent, but she was not. She had been much stirred. She had a strange feeling that something had happened to her while she had listened to Maxwell's speech. Some string had broken and her romance was out of tune.

She lay awake for a long time that night, thinking it over. She grew hot with the thought of the limitations of her previous conception of her lover. She had considered him a sort of background for the pleasant things he could do for her. She had fitted him to the measure of the boxes of candy that he had brought her, the luncheons in the House restaurant, the bountiful hospitality of the farm. How lightly she had looked down on him as he had stood below her on the stairs with her candle in his hand. How casually she had accepted his kiss. She had a sudden feeling that she must not let him kiss her again!

Early in the morning she went into Amy's room. "Amy," she said, "how soon do you think we can go to Aunt Elizabeth's?"

"Aunt Elizabeth's? Why, Anne?"

"I want to leave here."

"To leave here?" Amy sat up. Even in the bright light of the morning her face looked young. Good food and fresh air had done much for her. It had been quite heavenly, too, to let care slip away, to have no thought of what she should eat or what she should drink or what she should wear. "To leave here? I thought you loved it, Anne."

"I've got to get away. I'm not going to marry Maxwell, Amy."

"Anne! What made you change your mind?"

"I can't tell you. Please don't ask me. But I wish you would write to Aunt Elizabeth."

"I had a letter from her yesterday. She says we can come at any time. But—have you told Max?"

"Not yet."

"Has he done anything?"

"No. It's just—that I can't marry him. Don't ask me, Amy." She broke down in a storm of tears.

Amy, soothing her, wondered if after all Anne cared for Murray Flint. It was, she felt, the only solution possible. Surely a girl would not throw away a chance to marry a man like Maxwell Sears for nothing.

For Amy had learned in the days that she had spent at the farm that Maxwell Sears was a man to reckon with. She was very grateful for what he had done for her, and she had been glad of Anne's engagement. Murray would perhaps be disappointed, but there would still be herself and Ethel.

It was not easy to explain things to Maxwell.

"Why are you going now?" he demanded, and was impatient when they told him that Aunt Elizabeth expected them. "I don't understand it at all. It upsets all of my plans for you, Anne."

That night when he brought Anne's candle she was not on the stairs. Winifred and Amy had gone up.

"Anne! Anne!" he called softly.

She came to the top rail and leaned over. "I'm going to bed in the dark. There's a wonderful moon."

"Come down—for a minute."

"No."

"Then I'll come up," masterfully.

He mounted the stairs two at a time; but when he reached the landing the door was shut!

In the morning he asked her about it. "Why, dearest?"

"Max dear, I can't marry you."

"Nonsense!" His voice was sharp. He laid his hands heavily on her shoulders. "Why not? Look at me, Anne. Why not?"

"I'm not going to marry—anybody."

That was all he could get out of her. He pleaded, raged, and grew at last white and still with anger. "You might at least tell me your reasons."

She said that she would write. Perhaps she could say it better on paper. And she was very, very sorry, but she couldn't.

Winifred knew that something was up, but made no comment. Amy, carrying out their program of departure, had a sense of regret.

After all, it had been a lovely life, and there were worse things than being a sister to Maxwell Sears. Her voice broke a little as she tried to thank him on their last morning.

He wrung her hand. "Say a good word for me with Anne. I don't know what's the matter with her."

Neither did Amy. And if she was Maxwell's advocate how could she be Murray's? She flushed a little.

"Anne's such a child."

He remembered how he had called her a corking kid. She was more than that to him now. She stood in the doorway in her gray sailor hat and gray cape.

"Anne," he said, "you must have a last bunch of pansies from the garden. Come out and help me pick them."

In the garden he asked, "Are you going to kiss me good-bye?"

"No, Max. Please—"

"Then it's 'God bless you, dearest.'"

He forgot the pansies and they went back to where the car waited.

VII

Anne's letter, written from the Eastern Shore, was a long and childish screed. "We have always been beggars on horseback," she said. "Of course you couldn't know that, Max. We have gone without bread so that we could be grand and elegant. We have gone without fire so that we could buy our satin gowns for fashionable functions. We went without butter for a year so that Amy could entertain the Strangeways, whom she had met years ago in Europe. I wouldn't dare tell you what that dinner cost us, but we had a cabinet member or two, and the British Ambassador.

"You wondered why I liked Dickens. Well, I read him so that I could get a good meal by proxy. I used to gloat over the feasts at Wardle's, and Mr. Stiggins' hot toast. And when I met you you gave me—everything. Murray Flint thinks that because I am thin and pale I am all spirit, and I'm afraid you have the same idea. You didn't dream, did you, that I was pale because I hadn't had enough to eat? And when you told me that you wanted me to be your wife I looked ahead and saw the good food and the roaring fires, and I didn't think of anything else. I honestly didn't think of you for a moment, Max.

"There were days, though, when you meant more to me than just that. When we played at the Capitol—that night when we met Lafayette on the stairs! Nobody had ever played with me. But after we went to the farm I was smothered in ease. And I loved it. And I didn't love you. You were just—the man who gave me things. Do you see what I mean? And when you kissed me on the stairs it was as if I were being kissed by a nice old Santa Claus.

"Everybody saw it but you. I am sure Amy knew—and Winifred Reed. You—you ought to marry Winifred, Max. Perhaps you will. You won't want me after you read this letter. And Winifred is splendid.

"It was your speech to the men that waked me. I saw how big you were, and I just—shriveled up.

"And you mustn't worry about me. I am not hungry any more. I feel as if I should never want anything to eat. Perhaps it is because I am older and haven't a growing appetite. And I am not any of the things you thought me. And of course you would be disappointed, and it wouldn't be fair."

Having posted this, Anne had other things to do. She wrote mysterious letters, and finally came into a room where her sisters and Aunt Elizabeth were sewing, with an important-looking paper in her hand.

"I am going to work, Amy."

"To work!"

"Yes."

Amy and Ethel and Aunt Elizabeth wore white frocks, and looked very cool and feminine and high-bred. Aunt Elizabeth had a nose like Amy's and the same look of race.

It was Aunt Elizabeth who said in her commanding voice: "What are you talking about, Anne?"

"I am going to work in the War Risk Bureau, Aunt Elizabeth. I wrote to two senators, and they helped me."

No woman of the Merryman family had ever worked in an office.

Anne faced a storm of disapproval, but she stood there slim and defiant, and stated her reasons.

"We need money. I don't see how we can get through a winter like the last. I can't keep my self-respect if we go on living as we did last winter."

"Haven't you any pride, Anne?"

"I have self-respect."

She left the room a conqueror. After she had gone the three women talked about her. They did not say it openly, but they felt that there was really an ordinary streak in Anne. Otherwise she would not have wanted to work in an office.

There was, however, nothing to be done. Anne was twenty-one. She was to get a hundred dollars a month. In spite of herself, Amy felt a throb of the heart as she thought of what that hundred dollars would mean to them.

Murray Flint was much perturbed when he heard of Anne's decision. He wrote to her that of course she knew that there was no reason why she should go into an office—his home and hearthstone were hers. She wrote back that she should never marry! After that, Murray felt, with Amy and Ethel and Aunt Elizabeth, that there was an ordinary streak in Anne!

When he arrived in August at Aunt Elizabeth's he was astonished at the change in Amy. She looked really very young as she came to meet him, and Aunt Elizabeth's house was a perfect setting for her charms. Murray was very fond of Aunt Elizabeth's house. It was an ancient, stately edifice, and within there were the gold-framed portraits of men and women with noses like Amy's and Aunt Elizabeth's.

Murray had missed Amy very much and he told her so.

"It was a point of honor for me to ask Anne again. But when I thought I was going to lose you I learned that my life would be empty without you."

He really believed what he was telling her. If Amy did not believe it she made no sign. She was getting much more than she expected, and she accepted him graciously and elegantly, as became a daughter of the Merrymans.

It was when he told Anne of his engagement to Amy that Murray again offered her a home. "There will always be a place for Amy's sisters, Anne."

"You are very good, Murray—but I can't."

She had said the same thing to Maxwell, who had come hot-footed to tell her that her letter had made no difference in his feeling for her.

"How could you think it, Anne? My darling, you are making a mountain of a molehill!"

She had been tremulous but firm. "I've got to have my—self-respect, Max."

Because he understood men he understood her. And when he had left her he had said to himself with long-drawn breath, "She's a corking kid."

And this time there had been no laughter in his eyes.

All that winter Anne worked, a little striving creature, with her head held high!

Maxwell was in town, for Congress had convened. But he had not come to see her. Now and then when there was a night session she went up to the House and sat far back in the Gallery, where, unperceived, she could listen to her lover's voice. Then she would steal away, a little ghost, down the shadowy stairway; but there were no games now with Lafayette!

Amy and Murray were to be married in June. They had enjoyed a dignified and leisurely engagement, and Amy had bloomed in the sunshine of Murray's approbation. Anne's salary had helped a great deal in getting the trousseau together. Most of the salary, indeed, had been spent for that. The table was, as usual, meagre, but Anne had not seemed to care.

She was therefore rather white and thin when, on the day that Congress adjourned, Maxwell came out to Georgetown to see her. It had been a long session, and it was spring.

There were white lilacs in a great blue jar in the Merryman library, and through the long window a glimpse of a thin little moon in a faint green sky.

As he looked at Anne, Maxwell felt a lump in his throat. She had given him her hand and had smiled at him. "How are the kittens?" she had asked in an effort to be gay.

He did not answer her question. He went, rather, directly to the point. "Anne, why wouldn't you kiss me on that last night?"

She flushed to the roots of her hair. "It—it was because I loved you, Max."

"I thought so. But you had to prove it to yourself?"

"Yes."

"Anne, that's why I've let you alone all winter—so that you might prove it. But—I can't go on. It has been an awful winter for me, Anne."

It had been an awful winter for her. But she had come out of it knowing herself. And even when at last his arms were about her and he was telling her that he would never let her go, she had a plea to make:

"Don't let me live too softly, Max. Life isn't a feather bed—You belong to the world. I must go with you toward the big things. But now and then we'll run back to the farm."

"What do I care where we run, so that we run—together!"

Judy

CHAPTER I

THE JUDGE AND JUDY

There was a plum-tree in the orchard, all snow and ebony against a sky of sapphire.

Becky Sharp, perched among the fragrant blossoms, crooned soft nothings to herself. Under the tree little Anne lay at full length on the tender green sod and dreamed daydreams.

"Belinda," she said to her great white cat, "Belinda, if we could fly like Becky Sharp, we would all go to Egypt and eat our lunch on the top of the pyramids."

Belinda, keeping a wary eye on a rusty red robin on a near-by stump, waved her tail conversationally.

"They used to worship cats in Egypt, Belinda," Anne went on, drowsily, "and when they died they preserved them in sweet spices and made mummies of them—"

But Belinda had lost interest. The rusty red robin was busy with a worm, and she saw her chance.

As she sneaked across the grass, Anne sat up, "I'm ashamed of you,

Belinda," she said. "Becky, go bring her back!"

The tame crow fluttered from the tree with a squawk and straddled awkwardly to the stump, scaring the robin into flight, and beating an inky wing against Belinda's whiteness.

Belinda hit back viciously, but Becky flew over her head, and by several well-delivered nips sent the white cat mewing to the shelter of her mistress' arms.

"I suppose you can't help it, Belinda," said Anne, as she cuddled her, "but it's horrid of you to catch birds, horrid, Belinda."

Belinda curled down into Anne's blue gingham lap, and Becky Sharp climbed once more to the limb of the plum-tree, from which she presently sounded a discordant note.

Anne raised her head. "There is some one coming," she said, and rolled

Belinda out of her lap and stood up. "Who is it, Becky?"

But Becky, having given the alarm, blinked solemnly down at her mistress, and said nothing.

"It's Judge Jameson's horse," Anne informed her pets, "and there's a girl with him, with a white hat on, and they'll stay to lunch, and there isn't a thing but bread and milk, and little grandmother is cleaning the attic."

She picked up her hat and flew through the orchard with Belinda a white streak behind her, and Becky Sharp in the rear, a pursuing black shadow.

"Little grandmother, little grandmother," called Anne, when she reached a small gray house at the edge of the orchard.

At a tiny window set in the angle of the slanting roof, a head appeared—a head tied up just now in a clean white cloth, which framed a rosy, wrinkled face.

"Little grandmother," cried Anne, breathlessly, "Judge Jameson is coming, and there isn't anything for lunch."

"There's plenty of fresh bread and milk," said the little grandmother calmly.

"But we can't give the Judge just that," said Anne.

"It isn't what you give, it's the spirit you offer it in," said the little grandmother, reprovingly. "It won't be the first time that Judge Jameson has eaten bread and milk at my table, Anne, and it won't be the last," and with that the little grandmother untied the white cloth, displaying a double row of soft gray curls that made her look like a charming, if elderly, cherub.

"You go and meet him, Anne," she said "and I'll come right down."

So Anne and Belinda and Becky Sharp went down the path to meet the carriage.

On each side of the path the spring blossoms were coming up, tulips and crocuses and hyacinths. Against the background of the gray house, an almond bush flung its branches of pink and white, and the grass was violet-starred.

"Isn't that a picture, Judy," said the Judge to the girl beside him, as they drove up, "that little old house, with the flowers and Anne and her pets?"

But Judy was looking at Anne with an uplifting of her dark, straight eyebrows.

"She must be a queer girl," she said.

"This is my granddaughter, Judy Jameson," was the Judge's introduction, when he had shaken hands with Anne. "She is going to live with me now, and I want you two to be great friends."

To little country Anne, Judy seemed like a being from another world; she had never seen anything like the white hat with its wreath of violets, the straight white linen frock, the white cloth coat, and the low ribbon-tied shoes, and the unconscious air with which all these beautiful things were worn filled her with wonder. Why, a new ribbon on her own hat always set her happy heart a-flutter!

She gave Judy a shy welcome, and Judy responded with a self-possession that made Anne's head whirl.

"My dear Judge," said the little grandmother from the doorway, "I am glad you came. Come right in."

"You are like your grandmother, my dear," she told Judy, "she and I were girls together, you know."

Judy looked at the little, bent figure in the faded purple calico. "Oh, were you," she said, indifferently, "I didn't know that grandmother ever lived in the country before she was married."

"She didn't," explained the little grandmother, "but I lived in town, and we went to our first parties together, and became engaged at the same time, and we both of us married men from this county and came up here—"

"And lived happy ever after," finished the Judge, with a smile on his fine old face, "like the people in your fairy books, Judy."

"I don't read fairy books," said Judy, with a little curve of her upper lip.

"Oh," said Anne, "don't you, don't you ever read them, Judy?"

There was such wonder, almost horror, in her tone that Judy laughed. "Oh, I don't read much," she said. "There is so much else to do, and books are a bore."

Anne looked at her with a little puzzled stare. "Don't you like books—really?" she asked, incredulously.

"I hate them," said Judy calmly.

Before Anne could recover from the shock of such a statement, the Judge waved the young people away.

"Run along, run along," he ordered, "I want to talk to Mrs. Batcheller, you show Judy around a bit, Anne."

"Anne can set the table for lunch," said the little grandmother. "Of course you'll stay, you and Judy. Take Judy with you, Anne."

Belinda and Becky Sharp followed the two girls into the dining-room.

Becky perched herself on the wide window-sill in the sunshine, and

Belinda sat at Judy's feet and blinked up at her.

"Belinda is awfully spoiled," said Anne, to break the stiffness, as she spread the table with a thin old cloth, "but she is such a dear we can't help it."

Judy drew her skirts away from Belinda's patting paw. "I hate cats," she said, with decision.

Anne's lips set in a firm line, but she did not say anything. Presently, however, she looked down at Belinda, who rubbed against the table leg, and as she met the affectionate glance of the cat's green orbs, her own eyes said: "I am not going to like her, Belinda," and Belinda said, "Purr-up," in polite acquiescence.

Judy had taken off her hat and coat, and she sat a slender white figure in the old rocker. Around her eyes were dark shadows of weariness, and she was very pale.

"How good the air feels," she murmured, and laid her head back against the cushion with a sigh.

Anne's heart smote her. "Aren't you feeling well, Judy?" she asked, timidly.

"I'm never well," Judy said, slowly. "I'm tired, tired to death, Anne."

Anne set the little blue bowls at the places, softly. She had never felt tired in her life, nor sick. "Wouldn't you like a glass of milk?" she asked, "and not wait until lunch is ready? It might do you good."

"I hate milk," said Judy.

Anne sat down helplessly and looked at the weary figure opposite. "I am afraid you won't have much for lunch," she quavered, at last. "We haven't anything but bread and milk."

"I don't want any lunch," said Judy, listlessly. "Don't worry about me, Anne."

But Anne went to the cupboard and brought out a precious store of peach preserves, and dished them in the little glass saucers that had been among her grandmother's wedding things. Then she cut the bread in thin slices and brought in a pitcher of milk.

"Why don't you have some flowers on the table?" said Judy. "Flowers are better than food, any day—"

Like a flame the color went over Anne's fair face. "Oh, do you like flowers, Judy?" she said, joyously. "Do you, Judy?"

Judy nodded. "I love them," she said. "Give me that big blue bowl,

Anne, and I'll get you some for the table."

"Wouldn't you like a vase, Judy?" asked Anne. "We have a nice red one in the parlor."

Judy drew her shoulders together in a little shiver of distaste. "Oh, no, no," she shuddered, "this bowl is such a beauty, Anne."

"But it is so old," said Anne, "it belonged to my great-grandmother."

"That is why it is so beautiful," said Judy, as she went out of the door into the garden.

When she came in she had filled the bowl with yellow tulips, which, set in the center of the table, seemed to radiate sunshine, and to glorify the plain little room. "I should never have thought of the tulips, Judy," exclaimed Anne, "but they look lovely."

There was such genuine admiration in the tender voice, that Judy looked at Anne for the first time with interest—at the plain, straight figure in the unfashionable blue gingham, at the freckled face, with its tip-tilted nose, and at the fair hair hanging in two neat braids far below the little girl's waist.

"Do you like to live here, Anne?" she asked, suddenly.

Anne, still bending over the tulips, lifted two surprised blue eyes.

"Of course," she said. "Of course I do, Judy."

"I hate it," said Judy. "I hate the country, Anne—"

And this time she did not express her dislike indifferently, but with a swift straightening of her slender young body, and a nervous clasping of her thin white fingers.

"I hate it," she said again.

Anne stood very still by the table. What could she say to this strange girl who hated so many things, and who was staring out of the window with drawn brows and compressed red lips?

"Perhaps I like it because it is my home," she said at last, gently.

Judy caught her breath quickly. "I am never going back to my home,

Anne," she said.

"Never, Judy?"

"No—grandfather says that I am to stay here with him—" There was despair in the young voice.

Anne went over to the window. "Perhaps you will like it after awhile," she said, hopefully, "the Judge is such a dear."

"I know—" Judy's tone was stifled, "but he isn't—he isn't my mother—Anne—"

For a few minutes there was silence, then Judy went on:

"You see I nursed mother all through her last illness. I was with her every minute—and—and—I want her so—I want my mother—Anne—"

But so self-controlled was she, that though her voice broke and her lips trembled, her eyes were dry. Anne reached out a plump, timid hand, and laid it over the slender one on the window-sill.

"I haven't any mother either, Judy," she said, and Judy looked down at her with a strange softness in her dark eyes.

Suddenly she bent her head in a swift kiss, then drew back and squared her shoulders.

"Don't let's talk about it," she said, sharply. "I can't stand it—I can't stand it—Anne—"

But in spite of the harshness of her tone, Anne knew that there was a bond between them, and that the bond had been sealed by Judy's kiss.

CHAPTER II

ANNE GOES TO TOWN

"Grandfather," said Judy, at the lunch-table, "I want to take Anne home with us."

A little shiver went up and down Anne's spine. She wasn't sure whether it would be pleasant to go with Judy or not. Judy was so different.

"I don't believe Anne could leave Becky and Belinda," laughed the

Judge. "She would have to carry her family with her."

"Of course she can leave them," was Judy's calm assertion, "and I want her, grandfather."

She said it with the air of a young princess who is in the habit of having her wishes gratified. The Judge laughed again.

"How is it, Mrs. Batcheller?" he asked.

"May Anne go?"

The little grandmother shook her head.

"I don't often let her leave me," she said.

"But I want her," said Judy, sharply, and at her tone the little grandmother's back stiffened.

"Perhaps you do, my dear," was her quiet answer, "but your wants must wait upon my decision."

The mild blue eyes met the frowning dark ones steadily, and Judy gave in. Much as she hated to own it, there was something about this little lady in faded calico that forced respect.

"Oh," she said, and sat back in her chair, limply.

The Judge looked anxiously at her disappointed face.

"Judy is so lonely," he pleaded, and Mrs. Batcheller unbent.

"Anne has her lessons."

"But to-morrow is Saturday."

"Well—she may go this time. How long do you want her to stay?"

"Until Sunday night," said the Judge. "I will bring her back in time for school on Monday."

Anne went up-stairs in a flutter of excitement. Visits were rare treats in her uneventful life, and she had never stayed at Judge Jameson's overnight, although she had often been there to tea, and the great old house had seemed the palace beautiful of her dreams.

But Judy!

"She is so different from any girl I have ever met," she explained to the little grandmother, who had followed her to her room under the eaves, and was packing her bag for her.

"Different? How?"

"Well, she isn't like Nannie May or Amelia Morrison."

"I should hope not," said the little grandmother with severity. "Nan is a tomboy, and Amelia hasn't a bit of spirit—not a bit, Anne."

Anne changed the subject, skilfully. "Do you like Judy?" she questioned.

"She is very much spoiled," said the little grandmother, slowly, "a very spoiled child, indeed. Her mother began it, and the Judge will keep it up. But Judy is like her grandmother at the same age, Anne, and her grandmother turned out to be a charming woman—it's in the blood."

"She says she is going to live with the Judge." Anne was folding her best blue ribbons, with quite a grown-up air.

"Yes. I have never told you, Anne, but the Judge's son was in the navy, and four years ago he went for a cruise and never came back."

"Was he drowned?"

"He was washed overboard during a storm, and every one except Judy believes that he was drowned. Even Judy's mother believed it in time, but Judy won't. She thinks he will come back, and so she has lived on in her old home by the sea, with a cousin of her father's for a companion—always with the hope that he will come back. But the cousin was married in the winter, and so Judy is to live with the Judge. He has always wanted it that way—but Judy clung desperately to the life in the old house by the sea. The Judge will spoil her—he can't deny her anything."

"What pretty things she has," said Anne, looking down distastefully at the simple gown and neat but plain garments that the little grandmother was packing into a shiny black bag.

The little grandmother gave her a quick look. "Never mind, dearie," she said, "just remember that you are a gentlewoman by birth, and try to be sweet and loving, and don't worry about the clothes."

But as she tied the shabby old hat with its faded roses on the fair little head, her own old eyes were wistful. "I wish I could give you pretty things, my little Anne," she whispered.

Anne gave a remorseful cry. "I don't mind, little grandmother," she said, "I don't really," and for a moment her warm young cheek lay against the soft old one.

A tiny mirror opposite reflected the two faces. "How much we look alike," cried Anne, noticing it for the first time. Then she sighed. "But my hair doesn't curl like yours, little grandmother," and in that lament was voiced the greatest trial, that had, as yet, come to Anne.

"Neither does Judy's," said Mrs. Batcheller, and Anne brightened up, but when she went down-stairs and saw Judy's bronze locks giving out wonderful lights where they were looped up with a broad black ribbon she sighed again.

When the carriage drove around, Anne caught Belinda up in her arms.

"Good-bye, pussy cat, pussy cat," she cried, "take care of grandmother, and don't catch any birds."

Belinda crooned a loving song, and tucked her pretty head under her little mistress' chin.

"You're a dear, Belinda," said Anne, "and so is Becky," and at the sound of her name the tame crow flew to Anne's shoulder and gave her a pecking kiss.

"Oh, come on," said Judy, impatiently, and the Judge lifted the shiny bag and put it on the front seat; then they waved their hands to the little grandmother and were off.

It was five miles to town, but the ride did not seem long to Anne. She pointed out all the places of interest to Judy.

"That is where I go to school," she said, as they passed a low white building at the crossroads, and later when the setting sun shone red and gold on two low glass hothouses set in the corner of a scraggly lawn, she explained their use to Judy.

"That's where Launcelot Bart raises violets," she said.

"What a funny name!" was Judy's careless rejoinder.

"Launcelot is a funny boy," said Anne, "but I think you would like him, Judy."

"I hate boys," said Judy, and settled back in the corner of the carriage with a bored air.

But Anne was eager in the defence of her friend. "Launcelot isn't like most boys," she protested, "he is sixteen, and he lived abroad until his father lost all his money, and they had to come out here, and they were awfully poor until Launcelot began to raise violets, and now he is making lots of money."

"Well, I don't want to meet him," said Judy, indifferently, "he is sure to be in the way—all boys are in the way—"

327

Anne did not talk much after that; but when they reached the Judge's great red brick mansion, with the white pillars and with wistaria drooping in pale mauve clusters from the upper porch, she could not restrain her enthusiasm.

"What a lovely old place it is, Judy, what a lovely, lovely place."

But Judy's clenched fist beat against the cushions. "No, it isn't, it isn't," she declared in a tense tone, so low that the Judge could not hear, "it isn't lovely. It's too big and dark and lonely, Anne—and it isn't lovely at all."

As the Judge helped them out, there came over Anne suddenly a wave of homesickness. Judy was so hard to get along with, and the Judge was so stately, and after Judy's words, even the old mansion seemed to frown on her. Back there in the quiet fields was the little gray house, back there was peace and love and contentment, and with all her heart she wished that she might fly to the shelter of the little grandmother's welcoming arms.

Perhaps something of her feeling showed in her face, for as they went up-stairs, Judy said repentantly, "Don't mind me, Anne. I'm not a bit nice sometimes—but—but—I was born that way, I guess, and I can't help it."

Anne smiled faintly. She wondered what the little grandmother would have said to such a confession of weakness. "There isn't anything in this world that you can't help," the dear old lady would say, "and if you're born with a bad temper, why, that's all the more reason you should choose to live with a good one."

But Anne was not there to read moral lectures to her friend, and in fact as Judy opened the door of her room, the little country girl forgot everything but the scene before her.

"Oh, Judy, Judy," she cried, "how did you make it look like this? I have never seen anything like it. Never."

From where they stood they seemed to look out over the sea—a sea roughened by a fresh wind, so that tumbling whitecaps showed on the tops of the green waves. Not a ship was to be seen, not a gull swept across the hazy noon-time skies. Just water, water, everywhere, and a sense of immeasurable distance.

"It's a mirror," Judy explained, "and it reflects a picture on the other wall."

"It seems just as if I were looking out of a window," said Anne. "I have never seen the sea, Judy. Never."

"I love it," cried Judy, "there is nothing like it in the whole world—the smell of it, and the slap of the wind against your cheeks. Oh, Anne, Anne, if we were only out there in a boat with the wind whistling through the sails." Her face was all animation now, and there was a spot of brilliant color in each cheek.

"How beautiful she is," Anne thought to herself. "How very, very beautiful."

"You must have hated to leave it," she said, presently.

"I shall never get over it," said Judy with a certain fierceness. "I want to hear the 'boom—boom—boom' of the waves—it is so quiet here, so deadly, deadly quiet—"

"How sweet your room is," said tactful little Anne, to change the subject.

"Yes, I do like this room," admitted Judy reluctantly.

There were pictures everywhere——here a dark little landscape, showing the heart of some old forest, there a flaming garden, all red and blue and purple in a glare of sunlight. In the alcove was an etching—the head of a dream-child, and a misty water-color hung over Judy's desk.

"I did that myself," she said, as Anne examined it.

"Oh, do you paint?"

"Some," modestly.

"And play?" Anne's eyes were on the little piano in the alcove.

"Yes."

"Play now," pleaded Anne.

But Judy shook her head. "After dinner," she said. "The bell is ringing now."

Dinner at Judge Jameson's was a formal affair, commencing with soup and ending with coffee. It was served in the great dining-room where silver dishes and tankards twinkled on the sideboard, and where the light came in through stained-glass windows, so that Anne always had a feeling that she was in church.

The Judge sat at the head of the table, and his sister, Mrs. Patterson, at the foot. Judy was on one side and Anne on the other, and back of them, a silent, competent butler spirited away their plates, and substituted others with a sort of sleight-of-hand dexterity that almost took Anne's breath away.

Anne and the Judge chatted together happily throughout the meal. The Judge was very fond of the earnest maiden, whose grandmother had been the friend of his youth, and his eyes went often from her sunny face to that of the moody, silent Judy. "It will do Judy good to be with Anne," he thought. "I am going to have them together as much as possible."

"Why don't you get up a picnic to-morrow?" he suggested, as Perkins passed the fingerbowls—a rite which always tried Anne's timid, inexperienced soul, as did the mysteries of the half-dozen spoons and forks that had stretched out on each side of her plate at the beginning of the meal.

"You could get some of Anne's friends to join you," went on the Judge, "and I'll let you have the three-seated wagon and Perkins; and Mary can pack a lunch."

Judy raised two calm eyes from a scrutiny of the table-cloth.

"I hate picnics," she said.

Then as the Judge, with a disappointed look on his kind old face, pushed back his chair, Judy rose and trailed languidly through the dining-room and out into the hall.

Anne started to follow, but the hurt look on the Judge's face was too much for her tender heart, and as she reached the door she turned and came back.

"I think a picnic would be lovely," she said, a little surprised at her own interference in the matter, "and—and—let's plan it, anyhow, and Judy will have a good time when she gets there."

"Do you really think she will?" said the Judge, with the light coming into his eyes.

"Yes," said Anne, "she will, and you'd better ask Nannie May and Amelia
Morrison."

"And Launcelot Bart?" asked the Judge. For a moment Anne hesitated, then she answered with a sort of gentle decision.

"We can't have the picnic without Launcelot. He knows the nicest places. You ask him, Judge, and—and—I'll tell Judy."

"We will have something different, too," planned the Judge. "I will send to the city for some things—bonbons and all that. Perkins will know what to order. I haven't done anything of this kind for so long that I don't know the proper thing—but Perkins will know—he always knows—"

"Anne, Anne," came Judy's voice from the top of the stairway.

Anne fluttered away, rewarded by the Judge's beaming face, but with fear tugging at her heart. What would Judy say? Judy who hated picnics and who hated boys?

"Don't you want to come down and take a walk?" she asked coaxingly, from the foot of the stairs. It would be easier to break the news to Judy out-of-doors, and then the Judge would be in the garden, a substantial ally.

"I hate walks," said Imperiousness from the upper hall.

"Oh," murmured Faintheart from the lower hall, and sat down on the bottom step.

"I won't tell her till we are ready for bed," was her sudden conclusion.

It was getting dark, but Judy hanging over the rail could just make out the huddled blue gingham bunch.

"Aren't you coming up?" she asked, ominously.

"Yes," and with her courage all gone, Anne rose and began the long climb up the stately stairway.

CHAPTER III

IN THE JUDGE'S GARDEN

The Judge's garden was not a place of flaming flower beds and smooth clipped lawns open to the gaze of every passer-by. It was a quiet spot. A place where old-fashioned flowers bloomed modestly in retired corners, veiled from curious stares by a high hedge of aromatic box.

There was a fountain in the Judge's garden, half-hidden by an encircling border of gold and purple fleur-de-lis, where a marble cupid rode gaily on the back of a bronze dolphin, from whose mouth spouted a stream of limpid water.

There was, too, in summer, a tangled wilderness of roses—hundred-leaved ones, and little yellow ones, and crimson ones whose tall bushes topped the hedge, and great white ones that clung lovingly to the old stone wall that was the western barrier of the garden. And there was a bed of myrtle, and another one of verbenas, over which the butterflies hovered on hot summer days, and another of pansies, and along the wall great clumps of valley lilies. And at the end of the path was a lilac bush that the Judge's wife had planted in the first days of bridal happiness.

For years it had been a lonely garden, as lonely as the old Judge's heart—for fifteen years, ever since the death of his wife, and the departure of his only son to sail the seas, the darkened windows of the old house had cast a shadow on the garden, a shadow that had fallen upon the Judge as he had walked there night after night in solitude.

But this evening as he sat on the bench under the lilac bush, a broad bar of golden light shone down upon the gay cupid and the sleeping flowers, and from the open window came the lilt of girlish laughter and the rippling strain of the "Spring Song," as Judy's fingers touched the keys of the little piano lightly.

Presently the music changed to a wild dashing strain.

"It's a Spanish dance," Judy explained to Anne. She was swaying back and forth, keeping time with her body to the melodies that tinkled from her fingers.

"I can dance it, too," she added.

"Oh, do dance it, Judy—please," cried Anne. She was living in a sort of Arabian Nights' dream. Hitherto the girls that she had known had been demure and unaccomplished, so that Judy seemed a brilliant creature, fresh from fairyland.

With a crash the music stopped, as Judy jumped up from the bench, and went into the hall.

"Move the chairs back," she directed over her shoulder, and Anne bustled about, and cleared a space in the centre of the polished floor.

In the meantime Judy bent over a great trunk in the hall.

"Oh, dear," she cried, as she piled a bewildering array of things on the floor—bright hued gowns, picturesque hats, and a miscellaneous collection of fans and ribbons. "Oh, dear, of course they are at the very bottom."

"They" proved to be a scarlet silk shawl and a pair of high-heeled scarlet slippers. Judy wound the shawl about her in the Spanish manner, put on the high-heeled slippers, stuck an artificial red rose in her dark hair, and stepped forth as dashing a señorita as ever danced in old Seville.

"Oh, Judy," was all that Anne could say. She plumped herself down in a big chair, too happy for words, and waved to Judy to go on, while she held her breath lest she might wake from this marvelous enchantment.

Out in the garden, the Judge heard the click of castanets and the tap of the high heels.

"What is the child doing," he wondered.

As the dance proceeded, the sound of the castanets grew wilder and wilder, and the high heels beat double raps on the floor. Then, suddenly, with one sharp "click-ck" the dance ended, and there was silence.

Then Anne cried, "Do it again, do it again, Judy," and the Judge clapped his applause from the garden below.

At the sound the girls poked their heads out of the window.

"You ought to see her, Judge," Anne's tone was rapturous, "you just ought to see her."

"Shall I come down?" Judy asked. She was glowing, radiant.

"Yes, indeed. Come and dance on the path."

Five minutes later Judy was whirling, wraithlike in the white light of the moon, which turned her scarlet trappings to silver. Anne sat by the Judge and made admiring comments.

"Isn't it fine?" she asked.

The Judge nodded.

"I saw the Spanish girls do it when I was young," he said, beating time with his cane, "and Judy lived in Spain with her mother for a year, you'd think the child was born to it," and he chuckled with pride.

But when Judy came up after the last wild dash, he was more moderate in his praises. The Judge had been raised in the days when children heard often the rhyme, "Praise to the face, is open disgrace," and at times he reminded himself of the merits of such early discipline.

"I don't know what your grandmother would have thought of it, my dear," he said, with a doubtful shake of his head, "in her days, young ladies didn't do such things."

"Didn't grandmother dance?" asked Judy.

"Indeed she did," said the Judge with enthusiasm. "Why, Judy, there wasn't a couple that could beat your grandmother and me when we danced the Virginia reel."

Judy threw herself down on the bench beside him, and fanned herself with the end of her shawl.

"Can you dance," she asked, "can you really dance, grandfather? I'm so glad. Some day I shall give a party, and have all the people of the neighborhood, and we will end it with the reel. May I, grandfather?"

"You may do anything you wish," was the Judge's rash promise, and with a quick laugh, Judy saw her opportunity and took advantage of it.

"Then let's go down to the kitchen," she said, "and get something to eat now. I didn't eat much dinner, and I am starved. Aren't you, Anne?"

But Anne had been trained in the way she should go. "I—I haven't thought of being hungry," she hesitated. "I never eat before I go to bed."

"Oh, I do," said Judy, scornfully. "And dancing makes me ravenous."

"But Perkins has retired, and Mary, and everybody—" expostulated the
Judge.

"Who cares for Perkins?" asked Judy with her nose in the air.

"Well," said the Judge, who was hopelessly the slave of his servants, "he might not like it—"

"Judge Jameson," said Judy, shaking a reproachful finger at him, "I believe you are afraid of your butler."

"Well, perhaps I am, my dear," said the Judge, weakly, "but Perkins is an individual of a great deal of firmness, and he carries the keys, and I don't believe you will find anything, anyhow. And if you eat up anything that he has ordered for breakfast, you will have an unpleasant time accounting for it in the morning. I know Perkins, my dear—and he is rather difficult—rather difficult. But he is a very fine servant," he amended hastily.

"You leave him to me in the morning," said Judy, "I'll make the peace, grandfather, and I simply can't be starved to-night."

"But Perkins—"

"Perkins won't say a word to you," said Judy, "and if he does, you can say you were not in the kitchen, because you are to stay right here, and Anne and I will bring things up, and make you a receiver of stolen goods."

330

She was very charming in spite of her wilfulness, and when she ended her little speech, by tucking her hand through the Judge's arm, and looking up at him mischievously, the old gentleman gave in.

The two girls were gone for a long time, so long that the Judge nodded on his bench.

He was waked by a shriek that seemed to come from the depths of the earth.

"What—is the matter, what's the matter, my dear?" he cried, starting up.

There was another subdued shriek, then a hysterical giggle.

"Judy is shut up in the ice-box," announced Anne, hurrying up from the basement.

"Bless my soul," ejaculated the Judge.

"We hunted around and found the key," explained Anne, as the Judge stumped distractedly through the lower hall, "and Judy unlocked the door of the ice-box and got inside, and she still had the key in her hand, and I hit the door accidentally and it slammed on her, and it has a spring lock and we can't open it."

"Bless my soul," said the Judge again.

The ice-box was a massive affair, almost like a small room. It was in a remote corner of the lower hallway, and its walls were thick and impenetrable.

"Let me out, oh, let me out," came in muffled tones, as the Judge and
Anne came up.

"My dear child, my dear child," said the Judge, "how could you do such a thing?"

"I shall freeze. I shall freeze," wailed Judy.

"Are you very cold, Judy?" shivered Anne, sympathetically.

"It's so dark—and damp. Let me out, let me out," and Judy's voice rose to a shriek.

"Now, my dear, be calm," advised the Judge, whose hands were shaking with nervousness, "I shall call Perkins—yes, I really think I shall have to call Perkins—" and he hurried through the hall to the speaking tubes.

"Is there anything to eat in there?" Anne asked through the keyhole.

"Lots of things," said Judy. "I lighted a match as I came in, and there are lots of things. But I don't want anything to eat—I want to get out—I want to get out."

"Don't cry, Judy," advised Anne soothingly, "the Judge has called
Perkins and he is coming down now."

Perkins emerged into the light of the lower hallway in a state of informal attire and unsettled temper. His dignity was his stock in trade, and how could one be dignified in an old overcoat and bedroom slippers? But the Judge's summons had been peremptory and there had been no time for the niceties of toilet in which Perkins' orderly soul revelled.

"There ain't no other key," he said, severely. "I guess we will have to wait until mornin', sir."

"But we can't wait until morning," raged the Judge, "the young lady will freeze."

"Oh, no, sir," said Perkins, loftily, "oh, no, sir, she won't freeze.
Nothing freezes in that there box, sir."

"Well, she will die of cold," said the Judge. "Don't be a blockhead,
Perkins, we have got to get her out now—at once—Perkins."

"All right, sir," said Perkins, "then I'll have to go for a locksmith, sir—"

"Can't you take off the lock?" asked the Judge.

Perkins drew himself up. "That's not my work, sir," he said, stiffly, "no, sir, I can't take off no locks, sir," and so the Judge had to be content, while the independent Perkins hunted up a locksmith and brought him to the scene of disaster.

It was a white and somewhat cowed Judy that came out of the ice-box.

"Make her a cup of strong coffee, Perkins," commanded the Judge, as he received the woebegone heroine in his arms, "and take it up to her room, with something to eat with it."

"I don't want anything to eat," Judy declared. "There's everything to eat in that awful box—enough for an army—but I don't feel as if I could ever eat again," in a tone of martyr-like dolefulness.

"Them things in there is for the picnic, miss," said Perkins. "It's lucky you and Miss Anne didn't eat them," and he cast on the culprit a look of utter condemnation.

At the word "picnic," Anne's soul sank within her. She had forgotten all about the picnic in the excitement of the evening, all about Judy's anger and the confession she was to make of the plans for Saturday.

She and the Judge eyed each other guiltily, as Judy sank down on the bench and stared at Perkins.

"What picnic?" she demanded fiercely.

"The Judge said I was to get things ready, miss," said Perkins, dismally, and looked to his master for corroboration.

"Didn't you tell her, Anne?" asked the Judge, helplessly.

Anne felt as if she were alone in the world. Perkins and the Judge and
Judy were all looking at her, and the truth had to come.

"We decided to have the picnic to-morrow, anyhow, Judy," she said. "We thought maybe you would like it after it was all planned."

Judy jumped up from the bench and began a rapid ascent of the stairway. Half-way up she turned and looked down at the three conspirators. "I sha'n't like it," she cried, shrilly, "and I sha'n't go."

"Judy!" remonstrated the Judge.

"Oh, Judy," cried poor little Anne.

But Perkins, who had lived with the Judge in the days of Judy's lady grandmother, turned his offended back on this self-willed and unworthy scion of a noble race, and marched into the kitchen to make the coffee.

CHAPTER IV

"YOUR GRANDMOTHER, MY DEAR"

Judy had reached the door of her room when the Judge called her.

"Come down," he said, "I want to talk to you."

"I'm tired," said Judy, in a stifled voice, and Anne, who had followed her, saw that she was crying.

"I know," the Judge's voice was gentle, "I know, but I won't keep you long. Come."

Judy went reluctantly, and he led the way to the garden bench.

It was very still out there in the garden—just the splash of the little fountain, and the drone of lazy insects. The moon hung low, a golden disk above the distant line of dark hills.

"Judy," began the Judge, "do you know, my dear, that you are very like your grandmother?"

Judy looked at him, surprised at the turn the conversation was taking.

"Am I?" she asked.

"Yes," continued the Judge, "and especially in two things." His eyes were fixed dreamily on a bed of tall lilies that shone pale in the half light.

"What things?" Judy was interested. She had expected a lecture, but this did not sound like one.

"In your love of flowers—and in your temper—my dear."

Judy's head went up haughtily. "Grandfather!"

"You don't probably call it temper. But your grandmother did, and she conquered hers—and I am going to tell you how she did it, because I know she would want me to tell you, Judy."

Judy sat sulkily as far from her grandfather as she could get. Her hands were clasped around her knees and she stared out over the dusky garden, wide-eyed, and it must be confessed a little obstinate. Judy knew she had faults, but if the truth must be told, she was a little proud of her temper—"I have an awful temper," she had confessed on several occasions, and when meek admirers had murmured, "How dreadful," she had tossed her head and had said, "But I can't help it, you know, all of my family have had tempers," and as Judy's family was known to be aristocratic and exclusive, her more plebeian friends had envied and had tried to emulate her, generally with disastrous results.

She was not quite sure that she wanted to conquer it. It often gave her what she wanted, and that was something.

"The first time I had a taste of your grandmother's temper," the Judge related, "we had had an argument about a gown. We had been invited to a great dinner at the Governor's, and she had nothing to wear. She took me to the shop to see the stuff she wanted. It was heavy blue satin with pink roses all over it, and there was real lace to trim it with. It was beautiful and I wanted her to have it, but when they named the price it was more than I could pay—I was a poor lawyer in those days, Judy—so I said we would think it over, and we went home. All the way there your grandmother was very quiet and very white, but when we reached home and I tried to explain, she simply would not listen. She would not go to the Governor's, she said, unless she could have that gown. You can imagine the embarrassment it caused me—it was as much as my career was worth to stay away from that dinner, and I couldn't go without her.

"'I won't go. I won't go,' she said over and over again, and when I had coaxed and coaxed to no effect, I sat down and looked at her helplessly, and troubled as I was, I could not help thinking that she was the loveliest creature in the world—with her rose red cheeks and her flashing eyes.

"She said many cutting things to me, but suddenly she stopped and ran out of the room, and presently I saw her in the garden, this garden, my dear, and she was flying around the oval path, as if she were walking for a wager, her thin ruffles swirling around her, and the strings of her bonnet fluttering in the wind.

"Around and around she went, and I just sat there and stared. When she started in there was a deep frown on her forehead, but as she walked I saw her face clear, and when she had completed the round a dozen times or more, I saw her throw back her head in a light-hearted way, and then she ran into the house.

"She came straight to me and threw her arms around my neck. 'John,' she said, 'John, dear,' and there was the tenderest tremble in her voice, 'John Jameson, I was a hateful thing.' I tried to stop her, but she insisted. 'Oh, yes, I was. And I don't want the dress, I will wear an old one—and I'll make you proud of me—'

"Then all at once she began to sob, and her head dropped on my shoulder. 'Oh,' she cried, 'how could I say such things to you—how could I—?'

"'What made you change, sweetheart?' I asked, and she whispered, 'Oh, your face and the trouble in it.'

"'I made up my mind that I wouldn't say another word until I could get control of my temper, and so I went into the garden and walked and walked, and do you know, John Jameson, that I walked around that oval sixteen times before I could give up that dress.'

"It wasn't the last time she walked around that oval, Judy," the Judge finished, with a reminiscent smile on his old face, "and so perfectly did she conquer herself, that when she left me, it was just an angel stepping from earth to the place where she belonged."

Judy had listened breathlessly. So vivid had been the description, that she had seemed to see on the garden walk, the slender, imperious figure, the intent girlish face, and out of her knowledge of her own nature, she had entered into the struggle that had taken place in her grandmother's heart, as she flew around the oval of the old garden.

"Oh, grandfather," she said, when the Judge's quavering voice dropped into silence, "how lovely she was—"

"She was, indeed, and I want you to be as strong."

Judy tucked her hand into his. "I'll try," she said, simply, "thank you for telling me, grandfather."

"I want you to be happy here, too," said the old man wistfully, and then as she did not answer, "do you think you can, Judy?"

Judy caught her breath quickly. With all her faults she was very honest.

She bent and kissed the Judge on his withered cheek. "You are so good to me," she said, evasively, and with another kiss, she ran up-stairs to Anne.

Anne was in bed and Judy thought she was asleep, but an hour later as she lay awake lonely and restless, with her eyes fixed longingly on the great picture of the sea, a soft seeking hand curled within her own, and Anne whispered, "I didn't mean to make you unhappy, Judy," and Judy, clear-eyed and repentant in the darkness of the night, murmured back, "I was hateful, Anne," and a half hour later, the moon, peeping in, saw the two serene, sleeping faces, cheek to cheek on the same pillow.

CHAPTER V

TOO MANY COOKS

In spite of herself Judy was having a good time.

"I know you will enjoy it," had been Anne's last drowsy remark, and

Judy's final thought had been, "I'll go, but it will be horrid."

But it wasn't horrid.

There had been Anne's happiness in the first place. Judy had wondered at it until she found out that Anne's picnic experiences had been limited to little jaunts with the children of the neighborhood, and an occasional Sunday-school gathering. The Judge had lived his lonely life in his lonely house, and except when Anne and her little grandmother had been invited to formal meals, he had not interested himself in any festivities.

There had been the early start, the meeting of the queer boy at the crossroads—the boy with the lazy air and the alert eyes; the crowding of the big carriage with two rather dowdy little country girls, one of whom was, in Judy's opinion, exceedingly pert, and the other exasperatingly placid; the laughter and the light-heartedness, the beauty of the blossoming spring world, the restfulness of the dim forest aisles, the excitement of the arrival on the banks of the stream, and the arrangement of the camp for the day.

And now Judy, having declined more active occupation, was in a hammock, swung in a circle of pines. The softened sunlight shone gold on the dried needles under foot, and everywhere was the aromatic fragrance of the forest. Now and then there was a flutter of wings as a nesting bird swooped by with scarcely a note of song. A pair of redbirds came and went—flashes of scarlet against the whiteness of a blossoming dogwood-tree. Far away the squalling of a catbird mingled with the mellow cadences of the mountain stream.

There was the sound of laughter, too, and the chatter of gay voices in the distance, where the young people fished from the banks.

Judy could just see them through an opening in the pines. The three girls perched on the bent trunk of an old tree, which hung over the water, were dangling their lines and watching the corks that bobbed on the surface. The Judge, with a big hat pushed away from his warm, red face, held the can of bait and discoursed entertainingly on his past angling experiences.

Perkins in the foreground was opening the lunch-hampers, and just outside of Judy's circle of pines, a brisk little fire sent up its pungent smoke, and beside the fire, Launcelot Bart was cutting bacon.

Judy watched him with interest. He was tall and thin, but he carried himself with a lazy grace, and in spite of his old corduroy suit, there was about him a certain air of distinction.

He was whistling softly as he put the iron pan over the coals, and dropped into it a half-dozen slices of the bacon.

"Watch these, Perkins," he called, "I'll be back in a minute," and he started towards the hammock.

As he came up, Judy closed her eyes, with an air of indifference.

"Asleep?" asked Launcelot, a half-dozen steps from her.

Judy opened her eyes.

"Oh—is that you?" she asked.

"Yes. Don't you want to come and help me cook?" He was smiling down at her pleasantly.

"I hate cooking." Judy's voice was cold. She hoped he would go away.

Launcelot leaned against a tree to discuss the question.

"Oh," he said. "I don't hate it. It's rather a fine art, you know."

"Anybody can cook," murmured Judy with decision.

"H-m. Can you, little girl?"

Judy sat up at that. "I'm fourteen," she flashed.

Launcelot laughed, such a contagious laugh, that in spite of herself

Judy felt the corners of her lips twitch.

"That waked you up," he said, "you didn't like to have me call you 'little girl.' Well, am I to say Miss Jameson or Judy?"

Judy pondered.

"Neither," she said at last.

"Then what—?" began Launcelot. "Oh, by Jove, the bacon's burning.

I'll be back in a minute."

When he had taken the bacon out of the pan, and had laid the fish in a corn-mealed symmetrical row in the hot fat, he again turned the pan over to Perkins and came back to Judy.

"Well?" he asked, as he came up.

"Call me Judith," said the incensed young lady. "Judy is my pet name, and I keep it for—my friends."

Launcelot gave a long whistle.

"Say, do you talk like this to Anne?" he asked.

"Like what?"

"In this—er—straight from the shoulder sort of fashion?"

"No. Anne is my friend."

Launcelot shook his head. "You can't have Anne for a friend unless you have me."

"Why not?"

"She was my friend first."

"Oh, well," Judy shrugged her shoulders and shut her eyes again, "it is too hot to argue."

There was a long silence, and then Launcelot said: "Don't you want to fish?"

"I hate fishing."

"Or to pick wild flowers?"

"I hate—" Judy had started her usual ungracious formula, before she recognized its untruth. "Well, I don't want to pick them now," she amended, "I'd rather stay here."

"But you are not going to stay here."

"Why not?"

"You are going to help me cook those fish."

"I won't."

"Oh, yes you will. Come on."

"Oh, well. If you won't let me alone."

She slipped out of the hammock and picked up her hat. There was a tired droop to her slender young figure. "No, I am not going to let you alone," said Launcelot quietly. "You poor little thing."

She looked at him, startled.

"Why?" she breathed.

"You are lonely. That's why. You've got to do something. You just think and think and think—and get miserable—I know—I've been there."

It came out haltingly, the boyish expression of sympathy and understanding. And the sympathy combined with a hitherto unmet masterfulness conquered Judy. For a moment she stood very still, then she turned to him an illumined face.

"You may call me—Judy," she said shyly, then slipped past him and ran to the fire.

When he reached her, she was bending over the pan.

"How nice they look," she said, as Launcelot turned the fish, and they lay all crisp and brown in an appetizing row.

"You shall do the next," said Launcelot, smiling a little as he glanced at her absorbed face.

So while he made the coffee, Judy fried more bacon, and they slipped six fish into the big pan.

"Mine don't seem to brown as yours did," she told him, anxiously.

"Perhaps the fat wasn't hot enough," was Launcelot's suggestion. "It has to be smoking."

"Oh, dear," sighed Judy, "mine are going to look light brown instead of lovely and golden like yours."

"Put on some more wood." Launcelot's tone was abstracted. He was measuring the coffee, and it took all of his attention.

Judy poked a stick into the centre of the fire. For a moment it seemed to die down, then suddenly the big black pan seemed held aloft by a solid cone of yellow flame.

The grease in the pan snapped, and little burnt bits of corn-meal flew in all directions.

"Now they are cooking all right," and Judy shielded her face with her hand, as she held the long handle and watched complacently.

Suddenly Launcelot dropped the coffee-pot.

"Take them off, take them off," he cried.

Judy, with her fork upraised, stared at him as if petrified.

"Why?" she stammered.

He snatched the pan from the fire.

"They're burning," he cried, and turned the fish up one by one.

They were as black as coals down to the very tips of their crisp little tails!

CHAPTER VI

A RAIN AND A RUNAWAY

At her cry of dismay, Perkins strolled over to take a look.

"They're burnt, Miss," he announced, bending over the pan.

"Of course they are," snapped Judy, "any one could see that, Perkins."

Perkins looked over her head, loftily.

"Yes, Miss, of course," he said, "but it's mostly always that way when there are too many cooks. I'm afraid there won't be enough to go around, Miss."

"Are these all?" asked Judy, anxiously.

"Yes," said Launcelot, "I cooked four and you burned six, and there are the Judge and Anne and Nannie and Amelia and Perkins and you and I to be fed."

"You needn't count me, sir," said Perkins. "I never eats, sir."

With which astounding statement, he carried away the charred remains.

"Does he mean that he doesn't eat at all?" questioned Judy, staring after the stout figure of the retiring butler.

Launcelot laughed. "Oh, he eats enough," he said, "only he doesn't do it in public. He knows his place."

"I wish he did," said Judy, dubiously. "Oh, dear, what shall we do about the fish?"

"There will be one apiece for the others," said Launcelot. "I guess you and I will have to do without—Judy—"

He spoke her name with just the slightest hesitation, and his eyes laughed as they met hers.

"And I said any one could cook!" Judy's tone was very humble. "What a prig you must have thought me, Launcelot."

"Oh, go and get some flowers for the table and forget your troubles," was Launcelot's off-hand way of settling the question, and as Judy went off she decided that she should like him. He was different from other boys. He was a gentleman in spite of his shabby clothes, and his masterfulness rather pleased her—hitherto Judy had ruled every boy within her domain, and Launcelot was a new experience.

It was a hungry crowd that trooped to the great gray rock where the table was spread.

"How beautiful you have made it look, Judy," cried Anne, as she came up, blissfully unconscious of a half-dozen new freckles and a burned nose.

335

Nannie May sniffed. "Fish," she said, ecstatically, "our fish, oh,
Amelia, don't things look *good*."

Amelia surveyed the table solemnly. She was a fat, rather dumpy girl of twelve. She was noted principally for two things, her indolence and her appetite, and it was in deference to the latter that she sighed rapturously as she surveyed the table. She had never seen anything just like it. The country picnics of the neighbors always showed an amazing array of cakes and pies and chicken, but these were here, and added to them were sandwiches of wonderful and attractive shapes, marvelous fruits, bonbons, and chocolates, and salads garnished with a skill known to none other in the village but the accomplished Perkins.

As her eyes swept over the table, they were arrested by the platter of fish. In spite of Perkins' overplentiful border of cress and sliced lemon—put on to hide deficiencies, the four fish looked pitifully inadequate.

"I caught four myself," said Amelia, heavily, pointing an accusing finger at the platter, "and Anne caught three and Nan three—there were ten."

Launcelot groaned. "I wish you weren't quite so good at arithmetic, Amelia," he said, "we shall have to confess—we burned the rest up—and please ma'am, we are awfully sorry."

They all laughed at the funny figure he made as he dropped on his knees before the stolid Amelia—but into Judy's cheeks crept a little flush—"I—" she began, with a tremble in her voice; but Launcelot interrupted; "we will never do it again," he promised, and then as they laughed again, he rose and stood at Judy's side.

"Don't you dare tell them that you did it," he whispered, and once more she felt the masterfulness of his tone. "I should have watched the fire—it was as much my fault as yours," and with that he picked up a pile of cushions, and went to arrange a place for her at the head of the table.

Amelia ate steadily through the menu. She was not overawed by Perkins, nor was her attention distracted by the laughter and fun of the others. It was not until the ice-cream was served—pink and luscious, with a wreath of rosy strawberries encircling each plate—that she spoke.

"Well," she said, "I don't know's I mind now about those fish being burned," with which oracular remark, she helped herself to two slices of cake, and ate up her ice in silence.

Nannie May was thirteen and looked about eleven. She was red-haired and fiery-tempered, and she loved Anne with all the strength of her loyal heart. As yet she did not like Judy. It was all very well to look like a princess, but that was no reason why one should be as stiff as a poker. She hoped Anne would not love Judy better than she did her, and she noted jealously the rapt attention with which Anne observed the newcomer and listened to all she said.

Judy was telling the episode of the ice-box. She told it well, and in spite of herself Nannie had to laugh.

"When I went in there were salads to right of me, cold tongue to the left of me, and roast chicken in front of me," said Judy, gesticulating dramatically, "and I was so hungry that it seemed too good to be true that Perkins should have provided all of those things. And just then the door slammed and my match went out—and there I was in the cold and the dark—and I just screamed for Anne."

"Why didn't you put the latch up when you went in?" asked Nannie, scornfully. "It seems to me 'most anybody would have thought of that."

Anne came eagerly to her friend's defence.

"Neither of us knew it was a spring latch," she said, "and I was as surprised as Judy was."

"Why didn't you eat up all the things?" asked Amelia, as she helped herself to another chocolate.

"I didn't have any light—" began Judy.

"Well, I should have eaten them up in the dark," mused Amelia, as
Perkins passed her the salted almonds for the sixth time.

"It was a good thing I didn't," laughed Judy, "or you wouldn't have had anything to eat to-day. Would they, Perkins?"

For once in his life Perkins was in an affable mood. The lunch had gone off well, there had been no spiders in the cream or red ants in the cake. The coffee had been hot and the salads cold, and now that lunch was over he could pack the dishes away to be washed by the servants at home, and rest on his laurels.

"I should have found something, Miss," he said, cheerfully; then as a big drop splashed down on his bald head, he leaned over the Judge.

"I think it is going to rain, sir," he murmured, confidentially.

"By George," gasped the Judge, as a bright flash of light and a low rumble emphasized Perkins' words, "by George, I believe it is.

"Oh, oh, oh," screamed Amelia, and threw her arms frantically around
Nannie.

"Don't be silly," said Nannie, and gave her a little shake.

"We shall have to run for it," said Launcelot, gathering up wraps and hats, as a sudden gust of wind picked up the ends of the tablecloth and sent the napkins fluttering across the ground like a flock of white geese.

"You'd better get the young ladies to the carriage, sir," said Perkins, packing things into hampers in a hurry.

336

"They will get wet. It's going to be a heavy wind storm," said the
Judge with an anxious look at Judy.

"Let's run for the Cutter barn," cried Anne, with sudden inspiration.

"Good for you, Anne," said Launcelot, "that's the very thing."

"Where is the Cutter barn?" asked Judy.

"Across that stream and beyond the strip of woods. Over in the field."

"Come on, Anne, come on. Oh, isn't this glorious. I love the wind. I love it, I love it." Judy's cry became almost a chant as she led the way across the little bridge and through the fast-darkening bit of woodland. The wind fluttered her white garments around her, her long hair streamed out behind, and her flying feet seemed scarcely to touch the ground. Behind her came Anne, less like a wood-nymph, perhaps, but fresh and fair, and not at all breathless, then Nannie, bareheaded and with her best hat wrapped carefully in her short skirts, then Amelia, plunging heavily.

Launcelot waited to help Perkins with the horses and hampers and then he followed the girls.

The rain came before he was half-way across the stream, and the world grew dark for a moment in the heavy downpour that drenched him. There was a blaze of blue-white light, and a crash that seemed to shake the universe.

"They will be scared half to death," was Launcelot's thought as he forged ahead.

Just at the edge of the woods he came upon Anne and Judy. Judy had dropped down in a white huddled bunch, and Anne was bending over her.

"She ran too fast," she explained, while the rain beat down on her fair little head, "and she can't get her breath. Nannie and Amelia got to the barn before the rain came, but I couldn't leave Judy."

"I'm all right," gasped Judy, "you run on, Anne. I'm all right."

"Yes, run on, Anne," commanded Launcelot. "I'll take care of Judy, and you must not get wet," and with a protest Anne disappeared behind the curtain of driving rain.

Judy staggered to her feet and attempted to walk two or three steps.

"Stop it," said Launcelot, firmly, "you must not."

"But I can't stay here," cried poor Judy, desperately.

Her lips were blue and her cheeks were white, so that Launcelot wavered no longer. Without any warning, he picked her up as if she had been a child, and ran with her across the field.

"Put me down, Launcelot. Put me down." Judy's tone was imperious.

But she had met her match. Launcelot plodded on doggedly.

"I shall never forgive you," she sobbed, as they reached the door of the Cutter barn.

"Yes, you will," said Launcelot, and his lips were set in a firm line.

"I had to do it, Judy."

He laid her on a pile of hay in the corner.

Her eyes were closed, and her dark lashes swept across her pallid cheeks.

"She isn't strong," whispered the worried Anne, her tender fingers pushing back Judy's wet hair.

"No," said Launcelot, his deep young voice softening to a gentler key as he looked down at her, "she isn't. Poor little thing!"

Judy heard, and her lashes fluttered. "How good they are," she thought, remorsefully, and then she seemed to float away from realities.

When she came to herself, Launcelot had gone, and the three little girls were rubbing her hands and trying to get her to drink some water.

"Oh, Judy, do you feel better?" Anne whispered; "we were so frightened."

"Yes," murmured Judy, and the color began to come into her face.

"Launcelot went to see if he could get something from Perkins for you to take," said Anne; "he told us to build a fire in the old stove, but we have been so worried about you that we haven't done anything."

"Is there a stove?" asked Judy, listlessly.

"Yes. Mr. Cutter put it in here to heat milk for the lambs, and once when we had a picnic we made our coffee here."

"There isn't any wood," said Amelia, hopelessly.

"There is some up in the loft," said Nannie, "Don't you remember the boys put it there, so that no one but ourselves could find it?"

She went swiftly up the narrow steps, but came flying back in a panic.

"*There's some one up there*," she whispered, all the color gone from her face.

"Hush," said Anne, with her eyes on Judy.

Judy was not afraid. She was still weak and wan, but she was braver than the little country girls, and not easily frightened.

"It is probably a pussy cat," she scoffed.

"Or a hen," giggled Amelia.

Anne said nothing. The darkness, the crashing storm outside, and Judy's illness had upset her, and she shivered with apprehension.

"No," Nannie flared, with a scornful look at Amelia and Judy, "it isn't a cat and it isn't a hen. IT sneezed!"

"Ask who's there," advised Judy from her couch.

"I don't dare," said Nannie.

"I don't dare," said Amelia.

So that it was little timid Anne, after all, who gathered up her courage and went to the foot of the stairs and said in a trembling voice:

"Please, who is up there?"

For a moment there was silence, and then some one said in sepulchral tones:

"You won't ever tell?"

The girls stared at each other.

"What shall we say?" whispered Anne.

"Say 'never,'" suggested Judy, wishing she were well enough to manage this exciting episode.

"NEVER," said the little girls all together.

There was a rustling in the hay in the loft, then cautious steps, and a figure appeared at the top of the stairs.

At sight of it, Amelia shrieked and Nannie giggled, but Anne ran forward with both hands out, and with her fair little face alight with welcome.

"Why, Tommy Tolliver, Tommy Tolliver," she said, "is it really you, is it really, really you?"

CHAPTER VII

TOMMY TOLLIVER: SEAMAN

Tommy shook hands with Anne, then sat down disconsolately on the bottom step.

"Yes," he said, "it's me."

After a moment's uncomfortable silence, Anne asked, "Didn't you like it, Tommy?"

Tommy looked gloomy.

"Aw," he burst out, "they thought I was too young—"

"Did you go as far as China?" questioned Amelia, eagerly.

"Of course he didn't, Amelia," said Nannie with a superior air; "he has only been away three weeks."

"Then you didn't get me any preserved ginger," pouted Amelia.

"How could I?" But Tommy looked sheepish, as the memory of certain boastful promises came to him.

"Anyhow," he announced suddenly, "I'm not going to give up. I am going to be a sailor some day—if I have to run away again."

At that Judy sat up and fixed him with burning eyes.

"Did you go to sea?" she asked, intensely.

"I tried to."

"How far did you get?"

"To Baltimore."

"And they wouldn't have you?"

"No. And I had used up all my money, so I had to come back."

"Have you ever been on the ocean?"

"No. Have you?"

"Yes. My father was in the navy."

"Gee—" Tommy drew near to this fascinating stranger.

"The next time you want to run away, you tell me," said Judy, and sank back on the hay, "and I'll help you."

"But, Judy," said horrified little Anne, "he isn't going to run away any more—he is going to stay here, and please his father and go to school—aren't you, Tommy?"

Tommy looked from the fair little girl to the dark thin one. Hitherto Anne had been his ideal of gentle girlhood, but in Judy he now found a kindred spirit, a girl with a daring that more than matched his own—a girl who loved the sea—who knew about the sea—who could tell him things.

"Aw—I don't know," he said, uncertainly. "I guess I can run away if I want to, Anne."

"No, you can't," cried Anne. "You ought not to encourage him, Judy."

338

"I'm not encouraging him," said Judy, but there was a wicked sparkle in her eyes.

Tommy saw it and swaggered a little. He had returned home in the spirit of the prodigal son. He was ready to be forgiven. To eat of the fatted calf—if he should be so lucky. If not, to eat humble pie. The sight of the familiar fields and roads had even brought tears to his eyes. But now—!

"A fellow can't be tied to a little old place like this all his life," he said, toploftically, "you can't expect it, Anne."

"I don't expect it," said little Anne, quietly, "but if you had seen your mother after you ran away, Tommy—"

At that Tommy lowered his head.

"I know—" he stammered, huskily, "poor little mother."

"Tell me about her," he said. And now he turned his back on the dark young lady on the hay.

But Launcelot's voice broke in on Anne's story. He came in all wet and dripping.

"How's Judy?" he began, then stopped and whistled.

"Hello," he exclaimed, "hello, Bobby Shafto."

"Oh, I say," said Tommy, very red.

"I thought you were on the high seas by now," said Launcelot.

"Well, I wanted to be," said Tommy, resentfully.

"I am glad you're back. We have missed you awfully, old chap," and Launcelot slapped him on the shoulder in hearty greeting.

"How is Judy?" he asked.

"Better, thank you," said the young lady in the corner. "Tommy was a tonic and came just in time."

"Well, I am glad you found some kind of tonic. Perkins didn't have a thing but some mustard and red pepper, and I was feeling for you if we had to dose you with either of those."

Judy started to laugh, but stopped suddenly.

"I forgot," she said, "I am mad at you—"

"Oh, no, you're not."

"But I am—"

"Because I carried you across the field when you didn't want me to?"

"Yes."

"My child," advised Launcelot, "don't be silly."

"Oh," raged Judy, and turned her back to him.

Launcelot looked down at her for a moment.

"You know that tree where you fainted?" he asked.

A little shrug of Judy's shoulder was the only answer.

"Well, it was struck by lightning before I got back—"

"Really—?" Judy was facing him now, breathless with interest.

"Really, Judy." His face was very grave.

"Oh, oh," she wailed, softly, "oh, and I might have been there—"

"Yes."

She shivered and sat up. Her wet hair, half braided, trailed its dark length over her shoulder. Her eyes were big, and her face was white.

"What a baby I was," she said, nervously, "what a baby, Launcelot—not to see the danger—"

"You trust to your Uncle Launcelot, next time, little girl, and don't get fussy," was the big boy's way of stopping her thanks.

"I will," she promised, and the smile she gave him meant more than the words.

"It has stopped raining," said Anne from the door.

The cool spring air blew across the fields softly, bringing with it the fresh smell of the sodden earth and the scent of the wet pines.

"The Judge will be here in a minute," said Launcelot; "he stayed in the carriage, and Perkins put up the curtains, so that they managed to keep pretty dry.

"I wonder if there will be room for me to ride home?" Tommy asked. "I am dead tired."

"I guess so. The Judge has the big wagon with the three seats. Pretty long tramp you had, didn't you?" and Launcelot looked at the boy's dusty shoes.

"Awful," said Tommy, with a quiver in his voice at the remembrance.

"Hungry?" questioned Launcelot, briefly.

"Awful," said Tommy again. "I haven't had a square meal for a week," and now the quiver was intensified.

Amelia clasped her hands tragically. "Oh, Tommy," she asked in a stricken tone, "didn't you almost die?"

But just then Tommy caught Judy's eye on him, and was forced to continue his character of bold adventurer.

"Oh, a man must expect things like that," he asserted. "Suppose it had been a desert island—"

"Or a shipwreck," said Amelia, "with bread and water for a week."

"Or pirates," ventured Nannie.

"Oh, pirates," sniffed the dark young lady on the hay; "there aren't any pirates now."

"Well, there are shipwrecks," defended Tommy.

"Yes, but they are not half as interesting as they used to be."

"And desert islands."

"A few maybe. But it is such an old story to hear about Robinson Crusoes."

Tommy looked blank. He had always implicitly believed the marvelous tales of yarn spinners, and his soul had been fired by the thought of a life of adventure on the deep. He had talked to the little girls until they had accounted him somewhat of a hero and looked to him to perform great feats of bravery.

"I don't see any fun in going to sea, then," he said, dolefully, "if there ain't any pirates and shipwrecks and things like that—"

"It isn't those things that make you love the sea, Tommy," cried Judy. "It is the smell of it, and the wind, and the wide blue water and the wide blue sky. It is something in your blood. I don't believe you really love it at all, Tommy Tolliver."

She got up from the couch and began to gather up her wet hair, and only Launcelot saw that she did it to hide her tears.

But Tommy was blind to her emotion. "Yes, I do," he asserted, stoutly.

"I do love it, and I bet I could find a treasure island if I tried."

Judy stamped her foot impatiently. "Oh, you couldn't," she blazed, "you couldn't, Tommy Tolliver; you could just go to work like a common seaman and get your tobacco and your grog, and be frozen and stiff in the winter storms and hot and weary in the summer ones. But if you really loved the sea you wouldn't care—you wouldn't care, just so you could be rocked to sleep by it at night, and wake to hear it ripple against the sides of the boat—"

"Gee—" said Tommy, open-mouthed at this outburst.

"Tommy," said Launcelot, with a glance at Judy's excited face and at the trembling hands that could scarcely fasten her hair, "you don't know a sailboat from a scow."

"I do," cried the indignant Tommy, switching his attention from Judy to Launcelot, with whom he was deep in the argument when the carriage came.

The Judge read Tommy a little lecture as he welcomed him back, and then he ordered Perkins to give the runaway something to eat, and thereby tempered justice with mercy. And as Tommy had expected the scolding and had not expected the good things, it is to be feared that the latter made the greater impression.

"And how is my girl?" asked the Judge, beaming on Judy.

"All right," said Judy, and tucked her hand into his, "only I am a little tired, grandfather."

"Of course you are. Of course you are," said the Judge. "We must go right home. Perkins and I will sit on the front seat, and you can all crowd in behind—I guess there will be room enough."

"Oh, I say," said Launcelot, as Tommy and Anne sat down on the floor at the back, with their feet on the step, "that won't do. You sit with Judy, Anne."

But Anne shook her head.

"Tommy and I are going to sit here," she said. "He wants me to tell him all the news."

But that was not all that Tommy wanted, for when they were alone and unseen by those in the front of the wagon, he opened a handkerchief which he had carried knotted into a bundle.

"I brought you some things. They ain't much, but I thought you would like to have them."

There were a half-dozen pink and white shells, a starfish, and a few pretty pebbles.

"I picked them up on the beach," said Tommy, "and I thought you might like them."

"It was awfully good of you to think of me," said little Anne, gratefully.

"I wanted to buy you something," apologized Tommy. "There was some lovely jewelry made out of fish-scales, but I didn't have a cent to spare."

"I would rather have these, really, Tommy," said Anne, with appreciation, "because you found them yourself."

She tied them up carefully in her little clean white handkerchief, and then she folded her hands in her lap and told Tommy everything that had happened since he left home.

The sky was red with the blaze of the setting sun when the carriage started. Overhead the crows were flying in a straight black line to the woods to roost. As Anne talked on, the fireflies began to shine against the blue-gray of the twilight; then came darkness and the stars.

"It seems awfully good to be at home," confessed Tommy, as the lights began to twinkle in the nearest farmhouse, "if only father won't scold."

"I think he will scold, Tommy—he was awfully angry—but your mother will be so pleased."

"It was horrid sleeping out at night and tramping days." Tommy was unburdening his soul. It was so easy to tell things to gentle, sympathetic Anne. "And the men around the wharf were so rough—"

"I am sure you won't want to go again," said little Anne, "not for a long time, Tommy."

Tommy looked around cautiously. He didn't want Judy to hear, somehow.

He was afraid of her teasing laugh. Then he leaned down close to

Anne's ear:

"I'll stay here for awhile, Anne."

"I'm so glad, Tommy," said Anne, with a sigh of relief.

But as they drove into the great gateway, and the lights from the big house shone out in welcome, Tommy sighed:

"But I would like to find a treasure island, Anne," he said.

CHAPTER VIII

A WHITE SUNDAY

Anne was feeling very important. She was wrapped in a pale blue kimona of Judy's, and she had had her breakfast in bed! Piled up ten deep at her side were books—a choice collection from the Judge's bookcases, into which she dipped here and there with sighs of deep content and anticipation.

At the end of the room was a mirror, and Anne could just see herself in it. It was a distracting vision, for Judy had done Anne's hair up that morning, and had puffed it out over her ears and had tied it with broad black ribbon, and this effect, in combination with the sweeping blue robe, made Anne feel as interesting as the heroine of a book—and she had never expected that!

Judy in a rose-pink kimona lay on the couch, looking out of the window. The peace of the Sabbath was upon the world; and the house was very still.

Suddenly with a "click" and a "whirr-rr," the doors of the little carved clock on the wall new open and a cuckoo came out and piped ten warning notes.

"Goodness," cried Anne, and shut her book with a bang, "it is almost church time, and we aren't dressed."

But Judy did not move. "We are not going to church," she said, lazily.

Not going to church! Anne faced Judy in amazement. Never since she could remember had she stayed away from church—except when she had had the measles and the mumps!

"I told grandfather last night that we should be too tired," explained

Judy, "and he won't expect us to go."

"Oh," said Anne, and picked up her book, luxuriating in the prospect of a whole morning in which to read.

She wasn't quite comfortable, however. She was not a bit tired, and she had never felt better in her life—and yet she was staying away from church.

But the book she had opened was a volume of Dickens' Christmas stories, and in three minutes she was carried away from the little town of Fairfax to the heart of old London, and from the warmth of spring to the bitterness of winter, as she listened with Toby Veck to the music of the chimes that rang from the belfry tower.

It seemed only a part of the tale, therefore, when the bell of Fairfax church pealed out the first warning of the Sunday service to all the countryside.

"Ding dong, din, all come in, all come in," the bell had said to Anne since childhood, and now it called her, until it silenced the crashing voices of the bells of old London, and she had to listen.

She laid down her book. "The church bell is ringing," she said to Judy.

"I hear it," said Judy, indifferently.

Anne stood up—with a sidelong glance at the enchanting vision in the mirror. "I think I ought to go," she hesitated.

Judy turned to look at her.

"Don't be so good, Anne," she said, with a teasing laugh; "be wicked like I am, just for one day—"

"You are not wicked."

"Well, I haven't a proper sense of duty."

"You have too. You just like to say such things, Judy, just to shock people."

Which shows that in two days, wise little Anne had found Judy out!

"Well, I'm not going to church, anyhow," and Judy settled back and closed her eyes.

Anne's book was open at the fascinating place where Toby Veck eats his dinner on the church steps; the deep rose-cushioned chair opened its wide arms in comfortable invitation. It was the little girl's first taste of the temptation of ease,—

and she yielded. But as she picked up her book again, she soothed her conscience with the righteous resolve—"I will go to service this afternoon."

As she settled back, the girl reflected in the mirror looked at her.

"Your hair looks beautiful," said the reflection.

Anne dropped her eyes to her book.

Presently she raised them.

"If only the people in church could see," said the charming reflection.

Anne imagined the sensation she would make as she walked up the aisle. None of the girls in Fairfax or the country around had ever worn their hair puffed over their ears or tied with broad black ribbon. There would be a little flutter, and during church time the girls would look at nothing else, and it would be delightful to feel that for once she, little plain Anne Batcheller, was the center of attraction.

She dropped her book. "I think I will go, after all," she said virtuously, and Judy, not knowing her motive, looked at her with envy.

"You are a good little thing, Anne," she said, and at the praise Anne's face flamed.

She dressed hurriedly, in her one white dress, with a sigh for the becomingness of the blue kimona. When she was ready to tie on her old hat, she went to the mirror.

"It is because your hair is so pretty that you are going to church," said the reflection, accusingly.

"It is because of my conscience," defended Anne, but she did not dare to meet the eyes in the mirror, and she turned away quickly.

"You look awfully nice," Judy assured her, as Anne said "Good-by." "Take my blue parasol. It is on the parlor sofa. Go and be good for both of us, Annekins."

Anne ran down-stairs to the great dim room. There were four mirrors in the parlor, and each mirror seemed to say to the little girl as she passed, "It is because of your hair," and when she had picked up the pretty parasol, the mirrors said again, as she passed them going back, "It is because of your hair, oh, Anne, it is because of your hair that you are going to church!"

The hands of the big clock in the hall were on eleven as Anne opened the front door—and as she stepped out into the glare of sunshine, the church bell rang for the last time.

Anne loved the sweet old bell. Even when she had been ill, she had been able to hear just the end of its distant peal—like the ringing of a fairy chime, and when she was very little, the time she had the mumps, she had thought of it as being up in the clouds, calling the angels to worship.

She listened to it for a moment, standing perfectly still on the path, then she went back into the house, and laid the parasol carefully on the sofa. After that she ran quickly upstairs, untying her hat-strings as she went.

"What in the world are you doing?" asked Judy in amazement, as Anne pulled out hairpins, and took the big black bow from her looped-up hair.

"I was thinking too much about it," said Anne, soberly. "I shouldn't have heard a word of the sermon if I had worn my hair that way," and she went on braiding it into its customary tight and unbecoming pigtails.

"Well, of all things," ejaculated Judy, gazing at her spellbound.

But when Anne had gone, Judy stood up and watched her from the window. "What a queer little thing she is," she murmured, as the bobbing figure went up and down the village path, "what a queer little thing she is."

But somehow the actions of the queer girl distracted her mind so that she could not go back to her attitude of lazy indifference. She had thought Anne a little commonplace until now; but it had not been a commonplace thing, that changing from prettiness to plainness. She even wondered if Anne had not done a finer act than she could have done herself.

"She is a queer little thing," she said again, thoughtfully, and after a long pause, "but she is good—"

She went to her wardrobe and took out a white dress. Then she got out her hat and gloves and laid them on the bed. And then she sat and looked at them, and then she began to dress.

And so it came about that Fairfax church had that morning two sensations. In the first place Anne Batcheller came in late for the only time in her life, and in the second place, when the service was half over, a slender, distinguished maiden in a violet-wreathed white hat, slipped along the aisle, flashing a glance at Anne as she passed, and smiling at the delighted Judge as she entered the pew.

She fixed her eyes on the minister—and straightway forgot Anne and the Judge and Fairfax, for the minister was reading the 107th Psalm, and the words that fell on Judy's ears were pregnant with meaning to this daughter of a sailor—"They that go down to the sea in ships—"

Dr. Grennell was a plain man, a man of rugged exterior—but he was a man of spiritual power—and he knew his subject. His father had been a sea-captain, and back of that were generations of Newfoundland fishermen—men who went out in the glory of the morning to be lost in the mists of the evening—men who worked while women wept—men to whom this Psalm had been the song of hope—women to whom it had been the song of comforting.

To Judy the sea meant her father. It had taken him away, it would bring him back some day, and was not this man saying it, as he ended his sermon, "He bringeth them into their desired haven—"?

Dr. Grennell had never seen Judy, but he knew the tragedy in the Judge's life, and as she listened to him, Judy's face told him who she was.

She went straight up to him after church.

"I am Judy Jameson," she said, "and I want to tell you how much I liked the sermon."

The doctor looked down into her moved young face. "I am the son of a sailor," he said, "and I love the sea—"

"I love it—" she said, with a catch of her breath, "and it is not cruel—is it?"

"No—" he began. But with a man of his fiber the truth must out; "not always," he amended, and took her hands in his, "not always—"

"And men do come back," she said, eagerly; "the one you told about in your sermon—"

He saw the hope he had raised. "Yes, men do come back—but not always, Judy."

Her lip quivered. "Let me believe it," she pleaded, and in that moment, Judy's face foreshadowed the earnestness of the woman she was to be. "Let me believe that my father will come some day—"

"Indeed, I will," said the doctor, and there was a mist in his eyes as he clasped her hand, "and you must let me be your friend, Judith, as I was your father's."

"I shall be glad—" she said, simply, and then and there began a friendship that some day was to bring to Judy her greatest happiness.

That afternoon the Judge and Judy drove Anne home.

"It seems just like a dream," said Anne, as they came in sight of the little gray house, with Belinda chasing butterflies through the clover, and Becky Sharp on the lookout in the plumtree. "It seems just like a dream—the good times and all, since Friday, Judy."

"A good dream or a bad dream, Annekins?" asked Judy.

"Oh, a good one, a lovely dream, and you are the Princess in it, Judy," said the adoring Anne.

"Well, you are the good little fairy godmother," said Judy. "Isn't she good, grandfather?"

"Oh, I am not," said Anne, greatly embarrassed at this overwhelming praise, "I am not—"

"I never could have changed my hair," affirmed Judy.

"What's that?" asked the Judge.

"Oh, a little secret," said Judy, smiling. "Shall I tell him, Anne?"

"No, indeed," Anne got very red, "no, indeed, Judy Jameson."

There was a little pause, and then the Judge said:

"I am sorry the picnic was such a failure."

"Oh, but it wasn't," cried Judy, "it wasn't a failure."

Anne and the Judge stared at her. "Did you enjoy it, Judy?" they asked in one breath.

"Of course I did," said the calm young lady.

"But the rain," said the Judge.

"That was exciting."

"And your fainting—" said Anne.

"Just an episode," said Judy, wafting it away with a flirt of her finger-tips.

"And Amelia, and Nannie, and Tommy, did you like them?" asked Anne.

"Oh, Amelia is funny, and Nannie is clever, and Tommy is a curiosity. Oh, yes, I liked them," summed up Judy.

"And Launcelot—"

Judy smiled an inscrutable smile, as she pulled her hat low over her sparkling eyes.

"He's bossy," she began, slowly, "and we are sure to quarrel if we see much of each other—but he is interesting—and I think I shall like him, Anne."

And then Belinda and Becky discovered them, and made for their beloved mistress, and conversation on the picnic or any other topic was at an end.

CHAPTER IX

A BLUE MONDAY

There was a noisy scrambling in the vines outside of Anne's window early on Monday morning, and the little maid opened her eyes to see Belinda's white head peeping over the sill, and Belinda's white paws holding on like grim death to the ledge.

"You darling," cried Anne, sitting up, "come here," and Belinda with a plaintive mew made one last effort, pulled herself into the room, and flew to her mistress' arms.

"Where's Becky?" asked Anne, wondering why the tame crow did not follow, for in spite of their constant feuds, the two pets were inseparable.

Belinda blinked sagely, while from a shadowy corner of the room came a sepulchral croak.

"Are you there, Becky?" called Anne, peering into the darkness, and with a flap and a flutter, Becky swooped from the top of the bookcase, where she had been perched for a half-hour, waiting for Anne to wake.

Anne's bookcase was the one thing of value in the little house. It was of rich old mahogany, with diamond-shaped panes in its leaded doors, and behind the doors were books—not many of them, but very choice ones, culled from a fine library which had been sold when ruin came to Anne's grandfather and father one disastrous year.

It happened, therefore, that Anne had read much of poetry and history, and the lives of famous people, to say nothing of fairy-tales and legends, so that in the companionship of her books and pets, she had missed little in spite of her poverty and solitary life.

"How good it is to be at home," she said, as the sunlight, creeping around the room, shone on the green cover of a much-thumbed book of French fairy-tales, and then slanted off to touch the edge of a blue and gold Tennyson; "how good it is to be at home."

"How good it is to be at home," she said again, as followed by Belinda and Becky, she came, a half-hour later, into the sunlit kitchen, where the little grandmother, smiling and rosy, was pouring the steaming breakfast food into a blue bowl.

"I was afraid you might find it dull," said the little grandmother, as she kissed her, "after the good times at the Judge's."

"Oh, I did have such lovely times," sighed Anne, blissfully. She had sat up late in the moonlight the night before, telling her grandmother of them. "But they didn't make up for you and Becky and Belinda and the little gray house," and she hugged the little grandmother tightly while Belinda and Becky circled around them in great excitement, mingled with certain apprehensions for the waiting breakfast.

"But I do hate to start to school again," said Anne, when she finished breakfast, and had given Belinda a saucer of milk and Becky a generous piece of corn bread.

"Are the children going to speak their pieces this week?" asked Mrs. Batcheller, as Anne tied on her hat and went out into the garden to gather some roses for the teacher.

"Yes, on Saturday," said Anne; "it's going to be awfully nice. I have asked Launcelot and Judy to come to the entertainment, and they have promised to."

"I am going to be 'Cinderella' in the tableaux," she went on, as her grandmother brought out the tiny lunch-basket and handed it to her, "and Nannie and Amelia are to be the haughty sisters. We haven't found any boy yet for the prince. I wish Launcelot went to school."

"He knows all that Miss Mary could teach him now," said the little grandmother; "his father is preparing him for college, if they ever get money enough to send him there."

"Well, if Launcelot's violets sell as well next winter as they did this, he can go, 'specially if his mother keeps her boarders all summer. He told me so the other day, grandmother."

"But he would make a lovely prince," she sighed. "Judy is going to lend me a dress. She has a trunk full of fancy costumes."

"I hope you know your lessons," said the old lady, as Anne, escorted by her faithful pets, started off.

"Oh, I studied them on Friday, before Judy came—how long ago that seems—" and with a rapturous sigh in memory of her three happy days, and with a wave of her hand to the little grandmother, Anne went on her way.

Tommy Tolliver came to school that morning in a chastened spirit. He had been lectured by his father, and cried over by his mother, and in the darkness of the night he had resolved many things.

But it is not easy to preserve an attitude of humility when one becomes suddenly the center of adoring interest to twenty-five children in a district school. From the babies of the A, B, C, class to the big boys in algebra, Tommy's return was an exciting event, and he was received with acclaim.

Hence he boasted and swaggered for them as on Saturday he had boasted and swaggered for Judy's admiration.

"You ought to go," he was saying to a small boy, as Anne came up, but when he caught her reproachful eye on him, he backed down, "but not until you are a man, Jimmie," he temporized.

During the morning session he was a worry and an aggravation to Miss Mary. The little girls could look at nothing else, for had not Tommy been a sailor, and had he not had experiences which would set him apart from the commonplace boys of Fairfax? And the boys, a little jealous, perhaps, were yet burning with a desire to be the bosom friend of this bold, bad boy, while the luster of his daring lasted.

And so they were all restless and inattentive, until finally Miss Mary, who had a headache, lost patience.

"You are very noisy," she said, "and I am ashamed of you. I am going to put a list of words on the board, and I want you to copy them five times, while I take the little folks out into the yard for their recess. The rest of you don't deserve any, and will have to wait until noon."

That was the first piece of injustice to Anne. She had been as quiet as a mouse all the morning, and Miss Mary should have seen it and not have punished the innocent with the guilty. But Anne was a cheery little soul and never thought of questioning Miss Mary's mandates, and so she went on patiently writing with the rest.

Miss Mary stopped in the door long enough to issue an ultimatum.

"I shall put you on your honor," she said, "not to talk. And any one who disobeys will be punished."

And she went out.

For a little while there was perfect decorum. Then Tommy grew restless. Six weeks out of school had made sitting still almost impossible. He wiggled around in his seat, and began to whistle, "A Life on an Ocean Wave."

That was a signal for general disorder among the boys. Without speaking a word, and so preserving the letter of the rule, if not the spirit, they, with Tommy as leader, went through various pantomimic performances. They hitched up their trousers in seamanlike fashion, they pretended to row boats, they spit on their hands and hauled in imaginary ropes, and as a climax, Tommy danced a hornpipe on his toes.

And then Anne spoke right out—"Oh, Tommy, *don't*," she said, in an agony of fear lest Miss Mary should come in and catch him at it.

But Miss Mary did not come, and the little girls giggled and the boys capered, and Anne in despair went on writing her words.

When Miss Mary came back finally, with the little people trooping in a rosy row behind her, twenty-five virtuous heads were bent over twenty-five papers.

"Did any one speak while I was out?" asked the teacher.

A wave of horror swept over Anne. She had not meant to do it, but she had spoken, and to try to explain would be to condemn Tommy and the rest of the school.

"Did any one speak?" asked Miss Mary again.

Anne stood up, her face flaming.

"I—I—did—" she faltered.

"Oh, Anne—" said Miss Mary, while the girls and boys dropped their eyes for very shame. "Oh, Anne, why did you do it—"

"I just did it—" stammered Anne, who would rather have died than have blamed Tommy, and Nannie, and Amelia, and the rest of her friends.

"Well, then," said Miss Mary, firmly, "I'm sorry, but you will have to sit on the platform the rest of the morning, and I can't let you take part in the Saturday's entertainment. I must have order and I will have it."

And that was Miss Mary's second piece of injustice. But then she had a headache, and children on Monday mornings are troublesome.

For one hour Anne sat with her head held high and her fair little face flushed and burning. But she did not cry. And Tommy, bowed to the ground by his sense of guilt in the matter, did not dare to look at the patient, suffering martyr.

It was thus that Launcelot Bart, coming in just before twelve o'clock to see Tommy, found her.

As soon as he got Tommy outside of the schoolroom he collared him.

"What's the matter with Anne?" he demanded.

"She talked in school," said Tommy, doggedly.

"I don't believe it."

"Well, she did, anyhow."

"Whose fault was it?"

"Hers, I suppose."

"You don't suppose anything of the kind. Anne Batcheller never broke a rule in her life willingly, and you know it, Tommy Tolliver."

The children were coming out of the schoolroom in little groups of twos and threes—the girls discussing Anne's martyrdom sympathetically, the boys with hangdog self-consciousness.

Inside the room, Anne, released from her ordeal, had gone to her desk and was sitting there with her head up. Her face was white now, the little lunch-basket was open before her, but the cookie and the apple were untouched.

Launcelot looked in through the window.

"Poor little soul," he murmured.

And then Tommy blubbered.

"It was really my fault, Launcelot," he confessed.

"What!"

Tommy explained.

345

"And you let Anne bear it—you let Anne be punished—oh, you miserable—little—little—cur," said the indignant squire of dames, in a white heat.

"Aw, what could I do?" whimpered Tommy.

"Go in and tell Miss Mary," said Launcelot.

"Aw—Launcelot—"

"*Go in and tell Miss Mary!*"

Tommy went.

But Miss Mary did not wish to be bothered.

"I made a rule and Anne broke it," she said, when Tommy tried to straighten things out, "and that is all there is to it. Don't talk about it any more, Tommy," and she dismissed him peremptorily.

When Tommy told Launcelot the result of the interview, the big boy set his lips in a firm line, and started off down the dusty road.

He went straight to town and to Judy.

"Oh, oh," said Judy, when she had listened to his tale of woe, "what a mean old thing she is—I hate her—" and her dark eyes flashed.

"I don't think Miss Mary is mean," said Launcelot, "but the children *are* restless, and she isn't very strong, and when she feels badly she takes it out on the scholars."

"But to punish Anne," said Judy, and her voice trembled, "dear little Anne—"

"She might at least have listened to Tommy's explanation," said Launcelot.

After a pause he said: "I came to you because I thought you might go and see Anne after school. It would do her a lot of good. She will be all broken up."

"I will go to school and get her," cried Judy, eagerly. "Is it very far?"

"I am afraid you couldn't walk," said Launcelot, doubtfully.

"I'll drive over in the trap," said Judy. "Grandfather says I can use Vic whenever I want to."

"It was pretty mean of Miss Mary to pile it on, I must say," said Launcelot, as he rose to go. "She might have let Anne be in the entertainment."

"What?"

"She isn't going to let Anne be in it."

"Not be 'Cinderella'?" Judy's tone was ominous.

"No."

"Oh, oh, oh." Judy's hands were clenched fiercely. "I'll get even with her, Launcelot. I'll get even with that teacher yet."

Launcelot smiled at her vehemence.

"But you can't," he said.

"Can't I?" with a shrug of her shoulders.

"No."

"Wait," said Judy, and not another word could he get out of her on the subject.

The afternoon dragged along its interminable length, and Anne, with bursting head, thought that it would never end.

"Tick, tock," proclaimed the old school clock, as the hands crept slowly to one, to two, to three.

"In five minutes I can go," thought poor little Anne wildly, and just then the school-room door opened, and on the threshold appeared a self-contained young lady in pale violet gingham, and the young lady was asking for Anne Batcheller!

"Judy!" said Anne's heart, with a bound, but her lips were still.

Miss Mary had seen the Judge's grand-daughter at church the day before, and had been much impressed, and now when Judy asked sweetly if Anne could go, she gave immediate consent.

"Of course she may," she said. "Anne, you are dismissed."

But her eyes did not meet Anne's eyes as she said it, for Miss Mary's head was better, and she was beginning to wonder if she should not have investigated before she condemned Anne so harshly.

Twenty-four heads turned towards the window as Anne and Judy climbed into the fascinating trap with the fawn cloth cushions, and twenty-four pairs of lungs breathed sighs of envy, as Judy picked up the reins, and the two little girls drove away together in the sunshine.

CHAPTER X

MISTRESS MARY

No one ever knew how Judy managed to get the Judge's consent, but on Wednesday, when the children on their way home from school called at the post-office for the mail, they found small square envelopes addressed to themselves, and each envelope contained a card, and on the card was written an invitation to every child to be present at a lawn party to be given at Judge Jameson's on the following Saturday, from one until five o'clock.

But this was not all. For during the evening, rumors, started by the wily Launcelot, leaked out, that never in the history of Fairfax had there been such a party as the one to be given by Judge Jameson in honor of his grand-daughter, Judith, and her friend, Anne Batcheller.

"For it is as much Anne's party as Judy's," Launcelot stated, as one having authority.

After the first jubilation, however, the young people looked at each other with blank faces.

"It is the same afternoon as the school entertainment," wailed Amelia
Morrison.

"An' we've got to speak our pieces," said little Jimmie Jones.

But Nannie May cut the Gordian knot with her usual impetuosity.

"I am going to Judy's party," she declared, "and I am going to get mother to write a note to Miss Mary."

Many were the notes that went to Miss Mary that day. All sorts of excuses were given by the ambitious mothers, who would not have had their offspring miss the opportunity of seeing the inside of the most exclusive house in Fairfax for all the school entertainments in the world!

And Miss Mary!

She had invited the school board and a half-dozen pedagogues from neighboring districts. She had trained the children until they were letter perfect. She had drilled them in their physical exercises until they moved like machines, and now at the eleventh hour they were fluttering away from her like a flock of unruly birds, and she recognized at once that Judy had championed Anne's cause, and that in her she had an adversary to be feared.

In vain she expostulated with the mothers.

"Saturday isn't a regular school-day, you know, Miss Mary," said Mrs. Morrison, sitting down ponderously to argue the question with the teacher, "and of course the Judge couldn't know that it would interfere with your plans."

Miss Mary was convinced that the Judge *did* know, but she didn't quite dare to argue the question with him. She was conscious that she had been over-severe, and that the Judge, who believed in justice first, last, and all the time, would not uphold her.

And so the plans for the party went on.

"We will have games," said Judy, "and we won't have anything old like
'Cinderella.' Has anybody got an idea?"

She and Anne and Launcelot were in the Judge's garden, and it was Thursday evening, and there wasn't a great deal of time to get ready for Saturday's festivities.

"We might have some one read poems, and have living pictures to illustrate them," suggested Anne.

"What poems?" asked Judy, not quite sure that she liked the idea.

"There are some lovely things in Tennyson," said the little girl; "there's the Sleeping Beauty for one. You could be the Beauty, Judy, and Launcelot could be the prince—it would be just lovely—we could have little Jimmie Jones for the page, and Nannie and Amelia for ladies-in-waiting, and you could be asleep on the couch, while some one read:

"Year after year unto her feet,
She lying on her couch alone,
Across the purple coverlet,
The maiden's jet-black hair has grown."

Anne quoted with ease, for the little blue and gold volume in her bookcase had yielded up its treasures to her, and she knew the loved verses better than she knew her "Mother Goose."

"Oh," Judy's eyes were alight, "how lovely that is—I never read that,
Anne."

"Well, you hate books, you know," and Anne dimpled at her retort.

"I shouldn't hate that kind," and Judy resolved that she would know more about that princess.

"And we could have the arrival of the prince, and the awakening, and their departure:

"And o'er the hills and far away,
Beyond their utmost purple rim,
Beyond the night, across the day,
Through all the world she followed him,"

chanted Anne like one inspired.

Then she blushed and blushed as the astonished Launcelot and Judy praised her.

"I never dreamed that you knew so much poetry," cried Launcelot, seeing her in a new and more respectful light.

"Oh, it just sings itself," said Anne. "When you read it a few times you can't help reciting it."

"But I am not going to be the only one," said Judy. "What part will you take, Anne?"

"I don't know."

"Who's your favorite heroine in Tennyson, Anne?" asked Launcelot.

"Elaine."

"Then Elaine it shall be—"

"And you must be Lancelot," cried Anne, eagerly.

"But he *is* Launcelot," said puzzled Judy.

Anne and Launcelot laughed. "Well, you see," said Anne, "in the poem Elaine is in love with a knight named Lancelot, and he doesn't love her, and she dies, and when she is dead they put her on a barge and send her to the court of King Arthur, where Lancelot is one of the knights, and there is a letter to him in her hand, and a lily, and it's lovely," she finished breathlessly.

"We shall have a hard time to build a barge," said Launcelot, with a shake of his head.

"But we must have that scene, Launcelot," insisted Anne.

"Never mind," said Judy, who believed that all difficulties could be surmounted in this line, "we will find something. How many pictures shall we have for 'Elaine,' Anne?"

"We could have her giving him the 'red sleeve broider'd with pearls,' and then we could have him ill in the cave, and the scene in the garden, and at her window when he rides away, and then on the barge."

"We'll have to outline the story," said Launcelot; "the poem would be too long."

"But we could get in some of it, like the little song about Love and Death," said Anne, anxiously, for being too young to know tragedy or love, she was yet enamoured by that which was beyond her comprehension.

It took all the next day for them to get things ready, but everything went beautifully. Dr. Grennel promised to read the poems. Perkins, though depressed at the prospect of more undignified gayety, gave permission to use the dining-room for the tableaux, and the little grandmother promised to spend all of Saturday with the Judge and his sister, thus giving Anne a crowning delight.

And then, at the last minute, Anne spoiled everything!

"I can't bear to think of poor Miss Mary," she sobbed, late on Saturday morning, when Judy found her crouched up in the window-seat overlooking the garden.

"What?"

"I can't bear to think about poor Miss Mary," repeated Anne, dabbing her eyes with her wet handkerchief.

"What's the matter?" asked Launcelot, as Judy stood speechless. He was outside of the window, where he was helping Perkins place the tables and arrange the chairs in the garden.

Anne's woebegone face bobbed up over the window-sill.

"I can't bear to think of Miss Mary. All alone while we shall be having such a good time," she wailed. "I wish we could invite her."

Judy stamped her foot. "Anne Batcheller," she cried, tempestuously, "you are too good to live," and she went out of the room like a whirlwind.

She went straight to the Judge and Mrs. Batcheller, who were chatting together in the dimness and quiet of the great parlor.

"I sha'n't have anything to do with the lawn party, grandfather," she blazed, after she had told her story, "if that teacher is to be invited!"

But the Judge's eyes were dreamy. "Dear little tender-heart," he said.

"She teaches us a lesson of forgiveness," said Mrs. Batcheller, who with the Judge had deeply resented the treatment accorded Anne on that fateful Monday morning.

"Perhaps it would be best to ask Miss Mary," ventured the Judge.

"If she would come," said Mrs. Batcheller, doubtfully.

But Judy would not listen to reason or argument.

"Do you think we ought to back down now," she demanded of Launcelot, who, with Anne, had followed her to the parlor to talk things over.

"No," he said, slowly, "I don't think we ought to back down. But I guess we shall have to."

"Why?"

Launcelot's eyes went to the sobbing figure in the little grandmother's arms.

"We can't make her unhappy," he said in a low voice.

"Anne?"

"Yes."

"Everything is spoiled now," said Judy, chokingly, "everything. And I took such an interest. I think it's mean—mean—mean—"

Her voice grew very shrill, and her face was red. Mrs. Batcheller started to speak, but the Judge raised his hand to stop the untimely lecture.

"Wait!" he said.

Something in his kind old face reminded Judy suddenly of the story he had told her just a week before—of her grandmother and how she had conquered her temper.

With a strong effort she kept back the words of furious disappointment that she had intended to hurl at these weak-spirited people. Then she whisked out of the room and down the hall, and presently Launcelot, who had followed her, came back laughing but mystified.

"She is walking around the oval in the garden," he said, "as fast as she can go, and she won't stop."

The Judge slapped his hand on his knee. "By George," he said, with a sigh of relief, "she's done it!" But when Anne asked him to explain, he shook his head. "That's a secret between Judy and me," he said, "and I can't tell it," and over her head he smiled at Mrs. Batcheller, who knew the story, and had often laughed with Judy's grandmother over it.

Judy came in, finally, rosy and breathless.

"Oh, invite your Miss Mary if you want to," she panted, as she kissed the tear-streaked face. "But don't expect me to act too saint-like. I am not made of the same stuff that you are, Anne."

"You are a brick," Launcelot pronounced later, when they were alone in the dining-room superintending the putting up of the stage; "it was harder for you to give up than for Anne."

"No, I'm not a brick." said Judy, a little wearily, "I am just hateful. But I do try," and his praise meant much to her, and helped her afterwards.

Miss Mary sat alone and discouraged when the note of invitation was handed to her. She had sent letters to the school board and the other teachers, pleading "unavoidable postponement," and now she was correcting papers with an aching head.

"Dear Miss Mary,"—said Anne's little note,—"Please come to our party to-day. It is going to be very nice, and we are sorry we set the same day as the school entertainment, and we won't be happy if you are not here. Please forgive us, and come. Your affectionate scholar, Anne." And below the Judge had added, "I am anxious to supplement Anne's invitation and apology and to say with her, 'Please forgive us and come.'"

"I won't go," said Miss Mary at first, bitterly.

But when she had read the little letter again, she changed her mind.

"She is a dear child," she said.

And she washed her face and combed her hair, and put on her best white dress and her new summer hat with the roses in it, and went out looking young and pretty and with her headache forgotten.

And when she arrived at the Judge's she was escorted to a seat of honor in the front row, with the Judge on one side, and the little grandmother on the other, and with the astonished children smiling welcomes to her as she went up the aisle.

CHAPTER XI

THE PRINCESS AND THE LILY MAID

As the children arrived they were shown at once into the great dining-room, where at one end a stage had been erected and a curtain hung, from behind which came the sounds of hammering and subdued directions, given in Launcelot's voice.

"Amelia Morrison and Nannie May are in it," explained Tommy who had yearned for an important part, but Judy had declared against him.

"You shouldn't have been asked at all," she said, witheringly, "if it hadn't been that Anne begged that you might. You acted dreadfully the other day. Anne wouldn't have been punished if you had spoken right out, Tommy, and had said that it was your fault."

"Aw—yes, she would, too," stammered Tommy.

"I never could stand a coward," was Judy's fling, and at that Tommy subsided.

Behind the scenes Anne, in an entrancing trailing gown of pale blue with pearls wound in her long fair braids was trying to get Jimmie Jones to shut his eyes without opening his mouth.

"But I always sleep with my mouth open," persisted Jimmie, who, in spite of his yellow curls and his page's costume of green satire was at heart just plain boy.

349

"Well, you shouldn't," scolded Anne, as she tripped over her train. "You will simply spoil the picture. Just see how nice Judy and Amelia and Nannie look."

On the couch lay Judy all in soft, shining, satiny white, her dark hair spreading over the pillow, and one hand under her cheek; and at each end, Nannie and Amelia, in rose color and in violet, blissfully happy, and, though their eyes were closed, wide awake to the charms of the situation.

"Now—ready," whispered Anne, as Dr. Grennell's fine voice rolled out the last lines of the "Prologue." "Now—" and the curtain went up on "The Sleeping Princess."

Jimmie's mouth flew open and Amelia smiled, but little cared the gaping audience for such trifles. Breathless they stared as one scene followed another. Launcelot was a Prince that set all the little girls' hearts a-flutter, as he knelt beside the couch, with a great bunch of dewy roses in his arms, which, in the next picture, lay all scattered over Judy, when she waked and gazed at him dreamily. Jimmie came out strongly at this point, with a prodigious yawn that almost broke him in two, and was so expressive of great weariness that little Bobbie Green, his bosom friend, was carried away by the realism of it, and asked in awe, "Did he really sleep a hundred years?" and was not quite brought back to earth by Tommy Tolliver's exclamation, "Why you saw him awake this morning, Bobbie, didn't you?"

The Prince and the Princess went away together at last; she with a long velvet cloak covering the whiteness of her gown, and a hat with white plumes, and he with a sword at his side, that made Tommy Tolliver turn green with envy.

Jimmie Jones came down and sat by Bobbie Green during the intermission, in which lemonade was passed and the pictures discussed.

Bobbie gazed upon him as one who has come from a strange country.

"Say, say," he whispered eagerly, "how could you sleep when we was makin' all that noise, Jimmie—clappin'?"

Jimmie took a long blissful gulp of lemonade, and then fished out the strawberry from the bottom of the glass. "Ho," he said, "that wasn't nothin'. It wasn't really me that was asleep, it was just my eyes," and Bobbie, though still hazy, accepted the explanation and fished for his strawberry in imitation of his distinguished friend and actor, Jimmie Jones!

Most of the children had read parts of "Elaine" at school, and they

"Oh-ed" and "Ah-ed" as the fair-haired heroine appeared.

Anne was very sweet, very appealing, as she went through the sad little scenes, and when at last she sat at the window. Dr. Grennell did not read Elaine's song, but Anne sang it, to Judy's accompaniment, played softly behind the scenes.

"Sweet is true love, tho' given in vain, in vain;
And sweet is death who puts an end to pain:
I know not which is sweeter, no, not I."

And all the little girls wept into their handkerchiefs, while the boys sniffed audibly.

"Bless their hearts," said Mrs. Batcheller to Miss Mary, "it's too bad to have them cry."

But the Judge, who was a keen observer of human nature, shook his head. "A little sadness now and then won't hurt them," he said. "It is the shadows that make us appreciate the sunshine, you know."

There was a long wait before the curtain was raised on the last picture in the poem: "The dead steer'd by the dumb."

The barge had been a problem, until Judy solved it by placing an ironing-board across two chairs, and draping the whole into the semblance of a boat-like bier.

Perkins, under protest, was pressed into service as the dumb boatman, and with a long beard of white cotton, and a cloak and hood of funereal black, he was a picturesque and pessimistic figure.

"It's so wobbly," said Anne, powdered with corn-starch to an interesting paleness and draped all in white. "It's so wobbly, Judy," and she shrieked softly, as she laid herself flat on the ironing-board.

"Steady," advised Launcelot, as he shifted her carefully to the center, "now for the lily and the letter, Judy," and he threw over the prostrate Anne a yellow silk shawl of Judy's which was to serve as cloth of gold.

"Now, Perkins," and Perkins climbed to the high stool, which had been set in an armchair and formed the bow of the boat.

"If I falls, I falls," said Perkins, classically, "and my blood be on your head, sir," and while Judy writhed in agonies of laughter, Launcelot turned off the lights and adjusted the great lantern, which was to throw on the barge the effect of moonlight, while all else was to be in shadow.

The illusion from the front was perfect. Even the green piano cover with its dots of white cotton foamed up around the barge like real waves.

"How lovely she is," whispered all the children, as Anne lay there so still and quiet, with her fair hair streaming over the blackness of the bier.

"I don't like it. I don't like it," whimpered Bobbie Green, whose imagination was a thing to be reckoned with. "I don't like it. Anne, oh, Anne—"

And Anne's tender heart could not withstand that cry of fear.

"I'm all right, darling," she said, right out, and then the tension was broken, and all the children laughed, with relief, as Elaine sat up smiling and waving her hand to them.

"Bobbie Shafto" came next and was a dig at Tommy.

Judy's great marine picture made the background, and on the shore little Mary Morrison bade little Jimmie Jones "Good-bye" with heartrending sobs. But this Bobbie Shafto never went to sea. As picture followed picture, he was shown pulling at a rowing machine, sailing toy ships in a tub, fishing in a pail, and digging for treasure in a tiny sand pile—and after each funny scene, the curtain would drop, and tiny Mary Morrison would come to the front and wail:

"*Tommy* Shafto's gone to sea,
 Silver buckles on his knee,
 He'll come back and marry me,
 Pretty *Tommy* Shafto!"

It brought down the house, but Tommy got very red and murmured in Bobbie's ear that "They might think it was funny, but *he* didn't," which Bobbie Green did not understand in the least.

"That's all," and Launcelot gave a sigh of relief, as Mary and Jimmie made their bows amid uproarious applause. He had been stage manager as well as actor, and he was tired.

"No, no," whispered Judy, as she came on the stage dressed as a fishermaid, and dragging a great net behind her. "No, no. Dr. Grennell is going to read 'Break, break, break.' I sha'n't need any change of scene. Just leave the big picture, and put this net and the shells around, and smooth out that sand to look like the beach."

She was making a rock out of two boxes covered with a gray mackintosh as she spoke. "Now, if you could just whistle like the wind," she said. "Do you think you could, Launcelot?"

"I'll try," and he did whistle, so effectively, that he did not get his breath for five minutes.

Judy had read the poem one day when she was helping Anne to plan the pictures, and it had, like all songs of the sea, sung itself into her heart.

Again the big picture with its stretch of sea made the background, and Judy sat on the rock looking at it. The plaid lining of her mackintosh showed, and the wind sounded wheezy, but the pathos in Judy's face, the tragedy in her eyes as the third verse was read:

"And the stately ships go on,
 To the haven under the hill,
 But oh, for the touch of a vanished hand,
 And the sound of a voice that is still!"

made the Judge wipe his eyes, and Mrs. Batcheller say hurriedly, "She should not have done it. She should not."

And behind the dropped curtain Judy was saying to Dr. Grennell, "I want to go back to the sea. I hate the country. I want to go back to the wind and waves. I can't stand it here."

But the doctor put his hand on her shoulder and looked down into her troubled face with grave eyes.

"Not now," he said, quietly, "not while your grandfather needs you, Judy."

Judy drew a long breath, then she put out her hand as if to make him a promise.

"No, not while grandfather needs me," she said, "not while he needs me, Doctor."

CHAPTER XII

LORDLY LAUNCELOT

The children of the town of Fairfax never forgot that afternoon at Judge Jameson's. For years they had peeped through the hedge at the fascinating Cupid of the Fountain, but never had one of them put foot in the old garden, with its mysterious nooks and formal paths, which lay in the shadow of the Great House.

But to-day with its gipsy band playing wild music, with its gaily decorated tables, its awe-inspiring Perkins,—who with his satellites offered food fit for the gods,—with its riot of spring color, it was beyond their wildest dreams.

Before they went home they all assembled again in the great dining-room from which the chairs had been taken, and on the polished floor every one, old and young, danced the Virginia Reel, the Judge leading with Miss Mary, and Mrs. Batcheller bringing up at the end of the line with Jimmie Jones.

"It was a success, wasn't it," said Launcelot, when the children had trooped away, and Anne and Mrs. Batcheller and the smiling Miss Mary had been driven home in the Judge's carriage.

"Yes," said Judy, abstractedly, watching the musicians, who were having their refreshments under the lilac bushes.

"What handsome faces they have," she said, "so dark and wild. And their lives are so free—grandfather says they just roam around from place to place, living in the woods and picking up a little money here and there. He says their camp is just outside, and when he was driving yesterday, he saw one of them playing and asked them if they wouldn't come here to-day."

When the gipsies had finished they rose and went down the path towards the gate. They were talking and laughing with a vivacious play of feature and a recklessness of gesture that proclaimed them the unconscious children of nature.

"How I wish I could go with them," said Judy, impulsively, as the young leader of the band took off his hat and waved them a debonair "good-bye." "How I wish I could go!"

But Launcelot shook his head. "It's all very romantic from the outside," he said, "but the women don't have a very good time. They tramp the dusty roads in summer and almost freeze in their open wagons in the winter, and they bear most of the burdens. Those men are handsome, all right, but some of them are brutes."

As he spoke the leader of the band came back up the path.

"Come to our camp, pretty lady," he said, flashing his dark eyes upon Judy, "and our queen will tell your fortune. For a piece of silver she will tell you the things that are past and the things that are to come."

"Oh, will she?" asked Judy, eagerly. "Will you be at the camp next

Saturday?"

"We will be there until you come," said the gipsy with a glance of admiration at her vivid face.

But Launcelot's hand was clenched at his side. He did not like that fellow's face or his manner, he told himself, and Judy should not go near that camp if he could help it.

"You don't want to have your fortune told, Judy," he said, a little roughly.

Judy's eyebrows went up in surprise. "I do," she said. "It's fun."

"It's silly," contended Launcelot, doggedly.

The gipsy's eyes flashed from one to the other.

"You will come," he urged, ignoring Launcelot, and addressing his question to Judy.

"Yes."

"On Saturday?"

"Yes."

"Good; we will welcome you, pretty lady." And with a defiant glance at the big angry boy, the dark Hungarian swung down the path, singing as he went.

"You are not going," said Launcelot, when the man was out of sight.

"I am."

"Then I shall tell the Judge."

"Telltale."

Launcelot stood up and glowered at her.

"Who do you think will go with you?"

"You." There was a laugh in Judy's eyes, as she made the impertinent answer.

"I won't."

"Not if I ask you?"

"Not under any circumstances. It isn't the place for you, Judy."

Then he sat down beside her. "Look here," he said, in a wheedling tone, "if I were really your big brother, I wouldn't let you go. Can't you let me order you around a little, just as if I were—?"

Judy caught her breath. Why would he use that tone? It always made her feel as if she wanted to give in—but she wouldn't.

"I am going," she said, slowly, although she did not look at him, "if I have to go alone."

"Then I shall tell the Judge."

"Oh," Judy's tone was cutting, "I always did hate boys."

For a moment Launcelot's face flamed, then most unexpectedly he laughed.

"You don't hate me, Judy," he said, "you know you don't."

"I do."

"No, you don't," he went on, and there was no anger in his voice, only good-natured tolerance that made Judy's temper seem very childish. "You are angry now. But you are not that kind of girl—"

"What kind of girl?"

"Changeable."

"Oh, I don't know."

But Launcelot insisted. "You are not changeable, Judy, and you know it."

And finally Judy gave in. "No, I'm not, and I don't hate you, but I hate to be told I can't do things."

"You will have to get used to it—" daringly.

"Oh—you needn't think *you* can order me around, Launcelot, in that lordly way—"

She faced him defiantly. Her eyes were glowing with excited feeling. She looked like a young duchess in her anger. After the pictures, she had twisted her hair on top of her head in shining coils, and the dress she wore was a quaint mull that had been her grandmother's, a thing of creamy folds and laces that swept the floor. Launcelot felt suddenly very crude and impertinent to be dictating to this very stately young lady. But her next remark made her a child again, and brought him confidence.

"I have always had my own way—and I shall do as I please."

Launcelot got up lazily. "All right," he said, and held out his hand, "good-bye. I promised mother that I wouldn't be late."

But Judy did not seem to see the hand. She leaned against one of the big pillars indifferently, and looked out over the garden, Launcelot waited a moment, and then his hand dropped.

"Oh, I suppose you and I will have to quarrel now and then," he said, "we are both so obstinate," and he smiled to himself as Judy frowned darkly at the word, "but I don't see any use in doing it now, when we have had such a nice day—"

With one of her quick changes of mood Judy beamed on him. "Oh, hasn't it been nice," she said. And then she held out her hand. "Good-bye," she smiled.

But as he went down the path she called after him.

"If you meet Tommy Tolliver, tell him I want to see him."

He stopped. "What do you want him for?" he asked, suddenly suspicious.

"I sha'n't tell you."

"You needn't think you can get him to take you to the gipsy camp," said Launcelot.

"He will take me if I ask him."

"No, he won't."

"Why not?"

"Because I shall tell him beforehand that if he takes you out there I shall thrash him within an inch of his life."

"What?" gasped Judy.

"I shall do it," said Launcelot, and as he swung down the path, Judy, looking after the straight, strong figure, knew that his threat was not an idle one.

And yet, after all, if it had not been for Launcelot, Judy would never have gone to the camp. She had debated the question and had decided that the game was not worth the candle. She had approached Tommy Tolliver, and his numerous excuses convinced her that Launcelot had been before her. She had hinted her wishes to Anne, only to be met by that virtuous maiden with "Oh, Judy, I should be afraid—they look so dark and wild—and besides we ought not to go—" She even suggested a drive to the camp to the Judge, but he had said: "It is not a place for you, my dear," as if that settled the question.

Then, too, she had other plans for Saturday, for Launcelot planned to drive his mother and Judy and Anne to Lake Limpid, and they were to take an early boat for a little resort where they were to meet some of Mrs. Bart's friends.

Judy stayed with Anne all night, so as to be as near the Barts as possible, for there was a drive of five miles, and the boat left at eight o'clock.

"Do get up, Judy," begged Anne, on Saturday morning, as she stood in front of her little mirror, her hair combed, her shoes polished, and her last bow tied.

But Judy dug her rumpled head deeper into the pillow.

"'If you're waking, call me early, call me early, mother, dear,'" she murmured, having improved her acquaintance with Tennyson during the week.

"Well, it isn't early," said Anne, sharply. "You will be late, Judy, and we must catch the boat."

Judy sat up rubbing her eyes. "Oh, it won't hurt Launcelot to wait a little. He thinks he can manage everybody—but he can't dictate to me, Anne. I am not as meek as you are."

"I'm not meek," flared Anne, whose usually sweet temper had been somewhat ruffled in her efforts to wake Judy. "But Launcelot is a very sensible boy."

"Oh, sensible," groaned Judy. "I *hate* sensible people."

"What kind of people do you like?" demanded Anne, indignantly.

"Unsensible ones?"

"Yes. Dashing people and lively people and funny people—and—and—romantic people—but sensible people, oh, dear," and she buried her head again in the pillow.

"Judy, *get up*."

"I'll be ready in time."

"No, you won't. And breakfast is ready. Judy, get up."

A gentle snore was the only answer.

"Oh," and Anne flung herself out of the room, "if you are late, Judy Jameson, I can't help it."

She went down-stairs and ate her breakfast. But no sign of Judy.

"Judee—ee!" she called up the stairway, and "Judee—ee!" she called again from the garden, where, with Belinda and Becky, she stood awaiting the arrival of the carriage.

"Judith, my dear," expostulated the little grandmother, climbing the stairway slowly, "Judith, my dear, you really must hurry. You will have to go without any breakfast—I—"

She opened the door of the little bedroom and stopped short.

The bedclothes had been thrown over the foot-board, the pillows were on the floor, Judy's clothes were gone, and the room was empty!

CHAPTER XIII

A FORTUNE AND A FRIGHT

"She is hiding," said Anne.

But though they hunted and called, not a sign of the missing girl could they find.

When Launcelot came, Anne was almost in tears.

"She must be here somewhere," she said. "It's too bad. We shall be late."

"No, we won't," said Launcelot, who had listened without a word to the tale of Judy's shortcomings and final disappearance. "We will not be late, Anne, for if Judy doesn't come in just three minutes, we will go without her."

"Oh, no, no, no," protested Anne, all her grievances against Judy forgotten in the face of such a calamity. "We can't leave her behind."

"She will leave herself behind," said Launcelot, "for mother can't miss the boat. She has promised her friends that she will meet them."

"But my dear," protested gentle Mrs. Bart, "we can surely wait until the last minute. Judy only intends it as a joke, and it is too bad to leave her."

But Launcelot was in an explosive mood. The morning had been a trying one for him. He had hurried through a half-day's work in an hour and a half, he had eaten hardly any breakfast for fear he should keep the girls waiting, and now—to be treated like this!

"We can't wait any longer," he said, looking at his watch. "I am sorry, Anne, but we shall just have to leave Judy behind."

Again Anne started to protest, but the little grandmother shook her head. "Judy deserves it," she said. "She is too old to be so childish."

"Maybe she is waiting down the road somewhere," said Anne, hopefully.

"I think she is trying to fool us."

But Judy was not waiting down the road. She was in the orchard behind the plum-tree.

"It won't hurt Launcelot to wait," she had, thought as she hid herself,

"I will make him think I am not going—"

But she had not dreamed that they would go without her, and when she saw Anne climb in and the carriage start off, she ran forward wildly.

"Wait," she called, "wait for me."

But the carriage whirled on in a cloud of dust, and her voice echoed on the empty air.

By the time Judy reached the house Mrs. Batcheller had gone in, and so the little girl ran down the road unseen. "Perhaps they will stop for me," she thought, and her eyes were strained after the flying vehicle.

But it did not stop, and at last warm and tired Judy dropped down by the roadside, a forlorn figure.

"I didn't think they would leave me," she thought disconsolately.

After a while she got up and started towards the house. She dreaded to face Mrs. Batcheller, however, and she sat down again to decide upon a plan for spending the day.

She would not stay in the little gray cottage, that was a sure thing, and to go back to the Judge's meant a dull day by herself.

As she mused, a cheery whistle sounded down the road. "A Life on the Ocean Wave" was the tune and Judy started to her feet.

"Oh, Tommy Tolliver, Tommy Tolliver," she called, "come here."

Tommy rounded the curve in the road and stared at her.

"Say, I thought you were going with Anne," he said. "They just passed me down the road."

"Did they?" asked Judy, indifferently. "Well, at the last minute I thought I wouldn't go."

"Well, you missed it," said Tommy, aggravatingly. "Lake Limpid's great—and Launcelot can sail a boat like anything."

"Oh, can he?" said Judy, faintly. She loved to sail, and Tommy's words brought before her a vision of the pleasure she had forfeited.

There was silence for several minutes, then Judy said:

"Tommy, do you know where the gipsies are camping?"

Tommy waved her away.

"I can't take you there," he said, "I have promised I won't."

"'Nobody asked you, sir, she said,'" Judy's tone was withering. "I asked you where it was."

"Oh."

"Well, tell me."

Tommy wriggled.

"Are you going there?"

"Perhaps."

"Well, you'd better not. Launcelot won't like it."

"Oh, Launcelot, Launcelot." Judy's voice was scornful. "I don't care what Launcelot likes, Tommy Tolliver."

"Oh, don't you?" cried Tommy, brightening. "Well, then—"

But he stopped suddenly. "No, I can't tell you," he said, miserably.

"Why not?"

"I can't.

"Oh, well, you needn't," said Judy. "But I can find out. And I'm going."

"You'd better not," warned Tommy, yet hoping she would do it.

"I'll go with you," he agreed, "if you will promise not to tell."

"I don't want you to go," asserted Judy. "I want you to tell me how to get there."

Tommy told her as well as he could.

"That doesn't seem very clear," said Judy, when he had finished. "But I guess I can find it—and Tommy"—she fixed him with a stern glance—"don't you tell any one where I am—not any one—or I sha'n't ever speak to you again—"

"All right," said Tommy. "And don't you let on to Launcelot that I told you which way to go."

"Good-bye," said Judy.

"Good-bye," said Tommy.

And off they started in different directions, feeling like a pair of conspirators.

For the first half-mile Judy enjoyed her walk. The sky was blue, and the air was soft, and there were violets on the banks and forget-me-nots in the field, and the orchards were pink with bloom.

There were birds everywhere, from the great black crows, strutting over the red hills of newly planted corn, to the tiny gray sparrows, that slipped through the dusty grass at the roadside.

And in spite of the fact that she had started on a forbidden quest, Judy was happy. For the first time since she had come to the Judge's she was alone and free—with no reckoning to come until evening.

She stepped along lightly, but after a while she went more slowly, and by the time she reached the thick piece of woodland where the gipsies were encamped, she was tired out. They were not far from the road, for she could hear the thrum of the guitars, and voices raised as if in a quarrel.

The voices were stilled as Judy's white-gowned figure appeared under the over-arching oaks.

The dark young leader, who had been at the Judge's, uttered something in a warning voice to a sullen young woman who lounged against a pile of bright-colored rugs, and with whom he had been having evidently a fierce argument. She wore a soiled, silken cap, loaded with gilt coins, and her dress was in tawdry reds and yellows, yet picturesque and becoming to her dark beauty. She stared insolently at Judy as the latter came forward, but the young leader was smiling and profuse in his welcome.

"You have come," he said, "and alone?"

Something in his tone made Judy draw away from him.

"Yes," she said, and then, peremptorily, "I want my fortune told."

"I will speak to the queen," he said, and left her, with another of his flashing smiles.

The camp life as Judy looked upon it presented an alluring picture to one of her romantic turn of mind. Back in the darkness and dimness of a cave-like opening in the rocks, an old woman bent over a charcoal brazier. Her hair, gray and grizzled, fell over a yellow face that, lighted by the blue flames, took on a hag-like aspect. Her skinny hands moved as if in incantations, and Judy shivered with the mystery of it until the strong and unmistakable odor of beef and onion stew rose on the air and relieved her mind as to the nature of the brew which might have been of "wool of bat and tongue of dog" for all she knew to the contrary.

A group of swarthy men lounged under the trees and down by the stream a half-dozen children played with a half-dozen dogs. The children were fat and rosy, and the curs lean and cadaverous, and the dozen of them had stared at Judy as she came into the camp in animal-like curiosity, and then had gone on with their playing.

From one of the two big wagons drawn up near the road came the wailing of an infant, and in the other a woman, half-hidden by the curtain, sat weaving a bright-colored basket.

"Do you all work at basket weaving?" Judy asked the silent girl on the rugs.

"I do not work," was the answer. Then she tossed her head, defiantly.

"I will not work. They cannot make me."

She started to say more, but she stopped as the dark young leader came back.

He had spoken to the old woman who presided at the fire, and Judy saw her wipe her hands and make for a dilapidated tent under an oak.

It was to this tent that she was directed, and when she was once within and her eyes had grown accustomed to the darkness, she saw the old hag, looking more witch-like than ever, with her head tied up in a flaming yellow bandanna, and her shoulders wrapped in a great cloak covered with cabalistic signs.

"Cross my hand with silver," she murmured, and Judy took out the only piece of money she had with her—a silver quarter of a dollar.

The old woman looked at it with dissatisfaction. "That is not enough," she said. "I can tell you nothing for that."

"But I haven't any more," said Judy, in dismay. "I didn't expect to come, and it is all I have."

"Oh, well," grudgingly, "I will tell you a little."

She took Judy's hand in hers and studied the palm.

"You will live to be old," she said, monotonously. "There are double rings around your wrist. You will marry a man with wealth and with gray eyes."

"I don't want to know that—" said Judy, impatiently, to whom such matters were as yet unimportant. "Tell me about—about—other things."

"Hush," said the gipsy, "I must say, what I must say. You will go on a long journey. It will be on the sea. You will look for one who is lost. You are a child of the sea—" She flung Judy's hand away from her. "That is all," she said, heavily, "I can tell you no more without more money."

"Oh, oh," cried Judy, breathlessly, "how did you know it. How did you know that I was a child of the sea—"

"What I tell, I know," crooned the old woman, theatrically. "I can tell nothing without silver."

"But I haven't any more money," cried poor Judy.

"But a ring, a pin, they will do as well,'" the old woman looked at her greedily.

"I don't wear jewelry," said Judy, "I don't care for it."

"A chain, a charm, then," urged the old woman, whose eagle eyes had caught the outline of something that glittered beneath the thin lace collar of Judy's gown.

"I have nothing."

"There, there,—what have you there?" and the yellow finger tapped
Judy's throat.

Judy drew back with a little shudder, and shook her head as she showed the thin gold chain with a pearl clasp on the end of which was a quaint silver coin.

"I couldn't let you have this," she said. "My mother always wore it. It is a Spanish coin. My father found two of them on the beach near our home, and he gave mother one, and he kept the other—they are just alike. Oh, no, I couldn't give you that—"

"I will tell you many things—about one who has gone away," tempted the old woman.

For a moment Judy wavered. "Oh, I can't," she decided. "I can't let you have this."

The old woman got up. "Then go," she said roughly.

All at once there came over Judy a feeling of fear. She turned quickly and saw the young leader in the door behind her.

There was something sinister in his looks, and between the two she felt trapped.

"Let me out," she panted. "Let me out."

With a smile, the man in the door drew aside, and she stepped out into the daylight. As she did so, he whispered to the old woman, "What did you get?"

"Nothing. But the girl has on a chain with a pearl in it that would buy us food for a year."

"Oh!"

He followed Judy quickly.

"Stay, and we will play for you," he urged.

But her nerves were shaken.

"No, no," she said, hurriedly, "I must go home."

"You must stay until we play," he insisted, and called the men together, and Judy, still trembling from the moment of dread in the dark tent, sank down once more beside the sullen girl on the rugs.

But the leader called the girl away for a moment, and when she came back she sat closer to Judy than before, and her hand was busy with the fastening of the chain at the back—but so lightly, so deftly, that Judy sat unconscious.

And in the intervals of the music the girl laughed and chatted, telling

Judy of the life on the road, of anything to hold her attention.

"You would look like one of us," she said, "if you wore one of these," and she threw across Judy's shoulders a scarf of red silk.

"I believe I am half gipsy," said Judy, trying to be agreeable, but shrinking with a feeling of repulsion from the untidy creature so near her.

The girl drew away the scarf with a loud laugh and a triumphant nod and a wink to the leader, and presently the music stopped.

"I must go," said Judy, more and more in dread of these strange people.

Once more the old woman bent over the blue flames; but the children had gone deeper into the wood, and the place was silent except for the occasional guttural remark of one of the men, or a wail from the baby in the wagon.

"I must go," she said again, and started off.

But when she reached the road, the young leader caught up with her.

"You are beautiful," he said, when he was beyond the hearing of the others.

Judy hurried on in silence, but he kept by her side. "You are beautiful," he said again, and laid his hand on her arm.

Then Judy whirled around on him. "Don't speak to me that way again," she said, imperiously. "I may be alone and helpless, and I know now that I was very foolish to come. But my grandfather is a Judge. If anything happens to me, he will call you to account. Go back to the camp. Go back and let me alone."

The man stopped short and gazed at her.

"You are brave," he said, in a more respectful tone.

"None of my family have ever been cowards," said Judy, who was herself again. "I am not afraid of you."

His bold eyes dropped before the fearlessness in hers.

"Good-bye," he said, humbly, and when he reached the edge of the camp he turned and looked after her, and there was a shadow on his swarthy face.

The girl on the pile of rugs called him.

"I got it," she said.

"Give it to me," he ordered, roughly. But she held the necklace away from him with a teasing laugh. "It is mine, it is mine," she cried, then shrieked, as he wrenched it out of her hand, twisting her wrist cruelly.

Judy, alone once more and with her courage all gone, so that she was so weak that she could hardly stand, ran on and on, blindly. She dared not go back the way she had come for fear of meeting again some of the hated band.

"I will keep ahead," she thought. "There must be a house somewhere, and I can get them to drive me home."

But though she walked on and on, no house appeared. She was faint with fatigue and hunger, and at last, as she came to the end of a road and found herself stranded in a great pasture, a sob caught in her throat.

She sat down on a rock and looked around. There seemed to be nothing in sight but rocks and scrubby bushes, and already twilight was descending over the land.

"I believe I am lost," she owned at last, "and if some one doesn't find me pretty soon, I shall have to stay out all night."

CHAPTER XIV

A PRECIOUS PUSSY CAT

The moon was out and the stars when Judy discovered a flock of sheep in the middle of the great pasture.

They were gathered together in a close woolly bunch as she came upon them, and they turned to her their mild white faces, but did not get up from the ground. It was nice to be near something alive, even if it was only such meek, silly creatures, and Judy sat down on a stone near them.

"I will stay here," she decided. "I simply cannot walk another step."

It was very lonely and she was very frightened. The moon lighted the world with a white light, but the shadows were black under the trees; somewhere in the distance a whippoorwill uttered a plaintive note, and from the gloomy woods beyond came the mournful hoot of an owl.

Judy slipped down to the softer grass, and resting her head on her arm gazed up at the sky, and gradually her fear went from her in the silence of the perfect night. A line marked in one of her father's books came to her:

"God's in his heaven
All's right with the world."

Judy did not know that Browning had said that—she didn't care who had said it, but it comforted her. If everything had seemed to go wrong in her own little world, it was because she had made it wrong. Here under the wonderful sky was peace, and if she was afraid and out of harmony it was her own fault.

"If I hadn't gone where I ought not to have been, nothing would have happened," was her rather mixed, if perfectly correct, summing up.

The little lambs bleated now and then:

"Maa-a-a, Maa-aa-a."

And the old ewes responded comfortingly,

"Baa-aa—" which Judy interpreted as meaning, "I am here, little one, don't be afraid."

"I won't be afraid either, you dear old thing," said Judy to the motherly creature near her, who had turned upon her now and then inquiring gentle eyes. "I won't be afraid, and I am going to sleep."

She did go to sleep, and when she waked, the world was dark. The moon had sailed away like a golden boat, and the stars seemed very far off.

Judy sat up and shivered. A cool wind had risen, but that was not what had roused her.

She had heard something!

Something that just at the right of the flock of sheep moved silently, something blacker than the darkness that enveloped it!

She thought of wild animals, of tramps, of everything natural that might invade a pasture; then as a sepulchral cry broke once more upon the air, she remembered all the tales she had ever heard of Things that visited one in the night.

"Judy Jameson, you know you don't believe in ghosts," she tried to reassure herself, "you know you don't, Judy Jameson," but all the same her heart went "thumpety-thump."

She cowered back against the rock as a white figure appeared beside the black one, and the two bore down upon her.

There was a sudden bewildering chorus:

"Caw—caw—caw—"

"Purr—rr—meow—"

And then Judy screamed, joyfully, "Oh, Belinda, Belinda, you precious pussy cat," and in her relief she hugged the great white animal, as if she were not the same girl who, not many days before, had said, "I hate cats."

Becky walked around in a circle and inspected Judy.

"So it was you, Becky, was it?" asked Judy, "that I saw first? But what made you look so tall?"

She went to the place where she had first seen the apparition, and found the slender stump of a tree, on top of which Becky had been perched.

"What are you doing here, so far from home, Belinda," asked Judy, as she sat down and took the purring, gentle creature in her lap.

But Belinda could not talk, although she patted Judy's hand with her paw and curled down with her head in the crook of Judy's arm.

"My, it's good to have you here," said Judy, "but I wonder how it happened."

She gathered the big cat close to her, grateful for the warmth of the soft body, and with Becky perched up on a rock behind, she sat very still, comforted by the sound of Belinda's sleepy song, and by Becky's sentinel-like watchfulness.

It was in the black darkness that precedes the dawn that she was roused by a lantern flashing across her eyes.

"Grandfather," she said, sleepily, as a haggard old face bent above her. "Grandfather."

"Judy," he said, with a break in his voice.

Wide-awake now, she saw that his hands trembled so that he had to set the lantern down.

"Oh," she said, remorsefully, as she sat up, "how tired you look, grandfather."

"We have hunted for you all night," he said, and the dim rays from the lantern showed the droop of his figure and the lines in his face.

"Oh, grandfather," she said again, and clung to him, sobbing softly.

"Hush," he said, holding her close. "Hush, Judy. You are all right now."

"Oh, I am all right," she sobbed, despairingly, "but it is you, grandfather, you are all tired out, and just because I was such—such—a silly goose—"

"Never mind, never mind," said the Judge, hastily, "I have found you now."

"I am not worth finding," said Judy, miserably, "I am not, grandfather."

But the Judge laughed at that, and smoothed her hair away from her forehead with a loving touch. "You are always my dear little girl," he assured her, "whatever you do—you know that, don't you?"

"Yes," she whispered, and laid her face against his sleeve.

"Now we will go back," he said presently, and with Belinda and Becky in close attendance, they went up the hill together. At the top Judy gave a cry of astonishment, for right in front of her, on the other side of the hill, was the little gray house, ablaze with light.

"And I have been right back of it all night. If I had just walked a few steps farther," exclaimed Judy. "I must have gone in a circle, and I thought I was miles from here—"

As they came to the door the little grandmother met them, and Anne, and in the background Tommy Tolliver.

"We didn't know you were lost," explained Anne as she received the returned wanderer in her arms, "until we got back from Lake Limpid. Grandmother thought you had joined us down the road, and we thought you had stayed at home, and the Judge, of course, thought you were with me, and so none of us worried until we came back to-night and found you had been gone all day."

"And then Tommy told us that you had gone to the gipsy camp," went on

Anne.

At Judy's reproachful glance Tommy burst out:

"I couldn't help telling, Judy. Launcelot made me."

"I should say I did," said a voice from the doorway, and Launcelot came in with Dr. Grennell. "I was sure he knew something about it."

Judy greeted them from the big rocking chair—where she sat big-eyed and weary, but a most interesting spectacle.

"Launcelot went to the camp and found that the gipsies had gone, so we knew you couldn't have seen them—" began the Judge, and at that Judy interrupted him.

"But I *did* see them, grandfather," she said, "I went to the camp."

"And were they there?" asked Launcelot

"Yes."

"Were they packing while you were there?"

"No."

"I wonder what made them leave so suddenly," and Launcelot and the

Judge and Dr. Grennell looked at each other.

"Did you give them anything, Judy?" asked the Judge.

"Nothing but twenty-five cents. They were horrid, and the old woman wanted me to give my chain and Spanish coin. She knew an awful lot and I was crazy to hear the rest of my fortune, but I couldn't give away my coin."

"What coin, Judy?" asked Tommy, curiously.

"This one—" Judy put her hand to her neck, then she screamed:

"It's gone, grandfather. Launcelot, it's gone."

"What?" They all bent forward in excitement.

"I thought so," said the Judge, settling back in his chair, "when she said she had seen them, and then they disappeared before we could get to them. I thought they had been up to something."

"It was my chain with the pearl in it," said Judy, "the one you gave mother."

"Yes, and the rascals knew that the pearl was worth more than their whole outfit."

Launcelot picked up his hat. "I'm going to get it for you," he said, "they can't play any tricks like that."

"I'll go with you," said Dr. Grennell, "you may need an older man to help you. I think we can catch them with good horses."

He bent over Judy before he went out. "I wish you had come to me to have your fortune told," he said, "I could have told you more than that old hag."

"How?" asked Judy, puzzled.

"I should have told you that life is what we make it. And your fortune will be good or bad as you live it. It will not be a gipsy queen but Judy Jameson who shall decide the final issue."

"But, doctor, she knew that I loved the sea, and—and—that I had lost some one that I loved—"

"Oh, Judy," Launcelot's tone was impatient, "didn't you tell that fellow that you were coming, and didn't they have lots of time to find out about you."

"I didn't think of that." said Judy meekly.

But as he went out of the door, she had a little flash of temper.

"If you had waited for me this morning, I shouldn't have gone to the camp."

"If you had been ready, I shouldn't have left you," was Launcelot's reply, as his quiet eyes met Judy's stormy ones.

"Oh," she said, helplessly, and turned her gaze away, feeling that, as usual, he had the best of it.

And at that he whispered, "But I didn't have a good time, Judy—we—we missed—you—" and he followed Dr. Grennell.

"And now," said the little grandmother, "every one go home, and let me put this naughty girl to bed," but she smiled at Judy as she said it, and the tired little maid put her arms around her, and buried her face in the motherly bosom, and shook in a sudden chill.

"I am afraid she is going to be ill," said the Judge, anxiously, but the little grandmother tried to cheer him.

"She will be all right when she is rested," she said, with a confidence she did not really feel.

But when Anne was fast asleep, and Judy lay awake, tossing restlessly in the gray light of the dawn, the little grandmother came in, in a flannel wrapper, with her curls tucked away under a hand-made lace nightcap.

"Can't you sleep, dearie?" she whispered, as she sat down beside the bed.

"No. I think, and think, and think—about grandfather, and what a worry I am—" and Judy gave a great sigh.

"He has so many cares." The little grandmother's tone was gentle but it carried reproof, and Judy sat up and looked at her with troubled eyes.

"But I can't help my nature," she cried, tempestuously. "I can't bear to do things like other people, and when I get restless it seems as if I must go, and when I am angry I just have to say things—"

But the little grandmother shook her head. "You don't have to be anything you don't want to be, Judy," she said.

"But it seems so easy for Anne to be good," pursued Judy, "and so hard to me."

"It isn't always easy for Anne," said the little grandmother.

"Isn't it?" with astonishment.

"No, indeed. Anne has fought out many little fights of temper and wilfulness right here in this little room—she is a dear child."

"Indeed she is," agreed Judy, glancing at the serene face on the pillow.

"But Anne has learned to think for others. That is the secret, dearie. Think of your grandfather, think of your friends, and it will be wonderful how little time you will have to think of Judy Jameson."

"If I had my mother." Judy's lip quivered.

The little grandmother laid her old cheek against the flushed one.

"Dear heart," she said, "I can't take her place, but if you will try to talk to me as Anne does, maybe I can help—"

"I will," said Judy, and kissed her; but when the little grandmother had gone away, Judy could not sleep, and finally she got up and put on her red dressing-gown and sat by the window and looked out upon the waking world.

The robins were up and out on the dewy lawn, safe for once from Belinda, who was curled up sound asleep on the foot of Anne's bed.

Becky with her head under her wing was on top of the little bookcase, and the house was very quiet.

Suddenly through the mists of the morning Judy saw a carriage coming down the road.

It stopped at the gate and Launcelot leaped out.

Judy spoke to him from the window. "Hush," she said, "every one is asleep. I will come down."

As she met him at the lower door, he swung something bright and shining in front of her eyes.

"We found it," he whispered, excitedly, as Judy took her chain with a cry of delight. "We came across the gipsies on the Upper Fairfax road. The man tried to bluff it out, but the girl gave him away. While he was talking to Dr. Grennell she told me that he had it. I think she was mad at him about something, but she said he would kill her if he knew she told. So I just went on about the Judge and how he intended to put the police on the case if we didn't bring back the chain, and that he would be willing to hush it up if we got it, and so he handed it out—said it had been found on the ground after you left."

"Where is Dr. Grennell?" asked Judy.

"I dropped him at the manse," said Launcelot, "but I couldn't wait to bring this to you. I thought you would want to know about it."

"I couldn't sleep," explained Judy, "I was so afraid I had lost it."

"It's a funny coin, isn't it," said Launcelot. "Dr. Grennell knows a lot about such things, and he says it is a very old one."

"Yes," she told him. "Father found two of them on the beach in front of our house, 'The Breakers.' There have been others found on the Maryland coast near it, and they say that a Spanish vessel was shipwrecked off there years ago, and that now and then some of the money washes in. The fishermen along the shore dig holes in the sand, and occasionally they find one of these."

"Well, you had better leave it at home the next time you go on a wild goose chase."

"There won't be any next time," said Judy, with a sober face.

Launcelot looked up from the coin with a quick smile, which faded as she gave a hoarse little cough.

"Go into the house, child," he ordered, "you will take cold out here—"

"Oh," in that moment Judy was herself again, tempestuous, defiant, "don't be so bossy, Launcelot."

"Go in," he said again, but she threw up her head and lingered.

"What a beautiful morning it is," she said. "Look, Launcelot, the sun, it is like a ball of gold through the mist."

360

But Launcelot was looking at her—at the melancholy little figure in the trailing red gown, with the dark hair braided down on each side of the white face, and hanging in a long braid at the back.

"Go in," he said, for the third time, peremptorily. "You are tired to death, and you will be sick—"

CHAPTER XV

THE SPANISH COINS

Three weeks after Judy's exciting experience at the gipsy camp, an interesting party of travellers were gathered on the platform at Fairfax station.

There was a stately old man, imposing in spite of a tweed cap and sack coat. By his side stood a slender girl in gray, who coughed now and then, and near them, perched on a brand-new trunk, which bore the initials "A. B." was a small maiden, resplendent in a modish blue serge, a scarlet reefer, a stiff sailor hat of unquestionable up-to-dateness, and tan shoes!

And the resplendent maiden was Anne!

"You must let her go to the seashore with us," the Judge had said to Mrs. Batcheller. "Judy hasn't been well since she took that heavy cold the night she stayed out in the pasture—and I know the child pines for the sea, although she doesn't say a word. And I don't want her separated from Anne. She needs young company."

The little grandmother consented reluctantly. She was very proud, and although for years the Judge had tried to do something substantial to help his old friend in her poverty, he had so far been unsuccessful in breaking down the barrier of independence which she had set up.

One promise he had wrung from her, however, that when Anne was old enough, he was to send her away to school, where she would be fitted to take her place worthily in a long line of cultured people. This he had demanded and obtained by virtue of his friendship for her father and grandfather, and for the "sake of Auld Lang Syne."

"But Anne's things will do very well," said Mrs. Batcheller, when the Judge tried tactfully to suggest that he be allowed to send Anne's order with Judy's.

"No, they won't," the Judge had insisted, bluntly, "Judy's old home at The Breakers is somewhat isolated, but there will be trips that the girls will take together, and friends will call, and I can't have little Anne unhappy because she hasn't a pretty gown to wear."

"Oh, well," sighed Mrs. Batcheller, "if you look at it that way. Now in my day, if a girl had a sweet temper and nice manners, that was all that was necessary."

"Hum—" mused the Judge. "But I remember somebody in a little white gown with green sprigs, and a hat with pink roses under the brim."

"Judith and I had them just alike," smiled the blushing little grandmother.

"And you looked like two sweet old-fashioned roses," said the old man, "and you knew it, too. The world hasn't changed so very much, or girl nature."

"Perhaps not," confessed the little grandmother, her eyes still bright with the memories of youthful vanities; "perhaps not, and you may have your way, Judge, only you mustn't spoil my little girl."

"She can't be spoiled," said the Judge promptly, and went away triumphant.

And so it came about that in the trunk on which Anne sat were five frocks—two white linen ones like Judy's; a soft gray for cool days, an organdie all strewn with little pink roses, and an enchanting pale blue mull for parties.

No wonder that Anne sat on that trunk!

It was a treasure casket of her dreams—and with the knowledge of what it contained, she did not envy Cinderella her godmother, nor Aladdin his lamp!

"Amelia and Nannie are coming to say 'good-bye,'" said Anne, as two figures appeared far up the road, "they'd better hurry."

"Tommy is coming, too," said Judy. "I wish I could take them all with me."

"Why not invite them all down to The Breakers," suggested the Judge, who was eager to do anything for this fragile, big-eyed granddaughter, who was creeping into his heart by gentle ways and loving consideration, so that he sometimes wondered if the old, tempestuous Judy were gone for ever.

"Not now," said Judy, thoughtfully. "I just want you and Anne for a while, but I should love to have them some time—and Launcelot, too."

"Can you?" she asked Launcelot, as he came out of the baggage room with their checks in his hand, followed by Perkins with the bags.

"Can I what?" he asked, standing before her with his hat in his hand, a shabby figure in shabby corduroy, but a gentleman from the crown of his well-brushed head to the soles of his shining boots.

"Will you come down to The Breakers sometime?—I am going to ask Amelia and Nannie and Tommy, and I want you, too—"

"Will I come? Well, I should say I would—" but suddenly his smile faded. "I am awfully afraid I can't, though. There is so much to do around our place, and father isn't well."

Now in spite of the affectionate dutifulness with which of late Judy treated her grandfather, she still showed her thorny side to Launcelot.

"Oh, well, of course, if you don't want to come"—she snapped, tartly, and went forward to meet the young people, who were hurrying up, Amelia puffing and out of breath, Nannie with her red curls flying, and Tommy laden with a parting gift of apples, an added burden for the martyred Perkins.

Far down the road the train whistled. Anne was surrounded by a little circle of sorrowing friends. Even Launcelot was in the group, and Judy and the Judge stood alone.

"How they love her," said Judy, with a little ache of envy in her heart.

"How she loves them," said the wise old Judge. "That is the secret, Judy."

Amelia had brought Anne a box of fudge, Nannie a handkerchief made by her own stubby and patient fingers, and Launcelot made her happy with a book of fairy-tales, worn as to cover, but with rich things within—a book of his that she had long coveted.

"By-by, little Anne," he said, with a brotherly pat on her shoulder. Then he shook hands with the Judge. "I hope you will have a fine time, sir," he said. Then as he and Judy stood together for a moment, he handed her something wrapped carefully in tissue-paper.

"These are for you," he said, a little awkwardly.

She unwound the paper and gave a little cry of delight.

"Violets, oh, Launcelot—how did you know I loved them?"

"Guessed it—you had them on your hat, and I liked that violet colored dress you wore."

"And they are so sweet and fragrant. Where could you get them this time of year?"

"In my little hothouse. I forced them for you."

But he did not tell her of the hours he had spent over them.

She was silent for a moment. "It was lovely of you," she said, at last, with a little flush and with a sweetness that she rarely revealed. "It was lovely of you—and I was so hateful just now."

She reached out her hand to him, and his grasp was hearty, reassuring.

"It wouldn't seem natural if you and I didn't fuss a little, would it, Judy?" and then the train pulled in.

"All aboard!" shouted the conductor.

Anne and Judy went through the Pullman, and came out on the observation platform.

"Tell little grandmother to take good care of Belinda and Becky," called Anne, whose heart yearned for her pets.

"And all of you come and see me," cried Judy, hoping that she might win some of the love that was extended to Anne.

"We will," they cried, "we will."

"We will," echoed Launcelot, with his eyes on the violets pinned on Judy's gray coat, "we will if we have to sit up nights to do it."

A flutter of handkerchiefs, a blur of gray coat and red one, a trail of blue smoke, and the train was gone, and life to those left in Fairfax seemed suddenly a monotonous blank. As Launcelot turned away from the station, he ran into Dr. Grennell, who was rushing breathlessly up the steps.

"Has the train gone?" panted the minister.

"Yes."

Dr. Grennell wiped his heated forehead.

"I am sorry for that," he said, "I wanted especially to see the Judge."

He had a letter in his hand, and he stood looking at it perplexedly.

"To tell the truth, Launcelot," he began slowly, "I have something strange to tell the Judge, and I didn't want him to get away before I saw him. It isn't a thing to write about—and oh, why did I miss that train—"

Launcelot waited while the minister stared wistfully down the shining track.

"Look here, Launcelot," he asked, suddenly, "do you remember that Spanish coin of Judy's?"

"Well, I should say I did," replied the boy.

"It's the strangest thing—the strangest thing—oh, I'm going to tell you all about it, and see if you can help me out. Is there any place that we can be quite alone? I want to read this letter to you."

"There isn't a soul in the waiting-room," said Lancelot, "we can go in there. You'd better run on without me, Tommy," he called, "the doctor wants me. You can catch up with the girls if you hurry," and Tommy, who had eyed the pair with curiosity, departed crestfallen.

"I received this letter this morning," explained Dr. Grennell, as they sat down in the stuffy little room. "Read it. It's from an old friend of mine in Newfoundland—a physician."

The letter opened with personal matters, but the paragraph that the minister pointed out to Lancelot read thus:

"We have had a rather unusual case here lately. You know how often we have men brought to the hospital who have been shipwrecked, and as a rule there is little that is interesting about them—most of them are the type of ordinary seamen. Our latest case, however, was entered by the captain of a sailing vessel, who reported that they had picked the man up from a raft. That he was delirious then, and had never been able to tell them who he was or whence he came. He is still very ill and unconscious, and there is not a paper about him of identification. He is a gentlemen—I am sure of that, for his broken sentences are uttered in perfect English, and his hands tell it, too. As I have said, there isn't a letter or a paper about him, but around his neck on a silver chain we found the coin which I enclose. I know your fancy for odd coins, and so I send it, thinking perhaps you may give us some clue to our patient's identity."

Launcelot's eyes were bright with excitement as he finished reading.

"Let me see the coin," he begged, eagerly, and as the doctor handed it to him, he jumped to his feet.

"I thought so," he shouted, "it's a Spanish coin, like Judy's."

"Well," said the minister, quietly, but his hand beating against his knee showed that his agitation matched Launcelot's— "What then?"

"Why, the man must be Judy's father!" said Launcelot, and when he had thus voiced the doctor's thought, the two stared at each other with white faces.

"She always believed he was alive," said Launcelot at last.

"Pray God that it is really he?" said Dr. Grennell, reverently.

"And now what can we do?" asked the boy.

"We must not say a word to Judy yet. In fact I don't know whether we ought to tell the Judge. We musn't raise false hopes."

"Have you ever seen Captain Jameson?"

"We were at college together," said Dr. Grennell; "that is the way I happened to come to Fairfax. I got my appointment to this church through Captain Jameson and his father."

"Then couldn't you go on and see if he is really Judy's father?"

"By George," said the doctor, "of course I can. I can make the excuse that I want to visit my old friends. I need an outing, too."

"I wish I could go with you," said Launcelot, wistfully, as the two walked down the road, after having perfected plans for the doctor's trip. "I am getting awfully tired of this place, doctor. You see my life abroad was so different, and I feel as if I ought to be doing something worth while."

"Just now the thing that is worth while is for you to be a good son and stay here," said Dr. Grennell. "You can be nothing greater than that. And you are doing it like a hero," and his hand dropped affectionately on the boy's shoulder.

"Well, it's deadly dull," said the hero resignedly, as he thought of Anne and Judy speeding away to the coolness of the sea. But presently he cheered up. "It will be great if it does happen to be Captain Jameson," he said, "and just think if Judy hadn't run away we wouldn't have seen her coin, and if I had waited that morning she wouldn't have run away, and if I hadn't been cross I would have waited—how about that for a moral, Doctor."

"There is no moral," said the minister, "but all bad tempers don't turn out so well."

"It sounds like,
  "'Fire, fire burn stick,
  Stick, stick beat dog,
  Dog, dog bite pig—'
doesn't it?" said Launcelot with a laugh, as they parted at the crossroads.

CHAPTER XVI

THE WIND AND THE WAVES

It was dark and raining when the travellers reached The Breakers, but a light streamed out from the doorway, and Mrs. Adams, the caretaker, met them on the step.

"I couldn't get any maids to help me," she explained to the Judge, as she led the way in, "but my sister is coming over in the morning, and Jim will build the fires—and I've set out supper in the hall."

"That's all right, Mrs. Adams," said the Judge, heartily, "Perkins will serve us, and you needn't stay up. I know you are tired after hurrying to get the house ready for us."

"Being tired ain't nothin' so that things suits," said Mrs. Adams, with an awed glance at the expert Perkins, who having relieved the Judge of his hat and raincoat was carrying the bags up-stairs under the guidance of Mr. Adams.

"Everything is just right, Mrs. Adams," said Judy, with eyes aglow. "I am so glad you set the supper-table in front of the big fireplace—we used to sit here so often."

Her voice trembled a little over the "we," for the sight of the little round table with its shining glass and silver had unnerved her. But she had made up her mind to be brave, and in a minute she was herself again, leading the way to her room, which Anne was to share, and doing the honors of the house generally.

The Breakers was a cottage built half of stone and half of shingles. It was roomy and comfortable, but not as magnificent as the Judge's great mansion in Fairfax. To Judy it was home, however, and when she came down again, she sighed blissfully as she dropped into a chair in front of the blazing fire.

"Listen, Anne," she said to the little fair-haired girl, "listen—do you hear them—the wind and the waves?"

Anne was not quite sure that she liked it—the moaning of the wind, and the ceaseless swish—boom, crash of the waves.

"I wish it was daylight so that I could see the ocean," she said, politely, "I think it must be lovely and blue and big—"

"It is lovely now," said Judy, and went to the window and drew back the curtain.

"Look out here, Anne—"

As Anne looked out, the moon showed for an instant in a ragged sky and lighted up a wild waste of waters, whose white edge of foam ran up the beach half-way to the cottage.

"How high the waves are," said little Anne.

"I have seen them higher than that," exulted Judy. "I have seen them so high that they seemed to tower above our roof."

"Weren't you afraid?"

"They couldn't hurt me, and it was grand."

"Supper is served, miss," announced Perkins, coming in with a chafing-dish and a half-dozen fresh eggs on a silver tray.

"I thought you might like something hot, sir," he said to the Judge with a supercilious glance at the cold collation which Mrs. Adams had provided, and with that he proceeded on the spot to make an omelette—puffy, fluffy, and perfect.

It was a cozy scene—the old butler in his white coat bending over the shining silver dish with the blue flame underneath. The polished mahogany of the table giving out rich reflections as the ruddy light of the fire played over it. The sparkling glass, the quaint old silver, Judy's violets all fragrant and dewy in the center, and at the head of the table the Judge in a great armchair, and on each side the two girls, the dark-haired and the fair-haired, in white gowns and crisp ribbons.

But Judy ate nothing, although Perkins tempted her with various offers.

"I'm not a bit hungry," she said, over and over again, and Anne, who was ravenous, felt positively greedy in the face of such daintiness.

"You are tired," said the Judge at last, as Judy sat with her chin in her hand, gazing at a picture of her father which hung over the fireplace—a full-length portrait in uniform. "Go to bed, dear." And in spite of protests, as soon as Anne had finished her supper, he ordered them both to bed.

"What are we going to do about her, Perkins?" the Judge asked in a worried tone, when he and the old servant were alone.

"Miss Judy, sir?"

"Yes. She isn't well, Perkins."

"She will be better down here, sir," said Perkins. "She is like her father, you know, sir—likes the water—"

"Perkins—" after a pause.

"Yes, sir."

"Do you think—he is alive?"

It was the first time in years that the Judge had spoken of his son. Perkins stopped brushing the crumbs from the table, and came and stood beside his master, looking into the fire thoughtfully.

"Miss Judy thinks he is, sir," he said at last.

"I know—"

"And I find that it's the women that's mostly right in such things," went on Perkins. "A man now only knows what he sees, but, Lord, sir, a woman knows things without seein'. Sort of takes them on faith, sir."

"The uncertainty is bad for Judy," said the Judge, the deep lines showing in his care-worn face.

Perkins laid a respectful hand on the back of his chair. "You'd best go to bed yourself, sir," he said, gently, "you're tired, sir."

"Yes—yes." But he did not move until Perkins had drawn the water for his bath and had laid out his things, and had urged him, "Everything is ready, sir." Then he got up with a sigh, "I wish I knew."

"I wish I knew," he said, a half-hour later, as the careful Perkins covered him with an extra blanket. "I wish I knew where he is—to-night."

Outside the wind moaned, the rain beat against the windows and the waves boomed unceasingly. Perkins drew the curtain tight, and laid the Judge's Bible on the little table by the bed, where his hand could reach it the first thing in the morning; then he picked up the lamp and went to the door.

"I think wherever he is, he's bein' took care of, sir," he said, comfortingly, and with an affectionate glance at the gray head on the pillow, he went out and closed the door.

In the morning Anne slept soundly, but Judy slipped out of bed early, put on her bathing-suit and a raincoat, and with a towel in her hand went down-stairs.

She found Perkins in the lower hall.

"You are early, Miss," he said.

"Yes, I am going to take a dip in the waves," said Judy.

"You're sure it's safe, Miss?" asked Perkins anxiously.

"I have done it all my life," asserted Judy, "and it gives me an awful appetite for breakfast."

Perkins brightened. "Does it now, Miss," he asked. "Is there anything you would like cooked, Miss Judy—I could speak to Mrs. Adams."

But Judy shook her head. "I am not hungry now," she said gaily, as she went off, "but I know I shall have an appetite when I come in."

She tripped away to the bath-house, and as she came out of the door looking like a sea-nymph in her white-bathing suit and white rubber cap she saw Anne, also towel laden and rain-coated, flying down towards her.

"Why didn't you wake me up," scolded the younger girl. "Oh, Judy, isn't it lovely," and she dropped down on the beach, panting.

The morning sun cast rosy shadows over the sea, there was a touch of amethyst in the clouds, and the waves as they curled over the golden beach were gray-green in the hollows and silver-white on their crests.

"I just know I sha'n't dare to stick my toes into the water," said Anne with a shiver. "It is so—so big, Judy."

"You look just dear," declared Judy, as Anne dropped her raincoat and came forth in a scarlet suit, "that red suits you."

Anne clasped her hands. "Oh, Judy, does it," she sighed rapturously.

"Yes."

"You don't think I am getting vain, do you, Judy?" inquired Anne, anxiously, "but I do love pretty things."

"I think you are a goosie," said Judy with a little laugh, then she caught hold of Anne with impatient hands. "Come on in, little red bird," she urged, "it's lovely in the water."

Anne squealed and struggled, and finally waded in until the water came up to her knees.

"Don't take me any farther, Judy," she begged, and when Judy saw her frightened face, she let her go.

"Sit on the sand, then, and watch me, Annekins," she advised. "You will get used to this after a while and enjoy it as much as I do."

She was off with a run and a leap, and for fifteen minutes or more she was over and under and up and down on the waves like a snowy mermaid.

"And now for breakfast," said the young lady in white, as she dashed up the sands, with raincoat flying and towel fluttering in the breeze.

Ten minutes later two red-cheeked, wet-haired damsels rushed into the dining-room and kissed the Judge, who sat at the head of the table with his newspaper propped up in front of him.

"Bless my soul," he said, gazing at them over his spectacles, "are you really up?"

"We have been up for an hour," gurgled Anne, happily, "and in bathing."

But Judy did not stop for explanations, "Oh, waffles, waffles.

Perkins, I love you. How did you know I wanted waffles?"

"You said you would have an appetite, Miss," said the beaming Perkins, "and there's nothing that touches the spot on a cool morning like waffles."

He exchanged satisfied glances with the Judge as Judy finished her sixth section, having further supplemented the waffles with a dish of berries and a lamb chop.

"We are going down to the bay after breakfast," announced Judy.

"And I am going to take a book and read on the sand," planned Anne.

"Books, nothing," said Judy, slangily. "We are going to sail and catch crabs."

"Little red crabs?" asked Anne with interest.

"No, big blue ones, you goosie, and then Perkins will cook them for us.

Won't you, Perkins?"

"Anything you say, Miss," said Perkins, resignedly.

But it rained the next day, and after that they went sailing in Judy's own sailboat "The Princess," which she could manage as well as any man, and after that they drove to town with the Judge, so that it was over a week before the crabbing expedition came to pass.

The Breakers stood on a strip of land between the bay and the ocean. It was on a peninsula, but the connecting link with the mainland was many miles away, so that for all practical purposes the house was on an island, with the ocean in front and the bay behind, and all the pleasures that both made possible.

Anne was entranced with the delights of crabbing. It was very exciting to get the great rusty fellows on the line, tow them up to the top of the water, where the competent Perkins nabbed them with the crab-net.

Perkins caught crabs as he did everything else, expertly, and with dignity. His only concession to the informality of the sport was a white yachting cap and a white linen coat, and it was a sight worth going miles to see, to watch him officiate at a catch. The great vicious fellows might clash their claws in vain, for Perkins subdued them with a scientific clutch at the back that rendered them helpless.

"We are going to cook them as soon as we get home," Judy told Anne. "Perkins knows all about fixing them, and Mrs. Adams is going to give up the kitchen to us—it's lots of fun to eat the meat out of the claws."

"Do you want them—devilled, Miss?" and Perkins coughed discreetly before the word.

"Yes. In their shells, with parsley stuck in the top. They are delicious that way, Anne."

Anne had her doubts as to the deliciousness of anything so spidery-looking as those strange fish, but she said nothing.

"Is there anything Perkins can't do?" she asked Judy, as Perkins went on ahead, bearing the great basket of crabs, and the net.

"I don't believe there is," laughed Judy. "He is supposed to be grandfather's butler, but he won't let any one do a thing for grandfather, and he plays valet and cook half the time when the other servants don't suit him."

Once in the kitchen, Anne eyed the big basket shiveringly. The fierce creatures stared at her with protruding bead-like eyes, and in a way that seemed positively menacing.

"If they should get out," she thought, as she was left alone with them for a moment.

She never knew how it happened, but Perkins must have left the basket too near the edge of the chair on which he had placed it, for as she took hold of the cover to shut it, the basket tipped, and down came the living load, and in another moment, the desperate shell-fish were scuttling across the floor in all directions.

With a shriek Anne took refuge on top of the stationary wash-tubs.

"Come up here, Judy," she cried, frantically, and Judy who had reached the middle of the room, and was surrounded by pugilistic creatures before she realized the catastrophe, drew herself up beside Anne, and together they shrieked for Perkins.

Perkins came and saw and conquered as usual. The girls laughed until the tears ran down their cheeks to see the battle. One by one the crabs were picked up and dropped into a big kettle until at last it was full.

"And now you young ladies had best go out," said Perkins, firmly, "while I cook them."

It is well to draw a veil over the tragic fate of the kettleful of blue crabs, but when Anne next saw them they were beautifully boiled, and red—red as the scarlet of her bathing-suit.

All the afternoon the little girls, under Perkins' skilful guidance learned a lesson in expert cookery, and at last, as a dozen perfectly browned and parsley-decorated beauties were laid on a platter, Judy breathed an ecstatic sigh. "Aren't they beautiful?" she murmured.

"Yes, Miss, that they are," and Perkins surveyed them as an artist lets his glance linger on a finished masterpiece. He raised the platter to carry it to the dining-room, but as he turned towards the door he stopped and set it down quickly.

"What's the matter, sir," he asked sharply, "has anything gone wrong?"

The Judge stood on the threshold, his face white with excitement. In his hands was a letter, and his voice shook as he spoke.

"It's nothing bad, Perkins," he said, and Judy, as she faced him, saw that his eyes were bright with some new hope. "It's nothing bad. But I've had a letter—a strange, strange letter, Perkins—and I must go on a journey to-night—a journey to the north—to Newfoundland, Perkins."

CHAPTER XVII

MOODS AND MODELS

Anne and Judy were almost overcome by the mystery of the Judge's departure. Not a word could they get out of the reticent Perkins, however, as to the reasons for the sudden flitting, and the Judge had simply said when pressed with questions: "Important business, my dear, which may result rather pleasantly for you. Mrs. Adams will take care of you and Anne while I am gone, which I hope won't be long."

The day that he left it rained, and the day after, and the day after that, and on the fourth day, when the sea was gray and the sky was gray and the world seemed blotted out by the blinding torrents, Judy, who had been pacing through the house like a caged wild thing, came into the library, and found Anne curled up in the window-seat with a book.

"I came down here with all sorts of good resolutions," she said, fiercely, as she stood by the window, looking out, "but if this rain doesn't stop, I shall do something desperate. I hate to be shut in."

Anne did not look up. She was reading a book breathlessly, and not until Judy had jerked it out of her hand and had flung it across the room did she come to herself with a little cry.

"I shall do something desperate," reiterated Judy, stormily. "Do you hear, Anne?"

Anne smiled up at her—a preoccupied smile.

"Oh, Judy," she said, still seeing the visions conjured up by her book.

"Oh, Judy, you ought to read this—"

"You know I don't like to read, Anne." Judy's tone was irritable.

"You would like this," said Anne, gently, as she drew Judy down beside her. "It's about the sea." She opened the despised book at the place where she had been reading when Judy plucked it out of her hand. "Listen."

Judy did listen, but with her sullen eyes staring out of the window and her shoulders hunched up aggressively. When Anne stopped however, she said: "Go on," and when the chapter was finished, she asked, "Who wrote that?"

"Robert Louis Stevenson. He was a lovely man, and he wrote lovely books, and he died, and they buried him in Samoa on the top of a mountain. He wrote some verses called 'Requiem.' I think you would like them, Judy."

"What are they?"

Anne quoted softly, her sweet little voice deep with feeling, and her blue eyes dark with emotion.

"'Under the wide and stormy sky,
  Dig the grave and let me lie,
Glad did I live and gladly die,
  And I laid me down with a will.
  "'This be the verse you grave for me:
  "Here he lies where he longed to be;
Home is the sailor—home from the sea,
  And the hunter home from the hill.'"

"'Home is the sailor, home from the sea—'" echoed Judy, under her breath. "How fine that he could say it like that, Anne. Tell me about him."

All the discontent had gone from her face, and she lay back among the cushions of the window-seat quietly, while Anne told her of the young life that had ended in a land of exile. Of a singer whose song had been stilled so soon, but who would not be forgotten as long as men honor a brave heart and a gentle spirit.

"Let me see the book," and Judy stretched out her hand, and Anne gave her "Kidnapped" unselfishly, glad to see the softened look in Judy's eyes, and as the morning passed and the two girls read on and on, they did not notice that the rain had stopped and that the parted clouds showed a gleam of watery sun.

And when lunch was announced, Judy laid her book down with a sigh, and after lunch, in spite of clearing weather, she read until twilight, and having finished one book, would have started another, if Anne had not protested.

"You will wear yourself out," she said, as the intense Judy looked up with blurred eyes and wrinkled forehead. "Let's have a run on the beach."

Judy never did anything by halves, and after her introduction to books that she liked, she outread Anne. And as time went on it was her books that soothed her in her restless moods, and because there were in her father's library the writings of the greatest men and the best men who have given their thoughts to the world, Judy was gradually molded into finer girlhood, finer womanhood, than could have come to her by any other association.

She read Stevenson through in a week, and then began on Ruskin; for her thoughtful mind, starved so long of food that it needed, craved solid things, and Judy, who knew much of pictures and paintings, found in Ruskin's theories a great deal that delighted and interested her.

"You'll never get through," said Anne, with a dismayed glance at the long rows of brown volumes high up on the shelves. "I don't like anything but stories, and Ruskin preaches awfully."

"You ought to like him, then," said Judy, wickedly, "you good little
Anne."

"Oh, don't," protested Anne, reproachfully, "don't call me that, Judy."

"Well, bad little Anne, then," said Judy, composedly, from the top of the step-ladder, where she was examining the titles of the books and enjoying herself generally.

"You're such a tease," said Anne with a sigh.

"And you are so serious, little Annekins," and Judy smiled down at her.

"I like Ruskin," she announced, later. "He's a little hard to understand sometimes, but he knows a lot about art. I am going to take up my drawing again. He says that youth is the time to do things, and a girl ought not to fritter away her time."

"No, indeed," said Anne, virtuously. "Only don't get too tired, Judy."

But it was Anne who was tired, before Judy's enthusiasm wore itself out, for she was pressed into service as a model, and she served in turn as A Blind Girl, A Dancing Girl, A Greek Maiden, Rebecca at the Well, Marguerite, and Lorelei.

The last was an inspiration. Anne perched on a rock around which the breakers dashed appropriately, with her hair down, and with filmy garments fluttering in the wind, combed her golden locks in the heat of the blazing sun.

"It's broiling hot out here, Judy," she complained as that indefatigable artist sat on the beach with her easel before her, in a blue work-apron, and with a dab of charcoal on her nose.

"Oh, you look just lovely, Anne," Judy assured her, with the cruel indifference of genius. "You're just lovely. I think this is the best I have done yet. Think what a picture you will make."

"Think how my nose will peel," mourned Anne, forlornly.

"Die schönste Jungfrau sitzet
Dort oben wunderbar,
Ihr goldnes Geschmeide blitzet,
Sie kämmt ihr gold'nes Haar."

sang Judy, whose residence abroad had made her familiar with many folk-songs.

"Sie kämmt es mit gold'nem Kamme,
Und singt ein Lied dabei;"

"—Anne, you have the loveliest hair," she interrupted her song to say.

But Anne was tired. "I don't think that the Lorelei was very nice," she said, "to make men drown themselves just because she wants to comb her hair on a rock—"

"She didn't care," said Judy, sagely. "The men didn't have to let their old boats be wrecked."

"But her voice was so wonderful they just had to follow—"

"No, they didn't," declared Judy. "You just ask your grandmother. She says nobody has to go where they don't want to go, and I think she is right, and if those sailors had sailed away the minute they heard the Lorelei begin to sing they would have been safe."

"Well, maybe they would," agreed Anne, hastily, for Judy had stopped work to talk. "Judy, I shall fall off this rock if you don't finish pretty soon."

"All right, Annekins, just one minute," and Judy dashed in a drowning sailor or two, fluffed the heroine's hair into entrancing curliness, added a few extra rays to the sparkling comb, and held up the sketch.

"There," she said, triumphantly.

Anne slid from the rock, and waded in to look.

"It isn't a bit like me," she criticized, holding up her wet and flowing draperies.

"Well, you see I couldn't put in your dimples and your chubbiness, for although they are dear in you, Anne, they are not suitable for the purposes of art," and Judy stood back with a grown-up air and gazed upon her masterpiece. Then she caught Anne around the waist and danced with her on the beach.

"Ich glaube, die Wellen verschlingen
Am Ende Schiffer und Kahn;
Und das hat mit ihrem Singen
Die Lorelei gethan."

"You wicked little Lorelei," she panted, as they sat down on the sand.

"I'm not wicked," said Anne, composedly, "and the next time you use me for a model, Judy, I wish you would get an easier place than on that old rock."

"You shall be Juliet in the tomb," promised Judy, "and you can go to sleep if you want to."

But she let Anne rest for awhile, and used Perkins as a model.

Her first sketch of him was very clever—a sketch in which the stately butler posed as "The Neptune of the Kitchen." He sat on a great turtle, with a toasting-fork instead of a trident, with a necklace of oyster crackers, a crown of pickles, and a smile that was truly Perkins's own.

That sketch taught Judy her niche in the temple of art. She was not destined to be a great artist, but she had a keen wit, and a knack of discovering fun in everything, and in later years it was in caricature, not unkind, but truly humorous, that Judy made her greatest successes, and achieved some little fame.

CHAPTER XVIII

JUDY KEEPS A PROMISE

"What's your talent, Anne?" asked Judy, one evening, as she lay on the couch reading "Sesame and Lilies." It was raining again outside, but in the fireplace a great fire was blazing, and rosy little Anne was in front of it, popping corn.

"Haven't any," said Anne, watching the white kernels bob up and down. "I can't draw and I can't play, and I can't sing or converse—or anything."

Judy looked at her thoughtfully. "Well, we will have to find something that you can do," she said, for Judy liked to lead and have others follow, and having decided upon art as her life-work, she wanted Anne to choose a similar path. "I wish I could take up bookbinding or wood-carving, or—or dentistry—"

"Why, Judy Jameson." Anne turned an amazed hot face towards her.

"Why, Judy, you wouldn't like to pull teeth, would you?"

"It isn't what we like to do, Ruskin says," said Judy, calmly, "it's usefulness that counts."

"Oh, well, I can wash dishes and dust and take care of old people and pets," said placid Anne, opening the cover of the popper and letting out delicious whiffs of hot corn.

Judy shuddered. "I hate those things," she said. "I couldn't wash dishes, Anne. It is so dreadful for your hands."

She went back to her book, and Anne poured the hot corn into a big bowl and salted it.

"Have some?" she asked the absorbed reader.

Without taking her eyes from her book, Judy stretched out her hand, then all at once she flashed a glance into the rosy face so close to her own.

"Anne," she said, almost humbly, "do you know you are more of a Ruskin girl than I am? He says that every girl, every day, should do something really useful about the house—go into the kitchen, and sew, and learn how to fold table-cloths, and things, like that. And you know all of those things—and how to help the poor—and I—I am always trying to do some great thing, and I never really help any one. Not any one, Anne—not a single soul—"

"But you are so clever," said little Anne.

"But people don't love you just because you are clever, and it isn't clever people that make others the happiest," and Judy dropped her book and gazed deep into the flames as if seeking there an answer to the problems of life.

"People love you, Judy."

"Sometimes they do, and some people—but my awful temper, Anne," and Judy sighed.

"You don't flare up half as much as you used." Anne's tone was consoling. She had finished popping the corn, and she sat down on the floor beside the couch on which Judy lay, and munched the crisp kernels luxuriously.

"No, I don't," confessed Judy, "but it's an awful fight, Anne. You have helped me a lot."

"Me?" asked the rosy maiden in astonishment. "Why, how have I helped you, Judy?"

"By your example, Annekins," said Judy, sitting up. "You're such a dear."

At which praise the rosy maiden got rosier than ever, and shook her loosened hair over her happy eyes.

The firelight flickered on the beautiful dark face on the cushions, and on the fair little one that rested against Judy's dress.

"We are such friends, aren't we, Judy?" whispered Anne, as she reached up and curled her plump hand into Judy's slender fingers. "Almost like sisters, aren't we, Judy?"

"Just like sisters, Annekins," said Judy, dreamily, with a responsive pressure.

Outside the wind moaned and groaned, and the rain beat against the panes. "I have never seen such a rainy season," said Judy, as a blast shook the house. "But I rather like it when we are so cozy and warm and happy, Anne."

The pop-corn was all eaten, and Anne was gazing into the fire, half asleep, when suddenly she started up.

"What's that, Judy?" she cried.

Judy raised her eyes from her book.

"What?" she asked, abstractedly.

"That sound at the window."

"I didn't hear anything."

"It was like a rap."

"It was the rain."

"Well, maybe it was," and Anne settled back again. Presently her hand slipped and dropped, and Judy, feeling the movement, looked down and smiled, for little Anne was asleep.

Judy tucked a cushion behind the weary head, and was settling back for another quiet hour with her book, when all at once she sat up straight, listening.

Then she rolled from the couch quickly, without waking Anne, and went to the window and peered out. She could see nothing but the driving rain, but as she turned to leave there came again the sound that had startled her.

The window was a French one, opening outward. Very softly she unlatched it.

"Who's there?" she asked, wondering if she should have called Perkins.

"Come to the door," said a voice, and a dripping figure appeared within the circle of light. "Come out a minute. It's me—Tommy Tolliver."

Anne slept on as Judy went out and closed the door behind her.

"Why, Tommy," she said, trying to see him in the darkness, "how in the world did you get down here?"

"I have run away again," said Tommy, defiantly, "and I've come to you to help me, Judy."

"What!"

"You said you would help me, Judy. That's why I came."

"But—"

"Oh, don't try to get out of it," blazed Tommy, who was wet and tired and shivering, "you said you would. And if you back down now—well—" He left the sentence unfinished and his voice broke.

"*When* did I promise, Tommy?" asked poor Judy, in a dazed way.

"The day I came back to Fairfax."

It seemed like a dream to Judy, that day in the woods when she had first met the children of Fairfax,—Launcelot and Amelia and Nannie,—and she had entirely forgotten her reckless promise.

"Sit down," she faltered, "and tell me what you want me to do."

At the side of the house where they were sheltered somewhat from the rain Tommy outlined his plan.

"I want you to take me down the bay in your sailboat. I had money enough to get here, and if you can help me to get to the Point, a friend of mine has promised me a place on one of the ocean liners."

"But Tommy—"

"Don't say 'but' to me, Judy," and Judy recognized a new note in Tommy's voice. There was less of the old, weak swagger, and more determination. "I am going, and that's all there is to it."

"When do you want to start?" she asked, after a pause.

"The first thing in the morning, if you can get away," said Tommy.

"I can't go until evening. We are to spend the day with some friends of ours, the Bartons. But I can take you down by moonlight. It's a couple of hours' ride. I suppose we shall have to tell Anne."

"I hate to," said Tommy.

"Why?"

"Oh, Anne is such a good little thing—and—and—she believes in me—Judy."

"But if it is right for you to go, you shouldn't care—"

"I don't know whether it is right or not," said Tommy, doggedly, "and what's more, I don't care, Judy. I am going and that's the end of it."

"Well!" Judy stood up, shivering. "It's awfully cold out here, Tommy; you'd better come in."

"Are you going to help me?" demanded Tommy. "I sha'n't go in unless you are."

"What will you do?"

"Tramp on. Guess I can manage for another day. I've only had a slice of bread and a tomato to-day."

"Tommy Tolliver!" said Judy, shocked. "Why, you must be starved. I'll go right in and get you something."

"Are you going to help me to get away?" he insisted.

"I must think about it."

"But you promised."

"I am not sure that I exactly promised," hesitated Judy.

"You're afraid."

"I am not."

"Aw, you are—or you'd do it."

That was touching Judy on a tender point. She was proud of her courage—none of her race had ever been cowards. Besides, as she stood there with the wind and the waves beating their wild song into her ears, all the recklessness of her nature came uppermost. It would be glorious to sail down the bay. The water would be rough, and the wind would fill out the white sails of the little boat, and they would fly, fly, and the goal for Tommy would be freedom.

"I'll do it," she said, suddenly. "I'll do it, Tommy. We Jamesons never break a promise, and I'm not afraid."

They decided not to tell Anne.

"It would just worry her," said Judy, decidedly, "and I can get some food and things out to you after Anne goes to bed, and you can sleep in the boat-house. We can start in the morning."

It was a wild scheme, but before they had finished they felt quite uplifted. In their youth and inexperience, they imagined that Tommy's last dash for liberty was positively heroic, and Judy went in, feeling like one dedicated to a cause.

She found Anne rubbing her eyes sleepily.

"Why, have you been out, Judy?" she gasped, wide awake. "You are all wet."

370

"It's fine on the porch," said Judy, putting her soaked hair back from her face. "I—I was tired of the heat of the room, and—it was stifling. Let's go to bed, Anne."

"Aren't you going to finish your book?" Anne asked, wondering, for Judy was something of a night-owl, and hated early hours.

Judy picked up "Sesame and Lilies," which lay open on the couch, and shut it with a bang.

"No," she said, shortly, "I am not going to finish it to-night—I don't know whether I shall ever finish it, Anne. I'm not Ruskin's kind of girl, Anne. I can't 'sit on a cushion and sew a fine seam,' and I don't think it is any use for me to try."

Anne stared at the change that had come over her. "Well, you are my kind of girl," she said at last, and as they went up-stairs together, she slipped her hand into Judy's arm. "I love you, dearly, Judy," she said.

But Judy smiled down at her vaguely, for her mind was on Tommy, crouched out there in the rain, and in imagination she was not Judy Jameson, commonplacely going to bed at nine o'clock, but a heroine of history, dedicated to the cause of one Thomas, the Downtrodden.

CHAPTER XIX

PERKINS CLEANS THE SILVER

All the next day, Tommy skulked in the shadow of the pier and in the boat-house, whence during the morning Judy made her way laden with mysterious bundles and various baggage. At noon she departed for Lutie Barton's, leaving Anne, who had a cold, at home.

After Judy's departure, Anne wandered listlessly about the house. She tried to read, to sew a little, to pick out some simple tunes on Judy's piano, but thoughts of the little gray house, of the little grandmother, of Becky and Belinda, came between her and her occupations, so that at last, late in the afternoon, she sought the society of Perkins, who was in the dining-room cleaning silver.

"I believe I am homesick, Perkins," said Anne, perching herself in a great mahogany chair opposite him.

"Well, it ain't to be wondered at," said Perkins, as he picked up a huge cake-dish and began to work on it, energetically. "It ain't to be wondered at. You ain't ever been away from home much, Miss Anne."

"It is lovely not to have anything to do," said Anne. "That is, it is nice in a way, but do you know, Perkins, I sometimes just wish there were some rooms to dust or something, but you and the maids keep everything so clean," and Anne sighed a sigh that came from the depths of her housewifely soul.

"You might dip these cups in hot water and wipe them as I gets them finished," suggested Perkins, handing her several quaint little mugs, which he had placed in a row in front of him.

"Aren't they dear," Anne said, enthusiastically. "Why this one says 'Judith.' Is it Judy's, Perkins?"

"No, Miss, that was her great-grand-mother's, and that one with 'John' on it is the Judge's, and the one with 'Philip' is Miss Judy's father's—they are christening cups, Miss—six generations of them."

"Oh, how lovely," said Anne, and she handled them lovingly, dipping them into clear hot water, and polishing them until they shone.

"Judy never speaks of her father, lately," she said, as she placed the "Philip" cup on the sideboard.

"No, Miss, but she thinks of him a lot," said Perkins, with a shake of his old head. "I saw her this morning, Miss, standing in front of his picture in the hall, and there were tears in her eyes, Miss, and then all at once she whirled around and ran away, and her face had a wild look on it, Miss."

"Do you know, Perkins," said little Anne, stopping work for a minute and speaking earnestly, "do you know that I think Judy would be different if she only knew something about him. The uncertainty makes her unhappy, and then she does reckless things just to get away from herself."

"Yes, Miss," said Perkins, "and there ain't a morning that she don't put fresh flowers in front of that there picture, and there ain't a night that she don't kiss her hand to it from the top of the stairs."

"I know," sighed Anne. "Poor Judy."

"When will the Judge be back?" she asked after awhile.

But at that Perkins shut up like a clam. "I don't know, Miss," he snapped. "It's best for you not to ask too many questions, Miss."

Anne flushed. "Oh, of course I won't, Perkins," she said, "if you don't like to have me—" and she was very quiet, until the old butler, with a glance at her troubled face, said, "I don't care how many questions you axes, Miss, but the Judge might."

And Anne smiled at him, with radiant forgiveness.

"Isn't all this silver a lot of care, Perkins?" she asked, to clear the air.

"It is that," answered Perkins, "and yet there isn't half as much of it as there is at the Judge's in Fairfax. Only the Judge keeps his locked up in a safe, all except the things we uses every day. But here they just puts it on the sideboard, where it is a temptation to burglars—with them long windows opening out on the porch, and the curtains drawn back half the time. I don't call it safe, Miss, I surely don't."

"But there aren't any burglars around here, are there, Perkins?" and Anne stopped rubbing the cups to look at him anxiously.

"Nobody knows whether there is or not," grumbled Perkins. "There might be for all they know. It ain't fair to the servants, Miss, for to let them lie around loose this way. Mrs. Adams says so, too, but the Judge don't pay no attention to things since the Captain left, and Miss Judy is too young to bother."

"They wouldn't like to lose these cups," said Anne, as she finished the last one, and arranged them in a squat little row on the shelf.

"They wouldn't like to lose any of it," returned Perkins, putting a great soup-ladle back into its flannel bag. "It's all old and it's all family silver, and people ought to take care of it, and when the Judge comes back I am going to tell him so, Miss."

"Anne," said Judy, peeping in at the door, "I'm back, and Lutie Barton is with me. Come on in and see her."

"Oh, dear," said Anne, with a dismayed glance at her spattered apron, "I look like a sight."

"Run up the back way and fix up," said Judy, "and I'll talk to her until you come down."

Lutie Barton brought with her the gossip of the town. There had been a dance at the big hotel the night before, a sailing party down the bay in the afternoon had been caught in a thunder shower, and all the girls' hats had been ruined, and there had been a burglary at one of the cottages in an outlying district.

Anne jumped when they said that. "What did they steal?" she faltered, with her conversation with Perkins fresh in her mind.

"*Everything*, my dear," said Lutie, who did everything by extremes, and who wore the highest pompadour, and the highest heels, and who had the smallest waist and the largest hat that Anne had ever seen, and who always used the superlative when telling a tale.

"They stole *every single thing* down to the very shoes, and the kitten from the rug."

"Oh," said Anne, thinking of Belinda, "the dear little kitten. What did they want with it?"

"It was a Persian, and this morning it came back, but the silver collar was gone from its neck, and they took even a thimble from a work-basket, and a box of candy and a cake!"

"Did they get anything valuable?" asked Anne.

"All of Mrs. Durant's diamonds and the family silver," said Lutie. "My dear, Mrs. Durant is ill, *absolutely ill*, and the worst of it is that she saw the burglar, and it frightened her so that she hasn't gotten over it yet."

"How dreadful," said little Anne, thinking of the great sideboard and all of the Jameson silver that she and Perkins had cleaned. "Oh, Judy, suppose they should come here!"

But Judy was standing by the window, watching a figure that slipped from the boat-house to the wharf with a bundle on his shoulder, the figure of a small boy, with his cap pulled low.

"Such things are like lightning; they never strike twice in the same place," she said, indifferently. "Don't go, Lutie."

"Oh, I *must*," gushed Lutie. "I was just *dying* to see you, Anne, for a minute, so I came with Judy. But I *must* go. They will think I am *dead*."

But she stopped to ask a giggling question. "Tell me about Launcelot Bart, Anne," she begged. "Judy happened to mention him, but she wouldn't tell me a *thing*. I think they must have an *awful* case, for she is too quiet about him for *anything*. Is he nice?"

"He is the nicest boy I know," said Anne, enthusiastically.

"Oh, oh," gurgled silly Lutie, shaking her finger at the two girls as they stood together on the top step of the porch. "Don't get jealous of each other, you two."

"Jealous?" asked Anne's innocent eyes.

"Jealous?" blazed Judy's indignant eyes.

"Don't be a goose, Lutie." Judy was trying to control her temper. "Anne and I aren't grown up yet, and I hope we never will grow up and be horrid and self-conscious. Launcelot is our friend, and I didn't talk about him because I had plenty of other subjects."

"Oh," murmured Lutie, subdued for the moment; but she recovered as she went down the walk. "Oh, *good-bye*," she gushed; "let me know when it is to be, and I will dance at your wedding."

"Anne," said Judy, darkly, as the high heels tilted down the beach, and the feathers of the big hat fluttered in the breeze, "Anne, she hasn't talked a thing to-day but boys—and she reads the silliest books and writes the silliest poetry, about flaming hearts and Cupid's darts. Oh," and Judy stretched out her arms in a tense movement, "I don't want to grow up—I want to stay a little girl as long as I can and not think about lovers or getting married, or—or—anything—"

"You are lover enough for me," said Anne.

"And you for me," said Judy.

And arm in arm they went into the house. But as they went through the darkening hall, Anne clung tightly to Judy.

"Wouldn't it be dreadful, Judy, if burglars should come here," she quavered.

But Judy laughed. "I think it would be fun," she jested. "Bring on your burglars, Anne. I'm *dying* for excitement, as Lutie Barton would say." And then she touched a button, and the lights flared up, chasing away the shadows, and chasing away with them, for the moment, the fears of little Anne.

CHAPTER XX

ANNE HEARS A BURGLAR

Anne was wakened that night by a sense of utter loneliness.

"Judy," she called, softly.

No answer.

"Judy."

Anne reached over and found that the covers of the little white bed that stood beside her own had not been disturbed.

"She hasn't come up-stairs," thought Anne, who had left Judy reading in the library when she went to bed.

There was no light in the room, and as little Anne lay there, trembling and listening, her breath came quickly, for she was a timid little soul, and the talk of burglars that day had upset her; and without the wind howled, and within the house was very, very still.

At last she heard a sound. "She's coming," she thought, thankfully, but all at once she became conscious that the sound was not in the upper hall, but down-stairs on the porch.

There was the quick patter of little feet, and then an appealing whine.

"Why, it's a dog," said Anne, sitting up straight, "It's a dog."

She got up and looked out of the window. A little short-eared, stubby-tailed Boston terrier was running back and forth on the sand, anxiously.

Anne was a tender-hearted lover of animals, and his apparent distress appealed to her.

"I'll go down and see what's the matter with him," she decided, thrusting her feet into her slippers and tying the ribbons of her pink dressing-gown.

She flew down the long dark hall to the top of the steps that led below, and there she stopped still, with her hand on her heart.

The fire in the hall was still burning, and the flames wavered fitfully over the great picture above the mantel, and on the jar of red roses in front of it. The rest of the hall was in the shadow, and darker than the shadows, Anne had made out the figure of a man standing on the threshold.

As she gazed, he crossed the room and stood in front of the fire, his eyes raised to the great picture. Suddenly he leaned forward and took one of the red roses from the jar.

"He is even stealing the roses," thought Anne, indignantly, but then, what could you expect of a man who would carry off boxes of candy and thimbles and kittens?

She was sure it was the Durant burglar, and she dropped to the floor cautiously, and crouched there. Outside she could still hear the whine of the dog, but she had no thought of going to him now—she could not pass that silent figure on the rug.

Then, all at once, she thought of Judy. She was in the library, and there was just one room between her and the burglar!

Anne wasn't brave, and never had been, but in that moment she forgot herself, forgot everything but that Judy was not well and must not be frightened at any cost. Judy must not see the burglar.

As the man moved across the hall Anne staggered to her feet, feeling along the wall for the electric button, and then suddenly the lights flared up, and the little girl, a desperate pink figure clinging to the stair-rail, looked down into the upraised face of the man below.

"Don't," she said, with white lips, "don't—go—in—there—"

As she stared at him in a blur of fright she was conscious of wondering if all burglars looked so gentlemanly—if—why, *where had she seen his face*?

"Judy," breathed the man, and his whisper seemed to thunder in her ears as he came up the stairway two steps at a time.

Anne gave a little scream, half fright, half delight.

"Oh—" Why, his face was familiar—it was the face of the man in the picture over the fireplace!

"Judy," he said, again, as he reached her and caught her in his arms.

But as her yellow hair flowed over his coat, he laughed excitedly and put her from him. "I beg pardon," he apologized. "I thought you were Judy."

"And I thought you were a burglar," quavered Anne, as she sat down on the top step weakly.

Her fair little face was alight with joy as she held out her hand. "Oh," she said, "you are Judy's father, and you are alive, you are really alive!"

"And you are Anne," said the Captain.

"How did you know?" wondering.

"The Judge told me."

"Where did you see the Judge?" she asked.

"He has been with me ever since he left here," said the Captain. "Dr. Grennell discovered me in a hospital in Newfoundland, and I was very ill, and he sent for father, and he has been with me ever since. And he has gone straight to Fairfax, for he isn't very well. But I had to see my girl. Did I wake you?"

"I heard the dog."

"Terry? I brought him to Judy, and left him outside so he wouldn't startle the house. Where is my girl—where is she, Anne?"

"Oh, she's in the library," said Anne. "I'll call her. Oh, how happy she will be! How happy she will be!" She sang it like a little song, as she flitted through the hall.

At the same moment the electric bell of the front door thrilled through the house, and the Captain opened the door quickly. Preceded by a blast of wind, and the scurrying Terry-dog, Launcelot Bart came in. He stood irresolute as he saw the strange man on the rug, and before either could speak, Anne came running back.

Her face was white and her hands were shaking. She did not seem to see Launcelot, but went straight up to Captain Jameson.

"Oh, where is Judy, where is Judy?" she wailed, "she isn't there."

"And where is Tommy Tolliver?" demanded Launcelot Bart.

CHAPTER XXI

CAPTAIN JUDY

"Gee, Judy, but you can sail a boat."

Judy with the salt breeze blowing her hair back from her face, with her hand on the tiller, and with her eager eyes sweeping the surface of the moonlighted waters, smiled a little.

"I ought to," she declared, "father taught me. He said that he didn't have a son, so he intended that I should know as much as a boy about such things."

"It's mighty windy weather." Tommy was hunched up in the bottom of the boat—and his face had the woebegone look of the inexperienced sailor.

"It's going to be windier," said Judy, wisely, "it's coming now. Look at those clouds."

Back of the moon a heavy bank of clouds was crested with white, and the waters of the bay heaved sullenly.

Tommy, ignorant little landlubber that he was, began to wish that he had stayed at home, but Judy was exalted, uplifted by the thought of a coming battle with wind and waves. She had fought them so often in the little white boat, but one thing she forgot, that she was not as strong as she had been, and that Tommy was not as helpful as her father.

The start had been very exciting. Judy had pretended to read in the library, and little Anne had gone to bed, and then when the house was still she had crept out, and had met Tommy, and together they had gotten "The Princess" under sail.

But more than once that day Judy's heart had failed her. The Cause had looked rather silly on second thoughts, and Tommy was *so* commonplace—but, oh, well, she had promised, and that was the end of it.

Tommy was dreadfully awkward about a boat, too. In spite of his eagerness for a life on the ocean wave, he had never had any practical training and Judy grew impatient more than once at the slow way in which he followed out her orders.

"I would do it myself," she scolded finally, "only I must save my strength for the trip back. I shall be all alone then, you know."

Tommy sat down suddenly. "Gracious," he gasped, "I never thought of that. Oh, we will have to go back. You can't take this boat home alone, Judy."

Judy's head went up. "I am captain of this ship, Tommy Tolliver," she declared, "and I am going to sail into port and put you ashore. Then I shall do as I like."

"Aw—" said Tommy, appalled at this display of nautical knowledge, "aw—all right, Captain Judy."

The wind came as Judy had said it would, filling the little sail until it looked like a white flower, and carrying "The Princess" along at a pace that made Tommy feel weak and faint.

"Isn't it fine," cried Judy, leaning forward, and drinking in the strong air with delight. "Isn't it glorious, Tommy?"

"Yes," said Tommy, doubtfully. He was pale, and presently he lay down in the bottom of the boat.

"Suck a lemon," suggested Judy, practically, "there are some in that little locker," and after following her advice, Tommy recovered sufficiently to sit up, and in the lulls of the gale he and Judy shrieked at each other, and sang songs of the sea.

They ate a little lunch, intermittently—a bite of sandwich while Tommy pulled at the ropes or adjusted the sail, or a wing of chicken as Judy swung the boat with her head to the wind. It was all very exciting and Judy forgot care and the worried hearts that she had left behind, and Tommy, reckless in a new-found courage, felt that he was a true sailor and a son of the sea.

But as the night wore on, and the wind settled into a steady blow, it took all Judy's science and Tommy's strength to keep the little boat in her course. The waves ran higher and higher, and Judy grew quiet, and her face was pale with fatigue. Tommy began to have doubts. A life on the ocean wave wasn't all that it was cracked up to be, and anyhow, Judy was only a girl!

"How long before we get there," he shouted amid the tumult.

"We ought to reach the Point in a little while," said Judy, "but—but I am not quite sure where we are, Tommy. I have always kept within sight of land before—"

There was no land to be seen now. The moon was hidden by the clouds, and on each side of them black water stretched out to meet black sky, broken only by leaping lengths of white foam.

But they were not fated to reach the Point that night, for the wind changed, and in spite of all efforts to keep on their way, the little boat was blown farther and farther out into the great, wide waters of the bay.

"Is there any danger?" questioned Tommy as the foam boiled up on each side of the boat, drenching both himself and Judy, whose face, white as a pearl, showed through the gloom.

But Judy did not answer at once. She waited until she could make herself heard in a lull of the wind, and then she admitted, "We shall have to stay out all night, I am afraid."

"All night," gasped Tommy. "Oh, Judy, ain't it awful."

"No," said Judy, calmly, "not if we are not silly and afraid."

"Oh, I'm not afraid," swaggered Tommy, "only I wish we hadn't come," he ended, weakly, as the boat swooped down into the trough of a wave, and then rose high in the air.

"You should have told me it wasn't safe," he complained presently, "you knew it was going to storm, didn't you?"

"Well, I like that—" Judy stared at him. "Oh, try to be a man, Tommy, if you are a coward."

Tommy winced. "I'm not afraid," he defended.

"Perhaps not," said Judy, slowly, "but—but—if you had been a man you would have said, 'I am sorry I asked you to bring me, Judy.'"

"But—"

"Oh, we won't argue." Judy raised her voice as another blast came.

"I—I'm too tired to—to argue—Tommy—"

She swayed back and forth, holding on to the tiller weakly.

"I—I am so—tired," she tried to laugh, but her face was ghastly.

"I—I guess I wasn't very nice just now, Tommy,—but I—am—so tired. You will have to steer, Tommy."

"But I don't know how," blubbered Tommy.

"You will just have to do it. I can't sit up—" and Judy tumbled down into the bottom of the boat, completely worn out from the unaccustomed strain.

Tommy whimpered in a frightened monotone as he grasped the tiller with inexperienced hands. What if Judy were dead? What—? "I'll never do it again. I'll never run awa—" but Judy did not hear, for she lay with her eyes shut in a sort of stupor in the bottom of the boat.

She was waked by a bump and the wash of the waves over the boat.

"We've struck somewhere, Tommy," she shrieked.

"Oh, oh," howled Tommy, "we'll drown, Judy!"

"We won't," she said, tensely. "Hush, Tommy. *Hush*—do you hear? Can you swim?"

"No," and he clutched hold of her as another wave broke over the boat.

"There's a life-belt here somewhere," and Andy threw things out in frantic haste. "Here. Take hold of it, Tommy."

"But—what are you going to do?"

"I can swim. Don't mind about me, and if you keep quiet I will tow you in if we are near land."

She said it quietly, but in her heart she wondered where she would tow him.

"Don't take hold of me," she insisted, peremptorily, as she felt Tommy grab her arm, "or we shall both go under—oh—"

In that moment the boat keeled over, and when Judy came to the top of the water, she knew that between her and death in the green depths beneath, there was nothing but the strength of her frail limbs.

"Tommy," she called, as soon as she could get the salt water out of her mouth.

"Here," came shiveringly over the face of the waters.

"Are you all right?"

"No, no, it's horrid. Oh, I wish I was home—I wish I was home"—wailed Tommy, clinging to the belt for dear life.

The clouds had parted and one little star showed in the blackness, in the dim light Judy could just see Tommy's eyes glowing from out of his pallid face.

"He is afraid," she thought to herself, curiously. She was not afraid.

She had never been afraid of the water—poor Tommy.

She felt strangely weak, however, and all at once there came to her the knowledge that she could not keep up any longer. The strength of the old days was not hers—and she was tired—so tired—

She caught hold of the life-belt, and as she did so Tommy screamed,

"Don't, Judy. It won't hold us both. Don't—"

"He is afraid," she thought again, pityingly, "and I am not, and we can't both hold on to that belt—"

Tommy babbled crazily, bemoaning his danger, sobbing now and then—but

Judy was very still.

"I can't keep up much longer. I mustn't try to hold on with Tommy. He is afraid—poor Tommy—" she looked up at the little star, "and I'm not afraid—I love the sea," she thought, dreamily. Then for one moment she came out of her trance.

"Tommy, Tommy!" she cried sharply.

"What?"

"Don't let go of the belt. Hold on, no matter how tired you are. In the morning—some one—will save you—"

"But you—wh-wh-at are you going to do, Judy?"

"Oh, I—?" she laughed faintly. "Oh, I shall be all right—all right,

Tommy," and her voice died away in an awful silence.

CHAPTER XXII

THE CASTAWAYS

"Judy—" shrieked Tommy, and suddenly the answer came in a choking cry of joy.

"I can touch bottom, Tommy, I thought I was sinking, but it isn't over our heads at all. We must be near shore."

Tommy put his feet down gingerly. He had hated to think of the untold fathoms beneath him—depths which in his imagination were strewn with shipwrecks and the bones of lost mariners.

So when his feet came in contact with good firm sand, he giggled hysterically.

"Gee, but it feels good," he said. "Are you all right, Judy?"

But Judy had waded in and dropped exhausted on the beach.

"I don't know," she said, feebly, "I guess so."

"Where are we?" asked Tommy, splashing his way to her side.

He surveyed the land around them. In the moonlight it showed nothing but wide beach and back of that stiff rustling sea-grass and mounds of sand like the graves of sailors dead and gone. Not a house was in sight—not a sign of life.

"I don't know where we are," Judy raised her head for a second, then dropped it back, "but we are safe, Tommy Tolliver, and that's something to be thankful for.

"I knew the sea wouldn't hurt me," she went on—a little wildly, perhaps, which was excusable after the danger she had escaped. "I knew it wouldn't hurt me."

"Oh, the sea," whined Tommy, disgustedly, "this isn't the ocean, and if just an old bay can act like this, why, I say give me land. No more water for me, thank you. I am going home and plow—yes, I am, I am going to plow, Judy Jameson, and take care of the cows—and—and weed the garden," naming the thing he hated most as a climax, "and when I get to thinking things are hard, I will remember this night—when I was a shipwrecked mariner."

In imagination he was revelling in the story he would tell at home. Of the adventures that he would relate to the eager ears of the youth of Fairfax. "Yes, indeed, I will remember the time when I was a shipwrecked mariner," he said with gusto, "and lived on a desert island."

"Oh, Tommy," in spite of faintness and hunger and exhaustion, Judy laughed. "Oh, Tommy, you funny boy—this isn't a desert island."

"How do you know it isn't?" asked Tommy, stubbornly.

"There aren't any desert islands in the bay."

"I'll bet this is one."

"I hope not."

"Why?"

"We haven't anything to eat."

"Oh, well, we will find things in the morning."

"Where?"

"On the trees. Fruit and things."

"But there aren't any trees."

"Oh, well, oysters then."

"How will you get them—"

"And fish," ignoring difficulties.

"We haven't any lines or hooks."

"And things from the wreck."

"The boat tipped over," said Judy, with a little sobbing sigh for the capsized "Princess," "and anyhow there was nothing left to eat but some lemons and a box of crackers."

"Don't be so discouraging," grumbled Tommy, "you know people always find something."

They sat in silence for a time, and then Judy said:

"I hope they are not worrying at home."

"Gee—they will be scared, when they wake up in the morning and find you gone," said Tommy, consolingly.

"I left a note for Anne in the library, telling her where I had gone—but I thought I would get back before she found it," said Judy—"poor little Anne."

"I think it is poor Tommy and poor Judy," said the cause of all the trouble.

"But we deserve it and Anne doesn't. And that's the difference," said Judy, wisely.

"Aw—don't preach."

"Couldn't if I tried," and Judy clasped her hands around her knees and gazed out on the dark waters, and again there was a long silence.

"Well, what are we going to do?" demanded Tommy as the night wind blew cold against his wet garments and made him shiver.

"Do?"

"Yes. We can't sit like this all night."

"Guess we shall have to."

Another silence.

"Gee, I'm hungry."

"So am I."

"But there isn't anything to eat."

"No."

Silence again.

"Gee—I'm sleepy."

"Find some place out of the wind and go to sleep. I'll watch."

"All night?"

"Perhaps. You go to sleep, Tommy."

"Won't you be lonesome?"

Judy smiled wearily. "No," she said, "you go to sleep, Tommy."

And Tommy went.

But it was not until the cold light of dawn touched the face of the waters, that the sentinel-like figure on the beach relaxed from its strained position, and then the dark head dropped, and with a sigh Judy stretched her slender body on the hard sand, and she, too, slept.

IN A SILVER BOAT

The tide coming in the next morning brought with it on the blue surface of the waves two bobbing lemons. Many times the golden globes rolled up the beach only to be carried back by the under-wash of the waters, but finally one wave rolling farther than the rest left them high and dry on the sand, and the same wave splashing over an inert and huddled up figure waked it to consciousness.

Judy sat up stiffly and stared around her. "Oh," she sighed, as she remembered all that had happened in the darkness of the night.

She clasped her hands around her knees and gazed out forlornly over the empty waters. Not a sail, not a trail of smoke broke the blueness of the bay. With another sigh, this time of disappointment, she turned her gaze landward, and beheld there nothing but lank marsh grass and sand and driftwood.

And then at her feet she spied the lemons. She picked them up—they were the only salvage from the sunken boat. She looked around for Tommy. On the other side of a mound of sand, she could just see the top of his head, and as he did not move she decided that he was still asleep.

Her eyes twinkled, as with stealthy steps she crept up the beach until she reached a low bush with scrubby sage-green foliage. On its spiky branches she stuck the lemons, and then ran swiftly back.

Tommy was still sleeping, so she dipped her hands into the cold water, took off her stiffened shoes and bathed her swollen feet. Her dress had dried in the night winds, and when she had combed her hair she looked fairly presentable.

Barefooted she tripped over the cool wet sands, glorying in the broad expanse of blue, with white gulls dipping to it from a bluer sky.

"Tommy," she called, "Tommy."

A towsled head appeared over the top of the mound.

"Oh, dear," said Tommy, lugubriously, as he saw her sparkling face, "you act as if being shipwrecked was a good joke, Judy."

"The sun is shining and it is perfectly fine."

"It's perfectly horrid," said Tommy.

Judy looked at him for a moment, and a lump came in her throat.

"Well, it seems so much better to laugh over our troubles than to cry. Don't you think so, Tommy?" she said, wistfully, and tears welled up into her brave eyes.

"Oh, don't cry, Judy," begged Tommy, who felt that all the world would grow dark if Judy's staunch heart should fail.

"Don't cry, Judy." She brushed away her tears and smiled at him. "Well, get up, lazy boy," she said.

"I'm hungry."

"Well, go and hunt for something to eat."

"Don't know where to look."

"Neither did Robinson Crusoe."

"Oh, well, what are you going to do?"

"Watch for some one to come and take us off."

It began to be exciting. If Tommy had not been so hungry, he really believed that he might have appreciated the adventure. But his soul yearned for hot cakes and maple syrup, or beefsteak and waffles—or at least for plain bread and butter.

"Gee, but it would taste good," he said aloud.

"What?"

"I was thinking of breakfast," said poor Tommy, "hot rolls and things like that, Judy."

"O-o-oh," said Judy, "how about some hot biscuit, with one of Perkins' omelettes—and—creamed potatoes?"

"Oh, don't," groaned hungry Tommy, and fled.

He came back in about two minutes, swaggering with importance.

"This island isn't so barren as it looks," he said, pompously. "You don't know everything, Judy."

"Don't I?"

"No. Now what do you think of these," and he produced the two lemons triumphantly.

"Where did you find them?"

"Growing over there," and he pointed to the scrubby, sage-green spiky bush.

"Who would have believed it?" Judy's eyes were round and solemn, but the expression in them should have warned Tommy.

"You see there are some things you don't know. I'm going to look for oysters now."

"Oysters—"

"Yes. To eat with our lemons."

"You might find some cracker fruit, and a coffee vine, and maybe there will be a salt and pepper tree somewhere—and Tommy, *please* discover a Tabasco bush—I never could eat my oysters without Tabasco."

Tommy looked at her wrathfully. "Aw, Judy," he said, with a red face, "you're foolin'—and I think it's mean."

Then a thought struck him, and he examined the lemons carefully.

"You stuck them on that bush," he accused, excitedly. "There are holes in them. You did it to fool me, didn't you, Judy?" She nodded.

"An' you think it's a joke—I—I—" He could think of nothing sufficiently crushing to say. "Well, I don't," he finished sulkily, and plumped himself down on the sand, with his face away from her.

"Tommy," she said, after a long silence, "Tommy."

"Huh?"

"Please be good-natured."

"Be good-natured yourself," said Tommy, with a half-sob.

"I'm—I'm—perfectly mis'able, Judy Jameson—"

It was then that Judy showed that she could be womanly and sympathetic. "I'm sorry I teased you, Tommy," she said, softly. "Let's make ourselves comfortable here on the sand, and I'll tell you about when I used to live in Europe."

Tommy liked that, and all the morning Judy talked, although she was so tired, that her head felt light, and her eyes blurred, but Tommy was happy and she tried to forget about herself.

She made him suck both of the lemons.

"I don't want any," she said, although her throat was so dry that she could hardly speak. "I don't want any."

"Whew, but they are sour," said Tommy, and made a wry face, but he did not insist upon her having one.

That was the worst of it, the thirst, for there was no fresh water.

"Let's explore," said Tommy, as the afternoon waned and no relief came.

"Maybe we will find a house back there somewhere."

But Judy shook her head. "No," she said, "we are on the end of the peninsula, between the bay and the ocean. It is just salt marshes from one end to the other, and no one lives on them. The best thing we can do is to hail a boat."

"But there ain't any boats."

"There will be," said Judy, stoutly. "There are lots of little schooners that take fruit and vegetables to the markets. Not many of them come this way, but some of them do, and if we wait they will rescue us."

After that they saw several sails, and waved Tommy's coat frantically, but no one responded. As the twilight darkened into the night, a steamer went by, her lights shining like jewels against the purple background—red and green and yellow.

"If we only had a lantern," groaned Judy, as Tommy shouted himself hoarse, and the steamer kept on her majestic way, leaving them hopelessly behind.

"Maybe some one will see us in the morning." Judy was trying to encourage Tommy, who had dropped down on the sand with his back to her, but not before she had seen his working face, and his knuckles rubbing his red eyes.

"I'm going to sleep," he muttered, still with his face away from her, and with that he curled himself up against the big mound, as he had done the night before, and forgot his troubles.

Judy lay on the sand watching the waves roll in, and thinking long thoughts. She thought of her father, living, perhaps, on some such lonely beach as this, but farther away from the haunts of men—alone, looking at the same stars, searching a vaster expanse for the ship that never came. She thought, too, of her mother, the gentle mother, whose guarding presence she seemed to feel in the wonderful stillness. She thought of their plans for her; that she might grow to gracious womanhood, following in the footsteps of the women of her race, and here she was—a runaway, reckless little girl, away from home at midnight, chaperoned only by the wind and the waves, and with no roof above her but the sky!

Under the solemn canopy of the night she made many resolves, cried a little, and lay there with her eyes shut, but not asleep, feeling very wicked, and very forlorn, and very, very hopeless.

When she opened her eyes again, the night was glorious. The moon had risen, and its light made a silver pathway across the darkness of the waters, and sailing straight towards her, its sails set to the fair winds of heaven, came a little boat, dark against the shining background.

Some one stood in the bow, straight and strong and young, and as Judy watched in a half-dream, she remembered an opera she had seen once upon a time; where a knight in silver armor had come on the back of a silver swan to the lady he loved. She had hoped, mistily, that when she was old enough for such things, that Love might come to her like that—over the sea in silver armor, and sail away with her in a silver boat to the end of the world!

The boat came nearer, the boat with the silver sails! She stood up to watch, and as her slim figure was etched sharply against the background of white sand, there came to her upon the wings of the night the cry—

"Judy!"

Her hand went to her heart. Was it real? Where did he come from, that youth in the silver boat. But even as she wondered, the cry went back to him, an answering cry, joyous, welcoming—

"Launcelot, oh, Launcelot."

379

CHAPTER XXIV

"HOME IS THE SAILOR FROM THE SEA"

Judy's cry did not wake Tommy, and still in a half-dream she went down to the edge of the water and stood ghost-like in the moonlight, waiting. There was another figure in the boat, half-hidden by the shadowy sails, but it was Launcelot who, when the shallow water was reached, jumped out and waded to shore.

"Judy, Judy," he said, as he came up to her, "I knew I should find you."

She looked at him with wide eyes. "Where—where did you come from," she whispered, while her white hands fluttered across his coat sleeve as if to see that he was real.

There was sympathy and tenderness in his boyish face, but seeing her condition, he spoke cheerfully. "I came down to The Breakers after Tommy. His mother was ill, and his father had to stay with her, so they sent me. And when I got there I found Anne and—and—" he checked himself hurriedly, "I found Anne almost frantic because you had gone, and then when she found your note I started out, for I knew I should find you, Judy. I knew I should sail straight to you."

For one little moment as they stood together in the moonlight, he looked down at her with the eyes of the lover he was to be, but as yet they were only boy and girl and the moment passed.

"Where's Tommy?" asked Launcelot, coming out of his dream.

He was answered by a shout as Tommy came plunging over the sand.

"Why didn't you wake me, Judy?" he complained, bitterly, "when you first saw the boat."

"Stop that," commanded Launcelot. "Why weren't you keeping watch?

What kind of sailor do you call yourself, Tommy?"

"Oh, well," Tommy excused, "I was sleepy."

"And so you let a girl watch," was Launcelot's hard way of putting it, and Tommy's eyes shifted.

"Oh, well," he began again.

"I made him let me watch, Launcelot," Judy interrupted, feeling sorry for the small boy, "and I told him to go to sleep."

"Oh, of course you did," said Launcelot, shortly, "and of course he went, he's a nice sort of sailor."

"I'm not going to be a sailor," Tommy announced, sulkily. "I'm going home—"

"Right-o," agreed Lancelot, "and the quicker the better."

"Miss Judy," came a sepulchral voice from the boat, "Miss Judy, we thought you were drownded."

"Oh, Perkins," cried Judy, "is that you, Perkins?"

"What's left of me, Miss," and Perkins' bald head came into view as he stood up in the boat.

Judy and Tommy climbed in, amid excited questions and explanations, which presently settled into a continuous monotone of complaint from Tommy. "I'm half-starved. Haven't you anything to eat, Perkins?"

Now Tommy grated on Perkins' nerves. The old butler had always been treated by the Jamesons with the gentle consideration due his age and long and faithful service, in the light of which Tommy's dictation seemed nothing less than impertinent.

And so it came about that Judy was served with good things first, while

Tommy was made to wait.

"Oh, Perkins, can't you hurry," growled the small rude boy.

And then Judy turned on him. "You may be hungry, Tommy," she blazed, "but don't speak to Perkins that way again."

"Oh, Miss," deprecated Perkins, although in his old heart he was glad of her defense.

"Perkins has been out all night hunting for us," Judy's voice quivered, "and—and—he is just as tired as we are, Tommy Tolliver."

But Tommy had his sandwich, and blissfully munching it, cared little for Judy's reproof. After he had finished he went to sleep comfortably in the bottom of the boat, his troubles forgotten.

There was about Launcelot and Perkins an air of subdued excitement that finally attracted Judy's attention.

"What's the matter with you all?" she asked, curiously, as she looked up suddenly from her pile of comfortable cushions, and caught Perkins smiling at Launcelot over her head.

"Oh, nothing, Miss, nothing at all," coughed Perkins.

"Has anything happened?"

Launcelot, who was steering, smiled down at her.

"Miss Curiosity," he teased.

"I'm not curious. I just want to know."

"Oh, well, that's one way to put it."

"Tell me. Has anything happened?"

"Yes."

"What?"

"Something splendid."

Judy sat up. "Tell me," she begged.

But Launcelot was inflexible. "Not now," and Judy sank back with a sigh, for she was getting to know that when the big boy said a thing he meant it.

"When will I know?" she asked after a while.

"When you get to The Breakers."

"Oh."

She was silent for a little, then she said:

"I know you think it was awful for me to run away with Tommy—"

"It would have been better if you had sent him home."

"But I wanted to help him—he has such a hard time."

"He would have a harder time if he went to sea, Judy. He isn't like you, he doesn't like the sea for its own sake. He has read a lot of stuff about sailors and adventures, and his head is full of it. He isn't the kind that makes a brave man."

"I know that," said Judy, for the little voyage had proved Tommy and had found him wanting.

"He ought to stay at home and fight things out," said Launcelot, "as the rest of us have to."

Judy looked up at him, surprised. "Are you fighting things out?" she asked.

"Oh, yes. I want to go to college, and I can't and that's the end of it," and Launcelot's lips were set in a stern line.

"Why not?"

"Father's too sick for me to leave—I've got to run the farm," was

Launcelot's simple statement of the bitter fact.

"I am always trying to do great things," mourned Judy, with a sigh for the Cause of Thomas the Downtrodden, from which the romance seemed to have fled, "but they just fizzle out."

"Don't be discouraged. You'll learn to look before you leap yet, Judy," and Launcelot laughed, his own troubles forgotten in his interest in hers.

"What are you going to take up for a life work?" asked Judy, remembering Ruskin.

"I am going to be a lawyer," announced Launcelot, promptly, "and a good one like the Judge. My grandfather was a Judge, too, but father chose business, and failed because he wasn't fitted for it, and that's why we are on the farm, now."

"I'm going to be an artist," announced Judy, toploftically, "and paint wonderful pictures."

But Launcelot looked at her doubtfully. "I'll bet you won't," he said with decision. "I'll bet you won't paint pictures and be an artist."

"Why not?"

"Because you'll get married, and—"

Judy shrugged an impatient shoulder. "I am never going to marry," she declared.

"Why not?"

"Because I want my own way," said wilful Judy.

"Oh," said "bossy" Launcelot.

The waves were twinkling in the gold of the morning sun when the tired party sighted the beach below The Breakers.

Judy standing up in the boat with her dark hair blowing around her spied a little waiting group.

"There's Anne—dear Anne—and, why, Launcelot, there's a dog."

"Is there?"

"Yes, and—and—a man—"

"Yes." Launcelot's voice was calm, but his hand on the tiller trembled.

She turned on him her startled eyes. "Do you know who it is?" she demanded.

"Yes."

"Who?"

"Look and see."

The man on the beach was gazing straight out across the bay, and in the clearness of the morning air, Judy made out his features, the pale dark face, the waving hair.

She clutched Launcelot's arm. "Who is it?" she demanded, looking as if she had seen a spirit. "Who is it, Launcelot?"

And then Launcelot gave a shout that woke Tommy.

"It's, oh, *who* do you think it is, Judy Jameson?"

And Judy whispered with a white face, "It looks like—my father. Is it really—my father—Launcelot?" and Launcelot let the tiller go, and caught hold of her hands, and said: "It really is, it really and truly is, Judy Jameson."

Judy never knew how the boat reached the wharf, nor how she came to be in her father's arms. But she knew that she should never be happier this side of heaven than she was when he held her close and murmured in her ear, "My own daughter, my own dear little girl."

It was an excited group that circled around them—Perkins and Launcelot, and the dog, Terry, and last but not least, Anne, red-eyed and dishevelled.

"Oh, Judy, Judy," she sobbed, when at last Judy came down to earth and beamed on her. "We thought you were drowned, and I have cried all night."

And at that Judy cried, too, and they sat down on the sand and had a little weep together, comfortably, as girls will, when the danger is over and every one is safe and happy.

"I'm all right," gasped Judy at last, mopping her eyes with a clean handkerchief, offered her by the ever-useful Perkins. "I'm all right—but—but—Anne was such a goosie,—and I am so happy—" And with that she dropped her head on Anne's shoulder again and cried harder than ever.

"Dear heart, don't cry," begged the Captain.

"She is tired to death," explained Launcelot.

"She needs her breakfast, sir," suggested Perkins.

"So do I," grumbled Tommy Tolliver, who stood in the background feeling very much left out.

But even as they spoke, Judy slipped into her father's arms again, and lay there quietly, as she murmured, so that no one else heard:

"'Home is the sailor from the sea'—oh, father, father, I knew you would come back to me—I knew you would come back some day."

CHAPTER XXV

LAUNCELOT BUYS A COW

Never had Fairfax seen so many interesting arrivals as during that second week in August.

On Monday came Dr. Grennell, mysterious and smiling; on Tuesday, Judge Jameson, pale but radiant; on Wednesday, Tommy and Launcelot, bursting with important news; on Thursday, Captain Jameson, with a joyful dark maiden on one side of him, and a joyful fair maiden on the other; on Friday, Perkins, beaming with the baggage, and on Saturday, the Terry-dog, resignedly, in a crate.

And every one, except Terry, the dog, had a story to tell, and the story was one that was to become a classic in the annals of Fairfax. How Captain Jameson had been washed overboard in southern seas, how he had been rescued by natives and had lived among them; how he had been found by a party searching for gold; how he had started with them for home, had become ill as soon as they put to sea, and because of his illness had been the only one left when the ship caught on fire; how the fire had gone out, and he had floated on the deserted vessel until picked up by a fishing-boat, and how he had been brought to Newfoundland and how Dr. Grennell had discovered him by means of the Spanish coins.

But in the eyes of the children of Fairfax his adventures paled before those of Tommy Tolliver. To a gaping audience that small boy talked of the things he had done—of shipwrecks, of desert islands, of hunger and thirst until the little girls gazed at him with tears in their eyes, although the effect was somewhat spoiled by Jimmie Jones' artless remark, "But you were only away four days, Tommy!"

All Fairfax rejoiced with the Judge and Judy, but only little Anne knew what Judy really felt, for in the first moment that they were alone together after that eventful morning at The Breakers, Judy, with her eyes shining like stars, had thrown her arms around the neck of her fair little friend, and had whispered, "Oh, Anne, *Anne*, I don't deserve such happiness, but I am so thankful that I feel as if I should be good for the rest of my life."

And no one but Anne knew why Judy put everything aside to be with her father, to anticipate every desire of his, to cheer every solitary minute.

"I must try to take mother's place," she confided to her sympathetic listener in the watches of the night. "He misses her so—Anne."

Anne went back to the little gray house, where the plums were purple on the tree in the orchard, and where Becky on her lookout limb was hidden by the thickness of the foliage. The robins were gone, and so was Belinda's occupation, but she had more important things on hand, and after the first joy of greetings, the little grandmother led Anne to a cozy corner of the little kitchen, where in a big basket, Belinda sang lullabies to four happy, sleepy balls of down as white as herself.

"Oh, the dear little pussy cats," gurgled Anne, as Belinda welcomed her with a gratified "Purr-up," "what does Becky think of them, grandmother?"

"She takes care of them when Belinda goes out," said the little grandmother. "It's too funny to see them cuddle under her black wings."

"I wonder if she will make friends with Terry, Judy's dog," chatted Anne, as she cuddled the precious kittens. "He's the dearest thing, and he took to Judy right away, and follows her around all the time."

The little grandmother sat down in an old rocker with a red cushion and took off her spectacles with trembling hands. "Belinda will have to get used to him, I guess," she said.

"Of course," said Anne, not looking up, "Judy will bring him here when she comes."

"I don't mean that," said the little grandmother.

Something in the old voice made Anne look up.

"What's the matter, little grandmother?" she asked, anxiously.

"I mean that we are going to leave the little gray house, Anne, you and I and Belinda and Becky," and with that the little grandmother put on her spectacles again, to see how Anne took the news.

Anne stared. "Leave the little gray house," she said, slowly. "Why what do you mean, grandmother?"

"We are going to live at the Judge's," and at that Anne's face changed from dismay to happiness, and she turned the kittens over to Belinda and flung her arms around the little old lady's neck.

"Oh, am I really going to live with Judy?" she shrieked joyfully, "and you and Becky and Belinda—oh, it's too good to be true."

"We really are," said Mrs. Batcheller. "The Judge and I had a long talk together, the day he came down, and he wants you to go away to school with Judy, and have me come and help Aunt Patterson to manage his house. He says she is too feeble for so much care and that it will be an accommodation to him."

But Mrs. Batcheller did not tell how the Judge had argued for hours to break down the barriers of pride which she had raised, and that he had finally won, because of his insistence that Anne must have the opportunities due one of her name and race.

"You are to go to Mrs. French's school in Richmond, with Judy. She is a gentlewoman, a Southerner, and an old friend of the Judge's and mine, and we think it will be exactly the place for you two for a time."

"It will be lovely," cried little Anne, as the plans for her future were unfolded, but late that evening when she was ready to say "good night" she stood for a moment with her cheek against her grandmother's soft old one.

"I shall miss you and the little gray house, grandmother," she whispered, "I was hungry for you at The Breakers, although it was lovely there, and every one was so kind."

"I shall miss you too, dear heart," said the little grandmother, but she did not say how much, for she wanted Anne to go away happily, and she felt that she must not be selfish.

It was wonderful the planning that went on after that. Anne spent many days at the big house in Fairfax, and each time she went it was a tenderer, dearer Judy that welcomed her.

"Father will stay with grandfather this winter. I begged to stay, too, but they both think the schools here are not what I need, and so I am to go away," she explained one morning as she and Anne were getting ready to go with a party of young people to pick goldenrod.

"Yes," said Anne, putting her red reefer over her white dress, and admiring the effect.

"I hate school," began Judy, sticking in a hat-pin viciously, then she stopped and laughed, "No, I don't, either. I don't hate anything since father came back."

"Not even cats?" asked Anne, demurely.

"No. You know I love Belinda."

"Nor picnics?"

"Not Fairfax ones."

"Nor books?"

"I just love 'em—thanks to you."

"Nor—nor boys—?" mischievously.

"Oh, do stop your questions," and Judy put her hands over her ears.

But Anne persisted, "Nor boys, Judy?"

"I like Launcelot Bart—and—little Jimmie Jones, but I am not sure about Tommy Tolliver, Anne."

And then they both laughed light-heartedly, and tripped down-stairs to find Amelia and Nannie and Tommy waiting for them.

"Launcelot couldn't come," explained Tommy. "He had to go to Upper Fairfax, and he said he was awfully sorry, but he didn't dare to take so much time away from the farm."

"Poor fellow," sighed tender-hearted little Anne. "He is always so busy."

"I don't think he is to be pitied," said Judy, with a scornful glance at Tommy. "He has work to do and he does it, which is more than most people do."

There was gold in the sunshine, and gold in the changing leaves, and gold in the ripened grain in the fields, and gold in the goldenrod which they had come to pick.

Tommy gathered great armfuls of the feathery bloom, and the girls made it into bunches, while Terry, who had come with them, whuffed at the chipmunks on the gray fence-rails.

"What do you want it for?" asked Tommy, sitting down beside the busy maidens and wiping his warm forehead.

"To-morrow is Judy's birthday," said Anne, "and we are going to decorate the house."

"Oh, is it?" asked Amelia and Nannie together.

"Yes," said Judy, "and I want you to come to dinner and spend the evening with us. I am not going to have a party, because father isn't feeling as if he wanted to join in any gay things yet, but we can have a nice time together, and it may be the last before Anne and I go away to school."

"*Go where?*" gasped Nannie and Amelia and Tommy.

Judy explained. "We leave the first week in September," she ended.

"Oh, oh," cried the stricken three, "what shall we do. All winter—and we can't have any fun—if Anne isn't here, nor you, Judy, and we had planned so many things."

"Will you really miss *me*?" Judy asked a little wistfully, and at that Nannie's hand was laid on hers, as the little girl murmured, "We shall miss you awfly, Judy," while Amelia sighed a great, gusty sigh, as she said, "Oh, dear, now everything's spoiled!"

"Do you want me to come to your birthday dinner, too?" asked Tommy, anxiously, when the first shock of the coming separation was over, "or ain't you goin' to have any boys."

"Yes, I want you and Launcelot," said Judy, who had debated the question of being friendly with Tommy, for he hadn't seemed worth it, but Anne had pleaded for him. "He really means well, Judy," she had protested, "and I think he is going to turn over a new leaf."

"Well, I hope he will," said Judy, and forgave him.

When the big gate was reached, Nannie and Amelia and Tommy went on, and as Judy and Anne went into the old garden, they found the Judge and the Captain, both still semi-invalids, sitting there, amid a riot of late summer blossoms.

As he greeted them, Captain Jameson's eyes went from the rosy, fair face of little Anne to the pale but happy one of his daughter. "Father is right," he thought, "Anne does her good."

"Isn't it lovely here," said Judy, dropping her great golden bunch with a sigh as she sat down on the bench under the lilac bush. "It's so cool."

"What a lot of goldenrod," said the Judge. "Aren't you tired?"

"A little," said Judy, as she took off her hat.

"Launcelot couldn't go," Anne started to explain, when Terry, who had been investigating the hedge, barked.

"What's the matter with him?" asked Judy, as the small dog growled in what might be called a perfunctory fashion, for he was so good natured that he was in a chronic state of being at peace with the world.

She went to the gate and looked over.

"Why, it's a cow," she cried, "a beautiful little brown-eyed cow."

Terry barked again, and then a voice outside the hedge said: "Yes, and
I've just bought her."

"Launcelot," screamed both of the girls, delightedly, and opened the gate wide.

CHAPTER XXVI

JUDY PLAYS LADY BOUNTIFUL

"Down, Terry," commanded the Captain, as the little dog went for the mild-eyed cow, but the mild-eyed cow seemed perfectly able to take care of herself, and as she lowered her horns, Terry retired discreetly to a safe place between the Captain's knees, where he wagged an ingratiating tail.

Launcelot and the cow stood framed in the rose-covered gateway.

"Yes, I've bought a cow," explained the big boy, who was dusty but cheerful, "and we are going to have our own butter and milk, and if there is any over, I'll sell it."

"You have my order now," said the Judge, handsomely.

"Thank you, sir," said Launcelot, and Anne cried:

"Oh, Launcelot, make it in little pats stamped with a violet, and label it, 'From the Violet Farm.'"

"That's not a bad idea," commended the Captain, "novelties like that take, and if the butter is good, you may get a market for more than you can make."

"Then I will get another cow and enlarge my hothouse, and between the butter and the violets I guess I can bring up my college fund," and Launcelot looked so hopeful that they all smiled in sympathy.

"Where did you get her?" asked Judy, as she patted the pretty creature on the head.

"I bought her a mile or so out in the country, and I tell you I hated to take her after I had paid the money."

"Why?" asked Anne.

"Oh, they were so poor, and the cow was the only thing they had. There is a widow, named McSwiggins, with six children, and I guess they have had a pretty hard time, and now their taxes are due and the interest and two of them have had the typhoid fever, and are just skin and bone, and they had to sell the cow, and they cried, and I felt like a thief when I carried her off."

"Oh, poor things," cried Judy, when Launcelot finished his breathless recital, "poor things."

"I didn't want to take her, after I found out, but Mrs. McSwiggins said that they needed the money awfully, and that I was doing them a favor—only it was hard, and then she cried and the children all cried, too."

"Why haven't they told some one before this?" asked the Judge, wiping his eyes.

"I guess the mother is too proud. They are from the South and they haven't been in this neighborhood long, and she don't know any one."

"What's the cow's name?" asked Anne, whose eyes were like dewy forget-me-nots.

"Sweetheart. The biggest girl named her, and when I went out of the gate she just sat down on the step and looked after us, and her eyes hurt me, they were so sad."

The little cow moved restlessly. "I guess I'll have to go," sighed Launcelot, standing like a Peri outside the gates of Paradise, and contrasting the coolness and quiet of the old garden with the heat and dust of the long white road. "I guess I'll have to take Sweetheart on."

But just then down the path came Perkins, dignified in white linen, and in his hand he bore a tray on which a glass pitcher, misty with coolness and showing ravishing glimpses of lemon peel and ice, promised delicious refreshment.

"You come and have some lemonade, Mr. Launcelot," said Perkins, as he set the tray on the table, "I'll hold the cow."

And, as they all insisted, Launcelot came in, and Perkins went without the gate.

But, alas, Sweetheart was a cow of many moods, and as the gay little party in the garden sipped the cooling drink in the shade of the trees, the little cow, growing restive out there in the sun with the flies worrying her, suddenly ducked her head and ran.

And after her, still holding the rope, went the immaculate Perkins, to be dragged hither and thither by her erratic movements, while he shouted desperately, "Whoa."

And after Perkins went the excited Terry-dog, and after Terry went Launcelot, and after Launcelot went Judy, and then Anne, and then far in the rear, the Judge, while Captain Jameson, too weak to run, stood at the gate and watched.

It was a brave race. Perkins had grit and he would not let go of the rope, and Sweetheart wanted to go home and she would not stop running, and so the procession went up the dusty road and down a dusty hill, and then up another dusty hill, and down a cool green bank, where seeing ahead of her a murmuring limpid stream, Sweetheart dashed into it, stood still, and placidly drank in long sighing gulps.

Perkins went in after her, and was rescued by Launcelot, while Judy and Anne stood on the bank and laughed until the tears ran down their cheeks.

Perkins laughed, too, as he emerged wet and dripping, but beaming.

"I didn't let her go," he chuckled, a little proud of his agility in his old age, and Launcelot said admiringly, "I didn't think you had it in you, Perkins," and at that Perkins chuckled more than ever.

They went back in a triumphal procession, and then Lancelot took Sweetheart away with him, and the little girls went up-stairs to dress.

The Captain and the Judge were left alone, and presently the former said:

"Why can't we put Launcelot through college, father? It's a shame he should have to work so hard."

But the Judge shook his head. "He is having something better than college, Philip," he said. "He is learning self-reliance and he will get to college if he keeps on like this and be better for the struggle. I've told Grennell a half-dozen times that I would put up the money, for I like the boy—but there is one very good reason why we can't pay his way."

"What's that?" asked the Captain, with interest.

"He won't take a cent from anybody," said the Judge, "and I like his independence."

"So do I," said the Captain, heartily, "but we will keep an eye on him, father, and help him out when we can."

An hour later as the Captain sat alone under the lilac bush, Judy came down with white ruffles a-flutter and with her brown locks beautifully combed and sat beside him.

"To-morrow is my birthday," she said, superfluously.

"My big girl," smiled the Captain, "you make me feel old, Judy mine."

She smiled back, abstractedly. "Are—are you going to give me a present, father?" she stammered.

It was a queer question, and the Captain was not sure that he liked it.

Birthday presents were not to be talked about beforehand.

"Of course I am," he said, finally. "Why?"

"Will it—cost—as much as—Launcelot's cow?" asked Judy, still blushing.

"As Launcelot's cow?"

He stared at her. "Why do you want to know?" he asked.

"Well," she patted his coat collar, coaxingly, "I want you to give me the money, and let me buy back the McSwiggins cow.

"I'll buy it myself."

But she shook her head. "No, I want to give it myself. I feel—so—so—thankful, father, for my happiness, that I want to do something for somebody else, who isn't happy."

He put his hand under her chin and turned her face with its earnest eyes up to him. "You are sure you would rather have that than any other birthday present, Judy mine?" he asked, thinking how much she looked like her mother.

"I am very sure, father."

They sent for Launcelot that evening, and he entered into the plan with enthusiasm. "I can get another cow," he said, "and if they have the money and the cow both they will get along all right."

"I don't want them to know who gives it," said Judy. "I hate that way of giving. I don't want to go and stare at them and talk to them about their poverty. I think it would be nice to tie a note to Sweetheart's horns and just leave her there."

The next day about noon, a mysterious party, with a strange and unusual looking cow in their midst, crept to the back of the McSwiggins barn. Sweetheart lowed softly, as she recognized the familiar surroundings.

"Gracious, I hope they won't hear," said little Anne, "that would spoil it all."

Perkins set a heavy basket down and wiped his forehead.

"You go and look, Mr. Launcelot," he said, "and if there ain't any one around you tie her to the hitching-post, and then bring the ends of those pink ribbons back with you."

When that was accomplished, the Mysterious Four hid themselves in some bushes by the side of the road to await developments.

Presently Johnny McSwiggins, trailing listlessly towards the barn, gave one look and rushed back into the house.

"They's somethin' out thar," he said, with his eyes bulging.

Mary McSwiggins, the oldest girl, looked at him hopelessly. "I don' care ef they is. We alls too po' fer anythin' to hurt."

"But hit looks lak Sweetheart's ghos'," declared Johnny, "an' hit's got pink ribbin on. I declar' hit look lak Sweetheart's ghos', Sistuh Ma'y."

At that beloved name, Mary rushed out, while the family trailed behind,

Mrs. McSwiggins bringing up the rear with the wan baby in her arms.

Tied to the post was Sweetheart, but such a cow had never been seen before in the history of Fairfax, for Judy was nothing if not original, and with the help of Anne and Launcelot she had decked the little cow gorgeously.

Around her neck was a huge wreath of roses, pink ribbons were tied to her horns, and two long pink streamers like reins went over her back and across the path and around the barn, where the ends were hidden.

"Gee," said Johnny McSwiggins, but the rest of them were silent, gazing at this transformed and glorified Sweetheart, while Mary laid her head against the sleek neck and murmured love names to her dear little cow.

"They's somethin' at the end of them ribbins," said Mrs. McSwiggins, after awhile, "you all go an' look."

And when they looked they found two huge baskets, one filled with wonderful things all ready to eat (Perkins had packed that), and the other filled with fruits and vegetables (Launcelot had raised them), and on top of one basket was a box of candy (Anne sat up to make it), and on the other a package of raisin cookies (from the little grandmother).

The little McSwiggins squealed and gurgled with delight, and then ate as only people can who have seen the gaunt wolf of starvation at the door, and as they ate they asked the question unceasingly:

"Who sent it?"

"They's a letter tied to her horn," volunteered Johnny McSwiggins after he had devoured two cookies and three sandwiches and a chicken leg. "I seen it."

They found it under the roses, and when they opened it, there dropped out two yellow-backed bills (from the Judge and the Captain), and a note (and that was from Judy), and the note said:

"I waved my wand and commanded that Sweetheart be brought back to you. Also these other gifts. If you wish to keep them, and to keep my favor, you must never ask whence they came.

  "Your guardian fairy,

    "JUANNLOT."

Then all the little McSwiggins stared, and the littlest McSwiggins—except the baby, asked, "Was it really a fairy, mother?" and Mrs. McSwiggins wiped her eyes and sobbed, "I reckon it was, honey," but Mary McSwiggins with her eyes shining as they had never shone before in her sad little life said softly to her mother, "I'll bet it was them girls and that Bart boy. I'll bet it was—"

"What girls?" asked Mrs. McSwiggins.

"Them girls down at the Judge's in the big house. They wears white dresses, and one's got yaller hair and the other's got brown, and I was behin' the fence yustiddy when they was pickin' flowers, and that's how I foun' out they names—the dark one's Judy, and the light one's Anne—and the boy's named Launcelot. And that's how they got that fairy name—you look here," and she held up the note to her mother, "'Ju—ann—lot'—it's jes' them names strung together."

"Well, now," said Mrs. McSwiggins, "if that ain' bright, honey. But I don't know's we ought to take all them things."

"Sweetheart ain't goin' away from yer no more," said Mary, firmly, "and they'd feel mighty bad if we didn't take the other things."

"Well, mebbe they would," said Mrs. McSwiggins, "and anyhow they's saved us from the po'house, and that's a fact, Mary, and don' you forget it when you say yo' prayers."

Far down the road the Mysterious Four gloated over their success.

"Wasn't it fun?" gasped Anne.

"Here's to the fairy Juannlot," cried Launcelot.

"May she never cease to do good," cried Judy, beaming on her fellow conspirators.

But Perkins merely nodded approval. For had not all the good ladies of the house of Jameson played the role of Lady Bountiful, and was not Judy thus proving herself worthy of their name and fame?

CHAPTER XXVII

THE SUMMER ENDS

In the softened light of the candles, the big mirrors reflected that night four misty groups of happy people.

A blur of pink down at one end, was Anne in rosy organdie, playing games with Tommy and Amelia and Nannie; a little fire flickered in the open grate, for the evening was cool, and one side of it sat the little grandmother and her old friend, the Judge, and on the other Dr. Grennell and Captain Jameson, engaged in an animated discussion; while in the window-seat, Judy and Launcelot gazed out upon the old garden.

"I shall miss it awfully," said Judy, with a little sigh.

Launcelot turned on her a startled glance.

"Why?" he asked, "where are you going?"

"Away to school," said Judy, "didn't Anne tell you?"

"Oh, I say—oh, I say, you're not, really?" Launcelot's voice had a queer break in it, that made Judy say quickly:

"We are coming back for Christmas."

"Well, this is my finish," said Launcelot, moved to slang, by the intensity of his feelings. "I thought it was bad enough to be cut out of going to college, but if you and Anne go away, I will give up."

"No, you won't," said Judy, quickly.

"Why not?"

"Because I should be so disappointed in you, Launcelot."

For a moment they looked at each other in silence. The light wind came in through the open window and stirred the laces of Judy's dress, and blew a wisp of dark hair across her earnest eyes, which shone with a depth of feeling that Launcelot had never seen there before, and as he looked, the boy was suddenly possessed with the spirit that animated the knights of old who yearned to prove themselves worthy of their ladies.

"Would you be disappointed, Judy?" he asked, very low.

"Yes," she leaned forward, speaking eagerly. "You—you don't know what this summer has meant to me, Launcelot. I came here so miserable, so unhappy, and I found you and Anne—and because you were both so brave when you have so many things to make life hard, I think it made me a little braver, and I could bear things better, because of you, and Anne, Launcelot.

"And so—I want always to think of you as brave," she went on, "I want to feel though there are cowards in the world, that you aren't one; though there are boys who fail and boys who are not what they ought to be, that you are really brave and true and good, Launcelot—always brave and true and good—"

For a moment he could not speak, and then he said in a moved voice:

"Do you really think that, Judy?"

"Really, Launcelot."

"It helps me to know it—it will help me all my life," he said, simply, and for a moment his hand touched hers, as if a promise were given and taken.

All his life he carried the picture of her as she sat there with the silver light of the moon making a halo for her head—and though after that she was many times her old tempestuous self, yet the vision of little St. Judith, as he named her then, stayed with him, and led him to the heights.

Judy went out to dinner on Dr. Grennell's arm. She looked very grown up with her long white dress, with her hair twisted high, with pearl sidecombs that had belonged to her grandmother, and with a bunch of violets—Launcelot's birthday gift to her, in her belt.

"How old are you, little lady?" asked the doctor, as they took their seats at the table.

"As old as I look," flashing a demure glance.

"Then you are ten," he decided, "in spite of your hair on top of your head. Your eyes give you away. They are child-eyes."

"I hope she will always keep child-eyes," said the Judge, who at the head of the table was serving the soup from an old-fashioned silver tureen, with Perkins at his elbow to pass the plates. "I don't want her to grow up."

"I shall always be your little girl, grandfather," and Judy nodded happily to him from the foot of the table, where she was taking Aunt Patterson's place, "even when I am forty."

"Aw, forty," said Tommy Tolliver, unexpectedly, "that's awful old.

You'll be an old maid, Judy."

"That's what I intend to be," said that independent young lady. "I am going to be an artist."

"Oh, Judy," said little Anne, "you know you won't. You will marry Prince Charming and live happy ever after, as the fairy books say, and it will be lovely."

But Judy shrugged her shoulders, as they all laughed.

"We will see," she said, "and anyhow I am too young to think about such things," and at that the little grandmother nodded approval.

Tommy, having made his one contribution to the general conversation, ate steadily through the menu, accompanied by Amelia, whose sigh when the last course of ice-cream was served in little melons with candied cherries on top was expressive of great bliss.

But the crowning surprise of the dinner was the birthday cake.

Perkins brought it in on a great silver platter, and placed it in front of Judy with a flourish.

"Oh, oh, isn't it lovely," cried all the little girls.

"That's great," from Launcelot and Tommy.

"Perkins' *chef d'oeuvre*," was the Captain's comment, and the Judge and the doctor and Mrs. Batcheller added their praises. It really was a beautiful cake. The icing foamed up all over it like waves, and on the very top of the sugary billows was placed a little candy sailboat, as nearly like the lost "Princess" as Perkins could procure.

"Oh, how perfectly beautiful," said Judy. "How did you think of it, Perkins?" and she smiled at him in a way that set his old heart a-beating.

"You're to cut it, Miss," he said, handing her a great silver-handled knife. "There's a ring in it, and a thimble and a piece of money."

"Oh, I hope I'll get the ring," said little Anne, then blushed as

Perkins said: "That means you'll get married, Miss."

"And the one who gets the thimble will work for a living, and the one who gets the money will be rich, isn't that it?" asked Judy, as she stuck the knife in. "Oh, it seems a shame to cut it, Perkins. It is so pretty."

Launcelot found the thimble in his slice, the money—a tiny gold dollar—was in Nannie's, while to Judy came the turquoise ring.

"You see you can't escape," said Launcelot, softly, as she turned the blue hoop on her finger. "Fate doesn't intend you for an artist."

"Well, I intend to be, whether fate does or not," she insisted. "I guess I can do as I please."

"Anne, you can have the thimble," said Launcelot, rolling it across the table-cloth to her. It was a beautiful little gold affair, and she loved to sew.

"I shouldn't mind being an old maid and working for a living," she said, surveying it contentedly, "if I could have Becky and Belinda to live with me."

"I'm glad I am going to be rich," said Nannie. "I shall travel and have a new dress every week."

"Huh," boasted Tommy, "I am going to get rich, if I didn't find the money in the cake."

"Sailors don't get rich," said the Captain. "It's a poor profession."

"Aw, a sailor," stammered Tommy, getting very red, "I'm not going to be a sailor. I'm going to learn typewriting, and go to the city in an office."

And thus ended the Cause of Thomas, the Downtrodden!

But Amelia's plans proved the most interesting.

"I'm going to write," she announced, placidly. "I wrote a poem for Judy's birthday."

"Read it," they demanded, and Amelia, feeling very important, delivered the following:

"Oh, candy, oh, sugar, oh, cake, and oh, pie,
Are not half so sweet as dear J-U-D-Y."

It brought down the house, and Amelia was overcome by the honors heaped upon her.

"It isn't very good poetry," she confessed modestly, "but it means a lot."

And then the Captain made a little speech, in which he thanked Judy's friends for the happy summer she had spent among them. And then Launcelot made a speech and thanked Judy for the good times she had given them. And while Launcelot's speech wasn't as polished as the Captain's, it was so earnestly spoken that Judy was proud of her boy friend.

And after that they filed out to the old garden, the Judge and Mrs. Batcheller, and the Captain and Judy, Launcelot with his fair little friend Anne, and behind them the smaller fry, and Perkins—the wonderful Perkins at the end, with the coffee.

And there we will leave them, there in the old garden, where Judy had found hope and happiness, and where the little fountain sang ceaselessly to the nodding roses, of life and love, and of the things that had been and of the things that were to be.

Mistress Anne

CHAPTER I

In Which Things Are Said of Diogenes and of a Lady With a Lantern.

The second day of the New Year came on Saturday. The holiday atmosphere had thus been extended over the week-end. The Christmas wreaths still hung in the windows, and there had been an added day of feasting. Holidays always brought people from town who ate with sharp appetites.

It was mostly men who came, men who fished and men who hunted. In the long low house by the river one found good meals and good beds, warm fires in winter and a wide porch in summer. There were few luxuries, but it pleased certain wise Old Gentlemen to take their sport simply, and to take pride in the simplicity. They considered the magnificence of modern camps and clubs vulgar, and as savoring somewhat of riches newly acquired; and they experienced an almost æsthetic satisfaction in the contrast between the rough cleanliness of certain little lodges along the Chesapeake and its tributary tide-water streams, and the elegance of the Charles Street mansions which they had, for the moment, left behind.

It was these Old Gentlemen who, in khaki and tweed, each in its proper season, came to Peter Bower's, and ate the food which Peter's wife cooked for them. They went out in the morning fresh and radiant, and returned at night, tired but still radiant, to sit by the fire or on the porch, and, in jovial content, to tell of the delights of earlier days and of what sport had been before the invasion of the Philistines.

They knew much of gastronomic lore, these Old Gentlemen, and they liked to talk of things to eat. But they spoke of other things, and now and then they fell into soft silences when a sunset was upon them or a night of stars.

And they could tell stories! Stories backed by sparkling wit and a nice sense of discrimination. On winter nights or on holiday afternoons like this, as, gathered around the fire they grew mildly convivial, the sound of their laughter would rise to Anne Warfield's room under the eaves; she would push back the papers which held her to her desk, and wish with a sigh that the laughter were that of young men, and that she might be among them.

To-day, however, she was not at her desk. She was taking down the decorations which had made the little room bright during the brief holiday. To-morrow she would go back to school and to the forty children whom she taught. Life would again stretch out before her, dull and uneventful. The New Year would hold for her no meaning that the old year had not held.

It had snowed all of the night before, and from her window she could see the river, slate-gray against the whiteness. Out-of-doors it was very cold, but her own room was hot with the heat of the little round stove. With her holly wreaths in her arms, she stood uncertain in front of it. She had thought to burn the holly, but it had seemed to her, all at once, that to end thus the vividness of berry and of leaf would be desecration. Surely they deserved to die out in that clear cold world in which they had been born and bred!

It was a fanciful thought, but she yielded to it. Besides, there was Diogenes! She must make sure of his warmth and comfort before night closed in.

She put on her red scarf and cap and, with the wreaths in her arms, she went down-stairs. The Old Gentlemen were in the front room and she had to pass through. They rose to a man. She liked the courtliness, and gave in return her lovely smile and a little bow.

They gazed after her with frank admiration. "Who is she?" asked one who was not old, and who, slim and dark and with a black ribbon for his eye-glasses, seemed a stranger in this circle.

"The new teacher of the Crossroads school. There wasn't any place for her to board but this. So they took her in."

"Pretty girl."

The Old Gentlemen agreed, but they did not discuss her charms at length. They belonged to a generation which preferred not to speak in a crowd of a woman's attractions. One of them remarked, however, that he envied her the good fortune of feasting all the year round at Peter Bower's table.

Anne, trudging through the snow with the wreaths in her arms, would have laughed mockingly if she had heard them. It was not food that she wanted, not the game and oysters and fish over which these old gourmands gloated. What she wanted was the nectar and ambrosia of life, the color and glow—the companionship of young things like herself!

Of course there were the school children and there was Peggy. But to the children and Peggy she was a grown-up creature. Loving her, they still made her feel age's immeasurable distance, as she had felt her own distance from the Old Gentlemen.

It was Peggy, who, wound in her mother's knitted white shawl until she looked like a dingy snowball, bounced from the kitchen to meet her.

"Where are you going?" she asked.

The young teacher laughed. "Peggy," she said, "if you will never tell, you may come with me."

"Where?" demanded Peggy.

"Across the road and into the woods and down to the river."

"What are you carrying the wreaths for?"

"Wait and see."

The road which they crossed was the railroad. Over the iron rails the trains thundered from one big city to another, with a river to cross just before they reached Peter Bower's. Very few of the trains stopped at Peter's, and it was this neglect of theirs, and the consequent isolation, which constituted the charm of Bower's for town-tired folk. Yet Anne Warfield always wished that some palatial express might tarry for a moment to take her aboard, and whirl her on to the world of flashing lights, of sky-scraping towers and streaming crowds.

"What are you going to do with the wreaths?" Peggy was still demanding as they entered upon the frozen silence of the pine woods.

"I am going down as close as I can to the water's edge, and I am going to fling them out as far as I can into the river. And perhaps the river will carry them down to the sea, and the sea will say, 'Whence came you?' and the wreaths will whisper, 'We came from the forest to die on your breast, the river brought us, and the winds sang to us, and above us the sky smiled. And now we are ready to die, for we have seen life and its loveliness. It would have been dreadful if we had come to our end in the ashes of a little round stove.'"

Peggy stared, open-eyed. She had missed the application, but she liked the story.

"Let me throw one of them," she said.

"You couldn't throw them far enough, dear heart. But you shall count, 'one, two, three' for me. And when you say 'three' I'll throw one of them away, and then you must count again, and I will throw the others."

So Peggy, quite entranced by the importance of her office, took her part in the ceremony, and Anne Warfield stood on top of the snowy bank above the river, and cast upon its tumbling surface the bright burden which it was to carry to the sea.

It was at this moment that there crossed the bridge the only train from the north which stopped by day at Peter Bower's. The passengers looking out saw, far below them, sullen stream, somber woods, and a girl in a gay red scarf. They saw, too, a dingy white dot of a child who danced up and down. When the train stopped a few minutes later at Bower's, six of the passengers stepped from it, three men and three women, a smartly-dressed, cosmopolitan group, quite evidently indifferent to the glances which followed them.

Anne and Peggy had no eyes for the new arrivals. If they noticed the train at all, it was merely to give it a slurring thought, as bringing more Old Gentlemen who would eat and be merry, then hurry back again to town. As for themselves, having finished the business of the moment, they had yet to look after Diogenes.

Diogenes was a drake. He lived a somewhat cloistered life in the stable which had been made over into a garage. He had wandered in one morning soon after Anne had come to teach in the school. Peter had suggested that he be killed and eaten. But Anne, lonely in her new quarters, had appreciated the forlornness of the old drake and had adopted him. She had named him Diogenes because he had an air of searching always for something which could not be found. Once when a flock of wild ducks had flown overhead, Diogenes had listened, and, as their faint cries had come down to him, he had stretched his wings as if he, too, would fly. But his fat body had held him, and so still chained to earth, he waddled within the limits of his narrow domain.

In a cozy corner of the garage there was plenty of straw and a blanket to keep off draughts. Mrs. Bower had declared such luxury unsettling. But Anne had laughed at her. "Why should pleasant things hurt us?" she had asked, and Mrs. Bower had shaken her head.

"If you had seen the old men who come here and stuff, and die because their livers are wrong, you'd know what I mean. Give him enough, but don't pamper him."

In the face of this warning, however, Anne fed the old drake on tidbits, and visited him at least once a day. He returned her favors by waiting for her at the gate when it was not too cold and, preceding her to the house, gave a sort of major-domo effect to her progress.

Entering the stable, they found a lantern lighting the gloom, and Diogenes in a state of agitation. His solitude had been invaded by an Irish setter—a lovely auburn-coated creature with melting eyes, who, held by a leash, lay at length on Diogenes' straw with Diogenes' blanket keeping off the cold.

The old drake from some remote fastness flung his protest to the four winds!

"He's a new one." Peggy patted the dog, who rose to welcome them. "He ought to be in the kennels. Somebody didn't know."

Somebody probably had not known, but had learned. For now the door opened, and a young man came in. He was a big young man with fair hair, and he had arrived on the train.

"I beg your pardon," he said, as he saw them, "but they told me I had put my dog in the wrong place."

Peggy was important. "He belongs at the kennels. He's in Diogenes' corner."

"Diogenes?"

The old drake, reassured by the sound of voices, showed himself for a moment in the track of the lantern light.

"There he is," Peggy said, excitedly; "he lives in here by himself."

Anne had not spoken, but as she lifted the lantern from its nail and held it high, Richard Brooks was aware that this was the same girl whom he had glimpsed from the train. He had noted then her slenderness of outline, the grace and freedom of her pose; at closer range he saw her delicate smallness; the bloom on her cheek; the dusky softness of her hair; the length of her lashes; the sapphire deeps of her eyes. Yet it was not these charms which arrested his attention; it was, rather, a certain swift thought of her as superior to her surroundings.

"Then it is Diogenes whose pardon I must beg," he said, his eyes twinkling as the old drake took refuge behind Anne's skirts. "Toby, come out of that. It's you for a cold kennel."

392

"It's not cold in the kennels," Peggy protested; "it is nice and warm, and the food is fixed by Eric Brand."

"And where can I find Eric Brand?"

"He isn't here." It was Anne who answered him. "He is away for the New Year. Peggy and I have been looking after the dogs."

She did not tell him that she had done it because she liked dogs, and not because it was a part of her day's work. And he did not know that she taught school. Hence, as he walked beside her toward the kennels, with Peggy dancing on ahead with Toby, and with Diogenes left behind in full possession, he thought of her, quite naturally, as the daughter of Peter Bower.

It was an uproarious pack which greeted them. Every Old Gentleman owned a dog, and there was Peter's Mamie, two or three eager-eyed pointers, setters, hounds and Chesapeake Bay dogs. Old Mamie was nondescript, and was shut up in the kennels to-night only because Eric was away. She was eminently trustworthy, and usually ran at large.

Toby, given a box to himself, turned his melting eyes upon his master and whined.

"He was sent to me just before I left New York," Richard explained. "I fancy he is rather homesick. I am the only thing in sight that he knows."

"You might take him into the house," Anne said doubtfully, "only it is a rule that if there are many dogs they all have to share alike and stay out here. When there are only two or three they go into the sitting-room with the men."

"He can lie down behind the stove in the kitchen," Peggy offered hospitably. "Mamie does."

Richard shook his head. "Toby will have to learn with the rest of us that life isn't always what we want it to be."

He was startled by the look which the girl with the lantern gave him. "Why shouldn't it be as we want it?" she said, with sudden fire; "if I were Providence, I'd make things pleasant, and you are playing Providence to Toby. Why not let him have the comfort of the kitchen stove?"

CHAPTER II

In Which a Princess Serving Finds That the Motto of Kings is Meaningless.

Toby, safe and snug behind the kitchen stove, was keenly alive to the fact that supper was being served. He had had his own supper, so that his interest was purely impersonal.

Mrs. Bower cooked, and her daughter Beulah waited on the table. The service was not elaborate. Everything went in at once, and Peter helped the women carry the loaded trays.

Anne Warfield ate usually with the family. She would have liked to sit with the Old Gentlemen at their genial gatherings, but it would not, she felt, have been sanctioned by the Bowers. Their own daughter, Beulah, would not have done it. Beulah had nothing in common with the jovial hunters and fishers. She had her own circle of companions, her own small concerns, her own convictions as to the frivolity of these elderly guests. She would not have cared to listen to what they had to say. She did not know that their travels, their adventures, their stored-up experience had made them rich in anecdote, ready of tongue to tell of wonders undreamed of in the dullness of her own monotonous days.

But Anne Warfield knew. Now and then from the threshold she had caught the drift of their discourse, and she had yearned to draw closer, to sail with them on unknown seas of romance and of reminiscence, to leave behind her for the moment the atmosphere of schoolhouse, of small gossip, of trivial circumstance.

It was with this feeling strong upon her that to-night, when the supper bell rang, she came into the kitchen and asked Mrs. Bower if she might help Beulah. She had no feeling that such labor was beneath her. If a princess cared to serve, she was none the less a princess!

Secure, therefore, in her sense of unassailable dignity, she entered the dining-room. She might have been a goddess chained to menial tasks—a small and vivid goddess, with dusky hair. Richard Brooks, observing her, had once more a swift and certain sense of her fineness and of her unlikeness to those about her.

The young man with the black ribbon on his eye-glass also observed her. Later he said to Mrs. Bower, "Can you give me a room here for a month?"

"I might. Usually people don't care to stay so long at this time of year."

"I am writing a book. I want to stay."

Beside Richard Brooks at the table sat Evelyn Chesley. With the Dutton-Ames, and Philip Meade, she had come down with Richard and his mother to speed them upon their mad adventure.

Evelyn had taken off her hat. Her wonderful hair was swept up in a new fashion from her forehead, a dull gold comb against its native gold. She wore a silken blouse of white, slightly open at the neck. On her fingers diamonds sparkled. It seemed to Anne, serving, as if the air of the long low room were charged with some thrilling quality. Here were youth and beauty, wit and light laughter, the perfume of the roses which Evelyn wore tucked in her belt. There was the color, too, of the roses, and of the cloak in which Winifred Ames had wrapped her shivering fairness. The cloak was blue, a marvelous pure shade like the Madonna blue of some old picture.

Even Richard's mother seemed illumined by the radiance which enveloped the rest. She was a slender little thing and wore plain and simple widow's black. Yet her delicate cheeks were flushed, her eyes were shining, and her son had made her, too, wear a red rose.

The supper was suited to the tastes of the old epicures for whom it had been planned. There were oysters and ducks with the juices following the knife, hot breads, wild grape jelly, hominy and celery.

The fattest Old Gentleman carved the ducks. The people who had come on the train were evidently his friends. Indeed, he called the little lady with the shining eyes "Cousin Nancy."

"So you've brought your boy back?" he said, smiling down at her.

"Oh, yes, yes. Cousin Brin, I feel as if I had reached the promised land."

"You'll find things changed. Nothing as it was in your father's time. Foreigners to the right of you, foreigners to the left. Italians, Greeks—barbarians—cutting the old place into little farms—blotting out the old landmarks."

"I don't care; the house still stands, and Richard will hang out my father's sign, and when people want a doctor, they will come again to Crossroads."

"People in these days go to town for their doctors."

Richard's head went up. "I'll make them come to me, sir. And you mustn't think that mother brought me back. I came because I wanted to come. I hate New York."

The listening Old Gentlemen, whose allegiance was given to a staid and stately town on the Patapsco, quite glowed at that, but Evelyn flamed:

"You might have made a million in New York, Richard."

"I don't want a million."

"Oh," she appealed to Brinsley Tyson, "what can you do with a man like that—without red blood—without ambition?"

And now it was Richard who flamed. "I am ambitious enough, Eve, but it isn't to make money."

"He has some idea," the girl proclaimed recklessly to the whole table, "of living as his ancestors lived; as if one could. He believes that people should go back to plain manners and to strict morals. His mission is to keep this mad world sane."

A ripple of laughter greeted her scorn. Her own laughter met it. The slim young man at the other end of the table swung his eye-glasses from their black ribbon negligently, but his eyes missed nothing.

"It is my only grievance against you, Mrs. Nancy," Eve told the little shining lady. "I love you for everything else, but not for this."

"I am sorry, my dear. But Richard and I think alike. So we are going to settle at Crossroads—and live happy ever after."

Anne Warfield, outwardly calm, felt the blood racing in her veins. The old house at Crossroads was just across the way from her little school. She had walked in the garden every day, and now and then she had taken the children there. They had watched the squirrels getting ready for the winter, and had fed the belated birds with crumbs from the little lunch baskets. And there had been the old sun-dial to mark the hour when the recess ended and to warn them that work must begin.

She had a rapturous vision of what it might be to have the old house open, and to see Nancy Brooks and her son Richard coming in and out.

Later, however, alone in her dull room, stripped of its holiday trappings, the vision faded. To Nancy and Richard she would be just the school-teacher across the way, as to-night she had been the girl who waited on the table!

There was music down-stairs. The whine of the phonograph came up to her.

Peggy, knocking, brought an interesting bulletin.

"They are dancing," she said. "Let's sit on the stairs and look."

From the top of the stairs they could see straight into the long front room. The hall was dimly lighted so that they were themselves free from observation. Philip Meade and Eve were dancing, and the Dutton-Ames. Eve had on very high shoes with very high heels. Her skirt was wide and flaring. She dipped and swayed and floated, and the grace of the man with whom she danced matched her own.

"Isn't it lovely," said Peggy's little voice, "isn't it lovely, Anne?"

It was lovely, lovely as a dream. It was a sort of ecstasy of motion. It was youth and joy incarnate. Anne had a wild moment of rebellion. Why must she sit always at the head of the stairs?

The music stopped. Eve and Philip became one of the circle around the fireplace in the front room. Again Eve's roses and Winifred's cloak gave color to the group. There was also the leaping golden flame of the fire, and, in the background, a slight blue haze where some of the Old Gentlemen smoked.

The young man with the eye-glasses was telling a story. He told it well, and there was much laughter when he finished. When the music began again, he danced with Winifred Ames. Dutton Ames watched them, smiling. He always smiled when his eyes rested on his lovely wife.

Evelyn danced with Richard. He did not dance as well as Philip, but he gave the effect of doing it easily. He swung her finally out into the hall. The whine of the phonograph ceased. Richard and Eve sat down on a lower step of the stairway.

The girl's voice came up to the quiet watchers clearly. "When are you coming to New York to dance with me again, Dicky Boy?"

395

"You must come down here. Pip will bring you in his car for the week-ends, with the Dutton-Ames. And I'll get a music box and a lot of new records. The old dining-room has a wonderful floor."

"I hate your wonderful floor and your horrid old house. And when I think of Fifth Avenue and the lights and the theaters and you away from it all——"

"Poor young doctors have no right to the lights and all the rest of it. Eve, don't let's quarrel at the last moment. You'll be reconciled to it all some day."

"I shall never be reconciled."

And now Philip Meade was claiming her. "You promised me this, Eve."

"I shall have all the rest of the winter for you, Pip."

"As if that made any difference! I never put off till to-morrow the things I want to do to-day. And as for Richard, he'll come running back to us before the winter is over."

Richard shrugged. "You're a pair of cheerful prophets. Go and fox-trot with him, Eve."

Left alone, the eyes of the young doctor went at once to the top of the stairs.

"Come down and dance," he said.

"Do you mean me?" Peggy demanded out of the dimness.

"I mean both of you."

"I can't dance—not the new dances." Anne was conscious of an overwhelming shyness. "Take Peggy."

"How did you know we were up here?" Peggy asked.

"Well, I heard a little laugh, and a little whisper, and I looked up and saw a little girl."

"Oh, oh, did you really?"

"Really."

"Well, I can't dance. But I can try."

So they tried, with Richard lifting the child lightly to the lilting tune.

When he brought her back, he sat down beside Anne. Shyness still chained her, but he chatted easily. Anne could not have told why she was shy. In the stable she had felt at her ease with him. But then she had not seen Eve or Winifred. It was the women who had seemed to make the difference.

Presently, however, he had her telling of her school. "It begins again to-morrow."

"Do you like it?"

"Teaching? No. But I love the children."

"Do you teach Peggy?"

"Yes. She is too young, really, but she insists upon going."

"There used to be a schoolhouse across the road from my grandfather's. A red brick school with a bell on top."

"There is still a bell. I always ring it myself, although the boys beg to do it. But I like to think of myself as the bell ringer."

It was while they sat there that Eric Brand came in through the kitchen-way to the hall. He stood for a moment looking into the lighted front room where Eve still danced with Philip Meade, and where the young man with the eye-glasses talked with the Dutton-Ames. Anne instinctively kept silent. It was Peggy who revealed their hiding place to him.

"Oh, Eric," she piped, "are you back?" She went flying down the stairs to him.

He caught her, and holding her in his arms, peered up. "Who's there?"

Peggy answered. "It's Anne and the new doctor. I danced with him, and he came on the train with those other people in there—and he has a dog named Toby—it's in the kitchen."

"So that's his dog? It will have to go to the kennels for the night."

Richard, descending, apologized. "I shouldn't have let Toby stay in the house, but Miss Bower put in a plea for him."

"Beulah?"

"He means Anne," Peggy explained. "Her name is Warfield. It's funny you didn't know."

"How could I?" Richard had a feeling that he owed the little goddess-girl an explanation of his stupidity. He found himself again ascending the stairs.

But Anne had fled. Overwhelmingly she realized that Richard had believed her to be the daughter of Peter Bower. Daughter of that crude and common man! Sister of Beulah! Friend of Eric Brand!

Well, she had brought it on herself. She had looked after the dogs and she had waited on the table. People thought differently of these things. The ideals she had tried to teach her children were not the ideals of the larger world. Labor did not dignify itself. The motto of kings was meaningless! A princess serving was no longer a princess!

Sitting very tense and still in the little rocking-chair in her own room, she decided that of course Richard looked down on her. He had perceived in her no common ground of birth or of breeding. Yet her grandfather had been the friend of the grandfather of Richard Brooks!

When Peggy came up, she announced that she was to sleep with Anne. It was an arrangement often made when the house was full. To-night Anne welcomed the cheery presence of the child. She sang her to sleep, and then sat for a long time by the little round stove with Peggy in her arms.

She laid her down as a knock sounded on her door.

"Are you up?" some one asked, and she opened it, to find Evelyn Chesley.

"May I borrow a needle?" She showed a torn length of lace-trimmed flounce. "I caught it on a rocker in my room. There shouldn't be any rocker."

"Mrs. Bower loves them," Anne said, as she hunted through her little basket; "she loves to rock and rock. All the women around here do."

"Then you're not one of them?"

"No. My grandmother was Cynthia Warfield of Carroll."

The name meant nothing to Evelyn. It would have meant much to Nancy Brooks.

"How did you happen to come here? I don't see how any one could choose to come."

"My mother died—and there was no one but my Great-uncle Rodman Warfield. I had to get something to do—so I came here, and Uncle Rod went to live with a married cousin."

Evelyn had perched herself on the post of Anne's bed and was mending the flounce. Although she was not near the lamp, she gave an effect of gathering to her all the light of the room. She was wrapped in a robe of rose-color, a strange garment with fur to set it off, and of enormous fullness. It spread about her and billowed out until it almost hid the little bed and the child upon it.

Beside her, Anne in her blue serge felt clumsy and common. She knew that she ought not to feel that way, but she did. She would have told her scholars that it was not clothes that made the man, or dress the woman. But then she told her scholars many things that were right and good. She tried herself to be as right and good as her theories. But it was not always possible. It was not possible at this moment.

"What brought you here?" Eve persisted.

"I teach school. I came in September."

"What do you teach?"

"Everything. We are not graded."

"I hope you teach them to be honest with themselves."

"I am not sure that I know what you mean?"

"Don't let them pretend to be something that they are not. That's why so many people fail. They reach too high, and fall. That's what Nancy Brooks is doing to Richard. She is making him reach too high."

She laughed as she bent above her needle. "I fancy you are not interested in that. But I can't think of anything but—the waste of it. I hope you will all be so healthy that you won't need him, and then he will have to come back to New York."

"I don't see how anybody could leave New York. Not to come down here." Anne drew a quick breath.

Eve spoke carelessly: "Oh, well, I suppose it isn't so bad here for a woman, but for a man—a man needs big spaces. Richard will be cramped—he'll shrink to the measure of all this—narrowness." She had finished her flounce, and she rose and gave Anne the needle. "In the morning, if the weather is good, we are to ride to Crossroads. Is your school very far away?"

"It is opposite Crossroads. Mrs. Brooks' father built it."

Anne spoke stiffly. She had felt the sting of Eve's indifference, and she was furious with herself for her consciousness of Eve's clothes, of her rings—of the gold comb in her hair.

When her visitor had gone, Anne took down her own hair, and flung it up into a soft knot on the top of her head. Swept back thus, her face seemed to bloom into sudden beauty. She slipped the blue dress from her shoulders and saw the long slim line of her neck and the whiteness of her skin.

The fire had died down in the little round stove. The room was cold. She thought of Eve's rose-color, and of the warmth of her furs.

Bravely, however, she hummed the tune to which the others had danced. She lifted her feet in time. Her shoes were heavy, and she took them off. She tried to get the rhythm, the lightness, the grace of movement. But these things must be taught, and she had no one to teach her.

When at last she crept into bed beside the sleeping Peggy, she was chilled to the bone, and she was crying.

398

Peggy stirred and murmured.

Soothing the child, Anne told herself fiercely that she was a goose to be upset because Eve Chesley had rings and wore rose-color. Why, she was no better than Diogenes, who had fumed and fussed because Toby had taken his straw in the stable.

But her philosophy failed to bring peace of mind. For a long time she lay awake, working it out. At last she decided, wearily, that she had wept because she really didn't know any of the worth-while things. She didn't know any of the young things and the gay things. She didn't know how to dance or to talk to men like Richard Brooks. The only things that she knew in the whole wide world were—books!

CHAPTER III

In Which the Crown Prince Enters Upon His Own.

It developed that the name of the young man with the eye-glasses was Geoffrey Fox. Mrs. Bower told Anne at the breakfast table, as the two women sat alone.

"He is writing a book, and he wants to stay."

"The little dark man?"

"I shouldn't call him little. He is thin, but he is as tall as Richard Brooks."

"Is he?" To Anne it had seemed as if Richard had towered above her like a young giant. She had scarcely noticed the young man with the eye-glasses. He had melted into the background of old gentlemen; had become, as it were, a part of a composite instead of a single personality.

But to be writing a book!

"What kind of a book, Mrs. Bower?"

"I don't know. He didn't say. I am going to give him the front room in the south wing; then he will have a view of the river."

When Anne met the dark young man in the hall an hour later, she discovered that he had keen eyes and a mocking smile.

He stopped her. "Do we have to be introduced? I am going to stay here. Did Mrs. Bower tell you?"

"She told me you were writing a book."

"Don't tell anybody else; I'm not proud of it."

"Why not?"

He shrugged. "My stories are pot-boilers, most of them—with everybody happy in the end."

"Why shouldn't everybody be happy in the end?"

"Because life isn't that way."

"Life is what we make it."

"Who told you that?"

399

She flushed. "It is what I tell my school children."

"But have you found it so?"

She faltered. "No—but perhaps it is my fault."

"It isn't anybody's fault. If the gods smile—we are happy. If they frown, we are miserable. That's all there is to it."

"I should hate to think that was all." She was roused and ready to fight for her ideals. "I should hate to think it."

"All your hating won't make it as you want it," his glance was quizzical, "but we won't quarrel about it."

"Of course not," stiffly.

"And we are to be friends? You see I am to stay a month."

"Are you going to write about us?"

"I shall write about the Old Gentlemen. Is there always such a crowd of them?"

"Only on holidays and week-ends."

"Perhaps I shall write about you——" daringly. "I need a little lovely heroine."

Her look stopped him. His face changed. "I beg your pardon," he said quickly. "I should not have said that."

"Would you have said it if I had not waited on the table?" Her voice was tremulous. The color that had flamed in her cheeks still dyed them. "I thought of it last night, after I went up-stairs. I have been trying to teach my little children in my school that there is dignity in service, and so—I have helped Mrs. Bower. But I felt that people did not understand."

"You felt that we—thought less of you?"

"Yes," very low.

"And that I spoke as I did because I did not—respect you?"

"Yes."

"Then I beg your pardon. Indeed, I do beg your pardon. It was thoughtless. Will you believe that it was only because I was thoughtless?"

"Yes." But her troubled eyes did not meet his. "Perhaps I am too sensitive. Perhaps you would have said—the same things—to Eve Chesley—if you had just met her. But I am sure you would not have said it in the same tone."

He held out his hand to her. "You'll forgive me? Yes? And be friends?"

She did not seem to see his hand. "Of course I forgive you," she said, with a girlish dignity which sat well upon her, "and perhaps I have made too much of it, but you see I am so much alone, and I think so much."

He wanted to ask her questions, of why she was there and of why she was alone. But something in her manner forbade, and so they spoke of other things until she left him.

Geoffrey went out later for a walk in the blinding snow. All night it had snowed and the storm had a blizzard quality, with the wind howling and the drifts piling to prodigious heights. Geoffrey faced the elements with a strength which won the respect of Richard Brooks who, also out in it, with his dog Toby, was battling gloriously with wind and weather.

"If we can reach the shelter of the pines," he shouted, "they'll break the force of the storm."

Within the wood the snow was in winding sheets about the great trees.

"What giant ghosts!" Geoffrey said. "Yet in a month or two the sap will run warm in their veins, and the silence will be lapped by waves of sound—the singing of birds and of little streams."

"I used to come here when I was a boy," Richard told him. "There were violets under the bank, and I picked them and made tight bunches of them and gave them to my mother. She was young then. I remember that she usually wore white dresses, with a blue sash fluttering."

"You lived here then?"

"No, we visited at my grandfather's, a mile or two away. He used to drive us down, and he would sit out there on the point and fish,—a grand old figure, in his broad hat, with his fishing creel over his shoulder. There were just two sports that my grandfather loved, fishing and fox-hunting; but he was a very busy doctor and couldn't ride often to hounds. But he kept a lot of them. He would have had a great contempt for Toby. His own dogs were a wiry little breed."

"My grandfather was blind, and always in his library. So my boyhood was different. I used to read to him. I liked it, and I wouldn't exchange my memories for yours, except the violets—I should like to pick them here in the spring—perhaps I shall—I told Mrs. Bower I would take a room for a month or more—and since we have spoken of violets—I may wait for their blooming."

He laughed, and as they turned back, "I have found several things to keep me," he said, but he did not name them.

All day Anne was aware of the presence in the house of the young guests. She was aware of Winifred Ames' blue cloak and of Eve's roses. She was aware of Richard's big voice booming through the hall, of Geoffrey's mocking laugh.

But she did not go down among them. She ate her meals after the others had finished. She did not wait upon the table and she did not sit upon the stairs. In the afternoon she wrote a long letter to her Great-uncle Rodman, and she went early to bed.

She was waked in the morning by the bustle of departure. Some of the Old Gentlemen went back by motor, others by train. Warmed by a hearty breakfast, bundled into their big coats, they were lighted on their way by Eric Brand.

It was just as the sun flashed over the horizon and showed the whiteness of a day swept clear by the winds of the night that the train for the north carried off the Dutton-Ames, Philip and Eve.

Evelyn went protesting. "Some day you are going to regret it, Richard."

"Don't croak. Wish me good luck, Eve."

But she would not. Yet when she stood at last on the train steps to say "Good-bye," she had in her hand one of the roses he had given her and which she had worn. She touched it lightly to her lips and tossed it to him.

By the time he had picked it up the train was on its way, and Evelyn, looking back, had her last glimpse of him standing straight and tall against the morning sky, the rose in his hand.

It was eight o'clock when Eric drove Anne and Peggy through the drifts to the Crossroads school. It was nine when Geoffrey Fox came down to a late breakfast. It was ten when Richard and his mother and the dog Toby in a hired conveyance arrived at the place which had once been Nancy's home.

Imposing, even in its shabbiness, stood the old house, at the end of an avenue of spired cedars.

As they opened the door a grateful warmth met them.

"David has been here," Nancy said. "Oh, Richard, Richard, what a glorious day to begin."

And now there came from among the shadows a sound which made them stop and listen. "Tick, tock," said the great hall clock.

"Mother, who wound it?"

Nancy Brooks laughed tremulously. "Cousin David had the key. In all these years he has never let the old clock run down. It seemed queer to think of it ticking away in this empty house."

There were tears in her eyes. He stooped and kissed her. "And now that you are here, you are going to be happy?"

"Very happy, dear boy."

It was nearly twelve when David Tyson came limping up the path. He had a basket in one hand, and a cane in the other. Behind him trotted a weedy-looking foxhound. The dog Toby, charging out of the door as Nancy opened it, fell, as it were, upon the neck of the hound. His overtures of friendship were met with a dignified aloofness which merged gradually into a reluctant cordiality.

Nancy held out both hands to the old man. "I saw you coming. Oh, how good it seems to be here again, Cousin David."

"Let me look at you." He set the basket down, and took her hands in his. Then he shook his head. "New York has done things to you," he said. "It has given you a few gray hairs. But now that you are back again I shall try to forgive it."

"I shall never forgive it," she said, "for what it has done to me and mine."

"But you are here, and you have brought your boy; that's a thing to be thankful for, Nancy."

They were silent in the face of overwhelming memories. The only sound in the shadowy hall was the ticking of the old clock—the old clock which had tick-tocked in all the years of loneliness with no one to listen.

Richard greeted him with heartiness. "This looks pretty good to me, Cousin David."

"It's God's country, Richard. Brin hates it. He loves his club and the city streets. But for me there's nothing worth while but this sweep of the hills and the river between."

He uncovered his basket. "Tom put up some things for you. I've engaged Milly, a mulatto girl, but she can't get here until to-morrow. She is about the best there is left. Most of them go to town. She'll probably seem pretty crude after New York servants, Nancy."

"I don't care." Nancy almost sang the words. "I don't care what I have to put up with, Cousin David. I shall sleep to-night under my own roof with nothing between me and the stars. And there won't be anybody overhead or underneath, and there won't be a pianola to the right of me, and a phonograph to the left, and there won't be the rumble of the subway or the crash of the elevated, and in the morning I shall open my eyes and see the sun rise over the river, and I shall look out upon the world that I love and have loved all of these years——"

And now she was crying, and Richard had her in his arms. Over her head he looked at the older man. "I didn't dream that she felt like this."

"I knew—as soon as I saw her. You must never take her back, Richard."

"Of course not," hotly.

Yet with the perverseness of youth he was aware, as he said it, of a sudden sense of revolt against the prospect of a future spent in this quiet place. Flashing came a vision of the city he had left, of crowded hospitals, of big men consulting with big men, of old men imparting their secrets of healing to the young; of limousines speeding luxuriously on errands of mercy; of patients pouring out their wealth to the men who had made them well.

All this he had given up because his mother had asked it. She had spoken of the place which his grandfather had filled, of the dignity of a country practice, of the opportunities for research and for experiment. At close range, the big town set between its rivers and the sea had seemed noisy and vulgar. Its people had seemed mad in their race for money. Its medical men had seemed to lack the fineness and finish which come to those who move and meditate in quiet places.

But seen from afar as he saw it now, it seemed a wonder city, its tall buildings outlined like gigantic castles against the sky. It seemed filled to the brim with vivid life. It seemed, indeed, to call him back!

While David and Nancy talked he went out, and, from the top of the snowy steps, surveyed his domain. Back and back in the wide stretch of country which faced him, beyond the valleys, on the other side of the hills, were people who would some day listen for the step of young Richard as those who had gone before had listened for the step of his grandfather. He saw himself going forth on stormy nights to fight pain and pestilence; to minister to little children, to patient mothers; to men beaten down by an enemy before whom their strength was as wax. They would wait for him, anxious for his verdict, yet fearing it, welcoming him as a saviour, who would stand with flaming sword between disease and the Dark Angel.

The schoolhouse was on the other side of the road. It was built of brick like the house. Richard's grandfather had paid for the brick. He had believed in public schools and had made this one possible. Children came to it from all the countryside. There were other schools in the sleepy town. This was the Crossroads school, as Richard Tyson had been the Crossroads doctor. He had given himself to a rural community—his journeys had been long and his life hard, but he had loved the labor.

The bell rang for the noon recess. The children appeared presently, trudging homeward through the snow to their midday dinners. Then Anne Warfield came out. She wore a heavy brown coat and soft brown hat. In her hand was a small earthen dish. She strewed seeds for the birds, and they flew down in front of her—juncoes and sparrows, a tufted titmouse, a cardinal blood-red against the whiteness. She was like a bird herself in all her brown.

When the dish was empty, she turned it upside down, and spread her hands to show that there was nothing more. On the Saturday night when she had waited on the table, Richard had noticed the loveliness of her hands. They were small and white, and without rings. Yet in spite of their smallness and whiteness, he knew that they were useful hands, for she had served well at Bower's. And now he knew that they were kindly hands, for she had fed the birds who had come begging to her door.

Peggy joined her, and the two came out the gate together. Anne looking across saw Richard. She hesitated, then crossed the road.

He at once went to meet her. She flushed a little as she spoke to him. "Peggy and I want to ask a favor. We've always had our little Twelfth Night play in the Crossroads stable. And we had planned for it this year—you see, we didn't know that you were coming."

"And we were afraid that you wouldn't want us," Peggy told him.

"Were you really afraid?"

"I wasn't. But Miss Anne was."

"I told the children that they mustn't be disappointed if we were not able to do this year as we had done before. I felt that with people in the house, it might not be pleasant for them to have us coming in such a crowd."

"It will be pleasant, and mother will be much interested. I wish you'd come up and tell us about it."

She shook her head. "Peggy and I have just time to get back to Bower's for our dinner."

"Aren't the roads bad?"

"Not when the snow is hard."

Peggy went reluctantly. "I think he is perfectly lovely," she said, at a safe distance. "Don't you?"

Anne's reply was guarded. "He is very kind. I am glad that he doesn't mind about the Twelfth Night play, Peggy."

Richard spoke to David of Anne as the two men, a few minutes later, climbed the hill toward David's house.

"She seems unusual."

"She is the best teacher we have ever had, but she ought not to be at Bower's. She isn't their kind."

David's little house, set on top of a hill, was small and shabby without, but within it was as compact as a ship's cabin. David's old servant, Tom, kept it immaculate, and there were books everywhere, old portraits, precious bits of mahogany.

From the window beside the fireplace there was a view of the river. It was a blue river to-day, sparkling in the sunshine. David, standing beside Richard, spoke of it.

"It isn't always blue, but it is always beautiful. Even when the snow flies as it did yesterday."

"And are you content with this, Cousin David?"

The answer was evasive. "I have my little law practice, and my books. And is any one ever content, Richard?"

Going down the hill, Richard pondered. Was Eve right after all? Did a man who turned his face away from the rush of cities really lack red blood?

Stopping at the schoolhouse, he found teacher and scholars still gone. But the door was unlocked and he went in. The low-ceiled room was charming, and the good taste of the teacher was evident in its decorations. There were branches of pine and cedar on the walls, a picture of Washington at one end with a flag draped over it, a pot of primroses in the south window.

There were several books on Anne's desk. Somewhat curiously he examined the titles. A shabby Browning, a modern poet or two, Chesterton, a volume of Pepys, the pile topped by a small black Bible. Moved by a sudden impulse, he opened the Bible. The leaves fell back at a marked passage:

"Let not your heart be troubled."

He shut the book sharply. It was as if he had peered into the girl's soul. The red was in his cheeks as he turned away.

That night Nancy Brooks went with Richard to his room. On the threshold she stopped.

"I have given this room to you," she said, "because it was mine when I was a girl, and all my dreams have been shut in— waiting for you."

"Mother," he caught her hands in his, "you mustn't dream too much for me."

"Let me dream to-night;" she was looking up at him with her shining eyes; "to-morrow I shall be just a commonplace mother of a commonplace son; but to-night I am queen, and you are the crown prince on the eve of coronation. Oh, Hickory Dickory, I am such a happy mother."

Hickory Dickory! It was her child-name for him. She had not often used it of late. He felt that she would not often use it again. He was much moved by her dedication of him to his new life. He held her close. His doubts fled. He thought no more of Eve and of her flaming arguments. Somewhere out in the snow her rose lay frozen and faded where he had dropped it.

And when he slept and dreamed it was of a little brown bird which sang in the snow, and the song that it sang seemed to leap from the pages of a Book, "Let not your heart be troubled, neither let it be afraid."

CHAPTER IV

In Which Three Kings Come to Crossroads.

Anne's budget of news to her Great-uncle Rod swelled to unusual proportions in the week following the opening of Crossroads. She had so much to say to him, and there was no one else to whom she could speak with such freedom and frankness.

By the Round Stove.
My Dear:

I am sending this as an antidote for my doleful Sunday screed. Now that the Lovely Ladies are gone, I am myself again!

I know that you are saying, "You should never have been anything but yourself." That's all very well for you who know Me-Myself, but these people know only the Outside-Person part of me, and the Outside-Person part is stiff and old-fashioned, and self-conscious. You see it has been so many months since I have hobnobbed with Lilies-of-the-Field and with Solomons-in-all-their-Glory. And even when I did hobnob with them it was for such a little time, and it ended so heart-breakingly. But I am not going to talk of that, or I shall weep and wail again, and that wouldn't be fair to you.

The last Old Gentleman left yesterday in the wake of the Lovely Ladies. Did I tell you that Brinsley Tyson is a cousin of Mrs. Brooks? His twin brother, David, lives up the road. Brinsley is the city mouse and David is the country one. They are as different as you can possibly imagine. Brinsley is fat and round and red, and David is thin and tall and pale. Yet there is the "twin look" in their faces. The high noses and square chins. Neither of them wears a beard. None of the Old Gentlemen does. Why is it? Is hoary-headed age a thing of the dark and distant past? Are you the only one left whose silver banner blows in the breeze? Are the grandfathers all trying to look like boys to match the grandmothers who try to look like girls?

Mrs. Brooks won't be that kind of grandmother. She is gentle and serene, and the years will touch her softly. I shall like her if she will let me. But perhaps little school-teachers won't come within her line of vision. You see I learned my lesson in those short months when I peeped into Paradise.

I wonder how it would seem to be a Lily-of-the-Field. I've never been one, have I? Even when I was a little girl I used to stand on a chair to wipe the dishes while you washed them. I felt very important to be helping mother, and you would talk about the dignity of labor—you darling, with the hot water wrinkling and reddening your lovely long fingers, which were made to paint masterpieces.

I am trying to pass on to my school children what you have given to me, and oh, Uncle Rod, when I speak to them I seem to be looking with you, straight through the kitchen window, at the sunset. We never knew that the kitchen sink was there, did we? We saw only the sunsets. And now because you are a darling dear, and because you are always seeing sunsets, I am sending you a verse or two which I have copied from a book which Geoffrey Fox left last night at my door.

"When Salomon sailed from Ophir,
With Olliphants and gold,
The kings went up, the kings went down,
Trying to match King Salomon's crown;
But Salomon sacked the sunset,
Wherever his black ships rolled.
He rolled it up like a crimson cloth,
And crammed it into his hold.
CHORUS: "Salomon sacked the sunset,
Salomon sacked the sunset,
He rolled it up like a crimson cloth,
And crammed it into his hold.
"His masts were Lebanon cedars,
His sheets were singing blue,
But that was never the reason why
He stuffed his hold with the sunset sky!

The kings could cut their cedars,
And sail from Ophir, too;
But Salomon packed his heart with dreams,
And all the dreams were true."
Now join in the chorus, you old dear—and I'll think that I am a little girl again—

"The kings could cut their cedars,
Cut their Lebanon cedars;
But Salomon packed his heart with dreams,
And all
the dreams
were true! "

In the Schoolroom.

I told you that Geoffrey Fox left a book for me to read. I told you that he wore eye-glasses on a black ribbon, that he is writing a novel, and that I don't like him. Well, he went into Baltimore this morning to get his belongings, and when he comes back he will stay until his book is finished. It will be interesting to be under the same roof with a story. All the shadows and corners will seem full of it. The house will speak to him, and the people in it, though none of the rest of us will hear the voices, and the wind will speak and the leaping flames in the fireplace, and the sun and the moon—and when the snow comes it will whisper secrets in his ear and presently it will be snowing all through the pages.

It snowed this morning, and from my desk I can see young Dr. Brooks shoveling a path from his front porch. He and his mother came to Crossroads yesterday, and they have been very busy getting settled. They have a colored maid, Milly, but no man, and young Richard does all of the outside work. I think I shall like him. Don't you remember how as a little girl I always adored the Lion-hearted king? I always think of him when I see Dr. Brooks. He isn't handsome, but he is broad-shouldered and big and blond. I haven't had but one chance to speak to him since he and his mother left Bower's. Perhaps I shan't have many chances to speak to him. But a cat may look at a king!

I am all alone in the schoolroom. The children went an hour ago. Eric and Beulah are to call for me on their way home from town. They took Peggy with them. Did I tell you that Eric is falling in love with Beulah? I am not sure whether it is the best thing for him, but I am sure it is for her. She is very happy, and blushes when he looks at her. He is finer than she, and bigger, mentally and spiritually. He is crude, but he will grow as so many American men do grow—and there are dreams in his clear blue eyes. And, after all, it is the dreams that count—as Salomon discovered.

Yet it may be that Eric will bring Beulah up to his level. She is an honest little thing and good and loving. Her life is narrow, and she thinks narrow thoughts. But he is wise and kind, and already I can see that she is trying to keep step with him—which is as it should be.

I like to think that father and mother kept step through all the years. She was his equal, his comrade; she marched by his side with her head up fitting her two short steps to his long stride.

King Richard has just waved to me. I stood up to see the sunset—a band of gold with black above, and he waved, and started to run across the road. Then somebody called him from the house. Perhaps it was the telephone and his first patient. If I am ever ill, I should like to have a Lion-hearted Doctor—wouldn't you?

At the Sign of the Lantern.

I am with Diogenes in the stable, with the lantern making deep shadows, and the loft steps for a desk. Eric and Beulah came for me before I had asked a question—an important question—so I am finishing my letter here, while Eric puts Daisy in her stall, and then he will post it for me.

Diogenes has had his corn, and is as happy as Brinsley Tyson after a good dinner. Oh, such eating and drinking! How these old men love it! And you with your bread and milk and your book propped up against the lamp, or your handful of raisins and your book under a tree!

But I must scribble fast and ask my question. It isn't easy to ask. So I'll put it in sections:

Do you
ever

see
Jimmie—Ford?

That is the first time that I have written his name since I came here. I had made up my mind that I wouldn't write it. But somehow the rose-colored atmosphere of the other night, and these men of his kind have brought it back—all those whirling weeks when you warned me and I wouldn't listen. Uncle Rod, if a woman hadn't an ounce of pride she might meet such things. If I had not had a grandmother as good as Jimmie's and better—I might have felt less—stricken. Geoffrey Fox spoke to me on Saturday in a way which—hurt. Perhaps I am too sensitive—but I haven't quite learned to—hold up my head.

You mustn't think that I am unhappy. Indeed, I am not, except that I cannot be with you. But it is good to know that you are comfortable, and that Cousin Margaret is making it seem like home. Some day we are to have a home, you and I, when our ship comes in "with the sunset packed in the hold." But now it is well that I have work to do. I know that this is my opportunity, and that I must make the most of it. There's that proverb of yours, "The Lord sends us quail, but he doesn't send them roasted." I have written it out, and have tucked it into my mirror frame. I shall have to roast my own quail. I only hope that I may prove a competent cook!

Eric is here, and I must say "Good-bye." Diogenes sends love, and a little feather that dropped from his wing. Some day he will send a big one for you to make a pen and write letters to me. I love your letters, and I love you. And oh, you know that you have all the heart's best of your own

Anne.
The Morning After the Magi Came.
I am up early to tell you about it. But I must go back a little because I have had so much else to talk about that I haven't spoken of the Twelfth Night play.

It seems that years ago, when old Dr. Brooks first built the schoolhouse, the children used his stable on Twelfth Night for a spectacle representing the coming of the Wise Men.

Mr. David had told me of it, and I had planned to revive the old custom this year, and had rehearsed the children. I thought when I heard that the house was to be occupied that I might have to give it up. But Peggy and I plucked up our courage and asked King Richard, and he graciously gave permission.

It was a heavenly night. Snow on the ground and all the stars out. The children met in the schoolhouse and we started in a procession. They all wore simple little costumes, just some bit of bright color draped to give them a quaint picturesqueness. One of the boys led a cow, and there was an old ewe. Then riding on a donkey, borrowed by Mr. David, came the oldest Mary in our school. I chose her because I wanted her to understand the sacred significance of her name, and our only little Joseph walked by her side. The children followed and their parents, with the wise men quite in the rear, so that they might enter after the others.

When we reached the stable, I grouped Joseph and Mary in one of the old mangers, where the Babe lay, and he was a dear, real, baby brother of Mary. I hid a light behind the straw, so that the place was illumined. And then my little wise men came in; and the children, who with their parents were seated on the hay back in the shadows, sang, "We Three Kings" and other carols. The gifts which the Magi brought were the children's own pennies which they are giving to the other little children across the sea who are fatherless because of the war.

It was quite wonderful to hear their sweet little voices, and to see their rapt faces and to know that, however sordid their lives might be, here was Dream, founded on the Greatest Truth, which would lift them above the sordidness.

Dr. Brooks and his mother and Mr. David were not far from me, and Dr. Brooks leaned over and asked if he might speak to the children. I said I should be glad, so he stood up and told them in such simple, fine fashion that he wanted to be to them all that his grandfather had been to their parents and grandparents. He wanted them to feel that his life and service belonged to them. He wanted them to know how pleased he was with the Twelfth Night spectacle, and that he wanted it to become an annual custom.

Then in his mother's name, he asked them to come up to the house—all of them—and we were shown into the Garden Room which opens out upon what was once a terraced garden, and there was a great cake with candles, and sandwiches, and coffee for the grown-ups and hot chocolate for the kiddies.

Wasn't that dear? I had little François thank them, and he did it so well. Why is it that these small foreigners lack the self-consciousness of our own boys and girls? He had been one of the wise men in the spectacle, and he still wore his white beard and turban and his long blue and red robes. Yet he wasn't in the least fussed; he simply made a bow, said what he had to say, made another bow, with never a blush or a quaver or giggle. His mother was there, and she was so happy—she is a widow, and sews in the neighborhood, plain sewing, and they are very poor.

I rode home with the Bowers, and as we drove along, I heard the children singing. I am sure they will never forget the night under the winter stars, nor the scene in the stable with the cow and the little donkey and the old ewe, and the Light that illumined the manger. I want them always to remember, Uncle Rod, and I want to remember. It is only when I forget that I lose faith and hope.

Blessed dear, good-night.
Your Anne.

CHAPTER V

In Which Peggy Takes the Center of the Stage.

The bell on the schoolhouse had a challenging note. It seemed to call to the distant hills, and the echo came back in answer. It was the voice of civilization. "I am here that you may learn of other hills and of other valleys, of men who have dreamed and of men who have discovered, of nations which have conquered and of nations which have fallen into decay. I am here that you may learn—ding dong—that you may learn, ding ding—that you may learn—ding dong ding—of Life."

As she rang the bell, Anne had always a feeling of exhilaration. Its message was clear to her. She hoped it would be clear to others. She tried at least to make it clear to her children.

And now they came streaming over the countryside, big boys with their little sisters beside them, big girls with their little brothers. Some on sleds and some sliding. All rosy-cheeked with the coldness of the morning.

As they filed in, Anne stood behind her desk. They had opening exercises, and then the work of the day began.

It began scrappily. Nobody had his mind upon it. The children were much excited over the events of the preceding night—over the play and the feast which had followed.

Anne, too, was excited. On the way to school she had met Richard, and he had joined her and had told her of his first patient.

"I had to walk at one o'clock in the morning. I must get a horse or a car. I am not quite sure that I ought to afford a car. And I like the idea of a horse. My grandfather rode a horse."

"Are you going to do all the things that your grandfather did?"

He was aware of her quick smile. He smiled back.

"Perhaps. I might do worse. He made great cures with his calomel and his catnip tea."

"Did you cure your patient with catnip tea?"

"Last night? No. It was a child. Measles. I told the rest of the family to stay away from school."

"It is probably too late. They will all have it."

"Have you?"

"No. I am never sick."

Her good health seemed to him another goddess attribute. Goddesses were never ill. They lived eternally with lovely smiles.

He felt this morning that the world was his. He had been called up the night before by a man in whose household there had been a tradition of the skill of Richard's grandfather. There had been the memory, too, in the minds of the older ones of the days when that other doctor had thundered up the road to succor and to save. It was a proud moment in their lives when they gave to Richard Tyson's grandson his first patient. They felt that Providence in sending sickness upon them had imposed not a penance but a privilege.

Richard had known of their pride and had been touched by it, and with the glow of their gratitude still upon him, he had trudged down the snowy road and had met Anne Warfield!

"You'd better let me come and look over your pupils," he had said to her as they parted; "we don't want an epidemic!"

He was to come at the noon recess. Anne, anticipating his visit, was quite thrillingly emphatic in her history lesson. Not that history had anything to do with measles, but she felt fired by his example to do her best.

She loved to teach history, and she had a lesson not only for her children, but for herself. She was much ashamed of her mood of Sunday. It had been easy enough this morning to talk to Richard; and with Evelyn away, clothes had seemed to sink to their proper significance. And if she had waited on the table she had at least done it well.

Her exposition gained emphasis, therefore, from her state of mind.

"In this beautiful land of ours," she said, "all men are free—and equal. You mustn't think this means that all of you will have the same amount of money or the same kind of clothes, or the same things to eat, or even the same kind of minds. But I think it means that you ought all to have the same kind of consciences. You ought to be equal in right doing. And in love of country. You ought to know when war is righteous, and when peace is righteous. And you can all be equal in this, that no man can make you lie or steal or be a coward."

Thus she inspired them. Thus she saw them thrill as she had herself been thrilled. And that was her reward. For in her school were not only the little Johns and the little Thomases and the little Richards—she found herself quite suddenly understanding why there were so many Richards—there were also the little Ottos and the little Ulrics and the little Wilhelms, and there was François, whose mother went out to sew by the day, and there were Raphael and Alessandro and Simon. Out from the big cities had come the parents of these children, seeking the land, usurping the places of the old American stock, doing what had been left undone in the way of sowing and planting and reaping, making the little gardens yield as they had never yielded, even in those wonder days before the war.

It was Anne Warfield's task to train the children of the newcomers to the American ideal. With the blood in her of statesmen and of soldiers it was given to her to pass on the tradition of good citizenship. She was, indeed, a torch-bearer, lighting the way to love of country. Yet for a little while she had forgotten it.

She had cried because she could not wear rose-color!

But now her head was high again, and when Richard came she showed him her school, and he shook hands first with the little girls and then with the little boys, and he looked down their throats, and asked them questions, and joked and prodded and took their temperature, and he did it all in such happy fashion that not even the littlest one was afraid.

And when Richard was ready to go, he said to her, "I'll look after their bodies if you'll look after their minds," and as she watched him walk away, she had a tingling sense that they had formed a compact which had to do with things above and beyond the commonplace.

It began to snow in the afternoon, and it was snowing hard when the school day ended. Eric Brand came for Anne and Peggy in the funny little station carriage which was kept at Bower's. Eric and Anne sat on the front seat with Peggy between them. The fat mare, Daisy, jogged placidly along the still white road. There was a top to the carriage, but the snow sifted in, so Anne wrapped Peggy in an old shawl.

"I don't need anything," she said, when Eric offered her a heavier covering. "I love it—like this——"

Eric Brand was big and blond and somewhat slow in his movements. But he had brains and held the position of telegraph operator at Bower's Station. He had, too, a heart of romance. The day before he had seen Evelyn toss the rose to Richard, and he had found it later where Richard had dropped it. He had picked it up, and had put it in water. It had seemed to him that the flower must feel the slight which had been put upon it.

He spoke now to Anne of Richard. "They say he is a good doctor."

"I can't see why he came here."

"His mother wanted him to come. She hates the city. She went there as a bride. Her husband was rich, but he was always speculating. Sometimes they were so poor that she had to do her own work, and sometimes they had a half dozen servants. But they never had a home. And then all at once he lost other people's money as well as his own—and he killed himself———"

She turned on him her startled eyes. "Richard's father?"

"Yes. And after that young Brooks decided that as soon as he finished his medical course he would come here. He thinks that he came because he wanted to come. But he won't stay."

"Why not?"

"You saw his friends. And the women. Some day he'll go back and marry that girl——"

"Evelyn Chesley?"

"Is that her name? She threw him a rose;" he forgot to tell her that he had seen it fade.

They had reached the stable garage. Diogenes welcomed them from his warm corner. The old dog Mamie who had followed the carriage shook the snow from her coat and flopped down on the floor to rest. The little horse Daisy steamed and whinnied. It was a homely scene of sheltered creatures in comfortable quarters. Anne knelt down by the old drake, and he bent his head under her caressing hand. Her face was grave. Eric, watching her, asked; "Has it been a hard day?"

"No;" but she found herself suddenly tired.

She went in with Eric presently. They had a good hot supper, and Anne was hungry. Gathered around the table were Peter and his wife, Beulah and Eric, with Peggy rounding out the half dozen. Geoffrey Fox had gone to town to get his belongings.

Anne had a vision of Richard and his mother in the big house. At their table would be lovely linen and shining silver, and some little formality of service. She felt that she belonged to people like that. She had nothing in common with Peter and his wife and with Eric Brand. Nor with Beulah.

Beulah was planning a little party for the evening. There was to have been skating, but the warmer weather and the snow had made that impossible.

"I don't know just what I'll do with them," she said; "we might have games."

"Anne knows a lot of things." This from Peggy, who was busy with her bread and milk.

"What things?"

"Oh, dancing——"

Anne flushed. "Peggy!"

"But we do. We make bows like this——"

Peggy slid out of her chair and bobbed for them—a most entrancing little curtsey, with all her curls flying.

"And the boys do this." She was quite stiff as she showed them how the little boys bowed.

Anne seemed to feel some need of defense. "Well, they must learn manners."

Peggy, wound up, would not be interrupted. "We dance like this," and away she went in a mad gallop.

Anne laughed. "It warms their blood when the fire won't burn. Peggy, it isn't quite as bad as that. Show them nicely."

So Peggy showed them some pretty steps, and then came back to her bread and milk.

"We might dance." Beulah's mind was on her party. "But some of them don't know how."

Anne offered no suggestions. She really might have helped if she had cared to do it. But she did not care.

When she had finished supper, Eric followed her into the hall. "You'll come down, won't you?"

"I'm not sure."

"Beulah would like it if you would."

"I have a lot of things to do."

"Let them go. You can always work. When you hear the fire roaring up the chimney, you will know that it is calling to you, 'Come down, come down!'"

He stood and watched her as she climbed the stairs. Then he went back and helped Beulah.

Beulah was really very pretty, and to-night her cheeks were pink as she made her little plans with him.

He gave himself pleasantly to her guidance. He moved the furniture for her into the big front room, so that there would be a space for dancing. And presently it became not a sanctum for staid Old Gentlemen, but a gathering place for youth and joy.

Eric made his rounds before the company came. He looked after the dogs in the kennels and at Daisy in her stall. He flashed his lantern into Diogenes' dark corner and saw the old drake at rest.

The snow was whirling in a blinding storm when at last he staggered in with a great log for the fire, and with a basket of cones to make the air sweet. And it was as he knelt to put the cones on the fire that Anne came in and stood beside him.

She had swept up her hair in the new way from her forehead. She wore white silk stockings and little flat-heeled black slippers, and a flounced white frock. She was not in the least in fashion, but she was quaintly childish and altogether lovely.

The big man looked up at her. "You look nice in that dress."

She smiled down at him. "I'm glad you like it, Eric."

411

When the young belles and beauties of the countryside came in later, Anne found herself quite eclipsed by their blooming charms. The young men, knowing her as the school-teacher, were afraid of her brains. They talked to her stiffly, and left her as soon as possible for the easier society of girls of their own kind. Peggy sat with Anne on the big settle beside the fire. The child's hand was hot, and she seemed sleepy.

"My eyes hurt," she said, crossly.

"You ought to be in bed, Peggy; shall I take you?"

"No. There's going to be an oyster stew. Daddy said I might sit up."

Beulah in pink and very important came over to them. "Could you show us some of the dances, Anne?"

"Oh, Beulah, can't they play games?"

"I think you might help us." Beulah's tone was slightly petulant.

Anne stood up. "There's a march I taught the children. We could begin with that."

She led the march with Eric. Behind her was the loud laughter of the brawny young men, the loud laughter of the blooming young women. Their merriment sounded a different note from that struck by the genial Old Gentlemen or by the gay group of young folk from New York. What was the difference? Training? Birth?

Anne felt suddenly much alone. She had not belonged to Evelyn Chesley's crowd, she did not belong with Beulah's friends. She wondered if she really belonged anywhere.

Yet as her mind went over and over these things, her little slippered feet led the march. Eric was not awkward, and he fell easily into the step.

"How nicely we do it together," he said, and beamed down on her, and because her heart was really a kind little heart and a womanly one, she smiled up at him and tried to be as fine and friendly as she would have wanted her children to be.

After the dance, the young folks played old-fashioned games—"Going to Jerusalem" and "Post Office." Anne fled to the settle when the last game was announced. Peggy was moping among the cushions.

"Let me take you up to bed, dearie."

"No, I won't. I want to stay here."

The fun was fast and furious. Anne had a little shivery feeling as she watched the girls go out into the hall and come back blushing. How could they give so lightly what seemed to her so sacred? A woman's lips were for her lover.

She sat very still among the cushions. The fire roared up the chimney. Outside the wind blew; far away in the distance a dog barked.

The barking dog was young Toby. At the heels of his master he was headed straight for the long low house and the grateful shelter of its warmth.

Richard stood for a moment on the porch, looking in through the lighted window. A romping game was in full progress. This time it was "Drop the Handkerchief" and a plump and pretty girl was having a tussle with her captor. Everybody was shouting, clapping. Everybody? On an old settle by the fire sat a slim girl in a white gown. Peggy lay in the curve of her arm, and she was looking down at Peggy.

Richard laughed a big laugh. He could not have told why he laughed, but he flung the door open, and stood there radiant.

"May I come in?" he demanded of Beulah, "or will I break up your party?"

"Oh, Dr. Brooks, as if you could. We are so glad to have you."

"I had a sick call, and we are half frozen, Toby and I, and we saw the lights——"

Now the best place for a half-frozen man is by the fire, and the best place for an anxious and shivering dog is in a warm chimney corner, so in a moment the young dog Toby was where he could thaw out in a luxurious content, and Richard was on the settle beside Anne, and was saying, "Isn't this great? Do you think I ought to stay? I'm not really invited, you know."

"There's never any formality. Everybody just comes."

"I like your frock," he said suddenly. "You remind me of a little porcelain figure I saw in a Fifth Avenue window not long ago."

"Tell me about it," she said with eagerness.

"About what?"

"New York and the shops. Oh, I saw them once. They were like—Heaven."

She laughed up at him as she said it, and he laughed back.

"You'd get tired of them if you lived there."

"I should never get tired. And if I had money I'd go on in and try on everything. I saw a picture of a gown I'd like—all silver spangles with a pointed train. Do you know I've never worn a train? I should like one—and a big fan with feathers."

He shook his head. "Trains wouldn't suit your style. Nor big fans. You ought to have a little fan—of sandalwood, with a purple and green tassel and smelling sweet. Mother says that her mother carried a fan like that at a White House ball."

"I've never been to a ball."

"Well, you needn't want to go. It's a cram and a jam and everybody bored to death."

"I shouldn't be bored. I should love it."

His eyes were on the fire. And presently he said, "It seems queer to be away from it—New York. There's something about it that gets into your blood. You want it—as you do—drink."

"Then you'll be going back."

He jerked around to look at her. "No," sharply; "what makes you say that?"

"Because—it—it doesn't seem possible that you could be—buried—here."

"Do you feel buried?"

She nodded. "Oh, yes."

His face was grave. "And doesn't the school work—help?"

She caught her breath. "That's the best part of it. You see I love—the children."

He flashed a quick glance at her. "Then you're lonely sometimes?"

"Yes."

"I fancy these people aren't exactly—your kind. I wish you'd come and see my mother. She's awfully worth while, you know. And she'd be so glad to have you."

She found herself saying, "My grandmother was Cynthia Warfield. She knew your grandfather. I have some old letters. I think your mother might like to see them."

"No wonder I've been puzzling over you! Cynthia Warfield's portrait hangs in our library. And you're like your grandmother. Only you're young and—alive."

Again his ringing laugh and her own to meet it. She felt so young and happy. So very, very young, and so very, very happy!

Mrs. Bower, appearing importantly, announced supper. Beyond the hall, through the open door of the dining-room they could see the loaded table with the tureens of steaming oysters at each end.

There was at once a rollicking stampede.

Anne leaned down to wake Peggy. The child opened her heavy eyes, and murmured: "I want a drink."

Richard glanced at her. "Hello, hello," he said, quickly. "What's the matter, Pussy?"

"I'm not Pussy—I'm Peggy." The child was ready for tears.

He picked her up in his arms and carried her to the light. With careful finger he lifted the heavy eyelids and touched the hot little cheeks. "How long has she been this way?" he asked Anne.

"Just since supper. Is there anything the matter with her? Is she really sick, Dr. Brooks?"

"Measles," he said succinctly. "You'd better get her straight to bed."

CHAPTER VI

In Which a Gray Plush Pussy Cat Supplies a Theme.

Anne at the top of the stairs talked to Geoffrey Fox at the foot.

"But you really ought not to stay."

"Why not?"

"Because if you haven't had the measles you might get them, and, besides, poor Mrs. Bower is so busy."

"Why not tell me the truth? You don't want me to stay."

"What difference can it possibly make to me?"

"It may make a great difference," Geoffrey said, quietly, "whether I go or stay, but we won't talk of that. I am here. All my traps, bag and baggage, typewriter and trunks—books and bathrobe—and yet you want to send me away."

"I haven't anything to do with it. But the house is closed to every one."

"And everything smells of antiseptics. I rather like that. I spent six weeks in a hospital once. I had a nervous breakdown, and the quiet was heavenly, and all the nurses were angels."

She would not smile. "Of course if you will stay," she said, "you must take things as they come. Mrs. Bower will send your meals up to you. She won't have time to set a company table."

"I'm not company; let me eat with the rest of you."

She hesitated. "You wouldn't like it. I don't like it. There's no service, you see—we all just help ourselves."

"I can help myself."

She shook her head. "It will be easier for Mrs. Bower to bring it up."

He climbed three steps and stopped. "Are you going to do all the nursing?"

"I shall do some of it. Peggy is really ill. There are complications. And Mrs. Bower and Beulah have so much to do. We shall have to close the school. Dr. Brooks wants to save as many as possible from having it."

"So Brooks is handling Peggy's case."

"Of course. Peter Bower knew his grandfather."

"Well, it is something to have a grandfather. And to follow in his footsteps."

But her mind was not on grandfathers. "Dr. Brooks will be here in an hour and I must get Peggy's room ready. And will you please look after yourself for a little while? Eric will attend to your trunks."

It took Geoffrey all the morning to settle. He heard Richard come and go. At noon Anne brought up his tray.

Opening the door to her knock, he protested. "You shouldn't have done it."

"Why not? It is all in the day's work. And I am not going to be silly about it any more."

"You were never silly about it."

"Yes, I was. But I have worked it all out in my mind. My bringing up the tray to you won't make me any less than I am or any more. It is the way we feel about ourselves that counts—not what other people think of us."

"So you don't care what I think of you?"

"No, not if I am doing the things I think are right."

"And you don't care what Richard Brooks thinks?"

The color mounted. "No," steadily.

"Nor Miss Chesley?"

"Of course not."

"Not of course. You do care. You'd hate it if you thought they'd criticize. And you'd cry after you went to bed."

She felt that such clairvoyance was uncanny. "I wouldn't cry."

"Well, you'd feel like it."

"Please don't talk about me in that way. It really doesn't make any difference how I feel, does it? And your lunch is getting cold."

"What made you bring it? Why didn't you let Mrs. Bower or Beulah?"

"Mrs. Bower is lying down, and Beulah has been ironing all the morning."

"The next time call me, and I'll wait upon myself."

"Perhaps I shall." She surveyed his tray. "I've forgotten the cream for your coffee."

"I don't take cream. Oh, please don't go. I want you to see my books and my other belongings."

He had brought dozens of books, a few pictures, a little gilded Chinese god, a bronze bust of Napoleon.

"Everything has a reason for being dragged around with me. That etching of Helleu's is like my little sister, Mimi, who is at school in a convent, and who constitutes my whole family. The gilded Chinese god is a mascot—the Napoleon intrigues the imagination."

"Do you think so much of Napoleon?" coldly. "He was a little great man. I'd rather talk to my children of George Washington."

"You women have a grudge against him because of Josephine."

"Yes. He killed something in himself when he put her from him. And the world knew it, and his downfall began. He forgot that love is the greatest thing in the world."

How lovely she was, all fire and feeling!

"Jove," he said, staring, "if you could write, you'd make people sit up and listen. You've kept your dreams. That's what the world wants—the stuff that dreams are made of. And most of us have lost ours by the time we know how to put things on paper."

For days the sound of Geoffrey's typewriter could be heard in the hall. "Does it disturb Peggy?" he asked Anne late one night as he met her on the stairs.

"No; her room is too far away. You were so good to send her the lovely toys. She adores the plush pussy cat."

"I like cats. They are coy—and caressing. Dogs are too frankly adoring."

"The eternal masculine." She smiled at him. "Is your work coming on?"

"I have a first chapter. May I read it to you?"

"Please—I should love it."

She was glad to sit quietly by the big fireplace. With eyes half-closed, she listened to the opening sentences. But as he proceeded, her listlessness vanished. And when he laid down the manuscript she was leaning forward, her slim hands clasped tensely on her knees, her eyes wide with interest.

"Oh, oh," she told him, "how do you know it all—how can you make them live and breathe—like that?"

For a moment he did not answer, then he said, "I don't know how I do it. No artist knows how he creates. It is like Life and Death—and other miracles. If I could keep to this pace, I'd have a masterpiece. But I shan't keep to it."

"Why not?"

"I never do."

"But this time—with such a beginning."

"Will you be my critic, Mistress Anne? Let me read to you now and then—like this?"

"I am afraid I should spoil you with praise. It all seems so—wonderful."

"You can't spoil me, and I like to be wonderful."

In spite of his egotism, she found herself modifying her first unfavorable estimate of him. His quick eager speech, his mobile mouth, his mop of dark hair, his white restless hands, his long-lashed near-sighted eyes, these contributed a personality which had in it nothing commonplace or conventional.

For three nights he read to her. On the fourth he had nothing to read. "It is the same old story," he burst out passionately. "I see mountain peaks, then, suddenly, darkness falls and my brain is blank."

"Wait a little," she told him; "it will come back."

"But it never comes back. All of my good beginnings flat out toward the end. And that's why I'm pot-boiling, because," bitterly, "I am not big enough for anything else."

"You mustn't say such things. We achieve only as we believe in ourselves. Don't you know that? If you believe that things are going to end badly, they will end badly."

"Oh, wise little school-teacher, how do you know?"

"It is what I teach my children. That they must believe in themselves."

"What else do you teach them?"

"That they must believe in God and love their country, and then nothing can happen to them that they cannot bear. It is only when one loses faith and hope that life doesn't seem worth while."

"And do you believe all that you teach?"

Silence. She was gazing into the fire thoughtfully. "I believe it, but I don't always live up to it. That's the hard part, acting up the things that we believe. I tell my children that, and I tell them, too, that they must always keep on trying."

She was delicious with her theories and her seriousness. And she was charming in the crisp blue gown that had been her uniform since the beginning of Peggy's illness.

He laughed and leaned toward her. "Oh, Mistress Anne, Mistress Anne, how much you have to learn."

She stood up. "Perhaps I know more than you think."

"Are you angry because I said that? But I love your arguments."

His frankness was irresistible; she could not take offense so she sat down again.

"Perhaps," she said, hesitating, "you might understand better how I feel if I told you about my Great-uncle Rodman Warfield. When he was very young he went to Paris to study art, and he attracted much attention. Then after a while he began to find the people interested him more than pictures. You see we come from old Maryland stock. My grandmother, Cynthia Warfield, was one of the proudest women in Carroll. But Uncle Rodman doesn't believe in family pride, not the kind that sticks its nose in the air; and so when he came back to America he resolved to devote his talents to glorifying the humble. He lived among the poor and he painted pictures of them. And then one day there was an accident. He saved a woman from drowning between a ferry-boat and the slip, and he hurt his back. There was a sort of paralysis that affected the nerves of his hand—and he couldn't paint any more. He came to us—when I was a little girl. My father was dead, and mother had a small income. We couldn't afford servants, so mother sewed and Uncle Rod and I did the housework. And it was he who tried to teach me that work is the one royal thing in our lives."

417

"Where is he now?"

"When mother died our income was cut off, and—I had to leave him. He could have a home with a cousin of ours and teach her children. I might have stayed with her, but there was nothing for me to do. And we felt that it was best for me to—find myself. So I came here. He writes to me—every day——" She drew a long breath. "I don't think I could live without letters from my Uncle Rod."

"So you are really a princess in disguise, and you would love to stick your nose in the air, but you don't quite dare?"

"I shouldn't love to do anything snobbish."

"There is no use in pretending that you are humble when you are not. And your Great-uncle Rodman is a dreamer. Life is what it is, not what we want it to be."

"I like his dreams," she said, simply, "and I want to be as good as he thinks I am."

"You don't have to be too good. You are too pretty. Do you know that Cynthia Warfield's granddaughter is a great beauty, Mistress Anne?"

"I know that I don't like to have you say such things to me."

"Why not?"

"I am not sure that you mean them."

"But I do mean them," eagerly.

"Perhaps," stiffly, "but we won't talk about it. I must go up to Peggy."

Peter Bower was with Peggy. He was a round and red-faced Peter with the kindest heart in the world. And Peggy was the apple of his eye.

"Do you think she is better, Miss Anne?"

"Indeed I do. And now you go and get some sleep, Mr. Bower. I'll stay with her until four, and then I'll wake Beulah."

He left her with the daily paper and a new magazine, and with the light shaded, Anne sat down to read. Peggy was sleeping soundly with both arms around the plush pussy which Geoffrey had given her. It was a most lifelike pussy, gray-striped with green glass eyes and with a little red mouth that opened and mewed when you pulled a string. Hung by a ribbon around the pussy cat's neck was a little brass bell. As the child stirred in her sleep the little bell tinkled. There was no sound except the sighing of the wind. All the house was still.

The paper was full of news of the great war. Anne read it carefully, and the articles on the same subject in the magazine. She felt that she must know as much as possible, so that she might speak to her children intelligently of the great conflict. Of Belgium and England, of France and Germany. She must be fair, with all those clear eyes focussed upon her. She must, indeed, attempt a sort of neutrality. But how could she be neutral, with her soul burning candles on the altar of the allies?

As she read on and on in the silence of the night, there came to her the thought of the dead on the field of battle. What of those shining souls? What happened after men went out into the Great Beyond? Hun and Norman, Saxon and Slav, among the shadows were they all at Peace?

Again the child stirred and the little bell tinkled. It seemed to Anne that the bell and the staring eyes were symbolic. The gay world played its foolish music and looked with unseeing eyes upon murder and madness. If little Peggy had lain there dead, the little bell would still have tinkled, the wide green eyes would still have stared.

But Peggy, thank God, was alive. Her face, like old ivory against the whiteness of her pillow, showed the ravages of illness, but the doctor had said she was out of danger.

The child stirred and spoke. "Anne," she whispered, "tell me about the bears."

Anne knelt beside the bed. "We must be very quiet," she said. "I don't want to wake Beulah."

So very softly she told the story. Of the Daddy Bear and the Mother Bear and the Baby Bear; of the little House in the Woods; of Goldilocks, the three bowls of soup, the three chairs, the three beds——

In the midst of it all Peggy sat up. "I want a bowl of soup like the little bear."

"But, darling, you've had your lovely supper."

"I don't care." Peggy's lip quivered. "I'm just starved, and I can't wait until I have my breakfast."

"Let me tell you the rest of the story."

"No. I don't want to hear it. I want a bowl of soup like the little bear's."

"Maybe it wasn't nice soup, Peggy."

"But you said it was. You said that the Mother Bear made it out of the corn from the farmer's field, and the cock that the fox brought, and she seasoned it with herbs that she found at the edge of the forest. You said yourself it was dee-licious soup, Miss Anne."

She began to cry weakly.

"Dearie, don't. If I go down into the kitchen and warm some broth will you keep very still?"

"Yes. Only I don't want just broth. I want soup like the little bear had."

"Peggy, I am not a fairy godmother. I can't wave my wand and get things in the middle of the night."

"Well, anyhow, you can put it in a blue bowl, you said the little bear had his in a blue bowl, and you said he had ten crackers in it. I want ten crackers——"

The kitchen was warm and shadowy, with the light of a kerosene lamp above the cook-stove. Anne flitted about noiselessly, finding a little saucepan, finding a little blue bowl, breaking one cracker into ten bits to satisfy the insistent Peggy, stirring the bubbling broth with a spoon as she bent above it.

And as she stirred, she was thinking of Geoffrey Fox, not as she had thought of Richard, with pulses throbbing and heart fluttering, but calmly; of his book and of the little bust of Napoleon, and of the things that she had been reading about the war.

She poured the soup out of the saucepan, and set it steaming on a low tray. Then quietly she ascended the stairs. Geoffrey's door was wide open and his room was empty, but through the dimness of the long hall she discerned his figure, outlined against a wide window at the end. Back of him the world under the light of the waning moon showed black and white like a great wash drawing.

He turned as she came toward him. "I heard you go down," he said. "I've been writing all night—and I've written—perfect rot." His hands went out in a despairing gesture.

Composed and quiet in her crisp linen, she looked up at him. "Write about the war," she said; "take three soldiers,— French, German and English. Make their hearts hot with hatred, and then—let them lie wounded together on the field of battle in the darkness of the night—with death ahead—and let each one tell his story—let them be drawn together by the knowledge of a common lot—a common destiny——"

"What made you think of that?" he demanded.

"Peggy's pussy cat." She told him of the staring eyes and the tinkling bell. "But I mustn't stay. Peggy is waiting for her soup."

He gazed at her with admiration. "How do you do it?"

"Do what?"

"Dictate a heaven-born plot to me in one breath, and speak of Peggy's soup in the next. You are like Werther's Charlotte."

"I am like myself. And we mustn't stay here talking. It is time we were both in bed. I am going to wake Beulah when I have fed Peggy."

He made a motion of salute. "The princess serves," he said, laughing.

But as she passed on, calm and cool and collected, carrying the tray before her like the famous Chocolate lady on the backs of magazines, the laugh died on his lips. She was not to be laughed at, this little Anne Warfield, who held her head so high!

CHAPTER VII

In Which Geoffrey Writes of Soldiers and Their Souls.

Eve chesley writing from New York was still in a state of rebellion.

"And now they all have the measles. Richard, it needed only your letter to let me know what you have done to yourself. When I think of you, tearing around the country on your old white horse, with your ears tied up—I am sure you tie up your ears—it is a perfect nightmare. Oh, Dicky Boy, and you might be here specializing on appendicitis or something equally reasonable and modern. I feel as if the world were upside down. Do children in New York ever have the measles? Somehow I never hear of it. It seems to me almost archaic—like mumps. Nobody in society ever has the mumps, or if they do, they keep it a dead secret, like a family skeleton, or a hard-working grandfather.

"Your letters are so short, and they don't tell me what you do with your evenings. Don't you miss us? Don't you miss me? And our good times? And the golden lights of the city? Winifred Ames wants you for a dinner dance on the twentieth. Can't you turn the measley kiddies over to some one else and come? Say 'yes,' Dicky, dear. Oh, you musn't be just a country doctor. You were born for bigger things, and some day you will see it and be sorry."

Richard's letter, dashed off between visits to the "measley kiddies," was as follows:

"There aren't any bigger things, Eve, and I shan't be sorry. I can't get away just now, and to be frank, I don't want to. There is nothing dull about measles. They have aspects of interest unknown to a dinner dance. I am not saying that I don't miss some of the things that I have left behind—my good friends—you and Pip and the Dutton-Ames. But there are compensations. And you should see my horse. He's a heavy fellow like a horse of Flanders; I call him Ben because he is big and gentle. I don't tie up my ears, but I should if I wanted to. And please don't think I am ungrateful because I am not coming to the Dutton-Ames dance. Why don't you and the rest drift down here for a week-end? Next Friday, the Friday after? Let me know. There's good skating now that the snows have stopped."

He signed it and sealed it and on the way to see little Peggy he dropped it into the box. Then he entirely forgot it. It was a wonderful morning, with a sky like sapphire above a white world, the dog Toby racing ahead of him, and big gentle Ben at a trot.

At the innocent word "compensations" Evelyn Chesley pricked up her ears. What compensations? She got Philip Meade on the telephone.

"Richard has asked us for the week-end, Pip. Could we go in your car?"

"Unless it snows again. But why seek such solitudes, Eve?"

"I want to take Richard a fur cap. I am sure he ties up his ears."

"Send it."

"In a cold-blooded parcel post package? I will not. Pip, if you won't go, I'll kidnap Aunt Maude, and carry her off by train."

"And leave me out? Not much. 'Whither thou goest——'"

"Even when I am on the trail of another man? Pip, you are a dear idiot."

"The queen's fool."

So it was decided that on Friday, weather permitting, they should go.

Aunt Maude, protesting, said, "It isn't proper, Eve. Girls in my day didn't go running around after men. They sat at home and waited."

"Why wait, dearest? When I see a good thing I go for it."

"Eve——!"

"And anyhow I am not running after Dicky. I am rescuing him."

"From what?"

"From his mother, dearest, and his own dreams. Their heads are in the clouds, and they don't know it."

"I think myself that Nancy is making a mistake."

"More of a mistake than she understands." The lightness left Eve's voice. She was silent as she ate an orange and drank a cup of clear coffee. Eve's fashionable and adorable thinness was the result of abstinence and of exercise. Facing daily Aunt Maude's plumpness, she had sacrificed ease and appetite on the altar of grace and beauty.

Yet Aunt Maude's plumpness was not the plumpness of inelegance. Nothing about Aunt Maude was inelegant. She was of ancient Knickerbocker stock. She had been petrified by years of social exclusiveness into something less amiable than her curves and dimples promised. Her hair was gray, and not much of it was her own. Her curled bang and high coronet braid were held flatly against her head by a hair net. She wore always certain chains and bracelets which proclaimed the family's past prosperity. Her present prosperity was evidenced by the somewhat severe richness of her attire. Her complexion was delicately yellow and her wrinkles were deep. Her eyes were light blue and coldly staring. In manner she seemed to set herself against any world but her own.

The money on which the two women lived was Aunt Maude's. She expected to make Eve her heir. In the meantime she gave her a generous allowance and indulged most of her whims.

The latest whim was the new breakfast room in which they now sat, with the winter sun streaming through the small panes of a wide south window.

For sixty odd years Aunt Maude had eaten her breakfast promptly at eight from a tray in her own room. It had been a hearty breakfast of hot breads and chops. At one she had lunched decently in the long dim dining-room in a mid-Victorian atmosphere of Moquet and marble mantels, carved walnut and plush curtains.

And now back of this sacred dining-room Eve had built out a structure of glass and of stone, looking over a scrap of enclosed city garden, and furnished in black and white, relieved by splashes of brilliant color. Aunt Maude hated the green parrot and the flame-colored fishes in the teakwood aquarium. She thought that Eve looked like an actress in the little jacket with the apple-green ribbons which she wore when she came down at twelve.

"Aren't we ever going to eat any more luncheons?" had been Aunt Maude's plaintive question when she realized that she was in the midst of a gastronomic revolution.

"Nobody does, dearest. If you are really up-to-date you breakfast and dine—the other meals are vague—illusory."

"People in my time——" Aunt Maude had stated.

"People in your time," Evelyn had interrupted flippantly, "were wise and good. Nobody wants to be wise and good in these days. We want to be smart and sophisticated. Your good old stuffy dining-rooms were like your good old stuffy consciences. Now my breakfast room is symbolic—the green and white for the joy of living, and the black for my sins."

She stood up on tiptoe to feed the parrot. "To-morrow," she announced, "I am to have a black cat. I found one at the cat show—with green eyes. And I am going to match his cushion to his eyes."

"I'd like a cat," Aunt Maude said, unexpectedly, "but I can't say that I care for black ones. The grays are the best mousers."

Eve looked at her reproachfully. "Do you think that cats catch mice?" she demanded,—"up-to-date cats? They sit on cushions and add emphasis to the color scheme. Winifred Ames has a yellow one to go with her primrose panels."

The telephone rang. A maid answered it. "It is for you, Miss Evelyn."

"It is Pip," Eve said, as she turned from the telephone; "he's coming up."

Aunt Maude surveyed her. "You're not going to receive him as you are?"

"As I am? Why not?"

"Eve, go to your room and put something on," Aunt Maude agonized; "when I was a girl——"

Evelyn dropped a kiss on her cheek. "When you were a girl, Aunt Maude, you were very pretty, and you wore very low necks and short sleeves on the street, and short dresses—and—and——"

Remembering the family album, Aunt Maude stopped her hastily. "It doesn't make any difference what I wore. You are not going to receive any gentleman in that ridiculous jacket."

Eve surveyed herself in an oval mirror set above a console-table. "I think I look rather nice. And Pip would like me in anything. Aunt Maude, it's a queer world for us women. The men that we want don't want us, and the men that we don't want adore us. The emancipation of women will come when they can ask men to marry them."

She was ruffling the feathers on the green parrot's head. He caught her finger carefully in his claw and crooned.

Aunt Maude rose. "I had twenty proposals—your uncle's was the twentieth. I loved him at first sight, and I loved him until he left me."

"Uncle was a dear," Eve agreed, "but suppose he hadn't asked you, Aunt Maude?"

"I should have remained single to the end of my days."

"Oh, no, you wouldn't, Aunt Maude. You would have married the wrong man—that's the way it always ends—if women didn't marry the wrong men half the world would be old maids."

Philip Meade was much in love. He had money, family, good looks and infinite patience. Some day he meant to marry Eve. But he was aware that she was not yet in love with him.

She came down gowned for the street. And thus kept him waiting. "It was Aunt Maude's fault. She made me dress. Pip, where shall we walk?"

He did not care. He cared only to be with her. He told her so, and she smiled up at him wistfully. "You're such a dear—I wish——"

She stopped.

"What do you wish?" he asked eagerly.

"For the—sun. You are the moon. May I call you my moon-man, Pip?"

He knew what she meant "Yes. But you must remember that some day I shall not be content to take second place—I shall fight for the head of your line of lovers."

"Line of lovers—Pip. I don't like the sound of it."

"Why not? It's true."

Again she was wistful. "I wonder how many of them really—care? Pip, it is the one-proposal girl who is lucky. She has no problems. She simply takes the man she can get!"

They were swinging along Fifth Avenue. He stopped at a flower shop and bought her a tight little knot of yellow roses which matched her hair. She was in brown velvet with brown boots and brown furs. Her skin showed pink and white in the clear cold. She and the big man by her side were a pair good to look upon, and people turned to look.

Coming to a famous jewel shop she turned in. "I am going to have all of Aunt Maude's opals set in platinum to make a long chain. She gave them to me; and there'll be diamonds at intervals. I want to wear smoke-colored tulle at Winifred Ames' dinner dance—and the opals will light it."

Philip Meade's mind was not poetic, yet as his eyes followed Evelyn, he was aware that this was an atmosphere which belonged to her. Her beauty was opulent, needing richness to set it off, needing the shine of jewels, the shimmer of silk——

If he married her he could give her—a tiara of diamonds—a necklace of pearls—a pendant—a ring. His eyes swept the store adorning her.

When they came out he said, "I think I am showing a greatness of mind which should win your admiration."

"Why?"

"In taking you to Crossroads."

"Why?"

"You know why. Shall you write to Brooks that we are coming?"

"No. I want it to be a surprise. That's half the fun."

But there was nothing funny about it, as it proved, for it was on that very Friday morning that Richard had found Peggy much better, and Anne very pale with circles under her eyes.

He went away, and later his mother called Anne up. She asked her to spend the day at Crossroads. Richard would come for her and would bring her home after dinner.

Anne, with a fluttering sense of excitement, packed her ruffled white frock in a little bag, and was ready when Richard arrived.

At the gate they met Geoffrey Fox. The young doctor stopped his horse. "Come and have lunch with us, Fox?"

"I'm sorry. But I must get to work. How long are you going to keep Miss Warfield?"

"As late as we can."

"To-night?"

"Yes."

"I have a chapter ready to read to her, and you ask her to eat with you as if she were any every-day sort of person. Did you know that she is to play Beatrice to my Dante?"

"Don't be silly," Anne said; "you mustn't listen to him, Dr. Brooks."

Richard's eyes went from one to the other. "What do you know of Fox?" he asked, as they drove on.

"Nothing, except that he is writing a book."

"I'll ask Eve about him; she's a lion-hunter and she's in with a lot of literary lights."

Even as he spoke Evelyn was speeding toward him in Philip's car. He had forgotten her and his invitation for the week-end. But she had not forgotten, and she sparkled and glowed as she thought of Richard's royal welcome. For how could she know, as she drew near and nearer, that he was welcoming another guest, taking off the little teacher's old brown coat, noting the flush on her young cheeks, the pretty appeal of her manner to his mother.

"You are sure I won't be in the way, Mrs. Brooks?"

"My dear, my dear, of course not. Richard has been telling me that your grandmother was Cynthia Warfield. Did you know that my father was in love with Cynthia before he married my mother?"

"The letters said so."

"I shall want to see them. And to hear about your Great-uncle Rodman. We thought at one time that he was going to be famous, and then came that dreadful accident."

They had her in a big chair now, with a high back which peaked over her head and Nancy had another high-backed chair, and Richard standing on the hearth-rug surveyed the two of them contentedly.

"Mother, I am going to give myself fifteen minutes right here and a half hour for lunch, and then I'll go out and make calls, and you and Miss Warfield can take a nap and be ready to talk to me to-night."

Anne smiled up at him. "Do you always make everybody mind?"

"I try to boss mother a bit—but I am not sure that I succeed."

Before luncheon was served Cynthia Warfield's picture, which hung in the library, was pointed out to Anne. She was made to stand under it, so that they might see that her hair was the same color—and her eyes. Cynthia was painted in pink silk with a petticoat of fine lace, and with pearls in her hair.

"Some day," Anne said, "when my ship comes in, I am going to wear stiff pink silk and pearls and buckled slippers and yards and yards of old lace."

"No, you're not," Richard told her; "you are going to wear white with more than a million ruffles, and little flat black shoes. Mother, you should have seen her at Beulah Bower's party."

"White is always nice for a young girl," said pleasant Nancy Brooks.

The dining-room looked out upon the river, with an old-fashioned bay window curving out. The table was placed near the window. Anne's eyes brightened as she looked at the table. It was just as she had pictured it, all twinkling glass and silver, and with Richard at the head of it. But what she had not pictured was the moment in which he stood to say the simple and beautiful grace which his grandfather had said years before in that room of many memories.

The act seemed to set him apart from other men. It added dignity and strength to his youth and radiance. He was master of a house, and he felt that his house should have a soul!

Anne, writing of it the next night to her Uncle Rod, spoke of that simple grace:

"Uncle Rod, it seemed to me that while most of the world was forgetting God, he was remembering Him. Nobody says grace at Bower's—and sometimes I don't even say it in my heart. He looked like a saint as he stood there with the window behind him. Wasn't there a soldier saint—St. Michael?

"Could you imagine Jimmie Ford saying grace? Could you imagine him even at the head of his own table? When I used to think of marrying him, I had a vision of eternal motor riding in his long blue car—with the world rushing by in a green streak.

"But I am not wanting much to talk of Jimmie Ford. Though perhaps before I finish this I shall whisper what I thought of the things you had to say of him in your letter.

"Well, after lunch I had a nap, and then there was dinner with David Tyson in an old-fashioned dress-suit, and Mrs. Nancy in thin black with pearls, and St. Michael groomed and shining.

"It was all quite like a slice of Heaven after my hard days nursing Peggy. We had coffee in the library, and then Dr. Richard and I went into the music-room and I played for him. I sang the song that you like about the 'Lady of the West Country':

" 'I think she was the most beautiful lady
That ever was in the West Country.
But beauty vanishes, beauty passes,
However rare, rare it be;
And when I crumble who shall remember
That Lady of the West Country?'
"He liked it and made me sing it twice, and then a dreadful thing happened. A motor stopped at the door and some one ran up the steps. We heard voices and turned around, and there were the Lovely Ladies back again with the two men, and a chauffeur in the background with the bags!

"It seems that they had motored down at Dr. Richard's invitation for a week-end, and that he had forgotten it!

"Of course you are asking, 'Why was it a dreadful thing, my dear?' Uncle Rod, I stood there smiling a welcome at them all, and Dr. Richard said: 'You know Miss Warfield, Eve,' and then she said, 'Oh, yes,' in a frigid fashion, and I knew by her manner that back in her mind she was remembering that I was the girl who had waited on the table!

"Oh, you needn't tell me that I mustn't feel that way, Uncle Rod. I feel it, and feel it, and feel it. How can I help feeling it when I know that if I had Evelyn Chesley's friends and Evelyn's fortune, people would look on Me-Myself in quite a different way. You see, they would judge me by the Outside-Person part of me, which would be soft and silky and secure, and not dowdy and diffident.

"Oh, Uncle Rod, is Geoffrey Fox right? And have you and I been dreaming all these years? The rest of the world doesn't dream; it makes money and spends it, and makes money and spends it, and makes money and spends it. Only you and I are still old-fashioned enough to want sunsets; the rest of them want motor cars and yachts and trips to Europe. That was what Jimmie Ford wanted, and that was why he didn't want me.

"There, I have said it, Uncle Rod. Your letter made me know it. Perhaps I have hoped and hoped a little that he might come back to me. I have made up scenes in my mind of how I would scorn him and send him away, and indeed I would send him away, for there isn't any love left—only a lot of hurt pride.

"To think that he saw you and spoke to you and didn't say one word about me. And just a year ago at Christmas time, do you remember, Uncle Rod? The flowers he sent, and the pearl ring—and now the flowers are dead, and the ring went back to him.

"Oh, I can't talk about it even to you!

"Well, all the evening Eve Chesley held the center of the stage. And the funny part of it was that I found myself much interested in the things she had to tell. Her life is a sort of Arabian Nights' existence. She lives with her Aunt Maude in a big house east of Central Park, and she told about the green parrot for her new black and white breakfast room, and the flame-colored fishes in an aquarium—and she is having her opals set in platinum to go with a silver gown that she is to wear at the Dutton-Ames dance.

"I like the Dutton-Ames. He is dark and massive—a splendid foil for his wife's slenderness and fairness. They are much in love with each other. He always sits beside her if he can, and she looks up at him and smiles, and last night I saw him take her hand where it hung among the folds of her gown, and he held it after that—and it made me think of father and mother—and of the way they cared. Jimmie Ford could never care like that—but Dr. Richard could. He cares that way for his mother—he could care for the woman he loved.

"He took me home in Mr. Meade's limousine. It was moonlight, and he told the chauffeur to drive the long way by the river road.

"I like him very much. He believes in things, and—and I rather think, that his ship is packed with dreams—but I am not sure, Uncle Rod."

It was when Anne had come in from her moonlight ride with Richard, shutting the door carefully behind her, that she found Geoffrey Fox waiting for her in the big front room.

"Oh," she stammered.

"And you really have the grace to blush? Do you know what time it is?"

"No."

"Twelve! Midnight! And you have been riding with only the chauffeur for chaperone."

"Well?"

"And you have kept me waiting. That's the worst of it. You may break all of the conventional commandments if you wish. But you mustn't keep me waiting."

His laugh rang high, his cheeks were flushed. Anne had never seen him in a mood like this. In his loose coat with a flowing black tie and with his ruffled hair curling close about his ears, he looked boyish and handsome like the pictures she had seen of Byron in an old book.

"Sit down, sit down," he was insisting; "now that you are here, you must listen."

"It is too late," she demurred, "and we'll wake everybody up."

"No, we shan't. The doors are shut. I saw to that. We are as much alone as if we were in a desert. And I can't sleep until I have read that chapter to you—please——"

426

Reluctantly, with her wraps on, she sat down.

"Take off your hat."

He stood over her while she removed it, and helped her out of her coat "Look at me," he said, peremptorily. "I hate to read to wandering eyes."

He threw himself into a chair and began:

"So they marched away—young Franz from Nuremberg and young George from London, and Michel straight from the vineyards on the coast of France."

That was the beginning of Geoffrey Fox's famous story: "The Three Souls," the story which was to bring him something of fortune as well as of fame, the story which had been suggested to Anne Warfield by the staring eyes of Peggy's pussy cat.

As she listened, Anne saw three youths starting out from home, marching gaily through the cities and steadily along the roads—marching, marching—Franz from Nuremburg, young George from London, and Michel from his sunlighted vineyards, drawing close and closer, unconscious of the fate that was bringing them together, thinking of the glory of battle, and of the honor of Kaiser and King and of the Republic.

The shadow of the great conflict falls gradually upon them. They meet the wounded, the refugees, they hear the roar of the guns, they listen to the tales of those who have been in the thick of it.

Then come privations, suffering, winter in the trenches—Franz on one side, young George on the other, and Michel; then fighting—fear——

Geoffrey stopped there. "Shall I have them afraid?"

"I think they would be afraid. But they would keep on fighting, and that would be heroic."

She added, "How well you do it!"

"This part is easy. It will be the last of it that I shall find hard—when I deal with their souls."

"Oh, you must show at the last that it is because of their souls that they are brothers. Each man has had a home, he has had love, each of them has had his hopes and dreams for the future, for his middle-age and his old age, and now there is to be no middle-age, no old age—and in their knowledge of their common lot their hatred dies."

"I am afraid I can't do it," he said, moodily. "I should have to swing myself out into an atmosphere which I have never breathed."

"What do you mean?"

"Oh, I am of the earth—earthy. I have sold my birthright, I have yearned for the flesh-pots, I have fed among—swine. I have done all of the other things which haven't Biblical sanction. And now you expect me to write of souls."

"I expect you to give to the world your best. You speak of your talent as if it were a little thing. And it is not a little thing."

"Do you mean that——?"

"I mean that it is—God given."

Out of a long silence he said: "I thank you for saying that. Nobody has ever said such a thing to me before."

427

He let her go then. And as she stood before her door a little later and whispered, "Good-night," he caught her hand and held it. "Mistress Anne—will you remember me—now and then—in your little white prayers?"

CHAPTER VIII

In Which a Green-Eyed Monster Grips Eve.

Evelyn, coming down late on the morning after her unexpected arrival, asked: "How did you happen to have her here, Dicky?"

"Who?"

"The little waitress?"

"Eve——" warningly.

"Well, then, the little school-teacher."

"Since when did you become a snob, Eve?"

"Don't be so sharp about it, Dicky. I'm not a snob. But you must admit that it was rather surprising to find her here, when the last time I saw her she was passing things at the Bower's table."

"She is a granddaughter of Cynthia Warfield."

"Who's Cynthia? I never heard of her."

"You have seen her portrait in our library."

"Which portrait?"

He led the way and showed it to her. Eve, looking at it thoughtfully, remarked, "Why should a girl like that lower herself by serving——?"

"She probably doesn't feel that she can lower herself by anything. She is what she is."

She shrugged. "You know as well as I that people can't do such things—and get away with it. She may be very nice and all that——"

"She is nice."

"Well, don't lose your temper over it, and don't fall in love with her, Dicky."

"Why not?"

"Haven't you done enough foolish things without doing—that?"

"Doing what?" ominously.

"Oh, you know what I mean," impatiently. "Aren't you ever going to come to your senses, Dicky?"

"Suppose we don't talk of it, Eve."

She found herself wanting to talk of it. She wanted to rage and rant. She was astonished at the primitiveness of her emotions. She had laughed her way through life and had prided herself on the dispassionateness of her point of view. And now it was only by the exercise of the utmost self-control that she was able to swing the conversation toward other topics.

The coming of the rest of the party eased things up a little. They had all slept late, and Richard had made a half dozen calls before he had joined Eve in the Garden Room. He had stopped at David's, and had heard that on Monday there was to be a drag-hunt and breakfast at the club. David hoped they would all stay over for it.

"Cousin David has a bunch of weedy-looking hounds," Richard explained; "he lets them run as they please, and they've been getting up a fox nearly every night. He thought you might like to ride up to the ridge in the moonlight and have a view of them. I can get you some pretty fair mounts at Bower's."

There was a note of wistful appeal in Eve's voice. "Do you really want us, Dicky?"

He smiled at her. "Of course. Don't be silly, Eve."

She saw that she was forgiven, and smiled back. She had not slept much the night before. She had heard Richard come in after his ride with Anne, and she had been waked later by the sound of the telephone. In the room next to hers Richard's subdued voice had answered. And presently there had been the sound of his careful footsteps on the stairs.

She had crept out of bed and between the curtains had looked out. The world was full of the shadowy paleness which comes with the waning of the moon. The road beyond the garden showed like a dull gray ribbon against the blackness of the hills. On this road appeared presently Richard on his big white horse, the dog Toby, a shadow among the shadows as he ran on ahead of them.

On and on they sped up the dull gray road, a spectral rider on a spectral horse. She had wondered where he might be going. It must have been some sudden and urgent call to take him out thus in the middle of the night. For the first time she realized what his life meant. He could never really be at his ease. Always there was before him the possibility of some dread adventure—death might be on its way at this very moment.

Wide-awake and wrapped in her great rug, she had waited, and after a time Richard had returned. The dawn was rising on the hills, and the world was pink. His head was up and he was urging his horse to a swift gallop.

When at last he reached his room, she had gone to bed. But when she slept it was to dream that the man on the white horse was riding away from her, and that when she called he would not come.

But now with his smile upon her, she decided that she was making too much of it all. The affair with the little schoolteacher might not be in the least serious. Men had their fancies, and Dicky was not a fool.

She knew her power over him, and her charm. His little boyhood had been heavy with sorrow and soberness; she had lightened it by her gaiety and good nature. Eve had taken her orphaned state philosophically. Her parents had died before she knew them. Her Aunt Maude was rich and gave her everything; she was queen of her small domain. Richard, on the other hand, had been early oppressed by anxieties—his care for his strong little mother, his real affection for his weak father, culminating in the tragedy which had come during his college days. In all the years Eve had been his good comrade and companion. She had cheered him, commanded him, loved him.

And he had loved her. He had never analyzed the quality of his love. She was his good friend, his sister. If he had ever thought of her as his sweetheart or as his wife, it had always been with the feeling that Eve had too much money. No man had a right to live on his wife's bounty.

He had a genuinely happy day with her. He showed her the charming old house which she had never seen. He showed her the schoolhouse, still closed on account of the epidemic. He showed her the ancient ballroom built out in a separate wing.

"A little money would make it lovely, Richard."

"It is lovely without the money."

Winifred Ames spoke earnestly from the window where, with her husband's arm about her, she was observing the sunset. "Some day Tony and I are going to have a house like this—and then we'll be happy."

"Aren't you happy now?" her husband demanded.

"Yes. But not on my own plan, as it were." Then softly so that no one else could hear, "I want just you, Tony—and all the rest of the world away."

"Dear Heart——" He dared not say more, for Pip's envious eyes were upon them.

"When I marry you, Eve, may I hold your hand in public?"

"You may—when I marry you."

"Good. Whenever I lose faith in the bliss of matrimony, I have only to look at Win and Tony to be cheered and sustained by their example."

Nancy, playing the little lovely hostess, agreed. "If they weren't so new-fashioned in every way I should call them an old-fashioned couple."

"Love is never out of fashion, Mrs. Nancy," said Eve; "is it, Dicky Boy?"

"Ask Pip."

"Love," said Philip solemnly, "is the newest thing in the world and the oldest. Each lover is a Columbus discovering an unknown continent."

In the hall the old clock chimed. "Nobody is to dress for dinner," Richard said, "if we are to ride afterward. I'll telephone for the horses."

He telephoned and rode down later on his big Ben to bring the horses up. As he came into the yard at Bower's he saw a light in the old stable. Dismounting, he went to the open door. Anne was with Diogenes. The lantern was set on the step above her, and she was feeding the old drake. Her body was in the shadow, her face luminous. Yet it was a sober little face, set with tired lines. Looking at her, Richard reached a sudden determination.

He would ask her to ride with them to the ridge.

At the sound of his voice she turned and her face changed. "Did I startle you?" he asked.

"No," she smiled at him. "Only I was thinking about you, and there you were." There was no coquetry in her tone; she stated the fact frankly and simply. "Do you remember how you put Toby in here, and how Diogenes hated it?"

"I remember how you looked under the lantern."

"Oh,"—she had not expected that,—"do you?"

"Yes. But I had seen you before. You were standing on a rock with holly in your arms. I saw you from the train throw something into the river. I have often wondered what it was."

"I didn't want to burn my holly wreaths after Christmas. I hate to burn things that have been alive."

"So do I. Eve would say that we were sentimentalists. But I have never quite been able to see why a sentimentalist isn't quite as worthy of respect as a materialist—however, I am not here to argue that. I want you to ride with me to the ridge. To see the foxes by moonlight," he further elucidated. "Run in and get ready. I am to take some horses up for the others."

She rose and reached for her lantern. "The others?" she looked an inquiry over her shoulder.

"Eve and her crowd. They are still at Crossroads."

She stood irresolute. Then, "I think I'd rather not go."

"Why not?" sharply.

She told him the truth bravely. "I am a little afraid of women like that."

"Of Eve and Winifred? Why?"

"We are people of two worlds, Dr. Brooks—and they feel it."

His conversation with Eve recurring to him, he was not prepared to argue. But he was prepared to have his own way.

"Isn't your world mine?" he demanded. "And you mustn't mind Eve. She's all right when you know her. Just stiffen your backbone, and remember that you are the granddaughter of Cynthia Warfield."

After that she gave in and came down presently in a shabby little habit with her hair tied with a black bow. "It's a good thing it is dark," she said. "I haven't any up-to-date clothes."

As they went along he asked her to go to the hunt breakfast on Monday.

"I can't. School opens and my work begins."

"By Jove, I had forgotten. I shall be glad to hear the bell. When I am riding over the hills it seems to call—as it called to my grandfather and to be saying the same things; it is a great inspiration to have a background like that to one's life. Do you know what I mean?"

She did know, and they talked about it—these two young and eager souls to whom life spoke of things to be done, and done well.

Eve, standing on the steps at Crossroads, saw them coming. "Oh, I'm not going," she said to Winifred passionately.

"Why not?"

"He has that girl with him."

"What girl?"

"Anne Warfield."

Winifred's eyes opened wide. "She's a darling, Eve. I liked her so much last night."

"I don't see why he has to bring her into everything."

"All the men are in love with her; even Tony has eyes for her, and Pip——"

"What makes you defend her, Win? She isn't one of us, and you know it."

"I don't know it. She belongs to older stock than either you or I, Eve. And if she didn't, don't you know a lady when you see one?"

Eve threw up her hands. "I sometimes think the world is going mad—there aren't any more lines drawn."

"If there were," said Winifred softly, and perhaps a bit maliciously, "I fancy that Anne Warfield might be the one to draw them—and leave us on the wrong side, Eve."

It was Winifred who welcomed Anne, and who rode beside her later, and it was of Winifred that Anne spoke repentantly as she and Richard rode together in the hills. "I want to take back the things I said about Mrs. Ames. She is just—heavenly sweet."

He smiled. "I knew you would like her," he said. But neither of them mentioned Eve.

For Evelyn's manner had been insufferable. Anne might have been a shadow on the grass, a cloud across the sky, a stone in the road for all the notice she had taken of her. It was a childish thing to do, but then Eve was childish. And she was having the novel experience of being overlooked for the first time by Richard. She was aware, too, that she had offended him deeply and that the cause of her offending was another woman.

When they came to the ridge Richard drew Anne's horse, with his own, among the trees. He left Eve to Pip. Winifred and her husband were with David.

Far off in the distance a steady old hound gave tongue—then came the music of the pack—the swift silent figure of the fox, straight across the open moonlighted space in front of them.

Anne gave a little gasp. "It is old Pete," Richard murmured; "they'll never catch him. I'll tell you about him on the way down."

So as he rode beside her after that perfect hour in which the old fox played with the tumultuous pack, at his ease, monarch of his domain, unmindful of silent watchers in the shadows, Richard told her of old Pete; he told her, too, of the traditions of a ghostly fox who now and then troubled the hounds, leading them into danger and sometimes to death.

He went on with her to Bower's, and when he left her he handed her a feathery bit of pine. "I picked it on the ridge," he said. "I don't know whether you feel as I do about the scrub pines of Maryland and of Virginia; somehow they seem to belong, as you and I do, to this country."

When Anne went to her room she stuck the bit of pine in her mirror. Then in an uplifted mood she wrote to Uncle Rod. But she said little to him of Richard or of Eve. Her own feelings were too mixed in the matter to permit of analysis. But she told of the fox in the moonlight. "And the loveliest part of it all was that nothing happened to him. I don't think that I could have stood it to have had him killed. He was so free—and unafraid——"

The next night Anne in the long front room at Bower's told Peggy and François all about it. François' mother was sewing for Mrs. Bower, and as the distance was great, and she could not go home at night, her small son was sharing with her the hospitality which seemed to him rich and royal in comparison with the economies practised in his own small home.

It was a select company which was gathered in front of the fire. François and Peggy and Anne and old Mamie, with the white house cat, Josephine, and three kittens in a basket, and Brinsley Tyson smoking his pipe in the background.

"And the old fox went tit-upping and tit-upping along the road in the moonlight, and Dr. Richard and I stood very still, and we saw him——"

"Last night?"

Anne nodded.

"And what did you do, Miss Anne?"

"We listened and heard the dogs——"

Little François clasped his hands. "Oh, were the dogs after him?"

"Yes."

"Did they get him?"

"No. He is a wise old fox. He lives up beyond the Crossroads garden. Dr. Brooks thought when they came there to live that he would go away but he hasn't. You see, it is his home. The hunters here all know him, and they are always glad when he gets away."

Brinsley agreed. "There are so few native foxes left in the county that most of us call off the dogs before a killing—we'd soon be without sport if we didn't. An imported fox is a creature in a trap; you want the sly old natives to give you a run for your money."

Little François, dark-eyed and dreamy, delivered an energetic opinion. "I think it is horrid."

Peggy, less sensitive, and of the country, reproved him. "It's gentleman's sport, isn't it, Mr. Brinsley?"

"Yes. To me the dogs and horses are the best part of it. The older I grow the more I hate to kill—that's why I fish. They are cold-blooded creatures."

Peggy, leaning on his knee, demanded a fish story. "The one you told us the last time."

Brinsley's fish story was a poem written by one of the Old Gentlemen, hunting now, it was to be hoped, in happier fields. It was an idyl of the Chesapeake:

"In the Chesapeake and its tribute streams,
Where broadening out to the bay they come,
And the great fresh waters meet the brine,
There lives a fish that is called the drum."
The drum fish and an old negro, Ned, were the actors in the drama. Ned, fishing one day in his dug-out canoe,

"Tied his line to his ankle tight,
To be ready to haul if the fish should bite,
And seized his fiddle——"
He played:

"But slower and slower he drew the bow,
And soft grew the music sweet and low,
The lids fell wearily over the eyes,
The bow arm stopped and the melodies.
The last strain melted along the deep,
And Ned, the old fisherman, sank to sleep.
Just then a huge drum, sent hither by fate,
Caught a passing glimpse of the tempting bait. . . .
. . . . One terrible jerk of wrath and dread
From the wounded fish as away he sped
With a strength by rage made double—
And into the water went old Ned.
No time for any 'last words' to be said,
For the waves settled placidly over his head,
And his last remark was a bubble."
The children's eyes were wide. Peggy was entranced, but François was not so sure that he liked it. Brinsley's hand dropped on the little lad's shoulder as he told how the two were found

"So looped and tangled together
That their fate was involved in a dark mystery
As to which was the catcher and which the catchee . . .
And the fishermen thought it could never be known
After all their thinking and figuring,
Whether the nigger a-fishing had gone,
Or the fish had gone out a-niggering."

433

There were defects in meter and rhythm, but Brinsley's sprightly delivery made these of minor importance, and the company had no criticism. François, shivering a little, admitted that he wanted to hear it again, and climbed to Brinsley's knee. The old man with his arm about him decided that to say it over would be to spoil the charm, and that anyhow the time had come to pop the corn.

To François this was a new art, but when he had followed the fascinating process through all its stages until the white grains boiled up in the popper and threatened to burst the cover, his rapture knew no bounds.

"Could I do it myself, Miss Anne?" he asked, and she let him empty the snowy kernels into a big bowl, and fill the popper for a second supply.

She bent above him, showing him how to shake it steadily.

Geoffrey Fox coming in smiled at the scene. How far away it seemed from anything modern—this wide hearth-stone with the dog and the pussy cat—and the little children, the lovely girl and the old man—the wind blowing outside—the corn popping away like little pistols.

"May I have some?" he asked, and Anne smiled up at him, while Peggy brought little plates and set the big bowl on a stool within reach of them all.

"What brings you up, sir?" Geoffrey asked Brinsley.

"The drag-hunt and breakfast at the club. I am too stiff to follow, but David and I like to meet old friends—you see I was born in this country."

That was the beginning of a string of reminiscences to which they all listened breathlessly. The fox hunting instinct was an inheritance in this part of the country. It had its traditions and legends and Brinsley knew them all.

If any one had told Geoffrey Fox a few weeks before that he would be content to spend his time as he was spending it now, writing all day and reading the chapters at night to a serious-eyed little school-teacher who scolded him and encouraged him by turns, he would have scoffed at such an impossible prospect. Yet he was not only doing it, but was glad to be swept away from the atmosphere of somewhat sordid Bohemianism with which he had in these later years been surrounded.

And as Brinsley talked, Geoffrey watched Anne. She had Peggy in her arms. Such women were made, he felt, to be not only the mothers of children, but the mothers of the men they loved—made for brooding tenderness—to inspire—to sympathize.

Yet with all her gentleness he knew that Anne was a strong little thing. She would never be a clinging vine; she was rather like a rose high on a trellis—a man must reach up to draw her to him.

As she glanced up, he smiled at her, and she smiled back. Then the smile froze.

Framed in the front doorway stood Eve Chesley! She came straight to Anne and held out her hand. "I made Richard bring me down," she said. "I want to talk to you about the Crossroads ball."

Eve repentant was Eve in her most charming mood. On Sunday morning she had apologized to Richard. "I was horrid, Dicky."

"Last night? You were. I wouldn't have believed it of you, Eve."

"Oh, well, don't be a prig. Do you remember how we used to make up after a quarrel?"

He laughed. "We had to go down on our knees."

She went down on hers, sinking slowly and gracefully to the floor. "Please, I'm sorry."

"Eve, will you ever grow up?"

"I don't want to grow up," wistfully. "Dicky, do you remember that after I had said I was sorry you always bought chocolate drops, and made me eat them all. You were such a good little boy, Richard."

"I was not," hotly.

"Why is it that men don't like to be told that they were good little boys? You are a good little boy now."

"I'm not."

"You are—and you are tied to your mother's apron strings."

"Dicky," she wailed, as he rose in wrath, "I didn't mean that. Honestly. And I'll be good."

Still, with her feet tucked under her, she sat on the floor. "I've been thinking——"

"Yes, Eve."

"You and I have a birthday in March. Why can't we have a big house-warming, and ask all the county families and a lot of people from town?"

"I'm not a millionaire, Eve."

"Neither am I. But there's always Aunt Maude."

She spread out her hands, palms upward. "All I shall have to do is to wheedle her a bit, and she'll give it to me for a birthday present. Please, Dicky. If you say 'yes' I'll go down to Bower's my very own self and ask Anne Warfield to come to our ball."

He stared at her incredulously. "You'll do what?"

"Ask your little—school-teacher. Win scolded me last night, and said that I was a selfish pig. That I couldn't expect to keep you always to myself. But you see I have kept you, Dicky. I have always thought that you and I could go on being— friends, with no one to break in on it."

Her eyes as she raised them to his were shadowed. He spoke heartily. "My dear girl, as if anything could ever come between us." He rose and drew her up from her lowly seat. "I'm glad we talked it out. I confess I was feeling pretty sore over the way you acted, Eve. It wasn't like you."

Eve stuck to her resolution to go to Bower's to seek out and conciliate Anne, and thus it happened that they found her making a Madonna of herself with Peggy in her arms, and Geoffrey Fox's eyes adoring her.

Little François told his mother later that at first he had thought the lovely lady was a fairy princess; for Eve was quite sumptuous in her dinner gown of white and shining satin, with a fur-trimmed wrap of white and silver. She wore, also, a princess air of graciousness, quite different from the half appealing impertinence of her morning mood when she had knelt at Richard's feet.

Anne, appeased and fascinated by the warmth of Eve's manner, found herself drawn in spite of herself to the charming creature who discussed so frankly her plans for their pleasure.

"Dicky and I were born on the same day," she explained, "and we always have a party together, with two cakes with candles, and this year it is to be at Crossroads."

She invited Brinsley and Geoffrey on the spot, and promised the children a peep into fairy-land. Then having settled the matter to the satisfaction of all concerned, she demanded a fresh popper of corn, insisted on a repetition of Brinsley's fish story, asked about Geoffrey's book, and went away leaving behind her a trail of laughter and light-heartedness.

Later Anne was aware that she had left also a feeling of bewilderment. It seemed incredible that the distance between the mood of last night and of to-night should have been bridged so successfully.

Brushing her hair in front of the mirror, she asked herself, "How much of it was real friendliness?" Uncle Rod had a proverb, "'A false friend has honey in his mouth, gall in his heart.'"

She chided herself for her mistrust. One must not inquire too much into motives.

The sight of Richard's bit of pine in the mirror frame shed a gleam of naturalness across the strangeness of the hour just spent. It seemed to say, "You and I of the country——"

Eve was of the town!

The weeks which followed were rare ones. Anne went forth joyous in the morning, and came home joyous at night. She saw Richard daily; now on the road, again in the schoolhouse, less often, but most satisfyingly, by the fire at Bower's.

Geoffrey, noting jealously these evenings that the young doctor spent in the long front room, at last spoke his mind.

"What makes you look like that?" he demanded, as having watched Richard safely out of the way from an upper window, he came down to find Anne gazing dreamily into the coals.

"Like what?"

"Oh, a sort of seventh-heaven look."

"I don't know what you mean."

"You won't admit that you know what I mean."

She rose.

"Sit down. I want to read to you."

"I am afraid I haven't time."

"You had time for Brooks. If you don't let me read to you I shall have to sit all alone—in the dark—my eyes are hurting me."

"Why don't you ask Dr. Brooks about your eyes?"

"Is Dr. Brooks the oracle?"

"He could tell you about your eyes."

"Does he tell you about yours?"

With a scornful glance she left him, but he followed her. "Why shouldn't he tell you about your eyes? They are lovely eyes, Mistress Anne."

"I hate to have you talk like that. It seems to separate me in some way from your friendship, and I thought we were friends."

Her gentleness conquered his mad mood. "Oh, you little saint, you little saint, and I am such a sinner."

So they patched it up, and he read to her the last chapter of his book.

"And now in the darkness they lay dying, young Franz from Nuremberg, and young George from London, and Michel straight from the vineyards on the coast of France."

In the darkness they spoke of their souls. Soon they would go out into the Great Beyond. What then, after death? Franz thought they might go marching on. Young George had a vision of green fields and of hawthorn hedges. But it was young Michel who spoke of the face of God.

Was this the Geoffrey who had teased her on the stairs? This man who wrote words which made one shake and shiver and sob?

"Oh, how do you do it, how do you do it?" The tears were running down her cheeks.

She saw him then as people rarely saw Geoffrey Fox. "God knows," he said, seriously, "but I think that your prayers have helped."

And after she had gone up-stairs he sat long by the fire, alone, with his hand shading his eyes.

The next morning he went to see Richard. The young doctor was in the Garden Room which he used as an office. It was on the ground floor of the big house, with a deer's horns over the fireplace, an ancient desk in one corner, a sideboard against the north wall. In days gone by this room had served many purposes. Here men in hunting pink had gathered for the gay breakfasts which were to fortify them for their sport. On the sideboard mighty roasts had been carved, and hot dishes had steamed. On the round table had been set forth bottles and glasses on Sheffield trays. Men ate much and rode hard. They had left to their descendants a divided heritage of indigestion and of strong sinews, to make of it what they could.

Geoffrey entering asked at once, "Why the Garden Room? There is no garden."

"There was a garden," Richard told him, "but there is a tradition that a pair of lovers eloped over the wall, and the irate father destroyed every flower, every shrub, as if the garden had betrayed him."

"There's a story in that. Did the girl ever come back to find the garden dead?"

"Who knows?" Richard said lightly; "and now, what's the matter with your eyes?"

There was much the matter, and when Richard had made a thorough examination he spoke of a specialist. "Have you ever had trouble with them before?"

"Once, when I was a youngster. I thought I was losing my sight. I used to open my eyes in the dark and think that the curse had come upon me. My grandfather was blind."

"It is rarely inherited, and not in this form. But there might be a predisposition. Anyhow, you'll have to stop work for a time."

"I can't stop work. My book is in the last chapters. And it is a great book. I've never written a great book before. I can talk freely to you, doctor. You know that we artists can't help our egotism. It's a disease that is easily diagnosed."

Richard laughed. "What's the name of your book?"

"'Three Souls.' Anne Warfield gave me the theme."

As he spoke her name it was like a living flame between them. Richard tried to answer naturally. "She ought to be able to write books herself."

Geoffrey shrugged. "She will live her life stories, not write them."

"Why not?"

"Because we men don't let such women live their own lives. We demand their service and the inspiration of their sympathy. And so we won't let them achieve. We make them light our torches. We are selfish beasts, you know, in the last analysis."

He laughed and rose. "I'll see a specialist. But nobody shall make me stop writing. Not till I have scribbled 'Finis' to my manuscript."

"It isn't well to defy nature."

"Defiance is better than submission. Nature's a cruel jade. You know that. In the end she gets us all. That's why I hate the country. It's there that we see Nature unmasked. I stayed three weeks at a farm last summer, and from morning to night murder went on. A cat killed a cardinal, and a blue jay killed a grosbeak. One of the servants shot a squirrel. And when I walked out one morning to see the sheep, a lamb was gone and we had a roast with mint sauce for dinner. For lunch we had the squirrel in a stew. A hawk swept down upon the chickens, and all that escaped we ate later fried, with cream gravy."

"In most of your instances man was the offender."

"Well, if man didn't kill, something else would. For every lamb there's a wolf."

"You are looking on only one side of it."

"When you can show me the other I'll believe in it. But not to-day when you tell me that my sun may be blotted out."

 Something in his voice made the young doctor lay his hand on his shoulder and say quietly: "My dear fellow, don't begin to dread that which may never come. There should be years of light before you. Only you'll have to be careful."

They stood now in the door of the Garden Room. The sun was shining, the snow was melting. There was the acrid smell of box from the hedge beyond.

"I hate caution," said young Geoffrey; "I want to do as I please."

"So does every man," said Richard, "but life teaches him that he can't."

"Oh, Life," scoffed Geoffrey Fox; "life isn't a school. It is a joy ride, with rocks ahead."

CHAPTER IX

In Which Anne, Passing a Shop, Turns In.

Anne had the Crossroads ball much on her mind. She spoke to Beulah about it.

"I don't know what to wear."

"You'd better go to town with me on Saturday and look for something."

"Perhaps I will. If I had plenty of money it would be easy. Beulah, did you ever see such clothes as Eve Chesley's?"

"If I could spend as much as she does, I'd make more of a show."

"Think of all the tailors and dressmakers and dancing masters and hair-dressers it has taken to make Eve what she is. And yet all the art is hidden."

"I don't think it is hidden. I saw her powder her nose right in front of the men that day she first came. She had a little gold case with a mirror in it, and while Dr. Brooks and Mr. Fox were sitting on the stairs with her, she took it out and looked at herself and rubbed some rouge on her cheeks."

Anne had a vision of the three of them sitting on the stairs. "Well," she said, in a fierce little fashion, "I don't know what the world is coming to."

Beulah cared little about Eve's world. For the moment Eric filled her horizon, and the dress she was to get to make herself pretty for him.

"Shall we go Saturday?" she asked.

Anne, rummaging in the drawer of her desk, produced a small and shabby pocketbook. She shook the money out and counted it. "With the check that Uncle Rod sent me," she said, "there's enough for a really lovely frock. But I don't know whether I ought to spend it."

"Why not?"

"Everybody ought to save something—I am teaching my children to have penny banks—and yet I go on spending and spending with nothing to show for it."

Beulah was quite placid. "I don't see why you should save. Some day you will get married, and then you won't have to."

"If a woman marries a poor man she ought to be careful of finances. She has to think of her children and of their future."

Beulah shrugged. "What's the use of looking so far ahead? And 'most any husband will see that his wife doesn't get too much to spend."

Before Anne went to bed that night she put a part of her small store of money into a separate compartment of her purse. She would buy a cheaper frock and save herself the afterpangs of extravagance. And the penny banks of the children would no longer accuse her of inconsistency!

The shopping expedition proved a strenuous one. Anne had fixed her mind on certain things which proved to be too expensive. "You go for your fitting," she said to Beulah desperately, as the afternoon waned, "and I will take a last look up Charles Street. We can meet at the train."

The way which she had to travel was a familiar one, but its charm held her—the street lights glimmered pale gold in the early dusk, the crowd swung along in its brisk city manner toward home. Beyond the shops was the Cardinal's house. The Monument topped the hill; to its left the bronze lions guarded the great square; to the right there was the thin spire of the Methodist Church.

She had an hour before train time and she lingered a little, stopping at this window and that, and all the time the money which she had elected to save burned a hole in her pocket.

For there were such things to buy! Passing a flower shop there were violets and roses. Passing a candy shop were chocolates. Passing a hat shop there was a veil flung like a cloud over a celestial chapeau! Passing an Everything-that-is-Lovely shop she saw an enchanting length of silk—as pink as a sea-shell—silk like that which Cynthia Warfield had worn when she sat for the portrait which hung in the library at Crossroads!

Anne did not pass the Lovely Shop; she turned and went in, and bought ten yards of silk with the money that she had meant to spend—and the money she had meant to save!

And she missed the train!

Beulah was waiting for her as she came in breathless. "There isn't another train for two hours," she complained.

Anne sank down on a bench. "I am sorry, Beulah. I didn't know it was so late."

"We'll have to get supper in the station," Beulah said, "and I have spent all my money."

"Oh, and I've spent mine." Anne reflected that if she had not bought the silk she could have paid for Beulah's supper. But she was glad that she had bought it, and that she had it under her arm in a neat package.

She dug into her slim purse and produced a dime. "Never mind, Beulah, we can buy some chocolates."

But they were not destined for such meager fare. Rushing into the station came Geoffrey Fox. As he saw the clock he stopped with the air of a man baffled by fate.

Anne moving toward him across the intervening space saw his face change.

"By all that's wonderful," he said, "how did this happen?"

"We missed our train."

"And I missed mine. Who is 'we'?"

"Beulah is with me."

"Can't you both have dinner with me somewhere? There are two hours of waiting ahead of us."

Anne demurred. "I'm not very hungry."

But Beulah, who had joined them, was hungry, and she said so, frankly. "I am starved. If I could have just a sandwich——"

"You shall have more than that. We'll have a feast and a frolic. Let me check your parcels, Mistress Anne."

Back they went to the golden-lighted streets and turning down toward the city they reached at last the big hotel which has usurped the place of the stately and substantial edifices which were once the abodes of ancient and honorable families.

Within were soft lights and the sound of music. The rugs were thick, and there was much marble. As they entered the dining-room, they seemed to move through a golden haze. It was early, and most of the tables were empty.

Beulah was rapturous. "I have always wanted to come here. It is perfectly lovely."

The attentive waiter at Geoffrey's elbow was being told to bring—— Anne's quick ear caught the word.

"No, please," she said at once, "not for Beulah and me."

His keen glance commanded her. "Of course not," he said, easily. Presently he had the whole matter of the menu settled, and could talk to Anne. She was enjoying it all immensely and said so.

"I should like to do this sort of thing every day."

"Heaven forbid. You would lose your dreams, and grow self-satisfied—and fat—like that woman over there."

Anne shuddered. "It isn't that she is fat—it's her eyes, and the way she makes up."

"That is the way they get when they live in places like this. If you want to be slender and lovely and keep your dreams you must teach school."

"Oh, but there's drudgery in that."

"It is the people who drudge who dream. They don't know it, but they do. People who have all they want learn that there is nothing more for life to give. And they drink and take drugs to bring back the illusions they have lost."

They fell into silence after that, and then it was Beulah who became voluble. Her fair round face beamed. It was a common little face, but it was good and honest. Beulah was having the time of her life. She did not know that she owed her good fortune to Anne, that if Anne had not been there, Geoffrey would not have asked her to dine. But if she had known it, she would not have cared.

"What train did you come in on?" she asked.

"At noon. Brooks thought I ought to see a specialist. He doesn't give me much encouragement about my eyes. He wants me to stop writing, but I shan't until I get through with my book."

He spoke recklessly, but Anne saw the shadow on his face. "You aren't telling us how really serious it is," she said, as Beulah's attention was diverted.

"It is so serious that for the first time in my life I know myself to be—a coward. Last night I lay in bed with my eyes shut to see how it would seem to be blind. It was a pretty morbid thing to do—and this morning finished me."

She tried to speak her sympathy, but could not. Her eyes were full of tears.

"Don't," he said, softly, "my good little friend—my good little friend."

She dabbed her eyes with her handkerchief. The unconscious Beulah, busy with her oysters, asked: "Is the Tobasco too hot? I'm all burning up with it."

Geoffrey was able later to speak lightly of his affliction. "I shall go to the Brooks ball as a Blind Beggar."

"Oh, how can you make fun of it?"

"It is better to laugh than to cry. But your tears were—a benediction."

Silence fell between them, and after a while he asked, "What shall you wear?"

"To the ball? Pink silk. A heavenly pink. I have just bought it, and I paid more than I should for it."

"Such extravagance!"

"I'm to be Cynthia Warfield—like the portrait in the Crossroads library of my grandmother. It came to me when I saw the silk in the shop window. I shall have to do without the pearls, but I have the lace flounces. They were left to my mother."

"And so Cinderella will go to the ball, and dance with the Prince. Is Brooks the Prince?"

She flushed, and evaded. "I can't dance. Not the new dances."

"I can teach you if you'll let me."

"Really?"

"Yes. But you must pay. You must give the Blind Beggar the first dance and as many more as he demands."

"But I can't dance all of them with you."

"You can dance some of them. And that's my price."

To promise him dances seemed to her quite delicious and delightful since she could not dance at all. But he made a little contract and had her sign it, and put it in his pocket.

441

Going home Anne had little to say. It was Geoffrey who talked, while Beulah slept in a seat by herself.

Anne made her own lovely gown, running over now and then to take surreptitious peeps at Cynthia's portrait. She had let Mrs. Brooks into her secret, and the little lady was enthusiastic.

"You shall wear my pearls, my dear. They will be very effective in your dark hair."

She brought the jewels down in an old blue velvet box—milk-white against a yellowed satin lining.

"My father gave them to me on my wedding day. Some day I shall give them to Richard's wife."

She could not know how her words stirred the heart of the girl who stood looking so quietly down at the pearls.

"I am almost afraid to wear them," Anne said breathlessly. She gave Nancy a shy little kiss. "You were dear to think of it."

And now busy days were upon her. There was the school with Richard running in after closing time, and staying, too, and keeping her from the work that was waiting at home. Then at twilight a dancing lesson with Geoffrey in the long front room, with Beulah playing audience and sometimes Eric, and with Peggy capering madly to the music.

Then the evening, with its enchanting task of stitching on yards of rosy silk. Usually Geoffrey read to her while she worked. His story was nearing the end. He was wearing heavy goggles which gave him an owl-like appearance, of which he complained.

"It spoils my beauty, Mistress Anne. I am just an ugly gnome who sits at the feet of the Princess."

"You are not ugly, and you know it. And men shouldn't be vain."

"We are worse than women. Do you know what you look like with all that silk around you?"

"No."

"Like Aurora. Do you remember that Stevenson speaks of a 'pink dawn'? Well, you are a pink dawn."

"Please stop talking about me, and read your last chapter. I am so glad that you have reached the end."

"Because you are tired of hearing it?"

"Because of your poor eyes."

He took off his goggles. "Do my eyes look different? Are they changed or—dim?"

"They are as bright as stars," and he sighed with relief.

"And now it was young Michel who whispered, 'God is good! In a moment we shall see his face, and we shall say to him, "We fought, but there is no hatred in our hearts. We cannot hate—our brothers——"'"

That was the end.

"It is a great book," Anne told him solemnly. "It will be a great success."

He seemed to shrink and grow small in his chair. "It will come—too late."

She looked up and saw the mood that was upon him. "Oh, you must not—not that," she said, hurriedly; "if you give up now it will be a losing fight."

"Don't you suppose that I would fight if I felt that I could win? But what can a man do with a thing like this that is dragging him down to darkness?"

"You mustn't be discouraged. Dr. Brooks says that it isn't—inevitable. You know that he said that, and that the specialist said it."

"I know. But something tells me that I am facing—darkness." He threw up his head. "Why should we talk of it? Let me tell you rather how much you have helped me with my book. If it had not been for you I could not have written it."

"I am glad if I have been of service." Her words sounded formal after the warmth of his own.

He laughed, with a touch of bitterness. "The Princess serves," he said, "always and always serves. She never grabs, as the rest of us do, at happiness."

"I shall grab when it comes," she said, smiling a little, "and I am happy now, because I am going to wear my pretty gown."

"Which reminds me," he said, quickly, and brought from his pocket a little box. "Your costume won't be complete without these. I bought them for you with the advance check which my publishers sent after they had read the first chapters of my book."

She opened the box. Within lay a little string of pearls. Not such pearls as Nancy had shown her, but milk-white none the less, with shining lovely lights.

"Oh," she gave a distressed cry, "you shouldn't have done it."

"Why not?"

"I can't accept them. Indeed I can't."

"I shall feel as if you had flung them in my face if you give them back to me," heatedly.

"You shouldn't take it that way. It isn't fair to take it that way."

"It isn't a question of fairness. It is a question of kindness on your part."

"I want to be kind."

"Then take them."

She thought for a moment with her eyes on the fire. When she raised them it was to say, "Would you—want your little sister, Mimi, to take jewels from any man?"

"Yes. If he loved her as I love you."

It was out, and they stood aghast. Then Geoffrey stammered, "Can't you see that my soul kneels at your feet? That to me these pearls aren't as white as your—whiteness?"

The rosy silk had slipped to the floor. She was like a very small goddess in a morning cloud. "I can't take them. Oh, I can't."

He made a quick gesture. But for her restraining hand he would have cast the pearls into the flames.

"Oh, don't," she said, the little hand tense on his arm. "Don't—hurt me—like that."

He dropped the pearls into his pocket. "If you won't wear them nobody shall. I suppose I seem to you like all sorts of a fool. I seem like all sorts of a fool to myself."

He turned and left her.

An hour later he came back and found her still sewing on the rosy silk. Her eyes were red, as if she had wept a little.

"I was a brute," he said, repentantly; "forgive me and smile. I am a tempestuous fellow, and I forgot myself."

"I was afraid we weren't ever going to be friends again."

"I shall always be your friend. Yet—who wants a Blind Beggar for a friend—tell me that, Mistress Anne?"

CHAPTER X

In Which a Blind Beggar and a Butterfly Go to a Ball.

In my Own Little Room.
Uncle rod, I went to the party!

I came home an hour ago, and since then I have been sitting all shivery and shaky in my pink silk. It will be daylight in a few minutes, but I shan't go to bed. I couldn't sleep if I did. I feel as if I shouldn't ever sleep again.

Uncle Rod, Jimmie Ford was at the Crossroads ball!

I went early, because Mrs. Nancy had asked me to be there to help with her guests. Geoffrey Fox went with me. He was very picturesque in a ragged jerkin with a black bandage over his eyes and with old Mamie leading him at the end of a cord. She enjoyed it immensely, and they attracted a lot of attention, as he went tap-tapping along with his cane over the polished floor, or whined for alms, while she sat up on her haunches with a tin cup in her mouth.

Well, Dr. Richard met us at the door, looking the young squire to perfection in his grandfather's old dress coat of blue with brass buttons. The people from New York hadn't come, so Mrs. Nancy put the pearls in my hair, and they made me stand under the portrait in the library, to see if I were really like my grandmother. I can't believe that I looked as lovely as she, but they said I did, and I began to feel as happy and excited as Cinderella at her ball.

Then the New York crowd arrived in motors, and they were all masked. I knew Eve Chesley at once and Winifred Ames, but it was hard to be sure of any one else. Eve Chesley was a Rose, with a thousand fluttering flounces of pink chiffon. She was pursued by two men dressed as Butterflies, slim and shining in close caps with great silken wings—a Blue Butterfly and a Brown one. I was pretty sure that the Brown one was Philip Meade. It was quite wonderful to watch them with their wings waving. Eve carried a pocketful of rose petals and threw them into the air as she went. I had never imagined anything so lovely.

Well, I danced with Dr. Richard and I danced with Geoffrey Fox, and I danced with Dutton Ames, and with some men that I had never met before. It seemed so good to be doing things like the rest. Then all at once I began to feel that the Blue Butterfly was watching me. He drifted away from his pursuit of Evelyn Chesley, and whenever I raised my eyes, I could see him in corners staring at me.

It gave me a queer feeling. I couldn't be sure, and yet—there he was. And, Uncle Rod, suddenly I knew him! Something in the way he carried himself. You know Jimmie's little swagger!

I think I lost my head after that. I flirted with Dr. Richard and with Geoffrey Fox. I think I even flirted a little with Dutton Ames. I wanted them to be nice to me. I wanted Jimmie to see that what he had scorned other men could value. I wanted him to know that I had forgotten him. I laughed and danced as if my heart was as light as my heels, and all the while I was just sick and faint with the thought of it—"Jimmie Ford is here, and he hasn't said a word to me. Jimmie Ford is here—and—he hasn't said a word——"

At last I couldn't stand it any longer, and when I was dancing with Geoffrey Fox I said, "Do you think we could go down to the Garden Room? I must get away."

He didn't ask any question. And presently we were down there in the quiet, and he had his bandage off, and was looking at me, anxiously. "What has happened, Mistress Anne?"

And then, oh, Uncle Rod, I told him. I don't know how I came to do it, but it seemed to me that he would understand, and he did.

When I had finished his face was white and set. "Do you mean to tell me that any man has tried to break your heart?"

I think I was crying a little. "Yes. But the worst of all is my—pride."

"My little Princess," he said softly, "that this should have come—to you."

Uncle Rod, I think that if I had ever had a brother, I should have wanted him to be like Geoffrey Fox. All his lightness and frivolity seemed to slip from him. "He has thrown away what I would give my life for," he said. "Oh, the young fool, not to know that Paradise was being handed to him on a platter."

I didn't tell him Jimmie's name. That is not to be spoken to any one but you. And of course he could not know, though perhaps he guessed it, after what happened later.

While we sat there, Dr. Richard came to hunt for us. "Everybody is going in to supper," he said. He seemed surprised to find us there together, and there was a sort of stiffness in his manner. "Mother has been asking for you."

We went at once to the dining-room. There were long tables set in the old-fashioned way for everybody. Mrs. Nancy wanted things to be as they had been in her own girlhood. On the table in the wide window were two birthday cakes, and at that table Dr. Richard sat with his mother on one side of him, and Eve Chesley on the other. Eve's cake had pink candles and his had white, and there were twenty-five candles on each cake.

Geoffrey Fox and I sat directly opposite; Dutton Ames was on my right, Mrs. Ames was on Geoffrey's left, and straight across the table, with his mask off, was Jimmie Ford, staring at me with all his eyes!

For a minute I didn't know what to do. I just sat and stared, and then suddenly I picked up the glass that stood by my plate, raised it in salute and drank smiling. His face cleared, he hesitated just a fraction of a second, then his glass went up, and he returned my greeting. I wonder if he thought that I would cut him dead, Uncle Rod?

And don't worry about what I drank. It was white grape juice. Mrs. Nancy won't have anything stronger.

Well, after that I ate, and didn't know what I ate, for everything seemed as dry as dust. I know my cheeks were red and that my eyes shone, and I smiled until my face ached. And all the while I watched Jimmie and Jimmie watched me, and pretty soon, Uncle Rod, I understood why Jimmie was there.

He was making love to Eve Chesley!

Making love is very different from being in love, isn't it? Perhaps love is something that Jimmie really doesn't understand. But he was using on Eve all of the charming tricks that he had tried on me. She is more sophisticated, and they mean less to her than to me, but I could see him bending toward her in that flattering worshipful way of his—and when he took one of her roses and touched it to his lips and then to her cheek, everything was dark for a minute. That kind of kiss was the only kind that Jimmie Ford ever gave me, but to me it had meant that he—cared—and that I cared—and here he was doing it before the eyes of all the world—and for love of another woman!

After supper he came around the table and spoke to me. I suppose he thought he had to. I don't know what he said and I don't care. I only know that I wanted to get away. I think it was then that Geoffrey Fox guessed. For when Jimmie had gone he said, very gently, "Would you like to go home? You look like your own little ghost, Mistress Anne."

But I had promised one more dance to Dr. Richard, and I wanted to dance it. If you could have seen at the table how he towered above Jimmie Ford. And when he stood up to make a little speech in response to a toast from Dutton Ames, his voice rang out in such a—man's way. Do you remember Jimmie Ford's falsetto?

445

I had my dance with him, and then Geoffrey took me home, and all the way I kept remembering the things Dr. Richard had said to me, such pleasant friendly things, and when his mother told me "good-night" she took my face between her hands and kissed me. "You must come often, little Cynthia Warfield," she said. "Richard and I both want you."

But now that I am at home again, I can't think of anything but how Jimmie Ford has spoiled it all. When you have given something, you can't ever really take it back, can you? When you've given faith and constancy to one man, what have you left to give another?

The river is beginning to show like a silver streak, and a rooster is crowing. Oh, Uncle Rod, if you were only here. Write and tell me that you love me.

Your
Little Girl.
In the Telegraph Tower.
My very Dear:

It is after supper, and Beulah and I are out here with Eric. He likes to have her come, and I play propriety, for Mrs. Bower, in common with most women of her class, is very careful of her daughter. I know you don't like that word "class," but please don't think I am using it snobbishly. Indeed, I think Beulah is much better brought up than the daughters of folk who think themselves much finer, and Mrs. Bower in her simple way is doing some very effective chaperoning.

Eric is on night duty in the telegraph tower this week; the other operator has the day work. The evenings are long, so Beulah brings her sewing, and keeps Eric company. They really don't have much to say to each other, so that I am not interrupted when I write. They seem to like to sit and look out on the river and the stars and the moon coming up behind the hills.

It is all settled now. Eric told me yesterday. "I am very happy," he said; "I have been a lonely man."

They are to be married in June, and the things that she is making are to go into the cedar chest which her father has given her. He found it one day when he was in Baltimore, and when he showed it to her, he shone with pleasure. He's a good old Peter, and he is so glad that Beulah is to marry Eric. Eric will rent a little house not far up the road. It is a dear of a cottage, and Peggy and I call it the Playhouse. We sit on the porch when we come home from school, and peep in at the windows and plan what we would put into it if we had the furnishing of it. I should like a house like that, Uncle Rod, for you and me and Diogenes. We'd live happy ever after, wouldn't we? Some day the world is going to build "teacherages" just as it now builds parsonages, and the little houses will help to dignify and uplift the profession.

Your dear letter came just in time, and it was just right. I should have gone to pieces if you had pitied me, for I was pitying myself dreadfully. But when I read "Little School-teacher, what would you tell your scholars?" I knew what you wanted me to answer. I carried your letter in my pocket to school, and when I rang the bell I kept saying over and over to myself, "Life is what we make it. Life is what we make it," and all at once the bells began to ring it:

"Life is—what we—make it—
Life is—what we—make it."
When the children came in, before we began the day's work, I talked to them. I find it is always uplifting when we have failed in anything to try to tell others how not to fail! Perhaps it isn't preaching what we practice, but at least it supplies a working theory.

I made up a fairy-story for them, too, about a Princess who was so ill and unhappy that all the kingdom was searched far and wide for some one to cure her. And at last an old crone was found who swore that she had the right remedy. "What is it?" all the wise men asked; but the old woman said, "It is written in this scroll. To-morrow the Princess must start out alone upon a journey. Whatever difficulty she encounters she must open this scroll and read, and the scroll will tell her what to do."

Well, the Princess started out, and when she had traveled a little way she found that she was hungry and tired, and she cried: "Oh, I haven't anything to eat." Then the scroll said, "Read me," and she opened the scroll and read: "There is corn in the fields. You must shell it and grind it on a stone and mix it with water, and bake it into the best bread that you can."

446

So the Princess shelled the corn and ground it and mixed it with water, and baked it, and it tasted as sweet as honey and as crisp as apples. And the Princess ate with an appetite, and then she lay down to rest. And in the night a storm came up and there was no shelter, and the Princess cried out, "Oh, what shall I do?" and the scroll said, "Read me." So she opened the scroll and read: "There is wood on the ground. You must gather it and stack it and build the best little house that you can." So the Princess worked all that day and the next and the next, and when the hut was finished it was strong and dry and no storms could destroy it. So the Princess stayed there in the little hut that she had made, and ate the sweet loaves that she had baked, and one day a great black bear came down the road, and the Princess cried out, "Oh, I have no weapon; what shall I do?" And the scroll said, "Read me." So she opened the scroll and read, "Walk straight up to the bear, and make the best fight that you can." So the Princess, trembling, walked straight up to the big black bear, and behold! when he saw her coming, he ran away!

Now the year was up, and the king sent his wise men to bring the Princess home, and one day they came to her little hut and carried her back to the palace, and she was so rosy and well that everybody wondered. Then the king called the people together, and said, "Oh, Princess, speak to us, and let us know how you were cured." So the Princess told them of how she had baked the bread, and built the hut, and conquered the bear; and of how she had found health and happiness. For the bread that you make with your own hands is the sweetest, and the shelter that you build for yourself is the snuggest, and the fear that you face is no fear at all.

The children liked my story, and I felt very brave when I had finished it. You see, I have been forgetting our sunsets, and I have been shivery and shaky when I should have faced my Big Black Bear!

Beulah is ready to go—and so—good-night. The moon is high up and round, and as pure gold as your own loving heart.

Ever your own
Anne.

CHAPTER XI

In Which Brinsley Speaks of the Way to Win a Woman.

And now spring was coming to the countryside. The snow melted, and the soft rains fell, and on sunny days Diogenes, splashing in the little puddles, picked and pulled at his feathers as he preened himself in the shelter of the south bank which overlooked the river.

Some of the feathers were tipped with shining green and some with brown. Some of them fell by the way, some floated out on blue tides, and one of them was wafted by the wind to the feet of Geoffrey Fox, as, on a certain morning, he, too, stood on the south bank.

He picked it up and stuck it in his hat. "I'll wear it for my lady," he said to the old drake, "and much good may it do me!"

The old drake lifted his head toward the sky, and gave a long cry. But it was not for Anne that he called. She still gave him food and drink. He still met her at the gate. If her mind was less upon him than in the past, it mattered little. The things that held meaning for him this morning were the glory of the sunshine, and the softness of the breeze. Stirring within him was a need above and beyond anything that Geoffrey could give, or Anne. He listened not for the step of the little school-teacher, but for the whirring wings of some comrade of his own kind. Again and again he sent forth his cry to the empty air.

Geoffrey's heart echoed the cry. His book was finished, and it was time for him to go. Yet he was held by a tie stronger than any which had hitherto bound him. Here in the big old house at Bower's was the one thing that his heart wanted.

"I could make her happy," he whispered to that inner self which warned him. "With her as my wife and with my book a success, I could defy fate."

The day was Saturday, and all the eager old fishermen had arrived the night before. Brinsley Tyson coming out with his rod in his hand and a broad-brimmed hat on his head invited Geoffrey to join him. "I've a motor boat that will take us out to the island after we have done a morning's fishing, and Mrs. Bower has put up a lunch."

"The glare is bad for my eyes."

"Been working them too hard?"

"Yes."

"There's an awning and smoked glasses if you'll wear them. And I don't want to go alone. David went back on me; he's got a new book. It's a puzzle to me why any man should want to read when he can have a day's fishing."

"If people didn't read what would become of my books?"

"Let 'em read. But not on days like this." Brinsley's fat face was upturned to the sun. With a vine-wreath instead of his broad hat and tunic in place of his khaki he might have posed for any of the plump old gods who loved the good things of life.

Geoffrey, because he had nothing else to do, went with him. Anne was invisible. On Saturday mornings she did all of the things she had left undone during the week. She mended and sewed and washed her brushes, and washed her hair, and gave all of her little belongings a special rub and scrub, and showed herself altogether exquisite and housewifely.

She saw Geoffrey start out, and she waved to him. He waved back, his hand shading his eyes. When he had gone, she cleaned all of her toilet silver, and ran ribbons into nicely embroidered nainsook things, and put her pillows in the sun and tied up her head and swept and dusted, and when she had made everything shining, she had a bit of lunch on a tray, and then she washed her hair.

Geoffrey ate lunch on the island with Brinsley Tyson. He liked the old man immensely. There was a flavor about his worldliness which had nothing to do with stale frivolities; it was rather a thing of fastidious taste and of tempered wit. He was keen in his judgments of men, and charitable in his estimates of women.

Brinsley Tyson had known Baltimore before the days of modern cities. He had known it before it had cut its hotels after the palace pattern, and when Rennert's in more primitive quarters had been the Mecca for epicureans. He had known its theaters when the footlight favorites were Lotta and Jo Emmet, and when the incomparable Booth and Jefferson had held audiences spellbound at Ford's and at Albaugh's. He had known Charles Street before it was extended, and he had known its Sunday parade. He had known the Bay Line Boats, the harbor and the noisy streets that led to the wharves. He had known Lexington Market on Saturday afternoons; the Baltimore and Ohio Railroad in the heyday of its importance, and more than all he had known the beauties and belles of old Baltimore, and it added piquancy to many of his anecdotes when he spoke of his single estate as a tragedy resulting from his devotion to too many charmers, with no possibility of making a choice.

It was of these things that he spoke while Geoffrey, lying in the grass with his arm across his eyes, listened and enjoyed.

"And you never married, sir?"

"I've told you there were too many of them. If I could have had any one of those girls on this island with 'tother dear charmers away, there wouldn't have been any trouble. But a choice with them all about me was—impossible." His old eyes twinkled.

"Suppose you had made a choice, and she hadn't cared for you?" said the voice of the man on the grass.

"Any woman will care if you go at it the right way."

"What is the right way?"

"There's only one way to win a woman. If she says she won't marry you, carry her off by force to a clergyman, and when you get her there make her say 'Yes.'"

Geoffrey sat up. "You don't mean that literally?"

448

Brinsley nodded. "Indeed I do. Take the attitude with them of Man the Conqueror. They all like it. Man the Suppliant never gets what he wants."

"But in these days primitive methods aren't possible."

Brinsley skipped a chicken bone expertly across the surface of the water. "Primitive methods are always possible. The trouble is that man has lost his nerve. The cult of chivalry has spoiled him. It has taught him to kneel at his lady's feet, where pre-historically he kept his foot on her neck!"

Geoffrey laughed. "You'd be mobbed in a suffrage meeting."

"Suffrage, my dear fellow, is the green carnation in the garden of femininity. Every woman blooms for her lover. It is the lack of lovers that produces the artificial—hence votes for women. What does the woman being carried off under the arm of conquering man care for yellow banners or speeches from the tops of busses? She is too busy trying to please him."

"It would be a great experiment. I'd like to try it."

Brinsley, uncorking a hot and cold bottle, boldly surmised, "It is the little school-teacher?"

Geoffrey, again flat on the grass, murmured, "Yes."

"And it is neck and neck between you and that young cousin of mine?"

"I am afraid he is a neck ahead."

"It all depends upon which runs away with her first."

Again Geoffrey murmured, "I'd like to try it."

"Why not?" said Brinsley and beamed over his coffee cup like a benevolent spider at an unsuspecting fly. He had no idea that his fooling might be taken seriously. It was not given to his cynicism to comprehend the mood of the seemingly composed young person who lay on the grass with his hat over his eyes—torn by contending emotions, maddened by despair and the dread of darkness, awakened to new impulses in which youth and hot blood fought against an almost reverent tenderness for the object of his adoration. Since the night of the Crossroads ball Geoffrey had permitted himself to hope. She had turned to him then. For the first time he had felt that the barriers were down between them.

"Now Richard," Brinsley was saying, as he smoked luxuriously after the feast, "ought to marry Eve. She'll get her Aunt Maude's money, and be the making of him."

Richard, who at that very moment was riding through the country on his old white horse, had no thought of Eve.

The rhythm of old Ben's even trot formed an accompaniment to the song that his heart was singing—

"I think she was the most beautiful lady,
That ever was in the West Country——"
As he passed along the road, he was aware of the world's awakening. His ears caught the faint flat bleating of lambs, the call of the cocks, the high note of the hens, the squeal of little pigs, and above all, the clamor of blackbirds and of marauding crows.

The trees, too, were beginning to show the pale tints of spring, and an amethyst haze enveloped the hills. The river was silver in the shadow and gold in the sun; the little streams that ran down to it seemed to sing as they went.

Coming at last to an old white farmhouse, Richard dismounted and went in. The old man bent with rheumatism welcomed him, and the old wife said, "He is always better when he knows that you are coming, doctor."

449

The old man nodded. "Your gran'dad used to come. I was a little boy an' croupy, and he seemed big as a house when he came in at the door. He was taller than you, and thin."

"Now, father," the old woman protested, "the young doctor ain't fat."

"He's fatter'n his gran'dad. But I ain't saying that I don't like it. I like meat on a man's bones."

Richard laughed. "Just so that I don't go the way of Cousin Brin. You know Brinsley Tyson, don't you?"

"He's the fat twin. Yes, I know him and David. David comes and reads to me, but Brinsley went to Baltimore, and now he don't seem to remember that we were boys together, and went to the Crossroads school."

After that they spoke of the little new teacher, and Richard revelled in the praise they gave her. She was worshipped, they said, by the people roundabout. There had never been another like her.

"I think she was the most beautiful lady,
That ever was in the West Country——"
was Richard's enlargement of their theme. In the weeks just past he had seen much of her, and it had seemed to him that life began and ended with his thought of her.

When he rose to go the old woman went to the door with him. "I guess we owe you a lot by this time," she remarked; "you've made so many calls. It cheers him up to have you, but you'd better stop now that he don't need you. It's so far, and we ain't good pay like some of them."

Richard squared his shoulders—a characteristic gesture. "Don't bother about the bill. I have a sort of sentiment about my grandfather's old patients. It is a pleasure to know them and serve them."

"If you didn't mind taking your pay in chickens," she stated as he mounted his horse, "we could let you have some broilers."

"You will need all you can raise." Then as his eyes swept the green hill which sloped down to the river, he perceived an orderly line of waddling fowls making their way toward the house.

"I'd like a white duck," he said, "if you could let me take her now."

He chose a meek and gentle creature who submitted to the separation from the rest of her kind without rebellion. Tucked under Richard's arm, she surveyed the world with some alarm, but presently, as he rode on with her, she seemed to acquiesce in her abduction and faced the adventure with serene eyes, murmuring now and then some note of demure interrogation as she nestled quite confidently against the big man who rode so easily his great white horse.

And thus they came to Bower's, to find Anne on the south bank, like a very modern siren, drying her hair, with Diogenes nipping the new young grass near her.

She saw them coming. Richard wore a short rough coat and an old alpine hat of green. His leggings were splashed with mud, and the white horse was splashed, but there was about the pair of them an air of gallant achievement.

She rose to greet them. She was blushing a little and with her dark hair blowing she was "the most beautiful," like the lady in the song.

"I thought no one would be coming," was her apology, "and out here I get the wind and sun."

"All the old fishermen will be wrecked on the rocks if they get a glimpse of you," he told her gravely; "you mustn't turn their poor old heads."

And now the white duck murmured.

"The lovely dear, where did you get her?" Anne asked.

"In the hills, to cheer up Diogenes."

He set the white duck down. She shook her feathers and again spoke interrogatively. And now Diogenes lifted his head and answered. For a few moments he rent the air with his song of triumph. Then he turned and led the way to the river. There was a quiet pool in the bend of the bank. The old drake breasted its shining waters, and presently the white duck followed. With a sort of restrained coquetry she turned her head from side to side. All her questions were answered, all her murmurs stilled.

Richard and Anne smiled at each other. "What made you think of it?" she asked.

"I thought you'd like it."

"I do." She began to twist up her hair.

"Please don't. I like to see it down."

"But people will be coming in."

"Why should we be here when they come? I'll put Ben in the stable—and we'll go for a walk. Do you know there are violets in the wood?"

From under the red-striped awning of Brinsley's boat Geoffrey Fox saw Anne's hair blowing like a sable banner in the breeze. He saw Richard's square figure peaked up to the alpine hat. He saw them enter the wood.

He shut his eyes from the glare of the sun and lay quietly on the cushions of the little launch. But though his eyes were shut, he could still see those two figures walking together in the dreamy dimness of the spring forest.

"What were the ethics of the primitive man?" he asked Brinsley suddenly. "Did he run away with a woman who belonged to somebody else?"

"Why not?" Brinsley's reel was whirring. "And now if you don't mind, Fox, you might be ready with the net. If this fish is as big as he pulls, he will weigh a ton."

Geoffrey, coming in, found Peggy disconsolate on the pier.

"What's the matter?" he asked.

"I can't find Anne. She said that after her hair dried she'd go for a walk to Beulah's playhouse, and we were to have tea. Beulah was to bring it."

"She has gone for a walk with some one else."

"Who?"

"Dr. Brooks. Let's go and look for her, Peggy, and when we find her we will tell her what we think of her for running away."

The green stillness of the grove was very grateful after the glare of the river. Geoffrey walked quickly, with the child's hand in his. He had a feeling that if he did not walk quickly he would be too late.

He was not too late; he saw that at a glance. Richard had dallied in his wooing. It had been so wonderful to be with her. Once when he had knelt beside her to pick violets, the wind had blown across his face a soft sweet strand of her hair. It was then that she had braided it, sitting on a fallen log under a blossoming dogwood.

"It is so long," she had said with a touch of pride, "that it is a great trouble to care for it. Cynthia Warfield had hair like mine."

"I don't believe that any one ever had hair like yours. It seems to me as if every strand must have been made specially in some celestial shop, and then the pattern destroyed."

How lovely she was when she blushed like that! How little and lovely and wise and good. He liked little women. His mother was small, and he was glad that both she and Anne had delicate hands and feet. He was aware that this preference was old-fashioned, but it was, none the less, the way he felt about it.

And now there broke upon the silence of the wood the sound of murmuring voices. Peggy and Geoffrey Fox had invaded their Paradise!

"We thought," Peggy complained, "that we had lost you. Anne, you promised about the tea."

"Oh, Peggy, I forgot."

"Beulah's gone with the basket and Eric, and we can't be late because there are hot biscuits."

Hurrying toward the biscuits and their hotness, Anne ran ahead with Peggy.

"How about the eyes?" Richard asked as he and Geoffrey followed.

"I've been on the water, and it is bad for them. But I'm not going to worry. I am getting out of life more than I hoped—more than I dared hope."

His voice had a high note of excitement. Richard glanced at him. For a moment he wondered if Fox had been drinking.

But Geoffrey was intoxicated with the wine of his dreams. With a quick gesture in which he seemed to throw from him all the fears which had oppressed him, he told his triumphant lie.

"I am going to marry Anne Warfield; she has promised to be eyes for me, and light—the sun and the moon."

Richard's face grew gray. He spoke with difficulty. "She has promised?"

Then again Geoffrey lied, meaning indeed before the night had passed to make his words come true. "She is going to marry me—and I am the happiest man alive!"

The light went out of Richard's world. How blind he had been. He had taken her smiles and blushes to himself when she had glowed with a happiness which had nothing to do with him.

He steadied himself to speak. "You are a lucky fellow, Fox; you must let me congratulate you."

"The world doesn't know," Geoffrey said, "not yet. But I had to tell it to some one, and a doctor is a sort of secular father confessor."

Richard's laugh was without mirth. "If you mean that it's not to be told, you may rely on my discretion."

"Of course. I told you she was to play Beatrice to my Dante, but she shall be more than that."

It was a rather silent party which had tea on the porch of the Playhouse. But Beulah and Eric were not aware of any lack in their guests. Eric had been to Baltimore the day before, and Beulah wore her new ring. She accepted Richard's congratulations shyly.

"I like my little new house," she said; "have you been over it?"

He said that he had not, and she took him. Eric went with them, and as they stood in the door of an upper room, he put his arm quite frankly about Beulah's shoulders as she explained their plans to Richard. "This is to be in pink and the other one in white, and all the furniture is to be pink and white."

She was as pink and white and pretty as the rooms she was planning, and to see her standing there within the circle of her lover's arm was heart-warming.

"You must get some roses from my mother, Beulah, for your little garden," the young doctor told her; "all pink and white like the rest of it."

He let them go down ahead of him, and so it happened that he stood for a moment alone in a little upper porch at the back of the house which overlooked the wood. The shadows were gathering in its dim aisles, shutting out the daylight, shutting out the dreams which he had lost that day in the fragrant depths.

When later he came with the rest of them to Bower's, the river was stained with the sunset. Diogenes and the white duck breasted serenely the crimson surface. Certain old fishermen trailed belatedly up the bank. Others sat spick and span and ready for supper on the porch.

Brinsley Tyson over the top of his newspaper hailed Richard.

"There's a telephone call for you. They've been trying to get you for an hour."

He went in at once, and coming out told Anne good-night. "Thank you for a happy afternoon," he said.

But she missed something in his voice, something that had been there when they had walked in the wood.

She watched him as he went away, square-shouldered and strong on his big white horse. She had a troubled sense that things had in some fateful and tragic way gone wrong with her afternoon, but it was not yet given to her to know that young Richard on his big white horse was riding out of her life.

It was after supper that Geoffrey asked her to go out on the river with him.

"Not to-night. I'm tired."

"Just a little minute, Mistress Anne. To see the moon come up over the island. Please." So she consented.

Helping her into the boat, Geoffrey's hands were shaking. The boat swept out from the pier in a wide curve, and he drew a long breath. He had her now—it would be a great adventure—like a book—better than any book.

Primitive man in prehistoric days carried his woman off captive under his arm. Geoffrey, pursuing modern methods, had borrowed Brinsley's boat. A rug was folded innocently on the cushions; in a snug little cupboard under the stern seat were certain supplies—a great adventure, surely!

And now the boat was under the bridge; the signal lights showed red and green. Then as they slipped around the first island there was only the silver of the moonshine spread out over the waters.

Geoffrey stopped the motor. "We'll drift and talk."

"You talk," she told him, "and I'll listen, and we mustn't be too late."

"What is too late?"

"I told you I would stay just a little minute."

"There is no real reason why we shouldn't stay as long as we wish. You are surely not so prim that you are doing it for propriety."

"You know I am not prim."

"Yes you are. You are prim and Puritan and sometimes you are a prig. But I like you that way, Mistress Anne. Only to-night I shall do as I please."

"Don't be silly."

"Is it silly to love you—why?"

He argued it with her brilliantly—so that it was only when the red and green lights of a second bridge showed ahead of them that she said, sharply, "We are miles away from Bower's; we must go back."

"It won't take us long," he said, easily, and presently they were purring up-stream.

Then all at once the motor stopped. Geoffrey, inspecting it with a flashlight, said, succinctly, "Engine's on the blink."

"You mean that we can't go on?"

"Oh, I'll tinker it up. Only you'll have to let me get into that box under the stern seat for the tools. You can hold the light while I work."

As he worked they drifted. They passed the second bridge. Anne, steering, grew cold and shivered. But she did not complain. She was glad, however, when Geoffrey said, "You'd better curl down among the cushions, and let me wrap you in this rug."

"Can you manage without me?"

"Yes. I've patched it up partially. And you'll freeze in this bitter air."

The wind had changed and there was now no moon. She was glad of the warmth of the rug and the comfort of the cushioned space. She shut her eyes, after a time, and, worn out by the emotions of the day, she dropped into fitful slumber.

Then Geoffrey, his hair blown back by the wind, stood at the wheel and steered his boat not up-stream toward the bridge at Bower's, but straight down toward the wider waters, where the river stretches out into the Bay.

CHAPTER XII

In Which Eve Usurps an Ancient Masculine Privilege.

Aunt maude chesley belonged to the various patriotic societies which are dependent on Revolutionary fighting blood, on Dutch forbears, or on the ancestral holding of Colonial office. The last stood highest in her esteem. It was the hardest to get into, hence there was about it the sanctity of exclusiveness. Any man might spill his blood for his country, and among those early Hollanders were many whose blood was red instead of blue, but it was only a choice few who in the early days of the country's history had been appointed by the Crown or elected by the people to positions of influence and of authority.

When Aunt Maude went to the meeting of her favorite organization, she wore always black velvet which showed the rounds of her shoulders, point lace in a deep bertha, the family diamonds, and all of her badges. The badges had bars and jewels, and the effect was imposing.

Evelyn laughed at her. "Nobody cares for ancestors any more. Not since people began to hunt them up. You can find anything if you look for it, Aunt Maude. And most of the crests are bought or borrowed so that if one really belongs to you, you don't like to speak of it, any more than to tell that you are a lady or take a daily bath."

"Our ancestors," said Aunt Maude solemnly, "are our heritage from the past—but you have reverence for nothing."

"They were a jolly old lot," Eve agreed, "and I am proud of them. But some of their descendants are a scream. If men had their minds on being ancestors instead of bragging of them there'd be some hope for the future of old families."

Aunt Maude, having been swathed by her maid in a silk scarf, so that her head was stiff with it, batted her eyes. "If you would go with me," she said, "and hear some of the speeches, you might look at it differently. Now there was a Van Tromp——"

"And in New England there were Codcapers, and in Virginia there were Pantops. I take off my hat to them, but not to their descendants, indiscriminately."

And now Aunt Maude, more than ever mummified in a gold and black brocade wrap trimmed with black fur, steered her uncertain way toward the motor at the door.

"People in my time——" floated over her shoulder and then as the door closed behind her, her eloquence was lost.

Eve, alone, faced a radiant prospect. Richard was coming. He had telephoned. She had not told Aunt Maude. She wanted him to herself.

When at last he arrived she positively crowed over him. "Oh, Dicky, this is darling of you."

A shadow fell across her face, however, when he told her why he had come.

"Austin wanted me with him in an operation. He telegraphed me and I took the first train. I have been here for two days without a minute's time in which to call you up."

"I thought that perhaps you had come to see me."

"Seeing you is a pleasant part of it, Eve."

He was really glad to see her; to be drawn away by it all from the somberness of his thoughts. The night before he had left the train on the Jersey side and had ferried over so that he might view once more the sky-line of the great city. There had been a stiff breeze blowing and it had seemed to him that he drew the first full breath since the moment when he had walked with Geoffrey in the wood. What had followed had been like a dream; the knowledge that the great surgeon wanted him, his mother's quick service in helping him pack his bag, the walk to Bower's in the fragrant dark to catch the ten o'clock train; the moment on the porch at Bower's when he had learned from a word dropped by Beulah that Anne was on the river with Geoffrey.

And now it all seemed so far away—the river with the moon's broad path, Bower's low house and its yellow-lighted panes, the silence, the darkness.

Since morning he had done a thousand things. He had been to the hospital and had yielded once more to the spell of its splendid machinery; he had talked with Austin and the talk had been like wine to a thirsty soul. In such an atmosphere a man would have little time to—think. He craved the action, the excitement, the uplift.

He came back to Eve's prattle. "I told Winifred Ames we would come to her little supper after the play. I was to have gone with her and Pip and Jimmie Ford. Tony is away. But when you 'phoned, I called the first part of it off. I wanted to have a little time just with you, Richard."

He smiled at her. "Who is Jimmie Ford?"

"A lovely youth who is in love with me—or with my money—he was at your birthday party, Dicky Boy; don't you remember?"

"The Blue Butterfly? Yes. Is he another victim, Eve?"

She shrugged. "Who knows? If he is in love with me, he'll get hurt; if he is in love with Aunt Maude's money, he won't get it. Oh, how can a woman know?" The lightness left her voice. "Sometimes I think that I'll go off somewhere and see if somebody won't love me for what I am, and not for what he thinks Aunt Maude is going to leave me."

"And you with a string of scalps at your belt, and Pip ready at any moment to die for you."

She nodded. "Pip is pure gold. Nobody can question his motives. And anyhow he has more money than I can ever hope to have. But I am not in love with him, Dicky."

"You are not in love with anybody. You are a cold-blooded little thing, Eve. A man would need much fire to melt your ice."

"Would he?"

"You know he would."

He swept away from her petulances to the thing which was for the moment uppermost in his mind. "I have had an offer, Eve, from Austin. He wants an assistant, a younger man who can work into his practice. It is a wonderful working opportunity."

"It would be wicked to throw it away," she told him, breathlessly, "wicked, Richard."

"It looks that way. But there's mother to think of, and Crossroads has come to mean a lot to me, Eve."

"Oh, but New York, Dicky! Think of the good times we'd have, and of your getting into Austin's line of work and his patients. You would be rolling in your own limousine before you'd know it."

Rolling in his own limousine! And missing the rhythm of big Ben's measured trot——!

"I think—she was the—most beautiful——"

As they motored to Winifred's, Eve spoke of his quiet mood. "Why don't you talk, Dicky?"

"It has been a busy day—I'll wake up presently and realize that I am here."

It was before he went down-stairs at the Dutton-Ames that he had a moment alone with Jimmie Ford.

Jimmie was not in the best of moods. Winifred had asked him a week ago to join a choice quartette which included Pip and Eve. Of course Meade made a troublesome fourth, but Jimmie's conceit saved him from realizing the real fact of the importance of the plain and heavy Pip to that group. And now, things had been shifted, so that Eve had stayed to talk to a country doctor, and he had been left to the callow company of an indefinite debutante whom Winifred had invited to fill the vacancy.

"When did you come down, Brooks?" he asked coldly.

"This morning."

"Nice old place of yours in Harford."

"Yes."

"Owned it long?"

"Several generations."

"Oh, ancestral halls, and all that——?"

"Yes."

"I saw Cynthia Warfield's picture on the wall—used to know the family down in Carroll—our old estates joined—Anne Warfield and I were brought up together."

They had reached the head of the stairway. Richard stopped and stood looking down. "Anne Warfield?"

"Yes. Surprised to find her teaching. I fancy they've been pretty hard up—grandfather drank, and all that, you know."

"I didn't know." It was now Richard's turn to speak coldly.

"Oh, yes, ran through with all their money. Years ago. Anne's a little queen. Engaged to her once myself, you know. Boy and girl affair, broken off——"

Below them in the hall, Richard could see the women with whom he was to sup. Shining, shimmering figures in silk and satin and tulle. For these, softness and ease of living. And that other one! Oh, the cheap little gown, the braided hair! Before he had known her she had been Jimmie's and now she was Geoffrey's. And he had fatuously thought himself the first.

He threw himself uproariously into the fun which followed. After all, it was good to be with them again, good to hear the familiar talk of people and of things, good to eat and drink and be merry in the fashion of the town, good to have this taste of the old tumultuous life.

He and Eve went home together. Philip's honest face clouded as he saw them off. "Don't run away with her, Brooks," he said, as he leaned in to have a last look at her. "Good-night, little lady."

"Good-night."

It was when they were motoring through the park that Eve said, "I am troubled about Pip."

"Why?"

"Oh, I sometimes have a feeling that he has a string tied to me—and that he is pulling me—his way. And I don't want to go. But I shall, if something doesn't save me from him, Richard."

"You can save yourself."

"That's all you know about it. Women take what they can get in this world, not what they want. Every morning Pip sends me flowers, sweetheart roses to-day, and lilies yesterday, and before that gardenias and orchids, and when I open the boxes every flower seems to be shouting, 'Come and marry me, come and marry me.'"

"No woman need marry a man she doesn't care for, Eve."

"Lots of them do."

"You won't. You are too sensible."

"Am I?"

"Of course."

She sighed a little. "I am not half as sensible as you think."

When they reached home, they found Aunt Maude before them. She had been unswathed from her veil and her cloak, released from her black velvet, and was comfortable before her sitting-room fire in a padded wisteria robe and a boudoir cap with satin bow. Underneath the cap there were no flat gray curls. These were whisked mysteriously away each night by Hannah, the maid, to be returned in the morning, fresh from their pins with no hurt to Aunt Maude's old head.

457

She greeted Richard cordially. "I sent Hannah down when I heard you. Eve didn't let me know you were here; she never lets me know. And now tell me about your poor mother."

"Why poor, dear lady? You know she loves Crossroads."

"How anybody can—— I'd die of loneliness. Now to-night—so many people of my own kind——"

"Everybody in black velvet or brocade, everybody with badges, everybody with blue blood," Eve interrupted flippantly; "nobody with ideas, nobody with enthusiasms, nobody with an ounce of originality—ugh!"

"My dear——!"

"Dicky, Aunt Maude's idea of Heaven is a place where everybody wears coronets instead of halos, and where the angel chorus is a Dutch version of 'God save the King.'"

"My idea of Heaven," Aunt Maude retorted, "is a place where young girls have ladylike manners."

Richard roared. It had been long since he had tasted this atmosphere of salt and spice. Aunt Maude and her sprightly niece were as good as a play.

"How long shall you be in town, Richard?"

"Three or four days. It depends on the condition of our patient. It may be necessary to operate again, and Austin wants me to be here."

"Aunt Maude, Dicky may come back to New York to live."

"He should never have left. What does your mother think of it?"

"I haven't told her of Austin's offer. I shall write to-night."

"If she has a grain of sense, she'll make you take it."

Eve was restless. "Come on down, Dicky. It is time that Aunt Maude was in bed."

"I never go until you do, Eve, and in my day young men went home before morning."

"Dearest, Dicky shall leave in ten minutes. I'll send him."

But when they were once more in the great drawing-room, she forgot the time limit. "Don't let your mother settle things for you, Dicky. Think of yourself and your future. Of your—manhood, Dicky—please."

She was very lovely as she stood before him, with her hands on his shoulders. "I want you to be the biggest of them—all," she said, and her laugh was tremulous.

"I know. Eve, I want to stay."

"Oh, Dicky—really?"

"Really, Eve."

Their hands came together in a warm clasp.

She let him go after that. There had been nothing more than brotherly warmth in his manner, but it was enough that in the days to come she was to have him near her.

Richard, writing to his mother, told her something of his state of mind. "I'll admit that it tempts me. It is a big thing, a very big thing, to work with a man like that. Yet knowing how you feel about it, I dare not decide. We shall have to face one thing, however. The Crossroads practice will never be a money-making practice. I know how little money means to you, but the lack of it will mean that I shall be tied to rather small things as the years go on. I should like to be one of the Big Men, mother. You see I am being very frank. I'll admit that I dreamed with you—of bringing all my talents to the uplift of a small community, of reviving at Crossroads the dignity of other days. But—perhaps we have dreamed too much—the world doesn't wait for the dreamers—the only way is to join the procession."

In the day which intervened between his letter and his mother's answer, he had breakfast with Eve in the room with the flame-colored fishes and the parrot and the green-eyed cat. He motored with Eve out to Westchester, and they had lunch at an inn on the side of a hill which overlooked the Hudson; later they went to a matinée, to tea in a special little corner of a down-town hotel for the sake of old days, then back again to dress for dinner at Eve's, with Aunt Maude at the head of the table, and Tony and Winifred and Pip completing the party. Then another play, another supper, another ride home with Eve, and in the morning in quiet contrast to all this, his mother's letter.

"Dear Boy," she said, "I am glad you spoke to me frankly of what you feel. I want no secrets between us, no reservations, no sacrifices which in the end may mean a barrier between us.

"Our sojourn at Crossroads has been an experiment. And it has failed. I had hoped that as the days went on, you might find happiness. Indeed, I had been deceiving myself with the thought that you were happy. But now I know that you are not, and I know, too, what it must mean to you to feel that from among all the others you have been chosen to help a great man like Dr. Austin, who was the friend of my father, and my friend through everything.

"But Richard, I can't go back. I literally crawled to Crossroads, after my years in New York, as a wounded animal seeks its lair. And I have a morbid shrinking from it all, unworthy of me, perhaps, but none the less impossible to overcome. I feel that the very stones of the streets would speak of the tragedy and dishonor of the past: houses would stare at me, the crowds would shun me.

"And now I have this to propose. That I stay here at Crossroads, keeping the old house open for you. David is near me, and any one of Cousin Mary Tyson's daughters would be glad to come to me. And you shall run down at week-ends, and tell me all about it, and I shall live in your letters and in the things which you have to tell. We can be one in spirit, even though there are miles between us. This is the only solution which seems possible to me at this moment. I cannot hold you back from what may be your destiny. I can only pray here in my old home for the happiness and success that must come to you—my boy—my little—boy——"

The letter broke off there. Richard, high up in the room of the big hotel, found himself pacing the floor. Back of the carefully penned lines of his mother's letter he could see her slender tense figure, the whiteness of her face, the shadow in her eyes. How often he had seen it when a boy, how often he had sworn that when he was the master of the house he would make her happy.

The telephone rang. It was Eve. "I was afraid you might have left for the hospital."

"I am leaving in a few minutes."

"Can you go for a ride with me?"

"In the afternoon. There's to be another operation—it may be very late before I am through."

"Not too late for dinner out of town somewhere and a ride under the May moon." Her voice rang high and happy.

For the rest of the morning he had no time to think of his own affairs. The operation was extremely rare and interesting, and Austin's skill was superb. Richard felt as if he were taking part in a play, in which the actors were the white clad and competent doctors and nurses, and the stage was the surgical room.

Eve coming for him, found him tired and taciturn. She respected his mood, and said little, and they rode out and out from the town and up and up into the Westchester hills, dotted with dogwood, pink and white like huge nosegays. As the night came on there was the fragrance of the gardens, the lights of the little towns; then once more the shadows as they swept again into the country.

"We will go as far as we dare," Eve said. "I know an adorable place to dine."

She tried more than once to bring him to speak of Austin, but he put her off. "I am dead tired, dear girl; you talk until we have something to eat."

"Oh," Eve surveyed him scornfully, "oh, men and their appetites!"

But she had a thousand things to tell him, and her light chatter carried him away from somber thoughts, so that when they reached at last the quaint hostelry toward which their trip had tended, he was ready to meet Eve's mood half-way, and enter with some zest upon their gay adventure. She chose a little table on a side porch, where they were screened from observation, and which overlooked the river, and there took off her hat and powdered her nose, and gave her attention to the selection of the dinner.

"A clear soup, Dicky Boy, and Maryland chicken, hot asparagus, a Russian dressing for our lettuce, and at the end red raspberries with little cakes. They are sponge cakes, Dicky, filled with cream, and they are food for the gods."

He was hungry and tired and he wanted to eat. He was glad when the food came on.

When he finished he leaned back and talked shop. "If you don't like it," he told Eve, "I'll stop. Some women hate it."

"I love it," Eve said. "Dicky, when I dream of your future you are always at the top of things, with smaller men running after you and taking your orders."

He smiled. "Don't dream. It doesn't pay. I've stopped."

She glanced at him. His face was stern.

"What's up, Dicky Boy?"

He laughed without mirth. "Oh, I'm beginning to think we are puppets pulled by strings; that things happen as Fate wills and not as we want them."

"Men haven't any right to talk that way. It's their world. If you were a woman you might complain. Look at me! Everything that I have comes from Aunt Maude. She could leave me without a cent if she chose, and she knows it. She owns me, and unless I marry she'll own me until I die."

"You'll marry, Eve. Old Pip will see to that."

"Pip," passionately. "Dicky, why do you always fling Pip in my face?"

"Eve——!"

"You do. Everybody does. And I don't want him."

"Then don't have him. There are others. And you needn't lose your temper over a little thing like that."

"It isn't a little thing."

"Oh, well——" The conversation lapsed into silence until Eve said, "I was horrid—and I think we had better be getting back, Dicky."

Again in the big limousine, with the stolid chauffeur separated from them by the glass screen, she said, softly, "Oh, Dicky, it seems too good to be true that we shall have other nights like this—other rides. When will you come up for good?"

460

"I am not coming, Eve."

She turned to him, her face frozen into whiteness.

"Not coming? Why not?"

"While mother lives I must make her happy."

"Oh, don't be goody-goody."

He blazed. "I'm not."

"You are. Aren't you ever going to live your own life?"

"I am living it. But I can't break mother's heart."

"You might as well break hers as—mine."

He stared down at her. Mingled forever after with his thoughts of that moment was a blurred vision of her whiteness and stillness. Her slim hands were crossed tensely on her knees.

He laid one of his own awkwardly over them. "Dear girl," he said, "you don't in the least mean it."

"I do. Dicky, why shouldn't I say it? Why shouldn't I? Hasn't a woman the right? Hasn't she?"

She was shaking with silent sobs, the tears running down her cheeks. He had not seen her cry like this since little girlhood, when her mother had died, and he, a clumsy lad, had tried to comfort her.

He was faced by a situation so stupendous that for a moment he sat there stunned. Proud little Eve for love of him had made the supreme sacrifice of her pride. Could any man in his maddest moment have imagined a thing like this——!

He bent down to her, and took her hands in his.

"Hush, Eve, hush. I can't bear to see you cry. I'm not the fellow to make you happy, dear."

Her head dropped against his shoulder. The perfumed gold of her hair was against his cheeks. "No one else can make me happy, Dicky."

Then he felt the world whirl about him, and it seemed to him as he answered that his voice came from a long distance.

"If you'll marry me, Eve, I'll stay."

It was the knightly thing to do, and the necessary thing. Yet as they swept on through the night, his mother's face, all the joy struck from it, seemed to stare at him out of the darkness.

CHAPTER XIII

In Which Geoffrey Plays Cave Man.

Mine own uncle:

I don't know whether to begin at the beginning or at the end of what I have to tell you. And even now as I think back over the events of the last twenty-four hours I feel that I must have dreamed them, and that I will wake and find that nothing has really happened.

But something has happened, and "of a strangeness" which makes it seem to belong to some of those queer old dime "thrillers" which you never wanted me to read.

Last night Geoffrey Fox asked me to go out with him on the river. I don't often go at night, yet as there was a moon, it seemed as if I might.

We went in Brinsley Tyson's motor boat. It is big and roomy and is equipped with everything to make one comfortable for extended trips. I wondered a little that Geoffrey should take it, for he has a little boat of his own, but he said that Mr. Tyson had offered it, and they had been out in it all day.

Well, it was lovely on the water; I was feeling tired and as blue as blue—some day I may tell you about that, Uncle Rod, and I was glad of the quiet and beauty of it all; and of late Geoffrey and I have been such good friends.

Can't you ever really know people, Uncle Rod, or am I so dull and stupid that I misunderstand? Men are such a puzzle— all except you, you darling dear—and if you were young and not my uncle, even you might be as much of a puzzle as the rest.

Well, I would never have believed it of Geoffrey Fox, and even now I can't really feel that he was responsible. But it isn't what I think but what you will think that is important—for I have, somehow, ceased to believe in myself.

It was when we reached the second bridge that I told Geoffrey that we must turn back. We had, even then, gone farther than I had intended. But as we started up-stream, I felt that we would get to Bower's before Peter went back on the bridge, which is always the signal for the house to close, although it is never really closed; but the lights are turned down and the family go to bed, and I have always known that I ought not to stay out after that.

Well, just as we left the second bridge, something happened to the motor.

Uncle Rod, that was last night, and I didn't get back to Bower's until a few hours ago, and here is the whole truth before I write any more——

Geoffrey Fox tried to run away with me!

It would seem like a huge joke if it were not so serious. I don't know how he got such an idea in his head. Perhaps he thought that life was like one of his books—that all he had to do was to plan a plot, and then make it work out in his own way. He said, in that first awful moment, when I knew what he had done, "I thought I could play Cave Man and get away with it." You see, he hadn't taken into consideration that I wasn't a Cave Woman!

When the engine first went wrong I wasn't in the least worried. He fixed it, and we went on. Then it stopped and we drifted: the moon went down and it was cold, and finally Geoffrey made me curl up among the cushions. I felt that it must be very late, but Geoffrey showed me his watch, and it was only a little after ten. I knew Peter wouldn't be going to the bridge until eleven, and I hoped by that time we would be home.

But we weren't. We were far, far down the river. At last I gave up hope of arriving before the house closed, but I knew that I could explain to Mrs. Bower.

After that I napped and nodded, for I was very tired, and all the time Geoffrey tinkered with the broken motor. Each time that I waked I asked questions but he always quieted me—and at last—as the dawn began to light the world, a pale gray spectral sort of light, Uncle Rod, I saw that the shore on one side of us was not far away, but on the other it was a mere dark line in the distance—double the width that the river is at Bower's. Geoffrey was standing up and steering toward a little pier that stuck its nose into shallow water. Back of the pier was what seemed to be an old warehouse, and in a clump of trees back of that there was a thin church spire.

I said, "Where are we?" and he said, "I am not sure, but I am going in to see if I can get the motor mended."

I couldn't think of anything but how worried the Bowers would be. "You must find a telephone," I told him, "and call Beulah, and let her know what has happened."

He ran up to the landing and fastened the boat, and then he helped me out. "We will sit here and have a bit of breakfast first," he said; "there's some coffee left in Brinsley's hot and cold bottle, and some supplies under the stern seat."

It was really quite cheerful sitting there, eating sardines and crackers and olives and orange marmalade. A fresh breeze was blowing, and the river was wrinkled all over its silver surface, and we could see nothing but water ahead of us, straight to the horizon, where there was just the faint streak of a steamer's smoke.

"We must be almost in the Bay," I said. "Couldn't you have steered up-stream instead of down?"

He sat very still for a moment looking at me, and then he said quickly and sharply, "I didn't want to go up-stream. I wanted to go down. And I came in here because I saw a church spire, and where there is a church there is always a preacher. Will you marry me, Mistress Anne?"

At first I thought that he had lost his mind. Uncle Rod, I don't think that I shall ever see a sardine or a cracker without a vision of Geoffrey with his breakfast in his hand and his face as white as chalk above it.

"That's a very silly joke," I said. "Why should I marry you?"

He looked at me, and—I didn't need any answer, for it came to me then that I had been out all night on the river with him, and that he was thinking of a way to quiet people's tongues!

I tried to speak, but my voice shook, and finally I managed to stammer that when we got back I was sure it would be all right.

"It won't be all right," he said; "the world will have things to say about you, and I'd rather die than have them say it. And I could make you happy, Anne."

Then I told him that I did not love him, that he was my dear friend, my brother—and suddenly his face grew red, and he came over and caught hold of my hands. "I am not your brother," he said. "I want you whether you want me or not. I could make you love me—I've got to have you in my life. I am not going on alone to meet darkness—and despair."

Oh, Uncle Rod, then I knew and I looked straight at him and asked: "Geoffrey Fox, did you break the motor?"

"It isn't broken," he said; "there has never been a thing the matter with it."

I think for the first time that I was a little afraid. Not of him, but of what he had done.

"Oh, how could you," I said, "how could you?"

And it was then that he said, "I thought that I could play Cave Man and get away with it."

After that he told me how much he cared. He said that I had helped him and inspired him. That I had shown him a side of himself that no one else had ever shown. That I had made him believe in himself—and in—God. That if he didn't have me in his life his future would be—dead. He begged and begged me to let him take me into the little town and find some one to marry us. He said that if we went back I would be lost to him—that—that Brooks would get me—that was the way he put it, Uncle Rod. He said that he was going blind; that I hadn't any heart; that he would love me as no one else could; that he would write his books for me; that he would spend his whole life making it up to me.

I don't know how I held out against him. But I did. Something in me seemed to say that I must hold out. Some sense of dignity and of self-respect, and at last I conquered.

"I will not marry you," I said; "don't speak of it again. I am going back to Bower's. I am not a heroine of a melodrama, and there's no use to act as if I had done an unpardonable thing. I haven't, and the Bowers won't think it, and nobody else will know. But you have hurt me more than I can tell by what you have done to-night. When you first came to Bower's there were things about you that I didn't like, but—as I came to know you, I thought I had found another man in you. The night at the Crossroads ball you seemed like a big kind brother—and I told you what I had suffered, and now you have made me suffer."

463

And then—oh, I don't quite know how to tell you. He dropped on his knees at my feet and hid his face in my dress and cried—hard dry sobs—with his hands clutching.

I just couldn't stand it, Uncle Rod, and presently I was saying, "Oh, you poor boy, you poor boy——" and I think I smoothed his hair, and he whispered, "Can't you?" and I said, "Oh, Geoffrey, I can't."

At last he got control of himself. He sat at a little distance from me and told me what he was going to do.

"I think I was mad," he said. "I can't even ask your forgiveness, for I don't deserve it. I am going up to town to telephone to Beulah, and when I come back I will take you up the river where you can get the train. I shall break the engine and leave it here, so that when Brinsley gets it back there will be nothing to spoil our story."

He was gone half an hour. When he came he brought me a hat. He had bought it at the one little store where he had telephoned, and he had bought one for himself. I think we both laughed a little when we put them on, although it wasn't a laughing matter, but we did look funny.

He unfastened the boat, and we turned up the river and in about an hour we came into quite a thriving port with the Sunday quiet over everything, and Geoffrey did things to the engine that put it out of commission, and then he left it with a man on the pier, and we took the train.

It seems that all night at Bower's they were looking for us. They even took other boats, and followed. And they called. I know that if Geoffrey heard them call he didn't answer.

Every one seemed to accept our explanation. Perhaps they thought it queer. But I can't help that.

Geoffrey is going away to-morrow. When we were alone in the hall for a moment he told me that he was going. "If you can ever forgive me," he said, "will you write and tell me? What I have done may seem unforgivable. But when a man dreams a great deal he sometimes thinks that he can make his dreams come true."

Uncle Rod, I think the worst thing in the whole wide world is to be disappointed in people. As soon as school closes I am coming back to you. Perhaps you can make me see the sunsets. And what do you say about life now? Is it what we make it? Did I have anything to do with this mad adventure? Yet the memory of it will always—smirch.

And if life isn't what we make it, where is our hope and where are our sunsets? Tell me that, you old dear.

Anne.
P.S. When I opened my door just now, I found that Geoffrey had left on the threshold his little Napoleon, and a letter. I am sending the letter to you. I cried over it, and I am afraid it is blurred—but I haven't time to make a copy before the mail goes.

What Geoffrey said:

My little Child:

I am calling you that because there is something so young and untouched about you. If I were an artist I should paint you as young Psyche—and there should be a hint of angels' wings in the air and it should be spring—with a silver dawn. But if I could paint should I ever be able to put on canvas the light in your eyes when you have talked to me by the fire, my kind little friend whom I have lost?

 I cannot even now understand the mood that possessed me. Yet I will be frank. I saw you go into the wood with Richard Brooks. I felt that if he should say to you what I was sure he wanted to say that there would be no chance for me—so I hurried after you. The thing which was going to happen must not happen; and I arrived in time. After that I told Brooks as we walked back that I was going to marry you, and I took you out in my boat intending to make my words come true.

These last few days have been strange days. Perhaps when I have described them you may find it in your heart to feel sorry for me. The book is finished. That of itself has left me with a sense of loss, as if I had put away from me something

464

that had been a part of me. Then—I am going blind. Do you know what that means, the desperate meaning? To lose the light out of your life—never to see the river as I saw it this morning? Never to see the moonlight or the starlight—never to see your face?

The specialist has given me a few months—and then darkness.

Was it selfishness to want to tie you to a blind man? If you knew that you were losing the light wouldn't you want to steal a star to illumine the night?—and you were my—Star.

I am going now to my little sister, Mimi. She leaves the convent in a few days. There are just the two of us. I have been a wayward chap, loving my own way; it will be a sorry thing for her to find, I fancy, that henceforth I shall be in leading strings.

It is because of this thing that is coming that I am begging you still to be my friend—to send me now and then a little letter; that I may feel in the night that you are holding out your hand to me. There can be no greater punishment than your complete silence, no greater purgatory than the thought that I have forfeited your respect. Looking into the future I can see no way to regain it, but if the day ever comes when a Blind Beggar can serve you, you will show that you have forgiven him by asking that service of him.

I am leaving my little Napoleon for you. You once called him a little great man. Perhaps those of us who have some elements of greatness find our balance in something that is small and mean and mad.

Will you tell Brooks that you are not bound to me in any way? It is best that you should do it. I shall hope for a line from you. If it does not come—if I have indeed lost my little friend through my own fault—then indeed the shadows will shut me in.

Geoffrey.
Uncle Rodman writes:

My beloved Niece:

Once upon a time you and I read together "The Arabian Nights," and when we had finished the first book you laid your little hand on my knee and looked up at me. "Is it true, Uncle Rod?" you asked. "Oh, Uncle Rod, is it true?" And I said, "What it tells about the Roc's egg and the Old Man of the Sea and the Serpent is not true, but what it says about the actions and motives of people is true, because people have acted in that way and have thought like that through all the ages, and the tales have lived because of it, and have been written in all languages." I was sure, when I said it, that you did not quite understand; but you were to grow to it, which was all that was required.

Blessed child, what your Geoffrey Fox has done, though I hate him for it and blame him, is what other hotheads have done. The protective is not the primitive masculine instinct. Men have thought of themselves first and of women afterward since the beginning of time. Only with Christianity was chivalry born in them. And since many of our youths have elected to be pagan, what can you expect?

So your Geoffrey Fox being pagan, primitive—primordial, whatever it is now the fashion to call it, reverted to type, and you were the victim.

I have read his letter and might find it in my heart to forgive him were it not that he has made you suffer; but that I cannot forgive; although, indeed, his coming blindness is something that pleads for him, and his fear of it—and his fear of losing you.

I am glad that you are coming home to me. Margaret and her family are going away, and we can have their big house to ourselves during the summer. We shall like that, I am sure, and we shall have many talks, and try to straighten out this matter of dreams—and of sunsets, which is really very important, and not in the least to be ignored.

But let me leave this with you to ponder on. You remember how you have told me that when you were a tiny child you walked once between me and my good old friend, General Ross, and you heard it said by one of us that life was what we made it. Before that you had always cried when it rained; now you were anxious that the rain might come so that you could see if you could really keep from crying. And when the rain arrived you were so immensely entertained that you didn't shed a tear, and you went to bed that night feeling like a conqueror, and never again cried out against the elements.

It would have been dreadful if all your life you had gone on crying about rain, wouldn't it? And isn't this adventure your rainy day? You rose above it, dearest child. I am proud of the way you handled your mad lover.

Life is what we make it. Never doubt that. "He knows the water best who has waded through it," and I have lived long and have learned my lesson. When I knew that I could paint no more real pictures I knew that I must have dream pictures to hang on the walls of memory. Shall I make you a little catalogue of them, dear heart—thus:

No. 1.—Your precious mother sewing by the west window in our shadowed sitting-room, her head haloed by the sunset.

No. 2.—Anne in a blue pinafore, with the wind blowing her hair back on a gray March morning.

No. 3.—Anne in a white frock amid a blur of candle-light on Christmas——

Oh, my list would be long! People have said that I have lacked pride because I have chosen to take my troubles philosophically. There have been times when my soul has wept. I have cried often on my rainy days. But—there have always been the sunsets—and after that—the stars.

I fear that I have been but little help to you. But you know my love—blessed one. And the eagerness with which I await your coming. Ever your own

Uncle.

CHAPTER XIV

In Which There is Much Said of Marriage and of Giving in Marriage.

Eve's green-eyed cat sat on a chair and watched the flame-colored fishes. It was her morning amusement. When her mistress came down she would have her cream and her nap. In the meantime, the flashing, golden things in the clear water aroused an ancient instinct. She reached out a quick paw and patted the water, flinging showers of sparkling drops on her sleek fur.

Aunt Maude, eating waffles and reading her morning paper, approved her. "I hope you'll catch them," she said, "especially the turtles and the tadpoles—the idea of having such things where you eat."

The green-eyed cat licked her wet paw, then she jumped down from the chair and trotted to the door to meet Eve, who picked her up and hugged her. "Pats," she demanded, "what have you been doing? Your little pads are wet."

"She's been fishing," said Aunt Maude, "in your aquarium. She has more sense than I thought."

Eve, pouring cream into a crystal dish, laughed. "Pats is as wise as the ages—you can see it in her eyes. She doesn't say anything, she just looks. Women ought to follow her example. It's the mysterious, the silent, that draws men. Now Polly prattles and prattles, and nobody listens, and we all get a little tired of her; don't we, Polly?"

She set the cream carefully by the green cushion, and Pats, classically posed on her haunches, lapped it luxuriously. The Polly-parrot coaxed and wheedled and was rewarded with her morning biscuit. The flame-colored fishes rose to the snowy particles which Eve strewed on the surface of the water, and then with all of her family fed, Eve turned to the table, sat down, and pulled away Aunt Maude's paper.

"My dear," the old lady protested.

"I want to talk to you," Eve announced. "Aunt Maude, I'm going to marry Dicky."

Aunt Maude pushed back her plate of waffles. The red began to rise in her cheeks. "Oh, of all the fools——"

"'He who calleth his brother a fool——'" Eve murmured pensively. "Aunt Maude, I'm in love with him."

"You're in love with yourself," tartly, "and with having your own way. The husband for you is Philip Meade. But he wants you, and so—you don't want him."

"Dicky wants me, too," Eve said, a little wistfully; "you mustn't forget that, Aunt Maude."

"I'm not forgetting it." Then sharply, "Shall you go to live at Crossroads?"

"No. Austin has made him an offer. He's coming back to town."

"What do you expect to live on?"

Silence. Then, uncertainly, "I thought perhaps until he gets on his feet you'd make us an allowance."

The old lady exploded in a short laugh. She gathered up her paper and her spectacles case and her bag of fancy work. Then she rose. "Not if you marry Richard Brooks. You may as well know that now as later, Eve. All your life you have shaken the plum tree and have gathered the fruit. You may come to your senses when you find there isn't any tree to shake."

The deep red in the cheeks of the old woman was matched by the red that stained Eve's fairness. "Keep your money," she said, passionately; "I can get along without it. You've always made me feel like a pauper, Aunt Maude."

The old woman's hand went up. There was about her a dignity not to be ignored. "I think you are saying more than you mean, Eve. I have tried to be generous."

They were much alike as they faced each other, the same clear cold eyes, the same set of the head, the only difference Eve's youth and slenderness and radiant beauty. Perhaps in some far distant past Aunt Maude had been like Eve. Perhaps in some far distant future Eve's soft lines would stiffen into a second edition of Aunt Maude.

"I have tried to be generous," Aunt Maude repeated.

"You have been. I shouldn't have said that. But, Aunt Maude, it hasn't been easy to eat the bread of dependence."

"You are feeling that now," said the old lady shrewdly, "because you are ready for the great adventure of being poor with your young Richard. Well, try it. You'll wish more than once that you were back with your old—plum tree."

Flash of eye met flash of eye. "I shall never ask for another penny," Eve declared.

"I shall buy your trousseau, of course, and set you up in housekeeping, but when a woman is married her husband must take care of her." And Aunt Maude sailed away with her bag and her spectacles and her morning paper, and Eve was left alone in the black and white breakfast room, where Pats slept on her green cushion, the Polly-parrot swung in her ring, and the flame-colored fishes hung motionless in the clear water.

Eve ate no breakfast. She sat with her chin in her hand and tried to think it out. Aunt Maude had not proved tractable, and Richard's income would be small. Never having known poverty, she was not appalled by the prospect of it. Her imagination cast a glamour over the future. She saw herself making a home for Richard. She saw herself inviting Pip and Winifred Ames and Tony to small suppers and perfectly served little dinners. She did not see herself washing dishes or cooking the meals. Knowing nothing of the day's work, how could she conceive its sordidness?

She roused herself presently to go and write notes to her friends. Triumphant notes which told of her happiness.

Her note to Pip brought him that night. He came in white-faced. As she went toward him, he rose to meet her and caught her hands in a hard grip, looking down at her. "You're mine, Eve. Do you think I am going to let any one else have you?"

"Don't be silly, Pip."

"Is it silly to say that there will never be for me any other woman? I shall love you until I die. If that is foolishness, I never want to be wise."

He was kissing her hands now.

"Don't, Pip, don't."

She wrenched herself away from him, and stood as it were at bay. "You'll get over it."

"Shall I? How little you know me, Eve. I haven't even given you up. If I were a story-book sort of hero I'd bestow my blessing on you and Brooks and go and drive an ambulance in France, and break my heart at long distance. But I shan't. I shall stay right here on the job, and see that Brooks doesn't get you."

"Pip, I didn't think you were so—small."

The telephone rang. Eve answered it. "It was Winifred to wish me happiness," she said, as she came in from the hall.

She was blushing faintly. He gave her a keen glance. "What else did she say?"

"Nothing."

"You're fibbing. Tell me the truth, Eve."

She yielded to his masterfulness.

"Well, she said—'I wanted it to be Pip.'"

"Good old Win, I'll send her a bunch of roses." He wandered restlessly about the room, then came back to her. "Why, Eve, I planned the house—our house. It was to have the sea in front of it and a forest behind it, and your room was to have a wide window and a balcony, and under the balcony there was to be a rose garden."

"How sure you were of me, Pip."

"I have never been sure. But what I want, I—get. Remember that, dear girl. When I shut my eyes I can see you at the head of my table, in a high gold chair—like a throne."

She stared at him in amazement. "Pip, it doesn't sound a bit like you."

"No. What a man thinks is apt to be—different. On the surface I'm a rather practical sort of fellow. But when I plan my future with you I am playing king to your queen, and I'm not half bad at it."

And now it was she who was restless. "If I married you, what would I get out of it but—money?"

"Thank you."

"You know I don't mean it that way. But I like to think that I can help Richard—in his career."

"You're not made of that kind of stuff. You want your own good time. Women who help men to achieve must be content to lose their looks and their figures and to do without pretty clothes, and you wouldn't be content. You want to live your own life, and be admired and petted and envied, Eve."

She faced him, blazing. "You and Aunt Maude and Win are all alike. You think I can't be happy unless I live in the lap of luxury. Well, I can tell you this, I'd rather have a crust of bread with Richard than live in a palace with you, Pip."

He stood up. "You don't mean it. But you needn't have put it quite that way, and some day you'll be sorry, and you'll tell me that you're sorry. Tell me now, Eve."

He put his hands on her shoulders, holding her with a masterful grip. Her eyes met his and fell. "Oh, I hate your—sureness."

"Some day you are going to love it. Look at me, Eve."

She forced herself to do so. But she was not at ease. Then almost wistfully she yielded. "I—am sorry, Pip."

His hands dropped from her shoulders. "Good little girl."

He kissed both of her hands before he went away. "I am glad we are friends"—that was his way of putting it—"and you mustn't forget that some day we are going to be more than that," and when he had gone she found herself still shaken by the sureness of his attitude.

Pip on his way down-town stopped in to order Winifred's roses, and the next day he went to her apartment and unburdened his heart.

"If it was in the day of duels I'd call him out. Just at this moment I am in the mood for pistols or poison, I'm not sure which."

"Why not try—patience?"

He glanced at her quickly. "You think she'll tire?"

"I think—it can never happen. For Richard's sake I—hope not."

"Why for his sake?"

Winifred smiled. "I'd like to see him marry little Anne."

"The school-teacher?"

"Yes. Oh, I am broken-hearted to think he's spoiling Nancy's dreams for him. There was something so idyllic in them. And now he'll marry Eve."

"You say that as if it were a tragedy."

"It is, for him and for her. Eve was never made to be poor."

"Don't tell her that. She took my head off. Said she'd rather have a crust of bread with Richard——"

"Oh, oh!"

"Than a palace with me."

"Poor Pip. It wasn't nice of her."

"I shall make her eat her words."

Winifred shook her head. "Don't be hard on her, Pip. We women are so helpless in our loves. Richard might make her happy if he cared enough, but he doesn't. Perhaps Eve will be broadened and deepened by it all. I don't know. No one knows."

"I know this. That you and Tony seem to get a lot out of things, Win."

"Of marriage? We do. Yet we've had all of the little antagonisms and differences. But underneath it we know—that we're made for each other. And that helps. It has helped us to push the wrong things out of our lives and to hold on to the right ones."

Philip's young face was set. "I wanted to have my chance with Eve. We are young and pretty light-weight on the surface, but life together might make us a bit more like you and Tony. And now Richard is spoiling things."

Back at Crossroads, Nancy was trying to convince her son that he was not spoiling things for her. "I have always been such a dreamer, dear boy. It was silly for me to think that I could stand between you and your big future. I have written to Sulie Tyson, and she'll stay with me, and you can run down for week-ends—and I'll always have David."

"Mother, let me go to Eve and tell her——"

"Tell her what?"

"That I shall stay—with you."

She was white with the whiteness which had never left her since he had told her that he was going to marry Eve.

"Hickory-Dickory, if I kept you here in the end you would hate me."

"Mother!"

"Not consciously. But I should be a barrier—and you'd find yourself wishing for—freedom. If I let you go—you'll come back now and then—and be—glad."

He gathered her up in his arms and declared fiercely that he would not leave her, but she stayed firm. And so the thing was settled, and as soon as he could settle his affairs at Crossroads he was to go to Austin.

Anne, writing to Uncle Rod about it, said:

"St. Michael is to marry the Lily-of-the-Field. You see, after all, he likes that kind of thing, though I had fancied that he did not. She is not as fine and simple as he is, and somehow I can't help feeling sorry.

"But that isn't the worst of it, Uncle Bobs. He is going back to New York. And now what becomes of his sunsets? I don't believe he ever had any. And oh, his poor little mother. She is fooling him and making him think that it is just as it should be and that she was foolish to expect anything else. But to me it is unspeakable that he should leave her. But he'll have Eve Chesley. Think of changing Nancy Brooks for Eve!"

It was at Beulah's wedding that Anne and Richard saw each other for the last time before his departure.

Beulah was married in the big front room at Bower's. She was married at six o'clock because it was easy for the farmer folk to come at that time, and because the evening could be given up afterward to the reception and a big supper and Beulah and Eric could take the ten o'clock train for New York.

She had no bridesmaids except Peggy, who was quite puffed up with the importance of her office. Anne had instructed her, and at the last moment held a rehearsal on the side porch.

"Now, play I am the bride, Peggy."

"You look like a bride," Peggy said. "Aren't you ever going to be a bride, Miss Anne?"

"I am not sure, Peggy. Perhaps no one will ever ask me."

"I'd ask you if I were a man," Peggy reassured her. "Now, go on and show me, Anne."

"You must take Beulah's bouquet when she hands it to you, and after she is married you must give it back to her, and———"

"And then I must kiss her."

"You must let Eric kiss her first."

"Why?"

"Because he will be her husband."

"But I've been her sister for ever and ever."

"Oh, but a husband, Peggy. Husbands are very important."

"Why are they?"

"Well, they give you a new name and a new house, and you have new clothes to marry them in, and you go away with them on a honeymoon."

"What's a honeymoon?"

"The honey is for the sweetness, and the moon is for the madness, Peggy, dear."

"Do people always go away on trains for their honeymoons?"

"Not always. I shouldn't like a train. I should like to get into a boat with silver sails, and sail straight down a singing river into the heart of the sunset."

"Well, of course, you couldn't," said the plump and practical Peggy, "but it sounds nice to say it. Does our river sing, Miss Anne?"

"Yes."

"What does it say?"

Anne stretched out her arms with a little yearning gesture. "It says—'Come and see the world, see the world, see the world!'"

"It never says that to me."

"Perhaps you haven't ears to hear, Peggy."

It was a very charming wedding. Richard was there and Nancy, and David and Brinsley. The country folk came from far and wide, and there was a brave showing of Old Gentlemen from Bower's who brought generous gifts for Peter's pretty daughter.

Richard, standing back of his mother during the ceremony, could see over her head to where Anne waited not far from Peggy to prompt her in her bridesmaid's duties. She was in white. Her dark hair was swept up in the fashion which she had borrowed from Eve. She seemed very small and slight against the background of Bower's buxom kinsfolk.

As he caught her eye he smiled at her, but she did not smile back. She felt that she could not. How could he smile with that little mother drooping before his very eyes? How could he?

She found herself later, when the refreshments were served, brooding over Nancy. The little lady tasted nothing, but was not permitted to refuse the cup of tea which Anne brought to her.

"I had it made especially for you," she said; "you looked so tired."

"I am tired. You see we are having rather strenuous days."

"I know."

"It isn't easy to let—him—go."

"It isn't easy for anybody to let him go."

The eyes of the two women went to where Richard in the midst of a protesting group was trying to explain his reasons for deserting Crossroads.

He couldn't explain. They had a feeling that he was turning his back on them. "It's hard lines to have a good doctor and then lose him," was the general sentiment. He was made to feel that it would have been better not to have come than to end by deserting.

He was aware that he had forfeited something precious, and he voiced his thought when he joined his mother and Anne.

"I'll never have a practice quite like this. Neighborhood ties are something they know little about in cities."

His mother smiled up at him bravely. "There'll be other things."

"Perhaps;" he patted her hand. Then he fired a question at Anne. "Do you think I ought to go?"

"How can I tell?" Her eyes met his candidly. "I felt when you came that I couldn't understand how a man could bury himself here. And now I am wondering how you can leave. It seems as if you belong."

"I know what you mean."

She went on: "And I can't quite think of this dear lady alone."

Nancy stopped her. "Don't speak of that, my dear. I don't want you to speak of it. It is right that Richard should go."

Anne was telling herself passionately that it was not right, when Beulah sent for her, and presently the little bride came down in her going-away gown, to be joined by Eric in the stiff clothes which seemed to rob him of the picturesqueness which belonged to him in less formal moments.

But Richard had no eyes for the bride and groom; he saw only Anne at the head of the stairway where he had first talked to her. How long ago it seemed, and how sweet she had been, and how shy.

The train was on the bridge, and a laughing crowd hurried out into the night to meet it. Peggy in the lead threw roses with a prodigal hand. "Kiss me, Beulah," she begged at the last.

Beulah bent down to her, then was lifted in Eric's strong arms to the platform. Then the train drew out and she was gone!

Alone on the stairway, Anne and Richard had a moment before the crowd swept back upon them.

"Dr. Brooks, take your mother with you."

"She won't go."

"Then stay with her."

He caught at the edge of her flowing sleeve, and held it as if he would anchor her to him. "Do you want me to stay?"

Her eyes came up to him. She saw in them something which lifted her above and beyond her doubts of him. She had an ineffable sense of having found something which she could never lose.

Then as he drew back he was stammering, "Forgive me. I have been wanting to wish you happiness. Geoffrey told me——"

And now Peggy bore down upon them and all the heedless happy crowd, and Richard said, "Good-night," and was gone.

Yet when she was left alone, Anne felt desperately that she should have shouted after him, "I am not going to marry Geoffrey Fox. I am not going to be married at all."

CHAPTER XV

In Which Anne Asks and Jimmie Answers.

"'A moneyless man,'" said Uncle Rod, "'goes quickly through the market.'"

He had a basket on his arm. Anne, who was at her easel, looked up. "What did you buy?"

He laughed. His laugh had in it a quality of youth which seemed to contradict the signs of age which were upon him. Yet even these signs were modified by the carefulness of his attire and the distinction of his carriage. Great-uncle Rodman had been a dandy in his day, and even now his Norfolk coat and knickerbockers, his long divided beard and flowing tie gave him an air half foreign, wholly his own.

In his basket was a melon, crusty rolls, peaches and a bottle of cream.

"Such extravagance!" Anne said, as he showed her the bottle.

"It was the price of two chops. And not a lamb the less for it. Two chops would have been an extravagance, and now we shall feast innocently and economically."

"Where shall we eat?" Anne asked.

"Under the oak?"

She shook her head. "Too sunny."

"In the garden?"

"Not till to-night—people can see us from the road."

"You choose then." It was a game that they had played ever since she had come to him. It gave to each meal the atmosphere of an adventure.

"I choose," she clapped her hands, "I choose—by the fish-pond, Uncle Rod."

The fish-pond was at the end of the garden walk. Just beyond it a wooden gate connected a high brick wall and opened upon an acre or two of pasture where certain cows browsed luxuriously. The brick wall and the cows and the quiet of the corner made the fish-pond seem miles away from the town street which was faced by the front of Cousin Margaret's house.

The fish-pond was a favorite choice in the game played by Anne and Uncle Rod. But they did not always choose it because that would have made it commonplace and would have robbed it of its charm.

Anne, rising to arrange the tray, was stopped by Uncle Rodman. "Sit still, my dear; I'll get things ready."

473

To see him at his housekeeping was a pleasant sight. He liked it, and gave to it his whole mind. The peeling of the peaches with a silver knife, the selection of a bowl of old English ware to put them in, and making of the coffee in a copper machine, the fresh linen, the roses as a last perfect touch.

Anne carried the tray, for his weak arm could not be depended upon; and by the fish-pond they ate their simple meal.

The old fishes had crumbs and came to the top of the water to get them, and a cow looking over the gate was rewarded by the remaining half of the crusty roll. She walked away presently to give place to a slender youth who had crossed the fields and now stood with his hat off looking in.

"If it isn't Anne," he said, "and Uncle Rod."

Uncle Rod stood up. He did not smile and he did not ask the slender youth to enter. But Anne was more hospitable.

"Come in, Jimmie," she said. "I can't offer you any lunch because we have eaten it all up. But there's some coffee."

Jimmie entered with alacrity. He had come back from New York in a mood of great discontent, to meet the pleasant news that Anne Warfield was in town. He had flown at once to find her. If he had expected the Fatted Calf, he found none. Uncle Rodman left them at once. He had a certain amount of philosophy, but it had never taught him patience with Jimmie Ford.

Jimmie drank a cup of coffee, and talked of his summer.

"Saw your Dr. Richard in New York, out at Austin's."

"Yes."

"He's going to marry Eve."

"Is he?"

"Yes. I don't understand what she sees in him—he isn't good style."

"He doesn't have to be."

"Why not?"

"Men like Richard Brooks mean more to the world than just—clothes, Jimmie."

"I don't see it."

"You wouldn't."

"Why shouldn't I?"

"Well, you look so nice in your clothes—and you need them to look nice in."

He stared at her. He felt dimly that she was making fun of him.

"From the way you put it," he said, with irritation, "from the way you put it any one might think that it was just my clothes——"

"That make you attractive? Oh, no, Jimmie. You have nice eyes and—and a way with you."

She was sewing on a scrap of fancy work, and her own eyes were on it. She was as demure as possible, but she seemed unusually and disconcertingly self-possessed.

And now Jimmie became plaintive. Plaintiveness had always been his strong suit with Anne. He was eager for sympathy. His affair with Eve had hurt his vanity.

"I have never seen a girl like her. She doesn't care what the world thinks. She doesn't care what any one thinks. She goes right along taking everything that comes her way—and giving nothing."

"Did you want her to give you—anything, Jimmie?"

"Me? Not me. She's a beauty and all that. But I wouldn't marry her if she were as rich as Rockefeller—and she isn't. Her money is her Aunt Maude's."

"Oh, Jimmie—sour grapes."

"Sour nothing. She isn't my kind. She said one day that if she wanted a man she'd ask him to marry her. That it was a woman's right to choose. I can't stand that sort of thing."

"But if she should ask you, Jimmie?"

Again he stared at her. "I jolly well shouldn't give her a chance. Not after the way she treated me."

"What way?"

"Oh, making me think I was the whole thing—and then—throwing me down."

"Oh, so you don't like being thrown down?"

"No. I don't like that kind of a woman. You know the kind of woman I like, Anne."

The caressing note in his voice came to her like an echo of other days. But now it had no power to move her.

"I am not sure that I do know the kind of woman you like—tell me."

"Oh, I like a woman that is a woman, and makes a man feel that he's the whole thing."

"But mustn't he be the whole thing to make her feel that he is?"

He flung himself out of his chair and stood before her. "Anne," he demanded, "can't you do anything but ask questions? You aren't a bit like you used to be."

She laid down her work and now he could see her eyes. Such steady eyes! "No, I'm not like myself. You see, Jimmie, I have been away for a year, and one learns such a lot in a year."

He felt a sudden sense of loss. There had always been the old Anne to come back to. The Anne who had believed and had sympathized. Again his voice took on a plaintive note. "Be good to me, girl," he said. Then very low, "Anne, I was half afraid to come to-day."

"Afraid—why?"

"Oh, I suppose you think I acted like a—cad."

"What do you think?"

"Oh, stop asking questions. It was the only thing to do. You were poor and I was poor, and there wasn't anything ahead of me—or of you—surely you can't blame me."

"How can I blame you for what was, after all, my great good fortune?"

475

"Your what?"

She said it again, quietly, "My great good fortune, Jimmie. I couldn't see it then. Indeed, I was very unhappy and sentimental and cynical over it. But now I know what life can hold for me—and what it would not have held if I had married you."

"Anne, who has been making love to you?"

"Jimmie!"

"Oh, no woman ever talks like that until she has found somebody else. And I thought you were constant."

"Constant to what?"

"To the thought—to—to the thought of what we might be to each other some day."

"And in the meantime you were asking Eve to marry you. Was it her money that you wanted?"

"Her money! Do you think I am a fortune-hunter?"

"I am asking you, Jimmie?"

"For Heaven's sake, stop asking questions. You know how a pretty woman goes to my head. And she's the kind that flits away to make you follow. I can't fancy your doing that sort of a thing, Anne."

"No," quietly, "women like myself, Jimmie, go on expecting that things will come to them—and when they don't come, we keep on—expecting. But somehow we never seem to be able to reach out our hands to take—what we might have."

He began to feel better. This was the wistful Anne of the old days.

"There has never been any one like you, Anne. It seems good to be here. Women like Eve madden a man, but your kind are so—comfortable."

Always the old Jimmie! Wanting his ease! After he had left her she sat looking out over the gate beyond the fields to the gold of the west.

When at last she went up to the house Uncle Rod had had his nap and was in his big chair on the front porch.

"Jimmie and I are friends again," she told him.

He looked at her inquiringly. "Real friends?"

"Surface friends. He is coming again to tell me his troubles and get my sympathy. Uncle Rod, what makes me so clear-eyed all of a sudden?"

He smoothed his beard. "My dear, 'the eyes of the hare are one thing, the eyes of the owl another.' You are looking at life from a different point of view. I knew that if you ever met a real man you'd know the difference between him and Jimmie Ford."

She came over, and standing behind him, put her hands on his shoulders. "I've found him, Uncle Rod."

"St. Michael?"

"Yes."

"Poor little girl."

476

"I am not poor, Uncle Rod. I am rich. It is enough to have known him."

The sunset was showing above the wooden gate. The cows had gone home. The old fish swam lazily in the shadowed water.

Anne drew her low chair to the old man's side. "Uncle Rod, isn't it queer, the difference between the things we ask for and the things we get? To have a dream come true doesn't mean always that you must get what you want, does it? For sometimes you get something that is more wonderful than any dream. And now if you'll listen, and not look at me, I'll tell you all about it, you darling dear."

It was in late August that Anne received the first proof sheets of Geoffrey's book. "I want you to read it before any one else. It will be dedicated to you and it is better than I dared believe—I could never have written it without your help, your inspiration."

It was a great book. Anne, remembering the moment the plot had been conceived on that quiet night by Peggy's bedside when she had seen the pussy cat and had heard the tinkling bell, laid it down with a feeling almost of awe.

She wrote Geoffrey about it. It was her first real letter to him. She had written one little note of forgiveness and of friendliness, but she had felt that for a time at least she should do no more than that, and Uncle Rod had commended her resolution.

"Hot fires had best burn out," he said.

"If you never do anything else," Anne wrote to Geoffrey, "you can be content. There isn't a line of pot-boiling in it. It is as if you had dipped your pen in magic ink. Rereading it to Uncle Rodman has brought back the nights when we talked it over, and I can't help feeling a little peacock-y to know that I had a part in it.

"And now I am going to tell you what Uncle Rod's comment was when I finished the very last word. He sat as still as a solemn old statue, and then he said, 'Geoffrey Fox is a great man. No one could have written like that who was sordid of mind or small of soul.'

"If you knew my Uncle Rodman you would understand all that his opinion stands for. He is never flattering, but he has had much time to think—he is like one of the old prophets—so that, indeed, I sometimes feel that he ought to sing his sentences like David, instead of saying wise things in an ordinary way. And his proverbs! he has such a collection, he is making a book of them, and he digs into old volumes in all sorts of languages—oh, some day you must know him!

"I am going back to Crossroads. It seems that my work lies there. And I have great news for you. I am to live with Mrs. Brooks. She has her cousin, Sulie Tyson, with her, but she wants me. And it will be so much better than Bower's.

"All through Mrs. Nancy's letters I can read her loneliness. She tries to keep it out. But she can't. She is proud of her son's success—but she feels the separation intensely. He has his work, she only her thoughts of him—and that's the tragedy.

"In the meantime, here we are at Cousin Margaret's doing funny little stunts in the way of cooking and catering. We can't afford the kind of housekeeping which requires servants, so it is a case of plain living and high thinking. Uncle Rod hates to eat anything that has been killed, and makes all sorts of excuses not to. He won't call himself a vegetarian, for he thinks that people who label themselves are apt to be cranks. So he does our bit of marketing and comes home triumphant with his basket innocent of birds or beasts, and we live on ambrosia and nectar or the modern equivalent. We are quite classic with our feasts by the old fish-pond at the end of the garden.

"Cousin Margaret's garden is flaming in the August days with phlox, and is fragrant with day lilies. There's a grass walk and a sun-dial, and best of all, as I have said, the fish-pond.

"And while I am on the subject of gardens, Uncle Rod rises up in wrath when people insist upon giving the botanical names to all of our lovely blooms. He says that the pedants are taking all of the poetry out of language, and it does seem so, doesn't it? Why should we call larkspur Delphinium? or a forget-me-not Myostis Palustria, and would a primrose by the river's brim ever be to you or to me primula vulgaris? Uncle Rod says that a rose by any other name would not smell as sweet; and it is fortunate that the worst the botanists may do cannot spoil the generic—rosa.

"And now with my talk of Uncle Rod and of Me, I am stringing this letter far beyond all limits, and yet I have not told you half the news.

"I had a little note from Beulah, and she and Eric are at home in the Playhouse. She loves your silver candlesticks. So many of her presents were practical and she prefers the 'pretties.'

"You have heard, of course, that Dr. Brooks is to marry Eve Chesley. The wedding will not take place for some time. I wonder if they will live with Aunt Maude. I can't quite imagine Dr. Richard's wings clipped to such a cage."

She signed herself, "Always your friend, Anne Warfield."

Far up in the Northern woods Geoffrey read her letter. He could use his eyes a little, but most of the time he lay with them shut and Mimi read to him, or wrote for him at his dictation. He had grown to be very dependent on Mimi; there were even times when he had waked in the night, groping and calling out, and she had gathered him in her arms and had held him against her breast until he stopped shaking and shivering and saying that he could not see.

He spoke her name now, and she came to him. He put Anne's letter in her hand. "Read it!" and when she had read, he said, "You see she says that I am great—and she used to say it. Am I, Mimi?"

"Oh, Geoffrey, yes."

"I want you to make it true, Mimi. Shall I begin my new book to-morrow?"

It was what she had wanted, what she had begged that he would do, but he had refused to listen. And now he was listening to another voice!

She brought her note-book, and sat beside him. Being ignorant of shorthand she had invented a little system of her own, and she was glad when she could make him laugh over her funny pot-hooks and her straggling sketches.

Thus in the darkness Geoffrey struggled and strove. "Speaking of candlesticks," he wrote to Anne, "it was as if a thousand candles lighted my world when I read your letter!"

CHAPTER XVI

In Which Pan Pipes to the Stars.

That Richard in New York should miss his mother was inevitable. But he was not homesick. He was too busy for that. Austin's vogue was tremendous.

"Every successful man ought to be two men," he told Richard, as they talked together one Sunday night at Austin's place in Westchester, "'another and himself,' as Browning puts it. Then there would be one to labor and the other to enjoy. I want to retire, and I can't. There's a selfish instinct in all of us to grip and hold. That is why I am pinning my faith to you. You can slip in as I slip out. I have visions of riding to hounds and sailing the seas some day, to say nothing of putting up a good game of golf. But perhaps that's a dream. A man can't get away from his work, not when he loves it."

"That's why you're such a success, sir," Richard told him, honestly; "you go to every operation as if it were a banquet."

Austin laughed. "I'm not such a ghoul. But there's always the wonder of it with me. I sometimes wish I had been a churchgoing man, Brooks. There isn't much more for me to learn about bodies, but there's much about souls. I have a feeling that some day in some physical experiment I shall find tangible evidence of the spiritual. That's why I say my prayers to Something every night, and I rather think It's God."

"I know it's God," said Richard, simply, "on such a night as this."

They were silent in the face of the evening's beauty. The great trees on the old estate were black against a silver sky. White statues shone like pale ghosts among them. Back of Richard and his host, in a semicircle of dark cedars, a marble Pan piped to the stars.

"And in the cities babies are sleeping on fire escapes," Austin meditated. "If I had had a son I should have sent him to the slums to find his work. But the Fates have given me only Marie-Louise."

And now his laugh was forced. "Brooks, the Gods have checkmated me. Marie-Louise is the son of her father. I had planned that she should be the daughter of her mother. I sowed some rather wild oats in my youth, and waked in middle age to the knowledge that my materialism had led me astray. So I married an idealist. I wanted my children to have a spiritual background of character such as I have not possessed. And the result of that marriage is—Marie-Louise! If she has a soul it is yet to be discovered."

"She is young. Give her time."

"I have been giving her time for eighteen years. I have wanted to see her mother in her, to see some gleam of that exquisite fineness. There are things we men, the most material of us, want in our women, and I want it in Marie-Louise. But she gives back what I have given her—nothing more. And I don't know what to do with her."

"Her mother?" Richard hinted.

"Julie is worn out with trying to meet a nature so unlike her own. Our love for each other has made us understand. But neither of us understands Marie-Louise. I sent her away to school, but she wouldn't stay. She likes her home and she hates rules. She loves animals, and if she were a boy she would practice medicine. Being a woman and having no outlet for her energies, she is freakish. You saw the way she was dressed at dinner."

"I liked it," Richard said; "all that dead silver with her red hair."

"But it is too—sophisticated, for a young girl. Why, man, she ought to be in white frocks and pearls, and putting cushions behind her mother's back."

"You say that because her mother wore white and pearls, and put cushions behind her mother's back. There aren't many of the white-frocks-and-pearls kind left. It's a new generation. Perhaps dead silver with red hair is an expression of it. And it is we who don't understand."

"Perhaps. But it's a problem." Austin rose. "If you'll excuse me, Brooks, I'll go to my wife. We always read together on Sunday nights."

He sent Marie-Louise out to Richard. She came through the starlight, a shining figure in her silver dress, with a silver Persian kitten hugged up in her arms. She sat on the sun-dial and swung her jade bracelet for the kitten to play with.

"Dad and mother are reading the Bible. He doesn't believe in it, and she gets him to listen once a week. And then she reads the prayers for the day. When I was a little girl I had to listen—but never again!"

"Why not?"

"Why should I listen to things that I don't believe? To-night it is the ten virgins and their lamps. And Dad's pretending that he's interested. I am writing a play about it, but mother doesn't know. The Wise Virgins are Bernard Shaw women who know what they want in the way of husbands and go to it. The Foolish Virgins are the old maids, who think it unwomanly to get ready, and find themselves left in the end!"

The silver kitten clawed at the silver dress, and climbed on her mistress's shoulder.

479

"All of the parables make good modern plots. Mother would be shocked if she knew I was writing them that way. So I don't tell her. Mother is a dear, but she doesn't understand. I should like to tell things to Dad, but he won't listen. If I were a boy he would listen. But he thinks I ought to be like mother."

She slipped from the sun-dial and came and sat in the chair which her father had vacated. "If I were a boy I should have studied medicine. I wanted to be a trained nurse, but Dad wouldn't let me. He said I'd hate having to do the hard work, and perhaps I should. I like to wear pretty clothes, and a nurse never has a chance."

"Perhaps you'll marry."

"Oh, no. I should hate to be like mother."

"Why?"

"She just lives for Dad. Now I couldn't do that. I am not going to marry. I don't like men. They ask too much. I like books and cats and being by myself. I am never lonesome. Sometimes I talk to Pan over there, and pretend he is playing to me on his pipes, and then I write poetry. Real poetry. I'll read it to you some time. There's one called 'The Rose Garden.' I wrote it about a woman who was a patient of father's. When she knew she was going to die she wrote him a little note and asked him to see that her body was cremated, and that the ashes were strewn over the roses in his garden. He didn't seem to see anything in it but just a sick woman's fancy. But I knew that she was in love with him. And my poem tells that her blessed dust gathered itself into a gentle wraith which lives and breathes near him."

"And you aren't afraid to feel that her gentle wraith is here in the garden?"

"Why should I be? I don't believe in ghosts. I don't believe in fairies, either, or Santa Claus. But I like to read about them and write about them, and—and wish that it might be so."

There was something almost wistful in her voice. Richard, aware suddenly of what a child she was, bent forward.

"I think I half believe in fairies, and Christmas wouldn't be anything without Santa Claus, and as for the soul of your gentle lady, I have a feeling that it is finding Heaven in the rose garden."

She was stroking the silver kitten which had curled up in her lap. "I wish I weren't such a—heathen," she said, suddenly. "I know what you mean. But it is only the poetic sense in me that makes me know. I can't believe anything. Not about souls—or prayers. Do you ever pray?"

"Every night. On my knees."

"On your knees? Oh, is it as bad as that?"

Richard, writing to his mother, said of Marie-Louise, "Her mind isn't in a healthy state. It hasn't anything to feed on. Her father is too busy and her mother too ill to realize that she needs companionship of a certain kind. I wish she might have been a pupil at the Crossroads school, with Anne Warfield for her teacher. But no hope of that."

He wrote, too, of his rushing days, and Nancy, answering, hid from him the utter hopelessness of her outlook. Her life began and ended with his letters and the week-ends which he was able to give her. But some of his week-ends had to be spent with Eve; a man cannot completely ignore the fact that he has a fiancée, and Richard would have been less than human if he had not responded to the appeal of youth and beauty. So he motored with Eve and danced with Eve, and did all of the delightful summer things which are possible in the big city near the sea. Aunt Maude went to the North Shore, but Eve stayed with Winifred, and wove about Richard her spells of flattery and of frivolity.

"I want to be near you, Dicky boy. If I'm not you'll work too hard."

"It is work that I like."

"I believe that you like it better than you do me, Dicky."

480

"Don't be silly, Eve."

"You are always saying that. Do you like your work better than you do me, Dicky?"

"Of course not." But he had no pretty things to say.

The life that he lived with her, however, and with Pip and Winifred and Tony was a heady wine which swept away regrets. He had no time to think. He worked by day and played by night, and often after their play there was work again. Now and then, as the Sunday night when he had first met Marie-Louise, he motored with Austin out to Westchester. Mrs. Austin spent her summers there. Long journeys tired her, and she would not leave her husband. Marie-Louise stayed at "Rose Acres" because she hated big hotels, and found cottage colonies stupid. The great gardens swept down to the river—the wide, blue river with the high bluffs on the sunset side.

The river at Bower's was not blue; it showed in the spring the red of the clay which was washed into it, and now and then a clear green when the rains held off, but it was rarely blue except on certain sapphire days in the fall, when a northwest wind swept all clouds from the sky.

And this was not a singing river. It was too near the sea, and too full of boats, and there was no reason why it should say, "Come and see—come and see—the world," when the world was at its feet!

And so the great Hudson had no song for Richard. Yet now and then, as he walked down to it in the warm darkness, his ears seemed to catch a faint echo of the harmonies which had filled his soul on the day that Anne Warfield had dried her hair on the bank of the old river at Bower's, and had walked with him in the wood.

Except at such moments, however, it must be confessed that he thought little of Anne Warfield. It hurt to think of her. And he was too much of a surgeon to want to turn the knife in the wound.

Marie-Louise, developing a keen interest in his affairs as they grew better acquainted, questioned him about Evelyn.

"Dad says you are going to marry her."

"Yes."

"Is she pretty?"

"Rather more than that."

"Why don't you bring her out?"

"Nobody asked me, sir, she said."

She flashed a smile at him.

"I like your nursery-rhyme way of talking. You are the humanest thing that we have ever had in this house. Mother is a harp of a thousand strings, and Dad is a dynamo. But you are flesh and blood."

"Thank you."

"I wish you'd ask your Evelyn out here, and her friends. For tea and tennis some Saturday afternoon. I want to see you together."

But after she had seen them together, she said, shrewdly, "You are not in love with her."

"I am going to marry her, child. Isn't that proof enough?"

"It isn't any proof at all. The big man is the one who really cares."

"The big man? Pip?"

"Is that what you call him? He looks at her like a dog waiting for a bone. And he brightens when she speaks to him. And her eyes are always on you and yours are never on her."

"Marie-Louise, you are an uncanny creature. Like your little silver cat. She watches mice and you watch me. I have a feeling that you are going to pounce on me."

"Some day I shall pounce," she poked her finger at him, "and shake you as my little cat shakes a mouse, and you'll wake up."

"Am I asleep, Marie-Louise?"

"Yes. You haven't heard Pan pipe." She was leaning on the sun-dial and looking up at the grinning god. "Men who live in cities have no ears to hear."

"Are you a thousand years old, Marie-Louise?"

"I am as old as the centuries," she told him gravely. "I played with Pan when the world was young."

They smiled at each other, and then he said, "My mother wants me to live in the country. Do you think if I were there I should hear Pan pipe?"

"Not if you were there because your mother wished it. It is only when you love it yourself that the river calls and you hear the fluting of the wind in the rushes."

It was an August Saturday, hot and humid. Marie-Louise was in thin white, but it was a white with a difference from the demure summer frocks of a former generation. The modern note was in the white fur which came high up about Marie-Louise's throat. Yet she did not look warm. Her skin was as pale as the pearls in her ears. Her red hair flamed, but without warmth; it rippled back from her forehead to a cool and classic coil.

"If you marry your Eve," she told Richard, "and stay with father, you'll grow rich and fat, and forget the state of your soul."

"I thought you didn't believe in souls."

She flushed faintly. "I believe in yours. But your Eve doesn't. She likes you because you don't care, and everybody else does. And that isn't love."

"What is love?"

She pondered. "I don't know. I've never felt it. And I don't want to feel it. If I loved too much I should die—and if I didn't love enough I should be ashamed."

"You are a queer child, Marie-Louise."

"I am not a child. Dad thinks I am, and mother. But they don't know."

There were day lilies growing about the sun-dial. She gathered a handful of white blooms and laid them at the feet of the piping Pan. "I shall write a poem about it," she said, "of a girl who loved a marble god, and who found it—enough. Every day she laid a flower at his feet. And a human came to woo her, and she told him, 'If I loved you, you would ask more of me than my marble lover. He asks only that I lay flowers at his feet.'"

He could never be sure whether she was in jest or earnest. And now she narrowed her eyes in a quizzical smile and was gone.

He spoke of Marie-Louise to Eve. "She hasn't enough to do. She ought to be busy with her fancy work and her household matters."

"No woman is busy with household matters in this age, Dicky. Nor with fancy work. Is that what you expect of a wife?"

He didn't know what he expected, and he told her so. But he knew he was expecting more than she was prepared to give. Eve had an off-with-the-old-and-on-with-the-new theory of living which left him breathless. She expressed it one night when she said that she shouldn't have "obey" in her marriage service. "I never expect to mind you, Dicky, so what's the use?"

There was no use, of course. Yet he had a feeling that he was being robbed of something sweet and sacred. The quaint old service asked things of men as well as of women. Good and loving and fine things. He was old-fashioned enough to want to promise all that it asked, and to have his wife promise.

Eve laughed, too, at Richard's grace before meat. "You mustn't embarrass me at formal dinners, Dicky. Somehow it won't seem quite in keeping with the cocktails, will it?"

Thus the spirit of Eve, contending with all that made him the son of his mother, meeting his spiritual revolts with material arguments, banking the fires of his flaming aspirations!

Yet he rarely let himself dwell upon this aspect of it. He had set his feet in a certain path, and he was prepared to follow it.

On this path, at every turning, he met Philip. The big man had not been driven from the field by the fact of Eve's engagement. He still asked her to go with him, he still planned pleasures for her. His money made things easy, and while he included Richard in most of his plans, he looked upon him as a necessary evil. Eve refused to go without her young doctor.

Now and then, however, he had her alone. "Dicky's called to an appendicitis case," she informed him ruefully, one night over the telephone, "and I am dead lonesome. Come and cheer me up."

He went to her, and during the evening proposed a week-end yachting trip which should take them to the North Shore and Aunt Maude.

"Is Dicky invited?"

"Of course. But I'm not sure that I want him."

"He wouldn't come if he knew that you felt like that."

"It isn't anything personal. And you know my manner is perfect when I'm with him."

"Yes. Poor Dicky. Pip, we are a pair of deceivers. I sometimes think I ought to tell him."

"There's nothing to tell."

"Nothing tangible,—but he's so straightforward. And he'd hate the idea that I'm letting you—make love to me."

"I don't make love. I have never touched the tip of your finger."

"Pip! Of course not. But your eyes make love, and your manner—and deep down in my heart I am afraid."

"Afraid of what?"

"That Fate isn't going to give me what I want. I don't want you, Pip. I want Dicky. And if you loved me—you'd let me alone."

"Tell me to go,—and I won't come back."

"Not ever?"

"Never."

She weakened. "But I don't want you to go away. You see, you are my good friend, Pip."

She should not have let him stay. She knew that. She found it necessary to apologize to Richard. "You see, Pip cares an awful lot."

Richard had little sympathy. "He might as well take his medicine and not hang around you, Eve."

"If you would hang around a little more perhaps he wouldn't."

"I am very busy. You know that."

His voice was stern. "If I am a busy husband, will you make that an excuse for having Pip at your heels?"

"Richard."

"I beg your pardon. I shouldn't have said that. But marriage to me means more than good times. Life means more than good times. When I am here in New York it seems to me sometimes that I am drugged by work and pleasure. That there isn't a moment in which to live in a leisurely thoughtful sense."

"You should have stayed at Crossroads."

"I can't go back. I have burned my bridges. Austin expects things of me, and I must live up to his expectations. And, besides, I like it."

"Really, Dicky?"

"Really. There's a stimulus about the rush of it and the big things we are doing. Austin is a giant. My association with him is the biggest thing that has ever come into my life."

"Bigger than your love for me?"

Thus she brought him back to it. Making always demands upon him which he could not meet. He found himself harassed by her continued harping on the personal point of view, yet there were moments when she swung him into step with her. And one of the moments came when she spoke of the yachting trip. It was very hot, and Richard loved the sea.

"Dicky, I'll keep Pip in the background if you I promise to come."

"How can you keep him in the background when he is our host?"

"He is going to invite Marie-Louise. And he'll have to be nice to her. And you and I——! Dicky, we'll feel the slap of the breeze in our faces, and forget that there's a big city back of us with sick people in it, and slums and hot nights. Dicky—I love you—and I am going to be your wife. Won't you come—because I want you—Dicky?"

There were tears on her cheeks as she made her plea, and he was always moved by her tears. It was his protective sense that had first tied him to her; it was still through his chivalry that she made her most potent appeal.

Marie-Louise was glad to go. "It will be like watching a play."

She and Richard were waiting for Pip's "Mermaid" to make a landing at the pier at Rose Acres. A man-servant with their bags stood near, and Marie-Louise's maid was coated and hatted to accompany her mistress. "It will be like watching a play," Marie-Louise repeated. "The eternal trio. Two men and a girl."

She waved to the quartette on the forward deck. "Your big man looks fine in his yachting things. And your Eve is nice in white."

Marie-Louise was not in white. In spite of the heat she was wrapped to the ears in a great coat of pale buff. On her head was a Chinese hat of yellow straw, with a peacock's feather. Yet in spite of the blueness and yellowness, and the redness of her head, she preserved that air of amazing coolness, as if her blood were mixed with snow and ran slowly.

Arriving on deck, she gave Pip her hand. "I am glad it is clear. I hate storms. I am going to ask Dr. Brooks to pray that it won't be rough. He is a good man, and the gods should listen."

CHAPTER XVII

In Which Fear Walks in a Storm.

The "Mermaid," having swept like a bird out of the harbor, stopped at Coney Island. Marie-Louise wanted her fortune told. Eve wanted peanuts and pop-corn. "It will make me seem a little girl again."

Marie-Louise, cool in her buff coat, shrugged her shoulders. "I was never allowed to be that kind of a little girl," she said, "but I think I'd like to try it for a day."

Eve and Marie-Louise got on very well together. They spoke the same language. And if Marie-Louise was more artificial in some ways, she was more open than Eve.

"You'd better tell Dr. Brooks," she told the older girl, as the two of them walked ahead of Richard and Pip on the pier. Tony and Winifred had elected to stay on board.

"Tell him what?"

"That you are keeping the big man in reserve."

Eve flushed. "Marie-Louise, you're horrid."

"I am honest," was the calm response.

Pip bought them unlimited peanuts and pop-corn, and Marie-Louise piloted them to the tent of a fat Armenian who told fortunes.

In spite of his fatness, however, he was immaculate in European clothing; he charged exorbitantly and achieved extraordinary results.

"He said the last time that I should marry a poet," Marie-Louise informed them, "which isn't true. I am not going to be married at all. But it amuses me to hear him."

The black eyes of the fat Armenian twinkled. "There will be a time when you will not be amused. You will be married."

He pulled out a chair for her. "Will your friends stay while I tell you the rest?"

"No, they are children; they want to buy peanuts and pop-corn—they want to play."

The others laughed. But the fat Armenian did not laugh. "Your soul is old!"

"You see," she asked the others, "what I mean? He says things like that to me. He told me once that in a former incarnation I had walked beside the Nile and had loved a king."

"A king-poet," the man corrected.

"Will you tell mine?" Eve asked suddenly.

"Certainly, madam."

"I am mademoiselle. You go first, Marie-Louise."

But Marie-Louise insisted on yielding to her. "We will come back for you."

 Coming back, they found Eve in an irritable temper. "He told me—nothing."

"I told you what you did not want to hear. But I told you the truth."

"I don't believe in such things." Eve was lofty. Her cold eyes challenged the Oriental. "I don't believe you know anything about it."

"If Mademoiselle will write it down——" He was fat and puffy, but he had a sort of large dignity which ignored her rudeness. "If Mademoiselle will write it down, she will not say—next year—'I do not believe.'"

She shivered. "I wish I hadn't come. Dicky boy, let's go and play. Pip and Marie-Louise can stay if they like it. I don't."

When Marie-Louise had had her imagination once more fed on poets, kings, and previous incarnations, she and Pip went forth to seek the others.

"I wonder what he told Eve?" Pip speculated.

Marie-Louise spoke with shrewdness. "He probably told her that she would marry you—only he wouldn't put it that way. He would say that in reaching for a star she would stumble on a diamond."

"And is Brooks the star?"

She nodded, grinning. "And you are the diamond. It is what she wants—diamonds."

"She wants more than that"—tenderness crept into his voice—"she wants love—and I can give it."

 "She wants Dr. Brooks. 'Most any woman would," said Marie-Louise cruelly. "We all know he is different. You know it, and I know it, and Eve knows it. He is bigger in some ways, and better!"

They found Eve and Richard in a pavilion dancing in strange company, to raucous music. Later the four of them rode on a merry-go-round, with Marie-Louise on a dolphin and Eve on a swan, with the two men mounted on twin dragons. They ate chowder and broiled lobster in a restaurant high in a fantastic tower. They swept up painted Alpine slopes in reckless cars, they drifted through dark tunnels in gorgeous gondolas. Eve took her pleasures with a sort of feverish enthusiasm, Marie-Louise with the air of a skeptic trying out a new thing.

"Mother would faint and fade away if she knew I was here," Marie-Louise told Richard as she sat next to him in a movie show, "and so would Dad. He would object to the germs and she would object to the crowd. Mother is like a flower in a sunlighted garden. She can't imagine that a lily could grow with its feet in the mud. But they do. And Dad knows it. But he likes to have mother stay in the sunlighted garden. He would never have fallen in love with her if her roots had been in the mud."

She was murmuring this into Richard's ear. Eve was on the other side of him, with Pip beyond.

"I've never had a day like this," Marie-Louise further confided, "and I am not sure that I like it. It seems so far away from—Pan—and the trees—and the river."

Her voice dropped into silence, and Richard sat there beside her like a stone, seeing nothing of the pictures thrown on the screen. He saw a road which led between spired cedars, he saw an old house with a wide porch. He saw a golden-lighted table, and his mother's face across the candles. He saw a girl in a brown coat scattering food for the birds with a kind little hand—he heard the sound of a bell!

When they reached the yacht, Winifred was dressed for dinner, and Eve and Marie-Louise scurried below to change. They dined on the upper deck by moonlight, and sat late enjoying the still warmth of the night. There was no wind and they seemed to sail through silver waters.

Marie-Louise sang for them. Strange little songs for which she had composed both words and music. They had haunting cadences, and Pip told her "For Heaven's sake, kiddie, cheer up. You are making us cry."

She laughed, and gave them a group of old nursery rhymes. Most of them had to do with things to eat. There was the Dame who baked her pies "on Christmas day in the morning," and the Queen who made the tarts, and Jenny Wren and her currant wine.

"They are what I call appetizing," she said quaintly. "When I was a tiny tot Dad kept me on a diet. I was never allowed to eat pies or tarts or puddings. So I used to feast vicariously on my nursery rhymes."

They laughed, as she had meant they should, and Pip said, "Give us another," so she chanted with increasing dramatic effect the story of King Arthur.

"A bag pudding the king did make,
And stuffed it well with plums,
And in it put great hunks of fat,
As big as my two thumbs——"
"Think of the effect of those hunks of fat," she explained amid their roars of laughter, "on my dieted mind."

"I hate to think of things to eat," Eve said. "And I can't imagine myself cooking—in a kitchen."

"Where else would you cook?" Marie-Louise demanded practically. "I'd like it. I went once with my nurse to her mother's house, and she was cooking ham and frying eggs and we sat down to a table with a red cloth and had the ham and eggs with great slices of bread and strong tea. My nurse let me eat all I wanted, because her mother said it wouldn't hurt me, and it didn't. But my mother never knew. And always after that I liked to think of Lucy's mother and that warm nice kitchen, and the plump, pleasant woman and the ham and eggs and tea."

She was very serious, but they roared again. She was so far away from anything that was homely and housewifely, with her red hair peaked up to a high knot, her thick white coat with its black animal skin enveloping her shoulders, the gleam of silver slippers.

"Dicky," Eve said, "I hope you are not expecting me to cook in Arcadia."

"I don't expect anything."

"Every man expects something," Winifred interposed; "subconsciously he wants a hearth-woman. That's the primitive."

"I don't want a hearth-woman," Pip announced.

Dutton Ames chuckled. "You're a stone-age man, Meade. You'd like to woo with a club, and carry the day's kill to the woman in your tent."

A quick fire lighted Pip's eyes. "Jove, it wouldn't be bad, would it? What do you think, Eve?"

"I like your yacht better, and your chef and your alligator pears, and caviar."

An hour later Eve and Richard were alone on deck. The others had gone down. The lovers had preferred the moonlight.

"Eve, old lady," Richard said, "you know that even with Austin's help I'm not going to be a Croesus. There won't be yachts—and chefs—and alligator pears."

487

"Jealous, Dicky?"

"No. But you've always had these things, Eve."

"I shall still have them. Aunt Maude won't let us suffer. She's a good old soul."

"Do you think I shall care to partake of Aunt Maude's bounty?"

"Perhaps not. But I am not so stiff-necked. Oh, Ducky Dick, do you think that I am going to let you keep on being poor and priggish and steady-minded?"

"Am I that, Eve?"

"You know you are."

Her laughing eyes challenged him. He would have been less than a man if he had not responded to the appeal of her youth and beauty. "Dicky," she said, "when we are married I am going to give you the time of your young life. All work and no play will make you a dull boy, Dicky."

In the night the clouds came up over the moon, and when the late and lazy party appeared on deck for luncheon, Marie-Louise complained. "I hate it this way. There's going to be a storm."

There was a storm before night. It blew up tearingly from the south and there was menace in it and madness.

Winifred and Eve were good sailors. But Marie-Louise went to pieces. She was frantic with fear, and as the night wore on, Richard found himself much concerned for her.

She insisted on staying on deck. "I feel like a rat in a trap when I am inside. I want to face it."

The wind was roaring about them. The sea was black and the sky was black, a thick velvety black that turned to copper when the lightning came.

"Aren't you afraid?" Marie-Louise demanded; "aren't you?"

"No."

"Why shouldn't you be? Why shouldn't anybody be?"

"My nerves are strong, Marie-Louise."

"It isn't nerves. It's faith. You believe that the boat won't go down, and you believe that if it did go down your soul wouldn't die."

Her white face was close to him. "I wish I could believe like that," she said in a high, sharp voice. Then she screamed as the little ship seemed caught up into the air and flung down again.

"Hush," Richard told her; "hush, Marie-Louise."

She was shaking and shivering. "I hate it," she sobbed.

Pip, like a yellow specter in oilskins, came up to them. "Eve wants you, Brooks," he shouted above the clamor of wind and wave.

"Shall we go in, Marie-Louise?"

"No, no." She cowered against his arm.

Over her head Richard said to Pip, "I shall come as soon as I can."

So Pip went down, and the two were left alone in the tumult and blackness of the night.

As Marie-Louise lay for a moment quiet against his arm, Richard bent down to her. "Are you still afraid?"

"Yes, oh, yes. I keep thinking—if I should die. And I am afraid to die."

"You are not going to die. And if you were there would be nothing to fear. Death is just—falling asleep. Rarely any terror. We doctors know, who see people die. I know it, and your father knows it."

By the light of a blinding flash he saw her white face with its wet red hair.

"Dad doesn't know it as you know," she said, chokingly. "He couldn't say it as you—say it."

"Why not?"

"He's like I am. Dad's afraid."

The storm swept on, leaving the waves rough behind it, and Richard at last put Marie-Louise to bed with a sleeping powder. Then he went to hunt up Eve. He was very tired and it was very late. The night had passed, and the dawn would soon be coming up over the horizon. He found Pip in the smoking room. Eve had gone to bed. Everybody had gone to bed. It had been a terrible storm.

Richard agreed that it had been terrible. He was glad that Eve could sleep. He couldn't understand why Austin had allowed Marie-Louise to take such a trip. Her fear of storms was evidently quite uncontrollable. And she was at all times hysterical and high-strung.

Pip was not interested in Marie-Louise. "Eve lost her nerve at the last."

Richard was solicitous. "I'm sorry. I wanted to come down, but I couldn't leave Marie-Louise. Eve's normal, and she'll be all right as soon as the storm stops. But Marie-Louise may suffer for days. The sooner she gets on shore the better."

He went on deck, and looked out upon a gray wind-swept world.

Then the sun came up, and there was a great light upon the waters.

All the next day Marie-Louise lay in a long chair. "Dad told me not to come," she confessed to Richard. "I've been this way before. But I wouldn't listen."

"If I had been your father," Richard said, "you would have listened, and you would have stayed at home."

She grinned. "You can't be sure. Nobody can be sure. I don't like to take orders."

"Until you learn to take orders you aren't going to amount to much, Marie-Louise."

"I amount to a great deal. And your ideas are—old-fashioned; that's what your Eve says, Dr. Dicky."

She looked at him through her long eyelashes. "What's the matter with your Eve?"

"What do you mean?"

"She is punishing you, but you don't know it. She is down-stairs playing bridge with Pip and Tony and Win, and leaving you alone to meditate on your sins. And you aren't meditating. You are talking to me. I am going to write a poem about a Laggard Lover. I'll make you a shepherd boy who sits on the hills and watches his sheep. And when the girl who loves him calls to him, he refuses to go—he still watches—his sheep."

489

He looked puzzled. "I don't know in the least what you are talking about."

"You are the shepherd. Your work is the sheep—Eve is the girl. Your work will always be more to you than the woman. Dad's work isn't. He never forgets mother for a minute."

"And you think that I'll forget Eve?"

"Yes. And she'll hate that."

There was a spark in his eye.

"I think that we won't discuss Eve, Marie-Louise."

"Then I'll discuss her in a poem. Lend me a pencil, please."

He gave her the pencil and a prescription pad, and she set to work. She read snatches to him as she progressed. It was remarkably clever, with a constantly recurring refrain.

"Let me watch my sheep," said the lover, "my sheep on the hills."

The verses went on to relate that the girl, finding her shepherd dilatory, turned her attention to another swain, and at last she flouts the shepherd.

"Go watch your sheep, laggard lover, your sheep on the hills."

She laid the verses aside as Tony and Win joined them.

"Three rubbers, and Pip and Eve are ahead."

"Isn't Eve coming?"

"She said she was coming up soon."

But she did not come, and Pip did not come. Marie-Louise, with a great rug spread over her, slept in her chair. Dutton Ames read aloud to his wife. Richard rose and went to look for Eve.

There was a little room which Pip called "The Skipper's own." It was furnished in a man's way as a den, with green leather and carved oak and plenty of books. Its windows gave a forward view of sky and water.

It was here that the four of them had been playing auction. Eve was now shuffling the cards for Solitaire.

Pip, watching her, caught suddenly at her left hand. "Why didn't Brooks give you a better ring?"

"I like my ring. Let go of my hand, Pip."

"I won't. What's the matter with the man that he should dare dream of tying you down to what he can give you? It seems to me that he lacks pride."

"He doesn't lack anything. Let go of my hand, Pip."

But he still held it. "How he could have the courage to ask—until he had made a name for himself."

She blazed. "He didn't ask. I asked him, Pip. I cared enough for that."

He dropped her hand as if it had stung him. "You cared—as much as that?"

She faced him bravely. "As much as that—it pleased me to say what it was my right to say."

"Oh! It was the queen, then, and the—beggar man. Eve, come back."

She was at the door, but she turned. "I'll come back if you will beg my pardon. Richard is not a beggar, and I am not the queen. How hateful you are, Pip."

"I won't beg your pardon. And let's have this out right now, Eve."

"Have what out?"

"Sit down, and I'll tell you."

Once more they were seated with the table between them. Pip's back was to the window, but Eve faced the broad expanse of sky and sea. A faint pink flush was on the waters: a silver star hung at the edge of a crescent moon. There was no sound but the purr of machinery and the mewing of gulls in the distance.

Eve was in pink—a straight linen frock with a low white collar. It gave her an air of simplicity quite unlike her usual elegance. Pip feasted his eyes on her.

"You've got to face it. Brooks doesn't care."

"He does care."

"He didn't care enough to come down last night when you were afraid—and wanted him. And you turned to me, just for one little minute, Eve. Do you think I shall ever forget the thrill of the thought that you turned to me?"

She was staring straight out at the little moon. "Marie-Louise was his patient—he had to stay with her."

"You are saying that to me, but in your heart you know you are resenting the fact that he didn't come when you called. Aren't you, Eve? Aren't you resenting it?"

She told him the truth. "Yes. But I know that when I am his wife, I shall have to let him think about his patients. I ought to be big enough for that."

"You are big enough for anything. But you are not always going to be content with crumbs from the king's table. And that's what you are getting from Brooks. And I have a feast ready. Eve, can't you see that I would give, give, give, and he will take, take, take? Eve, can't you see?"

She did see, and for the moment she was swayed by the force of his passionate eloquence.

She leaned toward him a little. "Pip, dear, I wish—sometimes—that it might have been—you."

It needed only this. He swept the card table aside with his strong arms. He was on his knees begging for love, for life. Her hair swept his cheek.

The little moon shone clear in the quiet sky. There was not much light, but there was enough for a man standing in the door to see two dark figures outlined against the silver space beyond.

And Richard was standing in the door!

Eve saw him first. "Go away, Pip," she said, and stood up. "I—I think I can make him understand."

When they were alone she said to Richard in a strained voice, "It was my fault, Dicky."

"Do you mean that you—let him, Eve?"

491

"No. But I let him talk about his love for me—and—and—he cares very much."

"He knows that you are engaged to me."

"Yes. But last night when you stayed on deck when I needed you and asked for you, Pip knew that you wouldn't come—and he was sorry for me."

"And he was sorry again this afternoon?"

"Yes."

"And he showed it by making love to you?"

"He thinks I won't be happy with you. He thinks that you don't care. He thinks——"

"I don't care what Meade thinks. I want to know what you think, Eve."

Their voices had come out of the darkness. She pulled the little chain of a wall bracket, and the room was enveloped in a warm wave of light. "I don't know what I think. But I hated to have you with Marie-Louise."

"She was very ill. You knew that. Eve, if we can't trust each other, what possible happiness can there be ahead?"

She had no answer ready.

"Of course I can't stay on Meade's boat after this," he went on; "I'll get them to run in here somewhere and drop me."

She sank back in the chair from which she had risen when Philip left them. His troubled eyes resting upon her saw a blur of pink and gold out of which emerged her white face.

"But I want you to stay."

"You shouldn't want me to stay, Eve. I can't accept his hospitality, after this, and call myself—a man."

"Oh, Dicky—I detest heroics."

She was startled by the tone in which he said, "If that is the way you feel about it, we might as well end it here."

"Dicky——"

"I mean it, Eve. The whole thing is based on the fact that I stayed with a patient when you wanted me. Well, I shall always be staying with patients after we are married, and if you are unable to see why I must do the thing I did last night, then you will never be able to see it. And a doctor's wife must see it."

She came up to him, and in the darkness laid her cheek against his arm. "Dicky, don't joke about a thing like that. I can't stand it. And I'm sorry about—Pip. Dicky, I shall die if you don't forgive me."

He forgave her. He even made himself believe that Pip might be forgiven. He exerted himself to seem at his ease at dinner. He said nothing more about leaving at the next landing.

But late that night he sat alone on deck in the darkness. He was a plain man, and he saw things straight. And this thing was crooked. The hot honor of his youth revolted against the situation in which he saw himself. He felt hurt and ashamed. It was as if the dreams of his boyhood had been dragged in the dust.

CHAPTER XVIII

In Which We Hear Once More of a Sandalwood Fan.

In the winter which followed Richard often wondered if he were the same man who had ridden his old Ben up over the hills, and had said his solemn grace at his own candle-lighted table.

It had been decided that he and Eve should wait until another year for their wedding. Richard wanted to get a good start. Eve was impatient, but acquiesced.

It was not Richard's engagement, however, which gave to his life the effect of strangeness. It was, rather, his work, which swept him into a maelstrom of new activities. Austin needed rest and he knew it. Richard was young and strong. The older man, using his assistant as a buffer between himself and a demanding public, felt no compunction. His own apprenticeship had been hard.

So Richard in Austin's imposing limousine was whirled through fashionable neighborhoods and up to exclusive doorways. He presided at operations where the fees were a year's income for a poor man. A certain percentage of these fees came to him. He found that he need have no fears for his financial future.

His letters from his mother were his only link with the old life. She wrote that she was well. That Anne Warfield was with her, and Cousin Sulie, and that the three of them and Cousin David played whist. That Anne was such a dear—that she didn't know what she would do without her.

Richard went as often as he could on Sundays to Crossroads. But at such times he saw little of Anne. She felt that no one should intrude on the reunions of mother and son. So she visited at Beulah's or Bower's and came back on Mondays.

Nancy persisted in her refusal to go back to New York. "I know I am silly," she told her son, "but I have a feeling that I shouldn't be able to breathe, and should die of suffocation."

Richard spoke to Dr. Austin of his mother's state of mind. "Queer thing, isn't it?"

"A natural thing, I should say. Your father's death was an awful blow. I often wonder how she lived out the years while she waited for you to finish school."

"But she did live them, so that I might be prepared to practice at Crossroads. As I think of it, it seems monstrous that I should disappoint her."

"Fledglings always leave the nest. Mothers have that to expect. The selfishness of the young makes for progress. It would have been equally monstrous if you had stayed in that dull place wasting your talents."

"Would it have been wasted, sir? There's no one taking my place in the old country. And there are many who could fill it here. There's a chance at Crossroads for big work for the right man. Community water supply—better housing, the health conditions of the ignorant foreign folk who work the small farms. A country doctor ought to have the missionary spirit."

"There are plenty of little men for such places."

"It takes big men. I could make our old countryside bloom like a rose if I could put into it half the effort that I am putting into my work with you. But it would be lean living—and I have chosen the flesh-pots."

"Don't despise yourself because you couldn't go on being poor in a big way. You are going to be rich in a big way, and that is better."

As the days went on, however, Richard wondered if it were really better to be rich in a big way. Sometimes the very bigness and richness oppressed him. He found himself burdened by the splendor of the mansions at which he made his morning calls. He hated the sleekness of the men in livery who preceded him up the stairs, the trimness of the maids waiting on the threshold of hushed boudoirs. Disease and death in these sumptuous palaces seemed divorced from reality as if the palaces were stage structures, and the people in them were actors who would presently walk out into the wings.

It was therefore with some of the feelings which had often assailed him when he had stepped from a dim theater out into the open air that Richard made his way one morning to a small apartment on a down-town side street to call on a little girl who had recently left the charity ward at Austin's hospital. Richard had operated for appendicitis, and had found himself much interested in the child. He had dismissed the limousine farther up. It had seemed out of place in the shabby street.

He stopped at the florist's for a pot of pink posies and at another shop for fruit. Laden with parcels he climbed the high stairs to the top floor of the tenement.

The little girl and her grandmother lived together. The grandmother had a small pension, and sewed by the day for several old customers. They thus managed to pay expenses, but poverty pinched. Richard had from the first, however, been impressed by their hopefulness. Neither the grandmother nor the child seemed to look upon their lot as hard. The grandmother made savory stews on a snug little stove and baked her own sweet loaves. Now and then she baked a cake. Things were spotlessly clean, and there were sunshine and fresh air. To have pitied those two would have been superfluous.

After he had walked briskly out into Fifth Avenue, he was thinking of another grandmother on whom he had called a few days before. She was a haughty old dame, but she was browbeaten by her maid. Her grandchildren were brought in now and then to kiss her hand. They were glad to get away. They had no real need of her. They had no hopes or fears to confide. So in spite of her magnificence and her millions, she was a lonely soul.

Snow had fallen the night before, and was now melting in the streets, but the sky was very blue above the tall buildings. Christmas was not far away, and as Richard went up-town the crowd surged with him, meeting the crowd that was coming down.

He had a fancy to lunch at a little place on Thirty-third Street, where they served a soup with noodles that was in itself a hearty meal. In the days when money had been scarce the little German café had furnished many a feast. Now and then he and his mother had come together, and had talked of how, when their ship came in, they would dine at the big hotel around the corner.

And now that his ship was in, and he could afford the big hotel, it had no charms. He hated the women dawdling in its alleys, the men smoking in its corridors, the whole idle crowd, lunching in acres of table-crowded space.

So he set as his goal the clean little restaurant, and swung along toward it with something of his old boyish sense of elation.

And then a strange thing happened. For the first time in months he found his heart marking time to the tune of the song which old Ben's hoofs had beaten out of the roads as they made their way up into the hills—

"I think she was the most beautiful lady,
That ever was in the West Country——"
He was even humming it under his breath, unheard amid the hum and stir of the crowded city street.

The shops on either side of him displayed in their low windows a wealth of tempting things. Rugs with a sheen like the bloom of a peach—alabaster in curved and carved bowls and vases, old prints in dull gilt frames—furniture following the lines of Florentine elaborateness—his eyes took in all the color and glow, though he rarely stopped for a closer view.

In front of one broad window, however, he hesitated. The opening of the door had spilled into the frosty air of this alien city the scent of the Orient—the fragrance of incense—of spicy perfumed woods.

In the window a jade god sat high on a teakwood pedestal. A string of scarlet beads lighted a shadowy corner. On an ancient and priceless lacquered cabinet were enthroned two other gods of gold and ivory. A crystal ball reflected a length of blue brocade. A clump of Chinese bulbs bloomed in an old Ming bowl.

Richard went into the shop. Subconsciously, he went with a purpose. But the purpose was not revealed to him until he came to a case in which was set forth a certain marvelous collection. He knew then that the old song and the scents had formed an association of ideas which had lured him away from the streets and into the shop, that he might buy for Anne Warfield a sandalwood fan.

He found what he wanted. A sweet and wonderful bit of wood, carved like lace, with green and purple tassels.

It was when he had it safe in his pocket, in a box that was gay with yellow and green and gold, that he was aware of voices in the back of the shop.

There were tables where tea was served to special customers—at the expense of the management. Thus a vulgar bargain became as it were a hospitality—you bought teakwood and had tea; carved ivories, and were rewarded with little cakes.

In that dim space under a low hung lamp, Marie-Louise talked with the fat Armenian.

He was the same Armenian who had told her fortune at Coney. He stood by Marie-Louise's side while she drank her tea, and spoke to her of the poet-king with whom she had walked on the banks of the Nile.

Richard approaching asked, "How did you happen to come here, Marie-Louise?"

"I often come. I like it. It is next to traveling in far countries." She indicated the fat Armenian. "He tells me about things that happened to me—in the ages—when I lived before."

A slender youth in white silk with a crimson sash brought tea for Richard. But he refused it. "I am on my way to lunch, Marie-Louise. Will you go with me?"

She hesitated and glanced at the fat Armenian. "I've some things to buy."

"I'll wait."

She flitted about the shop with the fat Armenian in her train. He showed her treasures shut away from the public eye, and she bought long lengths of heavy silks, embroideries thick with gold, a moonstone bracelet linked with silver.

The fat Armenian, bending over her, seemed to direct and suggest. Richard, watching, hated the man's manner.

Outside in the sunshine, he spoke of it. "I wouldn't go there alone."

"Why not?"

"I don't like to see you among those people—on such terms. They don't understand, and they're—different."

"I like them because they are different," obstinately.

He shifted his ground. "Marie-Louise, will you lunch with me at a cheap little place around the corner?"

"Why a cheap little place?"

"Because I like the good soup, and the clean little German woman, and the quiet and—the memories."

"What memories?"

"I used to go there when I was poor."

She entered eagerly into the adventure, and ordered her car to wait. Then away they fared around the corner!

Within the homely little restaurant, Marie-Louise's elegance was more than ever apparent. Her long coat of gray velvet with its silver fox winked opulently from the back of her chair at the coarse table-cloth and the paper napkins.

But the soup was good, and the German woman smiled at them, and brought them a special dish of hard almond cakes with their coffee.

"I love it," Marie-Louise said. "It is like Hans Andersen and my fairy books. Will you bring me here again, Dr. Richard?"

"I am glad you like it," he told her. "I wanted you to like it."

"I like it because I like you," she said with frankness, "and you seem to belong in the fairy tale. You are so big and strong and young. I don't feel a thousand years old when I am with you. You are such a change from everybody else, Dr. Dicky."

Richard spoke the next day to Austin of Marie-Louise and the fat Armenian. "She shouldn't be going to such shops alone. She has a romantic streak in her, and they take advantage of it."

"She ought never to go alone," Austin agreed, "and I have told her. But what am I going to do? I can rule a world of patients, Brooks, but I can't rule my woman child," he laughed ruefully. "I've tried having a maid accompany her, but she sends her home."

"I wish she might have gone to the Crossroads school, and have known the Crossroads teacher—Anne Warfield. You remember Cynthia Warfield, sir; this is her granddaughter."

Austin remembered Cynthia, and he wanted to know more of Anne. Richard told him of Anne's saneness and common sense. "I am so glad that she can be with my mother, and that the children have her in the school. She is so wise and good."

He thought more than once in the days that followed of Anne's wisdom and goodness. He decided to send the fan. He expected to go to Crossroads for Christmas, but he was not at all sure that he should see Anne. Something had been said about her going for the holidays to her Uncle Rod.

Was it only a year since he had seen her on the rocks above the river with a wreath in her hand, and in the stable at Bower's, with the lantern shining above her head?

CHAPTER XIX

In Which Christmas Comes to Crossroads.

Nancy's plans for Christmas were ambitious. She talked it over with Sulie Tyson. "I'll have Anne and her Uncle Rod. If she goes to him they will eat their Christmas dinner alone. Her cousins are to be out of town."

Cousin Sulie agreed. She was a frail little woman, with gray hair drawn up from her forehead above a high-bred face. She spoke with earnestness on even the most trivial subjects. Now and then she had flashes of humor, but they were rare. Her life had been sad, and she had always been dependent. The traditions of her family had made it impossible for her to indulge in any money-making occupation. Hence she had lived in other people's houses. Usually with one or the other of two brothers, in somewhat large households.

Her days, therefore, with Nancy were rapturous ones.

"There's something in the freedom which two women can have when they are alone," she said, "that is glorious. We are ourselves. When men are around we are always acting."

Nancy was not so subtle. "I am myself with Richard."

"No, you're not, Nancy. You are always trying to please him. You make him feel important. You make him feel that he is the head of the house. You know what I mean."

Nancy did know. But she didn't choose to admit it.

"Well, I like to please him." Then with a sudden burst of longing, "Sulie, I want him here all of the time—to please."

"Oh, my dear," Sulie caught Nancy's hands up in her own, "oh, my dear. How mothers love their sons. I am glad I haven't any. I used to long for children. I don't any more. Nothing can hurt me as Richard hurts you, Nancy."

Nancy refused to talk of it. "We will ask David and Brinsley; that will be four men and three women, Sulie."

"Well, I can take care of David if you'll look after Brinsley and Rodman Warfield. And that will leave your Richard for Anne."

Nancy's candid glance met her cousin's. "That is the way I had hoped it might be—Richard and Anne. At first I thought it might be—and then something happened. He went to New York and that was the—end."

"If you had been more of a match-maker," Sulie said, "you might have managed. But you always think that such things are on the knees of the gods. Why didn't you bring them together?"

"I tried," Nancy confessed. "But Eve—I hate to say it, Sulie. Eve was determined."

The two old-fashioned women, making mental estimates of this modern feminine product, found themselves indignant. "To think that any girl could——"

It was lunch time, and Anne came in. She had Diogenes under her arm. "He will come across the road to meet me. And I am afraid of the automobiles. When he brings the white duck and all of the little Diogenes with him he obstructs traffic. He stopped a touring car the other day, and the men swore at him, and Diogenes swore back."

She laughed and set the old drake on his feet. "May I have a slice of bread for him, Mother Nancy?"

"Of course, my dear. Two, if you wish."

Diogenes, having been towed by his beloved mistress out-of-doors, was appeased with the slice of bread. He was a patriarch now, with a lovely mate and a line of waddling offspring to claim his devotion. But not an inch did he swerve from his loyalty to Anne. She had brought him with her from Bower's, and he lived in the barn with his family. Twice a day, however, he made a pilgrimage to the Crossroads school. It was these excursions which Anne deprecated.

"He comes in when I ring for recess and distracts the children. He waddles straight up to my desk—and he is such an old dear."

She laughed, and the two women laughed with her. She was their heart-warming comrade. She brought into their lonely lives something vivid and sparkling, at which they drank for their soul's refreshment.

Nancy spoke of Rodman Warfield. "We want him here for Christmas and the holidays. Do you think he can come?"

Anne flashed her radiance at them. "I don't think. I know. Mother Nancy, you're an angel."

"Richard is coming, of course. It will be just a family party. Not many young people for you, my dear. Just—Richard."

There was holly and crow's-foot up in the hills, and David and Anne hitched big Ben to a cart and went after it. It was a winter of snow, and in the depths of the woods there was a great stillness. David chopped a tall cedar and his blows echoed and reëchoed in the white spaces. The holly berries that dropped from the cut branches were like drops of blood on the shining crust.

Nancy and Sulie made up the wreaths and the ropes of green, and fashioned ornaments for the tree. There was to be a bigger tree at the school for the children, but this was to be a family affair and was to be free from tawdry tinsel and colored glass. Nancy liked straight little candles and silver stars. "It shall be an old-fashioned tree," she said, "such as I used to have when I was a child."

Sulie's raptures were almost solemn in their intensity. Richard sent money, plenty of it, and Sulie and Nancy went to Baltimore and spent it. "I never expected," Sulie said, "to go into shops and pick out things that I liked. I've always had to choose things that I needed."

Now and then on Saturdays when Anne went with them, they rushed through their shopping, had lunch at the Woman's Exchange and went to a matinée.

Nancy was always glad to get back home, but Sulie revelled in the excitement of it all. Anne made her buy a hat with a flat pink rose which lay enchantingly against her gray hair.

"I feel sometimes as if I had been born again," Sulie said quaintly; "like a flower that had shriveled up and grown brown, and suddenly found itself blooming in the spring."

Thus the days went on, and Christmas was not far away. Anne coming in one afternoon found Nancy by the library fire with a letter in her hand.

"Richard hopes to get here on Friday, Anne, in time for the tree and the children's festival. Something may keep him, however, until Christmas morning. He is very busy—and there are some important operations."

"How proud you are of him," Anne sank down on the rug, and reached up her hand for Nancy, "and how happy you will be with your big son. Could you ever have loved a daughter as much, Mother Nancy?"

"I'm not sure; perhaps," smiling, "if she had been like you. And a daughter would have stayed with me. Men have wandering natures—they must be up and out."

"Women have wandering natures, too," Anne told her. "Do you know that last Christmas I cried and cried because I was tied to the Crossroads school and to Bower's? I wanted to live in the city and have lovely things. You can't imagine how I hated all Eve Chesley's elegance. I seemed so—clumsy and common."

Nancy stared at her in amazement. "But you surely don't feel that way now."

"Yes, I do. But I am not unhappy any more. It was silly to be unhappy when I had so much in my life. But if I were a man, I'd be a rover, a vagabond—I'd take to the open road rather than be tied to one spot."

There was laughter in her eyes, but the words rang true. "I want to see new things in new people. I want to have new experiences—there must be a bigger, broader world than this."

Nancy gazing into the fire pondered. "It's the spirit of the age. Perhaps it is the youth in you. I wanted to go, too. But oh, my dear, how I wanted to come back!"

There was silence between them, then Anne said, "Perhaps if I could have my one little fling I'd be content. Perhaps it wouldn't be all that I expected. But I'd like to try."

On Thursday Anne met the postman as he drove up. There were two parcels for her. One was square and one was long and narrow. There were parcels also for Nancy and Sulie. Anne delivered them, and took her own treasures to her room. She shut and locked her door. Then she stood very still in the middle of the room. Not since she had seen the writing on the long and narrow parcel had her heart ceased to beat madly.

When at last she sat down and untied the string a faint fragrance assailed her nostrils. Then the gay box with its purple and green and gold was revealed!

The little fan was folded about with many thicknesses of soft paper. But at last she had it out, the dear lovely thing that her love had sent!

In that moment all the barriers which she had built about her thoughts of Richard were beaten down and battered by his remembrance of her. There was not a line from him, not a word. Nothing but the writing on the wrapper, and the memory of their talk together by the big fire at Bower's on the night of Beulah's party when he had said, "You ought to have a little fan—of—sandalwood—with purple and green tassels and smelling sweet."

When she went down her cheeks were red with color. "How pretty you are!" Sulie said, and kissed her.

Anne showed the book which had come in the square parcel. It was Geoffrey Fox's "Three Souls," and it was dedicated to Anne.

She did not show the sandalwood fan. It was hidden in her desk. She had a feeling that Nancy and Sulie would not understand, and that Richard had not meant that she should show it.

Nancy, too, had something which she did not show. One of her letters was from Dr. Austin. He had written without Richard's knowledge. He wished to inquire about Anne Warfield. He had been much impressed by what Richard had said of her. He needed a companion for his daughter Marie-Louise. He wanted a lady, and Cynthia Warfield's grandchild would, of course, be that. He wanted, too, some one who was fearless, and who thought straight. He fancied that from what Richard had said that Anne would be the antidote for his daughter's abnormality. If Nancy would confirm Richard's opinion, he would write at once to Miss Warfield. A woman's estimate in such a matter would, naturally, be more satisfying. He would pay well, and Anne would be treated in every way as one of the family. Marie-Louise might at first be a little difficult. But in the end, no doubt, she would yield to tact and firmness.

And he was always devotedly, her old friend!

It had seemed to Nancy as she read that something gripped at her heart. It was Anne's presence which had kept her from the black despair of loneliness. Sulie was good and true, but she had no power to fill the void made by Richard's absence. If Anne went away, they would be two old women, gazing blankly into an empty future.

Yet it was Anne's opportunity. The opportunity which her soul had craved. "To see new things and new people." And she was young and wanting much to live. It would not be right or fair to hold her back.

She had, however, laid the letter aside. When Richard came she would talk it over with him, and then they could talk to Anne. She tried to forget it in the bustle of preparation, but it lay like a shadow in the back of her mind, dimming the brightness of the days.

Everybody was busy. Milly and Sulie and Nancy seeded and chopped and baked, and polished silver, and got out piles of linen, and made up beds, and were all beautifully ready and swept and garnished when Uncle Rodman arrived from Carroll and Brinsley from Baltimore.

The two old men came on the same train, and David brought them over from Bower's behind big Ben. By the time they reached Crossroads, they had dwelt upon old times and old friends and old loves until they were in the warm and genial state of content which is age's recompense for the loss of youthful ardors.

They were, indeed, three ancient Musketeers, who, untouched now by any flame of great emotion, might adventure safely in a past of sentiment from which they were separated by long years. But there had been a time when passion had burned brightly for them all, even in gentle David, who had loved Cynthia Warfield.

What wonder, then, if to these three Anne typified that past, and all it meant to them, as she ran to meet them with her arms outflung to welcome Uncle Rod.

She had them all presently safe on the hearth with the fire roaring, and with Milly bringing them hot coffee, and Sulie and Nancy smiling in an ecstasy of welcome.

"It is perfect," Anne said, "to have you all here—like this."

Yet deep in her heart she knew that it was not perfect. For youth calls to youth. And Richard was yet to come!

Brinsley had brought hampers of things to eat. He had made epicurean pilgrimages to the Baltimore markets. There were turkeys and ducks and oysters—Smithfield hams, a young pig with an apple in its mouth.

He superintended the unloading of the hampers when Eric brought them over. Uncle Rod shook his head as he saw them opened.

"I can make a jar of honey and a handful of almonds suffice," he said. "I am not keen about butchered birds and beasts."

Brinsley laughed. "Don't rob me of the joy of living, Rod," he said. "Nancy is bad enough. I wanted to send up some wine. But she wouldn't have it. Even her mince pies are innocent. Nancy sees the whole world through eyes of anxiety for her boy. I don't believe she'd care a snap for temperance if she wasn't afraid that her Dicky might drink."

"Perhaps it is the individual mother's solicitude for her own particular child which makes the feminine influence a great moral force," Rodman ventured.

"Perhaps," carelessly. "Now Nancy has a set of wine-glasses that it is a shame not to use." He slapped his hands to warm them. "Let's take a long walk, Rod. I exercise to keep the fat down."

"I exercise because it is a good old world to walk in," and Rodman swung his long lean legs into an easy stride.

They picked David up as they passed his little house. They climbed the hill till they came to the edge of the wood where David had cut the tree.

There was a sunset over the frozen river as they turned to look at it. The river sang no songs to-day. It was as still and silent as their own dead youth. Yet above it was the clear gold of the evening sky.

"The last time we came we were boys," Brinsley said, "and I was in love with Cynthia Warfield. And we were both in love with her, David; do you remember?"

David did remember. "Anne is like her."

Rodman protested. "She is and she isn't. Anne has none of Cynthia's faults."

Brinsley chuckled. "I'll bet you've spoiled her."

"No, I haven't. But Anne has had to work and wait for things, and it hasn't hurt her."

"She's a beauty," Brinsley stated, "and she ought to be a belle."

"She's good," David supplemented; "the children at the little school worship her."

"She's mine," Uncle Rod straightened his shoulders, "and in that knowledge I envy no man anything."

As they sat late that night by Nancy's fire, Anne in a white frock played for them, and sang:

"I think she was the most beautiful lady
That ever was in the West Country,
But beauty vanishes, beauty passes,
However rare, rare it be,
And when I am gone, who shall remember
That lady of the West Country?"
And when she sang it was of Cynthia Warfield that all of the Old Gentlemen dreamed.

When the last note had died away, she went over and stood behind her uncle. She was little and slim and straight and her soft hair was swept up high from her forehead. Her eyes above Uncle Rod's head met Nancy's eyes. The two women smiled at each other.

"To-morrow," Nancy said, and she seemed to say it straight to Anne, "to-morrow Richard will be here."

Anne caught a quick breath. "To-morrow," she said. "How lovely it will be!"

But Richard did not come on Christmas Eve. A telegram told of imperative demands on him. He would get there in the morning.

500

"We won't light the tree until he comes," was Nancy's brave decision. "The early train will get him here in time for breakfast."

David drove big Ben down to meet him. Milly cooked a mammoth breakfast. Anne slipped across the road to the Crossroads school to ring the bell for the young master's return. The rest of the household waited in the library. Brinsley was there with a story to tell, but no one listened. Their ears were strained to catch the first sharp sound of big Ben's trot. Sulie was there with a red rose in her hair to match the fires which were warming her old heart. Nancy was there at the window, watching.

Then the telephone rang. Nancy was wanted. Long distance.

It was many minutes before she came back. Yet the message had been short. She had hung up the receiver, and had stood in the hall in a whirling world of darkness.

Richard was not coming.

He had been sorry. Tender. Her own sweet son. Yet he had seemed to think that business was a sufficient excuse for breaking her heart. Surely there were doctors enough in that octopus of a town to take his patients off of his hands. And she was his mother and wanted him.

She had a sense of utter rebellion. She wanted to cry out to the world, "This is my son, for whom I have sacrificed."

And now the bell across the street began to ring its foolish chime—Richard was not coming, ding, dong. She must get through the day without him, ding, dong, she must get through all the years!

When she faced the solicitous group in the library, only her whiteness showed what she was feeling.

"Richard is detained by—an important—operation. And breakfast is—waiting. Sulie, will you call Anne, and light the little tree?"

CHAPTER XX

In Which a Dresden-China Shepherdess and a Country Mouse Meet on Common Ground.

Marie-louise's room at Rose Acres was all in white with two tall candlesticks to light it, and a silver bowl for flowers. It was by means of the flowers in the bowl that Marie-Louise expressed her moods. There were days when scarlet flowers flamed, and other days when pale roses or violets or lilies suggested a less exotic state of mind.

On the day when Anne Warfield arrived, the flowers in the bowl were yellow. Marie-Louise stayed in bed all of the morning. She had ordered the flowers sent up from the hothouse, and, dragging a length of silken dressing-gown behind her, she had arranged them. Then she had had her breakfast on a tray.

Her hair was nicely combed under a lace cap; the dressing-gown was faint blue. In the center of the big bed she looked very small but very elegant, as if a Dresden-China Shepherdess had been put between the covers.

She had told her maid that when Anne arrived she was to be shown up at once. Austin had suggested that Marie-Louise go down-town to meet her. But Marie-Louise had refused.

"I don't want to see her. Why should I?"

"She is very charming, Marie-Louise."

"Who told you?"

"Dr. Brooks. And I knew her grandmother."

"Will Dr. Dicky meet her?"

"Yes. And bring her out. I have given him the day."

"You might have asked me if I wanted her, Dad. I don't want anybody to look after me. I belong to myself."

"I don't know to whom you belong, Marie-Louise. You're a changeling."

"I'm not. I'm your child. But you don't like my horns and hoofs."

He gazed at her aghast. "My dear child!"

She began to sob. "I am not your dear child. But I am your child, and I shall hate to have somebody tagging around."

"Miss Warfield is not to tag. And you'll like her."

"I shall hate her," said Marie-Louise, between her teeth.

It was because of this hatred that she had filled her bowl with yellow flowers. Yellow meant jealousy. And she had shrewdly analyzed her state of mind. She was jealous of Anne because Dad and Dr. Richard and everybody else thought that Anne was going to set her a good example.

It was early in January that Anne came. The whole thing had been hurried. Austin had been peremptory in his demand that she should not delay. So Nancy, very white but smiling, had packed her off. Sulie had cried over her, and Uncle Rod had wished her "Godspeed."

Richard met her at the station in the midst of a raging blizzard, and in a sort of dream she had been whirled with him through the gray streets shut in by the veil of the falling snow. They had stopped for tea at a big hotel, which had seemed as they entered to swim in a sea of golden light. And now here she was at last in this palace of a house!

Therese led her straight to Marie-Louise.

The Dresden-China Shepherdess in bed looked down the length of the shadowed room to the door. The figure that stood on the threshold was somehow different from what she had expected. Smaller. More girlish. Lovelier.

Anne, making her way across a sea of polished floor, became aware of the Shepherdess in bed.

"Oh," she said, "I am sorry you are ill."

"I am not ill," said Marie-Louise. "I didn't want you to come."

Anne smiled. "Oh, but if you knew how much I wanted to come."

Marie-Louise sat up. "What made you want to come?"

"Because I am a country mouse, and I wanted to see the world."

"Rose Acres isn't the world."

"New York is. To me. There is so much that I haven't seen. It is going to be a great adventure."

The Dresden-China Shepherdess fell down flat. "So that's what you've come for," she said, dully, "adventures—here."

There was a long silence, out of which Anne asked, "How many miles is it to my room?"

"Miles?"

"Yes. You see, I am not used to such great houses."

"It is down the hall in the west wing."

"If I get lost it will be my first adventure."

Marie-Louise turned and took a good look at this girl who made so much out of nothing. Then she said, "Therese will show you. And you can dress at once for dinner. I am not going down."

"Please do. I shall hate going alone."

"Why?"

"Well, there's your father, you know, and your—mother. And I'm a country mouse."

Their eyes met. Marie-Louise had a sudden feeling that there was no gulf between them of years or of authority.

"What shall I call you?" she asked. "I won't say Miss Warfield."

"Geoffrey Fox calls me Mistress Anne."

"Who is Geoffrey Fox?"

"He writes books, and he is going blind. He wrote 'Three Souls.'"

Marie-Louise stared. "Oh, do you know him? I loved his book."

"Would you like to know how he came to write it?"

"Yes. Tell me."

"Not now. I must go and dress."

Some instinct told Marie-Louise that argument would be useless.

"I'll dress, too, and come down. Is Dr. Dicky going to be at dinner?"

"No. He had to go back at once. He is very busy."

Marie-Louise slipped out of bed. "Therese," she called, "come and dress me, after you have shown Miss Warfield the way."

Anne never forgot the moment of entrance into the great dining-room. There were just four of them. Dr. Austin and his wife, herself and Marie-Louise. But for these four there was a formality transcending anything in Anne's experience. Carved marble, tapestry, liveried servants, a massive table with fruit piled high in a Sheffield basket.

The people were dwarfed by the room. It was as if the house had been built for giants, and had been divorced from its original purpose. Anne, walking with Marie-Louise, wondered whimsically if there were any ceilings or whether the roof touched the stars.

Mrs. Austin was supported by her husband. She was a little woman with gray hair. She wore pearls and silver. Anne was in white. Marie-Louise in a quaint frock of gold brocade. There seemed to be no color in the room except the gold of the fire on the great hearth, the gold of the oranges on the table, and the gold of Marie-Louise's gown.

Mrs. Austin was pale and silent. But she had attentive eyes. Anne was uncomfortably possessed with the idea that the little lady listened and criticized, or at least that she held her opinion in reserve.

Marie-Louise spoke of Geoffrey Fox. "Miss Warfield knows him. She knows how he came to write his book."

Anne told them how he came to write it. Of Peggy ill at Bower's, of the gray plush pussy cat, and of how, coming up the hall with the bowl of soup in her hand, she had found Fox in a despairing mood and had suggested the plot.

Austin, watching her, decided that she was most unusual. She was beautiful, but there was something more than beauty. It was as if she was lighted from within by a fire which gave warmth not only to herself but to those about her.

He was glad that he had brought her here to be with Marie-Louise. For the moment even his wife's pale beauty seemed cold.

"We'll have Fox up," he said, when she finished her story.

Anne was sure that he would be glad to come. She blushed a little as she said it.

Later, when they were having coffee in the little drawing-room, Marie-Louise taxed her with the blush. "Is he in love with you?"

Anne felt it best to be frank. "He thought he was."

"Don't you love him?"

"No, Marie-Louise. And we mustn't talk about it. Love is a sacred thing."

"I like to talk about it. In summer I talk to Pan. But he's out now in the snow and his pipes are frozen."

The little drawing-room seemed to Anne anything but little until she learned that there was a larger one across the hall. Austin and his wife went up-stairs as soon as the coffee had been served, and Marie-Louise led Anne through the shadowy vastness of the great drawing-room to a window which overlooked the river. "You can't see the river, but the light over the doorway shines on my old Pan's head. You can see him grinning out of the snow."

The effect of that white head peering from the blackness was uncanny. The shaft of light struck straight across the peaked chin and twisted mouth. The snow had made him a cap which covered his horns and which gave him the look of a rakish old tipster.

"Oh, Marie-Louise, do you talk to him of love?"

"Yes. Wait till you see him in the spring with the pink roses back of him. He seems to get younger in the spring."

Anne, going to bed that night in a suite of rooms which might have belonged to a princess, wondered if she should wake in the morning and find herself dreaming. To have her own bath, a silk canopy over her head, to know that breakfast would be served when she rang for it, and that her mail and newspapers would be brought—these were unbelievable things. She had a feeling that if she told Uncle Rod he would shake his head over it. He had a theory that luxury tended to cramp the soul.

Yet her last thought was not of Uncle Rod but of Richard. She had come intending to give him a sharp opinion of his neglect of Nancy. But he had been so glad to see her, and had given her such a good time. Yet she had spoken of Nancy's loneliness.

"I hated to leave her," she said, "but it seemed as if I had to come."

"Of course," he agreed, with his eyes on her glowing face, "and anyhow, she has Sulie."

Marie-Louise, in the days that followed, found interest and occupation in showing the Country Mouse the sights of the city.

"If you want to see such things," she said rather grandly, "I shall be glad to go with you."

Anne insisted that they should not be driven in state and style. "People make pilgrimages on foot," she told Marie-Louise gravely, but with a twinkle in her eye. "I don't want to whirl up to Grant's tomb, or to the door of Trinity. And I like the subway and the elevated and the surface cars."

If now and then they compromised on a taxi, it was because distances were too great at times, and other means of transportation too slow. But in the main they stuck to their original plan, and Marie-Louise entered a new world.

"Oh, I love you for it," she said to Anne one night when they came home from the Battery after a day in which they had gazed down into the pit of the Stock Exchange, had lunched at Faunce's Tavern, had circled the great Aquarium, and ended with a ride on top of a Fifth Avenue 'bus in the twilight.

It was from the top of the 'bus that Anne for the first time since she had come to New York saw Evelyn Chesley.

She was coming out of a shop with Richard. It was a great shop with a world-famous name over the door. One bought furniture there of a rare kind and draperies of a rare kind and now and then a picture.

"They are getting things for their apartment," Marie-Louise explained, and her words struck cold against Anne's heart. "Eve is paying for them with Aunt Maude's money."

"When will they be married?"

"Next October. But Eve is buying things as she sees them. I don't want her to marry Dr. Dicky."

"Why not, Marie-Louise?"

"He isn't her kind. He ought to have fallen in love with you."

"Marie-Louise, I told you not to talk of love."

"I shall talk of anything I please."

"Then you'll talk to the empty air. I won't listen. I'll go up there and sit with that fat man in front."

Marie-Louise laughed. "You're such an old dear. Do you know how nice you look in those furs?"

"I feel so elegant that I am ashamed of myself. I've peeped into every mirror. They cost a whole month's salary, Marie-Louise. I feel horribly extravagant—and happy."

They laughed together, and it was then that Marie-Louise said, "I love it."

"Love what?"

"Going with you and being young."

In the days that followed Anne found herself revelling in the elegances of her life, in the excitements. It was something of an experience to meet Evelyn Chesley on equal grounds in the little drawing-room. Anne always took Mrs. Austin's place when there were gatherings of young folks. Marie-Louise refused to be tied, and came and went as the spirit moved her. So it was Anne who in something shimmering and silken moved among the tea guests, and danced later in slippers as shining as anything Eve had ever worn.

It was on this day that Geoffrey Fox came and met Marie-Louise for the first time.

"I can't dance," he told her; "my eyes are bad, and things seem to whirl."

"If you'll talk," she said, "I'll sit at your feet and listen."

She did it literally, perched on a small gold stool.

"Tell me about your book," she said, looking up at him. "Anne Warfield says that you wrote it at Bower's."

"I wrote it because she helped me to write it. But she did more for me than that." His eyes were following the shining figure.

"What did she do?"

"She gave me a soul. She taught me that there was something in me that was not—the flesh and the—devil."

The girl on the footstool understood. "She believes in things, and makes you believe."

"Yes."

"I hated to have her come," Marie-Louise confessed, "and now I should hate to have her go away. She calls herself a country mouse, and I am showing her the sights—we go to corking places—on pilgrimages. We went to Grant's tomb, and she made me carry a wreath. And we ride in the subway and drink hot chocolate in drug stores.

"She says I haven't learned the big lessons of democracy," Marie-Louise pursued, "that I've looked out over the world, but that I have never been a part of it. That I've sat on a tower in a garden and have peered through a telescope."

She told him of the play that she had written, and of the verses that she had read to the piping Pan.

Later she pointed out Pan to him from the window of the big drawing-room. The snow had melted in the last mild days, and there was an icicle on his nose, and the sun from across the river reddened his cheeks.

"And there, everlastingly, he makes music," Geoffrey said, "'on the reed which he tore from the river.'"

" 'Yes, half a beast is the great god, Pan,
To laugh as he sits by the river,
Making a poet out of a man.
The true gods sigh for the cost and pain,
For the reed that grows nevermore again,
As a reed with the reeds in the river.'"
His voice died away into silence. "That is the price which the writer pays. He is separated, as it were, from his kind."

"Oh, no," Marie-Louise breathed, "oh, no. Not you. Your writings bring you—close. Your book made me—cry."

She was such a child as she stood there, yet with something in her, too, of womanliness.

"When your three soldiers died," she said, "it made me believe something that I hadn't believed before—about souls marching toward a great—light."

Geoffrey found himself confiding in her. "I don't know whether you will understand. But ever since I wrote that book I have felt that I must live up to it. That I must be worthy of the thing I had written."

Richard, dancing in the music room with Anne, found himself saying, "How different it all is."

"From Bower's?"

"Yes."

"Do you like it?"

"Sometimes. And then sometimes it all seems so big—and useless."

The music stopped, and they made their way back to the little drawing-room.

"Won't you sit here and talk to me?" Richard said. "Somehow we never seem to find time to talk."

She smiled. "There is always so much to do."

But she knew that it was not the things to be done which had kept her from him. It was rather a sense that safety lay in seeing as little of him as possible. And so, throughout the winter she had built about herself barriers of reserve. Yet there had never been a moment when he had dined with them, or when he had danced, or when he had shared their box at the opera, that she had not been keenly conscious of his presence.

"And so you think it is all so big—and useless?" He picked up the conversation where they had dropped it when the dance stopped.

She nodded. "A house like this isn't a home. I told Marie-Louise the other day that a home was a place where there was a little fire, with somebody on each side of it, and where there was a little table with two people smiling across it, and with a pot boiling and a woman to stir it, and with a light in the window and a man coming home."

"And what did Marie-Louise say to that?"

"She wrote a poem about it. A nice healthy sane little poem—not one of those dreadful things about the ashes of dead women which I found her doing when I came."

"How did you cure her?"

"I am giving her real things to think of. When she gets in a morbid mood I whisk her off to the gardener's cottage, and we wash and dress the baby and take him for an airing."

Richard gave a big laugh. "With your head in the stars, you have your feet always firmly on the ground."

"I try to, but I like to know that there are always—stars."

"No one could be near you and not know that," he told her gravely.

It was a danger signal. She rose. "I have a feeling that you are neglecting somebody. You haven't danced yet with Miss Chesley."

"Oh, Eve's all right," easily; "sit down."

But she would not. She sent him from her. His place was by Eve's side. He was going to marry Eve.

It was late that night when Marie-Louise came into Anne's room. "Are you asleep?" she asked, with the door at a crack.

"No."

"Will you mind—if I talk?"

"No."

Anne was in front of her open fire, writing to Uncle Rod. The fire was another of the luxuries in which she revelled. It was such a wonder of a fireplace, with its twinkling brasses, and its purring logs. She remembered the little round stove in her room at Bower's.

507

Marie-Louise had come to talk of Geoffrey Fox.

"I adore his eye-glasses."

"Oh, Marie-Louise—his poor eyes."

"He isn't poor," the child said, passionately, "not even his eyes. Milton was blind—and—and there was his poetry."

 "Dr. Dicky hopes his eyes are getting better."

"He says they are. That he sees things now through a sort of silver rain. He has to have some one write for him. His little sister Mimi has been doing it, but she is going to be married."

"Mimi?"

"Yes. He found out that she had a lover, and so he has insisted. And then he will be left alone."

She sat gazing into the fire, a small humped-up figure in a gorgeous dressing-gown. At last she said, "Why didn't you love him?"

"There was some one else, Marie-Louise."

Marie-Louise drew close and laid her red head on Anne's knee. "Some one that you are going to marry?"

Anne shook her head. "Some one whom I shall never marry. He loves—another girl, Marie-Louise."

"Oh!" There was a long silence, as the two of them gazed into the fire. Then Marie-Louise reached up a thin little hand to Anne's warm clasp. "That's always the way, isn't it? It is a sort of game, with Love always flitting away to—another girl."

CHAPTER XXI

In Which St. Michael Hears a Call.

It was in April that Geoffrey Fox wrote to Anne.

"When I told you that I was coming back to Bower's, I said that I wanted quiet to think out my new book, but I did not tell you that I fancied I might find your ghost flitting through the halls, or on the road to the schoolhouse. I felt that there might linger in the long front room the glowing spirit of the little girl who sat by the fire and talked to me of my soldiers and their souls.

"And what I thought has come true. You are everywhere, Mistress Anne, not as I last saw you at Rose Acres in silken attire, but fluttering before me in your frock of many flounces, carrying your star of a lantern through the twilight on your way to Diogenes, scolding me on the stairs——! What days, what hours! And always you were the little school-teacher, showing your wayward scholars what to do with life!

"Perhaps I have done with it less than you expected. But at least I have done more with it than I had hoped. I am lining my pockets with money, and Mimi has a chest of silver. That is the immediate material effect of the sale of 'Three Souls.' But there is more than the material effect. The letters which I get from the people who have read the book are like wine to my soul. To think that I, Geoffrey Fox, who have frittered and frivoled, should have put on paper things which have burned into men's consciousness and have made them better. I could never have done it except for you. Yet in all humility I can say that I have done it, and that never while life lasts shall I think again of my talent as a little thing.

"For it is a great thing, Mistress Anne, to have written a book. In all of my pot-boiling days I would never have believed it. A plot was a plot, and presto, the thing was done! The world read and forgot. But the world doesn't forget. Not when we give our best, and when we aim to get below the surface things and the shallow things and call up out of men's hearts that which, in these practical days, they try to hide.

"I suppose Brooks has told you about my eyes, and of how it may happen that I shall, for the rest of my life, be able to see through a glass darkly.

"That is something to be thankful for, isn't it? It is a rather weird experience when, having adjusted one's self in anticipation of a catastrophe, the catastrophe hangs fire. Like old Pepys, I had resigned myself to the inevitable—indeed in those awful waiting days I read, more than once, the last paragraph of his diary.

"'And so I betake myself to that course which it is almost as much as to see myself go into my grave; for which, and all the discomforts that will accompany my being blind, the good God prepare me!'

"Yet Pepys kept his sight all the rest of his life, and regretted, I fancy, more than once, that he did not finish his diary. And, perhaps, I, too, shall be granted this dim vision until the end.

"It seems to me that there are many things which I ought to tell you—I know there are a thousand things which are forbidden. But at least I can speak of Diogenes. I saw him at Crossroads the other day, much puffed up with pride of family. And I can speak of Mrs. Nancy, who is a white shadow of herself. Why doesn't Brooks see it? He was down here for a week recently, and he didn't seem to realize that anything was wrong. Perhaps she is always so radiant when he comes that she dazzles his eyes.

"She and Miss Sulie are a pathetic pair. I meet them on the road on their errands of mercy. They are like two sisters of charity in their long capes and little bonnets. Evidently Mrs. Brooks feels that if her son cannot doctor the community she can at least nurse it. The country folks adore her, and go to her for advice, so that Crossroads still opens wide its doors to the people, as it did in the days of old Dr. Brooks.

"And now, does the Princess still serve? I can see you with your blue bowl on your way to Peggy, and stopping on the stairs to light for me the torch of inspiration. And now all of this service and inspiration is being spilled at the feet of—Marie-Louise! Will you give her greetings, and ask her how soon I may come and worship at the shrine of her grinning old god?"

Anne, carrying his letter to Marie-Louise, asked, "Shall I tell him to come?"

"Yes. I didn't want him to go away, but he said he must—that he couldn't write here. But I knew why he went, and you knew."

"You needn't look at me so reproachfully, Marie-Louise. It isn't my fault."

"It is your fault," Marie-Louise accused her, "for being like a flame. Father says that people hold out their hands to you as they do to a fire."

"And what," Anne demanded, "has all this to do with Geoffrey Fox?"

"You know," Marie-Louise told her bluntly, "he loves you and looks up to you—and I—sit at his feet."

There was something of tenseness in the small face framed by the red hair. Anne touched Marie-Louise's cheek with a tender finger. "Dear heart," she said, "he is just a man."

For a moment the child stood very still, then she said, "Is he? Or is he a god, like my Pan in the garden?"

Later she decided that Geoffrey should come in May. "When there are roses. And I'll have some people out."

It was in May that Rose Acres justified its name. The marble Pan piping on his reeds faced a garden abloom with beauty. At the right, a grass walk led down to a sunken fountain approached by wide stone steps.

It was on these steps that Marie-Louise sat one morning, weaving a garland.

"I am going to tie it with gold ribbon," she said. "Tibbs got the laurel for me."

"Who is it for?"

"It may be for—Pan," Marie-Louise wore an air of mystery, "and it may not."

She stuck it later on Pan's head, but the effect did not please her. "You are nothing but a grinning old marble doll," she told him, and Anne laughed at her.

"I hoped some day you'd find that out."

Richard, arriving late that afternoon, found Mrs. Austin on the terrace. "The young people are in the garden," she said; "will you hunt them up?"

"I want to talk to Dr. Austin, if I may."

"He's in the house. He was called to the telephone."

Austin, coming out, found his young assistant on the portico.

"Can you give me a second, sir? I've a letter from mother. There's a lot of sickness at Crossroads. And I feel responsible."

"Why should you feel responsible?"

"It's the water supply. Typhoid. If I had been there I should have had it looked into. I had started an investigation but there was no one to push it. And now there are a dozen cases. Eric Brand's little wife, Beulah, and old Peter Bower, and the mother of little François."

"And you are thinking that you ought to go down?"

"Yes."

"I don't see how I can let you go. It doesn't make much difference where people are sick, Brooks, there's always so much for us doctors to do."

"But if I could be spared——"

"You can't, Brooks. I am sorry. But I've learned to depend on you."

The older man laid his hand affectionately on the shoulder of the younger. If for the moment Richard felt beneath the softness of that touch the iron glove of one who expected obedience from a subordinate, he did not show it by word or glance.

They talked of other things after that, and presently Richard wandered off to find Eve. He passed beyond the terraces to the garden. He felt tired and depressed. The fragrance of the roses was heavy and almost overpowering. There was a stone bench set in the midst of a tangle of bloom. He sank down on it, asking nothing better than to sit there alone and think it out.

He felt at this moment, strongly, what had come to him many times during the winter—that he was not in any sense his own master. Austin directed, controlled, commanded. For the opportunity which he had given young Brooks he expected the return of acquiescence. Thus it happened that Richard found less of big things and more of little ones in his life than he had anticipated. There had been times when the moral side of a case had appealed to him more than the medical, when he had been moved by generosities such as had moved his grandfather, when he had wanted to be human rather than professional, and always he had found Austin blocking his idealistic impulses, scoffing at the things he had valued, imposing upon him a somewhat hard philosophy in the place of a living faith. It seemed to Richard that in his profession, as well as in his love affair, he was no longer meeting life with a direct glance.

He rose and went on. He must find Eve. He had promised and yet in that moment he knew that he did not want to see her. He wanted his mother's touch, her understanding, her love. He wanted Crossroads and big Ben—and the people who, because of his grandfather, had called him—"friend."

He found Anne and Geoffrey and Marie-Louise by the fountain at the end of the grass walk. Marie-Louise perched on the rim was, in her pale green gown, like some nymph freshly risen. Her hat was off, and her red hair caught the sunlight.

Anne was reading the first chapter of Geoffrey's new book. He sat just above her on the steps of the fountain. His glasses were off, and as he looked down at her his eyes showed a brilliancy which seemed to contradict his failing sight.

Marie-Louise held up a warning finger. "Sit down," she said, "and listen. It is such a wonder-book, Dr. Dicky."

So Richard sat down and Anne went on reading. She read well; her voice had a thrilling quality, and once it broke.

"Oh, why did you make it so sad?" she said.

"Could I make it glad?" he asked, and to Richard, watching, there came the jealous certainty that between the two of them there was some subtle understanding.

When at last Anne had read all that he had written Marie-Louise said, importantly, "Anne is the heroine, the Princess who serves. Will you ever make me the heroine of a book, Geoffrey Fox?"

"Perhaps. Give me a plot?"

"Have a girl who loves a marble god—then some day she meets a man—and the god is afraid he will lose her, so he wakes to life and says, 'If you love this man, you will have to accept the common lot of women, you will have to work for him and obey him—and some day he will die and your soul will be rent with sorrow. But if you love me, I shall be here when you are forgotten, and while you live my love will demand nothing but the verses that you read to me and the roses that lay at my feet.'"

Geoffrey gave her an eager glance. "Jove, there's more in that than a joke. Some day I shall get you to amplify your idea."

"I'll give it to you if you promise to write the book here. There's a balcony room that overlooks the river—and nobody would ever interrupt you but me, and I'd only come when you wanted me."

Marie-Louise's breath was short as she finished. To cover her emotion she caught up the wreath which she had made in the morning, and which lay beside her.

"I made it for you," she told Geoffrey, "and now that I've done it, I don't know what to do with it."

She was blushing and glowing, less of an imp and more of a girl than Richard had ever seen her.

Geoffrey rose to the occasion. "It shall be a mascot for my new book. I'll hang it on the wall over my desk, and every time I look up at it, it shall say to me, 'These are the laurels you are to win.'"

"You have won them," Marie-Louise flashed.

"No artist ever feels himself worthy of laurel. His achievement always falls short of his ambition."

"But 'Three Souls,'" Marie-Louise said; "surely you were satisfied?"

"I did not write it—the credit belongs to Mistress Anne. Your wreath should be hers."

But Marie-Louise's mind was made up. Before Geoffrey could grasp what she was about to do, she fluttered up the steps, and dropped the garland lightly on his dark locks.

511

It became him well.

"Do you like it?" he asked Anne.

"To the Victor—the spoils," she told him, smiling.

Richard felt out of it. He wanted to get away, and he knew that he must find Eve. Eve, who when he met her would laugh her light laugh, and call him "Dicky Boy," and refuse to listen when he spoke of Crossroads.

The path that he took led to a little tea house built on the bank, which gave a wide view of the river and the Jersey hills. He found Winifred and Tony side by side and silent.

"Better late than never," was Tony's greeting.

"I am hunting for Eve."

"She and Meade were here a moment ago," Winifred informed him. "Sit down and give an account of yourself. We haven't seen you in a million years."

"Just a week, dear lady. I have been horribly busy."

"You say that as if you meant the 'horribly.'"

"I do. It has been a 'bluggy' business, and I am tired." He laughed with a certain amount of constraint. "If I were a boy, I should say 'I want to go home.'"

Winifred gave him a quick glance. "What has happened?"

"Oh, everybody is ill at Crossroads. Beastly conditions. And they ought to have been corrected. Beulah's ill."

"The little bride?"

"Yes. And Eric is frantic. He has written me, asking me to come down. But Austin can't see it."

"Could you go for the day?"

"If I went for a day I should stay longer. There's everything to be done."

He switched away from the subject. "Crowd seems to have separated. Fox and Anne Warfield by the fountain. You and Tony here, and Eve and Pip as yet undiscovered."

"It is the day," Winifred decided, "all romance and roses. Even Tony and I were a-lovering when Eve found us."

Richard rose. "Tony, she wants to hold your hand. I'll get out."

Winifred laughed. "You'd better go and hold Eve's."

As he went away, Richard wondered if there was anything significant in her way of saying it.

Eve and Pip were in the enclosed space where Pan gleamed white against the dark cedars. Eve was seated on the sun-dial. Pip had lifted her there, and he stood leaning against it. Her lap was full of roses, and there were roses on her hat. The high note of color was repeated in the pink sunshade which lay open where the wind had wafted it to the feet of the piping Pan.

Pip straightened up as he saw Richard approaching. "There comes your eager lover, Eve. Give me a rose before he gets here."

"No."

"Why not?"

"I'm afraid."

"Of me?"

"No. But if I give you anything you'll take more. And I want to give everything to—Dicky."

He laughed a triumphant laugh. "I take all I can get. Give me a rose, Eve."

She yielded to his masterfulness. Out of the mass of bloom she chose a pink bud. "I shall give a red one to Dicky, so don't feel puffed up."

"I told you I should take what I could get, and Brooks isn't thinking of roses. Look at his face."

"I am sorry to be so late, Eve," Richard said, as he came up. "I am always apologizing, it seems to me."

"Little Boy Blue——! Dicky, what's the matter?"

"I want to go home." He tried to speak lightly—to follow her mood.

"Home—to Crossroads?"

"Yes."

"But why?"

"There's typhoid, and they don't know how to cope with it."

"Aren't there other doctors?"

"Yes, but not enough."

"Nonsense; what did they do before you came to the county? You must get rid of the feeling that you are so—important." She was angry. Little sparks were in her eyes.

"Don't worry, Eve. Austin doesn't want me to go. I can't get away. But it is on my mind."

"Put it off and come and help me with my roses. I gave Pip a bud. Are you jealous, Dicky?"

Still trying to follow her mood, he said, "You and the rest of the roses belong to me. Why should I care for one poor bud?"

She stuck a red rose in his coat, and when she had made her flowers into a nosegay, he lifted her down from the sun-dial. For a moment she clung to him. Meade had gone to rescue the sunshade which was blowing down the slope, and for the moment they were alone. "Dicky," she whispered, "I was horrid, but you mustn't go."

"I told you I couldn't, Eve."

Then Pip came back, and the three of them made their way to the fountain, picking up Winifred and Tony as they passed. Tea was served on the terrace, and a lot of other people motored out. There was much laughter and lightness—as if there were no trouble in the whole wide world.

Richard felt separated from it all by his mood, and when he went to the house to send a message for Austin to the hospital, he did not at once return to the terrace. He sought the great library. It was dim and quiet and he lay back in one of the big chairs and shut his eyes. The vision was before him of Pip leaning on the sun-dial against a rose-splashed background,

513

with Eve smiling down at him. It had come to him then that Pip should have married Eve. Pip would make her happy. The thing was all wrong in some way, but he could not see clearly how to make it right.

There was a sound in the room and he opened his eyes to find Marie-Louise on the ladder which gave access to the shelves of the great bookcases which lined the walls. She had not seen him, and she was singing softly to herself. In the dimness the color of her hair and gown gave a stained-glass effect against a background of high square east window.

Richard sat up. What was she singing?

"I think she was the most beautiful lady
That ever was in the West Country,
But beauty vanishes, beauty passes,
However rare, rare it be.
And when I am gone, who shall remember
That lady of the West Country? "
"Marie-Louise," he asked so suddenly that she nearly fell off of the shelves, "where did you learn that song?"

"From Mistress Anne."

"When you sing it do you think of—her?"

"Yes. Do you?"

"Yes."

Marie-Louise sat down on the top step of the ladder. "Dr. Dicky, may I ask a question?"

"Yes."

"Why didn't you fall in love with Anne?"

"I did."

"Oh! Then why didn't you marry her?"

"She is going to marry Geoffrey Fox."

Dead silence. Then, "Did she tell you?"

"No. He told me. Last spring."

"Before you came here?"

"Yes. That was the reason I came. I wanted to get away from everything that—spoke of her."

Marie-Louise slipped down from the ladder and came and stood beside him. "He told you," she said in a sharp whisper, "but there must be some mistake. She doesn't love him. She said that she didn't. I wonder why he lied."

There was nothing cold about her now. She was a fiery spark. "Only a—cad could do such a thing—and I thought—oh, Dr. Dicky, I thought he was a man——"

She flung herself at his feet like a stricken child. He went down to her. "Marie-Louise, stop. Sit up and tell me what's the matter."

She sat up. "I shall ask Anne. I shall go and get her and ask her."

He found himself calling after her, "Marie-Louise," but she was gone.

She came back presently, dragging the protesting Anne. "But Marie-Louise, what do you want of me?"

Richard, rising, said, "Please don't think I permitted this. I tried to stop her."

"I didn't want to be stopped," Marie-Louise told them. "I want to know whether you and Geoffrey Fox are going to be married."

Anne's cheeks were stained red. "Of course not. But it isn't anything to get so excited about, is it, Marie-Louise?"

"Yes, it is. He told Dr. Dicky that you were, and he lied. And I thought, oh, you know the wonderful things I thought about him, Mistress Anne."

Anne's arm went around the sad little nymph in green. "You must still think wonderful things of him. He was very unhappy, and desperate about his eyes. And it seemed to him that to assert a thing might make it come true."

"But you didn't love him?"

"Never, Marie-Louise."

And now Richard, ignoring the presence of Marie-Louise, ignoring everything but the question which beat against his heart, demanded:

"If you knew that he had told me this, why didn't you make things clear?"

"When I might have made things clear—you were engaged to Eve."

She turned abruptly from him to Marie-Louise. "Run back to your poet, dear heart. He is waiting for the book that you were going to bring him. And remember that you are not to sit in judgment. You are to be eyes for him, and light."

It was a sober little nymph in green who marched away with her book. Geoffrey sat on the stone bench a little withdrawn from the others. His lean face, straining toward the house, relaxed as she came within his line of vision.

"You were a long time away," he said, and made a place for her beside him, and she sat down and opened her book.

And now, back in the dim library, Anne and Richard!

"I stayed," she said, "because they were speaking out there of Crossroads. I have had a letter, too, from Sulie. She says that the situation is desperate."

"Yes. They need me. And I ought to go. They are my people. I feel that in a sense I belong to them—as my grandfather belonged."

"Do you mean that if you go now you will stay?"

"I am not sure. The future must take care of itself."

"Your mother would be glad if your decision finally came to that."

"Yes. And I should be glad. But this time I shall not go for my mother's sake alone. Something deeper is drawing me. I can't quite analyze it. It is a call"—he laughed a little—"such as men describe who enter the ministry,—an irresistible impulse, as if I were to find something there that I had lost in the city."

She held out her hand to him. "Do you know the name I had for you when you were at Crossroads?"

"No."

"I called you St. Michael—because it always seemed to me that you carried a sword."

He tightened his grip on the little hand. "Some day I shall hope to justify the name; I don't deserve it now."

Her eyes came up to him. "You'll fight to win," she said, softly.

He did not want to let her go. But there was no other way. But when she had joined the others on the terrace he made a wide detour of the garden, and wandered down to the river.

It was not a singing river, but to-day it seemed to have a song, "Go back, go back," it said; "you have seen the world, you have seen the world."

And when he had listened for a little while he climbed the hill to tell Austin and to tell—Eve.

CHAPTER XXII

In Which Anne Weighs the People of Two Worlds.

"Richard!"

"Yes, mother, I'm here. Austin thinks I am crazy, and Eve won't speak to me. But—I came. And to think you have turned the house into a hospital!"

"It seemed the only thing to do. François' mother had no one to take care of her—and there were others, and the house is big."

"You are the biggest thing in it. Mother, if I ever pray to a saint, it will be one with gray hair in a nurse's cap and apron, and with shining eyes."

"They are shining because you are here, Richard."

Cousin Sulie, in the door, broke down and cried, "Oh, we've prayed for it."

They clung to him, the two little growing-old women, who had wanted him, and who had worked without him.

He had no words for them, for he could not speak with steadiness. But in that moment he knew that he should never go back to Austin. That he should live and die in the home of his fathers. And that his work was here.

He tried, a little later, to make a joke of their devotion. "Mother, you and Cousin Sulie mustn't. I shall need a body-guard to protect me. You'll spoil me with softness and ease."

"I shall buckle on your armor soon enough," she told him. "Did Eric meet you at the station?"

"Yes, I shall go straight to Beulah's. I stopped in to see old Peter before I came up. I can pull him through, but I shall have to have some nurses."

And now big Ben, at an even trot, carried Richard to the Playhouse. Toby, mad with gladness at the return of his master, raced ahead.

Up in the pretty pink and white room lay Beulah. No longer plump and blooming, but wasted and wan with dry lips and hollow eyes.

Eric had said to Richard, "If she dies I shall die, too."

"She is not going to die."

And now he said it again, cheerfully, to the wasted figure in the bed. "I have come to make you well, Beulah."

But Beulah was not at all sure that she wanted to be—well. She was too tired. She was tired of Eric, tired of her mother, tired of taking medicine, tired of having to breathe.

So she shut her eyes and turned away.

Eric sat by the bed. "Dear heart," he said, "it is Dr. Dicky."

But she did not open her eyes.

In the days that followed Richard fought to make his words come true. He felt that if Beulah died it would, in some way, be his fault. He was aware that this was a morbid state of mind, but he could not help the way he felt. Beulah's life would be the price of his self-respect.

But it was not only for Beulah's life that he fought, but for the lives of others. He had nurses up from Baltimore and down from New York. He had experts to examine wells and springs and other sources of water supply. He had a motor car that he might cover the miles quickly, using old Ben only for short distances. Toby, adapting himself to the car, sat on the front seat with the wind in his face, drunk with the excitement of it.

When Nancy spoke of the expense to which Richard was putting himself, he said, "I have saved something, mother, and Eric and the rest can pay."

Surely in those days St. Michael needed his sword, for the fight was to the finish. Night and day the battle waged. Richard went from bedside to bedside, coming always last to Beulah in the shadowed pink and white room at the Playhouse.

There were nurses now, but Eric Brand would not be turned out. "Every minute that I am away from her," he told Richard, "I'm afraid. It seems as if when I am in sight of her I can hold her—back."

So, night after night, Richard found him in the chair by Beulah's bed, his face shaded by his hand, rousing only when Beulah stirred, to smile at her.

But Beulah did not smile back. She moaned a little now and then, and sometimes talked of things that never were on sea or land. There was a flowered chintz screen in the corner of the room and she peopled it with strange creatures, and murmured of them now and then, until the nurse covered the screen with a white sheet, which seemed to blot it out of Beulah's mind forever.

There was always a pot of coffee boiling in the kitchen for the young doctor, and Eric would go down with him and they would drink and talk, and all that Eric said led back to Beulah.

"If there was only something that I could do for her," he said; "if I could go out and work until I dropped, I should feel as if I were helping. But just to sit there and see her—fade."

Again he said, "I had always thought of our living—never of dying. There can be no future for me without her."

So it was for Eric's future as well as for Beulah's life that Richard strove. He grew worn and weary, but he never gave up.

Night after night, day after day, from house to house he went, along the two roads and up into the hills. Everywhere he met an anxious welcome. Where the conditions were unfavorable, he transferred the patient to Crossroads, where Nancy and Sulie and Milly and a trio of nurses formed an enthusiastic hospital staff.

The mother of little François was the first patient that Richard lost. She was tired and overworked, and she felt that it was good to fall asleep. Afterward Richard, with the little boy in his arms, went out and sat where they could look over the river and talk together.

"I told her that you were to stay with me, François."

517

"And she was glad?"

"Yes. I need a little lad in my office, and when I take the car you can ride with me."

And thus it came about that little François, a sober little François, with a band of black about his arm, became one of the Crossroads household, and was made much of by the women, even by black Milly, who baked cookies for him and tarts whenever he cried for his mother.

Cousin Sulie rose nobly to meet the new demands upon her. "It is a feeling I never had before," she said to Richard, as she helped him pack his bag before going on his rounds, "that what I am doing is worth while. I know I should have felt it when I was darning stockings, but I didn't."

She gloried in the professional aspect which she gave to everything. She installed little François at a small table in the Garden Room. He answered the telephone and wrote the messages on slips of paper which he laid on the doctor's desk. Cousin Sulie at another table saw the people who came in Richard's absence.

"Nancy can read to the patients up-stairs and cut flowers for them and cook nice things for them," she confided, "but I like to be down here when the children come in to ask for medicine, and when the mothers come to find out what they shall feed the convalescents. Richard, I never heard anything like their—hungriness—when they are getting well."

Beulah, emerging slowly from among the shadows, began to think of things to eat. She didn't care about anything else. She didn't care for Eric's love, or her mother's gladness, or Richard's cheerfulness, or the nurses' sympathy. She cared only to think of every kind of food that she had ever liked in her whole life, and to ask if she might have it.

"But, dear heart, the doctor doesn't think that you should," Eric would protest.

She would cry, weakly, "You don't love me, or you would let me."

She begged and begged, and at last he couldn't stand it.

"You are starving her," he told the nurses fiercely.

They referred him to the doctor.

Eric telephoned Richard.

"My dear fellow," was the response, "her appetite is a sign that she is getting well."

"But she is so hungry."

"So are they all. I have to steel my heart against them, especially the children. And half of the convalescents are reading cook books."

"Cook books!"

"Yes. In that way they get a meal by proxy. I tell them to pick out the things they are going to have when they are well enough to eat all they want. Their choice ranges from Welsh rarebits to plum puddings."

He laughed, but Eric saw nothing funny in the matter. "I can't bear to see her—suffer."

Richard was sobered at once. "Don't think that I am not sympathetic. But—Brand, I don't dare-feel. If I did, I should go to pieces."

Slowly the weeks passed. Besides François' mother, two of Richard's patients died. Slowly the pendulum of time swung the rest of the sick ones toward recovery. Nancy and Sulie and Milly changed the rooms at Crossroads back to their original uses. The nurses, no longer needed, packed their competent bags, and departed. Beulah at the Playhouse had her first square meal, and smiled back at Eric.

The strain had told fearfully on Richard. Yet he persisted in his efforts long after it seemed that the countryside was safe. He tried to pack into twelve short weeks what he would normally have done in twelve long months. He spurred his fellow physicians to increased activities, he urged authorities to unprecedented exertions. He did the work of two men and sometimes of three. And he was so exhausted that he felt that if ever his work was finished he would sleep for a million years.

It was in September that he began to wonder how he would square things up with Eve. At first she had written to him blaming him for his desertion. But not for a moment did she take it seriously. "You'll be coming back, Dicky," was the burden of her song. He wrote hurried pleasant letters which were to some extent bulletins of the day's work. If Eve was not satisfied she consoled herself with the thought that he was tearingly busy and terribly tired.

In her last letter she had said, "Austin doesn't know what to do without you. He told Pip that you were his right hand."

Austin had said more than that to Anne. He had found her one hot day by the fountain. Nancy had written to her of the death of François' mother. The letter was in her hand.

Austin had also had a letter. "Brooks is a fool. He writes that he is going to stay."

Anne shook her head. "He is not a fool," she said; "he is doing what he had to do. You would know if you had ever lived at Crossroads. Why, the Brooks family belongs there, and the Brooks doctors."

"So you have encouraged him?" Austin said.

"I have had nothing to do with it. I haven't heard from him since he left, and I haven't written."

"And you think he is—right to—bury—himself?"

Anne sat very still, her hands folded quietly. Her calm eyes were on the golden fish which swam in the waters at the base of the fountain.

"I am not sure," she said; "it all has so much to do with—old traditions—and inherited feelings—and ideals. He could be just as useful here, but he would never be happy. You can't imagine how they look up to him down there. And here he looked up to you."

"Then you think I didn't give him a free hand?"

"No. But there he is a Brooks of Crossroads. And it isn't because he wants the honor of it that he has gone back, but because the responsibility rests upon him to make the community all that it ought to be. And he can't shirk it."

"Eve Chesley says that he is tied to his mother's apron strings."

"She doesn't understand, I do. I sometimes feel that way about the Crossroads school—as if I had shirked something to have—a good time."

"But you have had a good time."

"Yes, you have all been wonderful to me," her smile warmed him, "but you won't think that I am ungrateful when I say that there was something in my life in the little school which carried me—higher—than this."

"Higher? What do you mean?"

"I was a leader down there. And a force. The children looked to me for something that I could give and which the teacher they have isn't giving. She just teaches books, and I tried to teach them something of life, and love of country, and love of God."

519

"But here you have Marie-Louise, and you know how grateful we are for what you have done for her."

"I have only developed what was in her. What a flaming little genius she is!"

"With a poem accepted by an important magazine, and Fox believing that she can write more of them."

Anne spoke quietly: "And now I am really not needed. Marie-Louise can go on alone."

He stopped her. "We want you to stay—my wife wants you—Marie-Louise can't do without you. And I want you to get Brooks back."

She looked her amazement. "Get him back?"

"He will come if you ask it. I am not blind. Eve Chesley is. The things she says make him stubborn. But you could call him back. You could call to life anything in any man if you willed it. You are inspirational—a star to light the way."

His voice was shaken. After a pause he went on: "Will you help me to get Brooks back?"

She shook her head. "I shall not try. He is among his own people. He has found his place."

Yet now that Richard was gone, Anne found herself missing him more than she dared admit. She was, for the first time, aware that the knowledge that she should see him now and then had kept her from loneliness which might otherwise have assailed her. The thought that she might meet him had added zest to her engagements. His week-ends at Rose Acres had been the goal toward which her thoughts had raced.

And now the great house was empty because of his absence. The city was empty—because he had left it—forever. She had no hope that he would come back. Crossroads had claimed him. He had, indeed, come into his own.

When the rest of his friends spoke of him, praised or blamed, she was silent. Geoffrey Fox, who came often, complained, "You are always sitting off in a corner somewhere with your work, putting in a million stitches, when I want you to talk."

"You can talk to Marie-Louise. She is your ardent disciple. She burns candles at your altar."

"She is a charming—child."

"She is more than that. When her poem was accepted she cried over the letter. She thinks that she couldn't have done it except for your help and criticism."

"She will do more than she has done."

When Marie-Louise joined them, Anne was glad to see Geoffrey's protective manner, as if he wanted to be nice to the child who had cried.

She had to listen to much criticism of Richard. When Eve and the Dutton-Ames dined one night in the early fall at Rose Acres, Richard's quixotic action formed the theme of their discourse.

Eve was very frank. "Somebody ought to tie Dicky down. His head is in the clouds."

Marie-Louise flashed: "I like people whose heads are in the clouds. He is doing a wonderful thing and a wise thing—and we are all acting as if it were silly."

Anne wanted to hug Marie-Louise, and with heightened color she listened to Winifred's defense.

"I think we should all like to feel that we are equal to it—to give up money and fame—for the thing that—called."

"There is no better or bigger work for him there than here," Austin proclaimed.

"No," Winifred agreed, and her eyes were bright, "but it is because he is giving up something which the rest of us value that I like him. Renunciation isn't fashionable, but it is stimulating."

"The usual process is to 'grab and git,'" her husband sustained her. "We always like to see some one who isn't bitten by the modern bacillus."

After dinner Anne left them and made her way down in the darkness to the river. The evening boat was coming up, starred with lights, its big search-light sweeping the shores. When it passed, the darkness seemed deeper. The night was cool, and Anne, wrapped in a white cloak, was like a ghost among the shadows. Far up on the terrace she could see the big house, and hear the laughter. She felt much alone. Those people were not her people. Her people were of Nancy's kind, well-born and well bred, but not smart in the modern sense. They were quiet folk, liking their homes, their friends, their neighbors. They were not so rich that they were separated by their money from those about them. They had time to read and to think. They were perhaps no better than the people in the big house on top of the terrace, but they lived at a more leisurely pace, and it seemed to her at this moment that they got more out of life.

She wanted more than anything in the world to be to-night with that little group at Crossroads, to meet Cousin Sulie's sparkling glance, to sit at Nancy's knee, to hear Richard's big laugh, as he came in and found the women waiting for the news of the outside world that he would bring.

She knew that she could have the little school if she asked for it. But a sense of dignity restrained her. She could not go back now. It would seem to the world that she had followed Richard. Well, her heart followed him, but the world did not know that.

She heard voices. Geoffrey and Marie-Louise were at the river's edge.

"It is as if there were just the two of us in the whole wide world," Marie-Louise was saying. "That's what I like about the darkness. It seems to shut everybody out."

"But suppose the darkness followed you into the day," Geoffrey said, "suppose that for you there were no light?"

A rim of gold showed above the blackness of the Jersey hills.

"Oh," Marie-Louise exulted, "look at the moon. In a moment there will be light, and you thought you were in the dark."

"You mean that it is an omen?"

"Yes."

"What a small and comfortable person you are," Geoffrey said, and now Anne could see the two of them silhouetted against the brightening sky, one tall and slim, the other slim and short. They walked on, and she heard their voices faintly.

"Do I really make you comfortable, Geoffrey Fox?"

"You make me more than that, Marie-Louise."

CHAPTER XXIII

In Which Richard Rides Alone.

"Eve."

"Yes, Pip."

"Can't you see that if he cared Richard would do the thing that pleased you—that New York would be Paradise if you were in it?"

"Why shouldn't Crossroads be Paradise to me—with him?"

"It couldn't be."

"I am going to make it. I talked it over last night with Aunt Maude. She's an old dear. And I shall be the Lady of the Manor. If Dicky won't come to New York, I'll bring New York down to him."

"It can't be done. And it's going to fail."

"What is going to fail?"

"Your marriage. If you are mad enough to marry Brooks."

She mused. "Pip, do you remember the fat Armenian?"

"At Coney? Yes."

"He said that—I had reached for something beyond my grasp. That my fingers would touch it, but that it would soar always above me."

"Sounds as if Brooks were some fat sort of a bird. I can't think of him as soaring. I should call him the cock that crowed at Crossroads. Oh, it's all rot, Eve, this idea that love makes things equal. I went to the Hippodrome not long ago and saw 'Pinafore.' Our fathers and mothers raved over it. But that was a sentimental age, and Gilbert poked fun at them. He made the simple sailor a captain in the end, so that Josephine shouldn't wash dishes and cook smelly things in pots and hang out the family wash. But your hero balks and won't be turned into a millionaire. If you were writing a book you might make it work out to your satisfaction, but you can't twist life to the happy ending."

"I shall try, Pip."

"In Heaven's name, Eve! It is sheer obstinacy. If everybody wanted you to marry Brooks, you'd want to marry me. But because Aunt Maude and Winifred and I, and a lot of others know that you shouldn't, you have set your heart on it."

She flashed her eyes at him. "Is it obstinacy, Pip, I wonder? Do you know I rather think I am going to like it."

Her letters said something of the sort to Richard. "I shall love it down there. But you must let me have my own way with the house and garden. Don't you think I shall make a charming chatelaine, Dicky, dear?"

He had a sense of relief in her unexpected acquiescence in his decision. If she had objected, he would have felt as if he had turned his back not only on the work that he hated but on the woman he had promised to marry. It would have looked that way to others. Yet no matter how it had looked, he could not have done differently. The call had been insistent, and the deeps of his nature been stirred.

He was thinking of it all as one morning in October he rode to the Playhouse on big Ben to see Beulah.

Dismounting at the gate, he followed the path which led to the kitchen. Beulah was not there, and, searching, he saw her under an old apple tree at the end of the garden. She wore a checked blue apron, stiffly starched, and she was holding it up by the corners. A black cat and three sable kittens frisked at her feet.

Some one was dropping red apples carefully into the apron, some one who laughed as he swung himself down and tipped Beulah's chin up with his hand and kissed her. Richard felt a lump in his throat. It was such a homely little scene, but it held a meaning that love had never held for himself and Eve.

Eric untied Beulah's apron string, and carrying the apples in this improvised bag, with his arm about her waist sustaining her, they came down the walk.

"This is Beulah's pet tree. When she was sick she asked for apples and apples and apples."

Beulah, sinking her little white teeth into a red one, nodded. "It is perfectly wonderful," she said when she was able to speak, "how good everything tastes, and I can't get enough."

Eric pinched her cheek. "Pretty good color, doctor. We'll have them matching the apples yet."

Richard wanted to ask Eric about the dogs. "Some of my friends are coming down to-morrow for the Middlefield hunt."

"If they start old Pete there'll be some sport," Eric said.

"I shall be half sorry if they do," Richard told him. "I am always afraid I shall lose him out of my garden. He is a part of the place, like the box hedge and the cedars."

He said it lightly, but he meant it. He had hunting blood in his veins, and he loved the horses and the dogs. He loved the cold crisp air, and the excitement of the chase. But what he did not love was the hunted animal, doubling on its tracks, pursued, panting, torn to pieces by the hounds.

"Old Pete deserved to live and die among the hills," Beulah said. "Is Miss Chesley coming down?"

"Yes, and a lot of others. They will put up at the club. Mother and Sulie aren't up to entertaining a crowd."

He wanted Eric's dogs for ducks. Dutton-Ames and one or two others did not ride to hounds, and would come to Bower's in the morning.

As he rode away, he was conscious that as soon as his back was turned Eric's arm would again be about Beulah, and Beulah's head would be on Eric's shoulder. And that he would lift her over the threshold as they went in.

That afternoon Richard motored over to the Country Club to welcome Eve. She laughed at his little car. "I'd rather see you on big Ben than in that."

"Ben can't carry me fast enough."

"Don't expect me to ride in it, Dicky."

"Why not?"

"Oh, Dicky, can you ask?"

Meade's great limousine which had brought them seemed to stare the little car out of countenance. But Richard refused to be embarrassed by the contrast. "She's a snug little craft, and she has carried me miles. What would Meade's car do on these roads and in the hills?"

Pip had come up and as the two men stood together Eve's quick eye contrasted them. There was no doubt of Richard's shabbiness. His old riding coat was much the worse for wear. He had on the wrong kind of hat and the wrong kind of shoes, and he seemed most aggravatingly not to care. He was to ride to-morrow one of the horses which had been sent down from Pip's stables. He hadn't even a proper mount!

Pip, on the other hand, was perfectly groomed. He was shining and immaculate from the top of his smooth head to the heel of his boots. And he wore an air of gay inconsequence. It seemed to Eve that Richard's shoulders positively sagged with responsibility.

There was a dance at the club that night. Richard, coming in, saw Eve in Pip's arms. They were a graceful pair, and their steps matched perfectly. Eve was all in white, wide-skirted, and her shoulders and arms were bare. She had on gold slippers, and her hair was gold. Richard had a sense of discomfort as he watched them. He was going to marry her, yet she was letting Pip look at her like that. His cheeks burned. What was Pip saying? Was he making love to Eve?

523

He had tried to meet the situation with dignity. Yet there was no dignity in Eve's willingness to let Pip follow her. To speak of it would, however, seem to crystallize his feeling into a complaint.

Hence when he danced with her later, he tried to respond to the lightness and brightness of her mood. He tried to measure up to all the requirements of his position as an engaged man and as a lover. But he did not find it easy.

When he reached home that night, he found little François awake, and ready to ask questions about the hunt.

"Do you think they will get him?" he challenged Richard, coming in small pink pajamas to the door of the young doctor's room.

 "Get who?"

"Old Pete."

"He is too cunning."

"Will he come through here?"

"Perhaps."

"I shall stick my fingers in my ears and shut my eyes. Are you going to ride with them?"

"Yes."

"You won't let them kill old Pete, will you?"

"Not if I can help it."

After that, the child was more content. But when Richard was at last in bed, François came again across the hall, and stood on the threshold in the moonlight. "It would be dreadful if it was his last night."

"Whose last night, François?" sleepily.

"Old Pete's."

"Don't worry. And you must go to bed, François."

Richard waked to a glorious morning and to the hunt. Pink coats dotted the countryside. It seemed as if half the world was on its way to the club. Richard, as he mounted one of Pip's hunters, a powerful bay, felt the thrill of it all, and when he joined Eve and her party he found them in an uproarious mood.

Presently over hills streamed a picturesque procession—the hounds in the lead, the horses following with riders whose pink blazed against the green of the pines, against the blue of the river, against the fainter blue of the skies above.

And oh, the music of it, the sound of the horn, the bell-like baying, the thud of flying feet!

Then, ahead of them all, as the hounds broke into full cry, a silent, swift shadow—the old fox, Pete!

At first he ran easily. He had done it so often. He had thrown them off after a chase which had stirred his blood. He would throw them off again.

In leisurely fashion he led them. As the morning advanced, however, he found himself hard pushed. He was driven from one stronghold to another. Tireless, the hounds followed and followed, until at last he knew himself weary, seeking sanctuary.

He came with confidence to Crossroads. Beyond the garden was his den. Once within and the thing would end.

Across the lawn he loped, and little François, anxious at the window, spied him. "Will he get to it, will he get to it?" he said to Nancy, his small face white with the fear of what might happen, "and when he gets there will he be safe?"

"Yes," she assured him; "and when they have run him aground, they will ride away."

But they did not ride away. It happened that those who were in the lead were unaware of the tradition of the country, and so they began to dig him out, this old king of foxes, who had felt himself secure in his castle!

They set the dogs at one end, and fetched mattocks and spades from the stable.

Pip and Eve were among them. Pip directing, Eve mad with the excitement of it all.

Little François, watching, clung to Nancy. "Oh, they can't, they mustn't!"

She soothed him, and at last sent Milly out, but they would not listen.

Nancy and Sulie were as white now as little François. "Oh, where is Richard?" Nancy said. "It is like murder to do a thing like that. It is bad enough in the open—but like a rat—in a trap."

The big bay was charging down the hill with Richard yelling at the top of his voice. The bay had proved troublesome and had bolted in the wrong direction, but Richard had brought him back to Crossroads just in time!

François screamed. "It is Dr. Dicky. He'll make them stop. He'll make them."

He did make them. His voice rang sharply. "Get the dogs away, Meade, and stop digging."

They were too eager at first to heed him. Eve hung on his arm, but he shook her off. "We don't like things like that down here. Our foxes are too rare."

It was a motley group which gathered later at the club for the hunt breakfast. There were fox-hunting farmers born on the land, of sturdy yeoman stock, and careless of form. There were the lords of newly acquired acres, who rode carefully on little saddles with short stirrups in the English style.

There were the descendants of the great old planters, daring, immensely picturesque. There was Eve's crowd, trained for the sport, and at their ease.

A big fire burned on the hearth. A copper-covered table held steaming dishes. Another table groaned under its load of cold meats and cheese. On an ancient mahogany sideboard were various bottles and bowls of punch.

Old songs were sung and old stories told. Brinsley beamed on everybody with his face like a round full moon. There were other round and red-faced gentlemen who, warmed by the fire and the punch, twinkled like unsteady old stars.

Eve was the pivotal center of all the hilarity. She sat on the table and served the punch. Her coat was off, and in her silk blouse and riding breeches she was like a lovely boy. The men crowded around her. Pip, always at her elbow, delivered an admiring opinion. "No one can hold a candle to you, Eve."

Richard was out of it. He sat quietly in a corner with David, old Jo at their feet, and watched the others. Eve had been angry with him for his interference at Crossroads. "I didn't know you were a molly-coddle, Dicky," she had said, "and I wanted the brush."

She was punishing him now by paying absolutely no attention to him. She was punishing him, too, by making herself conspicuous, which she knew he hated. The scene was not to his liking. The women of his household, Nancy, Sulie and Anne, had had a fastidious sense of what belonged to them as ladies. Eve had not that sense. As he sat there, it occurred to him that things were moving to some stupendous climax. He and Eve couldn't go on like this.

Far up in the hills a man was in danger of bleeding to death. He had cut himself while butchering a pig. The doctor was called.

Richard, making his way through the shouting and singing crowd which surrounded Eve, told her, "I shall have to go for a little while. There's a man hurt. I'll be back in an hour."

She looked down at him with hard eyes. "We are going to ride cross-country—to the Ridge. You might meet us there, if you care to come."

"You know I care."

"I'm not sure. You don't show it. I—I am tired of never having a lover—Dicky."

It was a wonderful afternoon. The heavy frost had chilled the air, the leaves were red, and the sky was blue—and there was green and brown and gold. But Richard as he rode up in the hills had no eyes for the color, no ears for the song beaten out by big Ben's hoofs. The vision which held him was of Eve in the midst of that shouting circle.

The man who had cut himself was black. He was thin and tall and his hair was gray. He had worked hard all of his life, but he had never worked out of himself the spirit of joyous optimism.

"I jes' tole 'um," he said, "to send for Dr. Brooks, and he'd beat the devil gettin' to me."

When Richard reached the Ridge, a flash of scarlet at once caught his eye. On the slope below Eve, far ahead of Meade, in a mad race, was making for a grove at the edge of the Crossroads boundaries. She was a reckless rider, and Richard held his breath as she took fences, leaped hurdles, and cleared the flat wide stream.

As she came to the grove she turned and waved triumphantly to Pip. For a moment she made a vivid and brilliant figure in her scarlet against the green. Then the little wood swallowed her up.

Pip came pounding after, and Richard, spurring his big Ben to unaccustomed efforts, circled the grove to meet them on the other side.

But they did not come. From the point where he finally drew up he could command a view of both sides of the slope. Unless they had turned back, they were still in the grove.

Then out of the woods came Pip, running. He had something in his arms.

"It is Eve," he said, panting; "there was a hole and her horse stumbled. I found her."

Poor honest Pip! As if she were his own, he held her now in his arms. Her golden head, swung up to his shoulder, rested heavily above his heart. Her eyes were shut.

Richard's practiced eye saw at once her state of collapse. He jumped from his horse. "Give her to me, Meade," he said, "and get somebody's car as quickly as you can."

And now the tiger in Pip flashed out. "She's mine," he said, breathing hoarsely. "I love her. You go and get the car."

"Man," the young doctor said steadily, "this isn't the time to quarrel. Lay her down, then, and let me have a look at her."

He had his little case of medicines, and he hunted for something to bring her back to consciousness. Pip, pale and shaken, folded his coat under her head and chafed her hands.

Presently life seemed to sweep through her body. She shivered and moved.

Her eyes came open. "What happened?"

"You fell from your horse. Meade found you."

There were no bones broken, but the shock had been great. She lay very still and white against Pip's arm.

Richard closed his medicine case and rose. He stood looking down at her.

"Better, old lady?"

"Yes, Dicky."

He spoke a little awkwardly. "I'll ride down if you don't mind, and come back for you in Meade's car." His eyes did not meet hers.

As he plunged over the hill on his heavy old horse, her puzzled gaze followed him. Then she gave a queer little laugh. "Is he running away from me, Pip?"

"I told him you were—mine," the big man burst out.

"You told him? Oh, Pip, what did he say?"

"That this was not the time to talk about it."

She lay very still thinking it out. Then she turned on his arm. "Good old Pip," she said. He drew her up to him, and she said it again, with that queer little laugh, "Good old Pip, you're the best ever. And all this time I have been looking straight over your blessed old head at—Dicky."

CHAPTER XXIV

In Which St. Michael Finds Love in a Garden.

The flowers in Marie-Louise's bowl were lilacs. And Marie-Louise, sitting up in bed, writing verses, was in pale mauve. Her windows were wide open, and the air from the river, laden with fragrance, swept through the room.

The big house had been closed all winter. Austin had elected to spend the season in Florida, and had taken all of his household with him, including Anne. He had definitely retired from practice when Richard left him. "I can't carry it on alone, and I don't want to break in anybody else," he had said, and had turned the whole thing over to one of his colleagues.

But April had brought him back to "Rose Acres" in time for the lilacs, and Marie-Louise, uplifted by the fact that Geoffrey Fox was at that very moment finishing his book in the balcony room, had decided that lilacs in the silver bowl should express the ecstatic state of her mind.

Anne, coming in at noon, asked, "What are you writing?"

"Vers libre. This is called, 'To Dr. Dicky, Dinging.'"

"What a subject, and you call it poetry?"

"Why not? Isn't he coming to dinner for the first time since—he left New York, and since he broke off with Eve, and since—a lot of other things—and isn't it an important occasion, Mistress Anne?"

Anne ignored the question. "What have you written?"

"Only the outline. He comes—has caviar, and his eyes are on the queen. He drinks his soup—and dreams. He has fish— and a vision of the future; rhapsodies with the roast," she twinkled; "do you like it?"

"As far as it goes."

"It goes very far, and you know it. And you are blushing."

"I am not."

"You are. Look in the glass. Mistress Anne, aren't you glad that Eve is married?"

"Yes," honestly, "and that she is happy."

"Pip was made for her. I loved him at Palm Beach, adoring her, didn't you?"

"Yes." Anne's mind went back to it. The marriage had followed immediately upon the announcement of the broken engagement. People had pitied poor young Dr. Brooks. But Anne had not. One does not pity a man who, having been bound, is free.

He had written to her a half dozen times during the winter, friendly letters with news of Crossroads, and now that she was again at Rose Acres, he was coming up.

The spring day was bright. Rich with possibilities. "Marie-Louise, don't stay in bed. Nobody has a right to be in the house on such a day as this."

But Marie-Louise wouldn't be moved. "I want to finish my verses."

So Anne went out alone into the garden. It was ablaze with spring bloom, the river was blue, and Pan piped on his reeds. Geoffrey waved to her from his balcony. She waved back, then went for a walk alone. She returned to have tea on the terrace. The day seemed interminable. The hour for dinner astonishingly remote.

At last, however, it was time to dress. The gown that she chose was of pale rose, heavily weighted with silver. It hung straight and slim. Her slippers were of silver, and she still wore her dark hair in the smooth swept-up fashion which so well became her.

Richard, seeing her approach down the length of the big drawing-room where he stood with Austin, was conscious of a sense of shock. It was as if he had expected that she would come to him in her old blue serge, or in the little white gown with the many ruffles. That she came in such elegance made her seem—alien. Like Eve. Oh, where was the Anne of yesterday?

Even when she spoke to him, when her hand was in his, when she walked beside him on the way to the dining-room, he had this sense of strangeness, as if the girl in rose-color was not the girl of whom he had dreamed through all the days since he had known that he was not to marry Eve.

The winter had been a busy one for him, but satisfying in the sense that he was at last in his rightful place. He had come into his own. He had no more doubts that his work was wisely chosen. But his life was as yet unfinished. To complete it, he had felt that he must round out his days with the woman he loved.

But now that he was here, he saw her fitted to her new surroundings as a jewel fitted to a golden setting. And she liked lovely things, she liked excitement, and the nearness of the great metropolis. There were men who had wanted to marry her. Marie-Louise had told him that in a gay little letter which she had sent from the South.

As he reviewed it now disconsolately, he reminded himself that he had never had any real reason to know that Anne cared for him. There had been a flash of the eye, a few grave words, a break in her voice, his answered letters; but a woman might dole out these small favors to a friend.

Thus from caviar to soup, and from soup to roast, he contradicted Marie-Louise's conception of his state of mind. Fear and doubt, discouragement, a touch of despair, these carried him as far as the salad.

And then he heard Austin's voice speaking. "So you are really contented at Crossroads, Brooks?"

"Yes. I wish you would come down and let me show you some of the things I am doing. A bit primitive, perhaps, in the light of your larger experience. But none the less effective, and interesting."

Austin shrugged. "I can't imagine anything but martyrdom in such a life—for me. What do you do with yourself when you are not working—with no theaters—opera—restaurants—excitements?"

"We get along rather well without them—except for an occasional trip to town."

"But you need such things," dogmatically; "a man can't live out of the world and not—degenerate."

"He may live in it, and degenerate." Anne was speaking. Her cheeks were as pink as her gown. She leaned a little forward. "You don't know all that they have at Crossroads, and Dr. Brooks is too polite to tell you how poor New York seems to those of us who—know."

"Poor?" Richard had turned to her, his face illumined.

"Isn't it? Think of the things you have that New York doesn't know of. A singing river—this river doesn't sing, or if it does nobody would have time to listen. And Crossroads has a bell on its school that calls to the countryside. City children are not called by a bell—that's why they are all alike—they ride on trolleys and watch the clocks. My little pupils ran across the fields and down the road, and hurried when I rang for them, and came in—rosy."

She was rosy herself as she recounted it.

"Oh, we have a lot of things—the bridge with the lights—and the road up to the Ridge—and Diogenes. Dr. Austin, you should see Diogenes."

She laughed, and they all laughed with her, but back of Richard's laugh there was an emotion which swept him on and up to heights beyond anything that he had ever hoped or dreamed.

After that, he could hardly wait for the ending of the dinner, hardly wait to get away from them all, and out under the stars.

It was when they were at last alone on the steps above the fountain, with the garden pouring all of its fragrance down upon them, that he said, "I should not have dared ask it if you had not said what you said."

"Oh, St. Michael, St. Michael," she whispered, "where was your courage?"

"But in this gown, this lovely gown, you didn't look like anything that I could—have. I am only a country doctor, Anne."

"Only my beloved—Richard."

They clung together, these two who had found Love in the garden. But they had found more than Love. They had found the meaning for all that Richard had done, and for all that Anne would do. And that which they had found they would never give up!

529

The Trumpeter Swan

CHAPTER I
A MAJOR AND TWO MINORS
I

It had rained all night, one of the summer rains that, beginning in a thunder-storm in Washington, had continued in a steaming drizzle until morning.

There were only four passengers in the sleeper, men all of them—two in adjoining sections in the middle of the car, a third in the drawing-room, a fourth an intermittent occupant of a berth at the end. They had gone to bed unaware of the estate or circumstance of their fellow-travellers, and had waked to find the train delayed by washouts, and side-tracked until more could be learned of the condition of the road.

The man in the drawing-room shone, in the few glimpses that the others had of him, with an effulgence which was dazzling. His valet, the intermittent sleeper in the end berth, was a smug little soul, with a small nose which pointed to the stars. When the door of the compartment opened to admit breakfast there was the radiance of a brocade dressing-gown, the shine of a sleek head, the staccato of an imperious voice.

Randy Paine, long and lank, in faded khaki, rose, leaned over the seat of the section in front of him and drawled, "'It is not raining rain to me—it's raining roses—down——'"

A pleasant laugh, and a deep voice, "Come around here and talk to me. You're a Virginian, aren't you?"

"By the grace of God and the discrimination of my ancestors," young Randolph, as he dropped into the seat opposite the man with the deep voice, saluted the dead and gone Paines.

"Then you know this part of it?"

"I was born here. In this county. It is bone of my bone and flesh of my flesh," there was a break in the boy's voice which robbed the words of grandiloquence.

"Hum—you love it? Yes? And I am greedy to get away. I want wider spaces——"

"California?"

"Yes. Haven't seen it for three years. I thought when the war was over I might. But I've got to be near Washington, it seems. The heat drove me out, and somebody told me it would be cool in these hills——"

"It is, at night. By day we're not strenuous."

"I like to be strenuous. I hate inaction."

He moved restlessly. There was a crutch by his side. Young Paine noticed it for the first time. "I hate it."

He had a strong frame, broad shoulders and thin hips. One placed him immediately as a man of great physical force. Yet there was the crutch. Randy had seen other men, broad-shouldered, thin-hipped, who had come to worse than crutches. He did not want to think of them. He had escaped without a scratch. He did not believe that he had lacked courage, and there was a decoration to prove that he had not. But when he thought of those other men, he had no sense of his own valor. He had given so little and they had given so much.

Yet it was not a thing to speak of. He struck, therefore, a note to which he knew the other might respond.

"If you haven't been here before, you'll like the old places."

"I am going to one of them."

"Which?"

"King's Crest."

A moment's silence. Then, "That's my home. I have lived there all my life."

The lame man gave him a sharp glance. "I heard of it in Washington—delightful atmosphere—and all that——"

"You are going as a—paying guest?"

"Yes."

A deep flush stained the younger man's face. Suddenly he broke out. "If you knew how rotten it seems to me to have my mother keeping—boarders——"

"My dear fellow, I hope you don't think it is going to be rotten to have me?"

"No. But there are other people. And I didn't know until I came back from France—— She had to tell me when she knew I was coming."

"She had been doing it all the time you were away?"

"Yes. Before I went we had mortgaged things to help me through the University. I should have finished in a year if I hadn't enlisted. And Mother insisted there was enough for her. But there wasn't with the interest and everything—and she wouldn't sell an acre. I shan't let her keep on——"

"Are you going to turn me out?"

His smile was irresistible. Randy smiled back. "I suppose you think I'm a fool——?"

"Yes. For being ashamed of it."

Randy's head went up. "I'm not ashamed of the boarding-house. I am ashamed to have my mother work."

"So," said the lame man, softly, "that's it? And your name is Paine?"

"Randolph Paine of King's Crest. There have been a lot of us—and not a piker in the lot."

"I am Mark Prime."

"Major Prime of the 135th?"

The other nodded. "The wonderful 135th—God, what men they were——" his eyes shone.

Randy made his little gesture of salute. "They were that. I don't wonder you are proud of them."

"It was worth all the rest," the Major said, "to have known my men."

He looked out of the window at the drizzle of rain. "How quiet the world seems after it all——"

Then like the snap of bullets came the staccato voice through the open door of the compartment.

"Find out why we are stopping in this beastly hole, Kemp, and get me something cold to drink."

Kemp, sailing down the aisle, like a Lilliputian drum major, tripped over Randy's foot.

"Beg pardon, sir," he said, and sailed on.

Randy looked after him. "'His Master's voice——'"

"And to think," Prime remarked, "that the coldest thing he can get on this train is ginger ale."

Kemp, coming back with a golden bottle, with cracked ice in a tall glass, with a crisp curl of lemon peel, ready for an innocuous libation, brought his nose down from the heights to look for the foot, found that it no longer barred the way, and marched on to hidden music.

"Leave the door open, leave it open," snapped the voice, "isn't there an electric fan? Well, put it on, put it on——"

"He drinks nectar and complains to the gods," said the Major softly, "why can't we, too, drink?"

They had theirs on a table which the porter set between them. The train moved on before they had finished. "We'll be in Charlottesville in less than an hour," the conductor announced.

"Is that where we get off, Paine?"

"One mile beyond. Are they going to meet you?"

"I'll get a station wagon."

Young Paine grinned. "There aren't any. But if Mother knows you're coming she'll send down. And anyhow she expects me."

"After a year in France—it will be a warm welcome——"

"A wet one, but I love the rain, and the red mud, every blooming inch of it."

"Of course you do. Just as I love the dust of the desert."

They spoke, each of them, with a sort of tense calmness. One doesn't confess to a lump in one's throat.

The little man, Kemp, was brushing things in the aisle. He was hot but unconquered. Having laid out the belongings of the man he served, he took a sudden recess, and came back with a fresh collar, a wet but faultless pompadour, and a suspicion of powder on his small nose.

"All right, sir, we'll be there in fifteen minutes, sir," they heard him say, as he was swallowed up by the yawning door.

II

Fifteen minutes later when the train slowed up, there emerged from the drawing-room a man some years older than Randolph Paine, and many years younger than Major Prime. He was good-looking, well-dressed, but apparently in a very bad temper. Kemp, in an excited, Skye-terrier manner, had gotten the bags together, had a raincoat over his arm, had an umbrella handy, had apparently foreseen every contingency but one.

"Great guns, Kemp, why are we getting off here?"

"The conductor said it was nearer, sir."

Randolph Paine was already hanging on the step, ready to drop the moment the train stopped. He had given the porter an extra tip to look after Major Prime. "He isn't used to that crutch, yet. He'd hate it if I tried to help him."

The rain having drizzled for hours, condensed suddenly in a downpour. When the train moved on, the men found themselves in a small and stuffy waiting-room. Around the station platform was a sea of red mud. Misty hills shot up in a circle to the horizon. There was not a house in sight. There was not a soul in sight except the agent who knew young Paine. No one having come to meet them, he suggested the use of the telephone.

In the meantime Kemp was having a hard time of it. "Why in the name of Heaven didn't we get off at Charlottesville," his master was demanding.

"The conductor said this was nearer, sir," Kemp repeated. His response had the bounding quality of a rubber ball. "If you'll sit here and make yourself comfortable, Mr. Dalton, I'll see what I can do."

"Oh, it's a beastly hole, Kemp. How can I be comfortable?"

Randy, who had come back from the telephone with a look on his face which clutched at Major Prime's throat, caught Dalton's complaint.

"It isn't a beastly hole," he said in a ringing voice, "it's God's country—— I got my mother on the 'phone, Major. She has sent for us and the horses are on the way."

Dalton looked him over. What a lank and shabby youth he was to carry in his voice that ring of authority. "What's the answer to our getting off here?" he asked.

"Depends upon where you are going."

"To Oscar Waterman's——"

"Never heard of him."

"Hamilton Hill," said the station agent.

Randy's neck stiffened. "Then the Hamiltons have sold it?"

"Yes. A Mr. Waterman of New York bought it."

Kemp had come back. "Mr. Waterman says he'll send the car at once. He is delighted to know that you have come, sir."

"How long must I wait?"

"Not more than ten minutes, he said, sir," Kemp's optimism seemed to ricochet against his master's hardness and come back unhurt. "He will send a closed car and will have your rooms ready for you."

"Serves me right for not wiring," said Dalton, "but who would believe there is a place in the world where a man can't get a taxi?"

Young Paine was at the door, listening for the sound of hoofs, watching with impatience. Suddenly he gave a shout, and the others looked to see a small object which came whirling like a bomb through the mist.

"Nellie, little old lady, little old lady," the boy was on his knees, the dog in his arms—an ecstatic, panting creature, the first to welcome her master home!

Before he let her go, the little dog's coat was wet with more than rain, but Randy was not ashamed of the tears in his eyes as he faced the others.

"I've had her from a pup—she's a faithful beast. Hello, there they come. Gee, Jefferson, but you've grown! You are almost as big as your name."

Jefferson was the negro boy who drove the horses. There was a great splashing of red mud as he drew up. The flaps of the surrey closed it in.

Jefferson's eyes were twinkling beads as he greeted his master. "I sure is glad to see you, Mr. Randy. Miss Caroline, she say there was another gemp'mun?"

"He's here—Major Prime. You run in there and look after his bags."

Randy unbuttoned the flaps and gave a gasp of astonishment:

"*Becky*—Becky Bannister!"

In another moment she was out on the platform, and he was holding her hands, protesting in the meantime, "You'll get wet, my dear——"

"Oh, I want to be rained on, Randy. It's so heavenly to have you home. I caught Jefferson on the way down. I didn't even wait to get my hat."

"IT'S SO HEAVENLY TO HAVE YOU HOME"

She did not need a hat. It would have hidden her hair. George Dalton, watching her from the door, decided that he had never seen such hair, bronze, parted on the side, with a thick wave across the forehead, it shaded eyes which were clear wells of light.

She was a little thing with a quality in her youth which made one think of the year at the spring, of the day at morn, of Botticelli's Simonetta, of Shelley's lark, of Wordsworth's daffodils, of Keats' Eve of St. Agnes—of all the lovely radiant things of which the poets of the world have sung——

Of course Dalton did not think of her in quite that way. He knew something of Browning and little of Keats, but he had at least the wit to discern the rareness of her type.

As for the rest, she wore faded blue, which melted into the blue of the mists, stubbed and shabby russet shoes and an air of absorption in her returned soldier. This absorption Dalton found himself subconsciously resenting. Following an instinctive urge, he emerged, therefore, from his chrysalis of ill-temper, and smiled upon a transformed universe.

"My raincoat, Kemp," he said, and strode forth across the platform, a creature as shining and splendid as ever trod its boards.

Becky, beholding him, asked, "Is that Major Prime?"

"No, thank Heaven."

Jefferson, steering the Major expertly, came up at this moment. Then, splashing down the red road whirled the gorgeous limousine. There were two men on the box. Kemp, who had been fluttering around Dalton with an umbrella, darted into the waiting-room for the bags. The door of the limousine was opened by the footman, who also had an umbrella ready.

Dalton hesitated, his eyes on that shabby group by the mud-stained surrey. He made up his mind suddenly and approached young Paine.

"We can take one of you in here. You'll be crowded with all of those bags."

"Not a bit. We'll manage perfectly, thank you," Randy's voice dismissed him.

533

He went, with a lingering glance backward. Becky, catching that glance, waked suddenly to the fact that he was very good-looking. "It was kind of him to offer, Randy."

"Was it?"

Nothing more was said, but Becky wondered a bit as they drove on. She liked Major Prime. He was an old dear. But why had Randy thanked Heaven that the other man was not the Major?

III

The Waterman motor passed the surrey, and Dalton, straining his eyes for a glimpse of the pretty girl, was rewarded only by a view of Randy on the front seat with his back turned on the world, while he talked with someone hidden by the curtains.

Perhaps the fact that she was hidden by the curtains kept Dalton's thoughts upon her. He felt that her beauty must shine even among the shadows—he envied Major Prime, who sat next to her.

The Major was aware that his position was enviable. It was worth much to watch these two young people, eager in their reunion. "Becky Bannister, whom I have known all my life," had been Randy's presentation of the little lady with the shining hair.

"Grandfather doesn't know that I came, or Aunt Claudia. They felt that your mother ought to see you first and so did I. Until the last minute. Then I saw Jefferson driving by—I was down at the gate to wave to you, Randy—and I just came——" her gay laugh was infectious—the men laughed with her.

"You must let me out when we get to Huntersfield, and you mustn't tell—either of you. We are all to dine together to-night at your house, Randy, and when you meet me, you are to say—*Becky*'—just as you did to-day, as if I had fallen from the skies."

"Well, you did fall—straight," Randy told her. "Becky, you are too good to be true; oh, you're too pretty to be true. Isn't she, Major?"

"It is just because I am—American. Are you glad to get back to us, Randy?"

"Glad," he drew a long breath. Nellie, who had wedged herself in tightly between her master and Jefferson, wriggled and licked his hand. He looked down at her, tried to say something, broke a little on it, and ended abruptly, "It's Heaven."

"And you weren't hurt?"

"Not a scratch, worse luck."

She turned to Major Prime and did the wise thing and the thing he liked. "You were," she said, simply, "but I am not going to be sorry for you, shall I?"

"No," he said, "I am not sorry for—myself——"

For a moment there was silence, then Becky carried the conversation into lighter currents. "Everybody is here for the Horse Show next week. Your mother's house is full, and those awful Waterman people have guests."

"One of them came down with us."

"The good-looking man who offered us a ride?"

"Oh, of course if you like that kind of looks, he's the kind of man you'd like," said Randy, "but coming down he seemed rather out of tune with the universe."

"How out of tune?"

"Well, it was hot and he was hot——"

"It *is* hot, Randy, and perhaps he isn't used to it."

"Are you making excuses for him?"

"I don't even know him."

Major Prime interposed. "His man was a corking little chap, never turned a hair, as cool as a cucumber, with everybody else sizzling."

They were ascending a hill, and the horse went slowly. Ahead of them was a buggy without a top. In the buggy were a man and a woman. The woman had an umbrella over her, and a child in her arms.

"It's Mary Flippin and her father. See if you can't overtake them, Jefferson. I want you to see Fiddle Flippin, Randy."

"Who is Fiddle Flippin?"

"Mary's little girl. Mary is a war bride. She was in Petersburg teaching school when the war broke out, and she married a man named Branch. Then she came home—and she called the baby Fidelity."

"I hope he was a good husband."

"Nobody has seen him, he was ordered away at once. But she is very proud of him. And the baby is a darling. Just beginning to walk and talk."

"Stop a minute, Jefferson, while I speak to them."

Mr. Flippin pulled up his fat horse. He was black-haired, ruddy, and wide of girth. "Well, well," he said, with a big laugh, "it is cert'n'y good to see you."

Mary Flippin was slender and delicate and her eyes were blue. Her hair was thick and dark. There was Scotch-Irish blood in the Flippins, and Mary's charm was in that of duskiness of hair and blueness of eye. "Oh, Randy Paine," she said, with her cheeks flaming, "when did you get back?"

"Ten minutes ago. Mary, if you'll hand me that corking kid, I'll kiss her."

Fiddle was handed over. She was rosy and round with her mother's blue eyes. She wore a little buttoned hat of white piqué, with strings tied under her chin.

"So," said Randy, after a moist kiss, "you are Fiddle-dee-dee?"

"Ess——"

"Who gave you that name?"

"It is her own way of saying Fidelity," Mary explained.

"Isn't she rather young to say anything?"

"Oh, Randy, she's a year and a half," Becky protested. "Your mother says that you talked in your cradle."

Randy laughed, "Oh, if you listen to Mother——"

"I'm glad you're in time for the Horse Show," Mr. Flippin interposed, "I've got a couple of prize hawgs—an' when you see them, you'll say they ain't anything like them on the other side."

"Oh, Father——"

"Well, they ain't. I reckon Virginia's good enough for you to come back to, ain't it, Mr. Randy——?"

"It is good enough for me to stay in now that I'm here."

"So you're back for good?"

"Yes."

"Well, we're mighty glad to have you."

Fiddle Flippin, dancing and doubling up on Randy's knee like a very soft doll, suddenly held out her arms to her mother. As Mary leaned forward to take her, Randy was aware of the change in her. In the old days Mary had been a gay little thing, with an impertinent tongue. She was not gay now. She was a Madonna, tender-eyed, brooding over her child.

"She has changed a lot," Randy said, as they drove on.

"Why shouldn't she change?" Becky demanded.

"Wouldn't any woman change if she had loved a man and had let him go to France?"

IV

It was still raining hard when the surrey stopped at a high and rusty iron gate flanked by brick pillars overgrown with Virginia creeper.

"Becky," said young Paine, "you can't walk up to the house. It's pouring."

"I don't see any house," said Major Prime.

"Well, you never do from the road in this part of the country. We put our houses on the tops of hills, and have acres to the right of us, and acres to the left, and acres in front, and acres behind, and you can never visit your neighbors without going miles, and nobody ever walks except little Becky Bannister when she runs away."

"And I am going to run now," said Becky. "Randy, there's a raincoat under that seat. I'll put it on if you will hand it out to me."

"You are going to ride up, my dear child. Drive on, Jefferson."

"Randy, *please*, your mother is waiting. She didn't come down to the station because she said that if she wept on your shoulder, she would not do it before the whole world. But she is *waiting*—— And it isn't fair for me to hold you back a minute."

He yielded at last reluctantly. "Remember, you are to act as if you had never met me," she said to Major Prime as she gave him her hand at parting, "when you see me to-night."

"Becky," Randy asked, in a sudden panic, "are the boarders to be drawn up in ranks to welcome me?"

"No, your mother has given you and Major Prime each two rooms in the Schoolhouse, and we are to dine out there, in your sitting-room—our families and the Major. And there won't be a soul to see you until morning, and then you can show yourself off by inches."

"Until to-night then," said Randy, and opened the gate for her.

"Until to-night," she watched them and waved her hand as they drove off.

"A beautiful child," the Major remarked from the shadow of the back seat.

"She's more than beautiful," said Randy, glowing, "oh, you wait till you really know her, Major."

V

The Schoolhouse at King's Crest had been built years before by one of the Paines for two sons and their tutor. It was separated from the old brick mansion by a wide expanse of unmowed lawn, thick now in midsummer with fluttering poppies. There was a flagged stone walk, and an orchard at the left, beyond the orchard were rolling fields, and in the distance one caught a glimpse of the shining river.

535

On the lower floor of the Schoolhouse were two ample sitting-rooms with bedrooms above, one of which was reached by outside stairs, and the other by an enclosed stairway. Baths had been added when Mrs. Paine had come as a widow to King's Crest with her small son, and had chosen the Schoolhouse as a quiet haven. Later, on the death of his grandparents, Randy had inherited the estate, and he and his mother had moved into the mansion. But he had kept his rooms in the Schoolhouse, and was glad to know that he could go back to them.

Major Prime had the west sitting-room. It was lined with low bookcases, full of old, old books. There was a fireplace, a winged chair, a broad couch, a big desk of dark seasoned mahogany, and over the mantel a steel engraving of Robert E. Lee. The low windows at the back looked out upon the wooded green of the ascending hill; at the front was a porch which gave a view of the valley.

Randolph's arrival had had something of the effect of a triumphal entry. Jefferson had driven him straight to the Schoolhouse, but on the way they had encountered old Susie, Jefferson's mother, who cooked, and old Bob, who acted as butler, and the new maid who waited on the table. These had followed the surrey as a sort of ecstatic convoy. Not a boarder was in sight but behind the windows of the big house one was aware of watching eyes.

"They are all crazy to meet you," Randy's mother had told him, as they came into the Major's sitting-room after those first sacred moments when the doors had been shut against the world, "they are all crazy to meet you, but you needn't come over to lunch unless you really care to do it. Jefferson can serve you here."

"What do you want me to do?"

"My dear, I'm so proud of you, I'd like to show you to the whole world."

"But there are so many of us, Mother."

"There's only one of you——"

"And we haven't come back to be put on pedestals."

"You were put on pedestals before you went away."

"I'll be spoiled if you talk to me like that."

"I shall talk as I please, Randy. Major Prime, isn't he as handsome as a—rose?"

"*Mother*——"

"Well, you are——"

"Mother, if you talk like this to the boarders, I'll go back and get shot up——"

She clung to him. "Randy, don't say such a thing. He mustn't talk like that, must he, Major?"

"He doesn't mean it. Paine, this looks to me like the Promised Land——"

"I'm glad you like it," said Mrs. Paine, "and now if you don't mind, I'll run along and kill the fatted calf——"

She kissed her son, and under a huge umbrella made her way through the poppies that starred the grass——

"*On Flanders field—where poppies blow*"—the Major drew a sudden quick breath—— He wished there were no poppies at King's Crest.

"I hate this hero stuff," Randy was saying, "don't you?"

"I am not so sure that I do. Down deep we'd resent it if we were not applauded, shouldn't we?"

Randy laughed. "I believe we should."

"I fancy that when we've been home for a time, we may feel somewhat bitter if we find that our pedestals are knocked from under us. Our people don't worship long. They have too much to think of. They'll put up some arches, and a few statues and build tribute houses in a lot of towns, and then they'll go on about their business, and we who have fought will feel a bit blank."

Randy laughed, "You haven't any illusions about it, have you?"

"No, but you and I know that it's all right however it goes."

Randy, standing very straight, looked out over the valley where the river showed through the rain like a silver thread.

"Well, we didn't do it for praise, did we?"

"No, thank God."

Their eyes were seeing other things than these quiet hills. Things they wanted to forget. But they did not want to forget the high exaltation which had sent them over, or the quiet conviction of right which had helped them to carry on. What the people at home might do or think did not matter. What mattered was their own adjustment to the things which were to follow.

Randy went up-stairs, took off his uniform, bathed and came down in the garments of peace.

"Glad to get out of your uniform?" the Major asked.

"I believe I am. Perhaps if I'd been an officer, I shouldn't."

"Everybody couldn't be. I've no doubt you deserved it."

"I could have pulled wires, of course, before I went over, but I wouldn't."

From somewhere within the big house came the reverberation of a Japanese gong.

Randy rose. "I'm going over to lunch. I'd rather face guns, but Mother will like it. You can have yours here."

"Not if I know it," the Major rose, "I'm going to share the fatted calf."

It was late that night when the Major went to bed. The feast in Randy's honor had lasted until ten. There had been the shine of candles, and the laughter of the women, the old Judge's genial humor. Through the windows had come the fragrance of honeysuckle and of late roses. Becky had sung for them, standing between two straight white candles.

"In the beauty of the lilies, Christ was born across the sea,
With the glory in his bosom which transfigures you and me.
As he died to make men holy, let us die to make men free
While God is marching on———"

The last time the Major had heard a woman sing that song had been in a little French town just after the United States had gone into the war. She was of his own country, red-haired and in uniform. She had stood on the steps of a stone house and weary men had clustered about her—French, English, Scotch, a few Americans. Tired and spent, they had gazed up at her as if they drank her in. To them she was more than a singing woman. She was the daughter of a nation of dreamers, *the daughter of a nation which made its dreams come true*! Behind her stood a steadfast people, and—God was marching on———!

He had had his leg then, and after that there had been dreadful fighting, and sometimes in the midst of it the voice of the singing woman had come back to him, stiffening him to his task.

And here, miles away from that war-swept land, another woman sang. And there was honeysuckle outside, and late roses—and poppies, and there was Peace. And the world which had not fought would forget. But the men who had fought would remember.

He heard Randy's voice, sharp with nerves. "Sing something else, Becky. We've had enough of war———"

The Major leaned across the table. "When did you last hear that song, Paine?"

"On the other side, a red-haired woman—whose lover had been killed. I never want to hear it again———"

"Nor I———"

It was as if they were alone at the table, seeing the things which they had left behind. What did these people know who had stayed at home? The words were sacred—not to be sung; to be whispered—over the graves of—France.

CHAPTER II
STUFFED BIRDS
I

The Country Club was, as Judge Bannister had been the first to declare, "an excrescence."

Under the old régime, there had been no need for country clubs. The houses on the great estates had been thrown open for the county families and their friends. There had been meat and drink for man and beast.

The servant problem had, however, in these latter days, put a curb on generous impulse. There were no more niggers underfoot, and hospitality was necessarily curtailed. The people who at the time of the August Horse Show had once packed great hampers with delicious foods, and who had feasted under the trees amid all the loveliness of mellow-tinted hills, now ordered by telephone a luncheon of cut-and-dried courses, and motored down to eat it. After that, they looked at the horses, and with the feeling upon them of the futility of such shows yawned a bit. In due season, they held, the horse would be as extinct as the Dodo, and as mythical as the Centaur.

The Judge argued hotly for the things which had been. Love of the horse was bred in the bone of Old Dominion men. He swore by all the gods that when he had to part with his bays and ride behind gasoline, he would be ready to die.

Becky agreed with her grandfather. She adored the old traditions, and she adored the Judge. She spent two months of every year with him in his square brick house in Albemarle surrounded by unprofitable acres. The remaining two months of her vacation were given to her mother's father, Admiral Meredith, whose fortune had come down to him from whale-hunting ancestors. The Admiral lived also in a square brick house, but it had no acres, for it was on the Main Street of Nantucket town, with a Captain's walk on top, and a spiral staircase piercing its middle.

The other eight months of the year Becky had spent at school in an old convent in Georgetown. She was a Protestant and a Presbyterian; the Nantucket grandfather was a Unitarian of Quaker stock, Judge Bannister was High Church, and it was his wife's Presbyterianism which had been handed down to Becky. Religion had therefore nothing to do with her residence at the school. A great many of the Bannister girls had been educated at convents, and when a Bannister had done a thing once it was apt to be done again.

Becky was nineteen, and her school days were just over. She knew nothing of men, she knew nothing indeed of life. The world was to her an open sea, to sail its trackless wastes she had only a cockle-shell of dreams.

"If anybody," said Judge Bannister, on the first day of the Horse Show, "thinks I am going to eat dabs of things at the club when I can have Mandy to cook for me, they think wrong."

He gave orders, therefore, which belonged to more opulent days, when his father's estate had swarmed with blacks. There was now in the Judge's household only Mandy, the cook, and Calvin, her husband. Mandy sat up half the night to bake a cake, and Calvin killed chickens at dawn, and dressed them, and pounded the dough for biscuits on a marble slab, and helped his wife with the mayonnaise.

When at last the luncheon was packed there was coffee in the thermos bottle. Prohibition was an assured fact, and the Judge would not break the laws. The flowing glass must go into the discard with other picturesque customs of the South. His own estate that had once been sold by John Randolph to Thomas Jefferson for a bowl of arrack punch———! Old times, old manners! The Judge drank his coffee with the air of one who accepts a good thing regretfully. He stood staunchly by the Administration. If the President had asked the sacrifice of his head, he would have offered it on the platter of political allegiance.

So on this August morning, an aristocrat by inheritance, and a democrat by assumption, he drove his bays proudly. Calvin, in a worn blue coat, sat beside him with his arms folded.

Becky was on the back seat with Aunt Claudia. Aunt Claudia was a widow and wore black. She was small and slight, and the black was made smart by touches of white crepe. Aunt Claudia had not forgotten that she had been a belle in Richmond. She was a stately little woman with a firm conviction of the necessity of maintaining dignified standards of living. She was in no sense a snob. But she held that women of birth and breeding must preserve the fastidiousness of their ideals, lest there be social chaos.

"There would be no ladies left in the world," she often told Becky, "if we older women went at the modern pace."

Becky, in contrast to Aunt Claudia's smartness, showed up rather ingloriously. She wore the stubbed russet shoes, a not too fresh cotton frock of pale yellow, and a brown straw sailor.

"You might at least have stopped to change your shoes," Aunt Claudia told her, as they left the house behind.

"I was out with Randy and the dogs. It was heavenly, Aunt Claudia."

"My dear, if a walk with Randy is heavenly, what will you call Heaven when you get to it?"

They drove through the first gate, and Calvin climbed down to open it. Beyond the gate the road descended gradually through an open pasture, where sheep grazed on the hillside or lay at rest in the shade. The bells of the leaders tinkled faintly, the ewes and the lambs were calling. Beyond the big gate, the highroad was washed with the recent rains. From the gate to the club was a matter of five miles, and the bays ate up the distance easily.

The people on the porch of the Country Club were very gay and gorgeous, so that Becky in her careless frock and shabby shoes would have been a pitiful contrast if she had cared in the least what the people on the porch thought of her. But she did not care. She nodded and smiled to a friend or two as the Judge stopped for a moment in the crush of motors.

George Dalton was on the porch. When he saw Becky he leaned forward for a good look at her.

"Some girl," he said to Waterman, as the surrey moved on, "the one in the sailor hat. Who is she?"

Oscar Waterman was a newcomer in Albemarle. He had bought a thousand acres, with an idea of grafting on to Southern environment his own ideas of luxurious living. The county families had not called, but he was not yet aware of his social isolation. He was rich, and most of the county families were poor—from his point of view the odds were in his favor—and it was never hard to get guests. He could always motor up to Washington and New York, and bring a crowd back with him. His cellars were well stocked, and his hospitality undiscriminating.

"I don't know the girl," he told Dalton, "but the old man is Judge Bannister. He's one of the natives—no money and oodles of pride."

In calling Judge Bannister a "native," Oscar showed a lack of proportion. A native, in the sense that he used the word, is a South Sea Islander, indigenous but negligible. Oscar was fooled, you see, by the Judge's old-fashioned clothes, and the high surrey, and the horses with the flowing tails. His ideas of life had to do with motor cars and mansions, and with everybody very much dressed up. He felt that the only thing in the world that really counted was money. If you had enough of it the world was yours!

II

Year after year the Bannisters of Huntersfield had eaten their Horse Show luncheon under a clump of old oaks beneath which the horses now stopped. The big trees were dropping golden leaves in the dryness. From the rise of the hill one looked down on the grandstand and the crowd as from the seats of an amphitheater.

Judge Bannister remembered when the women of the crowd had worn hoops and waterfalls. Aunt Claudia's memory went back to bustles and bonnets. There were deeper memories, too, than of clothes—of old friends and young faces—there was always a moment of pensive retrospect when the Bannisters stopped under the old oak on the hill.

Randolph Paine, his mother and Major Prime were to join them at luncheon. Separate plans had been made by the boarders who had packed themselves into various cars and carriages, and had their own boxes and baskets.

"Caroline Paine is always late," the Judge said with some impatience; "if we don't eat on time, we shall have to hurry. I have never hurried in my life and I don't want to begin now."

Claudia Beaufort was accustomed to impatience in men, and she was inflexible as a hostess. "Well, of course, we couldn't begin without them, could we?" she asked. "There they come now, Father. William, you'd better help Major Prime."

Randy was driving the fat mare, Rosalind. Nellie Custis, Randolph's wiry hound, loped along with flapping ears in the rear of the low-seated carriage. Major Prime was on the back seat with Mrs. Paine.

"My dear Judge," he said, as the old gentleman came to the side of the carriage, "I can't tell you how honored I am to be included in your party. This is about the best thing that has happened to me in a long time."

"I wanted you to get the old atmosphere. You can't get it at the Country Club. We Bannisters have lunched up here for sixty years—older than you are, eh?"

"Twenty years——"

"We used to call it the races, but now they tack on the Horse Show. It was different, of course, when all the old places were owned by the old families. But they can't change the oaks and the sweep of the hills, and the mettle of the horses, thank God."

"I am sorry I was late," said Caroline Paine, as they settled themselves under the trees, "but I went to town to have my hair waved."

"I wish you wouldn't, Caroline," Mrs. Beaufort told her, "your hair is nice enough without it."

Caroline Paine took off her hat, "I couldn't get it up to look like this, could I?"

The Judge surveyed the undulations critically. "Caroline," he said, "you are too pretty to need it."

"I want to keep young for Randolph's sake," Mrs. Paine told him, "then he'll like me better than any other girl."

"You needn't think you have to get your hair curled to make me love you," said her tall son; "you are ducky enough as you are."

Major Prime, delighting in their lack of self-consciousness, made a diplomatic contribution. "Why quarrel with such a charming coiffure?"

Mrs. Paine smiled at him, comfortably. "I feel much better," she said; "they are always trying to hold me back."

She was a woman of ample proportions and of leisurely habit. Life had of late hurried her a bit, but she still gave the effect of restful calm. She was of the same generation as Aunt Claudia, and a widow. But she wore her widowhood with a difference. She had on to-day a purple hat. Her hair was white, her dress was white, and her shoes. She was prettier than Aunt Claudia but she lacked her distinction of manner and of carriage.

"They always want to hold me back when I try to be up-to-date," she repeated.

Randy threw an acorn at her. "Nobody can hold you back, Mother," he said, "when you get your mind on a thing. Aunt Claudia, what do you hear from Truxton?"

"A letter came this morning," said Mrs. Beaufort, lighting up with the thought of it. "I hadn't heard for days before that. And I was worried."

"Truxton hasn't killed himself writing letters since he went over," the Judge asserted. "Claudia, can't we have lunch?"

"William is unpacking the hamper now, Father. And I think Truxton has done very well. It isn't easy for the boys to find time."

"Randy wrote to me every week."

"Now, Mother——"

"Well, you did."

"But I'm that kind. I have to get things off my mind. Truxton isn't. And I'll bet when Aunt Claudia does get his letters that they are worth reading."

Mrs. Beaufort nodded. "They are lovely letters. I have the last one with me; would you like to hear it?"

"Not before lunch, Claudia," the Judge urged.

"I will read it while the rest of you eat." There were red spots in Mrs. Beaufort's cheeks. She adored her son. She could not understand her father's critical attitude. Had she searched for motives, however, she might have found them in the Judge's jealousy.

It was while she was reading Truxton's letter that the Flippins came by—Mr. Flippin and his wife, Mary, and little Fidelity. A slender mulatto woman followed with a basket.

The Flippins were one of the "second families." Between them and the Paines of King's Crest and the Bannisters of Huntersfield stretched a deep chasm of social prejudice. Three generations of Flippins had been small farmers on rented lands. They had no coats-of-arms or family trees. They were never asked to dine with the Paines or Bannisters, but there had been always an interchange of small hospitalities, and much neighborliness, and as children Mary Flippin, Randy and Becky and Truxton had played together and had been great friends.

So it was now as they stopped to speak to the Judge's party that Mrs. Beaufort said graciously, "I am reading a letter from Truxton. Would you like to hear it?"

Mary, speaking with a sort of tense eagerness, said, "Yes."

So the Flippins sat down, and Mrs. Beaufort read in her pleasant voice the letter from France.

Randy, lying on his back under the old oak, listened. Truxton gave a joyous diary of the days—little details of the towns through which he passed, of the houses where he was billeted, jokes of the men, of the food they ate, of his hope of coming home.

"He seems very happy," said Mrs. Beaufort, as she finished.

"He is and he isn't——"

"You might make yourself a little clearer, Randolph," said the Judge.

"He is happy because France in summer is a pleasant sort of Paradise—with the cabbages stuck up on the brown hillsides like rosettes—and the minnows flashing in the little brooks and the old mills turning—and he isn't happy—because he is homesick."

Randy raised himself on his elbow and smiled at his listening audience—and as he smiled he was aware of a change in Mary Flippin. The brooding look was gone. She was leaning forward, lips parted—"Then you think that he is—homesick?"

"I don't *think*. I know. Why, over there, my bones actually ached for Virginia."

The Judge raised his coffee cup. "Virginia, God bless her," he murmured, and drank it down!

The Flippins moved on presently—the slender mulatto trailing after them.

"If the Flippins don't send that Daisy back to Washington," Mrs. Paine remarked, "she'll spoil all the negroes on the place."

Mrs. Beaufort agreed, "I don't know what we are coming to. Did you see her high heels and tight skirt?"

"Once upon a time," the Judge declaimed, "black wenches like that wore red handkerchiefs on their heads and went barefoot. But the world moves, and some day when we have white servants wished on us, we'll pray to God to send our black ones back."

Calvin was passing things expertly. Randy smiled at Becky as he filled her plate.

"Hungry?"

"Ravenous."

"You don't look it."

"Don't I?"

"No. You're not a bread and butter sort of person."

"What kind am I?"

"Sugar and spice and everything nice."

"Did you learn to say such things in France?"

"Haven't I always said them?"

"Not in quite the same way. You've grown up, Randy. You seem *years* older."

"Do you like me—older?"

"Of course." There was warmth in her voice but no coquetry. "What a silly thing to ask, Randy."

Calvin, having served the lunch, ate his own particular feast of chicken backs and necks under the surrey from a pasteboard box cover. Having thus separated himself as it were from those he served, he was at his ease. He knew his place and was happy in it.

Mary Flippin also knew her place. But she was not happy. She sat higher up on the hill with her child asleep in her arms, and looked down on the Judge's party. Except for an accident of birth, she might be sitting now among them. Would she ever sit among them? Would her little daughter, Fidelity?

III

"We are the only one of the old families who are eating lunch out of a basket," said Caroline Paine; "next year we shall have to go to the Country Club with the rest of them."

"I shall never go to the Country Club," said Judge Bannister, "as long as there is a nigger to fry chicken for me."

"We may have to swim with the tide."

"Don't tell me that you'd rather be up there than here, Caroline."

"I'd like it for some things," Mrs. Paine admitted frankly; "you should see the clothes that those Waterman women are wearing."

"What do you care what they wear. You don't want to be like them, do you?"

"I may not care to be like them, but I want to look like them. I got the pattern of this sweater I am knitting from one of my boarders. Do you want it, Claudia?"

Mrs. Beaufort winced at the word "boarders." She hated to think that Caroline must—— "I never wear sweaters, Caroline. They are not my style. But I am knitting one for Becky."

"Is it blue?" Randy asked. "Becky ought always to wear blue, except when she wears pale yellow. That was a heavenly thing you had on at dinner the night we arrived, wasn't it, Major?"

"Everything was heavenly. I felt like one who expecting a barren plain sees—Paradise."

It was not flattery and they knew it. They were hospitable souls, and in a week he had become, as it were, one of them.

Randy, returning to the subject in hand, asked, "Will you wear the blue if I come up to-night, Becky?"

"I will not." Becky was making herself a chaplet of yellow leaves, and her bronze hair caught the light. "I will not. I shall probably put on my old white if I dress for dinner."

"Of course you'll dress," said Mrs. Beaufort; "there are certain things which we must always demand of ourselves——"

Caroline Paine agreed. "That's what I tell Randy when he says he doesn't want to finish his law course. His father was a lawyer and his grandfather. He owes it to them to live up to their standards."

Randy was again flat on his back with his hands under his head. "If I stay at the University, it means no money for either of us except what you earn, Mother."

The war had taken its toll of Caroline Paine. Things had not been easy since her son had left her. They would not be easy now. "I know," she said, "but you wouldn't want your father to be ashamed of you."

Randy sat up. "It isn't that—but I ought to make some money——"

The word was a challenge to the Judge. "Don't run with the mob, my boy. The world is money-mad."

"I'm not money-mad," said Randy; "I know what I should like to do if my life was my own. But it isn't. And I'm not going to have Mother twist and turn as she has twisted and turned for the last fifteen years in order to get me educated up to the family standard."

"If you don't mind I shouldn't." Caroline Paine was setting her feet to a rocky path, but she did not falter. "You shouldn't mind if I don't."

Becky laid down the chaplet of leaves. She knew some of the things Caroline Paine had sacrificed and she was thrilled by them. "Randy," she admonished, with youthful severity, "it would be a shame to disappoint your mother."

Randolph flushed beneath his dark skin. The Paines had an Indian strain in them—Pocahontas was responsible for it, or some of the other princesses who had mixed red blood with blue in the days when Virginia belonged to the King. Randy showed signs of it in his square-set jaw, the high lift of his head, his long easy stride, the straightness of his black hair. He showed it, too, in a certain stoical impassiveness which might have been taken for indifference. His world was, for the moment, against him; he would attempt no argument.

"I am afraid this doesn't interest Major Prime," he said.

"It interests me very much," said the Major. "It is only another case of the fighting man's adjustment to life after his return. We all have to face it in one way or another." His eyes went out over the hills. They were gray eyes, deep set, and, at this moment, kindly. They could blaze, however, in stress of fighting, like bits of steel. "We all have to face it in one way or another. And the future of America depends largely on our seeing things straight."

"Well, there's only one way for Randy to face it," said Caroline Paine, firmly, "and that is to do as his fathers did before him."

"If I do," Randy flared, "it will be three years before I can make a living, and I'll be twenty-five."

Becky put on the chaplet of leaves. It fitted like a cap. She might have been a dryad, escaped for a moment from the old oak. "Three years isn't long."

"Suppose I should want to marry——"

"Oh, you—Randy——"

"But why shouldn't I?"

"I don't want you to get married," she told him; "when I come down we couldn't have our nice times together. You'd always be thinking about your wife."

<h1 style="text-align:center">IV</h1>

From the porch of the Country Club, George Dalton had seen the Judge's party at luncheon. According to George's lexicon no one who could afford to go to the club would eat out of a basket. He rather blushed for Becky that she must sit there in the sight of everybody and share a feast with a shabby old Judge, a lean and lank stripling with straight hair, a lame duck of an officer, and two middle-aged women, who made spots of black and purple on the landscape. Like Oscar, George's ideas of life had to do largely with motor cars and yachts, and estates on Long Island, palaces at Newport and Lenox and Palm Beach. During the war he had served rather comfortably in a becoming uniform in the Quartermaster's Department in Washington. Now that the war was over, he regretted the becomings of the uniform. He felt to-day, however, that there were compensations in his hunting pink. He was slightly bronzed and had blue eyes. He was extremely popular with the women of the Waterman set, but was held to be the especial property of Madge MacVeigh.

Madge had observed his interest in the party on the hill.

"George," she said, "what are you looking at?"

"I am looking at those people who are picnicking. They probably have ants in the salad and spiders in their coffee."

"They are getting more out of it than you and I," said Madge.

"How getting more?"

"We are tired of things, Georgie-Porgie."

"Speak for yourself, Madge."

"I am speaking for both of us. You are tired of me, for example."

"My dear girl, I am not."

"You are. And I am tired of you. It's not your fault, and it's not mine. It is the fault of any house-party. People see too much of each other. I am glad I am going away to-morrow, and you'll be glad. And when we have been separated a month, you will rush up to see me, and say you couldn't live without me."

541

She dissected him coolly. Madge had a modern way of looking at things. She was not in the least sentimental. But she had big moments of feeling. It was because of this deep current which swept her away now and then from the shallows that she held Dalton's interest. He never knew in what mood he should find her, and it added spice to their friendship.

"I didn't know you were going to-morrow."

"Neither did I till this morning, but I am bored to death, Georgie."

She did not look it. She was long-limbed, slender, with heavy burned-gold hair, a skin which was pale gold after a July by the sea. The mauve of her dress and hat emphasized the gold of hair and skin. Some one had said that Madge MacVeigh at the end of a summer gave the effect of a statue cast in new bronze. Dalton in the early days of their friendship had called her his "Golden Girl." The name had stuck to her. She had laughed at it but had liked it. "I should hate it," she had said, "if I were rich. Perhaps some day some millionaire will turn me into gold and make it true."

"Just because you are bored to death," Dalton told her, "is no reason why you should accuse me of it."

"It isn't accusation. It's condolence. I am sorry for both of us, George, that we can't sit there under the trees and eat out of a basket and have spiders and ants in things and not mind it. Here we are in the land of Smithfield hams and spoon-bread and we ate canned lobster for lunch, and alligator pear salad."

"Baked ham and spoon-bread—for our sins?"

"It is because you and I have missed the baked ham and spoon-bread atmosphere, that we are bored to death, Georgie. Everything in our lives is the same wherever we go. When we are in Virginia we ought to do as the Virginians do, and instead Oscar Waterman brings a little old New York with him. It's Rome for the Romans, Georgie, lobsters in New England, avocados in Los Angeles, hog and hominy here."

There were others listening now, and she was aware of her amused audience.

"If you don't like my little old New York," Waterman said, "I'll change it."

"No, I am going back to the real thing, Oscar. To my sky-scrapers and subways. You can't give us those down here—not yet. Perhaps some day there will be a system of camouflage by which no matter where we are—in desert or mountain, we can open our windows to the Woolworth Building on the skyline or the Metropolitan Tower, or to Diana shooting at the stars,—and have some little cars in tunnels to run us around your estate."

"By Jove, Jefferson nearly did it," said Waterman; "you should see the subterranean passages at Monticello for the servants, so that the guests could look over the grounds without a woolly head in sight."

"Great old boob, Jefferson," said Waterman's wife, Flora.

"No," Madge's eyes went out over the hills to where Monticello brooded over great memories, "he was not a boob. He was so big that little people like us can't focus him, Flora."

She came down from her perch. "I adore great men," she said; "when I go back, I shall make a pilgrimage to Oyster Bay. I wonder how many of us who weep over Great heart's grave would have voted for him if he had lived. In a sense we crucified him."

"Madge is serious," said Flora Waterman, "now what do you think of that?"

"I have to be serious sometimes, Flora, to balance the rest of you. You can be as gay as you please when I am gone, and if you perish, you perish."

George walked beside her as the party moved towards the grandstand. "I've half a mind to go to New York with you, Madge. I came down on your account."

"It's because you followed me that I'm tired of you, Georgie. If you go, I'll stay."

She was smiling as she said it. But he did not smile. "Just as you wish, of course. But you mustn't expect me to come running when you crook your finger."

"I never expect things, but you'll come."

Perhaps she would not have been so sure if she could have looked into his mind. The day that Becky had ridden away, hidden by the flaps of the old surrey, the spark of his somewhat fickle interest had been lighted, and the glimpse that he had had of her this morning had fanned the spark into a flame.

"Did you say the old man's name is Bannister?" he asked Oscar as the Judge's party passed them later on their way to their seats.

"Yes. Judge Bannister. I tried to buy his place before I decided on Hamilton Hill. But he wouldn't sell. He said he wouldn't have any place for his stuffed birds."

"Stuffed birds?"

"His hobby is the game birds of Virginia. He has a whole room of them. I offered him a good price, but I suppose he'd rather starve than take it."

The Judge's box was just above Oscar Waterman's. Becky, looking up, saw Dalton's eyes upon her.

"It's the man who came with you on the train," she told Randy.

"What's he wearing a pink coat for?" Randy demanded. "He isn't riding."

"He probably knows that he looks well in it."

"That isn't a reason."

Becky took another look. "He has a head like the bust of Apollo in our study hall."

"I'd hate to have a head like that."

"Well, you haven't," she told him; "you may hug that thought to yourself if it is any consolation, Randy."

V

Caroline Paine's boarders sat high up on the grandstand. If the boarders seem in this book to be spoken of collectively, like the Chorus in a Greek play, or the sisters and aunts and cousins in "Pinafore," it is not because they are not individually interesting. It is because, *en Massey* only, have they any meaning in this history.

Now as they sat on the grandstand, they discerned Mrs. Paine in the Judge's box. They waved at her, and they waved at Randy, they waved also at Major Prime. They demanded recognition—some of the more enthusiastic detached themselves finally from the main group and came down to visit Caroline. The overflow straggled along the steps to the edge of the Waterman box. One genial gentleman was forced finally to sit on the rail, so that his elbow stuck straight into the middle of the back of George's huntsman's pink.

George moved impatiently. "Can't you find any other place to sit?"

The genial gentleman beamed on him. "I have a seat over there. But we came down to see Mrs. Paine. She is in Judge Bannister's box and we board with her—at King's Crest. And say, she's a corker!"

George, surveying Becky with increasing interest, decided that she was a bit above her surroundings. She sat as it were with—Publicans. George may not have used the Scriptural phrase, but he had the feeling. He was Pharisaic ally thankful that he was not as that conglomerate group in the Bannister box. A cheap crowd was his estimate. It would be rather nice to give the little girl a good time!

Filled, therefore, with a high sense of his philanthropic purpose, he planned a meeting. With his blue eyes on the flying horses, with his staccato voice making quick comments, he had Becky in the back of his mind. He found a moment, when the crowd went mad as the county favorite came in, to write a line on the back of an envelope, and hand it to Kemp, who hovered in the background, giving him quiet instructions.

"Yes, sir," said Kemp guardedly, and stood at attention until the races were over, and the crowd began to move, and then he handed the note to Judge Bannister.

The Judge put on his glasses and read it. "Where is he?" he asked Kemp.

"In the other box, sir. The one above."

"Tell him to come down."

"Yes, sir, thank you, sir."

The Judge was as pleased as Punch. "That man up there in Waterman's box has heard of my collection," he explained to his party. "He wants me to settle a point about the Virginia partridge."

"Which man?" Randy's tone was ominous.

Dalton's arrival saved the Judge an answer. In his hunting pink, with his Apollo head, Dalton was upon them. The Judge, passing him around to the members of his party, came at last to Becky.

"My granddaughter, Becky Bannister."

With George's sparkling gaze bent full upon her, Becky blushed.

Randy saw the blush. "Oh, Lord," he said, under his breath, and stuck his hands in his pockets.

"I've always called it a quail," Dalton was saying.

"You would if you come from the North. To be exact, it isn't either, it's an American Bob-white. I'd be glad to have you come up and look at my collection. There is every kind of bird that has been shot in Virginia fields or Virginia waters. I've got a Trumpeter Swan. The last one was seen in the Chesapeake in sixty-nine. Mine was killed and stuffed in the forties. He is in a perfect state of preservation, and in the original glass case."

"I'd like to come," George told him. "Could I—to-night? I don't know just how long I shall be staying down."

"Any time—any time. To-night, of course. There's nothing I like better than to talk about my birds, unless it is to eat them. Isn't that so, Claudia?"

"Yes, Father." Mrs. Beaufort was studying Dalton closely. His manner was perfect. It was, indeed, she decided, too perfect. "He is thinking too much of the way he does it." The one sin in Aunt Claudia's mind was social self-consciousness. People who thought all of the time about manners hadn't been brought up to them. They must have them without thinking. George was not, she decided, a gentleman in the Old Dominion sense. Dalton would have been amazed could he have looked into Aunt Claudia's mind and have seen himself a—Publican.

"Father," she said, after Dalton had left them, "did I hear you invite him to dinner?"

"Yes, my dear, but he could not come——"

"I'm glad he couldn't."

"Why?"

"I'm not sure that he's—our kind——"

"Nonsense, he's a very fine fellow."

"How do you know?"

543

"Well, I know this," testily, "that I am not to be instructed as to the sort of person I can ask to my house."

"Oh, Father, I didn't mean that. Of course you can do as you please."

"Of course I shall, Claudia."

"I think he is charming," said Mrs. Paine. "He has lovely eyes."

"Hasn't he?" said little Becky.

CHAPTER III
THE WOLF IN THE FOREST
I

The Bird Room at Judge Bannister's was back of the library. It was a big room lined with glass cases. There hung about it always the faint odor of preservatives. The Trumpeter Swan had a case to himself over the mantel. He had been rather stiffly posed on a bed of artificial moss, but nothing could spoil the beauty of him—the white of his plumage, the elegance of his lines. He was one of a dying race—the descendants of the men who had once killed for food had killed later to gratify the vanity of women who must have swans down to set off their beauty, puffs to powder their noses. No more did great flocks wing an exalted flight, high in the heavens, or rest like a blanket of snow on river banks. The old kings were dead—the glassy eyes of the Trumpeter looked out upon a world which knew his kind no more.

In the other cases were the little birds and big ones—ducks, swimming on crystal pools, canvas-backs and redheads, mallards and teal; Bob-whites, single and in coveys; sandpipers, tip-ups and peeps, those little ghosts of the seashore, shadows on the sand; there were soar and other rails, robins and blackbirds, larks and sparrows, wild turkeys and wild geese, all the toll which the hunter takes from field and stream and forest.

It was in a sense a tragic room, but it had never seemed that to Becky. She came of a race of men who had hunted from instinct but with a sense of honor. The Judge and those of his kind hated wanton killing. Their guns would never have swept away the feathered tribes of tree and sky. It was the trappers and the pot-hunters who had done that. There had motored once to the Judge's mansion a man and his wife who had raged at the brutes who hunted for sport. They had worn fur coats and there had been a bird's breast on the woman's hat.

The Judge, holding on to his temper, had exploded finally. "If you were consistent," he had flung at them, "you would not be decked in the bodies of birds and beasts."

Becky loved the birds in the glass cases, the peeps and the tip-ups, the old owl who did not belong among the game birds, but who, with the great eagle with the outstretched wings, had been admitted because they had been shot within the environs of the estate. She loved the little nests of tinted eggs, the ducks on the crystal pools.

But most of all she loved the Trumpeter. Years ago the Judge had told her of the wild swans who flew so high that no eye could see them. Yet the sound of their trumpets might be heard. It was like the fairy tale of "The Seven Brothers," who were princes, and who were turned into swans and wore gold crowns on their heads. She was prepared to believe anything of the Trumpeter. She had often tiptoed down in the night, expecting to see his case empty, and to hear his trumpet sounding high up near the moon.

There was a moon to-night. Dinner was always late at Huntersfield. In the old days three o'clock had been the fashionable hour for dining in the county, with a hot supper at eight. Aunt Claudia, keeping up with the times, had decided that instead of dining and supping, they must lunch and dine. The Judge had agreed, stipulating that there should be no change in the evening hour. "Serve it in courses, if you like, and call it dinner. But don't have it before candle-light."

So the moon was up when Becky came down in her blue dress. She had not expected to wear the blue. In spite of the fact that Randy and his mother and Major Prime had come back with them for dinner, she had planned to wear her old white, which had been washed and laid out on the bed by Mandy. But the blue was more becoming, and the man with the Apollo head had eyes to see.

She came into the Bird Room with a candle in her hand. There was a lamp high up, but she could not reach it, so she always carried a candle. She set it down on the case where the Bob-whites were cuddled in brown groups. She whistled a note, and listened to catch the answer. It had been a trick of hers as a child, and she had heard them whistle in response. She had been so sure that she heard them—a far-off silvery call——

Well, why not? Might not their little souls be fluttering close? "You darlings," she said aloud.

Randy, arriving at that moment on the threshold, heard her. "You are playing the old game," he said.

"Oh, yes," she caught her breath, "do you remember?"

He came into the room. "I remembered a thousand times when I was in France. I thought of this room and of the Trumpeter Swan, and of how you and I used to listen on still nights and think we heard him. There was one night after an awful day—with a moon like this over the battlefield, and across the moon came a black, thin streak—and a bugle sounded—far away. I was half asleep, and I said, 'Becky, there's the swan,' and the fellow next to me poked his elbow in my ribs, and said, 'You're dreaming.' But I wasn't—quite, for the thin black streak was a Zeppelin——"

She came up close to him and laid her hand on his arm. He towered above her. "Randy," she asked, "was the war very dreadful?"

"Yes," he said, "it was. More dreadful than you people at home can ever grasp. But I want you to know this, Becky, that there isn't one of us who wouldn't go through it again in the same cause."

There was no swagger in his statement, just simple earnestness. The room was very still for a moment.

Then Becky said, "Well, it's awfully nice to have you home again," and Randy, looking down at the little hand on his arm, had to hold on to himself not to put his own over it.

But she was too dear and precious——! So he just said, gently, "And I'm glad to be at home, my dear," and they walked to the window together, and stood looking out at the moon. Behind them the old eagle watched with outstretched wings, the great free bird which we stamp on American silver, backed with "In God We Trust." It is not a bad combination, and things in this country might, perhaps, have been less chaotic if we had taught newcomers to link love of God with love of liberty.

"Mr. Dalton is coming to see the birds," said Becky, and in a moment she had spoiled everything for Randy.

"Is that why you put on your blue dress?"

She was honest. "I am not sure. Perhaps."

"Yet you thought the old white one was good enough for me."

"Well, don't you like me just as well in my old white as in this?"

"Yes, of course."

"Well, then," Becky was triumphant, "why should I bother to change for you, Randy, when you like me just as well in anything?"

The argument was unanswerable, but Randy was not satisfied. "It is a mistake," he said, "not to be as nice to old friends as new ones."

"But I am nice. You said so yourself this afternoon. That I was sugar and spice and everything—nice——"

He laughed. "You are, of course. And I didn't come all the way from France to quarrel with you——"

"We've always quarreled, Randy."

"I wonder why?"

"Sister Loretta says that people only argue when they like each other. Otherwise they wouldn't want to convince."

"Do you quarrel with Sister Loretta?"

"Of course not. Nuns don't. But she writes notes when she doesn't agree with me—little sermons—and pins them on my pillow. She's a great dear. She hates to have me leave the school. She has the feeling that the world is a dark forest, and that I am Red Riding Hood, and that the Wolf will get me."

II

Dalton found them all at dinner when he reached Huntersfield. He was not in the least prepared for the scene which met his eyes—shining mahogany, old silver and Sheffield, tall white candles, Calvin in a snowy jacket, Mrs. Beaufort and Mrs. Paine in low-necked gowns, the Judge and Randy in dinner coats somewhat the worse for wear, Becky in thin, delicate blue, with a string of pearls which seemed to George an excellent imitation of the real thing.

He had thought that the trail of Mrs. Paine's boarding-house might be over it all. He had known boarding-houses as a boy, before his father made his money. There had been basement dining-rooms, catsup bottles, and people passing everything to everybody else!

"I'm afraid I'm early," he said in his quick voice.

"Not a bit. Calvin, place a chair for Mr. Dalton."

There were fruit and nuts and raisins in a great silver Pegeen, with fat cupids making love among garlands. There was coffee in Severus cups.

Back among the shadows twinkled a priceless mirror; shutting off Calvin's serving table was a painted screen worth its weight in gold. It was a far cry from the catsup bottles and squalid service of George's early days. The Bannisters of Huntersfield wore their poverty like a plume!

The Judge carried Dalton off presently to the Bird Boom. George went with reluctance. This was not what he had come for. Becky, slim and small, with her hair peaked up to a topknot, Becky in pale blue, Becky as fair as her string of imitation pearls, Becky in the golden haze of the softly illumined room, Becky, Becky Bannister—the name chimed in his ears.

Dalton had had some difficulty in getting away from Hamilton Hill.

"It's my last night," Madge had said; "shall we go out in the garden and watch the moon rise?"

"Sorry," George had told her, "but I've promised Flora to take a fourth hand at bridge."

"And after that?" asked Madge softly.

"What do you mean?"

"Who is the new—little girl?"

It was useless to pretend. "She's a beauty, rather, isn't she?"

"Oh, Georgie-Porgie, I wish you wouldn't."

"Wouldn't what?"

"Kiss the girls—and make them—cry——"

"You've never cried——"

She laughed at that. "If I haven't it is because I know that afterwards you always—run away."

He admitted it. "One can't marry them all."

"I wonder if you are ever serious," she told him, her chin in her hand.

"I am always serious. That's what makes it—interesting——"

"But the poor little—hearts?"

"Some one has to teach, them," said George, "that it's a pretty game——"

"Will it be always a game—to you—Georgie?"

"Who knows?" he said. "So far I've held trumps——"

"Your conceit is colossal, but somehow you seem to get away with it." She smiled and stood up. "I'm going to bed early. I have been losing my beauty sleep lately, Georgie."

He chose to be gallant. "You are not losing your beauty, if that's what you mean."

Her dinner gown was of the same shade of mauve that she had worn in the afternoon. But it was of a material so sheer that the gold of her skin seemed to shine through.

"Good-night, Golden Girl," said Dalton, and kissed the tips of her fingers as she stood on the stairs. Then he went off to join the others.

Madge did not go to bed. She went out alone and watched the moon rise. Oscar Waterman's house was on a hill which gave a view of the whole valley. Gradually under the moon the houses of Charlottesville showed the outlines of the University, and far beyond the shadowy sweep of the Blue Ridge. What a world it had been in the old days—great men had ridden over these red roads in swaying carriages, Jefferson, Lafayette, Washington himself.

If she could only meet men like that. Men to whom life was more than a game—a carnival. From the stone bench where she sat she had a view through the long French windows of the three tables of bridge—there were slender, restless girls, eager, elegant youths. "Perhaps they are no worse than those who lived here before them," Madge's sense of justice told her. "But isn't there something better?"

From her window later, she saw Dalton's car flash out into the road. The light wound down and down, and appeared at last upon the highway. It was not the first time that George had played the game with another girl. But he had always come back to her. She had often wondered why she let him come. "Why do I let him?" she asked the moon.

<h2 style="text-align:center">III</h2>

It really was a great moon. It shone through the windows of the Bird Room at Huntersfield, wooing George out into the fragrant night. He could hear voices on the lawn—young Paine's laugh—Becky's. Once when he looked he saw them on the ridge, silhouetted against the golden sky. They were dancing, and Randy's clear whistle, piping a modern tune, came up to him, tantalizing him.

But the Judge held him. It took him nearly an hour to get through with the Bob-whites and the sandpipers, the wild turkeys, the ducks and the wild geese. And long before that time George was bored to extinction. He had little imagination. To him the Trumpeter was just a stuffed old bird. He could not picture him as blowing his trumpet beside the moon, or wearing a golden crown as in "The Seven Brothers." He had never heard of "The Seven Brothers," and nobody in the world wore crowns except kings. As for the old eagle, it is doubtful whether George had ever felt the symbolism of his presence on a silver coin, or that he had ever linked him in his heart with God.

Then, suddenly, the whole world changed. Becky appeared on the threshold.

"Grandfather," she said, "Aunt Claudia says there is lemonade on the lawn."

"In a moment, my dear."

George rose hastily. "Don't let me keep you, Judge——"

Becky advanced into the room. "Aren't the birds wonderful?"

"They are," said George, seeing them wonderful for the first time.

"I always feel," she said, "as if some time they will flap their wings and fly away—on a night like this—the swans going first, and then the ducks and geese, and last of all the little birds, trailing across the moon——" Her hands fluttered to show them trailing. Becky used her hands a great deal when she talked. Aunt Claudia deplored it as indicating too little repose. The nuns, she felt, should have corrected the habit. But the nuns had loved Becky's descriptive hands, poking, emphasizing, and had let her alone.

The three of them, the Judge and Becky and Dalton, went out together. The little group which sat in the wide moonlighted space in front of the house was dwarfed by the great trees which hung in masses of black against the brilliant night. The white dresses of the women seemed touched with silver.

The lemonade was delicious, and Aunt Claudia forced herself to be gracious. Caroline Paine was gracious without an effort. She liked Dalton. Not in the same way, perhaps, that she liked Major Prime, but he was undoubtedly handsome, and of a world which wore lovely clothes and did not have to count its pennies.

Major Prime had little to say. He was content to sit there in the fragrant night and listen to the rest. A year ago he had been jolted over rough roads in an ambulance. There had been a moon and men groaning. There had seemed to him something sinister about that white night with its spectral shadows, and with the trenches of the enemy wriggling like great serpents underground. The trail of the serpent was still over the world. He had been caught but not killed. There was still poison in his fangs!

He spoke sharply, therefore, when Dalton said, "It was a great adventure for a lot of fellows who went over——"

"Don't," said the Major, and sat up. "Does it matter what took them? *The thing that matters is how they came back*——"

"What do you mean?"

"A thousand reasons took them over. Some of them went because they had to, some of them because they wanted to. Some of them dramatized themselves as heroes and hoped for an opportunity to demonstrate their courage. Some of them were scared stiff, but went because of their consciences, some of them wanted to fight and some of them didn't, but whatever the reason, *they went*. And now they are back, and it is much more important to know what they think now about war than what they thought about it when they were enlisted or drafted. If their baptism of fire has made them hate cruelty and injustice, if it has opened their eyes to the dangers of a dreaming idealism which refuses to see evil until evil has had its way, if it has made them swear to purge America of the things which has made Germany the slimy crawling enemy of the universe, if they have come back feeling that God is in His Heaven but that things can't be right with the world until we come to think in terms of personal as well as of national righteousness—if they have come back thus illumined, then we can concede to them their great adventure. But if they have come back to forget that democracy is on trial, that we have talked of it to other nations and do not know it ourselves, if they have come back to let injustice or ignorance rule—then they had better have died on the fields of France——"

He stopped suddenly amid a startled silence. Not a sound from any of them.

"I beg your pardon," he laughed a bit awkwardly, "I didn't mean to preach a sermon."

"Don't spoil it, *please*," Aunt Claudia begged brokenly; "I wish more men would speak out."

"May I say this, then, before I stop? The future of our country is in the hands of the men who fought in France. On them must descend the mantles of our great men, Washington, Lincoln, Roosevelt—we must walk with these spirits if we love America——"

"Do you wonder," Randy said, under his breath to Becky, "that his men fought, and that they died for him?"

She found her little handkerchief and wiped her eyes. "He's a—perfect—darling," she whispered, and could say no more.

Dalton was for the time eclipsed. He knew it and was not at ease. He was glad when Mrs. Paine stood up. "I am sorry to tear myself away. But I must. I can't be sure that Susie has made up the morning rolls. There's a camp-meeting at Jessica, and she's lost the little mind that she usually puts on her cooking."

Randy and the Major went with her in the low carriage, with Rosalind making good time towards the home stable, and with Nellie Custis following with flapping ears.

Dalton stayed on. The Judge urged him. "It's too lovely to go in," he said; "what's your hurry?"

Aunt Claudia, who was inexpressibly weary, felt that her father was exceeding the bounds of necessary hospitality. She felt, too, that the length of Dalton's first call was inexcusable. But she did not go to bed. As long as Becky was there, she should stay to chaperon her. With a sense of martyrdom upon her, Mrs. Beaufort sat stiffly in her chair.

The Judge was talkative and brilliant, glad of a new and apparently attentive listener. Becky had little to say. She sat with her small feet set primly on the ground. Her hands were folded in her lap. Dalton was used to girls who lounged or who hung fatuously on his words, as if they had set themselves to please him.

But Becky had no arts. She was frank and unaffected, and apparently not unconscious of Dalton's charms. The whole thing was, he felt, going to be rather stimulating.

When at last he left them, he asked the Judge if he might come again. "I'd like to look at those birds by daylight."

Becky, giving him her hand, hoped that he might come. She had been all the evening in a sort of waking dream. Even when Dalton had been silent, she had been intensely aware of his presence, and when he had talked, he had seemed to speak to her alone, although his words were for others.

"I saw you dancing," he said, before he dropped her hand.

"Oh, did you?"

"Yes."

Back of the house the dogs barked.

"Will you dance some time with me?"

"Oh, could I?"

"Why not?"

A moment later he was gone. The light of his motor flashed down the hills like a falling star.

"I wonder what made the dogs bark," the Judge said as they went in.

"They probably thought it was morning," was Mrs. Beaufort's retort, as she preceded Becky up the stairs.

IV

547

The dogs had barked because Randy after a quick drive home had walked back to Huntersfield.

"Look here," he burst out as he and the Major had stood on the steps of the Schoolhouse, "do you like him?"

"Who? Dalton?"

"Yes."

"He's not a man's man," the Major said, "and he doesn't care in the least what you and I think of him."

"Doesn't he?"

"No, and he doesn't care for—stuffed birds—and he doesn't care for the Judge, and he doesn't care for Mrs. Beaufort——"

"Oh, you needn't rub it in. I know what he's after."

"Do you?"

"Yes——"

The Major whistled softly a lilting tune. He had been called "The Whistling Major" by his men and they had liked his clear piping.

He stopped abruptly. "Well, you can't build fences around lovely little ladies——"

"I wish I could. I'd like to shut her up in a tower——"

They left it there. It was really not a thing to be talked about. They both knew it, and stopped in time.

Randy, climbing the outside stairs, presently, to his bedroom, turned at the upper landing to survey the scene spread out before him. The hills were steeped in silence. The world was black and gold—the fragrance of the honeysuckle came up from the hedge below. On such a night as this one could not sleep. He felt himself restless, emotionally keyed up. He descended the stairs. Then, suddenly, he found himself taking the trail back towards Huntersfield.

He walked easily, following the path which led across the hills. The distance was not great, and he had often walked it. He loved a night like this. As he came to a stretch of woodland, he went under the trees with the thrill of one who enters an enchanted forest.

An owl hooted overhead. A whip-poor-will in a distant swamp sounded his plaintive call.

Randy could not have analyzed the instinct which sent him back to Becky. It was not in the least to spy upon her, nor upon Dalton. He only knew that he could not sleep, that something drew him on and on, as Romeo was drawn perchance to Capulet's orchard.

He came out from under the trees to other hills. He was still on his own land. These acres had belonged to his father, his grandfather, his great-grandfather, and back of that to a certain gallant gentleman who had come to Virginia with grants from the King. There had been, too, a great chief, whose blood was in his veins, and who had roamed through this land before Europe knew it. Powhatan was a rare old name to link with one's own, and Randy had a Virginian's pride in his savage strain.

So, as he went along, he saw canoes upon the shining river. He saw tall forms with feathers blowing. He saw fires on the heights.

The hill in front of him dipped to a little stream. He and Becky had once waded in that stream together. How white her feet had been on the brown stones. His life, as he thought of it, was bound up in memories of Becky. She had come down from school for blissful week-ends and holidays, and she and Randy had tramped over the hills and through the pine woods, finding wild-flowers in the spring, arbutus, flushing to beauty in its hidden bed, blood-root, hepatica, wind-flowers, violets in a purple glory; finding in the summer wild roses, dewberries, blackberries, bees and butterflies, the cool shade of the little groves, the shine and shimmer of the streams; finding in the fall a golden stillness and the redness of Virginia Creeper. They had ridden on horseback over the clay roads, they had roamed the stubble with a pack of wiry hounds at their heels, they had gathered Christmas greens, they had sung carols, they had watched the Old Year out and the New Year in, and their souls had been knit in a comradeship which had been a very fine thing indeed for a boy like Randy and a girl like Becky.

There had been, too, about their friendship a rather engaging seriousness. They had talked a great deal of futures. They had dreamed together very great dreams. Their dreams had, of course, changed from time to time. There had been that dream of Becky's when she first went to the convent, that she wanted some day to be a nun like Sister Loretto. The fact that it would involve a change of faith was thrashed over flamingly by Randy. "It is all very well for an old woman, Becky. But you'd hate it."

Becky had been sure that she would not hate it. "You don't know how lovely she looks in the chapel."

"Well, there are other ways to look lovely."

"But it would be nice to be—good."

"You are good enough."

"I am not really, Randy. Sister Loretto says her prayers all day——"

"How often do you say yours?"

"Oh, at night. And in the mornings—sometimes——"

"That's enough for anybody. If you say them hard enough once, what more can the Lord ask?"

He had been a rather fierce figure as he had flung his questions, but he had not swerved her in the least from her thought of herself as a novice in a white veil, and later as a full-fledged sister, with beads and a black head-dress.

This dream had, in time, been supplanted by one imposed upon her by the ambitions of a much-admired classmate.

"Maude and I are going to be doctors," Becky had announced as she and Randy had walked over the fields with the hounds at their heels. "It's a great opportunity for women, Randy, and we shall study in Philadelphia."

"Shall you like cutting people up?" he had demanded brutally.

She had shuddered. "I shan't have to cut them up very much, shall I?"

"You'll have to cut them up a lot. All doctors do, and sometimes they are dead."

She had argued a bit shakily after that, and that night she had slept badly. The next morning they had gone over it again.

"You fainted when the kitten's paw was crushed in the door."

"It was dreadful——"

"And you cried when I cut my foot with the hatchet and we were out in the woods. And if you are going to be a doctor you'll have to look at people who are crushed and cut——"

"Oh, please, Randy——"

Three days of such intensive argument had settled it. Becky decided that it was, after all, better to be an authoress. "There was Louisa Alcott, you know, Randy."

He was scornful. "Women weren't made for that—to sit in an attic and write. Why do you keep talking about doing things, Becky? You'll get married when you grow up and that will be the end of it."

"I am not going to get married, Randy."

"Well, of course you will, and I shall marry and be a lawyer like my father, and perhaps I'll go to Congress."

Later he had a leaning towards the ministry. "If I preached I could make the world better, Becky."

That was the time when she had come down for Hallowe'en, and it was on Sunday evening that they had talked it over in the Bird Room at Huntersfield. There had been a smouldering fire on the wide hearth, and the Trumpeter Swan had stared down at them with shining eyes. They had been to church that morning and the text had been, "The harvest is past, the summer is ended, and we are not saved."

"I want to make the world better, Becky," Randy had said in the still twilight, and Becky had answered in an awed tone, "It would be so splendid to see you in the pulpit, Randy, wearing a gown like Dr. Hodge."

But the pulpit to Randy had meant more than that. And the next day when they walked through the deserted mill town, he had said, "Everybody is dead who lived here, and once they were alive like us."

She had shivered, "I don't like to think of it."

"It's a thing we've all got to think of. I like to remember that Thomas Jefferson came riding through and stopped at the mill and talked to the miller."

"How dreadful to know that they are—dead."

"Mother says that men like Jefferson never die. Their souls go marching on."

The stream which ground the county's corn was at their feet. "But what about the miller?" Becky had asked; "does his soul march, too?"

Randy, with the burden of yesterday's sermon upon him, hoped that the miller was saved.

He smiled now as he thought of the rigidness of his boyish theology. To him in those days Heaven was Heaven and Hell was Hell.

The years at school had brought doubt—apostasy. Then on the fields of France, Randy's God had come back to him—the Christ who bound up wounds, who gave a cup of cold water, who fought with flaming sword against the battalions of brutality, who led up and up that white company who gave their lives for a glorious Cause. Here, indeed, was a God of righteousness and of justice, of tenderness and purity. To other men than Randy, Christ had in a very personal and specific sense been born across the sea.

It was in France, too, that the dream had come to him of a future of creative purpose. He had always wanted to write. Looking back over his University days, he was aware of a formative process which had led towards this end. It was there he had communed with the spirit of a tragic muse. There had been all the traditions of Poe and his tempestuous youth— and Randy, passing the door which had once opened and closed on that dark figure, had felt the thrill of a living personality—of one who spoke still in lines of ineffable beauty—"_Banners yellow, glorious, golden, On its roof did float and flow_——" and again "_A dirge for her the doubly dead, in that she died so young_——" with the gayety and gloom and grandeur of those chiming, rhyming, tolling bells—"_Keeping time, time, time, In a sort of Runic rhyme_——" and that "_grim and ancient Raven wandering from the Nightly shore_——"

"Do you think I could write?" Randy had asked one of his teachers, coming verse-saturated to the question.

The man had looked at him with somber eyes. "You have an ear for it—and an eye—— But genius pays a price."

"What do you mean?"

"It shows its heart to the world, dissects its sacred thoughts, has no secrets——"

"But think of leaving a thing behind you like—'To Helen——'"

"Do you think the knowledge that he had written a few bits of incomparable verse helped Poe to live? If he had invented a pill or a headache powder, he would have slept on down and have dined from gold dishes."

"I'd rather write 'Ulalume' than dine from gold dishes."

"You think that now. But in twenty years you will sigh for a—feather bed——"

"You don't believe that."

There had come a lighting of the somber eyes. "My dear fellow, if you, by the grace of God, have it in you to write, what I believe won't have anything to do with it. You will crucify yourself for the sake of a line—starve for the love of a rhythm."

Randy had not yet starved for love of a rhythm, but he had lost sleep during those nights in France, trying to put into words the things that gripped his soul. There had been beauty as well as horror in those days. What a world it had been, a world of men—a striving, eager group, raised for the moment above sordidness, above self——

He had not found verse his medium, although he had drunk eagerly of the golden cups which others had to offer him. But his prose had gained because of his belief in beauty of structure and of singing lovely words. As yet he had nothing to show for his pains, but practice had given strength to his pen—he felt that some day with the right theme he might do— wonders——

The trees had again closed in about him. A shadow flitted by—a fox, unafraid and in search of a belated meal. Randy remembered the days when he and Becky had thought that there might be wolves in the forest. He laughed a little, recalling Becky's words. "Sister Loretto has the feeling that the world is a dark forest, and that I am Red Riding Hood." Was it that which had brought him back? Was there, indeed, a Wolf?

When he reached Huntersfield, and the dogs barked, he had feared for the moment discovery. He was saved, however, by the friendly silence which followed that first note of alarm. The dogs knew him and followed him with wagging tails as he skirted the lawn and came at last to the gate which had closed a few minutes before on Dalton's car. He saw the Judge go in, Aunt Claudia, Becky—shadowy figures between the white pillars.

Then, after a moment, a room on the second floor was illumined. The shade was up and he saw the interior as one sees the scene of a play. There was the outline of a rose-colored canopy, the gleam of a mirror, the shine of polished wood, and in the center, Becky in pale blue, with a candle in her hand.

And as he saw her there, Randolph knew why he had come. To worship at a shrine. That was where Becky belonged— high above him. The flame of the candle was a sacred fire.

CHAPTER IV
RAIN AND RANDY'S SOUL
I

Madge came down the next morning dressed for her journey. "Oscar and Flora are going to take me as far as Washington in their car. They want you to make a fourth, Georgie."

Dalton was eating alone. Breakfast was served at small tables on the west terrace. There was a flagged stone space with wide awnings overhead. Except that it overlooked a formal garden instead of streets, one might have been in a Parisian café. The idea was Oscar's. Dalton had laughed at him. "You'll be a *boulevardier*, Oscar, until you die."

Oscar had been sulky. "Well, how do you want me to do it?"

"Breakfast in bed—or in a breakfast room with things hot on the sideboard, luncheon, out here on the terrace when the weather permits, tea in the garden, dinner in great state in the big dining-room."

"I suppose you think you know all about it. But the thing that I am always asking myself is, were you born to it, Dalton?"

"I've been around a lot," Dalton evaded. "Of course if you don't want me to be perfectly frank with you, I won't."

"Be as frank as you please," Oscar had said, "but it's your air of knowing everything that gets me."

Dalton's breakfast was a hearty one—bacon and two eggs, and a pile of buttered toast. There had been a melon to begin with, and there was a pot of coffee. He was eating with an appetite when Madge came down.

"I had mine in bed," Madge said, as George rose and pulled out a chair for her. "Isn't this the beastliest fashion, having little tables?"

"That's what I told Oscar."

"Oscar and Flora will never have too much of restaurants. They belong to the class which finds all that it wants in a jazz band and scrambled eggs at Jack's at one o'clock in the morning. Georgie, in my next incarnation, I hope there won't be any dansants or night frolics. I'd like a May-pole in the sunshine and a lot of plump and rosy women and bluff and hearty men for my friends—with a fine old farmhouse and myself in the dairy making butter——"

George smiled at her. "I should have fancied you an Egyptian princess, with twin serpents above your forehead instead of that turban."

"Heavens, no. I want no ardours and no Anthonys. Tell me about the new little girl, Georgie."

"How do you know there is a—new little girl?"

"I know your tricks and your manners, and the way you managed to meet her at the Horse Show. And you saw her last night."

"How do you know?"

"By the light in your eyes."

"Do I show it like that? Well, she's rather—not to be talked about, Madge——"

She was not in the least affronted. "So that's it? You always begin that way—putting them on a pedestal—— If you'd only keep one of us there it might do you good."

"Which one—you?" he leaned a little forward.

"No." Indignation stirred within her. How easy it was for him to play the game. And last night she had lain long awake, listening for the sound of his motor. She had seen the moon set, and spectral dawn steal into the garden. "No, I'm running away. I am tired of drifting always on the tides of other people's inclination. We have stayed down here where it is hot because Oscar and Flora like it, yet there's all the coolness of the North Shore waiting for us——"

She rose and walked to the edge of the terrace. The garden was splashed now with clear color, purple and rose and gold. The air was oppressive, with a gathering haze back of the hills.

"I'm tired of it. Some day I'm going to flap my wings and fly away where you won't be able to find me, Georgie. I'd rather be a wild gull to the wind-swept sky, than a tame pigeon—to eat from your hand——" She said it lightly; this was not a moment for plaintiveness.

There was a dancing light in his eyes. "You're a golden pheasant—and you'll never fly so far that I shan't find you."

Oscar arriving at this moment saved a retort. "Flora's not well. We can't motor up, Madge."

"I am sorry but I can take a train."

"There's one at three. I don't see why you are going," irritably; "Flora won't stay here long after you leave."

"I am not as necessary as you think, Oscar. There are plenty of others, and I must go——"

"Oh, very well. Andrews will drive you down."

"I'll drive her myself," said Dalton.

II

Aunt Claudia was going to Washington also on the three o'clock train. She had had a wireless from Truxton who had sailed from Brest and would arrive at New York within the week.

"Of course you'll go and meet him, Aunt Claudia," Becky had said; "I'll help you to get your things ready."

Aunt Claudia, quite white and inwardly shaken by the thought of the happiness which was on its way to her, murmured her thanks.

Becky, divining something of the tumult which was beneath that outward show of serenity, patted the cushions of the couch in Mrs. Beaufort's bedroom. "Lie down here, you darling dear. It was such a surprise, wasn't it?"

"Well, my knees are weak," Mrs. Beaufort admitted.

The nuns had taught Becky nice ways and useful arts, so she folded and packed under Aunt Claudia's eye and was much applauded.

"Most girls in these days," said Mrs. Beaufort, "throw things in. Last summer I stayed at a house where the girls sat on their trunks to shut them, and sent parcel-post packages after them of the things they had left out."

"Sister Loretto says that I am not naturally tidy, so she keeps me at it. I used to weep my eyes out when she'd send me back to my room—— But crying doesn't do any good with Sister Loretto."

"Crying is never any good," said Aunt Claudia. She was of Spartan mold. "Crying only weakens. When things are so bad that you must cry, then do it where the world can't see."

Becky found herself thrilled by the thought of Aunt Claudia crying in secret. She was a martial little soul in spite of her distinctly feminine type of mind.

Aunt Claudia's lingerie, chastely French-embroidered in little scallops, with fresh white ribbons run in, was laid out on the bed in neat piles. There was also a gray corduroy dressing-gown, lined with silk.

"This will be too warm," Becky said; "please let me put in my white crepe house-coat. It will look so pretty, Aunt Claudia, when Truxton comes in the morning to kiss you——"

Aunt Claudia had been holding on to her emotions tightly. The thought of that morning kiss which for three dreadful years had been denied her—for three dreadful years she had not known whether Truxton would ever breeze into her room before breakfast with his "Mornin' Mums." She felt that if she allowed herself any softness or yielding at this moment she would spoil her spotless record of self-control and weep in maudlin fashion in Becky's arms.

So in self-defense, she spoke with coldness. "I never wear borrowed clothes, my dear."

Becky, somewhat dishevelled and warm from her exertions, sat down to argue it. "I haven't had it on. And I'd love to give it to you——"

"My dear, of course not. It's very generous of you—very——" Aunt Claudia buried her face suddenly in the pillows and sobbed stormily.

Becky stood up. "Oh, Aunt Claudia," she gasped. Then with the instinctive knowledge that silence was best, she gave her aunt a little pat on the shoulder and crept from the room.

She crept back presently and packed the crepe house-coat with the other things. Then, since Aunt Claudia made no sign, she went down-stairs to the kitchen.

Mandy, the cook, who had a complexion like an old copper cent, and who wore a white Dutch cap in place of the traditional bandana, was cutting corn from the cob for fritters.

"If you'll make a cup of tea," Becky said, "I'll take it up to Aunt Claudia. She's lying down."

"Is you goin' wid her?" Mandy asked.

"To New York? No. She'll want Truxton all to herself, Mandy."

"Well, I hopes she has him," Mandy husked an ear of corn viciously. "I ain' got my boy. He hol's his haid so high, he ain' got no time fo' his ol' Mammy."

"You know you are proud of him, Mandy."

"I ain' sayin' I is, and I ain' sayin' I isn't. But dat Daisy down the road, she ac' like she own him."

"Oh, Daisy? Is he in love with her?"

"Love," with withering scorn, "_love_? Ain' he got somefin' bettah to do than lovin' when he's jes' fit and fought fo' Uncle Sam?" She beat the eggs for her batter as if she had Daisy's head under the whip. "He fit and fought fo' Uncle Sam," she repeated, "and now he comes home and camps hisse'f on Daisy's do'-step."

Against the breeze of such high indignation, any argument would be blown away. Becky changed the subject hastily.

"Mandy," she asked, "are you making corn fritters?"

"I is——"

"What else for lunch?"

"An omlec——"

"Mandy, I'm so hungry I could eat a house——"

"You look it," Mandy told her; "effen I was you, I'd eat and git fat."

"It isn't fashionable to be fat, Mandy."

"Skeletums may be in style," said Mandy, breaking eggs for the omelette, "but I ain' ever found good looks in bones."

"Don't you like _my_ bones, Mandy?"

"You ain't got none, honey."

"You called me a skeleton."

The kettle boiled. "Effen I called you a skeletum," Mandy said as she placed a cup and saucer on a small napkined tray, "my min' was on dat-ar Daisy. You ain' got no bones, Miss Becky. But Daisy, she's got a neck like a picked tukkey, and her shoulder-blades stan' out like wings."

III

Becky went to the train with her aunt. George Dalton drove Madge down and passed the old surrey on the way.

Later Madge met Mrs. Beaufort and Becky on the station platform, and it was when Dalton settled her in her chair in the train that she said, "She's a darling. Keep her on a pedestal, Georgie——"

"You're a good sport," he told her; "you know you'd hate it if I did."

"I shouldn't. I'd like to think of you on your knees——"

It was time for him to leave her. She gave him her hand. "Until we meet again, Georgie."

Her eyes were cool and smiling. Yet later as she looked out on the flying hills, there was trouble in them. There had been a time when Dalton had seemed to square with her girlish dreams.

And now, there was no one to warn this other girl with dreams in her eyes. George was not a vulture, he was simply a marauding bee——!

Becky was already in the surrey when George came back, and Calvin was gathering up his reins.

"Oh, look here, I wish you'd let me drive you up, Miss Bannister," George said, sparkling; "there's no reason, is there, why you must ride alone?"

"Oh, no."

"Then you will?"

Her hesitation was slight. "I should like it."

"And can't we drive about a bit? You'll show me the old places? It is such a perfect day. I hope you haven't anything else to do."

She had not. "I'll go with Mr. Dalton, Calvin."

Calvin, who had watched over more than one generation of Bannister girls, and knew what was expected of them, made a worried protest.

"Hit's gwine rain, Miss Becky."

Dalton dismissed him with a wave of the hand. "I won't let her get wet," he lifted Becky from the surrey and walked with her to his car.

Kemp, who had come down in the house truck with Madge's trunks, stood stiff and straight by the door. Being off with Miss MacVeigh he was on with Miss Bannister. Girls might come and girls might go in his master's life, but Kemp had an air of going on forever.

When he had seated Becky, Dalton stepped back and gave hurried instructions.

"At four, Kemp," he said, "or if you are later, wait until we come."

"Very well, sir." Kemp stood statuesquely at attention until the car whirled on. Then he sat down on the station platform, and talked to the agent. He was no longer a servant but a man.

As the big car whirled up the hill, Becky, looking out upon the familiar landscape, saw it with new eyes. There was a light upon it which had never been for her on sea or land. She had not believed that in all the world there could be such singing, blossoming radiance.

They drove through the old mill town and the stream was bright under the willows. They stopped on the bridge for a moment to view the shining bend.

"There are old chimneys under the vines," Becky said; "doesn't it seem dreadful to think of all those dead houses——"

George gave a quick turn. "Why think of them? You were not made to think of dead houses, you were made to live."

On and on they went, up the hills and down into the valleys, between rail fences which were a riot of honeysuckle, and with the roads in places rough under their wheels, with the fields gold with stubble, the sky a faint blue, with that thick look on the horizon.

George talked a great deal about himself. Perhaps if he had listened instead to Becky he might have learned things which would have surprised him. But he really had very interesting things to tell, and Becky was content to sit in silence and watch his hands on the wheel. They were small hands, and for some tastes a bit too plump and well-kept, but Becky found no fault with them. She felt that she could sit there forever, and watch his hands and listen to his clear quick voice.

At last George glanced at the little clock which hung in front of him. "Look here," he said, "I told Kemp to have tea for us at a place which I found once when I walked in the woods. A sort of summer house which looks towards Monticello. Do you know it?"

"Yes. Pavilion Hill. It's on Randy Paine's plantation—King's Crest."

"Then you've been there?"

"A thousand times with Randy."

"I thought it was Waterman's. We shan't be jailed as trespassers, shall we?"

"No. But how could you tell your man to have tea for us when you didn't know that I'd be—willing?"

"But I did—know——"

A little silence, then "How?"

"Because when I put my mind on a thing I usually get my way."

She sat very still. He bent down to her. "You're not angry?"

"No." Her cheeks were flaming. She was thrilled by his masterfulness. No man had ever spoken to her like that. She was, indeed, having her first experience of ardent, impassioned pursuit. So might young Juliet have given ear to Romeo. And if Romeo had been a Georgie-Porgie, then alas, poor Juliet!

The Pavilion had been built a hundred and fifty years before of cedar logs. There had been a time when Thomas Jefferson had walked over to drink not tea, but something stronger with dead and gone Paines. Its four sides were open, but the vines formed a curtain which gave within a soft gloom. They approached it from the east side, getting out of their car and climbing the hill from the roadside. They found Kemp with everything ready. The kettle was boiling, and the tea measured into the Canton teapot which stood in its basket——

"Aren't you glad you came?" Dalton asked. "Kemp, when you've poured the tea, you can look after the car."

The wind, rising, tore the dry leaves from the trees. Kemp, exiled, as it were, from the Pavilion, sat in the big car and watched the gathering blackness. Finally he got out and put up the curtains. Everything would be ready when Dalton came. He knew better, however, than to warn his master. George was apt to be sharp when his plans were spoiled.

And now throughout the wooded slope there was the restless movement of nature disturbed in the midst of peaceful dreaming. The trees bent and whispered. The birds, flying low, called sharp warnings. A small dog, spurning the leaves, as she followed a path up the west side of the hill, stopped suddenly and looked back at the man who followed her.

"We'll make the Pavilion if we can, old girl," he told her, and as if she understood, she went up and up in a straight line, disregarding the temptation of side tours into bush and bramble.

George and Becky had finished their tea. There had been some rather delectable sweet biscuit which Kemp kept on hand for such occasions, and there was a small round box of glacé nuts, which George had insisted that Becky must keep. The box was of blue silk set off by gold lace and small pink roses.

"Blue is your color," George had said as he presented it.

"That's what Randy says."

"You are always talking of Randy."

She looked her surprise. "I've always known him."

553

"Is he in love with you?"

She set down the box and looked at him. "Randy is only a boy. I am very fond of him. But we aren't either of us—silly."

She brought the last sentence out with such scorn that George had a moment of startled amaze.

Then, recovering, he said with a smile, "Is being in love silly?"

"I think it's rather sacred——"

The word threw him back upon himself. Love was, you understand, to George, a game. And here was Becky acting as if it were a ritual.

Yet the novelty of her point of view made her seem more than ever adorable. In his heart he found himself saying, "Oh, you lovely, lovely little thing."

But he did not say it aloud. Indeed he, quite unaccountably, found himself unable to say anything, and while he hesitated, there charged up the west hill a panting dog with flapping ears. At the arched opening of the Pavilion she paused and wagged a tentative question.

"It's Nellie Custis——" Becky rose and ran towards her. "Where's your master, darling? *Randy*——"

In response to her call came an eerie cry—the old war cry of the Indian chiefs. Then young Paine came running up.

"Becky! Here? There's going to be a storm. You better get home——"

He stopped short. Dalton was standing by the folding table.

"Hello, Paine," he said, with ease. "We're playing 'Babes in the Wood.'"

"You seem very comfortable," Randy was as stiff as a wooden tobacco sign.

"We are," Becky said. "Mr. Dalton waved his wand like the Arabian nights——"

"My man did it," said Dalton; "he's down there in the car."

Randy felt a sense of surging rage. The Pavilion was his. It was old and vine-covered, and hallowed by a thousand memories. And here was Dalton trespassing with his tables and chairs and his Canton teapot. What right had George Dalton to bring a Canton teapot on another man's acres?

Becky was pouring tea for him. "Two lumps, Randy?"

"I don't want any tea," he said ungraciously. His eyes were appraising the flame of her cheeks, the light in her eyes. What had Dalton been saying? "I don't want any tea. And there's a storm coming."

All her life Becky had been terrified in a storm. She had cowered and shivered at the first flash of lightning, at the first rush of wind, at the first roll of thunder. And now she sat serene, while the trees waved despairing arms to a furious sky, while blackness settled over the earth, while her ears were assailed by the noise of a thousand guns.

What had come over her? More than anything else, the thing that struck against Randy's heart was this lack of fear in Becky!

IV

Of course it was Dalton who took Becky home. There had been a sharp summons to Kemp, who came running up with raincoats, a rush for the car, a hurried "Won't you come with us, Randy?" from Becky, and Randy's curt refusal, and then the final insult from Dalton.

"Kemp will get you home, Paine, when he takes the tea things."

Randy wanted to throw something after him—preferably a tomahawk—as Dalton went down the hill, triumphantly, shielding Becky from the elements.

He watched until a curtain of rain shut them out, but he heard the roar of the motor cutting through the clamor of the storm.

"Well, they're off, sir," said Kemp cheerfully.

He was packing the Canton teapot in its basket and was folding up the chairs and tables. Randy had a sense of outrage. Here he was, a Randolph Paine of King's Crest, left behind in the rain with a man who had his mind on—teapots—— He stood immovable in the arched opening, his arms folded, and with the rain beating in upon him.

"You'll get wet," Kemp reminded him; "it's better on this side, sir."

"I don't mind the rain. I won't melt; I've had two years in France."

"You have, sir?" something in Kemp's voice made Randy turn and look at him. The little man had his arms full of biscuit boxes, and he was gazing at Randy with a light in his eyes which had not been for Dalton.

"I had three years myself. And the best of my life, sir."

Randy nodded. "A lot of us feel that way."

"The fighting," said Kemp, "was something awful. But it was—big—and after it things seem a bit small, sir." He drew a long breath and came back to his Canton teapot and his folding table and his plans for departure.

"I'll be glad to take you in the little car, Mr. Paine."

"No," said Randy; "no, thank you, Kemp. I'll wait here until the storm is over."

Kemp, with a black rubber cape buttoned about his shoulders and standing out over his load like a lady's hoopskirts, bobbed down the path and was gone.

554

Randy was glad to be alone. He was glad to get wet, he was glad of the roar and of the tumult which matched the tumult in his soul.

Somehow he had never dreamed of this—that somebody would come into Becky's life and take her away——

Nellie Custis shivered and whined. She hated thunder-storms. Randy sat down on the step and she crept close to him. He laid his hand on her head and fear left her—as fear had left Becky in the presence of Dalton.

After that the boy and the dog sat like statues, looking out, and in those tense and terrible moments a new spirit was born in Randolph Paine. Hitherto he had let life bring him what it would. He had scarcely dared hope that it would bring him Becky. But now he knew that if he lost her he would face—chaos——

Well, he would not lose her. Or if he did, it would not be to let her marry a man like Dalton. Surely she wouldn't.

She *couldn't*—— But there had been that light in her eyes, that flame in her cheek—that lack of fear—Dalton's air of assurance, the way she had turned to him.

"Oh, God," he said suddenly, out loud, "don't let Dalton have her."

He was shaken by an emotion which bent his head to his knees. Nellie Custis pressed close against him and whined.

"He shan't have her, Nellie. He shan't——"

He burned with the thought of Dalton's look of triumph. Dalton who had carried Becky off, and had left him with Kemp and a Canton teapot.

He recalled Kemp's words. "After it things seem a bit small, sir."

Well, it shouldn't be small for him. It had seemed so big—over there. So easy to—carry on.

If he only had a fighting chance. If he had only a half of Dalton's money. A little more time in which to get on his feet. But in the meantime here was Dalton—with his money, his motors, and his masterfulness. And his look of triumph——

In a sudden fierce reaction he sprang to his feet. He stood in the doorway as if defying the future. "Nobody shall take her away from me," he said, "she's mine——"

His arms were folded over his chest, his wet black locks almost hid his eyes. So might some young savage have stood in the long ago, sending his challenge forth to those same hills.

CHAPTER V
LITTLE SISTER
I

It is one thing, however, to fling a challenge to the hills, and another to live up to the high moment. Looking at it afterwards in cold blood, Randy was forced to admit that his chances of beating George Dalton in a race for Becky were small.

There seemed some slight hope, however, in the fact that Becky was a Bannister and ought to know a gentleman when she saw one.

"And Dalton's a—a bounder," said Randy to Nellie Custis.

Nellie Custis, who was as blue-blooded as any Bannister, cocked a sympathetic ear. Cocking an ear with Nellie was a weighty matter. Her ears were big and unmanageable. When she got them up, she kept them there for some time. It was a rather intriguing habit, as it gave her an air of eager attention which wooed confidence.

"He's a bounder," said Randy as if that settled it.

But it did not settle it in the least. A man with an Apollo head may not be a gentleman under his skin, but how are you to prove it? The world, spurning Judy O'Grady, sanctions the Colonel's lady, and their sisterhood becomes socially negligible. Randy should have known that he could not sweep George Dalton away with a word. Perhaps he did know it, but he did not care to admit it.

He and Nellie Custis were in the garage. It had once been a barn, but the boarders had bought cars, so there was now the smell of gasoline where there had once been the sweet scent of hay. And intermittently the air was rent with puffs and snorts and shrieks which drowned the music of that living chorus which has been sung in stables for centuries.

There were three cars. Two of them have nothing to do with this story, but the third will play its part, and merits therefore description.

It was not an expensive car, but it was new and shining, and had a perky snub-nosed air of being ready for anything. It belonged to the genial gentleman who used it without mercy, and thus the little car wove back and forth over the hills like a shuttle, doing its work sturdily, coming home somewhat noisily, and even at rest, seeming to ask for something more to do.

The genial gentleman was very proud of his car. He talked a great deal about it to Randy, and on this particular morning when he came out and found young Paine sitting on a wheelbarrow with Nellie Custis lending him a cocked ear, he grew eloquent.

"Look here, I've been thinking. There ought to be a lot of cars like this in the county."

To Randy the enthusiasms of the genial gentleman were a constant source of amazement. He was always wanting the world to be glad about something. Randy felt that at this moment any assumption of gladness would be a hollow mockery.

"Any man," said the genial gentleman, rubbing a cloth over the enamel of the little car, "any man who would start selling this machine down here would make a fortune."

Randy pricked up his ears.

"How could he make a fortune?"

"Selling cars. Why, the babies cry for them——" he chuckled and rubbed harder.

"How much could he make?" Randy found himself saying.

The genial gentleman named a sum, "Easy."

Randy got up from the wheelbarrow and came over. "Is she really as good as that?"

"Is she really? Oh, say——" the genial gentleman for the next ten minutes dealt in superlatives.

Towards the end, Randy was firing questions at him.

"Could I own a car while I was selling them?"

"Sure—they'd let you have it on installments to be paid for out of your commissions——"

"And I'd have an open field?"

"My dear boy, in a month you could have cars like this running up and down the hills like ants after sugar. They speak for themselves, and they are cheap enough for anybody."

"But it is a horse-riding country, especially back in the hills. They love horse-flesh, you know."

"Oh, they'll get the gasoline bug like the rest of us," said the genial gentleman and slapped him on the back.

Randy winced. He did not like to be slapped on the back. Not at a moment—when he was selling his soul to the devil—— For that was the way he looked at it.

"I shall have to perjure myself," he said to Major Prime later, as they talked it over in the Schoolhouse, "to go through the country telling mine own people to sell their horses and get cars."

"If you don't do it, somebody else will."

"But a man can't be convincing if he doesn't believe in a thing."

"No, of course. But you've got to look at it this way, the world moves, and horses haven't had an easy time. Perhaps it is their moment of emancipation. And just for the sake of a sentiment, a tradition, you can't afford to hold back."

"I can't afford to lose this chance if there is money in it. But it isn't what I had planned."

As he sat there on the step and hugged his knees, every drop of blood in Randy seemed to be urging "Hurry, hurry." He felt as a man might who, running a race, finds another rider neck and neck and strains towards the finish.

To sell cars in order to win Becky seemed absurd on the face of it. But he would at least be doing something towards solving the problem of self-support, and towards increasing the measure of his own self-respect.

"What had you planned?" the Major was asking.

"Well of course there is the law—— And I like it, but there would be a year or two before I could earn a living—— And I've wanted to write——"

"Write what? Books?"

"Anything," said Randy, explosively, "that would make the world sit up."

"Ever tried it?"

"Yes. At school. I talked to a teacher of mine once about it. He said I had better invent a—pill——"

The Major stared, "A pill?"

Randy nodded. "He didn't quite mean it, of course. But he saw the modern trend. A poet? A poor thing! But hats off to the pillmaker with his multi-millions!"

"Stop that," said the Major.

"Stop what?"

"Blaming the world for its sordidness. There is beauty enough if we look for it."

"None of us has time to look for it. We are too busy trying to sell cars to people who love horses."

II

In the end Randy got his car. And after that he, too, might have been seen running shuttle-like back and forth over the red roads. Nellie Custis was usually beside him on the front seat. She took her new honors seriously. For generations back her forbears had loped with flapping ears in the lead of a hunting pack. To be sitting thus on a leather seat and whirled through the air with no need of legs from morning until night required some readjustment on the part of Nellie Custis. But she had always followed where Randy led. And in time she grew to like it, and watched the road ahead with eager eyes, and with her ears perpetually cocked.

Now and then Becky sat beside Randy, with Nellie at her feet. The difference between a ride with Randy and one with George Dalton was, Becky felt, the difference a not unpleasant commonplace and the stuff that dreams are made of.

"It is rather a duck of a car," she had said, the first time he took her out in it.

"Yes, it is," Randy had agreed. "I am getting tremendously fond of her. I have named her 'Little Sister.'"

"Oh, Randy, you haven't."

"Yes, I have. She has such confiding ways. I never believed that cars had human qualities, Becky."

"They are not horses of course."

"Well, they have individual characteristics. You take the three cars in our barn. The Packard reminds one of that stallion we owned three years ago—blooded and off like the wind. The Franklin is a grayhound—and Little Sister is a—duck——"

"Mr. Dalton's car is a—silver ship——"

"Oh, does he call it that?" grimly.

"No——"

"Was it your own—poetic—idea?"

"Yes."

"And you called Little Sister a duck," he groaned. "And when my little duck swims in the wake of his silver ship, and he laughs, do you laugh, too?"

There was a dead silence. Then she said, "Oh, Randy——"

He made his apology like a gentleman. "That was hateful of me, Becky. I'm sorry——"

"You know I wouldn't laugh, Randy, and neither would he."

"Who?"

"Mr. Dalton."

"Wouldn't what?"

"Laugh."

He hated her defense of young Apollo—but he couldn't let the subject alone.

"You never have any time for me."

"Randy, are you going to scold me for the rest of our ride?"

"Am I scolding?"

"Yes."

"Then I'll stop it and say nice things to you or you won't want to come again."

Yet after that when he saw her in Dalton's car, her words would return to him, and gradually he began to think of her as sailing in a silver ship farther and farther away in a future where he could not follow.

Little Sister was a great comfort in those days. She gave him occupation and she gave him an income. He was never to forget his first sale. He had not found it easy to cry his wares. The Paines of King's Crest had never asked favors of the country-folk, or if they had, they had paid generously for what they had received. To go now among them saying, "I have something to sell," carried a sting. There had been nothing practical in Randy's education. He had no equipment with which to meet the sordid questions of bargain and sale.

He had thought of this as he rode over the hills that morning to the house of a young farmer who had been suggested by the genial gentleman as a good prospect. He turned over in his mind the best method of approach. It was a queer thing, he pondered, to visualize himself as a salesman. He wondered how many of the other fellows who had come back looked at it as he did. They had dreamed such dreams of valor, their eyes had seen visions. To Randy when he had enlisted had come a singing sense that the days of chivalry were not dead. He had gone through the war with a laugh on his lips, but with a sense of the sacredness of the crusade in his heart. He had returned—still dreaming—to sell snub-nosed cars to the countryside!

Why, just a year ago——! He remembered a black night of storm, when, hooded like a falcon—he had ridden without a light on his motorcycle, carrying dispatches from the Argonne, and even as he had ridden, he had felt that high sense of heroic endeavor. On the success of his mission depended other lives, the saving of nations—victory——!

And now he, with a million others, was faced by the problem of the day's work. He wondered how the others looked at it—those gallant young knights in khaki who had followed the gleam. Were they, too, grasping at any job that would buy them bread and butter, pay their bills, keep them from living on the bounty of others?

He felt that in some way the thing was all wrong. There should have been big things for these boys to do. There seemed something insensate in a civilization which would permit a man who wore medals of honor to sell ribbon over a counter, or weigh out beef at a butcher's. Yet he supposed that many of them were doing it. Indeed he knew that some of them were. The butcher's boy, who brought the meat over every morning to King's Crest, wore two decorations, and when Randy had stopped for breakfast supplies, the hero of Belleau Woods had cut off sausages as calmly as he had once bayonetted Huns.

Randy wondered what the butcher's boy was feeling under that apparently stolid surface. Was his horizon bounded by beef and sausages, or did his soul expand with memories of the shoulder-to-shoulder march, the comradeship of the trenches, the laughter and songs? Did his pulses thrill with the thought of the big things he might yet do in these days of peace, or was he content to play safe and snip sausages?

Randy felt that he was not content. It was not that he loved war. But he loved the visions that the war had brought him. There had seemed no limit then to America's achievement. She had been a laggard—he thanked God that he had not been a party to that delay. But when she had come in, she had come in with all her might and main. And her young men had

557

fought and the future of the whole world had been in their hands, and since peace had come the future of the world must still be reckoned in the terms of their glorious youth.

And now, something within Randy began to sing and soar. He felt that here were things to be put on paper—the questions which he flung at himself should be written for other men to read. That was what men needed—questions. Questions which demanded answers not only in words but in deeds. This was a moment for men of high thoughts and high purposes. And he was selling cars——!

Well, some day he would write. He was writing a little now, at night. In his room at the top of the Schoolhouse. Yet the things that he had written seemed trivial as he thought of them. What he wanted was to strike a ringing note. To have the fellows say when they read it, "If it is true for him it is true for me."

Yet when one came to think of it, there were really not any "fellows." Not in the sense that it had been "over there." They were scattered to the four winds, dispersed to the seven seas—the A. E. F. was extinct—as extinct—as the Trumpeter Swan!

And now his thoughts ran fast, and faster. Here was his theme. Where was that glorious company of young men who had once sounded their trumpets to the world? Gone, as the swans were gone—leaving the memory of their whiteness—leaving the memory of their beauty—leaving the memory of their—song——

He wanted to turn back at once. To drive Little Sister at breakneck speed towards pen and paper. But some instinct drove him doggedly towards the matter on hand. One might write masterpieces, but there were cars to be sold.

He sold one——; quite strangely and unexpectedly he found that the transaction was not difficult. The man whom he had come to see was on the front porch and was glad of company. Randy explained his errand. "It is new business for me. But I've got something to offer you that you'll find you'll want——"

He found that he could say many things truthful about the merits of Little Sister. He had a convincing manner; the young farmer listened.

"Let me take you for a ride," Randy offered, and away they went along the country roads, and through the main streets of the town in less time that it takes to say—"Jack Robinson."

When they came back, the children ran out to see, and Randy took them down the road and back again. "You can carry the whole family," he said, "when you go——"

The man's wife came out. She refused to ride. She was afraid.

But Randy talked her over. "My mother felt like that. But once you are in it is different."

She climbed in, and came back with her face shining.

"I am going to buy the car," her husband said to her.

Randy's heart jumped. Somehow he had felt that it would not really happen. He had had little faith in his qualities as salesman. Yet, after all, it had happened, and he had sold his car.

Riding down the hill, he was conscious of a new sense of achievement. It was all very well to dream of writing masterpieces. But here was something tangible.

"Nellie," he said, "things are picking up."

Nellie laid her nose on his knee and looked up at him. It had been a long ride, and she was glad they were on the homeward stretch. But she wagged her tail. Nellie knew when things were going well with her master. And when his world went wrong, her sky darkened.

III

The sale of one car, however, does not make a fortune. Randy realized as the days went on that if he sold them and sold them and sold them, Dalton would still outdistance him financially.

There remained, therefore, fame, and the story in the back of his mind. If he could lay a thing like that at Becky's feet! He had the lover's urge towards some heaven-kissing act which should exalt his mistress—— A book for all the world to read—a picture painted with a flaming brush, a statue carved with a magic instrument. It was for Becky that Randy would work and strive hoping that by some divine chance he might draw her to him.

He worked at night until the Major finally remonstrated.

"Do you ever go to bed?"

Randy laughed. "Sometimes."

"Are you writing?"

"Trying to."

"Hard work?"

"I like it,"—succinctly.

The Major smoked for a while in silence. Then he said, "I suppose you don't want to talk about it."

It was a starry night and a still one. The younger boarders had gone for a ride. The older boarders were in bed. The Major was stretched in his long chair. Randy sat as usual on the steps.

"Yes," he said, "I'd like to talk about it. I have a big idea, and I can't put it on paper."

He hugged his knees and talked. His young voice thrilled with the majesty of his conception. Here, he said, was the idea. Once upon a time there had been a race of wonderful swans, with plumage so white that when they rested in flocks on the river banks they made a blanket of snow. Their flight was a marvellous thing—they flew so high that the eye of man could not see them—but the sound of their trumpets could be heard. The years passed and the swans came no more to their old haunts. Men had hunted them and killed them—but there were those who held that on still nights they could be heard—sounding their trumpets——

"I want to link that up with the A. E. F. We were like the swans—a white company which flew to France—— Our idealism was the song which we sounded high up. And the world listened—and caught the sound—— And now, as a body we are extinct, but if men will listen, they may still hear our trumpets—sounding——!"

As he spoke the air seemed to throb with the passion of his phrases. His face was uplifted to the sky. The Major remembered a picture in the corridor of the Library of Congress—the Boy of Winander—— Oh, the boys of the world—those wonderful boys who had been drawn out from among the rest, set apart for a time, and in whose hands now rested the fate of nations!

"It is epic," he said, slowly. "Take your time for it."

"It's too big," said Randy slowly, "and I am not a genius—— But it is my idea, all right, and some day, perhaps, I shall make it go."

"You must make it clear to yourself. Then you can make it clear to others."

"Yes," Randy agreed, "and now you can see why I am sitting up nights."

"Yes. How did you happen to think of it, Paine?"

"I've been turning a lot of things over in my mind——; what the other fellows are doing about their jobs. There's that boy at the butcher's, and a lot of us went over to do big things. And now we have come back to the little things. Why, there's Dalton's valet—Kemp—taking orders from that—cad."

His scorn seemed to cut into the night. "And I am selling cars—— I sold one to-day to an old darkey, and I felt my grandsires turn in their graves. But I like it."

The Major sat up. "Your liking it is the biggest thing about you, Paine."

"What do you mean?"

"A man who can do his day's work and not whine about it, is the man that counts. That butcher's boy may have a soul above weighing meat and wrapping sausages, but at the moment that's his job, and he is doing it well. There may be a divine discontent, but I respect the man who keeps his mouth shut until he finds a remedy or a raise.

"I don't often speak of myself," he went on, "but perhaps this is the moment. I am as thirsty for California, Paine, as a man for drink. It is the dry season out there, and the hills are brown, but I love the brown, and the purple shadows in the hollows. I have ridden over those hills for days at a time,—I shall never ride a horse over them again." He stopped and went on. "Oh, I've wanted to whine. I have wanted to curse the fate that tied me to a chair like this. I have been an active man—out-of-doors, and oh, the out-of-doors in California. There isn't anything like it—it is the sense of space, the clear-cut look of things. But I won't go back. Not till I have learned to do my day's work, and then I will let myself play a bit. I'd like to take you with me, Paine—you and a good car—and we'd go over the hills and far away——

"I haven't told you much of my life. And there's not a great deal to tell. Fifteen years ago I married a little girl and thought I loved her. But what I really loved was the thought of doing things for her. I had money and she was poor. It was pleasant to see her eyes shine when I gave her things—— But money hasn't anything to do with love, Paine, and that is where we American men fall down. When we love a woman we begin to tell her of our possessions and to tempt her by them. And the thing that we should do is to show her ourselves. We should say, 'If I were stripped of all my worldly goods what would there be in me for you to like?' My little wife and I had not one thing in common. And one day she left me. She found a man who gave her love for love. I had given her cars and flowers and boxes of candy and diamonds and furs. But she wanted more than that. She died—two years ago. I think she had been happy in those last years. I never really loved her, but she taught me what love is—and it is not a question of barter and sale——"

He seemed to be thinking aloud. Randy spoke after a silence. "But a man must have something to offer a woman."

"He must have himself. Oh, we are all crooked in our values, Paine. The best that a man can give a woman is his courage, his hope, his aspiration. That's enough. I learned it too late. I don't know why I am saying all this to you, Paine."

But Randy knew. It was on such nights that men showed their souls to each other. It was on such nights that his comrades had talked to him in France. Under the moon they had seemed self-conscious. But beneath a sky of stars, the words had come to them.

As he sat at his desk later, he thought of all that the Major had said to him: that possessions had nothing to do with love; that the test must be, "What would there be in me to like if I were stripped of all my worldly goods?"

Well, he had nothing. There were only his hopes, his dreams, his aspiration—himself.

Would these weigh with any woman in the balance against George Dalton's splendid trappings?

The dawn crept in and found him still sitting at his desk. He had not written a dozen lines. But his thoughts had been the long, long thoughts of youth.

559

CHAPTER VI
GEORGIE-PORGIE
I

It would never have happened if Aunt Claudia had been there. Aunt Claudia would have built hedges about Becky. She would have warned the Judge. She would, as a last resort, have challenged Dalton. But Fate, which had Becky's future well in hand, had sent Aunt Claudia to meet Truxton in New York. And she was having the time of her life.

Her first letter was a revelation to her niece. "I didn't know," she told the Judge at breakfast, "that Aunt Claudia could be like this——"

"Like what?"

"So young and gay——"

"She is not old. And when she was young she was gayer than you."

"Oh, not really, Grandfather."

"Yes. And she looked like you—and had the same tricks with her hands, and her hair was bright and brown. And she was very pretty."

"She is pretty yet," said Becky, loyally, but she was quite sure that whatever might have been Aunt Claudia's likeness to herself in the past, her own charms would not in the future shrink to fit Aunt Claudia's present pattern. It was unthinkable that her pink and white should fade to paleness, her slenderness to stiffness, her youthful radiance to a sort of weary cheerfulness.

There was nothing weary in the letter, however. "Oh, my dear, my dear, you should see Truxton. He is so perfectly splendid that I am sure he is a changeling and not my son. I tell him that he can't be the bundle of cuddly sweetness that I used to carry in my arms. I wore your white house-coat that first morning, Becky, and he sent some roses, and we had breakfast together in my rooms at the hotel. I believe it is the first time in years that I have looked into a mirror to really like my looks. You were sweet, my dear, to insist on putting it in. Truxton must stay here for two weeks more, and he wants me to stay with him. Then we shall come down together. Can you get along without me? We are going to the most wonderful plays, and to smart places to eat, and I danced last night on a roof garden. Should I say 'on' or 'in' a roof garden? Truxton says that my step is as light as a girl's. I think my head is a little turned. I am very happy."

Becky laid the letter down. "Would anyone have believed that Aunt Claudia *could*——"

"You have said that before, my dear. Your Aunt Claudia wasn't born in the ark——"

"But, Grandfather, I didn't mean that."

"It sounded like it. I shall write to her to stay as long as she can. We can get along perfectly without her."

"Of course," said Becky slowly. She had a feeling that, at all costs, she ought to call Aunt Claudia back.

For Dalton, after that first ride in the rain from Pavilion Hill, had speeded his wooing. He had swept Becky along on a rushing tide. He had courted the Judge, and the Judge had pressed upon him invitation after invitation. Day and night the big motor had flashed up to Huntersfield, bringing Dalton to some tryst with Becky, or carrying her forth to some gay adventure. Her world was rose-colored. She had not dreamed of life like this. She seemed to have drunk of some new wine, which lighted her eyes and flamed in her cheeks. Her beauty shone with an almost transcendent quality. As the dove's plumage takes on in the spring an added luster, so did the bronze of Becky's hair seem to burn with a brighter sheen.

Yet the Judge noticed nothing.

"Did you ask him to dine with us?" he had demanded, when Dalton had called Becky up on the morning of the receipt of Aunt Claudia's letter.

"No, Grandfather."

"Then I'll do it," and he had gone to the telephone, and had urged his hospitality.

II

When Dalton came Becky met him on the front steps of the house.

"Dinner is late," she said, "let's go down into the garden."

The garden at Huntersfield was square with box hedges and peaked up with yew, and there were stained marble statues of Diana and Flora and Ceres, and a little pool with lily pads.

"You are like the pretty little girls in the picture books," said George, as they walked along. "Isn't that a new frock?"

"Yes," said Becky, "it is. Do you like it?"

"You are a rose among the roses," he said. He wondered a bit at its apparent expensiveness. Perhaps, however, Becky was skillful with her needle. Some women were. He did not care greatly for such skill, but he was charmed by the effect.

"You are a rose among the roses," he said again, and broke off a big pink bud from a bush near by.

"Bend your head a little. I want to put it in your hair."

His fingers caught in the bronze mesh. "It is wound around my ring." He fumbled in his pockets with his free hand and got his knife. "It may pull a bit."

He showed her presently the lock which he had cut. "It seems alive," he kissed it and put it in his pocket.

Her protest was genuine. "Oh, please," she said, "I wish you wouldn't."

"Wouldn't what?"

"Keep it."

"Shall I throw it away?"

"You shouldn't have cut it off."

"Other men have been tempted—in a garden——"

It might have startled George could he have known that old Mandy, eyeing him from the kitchen, placed him in Eden's bower not as the hero of the world's initial tragedy, but as its Satanic villain.

"He sutt'n'y have bewitched Miss Becky," she told Calvin; "she ain' got her min' on nothin' but him."

"Yo' put yo' min' on yo' roas' lamb, honey," Calvin suggested. "How-cum you got late?"

"That chile kep' me fixin' that pink dress. She ain' never cyard what she wo'. And now she stan' in front o' dat lookin'-glass an' fuss an' fiddle. And w'en she ain' fussin' an' fiddlin', she jus' moons around, waitin' fo' him to come ridin' up in that red car like a devil on greased light'in'. An' I say right heah, Miss Claudia ain' gwine like it."

"Why ain' she?"

"Miss Claudia know black f'um w'ite. An' dat man done got a black heart——"

"Whut you know 'bout hit, Mandy?"

"Lissen. You wait. He'll suck a o'ange an' th'ow it away. He'll pull a rose, and scattah the leaves." Mandy, stirring gravy, was none the less dramatic. "You lissen, an' wait——"

"W'en Miss Claudia comin'?"

"In one week, thank the Lord," Mandy pushed the gravy to the back of the stove and pulled forward an iron pot. "The soup's ready," she said; "you go up and tell the Jedge, Calvin."

All through dinner, Becky was conscious of that lock of hair in George's pocket. The strand from which the lock had been cut fell down on her cheek. She had to tuck it back. She saw George smile as she did it. She forgave him.

It was after dinner that George spoke of Becky's gown.

"It is perfect," he said, "all except the pearls——?"

She gave him a startled glance. "The pearls?"

"I want to see you without them."

She unwound them and they dripped from her hand in milky whiteness.

He made his survey. "That's better," he said, "if they were real it would be different—I don't like to have you cheapened by anything less than—perfect——"

"Cheapened?" She smiled inscrutably, then dropped the pearls into a small box on the table beside her. "Yes," she said, "if they were real it would be different——"

There was something in her manner which made him say hurriedly, "You must not think that I am criticizing your taste. If I had my way you should have everything that money can buy——"

Her candid eyes came up to his. "There are a great many things that money cannot buy."

"You've got to show me," George told her; "I've never seen anything yet that I couldn't get with money."

"Could you buy—dreams——"

"I'd rather buy—diamonds."

"And money can't buy happiness."

"It can buy a pretty good imitation."

"But imitation happiness is like imitation pearls."

He laughed and sat down beside her. "You mustn't be too clever."

"I am not clever at all."

"I believe you are. And you don't have to be. There are plenty of clever women but only one Becky Bannister."

It was just an hour later that Georgie-Porgie kissed her. She was at the piano in the music-room, and there was no light except the glimmer of tall white candles, and the silver moonlight which fell across the shining floor.

Her grandfather was nodding in the room beyond, and through the open window came the dry, sweet scent of summer, as if nature had opened her pot-pourri to give the world a whiff of treasured fragrance.

Becky had been singing, and she had stopped and looked up at him.

"Oh, you lovely—lovely, little thing," he said, and bent his head.

To Becky, that moment was supreme, sacred. She trembled with happiness. To her that kiss meant betrothal—ultimate marriage.

To George it meant, of course, nothing of the kind. It was only one of many moments. It was a romance which might have been borrowed from the Middle Ages. A rare tale such as one might read in a book. A pleasant dalliance—to be continued until he was tired of it. If he ever married, it must be a spectacular affair—handsome woman, big fortune, not an unsophisticated slip of a child from an impoverished Virginia farm.

III

In the days that followed, Becky's gay lover came and rode away, and came again. He sparkled and shone and worshipped, but not a word did he say about the future. He seemed content with this idyl of old gardens, scented twilights, starlight nights, with Beauty's eyes for him alone radiant eyes that matched the stars.

Yet as the days went on the radiance was dimmed. Becky was in a state of bewilderment which bordered on fear. George showed himself an incomparable lover, but always he was silent about the things which she felt cried for utterance. So at last one day she spoke to the Judge.

"Granddad, did you kiss Grandmother before you asked her to marry you?"

"Asking always comes first, my dear. And you are too young to think of such things."

Grandfather was, thus obviously, no help. He sat in the Bird Room and dreamed of the days when the stuffed mocking-bird on the wax branch sang to a young bride, and his ideal of love had to do with the courtly etiquette of a time when men knelt and sued and were rewarded with the touch of finger tips.

As for George, he found himself liking this affair rather more than usual. There was no denying that the child was tremendously attractive—with her youth and beauty and the reserve which like a stone wall seemed now and then to shut her in. He had always a feeling that he would like to climb over the wall. It had pricked his interest to find in this little creature a strength and delicacy which he had found in no other woman.

He had had one or two letters from Madge, and had answered them with a line. She gave rather generously of her correspondence and her letters were never dull. In the last one she had asked him to join her on the North Shore.

"I am sorry," she said, "for the new little girl. I have a feeling that she won't know how to play the game and that you'll hurt her. You will probably think that I am jealous, but I can't help that. Men always think that women are jealous when it comes to other women. They never seem to understand that we are trying to keep the world straight.

"Oscar writes that Flora isn't well, that all her other guests are gone except you—and that she wants me. But why should I come? I wish he wouldn't ask me. Something always tugs at my heart when I think of Flora. She has so much and yet so little. She and Oscar would be much happier in a flat on the West Side with Flora cooking in a kitchenette, and Oscar bringing things home from the delicatessen. He would buy bologna and potato salad on Sunday nights, and perhaps they would slice up a raw onion. It sounds dreadful, doesn't it? But there are thousands of people doing just that thing, Georgie, and being very happy over it. And it wouldn't be dreadful for Flora and Oscar because they would be right where they belong, and the potato salad and the bologna and the little room where Oscar could sit with his coat off would be much more to their liking than their present pomp and elegance. You and I are different. You could never play any part pleasantly but that of Prince Charming, and I should hate the kitchenette. I want wide spaces, and old houses, and deep fireplaces—my people far back were like that—I sometimes wonder why I stick to Flora—perhaps it is because she clung to me in those days when Oscar was drafted and had to go, and she cried so hard in the Red Cross rooms that I took her under my wing—— Take it all together, Flora is rather worth while and so is Oscar if he didn't try so hard to be what he is not.

"But then we are all trying rather hard to be what we are not. I am really and truly middle-class. In my mind, I mean. Yet no one would believe it to look at me, for I wear my clothes like a Frenchwoman, and I am as unconventional as English royalty. And two generations of us have inherited money. But back of that there were nice middle-class New Englanders who did their own work. And the women wore white aprons, and the men wore overalls, and they ate doughnuts for breakfast, and baked beans on Sunday, and they milked their own cows, and skimmed their own cream, and they read Hamlet and the King James version of the Bible, and a lot of them wrote things that will be remembered throughout the ages, and they had big families and went to church, and came home to overflowing hospitality and chicken pies—and they were the salt of the earth. And as I think I remarked to you once before, I want to be like my great-grandmother in my next incarnation, and live in a wide, low farmhouse, and have horses and hogs and chickens and pop-corn on snowy nights, and go to church on Sunday.

"I don't know why I am writing like this, except that I went to Trinity to vespers, when I stopped over in Boston. It was dim and quiet and the boys' voices were heavenly, and over it all brooded the spirit of the great man who once preached there—and who still preaches——

"And now it is Sunday again, and I am back at the Crossing, and I played golf all the morning, and bridge this afternoon, and all the women smoked and all the men, and I was in a blue haze, and I wanted to be back in the quiet church where the boys sang, and the lights were like stars——

"I wish you and I could go there some day and that you could feel as I do about it. But you wouldn't. You are always so sure and smug—and you have a feeling that money will buy anything—even Paradise. I wonder what you will be like on the next plane. You won't fit into my farmhouse. I fancy that you'll be something rather—devilish—like Don Juan—or perhaps you'll be just an 'ostler in a courtyard, shining boots and—kissing maids——

"Of course I don't quite mean that. But I do feel that you'd be rather worth while if you'd stop philandering and discover your soul.

"I am a bit homesick, and I haven't any home. If Dad hadn't married a second time, I believe he would still love me a bit. But his wife doesn't. And so here I am—and as restless as ever—seeking something—always seeking.

"And now, once more, don't break the heart of the new little girl. I don't need to warn you not to break your own. You are the greatest example of the truth of 'he who loves and runs away will live to love another day.' Oh, Georgie-Porgie, will you ever love any woman enough to rise with her to the heights?

"Perhaps there aren't any heights for you or me. But I should like to think there were. Different hilltops, of course, so that we could wave across. We shall never climb together, Georgie. Perhaps we are too much alike to help each other up the hills. We need stronger props.

"Tell me about Flora. Is she really ill? If she is, I'll come. But I'd rather not.

"I hope you won't read this aloud to Oscar. You might, you know, and it wouldn't do. He would hate to believe that he'd be happier buying things at a delicatessen, and he wouldn't believe it. But it's true, just as it is true that you would be happy shining boots and making love to the maids like a character in Dickens.

"Come on up, and we'll motor to Boston on Sunday afternoon and we'll go to Trinity; I want somebody to be good with me, Georgie, and there are so many of the other kind.

"Ever wistfully,

"Madge."

George knew that he ought to go, but he was not ready yet to run away. He was having the time of his life, and as for Becky, he would teach her how to play the game.

<h2 style="text-align:center">IV</h2>

Aunt Claudia was away for three weeks.

"I wish she would come home," young Paine said one morning to his mother.

"Why?" Caroline Paine was at her desk with her mind on the dinner. "Why, Randy?"

"Oh, Dalton's going there a lot."

Mrs. Paine headed her list with gumbo soup. "Do you think he goes to see Becky?"

"Does a duck swim? Of course he goes there to see her, and he's turning her head."

"He is enough to turn any woman's head. He has nice eyes." Mrs. Paine left the topic as negligible, and turned to more important things.

"Randy, would you mind picking a few pods of okra for the soup? Susie is so busy and Bob and Jefferson are both in the field."

"Certainly, Mother," his cool answer gave no hint of the emotions which were seething within him. Becky's fate was hanging in the balance, and his mother talked of okra! He had decided some weeks ago that boarders were disintegrating—and that a mother was not a mother who had three big meals a day on her mind.

He went into the garden. An old-fashioned garden, so common at one time in the South—with a picket fence, a little gate, orderly paths—a blaze of flowers to the right, and to the left a riot of vegetables—fat tomatoes weighing the vines to the ground, cucumbers hiding under their sheltering leaves, cabbages burgeoning in blue-green, and giving the promise of unlimited boiled dinners, onions enough to flavor a thousand delectable dishes, sweet corn running in countless rows up the hill, carrots waving their plumes, Falstaffian watermelons. It was evident with the garden as an index that the boarders at King's Crest were fed on more than milk and honey.

Randy picked the okra and carried it to the kitchen, and returning to the Schoolhouse found the Major opening his morning mail.

Randy sat down on the step. "Once upon a time," he said, "we had niggers to work in our gardens. And now we are all niggers."

The Major's keen eyes studied him. "What's the matter?"

"I've been picking okra—for soup, and I'm a Paine of King's Crest."

"Well, you peeled potatoes in France."

"That's different."

"Why should it be different? If a thing is for the moment your job you are never too big for it."

"I wish I had stayed in the Army. I wish I had never come back."

The Major whistled for a moment, thoughtfully. Then he said, "Look here, Paine, hadn't you better talk about it?"

"Talk about what?"

"That's for you to tell me. There's something worrying you. You are more tragic than—Hamlet——"

"Well—it's—Becky——"

"And Dalton, of course. Why don't you cut him out, Paine——"

"Me? Oh, look here, Major, what have I to offer her?"

"Youth and energy and a fighting spirit," the Major rapped out the words.

"What is a fighting spirit worth," Randy asked with a sort of weary scorn, "when a man is poor and the woman's rich?"

The Major had been whistling a silly little tune from a modern opera. It was an air which his men would have recognized. It came to an end abruptly.

"Rich? Who is rich?"

"Becky."

The Major got up and limped to the porch rail. "I thought she was as poor as——"

"The rest of us? Well, she isn't."

It appeared that Becky's fortune came from the Nantucket grandmother, and that there would be more when the Admiral died. It was really a very large fortune, well invested, and yielding an amazing income. One of the clauses of the grandmother's will had to do with the bringing up of Becky. Until she was of age she was to be kept as much as possible away from the distractions and temptations of modern luxury. The Judge and the Admiral had agreed that nothing could be better. The result, Randy said, was that nobody ever thought of Becky Bannister as rich.

"Yet those pearls that she wears are worth more than I ever expect to earn."

"It is rather like a fairy tale. The beggar-maid becomes a queen."

"You can see now why I can't offer her just youth and a fighting spirit."

"I wonder if Dalton knows."

"I don't believe he does," Randy said slowly. "I give him credit for that."

"He might have heard——"

"I doubt it. He hasn't mingled much, you know."

"It will be rather a joke on him——"

"To find that he has married—Mademoiselle Midas?"

"To find that she is Mademoiselle Midas, whether he marries her or not."

V

Of course Georgie-Porgie ran away. It was the inevitable climax. Flora's illness hastened things a bit.

"She wants to see her New York doctors," Waterman had said. "I think we shall close the house, and join Madge later at the Crossing."

George felt an unexpected sense of shock. The game must end, yet he wanted it to go on. The cards were in his hands, and he was not quite ready to turn the trick.

"When do we go?" he asked Oscar.

"In a couple of days if we can manage it. Flora is getting worried about herself. She thinks it is her heart."

George rode all of that afternoon with Becky. But not a word did he say about his departure. He never spoiled a thing like this with "Good-bye." Back at Waterman's, Kemp was packing trunks. In forty-eight hours there would be the folding of tents, and Hamilton Hill would be deserted. It added a pensiveness to his manner that made him more than ever charming. It rained on the way home, and it seemed to him significant that his first ride and his last with Becky should have been in the rain.

He stayed to dinner, and afterwards he and Becky walked together in the fragrance of the wet garden. A new moon hung low for a while and was then lost behind the hills.

"My little girl," George said when the moment came that he must go, "My dear little girl." He gathered her up in his arms—but did not kiss her. For once in his life, Georgie-Porgie was too deeply moved for kisses.

After he had gone, Becky went into the Bird Room, and stood on the hearth and looked up at the Trumpeter Swan. There was no one to whom she could speak of the ecstasy which surged through her. As a child she had brought her joys here, and her sorrows—her Christmas presents in the early morning—the first flowers of the spring. She had sat here often in her little black frock and had felt the silent sympathy of the wise old bird.

He gazed down at her now with an almost uncanny intelligence. She laughed a little and standing on tiptoe laid her cheek against the cool glass. "When I am married," was her wordless question, "will you sound your trumpet high up near the moon?"

CHAPTER VII
MADEMOISELLE MIDAS

I

There came to Huntersfield the next morning at about the same moment, Kemp in his little car with a small parcel for Becky, and Calvin with a big box from the express office.

Becky was in her room at breakfast when Calvin brought the boxes up to her. It was a sunshiny morning, and the Judge had gone a-fishing with Mr. Flippin. Becky, in a lace cap and a robe that was delicately blue, sat in a big chair with a low table in front of her.

There were white roses on the table in a silver bowl. The Judge had sent them to her. The Judge had for the women of his family a feeling that was almost youthfully romantic, and which was, unquestionably, old-fashioned. He liked to think that they had roses for their little noses, ribbons and laces for their pretty faces. He wanted no harsh winds to blow on them.

And in return for the softness and ease with which he would surround them, he wanted their deference to his masculine point of view.

With the box which George sent was a note. It was the first that Becky had ever received from her lover. George's code did not include much correspondence. Flaming sentiment on paper was apt to look silly when the affair ended.

To Becky, her name on the outside of the envelope seemed written in gold. She was all blushing expectation.

"There ain't no answer," Calvin said, and she waited for him to go before she opened it.

She read it and sat there drained of all feeling. She was as white as the roses on her table. She read the note again and her hands shook.

"Flora is very ill. We are taking her up to New York. After that we shall go to the North Shore. There isn't time for me to come and say, 'Good-bye.' Perhaps it is better not to come. It has been a wonderful summer, and it is you who have made it wonderful for me. The memory will linger with me always—like a sweet dream or a rare old tale. I am sending you a little token—for remembrance. Think of me sometimes, Becky."

That was all, except a scrawled "G. D." at the end. No word of coming back. No word of writing to her again. No word of any future in which she would have a part.

She opened the box. Within on a slender chain was a pendant—a square sapphire set in platinum, and surrounded by diamonds. George had ordered it in anticipation of this crisis. He had, hitherto, found such things rather effective in the cure of broken hearts.

Now, had George but known it, Becky had jewels in leather cases in the vaults of her bank which put his sapphire trinket to shame. There were the diamonds in which a Meredith great-grandmother had been presented at the Court of St. James, and there were the pearls of which her own string was a small part. There were emeralds and rubies, old corals and jade— not for nothing had the Admiral sailed the seas, bringing back from China and India lovely things for the woman he loved. And now the jewels were Becky's, and she had not cared for them in the least. If George had loved her she would have cherished his sapphire more than all the rest.

But he did not love her. She knew it in that moment. All of her doubts were confirmed.

The thing that had happened to her seemed incredible.

She put the sapphire back in its box, wrapped it, tied the string carefully and called Mandy.

"Tell Calvin to take this to Mr. Dalton."

Mandy knew at once that something was wrong. But this was not a moment for words. The Bannisters did not talk about things that troubled them. They held their heads high. And Becky's was high at this moment, and her eyes were blazing.

As she sat there, tense, Becky wondered what Dalton could have thought of her. If she had not had a jewel in the world, she would not have kept his sapphire. Didn't he know that?

But how could he know? To him it had been "a sweet dream—a rare old tale," and she had thought him a Romeo ready to die for her sake, an Aucassin—willing to brave Hell rather than give her up, a Lohengrin sent from Heaven!

She shuddered and hid her face in her hands. At last she crept into bed. Mandy, coming in to straighten the room, was told to lower the curtains.

"My—my head aches, Mandy."

Mandy, wise old Mandy, knew of course that it was her heart. "You res' an' sleep, honey," she said, and moved about quietly setting things in order.

But Becky did not sleep. She lay wide awake, and tried to get the thing straight in her mind. How had it happened? Where had she failed? Oh, why hadn't Sister Loretto told her that there were men like this? Why hadn't Aunt Claudia returned in time?

In the big box which Mandy had brought up were clothes—exquisite things which Becky had ordered from New York. She had thought it a miracle that George should have fallen in love with her believing her poor. It showed, she felt, his splendidness, his kingly indifference to—poverty. Yet she had planned a moment when he should know. When their love was proclaimed to the world he should see her in a splendor which matched his own. He had loved her in spite of her faded cottons, in spite of her shabby shoes. She had made up her list carefully, thinking of his sparkling eyes when he beheld her.

She got out of bed and opened the box. The lovely garments were wrapped in rosy tissue paper, and tied with ribbons to match. It seemed to Becky as if those rosy wrappings held the last faint glow of her dreams.

She untied the ribbons of the top parcel, and disclosed a frock of fine white lace—there was cloth of silver for a petticoat, and silver slippers. She would have worn her pearls, and George and she would have danced together at the Harvest Ball at the Merriweathers. It was an annual and very exclusive affair in the county. It was not likely that the Watermans and their guests would be invited, but there would have been a welcome for Dalton as her friend—her more than friend.

There was a white lace wrap with puffs of pink taffeta and knots of silver ribbon which went with the gown. Becky with a sudden impulse put it on. She stripped the cap from her head, and wound her bronze locks in a high knot. She surveyed herself.

Well, she was Becky Bannister of Huntersfield—and the mirror showed her beauty. And Dalton had not known or cared. He thought her poor, and had thrown her aside like an old glove!

Down-stairs the telephone rang. Old Mandy, coming up to say that Mr. Randy was on the wire, stood in amazement at the sight of Becky in the rosy wrap with her hair peaked up to a topknot.

"Ain' you in baid?" she asked, superfluously.

"No. Who wants me, Mandy?"

"I tole you—Mr. Randy."

Becky deliberated. "I'll go down. When I come up we'll unpack all this, Mandy."

Randy at the other end of the wire was asking Becky to go to a barbecue the next day.

"The boarders are giving it—it is Mother's birthday and they want to celebrate. It is to be on Pavilion Hill. They want you and the Judge——"

"To-morrow? Oh, I don't know, Randy."

"Why not? Have you another engagement?"

"No."

"Then what's the matter? Can't you tear yourself away from your shining knight?"

Silence.

"Becky—oh, I didn't mean that. I'm sorry—_Becky_——"

Her answer came faintly, "I'll come."

"What's the matter with the wire? I can't hear you."

There was nothing the matter with the wire. The thing that was the matter was Becky's voice. She found it suddenly unmanageable. "We'll come," she told him finally, and hung up the receiver.

She ascended the stairs as if she carried a burden on her back. Mandy was on her knees before the hamper, untying the rosy packages.

"Is you goin' to try 'em on, honey?" she asked.

Becky stood in the doorway, the lace wrap hanging from her shoulders and showing the delicate blue of the negligee beneath—her face was like chalk but her eyes shone. "Yes," she said, "there's a pink gingham I want to wear to the barbecue to-morrow. There ought to be a hat to match. Did the hats come, Mandy?"

"Calvin he say there's another box, but he ain' brought it up from the deepot. He was ridin' dat Jo-mule, and this yer basket was all he could ca'y."

In the pink frock Becky looked like a lovely child.

"Huc-cum you-all gettin' eve'y thing pink, Miss Becky?" Mandy asked.

"For a change," said Becky.

And how could she tell old Mandy that she had felt that in a rose-colored world everything should be rose-color?

She tried on each frock deliberately. She tried on every pair of slippers. She tried on the wraps, and the hats which came up finally with Calvin staggering beneath the bulkiness of the box. She was lovely in everything. And she was no longer the little Becky Bannister whom Dalton had wooed. She was Mademoiselle Midas, appraising her beauty in her lovely clothes, and wondering what Dalton would think if he could see her.

II

Becky did not, after all, wear the pink gingham. The Judge elected to go on horseback, so Becky rode forth by his side correctly and smartly attired in a gray habit, with a straight black sailor and a high stock and boots that made her look like a charming boy.

They came to Pavilion Hill to find the boarders like the chorus in light opera very picturesque in summer dresses and summer flannels, and with Mrs. Paine in a broad hat playing the part of leading lady. Mr. Flippin, who was high-priest at all of the county barbecues, was superintending the roasting of a whole pig, and Mrs. Flippin had her mind on hot biscuits. The young mulatto, Daisy, and Mandy's John, with the negroes from the Paine household, were setting the long tables under the trees. There was the good smell of coffee, much laughter, and a generally festive atmosphere.

The Judge, enthroned presently in the Pavilion, was the pivotal center of the crowd. Everybody wanted to hear his stories, and with this fresh audience to stimulate him, he dominated the scene. He wore a sack suit and a Panama hat and his thin, fine face, the puff of curled white hair at the back of his neck, the gayety of his glance gave an almost theatric touch to his appearance, so that one felt he might at any moment come down stage and sing a topical song in the best Gilbertian manner.

It was an old scene with a new setting. It was not the first time that Pavilion Hill had been the backgrounds of a barbecue. But it was the first time that a Paine of King's Crest had accepted hospitality on its own land. It was the first time that it had echoed to the voices of an alien group. It was the first time that it had seen a fighting black man home from France. The old order had changed indeed. No more would there be feudal lords of Albemarle acres.

Yet old loyalties die hard. It was the Judge and Mrs. Paine and Becky and Randy who stood first in the hearts of the dusky folk who served at the long tables. The boarders were not in any sense "quality." Whatever they might be, North, East and

West, their names were not known on Virginia records. And what was any family tree worth if it was not rooted in Virginia soil?

"Effen the Jedge was a king and wo' a crown," said Mandy's John to Daisy, "he couldn't look mo' bawn to a th'one."

Daisy nodded. "Settin' at the head o' that table minds me o' whut my old Mammy used to say, 'han'some is as han'some does.' The Bannisters *done* han'some and they *is* han'some."

"They sure is," John agreed; "that-all's whut makes you so good-lookin', Daisy."

He came close to her and she drew away. "You put yo' min' on passin' them plates," she said with severity, "or you'll be spillin' po'k gravy on they haids." Her smile took away the sting of her admonition. John moved on, murmuring, "Well, yo' does han'some and yo' is han'some, Daisy, and that's why I loves you."

There were speeches after dinner. One from Randy, in which he thanked them in the name of his mother, and found himself quite suddenly and unexpectedly being fond of the boarders. Major Prime was not there. He had been summoned back to Washington, but would return, he hoped, for the week-end.

It was after lunch that Randy and Becky walked in the woods. Nellie Custis followed them. They sat down at last at the foot of a hickory tree. Becky took off her hat and the wind blew her shining hair about her face. She was pale and wore an air of deep preoccupation.

"Randy," she asked suddenly out of a long silence, "did you ever kiss a girl?"

Her question did not surprise him. He and Becky had argued many matters. And they usually plunged in without preliminaries. He fancied that Becky was discussing kisses in the abstract. It never occurred to him that the problem was personal.

"Yes," he said, "I have. What about it?"

"Did you—ask her to marry you?"

"No."

"Why not?"

He pulled Nellie Custis' ears. "One of them wasn't a nice sort of girl—not the kind that I should have cared to introduce to—you."

"Yet you cared to—kiss her?"

Randy flushed faintly. "I know how it looks to you. I hated it afterwards, but I couldn't marry a girl—like that——"

"Who was the other girl?"

For a moment he did not reply, then he said with something of an effort, "It was you, Becky."

"Me? When?" She turned on him her startled gaze.

"Do you remember at Christmas—oh, ten years ago—and your grandfather had a party for you. There was mistletoe in the hall, and we danced and stopped under the mistletoe——"

"I remember, Randy—how long ago it seems."

"Yet ten years isn't really such a long time, is it, Becky? I was only a little boy, but I told myself then that I would never kiss any other girl. I thought then that—that some day I might ask you to marry me. I—I had a wild dream that I might try to make you love me. I didn't know then that poverty is a millstone about a man's neck." He gave a bitter laugh.

Becky's breath came quickly. "Oh, Randy," she said, "poverty wouldn't have had anything to do with it—not if we had—cared——"

"I care," said Randy, "and I think the first time I knew how much I cared was when I kissed that other girl. Somehow you came to me that night, a little white thing, so fine and different, and I loathed her."

He was standing now—tall and lean and black-haired, but with the look of race on his thin face, a rather princely chap in spite of his shabby clothes. "Of course you don't care," he said; "I think if I had money I should try to make you. But I haven't the right. I had thought that, perhaps, if no other man came that some time I might——"

Becky picked up her riding crop, and as she talked she tapped her boot in a sort of staccato accompaniment.

"That other man has come," *tap-tap*, "he kissed me," *tap-tap*, "and made me love him," *tap-tap*, "and he has gone away—and he hasn't asked me to marry him."

One saw the Indian in Randy now, in the lifted head, the square-set jaw, the almost cruel keenness of the eyes.

"Of course it is George Dalton," he said.

"Yes."

"I could kill him, Becky."

She laughed, ruefully. "For what? Perhaps he thinks I'm not a nice sort of girl—like the one you kissed——"

"For God's sake, Becky."

He sat down on a flat rock. He was white, and shaking a little. He wanted more than anything else in the wide world to kill George Dalton. Of course in these days such things were preposterous. But he had murder in his heart.

"I blame myself," Becky said, *tap-tap*, "I should have known that a man doesn't respect," *tap-tap*, "a woman he can kiss."

He took the riding crop forcibly out of her hands. "Look at me, look at me, Becky, do you love him?"

She whispered, "Yes."

567

"Then he's got to marry you."

But her pride was up. "Do you think I want him if he doesn't want—me?"

"He shall want you," said Randy Paine; "the day shall come when he shall beg on his knees."

Randy had studied law. But there are laws back of the laws of the white man. The Indian knows no rest until his enemy is in his hands. Randy lay awake late that night thinking it out. But he was not thinking only of Georgie. He was thinking of Becky and her self-respect. "She will never get it back," he said, "until that dog asks her to marry him."

He had faith enough in her to believe that she would not marry Dalton now if he asked her. But she must be given the chance.

CHAPTER VIII
ANCESTORS
I

The Judge and Mr. Flippin were fishing, with grasshoppers for bait. The fish that they caught they called "shiners." As an edible product "shiners" were of little account. But the Judge and Mr. Flippin did not fish for food, they fished for sport. It was mild sport compared to the fishing of other days when the Judge had waded into mountain streams with the water coming up close to the pocket of his flannel shirt where he kept his cigars, or had been poled by Bob Flippin from "riffle" to pool. Those had been the days of speckled trout and small-mouthed bass, and Bob had been a boy and the Judge at middle age. Now Bob Flippin had reached the middle years, and the Judge was old, but they still fished together. They were comrades in a very close and special sense. What Bob Flippin lacked in education and culture he made up in wisdom and adoration of the Judge. When he talked he had something to say, but as a rule he let the Judge talk and was always an absorbed listener.

There was in their relations, however, a complete adjustment to the class distinctions which separated them. The Judge accepted as his right the personal service with which Bob Flippin delighted to honor him. It was always Bob who pulled the boat and carried the basket. It was Bob who caught the grasshoppers and cooked the lunch.

There was one dish dedicated to a day's fishing—fried ham and eggs. Bob had a long-handled frying-pan, and the food was seasoned with the salt and savor of the out-of-doors.

There were always several dogs to bear their masters company. The Judge's three were beagles—tireless hunters of rabbits, and somewhat in disgrace as a species since Germany had gone to war with the world. Individually, however, they were beloved by the Judge because they were the children and grandchildren of a certain old Dinah who had slept in a basket by his bed until she died.

Bob Flippin had a couple of setters, and the five canines formed a wistful semicircle around the lunch basket.

The lunch basket was really a fishing-basket, lined with tin. In one end was a receptacle for ice. After the lunch was eaten, the fish were put next to the ice, and the basket thus served two purposes. Among the other edibles there were always corn-cakes for the dogs. They knew it, and had the patience of assured expectation.

"Truxton comes on Saturday," said the Judge as he watched Bob turn the eggs expertly in the long-handled pan, "and Claudia. I told Becky to ride over this morning and ask your wife if she could help Mandy. Mandy's all right when there's nobody but the family, but when there's company in prospect she moans and groans."

"Mollie's up at the Watermans'; Mrs. Waterman is worse. They expected to take her to New York, but she is too ill, and they are going to have the doctors bring another nurse."

"I had a note from Mr. Dalton," said the Judge, "saying they were going. It was rather sudden, and he was sorry. Nice fellow. He liked to come over and look at my birds."

Bob Flippin's eyes twinkled. "I reckon he liked to look at a pretty girl——"

The Judge stared at him. "At Becky?"

Flippin nodded. "Didn't you know it?"

"Bless my soul." The Judge was unquestionably startled. "But I don't know anything about him. I can't have him running after Becky."

"Seems to me he's been a-runnin'."

"But what would Claudia say? I don't know anything about his family. Maybe he hasn't any family. How do I know he isn't a fortune-hunter?"

"Well, he isn't a bird hunter, I can tell you that. I saw him kick one of your dogs. A man that will kick a dog isn't fit to hold a gun."

"No, he isn't," said the Judge, soberly. "I'm upset by what you've said, Flippin. Dalton's all right as far as I can see as a friend of mine. But when anybody comes courting at Huntersfield he's got to show credentials."

He ate his lunch without much appetite. He was guiltily aware of what Claudia would say if she knew what had happened. But perhaps nothing had happened and perhaps she need not know. He cheered up and threw a bit of ham to the waiting dogs. Perhaps Becky wasn't interested. Perhaps, after all, Dalton had been genuine in his interest in the stuffed birds.

"Becky's too young for things like that," he began hopefully.

But Bob Flippin shook his head. "Girls are queer, Judge, and you never can tell what they're goin' to do next. Now, there's my Mary—running off and getting married, and coming home and not talking much about it. She—didn't even bring her marriage certificate. Said that he had kept it. But she's never lied to me, and I know when she says she's married, she's—married—but it's queer. He ain't written now for weeks, but she ain't worried. She says she knows the reason, but she can't tell me. And when I try to ask questions, she just looks me straight in the eye and says, 'I never lied to you, Father, did I? And it's all right.'"

"He has a good name," said the Judge. "Branch—it's one of our names—my wife's family."

"But I reckon there ain't never been any Truelove Branches in your family tree. I laugh at Mary when she calls him that. '"Truelove" ain't any name for a man, Mary,' I tell her. But she says there couldn't be a better one. And she insisted on naming the child 'Fidelity.' But if anybody had told me that my little Mary—would take things into her own hands like that—why, Judge, before she went away to teach school, she leaned on me and her mother—and now she's as stiff as a poker when we try to ask about her affairs——"

"Does he support her?" the Judge asked.

"Sends her plenty of money. She always seems to have enough, even when he doesn't write. He'll be coming one of these days—and then we'll get the thing straight, but in the meantime there ain't any use in asking Mary."

He brought out the bag of corn-cakes and fed the dogs. They were a well-bred crew and took their share in turn, sitting in a row and going through the ceremony with an air of enjoying not only the food but the attention they attracted from the two men.

"Of course," said Mr. Flippin as he gathered up the lunch things, "I'm saying to you what I wouldn't say to another soul. Mary's my girl, and she's all right. But I naturally have the feelings of a father."

The Judge stretched himself on the grass, and pulled his hat over his eyes. "Girls are queer, and if that Dalton thinks he can court my Becky——" He stopped, and spoke again from under his hat, "Oh, what's the use of worrying, Bob, on a day like this?"

The Judge always napped after lunch, and Bob Flippin, stretched beside him, lay awake and watched the stream slip by in a sheet of silver, he watched a squirrel flattened on the limb above him, he watched the birds that fluttered down to the pools to bathe, he watched the buzzards sailing high above the hills.

And presently he found himself watching his own daughter Mary, as she came along the opposite bank of the stream. She was drawing Fiddle-dee-dee in a small red cart and was walking slowly.

She walked well. Country-born and country-bred, there was nothing about her of plodding peasant. All her life she had danced with the Bannisters and the Beauforts. Yet she had never been invited to the big balls. When the Merriweathers gave their Harvest Dance, Mary and her mother would go over and help bake the cakes, and at night they would sit in the gallery of the great ballroom and watch the dancers, but Mary would not be asked out on the floor.

Seeing the Judge asleep, Mary stopped and beckoned from the other side.

Flippin rose and made his way across the stream, stepping from stone to stone.

"Mother wants you to come right up to the Watermans', Father. Mrs. Waterman is to have an operation, and you are to direct the servants in fitting up a room for the surgeons. The nurse will tell you what to do."

Mr. Flippin rubbed his face with his handkerchief. "I don't like to wake the Judge."

"I'll stay here and tell him," Mary said. "And you can send Calvin down to carry the basket."

She was standing beside him, and suddenly she laid her cheek against his arm. "I love you," she said, "you are a darling, Daddy."

He patted her cheek. "That sounds like my little Mary."

"Don't I always sound like your little Mary?"

"Not always."

"Well—I've had things on my mind." Her blue eyes met his, and she flushed a bit. "Not things that I am sorry for, but things that I am worried about. But now—well, I am very happy in my heart, Daddy."

He smiled down at her. "Have you heard from T. Branch?"

"Yes, by wireless——"

He looked his astonishment. "Wireless?"

"Heart-wireless, Daddy. Didn't you get messages that way when you were young—from Mother?"

"How do I know? It's been twenty-five years since then, and we haven't had to send messages. We've just held on to each other's hands, thank God." He bent and kissed her. "You stay and tell the Judge, Mary. He'll sleep for a half-hour yet; he's as regular as the clock."

His own two dogs followed him, but the Judge's beagles lay with their noses on their paws at their master's feet. Now and then they snapped at flies but otherwise they were motionless.

Before the half hour was up Fiddle-dee-dee fell asleep, and the Judge waking, saw on the other side of a stream propped against the gray old oak, the young mother cool in her white dress, her child in her arms.

"Father had to go," she told him, and explained the need; "he'll send Calvin for the basket."

"I can carry my own basket, Mary; I'm not a thousand years old."

"It isn't that. But you've never carried baskets, Judge."

The Judge chuckled. "You say that is if it were an accusation."

"It isn't. Only some of us seem born to carry baskets and others are born to—let us carry them." Her smile redeemed her words from impertinence.

"Are you a Bolshevik, Mary?"

"No. I believe in the divine rights of kings and—Judges. I'd hate to see you carry a basket. It would rob you of something—just as I would hate to see a king without his crown or a queen without her scepter."

"Oh, Mary, Mary, your father has never said things like that to me."

"He doesn't feel them. Father believes in The God of Things as They are——"

"And don't you?"

"I believe in you," she rose and carrying her sleeping child, crossed the stream on the stones as easily as if she carried no burden; "you know I believe in you, don't you—and in all the Bannisters?"

It was said so lightly that he took it lightly. No one was so touchy as the Judge about his dignity if it were disregarded. But here was little Mary smiling up at him and telling him that he was a king with a crown and she liked it.

"Well, well. Let's sit down, Mary."

"Fish, if you want to, and I'll watch."

He baited his hook and cast his line into the stream. It had a bobbing red cork which fascinated Fiddle-dee-dee. She tried to wade out and get it, and had to be held by her very short skirts lest she drown in the attempt.

"So I'm a confounded autocrat," the Judge chuckled. "Nobody ever said that to me before, but maybe some of them have been thinking it."

"Maybe they have," said Mary gravely, "but they haven't really cared. Having the Bannisters at Huntersfield is like the English having a Victoria or an Edward or a George at Buckingham Palace or at Windsor; it adds flavor to their—democracy——"

"Mary—who's been saying all this to you?" he demanded.

"My husband."

"Truelove Branch?"

She nodded.

"I'd like to meet him, by Jove, I'd like to meet him. He has been teaching his wife to poke fun at her old friend——"

She faced him fearlessly. "I'm not poking fun. I—I'd hate to have the Bannisters lose one little bit of their beautiful traditions. I—I—— Some day I'm going to teach little Fiddle those traditions, and tell her what it means when—when people have race back of them. You see, I haven't it, Judge, but I know what it's worth."

He was touched by her earnestness. "My dear Mary," he said, "I wish my own grandson looked at it that way. His letters of late have been very disturbing."

A little flush crept into her cheeks. "Disturbing?"

"He writes that we Americans have got to fit our practice to our theories. He says that we shout democracy and practice autocracy. That we don't believe that all men are free and equal, and that, well, in your words, Mary—we let other people carry our baskets."

Mary was smiling to herself. "You are glad he is coming home?"

"Truxton? Yes. On Saturday."

"Becky told me. She rode over to get Mother to help Mandy."

"I am going to have a lot of people to dine the day he arrives," said the Judge, "and next week there'll be the Merriweathers' ball. He will have a chance to see his old friends."

"Yes," said Mary, "he will."

They talked a great deal about Truxton after that.

"I wish he bore the Bannister name," said the Judge. "Becky is the only Bannister."

After the death of her husband Mrs. Beaufort had come to live with the Judge. Truxton's boyhood had been spent on the old estate. The Judge's income was small, and Truxton had known few luxuries. Like the rest of the boys of the Bannister family he was studying law at the University. He and Randy had been classmates, but had gone into different branches of the service.

"When he comes back," the Judge told Mary, "he must show the stuff he is made of. I can't have him selling cars around the county like Randy Paine."

"Well, Randy has sold a lot of them," said Mary. "Father has given him an order——"

"You don't mean to say that Bob Flippin is going to buy a car——"

"He is."

"He didn't dare tell me," the Judge said; "what's he going to do with his horses?"

"Keep them," said Mary serenely; "the car is for Mother—she's going to drive it herself."

The Judge, with a vision of Mollie Flippin's middle-aged plumpness upon him, exclaimed: "You don't mean that your mother is going to—drive a car?"

"Yes," said Mary, "she is."

"I would as soon think of Claudia——"

"No," said Mary, "Mrs. Beaufort will never drive her own car. She has the coachman habit, and if she ever gets a car, there'll be a man at the wheel."

She brought the conversation back to Truxton. "Do you remember how we had a picnic here years ago, Mother packed the lunch, and Truxton ate up all the raspberry tarts?"

"He loved tarts," said the Judge, "and chocolate cake. Well, well, I shall be glad to see him."

"Perhaps—perhaps when he gets here you'll be disappointed."

"Why," sharply, "why should I?"

Mary did not answer. She stood up with Fiddle in her arms. "Calvin's coming for the basket," she said, "and I shall have to go up on the other side—I left the cart."

She said "good-bye" and crossed by the stepping-stones. The Judge wound up his fishing tackle. The day's sport resulted in three small "shiners." But he had enjoyed the day—there had been the stillness and the sunlight, and the good company of Bob Flippin and his daughter Mary.

The dogs followed, and Mary from the other side of the stream watched the little procession, Calvin in the lead with the load, the Judge straight and slim with his fluff of white hair, the three little dogs paddling on their short legs.

"Judge Bannister of Huntersfield," said Mary Flippin. Then she raised Fiddle high in her arms. "Say *Granddad*, Fiddle," she whispered, "say *Granddad*."

II

The Flippin farmhouse was wide and rambling. It had none of the classic elegance of the old Colonial mansions, but it had a hall in the middle with the sitting-room on one side and on the other an old-fashioned parlor with a bedroom back of it. The dining-room was back of the sitting-room, and beyond that was the kitchen, and a succession of detached buildings which served as dairy, granary, tool-house and carriage house in the old fashion. There was much sunlight and cleanliness in the farmhouse, and beauty of a kind, for the Flippins had been content with simple things, and Mary's taste was evidenced in the restraint with which the new had been combined with the old. She and her mother did most of the work. It was not easy in these days to get negroes to help. Daisy, the mulatto, had come down for the summer, but they had no assurance that when the winter came they could keep her. Divested of her high heels and city affectations, Daisy was just a darkey, of a rather plain, comfortable, efficient type. When Mary went in, she was getting supper.

"Has Mother come, Daisy?"

"No, Miss, she ain', an' yo' Poppa ain' come. An' me makin' biscuits."

"Your biscuits are always delicious, Daisy."

"An' me and John wants to go to the movies, Miss Mary. An' efen the supper is late."

"You can leave the dishes until mornin', Daisy."

Mary smiled and sighed as she went on with Fiddle to her own room. The good old days of ordered service were over. She went into the parlor bedroom. It was the one which she and Fiddle occupied. She bathed and dressed her baby, and changed her own frock. Then she entered the long, dim parlor. There was a family Bible on the table. It was a great volume with steel engravings. It had belonged to her father's father. In the middle of the book were pages for births and deaths. The records were written legibly but not elegantly. They went back for two generations. Beyond that the Flippins had no family tree.

Mary had seen the family tree at Huntersfield. It was rooted in aristocratic soil. There were Huguenot branches and Royalist branches—D'Aubignes and Moncures, Peytons and Carys, Randolphs and Lees. And to match every name there was more than one portrait on the walls of Huntersfield.

Mary remembered a day when she and Truxton Beaufort had stood in the wide hall.

"A great old bunch," Truxton had said.

"If they were my ancestors I should be afraid of them."

"Why, Mary?"

"Oh, they'd expect so much of me."

"Oh, that," Truxton said airily, "who cares what they expect?"

Mr. and Mrs. Flippin came home in time for supper. The nurse had arrived and the surgeons would follow in the morning. "It's dreadful, Mary," Mrs. Flippin said, "to see her poor husband; money isn't everything. And he loves her as much as if they were poor."

Daisy washed the dishes in a perfect whirl of energy, donned her high-heeled slippers and her Washington manner, and went off with John. It was late that night when Mrs. Flippin went out to find Mary busy.

"My dear," she said, "what are you doing?"

Mary was rolling out pastry, with ice in a ginger-ale bottle. "I am going to make some tarts. There was a can of raspberries left—and—and well—I'm just hungry for—raspberry tarts, Mother."

III

It was the Judge who told Becky that Dalton had not gone. "Mrs. Waterman is very ill, and they are all staying down."

Becky showed no sign of what the news meant to her, but that night pride and love fought in the last ditch. It seemed to Becky that with Dalton at King's Crest the agony of the situation was intensified.

"Oh, why should I care?" she kept asking herself as she sat late by her window. "He doesn't. And I have known him only three weeks. Why should he count so much?"

She knew that he counted to the measure of her own constancy. "I can't bear it," she said over and over again pitifully, as the hours passed. "I think I shall—die."

It seemed to her that she wanted more than anything in the whole wide world to see him for a moment—to hear the quick voice—to meet the sparkle of his glance.

Well, why not? If she called him—he would come. She was sure of that. He was staying away because he thought that she cared. And he didn't want her to care. But he was not really—cruel—and if she called him——

She wandered around the room, stopping at a window and going on, stopping at another to stare out into the starless night. There had been rain, and there was that haunting wet fragrance from the garden. "I must see him," she said, and put her hand to her throat.

She went down-stairs. Everybody was in bed. There was no one to hear. Her grandfather's room was over the library; Mandy and Calvin slept in servants' quarters outside. To-morrow the house would be full of ears—and it would be too late.

A faint light burned in the lower hall. The stairway swept down from a sort of upper gallery, and all around the gallery and on the stairs and along the lower hall were the portraits of Becky's dead and gone ancestors.

They were really very worth-while ancestors, not as solid and substantial perhaps as those whose portraits hung in the Meredith house on Main Street in Nantucket, but none the less aristocratic, with a bit of dare-devil about the men, and a hint of frivolity about the women—with a pink coat here and a black patch there, with the sheen of satin and the sparkle of jewels—a Cavalier crowd, with the greatest ancestor of all in his curly wig and his sweeping plumes.

They stared at Becky as she went down-stairs, a little white figure in her thin blue dressing-gown, her bronze hair twisted into a curly topknot, her feet in small blue slippers.

The telephone was on a small table under the portrait of the greatest grandfather. He had a high nose, and a fine clear complexion, and he looked really very much alive as he gazed down at Becky.

She found the King's Crest number. It was a dreadful thing that she was about to do. Yet she was going to do it.

She reached for the receiver. Then suddenly her hand was stayed, for it seemed to her that into the silence her greatest grandfather shouted accusingly:

"Where is your pride?"

She found herself trying to explain. "But, Grandfather——"

The clamour of other voices assailed her:

"Where is your pride?"

They were flinging the question at her from all sides, those gentlemen in ruffles, those ladies in shining gowns.

Becky stood before them like a prisoner at the bar—a slight child, yet with the look about her of those lovely ladies, and with eyes as clear as those of the old Governor who had accused her.

"But I love him——"

It was no defense and she knew it. Not one of those lovely ladies would have tried to call a lover back, not one of them but would have died rather than show her hurt. Not one of those slender and sparkling gentlemen but would have found swords or pistols the only settlement for Dalton's withdrawal at such a moment.

And she was one of them—one of that prideful group. There came to her a sense of strength in that association. What had been done could be done again. Other women had hidden broken hearts. Other women had held their heads high in the face of disappointment and defeat. There were traditions of the steadfastness of those smiling men and women. Some day, perhaps, she would have her portrait painted, and she would be—smiling.

She had no fear now of their glances, as she passed them on the stairs, as she met them in the upper hall. What she had to bear she must bear in silence, and bear it like a Bannister.

CHAPTER IX
"T. BRANCH"
I

Dalton felt that Fate had played a shabby trick. He had planned a graceful exit and the curtain had stuck; he had wanted to run away, and he could not. Flora was very ill, and it was, of course, out of the question to desert Oscar.

Madge had been sent for. She was to arrive on the noon train. He had promised Oscar that he would drive down for her. The house was in a hubbub. There were two trained nurses, and a half-dozen doctors. The verdict was unanimous, Flora could not be moved, and an operation was imperative.

And in the meantime there was the thought of Becky beating at his heart. With miles between them, the thing would have been easy. Other interests would have crowded her out. But here she was definitely within reach—and he wanted her. He wanted her more than he had ever wanted Madge, more than he had ever wanted any other woman. There had been a sweetness about her, a dearness.

He thought it over as he lay in bed waiting for his breakfast. Since waking, he had led Kemp a life of it.

"Of all the fools," he said, when at last the tray came.

"Anything the matter, sir?"

George lifted a silver cover. "That's not what I ordered."

"You said a kidney omelette, sir."

"I wanted the kidney broiled—not in a messy sauce. Take it away."

"I'll get you another."

"I don't want another. Take it away." He flung his napkin on the tray and turned his face to the wall. "I've got a headache. Tell Waterman that if he asks for me, that I've told you to go down and meet Miss MacVeigh."

Kemp stood and looked at the figure humped up under the light silk cover. He had long patience. He might have been a stick or stone under his master's abuse. But he was not a stick or a stone. It seemed too that suddenly his soul expanded. No man had ever called him a fool, and he had worn a decoration in France. He knew what he was going to do. And for the first time in many months he felt himself a free man.

George's decision to have Kemp meet Madge had been founded on the realization that it would be unbearably awkward if he should pass Becky on the road. She had sent back his pendant without a word, and there was no telling how she was taking it. If the thing were ever renewed—and his mind dwelt daringly on that possibility, explanations would be easy—but he couldn't make explanation if she saw him first in a car with another woman.

It was thus that Madge, arriving on the noon train, found Kemp waiting for her. Kemp was very fond of Miss MacVeigh. She was not a snob and there were so many snobs among Dalton's friends. She talked to him as if he were a man and not a mechanical toy. Dalton, on the other hand, treated his valet as if he were a marionette to be pulled by strings, an organ controlled by stops, or a typewriter operated by keys.

Major Prime had come down on the same train. Randy, driving Little Sister, was there to meet him.

"It is good to get back," the Major said. "I've been homesick."

"We missed you a lot. Yesterday we had a barbecue, and you should have been here——"

"I wanted to be, Randy. I hope you are not going to turn me out with the rest of the boarders when you roll in affluence."

"Affluence, nothing—but I sold two cars yesterday——"

"Not bad for a poet."

"It is a funny sort of game," said Randy soberly; "all day I run around in this funny little car, and at night I think big thoughts and try to put them on paper."

He could not tell the Major that the night before his thoughts had not been the kind to put on paper. He had been in a white fury. He knew that if he met Dalton nothing could keep him from knocking him down. He felt that a stake and burning fagots would be the proper thing, but, failing that, fists would do. Yet, there was Becky's name to be considered. Revenge, if he took it, must be a subtle thing—his mind had worked on it in the darkness of the night.

Kemp was helping Madge into the Waterman car. "Who is she?" the Major asked. "She came down on my train."

"Miss MacVeigh. Mrs. Waterman is very ill. There is to be an operation at once."

"I watched her on the train," the Major confessed as he and Randy drove off. "She read all the way down, and smiled over her book. I saw the title, and it was 'Pickwick Papers.' Fancy that in these days. Most young people don't read Dickens."

"Well, she isn't young, is she?"

"Not callow, if that's what you mean, you ungallant cub. But she is young in contrast to a Methuselah like myself."

Kemp had to look after Miss MacVeigh's trunks, so Randy's little car went on ahead. Thus again Fate pulled wires, or Providence. If the big car had had the lead Madge would have gone straight as an arrow to Hamilton Hill. But as it happened, Little Sister barred the way to the open road.

II

The two cars had to pass the Flippins. Mrs. Flippin and Mary were baking cakes for the feast at Huntersfield. Mrs. Flippin was to go over in the afternoon and help Mandy, and to-morrow Truxton and his mother would arrive.

"The Judge is like a boy," said Mrs. Flippin; "he's so glad to have Truxton home."

"Perhaps he won't be so glad when he gets here——"

"Why not?" Mrs. Flippin turned and stared at her daughter.

Mary was seeding raisins, wetting her fingers now and then in a glass of water which stood on a table by her side. "Well, Truxton may be changed—most of the men are, aren't they?"

"Is Randy Paine changed?"

"Yes, Mother."

"How?"

"He's a grown-up."

"Well, he needed to grow, and it wouldn't hurt Truxton either."

"But if Truxton has grown up and wants his own way—the Judge won't like it. The Judge has always ruled at Huntersfield."

"Well, he supports Truxton; why shouldn't he?"

A bright flush stained Mary's skin. "Truxton has his officer's pay now."

"He won't have it when he gets out of the Army."

Mary rose and went to the stove. She came back with a kettle and poured boiling water over a dish of almonds to blanch them.

"We ought to have made this fruit cake a week ago to have it really good," she said, and shelved the subject of Truxton Beaufort.

"It will be good enough as it is," said Mrs. Flippin; "there isn't anybody in the county that can beat me when it comes to baking cakes."

"Where's Fiddle," Mary said, suddenly; "can you see her from the window, Mother?"

Mrs. Flippin could not.

"Well, she's probably sailing her celluloid fish in the chickens' water pan," said Mary; "I'll go out and look her up in a minute."

But Fiddle was not sailing celluloid fish. Columbus-like she had decided that there were wider seas than the water pan. Once upon a time her grandmother had taken her to the bottom of the hill, and at the bottom of the hill there had been a lot of water, and Fiddle had walked in it with her bare feet, and had splashed. She had liked it much better than the chickens' pan.

So she had picked up her three celluloid fish and had trotted down the path. She wore her pink rompers, and as she bobbed along she was like a mammoth rose-petal blown by the wind.

At the foot of the hill she came upon a little brown stream. It was just a thread of a stream, very shallow with a lot of big flat stones. Fiddle walked straight into it, and the clear water swept over her toes. She put in her little fish, and quite unexpectedly, they swam away. She followed and came to where the stream was spanned by a rail-fence which separated the Flippin farm from the road. The lowest rail was about as high above the stream as her own fast-beating heart. She ducked under it and discovered one of her fish whirling in a small eddy. It was a red fish and she was very fond of it. She made a sudden grab, caught it, lost her balance and sat down in the water. After the first shock, she found that she liked it. The other fish had continued on their journey towards the river. Perhaps some day they would come to the sea. Fiddle forgot them. She held the little red fish fast and splashed the water with her heels.

Now on each side of the water was a road, which went up a hill each way, so that cars coming down, put on speed to go up, and forded the stream which was a mere thread of water except after high rains.

Randy was talking to the Major as he came down the hill. He did not see Fiddle until he was almost upon her. He was driving at high speed, and there was only a second in which to jam things down and pull things up and stop the car. Kemp was behind him. He was not prepared for Randy's sudden stop. He swerved sharply to the left, slammed into a telegraph pole—and came back to life to find somebody bending over him. "Who is looking after the lady, sir?" he managed to murmur.

"Young Paine and Mr. Flippin are carrying her to the house. You are cut a bit. Let me tie up your head." The Major gave efficient first aid and after that Kemp got to his feet painfully. "Is Miss MacVeigh badly hurt?"

"She is conscious, and not in great pain. I'm not much of a prop to lean on, but I think we can make that hill together." They climbed slowly, the man of crutches and the man with the bound-up head.

"It's like a little bit of over there, Kemp, isn't it?"

"Yes it is, sir—many's the time I've seen them helping each other—master and man."

When they got to the house, they found Madge on the sofa, and Mrs. Flippin bending over her. "My husband has gone for the doctor," she told the Major. "I think the blood comes from her hand; she must have put it up to save her face."

"I bent my head," murmured Madge, "and my hat was broad. Think what might have happened if I had worn a little hat." She had started the sentence lightly but she stopped with a gasp of pain. "Oh—my foot——" she said, "the pain—is—dreadful——"

The Major drew up a chair, and handed his crutches to Randy. "If you'll let us take off your shoe, it might help till the doctor comes."

She fainted dead away while they did it, and came back to life to find her foot bandaged, and her uncut hand held in the firm clasp of the man with the crutches. He was regarding her with grave gray eyes, but his face lighted as she looked up at him.

"Drink this," he told her. "The doctor is on the way, and I think it will help the pain until he comes."

She liked his voice—it had a deep and musical quality. She was glad he was there. Something in his strength seemed to reach out to her and give her courage.

When the pain began again, he gave her another drink from the glass, and when she drifted off, she came back to the echo of a softly-whistled tune.

"I beg your pardon," the Major said as she opened her eyes; "it is a bad habit that I permit myself when I have things on my mind. My men said they always knew by the tune I whistled the mood I was in. And that there was only one tune they were afraid of."

"What was that?"

"'Good-night, Ladies——'" He threw back his head and laughed. "When I began on that they knew it was all up with them——"

She tried to laugh with him, but it was a twisted grin. "Oh," she said and began to tremble. She saw his eyes melt to tenderness. "Oh, you poor little thing."

She was conscious after that of the firm hand which held hers. The deep voice which soothed. Through all that blinding agony she was conscious of his call to courage—she wondered if he had called his men like that—over there——

When the doctor came, he shook his head. "We'd better keep her here. She is in no condition to be moved to Hamilton Hill, not over these roads. Can you make room for her, Mrs. Flippin?"

"She can have my room," said Mary; "Fiddle and I can go up-stairs——"

They moved Madge, and Mrs. Flippin and Mary got her to bed. The Major sat in the sitting-room and talked to Randy, and as he talked he held Madge's hat in his hand. It had a brim of straw and a crown of mauve silk. The Major, turning it round and round on a meditative finger, thought of the woman who had worn it. She was a pretty woman, a very oddly pretty woman.

"Is she related to Mrs. Waterman, Kemp?" he asked.

"No, sir. But she's been there all summer. And then she went away, and they sent for her because Mrs. Waterman is ill." Randy rather indiscreetly flung out, "It seems as if the trail of that Waterman crowd is over our world. I suppose we shall have to get the news of this up to them somehow."

"I can telephone Mr. Dalton, sir."

"Is Dalton still there?"

"Yes, sir. And he had a headache this morning, and stayed in bed, or he would have been in the car, sir——"

Randy wished bloodthirstily that Dalton had been in the car. Why couldn't Dalton have been smashed instead of Madge?

"I might call up Mr. Waterman instead of Mr. Dalton," Kemp suggested. "If Mr. Dalton's in bed, he'll hate to be disturbed."

"Are you afraid of him, Kemp?"

Kemp's honest eyes met Randy's burning glance. "No, I am not afraid. I am leaving his service, sir."

They stared at him. "Leaving his service, why?" Randy demanded.

"He called me a fool this morning. And I am not a fool, sir."

"What made him say that?" Randy asked, with interest.

"He ordered a kidney omelette for breakfast, and I brought it, and he wouldn't eat it, and blamed me. I am willing to serve any man, but not without self-respect, sir."

"What are you going to do now, Kemp?" the Major asked.

"Find a better man to work for."

"It won't be hard," Randy interpolated.

"Work for me," said the Major.

Kemp was eager——! "For you, sir?"

"Yes. I need somebody to be legs for me—I'm only half a man. The place is open for you if you want it."

"I shall want it in a week," said Kemp; "I shall have to give him notice."

"There will be three musketeers in the old Schoolhouse, Paine. We have all seen service."

"It will be the best thing that ever happened to me, sir," said Kemp ecstatically, "to know that I can wait on a fighting man." He swung down the hall to the telephone as if he marched to the swirl of pipes.

"Isn't Dalton a brute?" said Randy.

"He that calleth his brother a fool——" mused the Major. He was still turning the mauve hat in his hands. "It is queer," he said unexpectedly, "how some women make you think of some flowers. Did you notice everything Miss MacVeigh wore was lilac—and there's the perfume of it about her things——"

"Becky's a rose," said Randy, "from her own garden. She's as fresh and sweet," his voice caught. "Oh, hang Dalton," he said, "I hate the whole tribe of them——"

Kemp came back to say that Oscar Waterman would be down at once. He insisted that Miss MacVeigh should be brought up to Hamilton Hill.

"He must talk with the doctor."

"He is bringing a doctor of his own. One who came down for Mrs. Waterman."

Randy picked up his hat. "I'm going home. The same house won't hold us——"

Kemp was discreet. "Can I help you with your car, sir?"

"I'll come over later and look at it." Randy, escaping by the back way, walked over the hills.

The Major stayed, and was in the sitting-room with the county doctor when the others arrived.

Dr. Dabney, the county doctor, was not old. He rode to hounds and he enjoyed life. But he was none the less a good doctor and a wise one. Waterman's physician confirmed the diagnosis. It would be very unwise to move Miss MacVeigh.

"But she can't stay here," said Dalton.

"Why not?"

"She can't be made comfortable." Dalton surveyed the Flippin sitting-room critically. He was aware that Mr. Flippin was in the doorway, and that Mrs. Flippin and Mary could not fail to catch his words. But he did not care who heard what he said. All was wrong with his world. It was bad enough to have Flora ill, but to have Madge out of commission would be to forge another chain to hold him to Hamilton Hill.

"She can be made very comfortable here," said Dr. Dabney. "Mrs. Flippin is a famous housekeeper. And anyone who has ever slept in that east room in summer knows that there is nothing better."

Dalton ignored him. "What do you think?" He turned to the Washington doctor. "What do you think?"

"I think it best not to move her. We can send a nurse, and with Dr. Dabney on the case, she will be in good hands."

"The only trouble is," said Dr. Dabney, unexpectedly, "that we may impose too much on Mrs. Flippin's hospitality."

"We will pay——" said Dalton with a touch of insolence.

From the doorway, Mr. Flippin answered him. "We don't want pay—— Neighbors don't ask for money when they—help out——"

There was a fine dignity about him. He was a rough farmer in overalls, but Dalton would never match the simple grace of his fine gesture of hospitality.

The Major, who had been silent, now spoke up. "You are having more than your share of trouble, Mr. Waterman. First your wife, and now your guest."

"Oh, I am, I am," said Oscar, brokenly. "I don't see what I've done to deserve it."

He was a pathetic figure. Whatever else he lacked, he loved his wife. If she died—he felt that he could not bear it. For the first time in his life Oscar faced a situation in which money did not count. He could not buy off Death—all the money in the world would not hold back for one moment the shadow of the Dark Angel from his wife's door.

III

The window of the east room looked out on the old orchard. There was a screened door which opened upon a porch and a stretch of lawn beyond which was the dairy.

Within the room there was a wide white bed, and a mahogany dresser with a scarf with crocheted trimming, above the dresser was an old steel engraving of Samson destroying the temple. The floor was spotless, a soft breeze shook the curtains. Madge, relieved from pain and propped on her pillows, watched a mother cat who with her kittens sat just outside the door.

She was a gray cat with white paws and breast, not fat at the moment but with a comfortable well-fed look. She alternately washed herself and washed her offspring. There were four of them, a rollicking lot not easy to keep in order.

"Aren't they—ripping?" Madge said to Mary.

"They always come up on the step about this time in the afternoon; they are waiting for the men to bring the milk to the dairy."

A little later Madge saw the men coming—two of them, with the foaming pails. The mother cat rose and went to meet them. Her tail was straight up, and the kittens danced after her.

"They will get a big dish of it, and then they will go around to the kitchen door to wait for supper and the table scraps. And after that Bessie will coax the kittens out to the barn and go hunting for the night."

"Is that her name—Bessie?"

"Yes, there has always been a Bessie-cat here. And we cling to old customs."

"I like old customs," said Madge, "and old houses."

After a little she asked, "Who makes the butter?"

"I do. It's great fun."

"Oh, when I am well, may I help?"

"You——?" Mary came over and stood looking down at her; "of course you may help. But perhaps you wouldn't like it."

"I am sure I should. And I don't think I am going to get well very soon——"

Mary was solicitous. "Why not?"

"I don't want to get well. I want to stay here. I think this place is—heavenly."

Mary laughed. "It is just a plain farmhouse. If you want the show places you should go to Huntersfield and King's Crest——"

"I want just this. Do you know I am almost afraid to go to sleep for fear I shall wake up and find it a—dream——"

A little later, she asked, "Are those apples in the orchard ripe?"

"Yes."

"May I have one?"

"The doctor may not want you to have it," said her anxious nurse.

"Just to hold in my hand," begged Madge.

So Mary picked a golden apple, and when the doctor came after dark, he found the room in all the dimness of shaded lamplight, and the golden girl asleep with that golden globe in her hand.

Up-stairs the mulatto girl, Daisy, was putting Fiddle-dee-dee to sleep.

"You be good, and Daisy gwine tell you a story."

Fiddle liked songs better. "Sing 'Jack-Sam bye.'"

Daisy, without her corsets and in disreputable slippers, settled herself to an hour of ease. She had the negro's love of the white child, and a sensuous appreciation of the pleasant twilight, the bedtime song, the rhythm of the rocking-chair.

"Well, you lissen," she said, and rocked in time to the tune.

Bye, oh, bye, little Jack-Sam, bye.

Bye, oh, bye, my baby,

When you wake, you shall have a cake—

And all the pretty little horses—

Her voice was low and pleasant, with queer, quavering minor cadences. But Fiddle-dee-dee was not sleepy.

"'Tory," she begged, when the song was ended.

So Daisy told the story of the three bears. Fiddle was too young to fully comprehend, but she liked the sound of Daisy's voice at the climaxes, "Who's been sittin' in *my* chair?" and "Who's been sleepin' in *my* bed?" and "Who's been eatin' *my* soup?" Daisy was dramatic or nothing, and she entered into the spirit of her tale. It was such an exciting performance altogether that Fiddle was wider awake than ever when the story was finished.

"Ain' you evah gwine shut yo' eyes?"

"Daisy, sing," said Fiddle.

"I'se sung twel my th'oat's dry," said Daisy. And just then Mary came in. "Isn't she asleep, Daisy?—I'll take her. Bannister's John is down-stairs and wants to see you."

"Well, I ain' wantin' to see him," Daisy tossed her head; "you jus' take Miss Fiddle whilst I goes down and settles *him*. I ain' dressed and I ain' ready, Miss Mary. You jes' look at them feet." She stuck them out for inspection. Her shoes were out at the toes and down at the heels. "This ain' my comp'ny night." As she went down-stairs, her voice died away in a querulous murmur.

Mary, with her child in her arms, sat by the window and looked out upon the quiet scene. There was faint rose in the sky, and a silver star. But while she watched the rose faded.

Fiddle, warm and heavy in her arms, slept finally. Then Mary took off her dress and donned a thin white kimono. She let down her hair and braided it——

There was no light in the room, and her mother, coming up, asked softly, "Are you there?"

"Yes."

"Fiddle asleep?"

"Yes, Mother."

Mrs. Flippin found her way to the window and sat down. "The nurse is here, and a lot of clothes and things just came over for Miss MacVeigh from Hamilton Hill. Mary, I wish you could see them."

"I shall in the morning, Mother."

"The nurse got her into a satin nightgown before I came up, with nothing but straps for sleeves—but she looked like a Princess——"

"Aren't you tired to death, dear?"

Mrs. Flippin laughed. "Me? I like it. I am sorry to have Miss MacVeigh hurt, but having her in the house with all those pretty things and people coming and going is better than a circus."

Mary laughed a little. "You are such a darling—making the best of things——"

"Well, making the best is the easiest way," said Mrs. Flippin. "I ain't taking any credit, Mary."

"You've had a hard day. You'd better go to bed."

"I'll have a harder one to-morrow. Nothing would do but I must go back to Huntersfield. Mandy's off her head, and the Judge wants the whole house turned upside down for Truxton."

"And Truxton comes—on the noon train."

"Yes."

There was a long silence. Then Mary said in a queer voice, "Mother, I've got to tell you something—to-night——"

"You ain't got anything to tell me, honey."

"But I have—something—I should have told you—months ago."

"There isn't anything you can tell me that I don't know."

"Mother——"

"Girls can't fool their mothers, Mary. Do you think that when Fiddle grows up, she is going to fool you?"

IV

The next morning Mr. Flippin was at the foot of the stairs when his daughter came down.

"So you lied to me, Mary."

She shook her head, "No."

"You said his name was Truelove Branch."

"He is my true love, Father. And his name is T. Branch—Truxton Branch Beaufort."

"What do you think the Judge is going to say about this?"

"He is going to hate it. He is going to think that your daughter isn't good enough for his grandson."

"You are good enough for anybody, Mary. But this wasn't the right way."

"It was the only way. Didn't Mother tell you that he begged me to let him write to you and go to the Judge, and I wouldn't?"

"Why not?"

"I wanted to have him here, so that we might face it together."

"Your mother says she guessed it long ago. But she didn't say anything. Talking might make it worse."

"Talking would have made it worse, Dad. We had done it—and I'd do it again," there was a lift of her head, a light in her eyes, "but it hasn't been easy—to know that you wondered—that other people wondered. But it wouldn't have been any better if I had told. Truxton had to be here to make it right if he could."

"Why didn't he come a-runnin' to you as soon as he got on this side?"

"He couldn't. His orders kept him in New York, and he wanted me to come. But I wouldn't. I made him ask his mother. I could spare him for three weeks,—he will be mine for the rest of his life—and he is to tell her before they get here."

"I wouldn't have had it happen for a thousand dollars," said troubled Bob Flippin. "I've always done everything on the square with the Judge."

"I know," said Mary, with the sudden realization of how her act had affected others, "I know. That's the only thing I am sorry about. But—I don't believe the Judge would be so silly as to let anything I did make any difference about you——"

"Where are you going to live?"

For the first time Mary's air of assurance left her. "He is hoping his grandfather will want us at Huntersfield——"

"He can keep on a-hoping," said Bob Flippin. "I know the Judge."

Mary flared. "We can find a little house of our own——"

Her father laid his hand on her shoulder. "Look at me, daughter," he said, and turned her face up to him. "Our house is yours, Mary," he said. "I don't like the way you did it, and I hate to think what will happen when the Judge finds out. But our home is yours, and it's your husband's. As long as you like to stay——"

And now Mary sobbed—a little slip of a thing in her father's arms. All the long months she had kept her secret, holding it safe in her heart, dreading yet longing for the moment when she could tell the world that she was the wife of Truxton Beaufort, whom she had adored from babyhood.

"I would have married him, Dad, if—if I had had to tramp the road."

Truxton came on the noon train. He drove at once to Huntersfield with his mother, was embraced by the Judge, kissed Becky, and suddenly disappeared.

"Where's he gone?" the Judge asked, irritably. "Where has he gone, Claudia?"

"He will be back in time for lunch," said Mrs. Beaufort. "May I speak to you in the library, Father?"

Becky, from the moment of her aunt's arrival, had known that something was wrong. She had expected to see Mrs. Beaufort glowing with renewed youth, radiant. Instead, she looked as if a blight had come upon her, shrivelled—old. When she smiled it was without joy; she was dull and flat.

It was a half hour before Aunt Claudia came out from the library. "My dear," she said, finding Becky still on the porch, "I have something to tell you. Will you go up-stairs with me?—I—think I should like to—lie down——"

Becky put a strong young arm about her and they went up together.

"It's—it's about Truxton," Aunt Claudia said, prone on the couch in her room. "Becky—he's married——"

"Married?"

"Married, my dear. He did not tell me until—last night. He wanted me to be happy—as long as I could. He's a dear boy, Becky—but—he's married——" She went on presently with an effort. "He has been married over two years—and, Becky—he has married—Mary Flippin."

"Aunt Claudia——"

"He married her in Petersburg—before he went to France with the first ambulance corps. They decided not to tell anyone. Mary took Truxton's middle name. When the baby came, Truxton was wild to write us, but Mary—wouldn't. She felt if he was here when it was told that we would forgive him—— If anything—happened to him—she didn't want him to die feeling that we had—blamed him—— I must say that Mary—was wise—but—to think that my son has married—Mary Flippin."

"Mary's a dear," said Becky stoutly.

"Yes," Aunt Claudia agreed, "but not a wife for my son. I had such hopes for him, Becky. He could have married anybody."

Becky knew the kind of woman that Aunt Claudia had wanted Truxton to marry—one whose ancestors were like those whose portraits hung in the hall at Huntersfield—a woman with a high-held head—a woman whose family traditions paralleled those of the Bannisters and Beauforts.

"Then Fiddle is Truxton's child."

"And I am a grandmother, Becky. Mrs. Flippin and I are grandmothers——" She said it with a sort of bitter mirth.

"What did Grandfather say?"

"I left him—raging. It was—very hard on me. I had hoped—he would make it easy. He declares that Mary Flippin shan't step inside of his front door. That he is going to recall all the invitations that he had sent out for to-night. I tried to show him that now that the thing is done—we might as well—accept it. But he wouldn't listen. If he keeps it up like this, I don't want Truxton to come back—to lunch. I had hoped that he might bring Mary with him—— She's his wife, Becky—and I've got to love her——"

"Aunt Claudia," Becky came over and put her arms about the pitiful black figure, "you are the best sport—ever——"

"No, I'm not," but Aunt Claudia kissed her, and for a moment they clung together; "you mustn't make me cry, Becky." But she did cry a little, wiping her eyes with her black-bordered handkerchief, and saying all the time, "He's my son, Becky. I—I can't put him away from me——"

"He loved her," said Becky, with a catch of her breath. "I—I think that counts a great deal, Aunt Claudia."

"Yes, it does. And they did no wrong. They were only foolish children."

"If anyone was to blame," she went on steadily, "it was Truxton. He had been brought up a—gentleman. He knew what was expected of a man of his birth and breeding. Secrecy is never honorable and I told him—last night—that I was sorry to be less proud of my son than of the men who had gone before him."

"Did you tell him that?"

"Yes. If pride of family means anything, Becky, it means holding on to the finest of your traditions. If you break the rules—you are a little less fine—a little less worthy——"

What a stern little thing she was. Yet one felt the stimulus of her strength. "Aunt Claudia," said Becky, tremulously, "if I could only be as sure of things as you are——"

"What things?"

"Of right and wrong and all the rest of it."

"I don't know what you mean by all the rest. But right is right, and wrong is wrong, my dear. There is no half-way, in spite of all the sophistries with which people try to salve their consciences."

She stopped, and plunged again into the discussion of her problem. "I must telephone to Truxton—he mustn't come—not until his grandfather asks him, Becky."

"He is coming now," said Becky, who sat by the window. "Look, Aunt Claudia."

Tramping up the hill towards the second gate was a tall figure in khaki. Resting like a rose-petal on one shoulder was a mite of a child in pink rompers.

"He is bringing Fiddle with him," Becky gasped. "Oh, Aunt Claudia, he is bringing Fiddle."

Aunt Claudia rose and looked out—— "Well," she said, "let her come. She's his child. If Father turns them out, I'll go with them."

Truxton saw them at the window and waved. "Shall we go down?" Becky said.

"No—wait a minute. Father's in the hall." Aunt Claudia stood tensely in the middle of the room. "Becky, listen over the stair rail to what they are saying."

"But——"

"Go on," Aunt Claudia insisted; "there are times when—one breaks the rules, Becky. I've got to know what they are saying——"

The voices floated up. Truxton's a lilting tenor——

"Are you going to forgive us, Grandfather?"

"I am not the grandfather of Mary Flippin's child," the Judge spoke evidently without heat.

"You are the grandfather of Fidelity Branch Beaufort," said Truxton coolly; "you can't get away from that——"

"The neighborhood calls her Fiddle Flippin," the Judge reminded him.

"What's in a name?" said Truxton, and swung his baby high in the air. "Do you love your daddy, Fiddle-dee-dee?"

"'Ess," said Fiddle, having accepted him at once on the strength of sweet chocolate, and an adorable doll.

"What are they saying?" whispered Aunt Claudia, still tense in the middle of the room.

"Hush," Becky waved a warning hand.

"There is," said the Judge, in a declamatory manner, "everything in a name. The Bannisters of Huntersfield, the Paines of King's Crest, the Randolphs of Cloverdale, do you think these things don't count, Truxton?"

"I think there's a lot of rot in it," said young Beaufort, "when we were fighting for democracy over there——"

The shot told. "Democracy has nothing to do with it——"

"Democracy," said Truxton, "has a great deal to do with it. The days of kings and queens are dead, they have married each other for generations and have produced offspring like—William of Germany. Class assumptions of superiority are withered branches on the tree of civilization. Mary is as good as I am any day."

"You wrote things like this," said the Judge, interested in spite of himself, and loving argument.

"I wrote them because I believed them. I am ready to apologize for not telling you of my marriage before this. I have no apologies to make for my wife——

"I have no apologies to make for my wife," Truxton repeated. "I fought for democratic ideals. I am practising them. Mary is a lady. You must admit that, Grandfather."

"I do admit it," said the Judge slowly, "in the sense that you mean it. But in the county sense? Do you think the Merriweathers will ask her to their ball? Do you think Bob Flippin will dine with my friends to-night?"

"I don't think he will expect to dine with you, Grandfather. I think if you ask him, he will refuse. But if you take your friendship from him it will break his heart——"

"Who said I would take my friendship away from Bob Flippin?"

"He is afraid—you may——"

"Because you married Mary?"

"Yes."

The Judge was breathing hard. "Whom does he think I'd go fishing with?"

"Do you think he'll want to go fishing with you if you cast off Mary?"

The Judge had a vision of life without Bob Flippin. On sunshiny days there would be no one to cut bait for him, no one to laugh with him at the dogs as they sat waiting for their corn-cakes, no one to listen with flattering attention to his old, old tales.

It had not occurred to him that Bob Flippin, too, might have his pride.

He sat down heavily in a porch chair.

"Go and get Mary," he exploded; "bring her here. The thing is done. The milk is spilled. And there's no use crying over it. And if you think you two young people can separate me and Bob Flippin——"

Mrs. Beaufort and Becky came down presently, to find the old man gazing, frowning, into space.

"I have told him to bring Mary, Claudia, but I must say that I am bitterly disappointed."

"Mary is a good little thing, Father." Aunt Claudia's voice shook.

The old man looked up at her. "It is hardest for you, my dear. And I have helped to make it hard."

He reached out his hand to her. She took it. "He is my son—and I love him——"

"And I love you, Claudia."

"May I get the blue room ready?"

The blue room was the bridal chamber at Huntersfield; kept rather sacredly at other times for formal purposes.

"Do as you please. The house is yours, my dear."

And so that night the lights of the blue room shone on Fiddle Flippin and her new grandmother.

"Do you think she would let me put her to bed?" Mrs. Beaufort had asked Mary.

"If you will sing, 'Jack-Sam Bye.'"

Mary pulled the last little garment from the pink plump body, and Fiddle, like a rosy Cupid, counted her toes gleefully in the middle of the wide bed.

"I told Truxton," Mary said suddenly, "that he might not want to call her 'Fiddle.' The whole neighborhood says 'Fiddle Flippin.'"

"It is a dear little name," Aunt Claudia was bending adoringly over the baby, "but Fidelity is better—Fidelity Branch Beaufort——"

"I want her to be as proud of her name as I am," Mary's voice had a thrilling note. "It is a great thing to know that my child has in her the blood of all those wonderful people whose portraits hang in the hall. I want her to be worthy of her name."

She could have said nothing better. Aunt Claudia's face was lighted by the warmth in her heart. "Such a lot of ancestors for one little fat Fidelity," she said; "put on her nightgown, Mary, and I'll rock her to sleep."

CHAPTER X
A GENTLEMAN'S LIE

Becky was not well. Aunt Claudia, perceiving her listlessness, decided that she needed a change. Letters were written to the Nantucket grandfather, and plans made for Becky's departure. She was to spend a month on the island, come back to Boston to the Admiral's big old house on the water-side of Beacon Street, and return to Huntersfield for Christmas.

Becky felt that it was good of everybody to take so much trouble. She really didn't care in the least. She occupied herself steadily with each day's routine. She bent her head over the fine embroidery of a robe she was making for Mary. She cut the flowers for the vases and bowls, she recited nursery rhymes to Fiddle, entrancing that captious young person with "Oranges and Lemons" and "Lavender's Blue." She read aloud to the Judge, planned menus for Aunt Claudia, and was in fact such an angel in the house that Truxton, after three days of it, protested.

"Oh, what's the matter with Becky, Mums?"

"Why?"

"She hasn't any pep."

"I know."

"Isn't she well?"

"I have tried to have her see a doctor. But she won't. She insists that she is all right——"

"She is not. She is no more like the old Becky than champagne is like—milk—— Becky was the kind that—went to your head—Mums. You know that—sparkling."

"I have wondered," Mrs. Beaufort said, slowly, "if anything happened while I was away."

"What could happen——"

His mother sighed. "Nothing, I suppose——" She let it go at that. Her intuitions carried her towards the truth. She had learned from Mandy and the Judge that Dalton had spent much time at Huntersfield in her absence. Becky never mentioned him. Her silence spoke eloquently, Mrs. Beaufort felt, of something concealed. Becky was apt to talk of things that interested her. And there had been no doubt of her interest in Dalton before her aunt had gone away.

Randy, coming often now to Huntersfield, had his heart torn for his beloved. No one except himself knew what had happened, and the knowledge stirred him profoundly. He held that burning torches and a stake were none too good for Dalton. He sighed for the old days in Virginia when gentlemen settled such matters in the woods at dawn, with pistols, seconds, a shot or two. Farther back it would have been an affair of knives and tomahawks—Indian chiefs in a death struggle.

But neither duels nor death struggles were in the modern mode, nor would any punishment which he might inflict on Dalton help Becky in this moment of deep humiliation. He knew her pride and the hurt that had come to her, he knew her love, and the deadly inertia which had followed the loss of illusion.

Randy's love was not a selfish love. In that tense moment of Becky's confession on the day of the barbecue, his own hopes had died. The boy in him had died, too, and he had reached the full stature of a man. He wanted to protect and shield—he was all tenderness. He felt that he would dare anything, do anything, if he could bring back to Becky the dreams of which Dalton robbed her.

Night after night he sat in his room up-stairs in the old Schoolhouse, and wrote on "The Trumpeter Swan." It was an outlet for his pent-up emotions, and something of the romance which was denied him, something of the indignation which stirred him, something of the passions of love and revenge which fought within him, drove his pen onward, so that his little tale took on color and life. Crude, perhaps, in form, it was yet a song of youth and patriotism. It was Randy's call to his comrades. There was to be no compromise. They must make men look up and listen—to catch the sound of their clear note. The ideals which had made them fight brutality and greed were living ideals. They were not to be doffed with their khaki and overseas caps. Their country called, the whole world called, for men with faith and courage. There was no place for pessimism, no place for materialism, no place for sordidness.

His hero was, specifically, a man who had come back from the fighting, flaming with the thought of his high future. He had found the world smiling and unconcerned. It was this world which needed to listen to the call of trumpets—high up —
——

The chapters in which he wrote of love—for there was a woman in the story—were more beautiful than Randy realized. It was of a boy's love that he told—delicately. It was his own story of love denied, yet enriching a life.

Yet—because man cannot live up always to the measure of his own vision, there came often between Randy and the written page the image of George Dalton, smiling and insolent. And he would lay down his pen, and lean his head on his hand, and gaze into space, and sometimes he would speak out in the silence. "I will make him suffer."

It was in one of these moments that he saw how it might be done. "He would let fruit drop to the ground and rot if no other man wanted it," he analyzed keenly, "but if another man tried to pick it up, he would fight for it."

Dalton was still at King's Crest. Mrs. Waterman had not responded satisfactorily to the operation. The doctors had grave doubts as to her recovery. Madge was convalescing at the Flippins'.

Randy had been content, hitherto, to receive bulletins indirectly from both of the invalids. But on the morning following the birth of his great idea he rode on horseback to King's Crest. He looked well on horseback, and in his corduroys, with a soft shirt and flowing tie, a soft felt hat, he was at his best.

He found George and Oscar on the west terrace, shaded by blue and white-striped awnings, with a macaw, red and blue on a perch—a peacock glimmering at the foot of the steps—and the garden blazing beyond.

There were iced drinks in tall glasses—a litter of cigarettes on smoking-stands, magazines and newspapers on the stone floors, packs of cards on a small table. Oscar, hunched up in a high-backed Chinese chair, was white and miserable. George looked bored to extinction.

Randy, coming in, gave a clear-cut impression of strength and youth.

"Mother sent some wine jelly for Mrs. Waterman," he said to Oscar. "It was made from an old recipe, and she thought it might be different. And there were some hundred-leaved roses from our bush. I gave them to your man."

Oscar brightened. He was grateful for the kindness of these queer neighbors of his who would have nothing to do with him and his wife when they were well, and who had seemed to care not at all for his money. But who, now that sickness had come and sorrow, offered themselves and their possessions unstintedly.

"I'll go and see that Flora gets them," he said. "She hasn't any appetite. She's—it's rather discouraging——"

Randy, left alone with Dalton, was debonair and delightful. George, looking at him with speculative eyes, decided that there was more to this boy than he would have believed. He had exceedingly good manners and an ease that was undeniable. There was of course good blood back of him. And in a way it counted. George knew that he could never have been at ease in old clothes in the midst of elegance.

It was Randy who spoke first of Becky. Dalton's heart jumped when he heard her name. Night after night he had ridden towards Huntersfield, only to turn back before he reached the lower gate. Once he had ventured on foot as far as the garden, and in the hush had called softly, "Becky." But no one had answered. He wondered what he would have done if Becky had responded to his call. "I am not going to be fool enough to marry her," he told himself, angrily, yet knew that if he played the game with Becky there could be no other end to it.

Randy said, quite naturally, that Becky was going away. To Nantucket. He asked if George had been there.

"Once, on Waterman's yacht. It's quaint—but a bit spoiled by summer people——"

"Becky doesn't know the summer people. Her great-grandparents were among the first settlers, and the Merediths have never sold the old home."

"She is a pretty little thing," George said. "And she's buried down here."

"I shouldn't call it exactly—buried."

George, with his eyes on the peacock, smiled and shrugged his shoulders.

Randy smiled and his eyes, too, were on the peacock. He was thinking that there were certain points of resemblance between the gorgeous bird and Dalton. They glimmered in the sunlight and strutted a bit——

He came back to say easily, "Has Becky told you of our happiness——"

George gave him a startled glance. "Happiness?"

"We are to be married when she comes back—at Christmas."

"Married——"

"Yes," coolly, "it was rather to be expected, you know. We played together as children—our fathers played together—our grandfathers—our great-grandfathers."

A cold wave seemed to sweep over George. So this young cub would have her beauty!

"Aren't you rather young——?" he demanded, "and what have you to give her?"

"Love," said Randy calmly, "a man's respect for her goodness and worth—for her innocence. She's a little saint in a shrine."

"Is she?" Georgie-Porgie asked, and smiled to himself; "few women are that."

After Randy had gone George Dalton walked the floor. He knew innocence when he saw it, and he knew that Randy had told the truth. Becky Bannister was as white as the doves that were fluttering down to the garden pool to drink. He had never cared particularly for innocence. But he cared for Becky. He knew now that he cared tremendously. Randy had made him know it. It had not seemed so bad to think of Becky as breaking her heart and waiting for a word from him. It seemed very bad, indeed, when he thought of her as married to Randy.

He felt that, of course, she did not love Randy; that he, Georgie-Porgie, had all that she had to give—— But woman-like, she had taken this way to get back at him. He wondered if she had sent Randy.

Up and down the terrace he raged like a lion. He wanted to show that cub—oh, if he might show him——!

Randy had known that he would rage, and as he rode home he had the serene feeling that he had stuck a splinter in George's flesh.

Oscar Waterman joined George on the terrace, but noticed nothing. His mind was full of Flora. "I am sorry young Paine went so soon. I wanted to thank him. Flora can't eat the jelly, but it was good of them to send it. She can't eat anything. She's worse, George. I don't know how I am going to stand it."

George was in no mood for condolence. Yet he was not quite heartless. "Look here," he said, "you mustn't give up."

"George, if she dies," Oscar said, wildly, "what do you think will happen to me? I never planned for this. I planned for a good time. I thought maybe that when we were old—one of us might go. But it wouldn't be fair to take her now—and leave me."

"I have given her—everything——" he went on. "I—I think I've been a good husband. I have always loved her a lot, George, you know that."

He was a plain little man, but at this moment he gained something of dignity. And there was this to say for him, that what he felt for Flora was a deeper emotion than George had ever known.

"The doctor says the crisis comes to-night. I am not going to bed. I couldn't sleep. George—I've been wondering if I oughtn't to call in—some kind of clergyman—to see her."

"People don't, nowadays, do they?" George asked rather uncomfortably.

"Well, I don't see why they shouldn't. There ought to be somebody to pray for Flora."

There was, it developed upon inquiry, a little old rector who lived not far away. George went for him in his big car.

The little man, praying beside Flora's gorgeous bed, felt that this was the hundredth sheep who had wandered and was found. The other ninety and nine were safely in the fold. He had looked after the spiritual condition of the county for fifty years. There had been much to discourage him, but in the main if they strayed they came back.

He prayed with fervor, the fine old prayers of his church.

"Look down from heaven, we humbly beseech thee, with the eyes of mercy upon this child now lying upon the bed of sickness: Visit her, O Lord, with thy salvation; deliver her in thy good appointed time from bodily pain, and save her soul for thy mercies' sake; that, if it shall be thy pleasure to prolong her days here on earth, she may live for thee, and be an instrument of thy glory, by serving thee faithfully, and doing good in her generation; or else receive her into those heavenly habitations, where the souls of those who sleep in the Lord Jesus enjoy perpetual rest and felicity."

Flora, lying inert and bloodless, opened her eyes. "Say it again," she whispered. "Say it again."

II

Randy rode straight from Hamilton Hill to Huntersfield. He found Becky in the Bird Room. She had her head tied up in a white cloth, and a big white apron enveloped her. She was as white as the whiteness in which she was clad, and there were purple shadows under her eyes. The windows were open and a faint breeze stirred the curtains. The shade of the great trees softened the light to a dim green. After the glare of Oscar's terrace it was like coming from a blazing desert to the bottom of the sea.

There was a wide seat under a window which looked out towards the hills. Becky sat down on it. "Everybody is out," she said, "except Aunt Claudia. She is taking a nap up-stairs."

"I didn't come to see everybody, Becky. I came to see you."

"I am glad you came. I can rest a bit."

"You work as hard as if you had to do it."

She leaned back against the green linen cushions of the window seat and looked up at him. "I do have to do it. There is nobody else. Mandy is busy, and, anyhow, Grandfather doesn't like to have the servants in here. And neither do I—— It is almost as if the birds were alive—and loved me."

Randy hugged his knee and meditated. "But there are lots of rich women who wouldn't dust a room."

She made a gesture of disdain. "Oh, *that* kind of rich people."

"What kind?"

"The kind that aren't used to their money. Who think ladies—are idle. Sister Loretto says that is the worst kind—the awful kind. She talked to me every day about it. She said that money was a curse when people used it only for their ease. Sister Loretto hates laziness. She had money herself before she took her vows, but now she works every hour of the day and she says it brings her happiness."

Randy shook his head. "Most of us need to play around a bit, Becky."

"Do we? I—I think most women would be better off if they were like Sister Loretto."

"They would not. Stop talking rot, Becky, and take that thing off your head. It makes you look like a nun."

"I know. I saw myself in the glass. I don't mind looking like a nun, Randy."

"Well, I mind. Turn your head and I'll take out that pin."

"Don't be silly, Randy."

He persisted. "Keep still while I take it out——"

He found the pin and unwound the white cloth. "There," he said, drawing a long breath, "you look like yourself again. You were so—austere, you scared me, Becky."

He was again hugging his knees. "When are you going away?"

"On the twenty-ninth. I shall stay over until next week for the Merriweathers' ball."

"I didn't know whether you would feel equal to it."

"I shall go on Mary's account. It will be her introduction to Truxton's friends, and if I am there it will be easier for her. She has a lovely frock, jade green tulle with a girdle of gold brocade. It came down for me with a lot of other clothes, and it needed only a few changes for her to wear it."

"You will be glad to get away?"

"It will be cooler—and I need the change. But it is always more formal up there—they remember that I have money. Here it is forgotten."

"I wish I could forget it."

"Why should you ever think of it?" she demanded with some heat. "I am the same Becky with or without it."

"Not quite the same," he was turning his hat in his hand. Then, raising his eyes and looking at her squarely, he said what he had come to say, "I have—I have just been to see Dalton, Becky."

A wave of red washed over her neck, touched her chin, her cheeks. "I don't see what that has to do with me."

"It has a great deal to do with you. I told him you were going to marry me."

The wave receded. She was chalk-white.

"Randy, how dared you do such a thing?"

"I dared," said Randy, with tense fierceness, "because a man like Dalton wants what other men want. He will think about you a lot, and I want him to think. He won't sleep to-night, and I want him to stay awake. He will wonder whether you love me, and he will be afraid that you do—and I want him to be afraid."

"But it was a lie, Randy. I am not going to marry you."

"Do you think that I meant that——? That I am expecting anything for myself?"

"No," unsteadily, her slender body trembling as if from cold, "but what did you mean?"

"I told you. Dalton's got to come back to you and beg—on his knees—and he will come when he thinks you are mine——"

"I don't want him to come. And when you talk like that it makes me feel—smirched——"

Dead silence. Then, "It was a gentleman's lie——"

"Gentlemen do not lie. Go to him this minute, Randy, and tell him that it isn't true."

"Give me three days, Becky. If in that time he doesn't try to see you or call you up, I'll go—— But give me three days."

She wavered. "What good will it do?"

He caught up her cold little hands in his. "You will have a chance to get back at him. And when you stick in the knife, you can turn it—until it hurts."

III

It was while the family at Huntersfield were at dinner that the telephone rang. Calvin answered, and came in to say that Miss Becky was wanted. She went listlessly. But the first words over the wire stiffened her.

It was George's voice, quick imploring. Saying that he had something to tell her. That he must see her——

"Let me come, Becky."

"Of course."

"You mean that I—may——?"

"Why not?"

He seemed to hesitate. "But I thought——"

Her laugh was light and clear. "I must get back to my dinner. I have only had my soup. And I am simply—*starving*——"

It was not what he had expected. Not in the least. As he hung up the receiver he was conscious too of a baffled feeling that Becky had, in a sense, held the reins of the situation.

In spite of her famished condition, Becky did not at once go to the dining-room. She called up King's Crest, and asked for Randy.

She wanted to know, she said, whether he had anything on for the evening. No? Then could he come over and bring the boarders? Oh, as many of them as would come. And they would dance. She was bored to *death*. Her laugh was still clear and light, and Randy wondered.

Then she went back to the dinner table and ate the slice of lamb which the Judge had carved for her. She ate mint sauce and mashed potatoes, she ate green corn pudding, and a salad, and watermelon. Her cheeks were red, and Aunt Claudia felt that Becky was looking much better. For how could Aunt Claudia know that everything that Becky ate was like sawdust to her palate. She found herself talking and laughing a great deal, and Truxton teased her.

After dinner she went up-stairs with Mary and showed her a new way to do her hair, and found an entrancing wisp of a frock for Mary to wear.

"It will be great fun having the boarders from King's Crest. There are a lot of young people of all kinds—and not many of them our kind, Mary."

Mary smiled at her. "I am not quite your kind, am I?"

"Why not? And oh, Mary, you are happy, happy. And you are lovely with your hair like that, close to your head and satin-smooth."

584

Mary, surveying herself in the glass, gave an excited laugh. "Do you know when I married Truxton I never thought of this?"

"Of what?" Becky asked.

"Of pretty clothes—and dances—and dinners. I just knew that he—loved me, and that he had to leave me. But I don't suppose I could make the world believe it."

"Truxton believes it, doesn't he, Mary?"

"Yes."

"And I believe it. And what do you care for the others? It is what we know of ourselves, Mary," she drew a quick breath. "It is what we know of ourselves——"

Becky was wearing the simple frock of pale blue in which George had seen her on that first night when he came to Huntersfield.

"Aren't you going to change?" Mary asked.

"No. It is too much trouble." Becky was in front of the mirror. Her pearls caught the light of the candles. Her bronze hair was a shining wave across her forehead. "It is too much trouble," she said, again, and turned from the mirror.

She had a dozen frocks that had come in the rosy hamper—frocks that would have made the boarders open their eyes. Frocks that would have made Dalton open his. But Becky had the feeling that this was not the moment for lovely clothes. She felt that she would be cheapened if she decked herself for George.

When the two girls went down-stairs Truxton was waiting for his wife. "I thought you would never come," he said. He drew her within the circle of his arm, and they went out into the garden. The Judge and Mrs. Beaufort were on the porch. Becky sat on the step and leaned her head against Aunt Claudia's knee.

"What in the world made you ask all those people over, Becky?" the Judge demanded.

"Oh, they're great fun, Grandfather, and I felt like it."

"Have you planned anything for them to eat, Claudia?"

"Watermelons. Calvin has put a lot of them in the spring."

The stars were thick overhead. Becky looked up at them and relaxed a little. Since Dalton had spoken to her over the wire she had gone through the motions of doing normal things. She had eaten and talked, and now she was sitting quite still on the step while Aunt Claudia smoothed her hair, and the Judge talked of things to eat.

But shut up within her was a clock which ticked and never stopped. *"He will come—when he thinks—you are mine—— He will come—when he thinks—you are mine——"*

Randy and his mother arrived in Little Sister, with two of the boarders for good measure in the back seat. They had dropped Major Prime at Flippins', where he was to make a call on Madge MacVeigh. He had promised to come later, however, if Randy would drive over and get him.

The rest of the boarders were packed variously into their cars and the surrey, and as soon as they arrived they proceeded to occupy the lawn and the porch, and to overflow the garden. They made a great deal of pleasant noise about it, and the white gowns of the women, and the white flannels of the men gave an impressionistic effect of faint blue against the deeper blue of the night.

Within the house, the rugs were up in the drawing-room, the library, the dining-room, and the wide hall; there sounded, presently, the tinkling music of the phonograph, and there was the unceasing movement of white-clad figures which seemed to float in a golden haze.

Becky danced a great deal, with Randy, with the younger boarders, and with the genial gentleman. She laughed with an air of unaffected gayety. And she felt that her heart stopped beating, when at last she looked up and saw Dalton standing in the door.

She at once went towards him, and gave him her hand. "I wonder if you know everybody?"

Her clear eyes met his without self-consciousness. He attempted a swagger. "I don't want to know everybody. How do they happen to be here?"

"I asked them. And they are really very nice."

He did not see the niceness. He had thought to find her in the setting which belonged to her beauty. The silent night, the fragrance of the garden, the pale statues among the trees, and himself playing the game with a greater sense of its seriousness than ever before.

Throughout the evening George watched for a chance to see Becky alone. Without conspicuously avoiding him, she had no time for him. He complained constantly. "I want to talk to you. Run away with me, Becky—and let these people go."

"It isn't proper for a hostess to leave her guests."

"Are you trying to—punish me?"

"For what?"

So—she too was playing——! She had let him come that he might see her—indifferent.

Becky had danced with George once, and with Randy three times. George had protested, and Becky had said, "But I promised him before you came——"

"You knew I was coming?"

"Yes."

"You might have kept a few——"

She seemed to consider that. "Yes, I might. But not from Randy——"

At last he said to her, "I have been out in the garden. There is a star shining in the little pool where the fishes are. I want you to see the star."

It was thus he had won her. He had always seen stars shining in little pools, or a young moon rising from a rosy bed. But it had never meant anything. She shook her head. "I should like to see your little star. But I haven't time."

"Are you afraid to come?"

"Why should I be?"

"Well, there's Love—in the garden," he was daring—his sparkling eyes tried to hold hers and failed.

She was looking straight beyond him to where Randy stood by a window, tall and thin with his Indian profile, and his high-held head.

"We are going to have watermelons in a minute," was her romantic response to Dalton's fire. "You'd better stay and eat some."

"I don't want to eat. And if you aren't afraid you'll come."

Calvin and Mandy and their son, John, with Flippins' Daisy, had assembled the watermelons on a long table out-of-doors. Above the table on the branch of a tree was hung an old ship's lantern brought by Admiral Meredith to his friend, the Judge. It gave a faint but steady light, and showed the pink and green and white of the fruit, the dusky faces of the servants as they cut and sliced, and handed plates to the eager and waiting guests.

Becky, standing back in the shadows with Randy by her side, watched the men surge towards the table, and retire with their loads of lusciousness. Grinning boys were up to their ears in juice, girls, bare-armed and bare-necked, reached for plates held teasingly aloft. It was all rather innocently bacchanal—a picture which for Becky had an absolutely impersonal quality. She had entertained her guests as she had eaten her dinner, outwardly doing the normal and conventional thing, while her mind was chaotic. This jumble of people on the lawn seemed unreal and detached. The only real people in the world were herself and Dalton.

"How did you happen to ask us?" Randy was saying.

"Because I wanted you——"

"That doesn't explain it. It has something to do with Dalton——"

"He said he was coming—and I wanted a crowd."

"Were you afraid to see him alone?"

"He says that I am."

"When did he say it?"

"Just now. He's in the garden, Randy."

"Waiting for you?"

"He says that he is waiting."

Randy gave a quick exclamation. "Surely you won't go."

"Why not? I've got to turn—the knife——"

He groaned. "So this is what I've let you in for——"

"Well, I shall see it through, Randy."

"Becky, don't go to him in the garden."

"Why not?"

"The whole thing is wrong," the boy said, slowly. "I lied to give you your opportunity, and now, I'd rather die than think of you out there——"

"Then you don't trust me, Randy?"

"My dear, I do. But I don't trust—him."

IV

George had known that she would come. Yet when he saw the white blur of her gown against the blackness of the bushes, his heart leaped. All through the ages men have waited for women in gardens—"*She is coming, my own, my sweet——*" and farther back, "*Make haste, my beloved,*" and in the beginning, as Mandy could have told, a serpent waited.

Dalton was not, of course, a serpent. He was merely a very selfish man, who had always had what he wanted, and now he wanted Becky. He was still, perhaps, playing the game, but he was playing it in dead earnest with Randy as his opponent and Becky the prize.

She recognized a new note in his voice and was faintly disturbed by it.

"So you are not afraid?"

"No."

She sat down on the bench. Behind them was the pale statue of Diana, the pool was at their feet with its little star.

"Why should I be afraid?" she asked.

"You are trying to shut me out of your heart, Becky—and you are afraid I may try to—open the door."

"Silly," she said, clearly and lightly, but with a sense of panic. Oh, why had she come? The darkness seemed to shut her in; his voice was beating against her heart——

He was saying that he loved her, *loved* her. Did she understand? That he had been *miserable*? His defense was masterly. He played on her imagination delicately, as if she were a harp, and his fingers touched the strings. He realized what a cad he must have seemed. But she was a saint in a shrine—it will be seen that he did not hesitate to borrow from Randy. She was a saint in a shrine, and well, he knelt at her feet—a sinner. "You needn't think that I don't know what I have done, Becky. I swept you along with me without a thought of anything serious in it for either of us. It was just a game, sweetheart, and lots of people play it, but it isn't a game now, it is the most serious thing in life."

There is no eloquence so potent as that which is backed by genuine passion. Becky coming down through the garden had been so sure of herself. She had felt that pride would be the rock to which she would anchor her resistance to his enchantments. Yet here in the garden——

"Oh, *please*," she said, and stood up.

He rose, too, and towered above her. "Becky," he said, hoarsely, "it's the real thing—for me——"

His spell was upon her. She was held by it—drawn by it against her will. Her cry was that of a frightened and fascinated bird.

He bent down. His face was a white circle in the dark, but she could see the sparkle of his eyes. "Kiss me, Becky."

"I shall never kiss you again."

"I love you."

"Love," she said, with a sort of tense quiet, "does not kiss and run away."

"My heart never ran away. I swear it. Marry me, Becky."

He had never expected to ask her. But now that he had done it, he was glad.

She was swayed by his earnestness, by the thought of all he had meant to her in her dreams of yesterday. But to-day was not yesterday, and George was not the man of those dreams. Yet, why not? There was the quick laughter, with its new ring of sincerity, the sparkling eyes, the Apollo head.

"Marry me, Becky."

Beyond the pool which reflected the little star was the dark outline of the box hedge, and beyond the hedge, the rise of the hill showed dark against the dull silver of the sky—a shadow seemed to rise suddenly in that dim brightness, the tall thin shadow of a man with a clear-cut profile, and a high-held head!

Becky drew a sharp breath—then faced Dalton squarely. "I am going to marry Randy."

His laugh was triumphant——

"Do you think I am going to let you? You are mine, Becky, and you know it. *You are mine*——"

V

Randy, having made a record run with Little Sister to the Flippins', had brought back Major Prime. When he returned Becky had disappeared. He looked for her, knowing all the time that she had gone down into the garden to meet Dalton. And he had brought Dalton back to her, he had given him this opportunity to plead his cause, had given him the incentive of a man of his kind to still pursue; he had, as he had said, let Becky in for it, and now he was raging at the thought.

BECKY DREW A SHARP BREATH—THEN FACED DALTON SQUARELY—"I AM GOING TO MARRY RANDY"

Nellie Custis, padding at his heels, had known that something disturbed him. He walked restlessly from room to room, from porch to porch, across the lawn, skirted the garden, stopped now and then to listen, called once when he saw a white figure alone by the big gate, "Becky!"

Nellie knew who it was that he wanted. And at last she instituted a search on her own account. She went through the garden, passed the pool, found Becky's feet in blue slippers, and rushed back to her master with an air of discovery.

But Randy would not follow her. He must, he knew, set a curb on his impatience. He walked beyond the gate, following the ridge of the hill to the box hedge. He was not in the least aware that his shadow showed up against the silver of the sky. Perhaps Fate guided him to the ridge, who knows? At any rate, it seemed so afterwards to Becky, who felt that the shadow of Randy against the silver sky was the thing that saved her.

She gave the old Indian cry, and he answered it.

His shadow wavered on the ridge. He was lost for a moment against the blackness of the hedge, and emerged on the other side of the pool.

"Randy," she was a bit breathless, "here we are. Mr. Dalton and I. I saw you on the ridge. You have no idea how tall your shadow seemed——"

She was talking in that clear light voice which was not her own. Dalton said sullenly, "Hello, Paine." And Randy's heart was singing, "She called me."

The three of them walked to the house together. Becky had insisted that she must go back to her guests. George left them at the step. He was for the moment beaten. As he drove his car madly back to King's Crest, he tried to tell himself that it was all for the best. That he must let Becky alone. He would be a fool to throw himself away on a shabby slender slip of a thing because she had clear eyes and bronze hair.

But it was not because of her slenderness and clear eyes and bronze hair that Becky held him, it was because of the force within her which baffled him.

The guests were leaving. They had had the time of their lives. They packed themselves into their various cars, and the surrey, and shouted "good-bye." The Major stayed and sat on the lawn to talk to the Judge and Mrs. Beaufort. Mary and Truxton ascended the stairs to the Blue Room, where little Fiddle slept in the Bannister crib that had been brought down from the attic.

Becky and Randy went into the Bird Room and sat under the swinging lamp. "I have something to tell you, Randy," Becky had said, and as in the days of their childhood the Bird Room seemed the place for confidences.

Becky curled herself up in the Judge's big chair like a tired child. Randy on the other side of the empty fireplace said, "You ought to be in bed, Becky."

"I shan't—sleep," nervously. There were deep shadows under her troubled eyes. "I shan't sleep when I go."

Randy came over and knelt by her side. "My dear, my dear," he said, "I am afraid I have let you in for a lot of trouble."

"But the things you said were true—he came—because he thought I—belonged to—you."

She hesitated. Then she reached out her hand to him. "Randy," she said, "I told him I was going to marry—you."

His hand had gone over hers, and now he held it in his strong clasp. "Of course it isn't true, Becky."

"I am going to make it true."

Dead silence. Then, "No, my dear."

"Why not?"

"You don't love me."

"But I like you," feverishly, "I like you, tremendously, and don't you want to marry me, Randy?"

"God knows that I do," said poor Randy, "but I must not. It—it would be Heaven for me, you know that. But it wouldn't be quite—cricket—to let you do it, Becky."

"I am not doing it for your sake. I am doing it for my own. I want to feel—safe. Do I seem awfully selfish when I say that?"

A great wave of emotion swept over him. She had turned to him for protection, for tenderness. In that moment Randy grew to the full stature of a man. He lifted her hand and kissed it. "You are making me very happy, Becky, dear."

It was a strange betrothal. Behind them the old eagle brooded with outstretched wings, the owl, round-eyed, looked down upon them and withheld his wisdom, the Trumpeter, white as snow, in his glass case, was as silent as the Sphinx.

"You are making me very happy, Becky, dear," said poor Randy, knowing as he said it that such happiness was not for him.

CHAPTER XI
WANTED—A PEDESTAL
I

The Major's call on Miss MacVeigh had been a great success. She was sitting up, and had much to say to him. Throughout the days of her illness and convalescence, the Major had kept in touch with her. He had sent her quaint nosegays from the King's Crest garden, man-tied and man-picked. He had sent her nice soldierly notes, asking her to call upon him if there was anything he could do for her. He had sent her books, and magazines, and now on this first visit, he brought back the "Pickwick" which he had picked up in the road after the accident.

"I have wondered," Madge said, "what became of it."

They were in the Flippin sitting-room. Madge was in a winged chair with a freshly-washed gray linen cover. The chair had belonged to Mrs. Flippin's father, and for fifty years had held the place by the east window in summer and by the fireplace in winter. Oscar had wanted to bring things from Hamilton Hill to make Madge comfortable. But she had refused to spoil the simplicity of the quiet old house. "Everything that is here belongs here, Oscar," she had told him, "and I like it."

She wore a mauve negligee that was sheer and soft and flowing, and her burnt-gold hair was braided and wound around her head in a picturesque and becoming coiffure.

As she turned the pages of the little book the Major noticed her hands. They were white and slender, and she wore only one ring—a long amethyst set in silver.

"Do you play?" he asked abruptly.

"Yes. Why?"

"Your hands show it."

She smiled at him. "I am afraid that my hands don't quite tell the truth." She held them up so that the light of the lamp shone through them. "They are really a musician's hands, aren't they? And I am only a dabbler in that as in everything else."

"You can't expect me to believe that."

"But I am. I have intelligence. But I'm a 'dunce with wits.' I know what I ought to do but I don't do it. I think that I have brains enough to write, I am sure I have imagination enough to paint, I have strength enough when I am well to"—she laughed,—"scrub floors. But I don't write or play or paint—or scrub floors—I don't believe that there is one thing in the world that I can do as well as Mary Flippin makes biscuits."

Her eyes seemed to challenge him to deny her assertion. He settled himself lazily in his chair, and asked about the book. "Tell me why you like Dickens, when nobody reads him in these days except ourselves."

"I like him because in my next incarnation I want to live in the kind of world he writes about."

He was much interested. "You do?"

She nodded. "Yes. I never have. My world has always been—cut and dried, conventional, you know the kind." The slender hand with the amethyst ring made a little gesture of disdain. "There were three of us, my mother and my father and myself. Everything in our lives was very perfectly ordered. We were not very rich—not in the modern sense, and we were not very poor, and we knew a lot of nice people. I went to school with girls of my own kind, an exclusive school. I went away summers to our own cottage in an exclusive North Shore colony. We took our servants with us. After my mother died I went to boarding-school, and to Europe in summer, and when my school days were ended, and I acquired a stepmother, I set up an apartment of my own. It has Florentine things in it, and Byzantine things, and things from China and Japan, and the colors shine like jewels under my lamps—you know the effect. And my kitchen is all in white enamel, and the cook does things by electricity, and when I go away in summer my friends have Italian villas—like the Watermans, on the North Shore, although all of my friends are not like the Watermans." She threw this last out casually, not as a criticism, but that he might, it seemed, withhold judgment of her present choice of associates. "And I have never known the world of good cheer that Dickens writes about—wide kitchens, and teakettles singing and crickets chirping and everybody busy with things that interest them. Do you know that there are really no bored people in Dickens except a few aristocrats? None of the poor people are bored. They may be unhappy, but there's always some recompense in a steaming drink or savory stew, or some gay little festivity;—even the vagabonds seem to get something out of life. I realize perfectly that I've never had the thrills from a bridge game that came to the Marchioness when she played cards with Dick Swiveller—by stealth."

She talked rapidly, charmingly. He could not be sure how much in earnest she might be—but she made out her case and continued her argument.

"When I was a child I walked on gray velvet carpets, and there were etchings on the wall, and chilly mirrors between the long windows in the drawing-room. And the kitchen was in the basement and I never went down. There wasn't a cozy spot anywhere. None of us were cozy, my mother wasn't. She was very lovely and sparkling and went out a great deal and my father sparkled too. He still does. But there was really nothing to draw us together—like the Cratchits or even the Kenwigs. And we were never comfortable and merry like all of these lovely people in Pickwick."

She went on wistfully, "When I was nine, I found these little books in our library and after that I enjoyed vicariously the life I had never lived. That's why I like it here—Mrs. Flippin's kettle sings—and the crickets chirp—and Mr. and Mrs. Flippin are comfortable—and cozy—and content."

It was a long speech. "So now you see," she said, as she ended, "why I like Dickens."

"Yes. I see. And so—in your next incarnation you are going to be like——"

"Little Dorrit."

He laughed and leaned forward. "I can't imagine—you."

"She really had a heavenly time. Dickens tried to make you feel sorry for her. But she had the best of it all through. Somebody always wanted her."

"But she was imposed upon. And her unselfishness brought her heavy burdens."

"She got a lot out of it in the end, didn't she? And what do selfish people get? I'm one of them. I live absolutely for myself. There isn't a person except Flora who gets anything of service or self-sacrifice out of me. I came down here because she wanted me, but I hated to come. The modern theory is that unselfishness weakens. And the modern psychologist would tell you that little Dorrit was all wrong. She gave herself for others—and it didn't pay. But does the other thing pay?"

"Selfishness?"

"Yes. I'm selfish, and Oscar is, and Flora, and George Dalton, and most of the people we know. And we are all bored to death. If being unselfish is interesting, why not let us be unselfish?" Her lively glance seemed to challenge him, and they laughed together.

"I know what you mean."

"Of course you do. Everybody does who *thinks*."

"And so you are going to wait for the next plane to do the things that you want to do?"

"Yes."

"But why—wait?"

"How can I break away? I am tied into knots with the people whom I have always known; and I shall keep on doing the things I have always done, just as I shall keep on wearing pale purples and letting my skin get burned so that I may seem distinctive."

It came to him with something of a shock that she did these things with intention. That the charms which seemed to belong to her were carefully planned.

Yet how could he tell if what she said was true, when her eyes laughed?

"I shall get all I can out of being here. Mary Flippin is going to let me help her make butter, and Mrs. Flippin will teach me to make corn-bread, and some day I am going fishing with the Judge and Mr. Flippin and learn to fry eggs out-of-doors——"

"So those are the things you like?"

She nodded. "I think I do. George Dalton says it is only because I crave a change. But it isn't that. And I haven't told him the way I feel about it—the Dickens way—as I have told you."

He was glad that she had not talked to Dalton as she had talked to him.

"I wonder," he said slowly, "why you couldn't shake yourself free from the life which binds you?"

"I'm not strong enough. I'm like the drug-fiend, who doesn't want his drug, but can't give it up."

"Perhaps you need—help. There are doctors of everything, you know, in these days."

"None that can cure me of the habit of frivolity—of the claims of custom——"

"If a man takes a drug, he is cured by substituting something else for a while until he learns to do without it."

"What would you substitute for—my drug?"

"I'll have to think about it. May I come again and tell you?"

"Of course. I am dying to know."

Mrs. Flippin entered just then with a tall pitcher of lemonade and a plate of delicate cakes. "I think Miss MacVeigh is looking mighty fine," she said; "don't you, Major?"

He would not have dared to tell how fine she looked to him.

He limped across the room with the plate of cakes, and poured lemonade into a glass for Madge. Her eyes followed his strong soldierly figure. What a man he must have been before the war crippled him. What a man he was still, and his strength was not merely that of body. She felt the strength too of mind and soul.

"I think," said Mrs. Flippin that night, "that Major Prime is one of the nicest men."

Madge was in bed. The nurse had made her ready for the night, and was out on the porch with Mr. Flippin. Mrs. Flippin had fallen into the habit of having a little nightly talk with Madge. She missed her daughter, and Madge was pleasant and friendly.

"I think that Major Prime is one of the nicest men," repeated Mrs. Flippin as she sat down beside the bed, "but what a dreadful thing that he is lame."

"I am not sure," Madge said, "that it is dreadful."

She hastened to redeem herself from any possible charge of bloodthirstiness.

"I don't mean," she said, "that it isn't awful for a man to lose his leg. But men who go through a thing like that and come out—conquerors—are rather wonderful, Mrs. Flippin."

Madge had hold of Mrs. Flippin's hand. She often held it in this quiet hour, and the idea rather amused her. She was not demonstrative, and it seemed inconceivable that she should care to hold Mrs. Flippin's hand. But there was a motherliness about Mrs. Flippin, a quality with which Madge had never before come closely in contact. "It is like the way I used to feel when I was a little girl and said my prayers at night," she told herself.

Madge did not say her prayers now. Nobody did, apparently. She thought it rather a pity. It was a comfortable thing to do. And it meant a great deal if you only believed in it.

"Do you say your prayers, Mrs. Flippin?" she asked suddenly.

Mrs. Flippin was getting used to Madge's queer questions. She treated them as a missionary might treat the questions of a beautiful and appealing savage, who having gone with him to some strange country was constantly interrogatory.

"She don't seem to know anything about the things we do," Mrs. Flippin told her husband. "She got the nurse to wheel her out into the kitchen this afternoon, and watched me frost a cake and cut out biscuits. And she says that she has never seen anything so sociable as the teakettle, the way it rocks and sings."

So now when Madge asked Mrs. Flippin if she said her prayers, Mrs. Flippin said, "Do you mean at night?"

"Yes."

"Bob and I say them together," said Mrs. Flippin. "We started on our wedding night, and we ain't ever stopped."

It was a simple statement of a sublime fact. For thirty years this plain man and this plain woman had kept alive the spiritual flame on the household altar. No wonder that peace was under this roof and serenity.

Madge, as she lay there holding Mrs. Flippin's hand, looked very young, almost like a little girl. Her hair was parted and the burnished braids lay heavy on her lovely neck. Her thin fine gown left her arms bare. "Mrs. Flippin," she said, "I wish I could live here always, and have you come every night and sit and hold my hand."

Her eyes were smiling and Mrs. Flippin smiled back. "You'd get tired."

"No," said Madge, "I don't believe anybody ever gets tired of goodness. Not real goodness. The kind that isn't hypocritical or priggish. And in these days it is so rare, that one just loves it. I am bored to death with near-bad people, Mrs. Flippin, and near-good ones. I'd much rather have them real saints and real sinners."

The nurse came in just then, and Mrs. Flippin went away. And after a time the house was very still. Madge's bed was close to the window. Outside innumerable fireflies studded the night with gold. Now and then a screech-owl sounded his mournful note. It was a ghostly call, and there was the patter of little feet on the porch as the old cat played with her kittens in the warm dark. But Madge was not afraid. She had a sense of great content as she lay there and thought of the things she had said to Major Prime. It was not often that she revealed herself, and when she did it was still rarer to meet understanding. But he had understood. She was sure of that, and she would see him soon. He had promised. And she would not have to go back to Oscar and Flora until she was ready. Flora was better, but still very weak. It would be much wiser, the doctor had said, if she saw no one but her nurses for several days.

II

Truxton Beaufort rode over to King's Crest the next morning, and sat on the steps of the Schoolhouse. Randy and Major Prime were having breakfast out-of-doors. It was ten o'clock, but they were apparently taking their ease.

"I thought you had to work," Truxton said to Randy.

"I sold a car yesterday——"

"And to-day you are playing around like a plutocrat. I wish I could sell cars. I wish I could do *anything*. Look here, you two. I wonder if you feel as I do."

"About what?"

"Coming back. I came home expecting a pedestal—and I give you my word nobody seems to think much of me except my family. And they aren't worshipful—exactly. They can't be. How can they rave over my one decoration when that young nigger John has two, and deserved them, and when the butcher and baker and candlestick-maker are my ranking officers? War used to be a gentleman's game. But it isn't any more."

"We've got to carve our own pedestals," said the Major. "We are gods of yesterday. The world won't stop to praise us. We did our duty, and we would do it again. But our laurel wreaths are doffed. Our swords are beaten into plowshares. Peace is upon us. If we want pedestals, we've got to carve them."

Truxton argued that it wasn't quite fair. The Major agreed that it might not seem so, but the thing had been so vast, and there were so many men involved, so many heroes.

"Every little family has a hero of its own," Truxton supplemented. "Mary thinks none of the others did *anything*—I won the *whole* war. That's where I have it over you two," he grinned.

"It is a thing," said the Major, cheerfully, "which can be remedied."

"It can," Truxton told him; "which reminds me that our young John is going to marry Flippins' Daisy, and our household is in mourning. Mandy doesn't approve of Daisy, and neither does Calvin. Mandy took to her bed when she heard the news, and young John cooked breakfast to the tune of his Daddy's lamentations. But it was a good breakfast."

"Marriage," said the Major, "seems rather epidemic in these days."

Randy rose restlessly and sat on the porch rail. "Why in the world does John want to marry Daisy——"

"Why not?" easily. "There's some style about Daisy——"

"But there are lots of nice, comfortable, hard-working girls in this neighborhood."

"Lead me to 'em," Truxton mimicked young John, "lead me to 'em. Mary says that Daisy is the best of the lot. She has plenty of good sense back of her foolishness, and she is one of the best cooks in the county. She and John are planning to go up to Washington and open an old-fashioned oyster house. She says that people are complaining that they can't get oysters as they did in the old days, and she is going to show them. I wouldn't be surprised if they made a success of it. And I tell you this—I envy John. He will have a paying business, and here I am without a thing ahead of me, and I have married a wife and the ravens won't feed us."

Randy stuck his hands in his pockets with an air of sudden resolution.

"Look here," he said, "why can't we go halves in this car business? It will pay our expenses, and we can finish our law course at the University."

"Law? Oh, look here, Randy, I thought you had given that up."

"I haven't, and why should you? We will finish, and some day we will open an office together."

The Major, whistling softly, listened and said nothing.

"I have been thinking a lot about it," Randy went on, "and I can't see much of a future ahead of me. Not the kind of future that our families are expecting of us. You and I have got to stand for something, Truxton, or some day the world will be saying that all the great men died with Thomas Jefferson."

The Major went on with his lilting tune. What a pair they were, these lads! Randy, afire with his dreams, and rather tragic in his dreaming. Truxton, light as a feather—laughing.

"Why can't we give to the world as much as the men who have gone before us?" Randy was demanding. "Are we going to take everything from our ancestors, and give nothing to our descendants?"

Truxton chuckled. "By Jove," he said, "now that I come to think of it, I am the head of a family—there's Fiddle-dee-dee, and I shall have to reckon with Fiddle-dee-dee's children and grandchildren and great-grandchildren—who will expect that my portrait will hang on the wall at Huntersfield."

"It is all very well to laugh," said Randy hotly, "but that is the way it looks to me; that we have got to show to the world that our ambitions are—big. It is all very well to talk about the day's work. I am going to do it, and pay my way, but there's got to be something beyond that to think about—something bigger than I have ever known."

He gained dignity through the sincerity of his purpose. The Major, still whistling softly, wondered what had come over the boy. He recognized a difference since he had last talked to him. Randy was not only roused; he was ready to look life in the face, to wrest from it the best. "If that is what love of the little girl is doing for him," said the Major to himself, "then let him love her."

Truxton continued to treat the situation lightly. "Look here," he said, "do you think you are going to be the only great man in our generation?"

Randy laughed; but the fire was still in his eyes. "The county will hold the two of us."

And now the Major spoke. "No man can be great by simply saying it. But I think most of our great men have expected things of themselves. They have dreamed dreams of greatness. I fancy that Lincoln did in his log cabin, and Roosevelt on the plains. And it wasn't egotism—it was a boy's wish to give himself to the world. And the wish was the urge. And the trouble with many of our men in these days is that they are content to dream of what they can get instead of what they can do. Paine has the right idea. There must be a day's work no matter how hard, and it must be done well, but beyond that must be a dream of bigger things for the future——"

Truxton stood up. "I asked for bread and you have given me—caviar. Sufficient unto the day is the greatness thereof. And in the meantime, Randy, I will make the grand gesture—and help you sell cars." He was grinning as he left them. "Good-bye, Major. Good-bye, T. Jefferson, Jr. Let me know when you want me in your Cabinet."

It was late that afternoon that Mary, looking for her husband, found him in the Judge's library.

"What are you doing?" she asked, with lively curiosity.

Truxton was sitting on the floor with a pile of calf-bound books beside him.

"What are you doing, lover?"

"Come here and I'll tell you." He made a seat for her of four of the big books. His arm went around her and he laid his head against her shoulder.

"Mary," he said, "I am carving a pedestal."

"You are what?"

He explained. He laughed a great deal as he gave her an account of his conversation with the Major and Randy that morning.

"You see before you," with a final flourish, "a potential great man. A Thomas Jefferson, up-to-date; a John Randolph of the present day; the Lincoln of my own time; the ancestor of Fiddle's great-grandchildren."

She rumpled his hair. "I like you as you are."

He caught her hand and held it. "But you'd like me on—a pedestal?"

"If you'll let me help you carve it."

He kissed the hand that he held. "If I am ever anything more than I am," he said, and now he was not laughing, "it will be because of you—my dearest darling."

CHAPTER XII
INDIAN—INDIAN
I

The Merriweather fortunes had not been affected by the fall of the Confederacy. There had been money invested in European ventures, and when peace had come in sixty-five, the old grey stone house had again flung wide its doors to the distinguished guests who had always honored it, and had resumed its ancient custom of an annual harvest ball.

The ballroom, built at the back of the main house, was connected with it by wide curving corridors, which contained the family portraits, and which had long windows which opened out on little balconies. On the night of the ball these balconies were lighted by round yellow lanterns, so that the effect from the outside was that of a succession of full moons. The ballroom was octagonal, and canopied with a blue ceiling studded with silver stars. There were cupids with garlands on the side walls, and faded blue brocade hangings. Across one end of the ballroom was the long gallery reserved for those whom the Merriweathers still called "the tenantry," and it was here that Mary and Mrs. Flippin always sat after baking cakes.

Mrs. Flippin had not baked the cakes to-day, nor was she in the gallery, for her daughter, Mary, was among the guests on the ballroom floor, and her mother's own good sense had kept her at home.

"I shall look after Miss MacVeigh," she had said. "I want Truxton to bring you over and show you in your pretty new dress."

When they came, Madge, who was sitting up, insisted that she, too, must see Mary. "My dear, my dear," she said, "what a wonderful frock."

"Yes," Mary said, "it is. It is one of Becky's, and she gave it to me. And the turquoises are Mrs. Beaufort's."

Madge, who knew the whole alphabet of smart costumers, was aware of the sophisticated perfection of that fluff of jade green tulle. The touch of gold at the girdle, the flash of gold for the petticoat. She guessed the price, a stiff one, and wondered that Mary should speak of it casually as "one of Becky's."

"The turquoises are the perfect touch."

"That was Becky's idea. It seemed queer to me at first, blue with the green. But she said if I just wore this band around my hair, and the ring. And it does seem right, doesn't it?"

"It is perfect. What is Miss Bannister wearing?"

"Silver and white—lace, you know. The new kind, like a cobweb—with silver underneath—and a rose-colored fan—and pearls. You should see her pearls, Miss MacVeigh. Tell her about them, Truxton."

"Well, once upon a time they belonged to a queen. Becky's great-grandfather on the Meredith side was a diplomat in Paris, and he bought them, or so the story runs. Becky only wears a part of them. The rest are in the family vaults."

Madge listened, and showed no surprise. But that account of lace and silver, and priceless pearls did not sound in the least like the new little girl about whom George had, in the few times that she had seen him of late, been so silent.

"If only Flora would get well, and let me leave this beastly hole," had been the burden of his complaint.

"I thought you liked it."

"It is well enough for a time."

"What about the new little girl?"

He was plainly embarrassed, but bluffed it out. "I wish you wouldn't ask questions."

"I wish you wouldn't be—rude—Georgie-Porgie."

"I hate that name, Madge. Any man has a right to be rude when a woman calls him 'Georgie-Porgie.'"

"So that's it? Well, now run along. And please don't come again until you are nice—and smiling."

"Oh, look here, Madge."

"Run along——"

"But there isn't any place to run."

Laughter lurked in her eyes. "Oh, Georgie-Porgie—for once in your life can't you run away?"

"Do you think you are funny?"

"Perhaps not. Smile a little, Georgie."

"How can anybody smile, with everybody sick?"

"Oh, no, we're not. We are better. I am so glad that Flora is improving."

"Oscar thinks it is because that little old man prayed for her. Fancy Oscar——"

Madge meditated. "Yet it might be, you know, George. There are things in that old man's petition that transcend all our philosophy."

"Oh, you're as bad as Oscar," said George. He rose and stood frowning on the threshold. "Well, good-bye, Madge."

"Good-bye, Georgie, and smile when you come again."

She had guessed then that something had gone wrong in the game with the new little girl. She had a consuming curiosity to know the details. But she could never force things with Georgie. Some day, perhaps, he would tell her.

And now here was news indeed! She waited until young Beaufort and his wife had driven away, and until Mrs. Flippin had time for that quiet hour by her bedside.

"Mary looked lovely," said Madge.

"Didn't she?" Mrs. Flippin rocked and talked. "You would never have known that dress was made for anybody but for Mary. Becky gave Mary another dress out of a lot she had down from New York. It is yellow organdie, made by hand and with little embroidered scallops."

Madge knew the house which made a specialty of those organdie gowns with embroidered scallops, and she knew the price.

"But how does—Becky manage to have such lovely things?"

"Oh, she's rich," Mrs. Flippin was rocking comfortably. "You would never know it, and nobody thinks of it much. But she's got money. From her grandmother. And there was something in the will about having her live out of the world as long as she could. That's why they sent her to a convent and kept her down here as much as possible. She ain't ever seemed to care for clothes. Shecould always have had anything she wanted, but she ain't cared. She told Mary that she had a sudden notion to have some pretty things, and she sent for them, and it was lucky for Mary that she did. She couldn't have gone to this ball, for there wasn't any time to get anything made. Mr. Flippin and I are going to buy her some nice things when she goes to Richmond. But they won't be like the things that Becky gets, of course."

Madge, listening to further details of the Meredith fortunes, wondered how much of this Georgie knew. "Becky's mother died when she was five, and her father two years later," Mrs. Flippin was saying. "She might have been spoiled to death if she had been brought up as some children are. But she has spent her winters at the convent with Sister Loretto, and she's never worn much of anything but the uniform of the school. You wouldn't think that she had any money to see her, would you, Miss MacVeigh?"

"No, you wouldn't," said Madge, truthfully.

It was after nine o'clock—a warm night—with no sound but the ticking of the clock and the insistent hum of locusts.

"Mrs. Flippin," said Madge, "I wish you'd call up Hamilton Hill and ask for Mr. Dalton, and tell him that Miss MacVeigh would like to have him come and see her if he has nothing else on hand."

Mrs. Flippin looked her astonishment. "To-night?"

"Oh, I am not going to receive him this way," Madge reassured her. "If he can come, I'll get nurse to dress me and make me comfy in the sitting-room."

Having ascertained that Dalton would be over at once, the nurse was called, and Madge was made ready. It was a rather high-handed proceeding, and both Mrs. Flippin and the nurse stood aghast.

The nurse protested. "You really ought not, Miss MacVeigh."

"I love to do things that I ought not to do."

"But you'll tire yourself."

"If you were my Mary," said Mrs. Flippin severely, "I wouldn't let you have your way——"

"I love to have my own way, Mrs. Flippin. And—I am not your Mary"—then fearing that she had hurt the kind heart, she caught Mrs. Flippin's hand in her own and kissed it,—"but I wish I were. You're such a lovely mother."

Mrs. Flippin smiled at her. "I'm as near like your mother as a hen is mother to a bluebird."

Madge, robed in the mauve gown, refused to have her hair touched. "I like it in braids," and so when George came there she sat in the sitting-room, all gold and mauve—a charming picture for his sulky eyes.

"Oh," she said, as he came in, in a gray sack suit, with a gray cap in his hand, "why, you aren't even dressed for dinner!"

"Why should I be?" he demanded. "Kemp has left me."

She had expected something different. "Kemp?"

"Yes."

"Why?"

"He didn't give any reason. Just said he was going—and went. He said he had intended to go before, and had only stayed until Mrs. Waterman was better. Offered to stay on a little longer if it would embarrass me any to have him leave. I told him that if he wanted to go, he could get out now. And he is packing his bags."

"But what will you do without him?"

"I have wired to New York for a Jap."

"Where will Kemp go?"

"To King's Crest. To work for that lame officer—Prime."

"Oh—Major Prime? How did it happen?"

"Heaven only knows. I call it a mean trick."

"Well, of course, Kemp had a right to go if he wanted to. And perhaps you will like a Jap better. You always said Kemp was too independent."

"He is," shortly, "but I hate to be upset. It seems as if everything goes wrong these days. What did you want with me, Madge?"

Her eyelashes flickered as she surveyed him. "I wanted to see you—smile, Georgie."

"You didn't bring me down here to tell me that——" But in spite of himself the corners of his lips curled. "Oh, what's the answer, Madge?" he said, and laughed in spite of himself.

"I wanted to talk a little about—your Becky."

His laughter died at once. "Well, I'm not going to talk about her."

"Please—I am dying of curiosity—I hear that she is very—rich, Georgie."

"Rich?"

"Yes. She has oodles of money——"

"I don't believe it."

"But it is true, Georgie."

"Who told you?"

"Mrs. Flippin."

"It is all—rot——"

"It isn't rot, Georgie. Mrs. Flippin knows about it. Becky inherits from her Meredith grandmother. And her grandfather is Admiral Meredith of Nantucket, with a big house on Beacon Street in Boston. And they all belong to the inner circle."

He stared at her. "But Becky doesn't look it. She doesn't wear rings and things."

"'Rings on her fingers and bells on her toes'? Oh, George, did you think it had to be like that when people had money? Why, her pearls belonged to a queen." She told him their history.

595

It came back to him with a shock that he had said to Becky that the pearls cheapened her. "If they were *real*," he had said. "It was rather strange the way I found it out," Madge was saying. "Mary Flippin had on the most perfect gown—with all the marks on it of exclusive Fifth Avenue. She was going to the Merriweather ball, and Becky is to be there."

She saw him gather himself together. "It is rather a Cinderella story, isn't it?" he asked, with assumed lightness.

"Yes," she said, "but I thought you'd like to know."

"What if I knew already?"

She laughed and let it go at that. "I'm lonesome, Georgie, talk to me," she said. But he was not in a mood to talk. And at last she sent him away. And when he had gone she sat there a long time and thought about him. There had been a look in his eyes which made her almost sorry. It seemed incredible as she came to think of it that anybody should ever be sorry for Georgie.

II

Since that night with Becky in the garden at Huntersfield George had been torn by conflicting emotions. He knew himself at last in love. He knew himself beaten at the game by a little shabby girl, and a lanky youth who had been her champion. He would not acknowledge that the thing was ended, and in the end he had written her a letter. He cried to Heaven that a marriage between her and young Paine would be a crime. "How can you love him, Becky—you are mine."

The letter had been returned unopened. His burning phrases might have been dead ashes for all the good they had done. She had not read them.

And now Madge had told him the unbelievable thing—that Becky Bannister, the shabby Becky of the simple cottons and the stubbed shoes, was rich, not as Waterman was rich, flamboyantly, vulgarly, with an eye to letting all the world know. But rich in a thoroughbred fashion, scorning display—he knew the kind, secure in a knowledge of the unassailable assets of birth and breeding and solid financial standing.

No wonder young Paine wanted to marry her. George, driving through the night, set his teeth. He was seeing Randy, poor as Job's turkey, with Becky's money for a background.

Well, he should not have it. He should not have Becky.

George headed his car for the Merriweathers'. Becky was there, and he was going to see Becky. How he was to see her he left to the inspiration of the moment.

He parked his car by the road, and walked through the great stone gates. The palatial residence was illumined from top to bottom, its windows great squares of gold against the night. The door stood open, but except for a servant or two there was no one in the wide hall. The guests were dancing in the ballroom at the back, and George caught the lilt of the music as he skirted the house, then the sound of voices, the light laughter of the women, the deeper voices of the men.

The little balconies, lighted by the yellow lanterns, were empty. As soon as the music stopped they would be filled with dancers seeking the coolness of the outer air. He stood looking up, and suddenly, as if the stage had been set, Becky stepped out on the balcony straight in front of him, and stood under the yellow lantern. The light was dim, but it gave to her white skin, to her lace frock, to the pink fan, a faint golden glow. She might have been transmuted from flesh into some fine metal. George had not heard the Major's name for her, "Mademoiselle Midas," but he had a feeling that the little golden figure was symbolic—here was the real Golden Girl for him—not Madge or any other woman.

Randy was with her, back in the shadow, but unmistakable, his lean height, the lift of his head.

George moved forward until, hidden by a bush, he was almost under the balcony. He could catch the murmur of their voices. But not a word that they said was intelligible.

They were talking of Mary. Her introduction to her husband's friends had been an ordeal for Bob Flippin's daughter. But she had gone through it simply, quietly, unaffectedly, with the Judge by her side standing sponsor for his son's wife in chivalrous and stately fashion, with Mrs. Beaufort at her elbow helping her over the initial small talk of her presentation. With Truxton beaming, and with Becky drawing her into that charmed circle of the younger set which might so easily have shut her out. More than one of those younger folk had had it in mind that at last year's ball Mary Flippin had sat in the gallery. But not even the most snobbish of them would have dared to brave Becky Bannister's displeasure. Back of her clear-eyed serenity was a spirit which flamed and a strength which accomplished. Becky was an amiable young person who could flash fire at unfairness or injustice or undue assumption of superiority.

The music had stopped and the balconies were filled. George, in the darkness, was aware of the beauty of the scene—the lantern making yellow moons—the golden groups beneath them. Mary and Truxton with a friend or two were in the balcony adjoining the one where Becky sat with young Paine.

"Isn't she a dear and a darling, Randy?" Becky was saying; "and how well she carries it off. Truxton is so proud of her, and she is so pretty."

"She can't hold a candle to you, Becky."

"It is nice of you to say it." She leaned on the stone balustrade and swung her fan idly.

"I am not saying it to be nice."

"Aren't you—oh——!" She gave a quick exclamation.

"What's the matter?"

"I dropped my fan."

"I'll go and get it," he said, and just then the music started.

"No," said Becky, "never mind now. This is your dance with Mary—and she mustn't be kept waiting."

"Aren't you dancing this?"

"It is Truxton's, and I begged off. Run along, dear boy."

When he was gone she leaned over the rail. Below was a tangle of bushes, and the white gleam of a stone bench. Beyond the bushes was a path, and farther on a fountain. It was a rather imposing fountain, with a Neptune in bronze riding a seahorse, with nymphs on dolphins in attendance. Neptune poured water from a shell which he held in his hand, and the dolphins spouted great streams. The splash of the water was a grateful sound in the stillness of the hot night, and the mist which the slight breeze blew towards a bed of tuberoses seemed to bring out their heavy fragrance. Always afterwards when Becky thought of that night, there would come to her again that heavy scent and the splash of streaming water.

"Becky," a voice came up from below, "I have your fan."

She peered down into the darkness, but did not speak.

"Becky, I am punished enough, and I am—starved for you——"

"Give me my fan——"

"I want to talk to you—I must—talk to you——"

"Give me my fan——"

"I can't reach——"

"You can stand on that bench."

He stood on it, and she could see his figure faintly defined.

"I am afraid I am still too far away. Lean over a bit, Becky—and I'll hand it to you."

She stretched her white arm down into the darkness. Her hand was caught in a strong clasp. "Becky, give me just five minutes by the fountain."

"Let me go."

"Not until you promise that you'll come."

"I shall never promise."

"Then I shall keep your fan——"

"Keep it—I have others."

"But you will think about this one, because I have it." There was a note of triumph in his soft laugh.

He kissed her finger-tips and reluctantly released her hand. "The fan is mine, then, until you ask for it."

"I shall never ask."

"Who knows? Some day you may—who knows?" and he was gone.

He could not have chosen a better way in which to fire her imagination. His voice in the dark, his laughing triumph, the daring theft of her fan. Her heart followed him, seeing him a Conqueror even in this, seeing him a robber with his rose-colored booty, a Robin Hood of the Garden, a Dick Turpin among the tuberoses.

The spirit of Romance went with him. The things that Pride had done for her looked gray and dull. She had promised to marry Randy, and felt that she faced a somewhat sober future. Set against it was all that George had given her, the sparkle and dash and color of his ardent pursuit.

He was not worth a thought, yet she thought of him. She was still thinking of him when Randy came back.

"Did you get your fan?" he asked.

"No. Never mind, Randy. I will have one of the servants look for it."

"But I do mind."

She hesitated. "Well, don't look for it now. Let's go in and join the others. Are they going down to supper?"

Supper was served in the great Hunt Room, which was below the ballroom. It was a historic and picturesque place, and had been the scene for over a century of merry-making before and after the fox-hunts for which the county was famous. There were two great fireplaces, almost hidden to-night by the heaped-up fruits of the harvest, orange and red and green, with cornstalks and goldenrod from the fields for decorations.

Becky found Mary alone at a small table in a corner. Truxton had left her to forage for refreshments and Randy followed him.

"Are you having a good time, Mary?"

Mary did not answer at once. Then she said, bravely, "I don't quite fit in, Becky. I am still an—outsider."

"Oh, Mary!"

"I am not—unhappy, and Truxton is such a dear. But I shall be glad to get home, Becky."

"But you look so lovely, Mary, and everybody seems so kind."

"They are, but underneath I am just plain—Mary Flippin. They know that, and so do I, and it will take them some time to forget it."

There was an anxious look in Becky's eyes. "It seems to me that you are feeling it more than the others."

"Perhaps. And I shouldn't have said anything. Don't let Truxton know."

"Has anyone said anything to hurt you, Mary?"

"No, but when I dance with the men, I can't speak their language. I haven't been to the places—I don't know the people. I am on the outside."

Becky had a sudden forlorn sense that things were wrong with the whole world. But she didn't want Mary to be unhappy. "Truxton loves you," she said, "and you love him. Don't let anything make you miserable when you have—that. Nothing else counts, Mary."

There was a note of passion in her voice which brought a pulsing response from Mary.

"It *is* the only thing that counts, Becky. How silly I am to worry."

Her young husband was coming towards her—flushed and eager, a prince among men, and he was hers!

As he sat down beside her, her hand sought his under the table.

He looked down at her. "Happy, little girl?"

"Very happy, lover."

III

Caroline Paine was having the time of her life. She wore a new dress of thin midnight blue which Randy had bought for her and which was very becoming; her hair was waved and dressed, and she had Major Prime as an attentive listener while she talked of the past and linked it with the present.

"Of course there was a time when the men drank themselves under the tables. Everybody calls them the 'good old times,' but I reckon they were bad old times in some ways, weren't they? There was hot blood, and there were duels. There's no denying it was picturesque, Major, but it was foolish for all that. Men don't settle things now by shooting each other, except in a big way like the war. The last duel was fought by the old fountain out there—one of the Merriweathers met one of the Paines. Merriweather was killed, and the girl died of a broken heart."

"Then it was Merriweather that she loved?"

"Yes. And young Paine went abroad, and joined the British army and was killed in India. So nobody was happy, and all because there was, probably, a flowing bowl at the harvest ball. I am glad they don't do it that way now. Just think of my Randy stripped to his shirt and with pistols for two. We are more civilized in these days and I'm glad of it."

"Are we?" said the Major; "I'm not sure. But I hope so."

Randy came by just then and spoke to them. "Are you getting everything you want, Mother?"

"Yes, indeed. The Major looked after me. I've had salad twice, and everything else——"

"That sounds greedy, but it isn't, not when you think of the groaning boards of other days. Has she been telling you about them, Major?"

"Yes, she has peopled the room with ghosts——"

"Now, Major!"

"Pleasant ghosts—in lace ruffles and velvet coats, smoking long pipes around a punch bowl; beautiful ghosts in patches and powder," he made an expressive gesture; "they have mingled with the rest of you—shadow-shapes of youth and loveliness."

"Well, if anybody can tell about it, Mother can," said Randy, "but I don't believe there were ever any prettier girls than are here to-night."

"Becky looks like an angel," Mrs. Paine stated, "but she's pale, Randy."

"She is tired, Mother. I think she ought to go home. I shall try to make her when I come back. She dropped her fan and I am going to get it."

He had not told Becky where he was going. He had slipped away—his mind intent on regaining her property. But when he reached the bushes and flashed his pocket-light on the ground beneath, there was no fan. It must have fallen here. He was sure he had made no mistake.

He decided finally that someone else had found it. It seemed unlikely, however, for the spot was remote, and the thickness of the bushes offered a barrier to anyone strolling casually through the grounds.

He went slowly back to the house. Ever since that night when Becky had said she would marry him he had lived in a dream. They were pledged to each other, yet she did not love him. How could he take her? And again, how could he give her up? She had offered herself freely, and he wanted her in his future. And there was a fighting chance. He had youth and courage and a love for her he challenged any man to match. Why not? Was it beyond the bounds of reason that some day he could make Becky love him?

They had agreed that no one was to be told. "Not until I come back from Nantucket," Becky had stipulated.

"By that time you won't want me, my dear."

"Well, I shan't if you talk like that," Becky had said with some spirit.

"Like what?"

"As if I were a queen and you were a slave. When you were a little boy you bossed me, Randy."

There had been a gleam in his eye. "I may again."

He wondered if, after all, that would be the way to win her. Yet he shrank from playing a game. When she came to him, if she ever came, it must be because she found something in him that was love-worthy. At least he could make himself worthy of love, whether she ever came to him or not.

He stopped by the fountain; just beyond it the long windows of the Hunt Room opened out upon the lawn. The light lay in golden squares upon the grass. Randy, still in the shadow, stood for a moment looking in. There were long tables and little ones, kaleidoscopic color, movement and light, and Becky back in her corner in the midst of a gay group.

He was aware, suddenly, that he was not the only one who watched. Half hidden by the shadows of one of the great pillars of the lower porch was a man in light flannels and a gray cap.

He was not skulking, and indeed he seemed to have a splendid indifference to discovery. He was staring at Becky and in his hand, a blaze of lovely color against his coat, was Becky's fan!

Randy took a step forward. George turned and saw him.

"I was looking for that," Randy said, and held out his hand for the fan.

But Dalton did not give it to him. "She knows I have it."

"How could she know?" Randy demanded; "she dropped it from the balcony."

"And I was under the balcony"—George's laugh was tantalizing,—"a patient Romeo."

"You picked it up."

"I picked it up. And she knew that I did. Didn't she tell you?"

She had not told him. He remembered now her unwillingness to have him search for it.

He had no answer for George. But again he held out his hand.

"She will be glad to get it. Will you give it to me?"

"She told me I might—keep it."

"Keep it——?"

"For remembrance."

There was a tense pause. "If that is true," said Randy, "there is, of course, nothing else for me to say."

He turned to go, but George stopped him. "Wait a minute. You are going to marry her?"

"Yes."

"And she is very—rich."

"Her money does not enter into the matter."

"Some people might think it did. There are those who might be unkind enough to call you a—fortune-hunter."

"I shall be called nothing of the kind by those who know me."

"But there are so many who don't know you."

"I wonder," said Randy, fiercely, "why I am staying here and letting you say such things to me. There is nothing you can say which can hurt me. Becky knows—God knows, that I wish she were as poor as poverty. Perhaps money doesn't mean as much to us as it does to you. I wish I had it, yes—so that I could give it to her. But love for us means a tent in the desert—a hut on a mountain—it can never mean what we could buy with money."

"Does love mean to her," George's tone was incisive, "a tent in the desert, a hut on a mountain?"

Randy's anger flamed. "I think," he said, "that I should beg Becky's pardon for bringing her name into this at all—— And now, will you give me her fan?"

"When she asks for it—yes."

Randy was breathing heavily. "Will you give me her—fan——"

The mist from the fountain blew cool against his hot cheeks. The water which old Neptune poured from his shell flashed white under the stars.

"Let her ask for it——" George's laugh was light.

It was that laugh which made Randy see red. He caught George's wrists suddenly in his hands. "Drop it."

George stopped laughing. "Let her ask for it," he said again.

Randy twisted the wrists. It was a cruel trick. But his Indian blood was uppermost.

"Drop it," he said, with another twist, and the fan fell.

But Randy was not satisfied. "Do you think," he said, "that I am through with you? What you need is tar and feathers, but failing that——" he did not finish his sentence. He caught George around the body and began to push him back towards the fountain.

George fought doggedly—but Randy was strong with the muscular strength of youth and months of military training.

"I'll kill you for this," George kept saying.

"No," said Randy, conserving his breath, "they don't—do it—in—these—days——"

He had Dalton now at the rim and with a final effort of strength he lifted him—there was a splash, and into the deeps of the great basin went George, while the bronze Neptune, and the bronze dolphins, and the nymphs with flowing hair, splashed and spouted a welcoming chorus that drowned his cry!

Randy, head up, eyes shining, marched into the house and had a servant brush him off and powder a scratch on his chin; then he went down-stairs to the Hunt Room and strode across the room until he came to where Becky sat in her corner. "I found your fan," he told her, and laid it, a blaze of lovely color, on the table in front of her.

CHAPTER XIII
THE WHISTLING SALLY
I

Becky, as she journeyed towards the north, had carried with her a vision of a new and rather disturbing Randy—a Randy who, striding across the Hunt Room with high-held head, had delivered her fan, and had, later, asked for an explanation. "How did he get it, Becky?"

She had told him.

"Why didn't you tell me when I came back and said I would go for it?"

"I was afraid he might still be there."

"Well?"

"And that something might happen."

Something had happened later by the fountain. But Randy did not speak of it. "I saw the fan in his hand and asked for it," grimly, "and he gave it to me——"

On the night before she went away, Randy had said, "I can't tell you all that you mean to me, Becky, and I am not going to try. But I am yours always—remember that——" He had kissed her hand and held it for a moment against his heart. Then he had left her, and Becky had wanted to call him back and say something that she felt had been left unsaid, but had found that she could not.

Admiral Meredith met his granddaughter in New York, and the rest of the trip was made with him.

Admiral Meredith was as different from Judge Bannister in his mental equipment as he was in physical appearance. He was a short little man, who walked with a sailor's swing, and who laughed like a fog-horn. He had ruddy cheeks, and the manners of a Chesterfield. If he lacked the air of aristocratic calm which gave distinction to Judge Bannister, he supplied in its place a sophistication due to his contact with a world which moved faster than the Judge's world in Virginia.

He adored Becky, and resented her long sojourn in the South. "I believe you love the Judge better than you do me," he told her, as he turned to her in the taxi which took them from the train to the boat.

"I don't love anybody better than I do you," she said, and tucked her hand in his.

"What have they been doing to you?" he demanded; "you are as white as paper."

"Well, it has been hot."

"Of all the fool things to keep you down there in summer. I am going to take you straight to 'Sconset to the Whistling Sally and keep you there for a month."

"The Whistling Sally" was the Admiral's refuge when he was tired of the world. It was a gray little house set among other gray little houses across the island from Nantucket town. It stood on top of the bluff and overlooked a sea which stretched straight to Spain. It was called "The Whistling Sally" because a ship's figure-head graced its front yard, the buxom half of a young woman who blew out her cheeks in a perpetual piping, and whose faded colors spoke eloquently of the storms which had buffeted her.

The Admiral, as has been indicated, had an imposing mansion in Nantucket town. For two months in the summer he entertained his friends in all the glory of a Colonial background—white pillars, spiral stairway, polished floors, Chinese Chippendale, lacquered cabinets, old china and oil portraits. He gave dinners and played golf, he had a yacht and a motor boat, he danced when the spirit moved him, and was light on his feet in spite of his years. He was adored by the ladies, lionized by everybody, and liked it.

But when the summer was over and September came, he went to Siasconset and reverted to the type of his ancestors. He hobnobbed with the men and women who had been the friends and neighbors of his forbears. He doffed his sophistication as he doffed his formal clothes. He wore a slicker on wet days, and the rain dripped from his rubber hat. He sat knee to knee with certain cronies around the town pump. He made chowder after a famous recipe, and dug clams when the spirit moved him.

His housekeeper, Jane, adjourned from the town house to "The Whistling Sally" when Becky was there; at other times the Admiral did for himself, keeping the little cottage as neat as a pin, and cooking as if he were born to it.

It seemed to Becky that as the long low island rose from the sea, the burdens which she had carried for so long dropped from her. There were the houses on the cliff, the glint of a gilded dome, and then, gray and blue and green the old town showed against the skyline, resolving itself presently into roofs, and church towers, and patches of trees, with long piers stretching out through shallow waters, boat-houses, fishing smacks, and at last a thin line of people waiting on the wharf. The air was like wine. The sky was blue with the deep sapphire which follows a wind-swept night. There was not a hint of mist or fog. Flocks of gulls rose and dipped and rose again, or rested unafraid on the wooden posts of the pier.

The 'Sconset 'bus was waiting and they took it. Until two years ago no automobiles had been allowed on the island, but there had been the triumph of utility over the picturesque and quaint, and now one motored across the moor on smooth asphalt, in one-half the time that the trip had been made in the old days.

The Admiral did not like it. He admitted that it was quicker. "But we used to see the pheasants fly up from the bushes, and the ducks from the pools, and now they are gone before we can get our eyes on them."

Becky was not in a captious mood. The moor was before her, rising and falling in low unwooded hills, amber with dwarf goldenrod, red with the turning huckleberry, purple with drying grasses, green with a thousand lovely growing things still unpainted by the brush of autumn. The color was almost unbelievably gorgeous. Even the pools by the roadside were almost unbelievably blue, as if the water had been dyed with indigo, and above all was that incredible blue sky———!

Then out of the distance clear cut like cardboard the houses lifted themselves above the horizon, with the sea a wall to the right, and to the left, across the moor, the Sankaty lighthouse, white and red with the sun's rays striking across it.

They entered the village between rows of pleasant informal residences, many of them closed until another season; they passed the tennis courts, and came to the post-office, with its flag flying. The 'bus stopped, and they found Tristram waiting for them.

"Tristram" is an old name in Nantucket. There was a Tristram among the nine men who had purchased the island from Thomas Mayhew in 1659 for "30 pounds current pay and two beaver hats." The present Tristram wore the name appropriately. Fair-haired and tall, not young but towards the middle-years, strong with the strength of one who lives out-of-doors in all weathers, browned with the wind and sun, blue-eyed, he called no man master, and was the owner of his own small acres.

Like the Admiral, he gave himself up for two months of the year to the summer people. If his association with them was a business rather than a social affair, it was, none the less, interesting. The occupation of Nantucket by "off-islanders" was a matter of infinite speculation and amusement. Into the serenity of his life came restless men and women who golfed and swam and rode and danced, who chafed when it rained, and complained of the fog, who seemed endlessly trying to get something out of life and who were endlessly bored, who wondered how Tristram could stand the solitudes and who pitied him.

Tristram knew that he did not need their pity. He had a thousand things that they did not have. He was never bored, and he was too busy to manufacture amusements. There were always things happening on the island—each day brought something different.

To-day, it was the winter gulls. "They are coming down—lots of them from the north," he told the Admiral as they drove through the quaint settlement with its gray little houses, "the big ones———"

There was also the *gerardia*, pale pink and shading into mauve. He had brought a great bunch to "The Whistling Sally," and had put it in a bowl of gray pottery.

When Becky saw the flowers, she knew whom to thank. "Oh, Tristram," she said, "you found them on the moor."

Tristram, standing in the little front room of the Admiral's cottage, seemed to tower to the ceiling. "The Whistling Sally" from the outside had the look of a doll's house, too small for human habitation. Within it was unexpectedly commodious. It had the shipshape air of belonging to a seafaring man. The rooms were all on one floor. There was the big front room, which served as a sitting-room and dining-room. It had a table built out from the wall with high-backed benches on each side of it, and a rack for glasses overhead. There was a window above the table which looked out towards the sea. The walls were painted blue, and there was an old brick fireplace. A model of a vessel from which the figure-head in the front yard had been taken was over the mantel, flanked by an old print or two of Nantucket in the past. There were Windsor chairs and a winged chair; some pot-bellied silver twinkled in a corner cupboard.

The windows throughout were low and square and small-paned and white-curtained. The day was cool, and there was a fire on the hearth. The blaze and the pink flowers, and the white curtains gave to the little room an effect of brightness, although outside the early twilight was closing in.

Jane came in with her white apron and added another high light. She kissed Becky. "Did your grandfather tell you that Mr. Cope is coming over to have chowder?" she asked.

It would be impossible to describe Jane's way of saying "chowder." It had no "r," and she clipped it off at the end. But it is the only way in the world, and the people who so pronounce it are usually the only people in the world who can make it.

"Who is Mr. Cope?" Becky asked.

Mr. Cope, it seemed, had a cottage across the road from the Admiral's. He leased it, and it was his first season at 'Sconset. His sister had been with him only a week ago. She had gone "off-shore," but she was coming back.

"Is he young?" Becky asked.

"Well, he isn't old," said Jane, "and he's an artist."

Becky was not in the least interested in Mr. Cope, so she talked to Tristram until he had to go back to his farm and the cows that waited to be milked. Then Becky went into her room, and took off her hat and coat and ran a comb through the bronze waves of her hair. She did not change the straight serge frock in which she had travelled. She went back into the front room and found that Mr. Cope had come.

He was not old. That was at once apparent. And he was not young. He did not look in the least like an artist. He seemed, rather, like a prosperous business man. He wore a Norfolk suit, and his reddish hair was brushed straight back from his forehead. He had rather humorous gray eyes, and Becky thought there was a look of delicacy about his white skin. Later he spoke of having come for his health, and she learned that he had a weak heart.

He had a pleasant laughing voice. He belonged to Boston, but had lived abroad for years.

"With nothing to show for it," he told her with a shrug, "but one portrait. I painted my sister, and she kept that. But before we left Paris we burned the rest——"

"Oh, how dreadful," Becky cried.

"No, it wasn't dreadful. They were not worth keeping. You see, I played a lot and made sketches and things, and then there was the war—and I wasn't very well."

He had had two years of aviation, and after that a desk in the War Department.

"And now I am painting again."

"Gardens?" Becky asked, "or the sea?"

"Neither. I am trying to paint the moor. I'll show you in the morning."

The Admiral was in the kitchen, superintending the chowder. Jane knew how to make it, and he knew that she knew. But he always went into the kitchen at the psychological moment, tied on an apron, and put in the pilot crackers. Then he brought the chowder in, in a big porcelain tureen which was shaped like a goose. Becky loved him in his white apron, with his round red face, and the porcelain goose held high.

"If you could paint him like that," she suggested to Archibald Cope.

"Do you think he would let me?" eagerly.

After supper the two men smoked by the fire, and Becky sat between them and watched the blaze. She heard very little of the conversation. Her mind was in Albemarle. How far away it seemed! Just three nights ago she had danced at the Merriweathers' ball, and George had held her hand as she leaned over the balcony.

"If you can bring yourself back for a moment, Becky, to present company," her grandfather was saying, "you can tell Mr. Cope whether you will walk with us to-morrow to Tom Never's."

"I'd love it."

"Really?" Cope asked. "You are sure you won't be too tired?"

"Not in this air. I feel as if I could walk forever."

"How about a bit of a walk to-night—up to the bluff? Is it too late, Admiral?"

"Not for you two. I'll finish my pipe, and read my papers."

The young people followed the line of the bluff until they came to an open space which looked towards the east. To the left of them was the ridge with a young moon hanging low above it, and straight ahead, brighter than the moon, whitening the heavens, stretching out and out until it reached the sailors in their ships, was the Sankaty light.

"I always come out to look at it before I go to bed," said Cope; "it is such a *living* thing, isn't it?"

The wind was rising and they could hear the sound of the sea. Becky caught her breath. "On dark nights I like to think how it must look to the ships beyond the shoals——"

"The sea is cruel," said Cope; "that's why I don't paint it."

"Oh, it isn't always cruel."

"When isn't it? Last year, with the submarines, it was—a monster. I saw a picture once in a gallery, 'The Eternal Siren,' just the sea. And a woman asked, 'Where's the Siren?'"

Becky laughed. "If you had sailor blood in you, you wouldn't feel that way. Ask Grandfather."

"The Admiral is prejudiced. He loves—the siren——"

"He would tell you that the sea isn't a siren. It's a bold, blustering lass like the Whistling Sally out there in the front yard. Man has tamed her even if he hasn't quite mastered her."

"He will never master her. She will go on and on, after we are dead, through the ages, wooing men to—destruction——"

Becky shivered. "I hate to think of things—after we are dead."

"Do you? I don't. I like to think way beyond the ages to the time when there shall be no more sea——"

He pulled himself up abruptly. "I am talking rather dismally, I am afraid, about death and destruction. You won't want to walk with me again."

"Oh, yes, I shall. And I want to see your pictures."

"You may not care for them. Lots of people don't. But I have to work in my own way——"

As they walked back, he told her what he was trying to do. As she listened, Becky seemed to have two minds, one that caught his words, and answered them, and another which went back and back to the things which had happened since she had last walked this bluff with the wind in her face and the sound of the sea in her ears.

It seemed to her as if a lifetime had elapsed since last she had looked at the Sankaty light.

II

When Becky wrote to Randy, she had a great deal to say about Archibald Cope.

"He is trying to paint the moor. He wants to get its meaning, and then make other people see what it means. He doesn't look in the least like that, Randy—as if he were finding the spirit of things. He has red hair and wears correct clothes, and says the right things, and you feel as if he ought to be in Wall Street buying bonds. But here he is, refusing to believe that anything he has done is worth while until he does it to his own satisfaction.

"We walked to Tom Never's Head yesterday. It was one of those clear silver days, a little cloudy and without much color. The cranberries are ripe, and the moor was carpeted with them. When we got to Tom Never's we sat on the edge of the bluff, and Mr. Cope told me what he meant about the moor. It has its moods, he said. On a quiet, cloudy morning, it is a Quaker lady. With the fog in, it is a White Spirit. There are purple twilights when it is—Cleopatra, and windy nights with the sun going down blood-red, when it is—Medusa—— He says that the trouble with the average picture is that it is just—paint. I am not sure that I understand it all, but it is terribly interesting. And when he had talked a lot about that, he talked of the history of the island. He said that he should never be satisfied until somebody put a bronze statue of an Indian right where we stood, with his back to the sea. And when I said, 'Why with his back to it?' he said, 'Wasn't the sea cruel to the red man? It brought a conquering race in ships.'

"I told him then about our Indians in Virginia, and that some of us had a bit of red blood in our veins, and I told him that you and I always used the old Indian war cry when we called to each other, and he asked, 'Who is Randy?' and I said that you were an old friend, and that we had spent much of our childhood together."

As a matter of fact, Cope had been much interested in her account of young Paine. "Do you mean to say that he is still living on all that land?"

"Yes."

"Master of his own domain. I can't see it. The way I like to live is with a paint box, and a bag, and nothing to keep me from moving on."

"We aren't like that in the South."

"Do you like to stay in one place?"

"I never have. I have always been handed around."

"Would you like a home of your own?"

"Of course—after I am married."

"North, south, east or west?"

She put the question to him seriously. "Do you think it would make any difference if you loved a man, where you lived?"

"Well, of course, there might be difficulties—on a desert island."

"Not if you loved him."

"My sister wouldn't agree with you."

"Why not?"

"She is very modern. She says that love has nothing to do with it. Not romantic love. She says that when she marries she shall choose a man who lives in New York, who likes to go to Europe, and who hates the tropics. He must fancy pale gray walls and willow-green draperies, and he must loathe Florentine furniture. He must like music and painting, and not care much for books. He must adore French cooking, and have a prejudice against heavy roasts. He must be a Republican and High Church. She is sure that with such a man she would be happy. The dove of peace would hover over the household, because she and her husband would have nothing to quarrel about."

"Of course she doesn't mean it."

"She thinks she does."

"She won't if she is ever really in love."

He glanced at her. "Then you believe in the desert island?"

"I think I do——"

She stood up. "Did you feel a drop of rain? And Grandfather is waving."

The Admiral on the porch of the closed Lodge was calling to them to come under shelter.

It was a gentle rain, and they decided to walk home in it. They went at a smart pace, which they moderated as Cope showed signs of fatigue. "It's a beastly nuisance," he said, "to give out. I wish you would go on ahead, and let me rest here——"

They rested with him. The two men talked, and Becky was rather silent. When they started on again, Cope said to her, "Are you tired? It is a long walk."

"No," she said, "I am not tired. And I have been thinking a lot about the things you said to me."

He was not a conceited man, and he was aware that it was the things which he had said to her which had set her mind to work, not any personal fascination. She was quaint and charming, and he was glad that she had come. He had been lonely since his sister left. And his loneliness had fear back of it.

It was because of this conversation with Cope that Becky ended her letter to Randy with the following paragraph:

"Mr. Cope has a sister, Louise. She thinks that people ought to marry because they like the same things. She thinks that if two people care for the same furniture and the same religion and the same things to eat, that life will be lovely. She couldn't love a man enough to live on a desert island with him, because she adores New York. Of course, there is something in that, and if it is so, you and I ought to be very happy, Randy. We like old houses and the Virginia hills, and lots of books, and fireplaces—and dogs and horses and hot biscuits and fried chicken. It sounds awfully funny to put it that way, doesn't it, and practical? But perhaps Louise Cope is right, and one isn't likely, of course, to have the desert island test. Do you *really* think that anybody could be happy on a desert island, Randy?"

Randy replied promptly.

"If you were in love with me, Becky, you wouldn't be asking questions. You would believe that we could be blissful on a desert island. I believe it. It may not be true, yet I feel that a hut on a mountain top would be heaven for me if you were in it, Becky. In a way Cope's sister is right. The chances for happiness are greatest with those who have similar tastes, but not fried chicken tastes or identical religious opinions. These do not mean so much, but it would mean a great deal that we think alike about honesty and uprightness and truth and courage——

"And now, Becky, I might as well say it straight from the shoulder. I haven't the least right in the world to let you feel that you are engaged to me. I shall never marry you unless you love me—unless you love me so much that you would have the illusion of happiness with me on a desert island.

"I have no right to let you tie yourself to me. The whole thing is artificial and false. You are strong enough to stand alone. I want you to stand alone, Becky, for your own sake. I want you to tell yourself that Dalton isn't worth one single thought of yours. Tell yourself the truth, Becky, about him. It is the only way to own your soul.

"You may be interested to know that the Watermans left Hamilton Hill yesterday. Dalton went with them. I haven't seen him since the night of the Merriweathers' ball. I didn't tell you, did I, that after I took the fan away from him, I dropped him into the fountain? I had much rather have tied him to a stake, and have built a fire under him, but that isn't civilized, and of course, I couldn't. But I am glad I dropped him in the fountain——"

Becky read Randy's letter as she sat alone on the beach. It was cool and sunshiny and she was wrapped in a red cape. The winter gulls were beating strong wings above the breakers, and their sharp cries cut across the roar of the waters.

There had been a storm the night before—wind booming out of the northeast and the sea still sang the song of it.

Becky felt, suddenly, that she was very angry with Randy. It was as if he had broken a lovely thing that she had worshipped. She hated to think of that struggle in the dark—— She hated to think of Randy as—the Conqueror. She hated to think of George as dank and dripping. She wanted to think of him as shining and splendid, and Randy had spoiled that. But she wanted to be fair. Hadn't George, after all, spoiled his own splendidness? He had wooed her and had run away. And he had not run back until he thought another man wanted her.

"Of course," said somebody behind her, "you won't tell me what you are thinking about. But if you will just let me sit here and think, by your side, it will be a great privilege."

It was Mr. Cope, and she was not sure that she wanted him at this moment. Perhaps something of her thought showed in her eyes, for when she said, "Oh, yes," he stood looking down at her.

"Would you rather be alone with your letters? Don't hedge and be polite. Tell me."

"Well," she admitted, "my letters are a bit on my mind. But if you don't care if I am stupid, you can stay——"

He sat down. He had known her for ten days, and dreaded to think that in ten days more she might be gone. "I won't talk if you don't wish it."

Becky's eyes were on the sea. "I think I should like to talk. I have been thinking—about that Indian that you want commemorated in bronze up there on the bluff. Do you think he was cruel?"

"Who knows? He was, perhaps, a savage. Yet he may have been tender-hearted. I hope so, if he is going to be fixed in bronze for the ages to stare at."

"Did you," Becky asked, deliberately, "ever want to tie a man to a stake and build a fire under him?"

He turned and stared at her. "My dear child, what ever put such an idea in your head?"

"Well, did you?"

He considered it. "There was a time in France when I wanted to do worse than that."

"But that was war."

"No, it was a brute in my own company. He broke the heart of a little girl that he met in Brittany. He—he—well he murdered her—dreams."

"Perhaps he didn't know what he was doing."

"He knew. Every man knows."

"And you wanted to make him—suffer——"

"Yes."

She shivered. "Are all men like that?"

"Like what?"

"Cruel."

"It can't be cruelty. It's a sense of justice."

"I hope it is." She kept thinking about George rising dank and dripping from the fountain. She hated to think about it. So she changed the subject. "I thought you were painting."

"I was. But the moor is fickle. Yesterday she billowed towards the south, all gray and blue. And last night the storm spoiled it; she is gorgeous and gay to-day, and I don't like her."

"Oh, why not?"

"She is too obvious. Anybody can paint a Persian carpet, but one can't put soul into a—carpet——"

He was petulant. "I shall never paint the pictures I want to paint. Life is too short."

"Life isn't short. Look at Grandfather. You will have forty years yet in which to paint."

And now it was he who changed the subject, quickly, as if he were afraid of it.

"My sister is coming to-morrow. I rather think you will like her."

"Will she like me, that's more important."

"She will love you, as I do, as everybody does, Becky."

They had reached that point in ten days that he could say such things to her and win her smile. She did not believe in the least that he loved her. He always laughed when he said it.

She liked him very much. She felt that the Admiral and Tristram and Archibald Cope were all of them the best of comrades. Except for Jane, she had had practically no feminine society since she came. And Jane was not especially inspiring, not like Tristram, who seemed to carry one's imagination back to Viking days.

Cope was immensely enthusiastic about Tristram. "If I could paint figures as I want to," he said, "I'd do Tristram as 'The Islander.' One feels that he belongs here as inevitably as the moors or the sands or the sea. Perhaps it is he who ought to be in bronze on the bluff, instead of the Indian."

"But he'd have to face the sea," said Becky.

"Yes," Cope agreed, "he would. He loves it and his ancestors lived by it. I'll stick to my Indian and the moor."

Becky gathered up her letters. "It is time for lunch, and Jane doesn't like to be kept waiting. Won't you lunch with us? Grandfather will be delighted."

"I shall get to be a perpetual guest. I feel as if I were taking advantage of your hospitality."

"We shouldn't ask you if we didn't want you."

"Then I'll come."

They walked up the beach together. Becky was muffled in her red cape, Cope had a sweater under his coat. The air was sharp and clear as crystal.

"How anybody can go in bathing in this weather," Becky shivered, as a woman ran down the sands towards the sea. She cast off her bathing cloak and stood revealed, slim and rather startling, in yellow.

"She goes in every day," said Cope, "even when it storms."

"Who is she?"

"A dancer—from New York. Haven't you seen her before?"

"No. Where is she staying?"

"At the hotel."

"I thought the hotel was closed."

"Not for three weeks. There aren't many guests. This one came up a month ago. She dances on the moor—practising for some play which opens in October."

"What's her name?"

"I don't know. They call her 'The Yellow Daffodil' because of that bathing suit."

The girl was swimming now beyond the breakers.

Becky was envious. "I wish I could swim like that."

"You can do other things—that she can't do."

"What things?"

"Well, be a lady, for example. That's not exactly cricket, is it, to draw a deadly parallel? But I don't want people like that dancing on my moor."

CHAPTER XIV
THE DANCER ON THE MOOR
I

Randy's letter had set Becky adrift. She was not in love with him. She was sure of that. And he had said he would not marry her without love. He had said that if she owned her soul she would think of Dalton as a cad and as a coward.

It seemed queer that Randy should be demanding things of her. He had always been so glad to take anything she would give, and now she had offered him herself, and he wouldn't have her. Not till she owned her soul.

She knew what he meant. The thought of George was always with her. She kept seeing him as she had first seen him at the station; as he had been that wonderful day when they had had tea in the Pavilion; the night in the music room when he had kissed her; the old garden with its pale statues and box hedges; and always there was his sparkling glance, his quick voice. She would never own her soul until she forgot George. Until she put him out of her life; until the thought of him would not make her burn hot with humiliation; until the thought of him would not thrill to her finger-tips.

She found Cope's easy and humorous companionship a balance for her hidden emotions. And when Louise Cope came, she proved to be a rather highly emphasized counterpart of her brother. Her red-gold hair was thick and she wore it bobbed. Her skin was white but lacked the look of delicacy which seemed to contradict constantly Cope's vivid personality. She seemed to laugh at the world as he did. She called Becky "quaint," but took to her at once.

"Archie has been writing to me of you," she told Becky; "he says you came up like a bird from the south."

"Birds don't fly north in the fall——"

"Well, you were the—miracle," Cope asserted.

Louise Cope's shrewd glance studied him. "He has fallen in love with you, Becky Bannister," was her blunt assurance, "but you needn't let it worry you. As yet it is only an æsthetic passion. But there is no telling what may come of it——"

"Does he fall in love—like that?" Becky demanded.

"He has never been in love," Louise declared, "not really. Except with me."

Becky felt that the Copes were a charming pair. When she answered Randy's letter she spoke of them.

"Louise adores her brother, and she thinks he would be a great artist if he would take himself seriously. But neither of them seems to take anything seriously. They always seem to be laughing at the world in a quiet way. Louise is not pretty, but she gives an effect of beauty—— She wears a big gray cape and a black velvet tam, and I am not sure that the color in her cheeks is real. She is different from other people, but it doesn't seem to be a pose. It is just because she has lived in so many places and has seen so many people and has thought for herself. I have always let other people think for me, haven't I, Randy?

"And now that I have done with the Copes, I am going to talk about the things that you said to me in your letter, and which are really the important things.

"I hated to think that you dropped Mr. Dalton in the fountain. I hated to think that you wanted to burn him at the stake—there was something—cruel—and—dreadful in it all. I have kept thinking of that struggle between you—in the dark—— I have hated to think that a few years ago if you had felt as you do about him—that you might have—killed him. But perhaps men are like that. They care more for justice than for—mercy.

"I am trying to take your advice and tell myself the truth about Mr. Dalton. That he isn't worth a thought of mine. Yet I think of him a great deal. I am being very frank with you, Randy, because we have always talked things out. I think of him, and wonder which is the real man—the one I thought he was—and I thought him very fine and splendid. Or is he just trifling and commonplace? Perhaps he is just between, not as wonderful as I thought him, nor as contemptible as I seem forced to believe.

"Yet I gave him something that it is hard to take back. I gave a great deal. You see I had always been shut up in a glass case like the bob-whites and the sandpipers in the Bird Room, and I knew nothing of the world. And the first time I tried my wings, I thought I was flying towards the sun, and it was just a blaze that—burned me.

"Of course you are right when you say that you won't marry me unless I love you. I had a queer feeling at first about it—as if you were very far away and I couldn't reach you. But I know that you are right, and that you are thinking of the thing that is best for me. But I know I shall always have you as a friend. I don't think that I shall ever love anybody. And after this we won't talk about it. There are so many other things that we have to say to each other that don't hurt——"

Becky could not, of course, know the effect of her letter on Randy. The night after its receipt, he roamed the woods. She had thought him cruel—and dreadful. Well, let her think it. He was glad that he had dropped George in the fountain. He should always be glad. But women were not like that—they were tender—and hated—hardness. Perhaps that was because they were—mothers——

And men were—hard. He had been hard, perhaps, in the things he had said in his letter. Her words rang in his ears. "I had a queer feeling at first that you were very far away, and that I could not reach you." And she had said that, when his soul ached to have her near.

Yet he had tried to do the best that he could for Becky. He had felt that she must not be bound by a tie that was no longer needed to protect her from Dalton. She was safe at 'Sconset, with the Admiral and her new friends the Copes. He envied them, their hours with her. He was desperately lonely, with a loneliness which had no hope.

He worked intensively. The boarders had gone from King's Crest, and he and the Major had moved into the big house. Randy spent a good deal of time in the Judge's library at Huntersfield. He and Truxton had great plans for their future. They read law, sold cars, and talked of their partnership. The firm was to be "Bannister, Paine and Beaufort"; it was to have brains, conscience, and business acumen.

"In the order named," Truxton told the Major. "The Judge has brains, Randy has a conscience. There's nothing left for me but to put pep into the business end of it."

Randy worked, too, on his little story. He did not know in the least what he was going to do with it, but it was an outlet for the questions which he kept asking himself. The war was over and the men who had fought had ceased to be important. He and the Major and Truxton talked a great deal about it. The Major took the high stand of each man's satisfaction in the thing he had done. Truxton was light-heartedly indifferent. He had his Mary, and his future was before him. But Randy argued that the world ought not to forget. "It was a rather wonderful thing for America. I want her to keep on being wonderful."

The Major in his heart knew that the boy was right. America must keep on being wonderful. Her young men must go high-hearted to the tasks of peace. It was the high-heartedness of people which had won the war. It would be the high-heartedness of men and women which would bring sanity and serenity to a troubled world.

"The difficulty lies in the fact that we are always trying to make laws to right the world, when what we need is to form individual ideals. The boy who says in his heart, 'I want to be like Lincoln,' and who stands in front of a statue of Lincoln, and learns from that rugged countenance the lesson of simple courage and honesty, has a better chance of a future than the boy who is told, 'There is evil in the world, and the law punishes those who transgress.' Half of our Bolsheviks would be tamed if they had the knowledge and love of some simple hero in their hearts, and felt that there was a chance for them to be heroic. The war gave them a chance. We have now to show them that there is beauty and heroism in orderly living——"

He was talking to Madge. She was still with the Flippins. The injury to her foot had been more serious than it had seemed. She might have gone with Oscar and Flora when they left Hamilton Hill. But she preferred to stay. Flora was to go to a hospital; Madge would not be needed.

"I am going to stay here as long as you will let me," she said to Mrs. Flippin; "you will tell me if I am in the way——"

Mrs. Flippin adored Madge. "It is like having a Princess in the house," she said, "only she don't act like a Princess."

The Major came over every afternoon. Kemp drove him, as a rule, in the King's Crest surrey. If the little man missed Dalton's cars, he said no word. He made the Major very comfortable. He lived a life of ease if not of elegance, and he loved the wooded hills, the golden air, the fine old houses, the serene autumn glory of this southern world.

On the afternoon when the Major talked to Madge of the world at peace, they were together under the apple tree which Madge had first seen from the window of the east room. There were other apple trees in the old orchard, but it was this tree that Madge liked because of its golden globes. "The red ones are wonderful," she said, "but red isn't my color. With my gold skin, they make me look like a gypsy. If I am to be a golden girl, I must stay away from red——"

"Is that what you are—a golden girl?"

"That was always George Dalton's name for me."

"I am sorry."

"Why?"

"Because I should like it to be mine for you. I should like to link my golden West with the thought of you."

"And you won't now, because it was somebody else's name for me?"

Kemp, before he went away, had made her comfortable with cushions in a chair-like crotch of the old tree. The Major was at her feet. He meditated a moment. "I shall make it my name for you. What do I care what other men have called you."

"Do you know what you called me—once?" she was smiling down at him.

"No."

"A little lame duck. It was when I first tried to use my foot. And you laughed, and said that it—linked us—together. And now you are trying to link me with your West——"

"You know why, of course."

"Yes, I do."

He drew a long breath. "Most women would have said, 'No, I don't know.' But you told the truth. I want to link you with my life in every way I can because I love you. And you know that I care—very much—that I want you for my wife—my golden girl in my golden West——?"

"You have never told me before that—you cared."

"There was no need to tell it. You knew."

"Yes. I was afraid it was true——"

He was startled. "Afraid? Why?"

"Oh, I oughtn't to let you care," she said. "You don't know what a slacker I've been. And I don't want you to find out——"

"The only thing that I want to find out is whether you care for me."

She flushed a little under his steady gaze, then quite unexpectedly she reached her hand down to him. He took it in his firm clasp. "I do care—an awful lot," she said, "but I've tried not to. And I shouldn't let you care for me."

"Why—shouldn't?"

"I'm not—half good enough. My life has always been lived at loose ends. Nothing bad, but a thousand things that you wouldn't—like to hear—I'm not a golden girl—I'm a gilded one——"

"Why should you tell me things like that? I don't believe it."

"Please believe it," she said earnestly, "don't whitewash things. Just let me begin again—loving you——"

Her voice broke. He drew himself up, and took her in his arms. "My dear girl," he said, "my dear girl——"

"I never met a man like you, I never believed there were—such men——" He felt her tears against his hand.

"Listen," he said quietly; "let me tell you something of my life." He told her the things he had told Randy. Of the little wife he had not loved. "Perhaps if it had not been for her, I should not have had the courage to offer to you my—maimed—self. When I married her I was strong and young and had wealth to give her. Yet I did not give her love. And love is more than all the rest. I have that to give you—you know it."

"Yes."

"I have some money. I don't think it is going to count much with either of us. What will count is the way we plan our future. I have a big old ranch, and we'll live in it—with the dairy and the wide kitchen that you've talked about—and you won't have to wait for another world, dearest, to get your heart's desire——"

"I have my heart's desire," she whispered; "you are—my world."

II

Madge wrote to George Dalton that she was going to marry Major Prime.

"There is no reason why we should put it off, Georgie. The clergyman who prayed for Flora will perform the ceremony, and the wedding will be at the Flippins' farm.

"It seems, of course, too good to be true. Not many women have such luck. Not my kind of women anyway. We meet men as a rule who want us to be gilded girls, and not golden ones. But Mark wants me to be gold all through. And I shall try to be—— We are to live on his ranch, a place that passes in California for a farm—a sort of glorified country place. Mrs. Flippin is teaching me to make butter, so that I can superintend my own dairy, and I have learned a great deal about chickens and eggs.

"I am going to be a housewife in what I call a reincarnated sense—loving my house and the things which belong to it, and living as a part of it, not above it, and looking down upon it. Perhaps all American women will come to that some day and I shall simply be blazing the way for them. I shall probably grow rosy and round, and if you ever ride up to my door-step, you will find me a buxom and blooming matron instead of a golden girl. And you won't like it in the least. But my husband will like it, because he thinks a bit as I do about it, and he doesn't care for the woman who lives for her looks.

"I shall come and see Flora before I go West. But I am going to be married first. We both have a feeling that it must be now—that something might happen if we put it off, and nothing must happen. I love him too much. Of course you won't believe that. I can hardly believe it myself. But I have someone to climb the heights with me, Georgie, and we shall ascend to the peak—together."

For a wedding present George sent Madge the pendant he had bought for Becky. To connect it up with Madge's favorite color scheme, he had an amethyst put in place of the sapphire. He was glad to give it away. Every time he had come upon it, it had reminded him of things that he wished to forget.

Yet he could not forget. Even as Becky had thought of him, he had thought of her; of her radiant youth on the morning that Randy had arrived; at the Horse Show in her shabby shoes and sailor hat; in the Bird Room in pale blue under the swinging lamp; in the music room between tall candles; in the garden, with a star shining into the still pool; that last night, on the balcony, leaning over, with a yellow lantern like a halo behind her.

There were other things that he thought of—of Randy, in khaki on the station platform; Randy, lean and tall among the boarders; Randy, left behind with Kemp in the rain; Randy, debonair and insolent, announcing his engagement on the terrace at Hamilton Hill; Randy, a shadow against a silver sky, answering Becky's call; Randy, in the dark by the fountain, with muscles like iron, forcing him inevitably back, lifting him above the basin, letting him drop——; Randy, the Conqueror, marching away with Becky's fan as his trophy——!

New York was, of course, at this season of the year, a pageant of sparkling crowds, and of brilliant window displays, of new productions at the theaters. People were coming back to town. Even the fashionable folk were running down to taste the elixir of the early days in the metropolis.

But George found everything flat and stale. He did the things he had always done, hunted up the friends he had always known. He spent week-ends at various country places, and came always back to town with an undiminished sense of his need of Becky, and his need of revenge on Randy.

He had heard before he left Virginia that Becky was at Nantucket. He had found some consolation in the fact that she was not at Huntersfield. To have thought of her with Randy in the old garden, on Pavilion Hill, in the Bird Room, would have been unbearable.

He had a feeling that, in a sense, Madge's marriage was a desertion. He did not in the least want to marry her, but there were moments when he needed her friendship very much. He needed it now. And she was going to marry Major Prime, and go out to some God-forsaken place, and get fat and lose her beauty. He wished that she would not talk about such things—it made him feel old, and worried about his waist-line.

Even Oscar was failing him. "When Flora gets well," the little man kept telling him, "we are going to do some good with our money. We have done nothing but think of ourselves——"

"Oh, for Heaven's sake, don't preach," George exploded. It seemed to him that the world had gone mad on the subject of reforms. Man was no longer master of his fate. The time would come when the world would be a dry desert, without a cocktail or a highball for a thirsty soul, and all because a lot of people had been feeling for some time as Flora and Oscar felt at this moment.

"I shall take Flora up to the Crossing in a few days," Oscar was saying; "the doctor thinks the sea air will do her good. I wish you would come with us."

George had no idea of going with Oscar and Flora. He had been marooned long enough with a sick woman and her depressed spouse. When Flora was better and she and Oscar got over their mood of piety and repentance, he would be glad to join them. In the meantime he searched his mind for some reasonable excuse.

"Look here," he said, "I'll join you later, Oscar. I've promised some friends at Nantucket that I'll come down for the hunting."

"I didn't know that you had friends in Nantucket," Oscar told him moodily.

"The Merediths," George remembered in the nick of time the name of Becky's grandfather. Oscar would not know the difference.

Having committed himself, his spirits soared. It had, he felt, been an inspiration to put it over on Oscar like that. Subconsciously he had known that some day he would follow Becky, and when the moment came, he had spoken out of his thoughts.

In the two or three days that elapsed between his decision and the date that he had set for his departure, he found himself enjoying the city—its clear skies, its hurrying crowds, its color and glow, the tingle of its rush and hurry, its light-hearted acceptance of the pleasure of the moment.

He telegraphed for a room at a hotel in Nantucket. Once there, he was confident that he could find Becky. Everybody would know Admiral Meredith.

He went by boat from New York to New Bedford, and enjoyed the trip. Later on the little steamer, *Sankaty*, plying between New Bedford and Nantucket, he was so shining and splendid that he was much observed by the other passengers. His Jap servant, trotting after him, was perhaps less martial in bearing than the ubiquitous Kemp, but he was none the less an ornament.

Thus George came, at last, to Nantucket, and to his hotel. Having dined, he asked the way to the Admiral's house. He did not of course plan to storm the citadel after dark, but a walk would not hurt him, and he could view from the outside the cage which held his white dove. For he had come to that, sentimentally, that Becky was the white dove that he would shelter against his heart.

The clerk at the hotel desk, directing him, thought that the Admiral was not in his house on Main Street. He was apt at this season to spend his time in Siasconset.

"'Sconset? Where's 'Sconset?"

"Across the island."

"How can I get there?"

"You can motor over. There's a 'bus, or you can get a car."

So the next morning, George took the 'bus. He saw little beauty in the moor. He thought it low and flat. His heart leaped with the thought that every mile brought him nearer Becky—his white dove—whom he had—hurt!

He was set down by the 'bus at the post-office. He asked his way, and was directed to a low huddle of gray houses on a grassy street. "It is the 'Whistling Sally,'" the driver of the 'bus had told him.

When George reached "The Whistling Sally," he felt that there must be some mistake. Here was no proper home for an Admiral or an heiress. His eyes were blind to the charms of the wooden young woman with the puffed-out cheeks, to the beauty of silver-gray shingles, of late flowers blooming bravely in the little garden.

He kept well on the other side of the street. It might perhaps be embarrassing if he met Becky while she was with her grandfather. He wanted to see her alone. With no one to interfere, he would be, he was sure, master of the situation.

He passed the house. The windows were open, and the white curtains blew out. But there was no one in sight. At the next corner, he accosted a tall man in work clothes, with bronzed skin and fair hair.

"Can you tell me," George asked, "whether Admiral Meredith lives in that cottage—'The Whistling Sally'?"

"Yes. But he isn't there. He's gone to Boston."

George was conscious of a sense of shock.

"Boston?"

"Yes. He wasn't very well and he wanted to see his doctor."

"Has his—granddaughter gone with him?"

"Miss Becky? Yes."

"But—the windows of the house are open——"

"I open them every morning. The housekeeper is in Nantucket. But they are all coming back at the end of the week."

"Coming back?" eagerly; "the Admiral, and Miss Bannister?"

"Yes."

George drew a long breath. He walked back with Tristram to the low gray house. "Queer little place," he said.

Tristram eyed him with easy tolerance. "Of course it seems queer if you aren't used to it——"

"I thought the Admiral had money."

"Well, he has. But he forgets it out here——"

"Is there a good hotel?"

"Yes. It is usually closed by now. But they are keeping it open for some guests who are up for the hunting."

The hotel was a pleasant rambling structure, and overlooked the sea. George engaged a room for Saturday—and said that his man would bring his bags. He would have his lunch and take the afternoon 'bus back to Nantucket.

As he waited for the dining-room doors to open, a girl wrapped in a yellow cape crossed the porch and descended the steps which led to the beach. She wore a yellow bathing cap and yellow shoes. George walked to the top of the bluff and watched her. She threw off the cape, and stood slim and striking for a moment before she dived into the sea. She swam splendidly. It was very cold, and George wondered how she endured it. When she came running back up the steps and across the porch, she was wrapped in the cape. She was rather handsome in a queer dark way. "It was cold," she said, as she passed George.

He took a step forward. "You were brave——"

She stopped and shrugged her shoulders. "One gets warm," she said, "in a moment."

She left him, and he went in to lunch. He stopped at the desk on the way out. "I have changed my mind. My man will bring my bags to-morrow."

It was still too early for the 'bus, so George walked back up the bluff, turning at last towards the left. Crossing a grassy space, there was ahead of him a ridge which marked the edge of the moor. A little fog was blowing in, and mistily through the fog he saw a figure which moved as light as smoke above the eminence. It was a woman dancing.

As he came nearer, he saw that she wore gray with a yellow sash. Her yellow cape lay on the ground. "I am not sure," George said, as he stopped beside her, "whether you are a pixie or a mermaid."

"Look," she said, smiling, "I'll show you what I am——"

She began with a light swaying motion, like a leaf stirred by a breeze. Then, whipped into action, she ran before the pursuing elements. She cowered, and registered defiance. Her loosened hair hung heavy about her shoulders, then wound itself about her, as she whirled in a cyclone of movement. Beaten to the ground, she rose languidly, swayed again to that light step and stopped.

Then she came close to George. "You see," she said, "I am not a pixie or a mermaid. I am the spirit of the storm."

CHAPTER XV
THE TRUMPETER SWAN
I

The Admiral's rheumatism had taken Becky to Boston. "There'll be treatments every morning," he said, "and we'll invite the Copes to visit us, and they will look after you while I am away."

The Copes were delighted. "Only it seems like an imposition——"

"The house is big enough for an army," the Admiral told them; "that's what we built houses for in the old days. To have our friends. Charles, my butler, and his wife, Miriam, who cooks, stay in the house the year round, so it is always open and ready."

"And you and I shall see Boston together," Archibald told Becky, triumphantly. "I wonder if you have ever seen Boston as I shall show it to you."

"Well, I've been to all the historic places."

"Bunker Hill and the embattled farmers, of course," said Archibald; "but have you seen them since the war?"

"No. Are they different?"

"They aren't, but you are. All of us are."

Louise was not quite sure that her brother ought to leave the island. "You are down here for the air, Arch, and the quiet." He was impatient. "Do you think I am going to miss this?"

She frowned and shook her head. "I don't want you to miss it. But it will be going against the doctor's orders."

"Oh, hang the doctor, Louise. Being in Boston with Becky will be like—wine——"

But she was not satisfied. "You always throw yourself into things so—desperately——"

"Well, when I lose my enthusiasm I want to—die."

"No, you don't, Arch. Don't say things like that." Her voice was sharp.

He patted her hand. "I won't. But don't curb me too much, old girl. Let me play—while I can——"

They arrived in Boston to find a city under martial law, a city whose streets were patrolled by khaki-clad figures with guns, whose traffic was regulated by soldierly semaphores, who linked intelligence with military training, and picturesqueness with both.

For a short season Boston had been in the hands of the mob. All of her traditions of law and order had not saved her. It had been her punishment perhaps for leaving law and order in the hands of those who cared nothing for them. People with consciences had preferred to keep out of politics. So for a time demagogues had gotten the ear of the people, and chaos had resulted until a quiet governor had proved himself as firm as steel, and soldiers had replaced the policemen who had for a moment followed false gods.

"It all proves what I brought you here to see," Cope told Becky eagerly.

Coffee was being served in the library of the Meredith mansion on Beacon Street. The Admiral's library was as ruddy and twinkling as the little man himself. He had furnished it to suit his own taste. A great davenport of puffy red velvet was set squarely in front of a fireplace with shining brasses. The couch was balanced by a heavy gilt chair also in puffy red. The mantel was in white marble, and over the mantel was an oil portrait of the Admiral's wife painted in '76. She wore red velvet with a train, and with the pearls which had come down to Becky. The room had been keyed up to her portrait, and had then been toned down with certain heavy pieces of ebony, a cabinet of black lacquer, the dark books which lined the wall to the ceiling. The room was distinctly nineteenth-century. If it lacked the eighteenth-century exquisiteness of the house at Nantucket, with its reminder of austere Quaker prejudices, it was none the less appropriate as a glowing background for the gay old Admiral.

Becky and Cope sat on the red davenport. It was so wide that Becky was almost lost in a corner of it. The old butler, Charles, served the coffee. The coffee service was of repoussé silver. The Admiral would have no other. It had been given him by a body of seamen when he had retired from active duty.

"It all proves what I brought you here to see," Archibald emphasized, "how the gods of yesterday are going to balance the gods of to-day."

The Admiral chuckled. "There aren't any gods of to-day."

"The gods of to-day are our young men," Cope flung out, glowingly; "the war has left them with their dreams, and they have got to find a way to make their dreams come true. And that's where the old gods will help. Those fine old men who dreamed, backed their dreams with deeds. Then for a time we were so busy making money that we forgot their dreams. And when foreigners came crowding to our shores, we didn't care whether they were good Americans or not. All we cared was to have them work in our mills and factories and in our kitchens, and let us alone in our pride of ancestry and pomp of circumstance. We forgot to show them Bunker Hill and to tell them about the old North Church and Paul Revere and the shot heard 'round the world, and what liberty meant and democracy, and now we've got to show them. I am going to take you around to-morrow, Becky, and pretend you are Olga from Petrograd, and that you are seeing America for the first time."

Archibald Cope was kindled by fires which gave color to his pale cheeks. "Will you be—Olga from Petrograd?"

"I'd love it."

But the next morning it rained. "And you can't, of course, be Olga of Petrograd in the rain. Bunker Hill must have the sun on it, and the waves of the harbor must be sparkling when I tell you about the tea."

They decided, therefore, to read aloud "The Autocrat of the Breakfast Table."

"Then if it stops raining," said Archibald, "we'll step straight out from its pages into the Boston that I want to show you." He read well. Louise sat at a little table sewing a pattern of beads on a green bag. Becky had some rose-colored knitting. The Admiral was in his big chair by the fire with his hands folded across his waistcoat and his eyes shut. The colorful work of the two women, the light of the fire, the glow of the little lamp at Cope's elbow, the warmth of the red furniture saved the room from dreariness in spite of the rain outside.

"'It was on the Common,'" read Cope, "'that we were walking. The mall, or boulevard of our Common, you know, has various branches leading from it in different directions. One of these runs down from opposite Joy Street southward across the whole length of the Common to Boylston Street. We called it the long path, and were fond of it.

"'I felt very weak indeed (though of a tolerably robust habit) as we came opposite the head of this path on that morning. I think I tried to speak twice without making myself distinctly audible. At last I got out the question, "Will you take the long path with me?" "Certainly," said the schoolmistress, "with much pleasure." "Think," I said, "before you answer: if you take the long path with me now, I shall interpret it that we are to part no more!" The schoolmistress stepped back with a sudden movement, as if an arrow had struck her.

"'One of the long granite blocks used as seats was hard by—the one you may still see close by the Gingko-tree. "Pray sit down," I said. "No, no," she answered, softly, "I will walk the *long path* with you!"

"'—The old gentleman who sits opposite met us walking arm in arm about the middle of the long path, and said, very charmingly,—"Good-morning, my dears!"'"

The reading stopped at luncheon time, and it was still raining. On the table were letters for Becky forwarded from Siasconset. An interesting account from Aunt Claudia of the wedding of Major Prime and Madge MacVeigh.

"They were married in the old orchard at the Flippins', and it was beautiful. The bride wore simple clothes like the rest of us. It was cool and we kept on our wraps, and she was in white linen with a loose little coat of mauve wool, and a hat to match. The only bride-y thing about her was a great bunch of lilacs that the Major ordered from a Fifth Avenue florist.

They are to stay in New York for a day or two, and then visit the Watermans on the North Shore. After that they will go at once to the West, where they are to live on the Major's ranch. He has been relieved from duty at Washington, and will have all of his time to give to his own affairs.

"There has been an epidemic of weddings. Flippins' Daisy waited just long enough to help Mrs. Flippin get Miss MacVeigh married; then she and young John had an imposing ceremony in their church, with Daisy in a train and white veil, and four bridesmaids, and Mandy and Calvin in front seats, and Calvin giving the bride away. I think the elaborateness of it all really reconciled Mandy to her daughter-in-law."

There was also, from Randy, a long envelope enclosing a thick manuscript and very short note.

"I want you to read this, Becky. It belongs in a way to you. I don't know what I think about it. Sometimes it seems as if I had done a rather big thing, and as if it had been done without me at all. I wonder if you understand what I mean—as if I had held the pen, and it had—come—— I have sent it to the editor of one of the big magazines. Perhaps he will send it back, and it may not seem as good to me as it does at this moment. Let me know what you think."

Becky, finishing the letter, felt a bit forlorn. Randy, as a rule, wrote at length about herself and her affairs. But, of course, he had other things now to think of. She must not expect too much.

There was no time, however, in which to read the manuscript, for Cope was saying, wistfully, "Do you think you'd mind a walk in the rain?"

"No." She gathered up her letters.

"Then we'll walk across the Common."

They shared one umbrella. And they played that it was over fifty years ago when the Autocrat had walked with the young Schoolmistress. They even walked arm in arm under the umbrella. They took the long path to Boylston Street. And Cope said, "Will you take the long path with me?"

And Becky said, "Certainly."

And they both laughed. But there was no laughter in Cope's heart.

"Becky," he said, "I wish that you and I had lived a century ago in Louisberg Square."

"If we had lived then, we shouldn't be living now."

"But we should have had our—happiness——"

"And I should have worn lovely flowing silk skirts. Not short things like this, and little bonnets with flowers inside, and velvet mantles——"

"And you would have walked on my arm to church. And we would have owned one of those old big houses—and your smile would have greeted me across the candles every day at dinner——" He was making it rather personal, but she humored his fancy.

"And you would have worn a blue coat, and a bunch of big seals, and a furry high hat——"

"You are thinking all the time about what we would wear," he complained; "you haven't any sense of romance, Becky———"

"Well, of course, it is all make-believe."

"Yes, it is all—make-believe," he said, and walked in silence after that.

The wind blew cold and they stopped in a pastry shop on Boylston Street and had a cup of tea.

Becky ate little cream cakes with fluted crusts, and drank Orange Pekoe.

"I am glad you don't wear flowing silks and velvet mantles," said Archibald, suddenly; "I shall always remember you like this, Becky, in your rough brown coat and your close little hat, and that your hand was on my arm when we walked across the Common. Do you like me as a playmate, Becky?"

"Yes."

"Do you—love me—as a playmate?" He leaned forward.

"Please—don't."

"I beg your—pardon——" he flushed. "I am not going to say such things to you, Becky, and spoil things for both of us—I know you don't want to hear them——"

"Make-believe is much nicer," she reminded him steadily.

"But I am not a make-believe friend, am I? Our friendship—that at least is—real?"

Her clear eyes met his. "Yes. We shall always be friends—forever——"

"How long is forever, Becky?"

She could not answer that. But she was sure that friendship was like love and lived beyond the grave. They were very serious about it, these two young people drinking tea.

II

It was when the four of them were gathered together that night in the library that Becky asked Archibald Cope to read "The Trumpeter Swan."

"Randy wrote it," she said, "and he sent the manuscript to me this morning."

The Admiral was at once interested. "He got the name from the swan in the Judge's Bird Room?"

"Yes."

"Has he ever written anything before?" Louise asked.

"Lots of little things. Lovely things——"

"Have they been published?"

"I don't think he has tried."

Becky had the manuscript in her work-bag. She brought it out and handed it to Archibald. "You are sure you aren't too tired?"

Louise glanced up from her beaded bag. "You've had a hard day, Arch. You mustn't do too much."

"I won't, Louise," impatiently.

She went back to her work. "It will be on your own head if you don't sleep to-night, not on mine."

"The Trumpeter Swan" was a story of many pages. Randy had confined himself to no conventional limits. He had a story to tell, and he did not bring it to an end until the end came naturally. In it he had asked all of the questions which had torn his soul. What of the men who had fought? What of their futures? What of their high courage? Their high vision? Was it all now to be wasted? All of that aroused emotion? All of that disciplined endeavor? Would they still "carry on" in the spirit of that crusade, or would they sink back, and forget?

His hero was a simple lad. He had fought for his country. He had found when he came back that other men had made money while he fought for them. He loved a girl. And in his absence she had loved someone else. For a time he was overthrown.

Yet he had been one of a glorious company. One of that great flock which had winged its exalted flight to France. Throughout the story Randy wove the theme of the big white bird in the glass case. His hero felt himself likewise on the shelf, shut-in, stuffed, dead—his trumpet silent.

"Am I, too, in a glass case?" he asked himself; "will my trumpet never sound again?"

The first part of the story ended there. "Jove," Cope said, as he looked up, "that boy can write——"

Louise had stopped working. "It is rather—tremendous, don't you think?"

Archibald nodded. "In a quiet way it thrills. He hasn't used a word too much. But he carries one with him to a sort of—upper sky——"

Becky, flushing and paling with the thought of such praise as this for Randy, said, "I always thought he could do it."

But even she had not known that Randy could do what he did in the second part of the story.

For in it Randy answered his own questions. There was no limit to a man's powers, no limits to his patriotism, if only he believed in himself. He must strive, of course, to achieve. But striving made him strong. His task might be simple, but its very simplicity demanded that he put his best into it. He must not measure himself by the rule of little men. If other men had made money while he fought, then let them be weighed down by their bags of gold. He would not for one moment set against their greed those sacred months of self-sacrifice.

And as for the woman he loved. If his love meant anything it must burn with a pure flame. What he might have been for her, he would be because of her. He would not be less a man because he had loved her.

And so the boy came in the end of the story to the knowledge that it was the brave souls who sounded their trumpets—— One did not strive for happiness. One strove for—victory. One strove, at least, for one clear note of courage, amid the clamor of the world.

Louise, listening, forgot her beads. The Admiral blew his nose and wiped his eyes. Becky felt herself engulfed by a wave of surging memories.

"That's corking stuff, do you know it?" Archibald was asking.

Louise asked, "How old is he?"

"Twenty-three."

"He is young to have learned all that——"

"All what, Louise?" Archibald asked.

"Renunciation," said Louise, slowly, "that's what it is in the final analysis," she went back to her beads and her green bag.

"Randy ought to do great things," said Becky; "the men of his family have all done great things, haven't they, Grandfather?"

"Randolph blood is Randolph blood," said the Admiral; "fine old Southerners; proud old stock."

"If I could write like that," said Archibald, and stopped and looked into the fire.

Louise rose and came and stood back of him. "You can paint," she said, "why should you want to write?"

"I can't paint," he reached up and caught her hand in his; "you think I can, but I can't. And I am not wonderful—— Yet here I must sit and listen while you and Becky sing young Paine's praises."

He flung out his complaint with his air of not being in earnest.

The Admiral got up stiffly. "I've a letter to write before I go to bed. Don't let me hurry the rest of you."

"Please take Louise with you," Archibald begged; "I want to talk to Becky."

His sister rumpled his hair. "So you want to get rid of me. Becky, he is going to ask questions about that boy who wrote the story."

"Are you?" Becky demanded.

"Louise is a mind reader. That's why I want her out of the way——"

"You can stay until the Admiral finishes his letter." Louise bent and kissed him, picked up her beaded bag, and left them together.

When she reached the threshold, she stopped and looked back. Archibald had piled up two red cushions and was sitting at Becky's feet.

"Tell me about him."

"Randy?"

"Yes. He's in love with you, of course."

"What makes you think that?"

"He sent you the story."

"Well, he is," she admitted, "but I am not sure that we ought to talk about it."

"Why not?"

"Is it quite fair, to him?"

"Then we'll talk about his story. It gripped me—— Oh, let's have it out, Becky. He loves you and you don't love him. Why don't you?"

"I can't—tell you——"

There was silence for a moment, then Archibald Cope said gently, "Look here, girl dear, you aren't happy. Don't I know it? There's something that's awfully on your mind and heart. Can't you think of me as a sort of—father confessor—and let me—help——?"

She clasped her hands tensely on her knees; the knuckles showed white. "Nobody can help."

"Is it as bad as that?"

"Yes." She looked away from him. "There is somebody else—not Randy. Somebody that I shouldn't think about. But I—do——"

She was dry-eyed. But he felt that here was something too deep for tears.

"Does Randy know?"

"Yes. I told him. We have always talked about things——"

"I see," he sat staring into the fire, "and of course it is Randy that you ought to marry——"

"I don't want to marry anyone. I shall never marry——"

"Tut-tut, my dear." He laid his hand over hers. "Do you know what I was thinking, Becky, to-day, as we walked the Boston streets? I was thinking of why those big houses were built, rows upon rows of them, and of the people who lived in them. Those old houses speak of homes, Becky, of people who wanted household gods, and neighborly gatherings, and community interests. They weren't the kind of people who ran around Europe with a paint box, as I have been doing. They had home-keeping hearts and they built for the future."

He was very much in earnest. She had, indeed, never seen him so much in earnest.

"It is all very well," he went on, "to talk of a tent in a desert or a hut on a mountain top, but when we walked across the Common this morning, it seemed to me that if I could really have lived the game we played—that life could have held nothing better in the world for me than that, my dear."

She tried to withdraw her hand, but he held it. "Let me speak to-night, Becky—and then forever, we'll forget it. I love you—very much. You don't love me, and I should thank the stars for that, although I am not sure that I do. I am not a man to deal in—futures. I'll tell you why some day." He drew a long breath and went on in a lighter tone: "But you, Becky—you've got to find a man whose face you will want to see at the other end of the table—for life. It sounds like a prisoner's sentence, doesn't it?"

But he couldn't carry it off like that, and presently he hid his face against her hands. "Oh, Becky, Becky," she heard him whisper.

Then there was the Admiral's step in the hall and Archibald was on his feet, staring in the fire when the little man came in. "Any letters for Charles to mail?"

"No, Grandfather."

The Admiral limped away. Becky stood up. Cope turned from the fire.

"If it doesn't rain to-morrow, I'll show America to Olga of Petrograd."

They smiled at each other, and Becky held out her hand. He bent and kissed it. "I shall sleep well to-night because of—to-morrow."

III

But when to-morrow came there was a telephone message for Becky that Major Prime and his wife were in town. They had messages for her from Huntersfield, and from King's Crest.

"And so our day is spoiled," said Archibald.

"We can come again," said the Admiral, "but we must be getting back to Siasconset to-morrow. I wrote to Tristram. We'll have Prime and his wife here for dinner to-night, and drive them out somewhere this afternoon. I remember Mark Prime well. I played golf with him one season at Del Monte. How did you happen to know him, Becky?"

Becky told of the Major's sojourn to King's Crest.

The Copes made separate plans for the afternoon. "If I can't have you to myself, Becky," Cope complained, "I won't have you at all——"

Madge, sitting later next to Becky in the Admiral's big car, was lovely in a great cape of pale wisteria, with a turban of the same color set low on her burnt-gold hair.

"I have brought you wonderful news of Randy Paine," she said to Becky. "He has sold his story, 'The Trumpeter Swan.' To one of the big magazines. And they have asked for more. He is by way of being rather—famous. He came on to New York the day after we arrived. They had telegraphed for him. We wanted him to come up here with us, but he wouldn't."

"Why wouldn't he?"

"He had some engagements, and after that——"

"He will never write another story like 'The Trumpeter Swan,'" said Becky.

"Why not?"

"It—it doesn't seem as if he could—— It is—wonderful, Mrs. Prime——"

"Well, Randy—is wonderful," said Madge.

A silence fell between them, and when Madge spoke again it was of the Watermans. "We go to the Crossing to-morrow. I must see Flora before I go West."

The blood ran up into Becky's heart. She wondered if George Dalton was with the Watermans. But she did not dare ask. So she asked about California instead. "You will live out there?"

"Yes, on a ranch. There will be chickens and cows and hogs. It sounds unromantic, doesn't it? But it is really frightfully interesting. It is what I have always dreamed about. Mark says this is to be my—reincarnation."

She laughed a little as she explained what she meant. "And when I was in New York, I bought the duckiest lilac linens and ginghams, and white aprons, frilly ones. Mark says I shall look like a dairy maid in 'Robin Hood.'"

The Major, who was in front of them with the Admiral, turned and spoke.

"Tell her about Kemp."

"Oh, he is going with us. It develops that there is a girl in Scotland who is waiting for him. And he is going to send for her—and they are to have a cottage on the ranch, and come into the house to help us, and there is an old Chinese cook that Mark has had for years."

Becky spoke sharply. "You don't mean Mr.—Dalton's Kemp?"

"Yes. He came to Mark. Didn't you know?"

Becky had not known.

"Why did he leave Mr.—Dalton?"

"He and Georgie had a falling out about an omelette. I fancy it was a sort of comic opera climax. So Mark got a treasure and Georgie-Porgie lost one——"

"Georgie-Porgie?"

"Oh, I always call him that, and he hates it," Madge laughed at the memory.

"You did it to—tease him?" slowly.

"I did it because it was—true. You know the old nursery rhyme? Well, George is like that. There were always so many girls to be—kissed, and it was so easy to—run away——"

She said it lightly, with shrugged shoulders, but she did not look at Becky.

And that night when she was dressing for dinner, Madge said to her husband, "It sounded—catty—Mark. But I had to do it. There's that darling boy down there eating his heart out. And she is nursing a dream——"

The Major was standing by his wife's door, and she was in front of her mirror. It reflected her gold brocade, her amethysts linked with diamonds in a long chain that ended in a jeweled locket. Her jewel case was open and she brought out the pendant that George had sent her and held it against her throat. "It matches the others," she said.

He arched his eyebrows in inquiry.

"I wouldn't wear it," she said with a sudden quick force, "if there was not another jewel in the world. I wish he hadn't sent it. Oh, Mark, I wish I hadn't known him before I found—you," she came up to him swiftly; "such men as you," she said, "if women could only meet them— first ——"

His arm went around her. "It is enough that we—met——"

Becky was also at her mirror at that moment. She had dressed carefully in silver and white with her pearls and silver slippers. Louise came in and looked at her. "I haven't any grand and gorgeous things, you know. And I fancy your Mrs. Prime will be rather gorgeous."

"It suits her," said Becky, "but after this she is going to be different." She told Louise about the ranch and the linen frocks and the frilled aprons. "She is going to make herself over. I wonder if it will be a success."

"It doesn't fit in with my theories," said Louise. "I think it is much better if people marry each other ready-made."

Becky turned from her mirror. "Louise," she said, "does anything ever fit in with a woman's theories when she falls in love?"

"One shouldn't fall in love," Louise said, serenely, "they should walk squarely into it. That's what I shall do, when I get ready to marry—— But I shall love Archibald as long as the good Lord will let me——"

She was trying to say it lightly, but a quiver of her voice betrayed her.

"Louise," Becky said, "what's the matter with Archibald? Is anything really the matter?"

Louise began to cry. "Archie saw the doctor to-day, and he won't promise anything—I made Arch tell me——"

"Oh, Louise." Becky's lips were white.

"Of course if he takes good care of himself, it may not be for years. You mustn't let him know that I told you, Becky. But I had to tell somebody. I've kept it all bottled up as if I were a stone image. And I'm not a stone image, and he's all I have."

She dabbed her eyes with a futile handkerchief. The tears dripped. "I must stop," she kept saying, "I shall look like a fright for dinner——"

But at dinner she showed no signs of her agitation. She had used powder and rouge with deft touches. She had followed Becky's example and wore white, a crisp organdie, with a high blue sash. With her bobbed hair and pink cheeks she was not unlike a painted doll. She carried a little blue fan with lacquered sticks, and she tapped the table as she talked to Major Prime. The tapping was the only sign of her inner agitation.

The Admiral's table that night seemed to Becky a circle of sinister meaning. There was Archibald, condemned to die—while youth still beat in his veins—— There was Louise, who must go on without him. There was the Admiral—the last of a vanished company; there was the Major, whose life for four years had held—horrors. There was Madge, radiant to-night in the love of her husband, as she had perhaps once been radiant for Dalton.

Georgie-Porgie!

It was a horrid name. "*There were always so many girls to be kissed—and it was so easy to run away——*"

She had always hated the nursery rhyme. But now it seemed to sing itself in her brain.

"Georgie-Porgie,
Pudding and pie,
Kissed the girls,
And made them cry——"

Cope was at Becky's right. "Aren't you going to talk to me? You haven't said a word since the soup."

"Well, everybody else is talking."

"What do I care for anybody else?"

Becky wondered how Archibald did it. How he kept that light manner for a world which he was not long to know. And there was Louise with rouge and powder on her cheeks to cover her tears—— That was courage—— She thought suddenly of "The Trumpeter Swan."

She spoke out of her thoughts. "Randy has sold his story."

He wanted to know all about it, and she repeated what Madge had said. Yet even as she talked that hateful rhyme persisted,

"When the girls
Came out to play,
Georgie-Porgie
Ran away——"

After dinner they went into the drawing-room so that Louise could play for them. A great mirror which hung at the end of the room reflected Louise on the piano bench in her baby frock. It reflected Madge, slim and gold, with a huge fan of lilac feathers. It reflected Becky—in a rose-colored damask chair, it reflected the three men in black. Years ago there had been other men and women—the Admiral's wife in red velvet and the same pearls that were now on Becky's neck—— She shuddered.

As they drove home that night, the Major spoke to his wife of Becky. "The child looks unhappy."

"She will be unhappy until some day her heart rests in her husband, as mine does in you. Shall I spoil you, Mark, if I talk like this?"

When they reached their hotel there were letters. One was from Flora: "You asked about George. He is not with us. He has gone to Nantucket to visit some friends of his—the Merediths. He will be back next week."

"The Merediths?" Madge said. "George doesn't know any—Merediths. Mark—he is following Becky."

"Well, she's safe in Boston."

"She is going back. On Wednesday. And he'll be there." Her eyes were troubled.

"Mark," she said, abruptly, "I wonder if Randy has left New York. Call him up, please, long distance. I want to talk to him."

"My darling girl, do you know what time it is?"

"Nearly midnight. But that's nothing in New York. And, anyhow, if he is asleep, we will wake him up. I am going to tell him that George is at Siasconset."

"But, my dear, what good will it do?"

"He's got to save Becky. I know Dalton's tricks and his manners. He can cast a glamour over anything. And Randy's the man for her. Oh, Mark, just think of her money and his genius——"

"What have money and genius to do with it?"

"Nothing, unless they love each other. But—she cares—— You should have seen her eyes when I said he had sold his story. But she doesn't know that she cares, and he's got to make her know."

"How can he make her know?"

"Let her see him—now. She has never seen him as he was in New York with us, sure of himself, knowing that he has found the thing that he can do. He was beautiful with that radiant boy-look. You know he was, Mark, wasn't he?"

"Yes, my darling, yes."

"And I want him to be happy, don't you?"

"Of course, dear heart."

"Then get him on the 'phone. I'll do the rest."

IV

Randy, in New York, acclaimed by a crowd of enthusiasts who had read his story as a gold nugget picked up from a desert of literary mediocrity. Randy, not knowing himself. Randy, modest beyond belief. Randy, in his hotel at midnight, walking the floor with his head held high, and saying to himself, "I've done it."

It seemed to him that, of course, it could not be true. The young editor who had eyed him through shell-rimmed glasses had said, "There's going to be a lot of hard work ahead—to keep up to this——"

Randy, in his room, laughed at the thought of work. What did hardness matter? The thing that really mattered was that he had treasure to lay at the feet of Becky.

He sat down at the desk to write to her, cheeks flushed, eyes bright, a hand that shook with excitement.

"I am to meet a lot of big fellows to-morrow—I shall feel like an ugly duckling among the swans—oh, the swans, Becky, did we ever think that the Trumpeter in his old glass case——"

The telephone rang. Randy, answering it, found Madge at the other end. There was an exchange of eager question and eager answer.

Then Randy hung up the receiver, tore up his note to Becky, asked the office about trains, packed his bag, and went swift in a taxi to the station.

It was not until he was safe in his sleeper, and racketing through the night, that he remembered the meeting with the literary swans and the editor with the shell-rimmed glasses. A telegram would convey his regrets. He was sorry that he could not meet them, but he had on hand a more important matter.

CHAPTER XVI
THE CONQUEROR
I

If Randy's train had not missed a connection, he would have caught the same boat that took the Admiral and his party back to the island. They motored down to Wood's Hole, and boarded the *Sankaty*, while Randy, stranded at New Bedford, was told there would not be another steamer out until the next day.

The Admiral was the only gay and apparently care-free member of his quartette. Becky felt unaccountably depressed. Louise sat in the cabin and worked on her green bag. There was a heavy sky and signs of a storm. It was not pleasant outside.

Archibald was nursing a grievance. "If your grandfather had only stayed over another day."

"He had written Tristram that we would come. He is very exact in his engagements."

"And he feels that fifty years in 'Sconset is better than a cycle anywhere else."

"Yes. It will be nice to get back to our little gray house, and the moor, don't you think?"

"Yes. But I wanted to show you Boston as if you had never seen it, and now I shall never show it."

They were on deck, wrapped up to their chins. "Tell me what you would have shown me," Becky said; "play that I am Olga and that you are telling me about it."

He looked down at her. "Well, you've just arrived. You aren't dressed in a silver-toned cloak with gray furs and a blue turban with a silver edge. That's a heavenly outfit, Becky. But what made you wear it on a day like this?"

"It is the silver lining to my—cloud," demurely; "dull clothes are dreadful when the sky is dark."

"I am not sure but I liked you better in your brown—in the rain with your hand on my arm—— That is—unforgettable——"

She brought him back to Olga. "I have just arrived——"

"Yes, and you have a shawl over your head, and a queer old coat and funny shoes. I should have to speak to you through an interpreter, and you would look at me with eager eyes or perhaps frightened ones."

"And first we should have gone to Bunker Hill, and I should have said, 'Here we fought. Not of hatred of our enemy, but for love of liberty. The thing had to be done, and we did it. We had a just cause.' And then I should have taken you to Concord and Lexington, and I would have said, 'These farmers were clean-hearted men. They believed in law and order, they hated anarchy, and upon that belief and upon that hatred they built up a great nation.' And thus ends the first lesson." He paused. "Lesson the second would have to do with the old churches."

They had stopped by the rail; the wind buffeted them, but they did not heed it. "It was in the churches that the ideals of the new nation were crystallized. No country prospers which forgets its God."

"Lesson number three," he went on, "would have had to do with the bookshops."

"The bookshops?"

He nodded. "The old bookshops and the new of Boston. I would have taken you to them, and I would have said, 'Here, Olga, is the voice of the nation speaking to you through the printed page. Learn to read in the language of your new country.' Oh, Becky," he broke off, "I wanted to show you the bookshops. It's a perfect pilgrimage——"

The Admiral, swaying to the wind, came up to them. "Hadn't you better go inside?" he shouted. "Becky will freeze out here."

They followed him. The cabin was comparatively quiet after the tumult. Louise was still working on the green bag. "What have you two been doing?" she asked.

"Playing Olga of Petrograd," said Archibald, moodily, "but Becky was cold and came in."

"Grandfather brought me in," said Becky.

"If you had cared to stay, you would have stayed," he told her, rather unreasonably. "Perhaps, after all, Boston to Olga simply means baked beans which she doesn't like, and codfish which she prefers—raw——"

"Now you have spoiled it all," said Becky. "I loved the things that you said about the churches and the bookshops and Bunker Hill."

"Did you? Well, it is all true, Becky, the part they have played in making us a nation. And it is all going to be true again. We Americans aren't going to sell our birthright for a mess of pottage!"

And now the island once more rose out of the sea. The little steamer had some difficulty in making a landing. But at last they were on shore, and the 'bus was waiting, and it was after dark when they reached "The Whistling Sally."

The storm was by that time upon them—the wind blew a wild gale, but the little gray cottage was snug and warm. Jane in her white apron went unruffled about her pleasant tasks—storms might come and storms might go—she had no fear of them now, since none of her men went down to the sea in ships.

Tristram in shining oilskins brought up their bags. He stood in the hall and talked to them, and before he went away, he said casually over his shoulder, "There's a gentleman at the hotel that has asked for you once or twice."

"For me?" the Admiral questioned.

"You and Miss Becky."

"Do you know his name?"

"It's Dalton. George Dalton——"

"I don't know any Daltons. Do you, Becky?"

Becky stood by the table with her back to them. She did not turn. "Yes," she said in a steady voice. "There was a George Dalton whom I met this summer—in Virginia."

II

There was little sleep for Becky that night. The storm tore around the tiny house, but its foundations were firm, and it did not shake. The wind whistled as if the wooden figure in the front yard had suddenly come to life and was madly making up for the silence of a half-century.

So George had followed her. He had found her out, and there was no way of escape. She would have to see him, hear him. She would have to set herself against the charm of that quick voice, those sparkling eyes. There would be no one to save her now. Randy was far away. She must make her fight alone.

She turned restlessly. Why should she fight? What, after all, did George mean to her? A chain of broken dreams? A husk of golden armor? _Georgie-Porgie_—who had kissed and run away.

She was listless at breakfast. The storm was over, and the Admiral was making plans for a picnic the next day to Altar Rock. "Hot coffee and lobster sandwiches, and a view of the sea on a day like this."

Becky smiled. "Grandfather," she said, "I believe you are happy because you keep your head in the stars and your feet on the ground."

"What's the connection, my dear?"

"Well, lobster sandwiches and a view of the sea. So many people can't enjoy both. They are either lobster-sandwich people, or view-of-the-sea people."

"Which shows their limitations," said the Admiral, promptly; "the people of Pepys' time were eloquent over a pigeon pie or a poem. The good Lord gave us both of them. Why not?"

It was after breakfast that a note was brought to Becky. The boy would wait.

"I am here," George wrote, "and I shall stay until I see you. Don't put me off. Don't shut your heart against me. I am very unhappy. May I come?"

She wrote an immediate answer. She would see him in the afternoon. The Admiral would be riding over to Nantucket. He had some business affairs to attend to—a meeting at the bank. Jane would be busy in her kitchen with the baking. The coast would be clear. There would be no need, if George came in the afternoon, to explain his presence.

Having dispatched her note, and with the morning before her, she was assailed by restlessness. She welcomed Archibald Cope's invitation from the adjoining porch. He sang it in the words of the old song,

"Madam, will you walk!
Madam, will you talk?
Madam, will you walk and talk
With me——"

"Where shall we go?"

"To Sankaty——"

She loved the walk to the lighthouse. In the spring there was Scotch broom on the bluffs—yellow as gold, with the blue beyond. In summer wild roses, deep pink, scenting the air with their fresh fragrance. But, perhaps, she loved it best on a day like this, with the breakers on the beach below, racing in like white horses, and with the winter gulls, dark against the brightness of the morning.

"Why aren't you painting?" she asked Archibald.

"Because," he said, "I am not going to paint the moor any more. It gets away from me—it is too vast—— It has a primal human quality, and yet it is not alive."

"It sometimes seems alive to me," she said, "when I look off over it—it seems to rise and fall as if it—breathed."

"That's the uncanny part of it," Archibald agreed, "and I am going to give it up. I am not going to paint it—— I want to paint you, Becky."

"Me? Why do you want to do that?"

He flashed a glance at her. "Because you are nice to look at."

"That isn't the reason."

"Why should you question my motives?" he demanded. "But since you must have the truth—it is because of a fancy of mine that I might do it well——"

"I should like it very much," she said, simply.

"Would you?" eagerly.

"Yes."

She had on her red cape, and a black velvet tam pulled over her shining hair.

"I shall not paint you like this," he said, "although the color is—superlative—— Ever since you read to me that story of Randy Paine's, I have had a feeling that the real story ought to have a happy ending, and that I should like to make the illustration."

"I don't know what you mean?"

"Why shouldn't the girl care for the boy after he came back? Why shouldn't she, Becky Bannister?"

Her startled gaze met his. "Let's sit down here," he said, "and have it out."

There was a bench on the edge of the bluff, set so that one might have a wider view of the sea.

"There ought to be a happy ending, Becky."

"How could there be?"

"Why not you—and Randy Paine? I haven't met him, but somehow that story tells me that he is the right sort. And think of it, Becky, you and that boy—in that big house down there, going to church, smiling across the table at each other," his breath came quickly, "your love for him, his for you, making a background for his—genius."

She tried to stop him. "Why should you say such things?"

"Because I have thought them. Last night in the storm—I couldn't sleep. I—I wanted to be a dog in the manger. I couldn't have you, and I'd be darned if I'd help anyone else to get you. You—you see, I'm a sort of broken reed, Becky. It—it isn't a sure thing that I am going to get well. And if what I feel for you is worth anything, it ought to mean that I must put your happiness—first. And that's why I want to make the picture for the—happy ending."

Her hand went out to him. "It is a beautiful thing for you to do. But I am not sure that there will be a—happy ending."

"Why not?"

She could not tell him. She could not tell—that between her and her thought of Randy was the barrier of all that George Dalton had meant to her.

"If you paint the picture," she evaded, "you must finish it at Huntersfield. Why can't you and Louise come down this winter? It would be heavenly."

"It would be Heaven for me. Do you mean it, Becky?"

She did mean it, and she told him so.

"I shall paint you," he planned, "as a little white slip of a girl, with pearls about your neck, and dreams in your eyes, and back of you a flight of shadowy swans——"

They rose and walked on. "I thought you were to be with the Admiral in Boston this winter."

"I stay until Thanksgiving. I always go back to Huntersfield for Christmas."

After that it was decided that she should sit for him each morning. They did not speak again of Randy. There had been something in Becky's manner which kept Archibald from saying more.

When they reached the lighthouse, the wind was blowing strongly. Before them was the sweep of the Nantucket Shoals—not a ship in sight, not a line of smoke, the vast emptiness of heaving waters.

Becky stood at the edge of the bluff, her red cape billowing out into a scarlet banner, her hair streaming back from her face, the velvet tam flattened by the force of the wind.

Archibald glanced at her. "Are you cold?"

"No, I love it."

He was chilled to the bone, yet there she stood, warm with life, bright with beating blood——

"What a beastly lot of tumbling water," he said with sudden overmastering irritation. "Let's get away from it, Becky. Let's get away."

Going back they took the road which led across the moor. The clear day gave to the low hills the Persian carpet coloring which Cope had despaired of painting. Becky, in her red cape, was almost lost against the brilliant background.

But she was not the only one who challenged nature. For as she and Archibald approached the outskirts of the town, they discerned, at some distance, at the top of a slight eminence, two figures—a man and a woman. The woman was dancing, with waving arms and flying feet.

"She calls that dance 'Morning on the Moor,'" Cope told Becky; "she has a lot of them—'The Spirit of the Storm,' 'The Wraith of the Fog.'"

"Do you know her?"

"No. But Tristram says she dances every morning. She is getting ready for an act in one of the big musical shows."

The man sat on the ground and watched the woman dance. Her primrose cape was across his knee. He was a big man and wore a cap. Becky, surveying him from afar, saw nothing to command closer scrutiny. Yet had she known, she might have found him worthy of another look. For the man with the primrose cape was Dalton!

III

George Dalton, entering the little sitting-room of "The Whistling Sally," had to bend his head. He was so shining and splendid that he seemed to fill the empty spaces. It seemed, indeed, to Becky, as if he were too shining and splendid, as if he bulked too big, like a giant, top-heavy.

But she was not unmoved. He had been the radiant knight of her girlish dreams—some of the glamour still remained. Her cheeks were touched with pink as she greeted him.

He took both of her hands in his. "Oh, you lovely, lovely little thing," he said, and stood looking down at her.

They were the words he had said to her in the music-room. They revived memories. Flushing a deeper pink, she drew away from him. "Why did you come?"

"I could not stay away."

"How long have you been here?"

"Five days——"

"Please—sit down"—she indicated a chair on the other side of the hearth. She had seated herself in the Admiral's winged chair. It came up over her head, and she looked very slight and childish.

George, surveying the room, said, "This is some contrast to Huntersfield."

"Yes."

"Do you like it?"

"Oh, yes. I have spent months here, you know, and Sally, who whistles out there in the yard, is an old friend of mine. I played with her as a child."

"I should think the Admiral would rather have one of those big houses on the bluff."

"Would you?"

"Yes."

"But he has so many big houses. And this is his play-house. It belonged to his grandfather, and that ship up there is one on which our Sally was the figure-head."

He forced himself to listen while she told him something of the history of the old ship. He knew that she was making conversation, that there were things more important to speak of, and that she knew it. Yet she was putting off the moment when they must speak.

There came a pause, however. "And now," he said, leaning forward, "let's talk about ourselves, I have been here five days, Becky—waiting——"

"Waiting? For what?"

"To ask you to—forgive me."

Her steady glance met his. "If I say that I forgive you, will that be—enough?"

"You know it will not," his sparkling eyes challenged her. "Not if you say it coldly——"

"How else can I say it?"

"As if—oh, Becky, don't keep me at long distance—like this. Don't tell me that you are engaged to Randy Paine. Don't——. Let this be our day——" He seemed to shine and sparkle in a perfect blaze of gallantry.

"I am not engaged to Randy."

He gave an exclamation of triumph. "You broke it off?"

"No," she said, "he broke it."

"What?"

She folded her hands in her lap. "You see," she said, "he felt that I did not love him. And he would not take me that way—unloving."

"He seemed to want to take you any way, the day he talked to me. I asked him what he had to offer you——" He gave a light laugh—seemed to brush Randy away with a gesture.

Her cheeks flamed. "He has a great deal to offer."

"For example?" lazily, with a lift of the eyebrows.

"He is a gentleman—and a genius——"

His face darkened. "I'll pass over the first part of that until later. But why call him a 'genius'?"

"He has written a story," breathlessly, "oh, all the world will know it soon. The people who have read it, in New York, are crazy about it——"

"Is that all? A story? So many people write nowadays."

"Well," she asked quietly, "what more have you to offer?"

"Love, Becky. You intimated a moment ago that I was not—a gentleman—because I failed—once. Is that fair? How do you know that Paine has not failed—how do you know——? And love hasn't anything to do with genius, Becky, it has to do with that night in the music-room, when you sang and when I—kissed you. It has to do with nights like those in the old garden, with the new moon and the stars, and the old goddesses."

"And with words which meant—nothing——"

"_Becky_," he protested.

"Yes," she said, "you know it is true—they meant nothing. Perhaps you have changed since then. I don't know. But I know this, that I have changed."

He felt back of her words the force which had always baffled him.

"You mean that you don't love me?"

"Yes."

"I—I don't believe it——"

"You must——"

"But——" he rose and went towards her.

"Please—we won't argue it. And—Jane is going to give us some tea." She left him for a moment and came back to sit behind the little table. Jane brought tea and fresh little cakes.

"For Heaven's sake, Becky," George complained, when the old woman had returned to her kitchen, "can you eat at a moment like this?"

"Yes," she said, "I can eat and the cakes are very nice."

She did not let him see that her hand trembled as she poured the tea.

George had had five days in the company of the dancer in yellow. He had found her amusing. She played the game at which he had proved himself so expert rather better than the average woman. She served for the moment, but no sane man would ever think of spending his life with her. But here was the real thing—this slip of a child in a blue velvet smock, with bows on her slippers, and a wave of bronze hair across her forehead. He felt that Becky's charms would last for a lifetime. When she was old, and sat like that on the other side of the hearth, with silver hair and bent figure, she would still retain her loveliness of spirit, the steadfast gaze, the vivid warmth of word and gesture.

For the first time in his life George knew the kind of love that projects itself forward into the future, that sees a woman as friend and as companion. And this woman whom he loved had just said that she did not love him.

"I won't give you up," he said doggedly.

"How can you keep me?" she asked quietly, and suddenly the structure of hope which he had built for himself tumbled. "Then this is the—end?"

"I am afraid it is," and she offered him a cup.

His face grew suddenly gray. "I don't want any tea. I want you," his hands went over his face. "I want you, Becky."

"Don't," she said, shakily, "I am sorry."

She was sorry to see him no longer shining, no longer splendid, but she was glad that the spell was broken—the charm of sparkling eyes and quick voice gone—forever.

She said again, as she gave him her hand at parting, "I'm sorry."

His laugh was not pleasant. "You'll be sorrier if you marry Paine."

"No," she said, and he carried away with him the look which came into her eyes as she said it, "No, if I marry Randy I shall not be sorry."

IV

Randy, arriving on the evening boat, caught the 'bus, and found the Admiral in it.

"It's Randy Paine," he said, as he climbed in and sat beside the old gentleman.

"My dear boy, God bless you. Becky will be delighted."

"I was in New York," was Randy's easy explanation, "and I couldn't resist coming up."

"We read your story, and Mrs. Prime told us how the editor received it. You are by way of being famous, my boy."

"Well, it's mighty interesting, sir," said young Randy.

It was late when they reached the little town, but the west was blood-red above the ridge, with the moor all darkling purple.

Becky was not in the house. "I saw her go down to the beach," Jane told them.

"In what direction?" Randy asked; "I'll go after her."

"She sometimes sits back of the blue boat," said Jane, "when there's a wind. But if you don't find her, Mr. Paine, she'll be back in time for supper. I told her not to be late. I am having raised rolls and broiled fish, and Mr. and Miss Cope are coming."

"I'll find her," said Randy, and was off.

The moon was making a path of gold across the purple waters, and casting sharp shadows on the sand. The blue boat, high on the beach, had lost its color in the pale light. But there was no other boat, so Randy went towards it. And as he went, he gave the old Indian cry.

Becky, wrapped in her red cape, deep in thoughts of the thing that had happened in the afternoon, heard the cry and doubted her ears.

It came again.

"Randy," she breathed, and stood up and saw him coming. She ran towards him. "Oh, Randy, Randy."

She came into his arms as if she belonged there. And he, amazed but rapturous, received her, held her close.

"Oh, oh," she whispered, "you don't know how I have wanted you, Randy."

"It is nothing to the way that I have wanted you, my dear."

"Really, Randy?"

"Really, my sweet."

The moon was very big and bright. It showed her face white as a rose-leaf against his coat. He scarcely dared to breathe, lest he should frighten her. They stood for a moment in silence, then she said, simply, "You see, it was you, after all, Randy."

"Yes," he said, "I see. But when did you find it out?"

"This afternoon. Let's sit down here out of the wind behind the boat, and I'll tell you about it——"

But he was not ready yet to let her go. "To have you here—like this."

"OH, OH, SHE WHISPERED, "YOU DON'T KNOW HOW I HAVE WANTED YOU"

He stopped. He could not go on. He lifted her up to him, and their lips met. Years ago he had kissed her under the mistletoe; the kiss that he gave her now was a pledge for all the years to come.

They were late for supper. Jane relieved her mind to the Admiral and his guests. "She had a gentleman here this afternoon for tea, and neither of them ate anything. And now there's another gentleman, and the rolls are spoiling."

"You can serve supper, Jane," the Admiral told her; "they can eat when they come."

When they came, Becky's cheeks were as red as her cape. As she swept within the radius of the candle-light, Archibald Cope, who had risen at her entrance, knew what had happened. Her eyes were like stars. "Did Jane scold about us?" she asked, with a quick catch of her breath; "it was so lovely—with the moon."

Back of her was young Randy—Randy of the black locks, of the high-held head and Indian profile, Randy, with his air of Conqueror.

"I've told them all about you," Becky said, "and they have read your story. Will you please present him properly, Grandfather, while I go and fix my hair?"

She came back very soon, slim and childish in her blue velvet smock, her hair in that bronze wave across her forehead, her eyes still lighted.

She sat between her grandfather and Archibald.

"So," said Cope softly, under cover of the conversation, "it has happened?"

"What has happened?"

"The happy ending."

"Oh—how did you know?"

"As if the whole world wouldn't know just to look at you."

The Randy of the supper table at "The Whistling Sally" was a Randy that Becky had never seen. Success had come to him and love. There was the ring of it in his young voice, the flush of it on his cheeks. He was a man, with a man's future.

He talked of his work. "If I am a bore, please tell me," he said, "but it is rather a fairy-tale, you know, when you've made up your mind to a hum-drum law career to find a thing like this opening out."

Becky sat and listened. Her eyes were all for her lover. Already she thought of him at King's Crest, writing for the world, with her money making things easy for him, but not spoiling the simplicity of their tastes. If she thought at all of George Dalton, it was to find the sparkle and shine of his splendid presence dimmed by Randy's radiance.

"I hate to say that he is—charming," Cope complained.

He was a good sport, and he wanted Becky to be happy. But it was not easy to sit there and see those two—with the pendulum swinging between them of joy and dreams, and the knowledge of a long life together.

"Why should it be?" he asked Louise, as he stood beside her, later, on their own little porch which overlooked the sea; "those two—did you see them? While I——"

Louise laid her hand on his shoulder. "Yes. I think it is something like this, Arch. They've got to live it out, and life isn't always going to be just to-night for them. And perhaps in the years together they may lose some of their dreams. They've got to grow old, and you, you'll go out—with all—your dreams——"

He reached up and took the kind hand.

"'They all go out like this—into the night—but what a fleet of—stars.' Is that it, Louise?"

"Yes."

The clearness of the moonlight was broken by long fingers of fog stretched up from the horizon.

"I'll wrap up and sit here, Louise," Archibald said; "I shan't sleep if I go in."

"Don't stay too long. Good-night, my dear, good-night."

Archibald, watching the fog shut out the moonlight, had still upon him that sense of revolt. Fame had never come to him, and love had come too late.

Yet for Randy there was to be fulfillment—the wife of his heart, the applause of the world. What did it all mean? Why should one man have all, and the other—nothing?

Yet he had had his dreams. And the dreams of men lived. That which died was the least of them. The great old gods of democracy—Washington, Jefferson, Adams—had seen visions, and the visions had endured. Only yesterday Roosevelt had proclaimed his gallant doctrines. He had died proclaiming them, and the world held its head higher, because of his belief in its essential rightness.

The mists enveloped Archibald in a sort of woolly dampness. He saw for a moment a dim and distant moon. If he could have painted a moon like that—with fingers of fog reaching up to it——!

His own dreams of beauty? What of them? His pictures would not live. He knew that now. But he had given more than pictures to the world. He had given himself in a crusade which had been born of high idealism and a sense of brotherhood. Day after day, night after night, his plane had hung, poised like an eagle, above the enemy. He had been one of the young gods who had set their strength and courage against the greed and grossness of gray-coated hordes.

And these dreams must live—the dreams of the young gods—as the dreams of the old gods had endured. Because men had died to make others free, freedom must be the song on the lips of all men.

He thought of Randy's story. The Trumpeter Swan was only a stuffed bird in a glass case. But once he had spread his wings—flown high in the upper air. There had been strength in his pinions—joy in his heart—thrilling life in every feather of him. Some lovely lines drifted through Archibald's consciousness—

"Upon the brimming water, among the stones
Are nine and fifty swans.
Unwearied still, lover by lover,
They paddle in the cold
Companionable streams or climb the air;
Their hearts have not grown old;
Passion and conquest, wander where they will.
Attend upon them still——"

From the frozen north the swan had come to the sheltered bay and some one had shot him. He had not been asked if he wanted to live; they had taken his life, and had set him up there on the shelf—and that had been the end of him.

But was it the end? Stuffed and quiet in his glass case, he had looked down on a little boy. And the little boy had seen him not dead, but sounding his trumpet. And now the whole world would hear of him. In Randy's story, the Trumpeter would live again in the hearts of men. The wind was rising—the fog blown back before it showed the golden track of the sea—light stretching to infinity! He rose and stood by the rail. Then suddenly he felt a hand upon his, and looking down, he saw Becky. "I ran away from Randy," she said, breathlessly, "just for a moment. I was afraid you might be alone, and unhappy." His hand held hers. "Just for this moment you are mine?"

"Yes."

"Then let me tell you this—that I shall never be alone as long as I may have your friendship—I shall always be happy because I have—loved you." He kissed her hand. "Run back to your Randy. Good-night, my dear, good-night." Her lover received her rapturously at the door of the little house. They went in together. And Archibald looked out, smiling, over a golden sea.

Made in the USA
Lexington, KY
04 January 2015